DETERMINANTS OF HEALTH

Determinants of Health

An Economic Perspective

Michael Grossman

COLUMBIA UNIVERSITY PRESS  New York

Columbia University Press
Publishers Since 1893
New York   Chichester, West Sussex
cup.columbia.edu
© 2017 Columbia University Press

Library of Congress Cataloging-in-Publication Data
Names: Grossman, Michael, 1942- author.
Title: Determinants of health : an economic perspective /
Michael Grossman.
Description: New York : Columbia University Press, 2017. |
Includes bibliographical references and index.
Identifiers: LCCN 2016046853 | ISBN 978-0-231-17812-9 (cloth : alk. paper) |
ISBN 978-0-231-54451-1 (e-book)
Subjects: | MESH: Health Status Indicators | Socioeconomic Factors |
Risk Factors | Models, Economic | Collected Works
Classification: LCC RA418 | NLM WA 900.1 | DDC 362.1—dc23
LC record available at https://lccn.loc.gov/2016046853

Cover design: Jordan Wannemacher

For my wife, Ilene, my daughters, Sandy and Barri, my sons-in-law, Steve and Dave, and my grandchildren, Zack, Ben, Alise, and John for increasing the efficiency of my health production, lowering its price, and causing me to demand a large quantity of quality-adjusted life years.

Contents

Foreword

John Mullahy

Had Michael Grossman never conceived and written his seminal paper, "On the Concept of Health Capital and the Demand for Health," it is unlikely that we—certainly economists, but in reality a much larger "we"—would understand the determinants and consequences of human health as well as we do today. Grossman's paper, which has received to date more than five thousand Google Scholar–reported citations, may not have technically launched the field of health economics,[1] but it certainly cemented the field's standing and relevance as a science oriented toward understanding and improving people's health. Indeed, only a rare student of health economics has not been exposed at some point in their training to "the Grossman model" of health developed in the paper, which appears as chapter 1 of this book.

Assembling Grossman's most important work in this one volume and reissuing alongside it his classic monograph, *The Demand for Health: A Theoretical and Empirical Investigation*, is not only a fitting testimonial to him and the importance of his scholarly work, but also serves to guarantee that current and future scholars in this field will have ready access to the ideas of one of the finest minds—and finest people—in our discipline. There is considerable value added by the commentary Grossman provides in the introductions and afterwords to each of the book's four main parts. This commentary situates Grossman's collected work in larger contexts, debates, and literatures, thus providing solid contextual foundations for scholars pursuing these topics further in their own work, and for health policy analysts aiming to better understand the determinants of the health outcomes and behaviors in Grossman's studies.

This book's title, *Determinants of Health*, is well chosen. Health economists study a spectrum of topics, many of them focusing attention on features of health-care markets (providers, patients, insurance, technology, etc.). Even those economists who do target specifically *health* in their research often ask questions about the "consequences" side of the determinants–consequences ledger; for example, how does an individual's health influence outcomes like their labor market behavior, family well-being, health-care utilization, and so on? While such inquiry is important, and while Grossman's work does not ignore consequence-side concerns, Grossman's efforts have been directed largely toward the determinants side of the spectrum. That is, his research seeks to understand how the choices people make determine how healthy they are, and how the structure of incentives, constraints, and resources confronting people determines such choices in the first place.

The book is organized into four parts that represent the impressive span of Grossman's scholarly thinking and writing over roughly forty-five years. Each part's introduction and afterword provide a more thoughtful perspective on Grossman's work than I could ever hope to. Instead, I offer here brief commentary on three related themes of his work that have had significant impact on the field of health economics and beyond.

The first theme is the one addressed in chapter 1 of this book and in the accompanying reissued monograph, *The Demand for Health*. Here, Grossman extends in several directions the seminal work of his own mentor, Gary S. Becker, on human capital investment. He considers how people's "health capital" might usefully be characterized as a special dimension of their overall human capital. People desire but cannot buy healthiness. Yet people make choices that are tantamount to investing in a stock of depreciating health capital from which healthiness flows. To a significant degree people are producers of their own health, and the investment choices they make can be health-enhancing ones ("healthy behaviors") or health-reducing ones ("unhealthy behaviors"). In the author's words, "consumers demand health, defined broadly to include illness-free days in a given year and life expectancy, and produce it with inputs of medical care services, diet, other market goods and services, and their own time. Hence, the demand for medical care and other health inputs is derived from the basic demand for health" (Grossman 2016).[2]

An often underappreciated feature of this framework is that health status or healthiness itself—as distinct from the health capital stocks that yield it—is properly characterized in time dimensions, e.g. "illness-free days in a given year."[3] Grossman imagines a fixed time budget (say 365 days in one year) within which the mutually exclusive time-use categories of time working, time engaged in other productive behaviors in the household, time investing in health—e.g. through the use of preventive medical care or exercise—and time spent unhealthy or dead account for all the time at someone's disposal that year. Time that is not spent waylaid unhealthy or dead is time to be productively devoted to work, to household production, or to further investment in human capital, including health capital. Understanding how such time budgets are allocated is ultimately key in understanding the outcomes arising from people's health production activities.

The second, related theme concerns the role of schooling in the production of health, explored in part 2 of this book. Grossman's framework posits that the marginal productivity of the health-investment choices made by people is determined in part by their education. Such a framework is consistent with the strong population-level correlations that are typically observed between different measures of schooling attainment and of healthiness or health capital. As Grossman notes in the closing words of this book,

> The positive relationship between more schooling and better health is one of the most fundamental ones in health economics. It is natural to explore complementarities between these two most important forms of human capital. Research that investigates the causal nature of the relationship and the mechanisms via which schooling influences health has played and should continue to play an extremely prominent role in the literature that explores the determinants of the health of the population from an economic perspective.

Strong correlations are one thing, but a great deal of Grossman's work over the years has been dedicated to understanding causal roles of schooling in the production of health. As reasonable as a causal relationship running from schooling to health may sound, such mechanisms are both controversial and enormously challenging to establish empirically. For example, some economists have argued against a direct, causal relationship and in favor of some "third variable" that encourages individuals to invest in both their general human capital (through schooling) as well as their health capital, again consistent with the observed positive correlations. Over the years Grossman has dedicated considerable effort to understanding and advocating empirical strategies that might allow such debates to be adjudicated by data. Understanding the driving force behind such strong correlations is essential for policy-making purposes.

The third theme of Grossman's work, explored in part four of this book, concerns the economics of healthy and unhealthy behaviors—that is, what determines the determinants. I suggest that at least two strands of this research are of particular interest for policy making. The first strand is Grossman's work on unhealthy behaviors that are considered addictive, including tobacco, alcohol, and illicit drug use.[4] The notion that even addictive behaviors may be responsive to economic incentives has been an area of some controversy. Grossman's empirical work in this area has advanced understanding of such phenomena, and has suggested that thoughtfully structured public policies might be used to modify these harmful behaviors. The second strand is related: when officials consider such ostensibly beneficial public policies, it is imperative to appreciate that people will respond in many different ways, not all of which are ultimately health enhancing. Laws restricting access to some forms of illicit drugs might encourage substitution to other forms that could be more harmful; higher tobacco taxes might well result in lower tobacco use but also in higher caloric intake (see chapter 19); impeding access to nicotine delivery technologies (e.g., e-cigarettes) might encourage tobacco use or discourage its cessation; and so on. Policies intended to change incentives often—perhaps even typically—will have unintended, often unwelcome consequences. In fact, such unintended consequences are nothing more than people substituting some behaviors for others in light of changes to the incentives they face. While such outcomes may certainly be unintended and unwelcome, they should not be unanticipated if thoughtful economic analysis undergirds policy design in the first instance.[5] Grossman's afterword to part 4 offers a discussion of such issues that should be required reading for policy makers working in this field.

The bottom line of virtually all of the conceptual and empirical work appearing in this book is this: incentives, constraints, and resources—particularly human-capital resources—influence health-related decisions and outcomes. If policy makers deem it desirable to change people's health-related behaviors or health outcomes, then thoughtful policy design that modifies incentives—and takes into account that unintended consequences will also follow—can affect behaviors and outcomes even if the behaviors are deeply entrenched. Whether such policy implementation is politically viable and, if so, whether it will get the incentives right is a vitally important yet altogether separate question, as is whether such change is socially desirable in the first place.

In closing—and particularly for readers who have not had the privilege of knowing him personally—I offer three brief reflections on Mike Grossman, the person. First, no one I know in the profession is a more dedicated, generous, and supportive mentor than Mike. As his former students will attest, this dedication—Mike's personal investment in the human capital of the next generation of health economists—is lifelong and resolute. Second, Mike is a steadfastly positive, thoughtful person; he manages to find a nugget of good in virtually any manuscript, professional presentation, or scholar he is reviewing, whether or not others would always concur. Finally, despite his considerable professional accomplishments and assured long-term scholarly legacy, Mike is one of the most humble people I have ever known. "Conduct your affairs with humility, and you will be loved more than a giver of gifts," Sirach 3:17 instructs. That, in a nutshell, is Mike Grossman.

NOTES

1. If asked to nominate a single paper, many economists would give this credit to Kenneth J. Arrow's 1963 publication in the *American Economic Review* (Arrow 1963).
2. Grossman did not undertake empirical work on the health production framework in the 1972 *Journal of Political Economy* paper (see chapter 1), but did undertake empirical work in the *Demand for Health* monograph. I believe he would credit the work of Mark R. Rosenzweig and T. Paul Schultz (Rosenzweig and Schultz, 1983) as a major advance in recognizing many of the empirical challenges involved in implementing the health production model and in devising empirical strategies to estimate it. Much of Grossman's own work appearing in parts 3 and 4 of this book relies on empirical strategies akin to those in the Rosenzweig-Schultz framework.
3. Willard G. Manning, Joseph P. Newhouse, and John E. Ware, Jr. (Manning et al., 1982) provide extensive discussion of such health measurement issues.
4. Grossman's paper with Gary S. Becker and Kevin M. Murphy on tobacco addiction (see chapter 16) is his second most highly cited journal publication, based on Google Scholar accounts.
5. This is a point many economists associate with the work of Sam Peltzman (e.g., Peltzman 1975).

REFERENCES

Arrow, Kenneth J. 1963. "Uncertainty and the Welfare Economics of Medical Care." *American Economic Review* 53(5): 941–973.

Grossman, Michael. 2016. " 'A Theory of the Allocation of Time' Turns Fifty: Its Impact on the Field of Health Economics." *Health Economics* 25(1): 3–7.

Manning, Willard G., Joseph P. Newhouse, and John E. Ware, Jr. 1982. "The Status of Health in Demand Estimation; or, Beyond Excellent, Good, Fair, and Poor." In *Economic Aspects of Health*, edited by Victor R. Fuchs, 143–184. Chicago: University of Chicago Press.

Peltzman, Sam. 1975. "The Effects of Automobile Safety Regulation." *Journal of Political Economy* 83(4): 677–726.

Rosenzweig, Mark R., and T. Paul Schultz. 1983. "Estimating a Household Production Function: Heterogeneity, the Demand for Health Inputs, and Their Effects on Birth Weight." *Journal of Political Economy* 91(5): 723–746.

Introduction and Acknowledgments

This book is motivated by a quotation by Joseph P. Newhouse in his introduction to *Moral Hazard in Health Insurance*, by Amy Finkelstein with Kenneth J. Arrow, Jonathan Gruber, Joseph P. Newhouse, and Joseph E. Stiglitz, published by Columbia University Press in 2015. Professor Newhouse, who is the founding editor of the *Journal of Health Economics,* writes: "Each academic year, I teach the first session of a one semester course in health economics for second-year graduate students. The reading for that session consists of two seminal works in health economics: Kenneth Arrow's 'Uncertainty and the Welfare Economics of Medical Care' and Michael Grossman's *The Demand for Health: A Theoretical and Empirical Investigation* [Arrow 1963; Grossman 1972]. These two works have resulted in two largely nonoverlapping streams of the by-now vast health economics literature. Arrow's article led . . . to a literature on the functioning of markets for medical services and health insurance. Grossman's book led to a literature on determinants of the health status of the population, only one determinant of which . . . is medical care (p. 1)."

As I rapidly approach the end of my fifth decade as a professional economist, I thought it would be useful to make available in one volume a compilation of my most important papers dealing with an economic perspective of the determinants of the health of the population. These papers can be classified under the following headings:

The Demand for Health: Theoretical Underpinnings and Empirical Results
The Relationship Between Health and Schooling
Determinants of Infant Health with Special Emphasis on Public Policies
    and Programs
The Economics of Unhealthy Behaviors.

Based on these headings, the book is divided into four parts or sections. Each section includes an introduction to the topic at issue and to the papers in the section. More important, it ends with an afterword that contains a brief discussion of research stimulated by the studies in that section. The focus is on selected papers by others that have advanced and extended my work, including some that do not agree with it. It also includes my thoughts on promising areas for future research.

I titled my June 2010 Presidential Address to the American Society of Health Economists at its third biennial conference at Cornell University "It's Better to Be the First or One of the First Even if You're Wrong (Especially if You Pick Interesting Problems on Which to Work)." That title reflects my research philosophy. Hence, it is not surprising that at least some of the research in the afterwords is critical of my contributions. I try to give a balanced view of the issues involved, encourage the reader to make up his or her own mind concerning the points of contention, and pursue research that will contribute to the debate as well as opening up new perspectives on economic determinants of the health of the population.

In the two papers in the first part of the book, I set out my model of the demand for health. I treat health as a durable capital stock that is demanded because it is a source of utility and because, as a component of the stock of human capital, it is a determinant of earnings. I also summarize key predictions of the model and the empirical evidence concerning these predictions.

In the four papers in the second part of the book, my coauthors and I focus on the positive relationship between more schooling and better health—one of the most fundamental relationships in economics. Because I view health as a form of human capital, it is natural to examine complementarities between health capital and other forms of human capital, the most important of which is knowledge capital, as proxied by the number of years of formal schooling completed. The emphasis of the papers is on the extent to which the positive relationship implies causality from schooling to health and on the mechanisms that may lead an increase in schooling to result in better health.

In the five papers in the third part of the book, my coauthors and I deal with infant health outcomes in the context of a rich analytical framework in which my demand for health model is combined with economic models of the family. We focus on infant mortality because death rates at this age are much higher than child and teenage mortality rates, and adult death rates do not exceed the infant mortality rate until the mid-fifties (Xu et al. 2016). Our studies were particularly timely when they were conducted in the 1980s because the U.S. infant mortality rate was very stable between 1955 and 1964 but fell rapidly for at least the next two decades. The period beginning in 1964 witnessed the legalization and diffusion of abortion, the widespread adoption of oral and intra-uterine contraceptive techniques, and dramatic advances in neonatal science. It also witnessed the introduction and rapid growth of programs associated with President Lyndon B. Johnson's War on Poverty: Medicaid, federally subsidized maternal and infant care projects and community health centers, federally sub-sidized family planning services for low-income women, and the Special Supplemental Food Program for Women, Infants, and Children (WIC program). Although other researchers had pointed to these developments in explanations of the acceleration in the downward trend in infant mortality, the question had not been studied in a multivariate context prior to our work.

In the ten papers in the fourth part of the book, my coauthors and I treat the economics of unhealthy behaviors: the consumption of goods and associated behaviors that are harmful to health. Examples include cigarette smoking; overeating, reflected by the body mass index and by obesity; excessive alcohol consumption; and the consumption of illegal drugs. These behaviors rank first, second, third, and tenth, respectively, as the leading causes of premature mortality in the United States (National Research Council 2015). Not only do consumers who engage in these behaviors harm themselves, but they also harm others. For instance, pregnant women who smoke or use cocaine may injure their fetuses, and drunk drivers may injure or kill other people. The existence of ignored internal costs (harm to self) and external costs (harm to others) explains why the governments of almost every developed country and many developing ones have chosen to intervene in the markets for these goods.

From a positive standpoint, those who focus on economic approaches to the determinants of health outcomes need to understand the behavioral underpinnings of consumer choices pertaining to the consumption of unhealthy goods. Do decisions to consume goods with negative marginal products in the health production function conform to or violate basic propositions in economics? In particular, do they violate the law of the downward sloping demand function? And how should one take account of the addictive properties of many of them: the positive relationship between past consumption and current consumption?

I have been trying to answer these questions and examining implications for public policy on a continuous basis since the late 1970s. I have published more papers on this topic than on the first three topics in this book, including many publications in each of the last four decades—the 1980s, 1990s, 2000s, and 2010s. That explains why the ten papers in this part of the book fall one short of the total number of eleven papers in the previous three parts combined.

I could not have produced the twenty-one papers in this volume without the great fortune of terrific teachers, classmates, work environments, students, and colleagues—many of whom are my former students. My greatest debt is to the late Gary S. Becker. When I entered the PhD program in economics at Columbia University in September 1964, I was going to specialize in public finance. Then I met Gary and decided to specialize in whatever interested him. He was by far the best economist I had the privilege to know. He had a profound impact on my professional career in economics, and I owed a debt to him that I could never repay. In his two-semester course in microeconomics and in his justly famous labor economics workshop, I learned that economists can study every aspect of human behavior. He suggested the topic of my PhD dissertation. Originally, it was supposed to be a study of the effects of education on health, but along the way he encouraged (some might say demanded) me to broaden it into a theoretical and empirical analysis of the demand for health. In the mid-1980s, Gary introduced me to Kevin M. Murphy, the second-best economist it has been my privilege to know, and invited me to work with Kevin and him on an empirical test of their theory of rational addiction. That collaboration resulted in three coauthored papers, two of which are in part 4 of this volume.

My second-greatest debt is to Victor R. Fuchs. Although he was not my teacher at Columbia, he introduced me to the field of health economics shortly after he hired me as a research assistant at the National Bureau of Economic Research in June 1966. At the time, I had just finished all my coursework and exams at Columbia University; I was thinking about getting married; and I did not have much money. At the end of the summer, he said that I could continue to work for him half time and have office space to work on my dissertation if I wrote in the health economics field. That is how I became interested in the field;

until then I had no exposure to it. In retrospect, in 1966 an investment in health economics certainly paid me the best interest. After I finished my dissertation, Vic encouraged me to study the relationship between health and schooling in detail. That is the subject of the second part of this book.

The late Jacob Mincer provided me with profound insights concerning human capital theory in his two-semester course in labor economics and in the labor workshop that he organized with Gary Becker at Columbia. I have drawn on many of those insights in my work on health as a form of human capital.

I learned almost as much from my classmates at Columbia as I did from Gary and Jacob. They include Robert T. Michael, Linda N. Edwards, Isaac Ehrlich, Arleen A. Leibowitz, the late Gilbert R. Ghez, the late C. Michael Rahm, Carl J. Hemmer, and Peter Sperling. In addition to interactions as students, Linda Edwards and I collaborated on a project dealing with economic aspects of children's health in the late 1970s and early 1980s that resulted in five publications. One of them is included in part 2 of this book. Linda always impressed on me the value of rewriting manuscripts, a task that I still have difficulty undertaking.

I often refer to myself as a "child" of two institutions: the National Bureau of Economic Research and the PhD program in economics at the City University of New York Graduate Center. I have worked at the NBER since Vic Fuchs hired me as a research assistant in 1966 and have been a bureau research associate since 1970. I have taught at the Graduate Center since 1972. The nurturing environment at the bureau enabled me to increase my training and skills in economics after I received my PhD. It also provided a setting in which I could interact with colleagues with similar research interests and develop and fund research projects.

The PhD program in economics, like the other Graduate Center PhD programs, takes the form of a consortium involving the center and the CUNY senior (four-year) colleges. There are two types of faculty. My position as a central appointment means that I have tenure at the Graduate Center and do all my teaching at the PhD level. On the other hand, college-based faculty members have tenure or are on tenure-track lines at one of the CUNY colleges. Most, but not all, of their teaching is to undergraduates. With an enrollment of approximately eighty students per year in the forty-five years in which I have taught at the Graduate Center, its PhD program in economics certainly is not small. But in all these years, there have never been more than two additional central appointments. As a result, I have been involved in more than two hundred fifty completed dissertations, and have supervised more than one hundred of them. This has been a tremendously rewarding experience. It has forced me to keep on learning new material in economics. More important, many of my coauthors have been and continue to be my former students.

I have coauthored papers with twenty-eight of my former students. I cannot acknowledge all of them here, but I do want to acknowledge a few. Henry Saffer, Ted Joyce, and Bob Kaestner have been my collaborators for the longest periods of time. Henry was a student in the very first class that I taught at the Graduate Center—a class in mathematics for economists during the fall semester of 1972. I have been working with him on the economics of unhealthy behaviors since the mid-1980s, and two of our coauthored papers appear in part 4 of this book. I have known Ted since he took my course in microeconomics during the fall semester of 1981 and have worked with him on the relationship between health and schooling and on the determinants of infant health outcomes. One of our coauthored papers appears in part 2 of this book and two appear in part 3. I have known Bob since he took my course in microeconomics during the spring semester of 1985. Although none of our published papers are contained in this book, I refer to a number of his papers in the afterwords to parts 3 and 4. Henry, Ted, and Bob have ensured and continue to ensure that my education in economics never ends. They constantly encourage me (some would say demand me) to rethink conclusions that I have drawn from past studies, to consider new approaches to consumer behavior, and to employ new econometric techniques. I do not always agree with them, but our discussions are immensely enjoyable and extremely rewarding. Perhaps they have prevented an old economist from becoming a "has been," or at least slowed the depreciation on his stock of knowledge capital.

Of my other former students who have made major contributions to the papers in this volume and related research, I want to acknowledge and thank Steven Jacobowitz and especially Hope Corman for our work on infant health outcomes; Fred Goldman for our studies of community health centers and interest rates on tax-exempt hospital bonds; Douglas Coate and Eugene M. Lewit for our early research on unhealthy behaviors; Greg Colman, Inas Rashad Kelly, Dhaval Dave, H. Naci Mocan, Ismail Sirtalan, Jesse Margolis, and especially Sara Markowitz and Frank J. Chaloupka for our later research on the same subject; Neeraj Kaushal for our study of the relationship between health and schooling; and Avi Dor for our research on hospital surgery prices.

I am indebted to a former student who is not a coauthor: Alan C. Monheit. He was the first person to write a PhD dissertation under my supervision and then to pursue a career as a health economist with great success. As alumni of Far Rockaway High School, Alan and I share something else in common in addition to our field of specialization in economics.

I also want to acknowledge and thank a coauthor who is not my former student: Shin-Yi Chou. I induced her to collaborate with Henry Saffer, Inas Rashad Kelly, and me on economic aspects of obesity in the early 2000s. She returned that favor by arousing my interest in "all things Taiwan" a year or two later. Our collaboration resulted in four papers in this volume: one each in parts 2 and 3, and two in part 4. Her optimism and "upbeat" personality have always been an effective antidote to my pessimism and "downbeat" personality.

I am indebted to Björn Lindgren who has served as series coeditor with me of *Advances in Health Economics and Health Services Research* (published by JAI, an imprint of Elsevier Ltd. from 2005 through 2008; and published by Emerald Group Publishing Ltd. since that year). He and I organized a conference entitled *Substance Use: Individual Behavior, Social Interactions, Markets, and Politics* that was held in Lund University in Sweden in August 2004. Subsequently, we coedited a volume with that title and published it in 2005. In 2016, Björn and I joined Kristian Bolin, Robert Kaestner, Dorte Gyrd-Hansen, Tor Iversen, and Jody L. Sindelar in organizing a conference entitled *Human Capital and Health Behavior*, which was held in Gothenburg University in Sweden in May. We coedited a volume with that title in the "Advances" series published in 2017. The papers in both volumes are intimately related to many of the papers in this book, and my interactions with Björn as series coeditors have advanced my own research agenda. I owe a second debt to him because he arranged for me to spend the months of March, April, and May 2016 as a guest professor in the Child, Family and Reproductive Health Research Group at the Lund University Medical School. I wrote a good many of the introductions and afterwords to the four parts of this book while I was at Lund. In addition to Björn, Inger Hallström, the director of the research group, and her staff were extremely helpful to me and provided a pleasant atmosphere for me to work. I also am indebted to Kristian Bolin for arranging partial funding for my stay at Lund.

I am grateful to John Mullahy for organizing a joint session sponsored by the American Economic Association and the International Health Economics Association titled "The Demand for Health, 30 Years Later: What Do We Know? What Do We Need to Know?" for the January, 2003 Allied Social Science Association Meeting in Washington, DC. The papers given at that session were published in the July 2004 volume of the *Journal of Health Economics*. John's efforts helped to familiarize newer cohorts of health economists with my research on the demand for health and on the relationship between health and schooling. That body of work forms the basis of parts 1 and 2 of this book.

I cannot thank Bridget Flannery-McCoy, my editor at Columbia University Press, enough. Like Shin-Yi Chou, she has an optimistic and upbeat personality. For a pessimistic and downbeat author who was hesitant to propose the project, her enthusiasm for the book has been contagious. She made many fine comments on the introductions and afterwords and greatly improved the contents of these sections. I also want to thank Ryan Groendyk, Bridget's assistant, for the care in which he assembled the papers in the book and for his efforts in obtaining permissions to reprint the papers from the journals and books in which they originally appeared.

How can I ever thank Marinella Moscheni, the Business Manager of the NBER New York office and the only administrator in the office? The answer is that it is impossible for me to do so. She makes the office run, and I cannot imagine it without her. She solves all my computer problems, proofreads all my papers (including many that appear in this volume as well as the introductions and afterwords to each section), finds references and exact citations, sends files to me when I am out of the office, and ensures that everything is in working order. And she does all of this for the other fourteen members of the research staff as well as for me.

I must acknowledge and thank the agencies that provided grants to the NBER to fund most of the papers in this book. They include the National Institutes of Health, the National Science Foundation, the Agency for Healthcare Research and Quality and its predecessors, the Robert Wood Johnson Foundation, the Ford Foundation, and the Henry J. Kaiser Family Foundation.

Finally, I want to thank Ilene, my wife of fifty years as of September 11, 2016, for things that are impossible to enumerate in one paragraph. Given my last acknowledgment, let me begin by thanking her for supporting me in the manner to which I am accustomed to being supported for a long time. Ilene and I are a real-world example of the foundation of Gary Becker's theory of marriage: based on the theory of comparative advantage and with other factors held constant, it is optimal for a high-wage individual to marry one with a much lower wage. For many years, her earnings as designer and manager of computer systems in financial services far exceeded mine. That gave me the luxury to teach and pursue research that was not nearly as rewarding from a monetary standpoint but paid me a good deal of psychic income. More seriously, Ilene has supported me in everything I wanted to do, has always given me good advice, and has tolerated me, especially when my research was not going as well as I had hoped.

REFERENCES

Arrow, Kenneth J. 1963. "Uncertainty and the Welfare Economics of Medical Care." *American Economic Review* 53(5): 941–973.

Finkelstein, Amy, with Kenneth J. Arrow, Jonathan Gruber, Joseph P. Newhouse, and Joseph E. Stiglitz. 2015. *Moral Hazard in Health Insurance.* New York: Columbia University Press.

Grossman, Michael. 1972. *The Demand for Health: A Theoretical and Empirical Investigation.* New York: Columbia University Press for the National Bureau of Economic Research.

National Research Council, Institute of Medicine. 2015. *Measuring the Risks and Causes of Premature Death.* Washington, DC: National Academies Press.

Xu, Jiaquan, Sherry L. Murphy, Kenneth D. Kochanek, and Brigham A. Bastian. 2016. "Deaths: Final Data for 2013." *National Vital Statistics Report* 64(2). Hyattsville, MD: National Center for Health Statistics.

The Demand for Health: Theoretical
Underpinnings and Empirical Results

PART 1

Introduction to Part 1

In the fall of 1966, Gary S. Becker was a member of a National Bureau of Economic Research (NBER) staff reading committee that reviewed a paper titled "The Production of Health: An Exploratory Study," by Richard Auster, Irving Leveson, and Deborah Sarachek. Gary's main comment on the paper was that it ignored that what people demand when they purchase medical care services are not these services per se but rather good health. The latter item enters the utility functions of consumers, and medical care is only one of many inputs into its production. He proceeded to specify a demand function for health whose arguments included the prices of health inputs, the efficiency of the production process as reflected by the number of years of formal schooling completed by the consumer, and income or, more precisely, the exogenous components of income.

When Gary wrote his review, I had just entered my third year in the PhD program in economics at Columbia University. He was a professor of economics at that university as well as an NBER research associate. I had completed all the courses and examinations and was searching for a dissertation topic. I also was working as a research assistant to Victor R. Fuchs at the NBER. Victor had encouraged me to select a topic in health economics for my dissertation. I had consulted Gary about a topic, but he had not worked in health economics and did not have any suggestions. His review changed all that. After Gary finished it, he gave it to me and said that it contained an idea for a PhD dissertation. Originally, it was supposed to be a study of the effects of education on health, but along the way he encouraged (some might say demanded) me to broaden it into a theoretical and empirical analysis of the demand for health.

It is not surprising that Gary emphasized the difference between health as an output that enters the utility function and medical care as one of a number of inputs into its production in his review. After all, he had published his seminal paper titled "A Theory of the Allocation of Time" in the *Economic Journal* the previous year (Becker 1965). In that paper, he developed the household production function model of consumer behavior by drawing a distinction between fundamental objects of choice (called commodities) that enter the utility function and market goods and services. Consumers produce commodities with inputs of market goods and services and their own time. Because goods and services are inputs into the production of commodities, the demand for these goods and services is a derived demand for a factor of production. Although most of the applications in his paper pertain to extensions of labor supply theory, Gary could easily have titled it "The Household Production Approach to Consumer Behavior" or "On the New Theory of Consumer Behavior" because the applications extended far beyond labor supply. Indeed, he published a paper with the latter title in the *Swedish Journal of Economics* in 1973 (Michael and Becker 1973).

In my dissertation (Grossman 1970) and the publications that resulted from it (Grossman 1972a, 1972b), I use the household production function approach as one of two building blocks to construct a model of the demand for health. I assume that consumers demand health, defined broadly to include illness-free days in a given year and life expectancy, and produce it with inputs of medical care services, diet, other market goods and services, and their own time. Hence, the demand for medical care and other health inputs is derived from the basic demand for health.

My second building block, also due to Gary, is the theory of investment in human capital (for example, Becker 1964). Health, like knowledge, is a durable capital stock; and both may be viewed as components of the stock of human capital. Consumers have incentives to invest in this stock in the present because it increases their earnings in the future. Indeed, in his *Economic Journal* paper, Gary pointed out that investment in human capital is a prominent use of a portion of the time allocated to nonmarket or household production. I proceeded to pursue a distinction between the returns to an investment in knowledge and the returns to an investment in health that he suggested to me. To be specific, investments in knowledge raise wage rates and investments in health raise the total amount of time available for market and household production in a given year and prolong length of life.[1]

The first paper in this section contains most of the theory in my dissertation. It appeared in the 1972 volume of the *Journal of Political Economy* with the title "On the Concept of Health Capital and the Demand for Health." It is my first publication of original material and is my most widely cited one. In the paper, I first develop a general model of the demand for health, which contains both an investment motive and a consumption motive for increasing the stock of health. I then focus on a pure investment model in which the consumption benefits of health are small enough to be ignored. I do so to contrast health capital with other forms of human capital and because the pure investment model generates powerful predictions from simple analyses. Moreover, the consumption aspects of the demand for health can be incorporated into empirical estimation without much loss in generality.

The other paper in this section is my contribution to Volume 1A of the *Handbook of Health Economics*, published by Elsevier (Grossman 2000). I include it as a substitute for my 1972 monograph titled *The Demand for Health: A Theoretical and Empirical Investigation*, published by the NBER.[2] The monograph and the paper spell out the differences between a pure investment model of the demand for health and a pure consumption model in which the investment returns are small enough to be ignored. The paper also summarizes the main empirical results in the 1972 monograph. In addition, because the paper was published almost three decades after the monograph, some extensions of the theoretical and empirical work in the monograph and some criticisms of the framework as of the late 1990s are discussed.

I would be remiss if I did not indicate the fate of the paper by Auster, Leveson, and Sarachek that led Gary Becker to suggest the topic of my PhD dissertation to me. I am delighted to report that it was published in an early volume of the *Journal of Human Resources* (Auster, Leveson, and Sarachek 1969). The authors concluded that the rate of return to investing in health by increasing education far exceeded the rate of return to investment in health by increasing medical care. That conclusion was responsible, in part, for the subsequent literature that has investigated whether more schooling causes better health. That issue serves as the subject of part 2 of this book.

NOTES

1. In the introductions and afterwords to the first two parts of this book, I refer to forms of human capital other than health capital as knowledge capital, which is most commonly measured at the empirical level by completed years of formal schooling.

2. I am very pleased that Columbia University Press, which distributed the monograph for the NBER, is reissuing the monograph as a companion to this book.

REFERENCES

Auster, Richard, Irving Leveson, and Deborah Sarachek. 1969. "The Production of Health: An Exploratory Study." *Journal of Human Resources* 4(4): 411–436.

Becker, Gary S. 1964. *Human Capital*. New York: Columbia University Press for the National Bureau of Economic Research.

Becker, Gary S. 1965. "A Theory of the Allocation of Time." *The Economic Journal* 75(299): 493–517.

Grossman, Michael. 1970. "The Demand for Health: A Theoretical and Empirical Investigation." PhD Dissertation, New York: Columbia University.

——. 1972a. "On the Concept of Health Capital and the Demand for Health." *Journal of Political Economy* 80(2): 223–255.

——. 1972b. *The Demand for Health: A Theoretical and Empirical Investigation*. New York: Columbia University Press for the National Bureau of Economic Research.

——. 2000. "The Human Capital Model." In *Handbook of Health Economics*, Volume 1A, ed. Anthony J. Culyer and Joseph P. Newhouse. Amsterdam: Elsevier Science B.V., North-Holland Publishing, 347–408.

Michael, Robert T., and Gary S. Becker. 1973. "On the New Theory of Consumer Behavior." *Swedish Journal of Economics* 75(4): 378–396.

On the Concept of Health Capital and the Demand for Health

ONE

Michael Grossman

ABSTRACT

The aim of this study is to construct a model of the demand for the commodity "good health." The central proposition of the model is that health can be viewed as a durable capital stock that produces an output of healthy time. It is assumed that individuals inherit an initial stock of health that depreciates with age and can be increased by investment. In this framework, the "shadow price" of health depends on many other variables besides the price of medical care. It is shown that the shadow price rises with age if the rate of depreciation on the stock of health rises over the life cycle and falls with education if more educated people are more efficient producers of health. Of particular importance is the conclusion that, under certain conditions, an increase in the shadow price may simultaneously reduce the quantity of health demanded and increase the quantity of medical care demanded.

1. INTRODUCTION

During the past two decades, the notion that individuals invest in themselves has become widely accepted in economics. At a conceptual level, increases in a person's stock of knowledge or human capital are assumed to raise his productivity in the market sector of the economy, where he produces money earnings, and in the nonmarket or household sector, where he produces commodities that enter his utility function. To realize potential gains in productivity, individuals have an incentive to invest in formal schooling or on-the-job training. The costs of these investments include direct outlays on market goods and the opportunity cost of the time that must be withdrawn from competing uses. This framework has been used by Gary Becker (1967) and by Yoram Ben-Porath (1967) to develop models that determine the optimal quantity of investment in human capital at any age. In addition, these models show how the optimal quantity varies over the life cycle of an individual and among individuals of the same age.

Although several writers have suggested that health can be viewed as one form of human capital (Mushkin 1962, 129–149; Becker 1964, 33–36; Fuchs 1966, 90–91), no one has constructed a model of the demand for health capital itself. If increases in the stock of health simply increased wage rates, such a task would not be necessary, for one could simply apply Becker's and Ben-Porath's models to study the decision to invest in health. This paper argues, however, that health capital differs from other forms of human capital. In particular, it argues that a person's stock of knowledge affects his market and nonmarket productivity, while his stock of health determines the total amount of time he can spend producing money earnings and commodities. The fundamental difference between the two types of capital is the basic justification for the model of the demand for health that is presented in the paper.

A second justification for the model is that most students of medical economics have long realized that what consumers demand when they purchase medical services are not these services per se, but "good health." Given that the basic demand is for good health, it seems logical to study the demand for medical care by first constructing a model of the demand for health itself. Since, however, traditional demand theory assumes that goods and services purchased in the market enter consumers' utility functions, economists have emphasized the demand for medical care at the expense of the demand for health. Fortunately, a new approach to consumer behavior draws a sharp distinction between fundamental objects of choice—called "commodities"—and market goods (Becker 1965; Lancaster 1966; Muth 1966; Michael 1972; Becker and Michael 1970; Ghez 1970). Thus, it serves as the point of departure for my health model. In this approach, consumers *produce* commodities with inputs of market goods and their own time. For example, they use traveling time and transportation services to produce visits; part of their Sundays and church services to produce "peace of mind"; and their own time, books, and teachers' services to produce additions to knowledge. Since goods and services are inputs into the production of commodities, the demand for these goods and services is a derived demand.

Within the new framework for examining consumer behavior, it is assumed that individuals inherit an initial stock of health that depreciates over time—at an increasing rate, at least after some stage in the life cycle—and can be increased by investment. Death occurs when the stock falls below a certain level, and one of the novel features of the model is that individuals "choose" their length of life. Gross investments in health capital are produced by household production functions whose direct inputs include the own time of the consumer and market goods such as medical care, diet, exercise, recreation, and housing. The production function also depends on certain "environmental variables," the most important of which is the level of education of the producer that influence the efficiency of the production process.

It should be realized that in this model the level of health of an individual is *not* exogenous but depends, at least in part, on the resources allocated to its production. Health is demanded by consumers for two reasons. As a consumption commodity, it directly enters their preference functions, or, put differently, sick days are a source of disutility. As an investment commodity, it determines the total amount of time available for market and nonmarket activities. In other words, an increase in the stock of health reduces the time lost from these activities, and the monetary value of this reduction is an index of the return to an investment in health.

Since the most fundamental law in economics is the law of the downward-sloping demand curve, the quantity of health demanded should be negatively correlated with its shadow price. The analysis in this paper stresses that the shadow price of health depends on many other variables besides the price of medical care. Shifts in these variables alter the optimal amount of health and also alter the derived demand for gross investment, measured, say, by medical expenditures. It is shown that the shadow price rises with age if the rate of depreciation on the stock of health rises over the life cycle and falls with education if more educated people are more efficient producers of health. Of particular importance is the conclusion that, under certain conditions, an increase in the shadow price may simultaneously reduce the quantity of health demanded and increase the quantity of medical care demanded.

2. A STOCK APPROACH TO THE DEMAND FOR HEALTH

2.1. The Model

Let the intertemporal utility function of a typical consumer be

$$U = U(\phi_0 H_0, \ldots, \phi_n H_n, Z_0, \ldots, Z_n), \tag{1}$$

where H_0 is the inherited stock of health, H_i is the stock of health in the ith time period, ϕ_i is the service flow per unit stock, $h_i = \phi_i H_i$ is total consumption of "health services," and Z_i is total consumption of another commodity in the ith period.[1] Note that, whereas in the usual intertemporal utility function n, the length of life as of the planning date is fixed, here it is an endogenous variable. In particular, death takes place when $H_i = H_{\min}$. Therefore, length of life depends on the quantities of H_i that maximize utility subject to certain production and resource constraints that are now outlined.

By definition, net investment in the stock of health equals gross investment minus depreciation:

$$H_{i+1} - H_i = I_i - \delta_i H_i, \tag{2}$$

where I_i is gross investment and δ_i is the rate of depreciation during the ith period. The rates of depreciation are assumed to be exogenous, but they may vary with the age of the individual.[2] Consumers produce gross investments in health and the other commodities in the utility function according to a set of household production functions:

$$\begin{aligned} I_i &= I_i(M_i, TH_i; E_i), \\ Z_i &= Z_i(X_i, T_i; E_i). \end{aligned} \tag{3}$$

In these equations, M_i is medical care, X_i is the goods input in the production of the commodity Z_i, TH_i and T_i are time inputs, and E_i is the stock of human capital.[3] It is assumed that a shift in human capital changes the efficiency of the production process in the nonmarket sector of the economy, just as a shift in technology changes the efficiency of the production process in the market sector. The implications of this treatment of human capital are explored in section 4 of this chapter.

It is also assumed that all production functions are homogeneous of degree 1 in the goods and time inputs. Therefore, the gross investment production function can be written as

$$I_i = M_{ig}(t_i; E_i), \tag{4}$$

where $t_i = TH_i/M_i$. It follows that the marginal products of time and medical care in the production of gross investment in health are

$$\frac{\partial I_i}{\partial TH_i} = \frac{\partial g}{\partial t_i} = g',$$

$$\frac{\partial I_i}{\partial M_i} = g - t_i g'.$$

$$(5)$$

From the point of view of the individual, both market goods and own time are scarce resources. The goods budget constraint equates the present value of outlays on goods to the present value of earnings income over the life cycle plus depreciation, initial assets (discounted property income):[4]

$$\sum \frac{P_i M_i + V_i X_i}{(1+r)^i} = \sum \frac{W_i TW_i}{(1+r)^i} + A_0.$$

$$(6)$$

Here P_i and V_i are the prices of M_i and X_i, W_i is the wage rate, TW_i is hours of work, A_0 is discounted property income, and r is the interest rate. The time constraint requires that Ω, the total amount of time available in any period, must be exhausted by all possible uses:

$$TW_i + TL_i + TH_i + T_i = \Omega,$$

$$(7)$$

where TL_i is time lost from market and nonmarket activities due to illness or injury.

Equation (7) modifies the time budget constraint in Becker's time model (Becker 1965). If sick time were not added to market and nonmarket time, total time would *not* be exhausted by all possible uses. My model assumes that TL_i is inversely related to the stock of health; that is, $\partial TL_i/\partial H_i < 0$. If Ω were measured in days ($\Omega = 365$ days if the year is the relevant period) and if ϕ_i were defined as the flow of healthy days per unit of H_i, h_i would equal the total number of healthy days in a given year.[5] Then one could write

$$TL_i = \Omega - h_i.$$

$$(8)$$

It is important to draw a sharp distinction between sick time and the time input in the gross investment function. As an illustration of this difference, the time a consumer allocates to visiting his doctor for periodic checkups is obviously not sick time. More formally, if the rate of depreciation were held constant, an increase in TH_i would increase I_i and H_{i+1} and would reduce TL_{i+1}. Thus, TH_i and TL_{i+1} would be negatively correlated.[6]

By substituting for TW_i from equation (7) into equation (6), one obtains the single "full wealth" constraint:

$$\sum \frac{P_i M_i + V_i X_i + W_i(TL_i + TH_i + T_i)}{(1+r)^i} = \sum \frac{W_i \Omega}{(1+r)^i} + A_0 = R. \qquad (9)$$

According to equation (9), full wealth equals initial assets plus the present value of the earnings an individual would obtain if he spent all of his time at work. Part of this wealth is spent on market goods, part of it is spent on nonmarket production time, and part of it is lost due to illness. The equilibrium quantities of H_i and Z_i can now be found by maximizing the utility function given by equation (1) subject to the constraints given by equations (2), (3), and (9).[7] Since the inherited stock of health and the rates of depreciation are given, the optimal quantities of gross investment determine the optimal quantities of health capital.

2.2. Equilibrium Conditions

First-order optimality conditions for gross investment in period $i - 1$ are[8]

$$\frac{\pi_{i-1}}{(1+r)^{i-1}} = \frac{W_i G_i}{(1+r)^i} + \frac{(1-\delta_i)W_{i+1}G_{i+1}}{(1+r)^{i+1}} + \cdots$$

$$+ \frac{(1-\delta_i)\cdots(1-\delta_{n-1})W_n G_n}{(1+r)^n}$$

$$+ \frac{Uh_i}{\lambda}G_i + \cdots + (1-\delta_i)\cdots(1-\delta_{n-1})\frac{Uh_n}{\lambda}G_n; \qquad (10)$$

$$\pi_{i-1} = \frac{P_{i-1}}{g - t_{i-1}g'} = \frac{W_{i-1}}{g'} \qquad (11)$$

The new symbols in these equations are $Uh_i = \partial U/\partial h_i =$ the marginal utility of healthy days; $\lambda =$ the marginal utility of wealth; $G_i = \partial h_i/\partial H_i = -(\partial TL_i/\partial H_i) =$ the marginal product of the stock of health in the production of healthy days; and $\pi_{i-1} =$ the marginal cost of gross investment in health in period $i - 1$.

Equation (10) simply states that the present value of the marginal cost of gross investment in period $i - 1$ must equal the present value of marginal benefits. Discounted marginal benefits at age i equal

$$G_i\left[\frac{W_i}{(1+r)^i} + \frac{Uh_i}{\lambda}\right],$$

where G_i is the marginal product of health capital—the increase in the number of healthy days caused by a one-unit increase in the stock of health. Two monetary magnitudes are necessary to convert this marginal product into value terms, because consumers desire health for two reasons. The discounted wage rate measures the monetary value of a one-unit increase in the total amount of time available for market and nonmarket activities, and the term Uh_i/λ measures the discounted monetary equivalent of the increase in utility due to a one-unit increase in healthy time. Thus, the sum of these two terms measures the discounted marginal value to consumers of the output produced by health capital.

While equation (10) determines the optimal amount of gross investment in period $i - 1$, equation (11) shows the condition for minimizing the cost of producing a given quantity of gross investment. Total cost is minimized when the increase in gross investment from spending an additional dollar on medical care equals the increase in gross investment from spending an additional dollar on time. Since the gross investment production function is homogeneous of degree 1 and since the prices of medical care and time are independent of the level of these inputs, the average cost of gross investment is constant and equal to the marginal cost.

To examine the forces that affect the demand for health and gross investment, it is useful to convert equation (10) into a slightly different form. If gross investment in period i is positive, then

$$\frac{\pi_i}{(1+r)^i} = \frac{W_{i+1}G_{i+1}}{(1+r)^{i+1}} + \frac{(1-\delta_{i+1})W_{i+2}G_{i+2}}{(1+r)^{i+2}} + \cdots$$

$$\frac{(1-\delta_{i+1})\cdots(1-\delta_{n-1})W_nG_n}{(1+r)^n} + \frac{Uh_{i+1}G_{i+1}}{\lambda} + \cdots$$

$$+ (1-\delta_{i+1})\cdots(1-\delta_{n-1})\frac{Uh_nG_n}{\lambda}. \qquad (12)$$

From (10) and (12),

$$\frac{\pi_{i-1}}{(1+r)^{i-1}} = \frac{W_iG_i}{(1+r)^i} + \frac{Uh_iG_i}{\lambda} + \frac{(1-\delta_i)\pi_i}{(1+r)^i}.$$

Therefore,

$$G_i\left[W_i + \left(\frac{Uh_i}{\lambda}\right)(1+r)^i\right] = \pi_{i-1}(r - \tilde{\pi}_{i-1} + \delta_i), \qquad (13)$$

where $\tilde{\pi}_{i-1}$ is the percentage rate of change in marginal cost between period $i - 1$ and period i.[9] Equation (13) implies that the undiscounted value of the marginal product of the optimal stock of health capital at any moment in time must equal the supply price of capital, $\pi_{i-1}(r - \tilde{\pi}_{i-1} + \delta_i)$. The latter contains interest, depreciation, and capital gains components and may be interpreted as the rental price or user cost of health capital.

Condition (13) fully determines the demand for capital goods that can be bought and sold in a perfect market. In such a market, if firms or households acquire one unit of stock in period $i - 1$ at price π_{i-1}, they can sell $(1 - \delta_i)$ units at price π_i at the end of period i. Consequently, $\pi_{i-1}(r - \tilde{\pi}_{i-1} + \delta_i)$ measures the cost of holding one unit of capital for one period. The transaction just described allows individuals to raise their capital in period i *alone* by one unit and is clearly feasible for stocks like automobiles, houses, refrigerators, and producer durables. It suggests that one can define a set of single-period flow equilibria for stocks that last for many periods.

In my model, the stock of health capital cannot be sold in the capital market, just as the stock of knowledge cannot be sold. This means that gross investment must be nonnegative. Although sales of health capital are ruled out, provided gross investment is positive, there exists a used cost of capital that in equilibrium must equal the value of the marginal product of the stock.[10] An intuitive interpretation of this result is that exchanges over time in the stock of health by an individual substitute for exchanges in the capital market. Suppose a consumer desires to increase his stock of health by one unit in period i. Then he must increase gross investment in period $i - 1$ by one unit. If he simultaneously reduces gross investment in period i by $(1 - \delta_i)$ units, then he has engaged in a transaction that raises H_i and H_i *alone* by one unit. Put differently, he has essentially rented one unit of capital from himself for one period. The magnitude of the reduction in I_i is smaller the greater the rate of depreciation, and its dollar value is larger the greater the rate of increase in marginal cost over time. Thus, the depreciation and capital gains components are as relevant to the user cost of health as they are to the user cost of any other durable. Of course, the interest component of user cost is easy to interpret, for if one desires to increase his stock of health rather than his stock of some other asset by one unit in a given period, $r\pi_{i-1}$ measures the interest payment he forgoes.[11]

A slightly different form of equation (13) emerges if both sides are divided by the marginal cost of gross investment:

$$\gamma_i + a_i = r - \tilde{\pi}_{i-1} + \delta_i. \tag{13'}$$

Here $\gamma_i = (W_i G_i)/\pi_{i-1}$ is the marginal monetary rate of return on an investment in health and

$$a_i = \left[\frac{\left(\dfrac{Uh_i}{\lambda} \right)(1+r)^i G_i}{\pi_{i-1}} \right]$$

is the psychic rate of return. In equilibrium, the total rate of return on an investment in health must equal the user cost of health capital in terms of the price of gross investment. The latter variable is defined as the sum of the real-own rate of interest and the rate of depreciation.

2.3. The Pure Investment Model

It is clear that the number of sick days and the number of healthy days are complements; their sum equals the constant length of the period. From equation (8), the marginal utility of sick time is $-Uh_i$. Thus, by putting healthy days in the utility function, one implicitly assumes that sick days yield *disutility*. If healthy days did not enter the utility function directly, the marginal monetary rate of return on an investment in health would equal the cost of health capital, and health would be solely an investment commodity.[12] In formalizing the model, I have been reluctant to treat health as pure investment because many observers believe the demand for it has both investment and consumption aspects (see, for example, Mushkin 1962, 131; Fuchs 1966, 86). But to simplify the remainder of the theoretical analysis and to contrast health capital with other forms of human capital, the consumption aspects of demand are ignored from now on.[13]

If the marginal utility of healthy days or the marginal disutility of sick days were equal to zero, condition (13') for the optimal amount of health capital in period i would reduce to

$$\frac{W_i G_i}{\pi_{i-1}} = \gamma_i = r - \tilde{\pi}_{i-1} + \delta_i. \tag{14}$$

Equation (14) can be derived explicitly by excluding health from the utility function and by redefining the full wealth constraint as[14]

$$R' = A_0 + \sum \frac{W_i h_i - \pi_i I_i}{(1+r)^i}. \tag{15}$$

Maximization of R' with respect to gross investment in periods $i - 1$ and i yields

$$\frac{\pi_{i-1}}{(1+r)^{i-1}} = \frac{W_iG_i}{(1+r)^i} + \frac{(1-\delta_i)W_{i+1}G_{i+1}}{(1+r)^{i+1}}$$
$$+ \cdots + \frac{(1-\delta_i)\cdots(1-\delta_{n-1})W_nG_n}{(1+r)^n}, \tag{16}$$

$$\frac{\pi_i}{(1+r)^i} = \frac{W_{i+1}G_{i+1}}{(1+r)^{i+1}} + \frac{(1-\delta_{i+1})W_{i+2}G_{i+2}}{(1+r)^{i+2}}$$
$$+ \cdots + \frac{(1-\delta_{i+1})\cdots(1-\delta_{n-1})W_nG_n}{(1+r)^n}. \tag{17}$$

These two equations imply that equation (14) must hold.

Figure 1.1 illustrates the determinations of the optimal stock of health capital at any age i. The demand curve MEC shows the relationship between the stock of health and the rate of return on an investment or the marginal efficiency of health capital, γ_i. The supply curve S shows the relationship between the stock of health and the cost of capital, $r - \tilde{\pi}_{i-1} + \delta_i$. Since the cost of capital is independent of the stock, the supply curve is infinitely elastic. Provided the MEC schedule slopes downward, the equilibrium stock is given by $H_i{}^*$, where the supply and demand curves intersect.

In the model, the wage rate and the marginal cost of gross investment do not depend on the stock of health. Therefore, the MEC schedule would be negatively inclined if and only if G_i, the marginal product of health capital, were diminishing. Since the output produced by health capital has a finite upper limit

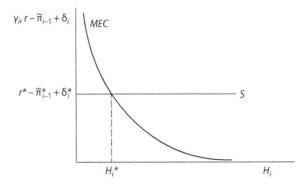

Figure 1.1

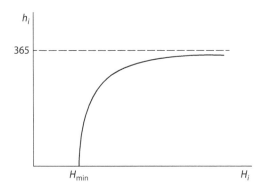

Figure 1.2

of 365 healthy days, it seems reasonable to assume diminishing marginal productivity. Figure 1.2 shows a plausible relationship between the stock of health and the number of healthy days. This relationship may be called the "production function of healthy days." The slope of the curve in the figure at any point gives the marginal product of health capital. The number of healthy days equals zero at the death stock H_{min}, so that $\Omega = TL_i = 365$ is an alternative definition of death. Beyond H_{min}, healthy time increases at a decreasing rate and eventually approaches its upper asymptote of 365 days as the stock becomes large.

In sections 3 and 4, later in this chapter, equation (14) and figure 1.1 are used to trace out the lifetime path of health capital and gross investment, to explore the effects of variations in depreciation rates, and to examine the impact of changes in the marginal cost of gross investment. Before I turn to these matters, some comments on the general properties of the model are in order. It should be realized that equation (14) breaks down whenever desired gross investment equals zero. In this situation, the present value of the marginal cost of gross investment would exceed the present value of marginal benefits for all positive quantities of gross investment, and equations (16) and (17) would be replaced by inequalities.[15] The remainder of the discussion rules out zero gross investment by assumption, but the conclusions reached would have to be modified if this were not the case. One justification for this assumption is that it is observed empirically that most individuals make positive outlays on medical care throughout their life cycles.

Some persons have argued that, since gross investment in health cannot be nonnegative, equilibrium condition (14) should be derived by using the optimal control techniques developed by Pontryagin and others. Kenneth Arrow (1968) employs these techniques to analyze a firm's demand for nonsalable physical capital. Since, however, gross investment in health is rarely equal to zero in the real world, the methods I use—discrete time maximization in the text and the calculus of variations in the Mathematical Appendix—are quite adequate. Some advantages of my methods are that they are simple, easy to interpret, and familiar to most economists. In addition, they generate essentially the same equilibrium condition as the Pontryagin method. Both Arrow and I conclude that, if desired gross investment were positive, then the marginal efficiency of nonsalable capital would equal the cost of capital. On the other hand, given zero gross investment, the cost of capital would exceed its marginal efficiency.

The monetary returns to an investment in health differ from the returns to investments in education, on-the-job training, and other forms of human capital, since the latter investments raise wage rates.[16] Of course, the amount of health capital might influence the wage rate, but it necessarily influences the time lost from all activities due to illness or injury. To emphasize the novelty of my approach, I assume that health is not a determinant of the wage rate. Put differently, a person's stock of knowledge affects his market and nonmarket productivity, while his stock of health determines the total amount of time he can spend producing money earnings and commodities. Since both market time and nonmarket time are relevant, even individuals who are not in the labor force have an incentive to invest in their health. For such individuals, the marginal product of health capital would be converted into a dollar equivalent by multiplying by the monetary value of the marginal utility of time.

Since there are constant returns to scale in the production of gross investment and since input prices are given, the marginal cost of gross investment and its percentage rate of change over the life cycle are exogenous variables. In other words, these two variables are independent of the rate of investment and the stock of health. This implies that consumers reach their desired stock of capital immediately. It also implies that the stock rather than gross investment is the basic decision variable in the model. By this I mean that consumers respond to changes in the cost of capital by altering the marginal product of health capital and not the marginal cost of gross investment. Therefore, even though equation (14) is not independent of equations (16) and (17), it can be used to determine the optimal path of health capital and, by implication, the optimal path of gross investment.[17]

Indeed, the major differences between my health model and the human capital models of Becker (1967) and Ben-Porath (1967) are the assumptions made about the behavior of the marginal product of capital and the marginal cost of gross investment. Both Becker and Ben-Porath assume that any one person owns only a small amount of the total stock of human capital in the economy. Therefore, the marginal product of his stock is constant. To rule out solutions in which the desired stock of capital is either zero or infinite, they postulate that the marginal cost of producing gross additions to the stock is positively related to the rate of gross investment. Since marginal cost rises, the desired stock of human capital is not reached immediately. Moreover, since the marginal product of capital is constant, gross investment is the basic decision variable in these models.[18] In my model, on the other hand, the marginal product of health capital falls because the output produced by this capital has a finite upper limit. Consequently, it is not necessary to introduce the assumption of rising marginal cost in order to determine the optimal stock.

To illustrate how the implications of the health and human capital models differ, suppose the rate of depreciation on either the stock of health or the stock of human capital rises. This upsets the equality between the cost of capital and its marginal efficiency. To restore this equality in the health model, the marginal product of health capital must rise, which would occur only if the stock of capital declines. To restore this equality in the human capital model, marginal cost must fall, which is possible only if gross investment declines.[19]

3. LIFE CYCLE VARIATIONS IN DEPRECIATION RATES

Equation (14) enables one to study the behavior of the demand for health and gross investment over the life cycle. To simplify the analysis, it is assumed that the wage rate, the stock of knowledge, the marginal cost of gross investment, and the marginal productivity of health capital are independent of age. These assumptions are not as restrictive as they may seem. To be sure, wage rates and human capital are undoubtedly correlated with age, but the effects of shifts in these variables are treated in section 4 of this chapter. Therefore, the results obtained in this section may be viewed as partial effects. That is, they show the impact of a pure increase in age on the demand for health, with all other variables held constant.

Since marginal cost does not depend on age, $\tilde{\pi}_{i-1} = 0$, and equation (14) reduce to

$$\gamma_i = r + \delta_i. \tag{18}$$

It is apparent from equation (18) that, if the rate of depreciation were independent of age, a single quantity of H would satisfy the equality between the marginal rate of return and the cost of health capital. Consequently, there would be no net investment or disinvestment after the initial period. One could not, in general, compare H_0 and H_1 because accumulation in the initial period would depend on the discrepancy between the inherited stock and the stock desired in period 1. This discrepancy in turn would be related to variations in H_0 and other variables across individuals. But, given zero costs of adjusting to the desired level immediately, H would be constant after period 1. Under the stated condition of a constant depreciation rate, individuals would choose an infinite life if they choose to live beyond period 1. In other words, if $H_1 > H_{min}$, then H_i would always exceed the death stock.[20]

To permit the demand for health to vary with age, suppose the rate of depreciation depends on age. In general, any time path of δ_i is possible. For example, the rate of depreciation might be negatively correlated with age during the early stages of the life cycle. Again, the time path might be nonmonotonic, so that δ_i rises during some periods and falls during others. Despite the existence of a wide variety of possible time paths, it is extremely plausible to assume that δ_i is positively correlated with age after some point in the life cycle. This correlation can be inferred because, as an individual ages, his physical strength and memory capacity deteriorate. Surely, a rise in the rate of depreciation on his stock of health is merely one manifestation of the biological process of aging. Therefore, the analysis focuses on the effects of an increase in the rate of depreciation with age.

Since a rise in δ_i causes the supply curve of health capital to shift upward, it would reduce the quantity of health capital demanded over the life cycle. Graphically, an increase in the cost of capital from $r + \delta_i$ to $r + \delta_{i+1}$ in figure 1.3 reduces the optimal stock from H_i to H_{i+1}. The greater the elasticity of the MEC schedule, the greater the decrease in the optimal stock with age. Put differently, the slower the increase in the marginal product of health capital as H falls, the greater the decrease in the optimal stock.

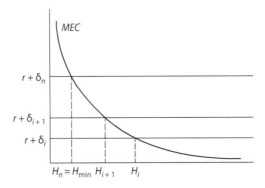

Figure 1.3

Differentiation of equation (18) with respect to age quantifies the percentage rate of decrease in the stock of health over the life cycle:

$$\tilde{H}_i = -s_i \varepsilon_i \tilde{\delta}_i. \tag{19}$$

In this equation, the tilde notation denotes a percentage time derivative ($\tilde{H}_i = (dH_i/di)(1/H_i)$, etc.), and the new symbols are $s_i = \delta_i/r + \delta_i =$ the share of depreciation in the cost of health capital and

$$\varepsilon_i = -\frac{\partial \ln H_i}{\partial \ln (r + \delta_i)} = -\frac{\partial \ln H_i}{\partial \ln \gamma_i} = -\frac{\partial \ln H_i}{\partial \ln G_i}$$

the elasticity of the *MEC* schedule (ln stands for natural logarithm).[21] Equation (19) indicates that the absolute value of the percentage decrease in H is positively related to the elasticity of the *MEC* schedule, the share of depreciation in the cost of health capital, and the percentage rate of increase in the rate of depreciation. If ε_i and $\tilde{\delta}_i$ were constant, the curve relating $\ln H_i$ to age would be concave unless $r = 0$, since[22]

$$\frac{d\tilde{H}_i}{di} = \tilde{H}_{ii} = -s_i(1 - s_i)\varepsilon\delta^2 < 0. \tag{20}$$

The absolute value of $\tilde{H}_i$ increases over the life cycle because depreciation's share in the cost of capital rises with age.

If δ_i grows continuously with age after some point in the life cycle, persons would choose to live a finite life. Since H declines over the life cycle, it would eventually fall to H_{min}, the death stock. When the cost of health capital is $r + \delta_n$ in figure 1.3, $H_n = H_{min}$, and death occurs. At death, no time is available for market and nonmarket activities, since healthy time equals zero. Therefore, the monetary equivalent of sick time in period n would completely exhaust potential full earnings, $W_n\Omega$. Moreover, consumption of the commodity Z_n would equal zero, since no time would be available for its production if total time equals sick time.[23] Because individuals could not produce commodities, total utility would be driven to zero at death.[24]

Having characterized the optimal path of H_i one can proceed to examine the behavior of gross investment. Gross investment's life cycle profile would not, in general, simply mirror that of health capital. In other words, even though health capital falls over the life cycle, gross investment might increase, remain constant, or decrease. This follows because a rise in the rate of depreciation not only reduces the amount of health capital *demanded* by consumers but also reduces the amount of capital *supplied* to them by a given amount of gross investment. If the change in supply exceeded the change in demand, individuals would have an incentive to close this gap by increasing gross investment. On the other hand, if the change in supply were less than the change in demand, gross investment would tend to fall over the life cycle.

To predict the effect of an increase in δ_i with age on gross investment, note that the net investment can be approximated by $H_i \tilde{H}_i$.[25] Since gross investment equals net investment plus depreciation,

$$\ln I_i = \ln H_i + \ln (\tilde{H}_i + \delta_i). \tag{21}$$

Differentiation of equation (21) with respect to age yields

$$\tilde{I}_i = \frac{\tilde{H}_i^2 + \delta_i \tilde{H}_i + \tilde{H}_{ii} + \delta_i \tilde{\delta}_i}{\tilde{H}_i + \delta_i}$$

Suppose $\tilde{\delta}_i$ and ε_i were constant. Then from equations (19) and (20), the expression for $\tilde{I}_i$ would simplify to

$$\tilde{I}_i = \frac{\tilde{\delta}(1 - s_i \varepsilon)(\delta_i - s_i \varepsilon \tilde{\delta}) + s_i^2 \varepsilon \tilde{\delta}^2}{\delta_i - s_i \varepsilon \tilde{\delta}}. \tag{22}$$

Since health capital cannot be sold, gross investment cannot be negative. Therefore, $\delta_i \geq -\tilde{H}_i$.[26] That is, if the stock of health falls over the life cycle, the absolute value of the percentage rate of net disinvestment cannot exceed the rate of depreciation. Provided gross investment does not equal zero, the term $\delta_i - s_i \varepsilon \tilde{\delta}$ in equation (22) must exceed zero. It follows that a sufficient condition for gross investment to be positively correlated with the depreciation rate is $\varepsilon < 1/s_i$. Thus, $\tilde{I}_i$ would definitely be positive at every point if $\varepsilon < 1$.

The important conclusion is reached that, if the elasticity of the *MEC* schedule were less than 1, gross investment and the depreciation rate would be positively correlated over the life cycle, while gross investment and the stock of health would be negatively correlated. Phrased differently, given a relatively inelastic demand curve for health, individuals would desire to offset *part* of the reduction in health capital caused by an increase in the rate of depreciation by increasing their gross investments. In fact, the relationship between the stock of health and the number of healthy days suggests that ε is smaller than 1. A general equation for the healthy-days production function illustrated by figure 1.2 is

$$h_i = 365 - BH_i^{-c}, \tag{23}$$

where B and C are positive constants. The corresponding *MEC* schedule is[27]

$$\ln \gamma_i = \ln BC - (C + 1) \ln H_i + \ln H_i + \ln W - \ln \pi. \tag{24}$$

The elasticity of this schedule is given by

$$\varepsilon = -\frac{\partial \ln H_i}{\partial \ln \gamma_i} = \frac{1}{(1+C)} < 1,$$

since $C > 0$.

Observe that with the depreciation rate held constant, increases in gross investment would increase the stock of health and the number of healthy days. But the preceding discussion indicates that, because the depreciation rate rises with age, it is not unlikely that unhealthy (old) people will make larger gross investments than healthy (young) people. This means that sick time, TL_i will be positively correlated with M_i and TH_i, the medical care and own time inputs in the gross investment function, over the life cycle.[28] In this sense, at least part of TL_i or TH_i may be termed "recuperation time."

Unlike other models of the demand for medical care, my model does not *assert* that "need" or illness, measured by the level of the rate of depreciation, will definitely be positively correlated with utilization of medical services. Instead, it derives this correlation from the magnitude of the elasticity of the *MEC* schedule and indicates that the relationship between the stock of health and the number of healthy days will tend to create a positive correlation. If ε is less than 1, medical care and "need" will definitely be positively correlated. Moreover, the smaller the value of ε, the greater the explanatory power of "need" relative to that of the other variables in the demand curve for medical care.

It should be realized that the power of this model of life cycle behavior is that it can treat the biological process of aging in terms of conventional economic analysis. Biological factors associated with aging raise the price of health capital and cause individuals to substitute away from future health until death is "chosen." It can be concluded that here, as elsewhere in economics, people reject a prospect—the prospect of longer life in this case—because it is too costly to achieve. In particular, only if the elasticity of the *MEC* schedule were zero would individuals fully compensate for the increase in δ_i and, therefore, maintain a constant stock of health.

4. MARKET AND NONMARKET EFFICIENCY

Persons who face the same cost of health capital would demand the same amount of health only if the determinants of the rate of return on an investment were held constant. Changes in the value of the marginal product of health capital and the marginal cost of gross investment shift the *MEC* schedule and, therefore, alter the quantity of health demanded even if the supply curve of capital does not change. I now identify the variables that determine the level of the *MEC* schedule and examine the effects of shifts in these variables on the demand for health and medical care. In particular, I consider the effects of variations in market efficiency, measured by the wage rate, and nonmarket efficiency, measured by human capital, on the *MEC* schedule.

Before beginning the analysis, two preliminary comments are in order. First, the discussion pertains to uniform shifts in variables that influence the rate of return across persons of the same age. That is, if the variable X_i is one determinant, then

$$\frac{d \ln X_i}{d \ln X_{i-1}} = 1, \text{ all } i.$$

Second, the discussion proceeds under the assumption that the real rate of interest, the rate of depreciation, and the elasticity of the *MEC* schedule are constant. These two comments imply that an increase in X_i will alter the amount of capital demanded but will not alter its rate of change over the life cycle.[29] Note from equation (21):

$$\frac{d \ln I}{dX} = \frac{d \ln H}{dX} \tag{25}$$

since the rate of depreciation and the percentage rate of net investment do not depend on X.[30] Equation (25) indicates that percentage changes in health and gross investment for a one-unit change in X are identical. Consequently, the effect of an increase in X on either of these two variables can be treated interchangeably.

4.1. Wage Effects

Since the value of the marginal product of health capital equals WG, an increase in the wage rate, W, raises the monetary equivalent of the marginal product of a given stock. Put differently, the higher a person's wage rate, the greater the value to him of an increase in healthy time. A consumer's wage rate measures his market efficiency or the rate at which he can convert hours of work into money earnings. Hence, it is obviously positively correlated with the benefits of a reduction in the time he loses from the production of money earnings due to illness. Moreover, a high wage rate induces an individual to substitute market goods for his own time in the production of commodities. This substitution continues until in equilibrium the monetary value of the marginal product of consumption time equals the wage rate. So the benefits from a reduction in time lost from nonmarket production are also positively correlated with the wage.

If an upward shift in the wage rate had no effect on the marginal cost of gross investment, a 1 percent increase in it would increase the rate of return, γ, associated with a fixed stock of capital by 1 percent. In fact, this is not the case because own time is an input in the gross investment function. If K is the fraction of the total cost of gross investment accounted for by time, then a 1 percent rise in W would increase marginal cost, π, by K percent. After one nets out the correlation between W and π, the percentage growth in γ would equal $1 - K$, which exceeds zero as long as gross investment is not produced entirely by time.

Since the wage rate and the level of the MEC schedule are positively correlated, the demand for health would be positively related to W. Graphically, an upward shift in W from W_1 to W_2 in figure 1.4 shifts the MEC schedule from MEC_1 to MEC_2 and, with no change in the cost of health capital, increases the optimal stock from H_1 to H_2. A formula for the wage elasticity of health capital is[31]

$$e_{H,W} = (1 - K)\varepsilon. \tag{26}$$

This elasticity is larger the larger the elasticity of the MEC schedule and the larger the share of medical care in total gross investment cost.

Although the wage rate and the demand for health or gross investment are positively related, W has no effect on the amount of gross investment supplied by a given input of medical care. Therefore, the demand for medical care would rise with the wage. If medical care and own time were employed in fixed proportions in the gross investment production function, the wage elasticity of M

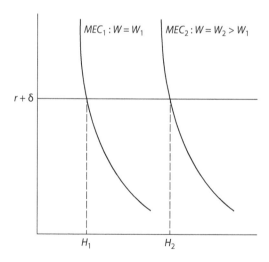

Figure 1.4

would equal the wage elasticity of H. On the other hand, given a positive elasticity of substitution, M would increase more rapidly than H. This follows because consumers would have an incentive to substitute medical care for their relatively more expensive own time. A formula for the wage elasticity of medical care is

$$e_{M,W} = K\sigma_p + (1 - K)\varepsilon, \qquad (27)$$

where σ_p is the elasticity of substitution between M and Th in the production of gross investment.[32] The greater the value of σ_p, the greater the difference between the wage elasticities of M and H.

Note that an increase in the price of either medical care or own time raises the marginal or average cost of gross investment. But the effects of changes in these two input prices are not symmetrical. In particular, an upward shift in the price of medical care lowers the *MEC* schedule and causes the demand for health to decline. This difference arises because the price of time influences the value of the marginal product of health capital while the price of medical care does not.

4.2. The Role of Human Capital

Up to now, no systematic allowance has been made for variations in the efficiency of nonmarket production. Yet it is known that firms in the market sector of an economy obtain varying amounts of output from the same vector of direct inputs. These differences have been traced to forces like technology and entrepreneurial capacity, forces that shift production functions or that alter the environment in which firms operate. Reasoning by analogy, one can say that certain environmental variables influence productivity in the nonmarket sector by altering the marginal products of the direct inputs in household production functions. This study is particularly concerned with environmental variables that can be associated with a particular person—his or her race, sex, stock of human capital, etc. While the analysis that follows could pertain to any environmental variable, it is well documented that the more educated are more efficient producers of money earnings. Consequently, it is assumed that shifts in human capital, measured by education, change productivity in the household as well as in the market, and the analysis focuses on this environmental variable.

The specific proposition to be examined is that education improves nonmarket productivity. If this were true, then one would have a convenient way to analyze and quantify what have been termed the nonmonetary benefits to an investment in education. The model can, however, treat adverse as well as beneficial effects and suggests empirical tests to discriminate between the two.[33]

To determine the effects of education on production, marginal cost, and the demand for health and medical care, recall that the gross investment production function is homogeneous of degree 1 in its two direct inputs—medical care and own time. It follows that the marginal product of E, the index of human capital, would be

$$\frac{\partial I}{\partial E} = M\frac{\partial(g - tg')}{\partial E} + TH\frac{\partial g'}{\partial E},$$

where $g - tg'$ is the marginal product of medical care and g' is the marginal product of time.[34] If a circumflex over a variable denotes a percentage change per unit change in E, the last equation can be rewritten as

$$r_H = \frac{\partial I}{\partial E}\frac{1}{I} = \left[\frac{M(g - tg')}{I}\right]\left(\frac{g\hat{g} - tg'\hat{g}'}{g - tg'}\right) + \left(\frac{THg'}{I}\right)(\hat{g}). \qquad (28)$$

Equation (28) indicates that the percentage change in gross investment supplied to a consumer by a one-unit change in E is a weighted average of the percentage changes in the marginal products of M and TH.[35]

If E increases productivity, then $r_H > 0$. Provided E raises both marginal products by the same percentage, equation (28) would simplify to

$$r_H = \hat{g} = \hat{g}'. \qquad (29)$$

In this case, education would have a "neutral" impact on the marginal products of all factors. The rest of the discussion assumes "factor neutrality."

Because education raises the marginal product of the direct inputs, it reduces the quantity of these inputs required to produce a given amount of gross investment. Hence, with no change in input prices, an increase in E lowers average or marginal cost. In fact, one easily shows that

$$\hat{\pi} = -r_H = -\hat{g} = -\hat{g}', \qquad (30)$$

where $\hat{\pi}$ is the percentage change in average or marginal cost.[36] So, if education increases the marginal products of medical care and own time by 3 percent, it would reduce the price of gross investment by 3 percent.

Suppose education does in fact raise productivity so that π and E are negatively correlated. Then, with the wage rate and the marginal product of a given stock of health held constant, an increase in education would raise the marginal efficiency of health capital and shift the *MEC* schedule to the right.[37] In figure 1.5, an increase in E from E_1 to E_2 shifts the *MEC* curve from

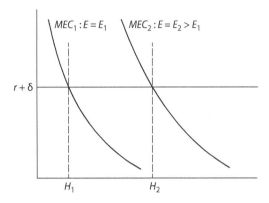

Figure 1.5

MEC_1 to MEC_2. If the cost of capital were independent of E, there would be no change in the supply curve, and the more educated would demand a larger optimal stock (compare H_1 and H_2 in figure 1.5).

The percentage increase in the amount of health demanded for a one-unit increase in E is given by[38]

$$\hat{H} = r_H \varepsilon. \tag{31}$$

Since r_H indicates the percentage increase in gross investment supplied by a one-unit increase in E, shifts in this variable would not alter the demand for medical care or own time if r_H equaled $\hat{H}$. For example, a person with ten years of formal schooling might demand 3 percent more health than a person with nine years. If the medical care and own time inputs were held constant, the former individual's one extra year of schooling might supply him with 3 percent more health. Given this condition, both persons would demand the same amounts of M and TH. As this example illustrates, any effect of a change in E on the demand for medical care or time reflects a positive or negative difference between $\hat{H}$ and r_H:[39]

$$\hat{M} = T\hat{H} = r_H (\varepsilon - 1). \tag{32}$$

Equation (32) suggests that, if the elasticity of the MEC schedule were less than unity, the more educated would demand more health but less medical care. Put differently, they would have an incentive to offset *part* of the increase in health caused by an increase in education by reducing their purchases of medical services. Note that if r_H were negative and ε were less than 1, H would be negative and M would be positive. Since education improves market productivity, I have examined the implications of the hypothesis that r_H is positive.

But the model is applicable whether r_H is positive or negative and gives empirical predictions in either case.

5. SUMMARY AND CONCLUSIONS

The main purpose of this paper has been to construct a model of the demand for the commodity "good health." The central proposition of the model is that health can be viewed as a durable capital stock that produces an output of healthy time. A person determines his optimal stock of health capital at any age by equating the marginal efficiency of this capital to its user cost in terms of the price of gross investment. Graphically, each person has a negatively inclined demand curve for health capital, which relates the marginal efficiency of capital to the stock, and an infinitely elastic supply curve. The equilibrium stock is determined by the intersection of these two functions. The demand curve slopes downward due to diminishing marginal productivity of health capital.

Although in recent years there have been a number of extremely interesting explorations of the forces associated with health differentials (Adelman 1963; Fuchs 1965; Larmore 1967; Newhouse 1968; Auster, Leveson, and Sarachek 1969), these studies have not developed behavioral models that can predict the effects that are in fact observed. Consequently, the framework I have developed is important because of its ability to bridge the existing gap between theory and empiricism in the analysis of health differentials. My model explains variations in both health and medical care among persons in terms of variations in supply and demand curves for health capital. This paper has traced upward shifts in the supply curve to increases in the rate of depreciation on the stock of health with age, and it has traced upward shifts in the demand curve to increases in the wage rate and education.

One prediction of the model is that if the rate of depreciation increases with age, at least after some point in the life cycle, then the quantity of health capital demanded would decline over the life cycle. At the same time, provided the elasticity of the marginal efficiency of capital schedule were less than unity, expenditures on medical care would rise with age. A second prediction is that a consumer's demand for health and medical care should be positively correlated with his wage rate. A third prediction is that if education increases the efficiency with which gross investments in health are produced, then the more educated would demand a larger optimal stock of health. On the other hand, given a relatively inelastic demand curve, the correlation between medical outlays and education would be negative. It should be noted that one of the advantages of the model is that it enables one to study the effects of demographic variables like age and education without assuming that these variables are positively or negatively correlated with consumers' "tastes" for health. Instead, these variables enter the analysis through their impact on either the cost of health capital or its marginal efficiency, and one can make strong predictions concerning their effects on health levels or medical care.

It must be admitted that this paper has made a number of simplifying assumptions, all of which should be relaxed in future work. A more general model would treat the depreciation rate as an endogenous variable and would not rule out periods in which the optimal amount of gross investment is zero. Most important of all, it would modify the assumption that consumers fully anticipate intertemporal variations in depreciation rates and, therefore, know their age of death with certainty. Since in the real world length of life is surely not known with perfect foresight, it might be postulated that a given consumer faces a probability distribution of depreciation rates in each period. This uncertainty would give persons an incentive to protect themselves against the "losses" associated with higher than average depreciation rates by purchasing various types of insurance and perhaps by holding an "excess" stock of health.[40] But whatever modifications are made, it would be a mistake to neglect the essential features of the model I have presented in this paper. Any model must recognize that health is a durable capital stock, that health capital differs in important respects from other forms of human capital, and that the demand for medical care must be derived from the more fundamental demand for "good health."

Appendix A

MATHEMATICAL APPENDIX

A1. Utility Maximization—Discrete Time

To maximize utility subject to the full wealth and production function constraints, form the Lagrangian expression

$$L = U(\phi_0 H_0, \dots, \phi_0 H_n, Z_0, \dots, Z_n)$$

$$+ \lambda \left(R - \sum_i \frac{C_i + C_{1i} + W_i TL_i}{(1 + r)^i} \right), \tag{A1}$$

where $C_i = P_i M_i + W_i TH_i$ and $C_{1i} = V_i X_i + W_i T_i$. Differentiating L with respect to gross investment in period $i - 1$ and setting the partial derivative equal to zero, one obtains

$$Uh_i \frac{\partial h_i}{\partial H_i} \frac{\partial H_i}{\partial I_{i-1}} + Uh_{i+1} \frac{\partial h_{i+1}}{\partial H_{i+1}} \frac{\partial H_{i+1}}{\partial I_{i-1}}$$

$$+ \ldots + Uh_n \frac{\partial h_n}{\partial H_n} \frac{\partial H_n}{\partial I_{i-1}} = \lambda \left[\frac{(dC_{i-1}/dI_{i-1})}{(1+r)^{i-1}} \right.$$

$$+ \frac{W_i(\partial TL_i/\partial H_i)/(\partial H_i/\partial I_{i-1})}{(1+r)^i}$$

$$+ \frac{W_{i+1}(\partial TL_{i+1}/\partial H_{i+1})/(\partial H_{i+1}/\partial I_{i-1})}{(1+r)^{i+1}}$$

$$+ \ldots + \left. \frac{W_n(\partial TL_n/\partial H_n)/(\partial H_n/\partial I_{i-1})}{(1+r)^n} \right].$$

(A2)

But

$$\frac{\partial h_i}{\partial H_i} = G_i, \quad \frac{\partial H_i}{\partial I_{i-1}} = 1, \quad \frac{\partial H_{i+1}}{\partial I_{i-1}} = (1 - \delta_i), \quad \frac{\partial H_n}{\partial I_{i-1}}$$

$$= (1 - \delta_i) \ldots (1 - \delta_{n-1}), \quad \frac{dC_{i-1}}{dI_{i-1}} = \pi_{i-1}, \text{ and } \frac{\partial TL_i}{\partial H_i} = -G_i.$$

Therefore,

$$\frac{\pi_{i-1}}{(1+r)^{i-1}} = \frac{W_i G_i}{(1+r)^i} + \frac{(1 - \delta_i)W_{i+1}G_{i+1}}{(1+r)^{i+1}}$$

$$+ \ldots + \frac{(1 - \delta_i) \ldots (1 - \delta_{n-1})W_n G_n}{(1+r)^n} + \frac{Uh_i}{\lambda} G_i$$

$$+ (1 - \delta_i) \frac{Uh_{i+1}}{\lambda} G_{i+1} + \ldots + (1 - \delta_i) \ldots (1 - \delta_{n-1}) \frac{Uh_n}{\lambda} G_n.$$

(A3)

A2. Utility Maximization—Continuous Time

Let the utility function be

$$U = \int m_i f(\phi_i H_i, Z_i) di,$$

(A4)

where m_i is the weight attached to utility in period i. Equation (A4) defines an additive utility function, but any monotonic transformation of this function could be employed.[41] Let all household production functions be homogeneous of degree 1. Then $C_i = \pi_i I_i$, $C_{1i} = q_i Z_i$,[42] and full wealth can be written as

$$R = \int e^{-ri}(\pi_i I_i + q_i Z_i + W_i TL_i)\,di. \tag{A5}$$

By definition,

$$I_i = \dot{H}_i + \delta_i H_i, \tag{A6}$$

where H_i is the instantaneous rate of change of capital stock. Substitution of equation (A6) into equation (A5) yields

$$R = \int e^{-ri}(\pi_i \delta_i H_i + \pi_i \dot{H}_i + q_i Z_i + W_i TL_i)\,di. \tag{A7}$$

To maximize the utility function, form the Lagrangian

$$L - \lambda R = \int \big[m_i f(\phi_i H_i, Z_i) - \lambda e^{-ri}\big(\pi_i \delta_i H_i$$
$$+ \pi_i \dot{H}_i + q_i Z_i + W_i TL_i)\big]\,di, \tag{A8}$$

or

$$L - \lambda R = \int Q(H_i, \dot{H}_i, Z_i, i)\,di, \tag{A9}$$

where

$$Q = m_i f(\phi_i H_i, Z_i) - \lambda e^{-ri}(\pi_i \delta_i H_i + \pi_i \dot{H}_i + q_i Z_i + W_i T_i L). \tag{A10}$$

Euler's equation for the optimal path of H_i is

$$\frac{\partial Q}{\partial H_i} = \frac{d}{di}\frac{\partial Q}{\partial \dot{H}_i}. \tag{A11}$$

In the present context,

$$\frac{\partial Q}{\partial H_i} = Uh_i G_i - \lambda e^{-ri}\pi_i \delta_i + \lambda e^{-ri} W_i G_i,$$
$$\frac{\partial Q}{\partial \dot{H}_i} = -\lambda e^{-ri}\pi_i, \tag{A12}$$
$$\frac{d}{di}\frac{\partial Q}{\partial H_i} = -\lambda e^{-ri}\dot{\pi}_i + \lambda e^{-ri} r\pi_i.$$

Consequently,

$$G_i\left[W_i + \left(\frac{Uh_i}{\lambda}\right)e^{ri}\right] = \pi_i(r - \tilde{\pi}_i + \delta_i), \tag{A13}$$

which is the continuous time analogue of equation (13).

A3. Wage Effects

To obtain the wage elasticities of medical care and the time spent producing health, three equations must be partially differentiated with respect to the wage. These equations are the gross investment production function and the two first-order conditions for cost minimization:

$$I(M, TH; E) = Mg(t; E) = (\tilde{H} + \delta)H,$$
$$W = \pi g',$$
$$P = \pi(g - tg').$$

Since I is linear homogenous in M and TH,

$$\frac{\partial(g - tg')}{\partial M} = -\frac{t\partial(g - tg')}{\partial TH},$$

$$\frac{\partial g'}{\partial TH} = -\frac{1}{t}\frac{\partial(g - tg')}{\partial TH},$$

$$\sigma_p = \frac{(g - tg')g'}{I\{[\partial(g - tg')]/\partial TH}.$$

Therefore, the following relationships hold:

$$\frac{\partial(g - tg')}{\partial M} = -\frac{t(g - tg')g'}{I\sigma_p},$$

$$\frac{\partial g'}{\partial TH} = -\frac{1}{t}\frac{(g - tg')g'}{I\sigma_p}, \qquad (A14)$$

$$\frac{\partial(g - tg')}{\partial TH} - \frac{(g - tg')g'}{Iq_p}.$$

Carrying out the differentiation, one gets

$$g'\frac{dTH}{dW} + (g - tg')\frac{dM}{dW} = -\frac{H(\tilde{H} + \delta)\varepsilon}{\pi}\left(\frac{d\pi}{dW} - \frac{\pi}{W}\right),$$

$$1 = g'\frac{d\pi}{dW} + \pi\left(\frac{\partial g'}{\partial TH}\frac{dTH}{dW} + \frac{\partial g'}{\partial M}\frac{dM}{dW}\right),$$

$$0 = (g - tg')\frac{d\pi}{dW} + \pi\left[\frac{\partial(g - tg')}{\partial TH}\frac{dTH}{dW} + \frac{\partial(g - tg')}{\partial M}\frac{dM}{dW}\right].$$

Using the cost-minimization conditions and equation (A14) and rearranging terms, one has

$$I\varepsilon\frac{d\pi}{dW} + W\frac{dTH}{dW} + p\frac{dM}{dW} = \frac{I\varepsilon\pi}{W},$$

$$I\sigma_p\frac{d\pi}{dW} - \frac{1}{t}p\frac{dTH}{dW} + p\frac{dM}{dW} = I\frac{\pi}{W}\sigma_p,$$

$$I\sigma_p\frac{d\pi}{dW} + W\frac{dTH}{dW} - tW\frac{dM}{dW} = 0.$$

(A15)

Since equation (A15) is a system of three equations in three unknowns—
dTH/dW, dM/dW, and dπ /dW—Cramer's rule can be applied to solve for, say,
dM/dW:

$$\frac{dM}{dW} = \frac{\begin{vmatrix} I\varepsilon + W & +\dfrac{I\varepsilon\pi}{W} \\[2ex] I\sigma_p - \left(\dfrac{1}{t}\right)P + I\left(\dfrac{\pi}{W}\right)\sigma_p \\[2ex] I\sigma_p + W & -0 \end{vmatrix}}{\begin{vmatrix} I\varepsilon + W & +P \\[2ex] I\sigma_p - \left(\dfrac{1}{t}\right)P + P \\[2ex] I\sigma_p + W & -tW \end{vmatrix}}.$$

The determinant in the denominator reduces to $(I\sigma_p\pi^2 I^2)/THM$. The determinant
in the numerator is

$$\frac{I\sigma_p}{THM}\left(I\pi\sigma_p THM + I\pi\varepsilon\frac{P}{W}M^2\right).$$

Therefore,

$$\frac{dM}{dW} = \frac{THM}{I\pi}\left(\sigma_p + \frac{\varepsilon PM}{WTH}\right).$$

In elasticity notation, this becomes

$$e_{M,W} = (1-K)\varepsilon + K\sigma_p.$$

(A16)

Along similar lines, one easily shows that

$$e_{TH,W} = (1-K)(\varepsilon - \sigma_p).$$

(A17)

A4. The Role of Human Capital

To convert the change in productivity due to a shift in human capital into a change in average or marginal cost, let the percentage changes in the marginal products of medical care and own time for a one-unit change in human capital be given by

$$\frac{\partial(g - tg')}{\partial E} \frac{1}{g - tg'} = \frac{g\hat{g} - tg'\hat{g}'}{g - tg'},$$

$$\frac{\partial g'}{\partial E} \frac{1}{g'} = \hat{g}'.$$

If a shift in human capital were "factor neutral," the percentage changes in these two marginal products would be equal:

$$\hat{g} = \frac{g\hat{g} - tg'\hat{g}'}{g - tg'},$$

or

$$\hat{g}' = \hat{g} = r_H. \tag{A18}$$

The average cost of gross investment in health is defined as

$$\bar{\pi} = (PM + WTH)I^{-1} = (P + Wt)g^{-1}.$$

Given factor neutrality,

$$\frac{d\bar{\pi}}{dE} \frac{1}{\pi} = -\hat{g} = -r_H. \tag{A19}$$

This coincides with the percentage change in marginal cost, since

$$\pi = P(g - tg')^{-1},$$

and

$$\frac{d\pi}{dE} \frac{1}{\pi} = -\left(\frac{g\hat{g} - tg'\hat{g}'}{g - tg'}\right) = -\hat{g}' = -\hat{g} = -r_H. \tag{A20}$$

Section 4.2 outlines a derivation of the human capital parameter in the demand curve for medical care but does not give a rigorous proof. Taking the *total* derivative of E in the gross investment function, one computes this parameter, thus:

$$\frac{dI}{dE}\frac{1}{I} = M\frac{(g - tg')}{I}M + \frac{THg'}{I}TH + r_H.$$

Since $\hat{M} = \widehat{TH}$ and $\hat{H} = \hat{I}$, the last equation can be rewritten as

$$\hat{H} = \hat{M} + r_H.$$

Solving for $\hat{M}$ and noting that $\hat{H} = r_H\varepsilon$, one gets

$$\hat{M} = r_H(\varepsilon - 1). \tag{A21}$$

Appendix B

GLOSSARY OF MATHEMATICAL TERMS

n	Total length of life
i	Age
H_0	Inherited stock of health
H_i	Stock of health in period i
H_{min}	Death stock
ϕ_i	Service flow per unit stock or number of healthy days per unit stock
h_i	Total number of healthy days in period i
Z_i	Consumption of an aggregate commodity in period i
I_i	Gross investment in health
δ_i	Rate of depreciation
M_i	Medical care
TH_i	Time input in gross investment function
X_i	Goods input in the production of Z_i
T_i	Time input in the production of Z_i
E_i	Stock of human capital
$g - t_i g'$	Marginal product of medical care in the gross investment production function
g'	Marginal product of time
P_i	Price of medical care
V_i	Price of X_i
W_i	Wage rate
A_0	Initial assets
r	Rate of interest

TW_i	Hours of work
TL_i	Sick time
Ω	Constant length of the period
R	Full wealth
G_i	Marginal product of health capital
Uh_i	Marginal utility of healthy days
λ	Marginal utility of wealth
π_i	Marginal cost of gross investment in health
$\tilde{\pi}_i$	Percentage rate of change of marginal cost
γ_i	Monetary rate of return on an investment in health or marginal efficiency of health capital
a_i	Psychic rate of return on an investment in health
$\tilde{v}$	A tilde over a variable denotes a percentage time derivative
s_i	Share of depreciation in the cost of health capital
ε	Elasticity of the *MEC* schedule
K	Fraction of the total cost of gross investment accounted for by time
σ_p	Elasticity of substitution between medical care and own time in the production of gross investment
$e_{H,W}$	Elasticity of H with regard to W
$e_{M,W}$	Elasticity of M with regard to W
$\hat{v}$	A circumflex over a variable denotes a percentage change per unit change in E
r_H	Percentage change in gross investment for a one-unit change in E
C_i	Total cost of gross investment in health in period i
C_{1i}	Total cost of Z_i
m_i	Weight attached to total utility in period i
q_i	Marginal cost of Z_i

NOTES

Originally published as Michael Grossman, "On the Concept of Health Capital and the Demand for Health," *Journal of Political Economy* 80, no. 2 (1972): 223–255. This paper is based on part of my Columbia University PhD dissertation, "The Demand for Health: A Theoretical and Empirical Investigation," which was published by the National Bureau of Economic Research (Grossman 1970, 1972). My research at the Bureau was supported by the Commonwealth Fund and the National Center for Health Services Research and Development (PHS research grant 2 P 01 HS 00451-04). Most of this paper was written while I was at the University of Chicago's Center for Health Administration Studies, with research support from the National Center for Health Services Research and Development (PHS grant HS 00080). A preliminary version of this paper was presented at the Second World Congress of the Econometric Society. I am grateful to Gary S. Becker, V. K. Chetty, Victor R. Fuchs, Gilbert R. Ghez, Robert T. Michael, and Jacob Mincer for their helpful comments on earlier drafts.

1. The commodity Z_i may be viewed as an aggregate of all commodities besides health that enter the utility function in period i. For the convenience of the reader, a glossary of symbols may be found in Appendix B.

2. In a more complicated version of the model, the rate of depreciation might be a negative function of the stock of health. The analysis is considerably simplified by treating this rate as exogenous, and the conclusions reached would tend to hold even if it were endogenous.

3. In general, medical care is not the only market good in the gross investment function, for inputs such as housing, diet, recreation, cigarette smoking, and alcohol consumption influence one's level of health. Since these inputs also produce other commodities in the utility function, joint production occurs in the household. For an analysis of this phenomenon, see Grossman (1970, chap. 6). To emphasize the key aspects of my health model, I treat medical care as the most important market good in the gross investment function in the present paper.

4. The sums throughout this study are taken from $i = 0$ to n.

5. If the stock of health yielded other services besides healthy days, φ_i would be a vector of service flows. This study emphasizes the service flow of healthy days because this flow can be measured empirically.

6. For a discussion of conditions that would produce a positive correlation between TH_i and TL_{i+1}, see section 3.

7. In addition, the constraint is imposed that $H_n \leq H_{\min}$.

8. Note that an increase in gross investment in period $i - 1$ increases the stock of health in all future periods. These increases are equal to

$$\frac{\partial H_i}{\partial I_{i-1}} = 1, \quad \frac{\partial H_{i+1}}{\partial I_{i-1}} = (1 - \delta_i), \dots, \frac{\partial H_n}{\partial I_{i-1}}$$
$$= (1 - \delta_i)(1 - \delta_{i+1}) \dots (1 - \delta_{n-1}).$$

For a derivation of equation (10), see Part A of the Mathematical Appendix.

9. Equation (13) assumes $\delta_i \tilde{\pi}_{i-1} \doteq 0$.

10. For similar conclusions with regard to nonsalable physical capital and with regard to a nonsalable stock of "goodwill" produced by advertising, see Arrow (1968) and Nerlove and Arrow (1962).

11. In a continuous time model, the user cost of health capital can be derived in one step. If continuous time is employed, the term $\delta_i \tilde{\pi}_{i-1}$ does not appear in the user cost formula. The right-hand side of (13) becomes $\pi_i (r - \tilde{\pi}_i + \delta_i)$, where $\tilde{\pi}_i$ is the instantaneous percentage rate of change of marginal cost at age i. For a proof, see section A2.

12. To avoid confusion, a note on terminology is in order. If health were entirely an *investment commodity,* it would yield monetary, but not utility, returns. Regardless of whether

health is investment, consumption, or a mixture of the two, one can speak of a *gross investment function* since the commodity in question is a durable.

13. Elsewhere, I have used a pure consumption model to interpret the set of phenomena that are analyzed in sections 3 and 4. In the pure consumption model, the marginal monetary rate of return on an investment in health is set equal to zero (see Grossman 1970, chap. 3).

14. Since the gross investment production function is homogeneous of the first degree, $P_i M_i + W_i TH_i = \pi_i I_i$.

15. Formally, $\gamma_i \leq r - \tilde{\pi}_{i-1} + \delta_i$, if $I_{i-1} = I_i = 0$.

16. This difference is emphasized by Mushkin (1962, 132–33).

17. This statement is subject to the modification that the optimal path of capital must always imply nonnegative gross investment.

18. For a complete discussion of these points, see Becker (1967, 5–12) and Ben-Porath (1967, 353–61). For models of the demand for physical capital by firms in which the marginal cost of investment and the amount of investment are positively correlated, see, for example, Eisner and Strotz (1963) and Gould (1968).

19. Section 3 demonstrates that an increase in the rate of depreciation on health capital might cause gross investment to increase.

20. The possibility that death can occur in period 1 is ruled out from now on.

21. From equation (18), $\ln (r + \delta_i) = \ln W + \ln G_i - \ln \pi$. Therefore,

$$\frac{\delta_i \tilde{\delta}_i}{r + \delta_i} = \frac{\partial \ln G_i}{\partial \ln H_i} \tilde{H}_i,$$

or

$$s_i \tilde{\delta}_i = -\frac{\tilde{H}_i}{\varepsilon_i}.$$

22. Differentiation of equation (19) with respect to age yields

$$H_{ii} = \frac{\varepsilon \tilde{\delta}[(r + \delta_i)\delta_i \tilde{\delta} - \delta_i(\delta_i \tilde{\delta})]}{(r + \delta_i)^2},$$

or

$$\tilde{H}_{ii} = -\frac{\delta_i r \varepsilon \tilde{\delta}^2}{(r + \delta_i)^2} = -s_i(1 - s_i)\varepsilon \tilde{\delta}^2.$$

23. The statement assumes that Z_i cannot be produced with X_i alone. This would be true if, say, the production function were Cobb-Douglas.

24. Utility would equal zero when $H = H_{\min}$ provided the death time utility function is such that $U(0) = 0$.

25. That is,

$$H_{i+1} - H_i = H_i \frac{dH_i}{di} \frac{1}{H_i} = H_i \tilde{H}_i.$$

The use of this approximation essentially allows one to ignore the one-period lag between a change in gross investment and a change in the stock of health.

26. Gross investment is nonnegative as long as $I_i = H_i(\tilde{H} + \delta_i) \geq 0$, or $\delta_i \geq -\tilde{H}_i$.

27. If equation (23) were the production function, the marginal product of health capital would be

$$G_i = BCH_i^{-C-1},$$

or

$$\ln G^i = \ln BC - (C+1)\ln H_i.$$

Since $\ln \gamma_i = \ln G_i + \ln W - \ln \pi$, one uses the equation for $\ln G_i$ to obtain equation (24).

28. Note that the time path of H_i or h_i would be nonmonotonic if the time path of δ_i were characterized by the occurrence of peaks and troughs. In particular, h_i would be relatively low and TH_i and M_i would be relatively high (if $\varepsilon < 1$) when δ_i was relatively high; these periods would be associated with relatively severe illness.

29. Strictly speaking, shifts in X_i would definitely have no effects on $\tilde{H}_i$ if and only if $\tilde{X}_i = 0$. Even though a uniform shift in X_i implies that there is no correlation between its level and rate of change, $\tilde{H}_i$ *might* be altered if $\tilde{X}_i \neq 0$. For a complete discussion of this point, see Grossman (1970, p. 49).

30. Since the analysis in this section deals with variations in X among individuals of the same age, time subscripts are omitted from now on. Note also that equation (25), like the expression for I_i, ignores the one-period lag between an increase in gross investment and an increase in the stock of health.

31. Differentiation of the natural logarithm of equation (18) with respect to ln W yields

$$\frac{d\ln(r+\delta)}{d\ln W} = 0 = 1 + \frac{\partial \ln G}{\partial \ln H}\frac{d\ln H}{d\ln W} - \frac{d\ln \pi}{d\ln W}$$

$$0 = 1 - K - \frac{e_{H,W}}{\varepsilon}.$$

32. For a proof, see section A3 of the Mathematical Appendix. The corresponding equation for the wage elasticity of the own time input is

$$e_{TH,W} = (1 - K)\left(\varepsilon - \sigma_p\right).$$

This elasticity is positive only if $\varepsilon > \sigma_p$.

33. The model developed here is somewhat similar to the one used by Michael (1969).

34. If I is homogeneous of degree 1 in M and TH, then from Euler's theorem

$$I = M(g - tg') + THg'.$$

Differentiation of this equation with respect to E, holding M and TH constant, yields the marginal product of human capital.

35. Instead of putting education in the gross investment production function, one could let it affect the rate of depreciation or the marginal productivity of health capital. This approach has not been taken because a general treatment of environmental variables like education must permit these variables to influence all household commodities. Since depreciation rates and stock-flow relationships are relevant only if a particular commodity is durable, a symmetrical development of the role of environmental variables requires

that they affect household production functions and not depreciation rates or stock-flow relationships. In a more complicated version of the model, the gross investment function, the rate of depreciation, and the marginal productivity of health capital might all depend on education. But the basic implications of the model would not change.

36. For a proof, see "The role of human capital" in the Mathematical Appendix, where the human capital formulas are developed in more detail.

37. It should be stressed that the model of nonmarket productivity variations presented here examines the *partial* effect of an increase in education with the wage rate held constant. Although these two variables are surely positively correlated, this correlation does not appear to be large enough to prevent one from isolating pure changes in nonmarket productivity at the empirical level. For some evidence on this point, see Grossman (1970, chap. 5) and Michael (1972, chaps. 4 and 5).

38. If W and $r + \delta$ are fixed and if G depends only on H, then

$$\frac{d \ln (r+\delta)}{dE} = 0 = \frac{\partial \ln G}{\partial \ln H} \frac{d \ln H}{dE} - \frac{d \ln \pi}{dE},$$

or

$$0 = -\frac{\hat{H}}{\varepsilon} + r_H.$$

39. The terms M and TH are equal because, by the definition of factor neutrality, E has no effect on the ratio of the marginal product of M to the marginal product of TH.

40. For an attempt to introduce uncertainty into a model that views health as a durable capital stock, see Phelps (1973).

41. Strotz (1955–56) has shown, however, that certain restrictions must be placed on m_i. In particular, the initial consumption plan will be fulfilled if and only if $m_i = (m_0)i$.

42. The variable q_i equals the marginal cost of Z_i.

REFERENCES

Adelman, Irma. 1963. "An Econometric Analysis of Population Growth." *American Economic Review* 53 (June): 314–349.

Arrow, Kenneth J. 1968. "Optimal Capital Policy with Irreversible Investment." In *Value, Capital and Growth: Papers in Honour of Sir John Hicks,* ed. J. N. Wolfe. Edinburgh: Edinburgh Univ. Press.

Auster, Richard D., Irving Leveson, and Deborah Sarachek. 1969. "The Production of Health: An Exploratory Study." *J. Human Resources* 4 (Fall): 411–436.

Becker, Gary S. 1964. *Human Capital.* New York: Columbia Univ. Press (for Nat. Bur. Econ. Res.).

——. 1965. "A Theory of the Allocation of Time." *Econ. J.* 75 (September): 493–517.

——. 1967. *Human Capital and the Personal Distribution of Income: An Analytical Approach.* W. S. Woytinsky Lecture no. 1. Ann Arbor: Univ. Michigan.

Becker, Gary S., and Robert T. Michael. 1970. "On the Theory of Consumer Demand." Unpublished paper.

Ben-Porath, Yoram. 1967. "The Production of Human Capital and the Life Cycle of Earnings." *J.P.E.* 75 (August): 353–367.

Eisner, Robert, and Robert H. Strotz. 1963. "Determinants of Business Investment." In *Impacts of Monetary Policy*. Englewood Cliffs, N.J.: Prentice-Hall (for Commission on Money and Credit).

Fuchs, Victor R. 1965. "Some Economic Aspects of Mortality in the United States." Mimeographed. New York: Nat. Bur. Econ. Res.

——. 1966. "The Contribution of Health Services to the American Economy." *Milbank Memorial Fund Q.* 44 (October): 65–102.

Ghez, Gilbert R. 1970. "A Theory of Life Cycle Consumption." PhD dissertation, Columbia Univ.

Gould, John P. 1968. "Adjustment Costs in the Theory of Investment in the Firm." *Rev. Econ. Studies* 25 (January): 47–55.

Grossman, Michael. 1970. "The Demand for Health: A Theoretical and Empirical Investigation." PhD dissertation, Columbia Univ.

Grossman, Michael. 1972. *The Demand for Health: A Theoretical and Empirical Investigation.* New York: Columbia Univ. Press (for *Nat. Bur. Econ. Res.*).

Lancaster, Kelvin J. 1966. "A New Approach to Consumer Theory." *J.P.E.* 74 (April): 132–157.

Larmore, Mary Lou. 1967. "An Inquiry into an Econometric Production Function for Health in the United States." PhD dissertation. Northwestern Univ.

Michael, Robert T. 1972. *The Effect of Education on Efficiency in Consumption.* New York: Columbia Univ. Press (for *Nat. Bur. Econ. Res.*).

Mushkin, Selma J. 1962. "Health as an Investment." *J.P.E.* 70, no. 2, suppl. (October): 129–157.

Muth, Richard. 1966. "Household Production and Consumer Demand Functions." *Econometrica* 34 (July): 699–708.

Nerlove, Marc, and Kenneth J. Arrow. 1962. "Optimal Advertising Policy under Dynamic Conditions." *Economica* 29 (May): 129–142.

Newhouse, Joseph P. 1968. "Toward a Rational Allocation of Resources in Medical Care." PhD dissertation, Harvard Univ.

Phelps, Charles E. 1973. "The Demand for Health Insurance: Theory and Empirical Results." PhD dissertation, Univ. Chicago .

Strotz, Robert H. 1955–1956. "Myopia and Inconsistency in Dynamic Utility Maximization." *Rev. Econ. Studies* 23: 165–180.

The Human Capital Model

TWO

Michael Grossman

ABSTRACT

This chapter contains a detailed treatment of the human capital model of the demand for health, which was originally developed in 1972. Theoretical predictions are discussed, and theoretical extensions of the model are reviewed. Empirical research that tests the predictions of the model or studies causality between years of formal schooling completed and good health is surveyed. The model views health as a durable capital stock that yields an output of healthy time. Individuals inherit an initial amount of this stock that depreciates with age and can be increased by investment. The household production function model of consumer behavior is employed to account for the gap between health as an output and medical care as one of many inputs into its production. In this framework, the "shadow price" of health depends on many variables besides the price of medical care. It is shown that the shadow price rises with age if the rate of depreciation on the stock of health rises over the life cycle and falls with education (years of formal schooling completed) if more educated people are more efficient producers of health. An important result is that, under certain conditions, an increase in the shadow price may simultaneously

*reduce the quantity of health demanded and increase the quantities of health
inputs demanded.*

1. INTRODUCTION

Almost three decades have elapsed since I published my National Bureau of Economic Research monograph (Grossman 1972b) and *Journal of Political Economy* paper (Grossman 1972a) dealing with a theoretical and empirical investigation of the demand for the commodity "good health."[1] My work was motivated by the fundamental difference between health as an output and medical care as one of a number of inputs into the production of health and by the equally important difference between health capital and other forms of human capital. According to traditional demand theory, each consumer has a utility or preference function that allows him or her to rank alternative combinations of goods and services purchased in the market. Consumers are assumed to select the combination that maximizes their utility function subject to an income or resource constraint: namely, outlays on goods and services cannot exceed income. While this theory provides a satisfactory explanation of the demand for many goods and services, students of medical economics have long realized that what consumers demand when they purchase medical services are not these services per se but rather better health. Indeed, as early as 1789, Bentham included relief of pain as one of fifteen "simple pleasures" which exhausted the list of basic arguments in one's utility function (Bentham 1931). The distinction between health as an output or an object of choice and medical care as an input had not, however, been exploited in the theoretical and empirical literature prior to 1972.

My approach to the demand for health has been labeled as the human capital model in much of the literature on health economics because it draws heavily on human capital theory (Becker 1964, 1967; Ben-Porath 1967; Mincer 1974). According to human capital theory, increases in a person's stock of knowledge or human capital raise his productivity in the market sector of the economy, where he produces money earnings, and in the nonmarket or household sector, where he produces commodities that enter his utility function. To realize potential gains in productivity, individuals have an incentive to invest in formal schooling and on-the-job training. The costs of these investments include direct outlays on market goods and the opportunity cost of the time that must be withdrawn from competing uses. This framework was used by Becker (1967) and by Ben-Porath (1967) to develop models that determine the optimal quantity of investment in human capital at any age. In addition, these models show how the optimal quantity varies over the life cycle of an individual and among individuals of the same age.

Although Mushkin (1962), Becker (1964), and Fuchs (1966) had pointed out that health capital is one component of the stock of human capital, I was the first person to construct a model of the demand for health capital itself. If increases in the stock of health simply increased wage rates, my undertaking would not have been necessary, for one could simply have applied Becker's and Ben-Porath's models to study the decision to invest in health. I argued, however, that health capital differs from other forms of human capital. In particular, I argued that a person's stock of knowledge affects his market and nonmarket productivity, while his stock of health determines the total amount of time he can spend producing money earnings and commodities.

My approach uses the household production function model of consumer behavior (Becker 1965; Lancaster 1966; Michael and Becker 1973) to account for the gap between health as an output and medical care as one of many inputs into its production. This model draws a sharp distinction between fundamental objects of choice—called commodities—that enter the utility function and market goods and services. These commodities are Bentham's (1931) pleasures that exhaust the basic arguments in the utility function. Consumers produce commodities with inputs of market goods and services and their own time. For example, they use sporting equipment and their own time to produce recreation, traveling time and transportation services to produce visits, and part of their Sundays and church services to produce "peace of mind." The concept of a household production function is perfectly analogous to a firm production function. Each relates a specific output or a vector of outputs to a set of inputs. Since goods and services are inputs into the production of commodities, the demand for these goods and services is a derived demand for a factor of production. That is, the demand for medical care and other health inputs is derived from the basic demand for health.

There is an important link between the household production theory of consumer behavior and the theory of investment in human capital. Consumers as investors in their human capital *produce* these investments with inputs of their own time, books, teachers' services, and computers. Thus, some of the outputs of household production directly enter the utility function, while other outputs determine earnings or wealth in a life cycle context. Health, on the other hand, does both.

In my model, health—defined broadly to include longevity and illness-free days in a given year—is both demanded and produced by consumers. Health is a choice variable because it is a source of utility (satisfaction) and because it determines income or wealth levels. That is, health is demanded by consumers for two reasons. As a consumption commodity, it directly enters their preference functions, or, put differently, sick days are a source of disutility. As an investment commodity, it determines the total amount of time available for market and nonmarket activities. In other words, an increase in the stock of health reduces the amount of time lost from these activities, and the monetary value of this reduction is an index of the return to an investment in health.

Since health capital is one component of human capital, a person inherits an initial stock of health that depreciates with age—at an increasing rate at least after some stage in the life cycle—and can be increased by investment. Death occurs when the stock falls below a certain level, and one of the novel features of the model is that individuals "choose" their length of life. Gross investments are produced by household production functions that relate an output of health to such choice variables or health inputs as medical care utilization, diet, exercise, cigarette smoking, and alcohol consumption. In addition, the production function is affected by the efficiency or productivity of a given consumer as reflected by his or her personal characteristics. Efficiency is defined as the amount of health obtained from a given amount of health inputs. For example, years of formal schooling completed plays a large role in this context.

Since the most fundamental law in economics is the law of the downward sloping demand function, the quantity of health demanded should be negatively correlated with its "shadow price." I stress that the shadow price of health depends on many other variables besides the price of medical care. Shifts in these variables alter the optimal amount of health and also alter the derived demand for gross investment and for health inputs. I show that the shadow price of health rises with age if the rate of depreciation on the stock of health rises over the life cycle and falls with education (years of formal schooling completed) if more educated people are more efficient producers of health. I emphasize the result that, under certain conditions, an increase in the shadow price may simultaneously reduce the quantity of health demanded and increase the quantities of health inputs demanded.

The task in this paper is to outline my 1972 model of the demand for health, to discuss the theoretical predictions it contains, to review theoretical extensions of the model, and to survey empirical research that tests the predictions made by the model or studies causality between years of formal schooling completed and good health. I outline my model in section 2 of this chapter. I include a new interpretation of the condition for death, which is motivated in part by analyses by Ehrlich and Chuma (1990) and by Ried (1996, 1998). I also address a fundamental criticism of my framework raised by Ehrlich and Chuma involving an indeterminacy problem with regard to optimal investment in health. I summarize my pure investment model in section 3, my pure consumption model in section 4, and my empirical testing of the model in section 5. While I emphasize my own contributions in these three sections, I do treat closely related developments that followed my 1972 publications. I keep derivations to a minimum because these can be found in Grossman (1972a, 1972b).[2] In section 6 I focus on theoretical and empirical extensions and criticisms, other than those raised by Ehrlich and Chuma and by Ried.

I conclude in section 7 with a discussion of studies that investigate alternative explanations of the positive relationship between years of formal schooling completed and alternative measures of adult health. While not all this literature is grounded in demand for health models, it is natural to address it in a paper of this nature because it essentially deals with complementary relationships between the two most important components of the stock of human capital. Currently, we still lack comprehensive theoretical models in which the stocks of health and knowledge are determined simultaneously. I am somewhat disappointed that my 1982 plea for the development of these models has gone unanswered (Grossman 1982). The rich empirical literature treating interactions between schooling and health underscores the potential payoffs to this undertaking.

2. BASIC MODEL

2.1. Assumptions

Let the intertemporal utility function of a typical consumer be

$$U = U(\phi_t H_t, Z_t), \quad t = 0, 1, \ldots, n, \tag{1}$$

where H_t is the stock of health at age t or in time period t, ϕ_t is the service flow per unit stock, $h_t = \phi_t H_t$ is total consumption of "health services," and Z_t is consumption of another commodity. The stock of health in the initial period (H_0) is given, but the stock of health at any other age is endogenous. The length of life as of the planning date (n) also is endogenous. In particular, death takes place when $H_t \leq H_{\min}$. Therefore, length of life is determined by the quantities of health capital that maximize utility subject to production and resource constraints.

By definition, net investment in the stock of health equals gross investment minus depreciation:

$$H_{t+1} - H_t = I_t - \delta_t H_t, \tag{2}$$

where I_t is gross investment and δ_t is the rate of depreciation during the t th period ($0 < \delta_t < 1$). The rates of depreciation are exogenous but depend on age.

Consumers produce gross investment in health and the other commodities in the utility function according to a set of household production functions:

$$I_t = I_t(M_t, TH_t; E),\tag{3}$$

$$Z_t = Z_t(X_t, T_t; E).\tag{4}$$

In these equations, M_t is a vector of inputs (goods) purchased in the market that contribute to gross investment in health, X_t is a similar vector of goods inputs that contribute to the production of Z_t, TH_t and T_t are time inputs, and E is the consumer's stock of knowledge or human capital exclusive of health capital. This latter stock is assumed to be exogenous or predetermined. The semicolon before it highlights the difference between this variable and the endogenous goods and time inputs. In effect, I am examining the consumer's behavior after he has acquired the optimal stock of this capital.[3] Following Michael (1972, 1973) and Michael and Becker (1973), I assume that an increase in knowledge capital raises the efficiency of the production process in the nonmarket or household sector, just as an increase in technology raises the efficiency of the production process in the market sector. I also assume that all production functions are linear homogeneous in the endogenous market goods and own time inputs.

In much of my modeling, I treat the vectors of goods inputs, M_t and X_t, as scalars and associate the market goods input in the gross investment production function with medical care. Clearly this is an oversimplification because many other market goods and services influence health. Examples include housing, diet, recreation, cigarette smoking, and excessive alcohol use. The latter two inputs have negative marginal products in the production of health. They are purchased because they are inputs into the production of other commodities such as "smoking pleasure" that yield positive utility. In completing the model, I will rule out this and other types of joint production, although I consider joint production in some detail in Grossman (1972b, 74–83). I also will associate the market goods input in the health production function with medical care, although the reader should keep in mind that the model would retain its structure if the primary health input purchased in the market was something other than medical care. This is important because of evidence that medical care may be an unimportant determinant of health in developed countries (Auster, Leveson, and Sarachek 1969) and because Zweifel and Breyer (1997) use the lack of a positive relationship between correlates of good health and medical care in micro data to criticize my approach.

Both market goods and own time are scarce resources. The goods budget constraint equates the present value of outlays on goods to the present value of earnings income over the life cycle plus initial assets (discounted property income):

$$\sum_{t=0}^{n} \frac{P_t M_t + Q_t X_t}{(1+r)^t} = \sum_{t=0}^{n} \frac{W_t TW_t}{(1+r)^t} + A_0. \tag{5}$$

Here P_t and Q_t are the prices of M_t and X_t, W_t is the hourly wage rate, TW_t is hours of work, A_0 is initial assets, and r is the market rate of interest. The time constraint requires that Ω, the total amount of time available in any period, must be exhausted by all possible uses:

$$TW_t + TH_t + T_t + TL_t = \Omega, \tag{6}$$

where TL_t is time lost from market and nonmarket activities due to illness and injury.

Equation (6) modifies the time budget constraint in Becker's (1965) allocation of time model. If sick time were not added to market and nonmarket time, total time would not be exhausted by all possible uses. I assume that sick time is inversely related to the stock of health; that is $\partial TL_t / \partial H_t < 0$. If Ω is measured in hours ($\Omega = 8{,}760$ hours or 365 days times 24 hours per day if the year is the relevant period) and if ϕ_t is defined as the flow of healthy time per unit of H_t, h_t equals the total number of healthy hours in a given year. Then one can write

$$TL_t = \Omega - h_t. \tag{7}$$

From now on, I assume that the variable h_t in the utility function coincides with healthy hours.[4]

By substituting for hours of work (TW_t) from equation (6) into equation (5), one obtains the single "full wealth" constraint:

$$\sum_{t=0}^{n} \frac{P_t M_t + Q_t X_t + W_t(TL_t + T_t)}{(1+r)^t} = \sum_{t=0}^{n} \frac{W_t \Omega}{(1+r)^t} + A_0. \tag{8}$$

Full wealth, which is given by the right-hand side of equation (8), equals initial assets plus the discounted value of the earnings an individual would obtain if he spent all of his time at work. Part of this wealth is spent on market goods, part of it is spent on nonmarket production, and part of it is lost due to illness. The equilibrium quantities of H_t and Z_t can now be found by maximizing the utility function given by equation (1) subject to the constraints given by equations (2), (3), and (8). Since the inherited stock of health and the rates of depreciation are given, the optimal quantities of gross investment determine the optimal quantities of health capital.

2.2. Equilibrium Conditions

First-order optimality conditions for gross investment in period $t - 1$ are[5]

$$
\frac{\pi_{t-1}}{(1+r)^{t-1}} = \frac{W_t G_t}{(1+r)^t} + \frac{(1-\delta_t)W_{t+1} G_{t+1}}{(1+r)^{t+1}} + \cdots
$$

$$
+ \frac{(1-\delta_t) \cdots (1-\delta_{n-1})W_n G_n}{(1+r)^n}
$$

$$
+ \frac{Uh_t}{\lambda} G_t + \cdots (1-\delta_t) \cdots (1-\delta_{n-1}) \frac{Uh_n}{\lambda} G_n, \tag{9}
$$

$$
\pi_{t-1} = \frac{P_{t-1}}{\partial I_{t-1} / \partial M_{t-1}} = \frac{W_{t-1}}{\partial I_{t-1} / \partial TH_{t-1}}. \tag{10}
$$

The new symbols in these equations are $Uh_t = \partial U / \partial h_t$, the marginal utility of healthy time; λ, the marginal utility of wealth; $G_t = \partial h_t / \partial H_t = -(\partial TL_t / \partial H_t)$, the marginal product of the stock of health in the production of healthy time; and π_{t-1}, the marginal cost of gross investment in health in period $t - 1$.

Equation (9) states that the present value of the marginal cost of gross investment in health in period $t - 1$ must equal the present value of marginal benefits. Discounted marginal benefits at age t equal

$$
G_t \left[\frac{W_t}{(1+r)^t} + \frac{Uh_t}{\lambda} \right],
$$

where G_t is the marginal product of health capital—the increase in the amount of healthy time caused by a one-unit increase in the stock of health. Two monetary magnitudes are necessary to convert this marginal product into value terms because consumers desire health for two reasons. The discounted wage rate measures the monetary value of a one-unit increase in the total amount of time available for market and nonmarket activities, and the term Uh_t / λ measures the discounted monetary value of the increase in utility due to a one-unit increase in healthy time. Thus, the sum of these two terms measures the discounted marginal value to consumers of the output produced by health capital.

Condition (9) holds for any capital asset, not just for health capital. The marginal cost as of the current period, obtained by multiplying both sides of the equation by $(1+r)^{t-1}$, must be equated to the discounted flows of marginal benefits in the future. This is true for the asset of health capital by labeling the marginal costs and benefits of this particular asset in the appropriate manner. As I will show presently, most of the effects of variations in exogenous variables can be traced out as shifting the marginal costs and marginal benefits of the asset.

While equation (9) determines the optimal amount of gross investment in period $t - 1$, equation (10) shows the condition for minimizing the cost of producing a given quantity of gross investment. Total cost is minimized when the increase in gross investment from spending an additional dollar on medical care equals the increase in total cost from spending an additional dollar on time. Since the gross investment production function is homogeneous of degree one in the two endogenous inputs and since the prices of medical care and time are independent of the level of these inputs, the average cost of gross investment is constant and equal to the marginal cost.

To examine the forces that affect the demand for health and gross investment, it is useful to convert equation (9) into an equation that determines the optimal stock of health in period t. If gross investment in period t is positive, a condition similar to equation (9) holds for its optimal value. From these two first-order conditions

$$G_t \left[W_t + \left(\frac{Uh_t}{\lambda} \right)(1 + r)^t \right] = \pi_{t-1}(r - \tilde{\pi}_{t-1} + \delta_t), \qquad (11)$$

where $\tilde{\pi}_{t-1}$ is the percentage rate of change in marginal cost between period $t - 1$ and period t.[6] Equation (11) implies that the undiscounted value of the marginal product of the optimal stock of health capital at any age must equal the supply price of capital, $\pi_{t-1}(r - \tilde{\pi}_{t-1} + \delta_t)$. The latter contains interest, depreciation, and capital gains components and may be interpreted as the rental price or user cost of health capital.

Equation (11) fully determines the optimal quantity at time t of a capital good that can be bought and sold in a perfect market. The stock of health capital, like the stock of knowledge capital, cannot be sold because it is imbedded in the investor. This means that gross investment cannot be nonnegative. Although sales of capital are ruled out, provided gross investment is positive, there exists a user cost of capital that in equilibrium must equal the value of the marginal product of the stock. In Grossman (1972a, 230; 1972b, 6–7), I provide an intuitive interpretation of this result by showing that exchanges over time in the stock of health by an individual substitute for exchanges in the capital market.

2.3. Optimal Length of Life[7]

So far I have essentially reproduced the analysis of equilibrium conditions in my 1972 National Bureau of Economic Research monograph and *Journal of Political Economy* article. A perceptive reader may have noted that an explicit condition determining length of life is absent. The discounted marginal benefits of an investment in health in period 0 are summed from periods 1 through n, so that the consumer is alive in period n and dead in period $n + 1$.[8] This means that H_{n+1} is equal to or less than H_{min}, the death stock, while H_n and H_t $(t < n)$ exceed H_{min}. But how do we know that the optimal quantities of the stock of health guarantee this outcome? Put differently, length of life is supposed to be an endogenous variable in the model, yet discounted income and expenditure flows in the full wealth constraint and discounted marginal benefits in the first-order conditions appear to be summed over a fixed n.

I was bothered by the above while I was developing my model. As of the date of its publication, I was not convinced that length of life was in fact being determined by the model. There is a footnote in my *Journal of Political Economy* article (Grossman 1972a, 228, footnote 7) and in my National Bureau of Economic Research monograph (Grossman 1972b, 4, footnote 9) in which I impose the constraints that $H_{n+1} \leq H_{min}$ and $H_n > H_{min}$.[9] Surely, it is wrong to impose these constraints in a maximization problem in which length of life is endogenous.

My publications on the demand for health were outgrowths of my 1970 Columbia University PhD dissertation. While I was writing my dissertation, my friend and fellow PhD candidate, Gilbert R. Ghez, pointed out that the determination of optimal length of life could be viewed as an iterative process. I learned a great deal from him, and I often spent a long time working through the implications of his comments.[10] It has taken me almost thirty years to work through his comment on the iterative determination of length of life. I abandoned this effort many years ago but returned to it when I read Ried's (1996, 1998) reformulation of the selection of the optimal stock of health and length of life as a discrete time optimal control problem. Ried (1998, 389) writes: "Since [the problem] is a free terminal time problem, one may suspect that a condition for the optimal length of the planning horizon is missing in the set of necessary conditions. . . . However, unlike the analogous continuous time problem, the discrete time version fails to provide such an equation. Rather, the optimal final period . . . has to be determined through the analysis of a sequence of fixed terminal time problems with the terminal time varying over a plausible domain." This is the same observation that Ghez made. I offer a proof below. I do not rely on Ried's solution. Instead, I offer a much simpler proof that has a very different implication than the one offered by Ried.

A few preliminaries are in order. First, I assume that the rate of depreciation on the stock of health (δ_t) rises with age. As we shall see in more detail later, this implies that the optimal stock falls with age. Second, I assume that optimal gross investment in health is positive except in the very last year of life. Third, I define V_t as $W_t + (Uh_t/\lambda)(1 + r)^t$. Hence, V_t is the undiscounted marginal value of the output produced by health capital in period t. Finally, since the output produced by health capital has a finite upper limit of 8,760 hours in a year, I assume that the marginal product of the stock of health (G_t) diminishes as the stock increases ($\partial G_t / \partial H_t < 0$).

Consider the maximization problem outlined in section 2.1 except that the planning horizon is exogenous. That is, an individual is alive in period n and dead in period $n + 1$. Write the first-order conditions for the optimal stocks of health compactly as

$$V_t G_t = \pi_{t-1}(r - \tilde{\pi}_{t-1} + \delta_t), \quad t < n, \tag{12}$$

$$V_n G_n = \pi_{n-1}(r + 1). \tag{13}$$

Note that equation (13) follows from the condition for optimal gross investment in period $n - 1$. An investment in that period yields returns in one period only (period n) since the individual dies after period n. Put differently, the person behaves as if the rate of depreciation on the stock of health is equal to 1 in period n.

I also will make use of the first-order conditions for gross investment in health in periods 0 and n:

$$\pi_0 = \frac{V_1 G_1}{(1 + r)} + \frac{d_2 V_2 G_2}{(1 + r)^2} + \cdots + \frac{d_n V_n G_n}{(1 + r)^n}, \tag{14}$$

$$I_n = 0. \tag{15}$$

In equation (14), d_t is the increase in the stock of health in period t caused by an increase in gross investment in period 0:

$$d_1 = 1, d_t(t > 1) = \prod_{j=1}^{t-1}(1 - \delta_j).$$

Obviously, gross investment in period n is 0 because the individual will not be alive in period $n + 1$ to collect the returns.

In order for death to take place in period $n + 1$ $H_{n+1} \leq H_{\min}$. Since $I_n = 0$,

$$H_{n+1} = (1 - \delta_n)H_n. \tag{16}$$

Hence, for the solution (death after period n) to be fully consistent,

$$H_{n+1} = (1 - \delta_n)H_n \leq H_{\min}. \tag{17}$$

Suppose that condition (17) is violated. That is, suppose maximization for a fixed number of periods equal to n results in a stock in period $n + 1$ that exceeds the death stock. Then lifetime utility should be re-maximized under the assumption that the individual will be alive in period $n + 1$ but dead in period $n + 2$. As a first approximation, the set of first-order conditions for H_t $(t < n)$ defined by equation (12) still must hold so that the stock in each of these periods is not affected when the horizon is lengthened by one period.[11] But the condition for the stock in period n becomes

$$V_n^* G_n^* = \pi_{n-1}(r - \tilde{\pi}_{n-1} + \delta_n), \tag{18}$$

where asterisks are used because the stock of health in period n when the horizon is $n + 1$ is not equal to the stock when the horizon is n (see below). Moreover,

$$V_{n+1}^* G_{n+1}^* = \pi_n(r + 1), \tag{19}$$

$$I_{n+1} = 0, \tag{20}$$

$$H_{n+2} = (1 - \delta_{n+1})H_{n+1}^*. \tag{21}$$

If the stock defined by equation (21) is less than or equal to $H_{\min}$, death takes place in period $n + 2$. If H_{n+2} is greater than $H_{\min}$, the consumer re-maximizes lifetime utility under the assumption that death takes place in period $n + 3$ (the horizon ends in period $n + 2$).

I have just described an iterative process for the selection of optimal length of life. In words, the process amounts to maximizing lifetime utility for a fixed horizon, checking to see whether the stock in the period after the horizon ends (the terminal stock) is less than or equal to the death stock ($H_{\min}$), and adding one period to the horizon and re-maximizing the utility function if the terminal stock exceeds the death stock.[12] I want to make several comments on this process and its implications. Compare the condition for the optimal stock of health in period n when the horizon lasts through period n [equation (13)] with the condition for the optimal stock in the same period when the horizon lasts through period $n + 1$ [equation (18)]. The supply price of health capital is smaller in the latter case because $\delta_n < 1$.[13] Hence, the undiscounted value of the marginal product of health capital in period n when the horizon is $n + 1$ ($V_n^* G_n^*$) must be smaller than the undiscounted value of the marginal product of health capital in period n when the horizon is n ($V_n G_n$). In turn, due to diminishing marginal productivity, the stock of health in period n must rise when the horizon is extended by one period ($H_n^* > H_n$).[14]

When the individual lives for $n + 1$ years, the first-order condition for gross investment in period 0 is

$$\pi_0 = \frac{V_1 G_1}{(1 + r)} + \frac{d_2 V_2 G_2}{(1 + r)^2} + \cdots + \frac{d_n V_n^* G_n^*}{(1 + r)^n} + \frac{d_n(1 - \delta_n)V_{n+1}^* G_{n+1}^*}{(1 + r)^{n+1}}. \tag{22}$$

Note that the discounted marginal benefits of an investment in period 0 are the same whether the person dies in period $n + 1$ or in period $n + 2$ [compare the right-hand sides of equations (14) and (22)] since the marginal cost of an investment in period 0 does not depend on the length of the horizon. This may seem strange because one term is added to discounted marginal benefits of an investment in period 0 or in any other period when the horizon is extended by one period—the discounted marginal benefit in period $n + 1$. This term, however, is exactly offset by the reduction in the discounted marginal benefit in period n. The same offset occurs in the discounted marginal benefits of investments in every other period except for periods $n - 1$ and n.

A proof of the last proposition is as follows. The first $n - 1$ terms on the right-hand sides of equations (14) and (22) are the same. From equations (13), (18), and (19),

$$V_n^* G_n^* = \frac{V_n G_n (r - \tilde{\pi}_{n-1} + \delta_n)}{(1 + r)},$$

$$V_{n+1}^* G_{n+1}^* = V_n G_n (1 + \tilde{\pi}_{n-1}).$$

Hence, the sum of the last two terms on the right-hand side of equation (22) equals the last term on the right-hand side of equation (14):[15]

$$\frac{d_n V_n^* G_n^*}{(1 + r)^n} + \frac{d_n (1 - \delta_n) V_{n+1}^* G_{n+1}^*}{(1 + r)^{n+1}} = \frac{d_n V_n G_n}{(1 + r)^n}. \tag{23}$$

Using the last result, one can fully describe the algorithm for the selection of optimal length of life. Maximize the lifetime utility function for a fixed horizon. Check to see whether the terminal stock is less than or equal to the death stock. If the terminal stock exceeds the death stock, add one period to the horizon and redo the maximization. The resulting values of the stock of health must be the same in every period except for periods n and $n + 1$. The stock of health must be larger in these two periods when the horizon equals $n + 1$ than when the horizon equals n. The stock in period t depends on gross investment in period $t - 1$, with gross investment in previous periods held constant. Therefore, gross investment is larger in periods $n - 1$ and n but the same in every other period when the horizon is increased by one year. A rise in the rate of depreciation with age guarantees finite life since for some j[16]

$$H_{n+j} = (1 - \delta_{n+j-1}) H_{n+j-1} \le H_{min}.$$

I have just addressed a major criticism of my model made by Ehrlich and Chuma (1990). They argue that my analysis does not determine length of life because it ". . . does not develop the required terminal (transversality) conditions needed to assure the consistency of any solutions for the life cycle path of health capital and longevity" [Ehrlich and Chuma (1990, 762)]. I have just shown that length of life is determined as the outcome of an iterative process in which lifetime utility functions with alternative horizons are maximized. Since the continuous time optimal control techniques employed by Ehrlich and Chuma are not my fields of expertise, I invite the reader to study their paper and make up his or her own mind on this issue.

As I indicated at the beginning of this subsection, Ried (1996, 1998) offers the same general description of the selection of length of life as an iterative process. He proposes a solution using extremely complicated discrete time optimal control techniques. Again, I leave the reader to evaluate Ried's solution. But I do want to challenge his conclusion that ". . . sufficiently small perturbations of the trajectories of the exogenous variables will not alter the length of the individual's planning horizon. . . . [T]he uniqueness assumption [about length of life] ensures that the planning horizon may be treated as fixed in comparative dynamic analysis. . . . Given a fixed length of the individual's life, it is obvious that the mortality aspect is entirely left out of the picture. Thus, the impact of parametric changes upon individual health is confined to the quality of life which implies the analysis to deal [sic] with a pure morbidity effect" (Ried 1998, p. 389).

In my view, it is somewhat unsatisfactory to begin with a model in which length of life is endogenous but to end up with a result in which length of life does not depend on any of the exogenous variables in the model. This certainly is not an implication of my analysis of the determination of optimal length of life. In general, differences in such exogenous variables as the rate of depreciation, initial assets, and the marginal cost of investing in health across consumers of the same age will lead to differences in the optimal length of life.[17]

To be concrete, consider two consumers: a and b. Person a faces a higher rate of depreciation in each period than person b. The two consumers are the same in all other respects. Suppose that it is optimal for person a to live for n years (to die in year $n + 1$). Ried argues that person b also lives for n years because both he and person a use equation (13) to determine the optimal stock of health in period n. That equation is independent of the rate of depreciation in period n. Hence, the stock of health in period n is the same for each consumer. For person a, we have

$$H_{n+1}^a = (1 - \delta_n^a)H_n^a \leq H_{\min},$$

where the superscript a denotes values of variables for person a. But for person b,

$$H_{n+1}^b = (1 - \delta_n^b)H_n^a.$$

Since $\delta_n^b < \delta_n^a$, there is no guarantee that $H_{n+1}^b \leq H_{min}$. If $H_{n+1}^b > H_{min}$, person b will be alive in period $n + 1$. He will then use equation (18), rather than equation (13), to pick his optimal stock in period n. In this case, person b will have a larger optimal stock in period n than person a and will have a longer length of life.

Along the same lines, parametric differences in the marginal cost of investment in health (differences in the marginal cost across people of the same age), differences in initial assets, and parametric differences in wage rates cause length of life to vary among individuals. In general, any variable that raises the optimal stock of health in each period of life also tends to prolong length of life.[18] Thus, if health is not an inferior commodity, an increase in initial assets or a reduction in the marginal cost of investing in health induces a longer optimal life. Persons with higher wage rates have more wealth; taken by itself, this prolongs life. But the relative price of health (the price of h_t relative to the price of Z_t) may rise as the wage rate rises. If this occurs and the resulting substitution effect outweighs the wealth effect, length of life may fall.

According to Ried, death occurs if $H_{n+1} < H_{min}$ rather than if $H_{n+1} \leq H_{min}$ The latter condition is the one that I employ, but that does not seem to account for the difference between my analysis and his analysis. Ried's only justification of his result is in the context of a dynamic model of labor supply. He assumes that a nonnegativity constraint is binding in some period and concludes that marginal changes in any exogenous variable will fail to bring about positive supply.

Ried's conclusion does not appear to be correct. To see this in the most simple manner, consider a static model of the supply of labor, and suppose that the marginal rate of substitution between leisure time and consumption evaluated at zero hours of work is greater than or equal to the market wage rate at the initial wage. Hence, no hours are supplied to the market. Now suppose that the wage rate rises. If the marginal rate of substitution at zero hours equaled the old wage, hours of work will rise above zero. If the marginal rate of substitution at zero hours exceeded the old wage, hours could still rise above zero if the marginal rate of substitution at zero hours is smaller than the new wage. By the same reasoning, while not every parametric reduction in the rate of depreciation on the stock of health will increase optimal length of life (see footnote 18), some reductions surely will do so. I stand by my statement that it is somewhat unsatisfactory to begin with a model in which length of life is endogenous and end up with a result in which length of life does not depend on any of the exogenous variables in the model.

2.4. "Bang-Bang" Equilibrium

Ehrlich and Chuma (1990, 762–768) assert that my "key assumption that health investment is produced through a constant-returns-to-scale . . . technology introduces a type of indeterminacy ('bang-bang') problem with respect to optimal investment and health maintenance choices. . . . [This limitation precludes] a systematic resolution of the choice of *both* (their italics) optimal health paths and longevity. . . . Later contributions to the literature spawned by Grossman . . . suffer in various degrees from these shortcomings. . . . Under the linear production process assumed by Grossman, the marginal cost of investment would be constant, and no interior equilibrium for investment would generally exist."[19]

Ried (1998) addresses this criticism by noting that an infinite rate of investment is not consistent with equilibrium. Because Ehrlich and Chuma's criticism appears to be so damaging and Ried's treatment of it is brief and not convincing, I want to deal with it before proceeding to examine responses of health, gross investment, and health inputs to evolutionary (life-cycle) and parametric variations in key exogenous variables. Ehrlich and Chuma's point is as follows: Suppose that the rate of depreciation on the stock of health is equal to zero at every age, suppose that the marginal cost of gross investment in health does not depend on the amount of investment, and suppose that none of the other exogenous variables in the model is a function of age.[20] Then the stock of health is constant over time (net investment is zero). Any discrepancy between the initial stock and the optimal stock is erased in the initial period. In a continuous time model, this means an infinite rate of investment to close the gap followed by no investment after that. If the rate of depreciation is positive and constant, the discrepancy between the initial and optimal stock is still eliminated in the initial period. After that, gross investment is positive, constant, and equal to total depreciation; while net investment is zero.

To avoid the "bang-bang" equilibrium (an infinite rate of investment to eliminate the discrepancy between the initial and the desired stock followed by no investment if the rate of depreciation is zero), Ehrlich and Chuma assume that the production function of gross investment in health exhibits diminishing returns to scale. Thus, the marginal cost of gross or net investment is a positive function of the amount of investment. Given this, there is an incentive to reach the desired stock gradually rather than instantaneously since the cost of gradual adjustment is smaller than the cost of instantaneous adjustment.

The introduction of diminishing returns to scale greatly complicates the model because the marginal cost of gross investment and its percentage rate of change over time become endogenous variables that depend on the quantity of investment and its rate of change. In section 6, I show that the structural demand function for the stock of health at age t in a model with costs of adjustment is one in which H_1 depends on the stock at age $t + 1$ and the stock at age $t - 1$. The solution of this second-order difference equation results in a reduced form demand function in which the stock at age t depends on all past and future values of the exogenous variables. This makes theoretical and econometric analysis very difficult.

Are the modifications introduced by Ehrlich and Chuma really necessary? In my view the answer is no. The focus of my theoretical and empirical work and that of others who have adopted my framework (Cropper 1977; Muurinen 1982; Wagstaff 1986) certainly is not on discrepancies between the inherited or initial stock and the desired stock. I am willing to assume that consumers reach their desired stocks instantaneously in order to get sharp predictions that are subject to empirical testing. Gross investment is positive (but net investment is zero) if the rate of depreciation is positive but constant in my model. In the Ehrlich–Chuma model, net investment can be positive in this situation. In both models, consumers choose an infinite life. In both models, life is finite and the stock of health varies over the life cycle if the rate of depreciation is a positive function of age. In my model, positive net investment during certain stages of the life cycle is not ruled out. For example, the rate of depreciation might be negatively correlated with age at early stages of the life cycle. The stock of health would be rising and net investment would be positive during this stage of the life cycle.

More fundamentally, Ehrlich and Chuma introduce rising marginal cost of investment to remove an indeterminacy that really does not exist. In figure 1 of their paper (Ehrlich and Chuma 1990, 768), they plot the marginal cost of an investment in health as of age t and the discounted marginal benefits of this investment as functions of the quantity of investment. The discounted marginal benefit function is independent of the rate of investment. Therefore, no interior equilibrium exists for investment unless the marginal cost function slopes upward. This is the basis of their claim that my model does not determine optimal investment because marginal cost does not depend on investment.

Why, however, is the discounted marginal benefit function independent of the amount of investment? In a personal communication, Ehrlich informed me that this is because the marginal product of the stock of health at age t does not depend on the amount of investment at age t. Surely that is correct. But an increase in I_t raises the stock of health in all future periods. Since the marginal product of health capital diminishes as the stock rises, discounted marginal benefits must fall. Hence, the discounted marginal benefit function slopes downward, and an interior equilibrium for gross investment in period t clearly is possible even if the marginal cost of gross investment is constant.

Since discounted marginal benefits are positive when gross investment is zero, the discounted marginal benefit function intersects the vertical axis.[21] Thus corner solutions for gross investment are not ruled out in my model. One such solution occurs if the rate of depreciation on the stock of health equals zero in every period. Given positive rates of depreciation, corner solutions still are possible in periods other than the last period of life because the marginal cost of gross investment could exceed discounted marginal benefits for all positive quantities of investment. I explicitly rule out corner solutions when depreciation rates are positive, and Ried and other persons who have used my model also rule them out. Corner solutions are possible in the Ehrlich–Chuma model if the marginal cost function of gross investment intersects the vertical axis. Ehrlich and Chuma rule out corner solutions by assuming that the marginal cost function passes through the origin.

To summarize, unlike Ried, I conclude that exogenous variations in the marginal cost and marginal benefit of an investment in health cause optimal length of life to vary. Unlike Ehrlich and Chuma, I conclude that my 1972 model provides a simple but logically consistent framework for studying optimal health paths and longevity. At the same time, I want to recognize the value of Ried's emphasis on the determination of optimal length of life as the outcome of an iterative process in a discrete time model. I also want to recognize the value of Ehrlich and Chuma's model in cases when there are good reasons to assume that the marginal cost of investment in health is not constant.

2.5. Special Cases

Equation (11) determines the optimal stock of health in any period other than the last period of life. A slightly different form of that equation emerges if both sides are divided by the marginal cost of gross investment:

$$\gamma_t + a_t = r - \tilde{\pi}_{t-1} + \delta_t. \qquad (24)$$

Here $\gamma_t \equiv W_t G_t / \pi_{t-1}$ defines the marginal monetary return on an investment in health and $a_t \equiv \left[(Uh_t/\lambda)(1 + r)^t G_t \right] / \pi_{t-1}$ defines the psychic rate of return.[22] In equilibrium, the total rate of return to an investment in health must equal the user cost of capital in terms of the price of gross investment. The latter variable is defined as the sum of the real-own rate of interest and the rate of depreciation and may be termed the opportunity cost of health capital.

In sections 3 and 4, equation (24) is used to study the responses of the stock of health, gross investment in health, and health inputs to variations in exogenous variables. Instead of doing this in the context of the general model developed so far, I deal with two special cases: a pure investment model and a pure consumption model. In the former model, the psychic rate of return is zero, while in the latter the monetary rate of return is zero. There are two reasons for taking this approach. One involves an appeal to simplicity. It is difficult to obtain sharp predictions concerning the effects of changes in exogenous variables in a mixed model in which the stock of health yields both investment and consumption benefits. The second is that most treatments of investments in knowledge or human capital other than health capital assume that monetary returns are large relative to psychic returns. Indeed, Lazear (1977) estimates that the psychic returns from attending school are negative. Clearly, it is unreasonable to assume that health is a source of disutility, and most discussions of investments in infant, child, and adolescent health (Currie 2000) stress the consumption benefits of these investments. Nevertheless, I stress the pure investment model because it generates powerful predictions from simple analyses and because the consumption aspects of the demand for health can be incorporated into empirical estimation without much loss in generality.

3. PURE INVESTMENT MODEL

If healthy time did not enter the utility function directly or if the marginal utility of healthy time were equal to zero, health would be solely an investment commodity. The optimal amount of H_t $(t < n)$ could then be found by equating the marginal monetary rate of return on an investment in health to the opportunity cost of capital:

$$\frac{W_t G_t}{\pi_{t-1}} \equiv \gamma_t = r - \tilde{\pi}_{t-1} + \delta_t. \tag{25}$$

Similarly, the optimal stock of health in the last period of life would be determined by

$$\frac{W_n G_n}{\pi_{n-1}} \equiv \gamma_n = r + 1. \tag{26}$$

Figure 2.1 illustrates the determination of the optimal stock of health capital at age t. The demand curve MEC shows the relationship between the stock of health and the rate of return on an investment or the marginal efficiency of health capital. The supply curve S shows the relationship between the stock of health and the cost of capital. Since the real-own rate of interest $(r - \tilde{\pi}_{t-1})$ and the rate of depreciation are independent of the stock, the supply curve is

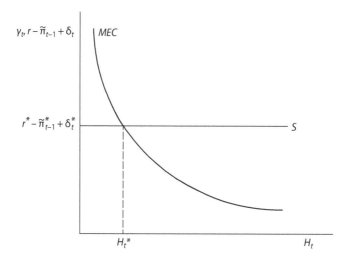

Figure 2.1

infinitely elastic. Provided the MEC schedule slopes downward, the equilibrium stock is given by H_t^*, where the supply and demand functions intersect.

The wage rate and the marginal cost of gross investment do not depend on the stock of health. Therefore, the MEC schedule would be negatively inclined if and only if the marginal product of health capital (G_t) diminishes as the stock increases. I have already assumed diminishing marginal productivity in section 2 and have justified this assumption because the output produced by health capital has a finite upper limit of 8,760 hours in a year. Figure 2.2 shows a plausible relationship between the stock of health and the amount of healthy time. This

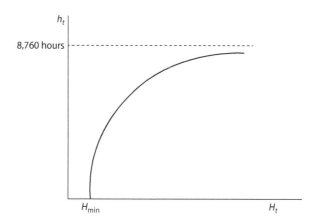

Figure 2.2

relationship may be termed a production function of healthy time. The slope of the curve in the figure at any point gives the marginal product of health capital. The amount of healthy time equals zero at the death stock, H_{min}. Beyond that stock, healthy time increases at a decreasing rate and eventually approaches its upper asymptote as the stock becomes large.

Equations (25) and (26) and figure 2.1 enable one to study the responses of the stock of health and gross investment to variations in exogenous variables. As indicated in section 2, two types of variations are examined: evolutionary (differences across time for the same consumer) and parametric (differences across consumers of the same age). In particular, I consider evolutionary increases in the rate of depreciation on the stock of health with age and parametric variations in the rate of depreciation, the wage rate, and the stock of knowledge or human capital exclusive of health capital (E).

3.1. Depreciation Rate Effects

Consider the effect of an increase in the rate of depreciation on the stock of health (δ_t) with age. I have already shown in section 2 that this factor causes the stock of health to fall with age and produces finite life. Graphically, the supply function in figure 2.1 shifts upward over time or with age, and the optimal stock in each period is lower than in the previous period.

To quantify the magnitude of percentage rate of decrease in the stock of health over the life cycle, assume that the wage rate and the marginal cost of gross investment in health do not depend on age so that $\tilde{\pi}_{t-1} = 0$. Differentiate equation (25) with respect to age to obtain[23]

$$\tilde{H}_t = - s_t \varepsilon_t \tilde{\delta}_t.$$ (27)

In this equation, the tilde notation denotes a percentage time or age derivative

$$\tilde{H}_t = \frac{dH_t}{dt} \frac{1}{H_t}, \quad etc.,$$

and the new symbols are $s_t = \delta_t/(r + \delta_t)$, the share of the depreciation rate in the cost of health capital; and

$$\varepsilon_t = - \frac{\partial \ln H_t}{\partial \ln(r + \delta_t)} = - \frac{\partial \ln H_t}{\partial \ln \gamma},$$

the elasticity of the MEC schedule.

Provided the rate of depreciation rises over the life cycle, the stock of health falls with age. The life cycle profile of gross investment does not, however, simply mirror that of health capital. The reason is that a rise in the rate of depreciation not only reduces the amount of health capital demanded by consumers but also reduces the amount of capital supplied to them by a given amount of gross investment. If the change in supply exceeds the change in demand, individuals have an incentive to close the gap by increasing gross investment. On the other hand, if the change in demand exceeds the change in supply, gross investment falls over the life cycle.

To begin to see why gross investment does not necessarily fail over the life cycle, first consider the behavior of one component of gross investment, total depreciation $(D_t = \delta_t H_t)$, as the rate of depreciation rises over the life cycle. Assume that the percentage rate of increase in the rate of depreciation with age $(\tilde{\delta}_t)$ and the elasticity of the MEC schedule (ε_t) are constant. Then

$$\tilde{D}_t = \tilde{\delta}(1 - s_t \varepsilon) \gtreqless 0 \quad \text{as } \varepsilon \lesseqgtr \frac{1}{s_t}.$$

From the last equation, total depreciation increases with age as long as the elasticity of the MEC schedule is less than the reciprocal of the share of the depreciation rate in the cost of health capital. A sufficient condition for this to occur is that ε is smaller than one.

If ε_t and $(\tilde{\delta}_t)$ are constant, the percentage change in gross investment with age is given by

$$\tilde{I}_t = \frac{\tilde{\delta}(1 - s_t \varepsilon)(\delta_t - s_t \varepsilon \tilde{\delta}) + s_t^2 \varepsilon \tilde{\delta}^2}{(\delta_t - s_t \varepsilon \tilde{\delta})}. \tag{28}$$

Since health capital cannot be sold, gross investment cannot be negative. Therefore, $\delta_t \geq -\tilde{H}_t$ or $\delta_t \geq -s_t \varepsilon \tilde{\delta}$. Provided gross investment is positive, the term $\delta_t - s_t \varepsilon \tilde{\delta}$ in the numerator and denominator of equation (28) must be positive. Thus, a sufficient condition for gross investment to be positively correlated with the depreciation rate is $\varepsilon < 1/s_t$. Clearly, $\tilde{I}_t$ is positive if $\varepsilon < 1$.

The important conclusion is reached that, if the elasticity of the MEC schedule is less than one, gross investment and the depreciation rate are positively correlated over the life cycle, while gross investment and the stock of health are negatively correlated. In fact, the relationship between the amount of healthy time and the stock of health suggests that ε is smaller than one. A general equation for the healthy time production function illustrated by figure 2.2 is

$$h_t = 8,760 - BH_t^{-C}, \tag{29}$$

where B and C are positive constants. The corresponding MEC schedule is

$$\ln \gamma_t = \ln BC - (C + 1)\ln H_t + \ln W + \ln \pi. \qquad (30)$$

The elasticity of this schedule is $\varepsilon = 1/(1 + C) < 1$ since $C > 0$.

Observe that with the depreciation rate held constant, increases in gross investment increase the stock of health and the amount of healthy time. But the preceding discussion indicates that because the depreciation rate rises with age it is likely that unhealthy (old) people will make larger gross investments in health than healthy (young) people. This means that sick time (TL_t) will be positively correlated with the market good or medical care input (M_t) and with the own time input (TH_t) in the gross investment production function over the life cycle.

The framework used to analyze life cycle variations in depreciation rates can easily be used to examine the impacts of variations in these rates among persons of the same age. Assume, for example, a uniform percentage shift in δ_t across persons so that the depreciation rate function can be written as $\delta_t = \delta_0 \exp(\tilde{\delta}_t)$ where δ_0 differs among consumers. It is clear that such a shift has the same kind of effects as an increase in δ_t with age. That is, persons of a given age who face relatively high depreciation rates would simultaneously reduce their demand for health but increase their demand for gross investment if $\varepsilon < 1$.

3.2. Market and Nonmarket Efficiency

Persons who face the same cost of health capital would demand the same amount of health only if the determinants of the rate of return on an investment were held constant. Changes in the value of the marginal product of health capital and the marginal cost of gross investment shift the MEC schedule and, therefore, alter the quantity of health capital demanded even if the cost of capital does not change. The consumer's wage rate and his or her stock of knowledge or human capital other than health capital are the two key shifters of the MEC schedule.[24]

Since the value of the marginal product of health capital equals WG, an increase in the wage rate (W) raises the monetary equivalent of the marginal product of a given stock. Put differently, the higher a person's wage rate the greater is the value to him of an increase in healthy time. A consumer's wage rate measures his market efficiency or the rate at which he can convert hours of work into money earnings. Hence, the wage is positively correlated with the benefits of a reduction in lost time from the production of money earnings due to illness. Moreover, a high wage induces an individual to substitute market goods for his own time in the production of commodities. This substitution continues until in equilibrium the monetary value of the marginal product of consumption time equals the wage rate. Thus, the benefits from a reduction in time lost from nonmarket production are also positively correlated with the wage.

If an upward shift in the wage rate had no effect on the marginal cost of gross investment, a 1 percent increase in the wage would increase the rate of return (γ) associated with a fixed stock of capital by 1 percent. In fact, this is not the case because own time is an input in the gross investment production function. If K is the fraction of the total cost of gross investment accounted for by time, a 1 percent rise in W would increase marginal cost (π) by K percent. After one nets out the correlation between W and π, the percentage growth in γ would equal $1 - K$, which exceeds zero as long as gross investment is not produced entirely by time. Hence, the quantity of health capital demanded rises as the wage rate rises as shown in the formula for the wage elasticity of capital:

$$e_{HW} = (1 - K)\varepsilon. \tag{31}$$

Although the wage rate and the demand for health or gross investment are positively related, W has no effect on the amount of gross investment supplied by a given input of medical care. Therefore, the demand for medical care rises with the wage. If medical care and own time are employed in fixed proportions in the gross investment production function, the wage elasticity of M equals the wage elasticity of H. On the other hand, given a positive elasticity of substitution in production (σ_p) between M and TH, M increases more rapidly than H because consumers have an incentive to substitute medical care for their relatively more expensive own time. This substitution is reflected in the formula for the wage elasticity of medical care:

$$e_{MW} = K\sigma_p + (1 - K)\varepsilon. \tag{32}$$

The preceding analysis can be modified to accommodate situations in which the money price of medical care is zero for all practical purposes because it is fully financed by health insurance or by the government, and care is rationed by waiting and travel time. Suppose that q hours are required to obtain one unit of medical care, so that the price of care is Wq. In addition, suppose that there are three endogenous inputs in the gross investment production function: M, TH, and a market good (X) whose acquisition does not require time. Interpret K as the share of the cost of gross investment accounted for by M and TH. Then equation (31) still holds, and an increase in W causes H to increase. Equation (32) becomes

$$e_{MW} = (1 - K)(\varepsilon - \sigma_{MX}), \tag{33}$$

where σ_{MX} is the partial elasticity of substitution in production between M and the third input, X. If these two inputs are net substitutes in production, σ_{MX} is positive. Then

$$e_{MW} \gtrless 0 \quad \text{as} \quad \varepsilon \gtrless \sigma_{MX}.$$

In this modified model the wage elasticity of medical care could be negative or zero. This case is relevant in interpreting some of the empirical evidence to be discussed later.

As indicated in section 2, I follow Michael (1972, 1973) and Michael and Becker (1973) by assuming that an increase in knowledge capital or human capital other than health capital (E) raises the efficiency of the production process in the nonmarket or household sector, just as an increase in technology raises the efficiency of the production process in the market sector. I focus on education or years of formal schooling completed as the most important determinant of the stock of human capital. The gross investment production function and the production function of the commodity Z are linear homogeneous in their endogenous inputs [see equations (3) and (4)]. Therefore, an increase in the exogenous or predetermined stock of human capital can raise output only if it raises the marginal products of the endogenous inputs.

Suppose that a one-unit increase in E raises the marginal products of M and TH in the gross investment production function by the same percentage (ρ_H). This is the Hicks-or factor-neutrality assumption applied to an increase in technology in the nonmarket sector. Given factor-neutrality, there is no incentive to substitute medical care for own time as the stock of human capital rises.

Because an increase in E raises the marginal products of the health inputs, it reduces the quantity of these inputs required to produce a given amount of gross investment. Hence, with no change in input prices, the marginal or average cost of gross investment falls. In fact, if a circumflex over a variable denotes a percentage change per unit change in E, one easily shows

$$\hat{\pi} = -\rho_H. \tag{34}$$

With the wage rate held constant, an increase in E would raise the marginal efficiency of a given stock of health. This causes the MEC schedule in figure 2.1 to shift upward and raises the optimal stock of health.

The percentage increase in the amount of health capital demanded for a one-unit increase in E is given by

$$\hat{H} = \rho_H \varepsilon. \tag{35}$$

Since ρ_H indicates the percentage increase in gross investment supplied by a one-unit increase in E, shifts in this variable would not alter the demand for medical care or own time if ρ_H equaled $\hat{H}$. For example, a person with ten years of formal schooling might demand 3 percent more health than a person with nine years of formal schooling. If the medical care and own time inputs were held constant, the former individual's one extra year of schooling might supply him with 3 percent more health. Given this condition, both persons would demand the same amounts of M and TH. As this example illustrates, any effect of a change in E on the demand for medical care or time reflects a positive or negative differential between $\hat{H}$ and ρ_H:

$$\hat{M} = \widehat{TH} = \rho_H(\varepsilon - 1). \tag{36}$$

Equation (36) suggests that the more educated would demand more health but less medical care if the elasticity of the MEC schedule were less than one. These patterns are opposite to those that would be expected in comparing the health and medical care utilization of older and younger consumers.

4. PURE CONSUMPTION MODEL

If the cost of health capital were large relative to the monetary rate of return on an investment in health and if $\tilde{\pi}_{t-1} = 0$, all t, then equation (11) or (24) could be approximated by

$$\frac{Uh_tG_t}{\lambda} = \frac{UH_t}{\lambda} = \frac{\pi(r + \delta_t)}{(1 + r)^t}. \tag{37}$$

Equation (37) indicates that the monetary equivalent of the marginal utility of health capital must equal the discounted user cost of H_t.[25] It can be used to highlight the differences between the age, wage, or schooling effect in a pure consumption model and the corresponding effect in a pure investment model. In the following analysis, I assume that the marginal rate of substitution between H_t and H_{t+1} depends only on H_t and H_{t+1} and that the marginal rate of substitution between H_t and Z_t depends only on H_t and Z_t. I also assume that one plus the market rate of interest is equal to one plus rate of time preference for the present (the ratio of the marginal utility of H_t to the marginal utility of H_{t+1} when these two stocks are equal minus one). Some of these assumptions are relaxed, and a more detailed analysis is presented in Grossman (1972b, Chapter III).

   With regard to age-related depreciation rate effects, the elasticity of substitution in consumption between H_t and H_{t+1} replaces the elasticity of the MEC schedule in equations (27) and (28). The quantity of health capital demanded still falls over the life cycle in response to an increase in the rate of depreciation. Gross investment and health inputs rise with age if the elasticity of substitution between present and future health is less than one.

Since health enters the utility function, health is positively related to wealth in the consumption model provided it is a superior good. That is, an increase in wealth with no change in the wage rate or the marginal cost of gross investment causes the quantity of health capital demanded to rise. This effect is absent from the investment model because the marginal efficiency of health capital and the market rate of interest do not depend on wealth.[26] Parametric wage variations across persons of the same age induce wealth effects on the demand for health. Suppose that we abstract from these effects by holding the level of utility or real wealth constant. Then the wage elasticity of health is given by

$$e_{HW} = -(1-\theta)(K-K_Z)\sigma_{HZ}, \tag{38}$$

where θ is the share of health in wealth, K_Z is the share of total cost of Z accounted for by time, and σ_{HZ} is the positive elasticity of substitution in consumption between H and Z.[27] Hence,

$$e_{HW} \lessgtr 0 \quad \text{as} \quad K \gtrless K_Z.$$

The sign of the wage elasticity is ambiguous because an increase in the wage rate raises the marginal cost of gross investment in health and the marginal cost of Z. If time costs were relatively more important in the production of health than in the production of Z, the relative price of health would rise with the wage rate, which would reduce the quantity of health demanded. The reverse would occur if Z were more time intensive than health. The ambiguity of the wage effect here is in sharp contrast to the situation in the investment model. In that model, the wage rate would be positively correlated with health as long as K were less than one.

Instead of examining a wage effect that holds utility constant, Wagstaff (1986) and Zweifel and Breyer (1997) examine a wage effect that holds the marginal utility of wealth constant. This analysis is feasible only if the current period utility function, $\psi(H, Z)$, is strictly concave:

$$\Psi_{HH} < 0, \Psi_{ZZ} < 0, \Psi_{HH}\Psi_{ZZ} - \Psi^2_{HZ} > 0.$$

With the marginal utility of wealth (λ) held constant, the actual change in health caused by a 1 percent increase in the wage rate is given by

$$\frac{\partial H}{\partial \ln W} = \frac{K\Psi_H\Psi_{ZZ} - K_Z\Psi_Z\Psi_{HZ}}{\Psi_{HH}\Psi_{ZZ} - \Psi^2_{HZ}}. \tag{39}$$

Equation (39) is negative if $\Psi_{HZ} \geq 0$. The sign of the wage effect is, however, ambiguous if $\Psi_{HZ} < 0$.[28]

The human capital parameter in the consumption demand function for health is

$$\hat{H} = \rho\eta_H + (\rho_H - \rho_Z)(1 - \theta)\sigma_{HZ}, \tag{40}$$

where ρ_Z is the percentage increase in the marginal product of the Z commodity's goods or time input caused by a one-unit increase in E (the negative of the percentage reduction in the marginal or average cost of Z), η_H is the wealth elasticity of demand for health, and $\rho = \theta\rho_H + (1 - \theta)\rho_Z$ is the percentage increase in real wealth as E rises with money full wealth and the wage rate held constant. The first term on the right-hand side of equation (40) reflects the wealth effect, and the second term reflects the substitution effect. If E's productivity effect in the gross investment production function is the same as in the Z production function, then $\rho_H = \rho_Z$ and $\hat{H}$ reflects the wealth effect alone. In this case, a shift in human capital, measured by years of formal schooling completed or education is "commodity-neutral," to use the term coined by Michael (1972, 1973). If $\rho_H > \rho_Z$, E is "biased" toward health, its relative price falls, and the wealth and substitution effects both operate in the same direction. Consequently, an increase in E definitely increases the demand for health. If $\rho_H < \rho_Z$, E is biased away from health, its relative price rises, and the wealth and substitution effects operate in opposite directions.

The human capital parameter in the consumption demand curve for medical care is

$$\hat{M} = \rho(\eta_H - 1) + (\rho_H - \rho_Z)\left[(1 - \theta)\sigma_{HZ} - 1\right]. \tag{41}$$

If shifts in E are commodity-neutral, medical care and education are negatively correlated unless $\eta_H \geq 1$. If, on the other hand, there is a bias in favor of health, these two variables will still tend to be negatively correlated unless the wealth and price elasticities both exceed one.[29]

The preceding discussion reveals that the analysis of variations in nonmarket productivity in the consumption model differs in two important respects from the corresponding analysis in the investment model. In the first place, wealth effects are not relevant in the investment model, as has already been indicated. Of course, health would have a positive wealth elasticity in the investment model if wealthier people faced lower rates of interest. But the analysis of shifts in education assumes money wealth is fixed. Thus, one could not rationalize the positive relationship between education and health in terms of an association between wealth and the interest rate.

In the second place, if the investment framework were utilized, then whether or not a shift in human capital is commodity-neutral would be irrelevant in assessing its impact on the demand for health. As long as the rate of interest were independent of education, H and E would be positively correlated.[30] Put differently, if individuals could always receive, say, a 5 percent real rate of return on savings deposited in a savings account, then a shift in education would create a gap between the cost of capital and the marginal efficiency of a given stock.

Muurinen (1982) and van Doorslaer (1987) assume that an increase in education lowers the rate of depreciation on the stock of health rather than raising productivity in the gross investment production function. This is a less general assumption than the one that I have made since it rules out schooling effects in the production of nondurable household commodities. In the pure investment model, predictions are very similar whether schooling raises productivity or lowers the rate of depreciation.[31] In the pure consumption model, the assumption made by Muurinen and van Doorslaer is difficult to distinguish from the alternative assumption that ρ_z is zero. Interactions between schooling and the lagged stock of health in the demand function for current health arise given costs of adjustment in the Muurinen–Van Doorslaer model. These are discussed in section 6.

5. EMPIRICAL TESTING

In Grossman (1972b), I present an empirical formulation of the pure investment model, including a detailed outline of the structure and reduced form of that model. I stress the estimation of the investment model rather than the consumption model because the former model generates powerful predictions from simple analysis and more innocuous assumptions. For example, if one uses the investment model, he or she does not have to know whether health is relatively time-intensive to predict the effect of an increase in the wage rate on the demand for health. Also, he or she does not have to know whether education is commodity-neutral to assess the sign of the correlation between health and schooling. Moreover, the responsiveness of the quantity of health demanded to changes in its shadow price and the behavior of gross investment depend essentially on a single parameter—the elasticity of the MEC schedule. In the consumption model, on the other hand, three parameters are relevant—the elasticity of substitution in consumption between present and future health, the wealth elasticity of demand for health, and the elasticity of substitution in consumption between health and the Z commodity. Finally, while good health may be a source of utility, it clearly is a source of earnings. The following formulation is oriented toward the investment model, yet I also offer two tests to distinguish the investment model from the consumption model.

5.1. Structure and Reduced Form

With the production function of healthy time given by equation (29), I make use of three basic structural equations (intercepts are suppressed):

$$\ln H_t = \varepsilon \ln W_t - \varepsilon \ln \pi_t - \varepsilon \ln \delta_t, \tag{42}$$

$$\ln \delta_t = \ln \delta_0 + \tilde{\delta} t, \tag{43}$$

$$\ln I_t \equiv \ln H_t + \ln(1 + \tilde{H}_t / \delta_t) = \rho_H E + (1 - K)\ln M_t + K \ln TH_t. \tag{44}$$

Equation (42) is the demand function for the stock of health and is obtained by solving equation (30) for $\ln H_t$. The equation contains the assumption that the real-own rate of interest is equal to zero. Equation (43) is the depreciation rate function. Equation (44) contains the identity that gross investment equals net investment plus depreciation and assumes that the gross investment production function is a member of the Cobb–Douglas class.

   These three equations and the least-cost equilibrium condition that the ratio of the marginal product of medical care to the marginal product of time must equal the ratio of the price of medical care to the wage rate generate the following reduced form demand curves for health and medical care:

$$\ln H_t = (1 - K)\varepsilon \ln W_t - (1 - K)\varepsilon \ln P_t + \rho_H \varepsilon E - \tilde{\delta}\varepsilon t - \varepsilon \ln \delta_0, \tag{45}$$

$$\ln M_t = \left[(1 - K)\varepsilon + K\right]\ln W_t - \left[(1 - K)\varepsilon + K\right]\ln P_t + \rho_H(\varepsilon - 1)E$$
$$+ \tilde{\delta}(1 - \varepsilon)t + (1 - \varepsilon)\ln \delta_0 + \ln(1 + \tilde{H}_t / \delta_t). \tag{46}$$

If the absolute value of the rate of net disinvestment ($\tilde{H}_t$) were small relative to the rate of depreciation, the last term on the right-hand side of equation (46) could be ignored.[32] Then equations (45) and (46) would express the two main endogenous variables in the system as functions of four variables that are treated as exogenous within the context of this model—the wage rate, the price of medical care, the stock of human capital, and age—and one variable that is unobserved—the rate of depreciation in the initial period. With age subscripts suppressed, the estimating equations become

$$\ln H = B_w \ln W + B_P \ln P + B_E E + B_t t + u_1, \tag{47}$$

$$\ln M = B_{WM} \ln W + B_{PM} \ln P + B_{EM} E + B_{tM} t + u_2, \tag{48}$$

where $B_W = (1 - K)\varepsilon$, et cetera, $u_1 = -\varepsilon \ln \delta_0$ and $u_2 = (1 - \varepsilon) \ln \delta_0$. The invest-ment model predicts $B_W > 0$, $B_P < 0$, $B_E > 0$, $B_t < 0$, $B_{WM} > 0$, and $B_{PM} < 0$. In addition, if $\varepsilon < 1$, $B_{EM} < 0$ and $B_{tM} > 0$.

The variables u_1 and u_2 represent disturbance terms in the reduced form equations. These terms are present because depreciation rates vary among peo-ple of the same age, and such variations cannot be measured empirically. Pro-vided $\ln \delta_0$ were not correlated with the independent variables in equations (47) and (48), u_1 and u_2 would not be correlated with these variables. Therefore, the equations could be estimated by ordinary least squares.

The assumption that the real-own rate of interest equals zero can be jus-tified by noting that wage rates rise with age, at least during most stages of the life cycle. If the wage is growing at a constant percentage rate of $\tilde{W}$ then $\tilde{\pi}_t = K\tilde{W}$, all t. So the assumption implies $r = K\tilde{W}$. By eliminating the real rate of interest and postulating that $-\tilde{H}_t$ is small relative to δ_t, $\ln H$ and $\ln M$ are made linear functions of age. If these assumptions are dropped, the age effect becomes nonlinear.

Since the gross investment production function is a member of the Cobb–Douglas class, the elasticity of substitution in production between medical care and own time (σ_p) is equal to one, and the share of medical care in the total cost of gross investment or the elasticity of gross investment with respect to medical care, $(1 - K)$, is constant. If σ_p were not equal to one, the term K in the wage and price elasticities of demand for medical care would be multiplied by this value rather than by one. The wage and price parameters would not be constant if σ_p were constant but not equal to one, because K would depend on W and P. The linear age, price, and wage effects in equations (47) and (48) are first-order approximations to the true effects.

I have indicated that years of formal schooling completed is the most important determinant of the stock of human capital and employ schooling as a proxy for this stock in the empirical analysis described in section 5.2. In real-ity, the amount of human capital acquired by attending school also depends on such variables as the mental ability of the student and the quality of the school that he or she attends. If these omitted variables are positively correlated with schooling and uncorrelated with the other regressors in the demand function for health, the schooling coefficient is biased upwards. These biases are more difficult to sign if, for example, mental ability and school quality are correlated with the wage rate.[33]

There are two empirical procedures for assessing whether the investment model gives a more adequate representation of people's behavior than the consumption model. In the first place, the wage would have a positive effect on the demand for health in the investment model as long as K were less than one. On the other hand, it would have a positive effect in the consumption model only if health were relatively goods-intensive ($K < K_z$). So, if the computed wage elasticity turns out to be positive, then the larger its value the more likely it is that the investment model is preferable to the consumption model. Of course, provided the production of health were relatively time intensive, the wage elasticity would be negative in the consumption model. In this case, a positive and statistically significant estimate of B_w would lead to a rejection of the consumption model.

In the second place, health has a zero wealth elasticity in the investment model but a positive wealth elasticity in the consumption model provided it is a superior good. This suggests that wealth should be added to the set of regressors in the demand functions for health and medical care. Computed wealth elasticities that do not differ significantly from zero would tend to support the investment model.[34]

In addition to estimating demand functions for health and medical care, one could also fit the gross investment function given by equation (44). This would facilitate a direct test of the hypothesis that the more educated are more efficient producers of health. The production function contains two unobserved variables: gross investment and the own time input. Since, however, $-\tilde{H}_t$ has been assumed to be small relative to δ_t, one could fit[35]

$$\ln H = \alpha \ln M + \rho_H E - \tilde{\delta}t - \ln \delta_0. \tag{49}$$

The difficulty with the above procedure is that it requires a good estimate of the production function. Unfortunately, equation (49) cannot be fitted by ordinary least squares because $\ln M$ and $\ln \delta_0$, the disturbance term, are bound to be correlated. From the demand function for medical care

$$\text{Covariance}(\ln M, \ln \delta_0) = (1 - \varepsilon)\text{Variance}(\ln \delta_0).$$

Given $\varepsilon < 1$, $\ln M$ and $\ln \delta_0$ would be positively correlated. Since an increase in the rate of depreciation lowers the quantity of health capital, the coefficient of medical care would be biased *downward*. The same bias exists if there are unmeasured determinants of efficiency in the production of gross investments in health.

The biases inherent in ordinary least squares estimates of health production functions were first emphasized by Auster, Leveson, and Sarachek (1969). They have been considered in much more detail in the context of infant health by Rosenzweig and Schultz (1983, 1988, 1991), Corman, Joyce, and Grossman

(1987), Grossman and Joyce (1990), and Joyce (1994). Consistent estimates of the production function can be obtained by two-stage least squares (TSLS). In the present context, wealth, the wage rates, and the price of medical care serve as instruments for medical care. The usefulness of this procedure rests, however, on the validity of the overidentification restrictions and the degree to which the instruments explain a significant percentage of the variation in medical care (Bound, Jaeger, and Baker 1995; Staiger and Stock 1997). The TSLS technique is especially problematic when the partial effects of several health inputs are desired and when measures of some of these inputs are absent. In this situation, the overidentification restrictions may not hold because wealth and input prices are likely to be correlated with the missing inputs.

In my monograph on the demand for health, I argued that "a production function taken by itself tells nothing about producer or consumer behavior, although it does have implications for behavior, which operate on the demand curves for health and medical care. Thus, they serve to rationalize the forces at work in the reduced form and give the variables that enter the equations economic significance. Because the reduced form parameters can be used to explain consumer choices and because they can be obtained by conventional statistical techniques, their interpretation should be pushed as far as possible. Only then should one resort to a direct estimate of the production function" (Grossman 1972b, 44). The reader should keep this position in mind in evaluating my discussion of the criticism of my model raised by Zweifel and Breyer (1997) in section 6.

5.2. Data and Results

I fitted the equations formulated in section 5.1 to a nationally representative 1963 United States survey conducted by the National Opinion Research Center and the Center for Health Administration Studies of the University of Chicago. I measured the stock of health by individuals' self-evaluation of their health status. I measured healthy time, the output produced by health capital, either by the complement of the number of restricted-activity days due to illness or injury or the number of work-loss days due to illness or injury. I measured medical care by personal medical expenditures on doctors, dentists, hospital care, prescribed and nonprescribed drugs, nonmedical practitioners, and medical appliances. I had no data on the actual quantities of specific types of services, for example the number of physician visits. Similarly, I had no data on the prices of these services. Thus, I was forced to assume that the price of medical care (P) in the reduced form demand functions either does not vary among consumers or is not correlated with the other regressors in the demand functions. Neither assumption is likely to be correct in light of the well-known moral hazard effect of private health insurance.[36] The main independent variables in the regressions were the age of the individual, the number of years of formal schooling he or she completed, his or her weekly wage rate, and family income (a proxy for wealth).

The most important regression results in the demand functions are as follows. Education and the wage rate have positive and statistically significant coefficients in the health demand function, regardless of the particular measure of health employed. An increase in age simultaneously reduces health and increases medical expenditures. Both effects are significant. The signs of the age, wage, and schooling coefficients in the health demand function and the sign of the age coefficient in the medical care demand function are consistent with the predictions contained in the pure investment model.

In the demand function for medical care, the wage coefficient is negative but not significant, while the schooling coefficient is positive but not significant. The sign of the wage coefficient is not consistent with the pure investment model, and the sign of the schooling coefficient is not consistent with the version of the investment model in which the elasticity of the MEC schedule is less than one. In Grossman (1972b, Appendix D), I show that random measurement error in the wage rate and a positive correlation between the wage and unmeasured determinants of nonmarket efficiency create biases that may explain these results. Other explanations are possible. For example, the wage elasticity of medical care is not necessarily positive in the investment model if waiting and travel time are required to obtain this care [see equation (33)]. Schooling is likely to be positively correlated with the generosity of health insurance coverage leading to an upward bias in its estimated effect.

When the production function is estimated by ordinary least squares, the elasticities of the three measures of health with respect to medical care are all *negative*. Presumably, this reflects the strong positive relation between medical care and the depreciation rate. Estimation of the production function by two-stage least squares reverses the sign of the medical care elasticity in most cases. The results, however, are sensitive to whether or not family income is included in the production function as a proxy for missing inputs.

The most surprising finding is that healthy time has a negative family income elasticity. If the consumption aspects of health were at all relevant, a literal interpretation of this result is that health is an inferior commodity. That explanation is, however, not consistent with the positive and significant income elasticity of demand for medical care. I offer an alternative explanation based on joint production. Such health inputs as cigarettes, alcohol, and rich food have negative marginal products. If their income elasticities exceeded the income elasticities of the beneficial health inputs, the marginal cost of gross investment in health would be positively correlated with income. This explanation can account for the positive income elasticity of demand for medical care. Given its assumptions, higher income persons simultaneously reduce their demand for health and increase their demand for medical care if the elasticity of the MEC schedule is less than one.

I emphasized in section 2 that parametric changes in variables that increase healthy time also prolong length of life. Therefore, I also examine variations in age-adjusted mortality rates across states of the United States in 1960. I find a close agreement between mortality and sick time regression coefficients. Increases in schooling or the wage rate lower mortality, while increases in family income raise it.

6. EXTENSIONS

In this section I deal with criticisms and empirical and theoretical extensions of my framework. I begin with empirical testing with cross-sectional data by Wagstaff (1986), Erbsland, Ried, and Ulrich (1995), and Stratmann (1999) in section 6.1. I pay particular attention to Wagstaff's study because it serves as the basis of a criticism of my approach by Zweifel and Breyer (1997), which I also address in section 6.1. I turn to empirical extensions with longitudinal data by van Doorslaer (1987) and Wagstaff (1993) in section 6.2. These studies introduce costs of adjustment, although in a rather ad hoc manner. I consider theoretical developments by Cropper (1977), Muurinen (1982), Dardanoni and Wagstaff (1987, 1990), Selden (1993), Chang (1996), and Liljas (1998) in section 6.3. With the exception of Muurinen's work, these developments all pertain to uncertainty.

6.1. Empirical Extensions with Cross-Sectional Data

Wagstaff (1986) uses the 1976 Danish Welfare Survey to estimate a multiple indicator version of the structure and reduced form of my demand for health model. He performs a principal components analysis of nineteen measures of nonchronic health problems to obtain four health indicators that reflect physical mobility, mental health, respiratory health, and presence of pain. He then uses these four variables as indicators of the unobserved stock of health. His estimation technique is the so-called MIMIC (multiple indicators-multiple causes) model developed by Jöreskog (1973) and Goldberger (1974) and employs the maximum likelihood procedure contained in Jöreskog and Sörbom (1981). His contribution is unique because it accounts for the multidimensional nature of good health both at the conceptual level and at the empirical level.

Aside from the MIMIC methodology, there are two principal differences between my work and Wagstaff's work. First, the structural equation that I obtain is the production function. On the other hand, the structural equation that he obtains is a conditional output demand function. This expresses the quantity demanded of a health input, such as medical care, as a function of health output, input prices, and exogenous variables in the production function such as schooling and age. In the context of the structure that I specified in section 5.1, the conditional output demand function is obtained by solving equation (44) for medical care as a function of health, the own time input, schooling, age, and the rate of depreciation in the initial period and then using the cost-minimization condition to replace the own time input with the wage rate and the price of medical care. Since an increase in the quantity of health demanded increases the demand for health inputs, the coefficient of health in the conditional demand function is positive.

Second, Wagstaff utilizes a Frisch (1964) demand function for health in discussing and attempting to estimate the pure consumption model. This is a demand function in which the marginal utility of lifetime wealth is held constant when the effects of variables that alter the marginal cost of investment in health are evaluated. I utilized it briefly in treating wage effects in the pure consumption model in section 4 but did not stress it either theoretically or empirically. The marginal utility of lifetime wealth is not observed but can be replaced by initial assets and the sum of lifetime wage rates. Since the data are cross-sectional, initial assets and wage rates over the life cycle are not observed. Wagstaff predicts the missing measures by regressing current assets and the current wage on age, the square of age, and age-invariant socioeconomic characteristics.

Three health inputs are contained in the data: the number of physician visits during the eight months prior to the survey, the number of weeks spent in a hospital during the same period, and the number of complaints for which physician-prescribed or self-prescribed medicines were being taken at the time of the interview. To keep my discussion of the results manageable, I will focus on the reduced form and conditional demand functions for physician visits and on the demand function for health. The reader should keep in mind that the latent variable health obtained from the MIMIC procedure is a *positive* correlate of good health. Good health is the dependent variable in the reduced form demand function for health and one of the right-hand side variables in the conditional demand function for physician visits.

Wagstaff estimates his model with and without initial assets and the sum of lifetime wage rates. He terms the former a pure investment model and the latter a pure consumption model. Before discussing the results, one conceptual issue should be noted. Wagstaff indicates that medical inputs in Denmark are heavily subsidized and that almost all of the total cost of gross investment is accounted for by the cost of the own time input. He then argues that the wage coefficient should equal zero in the pure investment demand function since K, the share of the total cost of gross investment accounted for by time, is equal to one. He also argues that the coefficient of the wage in the demand function for medical care should equal one [see the relevant coefficients in equations (45) and (46)].

Neither of the preceding propositions is necessarily correct. In section 3 I developed a model in which the price of medical care is zero, but travel and waiting time (q hours to make one physician visit) are required to obtain medical care as well as to produce health. I also assumed three endogenous inputs in the health production function: M, TH, and a market good whose acquisition does not require time. I then showed that the wage elasticity of health is positive, while the wage elasticity of medical care is indeterminate in sign [see equations (32) and (33), both of which hold q constant]. If there are only two inputs and no time required to obtain medical care, the wage elasticities of health and medical care are zero. The latter elasticity is zero because the marginal product of medical care would be driven to zero if its price is zero for a given wage rate. An increase in the wage rate induces no further substitution in production. With travel and waiting time, the marginal product of care is positive, but the price of medical care relative to the price of the own time input (Wq/W) does not depend on W.

An additional complication is that Wagstaff includes a proxy for Wq—the respondent's wage multiplied by the time required to travel to his or her physician—in the demand function for medical care. He asserts that the coefficient of the logarithm of this variable should equal the coefficient of the logarithm of the wage in the demand function for medical care in a model in which the price of medical care is not zero. This is not correct because the logarithm of W is held constant. Hence increases in Wq are due solely to increases in q. As q rises, H falls and M falls because the price of M relative to the price of $TH[(P + Wq)/W]$ rises.[37]

In Wagstaff's estimate of the reduced form of the pure investment model, the wage rate, years of formal schooling completed, and age all have the correct signs and all three variables are significant in the demand function for health. In the demand function for physician visits, the schooling variable has a negative and significant coefficient. This finding differs from mine and is in accord with the predictions of the pure investment model. The age coefficient is positive and significant at the 10 percent level on a one-tailed test but not at the 5 percent level.[38] The wage coefficient, however, is negative and not significant. The last finding is consistent with the three-input model outlined above and is not necessarily evidence against the investment model.

The time cost variable has the correct negative sign in the demand function for physician visits, but it is not significant. Wagstaff, however, includes the number of physicians per capita in the respondent's county of residence in the same equation. This variable has a positive effect on visits, is likely to be negatively related to travel time, and may capture part of the travel time effect.

Wagstaff concludes the discussion of the results of estimating the reduced form of the investment model as follows: "Broadly speaking . . . the coefficients are similar to those reported by Grossman and are consistent with the model's structural parameters being of the expected sign. One would seem justified, therefore, in using the . . . data for exploring the implications of using structural equation methods in this context" (p. 214). When this is done, the coefficient of good health in the conditional demand function for physician visits has the wrong sign. It is negative and very significant.

This last finding is used by Zweifel and Breyer (1997) to dismiss my model of the demand for health. They write: "Unfortunately, empirical evidence consistently fails to confirm this crucial prediction [that the partial correlation between good health and medical care should be positive]. When health status is introduced as a latent variable through the use of simultaneous indicators, all components of medical care distinguished exhibit a very definite and highly significant *negative* (their italics) partial relationship with health. . . . The notion that expenditure on medical care constitutes a demand derived from an underlying demand for health cannot be upheld because health status and demand for medical care are negatively rather than positively related" (pp. 60, 62).

Note, however, that biases arise if the conditional demand function is estimated with health treated as exogenous for the same reason that biases arise if the production function is estimated by ordinary least squares. In particular, the depreciation rate in the initial period (the disturbance term in the equation) is positively correlated with medical care and negatively correlated with health. Hence, the coefficient of health is biased downward in the conditional medical care demand function, and this coefficient could well be negative. The conditional demand function is much more difficult to estimate by two-stage least squares than the production function because no exogenous variables are omitted from it in the investment model. Input prices cannot be used to identify this equation because they are relevant regressors in it. Only wealth and the prices of inputs used to produce commodities other than health are omitted from the conditional demand function in the consumption model or in a mixed investment-consumption model. Measures of the latter variables typically are not available.

In his multiple indicator model, Wagstaff does not treat the latent health variable as endogenous when he obtains the conditional demand function. He is careful to point out that the bias that I have just outlined can explain his result. He also argues that absence of measures of some inputs may account for his finding. He states: "The identification of medical care with market inputs in the health investment production function might be argued to be a source of potential error. If non-medical inputs are important inputs in the production of health—as clearly they are—one might argue that the results stem from a fail-ure to estimate a *system* (his italics) of structural demand equations for health inputs" (p. 226). Although I am biased, in my view these considerations go a long way toward refuting the Zweifel–Breyer critique.

As I indicated above, Wagstaff estimates a reduced form demand function for health in the context of what he terms a pure consumption model as well as in the context of a pure investment model. He does this by including initial assets and the lifetime wage variable in the demand functions as proxies for the marginal utility of wealth. Strictly speaking, however, this is not a pure consumption model. It simply accommodates the consumption motive as well as the investment motive for demanding health. Wagstaff proposes but does not stress one test to distinguish the investment model from the consumption model. If the marginal utility of health does not depend on the quantity of the Z-commodity in the current period utility function, the wage effect should be negative in the demand function for health. Empirically, the current wage coef-ficient remains positive and significant when initial assets and the lifetime wage are introduced as regressors in this equation. As I noted in section 4, this result also is consistent with a pure consumption model in which the marginal utility of H is negatively related to Z.

The initial assets and lifetime wage coefficients are highly significant. As Wagstaff indicates, these variables are highly correlated with schooling, the cur-rent wage, and other variables in the demand function for health since both are predicted from these variables. These intercorrelations are so high that the school-ing coefficient becomes negative and significant in the consumption demand function. Wagstaff stresses that these results must be interpreted with caution.

Zweifel and Breyer (1997) have a confusing and incorrect discussion of theoretical and empirical results on wage effects. They claim that their dis-cussion, which forms part of the critique of my model, is based on Wagstaff's study. In the demand function for health, they indicate that the lifetime wage effect is negative in the pure consumption model and positive in the pure invest-ment model. If the current wage is held constant, both statements are wrong.

There is no lifetime wage effect in the investment model and a positive effect in the consumption model provided that health is a superior commodity.[39] If their statements pertain to the current wage effect, the sign is positive in the investment model and indeterminate in the consumption model whether utility or the marginal utility of wealth is held constant.

Zweifel and Breyer's (1997) discussion of schooling effects can be characterized in the same manner as their discussion of wage effects. They claim that the consumption model predicts a positive schooling effect in the demand function for health and a negative effect in the demand function for medical care. This is not entirely consistent with the analysis in section 4. They use Wagstaff's (1986) result that schooling has a positive coefficient in the conditional demand function for physician visits as evidence against my approach. But as Wagstaff and I have stressed, estimates of that equation are badly biased because health is not treated as endogenous.

A final criticism made by Zweifel and Breyer is that the wage rate does not adequately measure the monetary value of an increase in healthy time due to informal sick leave arrangements and private and social insurance that fund earnings losses due to illness. They do not reconcile this point with the positive effects of the wage rate on various health measures in my study and in Wagstaff's study. In addition, sick leave and insurance plans typically finance less than 100 percent of the loss in earnings. More importantly, they ignore my argument that ". . . 'the inconvenience costs of illness' are positively correlated with the wage rate. . . . The complexity of a particular job and the amount of responsibility it entails certainly are positively related to the wage. Thus, when an individual with a high wage becomes ill, tasks that only he can perform accumulate. These increase the intensity of his work load and give him an incentive to avoid illness by demanding more health capital" (Grossman 1972b, 69–70).

Erbsland, Ried, and Ulrich (1995) provide another example of the application of the MIMIC procedure to the estimation of a demand for health model. Their database is the 1986 West German Socio-economic Panel. The degree of handicap, self-rated health, the duration of sick time, and the number of chronic conditions, all as reported by the individual, serve as four indicators of the unobserved stock of health. In the reduced form demand function for health, schooling has a positive and significant coefficient, while age has a negative and significant coefficient. In the reduced form demand function for visits to general practitioners, the age effect is positive and significant, while the schooling effect is negative and significant. These results are consistent with predictions made by the investment model. The latent variable health, which is treated as exogenous, has a negative and very significant coefficient in the conditional demand function for physician visits. This is the same finding reported by Wagstaff (1986).

In my 1972 study (Grossman 1972b), I showed that the sign of the correlation between medical care and health can be reversed if medical care is treated as endogenous in the estimation of health production functions. Stratmann (1999) gives much more recent evidence in support of the same proposition. Using the 1989 US National Health Interview Survey, he estimates production functions in which the number of work-loss days due to illness in the past two weeks serves as the health measure and a dichotomous indicator for a doctor visit in the past two weeks serves as the measure of medical care. In a partial attempt to control for reverse causality from poor health to more medical care, he obtains separate production functions for persons with influenza, persons with impairments, and persons with chronic asthma.

In single equation tobit models, persons who had a doctor visit had significantly more work-loss than persons who did not have a visit for each of the three conditions. In simultaneous equations probit-tobit models in which the probability of a doctor visit is endogenous, persons who had a doctor visit had significantly less work-loss. The tobit coefficient in the simultaneous equations model implies that the marginal effect of a doctor visit is a 2.7 day reduction in work loss in the case of influenza.[40] The corresponding reductions for impairments and chronic asthma are 2.9 days and 6.9 days, respectively.

6.2. Empirical Extensions with Longitudinal Data

Van Doorslaer (1987) and Wagstaff (1993) fit dynamic demand for health models to longitudinal data. These efforts potentially are very useful because they allow one to take account of the effects of unmeasured variables such as the rate of depreciation and of reverse causality from health at early stages in the life cycle to the amount of formal schooling completed (see section 7 for more details). In addition, one can relax the assumption that there are no costs of adjustment, so that the lagged stock of health becomes a relevant determinant of the current stock of health.

Van Doorslaer (1987) employs the 1984 Netherlands Health Interview Survey. While this is a cross-sectional survey, respondents were asked to evaluate their health in 1979 as well as in 1984. Both measures are ten-point scales, where the lowest category is very poor health and the highest category is very good health.

Van Doorslaer uses the identity that the current stock of health equals the undepreciated component of the past stock plus gross investment:

$$H_t = (1 - \delta_{t-1})H_{t-1} + I_{t-1}. \tag{50}$$

He assumes that gross investment is a function of personal background variables (schooling, age, income, and gender). Thus, he regresses health in 1984 on these variables and on health in 1979. To test Muurinen's (1982) hypothesis that schooling lowers the rate of depreciation (see section 6.3), he allows for an interaction between this variable and health in 1979 in some of the estimated models.

Van Doorslaer's main finding is that schooling has a positive and significant coefficient in the regression explaining health in 1984, with health in 1979 held constant. The regressions in which schooling, past health, and an interaction between the two are entered as regressors are plagued by multicollinearity. They do not allow one to distinguish Muurinen's hypothesis from the hypothesis that schooling raises efficiency in the production of health.

Wagstaff (1993) uses the Danish Health Study, which followed respondents over a period of 12 months beginning in October 1982. As in his 1986 study, a MIMIC model is estimated. Three health measures are used as indicators of the unobserved stock of health capital in 1982 (past stock) and 1983 (current stock). These are a dichotomous indicator of the presence of a health limitation, physician-assessed health of the respondent as reported by the respondent, and self-assessed health.[41] Both of the assessment variables have five-point scales. Unlike his 1986 study, Wagstaff also treats gross investment in health as a latent variable. There are six health-care utilization indicators of gross investment: the number of consultations with a general practitioner over the year, the number of consultations with a specialist over the year, the number of days as an inpatient in a hospital over the year, the number of sessions with a physiotherapist over the year, the number of hospital outpatient visits over the year, and the number of hospital emergency room visits during the year.

Wagstaff explicitly assumes partial adjustment instead of instantaneous adjustment. He also assumes that the reduced form demand for health equation is linear rather than log-linear. He argues that this makes it compatible with the linear nature of the net investment identity (net investment equals gross investment minus depreciation). The desired stock in period t is a linear function of age, schooling, family income, and gender. A fraction (μ) of the gap between the actual and the desired stock is closed each period. Hence the lagged stock enters the reduced form demand function with a coefficient equal to $1 - \mu$. Solving equation (50) for gross investment in period $t - 1$ and replacing H_t by its demand function, Wagstaff obtains a demand function for I_{t-1} that depends on the same variables as those in the demand function for H_t. The coefficient of each sociodemographic variable in the demand function for H_t is the same as the corresponding coefficient in the demand function for I_{t-1}. The coefficient on the lagged stock in the latter demand function equals $- (\mu - \delta_{t-1})$. By estimating the model with cross-equation constraints, μ and δ_{t-1} are identified.

Wagstaff emphasizes that the same variables enter his conditional demand function for I_{t-1} in his cost-of-adjustment model as those that enter the conditional demand function for I_{t-1} in my instantaneous adjustment model. The interpretation of the parameters, however, differs. In my case, the contemporaneous health stock has a positive coefficient, whereas in his case the coefficient is negative if μ exceeds δ_{t-1}. In my case, the coefficient of schooling, for example, is equal to the negative of the schooling coefficient in the production function. In his case, it equals the coefficient of schooling in the demand function for H_t.

To allow for the possibility that the rate of depreciation varies with age, Wagstaff fits the model separately for adults under the age of forty-one and for adults greater than or equal to this age. For each age group, schooling has a positive and significant effect on current health with past health held constant. The coefficient of H_{t-1} in the demand function for I_{t-1} is negative, suggesting costs of adjustment and also suggesting that μ exceeds δ_{t-1}. The implied value of the rate of depreciation is, however, larger in the sample of younger adults than in the sample of older adults. Moreover, in the latter sample, the estimated rate of depreciation is *negative*. These implausible findings may be traced to the inordinate demands on the data attributed to the MIMIC methodology with two latent variables and cross-equation constraints.

Some conceptual issues can be raised in evaluating the two studies just discussed. Wagstaff (1993) estimates input demand functions which include availability measures as proxies for travel and waiting time (for example, the per capita number of general practitioners in the individual's district in the demand function for the number of consultations with general practitioners). Yet he excludes these variables from the demand functions for H_t and I_{t-1}. This is not justified. In addition, Wagstaff implies that the gross investment production function is linear in its inputs, which violates the cost-minimization conditions.

More fundamentally, both Van Doorslaer (1987) and Wagstaff (1993) provide ad hoc cost-of-adjustment models. I now show that a rigorous development of such a model contains somewhat different demand functions than the ones that they estimate. To simplify, I assume that the pure investment model is valid, ignore complications with cost-of-adjustment models studied by Ehrlich and Chuma (1990), and fix the wage rate at $1. I also make use of the exact form of the first-order condition for H_t in a discrete time model (see endnote 13):

$$G_t = (1+r)\pi_{t-1} - (1-\delta_t)\pi_t. \tag{51}$$

Note that π_{t-1} is the marginal cost of gross investment in health. Since marginal cost rises as the quantity of investment rises in a model with costs of adjustment, the marginal cost of investment exceeds the average cost of investment. Also, to simplify and to keep the system linear, I assume that G_t is a linear function of H_t and that π_{t-1} is a linear function of I_{t-1} and P_{t-1} (the price of the single market input used in the gross investment production function):

$$G_t = \varphi - \alpha H_t, \tag{52}$$

$$\pi_{t-1} = P_{t-1} + I_{t-1}. \tag{53}$$

Given this model, the optimal stock of health in period t is

$$H_t = \frac{\varphi}{\alpha} - \frac{(1+r)}{\alpha} P_{t-1} - \frac{(1+r)}{\alpha} I_{t-1} + \frac{(1-\delta_t)}{\alpha} P_t + \frac{(1-\delta_t)}{\alpha} I_t. \tag{54}$$

Since $I_{t-1} = H_t - (1 - \delta_{t-1})H_{t-1}$ and $I_t(1 - \delta_t) = (1 - \delta_t)H_{t+1} - (1 - \delta_t)^2 H_t,$

$$H_t = \frac{\varphi}{D} - \frac{(1+r)}{D} P_{t-1} + \frac{(1+r)(1-\delta_{t-1})}{D} H_{t-1}$$
$$+ \frac{(1-\delta_t)}{D} H_{t+1} + \frac{(1-\delta_t)}{D} P_t, \tag{55}$$

where $D = \alpha + (1 + r) + (1 - \delta_t)^2$. Alternatively, substitute equation (55) into the definition of I_{t-1} to obtain

$$I_{t-1} = \frac{\varphi}{D} - \frac{(1+r)}{D} P_{t-1} - \frac{(1-\delta_{t-1})\left[\alpha + (1-\delta_t)^2\right]}{D} H_{t-1}$$
$$+ \frac{(1-\delta_t)}{D} H_{t+1} + \frac{(1-\delta_t)}{D} P_t. \tag{56}$$

Equation (55) is the demand for health function obtained by Van Doorslaer (1987) and Wagstaff (1993). Their estimates are biased because the stock of health in period t depends on the stock of health in period $t + 1$ as well as on the stock of health in period $t - 1$ in a model with costs of adjustment. Equation (56) is the gross investment demand function obtained by Wagstaff. His estimate is biased because gross investment in period $t - 1$ depends on the stock of health in period $t + 1$ as well as on the stock of health in period $t - 1$. Note that this equation and equation (55) also depend on measured and unmeasured determinants of market and nonmarket efficiency in periods $t - 1$ and t.

The second-order difference equations given by equations (55) and (56) can be solved to express H_t or I_{t-1} as functions of current, past, and future values of all the exogenous variables. Similarly, H_{t-1} and H_{t+1} depend on this set of exogenous variables. Since one of the members of this set is the disturbance term in equation (55) or (56), the lagged and future stocks are correlated with the regression disturbance. Consequently, biases arise if either equation is estimated by ordinary least squares. Consistent estimates can be obtained by fitting the equations by two-stage least squares with past and future values of the exogenous variables serving as instruments for the one-period lead and the one-period lag of the stock.[42] Note that consistent estimates cannot be obtained by the application of ordinary least squares to a first-difference model or to a fixed-effects model. Lagged and future health variables do not drop out of these models and are correlated with the time-varying component of the disturbance term.

I conclude that cost-of-adjustment models require at least three data points (three observations on each individual) to be estimated. Calculated parameters of this model are biased if they are obtained by ordinary least squares. There is an added complication that arises even if all the necessary data are available because the procedure that I have outlined assumes that individuals have perfect information about the future values of the exogenous variables. This may or may not be the case.[43] While the two studies that I have reviewed are provocative, they do not contain enough information to compare instantaneous-adjustment models to cost-of-adjustment models.

6.3. Theoretical Extensions

Muurinen (1982) examines comparative static age, schooling, and wealth effects in the context of a mixed investment-consumption model with perfect certainty. This approach is more general than mine because it incorporates both the investment motive and the consumption motive for demanding health. In deriving formulas for the effects of increases in age and schooling on the optimal quantities of health capital and medical care, Muurinen assumes that the undiscounted monetary value of the marginal utility of healthy time in period t, given by $(Uh_t/\lambda)(1 + r)^t$, is constant for all t. If m_t is the marginal cost of the Z commodity and U_t is its marginal utility, the undiscounted monetary value of the marginal utility of healthy time also is given by $(Uh_t/U_t)m_t$. Hence, Muurinen is assuming that the marginal rate of substitution between healthy time and the Z commodity is constant or that the two commodities are perfect substitutes. Clearly, this is a very restrictive assumption.[44]

In my formal development of the demand for health, I ruled out uncertainty. Surely that is not realistic. I briefly indicated that one could introduce this phenomenon by assuming that a given consumer faces a probability distribution of depreciation rates in every period. I speculated, but did not prove, that consumers might have incentives to hold an excess stock of health in relatively desirable "states of the world" (outcomes with relatively low depreciation rates) in order to reduce the loss associated with an unfavorable outcome. In these relatively desirable states, the marginal monetary return on an investment in health might be smaller than the opportunity cost of capital in a pure investment model (Grossman 1972b, 19–21).

Beginning with Cropper (1977), a number of persons formally have introduced uncertainty into my pure investment model. Cropper assumes that illness occurs in a given period if the stock of health falls below a critical sickness level, which is random. Income is zero in the illness state. An increase in the stock of health lowers the probability of this state. Cropper further assumes that savings are not possible (all income takes the form of earnings) and that consumers are risk-neutral in the sense that their objective is to maximize the expected discounted value of lifetime wealth.[45]

In my view, Cropper's main result is that consumers with higher incomes or wealth levels will maintain higher stocks of health than poorer persons. While this may appear to be a different result than that contained in my pure investment model with perfect certainty, it is not for two reasons. First, an increase in the stock of health lowers the probability of illness but has no impact on earnings in non-illness states. Hence the marginal benefit of an increase in the stock is given by the reduction in the probability of illness multiplied by the difference between income and gross investment outlays. With these outlays held constant, an increase in income raises the marginal benefit and the marginal rate of return on an investment.[46] Therefore, this wealth or income effect is analogous to the wage effect in my pure investment model with perfect certainty. Second, consider a pure investment model with perfect certainty, positive initial assets but no possibility to save or borrow in financial markets. In this model, investment in health is the only mechanism to increase future consumption. An increase in initial assets will increase the optimal stock of health provided future consumption has a positive wealth elasticity.

Later treatments of uncertainty in the context of demand for health models have assumed risk-averse behavior, so that an expected utility function that exhibits diminishing marginal utility of present and future consumption is maximized. Dardanoni and Wagstaff (1987), Selden (1993), and Chang (1996) all employ two-period models in which the current period utility function depends only on current consumption. Uncertainty in the second period arises because the earnings-generating function in that period contains a random variable. This function is $Y_2 = Wh_2 (H_2, R) = F(H_2, R)$, where Y_2 is earnings in period two, h_2 is the amount of healthy time in that period, H_2 is the stock of health, and R is the random term. Clearly, $F_1 > 0$ and $F_{11} < 0$, where F_1 and F_{11} are the first and second derivatives of H_2 in the earnings function. The second derivative is negative because of my assumption that the marginal product of the stock of health in the production of healthy time falls as the stock rises. An increase in R raises earnings ($F_2 > 0$). In addition to income or earnings from health, income is available from savings at a fixed rate of return.

Given uncertainty, risk-averse individuals make larger investments in health than they would in its absence. Indeed, the expected marginal rate of return is smaller than the rate with perfect certainty. This essentially confirms a result that I anticipated in the brief discussion of uncertainty in my monograph.

The main impact of the introduction of uncertainty is that the quantities of health capital and gross investment depend on initial assets, with the wage rate held constant. The direction of these effects, however, is ambiguous because it depends on the way in which risk is specified. Dardanoni and Wagstaff (1987) adopt a multiplicative specification in which the earnings function is $Y_2 = RH_2$. They show that an increase in initial assets raises the optimal quantities of health and medical care if the utility function exhibits decreasing absolute risk aversion.[47] Selden (1993) adopts a linear specification in which the earnings function is $Y_2 = F(H_2 + R)$ and $\partial^2 Y_2/\partial(H_2 + R)^2 < 0$. He reaches the opposite conclusion: Health and medical care fall as assets rise given declining absolute risk aversion.

Chang (1996) generalizes the specification of risk. He shows that the sign of the asset effect depends on the sign of the second-order cross partial derivative in the earnings function (F_{12}). If F_{12} is positive and F_{11} is zero, the asset effect is positive. This is the case considered by Dardanoni and Wagstaff. In my view, it is not realistic because it assumes that the marginal product of the stock of health in the production of healthy time is constant. Given the more realistic case in which F_{11} is negative, the asset effect is negative if F_{12} is negative (Selden's case) and indeterminate in sign if F_{12} is positive.[48]

Dardanoni and Wagstaff (1990) introduce uncertainty into pure consumption models of the demand for health. Their study is a static one-period model. The utility function depends on the consumption of a composite commodity and health. Health is given by $H = R + I(M, R)$, where R is a random variable and $I(M, R)$ denotes the health production function. They consider two models: one in which $H = R + M$ and one in which $H = RM$. In the first model, an increase in the variance of R with the mean held constant increases the quantity of medical care demanded under plausible assumptions about the utility function (superiority of the composite consumption good and non-increasing absolute risk aversion with regard to that good). In the second model, the same effect is more difficult to sign, although it is positive if an increase in R leads to a reduction in M and an increase in the composite good if the utility function exhibits non-increasing relative risk aversion with regard to the composite good.[49]

Liljas (1998) considers uncertainty in the context of a multiperiod mixed investment-consumption model. Uncertainty takes the form of a random variable that affects the stock of health in period t in an additive fashion. He shows that the stock of health is larger in the stochastic case than in the certainty case. Presumably, this result pertains to the expected stock of health in period t. The actual stock should be smaller than the stock with certainty given a negative shock. Social insurance that funds part of the loss in income due to illness lowers the optimal stock. Private insurance that also funds part of this loss will not necessarily lower the stock further and may actually increase it if the cost of this insurance falls as the stock rises.

To summarize, compared to a model with perfect certainty, the expected value of the stock of health is larger and the optimal quantities of gross investment and health inputs also are larger in a model with uncertainty. In a pure investment model, an increase in initial assets can cause health and medical care to change, but the direction of these effects is ambiguous. Under reasonable assumptions, an increase in the variance of risk raises optimal medical care in a pure consumption model.

How valuable are these results? With the exception of the ambiguity of the asset effect, they are not very surprising. The variance of risk is extremely difficult to measure. I am not aware of empirical studies that have attempted to include this variable in a demand for health framework. The possibility that the asset effect can be nonzero in a pure investment model provides an alternative explanation of Wagstaff's (1986) finding that an increase in proxies for initial assets and lifetime earnings raise health. None of the studies has taken my suggestion to treat uncertainty in terms of a probability distribution of depreciation rates in a given period. This could be done by writing the stock of health in period t as

$$H_t = H_{t-1} - \bar{\delta}_{t-1} H_{t-1} + I_{t-1} + R_{t-1}, \tag{57}$$

where $\bar{\delta}_{t-1}$ is the mean depreciation rate and $R_{t-1} = (\bar{\delta}_{t-1} - \delta_{t-1})H_{t-1}$. I leave it to the reader to explore the implications of this formulation.

7. HEALTH AND SCHOOLING

An extensive review of the literature conducted by Grossman and Kaestner (1997) suggests that years of formal schooling completed is the most important correlate of good health. This finding emerges whether health levels are measured by mortality rates, morbidity rates, self-evaluation of health status, or physiological indicators of health, and whether the units of observation are individuals or groups. The studies also suggest that schooling is a more important correlate of health than occupation or income, the two other components of socioeconomic status. This is particularly true when one controls for reverse causality from poor health to low income. Of course, schooling is a causal determinant of occupation and income, so that the gross effect of schooling on health may reflect in part its impact on socioeconomic status. The studies reviewed, however, indicate that a significant portion of the gross schooling effect cannot be traced to the relationship between schooling and income or occupation.

In a broad sense, the observed positive correlation between health and schooling may be explained in one of three ways. The first argues that there is a causal relationship that runs from increases in schooling to increases in health. The second holds that the direction of causality runs from better health to more schooling. The third argues that no causal relationship is implied by the correlation; instead, differences in one or more "third variables," such as physical and mental ability and parental characteristics, affect both health and schooling in the same direction.

It should be noted that these three explanations are not mutually exclusive and can be used to rationalize an observed correlation between any two variables. But from a public policy perspective, it is important to distinguish among them and to obtain quantitative estimates of their relative magnitudes. Suppose that a stated goal of public policy is to improve the level of health of the population or of certain groups in the population. Given this goal and given the high correlation between health and schooling, it might appear that one method of implementation would be to increase government outlays on schooling. In fact, Auster, Leveson, and Sarachek (1969) suggest that the rate of return on increases in health via higher schooling outlays far exceeds the rate of return on increases in health via higher medical care outlays. This argument assumes that the correlation between health and schooling reflects only the effect of schooling on health. If, however, the causal relationship was the reverse, or if the third-variable hypothesis was relevant, then increased outlays on schooling would not accomplish the goal of improved health.

Causality from schooling to health results when more educated persons are more efficient producers of health. This efficiency effect can take two forms. Productive efficiency pertains to a situation in which the more educated obtain a larger health output from given amounts of endogenous (choice) inputs. This is the effect that I have emphasized throughout this paper. Allocative efficiency, discussed in detail by Kenkel (2000), pertains to a situation in which schooling increases information about the true effects of the inputs on health. For example, the more educated may have more knowledge about the harmful effects of cigarette smoking or about what constitutes an appropriate diet. Allocative efficiency will improve health to the extent that it leads to the selection of a better input mix.

Causality from schooling to health also results when education changes tastes or preferences in a manner that favors health relative to certain other commodities. In some cases, the taste hypothesis cannot be distinguished from allocative hypothesis, particularly when knowledge of health effects has been available for some time. But in a situation in which the new information becomes available, the allocative efficiency hypothesis predicts a more rapid response by the more educated.

Alternatively, the direction of causality may run from better health to more schooling because healthier students may be more efficient producers of additions to the stock of knowledge (or human capital) via formal schooling. Furthermore, this causal path may have long lasting effects if past health is an input into current health status. Thus, even for non-students, a positive relationship between health and schooling may reflect reverse causality in the absence of controls for past health.

The "third-variable" explanation is particularly relevant if one thinks that a large unexplained variation in health remains after controlling for schooling and other determinants. Studies summarized by Grossman and Kaestner (1997) and results in the related field of investment in human capital and the determinants of earnings [for example, Mincer (1974)] indicate that the percentage of the variation in health explained by schooling is much smaller than the percentage of the variation in earnings explained by schooling. Yet it also is intuitive that health and illness have larger random components than earnings. The third-variable explanation is relevant only if the unaccounted factors which affect health are correlated with schooling. Note that both the reverse causality explanation and the third-variable explanation indicate that the observed relationship between current health and schooling reflects an omitted variable. In the case of reverse causality, the omitted variable is identified as past or endowed health. In econometric terminology, both explanations fall under the general rubric of biases due to unobserved heterogeneity among individuals.

Kaestner and I (Grossman and Kaestner 1997) conclude from our extensive review of the literature that schooling does in fact have a causal impact on good health. In drawing this conclusion, we are sensitive to the difficulties of establishing causality in the social sciences where natural experiments rarely can be performed. Our affirmative answer is based on the numerous studies in the United States and developing countries that we have summarized. These studies employ a variety of adult, child, and infant health measures, many different estimation techniques, and controls for a host of third variables.

I leave it up to the reader to evaluate this conclusion after reading the Grossman-Kaestner paper and the studies therein. I also urge the reader to consult my study dealing with the correlation between health and schooling

(Grossman 1975) because I sketch out a framework in which there are complementary relationships between schooling and health—the principal components of the stock of human capital—at various stages in the life cycle. The empirical evidence that Kaestner and I report on causality from schooling to health as well as on causality from health to schooling underscores the potential payoffs to the formal development of a model in which the stocks of health and knowledge are determined simultaneously.

In the remainder of this section, I want to address one challenge of the conclusion that the role of schooling is causal: the time preference hypothesis first proposed by Fuchs (1982). Fuchs argues that persons who are more future oriented (who have a high degree of time preference for the future) attend school for longer periods of time and make larger investments in health. Thus, the effect of schooling on health is biased if one fails to control for time preference.

The time preference hypothesis is analogous to the hypothesis that the positive effect of schooling on earnings is biased upward by the omission of ability. In each case a well-established relationship between schooling and an outcome (earnings or health) is challenged because a hard-to-measure variable (ability or time preference) has been omitted. Much ink has been spilled on this issue in the human capital literature. Attempts to include proxies for ability in earnings functions have resulted in very modest reductions in the schooling coefficient (for example, Griliches and Mason 1972; Hause 1972). Proponents of the ability hypothesis have attributed the modest reductions to measurement error in these proxies (for example, Goldberger 1974). More recent efforts have sought instruments that are correlated with schooling but not correlated with ability (for example, Angrist and Krueger 1991). These efforts have produced the somewhat surprising finding that the schooling coefficient *increases* when the instrumental variables procedure is employed. A cynic might conclude that the way to destroy any empirical regularity is to attribute it to an unmeasured variable, especially if the theory with regard to the relevance of this variable is not well developed.[50]

Nevertheless, the time preference hypothesis is important because it is related to recent and potentially very rich theoretical models in which preferences are endogenous (Becker and Murphy 1988; Becker 1996; Becker and Mulligan 1997). Differences in time preference among individuals will not generate differences in investments in human capital unless certain other conditions are met. One condition is that the ability to finance these investments by borrowing is limited, so that they must be funded to some extent by foregoing current consumption. Even if the capital market is perfect, the returns on an investment in schooling depend on hours of work if schooling raises market productivity by a larger percentage than it raises nonmarket productivity.

Individuals who are more future oriented desire relatively more leisure at older ages. Therefore, they work more at younger ages and have a higher discounted marginal benefit on a given investment than persons who are more present oriented. If health enters the utility function, persons who discount the future less heavily will have higher health levels during most stages of the life cycle. Hence, a positive relationship between schooling and health does not necessarily imply causality.

Since the conditions that generate causal effects of time preference on schooling and health are plausible, attempts to control for time preference in estimating the schooling coefficient in a health outcome equation are valuable. Fuchs (1982) measures time preference in a telephone survey by asking respondents questions in which they chose between a sum of money now and a larger sum in the future. He includes an index of time preference in a multiple regression in which health status is the dependent variable and schooling is one of the independent variables. Fuchs is not able to demonstrate that the schooling effect is due to time preference. The latter variable has a negative regression coefficient, but it is not statistically significant. When time preference and schooling are entered simultaneously, the latter dominates the former. These results must be regarded as preliminary because they are based on one small sample of adults on Long Island and on exploratory measures of time preference.

Farrell and Fuchs (1982) explore the time preference hypothesis in the context of cigarette smoking using interviews conducted in 1979 by the Stanford Heart Disease Prevention Program in four small agricultural cities in California. They examine the smoking behavior of white non-Hispanics who were not students at the time of the survey, had completed twelve to eighteen years of schooling, and were at least twenty-four years old. The presence of retrospective information on cigarette smoking at ages seventeen and twenty-four allows them to relate smoking at these two ages to years of formal schooling completed by 1979 for cohorts who reached age seventeen before and after the widespread diffusion of information concerning the harmful effects of cigarette smoking on health.

Farrell and Fuchs find that the negative relationship between schooling and smoking, which rises in absolute value for cohorts born after 1953, does not increase between the ages of seventeen and twenty-four. Since the individuals were all in the same school grade at age seventeen, the additional schooling obtained between that age and age twenty-four cannot be the cause of differential smoking behavior at age twenty-four, according to the authors. Based on these results, Farrell and Fuchs reject the hypothesis that schooling is a causal factor in smoking behavior in favor of the view that a third variable causes both. Since the strong negative relationship between schooling and smoking developed only after the spread of information concerning the harmful effects of smoking, they argue that the same mechanism may generate the schooling-health relationship.

A different interpretation of the Farrell and Fuchs finding emerges if one assumes that consumers are farsighted. The current consumption of cigarettes leads to more illness and less time for work in the future. The cost of this lost time is higher for persons with higher wage rates who have made larger investments in human capital. Thus, the costs of smoking in high school are greater for persons who plan to make larger investments in human capital.

Berger and Leigh (1989) have developed an extremely useful methodology for disentangling the schooling effect from the time preference effect. Their methodology amounts to treating schooling as an endogenous variable in the health equation and estimating the equation by a variant of two-stage least squares. If the instrumental variables used to predict schooling in the first stage are uncorrelated with time preference, this technique yields an unbiased estimate of the schooling coefficient. Since the framework generates a recursive model with correlated errors, exogenous variables that are unique to the health equation are not used to predict schooling.

Berger and Leigh apply their methodology to two datasets: the first National Health and Nutrition Examination Survey (NHANES I) and the National Longitudinal Survey of Young Men (NLS). In NHANES I, health is measured by blood pressure, and separate equations are obtained for persons aged twenty through forty and over age forty in the period 1971 through 1975. The schooling equation is identified by ancestry and by average real per capita income and average real per capita expenditures on education in the state in which an individual resided from the year of birth to age six. These variables enter the schooling equation but are excluded from the health equation. In the NLS, health is measured by a dichotomous variable that identifies men who in 1976 reported that health limited or prevented them from working and alternatively by a dichotomous variable that identifies the presence of a functional health limitation. The men in the sample were between the ages of twenty-four and thirty-four in 1976, had left school by that year, and reported no health limitations in 1966 (the first year of the survey). The schooling equation is identified by IQ, Knowledge of Work test scores, and parents' schooling.

Results from the NLS show that the schooling coefficient rises in absolute value when predicted schooling replaces actual schooling, and when health is measured by work limitation. When health is measured by functional limitation, the two-stage least squares schooling coefficient is approximately equal to the ordinary least squares coefficient, although the latter is estimated with more precision. For persons aged twenty through forty in NHANES I, schooling has a larger impact on blood pressure in absolute value in the two-stage regressions. For persons over age forty, however, the predicted value of schooling has a positive and insignificant regression coefficient. Except for the last finding, these results are inconsistent with the time preference hypothesis and consistent with the hypothesis that schooling causes health.

In another application of the same methodology, Leigh and Dhir (1997) focus on the relationship between schooling and health among persons ages sixty-five and over in the 1986 wave of the Panel Survey of Income Dynamics (PSID). Health is measured by a disability index comprised of answers to six activities of daily living and by a measure of exercise frequency. Responses to questions asked in 1972 concerning the ability to delay gratification are used to form an index of time preference. Instruments for schooling include parents' schooling, parents' income, and state of residence in childhood. The schooling variable is associated with better health and more exercise whether it is treated as exogenous or endogenous.

Sander (1995a, 1995b) has applied the methodology developed by Berger and Leigh to the relationship between schooling and cigarette smoking studied by Farrell and Fuchs (1982). His data consist of the 1986–1991 waves of the National Opinion Research Center's General Social Survey. In the first paper the outcome is the probability of quitting smoking, while in the second the outcome is the probability of smoking. Separate probit equations are obtained for men and women ages twenty-five and older. Instruments for schooling include father's schooling, mother's schooling, rural residence at age sixteen, region of residence at age sixteen, and number of siblings.

In general schooling has a negative effect on smoking participation and a positive effect on the probability of quitting smoking. These results are not sensitive to the use of predicted as opposed to actual schooling in the probit regressions. Moreover, the application of the Wu-Hausman endogeneity test (Wu 1973; Hausman 1978) in the quit equation suggest that schooling is exogenous in this equation. Thus, Sander's results, like Berger and Leigh's and Leigh and Dhir's results, are inconsistent with the time preference hypothesis.

The aforementioned conclusion rests on the assumption that the instruments used to predict schooling in the first stage are uncorrelated with time preference. The validity of this assumption is most plausible in the case of measures such as real per capita income and real per capita outlays on education in the state in which an individual resided from birth to age six (used by Berger and Leigh in NHANES I), state of residence in childhood (used by Leigh and Dhir in the PSID), and rural residence at age sixteen and region of residence at that age (used by Sander). The validity of the assumption is less plausible in the case of measures such as parents' schooling (used by Sander and by Berger and Leigh in the NLS and by Leigh and Dhir in the PSID) and parents' income (used by Leigh and Dhir in the PSID).

Given this and the inherent difficulty in Fuchs's (1982) and Leigh and Dhir's (1997) attempts to measure time preference directly, definitive evidence with regard to the time preference hypothesis still is lacking. Moreover, Sander (1995a, 1995b) presents national data showing a much larger downward trend in the probability of smoking and a much larger upward trend in the probability of quitting smoking between 1966 and 1987 as the level of education rises. Since information concerning the harmful effects of smoking was widespread by the early 1980s, these results are not consistent with an allocative efficiency argument that the more educated are better able to process new information.

Becker and Murphy's (1988) theoretical model of rational addiction predicts that persons who discount the future heavily are more likely to participate in such addictive behaviors as cigarette smoking. Becker, Grossman, and Murphy (1991) show that the higher educated people are more responsive to changes in the harmful future consequences of the consumption of addictive goods because they are more future oriented. Thus, the trends just cited are consistent with a negative relationship between schooling and the rate of time preference for the present.

Proponents of the time preference hypothesis assume that a reduction in the rate of time preference for the present causes years of formal schooling to rise. On the other hand, Becker and Mulligan (1997) argue that causality may run in the opposite direction: namely, an increase in schooling may *cause* the rate of time preference for the present to fall (may *cause* the rate of time preference for the future to rise). In most models of optimal consumption over the life cycle, consumers maximize a lifetime utility function defined as the discounted sum or present value of utility in each period or at each age. The discount factor (β) is given by $\beta = 1/(1 + g)$, where g is the rate of time preference for the present. Becker and Mulligan point out that the present value of utility is *higher* the smaller is the rate of time preference for the present. Hence, consumers have incentives to make investments that *lower* the rate of time preference for the present.

Becker and Mulligan then show that the marginal costs of investments that lower time preference fall and the marginal benefits rise as income or wealth rises. Marginal benefits also are greater when the length of life is greater. Hence, the equilibrium rate of time preference falls as the level of education rises because education raises income and life expectancy. Moreover, the more educated may be more efficient in making investments that lower the rate of time preference for the present—a form of productive efficiency not associated with health production. To quote Becker and Mulligan: "Schooling also determines . . .

[investments in time preference] partly through the study of history and other subjects, for schooling focuses students' attention on the future. Schooling can communicate images of the situations and difficulties of adult life, which are the future of childhood and adolescence. In addition, through repeated practice at problem solving, schooling helps children learn the art of scenario simulation. Thus, educated people should be more productive at reducing the remoteness of future pleasures" (pp. 735–736).

Becker and Mulligan's argument amounts to a third causal mechanism in addition to productive and allocative efficiency in health production via which schooling can cause health. Econometrically, the difference between their model and Fuchs's model can be specified as follows:

$$H = \alpha_1 Y + \alpha_2 E + \alpha_3 g, \tag{58}$$

$$g = \alpha_4 Y + \alpha_5 E, \tag{59}$$

$$E = \alpha_6 g, \tag{60}$$

$$Y = \alpha_7 E. \tag{61}$$

In this system H is health, Y is permanent income, E is years of formal school-ing completed, g is time preference for the present, and the disturbance terms are suppressed. The first equation is a demand for health function in which the coefficient of E reflects productive or allocative efficiency or both. Fuchs assumes that α_5 is zero. Hence, the coefficient of E in the first equation is biased if g is omitted.

In one version of their model, Becker and Mulligan assume that α_6 is zero, although in a more general formulation they allow this coefficient to be non-zero. Given that α_6 is zero, and substituting the second equation into the first, one obtains

$$H = (\alpha_1 + \alpha_4 \alpha_3)Y + (\alpha_2 + \alpha_5 \alpha_3)E. \tag{62}$$

The coefficient of Y in the last equation reflects both the direct effect of income on health (α_1) and the indirect effect of income on health through time preference ($\alpha_4 \alpha_3$). Similarly, the coefficient of E reflects both the direct efficiency effect (α_2) and the indirect effect of schooling on health through time preference ($\alpha_5 \alpha_3$).

Suppose that the direct efficiency effect of schooling (α_2) is zero. In Fuchs's model, if health is regressed on income and schooling as represented by solving equation (60) for g, the expected value of the schooling coefficient is α_3/α_6. This coefficient reflects causality from time preference to schooling. In Becker and Mulligan's model the schooling coefficient is $\alpha_3 \alpha_5$. This coefficient reflects causality from schooling to time preference. The equation that expresses income as a function of schooling stresses that schooling has indirect effects on health via income. Becker and Mulligan would include health as a determinant of time preference in the second equation because health lowers mortality, raises future utility levels, and increases incentives to make investments that lower the rate of time preference.

Becker and Mulligan's model appears to contain useful insights in considering intergenerational relationships between parents and children. For example, parents can raise their children's future health, including their adulthood health, by making them more future oriented. Note that years of formal schooling completed is a time-invariant variable beyond approximately age thirty, while adult health is not time invariant. Thus, parents probably have a more important direct impact on the former than the latter. By making investments that raise their offsprings' schooling, parents also induce them to make investments that lower their rate of time preference for the present and therefore raise their adult health.

Becker and Mulligan suggest a more definitive and concrete way to measure time preference and incorporate it into estimates of health demand functions than those that have been attempted to date. They point out that the natural logarithm of the ratio of consumption between consecutive time periods ($\ln L$) is approximately equal to $\sigma[\ln(1 + r) - \ln(1 + g)]$, where σ is the intertemporal elasticity of substitution in consumption, r is the market rate of interest, and g is the rate of time preference for the present. If σ and r do not vary among individuals, variations in $\ln L$ capture variations in time preference. With panel data, $\ln L$ can be included as a regressor in the health demand function. Since Becker and Mulligan stress the endogeneity of time preference and its dependence on schooling, simultaneous equations techniques appear to be required. Identification of this model will not be easy, but success in this area has the potential to greatly inform public policy.

To illustrate the last point, suppose that most of the effect of schooling on health operates through time preference. Then school-based programs to promote health knowledge in areas characterized by low levels of income and education may have much smaller payoffs than programs that encourage the investments in time preference made by the more educated. Indeed, in an ever-changing world in which new information constantly becomes available, general interventions that encourage future-oriented behavior may have much larger rates of return in the long run than specific interventions designed, for example, to discourage cigarette smoking, alcohol abuse, or the use of illegal drugs.

There appear to be important interactions between Becker and Mulligan's theory of the endogenous determination of time preference and Becker and Murphy's (1988) theory of rational addiction. Such addictive behaviors as cigarette smoking, excessive alcohol use, and the consumption of illegal drugs have demonstrated adverse health effects. Increased consumption of these goods raises present utility but lowers future utility. According to Becker and Mulligan (1997, p. 744), "Since a decline in future utility reduces the benefits from a lower discount on future utilities, greater consumption of harmful substances would lead to higher rates of time preference by discouraging investments in lowering these rates . . ." This is the converse of Becker and Murphy's result that people who discount the future more heavily are more likely to become addicted. Thus, ". . . harmful addictions induce even rational persons to discount the future more heavily, which in turn may lead them to become more addicted" (Becker and Mulligan 1997, 744).

It is well known that cigarette smoking and excessive alcohol abuse begin early in life (for example, Grossman et al. 1993). Moreover, bandwagon or peer effects are much more important in the case of youth smoking or alcohol consumption than in the case of adult smoking or alcohol consumption. The two-way causality between addiction and time preference and the importance of peer pressure explain why parents who care about the welfare of their children have large incentives to make investments that make their children more future oriented. These forces may also account for the relatively large impact of schooling on health with health knowledge held constant reported by Kenkel (1991).

Some parents may ignore or be unaware of the benefits of investments in time preference. Given society's concern with the welfare of its children, subsidies to school-based programs that make children more future oriented may be warranted. But much more research dealing with the determinants of time preference and its relationship with schooling and health is required before these programs can be formulated and implemented in a cost-effective manner.

8. CONCLUSIONS

Most of the chapters in this book focus on various aspects of the markets for medical care services and health insurance. This focus is required to understand the determinants of prices, quantities, and expenditures in these markets. The main message of my paper is that a very different theoretical paradigm is required to understand the determinants of health outcomes. I have tried to convince the reader that the human capital model of the demand for health provides the framework to conduct investigations of these outcomes. The model emphasizes the difference between health as an output and medical care as one of many inputs into the production of health and the equally important difference between health capital and other forms of human capital. It provides a theoretical framework for making predictions about the impacts of many variables on health and an empirical framework for testing these predictions.

Future theoretical efforts will be especially useful if they consider the joint determination of health and schooling and the interactions between these two variables and time preference for the present. A model in which both the stock of health and the stock of knowledge (schooling) are endogenous does not necessarily generate causality between the two. Individuals, however, typically stop investing in schooling at relatively young ages but rarely stop investing in health. I have a "hunch" that a dynamic model that takes account of these patterns will generate effects of an endogenously determined schooling variable on health in the health demand function if schooling has a causal impact on productive efficiency or time preference.

Future empirical efforts will be especially useful if they employ longitudinal databases with a variety of health outputs, health inputs, and direct and indirect (for example, the rate of growth in total consumption) measures of time preference at three or more different ages. This is the type of data required to implement the cost-of-adjustment model outlined in section 6. It also is the type of data required to distinguish between the productive and allocative efficiency effects of schooling and to fit demand for health models in which medical care is not necessarily the primary health input. Finally, it is the type of data to fully sort out the hypothesis that schooling causes health from the competing hypothesis that time preference causes both using methods outlined in section 7.

These research efforts will not be easy, but their potential payoffs are substantial. Medical care markets in most countries are subject to large amounts of government intervention, regulation, and subsidization. I have emphasized the basic proposition that consumers demand health rather than medical care. Thus, one way to evaluate policy initiatives aimed at medical care is to consider their impacts on health outcomes in the context of a cost-benefit analysis of programs that influence a variety of health inputs. If this undertaking is to be successful, it must draw on refined estimates of the parameters of health production functions, output demand functions for health, and input demand functions for health inputs.

NOTES

Originally published as Michael Grossman, "The Human Capital Model," in *Handbook of Health Economics*, Volume 1A, ed. Anthony J. Culyer and Joseph P. Newhouse (Amsterdam: Elsevier Science B.V., North-Holland Publishing, 2000), 347–408. I am indebted to Robert Kaestner, Sara Markowitz, Tomas Philipson, and Walter Ried for helpful comments.

1. My monograph was the final publication in the Occasional Paper Series of the National Bureau of Economic Research. It is somewhat ironic that the publication of a study dealing with the demand for health marked the death of the series.

2. Grossman (1972b) is out of print but available in most libraries.

3. Equations (3) and (4) assume that E does not vary over the life cycle. In Grossman (1972b, 28–30), I consider the impacts of exogenous variations in this stock with age.

4. Clearly this is a simplification. No distinction is made between the quality and the quantity of healthy time. If the stock of health yielded other services besides healthy time, ϕ_t would be a vector of service flows. These services might or might not be perfect substitutes in the utility function.

5. An increase in gross investment in period $t - 1$ increases the stock of health in all future periods. These increases are equal to

$$\frac{\partial H_t}{\partial I_{t-1}} = 1, \ \frac{\partial H_{t+1}}{\partial I_{t-1}} = (1 - \delta_t), \ \ldots, \ \frac{\partial H_n}{\partial I_{t-1}} = (1 - \delta_t)(1 - \delta_{t+1})\ldots(1 - \delta_{n-1}).$$

6. Equation (11) assumes $\delta_t \tilde{\pi}_{t-1} \cong 0$.

7. First-time readers of this chapter can skip sections 2.3 and 2.4. The material in the remaining sections does not depend on them.

8. Since the initial period is period 0, a consumer who is alive in year n and dead in year $n + 1$ lives for $n + 1$ years.

9. Actually, I assert that I am assuming $H_n \leq H_{\min}$. That is incorrect because $H_n > H_{\min}$ if the consumer is alive in period n. The corrected footnote should read: "The constraints are imposed that $H_{n+1} \leq H_{\min}$ and $H_n > H_{\min}$."

10. Readers seeking a definitive and path-breaking treatment of the allocation of goods and time over the life cycle should consult Ghez's pioneering monograph on this topic with Becker (Ghez and Becker 1975). In the late 1970s and 1980s, there was a tremendous growth in the literature on life-cycle labor supply and consumption demand using the concept of demand functions that hold the marginal utility of wealth constant. All this literature can be traced to Ghez's treatment of the topic.

11. This is a first approximation because it assumes that λ does not change when the horizon is extended by one period. Consider the standard intertemporally separable lifetime utility function in which the current period utility function, $\Psi(h_t, Z_t)$, is strictly concave. With full wealth constant, an increase in the horizon causes λ to rise. But full wealth increases by $W_{n+1}\Omega/(1 + r)^{n+1}$, which causes λ to decline. I assume that these two effects exactly offset each other. This assumption is not necessary in the pure investment model described in sections 2.5 and 3 because V_t does not depend on λ in that model.

12. If $H_n \leq H_{\min}$, the utility function is re-maximized after shortening the horizon by 1 period.

13. It may appear that the supply price of capital given by the right-hand side of equation (18) is smaller than the one given by the right-hand side of equation (13) as long as $1 - \delta_n > - \tilde{\pi}_{n-1}$. But equation (18) is based on the assumption $\delta_n \tilde{\pi}_{n-1} \cong 0$. The exact form of equation (18) is

$$V_n^* G_n^* = \pi_{n-1}(r + 1) - (1 - \delta_n)\pi_n.$$

The difference between the right-hand side of this equation and the right-hand side of equation (13) is $- (1 - \delta_n)\pi_n < 0$.

14. While G_n^* is smaller than G_n, it is not clear whether V_n^* is smaller than V_n. The last term can be written

$$V_n = W_n + \frac{Uh_n}{U_n}m_t,$$

where U_n is the marginal utility of Z_n and m_n is the marginal cost of producing Z_n. The wage rate in periods n (W_n) and m_n are not affected when the length of the horizon is increased from n to $n + 1$. In equilibrium,

$$\frac{Uh_n}{U_n} = \left[\frac{(\pi_{n-1}(1 + r))/G_n - W_n}{m_n} \right]$$

and

$$\frac{Uh_n^*}{U_n^*} = \left[\frac{(\pi_{n-1}(1 + r) - \pi_n(1 - \delta_n))/G_n^* - W_n}{m_n} \right].$$

Suppose that

$$G_n^* = G_n \left[\frac{\pi_{n-1}(r + 1) - \pi_n(1 - \delta_n)}{\pi_{n-1}(r + 1)} \right].$$

Then $Uh_n^*/U_n^* = Uh_n/U_n$ and $V_n^* = V_n$. In this case there is no incentive to substitute healthy time for the other commodity in the utility function in period n when the horizon is increased by one period. In other cases this type of substitution will occur. If it does occur, I assume that the lifetime utility function is separable over time so that the marginal rate of substitution between h and Z in periods other than period n is not affected. Note the distinction between H_{n+1} and H_{n+1}^*. The former stock is the one associated with an n period horizon and $I_n = 0$. The latter stock is the one associated with an $n + 1$ horizon and $I_n > 0$. Clearly, $H_{n+1}^* > H_{n+1}$.

15. In deriving equation (23) I use the approximation that $\delta_n \tilde{\pi}_{n-1} \cong 0$. If the exact form of equation (18) is employed (see footnote 13), the approximation is not necessary.

16. If $W_{n+1} = W_n$ and $\pi_n = \pi_{n-1}$, then H_{n+1}^* (the optimal stock when the horizon is $n + 1$) $= H_n$ (the optimal stock when the horizon is n). Hence,

$$H_{n+2} = (1 - \delta_{n+1})H_n,$$
$$H_{n+1} = (1 - \delta_n)H_n.$$

Since $\delta_{n+1} > \delta_n$, H_{n+2} could be smaller than or equal to H_{min}, while at the same time H_n could exceed H_{min}. Note that one addition to the algorithm described is required. Return to the case when maximization for a fixed number of periods equal to n results in a stock in period $n + 1$ that is smaller than or equal to the death stock. The consumer should behave as if the rate of depreciation on the stock of health is equal to 1 in period n and consult equation (13) to determine I_{n-1} and H_n. Suppose instead that he behaves as if the rate of depreciation is the actual rate in period n ($\delta_n < 1$). This is the same rate used by the consumer who dies in period $n + 2$. Denote I_{n-1}^* as the quantity of gross investment that results from using equation (18) to select the optimal stock in period n. Under the alternative decision rule, the stock in period $n + 1$ could exceed the death stock. The difference in the stock in period $n + 1$ that results from these two alternative decision rules is

$$H_{n+1}^* - H_{n+1} = I_{n-1}^* + \delta_{n-1}(I_{n-1} - I_{n-1}^*),$$

where I assume that I_n (gross investment in period n when death takes place in period $n+2$) equals I_{n-1} (gross investment in period $n - 1$ when death takes place in period $n + 1$). This difference falls as I_{n-1}^* falls. In turn, I_{n-1}^* falls as δ_n rises with rates of depreciation in all other periods held constant.

17. Technically, I am dealing with parametric differences in exogenous variables (differences in exogenous variables across consumers) as opposed to evolutionary differences in exogenous variables (differences in exogenous variables across time for the same consumer). This distinction goes back to Ghez and Becker (1975) and is explored in detail by MaCurdy (1981).

18. Consider two people who face the same rate of depreciation in each period. Person b has higher initial assets than person a and picks a larger stock in each period. Suppose that person a dies after period n. Hence,

$$H_{n+1}^a = (1 - \delta_n)H_n^a \leq H_{\min}.$$

Suppose that person b, like person a, invests nothing in period n. Then

$$H_{n+1}^b = (1 - \delta_n)H_n^b.$$

Clearly, $H_{n+1}^b > H_{n+1}^a$ since $H_n^b > H_n^a$. But both people could die in period $n + 1$ if $H_{n+1}^a < H$ min. This is a necessary, but not a sufficient, condition. For this reason, I use the term "tends" in the text. This ambiguity is removed if the condition for death is defined by $H_{n+1} = H_{\min}$. That definition is, however, unsatisfactory because the rate of depreciation in period n does not guarantee that it is satisfied. That is, death takes place in $n + 1$ if $\delta_n \geq (H_n - H_{\min})/H_n$.

19. For an earlier criticism of my model along the same lines, see Usher (1975).

20. In addition, I assume that the market rate of interest is equal to the rate of time preference for the present. See section 4 for a definition of time preference.

21. This follows because

$$\frac{\partial h_{t+j}}{\partial I_t} = \frac{\partial h_{t+j}}{\partial H_{t+j}} \frac{\partial H_{t+j}}{\partial I_t},$$

or

$$\frac{\partial h_{t+j}}{\partial I_t} = G_{t+j}(1 - \delta_{t+1})(1 - \delta_{t+2}) \cdots (1 - \delta_{t+j-1}) = G_{t+j}\, d_{t+j}.$$

Clearly, d_{t+j} is positive and finite when I_t equals zero. Moreover, G_{t+j} is positive and finite when I_t equals zero as long as H_{t+j} is positive and finite.

22. The corresponding condition for the optimal stock in the last period of life, period n, is

$$\gamma_n + a_n = r + 1.$$

23. As Ghez and Becker (1975) point out, none of the variables in a discrete time model are differentiable functions of time. Equation (27) and other equations involving time or age derivatives are approximations that hold exactly in a continuous time model.

24. In this section I deal with uniform shifts in variables that influence the rate of return across persons of the same age. I also assume that these variables do not vary over the life cycle. Finally, I deal with the *partial* effect of an increase in the wage rate or an increase in knowledge capital, measured by the number of years of formal schooling completed, on the demand for health and health inputs. For a more general treatment, see Grossman (1972b, 28–30).

25. Solving equation (37) for the monetary equivalent of the marginal utility of healthy time, one obtains

$$\frac{Uh_t}{\lambda} = \frac{\pi(r + \delta_t)/G_t}{(1 + r)^t}.$$

Given diminishing marginal productivity of health capital, the undiscounted price of a healthy hour, $\pi(r + \delta_t)/G_t$, would be positively correlated with H or h even if π were constant. Therefore, the consumption demand curve would be influenced by scale effects. To emphasize the main issues at stake in the consumption model, I ignore these effects essentially by assuming that G_t is constant. The analysis would not be greatly altered if they were introduced.

26. For a different conclusion, see Ehrlich and Chuma (1990). They argue that wealth effects are present in the investment model given rising marginal cost of investment in health and endogenous length of life.

27. I assume that the elasticity of substitution in consumption between H_t and Z_t is the same in every period and that the elasticity of substitution between H_t and Z_j ($t \neq j$) does not depend on t or j. The corresponding equation for the wage elasticity of medical care is

$$e_{MW} = K\sigma_p - (1 - \theta)(K - K_Z)\sigma_{HZ}.$$

28. I assume that $\Psi_z \Psi_{HZ} > \Psi_H \Psi_{ZZ}$ so that the pure wealth effect is positive and a reduction in λ raises health. When Ψ_{HZ} is negative, this condition does not guarantee that equation (39) is negative because K_Z could exceed K.

29. The term $(1 - \theta)\sigma_{HZ}$ in equation (40) or equation (41) is the compensated or utility-constant price elasticity of demand for health.

30. I relax the assumption that all persons face the same market rate of interest in section 7.

31. If an increase in schooling lowers the rate of depreciation at every age by the same percentage, it is equivalent to a uniform percentage shift in this rate, a matter considered briefly in section 3.2 and in more detail in Grossman (1972b, pp. 19, 90). The only difference between this model and the productivity model is that a value of the elasticity of the MEC schedule smaller than one is a sufficient, but not a necessary, condition for medical care to fall as schooling rises.

32. Recall that $\delta_t > -\tilde{H}_t$ since gross investment must be positive. Given that the real rate of interest is zero

$$\frac{-\tilde{H}_t}{\delta_t} = \varepsilon\delta_t^2 \frac{d\delta_t}{dt}.$$

Since ε is likely to be smaller than one and the square of the rate of depreciation is small for modest rates of depreciation, δ_t is likely to be much larger than $-\tilde{H}_t$.

33. See section 7 for a detailed analysis of biases in the regression coefficient of schooling due to the omission of other variables.

34. Health would have a positive wealth elasticity in the investment model for people who are not in the labor force. For such individuals, an increase in wealth would raise the ratio of market goods to consumption time, the marginal product of consumption time, and its shadow price. Hence, the monetary rate of return on an investment in health would rise. Since my empirical work is limited to members of the labor force, a pure increase in wealth would not change the shadow price of their time.

35. In my monograph, I argue that a 1 percent increase in medical care would be accompanied by a 1 percent increase in own time if factor prices do not vary as more and more health is produced. Therefore, the regression coefficient α in equation (49) would reflect the sum of the output elasticities of medical care and own time. Given constant returns to scale, the true value of α should be unity (Grossman 1972b, p. 43). This analysis becomes much more complicated once joint production is introduced (see Grossman (1972b), Chapter VI, and the brief discussion of joint production below).

36. See Zweifel and Manning (2000) for a review of the literature dealing with the effect of health insurance on the demand for medical care.

37. The complete specification involves regressing H on W and q and regressing M on W and q, where it is understood that all variables are in logarithms. In the three-input model in which the money price of medical care is zero, the coefficients of q are negative in both equations. The coefficient of W is positive in the health equation and ambiguous in sign in the medical care equation.

38. A one-tailed test is appropriate since the alternative hypothesis is that the age coefficient is positive. The age coefficient is positive and significant at all conventional levels in the demand functions for hospital stays and medicines.

39. Joint production could account for a negative lifetime wage effect, but Zweifel and Breyer do not consider this phenomenon.

40. Stratmann identifies his model with instruments reflecting the price of visiting a physician which differs according to the type of health insurance carried by individuals. The specific measures are Medicaid coverage, private insurance coverage, membership in a Health Maintenance Organization, and whether or not the employer paid the health insurance premium.

41. The health limitation variable for 1982 is based on responses during October, November, and December of that year. The corresponding variable for 1983 is based on responses during the months of January through September. It is not clear which month is used for the self- and physician-rated health measures. I assume that the 1982 measures come from the October 1982 survey and the 1983 measure comes from the September 1983 survey.

42. The minimum requirements for instruments are measures of P_{t+1} and P_{t-2}. The one-period lead of the price has no impact on H_t with H_{t+1} held constant. Similarly, the two-period lag of the price has no impact on H_t with H_{t-1} held constant.

43. The same issue arises in estimating the rational addiction model of consumer behavior. For a detailed discussion, see Becker, Grossman, and Murphy (1994).

44. Ried (1998) also develops a framework for examining the impacts of changes in exogenous variables in the context of a mixed investment-consumption model. He uses Frisch (1964) demand curves to decompose the total effect into an effect that holds the marginal utility of wealth constant and an effect attributable to a change in the marginal utility of wealth. He obtains few, if any, unambiguous predictions. I leave it to the reader to evaluate this contribution.

45. Cropper begins with a model in which consumers are risk-averse, but the rate of depreciation on the stock of health does not depend on age. She introduces risk-neutrality when she allows the rate of depreciation to depend on age.

46. Cropper assumes that gross investment in health is produced only with medical care, but the above result holds as long as the share of the own time input in the total cost of gross investment is less than one.

47. A utility function $U = U(C)$ exhibits decreasing absolute risk aversion if $-U_{CC}/U_C$ falls as C rises.

48. Chang provides more results by assuming that the earnings function depends only on "post-shock health," $f(H_2, R)$. The finding that the sign of the asset effect is ambiguous holds in his formulation.

49. Garber and Phelps (1997), Meltzer (1997), and Picone, Echeverria, and Wilson (1998) also introduce uncertainty into a pure consumption model of the demand for health. I do not discuss the first two studies because they focus on cost-effectiveness analysis. I do not discuss the last one because it emphasizes the behavior of individuals in their retirement years.

50. See Grossman and Kaestner (1997) for a model in which ability should be omitted from the reduced form earnings function even though it enters the structural production function and has a causal impact on schooling.

REFERENCES

Angrist, J. D., and A. B. Krueger. 1991. "Does Compulsory School Attendance Affect Schooling and Earnings?" *Quarterly Journal of Economics* 106: 979–1014.

Auster, R., I. Leveson, and D. Sarachek. 1969. "The Production of Health: An Exploratory Study." *Journal of Human Resources* 4: 411–436.

Becker, G. S. 1964. *Human Capital*. New York: Columbia University Press for the National Bureau of Economic Research.

Becker, G. S. 1965. "A Theory of the Allocation of Time." *Economic Journal* 75: 493–517.

Becker, G. S. 1967. *Human Capital and the Personal Distribution of Income: An Analytical Approach*. Ann Arbor, MI: University of Michigan. Also available in: G. S. Becker. 1993. *Human Capital*, Third Edition. University of Chicago Press. 102–158.

Becker, G. S. 1996. *Accounting for Tastes*. Cambridge, MA: Harvard University Press.

Becker, G. S., M. Grossman, and K. M. Murphy. 1991. "Rational Addiction and the Effect of Price on Consumption." *American Economic Review* 81: 237–241.

Becker, G. S., M. Grossman, and K. M. Murphy. 1994. "An Empirical Analysis of Cigarette Addiction." *American Economic Review* 84: 396–418.

Becker, G. S., and C. B. Mulligan. 1997. "The Endogenous Determination of Time Preference." *Quarterly Journal of Economics* 112: 729–758.

Becker, G. S., and K. M. Murphy. 1988. "A Theory of Rational Addiction." *Journal of Political Economy* 96: 675–700.

Ben-Porath, Y. 1967. "The Production of Human Capital and the Life Cycle of Earnings." *Journal of Political Economy* 75: 353–367.

Bentham, J. 1931. *Principles of Legislation*. New York: Harcourt, Brace and Co.

Berger, M. C., and J. P. Leigh. 1989. "Schooling, Self-Selection, and Health." *Journal of Human Resources* 24: 433–455.

Bound, J., D. M. Jaeger, and R. M. Baker. 1995. "Problems with Instrumental Variables Estimation When the Correlation Between the Instruments and the Endogenous Explanatory Variable Is Weak." *Journal of the American Statistical Association* 90: 443–450.

Chang, F. R. 1996. "Uncertainty and Investment in Health." *Journal of Health Economics* 15: 369–376.

Corman, H., T. J. Joyce, and M. Grossman. 1987. "Birth Outcome Production Functions in the U.S." *Journal of Human Resources* 22: 339–360.

Cropper, M. L. 1977. "Health, Investment in Health, and Occupational Choice." *Journal of Political Economy* 85: 273–1294.

Currie, J. 2000. "Child Health in Developed Countries." In *Handbook of Health Economics*, ed. A. J. Culyer and J. P. Newhouse. Amsterdam: Elsevier: Chapter 19.

Dardanoni, V., and A. Wagstaff. 1987. "Uncertainty, Inequalities in Health and the Demand for Health." *Journal of Health Economics* 6: 283–290.

Dardanoni, V., and A. Wagstaff. 1990. "Uncertainty and the Demand for Medical Care." *Journal of Health Economics* 9: 23–38.

Ehrlich, I., and H. Chuma. 1990. "A Model of the Demand for Longevity and the Value of Life Extensions." *Journal of Political Economy* 98: 761–782.

Erbsland, M., W. Ried, and V. Ulrich. 1995. "Health, Health Care, and the Environment. Econometric Evidence from German Micro Data." *Health Economics* 4: 169–182.

Farrell, P., and V. R. Fuchs. 1982. "Schooling and Health: The cigarette Connection." *Journal of Health Economics* 1: 217–230.

Frisch, R. 1964. "Dynamic Utility." *Econometrica* 32: 418–424.

Fuchs, V. R. 1966. "The Contribution of Health Services to the American Economy." *Milbank Memorial Fund Quarterly* 44: 65–102.

Fuchs, V. R. 1982. "Time Preference and Health: An Exploratory Study." In *Economic Aspects of Health*, ed. V. R. Fuchs. Chicago: University of Chicago Press for the National Bureau of Economic Research: 93–120.

Garber, A. M., and C. E. Phelps. 1997. "Economic Foundations of Cost-Effectiveness Analysis." *Journal of Health Economics* 16: 1–31.

Ghez, G. R., and G. S. Becker. 1975. *The Allocation of Time and Goods Over the Life Cycle.* New York: Columbia University Press for the National Bureau of Economic Research.

Goldberger, A. S. 1974. "Unobservable Variables in Econometrics." In *Frontiers in* Econometrics, ed. P. Zarembreka. New York: Academic Press: 193–213.

Griliches, Z., and W. M. Mason. 1972. "Education, Income, and Ability." *Journal of Political Economy* 80: S74–S103.

Grossman, M. 1972a. "On the Concept of Health Capital and the Demand for Health." *Journal of Political Economy* 80: 223–255.

Grossman, M. 1972b. *The Demand for Health: A Theoretical and Empirical Investigation.* New York: Columbia University Press for the National Bureau of Economic Research.

Grossman, M. 1975. "The Correlation Between Health and Schooling." In *Household Production and Consumption*, ed. N.E. Terleckyj. New York: Columbia University Press for the National Bureau of Economic Research: 147–211.

Grossman, M. 1982. "The Demand for Health After a Decade." *Journal of Health Economics* 1: 1–3.

Grossman, M., and T. J. Joyce. 1990. "Unobservables, Pregnancy Resolutions, and Birth Weight Production Functions in New York City." *Journal of Political Economy* 98: 983–1007.

Grossman, M., and R. Kaestner. 1997. "Effects of Education on Health." In *The Social Benefits of Education*, ed. J. R. Behrman and N. Stacey. Ann Arbor, MI: University of Michigan Press: 69–123.

Grossman, M., J. L. Sindelar, J. Mullahy, and R. Anderson. 1993. "Policy Watch: Alcohol and Cigarette Taxes." *Journal of Economic Perspectives* 7: 211–222.

Hause, J. C. 1972. "Earnings Profile: Ability and Schooling." *Journal of Political Economy* 80: S108–S138.

Hausman, J. A. 1978. "Specification Tests in Econometrics." *Econometrica* 46: 1251–1271.

Jöreskog, K. G. 1973. "A General Method for Estimating a Linear Structural Equations System." In *Structural Equations Models in the Social Sciences*, ed. A. S. Goldberger and O. D. Duncan. New York: Seminar Press: 85–112.

Jöreskog, K. G., and D. Sörbom.1981. *LISREL: Analysis of Linear Structural Relationships by the Method of Maximum Likelihood.* Chicago: International Educational Services.

Joyce, T. J. 1994. "Self-Selection, Prenatal Care, and Birthweight Among Blacks, Whites, and Hispanics in New York City." *Journal of Human Resources* 29: 762–794.

Kenkel, D. S. 1991. "Health Behavior, Health Knowledge, and Schooling." *Journal of Political Economy* 99: 287–305.

Kenkel, D. S. 2000 "Prevention." In *Handbook of Health Economics*, ed. A. J. Culyer and J. P. Newhouse. Amsterdam: Elsevier: Chapter 31.

Lancaster, K. J. 1966. "A New Approach to Consumer Theory." *Journal of Political Economy* 74: 32–157.

Lazear, E. 1977. "Education: Consumption or Production?" *Journal of Political Economy* 85: 569–597.

Leigh, J. P., and R. Dhir. 1997. "Schooling and Frailty Among Seniors." *Economics of Education Review* 16: 45–57.

Liljas, B. 1998. "The Demand for Health with Uncertainty and Insurance." *Journal of Health Economics* 17: 153–170.

MaCurdy, T. E. 1981. "An Empirical Model of Labor Supply in a Life-Cycle Setting." *Journal of Political Economy* 89: 1059–1085.

Meltzer, D. 1997. "Accounting for Future Costs in Medical Cost-Effectiveness Analysis." *Journal of Health Economics* 16: 33–64.

Michael, R. T. 1972. *The Effect of Education on Efficiency in Consumption*. New York: Columbia University Press for the National Bureau of Economic Research.

Michael, R. T. 1973. "Education in Nonmarket Production." *Journal of Political Economy* 81: 306–327.

Michael, R. T., and G. S. Becker. 1973. "On the New Theory of Consumer Behavior." *Swedish Economic Journal* 75: 378–396.

Mincer, J. 1974. *Schooling, Experience, and Earnings*. New York: Columbia University Press for the National Bureau of Economic Research.

Mushkin, S. J. 1962. "Health as an Investment." *Journal of Political Economy* 70 (Supplement): 129–157.

Muurinen, J. 1982. "Demand for Health: A Generalised Grossman Model." *Journal of Health Economics* 1: 5–28.

Picone, G., M. U. Echeverría, and R. M. Wilson.1998. "The Effect of Uncertainty on the Demand for Medical Care, Health Capital and Wealth." *Journal of Health Economics* 17: 171–186.

Ried, M. 1996. "Willingness to Pay and Cost of Illness for Changes in Health Capital Depreciation." *Health Economics* 5: 447–468.

Ried, M. 1998. "Comparative Dynamic Analysis of the Full Grossman Model." *Journal of Health Economics* 17: 383–426.

Rosenzweig, M. R., and T. P. Schultz. 1983. "Estimating a Household Production Function: Heterogeneity, the Demand for Health Inputs, and Their Effects on Birth Weight." *Journal of Political Economy* 91: 723–746.

Rosenzweig, M. R., and T. P. Schultz. 1988. "The Stability of Household Production Technology: A Replication." *Journal of Human Resources* 23: 535–549.

Rosenzweig, M. R., and T. P. Schultz. 1991. "Who Receives Medical Care? Income, Implicit Prices, and the Distribution of Medical Services Among Pregnant Women in the United States." *Journal of Human Resources* 26: 473–508.

Sander, W. 1995a. "Schooling and Quitting Smoking." *Review of Economics and Statistics* 77: 191–199.

Sander, W. 1995b. "Schooling and Smoking." *Economics of Education Review* 14: 23–33.

Selden, T. M. 1993. "Uncertainty and Health Care Spending by the Poor: The Human Capital Model Revisited." *Journal of Health Economics* 12: 109–115.

Staiger, D., and J. A. Stock. 1997. "Instrumental Variables Regression with Weak Instruments." *Econometrica* 65: 557–586.

Stratmann, T. 1999 "What Do Medical Services Buy? Effects of Doctor Visits on Work Day Loss." *Eastern Economic Journal* 25: 1–16.

Usher, D. 1975. "Comments on the Correlation Between Health and Schooling." In *Household Production and Consumption*, ed. N. E. Terleckyj. New York: Columbia University Press for the National Bureau of Economic Research: 212–220.

van Doorslaer, E. K. A. 1987. *Health, Knowledge and the Demand for Medical Care*. Van Gorcum: Assen, Maastricht, The Netherlands.

Wagstaff, A. 1986. "The Demand for Health: Some New Empirical Evidence." *Journal of Health Economics* 5: 195–233.

Wagstaff, A. 1993. "The Demand for Health: An Empirical Reformulation of the Grossman Model." *Health Economics* 2: 189–198.

Wu, D. M. 1973. "Alternative Tests of Independence Between Stochastic Regressors and Disturbances." *Econometrica* 41: 733–750.

Zweifel, P., and F. Breyer. 1997. *Health Economics*. New York: Oxford University Press.

Afterword to Part 1

As reflected by almost any textbook in health economics, my demand for health model serves as the conceptual foundation for one of the two major branches of that field: the one dealing with the determinants of the health of the population (for example, Johnson-Lans 2006; Sloan and Hsieh 2012; Bhattacharya, Hyde, and Tu 2014; Phelps 2013; Santerre and Neun 2013; Folland, Goodman, and Stano 2016). It also is reflected in almost any issue of the two oldest journals in the field: the *Journal of Health Economics* and *Health Economics*. Finally, in their review of the field of health economics titled "Four Decades of Health Economics Through a Bibliometric Lens" in the 2012 volume of the *Journal of Health Economics*, Adam Wagstaff and Anthony J. Culyer list my 1972 *Journal of Political Economy* paper as the third most widely cited paper in the field as of 2011 (Wagstaff and Culyer 2012).[1]

The three remaining parts of this book highlight the application of my framework to studies dealing with the relationship between health and schooling, the determinants of infant mortality with special emphasis on the roles of public policies and programs, and the economics of unhealthy behaviors. Most of my papers in those sections and papers authored by others and discussed in the afterwords draw on the framework in my *JPE* paper and my NBER monograph. They also are much more empirical and much less theoretical than those two contributions. Therefore, in this first afterword, I want to address some key theoretical advances to my demand for health model. That focus is especially appropriate because my 2000 contribution to the *Handbook of Health Economics*, which is the second paper in this section, discusses important empirical developments as of the late 1990s. I want to deal with two types of theoretical advances. The first type is noncritical in that it adds components to the model that I explicitly stated that I would not incorporate and examines some of the implications of that exercise. The second type is critical in the sense that it includes objections to my model that, in my view, the field in general considers to be the most substantial. I will try to respond to these objections, a discussion that will lead naturally to suggestions for future research.

Noncritical extensions of my framework include the introduction of (1) a depreciation rate on the stock of health that depends on observed exogenous variables other than age; (2) uncertainty; and (3) the production of adult health in a family context. Jaana-Marja Muurinen (1982) and Eddy K. A. van Doorslaer (1987) assume that an increase in education lowers the rate of depreciation on the stock of health rather than raising productivity in the gross investment production function. This is a less general assumption than the one that I have made because it rules out schooling effects in the production of nondurable household commodities. In the pure investment model, predictions are very similar whether schooling raises productivity or lowers the rate of depreciation. In the pure consumption model, the assumption made by Muurinen and van Doorslaer is difficult to distinguish from the alternative assumption that schooling has a larger effect in the health production function than in the production of other household commodities.

Beginning with Maureen L. Cropper (1977), a number of persons have introduced uncertainty into my framework. Other important contributions have been made by Valentino Dardanoni and Adam Wagstaff (1987, 1990), Thomas M. Selden (1993), Fwu-Ranq Chang (1996), and Bengt Liljas (1998). Compared to a model with perfect certainty, the expected value of the stock of health is larger and the optimal quantities of gross investment and health inputs also are larger in a model with uncertainty. In a pure investment model, an increase in initial assets can cause health and medical care to change, but the direction of these effects is ambiguous. Under reasonable assumptions, an increase in the variance of risk raises optimal medical care in a pure consumption model.

Lena Jacobson (2000) and Kristian Bolin, Jacobson, and Björn Lindgren (2001, 2002) consider the production of and demand for adult health in the context of a family consisting of husband, a wife, and in some cases children. Jacobson (2000) assumes that the family has a common utility function. The time input of each spouse enters the gross investment production function of both spouses. As in other models of household production in a family setting (for example, Becker 1981), family members benefit from comparative advantage, which reduces the marginal cost of investment. In addition, marginal benefits are higher because an increase in the time, for example, that a wife allocates to the production of her husband's health raises his future healthy time and hence resources available to both spouses. With child health viewed as a measure of quality, inclusion of children in this setting creates a "marriage" between my demand for health framework and Becker's quantity-quality interaction model of family decision making.[2] Following literature in this area Bolin, Jacobson, and Lindgren (2001, 2002) introduce Nash-bargaining and strategic behavior between spouses. The main implication is that the possibility of divorce affects the distribution of health capital between family members.

There are three major contributions to the literature on the demand for health that contain substantial objections to my framework. The first deals with the appropriate way to view the demand for medical care. The second and third are related and address the determination of optimal length of life and the exact nature of the production function of gross investment in health.

Peter Zweifel and Fredrick Breyer (1997) assume that individuals lack control over their health status. Instead, health is governed solely by random shocks, and these shocks generate a demand function for medical care. This is in sharp contrast to my treatment of health as an endogenously determined variable and to the demand for medical care as being derived from the demand for health. Zweifel and Breyer justify their approach because my model assumes a positive relationship between health and health investment or medical care, but there is a negative relationship at the empirical level.

I dealt with the issue that Zweifel and Breyer raised in my *Handbook* paper and anticipated it in my 1972 monograph. The key point is that health and medical care are endogenous variables. For any number of reasons, the estimated coefficient of medical care will be downward biased if the production function is obtained by ordinary least squares. In the context of my model, the disturbance term in the production function is a measure of the rate of depreciation on the stock of health of a person of a given age (the rate net of the effects of age). An increase in that rate simultaneously lowers the optimal stock of health and increases the optimal amount of medical care.[3] A similar relationship can be generated in a model with costs of adjustment and exogenous shocks to health. Hence, consistent estimates of the production function require simultaneous equations techniques such as two-stage least squares, a point highlighted as early as 1969 by Richard Auster, Irving Leveson, and Deborah Sarachek (Auster, Leveson, and Sarachek 1969).[4]

I employed discrete time, elementary calculus, and a gross investment production function characterized by constant returns to scale to determine the optimal stock of health, optimal investment in health, the life cycle behavior of those variables, and optimal length of life in my demand for health model. Isaac Ehrlich and Hiroyuki Chuma (1990), Titus Galama (2011), Galama and Arie Kapteyn (2011), and Galama and Hans van Kippersluis (2016) examine these issues in a continuous time setting with optimal control theory and with a production function characterized by diminishing returns to scale. Their framework is more realistic than mine for a number of reasons. It allows for lagged, as opposed to instantaneous, responses to parametric variations in exogenous variables, to more realistic life-cycle patterns, and to a fuller treatment of the endogeneity of length of life. That treatment allows for a richer analysis of the behaviors of the stock of health, health investment, and health inputs as the end of life approaches.

In addition to these accomplishments, I am delighted that Galama and van Kippersluis took me seriously when I wrote in my paper in the *Handbook of Health Economics*, "Currently, we still lack comprehensive theoretical models in which the stocks of health and knowledge are determined simultaneously. . . . The rich empirical literature treating interactions between schooling and health underscores the potential payoff to this undertaking" (Grossman 2000, p. 351). Galama and van Kippersluis (2016) have accepted my challenge to construct such a model. It allows for a complex set of interactions between the two most important components of the stock of human capital. Moreover, it contains the intriguing prediction that complementarity effects among health capital, skill capital (reflected by schooling), and low costs of the production of skill capital (high-quality teachers, healthy students, modest tuition, and short distance to school) are reinforced by increases in longevity. The end results are a strong positive relationship between changes in life expectancy and changes in education in developed countries and an equally strong relationship between inequality in life expectancy and inequality in education.

I am extremely pleased by the advancements in my demand for health model made most forcefully by Ehrlich and Chuma (1990) and by Galama and van Kippersluis (2016). At the same time, I want to acknowledge that their contributions contain two objections to my model. The first is that the model does not determine optimal length of life. The second is that my assumption of constant returns to scale in the gross investment in health production function generates an indeterminacy problem with respect to optimal investment and the optimal stock of health even in a model in which length of life is exogenous. I will conclude this afterword by responding to these criticisms. The reader should keep in mind that the mathematical sophistication of my critics is much greater than mine, so much of my reply will be characterized by a heavy dose of intuition.

I admitted an uneasiness about whether my 1972 model did, in fact, determine optimal length of life in the *Handbook* paper. I proceeded to build on Walter Ried's extension of my model in which he attempts to determine it by maximizing lifetime utility over a sequence of alternative fixed time horizons (Ried 1998). I simplified his extremely complicated discrete time optimal control techniques because he begins with a model in which length of life is endogenous and ends up with a result in which it does not depend on any of the exogenous variables in the model.

How successful were my efforts? I think that the iterative algorithm that I developed for the selection of optimal length of life had some important insights with regard to the equilibrium conditions for the stock of health in each period in my original formulation. In particular, I revised the equilibrium condition for the stock in the last period of life because gross investment in the next to last period yields returns for only one period. Put differently, the person behaves as if the rate of depreciation on the stock is equal to 1 in the last period. I also showed that discounted marginal benefits of an investment in period 0 (the initial period) are the same whether the person dies in period $n + 1$ or in period $n + 2$ because the marginal cost of an investment in period 0 does not depend on the length of the horizon. This may seem strange because one term is added to discounted marginal benefits of an investment in period 0 or in any other period when the horizon is extended by one period—the discounted marginal benefit in period $n + 1$. This term, however, is exactly offset by the reduction in the discounted marginal benefit in period n. Finally, I showed that parametric variations in exogenous variables will affect optimal length of life.

Despite these accomplishments, Yan Qin, who completed a PhD dissertation under my supervision in 2009, pointed out to me in an unpublished note (Qin 2008) that my solution for optimal length of life still had some indeterminacy, especially if none of the exogenous variables changed when the horizon was extended by one period. In my view, Christoph Eisenring (2000) successfully addresses this issue. He shows that two additional conditions must be satisfied in order to conclude that a horizon of length n is optimal. One is that wealth, less the present value of investments in health, must fall when the horizon is extended by one year. That is a necessary, but not a sufficient, condition. Furthermore, the additional utility from prolonging life by one year must be less than the foregone utility due to the decrease in net earnings. My intuition for the last result is that it can be found in a simple model in which consumers maximize a lifetime utility function of the form

$$n(r) \; U \; (I - r),$$

where length of life (n) is positively related to an input (r) purchased at a price of $1, I is income, and U is current period utility. Eisenring's extension suggests that an increase in initial assets will extend length of life even if healthy time does not enter the utility function. The optimal stock, however, will not change in a given period unless some individuals would have died in that period absent the increase in assets.

The second objection to my framework is that my assumption of constant returns to scale in the gross investment in health production function generates an indeterminacy problem with respect to optimal investment and the optimal stock of health even in a model in which length of life is exogenous. The objection is made most forcefully by Ehrlich and Chuma who assert that the discounted marginal benefits of an investment in health at age t do not depend on the rate of investment at that age. Therefore, no interior equilibrium exists for investment unless the marginal cost function slopes upward. This is the basis of their claim that my model does not determine optimal investment because marginal cost does not depend on investment.

Why, however, is the discounted marginal benefit function independent of the amount of investment? In a personal communication, Ehrlich informed me that this is because the marginal product of the stock of health at age t does not depend on the amount of investment at age t. Surely that is correct. But an increase in investment at that age raises the stock of health in all future periods. Because the marginal product of health capital diminishes as the stock rises, discounted marginal benefits must fall. Hence, the discounted marginal benefit function slopes downward, and an interior equilibrium for gross investment in period t clearly is possible even if the marginal cost of gross investment is constant.

Where does that leave us? I certainly acknowledge that the assumption of diminishing returns to scale generates more realistic life-cycle profiles than the instantaneous adjustments characterized by a model with constant returns to scale. But I continue to be puzzled by Galama and van Kippersluis's (2016) endorsement of Ehrlich and Chuma's (1990) proposition that diminishing returns to scale is required to obtain an interior equilibrium for gross investment in health. And I want to emphasize that Yoram Ben-Porath had to make that assumption in his seminal 1967 model of optimal investment in knowledge or skill capital because he assumes that the marginal product of that stock in the production of earnings does not depend on the stock (Ben-Porath 1967).

Audrey Laporte (2015) has addressed health dynamics in a model with constant returns to scale. Her paper has the somewhat provocative title "Should the Grossman Model of Investment in Health Capital Retain Its Iconic Status?" If she had answered in the negative, Columbia University Press might not have agreed to publish this book. Fortunately for me, she answered in the positive, but I am not fully satisfied with some aspects of her analysis. She begins with a situation in which there is an exogenous increase in the endowed stock of health. Her conclusion that gross investment would increase if health is not a source of utility does not appear to be correct. Because she assumes constant returns to scale, the optimal stocks in period 1 of people with different endowments would have to be the same because the endowment has no impact on the marginal cost of investment. That implies a negative relationship between the endowed stock and gross investment in the initial period. If her conclusion is not correct, the results of her more complicated phase diagram analysis are difficult to assess. In general, she seems to allow for life-cycle profiles characterized by lagged adjustments when the assumption of constant returns to scale would suggest that the adjustments are instantaneous. Even if her analysis is correct, a more sophisticated mathematician than me is required to evaluate her paper.

I applaud Galama and van Kippersluis for including a fully endogenous length of life in their model. Yet I am puzzled as to exactly why length of life is finite in their analysis. To be sure, they do make the rate of depreciation on the stock a function of age but do not specify its behavior as an individual becomes older. In the Ehrlich-Chuma framework and in my framework, life is finite because of a rising rate of depreciation. Ehrlich, Galama, and I presented papers at the RAND Conference on Health, Aging, and Human Capital in December 2011. Galama's paper was a preliminary version of his 2016 study with van Kippersluis. I asked him whether life could be finite even if the rate of depreciation was constant. He replied that it could be. I whispered to Ehrlich, who was sitting next to me, whether that was possible in his model. He replied that it was not. I would love to witness a round table discussion by Ehrlich, Galama, van Kippersluis, and Laporte on this and other issues in demand for health models, especially since Laporte supports my constant returns to scale assumption and works with a fixed finite horizon form of my model. As part of their discussion, they might be willing to evaluate Eisenring's 2000 contribution, which has not received the attention that I think it deserves.

NOTES

1. Kenneth J. Arrow's 1963 paper in the *American Economic Review* ("Uncertainty and the Welfare Economics of Medical Care"), to which I referred in the introduction to this book, is the second most widely cited paper (Arrow 1963). The first is a 2001 paper in the *American Economic Review* ("The Colonial Origins of Comparative Development: An Empirical Investigation") by Daron Acemoglu, Simon Johnson, and James A. Robinson (Acemoglu,

Johnson, and Robinson 2001). This is an outstanding contribution to the fields of economic development and economic history. But it is not obvious that it should be classified as a contribution to the field of health economics. It shows that protection against appropriation risk in 1990, rather than location in Africa or distance from the equator, was the major determinant of differences in gross domestic product per capita among 64 countries in 1995. These countries were originally colonized by European countries. Protection against appropriation risk is treated as endogenous and instrumented with differences in mortality rates of European settlers among countries during the period in which those countries were colonized or shortly thereafter (the late 1700s through approximately 1840). The idea is that European countries were more likely to set up what the authors call "extractive states" in colonies characterized by high mortality rates. The institutions in these colonies offered little protection for private property or for checks and balances against government appropriation. Moreover, current and colonial institutions are positively correlated. None of the three authors of the paper appears in the list of the top 100 health economists based on the h-index compiled by Wagstaff and Culyer (2012, Table 5, pp. 423–424). The h-index is the most widely used measure of citations and reflects both the number of publications and the number of times they have been cited. For example, an author whose fiftieth most cited publication has been cited exactly fifty times has an h-index of 50.

2. See the introduction to part 3 for a more detailed discussion of this point.

3. This assumes that the price elasticity of demand for health is less than 1 in absolute value.

4. Unfortunately, Zweifel still is not convinced. See his exchange with Robert Kaestner in the *European Journal of Health Economics* (Zweifel 2012, 2013; Kaestner 2013).

REFERENCES

Acemoglu, Daron, Simon Johnson, and James A. Robinson. 2001. "The Colonial Origins of Comparative Development: An Empirical Investigation." *American Economic Review* 91(5): 1369–1401.

Arrow, Kenneth J. 1963. "Uncertainty and the Welfare Economics of Medical Care." *American Economic Review* 53(5): 941–973.

Auster, Richard, Irving Leveson, and Deborah Sarachek. 1969. "The Production of Health: An Exploratory Study." *Journal of Human Resources* 4(4): 411–436.

Becker, Gary S. 1981. *A Treatise on the Family*. Cambridge, MA: Harvard University Press.

Ben-Porath, Yoram. 1967. "The Production of Human Capital and the Life Cycle of Earnings." *Journal of Political Economy* 75(4): 353–367.

Bhattacharya, Jay, Timothy Hyde, and Peter Tu. 2014. *Health Economics*. London: Palgrave-MacMillan.

Bolin, Kristian, Lena Jacobson, and Björn Lindgren. 2001. "The Family as the Health Producer—When Spouses Are Nash-Bargainers." *Journal of Health Economics* 20(3): 349–362.

Bolin, Kristian, Lena Jacobson, and Björn Lindgren. 2002. "The Family as the Health Producer—When Spouses Act Strategically." *Journal of Health Economics* 21(3): 475–495.

Chang, Fwu-Ranq. 1996. "Uncertainty and Investment in Health." *Journal of Health Economics* 15(3): 369–376.

Cropper, Maureen L. 1977. "Health, Investment in Health, and Occupational Choice." *Journal of Political Economy* 85(6): 1273–1294.

Dardanoni, Valentino, and Adam Wagstaff. 1987. "Uncertainty, Inequalities in Health and the Demand for Health." *Journal of Health Economics* 6(4): 283–290.

Dardanoni, Valentino, and Adam Wagstaff. 1990. "Uncertainty and the Demand for Medical Care." *Journal of Health Economics* 9(1): 23–38.

Ehrlich, Isaac, and Hiroyuki Chuma. 1990. "A Model of the Demand for Longevity and the Value of Life Extension." *Journal of Political Economy* 98(4): 761–782.

Eisenring, Christoph. 2000. "Is There a Trade-off Between Longevity and Quality of Life in Grossman's Pure Investment Model?" *Health Economics* 9(8): 669–680.

Folland, Sherman, Allen C. Goodman, and Miron Stano. 2016. *The Economics of Health and Health Care*, Seventh Edition. London and New York: Routledge, an Imprint of the Taylor and Francis Group.

Galama, Titus. 2011. *A Theory of Socioeconomic Disparities in Health*. PhD Dissertation. Tilburg, the Netherlands: Tilburg University.

Galama, Titus, and Arie Kapteyn. 2011. "Grossman's Missing Health Threshold." *Journal of Health Economics* 30(5):1044–1056.

Galama, Titus, and Hans van Kippersluis. 2016. "A Theory of Education, Health and Longevity." Presented at the "Human Capital and Health Behavior" conference. Gothenburg University, Sweden, May 19–20.

Grossman, Michael. 2000. "The Human Capital Model." In *Handbook of Health Economics*, Volume 1A, ed. Anthony J. Culyer and Joseph P. Newhouse. Amsterdam: Elsevier Science B.V., North-Holland Publishing, 347–408.

Jacobson, Lena. 2000. "The Family as a Producer of Health—An Extended Grossman Model." *Journal of Health Economics* 19(5): 611–637.

Johnson-Lans, Shirley. 2006. *A Health Economics Primer*. Boston: Pearson Education, publishing as Addison-Wesley.

Kaestner, Robert. 2013. "The Grossman Model After 40 Years: A Reply to Peter Zweifel." *European Journal of Health Economics* 14(2): 356–360.

Laporte, Audrey. 2015. "Should the Grossman Model of Investment in Health Capital Retain Its Iconic Status?" Toronto: Canadian Center for Health Economics Working Paper No. 2014–04.

Liljas, Bengt. 1998. "The Demand for Health with Uncertainty and Insurance." *Journal of Health Economics* 17(2):153–170.

Muurinen, Jaana-Marja. 1982. "Demand for Health: A Generalised Grossman Model." *Journal of Health Economics* 1(1): 5–28.

Phelps, Charles E. 2013. *Health Economics*, Fifth Edition. London and New York: Routledge, an Imprint of the Taylor and Francis Group.

Qin, Yan. 2008. "Note on an Algorithm for Optimal Length of Life." Working Paper, PhD program in economics. New York: City University of New York Graduate Center.

Ried, Walter. 1998. "Comparative Dynamic Analysis of the Full Grossman Model." *Journal of Health Economics* 17(4): 383–426.

Santerre, Rexford E., and Stephen P. Neun. 2013. *Health Economics: Theories, Insights, and Industry Studies*, Sixth Edition. Mason, OH: South-Western Cengage Learning.

Selden, Thomas M. 1993. "Uncertainty and Health Care Spending by the Poor: The Human Capital Model Revisited." *Journal of Health Economics* 12(1):109–115.

Sloan, Frank A., and Chee-Ruey Hsieh. 2012. *Health Economics*. Cambridge, MA: MIT Press.

van Doorslaer, Eddy K. A. 1987. *Health, Knowledge and the Demand for Medical Care*. Assen/Maastricht, the Netherlands: Van Gorcum.

Wagstaff, Adam, and Anthony J. Culyer. 2012. "Four Decades of Health Economics Through a Bibliometric Lens." *Journal of Health Economics* 31(2): 406–439.

Zweifel, Peter. 2012. "The Grossman Model After 40 Years." *European Journal of Health Economics* 13(6): 677–682.

Zweifel, Peter. 2013. "The Grossman Model After 40 Years: Response to Robert Kaestner." *European Journal of Health Economics* 14(2): 361–362.

Zweifel, Peter, and Fredrich Breyer. 1997. *Health Economics*. New York: Oxford University Press.

The Relationship between
Health and Schooling

PART 2

Introduction to Part 2

For theoretical and empirical reasons, the positive relationship between more schooling and better health is one of the most fundamental relationships in health economics. Clearly, the relationship is part of the massive literature in health economics on the determinants of the health of the population, a literature that originates from a demand for health model that I developed and that serves as the basis of part 1 of this book. That model emphasizes that medical care is only one of many determinants of health, and it is natural to explore others. Moreover, my model views health as a form of human capital and therefore a determinant of earnings. Hence, it is natural to allow for and explore complementarities between health capital and other forms of human capital, the most important of which is knowledge capital, as proxied by the number of years of formal schooling completed.

Empirically, the importance of the relationship is highlighted by Gina Kolata (2007, p. 1): "The one social factor that researchers agree is consistently linked to longer lives in every country where it has been studied is education. It is more important than race; it obliterates any effects of income." It also is underscored by Ellen Meara, Seth Richards, and David Cutler (2008, p. 350): "With the exception of black males, all recent gains in life expectancy at age twenty-five have occurred among better educated groups, raising education differentials in life expectancy by 30 percent." Even more dramatically, Michael

L. Spittel, William T. Riley, and Robert M. Kaplan (2015) summarize evidence suggesting that the effects of schooling on life expectancy are much larger than mammography screenings or elevated LDL cholesterol. The increase in life expectancy experienced by women who undergo a yearly mammography screening compared to those who do not amounts to one month. The difference in that outcome between those with elevated LDL cholesterol compared to those with normal cholesterol is roughly six months. On the other hand, the difference in life expectancy between those with less than a high school degree and those with an advanced degree is at least ten years.

The relationship between schooling and health is more than just of theoretical and empirical interest. Improvements in health are widely accepted goals in developed and developing countries. In a 2002 issue of *Health Affairs* devoted primarily to the nonmedical determinants of health, Nobel Laureate Angus Deaton (2002) argues that policies to increase education in the United States, and to increase income in developing countries, are very likely to have larger payoffs in terms of health than those that focus on health care, even if inequalities in health rise. The same proposition, with regard to the United States, can be found in a much earlier study by Richard Auster, Irving Leveson, and Deborah Sarachek (1969). Because more education typically leads to higher income, policies to increase the former appear to have large returns for more than one generation throughout the world.

Efforts to improve the health of an individual by increasing the amount of formal schooling that he or she acquires, or that try to improve child health by raising parental schooling, assume that the schooling effects summarized previously imply that more schooling causes better health. Yet reverse causality from health to schooling may exist, and omitted "third variables" may cause schooling and health to vary in the same direction. Governments can employ a variety of policies to raise the educational levels of their citizens. These include compulsory schooling laws, new school construction, and targeted subsidies to parents and students. If the third-variable hypothesis and the hypothesis that health causes schooling have some validity, evaluations of the impacts of these policies on health should not be based on studies that simply correlate measures of health and schooling.

Students in poor health are almost certain to miss more days of school due to illness than their healthy peers and may also learn less while they are in school. Both factors suggest negative effects of poor health in childhood on school achievement and ultimately on years of formal schooling completed. Furthermore, this causal path may have long-lasting effects if past health is an input into current health status. Thus, even for nonstudents, a positive relationship between health and schooling may reflect causality from health to schooling in the absence of controls for past health. Health also may cause schooling because a reduction in mortality increases the number of periods over which the returns from investments in knowledge can be collected.

Productive and allocative efficiency models generate causality from education to health. In the former model, which is developed in detail in part 1 of this book, the more educated are assumed to obtain more health output from given amounts of medical care and other inputs. In the latter model, the more educated are assumed to pick a different input mix to produce health than the less educated. That mix gives them more output than the mix selected by the less educated. For example, the more educated may have more knowledge about the harmful effects of cigarette smoking or about what constitutes an appropriate diet.

Health and schooling are both endogenous, so unobserved "third variables" may cause both of these outcomes to vary in the same direction. Victor R. Fuchs (1982) identifies time preference as perhaps the key third variable. He argues that people who are more future oriented (who have a high degree of time preference for the future or discount it at a modest rate) attend school for longer periods of time and make larger investments in their own health and in the health of their children. Thus the effects of schooling on these outcomes are biased if one fails to control for time preference.[1]

The time preference hypothesis is analogous to the hypothesis that the positive effect of schooling on earnings may be biased upward by the omission of ability. The latter hypothesis and the general issue of whether more schooling causes higher earnings have generated a massive number of studies in the labor economics literature (see David Card 1999, 2001 for reviews of many of these studies). The related literature on the relationship between health and schooling in health economics is not as large but is rapidly growing. For example, in Grossman (2015), I counted thirty-eight such studies in the period from 2010 through 2014. And that count excludes the more than twenty papers that appeared in a special issue of *Social Science and Medicine* in February 2015 titled "Educational Attainment and Health: Contextualizing Causality (Jennifer Karas Montez and Esther M. Friedman 2015).

The studies that investigate whether more schooling causes better health employ one of three econometric procedures. The first one directly includes such hard-to-measure third variables as time preference, cognitive development, noncognitive development, and past health. The second procedure controls for unobserved genetic and environmental factors by examining the effects of differences in schooling obtained by identical twins on differences in their health outcomes. The third procedure employs the technique of instrumental variables. The idea here is to find exogenous variables that are correlated with schooling but not correlated with unmeasured variables that affect health. In addition, they have no effect on health, with schooling held constant. These variables serve as instruments for schooling in the estimation of health equations by two-stage least squares. One such instrument is the enactment of a law that increases the required amount of formal schooling.

In addition to employing three alternative econometric techniques, the health-schooling studies address three types of relationships: (1) the relationship between an individual's own schooling and his or her own health; (2) the relationship between parents' schooling and their children's health; and (3) the relationship between schooling and mechanisms that may lead to worse or better health outcomes. Examples are health knowledge, fertility choices, and such unhealthy behaviors as cigarette smoking, excessive alcohol consumption, and overeating and lack of exercise—sometimes reflected by a large body mass index (BMI) and obesity.[2]

I have been investigating whether more schooling causes better health since I began to work on my PhD dissertation in 1966. I have studied all three schooling–health relationships just mentioned using direct inclusion of third variables and instrumental variables. I have not employed twin differences in my research but summarize findings that do so in the afterword to this section of the book.

The first paper in this section (Grossman 1976) is my initial attempt to focus on the causality issue in a systematic fashion. It sets the stage for the large literature on this topic that has emerged since the mid- to late 1980s. My strategy in the paper is to try to control for as many hard-to-measure third variables as possible.

I conclude that schooling has a significant positive impact on the current self-rated health of middle-aged white males in the NBER-Thorndike sample. The estimated schooling effect controls for health in high school, parents' schooling, scores on physical and mental tests taken by the men when they were in their early twenties, current hourly wage rates, and property income. My finding is particularly notable because all the men graduated from high school. Hence, it suggests that the favorable impact of schooling on health persists even at high levels of schooling.

I also identify three endogenous mechanisms via which the schooling effect operates. More educated men marry more educated women, are more satisfied with their jobs, and are less likely to be overweight. In turn, these three factors have positive impacts on their health.

My analysis of the mortality experience of the Thorndike sample between 1955 and 1969 confirms the important role of schooling in health outcomes. This analysis is restricted to men who reported positive full-time salaries in 1955. In the fitted logit functions, schooling has a positive and statistically significant effect on the probability of survival. Indeed, schooling is the only variable whose logit coefficient differs from zero in a statistical sense. The schooling effect is independent of the level of median salary in 1955 and suggests that, in the vicinity of the mean death rate, a one-year increase in schooling lowers the probability of death by 0.4 percentage points or by 14 percent relative to the mean death rate of 2.8 percent in the fourteen-year period at issue.

Like the first paper, the second paper in this section is an early forerunner of the large literature on the schooling–health causality question (Shakotko, Edwards, and Grossman 1981). Although the empirical techniques are similar to those in the first paper, the focus shifts to some extent to the effects of parents' schooling on the health of their children. We use a panel that received physical examinations and took IQ and cognitive development tests when they were approximately ages eight and fourteen to investigate the nature–nurture controversy and to obtain estimates of the impact of cognitive development in childhood (an important precursor of the ultimate amount of schooling an individual obtains) on health in adolescence. We find that mother's schooling has a positive impact on a variety of health outcomes in adolescence (at age fourteen), with health in childhood (at age eight) and at birth held constant. We also find that an increase in cognitive development at age eight improves health at age fourteen.

The last two papers in the section, which are much more recent than the first two, employ the technique of instrumental variables to assess whether more educated parents have healthier infants and engage in health behaviors that contribute to this outcome (Chou, Liu, Grossman, and Joyce 2010; Dinçer, Kaushal, and Grossman 2014). Both studies use compulsory school reform as the instrument for schooling: the first in Taiwan and the second in Turkey. Chou et al. (2010) uncover negative effects of mother's schooling on low birth weight, neonatal mortality, postneonatal mortality, and infant mortality in Taiwan. Dinçer et al. (2014) find positive effects of mother's schooling on age at first marriage and at first birth, a negative effect on number of pregnancies, and weak evidence of negative effect on infant mortality in Turkey.

NOTES

1. For a detailed discussion of the framework employed to study the health–schooling relationship, see Grossman (2006) and the references that I cite in that paper. My discussion includes a model in which schooling causes health because it makes people more future oriented.
2. I consider fertility and mother's age at birth as outcomes because children in large families tend to have worse health outcomes than those in smaller families, and children born to teenage mothers have worse outcomes than those born to older mothers.

REFERENCES

Auster, Richard, Irving Leveson, and Deborah Sarachek. 1969. "The Production of Health: an Exploratory Study." *Journal of Human Resources* 4(4): 411–436.

Card, David. 1999. "The Causal Effect of Education on Earnings." In *Handbook of Labor Economics*, Volume 3, ed. Orley Ashenfelter and David Card. Amsterdam: Elsevier Science B.V., North-Holland Publishing: 1801–1863.

Card, David. 2001. "Estimating the Return to Schooling: Progress on Some Persistent Econometric Problems." *Econometrica* 69(5): 1127–1160.

Chou, Shin-Yi, Jin-Tan Liu, Michael Grossman, and Ted Joyce. 2010. "Parental Education and Child Health: Evidence from a Natural Experiment in Taiwan." *American Economic Journal: Applied Economics* 2(1): 33–61.

Deaton, Angus. 2002. "Policy Implications of the Gradient of Health and Wealth." *Health Affairs* 21(2): 13–20.

Dinçer, Mehmet Alper, Neeraj Kaushal, and Michael Grossman. 2014. "Women's Education: Harbinger of Another Spring? Evidence from a Natural Experiment in Turkey." *World Development* 64(December): 243–25.

Fuchs, Victor R. 1982. "Time Preference and Health: An Exploratory Study." *In Economic Aspects of Health*, ed. Victor R. Fuchs. Chicago: University of Chicago Press: 93–120.

Grossman, Michael. 1976. "The Correlation between Health and Schooling." In *Household Production and Consumption,* ed. Nestor E. Terleckyj. Studies in Income and Wealth, Volume 40, by the Conference on Research in Income and Wealth. New York: Columbia University Press for the National Bureau of Economic Research: 147–211.

Grossman, Michael. 2006. "Education and Nonmarket Outcomes." In *Handbook of the Economics of Education,* Volume 1, ed. Eric Hanushek and Finis Welch. Amsterdam: Elsevier Science B.V., North-Holland Publishing: 577–633.

Grossman, Michael. 2015. "The Relationship between Health and Schooling: What's New?" *Nordic Journal of Health Economics* 3(1): 7–17.

Karas Montez, Jennifer, and Esther M. Friedman, ed. 2015. "Special Issue: Educational Attainment and Adult Health: Contextualizing Causality." *Social Science and Medicine* 127(February): 1–206.

Kolata, Gina. 2007. "A Surprising Secret to Long Life: Stay in School." *New York Times*, January 3: 1.

Meara, Ellen, Seth Richards, and David M. Cutler. 2008. "The Gap Gets Bigger: Changes in Mortality and Life Expectancy by Education, 1980–2001." *Health Affairs* 27(2): 350–360.

Shakotko, Robert A., Linda N. Edwards, and Michael Grossman. 1981. "An Exploration of the Dynamic Relationship between Health and Cognitive Development in Adolescence." In *Contributions to Economic Analysis: Health, Economics, and Health Economics,* ed. Jacques van der Gaag and Mark Perlman. Amsterdam: North-Holland Publishing, 305–328.

Spittel, Michael L., William T. Riley, and Robert M. Kaplan. 2015. "Educational Attainment and Life Expectancy: A Perspective from the NIH Office of Behavioral and Social Science Research." *Social Science and Medicine* 127(February): 203–205.

The Correlation between

Health and Schooling

Michael Grossman

THREE

The relationship between health status and socioeconomic conditions is a subject of increasing concern for both medicine and social science. Several recent studies in the United States indicate that among socioeconomic variables, years of formal schooling completed is probably the most important correlate of good health (Stockwell 1963; Fuchs 1965; Hinkle et al. 1968; Kitagawa and Hauser 1968; Auster, Leveson, and Sarachek 1969; Breslow and Klein 1971; Grossman 1972b; Silver 1972). This finding emerges whether health levels are measured by mortality rates, morbidity rates, or self-evaluation of health status, and whether the units of observation are individuals or groups. The relationship is usually statistically significant at levels of confidence of .05 or better in both simple and partial correlations.

This chapter has two purposes. The first is to develop a methodological framework that can be used to introduce and discuss alternative explanations of the correlation between health and schooling. The second is to test these explanations empirically in order to select the most relevant ones and to obtain quantitative estimates of different effects. The empirical work is limited to one unique body of data and uses two measures of health that are far from ideal. The methodological framework can, however, serve as a point of departure for future research when longitudinal samples with more refined measures of current and past health and background characteristics become available.

In a broad sense, the observed positive correlation between health and schooling may be explained in one of three ways. The first argues that there is a causal relationship that runs from increases in schooling to increases in health. The second holds that the direction of causality runs from better health to more schooling. The third argues that no causal relationship is implied by the correlation. Instead, differences in one or more "third variables," such as physical and mental ability and parental characteristics, affect both health and schooling in the same direction.

It should be noted that these three explanations are not mutually exclusive and can be used to rationalize any observed correlation between two variables. But from both a public policy and a theoretical point of view, it is important to distinguish among them and to obtain quantitative estimates of their relative magnitudes. A stated goal of public policy in the United States is to improve the level of health of the population or of certain groups in the population. Given this goal and given the high correlation between health and schooling, it might appear that one method of implementing it would be to increase government outlays on schooling. In fact, Auster, Leveson, and Sarachek (1969) suggest that the rate of return on increases in health via higher schooling outlays far exceeds the rate of return on increases in health via higher medical care outlays. This argument assumes that the correlation between health and schooling reflects only the effect of schooling on health. If, however, the causality ran the other way or if the third-variable hypothesis were relevant, then increased outlays on schooling would not accomplish the goal of improved health.

From a theoretical point of view, recent new approaches to demand theory assume that consumers produce all their basic objects of choice, called commodities, with inputs of market goods and services and their own time (Becker 1965; Lancaster 1966; Muth 1966; Michael 1972; Ghez and Becker 1975; Michael and Becker 1973). Within the context of the household production function model, there are compelling reasons for treating health and schooling as jointly determined variables. It is reasonable to assume that healthier students are more efficient producers of additions to the stock of knowledge, or human capital, via formal schooling. If so, then they would tend to increase the quantity of investment in knowledge they demand as well as the number of years they attend school. Similarly, the efficiency with which individuals transform medical care and other inputs into better health might rise with schooling. This would tend to create a positive correlation between schooling and the quantity of health demanded. Moreover, genetic and early childhood environmental factors might be important determinants of both health and intelligence.[1] Since intelligence and parental characteristics are key variables in the demand curve for schooling, the estimated effect of schooling on health would, under certain conditions, be biased if relevant third variables were omitted from the demand curve for health.[2]

The plan of this chapter is as follows. In section 1 I formulate a recursive system whose two fundamental equations are demand curves for health and schooling. The former equation is based on a model of the demand for health that I have developed in previous work (Grossman 1972a, 1972b). The system as a whole is similar to those that have been used by Bowles (1972), Griliches and Mason (1972), Lillard (1973), and Leibowitz (1974) to study relationships among schooling, ability, and earnings. In section 2, I describe the empirical implementation of the model to data contained in the NBER-Thorndike sample, and in section 3, I present empirical estimates. In section 4, I expand the model by treating current health and current market wage rates as simultaneously determined variables and show the results of estimating wage and health functions by two-stage least squares. Finally, in section 5, I examine the mortality experience of the NBER-Thorndike sample between 1955 and 1969.

1. THE MODEL

1.1. Demand Curve for Health

Elsewhere (Grossman 1972a, 1972b), I have constructed and estimated a model of the demand for health. For the purpose of this chapter, it will be useful to summarize this model and to comment on the nature of the reduced-form demand curve for health capital that it generates. As a point of departure, I assume that individuals inherit an initial stock of health which depreciates with age, and which can be increased by investment. By definition, net investment in the stock of health equals gross investment minus depreciation:

$$H_{t+1} - H_t = I_t - \delta_t H_t \tag{1}$$

where H_t is the stock of health at age t, I_t is gross investment, and δ_t is the rate of depreciation. Direct inputs into the production of gross investments in health include the time expenditure of the consumer, medical care, proper diet, housing facilities, and other market goods and services as well.

In the model, consumers demand health for two reasons. As a consumption commodity, it directly enters their utility functions, or put differently, illness is a source of disutility. As an investment commodity, it determines the total amount of time available for work in the market sector of the economy, where consumers produce money earnings, and for work in the nonmarket or household sector, where they produce commodities that enter their utility functions. The investment motive for demanding health is present because an increase in the stock of health lowers the amount of time lost from market and nonmarket activities in any given period, say a year, due to illness and injury. The monetary value of this reduction in lost time measures the return to an investment in health.

In much of my work, I have ignored the consumption aspects of the demand for health and have developed in detail a pure investment version of the general model.[3] The pure investment model generates powerful predictions from simple analysis and innocuous assumptions and also emphasizes the difference between health capital and other forms of human capital. In particular, persons demand knowledge capital because it influences their market and nonmarket productivity. On the other hand, they demand health capital because it produces an output of healthy time that can then be allocated to the production of money earnings and commodities. Since the output of health capital has a finite upper limit of 8,760 hours in a year (365 days times 24 hours per day), the marginal product of this capital diminishes. This suggests a healthy-time production function of the form

$$h_t = 8,760 - BH_t^{-C} \tag{2}$$

where h_t is healthy time and B and C are positive constants. From equation (2), the marginal product of health capital would be

$$G_t = (\partial h_t / \partial H_t) = BCH_t^{-C-1} \tag{3}$$

In the pure investment model, given constant marginal cost of gross investment in health, the equilibrium stock of health at any age can be determined by equating the marginal monetary rate of return on health capital to the opportunity cost of this capital. If W_t is the hourly wage rate, and if π_t is the marginal cost of gross investment in health, then the rate of return or the marginal efficiency of health capital can be defined as

$$\gamma_t = W_t G_t / \pi_t \tag{4}$$

In equilibrium,

$$\gamma_t = r - \tilde{\pi}_t + \delta_t \tag{5}$$

where r is the rate of interest and $\tilde{\pi}_t$ is the continuously compounded percentage rate of change in marginal cost with age.[4] Equations (3), (4), and (5) imply a demand curve for health capital or a marginal efficiency of capital schedule of the form[5]

$$\ln H_t = \ln BC + \varepsilon \ln W_t - \varepsilon \ln \pi_t - \varepsilon \ln \delta_t \qquad (6)$$

where $\varepsilon = 1/(1 + C)$ is the elasticity of the schedule.

By making assumptions about the nature of the depreciation rate function and the marginal cost of gross investment function, I have used equation (6) to obtain and estimate a reduced-form demand curve for health capital. If $\tilde{\delta}$ is the constant continuously compounded rate of increase in the rate of depreciation with age, and if δ_1 is the rate of depreciation during some initial period, then

$$\ln \delta_t = \delta_1 + \tilde{\delta}_t \qquad (7)$$

It should be noted that δ_1 is not the rate of depreciation at the very beginning of the life cycle. Instead, it is the rate at an age, say age sixteen, when individuals rather than their parents begin to make their own decisions.

I develop an equation for marginal cost by letting the gross investment production function be a member of the Cobb-Douglas class:

$$\ln I_t = \alpha \ln M_t + (1 - \alpha) \ln T_t + \rho E \qquad (8)$$

The new variables in this equation are M_t, a market good or a vector of market goods used to produce gross investments in health; T_t, an input of the consumer's own time; and E, an index of the stock of knowledge, or human capital.[6] The new parameters are α, the output elasticity of M_t or the share of M_t in the total cost of gross investment; $(1 - \alpha)$, the output elasticity of T_t; and ρ, the percentage improvement in nonmarket productivity due to human capital. It is natural to view medical care as an important component of M_t, although studies by Auster, Leveson, and Sarachek (1969); Grossman (1972b), and Benham and Benham (1975) reach the tentative conclusion that medical care has, at best, a minor marginal impact on health.[7]

Equations (6), (7), and (8) generate a reduced-form demand curve for health capital given by[8]

$$\ln H_t = \alpha\varepsilon \ln W_t - \alpha\varepsilon \ln P_t + \rho\varepsilon E - \tilde{\delta}\varepsilon t - \varepsilon \ln \delta_1 \qquad (9)$$

where P_t is the price of M_t. It should be realized that although the subscript t refers to age, H_t will vary among individuals as well as over the life cycle of a given individual. It should also be realized that the functional form of equation (9) is one that is implied by the model rather than one that is imposed on data for "convenience." According to the equation, the quantity of health capital demanded should be positively related to the hourly wage rate and the stock of human capital and should be negatively related to the price of M_t, age, and the rate of depreciation in the initial period.

In previous empirical work (Grossman 1972b, Chapter V), I fitted equation (9) to data for individuals who had finished their formal schooling. I measured health by self-rated health status, and alternatively by sick time, and measured the stock of knowledge, or human capital, by years of schooling completed. Since I had no data on depreciation rates of persons of the same age, I assumed that $\ln \delta_1$ was not correlated with the other variables on the right-hand side of equation (9). Put differently, I treated $\ln \delta_1$ as the random disturbance term in the reduced-form demand curve.

In general, my empirical results were consistent with the predictions of the model. In particular, with age, the wage rate, and several other variables held constant, schooling had a positive and significant effect on health.[9] I interpreted this result as evidence in support of the hypothesis that schooling raises the efficiency with which health is produced. That is, I interpreted it in terms of a causal relationship that runs from more schooling to better health. If, however, the unobserved rate of depreciation on health capital in the initial period were correlated with schooling, or if schooling were an imperfect measure of the stock of human capital, then my finding would be subject to more than one interpretation.

1.2. A General Recursive System

I now show that a general model of life-cycle decision making would lead to a negative relationship between schooling and the rate of depreciation. Moreover, this model would predict positive relationships between schooling and other components of nonmarket efficiency; and between schooling and additional third variables that should, under certain conditions, enter equation (9). These relationships arise because, in the context of a life-cycle model, the amount of schooling persons acquire and their health during the time that they attend school are endogenous variables. I do not develop the model in detail but instead rely heavily on previous work dealing with the demand for preschool and school investments in human capital, and the demand for child quality.[10]

1.2.1. Demand Curve for Schooling

The optimal quantity of school investment in human capital in a given year and the number of years of formal schooling completed should be positive functions of the efficiency with which persons transform teachers' services, books, their own time, and other inputs into gross additions to the stock of knowl-edge. As Lillard (1973, 32) points out, efficiency in producing human capital via schooling is determined by factors such as physical ability, mental ability (intelligence), and health.[11] Another reason for expecting a positive effect of health on schooling is that the returns from an investment in schooling last for many periods. Since health status is positively correlated with life expectancy, it should be positively correlated with the number of periods over which returns can be collected. In addition to efficiency and to the number of periods over which returns accrue, the opportunity to finance investments in human capital, measured by parents' income or by parents' schooling, should be a key deter-minant of the quantity of schooling demanded.

Let the factors that determine variations in years of formal schooling com-pleted (S) among individuals be summarized by a demand curve of the form

$$S = a_1 \ln H_1 + a_2 X \tag{10}$$

where X is a vector of all other variables besides health that influences S. In a manner analogous to the interpretation of δ_1, H_1 may be interpreted as health capital at the age (age sixteen) when individuals begin to make their own deci-sions. I will assume, however, that a given person's health capital at age sixteen is highly correlated with his or her own health capital at the age (age five or six) when formal schooling begins. One justification for this assumption is that the rate of increase in the rate of depreciation might be extremely small and even zero at young ages.[12]

The demand curve for schooling given by equation (10) differs in a funda-mental respect from the demand curve for health given by equation (9). Since the production function of gross investment in health exhibits constant returns to scale and since input prices are given, the marginal cost of gross investment in health is independent of the quantity of investment produced. Therefore, con-sumers reach their desired stock of health capital immediately, and equation (9) represents a demand curve for an equilibrium stock of capital at age t. Implicit in this equation is the assumption that people never stop investing in their health.[13]

On the other hand, following Becker (1967) and Ben-Porath (1967), I allow the marginal cost of gross investment in knowledge to be a positive function of the rate of production of new knowledge.[14] Thus, consumers do not reach their equilibrium stock of knowledge immediately, and equation (10) represents a demand curve for the equilibrium length of the investment period, measured by the number of years of formal schooling completed. Since persons typically have left school by age thirty, investment in knowledge ceases after some point in the life cycle.[15]

1.2.2. Demand Curve for Children's Health

Although the health and intelligence of children depend partly on genetic inheritance, these variables are not completely exogenous in a life-cycle model. In particular, they also depend on early childhood environmental factors, which are shaped to a large extent by parents.[16] If children's health is viewed as one aspect of their quality, then one can conceive of a demand curve for H_1 whose key arguments are variables that determine the demand for child quality. Children's health should rise with their parents' income if quality has a positive income elasticity and should rise with their parents' schooling if persons with higher schooling levels are relatively more efficient producers of quality children than of other commodities. Most important for my purposes, the quantity of H_1 demanded should be negatively related to δ_1. This follows because, regardless of whether one is examining the demand for children's health capital or adults' health capital, an increase in the rate of depreciation raises the price of such capital.

Let the demand curve for children's health be given by

$$\ln H_1 = b_1 Y - \varepsilon' \ln \delta_1 \tag{11}$$

In equation (11), Y is a vector of all other variables in addition to δ_1 that affects H_1, and ε' is the price elasticity of H_1,[17] This elasticity will not, in general, equal the price elasticity of H_t (ε). Surely, in a developed economy such as the United States, a healthy child is primarily a consumption commodity. Since my model treats adult health as primarily an investment commodity, the substitution effect associated with a change in the price of H_1 will differ in nature from the substitution effect associated with a change in the price of H_1.

It should be realized that the stock of health capital inherited at birth does not enter equation (11) directly. Given constant marginal cost of gross investment in health, any discrepancy between the inherited stock of children's health and the stock that their parents demand in the period immediately following birth would be eliminated instantaneously. This does *not* mean that H_1 is independent of genetic inheritance and birth defects. Variations in these factors explain part of the variation in δ_1 among children of the same age. According to this interpretation, children with inferior genetic characteristics or birth defects would have above-average rates of depreciation, and their parents would demand a smaller optimal quantity of H_1.[18] Of course, one could introduce a direct relationship between current and lagged stock by dropping the assumption of constant marginal cost. Such a framework would, however, greatly complicate the interpretation and empirical estimation of demand curves for children's health and adults' health. Consequently, I will not pursue it in this chapter.

1.2.3. Human Capital Equation

To complete the analytical framework, it is necessary to specify an equation for the stock of knowledge, or human capital, after the completion of formal schooling. Recall that it is this stock that determines the efficiency with which adult health is produced. Assume that the stock (E) depends on years of formal schooling completed (S) and a vector of other variables (Z) as in[19]

$$E = c_1 S + c_2 Z \qquad (12)$$

The variables in Z include the initial or inherited stock of human capital and determinants of the "average" quantity of new knowledge produced per year of school attendance, such as ability, health, quality of schooling, and parental characteristics. In one important respect, equation (12) is misspecified, for the function that relates E to S and Z is almost certainly nonlinear.[20] In this chapter, I use equation (12) as a first approximation in assessing the biases that arise when determinants of human capital other than schooling are omitted from the demand curve for health. In future work, I plan to modify the assumption of linearity.

1.2.4. Comments and Interpretation of Health–Schooling Relationships

The system of equations that I have just developed provides a coherent framework for analyzing and interpreting health–schooling relationships and for obtaining unbiased estimates of the "pure" effect of schooling on health. Before I turn to these matters, it will be useful to make a few comments about the general nature of this system. The stock of knowledge is a theoretical concept and is difficult to quantify empirically. Because it will not, in general, be possible to estimate the human capital function given by equation (12), substitute it into the demand curve for adults' health given by equation (9). This reduces the system to three basic equations. They are demand curves for children's health and schooling, given by equations (11) and (10), respectively, and a modified demand curve for adults' health:[21]

$$\ln H_1 = \alpha \varepsilon \ln W - \alpha \varepsilon \ln P + c_1 \rho \varepsilon S + c_2 \rho \varepsilon Z - \tilde{\delta} \varepsilon t - \varepsilon \ln \delta_1 \qquad (9')$$

Since the endogenous variables are determined at various stages in the life cycle, these three equations constitute a recursive system rather than a full simultaneous-equations model. For example, although children's health is the endogenous variable in equation (11), it is predetermined when students select

their optimal quantity of schooling at age sixteen. Similarly, schooling is predetermined when adults select their optimal quantity of health capital at age t. It is
well known that estimation of each equation in a recursive system by ordinary
least squares is equivalent to estimation of the entire system by the method of
full-information maximum likelihood.[22]

I have specified demand curves for adults' health and for children's health,
but I have not specified a demand curve for health at an age when persons are
still in school but are making their own decisions. Formally, if the decision-
making process begins at age sixteen, and if schooling ends at age t^*, then I
ignore demand at age j, where $16 < j \leq t^*$. It might appear that I have done this
to avoid a problem of instability in the system. Specifically, variations in H_1
would cause the quantity of human capital produced in period 1 (Q_1) to vary.
An increase in Q_1 would raise the stock of human capital (E_2) in period 2,
which should raise efficiency in the production of health and the quantity of
H_2 demanded. In turn, the increase in H_2 would raise Q_2, and so on. Although
this process is potentially unstable, it is observed empirically that persons do
not attend school throughout their life cycles. Rather, the equilibrium quantities
of S and the stock of human capital ($E = E_t^*$) are reached at fairly young ages,
and the system would retain its recursive nature even if a demand curve for H_j
were introduced.

The simultaneous determination of health and knowledge in the age inter-
val $16 \leq j < t^*$ does suggest that E_t^* should depend either on all quantities of H,
or on an average quantity of H. in this interval. But such an average undoubtedly is highly correlated with the stock of health at age sixteen. This simultaneous determination also blurs to some extent the sharp distinction that I have
drawn between knowledge capital as a determinant of productivity and health
capital as a determinant of total time. Note, however, that E_t^* depends on H_1
rather than on the contemporaneous stock of health. Therefore, the distinction
between health and knowledge capital remains valid as long as it is applied to
contemporaneous stocks of the two types of capital at ages greater than t^*.

The wage rate and the stock of human capital obviously are positively correlated, yet I treat the wage rate as an exogenous variable in the recursive system. The wage rate enters the demand curve for adults' health in order to assess
the pure effect of schooling on nonmarket productivity, with market productivity held constant. The wage should have an independent and positive impact
on the quantity of health demanded, because it raises the monetary value of a
reduction in sick time by a greater percentage than it raises the cost of producing such a reduction. If market and nonmarket productivity were highly correlated, it would be difficult to isolate the pure nonmarket productivity effect,

but this is an empirical issue that can ultimately be decided by the data. As long as the current stock of health is not a determinant of the current stock of human capital, nothing would be gained by specifying an equation for the wage rate. Until section 4, I assume that, at ages greater than t^*, E_t and, therefore, W_t do not depend on H_t.

In the remainder of this section, I discuss the interpretation and estimation of health-schooling relationships within the context of the recursive system. Given an appropriate measure of the rate of depreciation in the initial period, an ordinary least squares fit of equation (9′) would yield an unbiased estimate of the pure effect of schooling on health. Now suppose that no measure of δ_1 is available. From equation (11), H_1 is negatively related to δ_1, and from equation (10), S is positively related to H_1. Therefore, S is negatively related to δ_1. Since an increase in δ_1 causes H_t to fall, the expected value of the regression coefficient of S in equation (9′) would be an upward-biased estimate of the relevant population parameter. This is the essence of the reverse causality interpretation of an observed positive relationship between schooling and health. Due to the prediction of the recursive system that healthier students should attend school for longer periods of time, the effect of schooling on health would be *overstated* if δ_1 were not held constant in computing equation (9′).

In general, it should be easier to measure the stock of health in the initial period empirically than to measure the rate of depreciation in this period. Therefore, the easiest way to obtain unbiased estimates of the parameters of equation (9′) would be to solve equation (11) for $\ln \delta_1$ and substitute the resulting expression into (9′):

$$\ln H_t = \alpha\varepsilon \ln W - \alpha\varepsilon \ln P + c_1\rho\varepsilon S + c_2\rho\varepsilon Z - \tilde{\delta}\varepsilon t$$
$$+ (\varepsilon / \varepsilon') \ln H_1 - (b_1\varepsilon / \varepsilon') Y \tag{9″}$$

A second justification for this substitution is that H_1 is one of the variables in the Z vector, because it is a determinant of the average quantity of new knowledge produced per year of school attendance. Consequently, $\ln H_1$ should enter the regression whether or not $\ln \delta_1$ can be measured, and the elimination of $\ln \delta_1$ from equation (9′) makes it simpler to interpret variations in key variables within the recursive system.[23]

Formally, if $Z = Z' + c_3 \ln H_1$, then the regression coefficient of $\ln H_1$, in equation (9″) would be $c_3c_2 \rho\varepsilon + (\varepsilon/\varepsilon')$. Although it would not be possible to isolate the two components of this coefficient, both should be positive. Therefore, one can make the firm prediction that H_1 should have a positive effect on H_t. This relationship arises not because of any direct relationship between current and lagged stock but because H_1 is negatively correlated with the depreciation rate in the initial period and is positively correlated with the equilibrium stock of human capital.

The "third variable" explanation of the observed positive correlation between health and schooling asserts that no causal relationship is implied by this correlation. Instead, differences in one or more third variables cause health and schooling to vary in the same direction. The most logical way to introduce this hypothesis and to examine its relevance within the context of the recursive system is to associate third variables with the Y vector in the demand curve for children's health and with the X vector in the demand curve for schooling. Many of the variables in these two vectors represent factors, such as parents' schooling and parents' income, that shape early childhood environment. If years of formal schooling completed were the only determinant of the stock of human capital, and if one had a perfect measure of δ_1 or H_1 then the third-variable effect would operate solely via the relationship between H_1 and H_t. That is, provided H_1 were held constant, the estimated schooling parameter in equation (9″) would not be biased by the omission of environmental variables that induce similar changes in schooling and children's health.[24]

The situation would be somewhat different if one had no measure of δ_1 or H_1. Then a variable in the Y vector might have a positive effect on H_t if it were negatively correlated with δ_1.[25] The assumption of a negative correlation between Y and δ_1 is not as arbitrary as it may seem, for δ_1 is not entirely an exogenous variable. To the extent that variations in δ_1 reflect variations in birth defects, these defects should depend in part on the quantity and quality of prenatal care, which in turn may be related to the characteristics of parents. For instance, at an empirical level, birth weight is positively correlated with mothers' schooling.[26] Moreover, there is evidence that physical health is influenced by mental well-being.[27] Some of the differences in δ_1 among individuals may be associated with differences in mental well-being that are created by early-childhood environmental factors.

In an intermediate situation, one may have some data on past health, but it may be subject to errors of observation. Then it would make sense to include Y in a regression estimate of equation (9″) in order to improve the precision with which past health is estimated. In general, Y would have a larger effect on current health, the greater is the error variance in H_t relative to the total variance.

If efficiency in the production of adults' health were not determined solely by years of formal schooling completed, then third variables could have effects on current health independent of their effects on past health. These effects are represented by the coefficients of the variables in the Z vector in equation (9″). Since some of these variables also enter the X vector in the demand curve for schooling, the estimated impact of schooling on current health would be biased if the Z variables were excluded from the demand curve for adults' health. I have interpreted the variables in this vector primarily as measures of a person's capacity to assimilate new knowledge in a given year of school attendance and have associated them with physical and mental ability, health, parental characteristics, and school quality. In general, it will not be possible to distinguish the effects of Y variables from those of Z variables in the demand curve for health. For example, given an imperfect measure of past health, parents' schooling may have a positive impact on current health because it is positively correlated with past health or because it is one determinant of the stock of human capital.

The overlap between elements in the Z vector and those in the X and Y vectors suggests that certain third variables must operate in an indirect manner only in the demand curve for adults' health. Clearly, it would not be feasible to vary schooling, with past health and all of the other variables in the X vector held constant. That is, one could not use schooling and all of its systematic determinants as independent variables in a regression with current health as the dependent variable. Specifically, intelligence, like children's health, is one aspect of the quality of children that depends on genetic inheritance and early childhood environment. Therefore, these factors may affect the current stock of health solely through their influence on intelligence.[28]

At this point, two caveats with regard to the third variable effect are in order. First, I have assumed that efficiency in health production is a function of a homogeneous stock of knowledge, or human capital. Efficiency may, however, depend on "general" human capital (knowledge) and on "specific" (health-related) human capital. It is plausible to associate schooling and mental intelligence with general capital and to associate physical characteristics with specific capital. Suppose that genetic inheritance affects physical and mental ability and suppose that an inferior genetic endowment is not reflected in poor health until later stages of the life cycle. Then, there is a rationale for including physical ability in the demand curve for health, even if this dimension of ability is not directly related to the quantity of schooling demanded. Indeed, given the health-specific nature of physical ability, it should have a larger effect on current health than mental ability. On the other hand, given the schooling-specific nature of mental ability, it should have a larger impact on schooling than physical ability.

Second, if one considers the production of health in a family context, then years of formal schooling completed by one's spouse becomes a relevant third variable. To anticipate the empirical work in the following sections of this chapter, consider the process by which the health of married men is produced. Typically, such men devote most of their time to market production, while their wives devote most of their time to nonmarket production. This suggests that wives' time should be an important input in the production of husbands' health. If an increase in wives' schooling raises their nonmarket productivity, then it would tend to raise the quantity of husbands' health demanded. To be sure, an increase in schooling should raise the value of time, measured by the potential market wage rate, as well as nonmarket productivity.[29] Suppose that wives' schooling but not their potential market wage were included in a demand curve for husbands' health. Then the wives' schooling parameter would be $\varepsilon(\rho_f - \alpha_f \hat{W}_f)$, where ρ_f is the percentage increase in wives' nonmarket productivity due to a one year increase in schooling, $\hat{W}_f$ is the percentage change in market productivity, and α_f is the share of wives' time in the total cost of gross investment in husbands' health. This parameter would be positive provided ρ_f exceeded $\alpha_f \hat{W}_f$. Thus, it would definitely be positive if schooling raised market and non-market productivity by the same percentage.[30]

To summarize, given data on current health, past health, and third variables for persons who had completed formal schooling, one could estimate the demand curves for adults' health and schooling given by equations (9″) and (10). The coefficient of schooling in equation (9″) would indicate the contribution of this variable to current health, with past health and third variables held constant. That is, it would measure the degree to which more schooling causes belter health. The coefficient of past health in equation (10) would measure the extent to which good health at young ages induces people to attend school for longer periods of time. Since the two equations constitute a recursive system rather than a full simultaneous-equations model, consistent estimates of each may be obtained by ordinary least squares.

2. EMPIRICAL IMPLEMENTATION OF THE MODEL

2.1. The Sample

I have used data contained in the NBER-Thorndike sample to estimate health and schooling functions. This is a sample drawn from a population of 75,000 white males who volunteered for, and were accepted as candidates for, Aviation Cadet status as pilots, navigators, or bombardiers in the Army Air Force in the last half of 1943.[31] To be accepted as a candidate, a man had to pass a physical examination and the Aviation Cadet Qualifying Examination, which measured scholastic aptitude and achievement. According to Thorndike and Hagen, the minimum passing score on the Qualifying Examination was "one that could be achieved by about half of high-school graduates (1959, 53)." Thus, the candidates were selected almost entirely from the upper half of the scholastic ability

(IQ) distribution of all draft-eligible white mates in the United States in 1943. After passing the Qualifying Examination, candidates were given seventeen specific tests that measured five basic types of ability: general intelligence, numerical ability, visual perception, psychomotor control, and mechanical ability.[32] A candidate's scores on these tests determined whether he was accepted as an Aviation Cadet for training in one of the programs, and his subsequent performance in training school determined whether he actually served in the Air Force.

In 1955, Robert L. Thorndike and Elizabeth Hagen collected information on earnings, schooling, and occupation for a civilian sample of 9,700 of these 75,000 men. In 1969, the National Bureau of Economic Research mailed a questionnaire to the members of the Thorndike-Hagen sample and received 5,085 responses. In 1971, the NBER sent a supplementary questionnaire to the persons who answered its initial questionnaire and received 4,417 responses. In section 5, I examine the mortality experience of the NBER-Thorndike sample between 1955 and 1969. Until then, my empirical analysis is limited to men who responded to both NBER questionnaires, were married in 1969, were members of the labor force in that year, and did not have unknown values for certain key variables.[33] The sample size of this group is 3,534.

The NBER resurveys greatly increased the amount of information available in the dataset. In particular, Thorndike and Hagen did not obtain any measures of health, parental characteristics, or spouses' characteristics. The NBER surveys included questions on all these variables and also updated the information on earnings, schooling, and work history since 1955. Most of this information was gathered in the 1969 survey. The 1971 survey collected several background characteristics that were omitted from the 1969 survey and also expanded the measures of health to include an index of past health as well as an index of current health. Since the measure of past health is available only for persons who responded to both the 1969 and 1971 surveys, I limit my analysis to such persons.

It should be emphasized that, for several reasons, the white males in the NBER-Thorndike sample by no means constitute a representative sample of all white males in the United States. First, everyone in the sample is around the same age. The mean age in 1969 was forty-seven years, and the age range was from forty-one years to fifty-five years. Second, these men are drawn mainly from the upper tails of the schooling, earnings, and scholastic ability distributions. All of them graduated from high school, and their mean full-time salary was approximately $18,000 in 1969. As I have already indicated, in order to pass the Aviation Cadet Qualifying Examination in 1943, one had to have a level of scholastic ability at least as high as half of all high-school graduates.

Third, since the men passed a physical examination in 1943, they were at least fairly healthy in that year. As I will show presently, their current health tends to exceed that of a random sample of white males.

It is plausible to postulate that the effect of past health on schooling and the effect of schooling on current health decline as the levels of these variables increase. Therefore, it may be more difficult to uncover significant health-schooling relationships in the NBER-Thorndike sample than in other samples. In particular, with past health held constant, any impact of schooling on current health represents the effect of college attendance versus completion of formal schooling after graduation from high school. As a corollary, if significant health-schooling relationships exist in the NBER-Thorndike sample, even more significant relationships may exist in the general population. The main advantage in using the sample to study these relationships is that data on past health and a fairly wide set of potential third variables are available.

2.2. Measurement of Health

The stock of health, like the stock of knowledge, is a theoretical concept that is difficult to define and quantify empirically. A proxy for it is, however, available in the 1969 NBER-Thorndike survey. The men in the sample were asked whether the state of their general health was excellent, good, fair, or poor. I use their response to this question as an index of the amount of health capital they possessed in 1969. This measure of health capital suffers from the defect that it depends on an individual's subjective evaluation of the state of his health: what one person considers to be excellent health may be viewed as good or only fair health by another. Moreover, it is not immediately obvious how to quantify the four possible responses. That is, one must determine exactly how much more health capital a man in, say, excellent health has compared to a man in poor health.

Table 3.1 contains a frequency distribution of health status in 1969 for married men in the NBER-Thorndike sample. For comparative purposes, the table also contains a frequency distribution of this variable for white married men in a 1963 health interview survey conducted by the National Opinion Research Center (NORC) and the Center for Health Administration Studies of the University of Chicago. The NORC sample is an area probability sample of the entire civilian noninstitutionalized population of the United States.[34] Therefore, its white male members are much more representative of the population at large than the members of the NBER-Thorndike sample.

In the table, I show that most of the men in the NBER-Thorndike sample are in either good or excellent health. I also show that the level of health of these

Table 3.1 Frequency Distributions of Health Status, Married Men

	Percentage Distribution	
Class	NBER-Thorndike Sample[a]	NORC Sample[b]
Excellent	59.51	48.54
Good	37.29	37.45
Fair	2.80	11.87
Poor	0.40	2.14

[a] Sample size is 3,534. Until section 5, all subsequent tables based on the NBER-Thorndike sample pertain to this sample size.
[b] Sample size is 1,028.

men is higher than that of men in the NORC sample. Approximately 97 percent of the former sample report that their health is at least good. The corresponding figure in the latter sample is approximately 86 percent.

In table 3.2, I present relationships between self-rated health status and more objective measures of health for both samples. These relationships take the form of regressions of number of work-loss weeks due to illness, medical expenditures, or number of symptoms reported from a checklist of twenty common symptoms[35] on three health status dummy variables ($HS1$, $HS2$, and $HS3$). The dummy variables are coded as follows: $HS1 = 1$ if health status is good, fair, or poor; $HS2 = 1$ if health status is fair or poor; and $HS3 = 1$

Table 3.2 Regressions of Work-Loss Weeks Due to Illness, Medical Expenditures, and Symptoms on Health Status Dummy Variables

		Regression Coefficient of:			
Dependent Variable	Intercept	$HS1$	$HS2$	$HS3$	R^2
Work-loss weeks[a]	.103	.235 (3.94)	.571 (3.23)	8.019 (16.55)	.102
Work-loss weeks[b]	.524	.584 (2.43)	1.749 (4.75)	4.929 (6.00)	.106
Medical expenditures[b]	55.854	61.235 (4.85)	75.231 (3.89)	49.089 (1.14)	.067
Symptoms[b]	.940	.741 (5.87)	1.401 (7.25)	3.463 (8.04)	.224

Note: t ratios in parentheses. R^2 is the unadjusted coefficient of multiple determination.
[a] Regression based on the NBER-Thorndike sample.
[b] Regression based on the NORC sample.

if health status is poor. All three dependent variables pertain to the year pre-ceding the survey.

Since there are no data on medical expenditures or symptoms in the NBER-Thorndike sample, only the first regression in table 3.2 is relevant for this sample. It shows that the number of work-loss weeks in 1968 rises as health status declines. The intercept of the regression indicates that the mean number of work-loss weeks for men in excellent health equals .1. The regression coefficient of $HS1$ indicates that men in good health have .2 more work-loss weeks on the average than men in excellent health. Similarly, men in fair health have .6 more work-loss weeks than men in good health, and men in poor health have 8.0 more work-loss weeks than men in fair health. These differences in work-loss by health status are statistically significant at all conventional levels of confidence.

The second regression in table 3.2 demonstrates a similar inverse relation-ship between work-loss and health status in the NORC sample. The third and fourth regressions show that medical expenditures and symptoms rise as health status falls. The negative relationship between medical expenditures, an input into the production of health, and health can be traced to a positive correlation between medical care and the rate of depreciation on health capital. An increase in the rate of depreciation would cause the quantity of health capital demanded to fall. At the same time, the quantity of medical care demanded would rise if the price elasticity of demand for health capital were less than one.[36]

Taken together, the regression results in table 3.2 give evidence that vari-ations in self-rated health status reflect true variations in more objective mea-sures of health. Additional considerations support the use of this variable as an index of health. Palmore (1969a, 1969b) reports that work satisfaction, itself an important correlate of self-rated health, and health status are key determinants of survival in a longitudinal sample of older persons. Rahe and Holmes (1965), Holmes and Masuda (1970), and Rahe (1972) find that physical illness is often associated with changes in life events that cause changes in mental well-being. Variations in mental well-being may cause current health status to vary but may affect work-loss and other measures of disability only with a long lag.

The first regression in table 3.2 and the production function of healthy time given by equation (2) can be employed to select a set of scales for health status. The scaling scheme is based on the proposition that health capital, like knowl-edge capital, is a units-free measure of an existing stock. Setting this index equal to one for men in poor health, one could then express the amount of health capital of men in one of the other three categories relative to that of men in poor health. To be specific, if time is measured in weeks, then the production function of healthy time given by equation (2) implies

$$52 - h = WLW = BH^{-C} \qquad (13)$$

where WLW denotes the number of work-loss weeks due to illness. Solve equation (13) for H to obtain

$$H = B^{1/C} WLW^{-1/C} \qquad (14)$$

and let WLW_P, WLW_F, WLW_G, and WLW_E be mean work-loss of men in poor, fair, good, and excellent health. Then, to express the stock of health in an index number form with $H_P = 1$, write $H_F/H_P = (WLW_P/WLW_F)^{1/C}$, et cetera.

According to regression 1 in table 3.2, $WLW_P/WLW_F = 9.82$, $WLW_P/WLW_G = 26.41$, and $WLW_P/WLW_E = 86.68$. Thus, the health capital series, termed $H69$ in subsequent analysis, is 1.00, 9.82, 26.41, and 86.68. The dependent variable in the demand curve for adults, health should be ln H_J/H_P ($J = P, F, G, E$). Therefore, the use of ln WLW_P/WLW_J as the dependent variable would generate regression coefficients that would exceed, equal, or fall short of the true coefficients as C exceeds, equals, or falls short of one. However, because C is a constant, the t ratios associated with these coefficients would be unaffected.

In most of my empirical analysis in the next two sections, I emphasize the qualitative effects of independent variables on $H69$. To examine the sensitivity of results to the scaling scheme, I estimate some equations with a dichotomous dependent variable ($EXCELL$) that is equal to one if a man is in excellent health and is equal to zero otherwise. In a few instances, I discuss quantitative effects in conjunction with $H69$, and in these instances, I assume that C is equal to one. Of course, the quantitative analysis is based on the specification of the production function of healthy time given by equation (13). This specification is not the only one that is consistent with diminishing marginal productivity to health capital and an upper asymptote of 52 healthy weeks in a year, but it is the most simple one. I have investigated the behavior of the health capital series with more complicated functional forms such as the logistic function. Provided that the mean number of work-loss weeks for the entire sample and the mean for men in poor health are relatively small, this series is almost unaffected.[37] The existence of other functional forms and the somewhat arbitrary assumption about the value of C does suggest, however, that quantitative results should be interpreted with caution.

I could have employed the actual number of work-loss weeks reported by an individual as a negative measure of health, but only 9 percent of the NBER-Thorndike sample reported positive work-loss in 1968.[38] Undoubtedly, there is a large random component in work-loss in a given year. Therefore, it is reasonable to associate variations in work-loss due to variations in health status with "permanent" differences in health. On the other hand, variations in work-loss not accounted for by variations in health status may be viewed as more "transitory" in nature.

The 1971 NBER-Thorndike resurvey contains a proxy variable for past health. The men in the sample were asked whether the state of their health during the years they were attending high school was excellent, good, fair, or poor. The frequency distribution of responses is as follows: excellent, 87.29 percent; good, 11.72 percent; fair, 0.88 percent; and poor, 0.11 percent. The men were also asked how many weeks per year they lost from high school, on the average, due to illness. I analyze the relationship between self-rated high-school health status and average school-loss weeks due to illness (SLW) in the same manner as I analyzed the relationship between current health status and work-loss weeks. Specifically, I estimate a regression of SLW on three dummy variables for high-school health status: $HSHS1 = 1$ if high-school health status is good, fair, or poor; $HSHS2 = 1$ if high-school health status is fair or poor; and $HSHS3 = 1$ if high-school health status is poor. The regression is as follows (t ratios in parentheses):

$$SLW = .403 + .384 \; HSHS1 + .907 \; HSHS2 + 1.306 \; HSHS3$$
$$(15.04) \qquad (10.00) \qquad\qquad (5.05)$$
$$R^2 = .132$$

Based on this regression, I create a series for health capital in high school the same way that I created a series for health capital in 1969. Let SLW_P, SLW_F, SLW_G, and SLW_E be mean school-loss of students in poor, fair, good, and excellent health. According to the regression, $SLW_P/SLW_F = 1.77$, $SLW_P/SLW_G = 3.81$, and $SLW_P/SLW_E = 7.44$. Thus, the past or high-school health capital series, termed HHS in subsequent analysis, is 1.00, 1.77, 3.81, and 7.44. This measure of past health suffers from the defect that it was obtained in a retrospective fashion. Note, however, that the information on current health was requested in 1969, while the information on past health was requested in 1971. Since the two variables were obtained at different points in time, the possibility of a spurious positive correlation between them is greatly mitigated. That is, respondents could not have used their answer to a question on current health status as the basis for an answer to a question on past health status.

2.3. Regression Specification

The most general versions of the health and schooling regressions that I estimate with the NBER-Thorndike sample are given by

$$\ln H69 = b_1 A + b_2 S + b_3\ SFAT + b_4\ SMOT + b_5 V + b_6 P + b_7\ MECH$$
$$+ b_8\ NUM + b_9\ GEN + b_{10}\ \ln HHS + b_{11}\ SWIFE$$
$$+ b_{12}\ JSAT + b_{13}\ WTDIF + b_{14}\ \ln\ W + b_{15}\ OTINC \qquad (15)$$

$$S = a_1\ A + a_2\ SFAT + a_3\ SMOT + a_4 V + a_5 P + a_6 MECH$$
$$+ a_7\ NUM + a_8\ GEN + a_9 \ln HHS \qquad (16)$$

Table 3.3 contains definitions of the variables in these two regressions, table A.1 in the appendix contains their means and standard deviations, and table A.2 contains a matrix of simple correlation coefficients. All variables except past health, mothers' schooling, and the test scores are taken from the 1969 survey. Mothers' schooling and past health are taken from the 1971 survey, and the 1943 test scores are taken from military records. I formulated specific hypotheses concerning the roles of most of the right-hand side variables in equations (15) and (16) in section 1. Therefore, in the remainder of this section, I clarify

Table 3.3 Definition of Variables, NBER-Thorndike Sample

Variable	Definition
ln $H69$	Natural logarithm of stock of health in 1969[a]
A	Age in 1969
S	Years of formal schooling completed
$SFAT$	Years of formal schooling completed by father
$SMOT$	Years of formal schooling completed by mother
V	Visual perception[a]
P	Psychomotor control[a]
$MECH$	Mechanical ability[a]
GEN	General intelligence[a]
NUM	Numerical ability[a]
ln HHS	Natural logarithm of stock of health while attending high school[a]
$SWIFE$	Years of formal schooling completed by wife
$JSAT$	Job satisfaction: 1 = lowest; 5 = highest[a]
$WTDIF$	Weight difference: absolute value of difference between actual weight and ideal weight for a given height[a]
ln W	Natural logarithm of hourly wage rate on current job[a]
$OTINC$	Nonearnings income of the family in 1968
$EXCELL$	Excellent health in 1969 = 1[b]

[a] See text for a more complete definition.
[b] See section 2.3 for a discussion of the use of this variable.

a few of the definitions in table 3.3 and comment on the predicted effects of several variables that I did not discuss insection 1.

The hourly wage rate equals a man's full-time salary on his current job divided by the product of fifty weeks and the average number of hours per week he worked on his main job in 1968. The five ability variables (*V*, *P*, *MECH*, *GEN*, *NUM*) are derived from Thorndike and Hagan's factor analysis (1959, 19) of scores on the seventeen specific tests that candidates for Aviation Cadet status were given in 1943. Based on their analysis, Thorndike and Hagan identified the five basic types of ability given in table 3.3. The tests included in each of these categories are listed in table 3.4.

I generate an aggregate index of visual perception, for example, by computing the first principal component of its three test scores, where each score is normalized to have a zero mean and a unitary standard deviation. Specifically, if X_i ($i = 1, 2, 3$) denotes the normalized value of the ith test score included in visual perception, then $V = \sum_{i=1}^{3} a_i X_i$, where the a_i are selected to maximize the variance in V subject to the constraint that $\sum_{i=1}^{3} a_i^2 = 1$.[39] I follow a similar procedure to aggregate the scores in the other four categories. One justification

Table 3.4 Categories of Ability

Category	Tests Included[a]
Visual perception	Speed of identification Spatial orientation I Spatial orientation II
Psychomotor control	Complex coordination Rotary pursuit Finger dexterity Aiming stress
Mechanical ability	Mechanical principles Two-hand coordination Biographical data-pilot[b]
General intelligence	Reading comprehension General information-Navigator[c] Arithmetic reasoning Mathematics
Numerical ability	Numerical operations I Numerical operations II Dial and table reading

[a] For a description of each test see Thorndike and Hagen (1959, 55–76).

[b] Items on a biographical data form that proved to be important predictors of performance in pilot training school of candidates who were accepted as Pilot Aviation Cadets.

[c] A vocabulary test that dealt with terminology in astronomy, trigonometry, and science.

for my procedure is that the units in which ability is measured are arbitrary. It should be noted that health functions estimated with, for example, visual perception defined as a simple average of its three test scores (not shown) do not differ in a qualitative sense from those estimated with the principal components measures in the next section.

When the men in the NBER-Thorndike sample took the seventeen tests in 1943, practically all of them had graduated from high school but had little additional schooling. Most of those who went on to college did so after World War II. Thus, in this dataset, one largely avoids the problem that a person's performance on a general intelligence test will depend on the amount of schooling he has had. A small percentage of the men, chiefly the older ones, did attend college prior to World War II. Moreover, high-school graduates who participated in the labor force for several years before the war might have scored lower on the general intelligence tests than recent high-school graduates. To eliminate a potential reverse causality relationship running from schooling to general intelligence, I include age in the schooling function. Due to the upward secular trend in years of formal schooling completed, age and schooling are negatively correlated in random samples of the population of the United States. This negative correlation is also present in the NBER-Thorndike sample ($r = -.172$) despite the narrow age range of the sample. Therefore, by including age in the schooling function, I control for the trend factor and avoid biasing the estimated effect of intelligence on schooling.

There are two reasons for employing a measure of job satisfaction as an independent variable in the health function. First, someone who is satisfied with his job and with his life style in general may also be more satisfied with the state of his health than someone who is dissatisfied with his job and life style. Thus, the first person may be more likely to report that his health status is good or excellent, even though the two persons may have the same level of physical health measured in an objective fashion. Consequently, by holding job satisfaction constant. I purge self-rated health status of some of its subjective elements. Second, the studies that I have already cited by Rahe and Holmes (1965), Palmore (1969a, 1969b), Holmes and Masuda (1970), and Rahe (1972) indicate that dissatisfaction with life style creates tensions that cause mental and ultimately physical health to deteriorate. In this context, Palmore's finding that job satisfaction is the most important correlate of longevity in a longitudinal sample of older persons is particularly striking. Along these lines, one can view job satisfaction as an input into the production of health and estimate the sensitivity of health output to variations in this input.

The men in the NBER-Thorndike sample were asked whether they enjoy their work, whether their work provides a challenge, and whether their work is interesting. Each question has five possible numerical responses that constitute a scale ranging from five (the highest) to one (the lowest). The job-satisfaction index that I use is simply an average of a man's responses to these three questions.

Obesity and malnutrition, like job satisfaction, may be treated as inputs into the production of health. By computing the absolute value of the difference between actual weight and ideal weight for a given height, I create one variable to measure these mutually exclusive states. The 1969 questionnaire included items on actual height and actual weight. I calculate ideal weight for a given height from estimates made by the Metropolitan Life Insurance Company.[40] These estimates take the form of ideal weights for men by height and body frame (small, medium, or large). Since there is no information on body frames of men in the NBER-Thorndike sample, I define ideal weight for a given height as an average of the weight given for each body frame.

The inclusion of two input variables, job satisfaction and weight difference, in the health function makes this function a mixture of a demand curve and a production function. If most of the variation in job satisfaction and weight difference were due to variation in the "prices" of these inputs, the estimated equation would be primarily a demand curve for health.[41] Under this interpretation, nonearnings income would enter the health function to take account of the pure consumption aspects of the demand for health. Alternatively, the wage rate and nonearnings income can be viewed as proxies for inputs besides job satisfaction and weight difference that affect health. Under this interpretation, the estimated equation would be primarily a production function of health. I do not emphasize one of these two extreme interpretations of the health function in the next section. I do, however, examine the extent to which the productivity effect of schooling on health operates via the impact of schooling on contemporaneous variables such as job satisfaction and weight difference.

3. EMPIRICAL RESULTS

3.1. Estimates of Recursive Health-Schooling System

Table 3.5 contains ordinary least squares estimates of health functions, and table 3.6 contains corresponding estimates of schooling functions. The empirical analysis reflected by the regressions in these two tables represents a compromise between rigorous hypothesis testing of the effects of given variables and attempts to come to grips with somewhat more broad issues. These issues include the answers to such questions as: Which components of ability are the major determinants of health or schooling? By how much is the estimated effect

Table 3.5 Ordinary Least Squares Estimates of Health Functions

Variable	Eq. 1 Regr. Coef.	Eq. 2 Regr. Coef.	Eq. 3 Regr. Coef.	Eq. 4 Regr. Coef.	Eq. 5 Regr. Coef.	Eq. 6 Regr. Coef.	Eq. 7 Regr. Coef.
A	−.017 (−3.31)	−.012 (−2.33)	−.011 (−2.07)	−.011 (−2.14)	−.010 (−1.92)	−.010 (−2.00)	−.011 (−2.17)
S	.035 (7.41)	.028 (5.51)	.028 (5.94)	.019 (3.76)	.019 (3.92)	.012 (2.26)	.012 (2.26)
SFAT		.005 (1.51)	.006 (1.58)	.004 (1.00)	.004 (1.23)	.003 (0.72)	.002 (0.65)
SMOT		.006 (1.57)	.007 (1.87)	.005 (1.30)	.006 (1.73)	.004 (1.21)	.003 (0.94)
V		.027 (2.81)	.036 (4.19)	.035 (4.19)	.033 (3.87)	.033 (3.91)	.027 (2.86)
P		.010 (1.02)					.008 (0.83)
MECH		.012 (1.16)					.013 (1.26)
NUM		.004 (0.42)					−.001 (−0.12)
GEN		.005 (0.60)					.002 (0.27)
ln HHS			.479 (11.05)	.481 (11.12)	.461 (10.74)	.459 (10.66)	.445 (10.39)	.445 (10.37)
SWIFE					.019 (3.25)		.018 (3.16)	.018 (3.16)
J SAT					.094 (6.67)		.082 (5.76)	.082 (5.72)
WTDIF					−.002 (−3.57)		−.002 (−3.52)	−.002 (−3.41)
ln W						.167 (7.00)	.146 (6.10)	.147 (6.05)
OTINC						−.001 (−0.29)	−.0005 (−0.28)	−.001 (−0.30)
R^2	.021	.064	.063	.080	.076	.090	.091

Note: Intercepts not shown, t ratios in parentheses. See table 3.3 for definitions of all variables.

Table 3.6 Ordinary Least Squares Estimates of Schooling Functions

Variable	Equation 1 Regression Coefficient	Equation 2 Regression Coefficient	Equation 3 Regression Coefficient
A	−.146 (−8.40)	−.124 (−7.08)	−.131 (−7.58)
SFAT	.067 (5.47)	.066 (5.52)	.067 (5.61)
SMOT	.032 (2.56)	.050 (4.03)	.050 (4.05)
V		.052 (1.65)	.030 (1.00)
P		.004 (0.11)	
MECH		−.339 (−9.98)	−.318 (−10.30)
NUM		−.082 (−2.62)	
GEN	.446 (18.40)	.534 (18.85)	.499 (19.94)
ln HHS	.419 (2.86)	.416 (2.87)	.396 (2.74)
R^2	.146	.173	.171

Note: t ratios in parentheses.

of schooling on current health biased when past health and third variables are omitted from the health function? Do contemporaneous variables such as wives' schooling, job satisfaction, weight difference, the hourly wage rate, and non-earnings income play a more important role in the health function than lagged variables such as parents' schooling, ability in 1943, and past health? Does the inclusion of the set of lagged variables have a greater impact on the coefficient of own schooling than the inclusion of the set of current variables? Which of the contemporaneous variables have the most significant effects on health and on the estimated coefficient of schooling? Which of the lagged variables influence health only indirectly, via their effects on schooling?

To examine these issues, in tables 3.5 and 3.6, I show alternative versions of health and schooling equations. In addition, in table 3.7, I show the percentage reduction in the coefficient of schooling when specific sets of variables are held constant.[42] My discussion of the regression results is organized as follows. First,

Table 3.7 Estimated Bias in Schooling Coefficients

Initial Variables	Variables Added	Initial Schooling Coefficient	Final Schooling Coefficient	Percentage Reduction[a]
A	SFAT, SMOT, V, ln HHS	.035	.028	20.00
A	SWIFE, JSAT, WTDIF	.035	.023	34.28
A	ln W, OTINC	.035	.021	40.00
A	SWIFE, JSAT, WTDIF, ln W, OTINC	.035	.014	60.00
A	SFAT, SMOT, V, ln HHS, SWIFE, JSAT, WTDIF, ln W, OTINC	.035	.012	65.71
A, SFAT, SMOT, V, ln HHS	SWIFE, JSAT, WTDIF	.028	.019	32.14
A, SFAT, SMOT, V, ln HHS	ln W, OTINC	.028	.019	32.14
A, SFAT, SMOT, V, ln HHS	SWIFE, JSAT, WTDIF, ln W, OTINC	.028	.012	57.14
A, SWIFE, JSAT, WTDIF	SFAT, SMOT, V, ln HHS	.023	.019	17.39
A, ln W, OTINC	SFAT, SMOT, V, ln HHS	.021	.019	9.52
A, SWIFE, JSAT, WTDIF, ln W, OTINC	SFAT, SMOT, V, ln HHS	.014	.012	14.28

[a]Defined as one minus the ratio of the final schooling coefficient to the initial schooling coefficient.

I comment on variations in the estimated schooling parameter in the health function as the set of independent variables varies. Then, I examine some specific health effects of current variables other than schooling. Finally, I discuss health effects of past variables and the roles of these variables in the schooling equation.[43]

Regardless of the other variables held constant, schooling has a positive effect on current health that is statistically significant at the .025 level of confidence on a one-tail test. Since past health is included in each equation in table 3.5 except the first, this finding may be interpreted as evidence in favor of a causal relationship that runs from schooling to current health. The actual regression coefficients indicate the continuously compounded percentage rate of increase in health capital associated with a one-year increase in schooling. These coefficients range from 3.5 percent, when only age is held constant, to 1.2 percent, when all relevant variables are held constant.

Suppose that the health functions were viewed primarily as demand curves, and suppose that the price elasticity of demand for health were equal to one-half. Then the schooling parameter estimates would imply that schooling raises health productivity by 2.4 percent at a minimum.[44] This may be compared to the approximately 5.5 percent increase in the *hourly* wage rate due to an additional year of formal schooling in the NBER-Thorndike sample.[45] Although the non-market productivity effect of schooling may appear to be small in an absolute sense, it is approximately 40 percent as large as the market productivity effect. Moreover, in assessing the magnitude of the effect, it should be realized that all of the men in the sample are high-school graduates. If the nonmarket productivity improvement falls as schooling rises, then my estimate would understate the effect that would be observed in a sample of men at all schooling levels.

In table 3.7, I reveal that the estimated bias in schooling coefficients is larger when current variables are excluded from the health function than when past variables are excluded. For example, the estimated bias due to the omission of parents' schooling, visual perception, and past health is 20 percent (line 1 of table 3.7).[46] The corresponding bias due to the omission of wives' schooling, weight difference, job satisfaction, the wage rate, and nonearnings income is 60 percent (line 4). When past variables are held constant initially but current variables are not, the bias is 57 percent (line 8). When this procedure is reversed, the bias is only 14 percent (line 11). These results arise because the set of current variables is more highly correlated with schooling than the set of past variables.

In table 3.7, I also reveal that the bias from omitting the subset of contemporaneous variables consisting of wives' schooling, job satisfaction, and weight difference is approximately the same as the bias that arises from omitting the subset consisting of the wage rate and nonearnings income. In particular, when past variables are included in the regressions, the bias due to the exclusion of each subset is 32 percent (lines 6 and 7). This is an important finding if one is seeking to uncover channels via which the pure effect of schooling on non-market productivity operates. If one does not control for any of the contemporaneous variables, then schooling may increase health simply because it raises market productivity and therefore command over market resources. If one takes account of this factor by holding the wage rate and nonearnings income constant, then part of the remaining effect of schooling on health may operate via the effect of this variable on spouses' characteristics, satisfaction with life style, and diet.

According to equation (6) or (7) in table 3.5, with the wage rate and non-earnings income held constant, an increase in wives' schooling, an increase in job satisfaction, or a reduction in the absolute value of the difference between actual and ideal weight causes health to rise. The regression coefficients of these three variables are statistically significant at all conventional levels of confidence. The effect of wives schooling is striking, because the coefficient of this variable exceeds the coefficient of own schooling. The difference between these two coefficients is not, however, statistically significant ($t = .68$ in both equations).

Even if the coefficients of husbands' and wives' schooling were the same, provided that the estimated health functions primarily reflected demand forces, one could conclude that wives' schooling has a larger impact on the efficiency with which husbands' health is produced than husbands' schooling. Since there is no specific measure of the value of wives' time, the demand parameter of their schooling would equal $\varepsilon(\rho_f - \alpha_f \hat{W}_f)$, where ε is the price elasticity of health. ρ_f is the percentage increase in wives' nonmarket productivity for a one-year increase in schooling, α_f is the share of wives' time in the total cost of gross investment in husbands' health, and $\hat{W}_f$ is the percentage increase in the "shadow price" of time due to schooling. On the other hand, since husbands' wage rates are held constant, the demand parameter of their schooling should equal $\varepsilon\rho$, where ρ is the percentage increase in their nonmarket productivity due to schooling. If these two demand parameters are identical, then

$$\rho_f = \rho + \alpha_f \hat{W}_f$$

Heckman (1974b) in "Shadow Prices, Market Wages, and Labor Supply,"[47] estimates that a one-year increase in wives' schooling raises the shadow price of time by 5.3 percent, and I have already estimated that ρ equals 2.4 percent. Therefore, ρ_f would equal 3.7 percent if α_f were one-quarter, and would equal 5.0 percent if α_f were one-half.

An alternative explanation of the effect of wives' schooling is that it reflects selective mating in the marriage market.[48] According to this interpretation, healthier men marry women with more schooling. Yet I control for important correlates of selective mating, such as general intelligence, parents' schooling, and past health.[49] Therefore, it is very unlikely that a significant part of the relationship between wives schooling and husbands' health can be traced to selective mating.

With regard to the other contemporaneous variables, age is negatively related to health, which reflects the positive impact of this variable on the rate of depreciation on health capital. The hourly wage rate has a positive and very significant effect on health, while nonearnings income has an insignificant negative effect. These two findings support the predictions of my pure investment model of the demand for health. In a production function sense, the weak negative coefficient of nonearnings income may represent a compromise between the consumption of beneficial and detrimental health inputs as income rises, with the wage rate held constant. Clearly this interpretation should not be pushed too far because the coefficient of nonearnings income is not statistically significant. But it may appeal to those who are surprised to learn that the pure income elasticity of health ranges from −.01 to −.02 at an income of $20,000.[50]

As shown by the *t* ratios associated with the regression coefficients of past health in table 3.5, the partial correlation between this variable and current health exceeds the partial correlation between current health and any of the other independent variables in the regressions. The elasticity of current health with respect to past health varies from .44 to .48. In a demand-curve sense, this elasticity should estimate the ratio of the price elasticity of adults' health to the price elasticity of children's health.[51] Since the coefficient of ln *HHS* is smaller than one, the demand curve for children's health is more elastic than the demand curve for adults' health. If, as I have assumed in other computations, the price elasticity of adults' health equals one-half, then the price elasticity of children's health would approximately equal one.

The equations in table 3.6 demonstrate that although past health is certainly not the most important determinant of schooling, it does have a statistically significant positive effect on years of formal schooling completed. Despite this, and despite the important role of past health in the current health function, the parameter estimate of schooling is not greatly affected by the inclusion of past health. This follows because schooling and past health are not nearly as highly correlated as schooling and the set of current variables. If the past health parameter estimate in the schooling function and the schooling parameter estimate in the health function are both converted into elasticities, then the elasticity of schooling with respect to past health would equal .03 and the elasticity of current health with respect to schooling would equal .18. It is clear that the latter elasticity dominates the former.

According to equation (7) in table 3.5, among the past variables other than health in high school, only visual perception has a statistically significant effect on current health when all relevant factors are held constant. According to equation (2), this is true even if the set of predictor variables is limited to age, schooling, parents' schooling, the test scores, and past health.[52] As the equations in table 3.6 reveal, parents' schooling and general intelligence are important determinants of schooling. Therefore, my results suggest that the effects of these variables on current health operate indirectly, via their effects on schooling. Once schooling is held constant, they have almost no direct impact on health.

In section 1 of this chapter, I argued that given the health-specific nature of physical ability, it should have a larger impact on current health than does mental ability. On the other hand, given the schooling-specific nature of mental ability, it should have a larger impact on schooling than does physical ability. Tables 3.5 and 3.6 contain some evidence in support of this hypothesis, provided visual perception is interpreted as a measure of health-specific ability and general intelligence is interpreted as a measure of schooling-specific ability. In interpreting the positive effect of visual perception on current health in this manner, I do not necessarily assume that this variable per se has a direct impact on current health. Rather, I assume that it is the best available proxy for genetic or biological characteristics that do influence the efficiency with which health is produced.[53]

Based on the above argument, and given that visual perception is the only component of ability that has a positive effect on health, I prefer a regression specification of the health function that omits the four other ability variables. Another reason for preferring such a specification is that, with general intelligence and parental characteristics held constant, it is not obvious what causes schooling to vary.[54] Since general intelligence plays a very important role in the estimated schooling function and plays an unimportant role in the estimated health function, it is logical to exclude it from the latter function. In theory, the appropriate way to take account of the insignificant effects of the four ability variables would be to reestimate the health function with another sample. Since this is not a feasible course of action at the present time, I omit these variables from the empirical analysis in the rest of this section and in section 4.

3.2. Decomposition Analysis

It is well established that schooling raises market productivity, and my results in section 3.1 suggest that it raises health productivity as well. Indeed, the recent work on the household production function approach to demand theory emphasizes the pervasive impact of schooling on many aspects of consumer behavior, including fertility, contraceptive knowledge, efficiency in producing quality children, and consumption patterns.[55] If schooling enhances productivity and knowledge in many areas, then it should increase a person's knowledge about an appropriate diet and raise his or her ability to select a productive mate and to produce a "high quality life style." Therefore, with market productivity, measured by the wage rate, and past variables held constant, the effect of schooling on health may be decomposed into direct and indirect components. The direct component represents the ability of those with additional schooling to obtain a larger health output from given amounts of all relevant inputs. The indirect component represents the ability of those with extra schooling to select a better input mix.[56]

Table 3.8 Estimates of Direct and First-Order Indirect Effects of Schooling on Health

Source of Effect	Magnitude	Percentage of Total Effect
Direct[a]	.012	63.16
First-order indirect:		
Wives' schooling	.005	26.32
Job satisfaction	.001	5.26
Weight difference	.001	5.26
Total[b]	.019	100.00

[a] Regression coefficient of schooling from equation (6) in table 3.5.
[b] Regression coefficient of schooling from equation (5) in table 3.5.

In table 3.8, I decompose an estimate of a total nonmarket productivity effect of schooling on health of 1.9 percent into a direct component of 1.2 percent and an indirect component of 0.7 percent. The total effect equals the regression coefficient of schooling in an equation that includes age, parents' schooling, visual perception, past health, the wage rate, and nonearnings income as independent variables. The direct component equals the regression coefficient of schooling in an equation that adds wives' schooling, weight difference, and job satisfaction to the set of independent variables. The three positive indirect components are present because an increase in husbands' schooling is associated with an increase in wives' schooling, an increase in job satisfaction, and a reduction in the absolute value of the difference between actual and ideal weight. In turn, each of these three factors causes current health to rise.

The statistical model that underlies this decomposition is a recursive system of the form:

$$SWIFE = a_1S + a_2Z$$

$$JSAT = c_1S + c_2Z + c_3SWIFE$$

$$WTDIF = d_1S + d_2Z + d_3SWIFE + d_4JSAT$$

$$\ln H69 - b_1S + b_2Z + b_3SWIFE + b_4JSAT + b_5WTDIF$$

where Z is a vector of predetermined variables. By substituting the first three equations into the fourth, one obtains an estimate of the total or reduced-form parameter of schooling. The direct component of this parameter estimate is given by b_1, the first-order indirect component due to wives' schooling by a_1b_3, the first-order indirect component due to job satisfaction by c_1b_4, and the first-order indirect component due to weight difference by d_1b_5.[57]

In table 3.8, I show that of the three indirect channels, the one due to wives' schooling is by far the most important. This channel accounts for 26.32 percent

Table 3.9 Ordinary Least Squares Estimates of Wives' Schooling, Weight Differences, and Job Satisfaction Functions

Variable	SWIFE Function Regression Coefficient	WTDIF Function Regression Coefficient	JSAT Function Regression Coefficient
A	.018 (1.21)	.032 (0.24)	.001 (0.23)
S	.302 (21.50)	−.282 (−2.15)	.014 (2.23)
SFAT	.077 (7.51)	−.157 (−1.73)	−.0001 (−0.02)
SMOT	.055 (5.20)	−.164 (−1.78)	.006 (1.37)
V	−.002 (−0.06)	−.172 (−0.80)	−.006 (−0.56)
ln HHS	.173 (1.39)	1.643 (1.51)	.177 (3.50)
ln W	.046 (0.67)	−.279 (−0.46)	.240 (8.54)
OTINC	.015 (2.80)	.014 (0.29)	−.003 (−1.52)
SWIFE		−.114 (−0.77)	.006 (085)
R^2	.189	.008	.036

Note: t ratios in parentheses.

of the total effect of husbands' schooling and 71.43 percent of the combined indirect effect. Table 3.9 contains modified estimates of the first three equations in the recursive system.[58] These equations may be viewed as demand curves for three inputs into the production of health although wives' schooling, weight difference, and job satisfaction also enter the production functions of other household commodities.

According to table 3.9, schooling is the only predictor variable that has a significant effect on all three inputs. For example, while the hourly wage rate is the best predictor of job satisfaction, it is not related to wives' schooling or weight difference. These results reveal the important role of schooling in many aspects of consumer behavior. Clearly, a more careful examination of the process by which schooling influences behavior and the mechanisms by which it operates should be given high priority on an agenda for future research.[59]

3.3. Estimates of Excellent Health Functions

To examine the sensitivity of the results in section 3.1 to the manner in which I scaled health status, I created a dichotomous variable (*EXCELL*) that is equal to one if a man is in excellent health and is equal to zero otherwise. This variable has a mean of .5951, which indicates that approximately 60 percent of the sample are in excellent health. Table 3.10 contains an ordinary least squares regression of the dichotomous excellent health variable on the same set of independent variables that enter equation (6) in table 3.5. For given values of the independent variables, the predicted value of the dependent variable can be interpreted as the conditional probability that a man is in excellent health. Similarly, the regression coefficient of a given independent variable shows the change in the conditional probability of being in excellent health for a one-unit (1 percent in the case of ln *HHS* or ln *W*) change in this variable.

The magnitudes of the regression coefficients in table 3.10 should and do differ from the magnitudes of the corresponding coefficients in table 3.5. The signs of these two sets of regression coefficients are, however, identical, and the same patterns of statistical significance emerge from the two equations. These findings should strengthen confidence in the results obtained with ln *H69* as the dependent variable in the current health function. This variable, like the theoretical index of health capital, is free of units. Moreover, there is some theoretical justification for the scales used to create it, and for the magnitudes of its regression coefficients.

Table 3.10 Ordinary Least Squares Estimate of Dichotomous Excellent Health Function

Variable	Regression Coefficient	Variable	Regression Coefficient
A	−.009 (−2.53)	SWIFE	.011 (2.75)
S	.010 (2.82)	JSAT	.053 (5.18)
SFAT	.001 (0.39)	WTDIF	−.002 (−3.97)
SMOT	.005 (1.76)	ln W	.101 (5.88)
V	.022 (3.71)	OTINC	−.001 (−0.55)
ln HMS	.314 (10.21)	R^2	.089

Note: t ratios in parentheses.

It is well known that certain statistical problems arise when the dependent variable in an ordinary least squares regression is dichotomous.[60] In particular, the regression in table 3.10 does not take account of the restriction that the conditional probability of being in excellent health should lie between zero and one. To take account of this restriction, I have estimated a dichotomous logit excellent health function by the method of maximum likelihood. This technique assumes that the probability that the ith individual is in excellent health (p_i) is given by the logistic function

$$p_i = 1/(1 + e^{-a}e^{-bx_i})$$

where x_i is an independent variable (or a vector of variables) and a and b are parameters to be estimated. With the logistic function, the predicted value of p_i must fall between zero and one. By solving for the logarithm of the odds of being in excellent health, one transforms the logistic function into a linear equation:

$$\ln\left[\, p_i /(1 - p_i)\,\right] = a + bx_i$$

which is called the logit function.[61] The logit coefficient b shows the percentage change in the odds for a one-unit change in x_1. The marginal effect of x_i on p_i (the change in p_i due to a one-unit change in x_i) is given by

$$(\partial p_i / \partial p_i) = bp_i(1 - p_i)$$

Table 3.11 contains an estimate of a dichotomous logit excellent health function.[62] The marginal effects in the table are computed at the mean value of p for the sample of .5951. A comparison of the results in tables 3.10 and 3.11 reveals that all variables have the same signs in the ordinary least squares excellent health function as they have in the logit function. Tests of statistical significance yield identical conclusions when applied to either function. Moreover, the marginal effects in table 3.11 are approximately equal to the corresponding regression coefficients in table 3.10. It should be noted that problems similar to those that are encountered when a dependent variable is dichotomous are also encountered when it is polytomous.[63] Since my health capital series has only four possible values, it generates a polytomous variable. Yet an extrapolation of the comparison between ordinary least squares and logit excellent health functions would suggest that one would gain little by using estimation techniques other than ordinary least squares simply because ln $H69$ is polytomous.

Table 3.11 Maximum Likelihood Estimate of Dichotomous Logit Excellent Health Function

Variable	Logit Coefficient	Marginal Effect	Variable	Logit Coefficient	Marginal Effect
A	−.041 (−2.49)	−.010	SWIFE	.053 (2.76)	.013
S	.046 (2.74)	.011	JSAT	.237 (5.12)	.057
SFAT	.004 (0.36)	.001	WTDIF	−.008 (−3.91)	−.002
SMOT	.020 (1.73)	.005	ln W	.466 (5.79)	.112
V	.101 (3.66)	.024	OTINC	−.003 (−0.54)	−.001
ln HHS	1.427 (9.56)	.344			

Note: Asymptotic t ratios in parentheses.

4. ESTIMATES OF A SIMULTANEOUS-EQUATIONS HEALTH–WAGE MODEL

4.1. Introduction

In previous sections of this chapter, I assumed that the current stock of health is not a determinant of the current stock of human capital, I now relax this assumption and examine the possibility that health capital, as one component of human capital, raises market productivity and the hourly wage rate. Empirically, I estimate a simultaneous-equations model by the method of two-stage least squares, in which current health and the hourly wage rate are endogenous variables.

There are both theoretical and empirical reasons for proceeding along these lines. At a theoretical level, the distinction that I have drawn between adults' health capital as a determinant of their total available time and their human capital as a determinant of their productivity may be too extreme. If, as I have postulated, students' health influences their productivity in school, then should not adults' health influence their productivity in the labor market? Moreover, Malkiel and Malkiel (1973) hypothesize that employers may lower the wage offered to employees who work fewer hours in a year due to illness and other reasons. Finally, Mincer (1970, 1974) stresses that investment in on-the-job training, measured by the total amount of time spent in such activity, plays a major role in the wage function. This variable is imperfectly measured in most datasets. The best available proxy is years of experience in the labor market, which itself is subject to measurement error. To the extent that poor health reduces the amount of time spent in the labor market, current health may affect the current wage via its impact on past investment in on-the-job training.

At an empirical level, studies by Boskin (1973); Hall (1973); and Luft (1972) suggest that health, treated as an exogenous variable, does have a positive effect on the wage rate, Benham and I (Grossman and Benham 1974) also find a positive impact of health on the wage when both variables are treated as endogenous in the NORC sample. Therefore, part of the positive relationship between these two variables in the regressions in section 3 may reflect causality from health to market productivity. The health-wage model that I estimate in this section may be viewed as an extension of the Grossman-Benham model, although the measure of health and the set of exogenous variables are somewhat different.

I want to emphasize that there are costs to be paid as well as benefits to be gained as a result of simultaneous-equations estimation. In particular, I have found in previous work that when this method is applied to microdata, results tend to be fairly sensitive to the manner in which equations are "identified," Although it might be clear in theory that a certain subset of exogenous variables should be included in one equation and excluded from another, key members of this subset might not be available in the data. Another problem in applying two-stage least squares, for example, to microdata is that coefficients of determination in the first stage rarely exceed 30 or 40 percent. Therefore, in selecting between two-stage least squares and ordinary least squares estimates, one is forced to make a tradeoff between consistency and efficiency.[64] Given these factors, and given the far from ideal way in which health is measured in the NBER-Thorndike sample, I view the model that is formulated and fitted in this section as an *illustration* of the kind of model that could be fitted with more refined data. The parameter estimates that I present are by no means definitive. For the same reasons, I also view the simultaneous-equations model as a complement to, rather than a substitute for, the ordinary least squares model.

4.2. Specification of Structural Equations

The structural equations for health and the hourly wage rate are as follows:

$$\ln H69 = b_1 A + b_2 S + b_3 V + b_4 \ln HHS + b_5 SWIFE$$
$$+ b_6 JSAT + b_7 WTDIF + b_8 \ln W^* + b_9 OTINC \qquad (17)$$

$$\ln W = a_1 \ln H69^* + a_2 S + a_3 EXP + a_4 GEN + a_5 SOUTH + a_6 CS1$$
$$+ a_7 CS2 + a_8 CS3 + a_9 CS4 + a_{10} CS5 \qquad (18)$$

Table 3.12 Definition of Supplementary Variables

Variable	Definition
EXP	Years of experience in the labor force[a]
SOUTH	Reside in South = 1
CS1[b]	Reside in a small town (2,500–10,000 people) = 1
CS2[b]	Reside in a town (10,000–50,000 people) = 1
CS3[b]	Reside in a moderate-sized city (50,000–250,000 people) = 1
CS4[b]	Reside in a large city (250,000–1 million people) = 1
CS5[b]	Reside in a major metropolitan area (over 1 million people) = 1

[a] See text for a more complete definition.
[b] The "reside in a rural area (under 2,500 people)" class is omitted.

An asterisk next to a variable in equation (17) or (18) means it is endogenous. Variables in the wage function that were not included in the analysis in section 3 are defined in table 3.12. The specification of the health function was fully discussed in previous sections of this chapter. Here, I would simply point out that I omit mothers' schooling and fathers schooling from this function. That is, I assume that any gross effects of these two variables on health operate solely via their effects on own schooling or past health.[65]

The wage function is based on work on wage determination by Becker and Chiswick (1966); Mincer (1970, 1974); and Lillard (1973). These authors emphasize that wage rates should be positively related to correlates of the stock of human capital, such as years of formal schooling completed, years of experience in the labor force, general intelligence, and current health. Obviously, years of formal schooling completed is a partial measure of the quantity of investment in knowledge via schooling, while years of experience in the labor market, defined as the number of years since a man was last in school, is a partial measure of the quantity of investment in on-the-job training. General intelligence and health may influence the quantities of both types of investment. Note that, if the dependent variable in equation (18) were annual earnings or weekly earnings, a positive health effect might simply mean that health raises weeks worked per year or hours worked per week but has no effect on market productivity. Since, however, the dependent variable in the equation is the natural logarithm of the *hourly* wage rate, one cannot interpret a positive health coefficient along these lines.[66]

I add dummy variables for region and city size to the basic set of human capital variables in the wage function. I assume that these variables mainly capture shifts in the demand curve for labor around a fairly stable supply curve among labor markets in the United States. Undoubtedly, part of the variation in wages by region and city size is due to differences in the cost of living. Since the health function should relate health to the wage rate, with the prices of medical care and other market goods used to produce health held constant, region and city size might also be entered in the health function. However, in that function, they might reflect other factors as well, such as variation in the availability of medical care, not associated with the price of care and climate. Some of these factors might offset differences in the cost of living. Moreover, the health components of an aggregate price index might not vary in the same manner as the index itself among regions and cities of various sizes. Since I have not emphasized region and city-size health differentials, and since predictions concerning these differentials are ambiguous, I do not include these variables in the health function. To the extent that the money wage rate is positively correlated with the prices of health inputs, the estimated wage elasticity of health would be biased *downward.*[67]

4.3. Results

Table 3.13 contains two-stage least squares estimates of health functions, and table 3.14 contains two-stage least squares estimates of wage functions.[68] The results in the latter table reveal that the endogenous current health variable has a positive and very significant effect on the hourly wage rate. As shown by its regression coefficient in equation (1), a 10 percent increase in the stock of current health causes the hourly wage rate to rise by approximately 4 percent. The signs of the regression coefficients of the other variables in the wage equation are consistent with a priori expectations.

In table 3.13, I demonstrate that when the wage is treated as an endogenous variable, a striking change occurs in the health function coefficient of this variable. In equation (6) in table 3.5, the wage elasticity of health equals .15. In equation (1) in table 3.13, this elasticity equals .30. This doubling in the wage elasticity occurs despite the presumed upward bias in the ordinary least squares estimate because it reflects causality from health to the wage as well as causality from the wage to health.[69] A possible explanation of this finding is that there might be measurement error in the computed hourly wage variable, which would bias the ordinary least squares parameter estimate downward. This bias should be reduced by the use of a set of instrumental variables via the method of two-stage least squares.

In the health-wage model that Benham and I (Grossman and Benham 1974) fit to the NORC sample, the endogenous wage rate has a *negative* effect on

Table 3.13 Two-Stage Squares Estimates of Health Functions

Variable	Equation 1 Regression Coefficient	Equation 2 Regression Coefficient	Equation 3 Regression Coefficient
A	−.013 (−2.56)	−.014 (−2.63)	−.014 (−2.63)
S	.004 (0.58)	.012 (1.66)	.013 (0.82)
V	.031 (3.62)	.032 (3.67)	.032 (3.71)
ln HHS	.427 (9.63)	.438 (9.72)	.440 (9.78)
SWIFE	.020 (3.42)		
J SAT	.070 (4.25)		
WTDIF	−.002 (−3.49)		
ln W*	.297 (3.03)	.325 (3.31)	.310 (3.39)
OTINC	−.003 (−1.18)	−.003 (−1.18)	
R^2	.082	.063	.063

Note: An asterisk next to a variable means that it is endogenous. Asymptotic *t* ratios in parentheses. See tables 3.3 and 3.12 for definitions of variables.

health rather than a positive effect. We argue that this might reflect a greater tendency to select occupations that are hazardous or otherwise detrimental to health as the wage rate rises, with schooling and experience held constant. It should be noted that Benham and I include proxy variables for preventive medical care in our health function. This is one source of the discrepancy between the signs of the wage elasticities in the NORC and NBER-Thorndike samples. Another source is that the NORC health function is estimated for all white men, while the NBER-Thorndike health function is estimated for a high-earnings, high-schooling, and high-ability sample. Variations in wages associated with harmful health characteristics of occupations might be much more important at low levels of earnings and schooling than at high levels.

In general, there are two theoretical reasons for an increase in the wage elasticity of health as the wage rate rises, First, if the elasticity of substitution between own time and market goods in the health production function exceeded one, then the share of market goods in the total cost of producing

Table 3.14 Two-Stage Least Squares Estimates of Wage Functions

	Equation 1	Equation 2[a]	Equation 3[b]
Variable	Regression Coefficient	Regression Coefficient	Regression Coefficient
ln $H69^*$	.403	.314	.254
	(7.83)	(5.23)	(4.31)
S	.043	.046	.048
	(9.10)	(10.15)	(10.80)
EXP	.007	.007	.007
	(4.35)	(4.90)	(4.98)
GEN	.031	.033	.034
	(5.46)	(5.98)	(6.35)
SOUTH	−.013	−.014	−.015
	(−0.63)	(−0.73)	(−0.79)
CS1	.157	.155	.154
	(4.56)	(4.73)	(4.81)
CS2	.182	.190	.195
	(5.75)	(6.25)	(6.58)
CS3	.207	.213	.217
	(6.24)	(6.71)	(7.00)
CS4	.224	.236	.243
	(6.23)	(6.80)	(7.18)
CS5	.348	.358	.365
	(9.86)	(10.56)	(11.03)
R^2	.166	.156	.153

Note: An asterisk next to a variable means it is endogenous. Asymptotic t ratios in parentheses.
[a] SWIFE, JSAT, and WTDIF excluded from the set of instrumental variables.
[b] SWIFE, JSAT, WTDIF, and OTINC excluded from the set of instrumental variables.

health (α) would rise with the wage. This would increase the wage parameter ($\alpha\varepsilon$) in the health demand curve. Second, the positive relationship between the wage rate and what I have termed "the inconvenience costs of illness" (Grossman 1972b, 69) might become stronger as the wage grows. This relationship arises because the complexity of a particular job and the amount of responsibility it entails certainly are positively correlated with the wage. Thus, when an individual with a high wage becomes ill, tasks that only he can perform accumulate. These increase the intensity of his work load and give him an incentive to avoid illness by demanding more health capital. I suspect that the importance of inconvenience costs in the NBER-Thorndike sample is the major source of the large wage elasticity of health that is observed in this sample. By using a set of instrumental variables for the wage rate,

I probably create a variable that more accurately reflects these costs than the measured wage.

With two exceptions, the health coefficients of variables other than the wage are not altered much when the wage is treated as endogenous. The two exceptions are that the coefficient of nonearnings income increases in absolute value and the coefficient of own schooling falls dramatically (compare equation [1] in table 3.13 to equation [6] in table 3.5). The pure income elasticity of health rises in absolute value from −.01 to −.06 at an income of $20,000 when the health function is estimated by two-stage least squares rather than by ordinary least squares. Although the pure income elasticity is still not statistically significant, its sign suggests that, at high income levels, the consumption of detrimental health inputs grows at least as rapidly as the consumption of beneficial inputs as income grows. In a statistical sense, the reduction in the coefficient of own schooling is due to multicollinearity between schooling and the predicted wage rate. These two variables are much more highly correlated than schooling and the actual wage rate ($r = .642$ versus $r = .289$). In a literal sense, according to equation (1) in table 3.13, schooling has no direct effect on health, with the wage rate and other variables held constant.

Even if the literal interpretation of the schooling coefficient in equation (1) is correct, this does *not* mean that schooling has no impact on health independent of its impact on the wage rate. In section 2.2 of this chapter, I showed that schooling influences health in part because of its effects on wives' schooling, weight difference, and job satisfaction. Equation (2) in table 3.13 allows the schooling coefficient to reflect these channels by omitting wives' schooling, job satisfaction, and weight difference from the model. The omission of these three variables causes the schooling coefficient to triple in magnitude and to achieve statistical significance at the .05 level of confidence on a one-tail test. Greenberg (1972) and Smith (1973) argue that it is not entirely appropriate to treat nonearnings income as an exogenous variable in the context of a model of life-cycle decision making. Therefore, (3) excludes this variable as well as the three excluded in equation (2). This results in a slightly larger and a slightly more significant schooling coefficient.[70]

Due to the importance of schooling as a policy variable from the point of view of both the individual and society, it is useful to examine the reduced-form health and schooling parameters of this variable. In table 3.15, I show estimates of these parameters based on a specification of the health function that omits wives' schooling, job satisfaction, weight difference, and nonearnings income, I also decompose each parameter into a direct component and an indirect component.[71] The reduced-form health parameter of schooling indicates that a one-year increase in this variable raises health by 3.0 percent. The indirect component, which is present because schooling raises the wage rate and the wage

Table 3.15 Estimates of Direct, Indirect, and Total Effects of Schooling on Health and the Wage Rate

	Health Effects	Wage Effects
Direct effect	.014	.052
Indirect effect	.016	.003
Total effect (reduced-form parameter)	.030	.055

rate raises health, is slightly larger than the direct component. The reduced-form wage parameter of schooling suggests a rate of return to investment in schooling via an expansion in market productivity of 5.5 percent. A small percentage of this increase (approximately 5.45 percent) can be attributed to the increase in health caused by an increase in schooling.

In a sense, the direct component of the reduced-form health parameter is itself an indirect component, because it measures the effects of schooling on health that operate via wives' schooling, job satisfaction, and weight difference. Regardless of the manner in which the direct component is interpreted, its magnitude suggests that schooling influences health by channels other than the wage rate. Given the high degree of multicollinearity between schooling and the predicted wage, this is an impressive finding. Future research is necessary in order to ascertain whether the direct nonmarket productivity component of the schooling coefficient in the health function is really as small as the simultaneous-equations model indicates, and whether the indirect non-market component is as large.

5. MORTALITY EXPERIENCE OF THE THORNDIKE SAMPLE BETWEEN 1955 AND 1969

5.1. Nature of the Analysis

Death is the most objective, although the most extreme, measure of ill health. Therefore, in this section I examine the mortality experience of the Thorndike sample between the year of the initial survey by Thorndike and Hagen (1959) and the year of the first resurvey by the NBER (1969). In particular, I want to see whether relationships that are observed when health is measured by self-rated health status are also observed when health is measured by mortality or survival.

Of the 9,700 men in the original Thorndike sample, 275 had died by 1969.[72] This gives a mortality rate of 2.84 percent over a period that extends roughly from 1956 through 1968. In 1955, the mean age of the sample was thirty-three years, and the age-specific death rate in the United States of white males ages thirty-five to forty-four was 0.34 percent (U.S. Department of Health, Education, and Welfare 1961). Since this age-specific death rate was practically constant between 1956 and 1968, 4.32 percent of the Thorndike sample would have died by 1968 if the sample had the same mortality experience as the population at large.[73] Thus, the survival rate in a sample drawn from the upper tails of the schooling, earnings, and scholastic-ability distributions exceeds the survival rate in the general population. This complements my finding that the levels of self-rated health status and healthy time in the NBER-Thorndike sample exceed the levels of these health indexes in the NORC sample.

To examine the partial effects of various factors on survival in the Thorndike sample, I have estimated a dichotomous logit survival function by the method of maximum likelihood.[74] If p_i is the probability that the ith individual survives, then this function is given by

$$\ln [p_t/(1 - p_t)] = b_1 S + b_2 V + b_3 P + b_4 MECH + b_5 GEN + b_6 NUM + b_7 JSAT55 + b_8 \ln SAL55$$

where S is years of formal schooling completed in 1955, $JSAT55$ is an index of job satisfaction in 1955, ln $SAL55$ is the natural logarithm of full-time salary in 1955, and the other variables are defined in section 2 of this chapter. The logit function contains only eight independent variables, because no information is available on people who died between 1955 and 1969 other than that collected by Thorndike and Hagen in 1955. Full-time salary rather than the hourly wage rate measures the value of time, because there are no data on hours worked per week in 1955. Job satisfaction in 1955 is simply the answer to the question: How well do you like the type of work you are doing now? The four possible numerical responses constitute a scale ranging from four (the highest) to one (the lowest).

I could have used all 9,700 men in the original sample as a base for estimating the logit function, but for two reasons, I have limited observations on survivors to men who responded to the 1969 NBER questionnaire. First, a significant fraction of the sample completed their formal schooling after 1955.[75] Therefore, a positive relationship between schooling in 1955 and survival might reflect the incentive of persons with a longer life expectancy and a higher level of general health to invest more in schooling. By using the 1969 survey as a base, I can restrict the survivors to men who had completed their formal schooling by 1955.

Second, Thorndike and Hagen did not obtain age as a variable in 1955. Since age and schooling are negatively correlated and age and survival are presumably negatively correlated, the effect of schooling on survival is biased upward by the omission of age from the survival function. By selecting survivors who had completed their formal schooling by 1955, I select a set whose mean age is somewhat greater than the mean age of all survivors. At the same time, I reduce the size of the correlation between age and schooling. This procedure mitigates, although it does not entirely eliminate, the bias caused by omitting age from the survival function.[76]

Note that men with zero or unknown full-time salaries in 1955 are excluded from the analysis. Therefore, persons who died shortly after 1955 and were not able to work at all in that year are eliminated from the survival function. To further reduce the magnitude of a possible relationship from survival to full-time salary, I estimate survival functions for men whose 1955 full-time salary exceeds one-half the median full-time salary of $6,000 and for men whose salary exceeds the median salary. This procedure alleviates problems that arise because I do not know whether decedents completed their formal schooling by 1955. It is unlikely that a decedent whose salary exceeded the median salary had not finished his schooling.

The sample size, number of deaths, and "adjusted mortality rate" in each of the three logit functions that I fit are shown in table 3.16. Since the response rate to the 1969 questionnaire was approximately 50 percent, the decedents in each sample represent 100 per cent of all decedents, but the survivors represent 50 percent of all survivors. Therefore, in computing the adjusted mortality rate, I give double weight to survivors. In calculating logistic functions, I do not give double weight to survivors, but I do estimate marginal effects at the adjusted mean probability of survival (one minus the adjusted death rate).[77]

5.2. Results

Table 3.17 contains maximum likelihood estimates of dichotomous logit survival functions. The three equations in the table reveal that schooling has a positive and statistically significant effect on the probability of survival. Indeed, schooling is the only variable whose logit coefficient differs from zero in a statistical sense. The schooling effect is independent of the level of median

Table 3.16 Characteristics of Samples in Survival Analysis

Sample	Size	Deaths	Adjusted Mortality Rate (%)
Positive salary in 1955	4,386	248	2.83
Salary exceeds one-half the median salary	4,277	238	2.78
Salary exceeds the median salary	2,013	107	2.66

Table 3.17 Maximum Likelihood Estimates of Dichotomous Logit Survival Functions

Variable	Equation 1[a]		Equation 2[b]		Equation 3[c]	
	Logit Coefficient	Marginal Effect	Logit Coefficient	Marginal Effect	Logit Coefficient	Marginal Effect
S	.135 (4.06)	.004	.142 (4.15)	.004	.147 (3.04)	.004
V	.037 (0.68)	.001	.037 (0.67)	.001	.058 (0.71)	.002
P	−.038 (−0.67)	−.001	−.034 (−0.59)	−.001	−.085 (−0.97)	−.002
MECH	.013 (0.22)	.0004	.015 (0.25)	.0004	.012 (0.13)	.0003
GEN	.056 (1.05)	.002	.070 (1.28)	.002	.032 (0.42)	.001
NUM	−.013 (−0.24)	−.0004	−.009 (−0.17)	−.0003	.014 (0.17)	.0004
JSAT55	.084 (0.84)	.002	.116 (1.14)	.003	.027 (0.17)	.001
In SAL55	.037 (0.21)	.001	−.087 (−0.46)	−.002	.129 (0.39)	.003

Note: Asymptotic t ratios in parentheses.
[a] Includes all men who completed schooling by 1955 and had a positive salary in that year. Sample size is 4,386.
[b] Includes men whose salary exceeded one-half the median salary. Sample size is 4,277.
[c] Includes men whose salary exceeded the median salary. Sample size is 2,013.

salary in 1955 and suggests that in the vicinity of the adjusted death rate a one-year increase in schooling lowers the probability of death by .4 percentage points. The important role of schooling in the survival function is a further justification for the emphasis that I have given to this variable as a determinant of health throughout this chapter.

Although none of the other variables has a statistically significant effect on survival, the signs of job satisfaction and visual perception are consistent with the signs of these variables in the self-rated health status functions. When the lower tail of the salary distribution is included in the analysis, general intelligence is a better predictor of survival than visual perception. This is not, however, the case when the sample is limited to the upper tail of the salary distribution. In general, the estimated schooling parameter and the estimated parameter of a given test score are not sensitive to the other test scores that are included in the survival function.

Two difficulties with the mortality analysis are that the men in the Thorn-dike sample were only in their thirties in 1955, and that relatively few variables are available for that year. The sample has now reached a point in the life cycle at which death rates in future years should be much higher than in the past. Consequently, one promising area for future research would be to trace the mortality experience of the sample for the next five or ten years. Mortality could then be related to a wide variety of factors that can be measured with the large set of variables that was collected by the NBER in 1969 and 1971.

6. SUMMARY AND CONCLUSION

In this chapter, I have used the household production function approach to con-sumer behavior to develop recursive and simultaneous models of decision mak-ing that can be used to formulate and estimate health-schooling relationships. In the theoretical section, I have shown how a recursive system whose princi-pal equations are demand curves for children's health, schooling, and adults' health generates causal relationships from schooling to health and from health to schooling. In addition, this system generates relationships from third variables to both health and schooling. In the main empirical section, I have estimated a recursive health-schooling model by ordinary least squares, using data contained in the NBER-Thorndike sample. In this model, I have measured health capital by self-rated health status. In other empirical sections, I have conducted "sensitivity analyses" that show how the ordinary least squares results are affected (1) when the health equation is specified as a dichotomous logit function and estimated by the method of maximum likelihood, and (2) when the health function is fitted in the context of a simultaneous-equations health-wage model. Finally, I have exam-ined the mortality experience of the Thorndike sample between 1955 and 1969.

The major empirical results of the recursive health-schooling model can be summarized as follows. With past health and third variables held constant, schooling has a positive and statistically significant effect on current health. This is evidence in favor of a causal relationship that runs from schooling to current health. The estimated bias in schooling coefficients is larger when cur-rent variables are omitted from the health function than when past variables are omitted. Current variables include the hourly wage rate, wives' schooling, weight difference, and job satisfaction; while past variables include past health, parents' schooling, and visual perception. Past health has an extremely sig-nificant positive effect on current health and also has a positive and significant effect on years of formal schooling completed. Yet the parameter estimate of schooling in the current health function is not greatly altered by the inclusion of past health. Current health is positively related to physical ability, measured by visual perception, but it is not related to mental ability, measured by general intelligence. A decomposition analysis of the effect of schooling on health, with the wage rate held constant, reveals that a substantial fraction of this effect operates via the impact of schooling on wives' schooling, job satisfaction, and weight difference. Indeed, these three channels of influence account for nearly 40 percent of the total nonmarket productivity effect of schooling on health.

The sensitivity analysis reveals that the qualitative results of the recursive model are not altered when the health equation is specified as a dichotomous logit function and estimated by the technique of maximum likelihood. In the context of the simultaneous-equations health-wage model, schooling has a somewhat smaller impact on health than it does in the pure recursive system. In fact, the simultaneous-equations model shows that, with the wage rate held constant, the entire effect of schooling on health operates via the channels of wives' schooling, job satisfaction, and weight difference. This model also shows that health is an important determinant of market productivity and the hourly wage rate. The mortality experience of the Thorndike sample between 1955 and 1969 confirms the important role of schooling in the health function.

I view the empirical work in this chapter as preliminary or ongoing rather than definitive or final. Given the uniqueness of the Thorndike sample and the less than ideal measures of health, the models that I have formulated and estimated should be treated as examples of the kinds of models that could be fitted with longitudinal samples that contain more refined measures of current and past health and back-ground characteristics. Due to the preliminary nature of my work, I have not hesitated to suggest alternative explanations of certain findings, to speculate and to be provocative in discussing results, and to propose a partial agenda for future research.

One topic on such an agenda would be a careful study of the process by which schooling influences health and other aspects of consumer behavior. In such a study, one would delineate in detail all channels through which the nonmarket productivity effect of schooling on health operates. A second topic would be an examination of the mortality experience of the NBER-Thorndike sample after 1969. A third topic, not previously mentioned, would be a study that takes full account of my notion that children's health is one aspect of their quality. In this research, one would formulate and estimate a demand curve for children's health. One would also use this demand curve to derive and estimate a demand curve for children's medical care along the same lines that I have used in the past to derive and fit a demand curve for adults' medical care (Grossman 1972b). At a somewhat deeper level, my empirical results suggest that what some persons might call "attitudinal variables," such as self-rated health status and job satisfaction, are amenable to economic analysis. Consequently, practitioners of the "new economics of the household" should not relegate the analysis of these variables to sociologists and psychologists, just as they do not relegate the analysis of fertility and contraception to demographers.

APPENDIX

The empirical analysis in sections 3 and 4 of this chapter is limited to men who responded to both the 1969 and the 1971 NBER questionnaires, were married in 1969, and were members of the labor force in that year. In addition to these restrictions, men were excluded from the analysis if there was no information on their current health status, age, height, actual weight, full-time salary, family income, wives' schooling, health status in high school, and school-loss weeks. In cases where there were unknown values of variables other than the ones just listed, the mean value of the relevant variable was substituted.

Table A.1 contains means and standard deviations of all variables that are used in sections 3 and 4 for the sample of 3,534 men. Table A.2 contains a matrix of simple correlation coefficients. Note that the principal components analysis of the test scores was performed on the entire sample of men who responded to the 1969 questionnaire. Therefore, the five ability variables do not necessarily have zero means.

Table A.1 Means and Standard Deviations, Married Men in NBER-Thorndike Sample

Variable	Mean	Standard Deviation
ln $H69$	3.938	.684
A	46.733	2.196
S	15.054	2.431
$SFAT$	9.812	3.528
$SMOT$	9.977	3.464
V	.035	1.330
P	.012	1.304
$MECH$	.019	1.301
NUM	.072	1.454
GEN	.072	1.595
ln HHS	1.917	.258
$SWIFE$	13.320	2.100
$JSAT$	4.415	.786
$WTDIF$	23.102	16.641
ln W	1.963	.498
$OTINC$[a]	1.508	5.896
$EXCELL$[b]	.595	
EXP	21.387	6.807
$SOUTH$[b]	.229	
$CS1$[b]	.153	
$CS2$[b]	.265	
$CS3$[b]	.195	
$CS4$[b]	.134	
$CS5$[b]	.148	

Note: Sample size is 3,534.

[a] Thousands of dollars.

[b] Standard deviations of dummy variables not shown.

Table A.2 Matrix of Simple Correlation Coefficients, Married Men in NBER-Thorndike Sample

	ln H69	A	S	SFAT	SMOT	V	P	MECH	NUM	GEN	ln HHS	SWIFE
ln H69	1.000											
A	-.078	1.000										
S	.135	-.172	1.000									
SFAT	.079	-.093	.76	1.000								
SMOT	.081	-.130	.63	.467	1.000							
V	.095	-.114	.094	.120	.125	1.000						
P	.047	.088	-.022	.039	.019	.294	1.000					
MECH	.048	.034	-.061	-.114	.196	.276	.387	1.000				
NUM	.055	.061	.130	.030	.036	.306	.197	-.031	1.000			
GEN	.089	-.077	.327	.155	.186	.273	.145	.255	.468	1.000		
ln HHS	.193	-.059	.063	.022	.018	.022	.027	-.008	.054	.026	1.000	
SWIFE	.118	-.067	.389	.235	.209	.058	-.009	.013	.060	.172	.048	1.000
JSAT	.134	-.023	.098	.040	.049	.012	-.002	.020	-.00002	-.012	.075	.060
WTDIF	-.064	.021	-.061	-.062	-.062	-.027	-.066	-.036	-.048	-.065	.020	-.046
ln W	.170	-.085	.289	.122	.104	.084	.027	.025	.163	.220	.088	.147
OTINC	.028	-.008	.020	.032	.059	.009	-.0005	.013	.037	.067	.013	.062
EXCELL	.927	-.087	.142	.077	.089	.093	.039	.050	.046	.100	.189	.114
EXP	-.067	.305	-.550	-.071	-.070	-.068	.020	.006	-.017	-.146	-.022	-.182
SOUTH	.004	-.037	.280	.0005	.085	-.017	-.007	.019	-.049	-.008	-.005	.048
CS1	-.056	.017	-.029	-.033	-.017	-.049	-.011	.017	-.029	-.016	-.037	.002
CS2	.019	.010	.004	.021	.008	.028	.052	-.008	.021	.008	.025	.006
CS3	.004	.006	.039	-.004	.002	.013	-.005	-.014	.005	-.007	.003	.038
CS4	.036	.008	.035	.033	.028	.010	-.018	.016	.012	.004	.006	.005
CS5	.038	-.040	.053	.015	-.004	.026	.012	-.056	.039	.064	.035	.018

	JSAT	WTDIF	ln W	OTINC	EXCELL	EXP	SOUTH	CS1	CS2	CS3	CS4	CS5
SWIFE												
JSAT	1.000											
WTDIF	.024	1.000										
ln W	.168	-.028	1.000									
OTINC	.010	-.001	.210	1.000								
EXCELL	.124	-.072	.166	.023	1.000							
EXP	.007	.013	-.096	-.005	-.069	1.000						
SOUTH	.040	-.029	.012	.024	.001	-.045	1.000					
CS1	-.005	-.012	-.068	-.021	-.054	.021	-.051	1.000				
CS2	-.038	.016	-.002	-.012	.017	.001	.075	.255	1.000			
CS3	.018	-.022	.021	-.008	.007	.006	.070	-.210	-.296	1.000		
CS4	.018	-.022	.047	-.002	.038	-.044	.053	-.167	-.236	-.194	1.000	
CS5	.023	.006	.162	.077	.034	-.044	.029	-.177	-.250	-.206	-.164	1.000

NOTES

Originally published as Michael Grossman, "The Correlation between Health and Schooling," in *Household Production and Consumption*, ed. Nestor E. Terleckyj, Studies in Income and Wealth, Volume 40, by the Conference on Research in Income and Wealth (New York: Columbia University Press for the National Bureau of Economic Research, 1976), 147–211. Research for this chapter was supported by PHS Grant Number 5 P01 HS 00451 from the Bureau of Health Services Research and Evaluation. I owe a special debt to Victor R. Fuchs for urging me to investigate the relationship between health and schooling in detail and for interacting with me many times while I was working on the chapter. I should also like to thank Gary S. Becker, Barry R. Chiswick, Reuben Gronau, F. Thomas Juster, William M. Landes, Robert T. Michael, Jacob Mincer, Melvin W. Reder, James P. Smith, Finis Welch, and Robert J. Willis for helpful comments and suggestions; and Carol Breckner, Janice Platt, and Elizabeth H. Rand for research assistance.

1. Early childhood environment is shaped, to a large extent, by parental characteristics such as schooling, family income, and socioeconomic status.

2. The effect of schooling on the health of adults would not be biased by the omission of third variables if one had a perfect measure of their health during the years that they attended school, and if schooling were the only determinant of the efficiency of nonmarket production. For a complete discussion of this point, see section 1.2.

3. In the pure investment model, the marginal utility of healthy time or the marginal disutility of sick time equals zero.

4. Equilibrium condition (5) assumes that gross investment in health is always positive. For a discussion of this point, see Grossman (1972a, 233–234).

5. From equation (3)

$$\ln G_t = \ln BC - (C + 1)\ln H_t$$

Substitute $\ln \gamma_i - \ln W_t$, $\ln \pi_t$ for $\ln G_t$ in this equation, and solve for $\ln H_t$ to obtain

$$\ln H_t = \ln BC + \varepsilon \ln W_t - \varepsilon \ln \pi_t - \varepsilon \ln \gamma_t$$

where $\varepsilon = 1/(1 + C)$. Replacing γ_t by $t - \tilde{\pi}_t + \delta_t$ in the last equation and assuming that the real own rate of interest, $r - \tilde{\pi}_t$, is equal to zero, one obtains equation 6. For a justification of the assumption that $r - \tilde{\pi}_t$ is zero, see Grossman (1972b, 42).

6. Note that certain inputs in the M vector, such as cigarette smoking and alcohol consumption, have negative marginal products in the gross investment function. They are purchased because they also produce other commodities, such as "smoking pleasure." Therefore, joint production occurs in the household. For an analysis of this phenomenon, see Grossman (1971). Note also that, if health were produced in a family context, then T_t might be a vector of time inputs of various family members.

7. Grossman and Benham (1974) produce some evidence to the contrary, but this evidence should also be viewed as tentative.

8. For a derivation of equation (9), see Grossman (1972b, Appendix D). This equation, as well as the remainder of those in this chapter, does not contain an intercept, because all variables are expressed as deviations from their respective means.

9. This finding complements the negative relationships among schooling and various age-adjusted mortality rates that are reported in a number of studies. See Stockwell (1963) Fuchs (1965); Hinkle et al. (1968); Kitagawa and Hauser (1968); Auster, Leveson, and Sarachek (1969); Breslow and Klein (1971); and Silver (1972).

10. For models of the determination of optimal investment in human capital, see, for example, Becker (1967); Ben-Porath (1967); and Lillard (1973). For models of the demand for child quality, see, for example, Leibowitz (1972); Ben-Porath (1973); De Tray (1973); and especially Willis (1973). For studies that view preschool investment in human capital as one aspect of child quality, see, for example, Lillard (1973) and Leibowitz (1974).

11. A common specification of the production function of new human capital at age t, due originally to Ben-Porath (1967), is

$$\ln Q_t = \ln B + \alpha_1 \ln s_t E_t + \alpha_2 \ln D_t$$

where s_t is the proportion of the existing stock of human capital allocated to the production of more human capital, D_t is an input of market goods and services, and $\alpha_1 + \alpha_2 < 1$. Following Lillard (1973), I assume that ability and health primarily affect the Hicks-neutral technology parameter B, rather than the stock of human capital that individuals possess when they first begin to make their own decisions. Leibowitz (1974) stresses the effect of ability on the preschool stock of human capital but reaches the same conclusion with regard to the effect of ability on schooling.

12. Indeed, at young ages, the rate of depreciation might fall rather than rise with age.

13. One justification for this assumption is that it is observed empirically that most individuals make positive outlays on medical care throughout their life cycles.

14. This assumption is required because, from the point of view of any one person, the marginal product of the stock of knowledge is independent of the stock. For a complete discussion of this point, see Becker (1967) and Ben-Porath (1967). Grossman (1972a, 234–235) compares and contrasts in detail the alternative assumptions made about the marginal products of health and knowledge capital and about the marginal costs of producing gross additions to these two stocks.

15. After leaving school, persons can continue to acquire human capital via investments in on-the-job training. I assume that human capital obtained in this manner is a much less relevant determinant of efficiency in the production of health than human capital obtained via formal schooling. For analyses of the forces that cause the quantity of investment in human capital to decline with age, see Becker (1967); Ben-Porath (1967); and Mincer (1970, 1974).

16. This point is emphasized by Lillard (1973) and especially by Leibowitz (1974).

17. Along similar lines, one could specify a demand curve for children's intelligence. For one specification and some empirical estimates, see Leibowitz (1974).

18. The same conclusion would be reached if an inferior genetic endowment or a birth defect lowered the amount of gross investment in health obtained from given amounts of medical care and other inputs.

19. The variable E does not have an age subscript, because it is the stock of knowledge after schooling ends. If the rate of depreciation on knowledge capital were positive, E would fall with age. I assume that this effect is small enough to be ignored, at least at most stages of the life cycle.

20. Employing Ben-Porath's model of investment in human capital, Lillard (1973) obtains a specific solution for the stock of human capital as a function of schooling, ability, and age. His equation is highly nonlinear.

21. From now on, age subscripts are deleted from all variables on the right-hand side of the demand curve for adults' health except the rate of depreciation in the initial period.

22. See, for example, Johnston (1963). This proposition is valid only if the unspecified disturbance terms in the equations are mutually independent.

23. If $\ln H_1$ varied with S and $\ln \delta_1$ held constant, then one would be imposing a negative correlation between Y and X. Since the variables in these two vectors primarily reflect childhood environment, such a correlation is not plausible.

24. Indeed, according to equation (9″), an increase in γ, with $\ln H_1$ constant, would cause $\ln H_1$ to fall. Note, however, that, if $\ln \delta_1$ and Y were independent, then Y should be omitted from equation (9′).

25. If equation (9′) were fitted with $\ln H_1$ omitted, the expected value of the regression coefficient of Y would be $(\varepsilon/\varepsilon')(b - b_1)$ where b is the partial regression coefficient of $\ln H_1$ on Y, with other variables in the demand curve for adults' health held constant, if b were positive, the expected value of the regression coefficient of $\ln H_1$ on Y would be positive provided $b > b_1$.

26. See, for example, Masland (1968).

27. See, for example, Palmore (1969a, 1969b).

28. For a similar discussion with regard to the effects of parental characteristics and intelligence on earnings, see Leibowitz (1974).

29. I do not consider here the difficult problem of measuring the value of time of persons not in the labor force. For discussions of this issue, see Gronau (1973) and Heckman (1974)

30. Since $a_t < 1, \rho_t > \alpha_t \hat{W}_t$ if $\rho_t = \hat{W}_t$.

31. For complete descriptions of the sample, see Thorndike and Hagen (1959) and Taubman and Wales (1974).

32. The identification of these five basic types of ability is due to Thorndike and Hagen (1959). It is discussed in more detail in section 2.3.

33. The specific sample that I utilize is described in more detail in the appendix.

34. Data were obtained from 2,367 families containing 7,803 persons. For a complete description of the NORC sample, see Andersen and Anderson (1967). I do not employ it to study health-schooling relationships in this chapter, because it has no data on past health and very limited data on third variables.

35. Examples of these symptoms include persistent cough, swelling in joints, frequent backaches, unexplained loss of weight, and repeated pains in or near the heart.

36. For a proof, see Grossman (1972b, 16–19). Given the production function of healthy time specified in equation (2), the price elasticity of demand for health capital is $\varepsilon = 1/(1 + C)$. This elasticity is smaller than one since C exceeds zero.

37. These two means arc small in the NBER-Thorndike sample: .3 weeks for the entire sample and 9.8 weeks for men in poor health.

38. The corresponding figure in the NORC sample is 33 percent. Although part of this difference reflects the higher level of health in the NBER-Thorndike sample, part of it is due to the manner in which the work-loss data were collected. The members of the NORC sample were asked for work-loss *days*, while the members of the NBER-Thorndike sample were asked for work-loss *weeks*. The mean number of work-loss days in the NORC sample is 5, and many persons reported 1 to 4 days. Therefore, at least some of the zero values in the NBER-Thorndike sample may represent positive amounts of work-loss days. This is another reason why I do not use work-loss itself as a measure of health.

39. The a_i coincide with the elements of the characteristic vector associated with the largest characteristic root of the correlation matrix of the X_i.

40. These estimates are reported by Netzer (1969, 129).

41. Admittedly, it would be difficult to define these input prices, although elsewhere (Grossman 1971) I have shown that the concept and theory of joint production would aid in accomplishing this task. The price of job satisfaction might be defined as the reduction in the wage rate required to increase this variable by one unit, with schooling held constant. But the partial correlation between job satisfaction and the wage is positive in the NBER-Thorndike sample possibly because the "income effect" dominates the "substitution effect."

42. The computations in table 3.7 are based on the regressions in table 3.5, as well as on some additional regressions not shown in the table. These computations do not depend on the value of the parameter C in the production function of healthy time given by equation (2) or equation (13).

43. My empirical analysis in sections 2.1. and 2.2 is similar to Griliches and Mason's (1972) analysis of interrelationships among schooling, ability, and earnings.

44. The price elasticity of health would equal one-half if C in the production function of healthy time given by equation (2) or (13) were equal to one. According to the reduced form demand curve for health given by equation (9″), the schooling parameter should be $c_1 \rho \varepsilon$, where c_1 gives the effect of schooling on the stock of human capital. My estimate of ρ assumes that c_1 equals one, but this assumption would not affect the comparison of market and nonmarket productivity effects.

45. This figure is based on a regression of the natural logarithm of the hourly wage rate on schooling, years of experience in the labor force, general intelligence, and several other variables.

46. The other test scores are omitted from the computations in table 3.7, because they have statistically insignificant effects on health. This procedure is justified in more detail when the effects of third variables are discussed below.

47. Heckman. 1974. *Econometrica* 42: 679–694.

48. See Becker (1973) for a general discussion of the economics underlying this phenomenon and Fuchs (1974) for a discussion of health differentials among married men in terms of selective mating and other factors.

49. Welch (1974) criticizes Benham (1974) for measuring the effect of wives' schooling on husbands' market productivity without controlling for husbands' ability and background characteristics.

50. The pure income elasticity is computed as the product of the regression coefficient of nonearnings income ($\partial \ln H69/\partial OTINC$) and total income in thousands of dollars.
51. See equation (9′).
52. The simple correlation coefficient between fathers' schooling and mothers' schooling is .467. If either of these two variables is excluded from the set of independent variables, the remaining one is statistically significant in equation (2), borders on significance in several other equations in table 3.5, but is not significant in equation (7). For this reason, I include both variables in the estimates of biases in schooling coefficients in table 3.7.
53. In this context, note that two of the scores in the mechanical ability component measure knowledge of mechanical principles rather than mechanical ability in a physical sense. Since persons may have acquired this knowledge in the labor force prior to 1943, the large negative effect of mechanical ability on schooling may be spurious.
54. One source of variation may be traced to complementarity between number of years of schooling completed and the quality of schooling.
55. See, for example, the references cited in the introductory section of this chapter.
56. This decomposition is due to Welch (1970), who terms the direct component the "worker effect" and the indirect component the "allocative effect."
57. There are also second- and higher-order indirect effects that arise, for example, because wives' schooling influences job satisfaction. But these are *extremely* small and are not shown in table 3.8. It may seem arbitrary to assume that the determination of *JSAT* precedes the determination of *WTDIF*. Since, however, the higher-order effects are very small, this assumption does not affect the computations in table 3.8.
58. Since the sequence in which job satisfaction and weight difference are determined is somewhat arbitrary, job satisfaction is omitted from the weight difference equation.
59. I have probably "contaminated" the NBER-Thorndike sample for research along these lines, but other datasets can be utilized.
60. For an extensive discussion of these problems and a complete description of alternative estimation techniques, see Nerlove and Press (1973).
61. See Berkson (1944, 1955) for detailed analyses of the properties of the logit function.
62. To see how this function is obtained, consider a sample in which, for simplicity, the first m men are in excellent health and the next $n - m$ are not. The natural logarithm of the likelihood function associated with this sample is

$$\ln L = \sum_{i=1}^{m} \ln p_i + \sum_{i=m+1}^{n} \ln(1 - p_i)$$

Assuming that the relationship between p_i and x_i is given by the logistic function and maximizing $\ln L$ with respect to a and b, one obtains the estimates in table 3.11. The ratios of logit coefficients to their standard errors do not have Student's t distribution. These ratios do, however, approach the normal distribution as the sample size becomes large. Therefore, the t test is an asymptotic one, which can be applied to the logit function I estimate, since there are over 3,500 observations.
63. See Nerlove and Press (1973).

64. Finis Welch has stressed this point to me on a number of occasions.

65. Two-stage least squares estimates obtained with these two variables in the health function (not shown) are almost identical to those presented in section 4.3.

66. I exclude the square of years of experience from equation (18), because the dependent variable is the hourly wage rate. Although theory and previous empirical research suggest that experience-earnings profiles or experience-weekly-wage profiles should be concave to the origin (Becker 1967; Ben-Porath 1967; Mincer 1970, 1974; Lillard 1973), I find no empirical evidence that experience-hourly-wage profiles are concave. This may be due in part to the limited age range in the NBER-Thorndike sample.

67. If the health demand curve given by equation (9′) is differentiated with respect to the wage rate, and if the composite price of medical care and other inputs (P) varies with the wage, then

$$(d \ln H/d \ln W) = \alpha \varepsilon [1 - (d \ln P/d \ln W)]$$

68. When two-stage least squares estimation is employed, the ratios of regression coefficients to their standard errors do not have a student's t distribution but do have an asymptotic normal distribution. Therefore, the t test is an asymptotic one. The unadjusted coefficients of multiple determination (R^2) in tables 3.13 and 3.14 should be interpreted with caution. I forced the R^2 to fail between zero and one, for example, by using the variance in the logarithm of the predicted wage rather than the variance in the logarithm of the actual wage in computing the ones in table 3.13. I used this procedure to get a rough approximation of "explanatory power." Since age, schooling, and experience are almost perfectly collinear, I omitted experience from the first-stage health equation. Similarly, I omitted age from the first-stage wage equation.

69. Suppose that the wage elasticity of health (b_8) and the health elasticity of the wage (a_1) are positive. Then the simultaneous-equations system given by equations (17) and (18) would have a stable solution if, and only if, the product of b_8 and a_1 were smaller than one. This follows because the reduced-form health parameter of ln HHS, for example, is $b_4/(1 - b_a a_1)$. Since b_8 equals .30 and a_1 equals .40, the stability condition is satisfied at an empirical level.

70. Clearly, within the context of a life-cycle model, wives' schooling, job satisfaction, weight difference, and nonearnings income are endogenous variables. If these variables are determined prior to the determination of current health and the current wage, it would be appropriate to use them as instruments in two-stage least squares. If, however, they are determined simultaneously with current health and the current wage, they should not be used as instruments. I have not tried to estimate equation (1) in table 3.13 by specifying separate equations for *SWIFE*, *JSAT*, *WTDIF*, and *OTINC*. I have estimated equation (1) with these variables entered in the second-stage health function but excluded from the first-stage. Coefficients obtained in this manner are almost identical to those shown in equation (1).

Equation (2) in table 3.14 gives the wage function that is obtained when *SWIFE*, *JSAT*, and *WTDIF* are excluded from the health function, and equation (3) gives the wage function that is obtained when these three variables and *OTINC* are excluded. The main impact of these exclusions is to reduce the elasticity of the wage with respect to health from approximately .4 to approximately .3. The smaller elasticity is still significant at all conventional levels of confidence.

71. Given the simultaneous-equations system specified by equations (17) and (18), the reduced-form health parameter of schooling equals $(b_2 + a_2b_8)/(1 - b_8a_1)$. The term $b_2/(1 - b_8a_1)$ gives the direct component, and the term $a_2b_8/(1 - b_8a_1)$ gives the indirect component. Similarly, the reduced-form wage parameter of schooling equals $(a_2 + b_2a_1)$ $/(1 - b_8a_1)$, where $a_2/(1 - b_8a_1)$ is the direct component and $b_2a_1/(1 - b_8a_1)$ is the indirect component.

72. Although the response rate to the 1969 questionnaire was only slightly higher than 50 percent, it is known with certainty that exactly 275 men died. This information was supplied by the Veterans Administration.

73. If the age-specific death rate of a cohort (d) is constant over time, then the fraction who die in a t-year period would equal $1 - (1 - d)^t$.

74. I have also estimated dichotomous survival functions by ordinary least squares. The results (not shown) are almost identical to those obtained with the logit functions in section 5.2.

75. Of the 5,085 respondents to the 1969 questionnaire, 11 percent completed schooling after 1955.

76. My procedure assumes that men who completed schooling by 1955 and responded to the 1969 questionnaire have the same characteristics as all men who survived and completed schooling by 1955. Taubman and Wales (1974) indicate that men who responded to the 1969 questionnaire reported slightly higher schooling levels in 1955 than the entire 1955 sample. But their comparison is *not* restricted to men who finished schooling by 1955.

77. In regression analysis, weighting is employed to produce efficient estimates rather than to produce consistent estimates. Consequently, it is by no means obvious that logistics survival functions should be weighted.

REFERENCES

Andersen, Ronald, and Odin W. 1967. *A Decade of Health Services: Social Survey Trends in Use and Expenditure.* Chicago: University of Chicago Press.

Auster, Richard D., Irving Leveson, and Deborah Sarachek. 1969. "The Production of Health: An Exploratory Study." *Journal of Human Resources* 4: 411–436. In *Essays in the Economics of Health and Medical Care*, ed. Victor R. Fuchs. NBER.

Becker, Gary S. 1965. "A Theory of the Allocation of Time." *Economic Journal* 75: 493–517.

——. 1967. *Human Capital and the Personal Distribution of Income: An Analytical Approach.* W. S. Woytinsky Lecture No. 1. Ann Arbor: University of Michigan.

——. 1973. "A Theory of Marriage: Part I." *Journal of Political Economy* 81: 813–846.

Becker, Gary S., and Barry R. Chiswick. 1966. "Education and the Distribution of Earnings." *American Economic Review, Papers and Proceedings* 56: 358–369.

Benham, Lee. 1974. "Benefits of Women's Education within Marriage." In *Marriage, Family Human Capital, and Fertility* ed. T. W. Schultz. Proceedings of a conference sponsored by the National Bureau of Economic Research and the Population Council. *Journal of Political Economy* 82, No. 2. Part II.

——., and Alexndra Benham. 1975. "The Impact of Incremental Medical Services on Health Status, 1963-1970." In Equity in Health Services ed. Ronald Andersen. Cambridge, MA: Ballinger Publishing Company.

Ben-Porath, Yoram. 1967. "The Production of Human Capital and the Life Cycle of Earnings." *Journal of Political Economy* 75: 353–367.

——. 1973. "Economic Analysis of Fertility in Israel: Point and Counterpoint." In *New Economic Approaches to Fertility*, ed. W. T. Schultz. Proceedings of a conference sponsored by the National Bureau of Economic Research and the Population Council. *Journal of Political Economy* 81. No. 2, Part II.

Berkson, Joseph.1944. "Application of the Logistic Function to Bio-Assay." *Journal of the American Statistical Association* 39): 357–365.

——. 1955. "Maximum Likelihood and Minimum X^2 Estimates of the Logistic Function." *Journal of the American Statistical Association* 50: 130–162.

Boskin, Michael J. 1973. "The Economics of the Labor Supply." In *Income Maintenance and Labor Supply*, ed. Glen G. Cain and Harold W. Watts. New York. Academic Press.

Bowles, Samuel. 1972. "Schooling and Inequality from Generation to Generation." In *Investment in Education: The Equity-Efficiency Quandary*, ed. T. W. Schultz. Proceedings of a conference sponsored by the Committee on Basic Research in Education of the National Research Council. *Journal of Political Economy* 80, No. 3, Part II.

Breslow, Lester, and Bonnie Klein. 1971. "Health and Race in California." *American Journal of Public Health* 61: 763–775.

De Tray, Dennis N. 1973. "Child Quality and the Demand for Children." In *New Economic Approaches to Fertility* ed. T. W. Schultz. Proceedings of a conference sponsored by the National Bureau of Economic Research and the Population Council. *Journal of Political Economy* 81, No. 2, Part II.

Fuchs, Victor R. 1965. "Some Economic Aspects of Mortality in the United States." New York: National Bureau of Economic Research Processed.

——. 1974. "Some Economic Aspects of Mortality in Developed Countries." In *The Economics of Health and Medical Care* ed. Mark Perlman. London: Macmillan.

Ghez, Gilbert R., and Gary S. Becker. 1975. "The Allocation of Time and Goods Over the Life Cycle." New York: National Bureau of Economic Research.

Greenberg, David H. 1972. "Problems of Model Specification and Measurement: The Labor Supply Function." Santa Monica: The RAND Corporation. Processed.

Griliches, Zvi, and William M. Mason. 1972. "Education, Income, and Ability." In *Investment in Education: The Equity-Efficiency Quandary*, ed. T. W. Schultz. Proceedings of a conference sponsored by the Committee on Basic Research in Education of the National Research Council. *Journal of Political Economy* 80, No. 3, Part II.

Gronau, Reuben. 1973. "The Effect of Children on the Housewife's Value of Time." In *New Economic Approaches to Fertility* ed. T. W. Schultz. Proceedings of a conference sponsored by the National Bureau of Economic Research and the Population Council. *Journal of Political Economy* 81, No. 2, Part II.

Grossman, Michael. 1972a. "On the Concept of Health Capital and the Demand for Health." *Journal of Political Economy* 80: 223–255.

——. 1972b. *The Demand for Health: A Theoretical and Empirical Investigation.* New York: NBER.

——. 1971. "The Economics of Joint Production in the Household." Center for Mathematical Studies in Business and Economics, University of Chicago. Processed.

Grossman, Michael, and Lee Benham. 1974. "Health, Hours, and Wages." In *The Economics of Health and Medical Care*, ed. Mark Perlman. London: Macmillan.

Hall, Robert E. 1973. "Wages, Income, and Hours of Work in the U.S. Labor Force." In *Income Maintenance and Labor Supply*, ed. Glen G. Cain and Harold W. Watts. New York: Academic Press.

Heckman, James J. 1974a. "Estimating Indifference Curves to Determine the Effect of Child Care Programs on Women's Work Effort." In *Marriage, Family Human Capital, and Fertility*, ed. T. W. Schultz. Proceedings of a conference sponsored by the National Bureau of Economic Research and the Population Council. *Journal of Political Economy* 82, No. 2, Part II.

——. 1974b. "Shadow Prices, Market Wages, and Labor Supply." *Econometrica* 42: 679–694.

Hinkle, Lawrence E., Jr. et al. 1968. "Occupation, Education, and Coronary Heart Disease." *Science* 161: 238–246.

Holmes, Thomas H., and Minoru Masuda. 1970. "Life Change and Illness Susceptibility." Paper presented at a symposium on "Separation and Depression: Clinical and Research Aspects." American Association for the Advancement of Science.

Johnston, J. 1963. *Econometric Methods.* New York: McGraw-Hill.

Kitagawa, Evelyn M., and Philip M. Hauser. 1968. "Education Differences in Mortality by Cause of Death: United States, 1960." *Demography* 5, no. 1: 318–353.

Lancaster, Kelvin J. 1966. "A New Approach to Consumer Theory." *Journal of Political Economy* 75: 132–157.

Leibowitz, Arleen S. 1972. "Women's Allocation of Time to Market and Nonmarket Activities: Differences by Education." PhD dissertation, Columbia University.

——. 1974. "Home Investments in Children." In *Marriage, Family Human Capital, and Fertility*, ed. T. W. Schultz. Proceedings of a conference sponsored by the National Bureau of Economic Research and the Population Council. *Journal of Political Economy* 82, No. 2, Part II.

Lillard, Lee A. 1973. "Human Capital Life Cycle of Earnings Models: A Specific Solution and Estimation." New York: National Bureau of Economic Research Working Paper No. 4.

Luft, Harold S. 1972. "Poverty and Health: An Empirical Investigation of the Economic Interactions." PhD dissertation. Harvard University.

Malkiel, Burton G., and Judith A. Malkiel. 1973. "Male-Female Pay Differentials in Professional Employment." *American Economic Review* 63: 693–705.

Masland, Richard L. 1968. Tables presented at Twelfth International Congress of Pediatrics, Mexico City.

Michael, Robert T. 1972. *The Effect of Education on Efficiency in Consumption.* New York: NBER.

Michael, Robert T., and Gary S. Becker. 1973. "On the New Theory of Consumer Behavior." *Swedish Journal of Economics* 4: 378–396.

Mincer, Jacob. 1970. "The Distribution of Labor Incomes: A Survey with Special Reference to the Human Capital Approach." *Journal of Economic Literature* 8: 1–26.

——. 1974. *Schooling, Experience and Earnings.* New York: NBER.

Muth, Richard. 1966. "Household Production and Consumer Demand Functions." *Econometrica* 34: 699–708.

Nerlove, Marc, and James S. Press. 1973. "Notes on the Log-Linear or Logistic Model for the Analysis of Qualitative Socioeconomic Data." Santa Monica: The RAND Corporation. Processed.

Netzer, Corinne T. 1969. *The Brand-Name Calorie Counter.* New York: Dell.

Palmore, Erdman B. 1969a."Physical, Mental, and Social Factors in Predicting Longevity." *The Gerontologist* 9: 103–108.

——. 1969b."Predicting Longevity: A Follow-up Controlling for Age." *The Gerontologist* 9: 247–250.

Rahe, Richard H. 1972. "Subjects' Recent Life Changes and Their Near-Future Illness Reports." *Annals of Clinical Research* 4): 250–265.

Rahe, Richard H., and Thomas H. Holmes. 1965. "Social, Psychologic, and Psychophysiologic Aspects of Inguinal Hernia." *Journal of Psychosomatic Research* 8: 487–491.

Silver, Morris. 1972. "An Econometric Analysis of Spatial Variations in Mortality by Race and Sex." In *Essays in the Economics of Health and Medical Care*, ed. Victor R. Fuchs. New York: NBER.

Smith, James P. 1973. "Family Decisionmaking over the Life Cycle: Some Implications for Estimating Labor Supply." Santa Monica: The RAND Corporation. Processed.

Stockwell, Edward G. 1963. "A Critical Examination of the Relationship Between Socioeconomic Status and Mortality." *American Journal of Public Health* 53: 956–964.

Taubman, Paul J., and Terence J. Wales. 1974. "Higher Education and Earnings: College as an Investment and a Screening Device." New York and Berkeley: National Bureau of Economic Research and Carnegie Commission of Higher Education.

Thorndike, Robert, L. and Elizabeth Hagen. 1959. *Ten Thousand Careers.* New York: John Wiley and Sons.

U.S. Department of Health, Education, and Welfare, Public Health Service, National Center for Health Statistics.1961. *Vital Statistics of the United States.* Volume 11: *Mortality,* Part A.

Welch, Finis. 1970. "Education in Production." *Journal of Political Economy* 78: 35–59.

——. 1974. "Comment: Benefits of Women's Education within Marriage, by Lee Benham." In *Marriage, Family Human Capital, and Fertility*, ed. T. W. Schultz. Proceedings of a conference sponsored by the National Bureau of Economic Research and the Population Council. *Journal of Political Economy* 82, No. 2, Part II.

Willis, Robert. 1973. "A New Approach to the Economic Theory of Fertility Behavior." In *New Economic Approaches to Fertility*, ed. T. W. Schultz. Proceedings of a conference sponsored by the National Bureau of Economic Research and the Population Council. *Journal of Political Economy* 81, No. 2, Part II.

FOUR

An Exploration of the Dynamic Relationship between Health and Cognitive Development in Adolescence

Robert A. Shakotko, Linda N. Edwards, and Michael Grossman

Recent studies of children have documented the existence of a relationship between health and cognitive development, reporting typically that good health is associated with higher levels of cognitive development (Edwards and Grossman, 1979, and the references cited therein).* This association may arise from causality running in one or both directions. Poor health may impede cognitive development in diverse ways. Children who had excessively low birth weights may experience defective brain functioning and abnormally low IQ's throughout their lives. Children who are frequently sick or who are undernourished may be less able to benefit from school instruction because they are either absent from school or lethargic and passive when present. A similar comment can be made about children with vision or hearing problems. Causality runs in the other direction when more intelligent children and adolescents are better able to manage or avoid health problems. Such children can better understand and follow instructions, and they may be more conscientious about taking prescribed medicine or following a specified treatment. In addition, they may better appreciate the importance of eating a nutritious diet and act appropriately.

While existing studies of childhood document this association between health and cognitive development, they do not provide much evidence concerning the direction of causality. This is because they rely almost exclusively on cross-sectional data. The use of cross-sectional data does not necessarily preclude the investigation of causality, of course, but in the present context the underlying theory does not yield enough prior restrictions to allow one to address this issue. Another stumbling block that arises when one tries to unravel the complicated health—cognitive development relationship with cross-sectional data is the impossibility of holding constant certain unmeasurable genetic factors which may be correlated with both health and cognitive development.

A partial remedy for these problems lies with the use of longitudinal data. With such data it is possible directly to model and estimate the dynamic relationship between health and cognitive development. Causality is probed by examining which attribute of children is statistically prior to the other. For example, if it is found that early health status influences later IQ but that early IQ does not influence later health status, it is concluded that health affects IQ but not vice versa. (This notion of causality is akin to that of Granger, 1969.) The problem of separating out the impact of unmeasured genetic factors is not so readily dealt with, but it may have less damaging consequences when longitudinal as opposed to cross-sectional data are used.

In this chapter we investigate the relationship between health and cognitive development using a longitudinal data set compiled from two nationally representative cross-sections of children: Cycles II and III of the Health Examination Survey (HES). Cycle II samples 7,119 noninstitutionalized children aged six to eleven years in the 1963–1965 period; and Cycle III samples 6,768 noninstitutionalized youths aged twelve to seventeen years in the 1966–1970 period. There are 2,177 children common to both cycles, and they were examined in both periods. These 2,177 children constitute the sample on which our longitudinal analysis is based. For these 2,177 children we have measures of health and cognitive development in both periods (childhood and adolescence) and an array of family background variables taken from the first period.

Two multivariate equations are estimated with these data. The first relates adolescent health to childhood health, childhood cognitive development, and family background; and the second relates adolescent cognitive development to childhood cognitive development, childhood health, and family background. Thus, the resulting estimates will enable us to compare the effect of prior health on current cognitive development with the effect of prior cognitive development on current health. As a byproduct, these equations provide sharper estimates of the environmental as opposed to genetically related impacts of selected family background variables on children's health and cognitive development.

1. SOME THEORETICAL CONSIDERATIONS

The general type of model estimated here can be represented by the following equation

$$y_{i,t} = Ay_{i,t-1} + Bx_{i,t-1} + \varepsilon_{i,t} \tag{1}$$

where $y_{i,t}$ represents a vector of health and cognitive development measures in period t for individual i, $X_{i,t}$ is a vector of economic and background variables for that individual in period t, and A and B are matrices of coefficients.[1] The variables in $x_{i,t}$ are those that determine the quantity and productivity of the various inputs in the health and cognitive development production functions: family income, parents' educational attainment, family size, and the prices of medical care, schooling and nutrition.[2] Some of these variables vary through time and some are assumed to be constant in all periods. In the special case where $y_{i,t}$ is a dichotomous measure (when it denotes the presence or absence of a particular illness, for example), equation (1) can be directly interpreted as a transition probability function; it gives the probability that individual i has a given health status in time t conditional on his health status in time $t-1$ and on the values of the other predetermined variables in $t-1$.

Estimation of this type of model improves on existing cross-sectional analysis of causality because it explicitly treats the time sequence of changes in health and cognitive development. Briefly, this approach, suggested by Granger (1969), relies on a temporal ordering of events: a variable x is said to cause y if predictions of y conditional on lagged values of both y and x are statistically superior to predictions conditional on lagged values of y alone. In this setting, causality between cognitive development and health can be discovered by examining the coefficients of childhood health in the adolescent cognitive development equation and the coefficients of childhood cognitive development in the adolescent health equation.

The problem raised by omitted genetic factors is less tractable. Nevertheless, if such factors can be assumed to operate once and for all by determining the "endowed" levels of health or cognitive development [$y_{i,0}$], past values of these variables will fully embody and control for all genetic effects. Under this assumption, the fact that one cannot directly measure genetic factors does not mar the above analysis of causality. Even as restrictive an assumption as this, however, cannot rescue cross-sectional work because cross-sectional data do not typically include past values of the dependent variable.[3]

An additional implication of this assumption is that the estimated impacts of the various family background measures and of early health or IQ represent true environmental (as opposed to genetic) effects. That is, they represent effects that operate through the parents' demand for health or cognitive development inputs or through the degree of productive efficiency. This is in contrast to estimates generated from cross-sectional data. In the latter case, the relationship between parents' educational attainment and children's IQ, for example, reflects both an environmental effect (more highly educated mothers do a better job of educating their children) and a genetic effect (more highly educated mothers have on average greater native intelligence, which is passed genetically to their children). When it is assumed that early health or cognitive development fully embodies the genetic contribution, family background variables will reflect only environmental influences.

Admittedly, this assumption concerning genetic impacts is very restrictive. With data like ours, however, which cover only two points in time, it is impossible to partition the effect of the unobservable genetic factors from other time-invariant factors without making some fairly restrictive assumptions. We choose to make this particular assumption for the balance of this chapter because it has the advantage of permitting us to use single-equation estimation techniques, a not insignificant consideration with a data set as large as this one.[4]

To illustrate better the exact nature of this assumption and its necessity, we present the following simplified two-period formulation, of which our model is a special case (the i's are suppressed for simplicity):

$$H_1 = a_1 GH + b_1 E + \varepsilon_1 \tag{2a}$$

$$H_2 = a_2 GH + b_2 E + c_2 H_1 + d_2 Q_1 + \varepsilon_2 \tag{2b}$$

$$Q_1 = \alpha_1 GQ + \beta_1 E + \varepsilon_1' \tag{3a}$$

$$Q_2 = \alpha_2 GQ + \beta_2 E + \gamma_2 Q_1 + \delta_2 H_1 + \varepsilon_2' \tag{3b}$$

In this two-period model H_t represents health, Q_t represents cognitive development, GH represents the time-invariant genetic health endowment, GQ represents the time-invariant cognitive endowment, and E represents a time-invariant background variable. Since GH and GQ are unobserved, we write H_2 and Q_2 in terms of the predetermined values of H and Q (assuming a_1 and α_1 do not equal zero):

$$H_2 = \left[\frac{a_2}{a_1} + c_2 \right] H_1 + b_2 \left[1 - \frac{a_2}{a_1} \frac{b_1}{b_2} \right] E$$

$$+ d_2 Q_1 + \left[\varepsilon_2 - \frac{a_2}{a_1} \varepsilon_1 \right] \tag{2c}$$

$$Q_2 = \left[\frac{\alpha_2}{\alpha_1} + \gamma_2 \right] Q_1 + \beta_2 \left[1 - \frac{\alpha_2}{\alpha_1} \frac{\beta_1}{\beta_2} \right] E$$
$$+ \delta_2 H_1 + \left[\varepsilon_2' - \frac{\alpha_2}{\alpha_1} \varepsilon_2' \right]. \tag{3c}$$

In the context of this model, the assumption of no direct genetic effects after the first period is equivalent to fixing a_2 and α_2 at zero. When these are not zero, one cannot determine directions of causality because the error terms in the equations are correlated with the explanatory variables and this correlation leads to biased estimates of both d_2 and δ_2. Nor can one obtain unbiased estimates of pure environmental effects, because the reduced form coefficients of the background variable (E) and of the lagged dependent variable (Q_1 or H_1) embody both genetic (a_1 and a_2 or α_1 and α_2) and environmental (b_2, c_2 or β_2, γ_2) impacts.[5]

2. EMPIRICAL IMPLEMENTATION

2.1. The Data

Equations (2) and (3b) are estimated (under the assumptions that $a_2 = 0$ and $\alpha_2 = 0$) using the longitudinal sample compiled from Cycles II and III of the HES. Both cycles are described in detail in National Center for Health Statistics (NCHS) (1967a and 1969, respectively). Ninety-nine percent of the youths in the longitudinal sample are between the ages of twelve and fifteen years at the time of Cycle III, and the remaining 1 percent are sixteen years old.

The HES data include medical histories of each youth provided by the parent, information on family socioeconomic characteristics, birth certificate information, and a school report with data on school performance and classroom behavior provided by teachers or other school officials. Most important, there are objective measures of health from detailed physical examinations and scores on psychological (including IQ and achievement) tests. The physical examinations were given to the children and youths by pediatricians and dentists, and the IQ and achievement tests were administered by psychologists, all of whom were employed by the Public Health Service at the time of each cycle of the HES.

This chapter uses only data for white adolescents who at the time of the Cycle II exam lived with either both of their parents or with their mothers only. Black adolescents are excluded from the empirical analysis because Edwards and Grossman (1979, 1980, and 1983) have found significant race differences in slope coefficients in cross-sectional research using Cycles II and III. Separate estimates for black adolescents are not presented because the black sample is too small to allow for reliable coefficient estimates. Our working sample also excludes observations for which data are missing.[6] The final sample size is 1,434.

The health and cognitive development measures are described below. In labeling these measures, we denote those that refer to childhood (from Cycle II) by the number 1 at the end of the variable name, and those that refer to adolescence (from Cycle III) by the number 2.

2.2. Measurement of Cognitive Development

Two measures of cognitive development are used: an IQ measure derived from two subtests of the Wechsler Intelligence Scale for Children (WISC1, WISC2), and a school achievement measure derived from the reading and arithmetic subtests of the Wide Range Achievement Test (WRAT1, WRAT2). Both measures are scaled to have means of 100 and standard deviations of 15 for each age-group (four-month cohorts are used for WISC and six-month cohorts are used for WRAT).[7] WISC is a common IQ test, similar to (and highly correlated with results from) the Stanford-Binet IQ test (NCHS, 1972). The full test consists of twelve subtests, but only two of these—vocabulary and block design—were administered in the HES. IQ estimates based on these two subtests are highly correlated with those based on all twelve subtests (NCHS, 1972). Similarly, a test score based on the reading and arithmetic subtests of Wide Range Achievement Test have been found to be highly correlated with the full test and with other conventional achievement tests (NCHS, 1967b).

2.3. Measurement of Health

The measures of childhood and adolescent health are the periodontal index (APERI1, APERI2); obesity (OBESE1, OBESE2); the presence of one or more significant abnormalities as reported by the examining physician (ABN1, ABN2); high diastolic blood pressure (HDBP1, HDBP2); the parent's assessment of the youth's overall health (PFGHEALTH1, PFGHEALTH2); and excessive school absence for health reasons during the past six months (SCHABS1, SCHABS2). These six measures are negative correlates of good health, and with the exception of the periodontal index, they are all dichotomous variables. Detailed definitions of these health measures (as well as the cognitive development measures) appear in table 4.1. All but two of the measures—APERI and ABN—are adequately explained by the table. Additional discussion of APERI and ABN follows.

Table 4.1 Definitions of Health and Cognitive Development Measures

Variable Name	Sample[a] Mean	Sample Standard Deviation	Definition[b]
Cognitive Development Measures			
WISC1[c]	103.508	13.924	Youth's IQ as measured by vocabu-
WISC2[c]	104.513	13.998	lary and block design subtests of the Wechsler Intelligence Scale for Children, standardized by the mean and standard deviation of four-month age cohorts, in Cycles II and III, respectively. (Source: 4)
WRAT1[c]	103.568	12.017	Youth's school achievement as mea-
WRAT2[c]	104.112	13.563	sured by the reading and arithmetic subtests of the Wide Range Achievement Test, standardized by the mean and standard deviation of six month age cohorts, in Cycles II and III, respectively. (Source: 4)
Health Measures			
APERI1[c]	−0.055	0.792	Periodontal Index, standardized by the
APERI2[c]	−0.138	0.852	mean and standard deviation for one-year age-sex cohorts, in Cycles II and III, respectively. (Source: 3)
ABN1	0.096	0.294	Dummy variables that equal one if the
ABN2	0.188	0.391	physician finds a significant abnormality in examining the youth, in Cycles II and III, respectively. (Source: 3)
HDBP1	0.054	0.226	Dummy variables that equal one if
HDBP2	0.054	0.227	youth's average diastolic blood pressure is greater than the 95th percentile for the youth's age and sex class, in Cycles II and III, respectively. (Source: 3)
OBESE1	0.11	0.312	Dummy variables that equal one if
OBESE2	0.094	0.292	youth's weight is greater than the 90th percentile for youth's age, sex, and height class, in Cycles II and III, respectively. (Source: 3)

Table 4.1 (*Continued*)

Variable Name	Sample[a] Mean	Sample Standard Deviation	Definition[b]
PFGHEALTH1	0.441	0.497	Dummy variables that equal one if
PFGHEALTH2	0.272	0.445	parental assessment of youth's health is poor, fair, or good in Cycles II and III, respectively. Variable equals zero if assessment is very good in Cycle II and very good or excellent in Cycle III; there is no excellent category in Cycle II. (Source: 1)
SCHABS1	0.033	0.178	Dummy variables that equal one if
SCHABS2[d]	0.054	0.221	youth has been excessively absent from school for health reasons during the past six months, in Cycles II and III, respectively. (Source: 5)
SCHABSUK1	0.068	0.252	Dummy variation that equals one if information about school absence in Cycle II is not available (see note 6). (Source: 5)

Source: Data from the Health Examination Survey, Cycles II and III.

[a] The means and standard deviations are for the sample of 1,434 white youths described in the text.

[b] The sources are the following: 1 = parents, 2 = birth certificate, 3 = physical examination, 4 = psychological examination, 5 = school form.

[c] The means of the cognitive development measures are not equal to 100, and the means of the periodontal indexes are not zero because standardizations were done using the entire Cycle II or Cycle III sample rather than the subsample reported here.

[d] The mean and standard deviation are based on a subsample of 1,321 youths for whom the school form was available.

The periodontal index (APERI1, APERI2) is a good overall indicator of oral health as well as a positive correlate of nutrition (Russell, 1956). It is obtained from an examination of the gums surrounding each tooth and is scored in such a way that a higher value reflects poorer oral health.[8] Because the periodontal index has marked age and sex trends, our measure is computed as the difference between the adolescent's (or child's) actual index and the mean index for his or her age-sex group, divided by the standard deviation for that age-sex group. Oral health is one of the few aspects of health for which a well-defined continuous index has been constructed.

Significant abnormalities (ABN1, ABN2) are defined to be heart disease; neurological, muscular, or joint conditions; other major diseases; and in Cycle III only, otitis media. This minor difference between the definitions of ABN1 and ABN2 will have little impact on our results because otitis media constitutes only a small percentage (about 1 percent) of all reported abnormalities in Cycle III.

In choosing these six particular health measures, our overriding consideration was diversity.[9] Indeed, it is the well-known multidimensional nature of health that led us to study a set of measures rather than a single composite index. Diversity is desired not only with respect to the systems of the body covered, but also with regard to the degree to which the health conditions can be affected by environmental influences. For example, both obesity and the periodontal index are greatly affected by life-style and preventive medical care. In the case of either of these measures, therefore, one would expect to observe a significant impact of family background variables. On the other hand, health problems like high blood pressure and significant abnormalities may not be responsive to family or medical intervention. Such measures may, however, have an impact on other aspects of health or on cognitive development. Subjective health measures like the parents' assessment of the child's health or school absenteeism have the advantage of reflecting people's perceptions about their health. But, at the same time, they may depend on the socioeconomic status of the family. For example, parents with low levels of income and schooling may be dissatisfied with many aspects of their lives including the health of their offspring. (This type of reporting bias is largely controlled for in our analysis, however, because we hold constant both a group of socioeconomic variables and the lagged value of the subjective measure.) A secondary criterion used in choosing the health measures was prevalence. In particular, we avoided health problems like abnormal hearing that have a relatively low prevalence in this cohort.

2.4. Measurement of Other Variables

In addition to lagged (i.e., childhood) cognitive and health development, each equation includes the set of family and youth characteristics defined in Appendix 1. *All family and youth characteristics are taken from Cycle II* (except for the variable INTERVAL which measures the elapsed time between the child's two examinations). The child's age as of the Cycle II exam and/or his sex are also included when the dependent variable is not age- and/or sex-adjusted (that is, for ABN, PFGHEALTH, SCHABS, WISC, and WRAT).[10]

The rationale for including each of these youth and family characteristics variables has been discussed extensively elsewhere (Edwards and Grossman, 1979b, 1980, and forthcoming) and will not be treated here. In section 3, we discuss the effects of only the most important family background variables: mother's schooling (MEDUCAT), father's schooling (FEDUCAT), and family income (FINC). We view parents' schooling as representing the parents' efficiency in the production of their offspring's health and cognitive development, and family income as representing the family's command over resources.

3. EMPIRICAL RESULTS

The results of the estimation of ordinary least squares multiple regression equations for the dependent variables WISC2, WRAT2, APERI2, ABN2, HDBP2, PFGHEALTH2, OBESE2, and SCHABS2 are discussed in this section. (The regression equations are available on request.) Since the six adolescent health measures are negative correlates of good health, negative (positive) effects of family background and lagged cognitive development in the health equations reflect factors associated with better (poorer) health outcomes. Alternatively, positive coefficients of lagged health in the current health equations signify that poor health in childhood is associated with poor health in adolescence. Finally, negative coefficients of lagged health in the current cognitive development equations mean that poor health in childhood reduces cognitive development in adolescence.

Although five of the eight dependent variables are dichotomous, the method of estimation is ordinary least squares. Preliminary investigation revealed almost no differences between ordinary least squares estimates and dichotomous logit estimates. Given the size of our sample and the minimal improvement in the accuracy of the estimates, we decided to rely on OLS estimation. When the dependent variable is dichotomous, the estimated equation can be interpreted as a linear probability function.

3.1. Causal Priorness

In order to address the issue of the direction of causality between health and cognitive development, we present in table 4.2 an 8×8 matrix of lagged coefficients from the eight equations. The off-diagonal elements of the matrix provide information with regard to mutual feedback between health and cognitive development, mutual feedback between various health conditions, and mutual feedback between IQ (WISC) and achievement (WRAT). The elements on the main diagonal of the matrix are the own-lagged effects, or the regression coefficients of the lagged dependent variable.

We begin by looking at the own-lagged effects. The size of the own-lagged coefficients is an indication of the persistence of each health condition. For

Table 4.2 Regression Coefficients of Lagged Health and Lagged Cognitive Development

Current \ Lagged	WISC1	WRAT1	APERI1	ABN1	HDBP1	PFGHEALTH1	OBESE1	SCHABS1
WISC2	.603 (27.35)	.231 (9.47)	-.164 (-0.54)	-1.619 (-2.15)	-1.791 (-1.82)	.388 (0.84)	.946 (1.33)	-.650 (-0.53)
WRAT2	.192 (9.79)	.728 (33.52)	-.073 (-0.27)	-.204 (-0.30)	-.740 (-0.85)	-.341 (-0.82)	.421 (0.66)	-.699 (-0.64)
APERI2	-.004 (-2.25)	-.005 (-2.35)	.340 (12.16)	-.005 (-0.07)	-.195 (-2.15)	.039 (0.90)	.114 (1.73)	.146 (1.28)
ABN2	-.001 (0.98)	-.002 (-2.00)	.020 (1.41)	.146 (4.16)	.042 (0.91)	.001 (0.03)	.049 (1.47)	.064 (1.11)
HDBP2	-.001 (-1.11)	-.0003 (-0.51)	-.003 (-0.41)	.030 (1.47)	.169 (6.38)	-.010 (-0.78)	.096 (4.97)	.033 (1.00)
PFGHEALTH2	-.001 (-0.92)	-.003 (-2.76)	.019 (1.22)	.139 (0.37)	.043 (0.86)	.243 (10.43)	.019 (0.52)	.096 (1.54)
OBESE2	.0001 (0.08)	-.001 (-1.45)	-.014 (-1.60)	-.020 (-0.91)	.013 (0.43)	-.016 (-1.15)	.512 (24.28)	.007 (0.18)
SCHABS2	.0002 (0.34)	-.001 (-1.78)	.004 (0.49)	.011 (0.49)	.009 (0.34)	.045 (3.45)	.020 (1.03)	.159 (4.60)

Source: Data from the Health Examination Survey, Cycles II and III.

Note: t-ratios are in parentheses. The critical t-ratios at the 5 percent level of significance are 1.64 for a one-tailed test and 1.96 for a two-tailed test.

example, if the coefficient of the lagged dependent variable is close to one, this signifies that the health condition (or the stochastic process governing the occurrence of that condition) has a relatively low frequency and is slow to change. Coefficients close to zero indicate a higher frequency process. For slowly changing conditions one would expect to find that other explanatory variables (besides the lagged dependent variable) will not have such large effects as they would for conditions that are more readily altered. When the dependent variable is dichotomous, the own-lagged coefficient can be directly interpreted as the degree of persistence in the particular aspect of health in question: in this case the lagged coefficient is the difference between the expected conditional probability of an adolescent health condition, given that the same condition was present in childhood, and the conditional probability given that the condition was absent in childhood. Each of the eight own-lagged effects is positive and statistically significant at all conventional levels of confidence.[11] The coefficients range from a high of .73 in the case of WRAT to a low of .15 in the case of ABN.[12] Among the dichotomous variables, obesity is the most persistent: obese children have approximately 50 percentage point higher probabilities of being obese adolescents than do non-obese children.

The cross-lagged effects, however, appearing off the diagonal in table 4.2, are the primary focus of this chapter. From these coefficients, it appears that causality runs more strongly from cognitive development to health than vice versa. When the two cognitive development measures are the dependent variables, only two of the six health measures (ABN1 and HDBP1) have significant impacts on WISC2; and none have significant impacts on WRAT2 (the latter statement holds whether the statistical test is done on each health variable separately or on the set of six). In the two cases where there is a significant impact, the effect is as expected, with poorer health being associated with lower values of WISC2. When the health measures are the dependent variables, one or both of the cognitive development measures have significant impacts for four of the six health measures: APERI2, ABN2, SCHABS2, and PFGHEALTH2 (these results hold whether the statistical test is done on WISC1 and WRAT1 separately or together). In all four cases, higher levels of WISC1 or WRAT1 are associated with better health. To conclude, while these off-diagonal elements affirm a two-way relationship between health and cognitive development, the link from cognitive development to health appears to be the stronger one.

Several other interesting relationships are evident in table 4.2. There is evidence of mutual feedbacks between IQ and achievement: childhood achievement has a significant impact on adolescent IQ even when childhood IQ is held constant; and childhood IQ has a significant impact on adolescent achievement when childhood achievement is held constant. There are also dependencies between some of the health measures: obesity in childhood is related to poorer oral health and high blood pressure in adolescence,[13] and a parental rating of health in childhood as poor, fair, or good (as opposed to very good) is associated with excessive school absence due to illness in adolescence. Finally, there is one seemingly "perverse" and statistically significant relationship in the table: high blood pressure in childhood is associated with better oral health in adolescence, although this may be due to excessive consumption of dairy products.

3.2. Family Background Effects

A secondary objective of this chapter is to obtain better estimates of the impacts of environmental factors on health and cognitive development. The three environmental measures we focus on are mother's schooling (MEDUCAT), father's schooling (FEDUCAT), and family income (FINC).

Coefficients of these three variables in the adolescent health and cognitive development functions are shown in table 4.3. Two types of estimates are reported. Those in the first three columns, labeled cross-sectional coefficients, are taken from multiple regressions that control for all of the family and youth characteristics listed in Appendix 1 but *exclude* all lagged (childhood) cognitive development and health measures. The estimates in the last three columns, labeled "dynamic" coefficients, are taken from multiple regressions that *include* all lagged cognitive development and health measures in addition to the family and youth characteristics. The first set of estimates shows background effects as typically computed in a cross-section. The second set shows background effects estimated in a dynamic context which controls for initial levels of cognitive development and health. As we argued in the first section, the "dynamic" estimates are free of genetic bias if genetic effects are fully embodied in the early health and cognitive development measures.[14] Under this assumption, then, the "dynamic" coefficients represent the pure contribution of the home environment to cognitive development and health outcomes in the interval between Cycles II and III.

Let us consider first the impacts of the three family background variables on cognitive development. In the cross-section estimates, all six family background coefficients are positive and statistically significant, and they tend to remain significant when the lagged variables are included. The magnitudes of the "dynamic" family background effects are, however, much smaller than the magnitudes of the cross-sectional effects. To be precise, the ratios of "dynamic" coefficients to the corresponding cross-sectional coefficients range from .15 in the case of mother's schooling in the WISC2 equation to .47 in the case of family income in the same equation.

Table 4.3 Regression Coefficients of Parent's Schooling and Family Income

Dependent Variable / Independent Variable	Cross-Section Coefficients			Dynamic Coefficients		
	MEDUCAT	FEDUCAT	FINC	MEDUCAT	FEDUCAT	FINC
WISC2	.986 (6.19)	.904 (6.80)	.288 (3.33)	.146 (1.32)	.207 (2.24)	.135 (2.27)
WRAT2	.942 (6.03)	.805 (6.18)	.271 (3.20)	.177 (1.79)	.136 (1.65)	.103 (1.94)
APERI2	−.039 (−3.67)	−.019 (−2.17)	0.005 (−0.91)	−.023 (−2.25)	−.006 (−0.75)	.0001 (0.00)
ABN2	−.002 (−0.36)	−.005 (−1.26)	.004 (1.60)	.003 (0.51)	−.003 (−0.65)	.005 (1.83)
HDBP2	−.005 (−1.84)	.002 (0.66)	−.001 (−0.33)	−.003 (−0.89)	.003 (1.07)	−.001 (−0.53)
PFGHEALTH2	−.015 (−2.71)	−.012 (−2.47)	−.007 (−2.21)	−.009 (−1.69)	−.006 (−1.23)	−.001 (−0.47)
OBESE2	−.012 (−3.19)	.00002 (0.00)	.001 (0.55)	−.005 (−1.42)	.001 (0.53)	.0004 (0.21)
SCHABS2	−.010 (−3.11)	.003 (1.09)	−.002 (−1.32)	−.008 (−2.46)	.004 (1.35)	−.001 (−0.66)

Source: Data from the Health Examination Survey, Cycles II and III.

Note: t-ratios are in parentheses. The critical t-ratios at the 5 percent level of significance are 1.64 for a one-tailed test and 1.96 for a two-tailed test. The cross-sectional coefficients are taken from multiple regressions that contain all family and youth characteristics. The dynamic coefficients are taken from multiple regressions that contain all variables.

In the case of adolescent health, the difference between cross-section and dynamic family background estimates is less dramatic. First, fewer of the cross-section estimates themselves show significant impacts: only mother's educational attainment is a consistently important variable (except when ABN2 is the dependent variable). Father's educational attainment has significant positive health impacts for the periodontal index and the subjective health rating, and family income is significant in determining only the subjective health rating. All of the statistically significant background effects are reduced in absolute value when childhood health and cognitive development are included in the equations. The ratios of the "dynamic" coefficients to the corresponding cross-sectional coefficients range from .14 in the case of family income in the PFG-HEALTH2 equation to .80 in the case of mother's schooling in the SCHABS2 equation. Moreover, there are only three statistically significant dynamic coefficients: those belonging to mother's schooling in the APERI2, PFGHEALTH2, and SCHABS2 equations.

A clear message in table 4.3 is that the "dynamic" estimates of family background effects on cognitive development and health are much smaller than the corresponding cross-sectional estimates. The important point here, however, is not that the "dynamic" estimates of background effects are smaller than the cross-sectional estimates. This decline is to be expected if our procedure does in fact remove many of the genetic effects otherwise embodied in the family background variables.[15] The main point, rather, is that after removing the genetic component from the family background variables, family background—especially mother's education—remains an important determinant of cognitive development and of some aspects of health. This finding is strong evidence that the family environment plays an important role in the overall development of adolescents.

An interesting sidelight to the discussion of family background effects is found in a comparison of the results for cognitive development versus health. First, regardless of which set of estimates is used, family background variables as a group are less likely to have significant impacts on adolescent health than on adolescent cognitive development. Second, according to the "dynamic" estimates, either one year of additional educational attainment for either parent or one thousand additional dollars of family income are associated with roughly the same increase in WISC2 or WRAT2. For the health measures, however, the "dynamic" estimates show that mother's educational attainment tends to have a larger impact than the other variables, and it is frequently the only statistically significant background variable. Taken together, these points suggest that there is more "home production" of health than of cognitive development—at least in the period between childhood and adolescence.

4. SUMMARY AND IMPLICATIONS

Our exploration of the dynamic relationship between health and cognitive development in adolescence has generated two important results. First, there is feedback both from health to cognitive development and from cognitive development to health, but the latter of these relationships is stronger. Second, estimates of family background effects taken from the dynamic model, which can be assumed to be less influenced by genetic factors–, smaller than their cross-sectional counterparts, but some still remain statistically significant.

The first finding calls attention to the existence of a continuing interaction between health and cognitive development over the life cycle. Since an individual's cognitive development (measured by IQ or achievement tests) is an important determinant of the number of years of formal schooling that he ultimately completes (see Grossman, 1975), our findings may be viewed as the early forerunner of the positive impact of schooling on good health for adults in the United States reported by Grossman (1975), Shakotko (1977), and others.

The second finding suggests that nurture "matters" in cognitive development and health outcomes. All three background variables are important contributors to cognitive development, but mother's schooling is singled out as the crucial component of the home environment in adolescent health outcomes. This is an especially strong result because, in the words of Keniston and the Carnegie Council on Children, "Doctors do not provide the bulk of health care for children; families do" (1977, 179). Since the mother typically spends more time in household production than the father, her characteristics should be the dominant factor in outcomes that are determined to a large extent in the home. The importance of mother's schooling in obesity and oral health is notable because these are outcomes that are neither irreversible or self-limiting. Instead, they can be modified by inputs of dental care, medical care, proper diet, and parents' time.

The two findings interact with each other. Cognitive development in childhood has a positive effect on health in adolescence, and cognitive development in childhood is positively related to parents' schooling and family income. Both findings imply that the health of adults is heavily dependent upon their home environment as youths. They also imply that public policies aimed at children's and adolescents' health must try to offset the problems encountered by offspring of mothers with low levels of schooling. In particular, they should try to improve the skills of uneducated mothers in their capacity as the main providers of health care for their offspring.

Appendix 1

FAMILY AND YOUTH CHARACTERISTICS

Variable Name	Sample[a] Mean	Sample Standard Deviation	Definition[b]
FEDUCAT[c]	11.310	3.355	Years of formal schooling completed by father
MEDUCAT	11.216	2.704	Years of formal schooling completed by mother
FINC	8.060	4.607	Continuous family income (in thousands of dollars) computed by assigning mid-points to the following closed income intervals, $250 to the lowest interval, and $20,000 to the highest interval. The closed income classes are:
			$500 – $999
			$1,000 – $1,999
			$2,000 – $2,999
			$3,000 – $3,999
			$4,000 – $4,999
			$5,000 – $6,999
			$7,000 – $9,999
			$10,000 – $14,999
LESS20	3.700	1.813	Number of persons in the household twenty years of age or less
MWORKFT	.149	.356	Dummy variables that equal one if the mother
MWORKPT	.149	.356	works full-time or part-time, respectively; omitted class is mother does not work
NEAST	.265	.442	Dummy variables that equal one if youth lives
MWEST	.315	.465	in Northeast, Midwest, or South, respectively;
SOUTH	.203	.402	omitted class is residence in West
URB1	.189	.392	Dummy variables that equal one if youth lives in
URB2	.126	.331	an urban area with a population of 3 million or
URB3	.200	.400	more (URB1); in an urban area with a population
NURB	.140	.347	between 1 million and 3 million (URB2); in an urban area with a population fewer than 1 million (URB3); or in a non-rural and non-urbanized area (NURB); omitted class is residence in a rural area
LIGHTA	.008	.091	Dummy variable that equals one if youth's birth weight was under 2,000 grams (under 4.4 pounds) (Source: 2)

Appendix 1 (*Continued*)

Variable Name	Sample[a] Mean	Sample Standard Deviation	Definition[b]
LIGHTB	.054	.227	Dummy variable that equals one if youth's birth weight was equal to or greater than 2,000 grams but under 2,500 grams (under 5.5 pounds) (Source: 2)
BWUK	.138	.345	Dummy variable that equals one if youth's birth weight is unknown (Source: 2)
FYPH	.068	.252	Dummy variable that equals one if parental assessment of child's health at one year was poor or fair and zero if it was good
BFED	.302	.459	Dummy variable that equals one if the child was breast fed
LMAG	.057	.231	Dummy variable that equals one if the mother was less than 20 years old at birth of youth
HMAG	.119	.324	Dummy variable that equals one if mother was more than 35 years old at birth of youth
NOFATH	.047	.213	Dummy variable that equals one if youth lives with mother only
FIRST	.292	.455	Dummy variable that equals one if youth is the first-born child in the family
TWIN	.028	.165	Dummy variable that equals one if youth is a twin
FLANG	.110	.312	Dummy variable that equals one if a foreign language is spoken in the home
MALE	.522	.500	Dummy variable that equals one if youth is a male
AGE	9.712	1.042	Age of youth
INTERVAL	42.327	6.404	Number of months between the physical examinations given for the Cycle II survey and the Cycle III survey (Source: 3)

Source: Health Examination Survey, Cycles II and III.

Note: All family and youth characteristics are from Cycle II unless otherwise stated.

[a]The means and standard deviations are for the sample of 1,434 white youths described in the text.

[b]Source for all is 1, parents, unless otherwise indicated; 2 = birth certificate; 3 = physical examination.

[c]For youths who were not currently living with their father, father's education was coded at the mean of the sample for which father's education was reported.

NOTES

Originally published as Robert A. Shakotko, Linda N. Edwards, and Michael Grossman, "An Exploration of the Dynamic Relationship between Health and Cognitive Development in Adolescence," in *Contributions to Economic Analysis: Health, Economics, and Health Economics*, ed. Jacques van der Gaag and Mark Perlman (Amsterdam: North-Holland Publishing, 1981), 305–328. Research for this chapter was supported by grants from the Ford Foundation, the Robert Wood Johnson Foundation, and the National Center for Health Services Research (PHS Grant No. 1 R01 HS02917) to the National Bureau of Economic Research. We are indebted to Ann Colle for research assistance and to Anthony Cassese and Lee Lillard for their comments on an earlier draft. This is a revision of a chapter presented at the fifty-fourth annual conference of the Western Economic Association, Las Vegas, Nevada, June 1979.

1. This is a reduced form equation derived by solving a system of equations that include a family utility function (with the health and development of each child in each period as arguments), a children's health production function, a production function for children's cognitive development, and a wealth constraint. Note that at any point in time, t, both $y_{i,t-1}$ and $x_{i,t-1}$ are predetermined variables.

2. A detailed discussion of the types of variables included in $x_{i,t}$ can be found in Edwards and Grossman (1979 and 1980).

3. One technique that has been used in cross-sectional analysis is to include indicators of the unobserved variable. These indicators, which are not themselves part of the original cross-section specification, are taken to be instruments for the unobserved variable. An example is the inclusion of test scores as a proxy for ability in earnings equations. Investigators generally acknowledge that this is a second-best procedure because it introduces an errors-in-variables bias which may be nearly as large as the original omitted-variables bias (Griliches, 1974).

4. See Shakotko (1979) for an alternative model formulated in the spirit of the ability-bias problem as described, for example, by Griliches (1977). While relaxing the restrictive assumption in the present chapter regarding genetic embodiment, Shakotko requires an alternative set of restrictions in order to identify and estimate a factor structure.

5. Since H_1 is correlated with the error term in equation (2c), the coefficient of Q_1 in this equation is biased unless the partial correlation between Q_1 and H_1 with E held constant is zero. This is extremely unlikely because GQ and GH are bound to be related, probably in a positive manner. The same comment applies to the coefficient of H_1 in equation (3c). Note that if the partial correlation between E and H_1 or between E and Q_1 is non-zero, ordinary least squares estimates of the reduced form environmental parameters, given by the coefficients of E in equation (2c) or (3c), are biased.

6. We did not, however, exclude observations from the analysis if data were missing for the school absenteeism variables (SCHABS1, SCHABS2) and birth-weight variables (LIGHTA, LIGHTB). Information on school absenteeism is taken from the school form completed by the child's school. This form is missing for roughly 7 percent of the sample. Since excessive absence due to illness is the only variable taken from this form, a

dummy variable that identifies youths with missing Cycle II school forms (SCHABSUKI) is included in all regression equations as an independent variable. Youths without a Cycle III school form are eliminated from the empirical analysis *only* when SCHABS2 is the dependent variable. Birth weight is taken from the child's birth certificate, which is missing for 14 percent of the sample. Since birth weight is the only variable taken from the birth certificate, we do not delete these observations, but rather we include a dummy variable that identifies youths with missing birth certificates (BWUK) in the regression equations.

7. Although these and other test scores have been widely criticized, they are used here and elsewhere because they are so readily obtainable and because they are roughly comparable across diverse populations. WISC and WRAT are adjusted for sex as well as for age in some studies, but the variables used here are *not* sex-adjusted.

8. Kelly and Sanchez (1972, 1–2) describe the periodontal index as follows:

Every tooth in the mouth . . . is scored according to the presence or absence of manifest signs of periodontal disease. When a portion of the free gingiva is inflamed, a score of 1 is recorded. When completely circumscribed by inflammation, teeth are scored 2. Teeth with frank periodontal pockets are scored 6 when their masticatory function is unimpaired and 8 when it is impaired. The arithmetic average of all scores is the individual's [periodontal index], which ranges from a low of 0.0 [no inflammation or periodontal pockets] to a high of 8.0 [all teeth with pockets and impaired function].

9. The choice of appropriate measures of health in childhood and adolescence is discussed in detail in Edwards and Grossman (1979, 1980, and 1983).

10. The periodontal index and the two cognitive development measures are continuous variables. In these cases we have experimented with the raw score as the dependent variable in a multiple regression that includes in the set of explanatory variables age in Cycle II, the square of age, the time interval between the Cycle II and III examinations, the square of the interval, the product of age and the interval, and a dummy variable for male adolescents. The results obtained (not shown) with respect to family background, lagged health, and lagged cognitive development effects are similar to those reported in the third section.

11. Statements concerning statistical significance in the text refer to the 5 percent level in a one-tailed test, except when the direction of the effect is unclear on a priori grounds or when the estimated effect has the "wrong sign." In the latter cases two-tailed tests are used.

12. If the dynamic processes that we study have the same structures over time and if cross-lagged effects are ignored, they all have stable long-run solutions. To be specific, if $H_t = aH_{t-1} + bE$, the long-run solution, obtained by setting $H_t = H_{t-1}$, is $H_t = (b/1-a) E$. This is a stable solution when a is positive and smaller than one.

13. This finding is consistent with cross-sectional results reported by the National Heart, Lung, and Blood Institute's Task Force (1977). The Task Force points out that obesity is a risk factor in the incidence of high blood pressure in adolescents.

14. Some evidence supporting the validity of this assumption appears in the regression results. In particular, the coefficients of birth weight, mother's age at the birth of the youth, and parental assessment of the youth's health in the first year of his life are almost

never statistically significant. These variables are proxy measures of the genetic endowment. If they had had large significant impacts in the dynamic equations, this would have thrown into question the validity of our assumption.

15. Even if the family background variables had no genetic components, we would still expect the "dynamic" coefficients to be smaller than the cross-sectional coefficients, because the "dynamic" estimates represent short-run effects in the sense that they hold constant the lagged values of health and cognitive development. Since these lagged values themselves depend on family background, the cumulative or long-run impacts of family background are likely to exceed the "dynamic" or short-run impacts. To be precise, if cross-lagged effects are ignored, a full representation of the dynamic health process that we study is (ignoring stochastic terms):

$$H_1 = \alpha GH + b_1 \, E, \text{. and}$$
$$H_t = a_t H_{t-1} + b_t E, t = 2, ..., n.$$

Solving recursively, one obtains

$$H_t = \left[\alpha \prod_{i=1}^{t} a_i \right] GH + \left[b_t + \sum_{i=1}^{t-1} b_i \prod_{j=t-1}^{i} a_j \right] E.$$

The parameter of E in the above equation is the cumulative environmental effect. If the b_i all have the same sign, the long-run parameter unambiguously exceeds b_t in absolute value. Of course, the long-run parameter estimate may be larger or smaller than the cross-sectional estimate if GH is omitted from the equation.

REFERENCES

Edwards, Linda N., and Michael Grossman. 1979. "The Relationship between Children's Health and Intellectual Development." In *Health: What is it Worth?*, ed. Selma Mushkin. Elmsford, New York: Pergamon Press, Inc.

——. 1980. "Children's Health and the Family." In Volume II of the *Annual Series of Research in Health Economics*, ed. Richard M. Scheffler. Greenwich, Connecticut: JAI Press.

——. 1983. "Adolescent Health, Family Background, and Preventive Medical Care." In Volume III of *Research in Human Capital and Development*, ed. Ismail Sirageldin, David Salkever, and Alan Sorkin. Greenwich, Connecticut: JAI Press, Inc.

Granger, C. W. J. 1969. "Investigating Causal Relations by Econometric Models and Cross-Spectral Methods." *Econometrica*, 37, No. 3.

Griliches, Zvi. 1974. "Errors in Variables and Other Unobservables." *Econometrica*, 42.

——. 1977. "Estimating the Returns to Schooling: Some Econometric Problems." *Econometrica*, 45, No. 1.

Grossman, Michael. 1975. "The Correlation Between Health and Schooling." In *Household Production and Consumption*, ed. Nestor E. Terleckyj. New York: Columbia University Press for the National Bureau of Economic Research.

Kelly, James E., and Marcus J. Sanchez. 1972. *Periodontal Disease and Oral Hygiene Among Children*. National Center for Health Statistics, U.S. Department of Health, Education and Welfare, Public Health Publication Series 11 - No. 117.

Keniston, Kenneth, and the Carnegie Council on Children. 1977. *All Our Children: The American Family under Pressure*. New York: Harcourt Brace Jovanovich.

National Center for Health Statistics. 1967a. *Plan, Operation, and Response Results of a Program of Children's Examinations*. U.S. Department of Health, Education, and Welfare, Public Health Service Publication No. 1000 - Series 1 - No. 5.

——. 1967b. *A Study of the Achievement Test Used in the Health Examination Survey of Persons Aged 6–17 Years*. U.S. Department of Health, Education, and Welfare, Public Health Service Publication No. 1000 - Series 2, No. 24.

——. 1969. *Plan and Operation of a Health Examination Survey of U.S. Youths 12–17 Years of Age*. U.S. Department of Health, Education, and Welfare, Public Health Service Publication No. 1000 - Series 1 - No. 8.

——. 1972. *Subtest Estimates of the WISC Full Scale IQ's for Children*. U.S. Department of Health, Education, and Welfare, Vital and Health Statistics - Series 2 -No. 47.

National Heart, Lung, and Blood Institute's Task Force on Blood Pressure Control in Children. 1977. "Report of the Task Force on Blood Pressure Control in Children." *Pediatrics*, 59, No. 5, Supplement.

Russell, A. L. 1956. "A System of Classification and Scoring for Prevalence Surveys of Periodontal Disease." *Journal of Dental Research*, 35.

Shakotko, Robert A. "Health and Economic Variables: An Empirical Investigation of the Dynamics." 1977. PhD dissertation, University of Minnesota.

——. 1979. "Dynamic Aspects of Children's Health, Intellectual Development, and Family Economic Status." Presented at a session sponsored by the American Economic Association and the Health Economics Research Organization at the annual meeting of the Allied Social Science Associations, Atlanta, Georgia, December.

Parental Education and Child Health

Evidence from a
Natural Experiment in Taiwan

Shin-Yi Chou, Jin-Tan Liu,
Michael Grossman, and Ted Joyce

FIVE

The one social factor that researchers agree is
consistently linked to longer lives in every country
where it has been studied is education. It is more
important than race; it obliterates any
effects of income.
—Gina Kolata, "A Surprising Secret to Long
Life: Stay in School," *New York Times*,
January 3, 2007

ABSTRACT

In 1968, the Taiwanese government extended compulsory education from six to nine years and opened over 150 new junior high schools at a differential rate among regions. Within each region, we exploit variations across cohorts in new junior high school openings to construct an instrument for schooling, and employ it to estimate the causal effects of mother's or father's schooling on infant birth outcomes in the years 1978–1999. Parents' schooling does cause favorable infant health outcomes. The increase in schooling associated with the reform saved almost 1 infant life in 1,000 live births.

This chapter is a contribution to the literature on the relationship between years of formal schooling completed and good health. In particular, we investigate whether the positive relationship between these two variables implies causality from the former to the latter. As the quotation from Kolata indicates, there is a large literature, reviewed in detail by Grossman and Robert Kaestner (1997) and Grossman (2000, 2006), that shows that an individual's own schooling is the most important correlate of his or her health, and that parents' schooling, especially mother's schooling, is the most important correlate of child health. This finding emerges whether health levels are measured by mortality rates, morbidity rates, self-evaluation of health status, or physiological indicators of health, and whether the units of observation are individuals or groups.

Improvements in child health are widely accepted public policy goals in developing and developed countries. The positive correlation between mother's schooling and child health in numerous studies was one factor behind the World Bank's campaign in the 1990s to encourage increases in maternal education in developing countries (World Bank 1993). In a 2002 issue of *Health Affairs* devoted primarily to the nonmedical determinants of health, Angus Deaton (2002) argues that policies to increase education in the United States, and to increase income in developing countries, are very likely to have larger payoffs in terms of health than those that focus on health care, even if inequalities in health rise. The same proposition, with regard to the United States, can be found in a much earlier study by Richard Auster, Irving Leveson, and Deborah Sarachek (1969). Since more education typically leads to higher income, policies to increase the former appear to have large returns for more than one generation throughout the world.

Efforts to improve the health of an individual by increasing the amount of formal schooling that he or she acquires, or that try to improve child health by raising maternal schooling, assume that the schooling effects reported in the literature are causal. A number of investigators have argued, however, that reverse causality from health to schooling, or omitted "third variables," may cause schooling and health to vary in the same direction. Governments can employ a variety of policies to raise the educational levels of their citizens. These include compulsory schooling laws, new school construction, and targeted subsidies to parents and students. If proponents of the third-variable hypothesis are correct, or if health causes schooling, evaluations of these policies should not be based on studies that relate adult health or child health to actual measures of schooling because these measures may be correlated with unmeasured determinants of the outcomes at issue.

In this chapter, we propose to use techniques that correct for biases due to the endogeneity of schooling to evaluate the effects of a policy initiative that radically altered the school system in Taiwan, and led to an increase in the amount of formal schooling acquired by the citizens of that country during a period of very rapid economic growth. In 1968, Taiwan extended compulsory schooling from six years to nine years. In the period 1968–1973, many new junior high schools were opened at a differential rate among regions of the country. We form treatment and control groups of women or men who, in

1968, were age twelve or younger on the one hand, and between the ages of thirteen and twenty or twenty-five on the other hand. Within each region, we exploit variations across cohorts in new junior high school openings to construct an instrument for schooling. We employ this instrument to estimate the causal effects of mother's or father's schooling on the incidence of low birthweight and mortality of infants born to women in the treatment and control groups, or the wives of men in these groups in the period 1978–1999.

The chapter proceeds as follows. Section 1 outlines a conceptual framework, followed by a review of the related literature. Section 2 provides some background on education reform in 1968 in Taiwan. Section 3 indicates how we exploit aspects of the reform to construct instruments for parents' schooling, presents estimates of the effects of the instrument on schooling, and discusses the specification of infant health outcome equations. Section 4 contains reduced form and structural estimates of these equations, and section 5 concludes.

1. ANALYTICAL FRAMEWORK AND REVIEW OF LITERATURE

Models that generate two-way causality between schooling and good health, and introduce third-variables that cause both outcomes to vary in the same direction, are discussed in detail by Grossman (2006). Consequently, they will be outlined briefly here. Causality from own schooling to own health, or from parents' schooling to child health, results when the more educated are more efficient producers of these outcomes, or when education changes tastes a manner that leads the more educated to allocate more resources toward health and away from other items in their utility function. The efficiency effect can take two forms. Productive efficiency pertains to a situation in which the more educated obtain a larger health output from given amounts of endogenous (choice) inputs. Allocative efficiency pertains to a situation in which schooling increases information about the true effects of the inputs on health. For example, the more educated may have more knowledge about the harmful effects of cigarette smoking or about what constitutes an appropriate diet.

Endogenous taste models also generate causality from schooling to health. For example, Gary S. Becker and Casey B. Mulligan (1997) show that the more educated have greater incentives to make investments that make them or their children more future oriented. The resulting reduction in the rate of time preference for the present raises optimal investment in health.

Now consider causality from health to schooling. In the case of these outcomes for the same person, healthier individuals have longer life expectancies, and greater payoffs to schooling investments, since the number of periods over which returns accrue is larger. Moreover, students in poor health are almost certain to miss more days of school due to illness than their healthy peers, and may also learn less while in school. Both factors suggest negative effects of poor health in childhood on school achievement and ultimately on years of formal schooling completed. In the case of child health, parents who demand higher levels of this outcome may obtain more schooling because it is a mechanism to achieve this goal.

Since health and schooling are endogenous, unobserved third variables may cause both of these outcomes to vary in the same direction. The third-variable hypothesis has received the most attention in the literature because it is related to the hypothesis that the positive effect of schooling on earnings, explored in detail by Jacob A. Mincer (1974), and in hundreds of studies since his seminal work (see David Card 1999, 2001 for reviews of these studies), is biased upward by the omission of ability. For example, Victor R. Fuchs (1982) identifies time preference as the third variable. He argues that persons who are more future oriented (who have a high degree of time preference for the future or discount it at a modest rate) attend school for longer periods of time, and make larger investments in their own health and in the health of their children. Thus, the effects of schooling on these outcomes are biased if one fails to control for time preference.

The forces just discussed can be summarized in the following two-equation structural model:

$$S = S(P_S, H, U) \tag{1}$$

$$H = H(P_H, S, U). \tag{2}$$

Here, S and H are positive correlates of completed schooling and health, P_S is the price of schooling (or the prices of a vector of schooling inputs), P_H is the price of health (or the prices of a vector of health inputs), and U is an unobserved third variable. The prices are uncorrelated with U. Solving equations (1) and (2) simultaneously, one obtains the reduced form schooling equation and health equations:

$$S = S(P_S, P_H, U) \tag{3}$$

$$H = H(P_S, P_H, U). \tag{4}$$

Our aim is to estimate equations (2), (3), and (4). We have no direct measures of the prices of health inputs, and assume either they are not correlated with P_S, or that they are captured by county and year indicators (see section 3 for more details). The application of ordinary least squares to equation (2) produces inconsistent coefficient estimates if S and U are correlated. Hence, we employ the program intensity variable described in sections 2 and 3 (a measure of P_S) as an instrument for schooling in a two-stage least squares estimation of equation (2).[1]

Our research strategy is related to that in a growing literature that employs instrumental variables (IV) techniques to estimate the causal impact of schooling on health. The earliest studies to employ these techniques are by Mark C. Berger and J. Paul Leigh (1989), William Sander (1995a, 1995b), and Leigh and Rachna Dhir (1997). All four studies employ U.S. data and pertain to adults. In almost all cases, the IV coefficients are at least as large, in absolute value, as the ordinary least squares coefficients. These findings point to causal impacts of schooling on health. This conclusion should be interpreted with caution because some of the instruments employed (parents' schooling, parents' income, and cognitive test scores) may be correlated with omitted third variables.

Very recent work by Adriana Lleras-Muney (2005); Scott J. Adams (2002); Jacob Nielsen Arendt (2005, 2008); Jasmina Spasojevic (2003); Philip Oreopoulos (2006); Damien de Walque (2007); Franque Grimard and Daniel Parent (2007); Piero Cipollone, Debora Radicchia, and Alfonso Rosolia (2007); Jeremy Arkes (2004); Donald Kenkel, Dean Lillard, and Alan Mathios (2006); Mary A. Silles (2009); Valerie Albouy and Laurent Lequien (2009); and Hans van Kippersluis, Owen O'Donnell, and Eddy van Doorslaer (2009) address the schooling-health relationship by using compulsory education laws, exemption from military service, unemployment rates during a person's teenage years, and requirements for high school completion and for the receipt of a General Educational Development High School Equivalency Diploma (GED) to obtain consistent estimates of the effect of schooling on adult health or on cigarette smoking (a key determinant of many adverse health outcomes). These variables, some of which result from quasi-natural experiments, are assumed to be correlated with schooling but uncorrelated with time preference and other third variables. Hence, they serve as instruments for schooling in the estimation of health equations by two-stage least squares and its variants. These fourteen second-generation studies improve on the four first-generation studies by employing instruments that are more likely to be uncorrelated with omitted third variables. Like the earlier studies, however, they conclude that the IV effects of schooling on health are at least as large as the ordinary least squares (OLS) effects.[2]

The IV studies just reviewed examine the effects of the amount of schooling an individual has completed on his or her health as an adult. There are only five corresponding IV studies that consider the effects of parents' schooling on child health or on the complementary outcome of fertility. Janet Currie and Enrico Moretti (2003) examine the relationship between maternal education and birthweight among U.S. white women with data from individual birth certificates from the Vital Statistics Natality files for 1970 to 2000. They use information on college openings between 1940 and 1990 to construct an availability measure of college in a woman's seventeenth year as an instrument for schooling. They find that the negative effect of maternal schooling on the incidence of low birthweight increases in absolute value when it is estimated by instrumental variables. They also find that the negative IV coefficient of maternal schooling in an equation for the probability of smoking during pregnancy exceeds the corresponding OLS coefficient in absolute value. Since it is well known that prenatal smoking is the most important modifiable risk factor for poor pregnancy outcomes in the United States, they identify a very plausible mechanism via which more schooling causes better birth outcomes. Their results suggest that the increase in maternal education between the 1950s and the 1980s accounts for 12 percent of the 6 percentage point decline in the incidence of low birthweight in that period.

Lucia Breierova and Esther Duflo (2004) capitalize on a primary school construction program in Indonesia between 1973–1974 and 1978–1979. In that period, 61,000 primary schools were constructed. Program intensity, measured by the total number of new schools constructed as of 1978–1979, per primary school age child in 1971, varied considerably across the country's 281 districts. In a study of the effects of schooling on earnings, Duflo (2000, 2001) shows that average educational attainment rose more rapidly in districts where program intensity was greater. She also argues that the program had a bigger effect for children who entered school later in the 1970s, and no effect for children who entered school before 1974. Therefore, she uses the interaction between year of birth and program intensity as an instrument for schooling in male wage functions in the 1995 intercensal survey of Indonesia. These functions are restricted to men who were between the ages of 2 and 24 in 1974. The instrument in question turns out to be an excellent predictor of schooling.

Breierova and Duflo (2004) use the instrument just described to estimate the effects of mother's and father's education on child mortality in the same survey employed by Duflo. They employ fertility and infant mortality histories of approximately 120,000 women between the ages of 23 and 50 in 1995. They find that mother's and father's schooling have about the same negative effects on infant mortality. Some, but not all, of the IV coefficients exceed the corresponding OLS coefficients. The authors treat their results as very preliminary.

Justin McCrary and Heather Royer (2006) use age-at-school entry policies to identify the effect of mother's schooling on the probability of a low-birthweight birth and the probability of an infant death for all births in Texas in the years 1989–2001, and on the probability of a low-birthweight birth for all births in California in 1989–2002. When combined with the effects of compulsory schooling laws on education and school entry age laws suggest that some children born one day after the school entry cutoff will obtain less schooling than comparable children born one day earlier. McCrary and Royer observe this effect for maternal education. They find little evidence, however, that the laws affect infant health outcomes either in the reduced form or in two-stage least squares (TSLS) with the law combined with the mother's exact date of birth used to form an instrument for schooling. They caution that their results may be heavily influenced by the experience of women from low socio-economic backgrounds, since other researchers have shown that the parents of these women are more likely to comply with school entry policies.

Maarten Lindeboom, Ana Llena-Nozal, and Bas van der Klaauw (2009) use compulsory school reform in 1947 in the United Kingdom, which raised the minimum age for leaving school from fourteen to fifteen years old, to assess the causal impact of parents' schooling on child health in the National Child Development Study. This is a panel of 17,000 babies born in Great Britain in the first week of March 1958. The authors consider a variety of health measures at birth and at ages seven, eleven, and sixteen, and include both mother's and father's schooling in most models. Like McCrary and Royer (2006), they find little evidence that schooling has beneficial effects on child health in the instrumental variable estimates, even when mother's schooling or father's schooling is omitted as a regressor.

Una Okonkwo Osili and Bridget Terry Long (2008) examine the effects of female schooling on fertility in Nigeria. In 1976, Nigeria introduced a nation-wide program that provided tuition-free primary education and increased the number of primary school classrooms at a differential rate among the nineteen states of Nigeria. Following Duflo (2001) and Breierova and Duflo (2004), Osili and Long (2008) employ the interaction between year of birth and program intensity, measured by the per capita amount of federal funds given to each state for classroom construction, as an instrument for mother's schooling, in an equation in which the number of births before age twenty-five in the 1999 Nigerian Demographic Health Survey is the dependent variable. Their TSLS estimate of the effect of mother's schooling on this outcome is negative and four times larger in absolute value than the OLS estimate. This is relevant to child health because the quantity-quality substitution model developed by Becker and H. Gregg Lewis (1973) predicts that the reduction in family size should be accompanied by an increase in health.

In summary, the majority of the studies reviewed conclude that schooling causes health and that the IV effects are at least as large as the TSLS effects. Only five of these studies, however, deal with children's health, and only the ones by Breierova and Duflo (2004) and Osili and Long (2008) deal with developing countries. Of course, there is a large literature, summarized by John Strauss and Duncan Thomas (1995), Grossman and Kaestner (1997), and Grossman (2006), that reports positive relationships between parents' schooling and child health in developing countries. The study by Yuyu Chen and Hongbin Li (2009), which considers the effect of mother's schooling on the health of adopted children in China, is a very recent example of this literature. Using height-for-age as the measure of health, they find that the positive effect of mother's schooling on this outcome in the adoptee sample is similar to that in the own birth sample, suggesting that it is not due to genetic factors. Like all previous studies in this literature, with the exception of the two mentioned above, Chen and Li do not employ instrumental variable techniques. Hence, they are careful to conclude that the evidence that the schooling effect is causal is tentative, especially since the sample of adoptees is relatively small.

2. 1968 EDUCATION REFORM IN TAIWAN

In 1968, the Taiwan government extended compulsory education from six to nine years, which required all school-age children (between six and fifteen years old) to attend elementary school for six year, and junior high school for three years. To accommodate the expected increase in enrollment in junior high schools, the government opened 150 new junior high schools, an increase of almost 50 percent, at the beginning of the school year 1968–1969 (September 1, 1968). This education reform created the largest expansion in junior high school construction and student enrollment in Taiwan's history (Diana E. Clark and Chang-Tai Hsieh 2000; Chris A. Spohr 2000, 2003; Wehn-Jyuan Tsai 2007a, 2007b; and the sources listed in table 5.1).

Primary school education in Taiwan was nearly universal by the mid-1960s, but approximately one-half of primary school graduates did not obtain additional education because enrollment in public junior high school was restricted by a competitive national examination, and by the limited number of junior high schools, especially in rural areas. The national examination was so difficult that parents had to enroll their primary school children in costly after-school tutoring classes if they wanted their children to be admitted to a nominally free public junior high school (Spohr 2003). There were a very small number of private junior high schools, but their tuition amounted to approximately 1 percent of per capita gross national product (Spohr 2003). The 1968 reform abolished the junior high school entrance examination and made it possible for all primary school graduates to continue their education. Children who had previously ended their education after primary school also were allowed to continue

Table 5.1 Cumulative Number of New Junior High School Openings per Thousand Children Aged 12–14, by School Year and County, 1968–1973

County	1968	1969	1970	1971	1972	1973
Taipei City	0.188	0.222	0.223	0.217	0.211	0.214
Taichung City	0.124	0.150	0.234	0.227	0.218	0.210
Keelung City	0.162	0.156	0.153	0.152	0.150	0.150
Tainan City	0.086	0.111	0.136	0.134	0.133	0.132
Kaohsiung City	0.018	0.052	0.081	0.078	0.075	0.101
Taipei County	0.135	0.186	0.189	0.254	0.214	0.204
Ilan County	0.062	0.153	0.211	0.240	0.265	0.266
Taoyuan County	0.100	0.134	0.130	0.144	0.191	0.182
Chaiyi County	0.070	0.125	0.167	0.168	0.183	0.200
Hsinchu County	0.045	0.133	0.154	0.174	0.193	0.190
Miaoli County	0.119	0.164	0.185	0.184	0.182	0.181
Taichung County	0.220	0.219	0.234	0.251	0.249	0.245
Nantou County	0.166	0.164	0.258	0.330	0.401	0.402
Changhua County	0.024	0.035	0.047	0.059	0.071	0.071
Yunlin County	0.106	0.106	0.152	0.169	0.200	0.200
Tainan County	0.229	0.228	0.228	0.228	0.255	0.257
Kaohsiung County	0.016	0.046	0.061	0.075	0.133	0.130
Pingtung County	0.195	0.193	0.222	0.221	0.220	0.219
Hualien County	0.385	0.410	0.408	0.408	0.408	0.408
Taitung County	0.424	0.540	0.578	0.579	0.578	0.578
Penghu County	0.529	0.516	0.708	0.803	0.904	0.911
Country as a whole	0.136	0.164	0.188	0.201	0.212	0.212

Sources: Ministry of Education, *Fourth Education Yearbook of the Republic of China*, 1974; and websites of selected schools for the number of new junior high schools, 1968–1972; the website of each individual school for 1973; and Directorate-General of Budgets, Accounts, and Statistics, Executive Yuan, *Statistical Abstract of the Republic of China*, 1983 for the population aged twelve to fourteen in 1968–1973.

Notes: Denominator pertains to children aged twelve to fourteen in a given year. The figure for the country as a whole is a weighted average of the figures for each county, where the set of weights is the county-specific number of children twelve to fourteen years old.

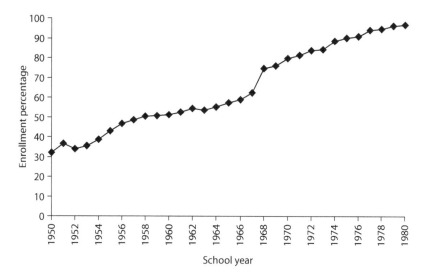

Figure 5.1 Percentage of primary school graduates entering junior high school

Note: Percentage of primary school graduates in June of school year $t - 1$ who entered junior high school in September of school year t.

Source: Directorate-General of Budgets, Accounts, and Statistics, Executive Yuan, *Statistical Abstract of the Republic of China*, 1983.

their education as long as they were under the age of fifteen in 1968, but were unlikely to do so as shown in section 3.

The sizable new junior high school openings in 1968 increased the number of these schools from 0.3 schools per 1,000 children aged twelve to fourteen in the school year 1967–1968 to 0.4 schools per thousand children aged twelve to fourteen in the school year 1968–1969 (see table 5.1 for sources).[3] The immediate impact was to increase the percentage of primary school graduates who entered junior high school from 62 percent in 1967, to 75 percent in 1968 (see figure 5.1). Spohr (2003) reports that there was no comparable jump in enrollment for senior high school or senior vocational school relative to underlying trends. He concludes that the large increase in junior high school enrollment in 1968 was due to the legislation rather than to other factors.

By 1973, an additional 104 public junior high schools had opened, increasing the total number of these schools from 311 in 1967 to 565 in 1973 (0.5 per thousand children aged twelve to fourteen). The junior high school entry percentage rose to 84 percent in the same year. Hence, the number of junior high schools almost doubled in a six-year period, the number per thousand children aged twelve to fourteen rose by almost 70 percent, and the junior high school entry percentage grew by 35 percent. After 1973, the government's six-year plan to implement the 1968 legislation ended. The growth in junior high schools slowed, with additional openings resulting mainly from population growth.

A notable aspect of the school construction program was that its intensity varied across regions of Taiwan. Table 5.1 contains the number of new junior high schools that opened in 1968 per thousand children between the ages of twelve and fourteen in that year in each of the twenty-one cities or counties of Taiwan.[4] The table also contains the cumulative number of new junior high schools in each of the years 1969–1973 per thousand children between the ages of twelve and fourteen in that year. In 1968, program intensity varied from 0.02 in Kaohsiung City and Kaohsiung County to 0.53 in Penghu County. By 1973, intensity varied from 0.07 in Changhua County to 0.91 in Penghu County.

Hence, the nine-year compulsory schooling legislation provides a "natural experiment" to evaluate the impact of parents' schooling on the health of their children. In particular, those over the age of twelve on September 1, 1968, when the school year began, were not affected by school reform, and constitute a control group. On the other hand, those twelve years of age and under on September 1, 1968, were very likely to have been affected by school reform, and constitute a treatment group.[5] Moreover, the effects of school reform on the number of years of formal schooling completed in the treatment group should be larger, the larger the program intensity measure is in city or county of birth. (Hereafter, the term county refers to city or county of birth.) We employ the products of cohort indicators and the program intensity measure in table 5.1 as instruments for schooling. Greater intensity among younger cohorts should lead to more schooling but should be uncorrelated with unmeasured determinants of the well-being of the offspring of these cohorts. We employ this instrument to estimate the causal effects of mother's or father's schooling on the incidence of low birthweight and mortality of infants born to women in the treatment and control groups, or the wives of men in these groups in the period 1978–1999.

We describe the instrument in more detail in section 3. Here, we want to point out that our methodology follows the one developed by Duflo (2001) to obtain an instrument for schooling in male wage earnings functions in Indonesia. As noted in section 1, her instrument is the product of cohort indicators and the per capita number of new primary schools constructed in each county in Indonesia in the period from 1973–1974 through 1978–1979. Breierova and Duflo (2004) use the same instrument to estimate the effects of mother's and father's schooling on self-reported infant mortality. Osili and Long (2008) adopt this identification strategy to obtain an instrument for mother's schooling in fertility equations in Nigeria. Clark and Hsieh (2000) apply Duflo's methodology to the 1968 school reform in Taiwan. They obtain an instrument similar to ours in their study of the impacts of schooling on male earnings in that country.

Spohr (2000, 2003) was the first economist to employ the 1968 school reform in Taiwan as an instrument for schooling in his study of the impacts of schooling on labor force participation and earnings of men and women.

Given the five studies just mentioned, our chapter, obviously, is not the first to use school reform in Taiwan and an identification strategy based on cohort-program intensity interactions. Our study does, however, have unique aspects. Unlike Spohr (2003), we exploit both reform and program intensity. Clark and Hsieh (2000) are forced to predict schooling based on county of current residence of males between the ages of 30 and 50 in the years 1990–1997, while we have information on county of birth. Based on our computations from the Taiwan Panel Survey of Family Dynamics, less than 10 percent of the population attended junior high school in a county that differed from their county of birth in the period after 1968. In contrast to Osili and Long (2008), we consider infant health rather than fertility. Unlike Breierova and Duflo (2004), we employ objective measures of infant health from birth certificates and from merging these certificates with infant death certificates. This is in contrast to Breierova and Duflo, who rely on women's reports of deaths of their infants. These reports are likely to contain errors.

3. EMPIRICAL IMPLEMENTATION

3.1. Data

Our data collection consists of all birth certificates and infant death certificates for the years 1978–1999. There were more than 300,000 births each year in Taiwan during this period. Birth and death certificates are linked through national identification numbers received by each person born in Taiwan. We consider the following outcomes from these data: the probability of a low-weight (less than 2,500 grams) birth, the probability of a neonatal death, the probability of a postneonatal death, and the probability of an infant death.

Low birthweight has extremely strong positive associations with infant morbidity and mortality. Neonatal deaths pertain to deaths within the first twenty-seven days of life, while postneonatal deaths pertain to deaths between the ages of twenty-eight days and 364 days. Infant deaths are the sum of those occurring in the neonatal and postneonatal periods. We distinguish between neonatal and postneonatal mortality because their causes are very different. Most neonatal deaths are caused by congenital anomalies, prematurity, and complications of delivery, while most postneonatal deaths are caused by infectious diseases and accidents. Infants who die within the first twenty-seven days of life are excluded when the probability of postneonatal death is the outcome.

In addition to birthweight, birth certificates contain the following information that is relevant for our research: infant's date of birth, mother's date of birth, mother's city or county of birth, father's date of birth, father's city or county of birth, mother's schooling, and father's schooling. Observations with missing values are deleted. Birthweights under 400 grams or over 6,500 grams are treated as missing. These cases are excluded when the probability of low birthweight is the outcome, but are included with the three other outcomes.[6]

When we estimate the effects of mother's schooling on infant health, we consider births to women who were between the ages of less than one and twenty in 1968 and between the ages of twenty-two and forty-five when they gave birth in the period 1978–1999. We do not include births to women under the age of twenty-two because we do not have birth certificates prior to 1978. The youngest women in the control group were thirteen in 1968 and twenty-three in 1978. When we estimate the effects of father's schooling on infant health, we consider births to the wives of husbands who were between the ages of less than one and twenty-five in 1968, and between the ages of twenty-two and fifty when their wives gave birth in the years 1978–1999.[7] Recall that age in 1968 pertains to age as of September 1. We select a wider age range for fathers than for mothers because husbands typically are older than their wives. Father's schooling and mother's schooling are too highly correlated to include both variables in the same regression, especially since the data are aggregated for reasons explained below.

We aggregate the data into mother's or father's county of birth, mother's or father's cohort in 1968, and child's year of birth cells. For mothers, there are 21 cells for their country of birth, 21 cells for their cohort (ages less than one to twenty in 1968), and 22 cells for their child's year of birth (1978–1999). This gives 9,702 potential cells, but 1,849 have no births. Hence, there are 7,853 observations in the regressions with mother's schooling. For fathers, there are 26 cohorts (ages less than one through twenty-five in 1968), resulting in 12,012 potential cells. Of these, 1,770 have no births, and there are 10,242 observations in the regressions with father's schooling.

We aggregate the data for several reasons. First, aside from parents' schooling, no individual-level variables are employed as regressors. Second, and more importantly, ordinary least squares estimates of the effects of schooling on the infant health outcomes that we consider are much bigger in absolute value in the aggregate data than they are in the individual data. In our view, the most compelling explanation of this result is that there is random measurement error in the schooling variables, which are obtained from parents. These errors are greatly reduced or eliminated in the aggregate data.

In the infant health outcome equations, variations in predicted schooling are based on an instrument that varies only at the county and cohort levels.

Hence, a comparison of the IV estimate of the effect of mother's or father's schooling on infant health to the corresponding OLS estimate obtained from the aggregate data reflects inconsistencies due to omitted third variable or reverse causality. On the other hand, the corresponding comparison of the IV estimate to the OLS estimate obtained from individual data reflects inconsistencies due to measurement error in addition to those associated with the two factors just mentioned.[8] Since our focus is on inconsistencies due to these two factors, we focus on the aggregate data. We want to emphasize that this point pertains to a comparison of individual and aggregate coefficients and not to a comparison of individual and aggregate standard errors of regression coefficients. The two types of standard errors can be made comparable by correcting both types for clustering by county. That is exactly what we did.

To be sure, the finding just described (larger OLS schooling effects in the grouped data than in the individual data) may be due to omitted variables that are reflected by county-cohort interactions. If that were the case, our identification strategy would be compromised since the instrument for schooling varies only by county and cohort. To examine this issue, we included a full set of county-cohort interactions in the individual and aggregate regression. The inclusion of these variables could not account for the discrepancy between the individual-level and the aggregate-level schooling coefficients. These results are available on request.

3.2. Construction of Instrument and Its Impacts on Schooling

We begin by defining the program intensity measure in a manner that is analogous to Duflo's (2001) measure. Consider the model for female schooling. We have twenty-one female cohorts who were between the ages of less than one and twenty in 1968. Those between the ages of less than one and twelve were subject to the 1968 school reform and comprise the treatment group. Those between the ages of thirteen and twenty were not subject to the increase in compulsory schooling mandated by the law, and form the control group. The idea is to interact a program intensity measure that has the same value for each cohort in a given county with a dichotomous indicator for each cohort except twenty-year-olds. These twenty cohort-intensity variables serve as instruments for years of formal schooling completed in a model that includes dichotomous indicators for each cohort except one, and for each county except one. Program intensity is given by the cumulative number of new junior high schools that opened as of 1973 (the total number that opened between 1968 and 1973) per thousand children aged twelve to fourteen in 1968. We interpret this measure as the intended number of new junior high school openings. Following Duflo

(2001), we assume that the coefficients of the interaction terms should be negatively correlated with age (should be largest for the youngest cohorts) and should fall to zero for the control cohorts. The cohort dummies capture trends in schooling not associated with reform or program intensity. The county dummies control for cohort-invariant unmeasured factors that vary among counties and may be correlated with schooling and program intensity.

The dependent variable in the regression model is years of formal schooling completed because Chou et al. (2007) present evidence that the reform had effects on the probabilities of completing schooling levels beyond junior high school. With the intercept and the disturbance term suppressed, the full model that we estimate for mean years of formal schooling completed by women in cohort a ($a = 0, 1, \ldots, 19$, with twenty-year-olds in 1968 the omitted cohort), born in county j ($j = 1, 2, \ldots, 20$), and giving birth to a child in a year (t) from 1978 through 1999 ($t = 1, 2, \ldots, 21$, with 1999 the omitted year) is

$$S_{ajt} = \sum_{a=0}^{19} \alpha_a C_a + \sum_{j=1}^{20} \varphi_j X_j + \sum_{a=0}^{19} \beta_a C_a P_j + \sum_{t=1}^{21} \theta_t Z_t + \sum_{j=1}^{20} \sum_{t=1}^{21} \lambda_{jt} X_j Z_t$$

$$+ \sum_{a=0}^{19} \delta_a C_a J_j + \sum_{a=0}^{19} \eta_a C_a A_j. \tag{5}$$

Here, C_a is a dummy variable for cohort a, X_j is a dummy variable for county j, P_j is program intensity in county j, Z_t is a dummy variable for year of birth of child t, J_j is the fraction of twelve- to fourteen-year-olds enrolled in junior high school in 1966 in county j (hereafter termed the junior high school enrollment rate), and A_j is the fraction of workers in agriculture in 1966 in county j. Clearly, we want to take account of year of birth effects when one of the four infant health measures is the outcome. In part, these effects reflect advances in medical technology, changes in the nature of health insurance coverage for prenatal and neonatal care due to the introduction of National Health Insurance in 1995, the legalization of abortion in 1985, and increases in its availability. The interactions allow these developments to have differential impacts over time in different counties.[9] Given the two-stage least squares methodology, year and county-year interactions must be included in the first-stage equation that predicts schooling if they appear in the second stage. In addition, they control for changes in the composition of births over time.

Taiwanese authorities planned to allocate more new junior high schools to counties where initial enrollment in junior high schools was low. There is some evidence that this allocation was achieved. The simple correlation coefficient between the cumulative per capita number of new junior high schools in 1973, and the junior high school enrollment rate in 1966, across the twenty-one counties in table 5.1 is −0.27, and the corresponding correlation coefficient between the program intensity variable and the fraction of workers in agriculture (an alternative measure of education needs) in 1967 is 0.37.[10] While these correlation coefficients are not significant at conventional levels, they are based on a small number of observations. Moreover, different magnitudes might emerge in the birth certificate data that we utilize and in the specifications that we employ. For these reasons, we include interactions between the cohort indicators and the fraction of workers in agriculture in 1967, and between the cohort indicators and the junior high school enrollment rate in 1966 in equation (5).[11] The 1968 legislation was preceded by the introduction of a nationwide family planning program beginning in 1964. The main aspect of the program consisted of the employment of two types of fieldworkers (village health education nurses and pre-pregnancy health workers) to disseminate information concerning family planning (Ronald Freedman and John Y. Takeshita 1969; T. Paul Schultz 1973). The number of person-months of these personnel per thousand women ages fifteen to forty-nine varied among counties and was higher in rural agricultural areas than in urban areas. Schultz (1973) reports that increases in the measure just described had negative effects on total fertility rates and age-specific birth rates. It is possible that this family planning variable is positively correlated with junior high school program intensity. To examine this possibility, we included interactions between the cohort indicators and the county-specific number of person-months of each type of family planning worker, per thousand women ages fifteen to forty-nine, in 1968 in preliminary regressions. These variables had small and statistically insignificant effects in the regressions and almost no impact on the coefficients of interest. Therefore, they were excluded from our final specifications.[12]

Panel A of figure 5.2 plots the coefficients of the interactions between age in 1968 and program intensity in county of birth in the mother's schooling equation. Panel B plots the corresponding coefficients in the father's schooling equation. The ninety-fifth percent confidence interval is also shown. For each gender, the coefficients are largest for the youngest cohorts, and decline with age in 1968. For females, the coefficients fall from 1.30 at age less than one to 0.58 at age nineteen. The mean coefficient in the treatment group is 1.17, while the mean coefficient in the control group is 0.54. There is a sharp break from a coefficient of 1.05 at age twelve to a coefficient of 0.70 at age thirteen. The ninety-fifth percent confidence interval contains a coefficient of zero for each cohort in the control group.

For males, the oldest members of the control cohort are twenty-five years old (the omitted category in the regression), as indicated in section 3.1. Hence, twenty-five coefficients are plotted in panel A compared to twenty in panel B.

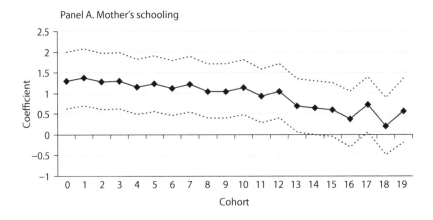

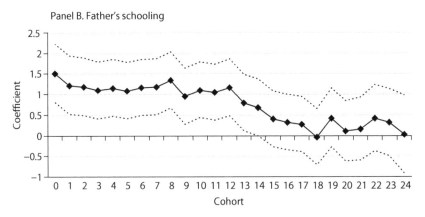

Figure 5.2 Coefficients of the interactions between age in 1968 and program intensity in county of birth in schooling equation with ninety-fifth percent confidence interval bands

Nevertheless, the patterns in panel B mirror those in panel A. The coefficients decline from 1.50 at age less than one to 0.11 at age twenty and to 0.02 at age twenty-four. The mean coefficient in the treatment group is 1.17, and the corresponding mean in the control group is 0.32 (0.41 if the control group is limited to thirteen- to twenty-year-olds). The coefficient at age twelve is 1.16, while that at age thirteen is 0.79. The ninety-fifth percent confidence interval contains a coefficient of 0.11 at age thirteen and a coefficient of 0 above age thirteen.

The results just discussed suggest gains to a specification in which program intensity effects are restricted to the treatment group. In theory, the cohorts in the control group should not have been affected by the 1968 legislation, and the findings in figure 5.2 justify this proposition. By assuming that the coefficients of the interactions between control group cohort dummies and program intensity are zero (which is equivalent to setting program intensity equal to zero for each cohort in the control group), we reduce the large number of program intensity coefficients that must be estimated. This has the advantage of reducing the degree of multicollinearity among the regressors and improving the efficiency of the estimates.

The precision of the program intensity effects also can be improved by accounting for within-county variation in the intensity variable among treatment cohorts (see table 5.1). For cohorts ages twelve and younger in 1968, our specific procedure is to interact a dichotomous indicator for each of these thirteen cohorts with the county-specific cumulative number of new junior high schools per thousand children ages twelve to fourteen in the year in which the cohort entered junior high school (hereafter termed program intensity, P_{aj}). To be specific, twelve-year-olds are assigned the program intensity measure in 1968, eleven-year-olds are assigned the intensity measure in 1969, ten-year-olds are assigned the measure in 1970, nine-year-olds are assigned the measure in 1971, eight-year-olds are assigned the measure in 1972, and those seven years old and younger are assigned the measure in 1973.

The intensity variable employed to obtain the coefficients in figure 5.2 has twenty-two unique values, one for each of the twenty-one counties and a value of zero for the oldest cohort regardless of county. On the other hand, the variable just defined has 127 unique values, 126 defined by the product of twenty-one counties and six years from 1968 through 1973, and a value of zero for each cohort in the control group regardless of county and year. Obviously, there is more variation in the latter measure than in the former.

While the 1968 legislation called for compulsory education through the ninth grade, the percentage of primary school graduates who entered junior high school was only 84 percent in 1973 and did not reach 95 percent until 1978 (see figure 5.1). The factors responsible for this lagged response to the legislation are unclear, but candidates include lack of enforcement and capacity constraints. Moreover, while enrollment in junior high school was mandatory as of September 1, 1968, attendance was not compulsory until May 12, 1982 (Tsai 2007a). These factors highlight an identification strategy that take into account program intensity in the year in which each treatment cohort enters junior high school as well as treatment status. By including the junior high school enrollment rate in 1966 and the percentage of workers in agriculture in 1967, each interacted with the thirteen treatment cohort dummies, we control for obvious factors that may be correlated with intensity and schooling.

Table 5.2 contains coefficients of the interactions between cohort dummies in the treatment group and program intensity from estimates of regressions just specified for mother's schooling and father's schooling. The regressions are

Table 5.2 Effects of Educational Reform on Parents' Years of Formal Schooling Completed

Program Intensity × Cohort	Mother's Schooling (Mean = 9.53)		Father's Schooling (Mean = 10.12)	
Age < 1 in 1968	0.707	(0.608)	1.013	(0.481)**
Age = 1 in 1968	0.789	(0.551)	0.731	(0.413)*
Age = 2 in 1968	0.685	(0.505)	0.696	(0.458)
Age = 3 in 1968	0.703	(0.464)	0.606	(0.397)
Age = 4 in 1968	0.557	(0.361)	0.666	(0.393)
Age = 5 in 1968	0.636	(0.386)	0.597	(0.421)
Age = 6 in 1968	0.526	(0.311)	0.682	(0.394)*
Age = 7 in 1968	0.615	(0.282)*	0.699	(0.401)*
Age = 8 in 1968	0.478	(0.309)	0.871	(0.403)**
Age = 9 in 1968	0.489	(0.254)*	0.572	(0.381)
Age = 10 in 1968	0.611	(0.240)**	0.726	(0.301)**
Age = 11 in 1968	0.486	(0.222)**	0.710	(0.281)**
Age = 12 in 1968	0.511	(0.259)*	0.825	(0.331)**
F-test 0, . . ., 12 = 0	28.58		16.62	
Observations	7,853		10,242	
R^2	0.96		0.92	

Notes: Standard errors, reported in parentheses, are adjusted for clustering at the county level. All regressions include twenty cohort dummies, twenty county dummies, twenty-one year-of-birth-of-child dummies, interactions between each of the treatment cohort dummies and the county-specific junior high school enrollment rate in 1966, and between each of the treatment cohort dummies and the fraction of workers in agriculture in 1967, and interactions between the county and year-of-birth-of-child dummies.
*** Significant at the 1 percent level (two-tailed test).
** Significant at the 5 percent level (two-tailed test).
* Significant at the 10 percent level (two-tailed test).

estimated across 7,853 county-cohort-year of birth cells for mother's schooling and across 10,242 cells for father's schooling, and are weighted by the square root of the number of births in each cell. The standard errors of regression coefficients are clustered at the county level.[13]

Recall that thirteen- and fourteen-year-olds who had previously ended their education after primary school were allowed to return to school as part of the 1968 reform. To examine whether it is appropriate to include them in the control or treatment groups, we estimated a regression (not shown) for each gender in which program intensity as of 1968 was interacted with indicators for each of these two cohorts, and an F-test was performed on the significance of these two coefficients as a set.[14] The F values were 0.14 for females and 1.14 for males. Hence, we accept the hypothesis that thirteen- and fourteen-year-olds should be included in the control group.

The results in table 5.2 indicate that for females, five of the thirteen program intensity coefficients are significant at the 10 percent level on a two-tailed test, and two are significant at the 5 percent level.[15] More importantly, the F-ratio associated with the test that the thirteen coefficients are significant as a set equals 28.58. This is much larger than the critical F-ratio of 10 used to assess whether instruments are weak (for example, Douglas Staiger and James H. Stock 1997; A. Colin Cameron and Pravin K. Trivedi 2005). The Stata Corporation (2005) and William Sribney (1997) recommend an adjustment to the F-ratio when the number of clusters is less than one hundred.[16] Their adjustment results in an F of 11.43, which still exceeds 10. For males, eight of the thirteen program coefficients are significant at the 10 percent level, and five at the 5 percent level. Unadjusted and adjusted F-ratios associated with the test that the thirteen coefficients are significant as a set are 16.62 and 6.65, respectively. Both reject the hypothesis that intensity coefficients are not significant as a set. The latter is somewhat smaller than ten, but does exceed the value of five, which Cameron and Trivedi (2005) propose as a less strict rule of thumb.

For each gender, there is not much variation in the program intensity coefficients. For females, they range from 0.48 to 0.79, with a mean of 0.61. For males, the corresponding range is from 0.57 to 1.01, with a mean of 0.92. Multiplication of the program intensity coefficient for a given cohort by the mean value of program intensity for that cohort yields an estimate of the increase in schooling due to the 1968 compulsory school reform and its aftermath. For females, these increases range from 0.17 years for those one year old in 1968 to 0.07 years for those twelve years old in 1968. The mean gain is 0.11 years. For males, the increases range from 0.22 for those less than one year old in 1968 to 0.11 for those twelve years old in that year. The mean gain is 0.16 years. Given mean levels of female and male schooling of 9.53 years and 10.12 years, respectively, these estimates imply that the program raised female schooling by approximately 1.2 percent and raised male schooling by approximately 1.6 percent.

Since the thirteen program coefficients are very similar for each gender, additional gains in precision and efficiency can be obtained by restricting these coefficients to be the same. This can be accomplished by fitting a regression of the form

$$S_{ajt} = \sum_{a=0}^{19} \alpha_a C_a + \sum_{j=1}^{20} \varphi_j X_j + \beta T_a P_{aj} + \sum_{t=1}^{21} \theta_t Z_t + \sum_{j=1}^{20} \sum_{t=1}^{21} \lambda_{jt} X_j Z_t$$
$$+ \delta T_a J_j + \eta T_a A_j. \tag{6}$$

Here, T_a is a dummy variable that equals one for those between the ages of less than one and twelve in 1968, and equals zero otherwise. In addition to precision and efficiency criteria, equation (6) is appealing because it recognizes that, in a fundamental sense, there is one instrument for schooling rather than thirteen. At the same time, it allows for variations in the effect of the program (βP_{aj}) on different treatment cohorts. A final advantage of equation (6) is that it avoids discrepancies between t-tests of single coefficients and F-tests of sets of related coefficients that can arise when the number of variables in the set and the number of clusters are similar. We adopt this specification in obtaining estimates of the reduced form schooling and health equations and the structural health equation in the next section.[17] One of the four health outcomes replaces schooling as the dependent variable in the health reduced form equation, and the actual or predicted value of schooling replaces program intensity in the structural health equation.

3.3. Cox's Modified Logistic Specification

The last issue we address before presenting the full set of results is that of functional form. The infant health outcomes that we investigate are rare events. For example, in the dataset for mothers, the percentage of light births is 4.30 percent. The neonatal and infant mortality rates expressed as deaths per thousand live births are 2.32 and 5.89, respectively. The postneonatal mortality rate expressed as deaths per thousand infants who survive the neonatal period is 3.57.[18] These figures, which are very similar in the dataset for fathers, translate into probabilities of a light birth, a neonatal death, a postneonatal death, and an infant death of 0.04303, 0.00232, 0.00357, and 0.00589, respectively. Since the outcomes range between zero and one, and are uncommon, we apply a logistic transformation to our grouped data. One problem is that a number of cells have no low-weight births or no deaths. Again, with reference to the dataset for mothers, 8 percent of the 7,853 cells have no low-weight births, 44 percent have no neonatal deaths, 38 percent have no postneonatal deaths, and 28 percent have no infant deaths.[19]

Given the nature of the data, we employ David R. Cox's (1970) modified logistic transformation to the dependent variables in the health outcome equations. Let $Y_i \equiv N_i/D_i$ be one of the four health outcomes in the ith cell. For example, in the case of low birthweight, N_i is the number of light births, and D_i is the total number of births. Then the dependent variable is

$$\ln Z_i = \ln \frac{Y_i + \dfrac{1}{2D_i}}{1 - Y_i + \dfrac{1}{2D_i}} = \ln \frac{N_i + 0.5}{D_i - N_i + 0.5}. \tag{7}$$

The regression employs a set of weights given by

$$W_i = \left[\frac{D_i(N_i + 1)(D_i - N_i + 1)}{(D_i + 1)(D_i + 2)} \right]^{1/2}. \tag{8}$$

We want to make several comments on the procedure just described. First, we have compared the results to those obtained when the cells with the zeros are deleted and a grouped logit with weights given by $[D_i Y_i (1 - Y_i)]^{1/2}$ is fit. These results, which are available on request, are very similar. Second, the latter estimates are not sensitive to weighting by predicted, as opposed to actual values of Y_i. In the Cox procedure, weights must be based on actual values. Third, our procedure is not subject to Cameron and Trivedi's (2005) criticism that grouped logits should not be obtained when variation in some of the regressors is eliminated by aggregation into cells. In our case, schooling is the only right-hand-side variable for which variation is reduced by grouping. As we have previously indicated, this is desirable because it reduces measurement error. Finally, there are four sets of weights, one each for low birthweight, neonatal mortality, postneonatal mortality, and infant mortality. Therefore, four reduced form equations for schooling are obtained since the same set of weights is employed in the first and second stages of two-stage least squares estimation.

4. RESULTS

Table 5.3 contains means and standard deviations of key variables in the mother's sample and in the father's sample. Table 5.4 contains estimates of the effects of educational reform on mother's and father's years of formal schooling completed from the specification given by equation (6). This specification obtains a single program coefficient from the interaction between program intensity and the dichotomous indicator for treatment status. As explained in the previous section, four regressions are estimated for each gender because the weights employed in each of the four health outcome equations differ. Standard errors of regression coefficients are clustered at the county level.

For females, all four program coefficients are positive and significant at the 1 percent level. More importantly, the F-ratios associated with the test for weak instruments all exceed the critical value of 10 used to assess whether instruments are weak (for example, Staiger and Stock 1997; Cameron and Trivedi 2005). Since the structural health equation is exactly identified, these F-ratios are given by the square of the corresponding t-ratios. They are 12.74 with the

Table 5.3 Means and Standard Deviations of Variables

	Mothers	Fathers
Years of formal schooling completed by mother or father	9.53	10.18
	(1.46)	(1.15)
Fraction of births in treatment group	0.75	0.62
	(0.43)	(0.48)
Program intensity[a,b]	0.20	0.20
	(0.11)	(0.11)
Percentage of low-birthweight births	4.30	4.45
	(1.24)	(1.25)
Neonatal mortality (deaths per thousand births)	2.32	2.34
	(2.38)	(2.38)
Postneonatal mortality (deaths per thousand neonatal survivors)	3.57	3.63
	(2.56)	(2.71)
Infant mortality (deaths per thousand births)	5.89	5.97
	(3.58)	(3.67)
Junior high school enrollment rate, 1966[a]	0.31	0.31
	(0.13)	(0.13)
Fraction of workers in agriculture, 1967[a]	0.47	0.47
	(0.23)	(0.23)

Notes: Standard deviations in parentheses. All means and standard deviations except for the postneonatal mortality rate are weighted by the cell-specific number of births. The mean and standard deviation of the postneonatal mortality rate are weighted by the cell-specific number of infants who survive the neonatal period. The mean and standard deviation of the fraction of births in the treatment group are not weighted.

[a] Mean and standard deviation pertain to the treatment group.

[b] County-specific cumulative number of new junior high schools per thousand children ages twelve to fourteen in the year in which each cohort in the treatment group entered junior high school. See text for more details.

weights for low birthweight, 10.18 with the weights for neonatal mortality, and 13.76 with the weights for postneonatal or infant mortality.

For males, the program coefficients are somewhat smaller than for females. Three of the four coefficients are significant at the 5 percent level, but only one is significant at the 1 percent level. Moreover, the coefficient with the weights for neonatal mortality is not significant at the 10 percent level. The F-ratios associated with the test for weak instruments are 8.58 with the weights for low birthweight, 2.76 with the weights for neonatal mortality, 5.15 with the weights for postneonatal mortality, and 5.62 with the weights for infant mortality. All of these fall short of the critical value of 10, but three of them exceed the value of 5, which Cameron and Trivedi (2005) propose as a less strict rule of thumb.

Table 5.4 Effects of Educational Reform on Parents' Years of Formal Schooling Completed, Single Program Intensity Measure

	Mother's Schooling				Father's Schooling			
	Model 1	Model 2	Model 3	Model 4	Model 1	Model 2	Model 3	Model 4
Treatment × program intensity	1.288***	1.045***	1.302***	1.240***	1.143***	0.805*	1.087**	1.094**
	(0.361)	(0.328)	(0.351)	(0.334)	(0.390)	(0.485)	(0.478)	(0.462)
R^2	0.926	0.844	0.856	0.882	0.889	0.800	0.812	0.838
Observations	7,853	7,853	7,853	7,853	10,242	10,242	10,242	10,242

Notes: Each of the four models employs a different set of weights. Model 1 uses the weights in the Cox modified logistic equation for low birthweight. Model 2 uses the weights in the equation for neonatal mortality. Model 3 uses the weights in the equation for postneonatal mortality. Model 4 uses the weights in the equation for infant mortality. See equation (8) for more details. Standard errors, reported in parentheses, adjust for clustering at the county level. All regressions include twenty cohort dummies, twenty county dummies, twenty-one year-of-birth-of-child dummies, interactions between the treatment dummy and the county-specific junior high school enrollment rate in 1966, interactions between the treatment dummy and the fraction of workers in agriculture in 1967, and interactions between the county and year-of-birth-of-child dummies.

*** Significant at the 1 percent level (two-tailed test).
** Significant at the 5 percent level (two-tailed test).
* Significant at the 10 percent level (two-tailed test).

For both females and males in the treatment group, the cumulative number of new junior high school openings per thousand children ages twelve to fourteen has a mean of 0.20 (see table 5.3). Hence, for females, the effect of the 1968 school reform legislation on years of completed schooling is 0.26 years in models 1 and 3, 0.21 years in model 2, and 0.25 years in model 4. For males, the increases are 0.23 years in model 1, 0.16 years in model 2, and 0.22 years in models 3 and 4. An average of these effects gives an increase of approximately one-fourth of a year for females and approximately one-fifth of a year for males. Put differently, the legislation induced 25 percent of women in the treatment group to attend school for an additional year, while it induced 20 percent of men in the treatment group to gain an additional year of schooling.

The smaller F-ratios for males than for females in the weak instruments test suggest that program intensity is a better instrument for mother's schooling than for father's schooling. Given these results, and the somewhat larger impacts on completed schooling for females, we put more weight on the reduced form and structural infant health equations that contain either mother's program intensity or mother's schooling, and discuss them first. These estimates are presented in table 5.5.

In each of the four infant health outcome equations, the logit coefficient of mother's program intensity is negative and significant at the 5 percent level (see table 5.5, panel A). All three mortality coefficients are significant at the 1 percent level. All four mother's schooling coefficients are significant at the 1 percent level in the structural infant health equations estimated by weighted least squares (WLS, see panel B). The estimates in table 5.5, panel B treat mother's schooling as exogenous and ignore the possibility that it is correlated with the disturbance term in the equation.

Perhaps the most interesting set of results in the table pertains to the structural infant health equations estimated by weighted two-stage least squares (WTSLS, see panel C). These estimates treat schooling as endogenous and employ the interaction between treatment status and program intensity as an instrument. Although the schooling coefficients have much larger standard errors in the WTSLS regressions, all are negative and all are significant at the 10 percent level. Only the neonatal mortality coefficient loses its significance at the 5 percent level. Moreover, the WTSLS and WLS coefficients are similar in magnitude. The ratio of the former coefficient to the latter is 0.86 for low birthweight, 0.75 for neonatal mortality, 1.38 for postneonatal mortality, and 1.31 for infant mortality. Finally, the F-ratio resulting from the De-Min Wu (1973)-Jerry A. Hausman (1978) test suggests the estimates that treat schooling as exogenous are consistent. We want to emphasize that this finding cannot be traced to the use of a weak instrument for schooling.

Table 5.5 Effects of Program Intensity and Mother's Schooling on Infant Health

	Low Birthweight	Neonatal Mortality	Postneonatal Mortality	Infant Mortality
Panel A. Reduced form infant health Cox-modified logit regressions, weighted least squares				
Treatment × program intensity	−0.249**	−0.333***	−0.835***	−0.626***
	(0.089)	(0.099)	(0.152)	(0.111)
R^2	0.445	0.499	0.333	0.365
Mean × 100 (or 1,000)	4.30	2.32	3.57	5.89
Panel B. Structural infant health Cox-modified logit regressions, weighted least squares				
Mother's schooling	−0.226***	−0.426***	−0.463***	−0.386***
	(0.030)	(0.019)	(0.017)	(0.034)
R^2	0.534	0.571	0.453	0.463
Panel C. Structural infant health Cox-modified logit regressions, weighted two-stage least squares				
Mother's schooling	−0.194**	−0.318*	−0.641**	−0.505**
	(0.082)	(0.158)	(0.258)	(0.206)
R^2	0.532	0.566	0.435	0.454
Wu-Hausman *F*-ratio	0.23	0.32	0.69	0.46

Notes: Sample size is 7,853 in all regressions. Weights are given by equation (8). Standard errors, reported in parentheses, adjust for clustering at the county level. All regressions include twenty cohort dummies, twenty county dummies, twenty-one year-of-birth-of-child dummies, interactions between the treatment dummy and the county-specific junior high school enrollment rate in 1966, interactions between the treatment dummy and the fraction of workers in agriculture in 1967, and interactions between the county and year-of-birth-of-child dummies. All means, except for the postneonatal mortality rate, are weighted by the cell-specific number of births. The mean of the latter variable is weighted by the cell-specific number of infants who survive the neonatal period. For low birthweight, the mean is the percentage of light births. For neonatal and infant mortality, the means are deaths per thousand live births. For postneonatal mortality, the mean is deaths per thousand survivors of the neonatal period.
*** Significant at the 1 percent level (two-tailed test).
** Significant at the 5 percent level (two-tailed test).
* Significant at the 10 percent level (two-tailed test).

The corresponding estimates of infant health equations that contain either father's program intensity or father's schooling are given in table 5.6. All four logit coefficients of father's program intensity are negative, but the neonatal mortality coefficient is not significant at the 10 percent level. The three other coefficients are significant at the 1 percent level (see panel A). This differs from the results for mother's program intensity in which all four coefficients are significant at 5 percent. Moreover, the father's coefficients are smaller in absolute value than the corresponding mother's coefficients. The ratio of the former to the latter ranges from 0.59 in the case of neonatal mortality to 0.87 in the case of low birthweight.

Table 5.6 Effects of Program Intensity and Father's Schooling on Infant Health

	Low Birthweight	Neonatal Mortality	Postneonatal Mortality	Infant Mortality
Panel A. Reduced form infant health Cox-modified logit regressions, weighted least squares				
Treatment × program intensity	−0.216***	−0.196	−0.634***	−0.469***
	(0.060)	(0.137)	(0.117)	(0.095)
R^2	0.374	0.461	0.353	0.371
Mean × 100 (or 1,000)	4.45	2.34	3.63	5.97
Panel B. Structural infant health Cox-modified logit regressions, weighted least squares				
Father's schooling	−0.253***	−0.434***	−0.442***	−0.369***
	(0.027)	(0.020)	(0.019)	(0.018)
R^2	0.483	0.526	0.443	0.450
Panel C. Structural infant health Cox-modified logit regressions, weighted two-stage least squares				
Father's schooling	−0.189**	−0.243	−0.584*	−0.429*
	(0.077)	(0.025)	(0.357)	(0.251)
R^2	0.476	0.514	0.434	0.448
Wu-Hausman *F*-ratio	0.53	0.25	0.23	0.07

Notes: Sample size is 10,242 in all regressions. Weights are given by equation (8). Standard errors, reported in parentheses, adjust for clustering at the county level. All regressions include twenty cohort dummies, twenty county dummies, twenty-one year-of-birth-of-child dummies, interactions between the treatment dummy and the county-specific junior high school enrollment rate in 1966, interactions between the treatment dummy and the fraction of workers in agriculture in 1967, and interactions between the county and year-of-birth-of-child dummies. All means except for the postneonatal mortality rate are weighted by the cell-specific number of births. The mean of the latter variable is weighted by the cell-specific number of infants who survive the neonatal period. For low birthweight, the mean is the percentage of light births. For neonatal and infant mortality, the means are deaths per thousand live births. For postneonatal mortality, the mean is deaths per thousand survivors of the neonatal period.

*** Significant at the 1 percent level.
** Significant at the 5 percent level.
* Significant at the 10 percent level.

When father's schooling is treated as exogenous, all four coefficients are negative, significant at the 1 percent level, and similar in magnitude to the corresponding mother's coefficients (see panel B). These coefficients retain their negative signs in WTSLS, but only the low-birthweight coefficient is significant at the 10 percent level, and none of the coefficients are significant at the 5 percent level (see panel C). There is more variability in the ratio of WTSLS to WLS coefficients for fathers than for mothers. The former ratio ranges from 0.56 for neonatal mortality to 1.32 for postneonatal mortality. The mother WTSLS coefficients are larger in absolute value than the father WTSLS coefficients The Wu-Hausman test supports the consistency of estimates that treat schooling as exogenous. Some caution is required here because the instrument for father's schooling does not have an F-ratio in excess of 10.

To gauge the magnitude of the effects of mother's or father's schooling on each of the infant health outcomes, we compute the reduction in each adverse outcome associated with the increase in schooling caused by the 1968 school reform legislation. Refer to equation (7), let $K_i \equiv 1/2D_i$, let a bar over a variable denote a mean, and let γ be the logit coefficient of schooling in one of the four health outcome equations.

Then we compute

$$Y_1 = \frac{e^{\gamma\Delta S}(\bar{Y} + \bar{K}\bar{Y} + \bar{K} + \bar{K}^2) - \bar{K} + \bar{K}\bar{Y} - \bar{K}^2}{e^{\gamma\Delta S}(\bar{Y} + \bar{K}) + 1 - \bar{Y} + \bar{K}}. \tag{9}$$

In this equation, $\Delta S = \beta\bar{P}$, where β is the regression coefficient of program intensity in the schooling equation (equation [6]), and $\bar{P}$ is the mean of program intensity in the treatment group. The absolute difference between Y_1 and $\bar{Y}$ shows the reduction in one of the four adverse infant health outcomes associated with an increase in schooling of ΔS years.

Table 5.7 contains the results of the computations just described. For a given parent and a given health outcome, two estimates are shown. The first employs the WLS value of γ, while the second employs the WTSLS value of that coefficient. Our results imply that the WLS value is consistent. Nevertheless, we show both estimates because the Wu-Hausman test may have relatively low power given the loss in efficiency associated with two-stage least squares.

Focusing on the results for mother's schooling, one sees that the percentage of low-birthweight births falls by 0.24 percentage points when the WLS coefficient is employed in the computation. This translates into a percentage reduction in the number of light births in a fixed population of births of 5.5 percent. The WTSLS figures are slightly smaller. The percentage of light births falls by 0.20 percentage points or by 4.74 percent. Reductions in mortality range from a decline of 0.20 neonatal deaths per thousand live births to a decline of 0.77 infant deaths per thousand live births. In percentage terms, the smallest decline is an 8.41 percent fall in the number of neonatal deaths. The largest decline is an 18.63 percent reduction in the number of postneonatal deaths. These absolute and percentage reductions in mortality emerge from WTLS.

With one exception, the reductions associated with increases in father's schooling are smaller than those associated with mother's schooling. The exception is the percentage point reduction in the percentage of light births in WLS. Here, the reduction for father's schooling exceeds that for mother's schooling by only 0.01 percentage points.

Table 5.7 Reductions in Low Birthweight and Mortality Due to Increases in Schooling

Outcome	Mother's Schooling		Father's Schooling	
	Weighted Least Squares	Weighted Two-Stage Least Squares	Weighted Least Squares	Weighted Two-Stage Least Squares
Low birthweight				
Percentage point reduction	0.237	0.204	0.246	0.185
Percentage reduction in number of light births	5.512	4.744	5.528	4.157
Neonatal mortality				
Reduction in number of deaths per thousand live births	0.258	0.195	0.211	0.120
Percentage reduction in number of deaths	11.121	8.405	9.017	5.128
Postneonatal mortality				
Reduction in number of deaths per thousand neonatal survivors	0.492	0.665	0.404	0.526
Percentage reduction in number of deaths	13.782	18.627	11.129	14.490
Infant mortality				
Reduction in number of deaths per thousand live births	0.600	0.774	0.521	0.602
Percentage reduction in number of deaths	10.187	13.141	8.727	10.084

Notes: Reduction in outcome due to increase in schooling is computed by multiplying the coefficient of program intensity in the schooling regression by the mean value of intensity in the treatment group. Percentage reduction assumes no change in the denominator of the relevant outcome.

Can one conclude from these results that mother's schooling is a more important determinant of infant health outcomes than father's schooling? For several reasons, the answer is no. First, the mother's schooling effects are larger than the corresponding father's schooling effects, in part, because the coefficient of program intensity in the reduced form for mother's schooling is larger than the corresponding coefficient in the reduced form for father's schooling.

Second, and more importantly, we exclude father's schooling from the infant health outcome equations when mother's schooling is included, and exclude mother's schooling when father's schooling is included. Given the strong positive correlation between these two schooling variables in our data and in data for practically every developing and developed country, the estimate of the effect of either one on infant health is biased by the omission of the other. As was pointed out in section 3, the two schooling variables are too highly correlated to include both in the same regression.

5. DISCUSSION

Our results suggest that parents' schooling causes favorable infant health out-comes. In particular, an increase in schooling lowers the probability that an infant will be born light or will die in the neonatal or postneonatal periods. Our results also suggest that schooling can be treated as exogenous in estimating these effects.

The last result may seem puzzling because schooling clearly is an endoge-nous variable. If one recognizes this a priori, then a literal interpretation of our findings is that the schooling-health system is recursive rather than simulta-neous and that the disturbance terms in the two equations are not correlated. Lack of simultaneity means that parents ignore the impacts of their schooling on the health of their offspring when they make optimal schooling decisions. Uncorrelated disturbance terms mean that unobserved factors that govern schooling outcomes are not related to unobserved factors that govern infant health outcomes.

This literal interpretation may be too narrow and naïve. Parents play an important role in the schooling outcomes of their children and may take account of all potential benefits in allocating resources to their own schooling. But the infant health benefits associated with investments in schooling may be small rel-ative to other benefits in these investments. In this case, a recursive specification may approximate reality.

Even if the recursive specification is correct, the disturbance terms in the two equations may share a common element. Time preference is an obvious candidate, as suggested by Fuchs (1982). In the schooling equation, however, variations in time preference may be small relative to variations in observed determinants of this outcome such as its price. If a minor part of the variation in schooling is due to time preference, the bias introduced by treating it as exogenous will be small.

The endogenous time preference hypothesis proposed by Becker and Mul-ligan (1997) complicates the situation. If causality runs solely from schooling to time preference, one does not want to control for the latter in estimating the effect of the former on health. Now, suppose there is two-way causality between schooling and time preference and that time preference is replaced by its determinants in the health equation. Then the correlation that determines biases is that between schooling and the disturbance term that results from this substitution rather than the correlation between schooling and time preference itself. The former correlation is likely to be smaller than the latter.

An alternative approach to our results is possible. Two-stage least squares estimation results in a loss of efficiency. For example, in the infant mortality logit, the standard error of mother's schooling rises by a factor of 12 when it is treated as endogenous. Hence, one may want to interpret Wu-Hausman consistency tests with some caution. If that approach is taken, our two-stage least squares estimates should be stressed. These estimates allow us to conclude that mother's schooling causes favorable infant health outcomes without having to dismiss any of the factors that generate inconsistencies when schooling is treated as exogenous. The two-stage least squares estimates do not allow us to conclude that father's schooling causes favorable infant health outcomes. The conclusions with regard to the TSLS estimates are, however, tentative because we do not control for father's schooling in the equations that include mother's schooling and vice versa.

Our findings should be placed in the context of the Taiwan experience. One factor that may make them different from results for the United States is that postneonatal deaths accounted for 60 percent of all infant deaths in Taiwan during our sample period. By contrast, they accounted for only 36 percent of all infant deaths in the United States. Parents may play an important role in preventing or dealing with the infectious diseases and accidents that are the major causes of postneonatal mortality.

A second and related factor is that a large percentage of Taiwanese women and children lacked health insurance prior to the enactment of National Health Insurance in March 1995 (see Tung-Liang Chiang 1997 for details). Parents' education may be an especially important factor in postneonatal infant health outcomes in this setting. The larger absolute and percentage impacts schooling on postneonatal mortality than on neonatal mortality (see table 5.7) provide evidence in support of this proposition.

A third factor is that our estimating equation allows the effects of school reform to be larger in counties with more new school construction. These counties had lower junior high school enrollment rates and larger fractions of workers in agriculture. Income is positively correlated with the former variable and negatively correlated with the latter. Hence, the impacts of the school reform that we have studied are larger in poorer areas and in rural areas, which, by definition, have more workers in agriculture. Our results may not generalize to legislation that has a different focus.

In summary, we have used a natural experiment in Taiwan to answer the question: Do increases in parents' schooling cause better infant health? Our answer to this question is yes. Beyond that we have not investigated the mechanisms via which schooling operates because we lack data on infant health inputs. Studies that examine this issue, and that try to sort out the partial effects of mother's and father's schooling, deserve high priority on an agenda for future research.

NOTES

Originally published as Shin Yi Chou, Jin Tan Liu, Michael Grossman, and Ted Joyce, "Parental Education and Child Health: Evidence from a Natural Experiment in Taiwan," *American Economic Journal: Applied Economics* 2, no. 1 (2010): 33–61. This chapter was presented at the Sixth World Congress of the International Health Economics Association in Copenhagen, Denmark, July 9–11, 2007. Research for the chapter was supported by grant number 5 R01 HD045603 from the National Institute of Child Health and Human Development to the National Bureau of Economic Research. The chapter has had a long gestation period due to problems encountered in using Taiwanese birth and infant death certificates, and in accurately measuring new junior high school openings. Preliminary versions of the chapter, with empirical results that turned out to be incorrect after inconsistencies in the data were uncovered and resolved, were presented at the 2004 Annual Meeting of the Population Association of America, the Fourth World Congress of the International Health Economics Association, the 2005 NIA/NICHD Intergenerational Research Workshop, and at seminars at Harvard University, Cornell University, the State University of New York at Buffalo, National Taiwan University, the University of South Florida, and the University of Medicine and Dentistry of the New Jersey School of Public Health. More recent seminars with correct empirical results were presented at Louisiana State University, Kansas State University, the New School University, Columbia University, McMaster University, the Sixth Summer Workshop in Health Economics sponsored by the Centre for Applied Economic Research at the University of New South Wales, the Melbourne Institute of Applied Economic and Social Research at the University of Melbourne, the University of Canterbury, and the University of Auckland. We wish to thank the participants in those forums for helpful comments and suggestions. We also wish to thank Silvie Colman, Ryan Conrad, Danielle Ferry, and Wehn-Jyuan Tsai for research assistance. Finally, we wish to thank two anonymous referees for extremely helpful comments on an earlier draft. Any opinions expressed are those of the authors and do not necessarily reflect the views of NICHD or NBER.

1. Note that we do not attempt to distinguish between the productive and allocative efficiency effects of education. In addition, we do not attempt to test the efficiency hypothesis against the alternative hypothesis that education causes health because it is a determinant of time preference. Note, also, that in the Becker-Mulligan (1997) model, schooling might have no effect on health with an endogenous measure of time preference held constant, but schooling might have a very important indirect or reduced form impact that operates through time preference. Even with an adequate measure of time preference, estimation of their model would be difficult if one wanted to allow that measure and schooling to be endogenous, and to allow schooling to enter the structural health equation.

2. The study by Albouy and Lequien (2009) is an exception.

3. Hereafter, school year t denotes the school year that starts in September of year t and ends in June of year $t + 1$.

4. In Taiwan, large cities are separate local entities. Hence, Taipei County pertains to the region outside of Taipei City. Unlike Clark and Hsieh (2000), we present separate

program intensity data for Taipei City, Kaohsiung City, Taichung City, and Tainan City. This is appropriate because children who reside in Kaohsiung City, for example, do not attend school in the part of Kaohsiung County that is outside the city.

5. In Taiwan, children must be six years old on September 1 of year t to enter the first grade in that year, and must be twelve years old on September 1 to enter the seventh grade. We have the exact date of birth (day, month, and year) of all individuals in our data. Hence, age in 1968 pertains to age as of September 1. To be specific, an individual born on September 2, 1956, is assigned an age of eleven in 1968, while an individual born on September 1, 1956, is assigned an age of twelve. Individuals born between September 2, 1967, and September 1, 1968, are assigned an age of zero or less than one in 1968. Individuals born from September 2, 1968, through December 31, 1968, are excluded from the data.

6. Unlike U.S. birth certificates, Taiwanese certificates do not contain such prenatal health inputs and behaviors as month in which prenatal medical care began, number of prenatal care visits, and maternal cigarette smoking and alcohol use during pregnancy. Marital status and parity are available, but births to unmarried women accounted for less than 2 percent of all births in our sample period, and that indicator and parity are potentially endogenous.

7. Preliminary results with a control group of men between the ages of thirteen and twenty were very similar to the ones presented in sections 3.2 and 4.

8. Card (1999, 2001) and others point to random measurement error as an explanation of the larger IV than OLS estimates of the effect of schooling on earnings. Our results suggest that the IV coefficient should be compared to the OLS coefficient obtained at the level of aggregation of the instrument. A second explanation of our results is that there may be spillover effects in the sense that the health outcome of a child depends on the average schooling of parents in his or her area as well as on the schooling of the infant's own parents. Note that the aggregate regressions described in the text were weighted by the square root of the number of births in each cell.

9. The mother's age in 1968, and the year in which she gave birth, determine her age at birth. Thus, the cohort and year effects partially reflect the impacts of age at birth. While age at birth could be included in the regressions, we did not do so because it is potentially endogenous.

10. The corresponding weighted (by the number of children ages twelve to fourteen in 1967) correlation coefficients are −0.26 and 0.20, respectively.

11. In alternative specifications, we omitted the interactions just mentioned. The results in section 4 are not sensitive to these omissions. The results from the alternative specifications are available on request.

12. It is possible that the findings just described are due to the inclusion of county indicators and interactions between cohort dummies and the percentage of workers in agriculture in 1967, and between cohort dummies and the junior high school enrollment rate in 1966. Note that the family planning measure described in the text could have a positive causal effect on schooling as predicted by the quantity-quality substitution model developed by Becker and Lewis (1973). In that case, it would be an additional valid instrument. If,

however, infants born to women in the treatment cohort experienced better health outcomes because the parents of these women had smaller families and gave their children more information about family planning and prenatal care, these improved outcomes could not be attributed to increases in schooling. In any case, our preliminary results suggest that these issues are not relevant.

13. Since there are twenty-one clusters, t-tests of the significance of regression coefficients assume 20 degrees of freedom (Stata Corporation 2005).

14. Given the cluster procedure in Stata (2005), the F-ratio is computed as W/q, where W is the Wald test statistic and q is the number of restrictions (two in the test described in the text). The significance of the F-ratio is based by comparing it to the critical $F(q, d)$, where d is the number of clusters minus one.

15. We follow the convention in most of the empirical economics literature of reporting significance of regression coefficients based on two-tailed tests. Note, however, that the alternative hypothesis is that each program coefficient is positive when schooling is the outcome. This suggests that one-tailed tests are relevant. If these are applied, twelve of the thirteen program intensity coefficients are significant at the 10 percent level; four are significant at the 5 percent level; and one is significant at the 1 percent level. For readers who prefer one-tailed tests, the critical t-ratios with 20 degrees of freedom are 1.32 at the 10 percent level, 1.72 at the 5 percent level, and 2.52 at the 1 percent level. In the specification with a single intensity variable in the next section, the alternative hypotheses are as follows: the program intensity coefficients are positive when schooling is the outcome; the program intensity coefficients are negative when one of the four negative correlates of infant health is the outcome; and the schooling coefficients are negative when one of the four negative correlates of infant health is the outcome.

16. Refer to endnote 14. The formula that relates the adjusted F (F') to the unadjusted F is

$$F' = F\,[(d - q + 1)/d].$$

In our case $d = 20$ and $q = 13$. Hence, $F' = (8/20) \times 28.58 = 11.43$.

17. To be consistent, the junior high school enrollment rate in 1966 and the percentage of workers in agriculture in 1967 are interacted with the single treatment dummy.

18. Let π_i be the infant mortality rate (deaths within the first 364 days of life divided by births), π_n be the neonatal mortality rate (deaths within the first 27 days of life divided by births), and π_p be the postneonatal mortality rate (deaths between 28 and 364 days of life divided by infants who survive the neonatal period). Then

$$\pi_i = \pi_n + f\pi_p,$$

where f is the ratio of neonatal survivors to total births. Since f is less than 1, π_i is less than the sum of π_n and π_p. The ratio in question is, however, so close to 1 that the discrepancy between the infant mortality rate and the sum of the neonatal and postneonatal mortality rates is noticeable only if the rates are expressed with more than five decimal places.

19. For fathers, 9 percent of the 10,242 cells have no low-weight births, 47 percent have no neonatal deaths, 38 percent have no postneonatal deaths, and 29 percent have no infant deaths.

REFERENCES

Adams, Scott J. 2002. "Educational Attainment and Health: Evidence from a Sample of Older Adults." *Education Economics*, 10(1): 97–109.

Albouy, Valerie, and Laurent Lequien. 2009. "Does Compulsory Education Lower Mortality?" *Journal of Health Economics*, 28(1): 155–68.

Arendt, Jacob Nielsen. 2005. "Does Education Cause Better Health? A Panel Data Analysis Using School Reforms for Identification." *Economics of Education Review*, 24(2): 149–60.

——. 2008. "In Sickness and in Health—Till Education Do Us Part: Education Effects on Hospitalization." *Economics of Education Review*, 27(2): 161–72.

Arkes, Jeremy. 2004. "Does Schooling Improve Adult Health?" Unpublished.

Auster, Richard, Irving Leveson, and Deborah Sarachek. 1969. "The Production of Health, an Exploratory Study." *Journal of Human Resources*, 4(4): 411–36.

Becker, Gary S., and H. Gregg Lewis. 1973. "On the Interaction between the Quantity and Quality of Children." *Journal of Political Economy*, 81(2): S279–88.

Becker, Gary S., and Casey B. Mulligan. 1997. "The Endogenous Determination of Time Preference." *Quarterly Journal of Economics*, 112(3): 729–58.

Berger, Mark C., and J. Paul Leigh. 1989. "Schooling, Self-Selection, and Health." *Journal of Human Resources*, 24(3): 433–55.

Breierova, Lucia, and Esther Duflo. 2004. "The Impact of Education on Fertility and Child Mortality: Do Fathers Really Matter Less Than Mothers?" National Bureau of Economic Research Working Paper 10513.

Cameron, A. Colin, and Pravin K. Trivedi. 2005. *Microeconometrics: Methods and Applications*. Cambridge, UK: Cambridge University Press.

Card, David. 1999. "The Causal Effect of Education on Earnings." In *Handbook of Labor Economics*, Vol. 3A, ed. Orley Ashenfelter and David Card, 1801–63. Amsterdam: Elsevier Science.

——. 2001. "Estimating the Return to Schooling: Progress on Some Persistent Econometric Problems." *Econometrica*, 69(5): 1127–60.

Chen, Yuyu, and Hongbin Li. 2009. "Mother's Education and Child Health: Is There a Nurturing Effect?" *Journal of Health Economics*, 28(2): 413–26.

Chiang, Tung-Liang. 1997. "Taiwan's 1995 Health Care Reform." *Health Policy*, 39(3): 225–39.

Chou, Shin-Yi, Jin-Tan Liu, Michael Grossman, and Theodore J. Joyce. 2007. "Parental Education and Child Health: Evidence from a Natural Experiment in Taiwan." National Bureau of Economic Research Working Paper 13466.

Cipollone, Piero, Debora Radicchia, and Alfonso Rosolia. 2007. "The Effect of Education on Youth Mortality." Unpublished.

Clark, Diana E., and Chang-Tai Hsieh. 2000. "Schooling and Labor Market Impact of the 1968 Nine-Year Education Program in Taiwan." Unpublished.

Cox, David R. 1970. *The Analysis of Binary Data*. London: Methuen and Company Ltd.

Currie, Janet, and Enrico Moretti. 2003. "Mother's Education and the Intergenerational Transmission of Human Capital: Evidence from College Openings." *Quarterly Journal of Economics*, 118(4): 1495–1532.

Deaton, Angus. 2002. "Policy Implications of the Gradient of Health and Wealth." *Health Affairs*, 21(2): 13–30.

de Walque, Damien. 2007. "Does Education Affect Smoking Behaviors? Evidence Using the Vietnam Draft as an Instrument for College Education." *Journal of Health Economics*, 26(5): 877–95.

Duflo, Esther. 2000. "Schooling and Labor Market Consequences of School Construction in Indonesia: Evidence from an Unusual Policy Experiment." National Bureau of Economic Research Working Paper 7860.

——. 2001. "Schooling and Labor Market Consequences of School Construction in Indonesia: Evidence from an Unusual Policy Experiment." *American Economic Review*, 91(4): 795–813.

Freedman, Ronald, and John Y. Takeshita. 1969. *Family Planning in Taiwan: An Experiment in Social Change*. Princeton, NJ: Princeton University Press.

Fuchs, Victor R. 1982. "Time Preference and Health: An Exploratory Study." In *Economic Aspects of Health*, ed. Victor R. Fuchs, 93–120. Chicago: University of Chicago Press.

Grimard, Franque, and Daniel Parent. 2007. "Education and Smoking: Were Vietnam War Draft Avoiders Also More Likely to Avoid Smoking?" *Journal of Health Economics*, 26(5): 896–926.

Grossman, Michael. 2000. "The Human Capital Model." In *Handbook of Health Economics*, Vol. 1A, ed. Anthony J. Culyer and Joseph P. Newhouse, 347–408. Amsterdam: Elsevier Science.

——. 2006. "Education and Nonmarket Outcomes." In *Handbook of the Economics of Education*, Vol. 1, ed. Eric A. Hanushek and Finis Welch, 577–633. Amsterdam: Elsevier Science.

Grossman, Michael, and Robert Kaestner. 1997. "Effects of Education on Health." In *The Social Benefits of Education*, ed. Jere R. Behrman and Nevzer Stacey, 69–123. Ann Arbor, MI: University of Michigan Press.

Hausman, Jerry A. 1978. "Specification Tests in Econometrics." *Econometrica*, 46(6): 1251–71.

Kenkel, Donald, Dean Lillard, and Alan Mathios. 2006. "The Roles of High School Completion and GED Receipt in Smoking and Obesity." *Journal of Labor Economics*, 24(3): 635–60.

Leigh, J. Paul, and Rachna Dhir. 1997. "Schooling and Frailty among Seniors." *Economics of Education Review*, 16(1): 45–57.

Lindeboom, Maarten, Ana Llena-Nozal, and Bas van der Klaauw. 2009. "Parental Education and Child Health: Evidence from a Schooling Reform." *Journal of Health Economics*, 28(1): 109–31.

Lleras-Muney, Adriana. 2005. "The Relationship between Education and Adult Mortality in the United States." *Review of Economic Studies*, 72(1): 189–221.

McCrary, Justin, and Heather Royer. 2006. "The Effect of Female Education on Fertility and Infant Health: Evidence from School Entry Policies Using Exact Date of Birth." National Bureau of Economic Research Working Paper 12329.

Mincer, Jacob A. 1974. *Schooling, Experience, and Earnings*. New York: Columbia University Press.

Oreopoulos, Philip. 2006. "Estimating Average and Local Average Treatment Effects of Education When Compulsory Schooling Laws Really Matter." *American Economic Review*, 96(1): 152–75.

Osili, Una Okonkwo, and Bridget Terry Long. 2008. "Does Female Schooling Reduce Fertility? Evidence from Nigeria." *Journal of Development Economics*, 87(1): 57–75.

Sander, William. 1995a. "Schooling and Quitting Smoking." *Review of Economics and Statistics*, 77(1): 191–99.

——. 1995b. "Schooling and Smoking." *Economics of Education Review*, 14(1): 23–33.

Schultz, T. Paul. 1973. "Explanation of Birth Rate Changes over Space and Time: A Study of Taiwan." *Journal of Political Economy*, 81(2): S238–74.

Silles, Mary A. 2009. "The Causal Effect of Education on Health: Evidence from the United Kingdom." *Economics of Education Review*, 28(1): 122–28.

Spasojevic, Jasmina. 2003. "Effects of Education on Adult Health in Sweden: Results from a Natural Experiment." PhD diss. City University of New York.

Spohr, Chris A. 2000. "Essays on Household and Workforce in Taiwan." PhD diss. MIT.

——. 2003. "Formal Schooling and Workforce Participation in a Rapidly Developing Economy: Evidence From 'Compulsory' Junior High School in Taiwan." *Journal of Development Economics*, 70(2): 291–327.

Sribney, William. 1997. "Chi-Squared Test for Models Estimated with Robust Standard Errors." StataCorp, August. http://www.stata.com/support/faqs/stat/chi2.html.

Staiger, Douglas, and James H. Stock. 1997. "Instrumental Variables Regression with Weak Instruments." *Econometrica*, 65(3): 557–86.

Stata Corporation. 2005. *Stata Base Reference Manual*, Vol. 3, Reference R-Z, Release 9. College Station, TX: Stata Press.

Strauss, John, and Duncan Thomas. 1995. "Human Resources: Empirical Modeling of Household and Family Decisions." In *Handbook of Development Economics*, Vol. 3A, ed. Jere Behrman and T. N. Srinivasan, 1883–2023. Amsterdam: Elsevier Science.

Tsai, Wehn-Jyuan. 2007a. "Does Educational Expansion Encourage Female Workforce Participation? A Study of the 1968 Reform in Taiwan." In "Three Essays in Applied Microeconomics." PhD diss. National Taiwan University.

——. 2007b. "Intergenerational Transmissions of Human Capital: Natural Experiment from Compulsory Education Reform in Taiwan." In "Three Essays in Applied Microeconomics." PhD diss. National Taiwan University.

van Kippersluis, Hans, Owen O'Donnell, and Eddy van Doorslaer. 2009. "Long Run Returns to Education: Does Schooling Lead to an Extended Old Age?" Tinbergen Institute Discussion Paper TI 2009-037/3.

World Bank. 1993. *World Development Report 1993: Investing in Health*. New York: Oxford University Press.

Wu, De-Min. 1973. "Alternative Tests of Independence between Stochastic Regressors and Disturbances." *Econometrica*, 41(4): 733–50.

Women's Education: Harbinger of Another Spring?

Evidence from a Natural Experiment in Turkey

Mehmet Alper Dinçer, Neeraj Kaushal, and Michael Grossman

ABSTRACT

We use Turkey's 1997 Education Law that increased compulsory schooling from five to eight years to study the effect of education on women's fertility and empowerment. Using an instrumental variables methodology, we find that a 10 percentage-point increase in the proportion of ever-married women with eight years of schooling lowered pregnancies by 0.13 per woman; increased the proportion paying an antenatal visit during the first trimester by 6 percentage points; using contraceptives by eight points and with knowledge of the ovulation cycle by five points. There is weak evidence that schooling decreased child mortality; no evidence that it changed attitudes toward gender inequality.

1. INTRODUCTION

The impacts of women's education on their well-being and the well-being of their children have been widely documented.[1] But almost all of the research is based on non-Middle Eastern countries. Cultural norms and social environments in Middle Eastern societies discriminate against women, limit their economic and educational opportunities, and relegate them to a lesser status than men (UNDP 2005). The returns to women's education may be different in a social and cultural environment that discriminates against them than in societies that accord them a more equal status. Despite its significance, there is limited empirical research to estimate the effects of women's education within the social and cultural settings of a Middle Eastern country. Such research is critical in light of recent papers that cast doubt on previous findings of negative effects of maternal education on fertility and infant health (Lindeboom, Llena-Nozal, and van Der Klaauw 2009; McCrary and Royer 2011; Zhang 2012).

In this chapter, we take advantage of Turkey's Compulsory Education Law, and variation in the intensity of its implementation across regions in Turkey, to study the effect of women's formal years of schooling on a range of measures that capture women's fertility, empowerment, and child mortality. Turkey is the largest economy in the Middle East and by many measures, a relatively modern society. Despite its growing economic and geopolitical influence, the position of women in Turkey continues to be defined along traditional lines: In 2010, only 27 percent of women (*versus* 47 percent of men) had a secondary or higher education, and a mere 24 percent worked for wages (*versus* 70 percent of men)—a proportion that declined from 32 percent in 1990 (UNDP 2011). Surveys indicate that a third of women in Turkey have been exposed to physical violence at home (Altınay and Arat 2007). In 2011, Turkey was ranked 124th (out of 135 countries) in the gender equality index of the World Economic Forum (Hausmann, Tyson, and Zahidi, 2012). Gender inequality portends poor child wellbeing: In 2010, infant mortality in Turkey was 15.8 per 1,000 births compared to 5.1 in the European Union and 27.6 for the Middle East and North Africa.[2] Whether women's education can improve child health and women's reproductive health and empowerment, the focus of our study, is therefore an issue of considerable policy relevance not just for Turkey, but for the entire MiddleEast.

In 1997, Turkey passed the Compulsory Education Law that increased mandatory formal schooling from five to eight years. Individuals born after 1985 (who were eleven or less in 1997) were the target of the Compulsory Education Law. Its primary objective was to prepare Turkey's entry into the European Union (EU) by increasing educational attainment and reducing geographic and gender-specific educational disparity. Access to education has been widely acknowledged by the EU as a means of enhancing economic and social development in Turkey as well as in bringing economic and social cohesion across its eastern and western regions. To accommodate the expected increase in enrollment, the government devoted additional resources on school infrastructure and in hiring new teachers leading to a 36 percent increase in primary school teachers during 1996–2003 (Dülger 2004; State Institute of Statistics 1999; Turkish Statistical Institute 2006).

We capitalize on the 1997 compulsory school reform legislation to estimate the causal effect of women's schooling on a range of outcomes relating to child mortality, women's reproductive health, and measures of empowerment, including age at first marriage, age at first childbirth, contraceptive use, antenatal visits, fertility, and attitudes toward gender equality. We form a treatment group of women who were born during 1986–1990 and were affected by the legislation and a corresponding comparison group of women who were born during 1979–1985 and were not affected. Investment in new teachers varied across the subregions of Turkey. Within each subregion, we exploit variations across cohorts in the number of primary school teachers in the subregion of residence at age eleven to construct an instrument to predict the educational attainment of young women. The predicted education variable is then used to estimate the effect of education on a variety of outcomes experienced by the treatment group of women and their offspring from information obtained when the treatment cohort was between the ages of eighteen and twenty-two and the comparison cohort was between the ages of twenty-three and twenty-nine.

2. REVIEW OF LITERATURE

Economists argue that more educated individuals are more efficient producers of health and more educated parents are more efficient in producing healthy children (Grossman 2006). Knowledge helps parents make informed decisions on their children's nutrition and health care. It influences health-related behaviors (such as smoking, drug abuse, and binge drinking) and lifestyles (e.g., physical exercise), and parents', in particular mother's, health behavior and lifestyle impact child health (e.g., birth weight). Parental education is also the most basic component of socio-economic status, which according to epidemiologists is the key determinant of own and child health (Adler and Newman 2002). Further, education may affect attitudes toward gender equality empowering women (Mocan and Cannonier 2012). Because mothers are often the primary caregiver for infants and young children, their empowerment is likely to channel family resources toward mother-and child well-being.

There is extensive empirical evidence of the association between parental education and child health.[3] Because genetic endowments are a key determinant of a child's health, it is challenging to provide convincing evidence that the correlation between parental education and child health implies causality: that parental education improves child health. Arguably, heritable ability may result in more able women seeking higher education and having more able children who have better health (Behrman and Rosenzweig 2002). Further, a future orientation may cause mothers to acquire more education and invest in their children's health (Fuchs 1982). In short, an unobserved third factor may be causing both higher education among women and better health of their children.

Two studies have applied increases in parental education resulting from policy changes to study the effect of an exogenous increase in parental education on the health outcomes of their children. Breierova and Duflo (2004) exploit a large-scale school construction program in Indonesia and Chou, Liu, Grossman, and Joyce (2010) use changes in compulsory education laws in Taiwan. Both studies conclude that parent's education has a negative effect on child and infant mortality. In contrast to the findings of these investigations, a recent innovative study that uses the decline in maternal education triggered by high-school closures during the Cultural Revolution in China from 1977 to 1984 finds that women who completed high-school were more likely to use prenatal care and were more likely to work off-farm, but their high-school completion had no effect on premature-births, low-birth weight, neonatal mortality, and infant mortality (Zhang 2012).[4] Two other studies, one based on U.S. data and the other on British data, reached similar conclusions. McCrary and Royer (2011) used school entry policies in the U.S. to identify the effect of mother's education on fertility and infant health and found these effects to be small and possibly heterogeneous. Lindeboom, Llena-Nozal, and van Der Klaauw. (2009) used British compulsory schooling laws and found that postponing the school leaving age of parents by one year had little effect on the health of their children. These findings thus cast doubt on previous research on the effects of mother's education on child health and its applicability across diverse cultural and institutional settings.

Researchers have also investigated the effect of education on early marriage and childbearing in adolescence—both are known to have adverse consequences on mother and child health (WHO 1995). This is an important issue in many Middle Eastern countries where marriage and child bearing in adolescence are high. For instance, approximately 17 percent of ever-married women aged twenty to forty-five in Turkey are married before the age of sixteen and 13 percent have a child before they turn seventeen.[5] A reduction in childbearing in adolescence is likely to improve birth outcomes and mother's and child's health. Becker's human capital model, for instance, predicts that education results in a quantity-quality trade off in fertility: more educated parents opting for fewer children of higher quality—e.g., better health (Becker and Lewis 1973).

Empirical studies also suggest that more educated couples have wider knowledge, and make more efficient use of contraceptive methods (Breierova and Duflo

2004; Rosenzweig and Schultz 1989). If mother's education causes a reduction in early marriage and childbearing and improves fertility outcomes, it will improve mother and child health. Establishing causality between mother's education and early marriage, early childbearing, and fertility outcomes is also a challenge because low level of empowerment and high dependency may result in women marrying early and having children thus forgoing education. While this phenomenon may be more prevalent in Middle Eastern countries, in western societies too, teenage pregnancy may limit the options of young mothers and interrupt their schooling.[6] In this context, fertility will be endogenously affecting schooling (Angrist and Evans 1998). In general, the observed association between low education and early marriage and fertility could simply be on account of reverse causality or an unobserved third factor causing both low education and early childbearing.

Here again researchers have used "natural experiments" to determine the direction of causality between education and marriage and education and teenage fertility. Currie and Moretti (2003) use data on opening of two- and four-year colleges during 1940–1990 in the U.S. as an instrument to predict maternal education to study the effect of the predicted education variable on mother's marriage, infant health, use of prenatal care, and smoking and find that mother's education has a positive impact on infant health, prenatal care and a negative impact on smoking. Similarly, Osili and Long (2008) exploited the Universal Primary Education Program introduced in Nigeria in 1976 and exposure to this program by age and region to study the effect of women's education on their fertility and found that increasing female education by one year reduced early fertility by 0.26 births. Using the extension of compulsory education from sixth to ninth grade in Mexico in 1993, Andalon, Grossman, and Williams (2013) find that raising women's education beyond the sixth grade improved their knowledge and use of contraception. Again, whether findings from these studies can be generalized across cultural and institutional settings is an empirical issue and we investigate that in the context of a Middle Eastern country.

Our study builds on the existing literature and makes three contributions. One, we study the effect of education on a range of outcomes, including women's empowerment, utilization of modern family planning methods, and knowledge of the ovulation cycle, that have not been widely studied in previous research. Two, we study the effect of education on child mortality and fertility—two outcomes on which previous studies have found mixed results: Whereas some researchers have found that mothers' education lowered fertility and infant mortality, others have found modest to no effects. Finally, we study the returns to women's education in a Middle Eastern country within a social and cultural environment that discriminates against them to investigate if the effects differ across cultures.

2.1. Previous Research on Effects of Education in Turkey

Earlier research based on single waves of the Turkey Demographic and Health Surveys (TDHS) has found education to be positively correlated with contraceptive use and use of health-care services (Celik 2000; Celik and Hotchkiss 2000; Koç 2000). More recent studies have applied multiple waves TDHS to reach similar conclusions (Atun et al. 2013; Koç et al. 2010). The last two chapters also find a negative correlation between mother's education and child mortality. These studies, however, do not establish causality between mother's education and child mortality, use of contraceptives, and health-care services.

There is no published research on the effects of mother's formal education on child mortality in Turkey.[7] A number of researchers have studied the effects of Turkey's Compulsory Education Law on marriage and fertility (Güneş 2013a; Kırdar, Dayıoğlu, and Koç 2009, 2011), on birth weight, height-for-age, weight-for-age, and preventive care initiation (Güneş 2013b) and on religious tolerance and attitudes toward women's empowerment (Gulesci and Meyersson 2014). These studies use the 2008 TDHS and fail to adjust for confounding factors correlated with the policy as they are based on changes in outcomes from the pre-to post-policy periods. There were several economic and social factors and policy changes coinciding with the education reform that could potentially confound these estimates. For instance, this is a period of a steady decline in women's employment in Turkey.[8] The decline is often attributed to urbanization and shifts in family activities away from agriculture to sectors where women's participation is relatively low (World Bank, 2009). Further, the 1990s is a decade of financial instability in Turkey that culminated in the 2001 financial crisis (Görmez and Yiğit 2010). Such national trends in women's employment, urbanization, and overall economic growth are likely to confound estimates of the effect of education reform in a research design that is based on pre- to post-policy changes in outcomes.

In addition, changes in social policy may also have a con-founding effect. For instance, in 2002, a change in the Civil Code raised the minimum marriage age of women in Turkey from fifteen to seventeen years, making it equal to the minimum marriage age of men. Nationwide women aged eleven or less in 1997, the target of the Compulsory Education law, are also affected by the change in the Civil Code since they were all less than seventeen in 2002. Indeed, any methodology based on comparisons of outcomes of women born before and after 1986 will not be able to distinguish the effect of the Compulsory Education Law from the effect of the change in legal minimum marriage age.

Gulesci and Meyersson use a regression discontinuity model and assume that women born on or after September 1986 are bound by the Compulsory

Schooling Law to acquire eight years of schooling. The Bylaw of Primary Education in Turkey, however, counts age by calendar year, and not school year.[9] Thus it is likely that Gulesci and Meyersson measured the target group of the Compulsory School Law with some degree of error.[10]

In our analysis, we assume that schools in Turkey follow the Bylaw of Primary Educations Institutions for admission and in the implementation of Compulsory Schooling Law. Individuals born in 1986 or later are considered the target of education reform. Further, we apply changes in Compulsory Education Law and geographic differences in the intensity of its implementation, described in detail below, to identify the effects of ever-married women's education on child health, use of health-care services, and a range of measures capturing the fertility and empowerment of ever-married women. This methodology allows us to control for, in a parsimonious manner, unobserved national economic and social trends and policy changes that are correlated with education reform.

3. TURKEY'S COMPULSORY EDUCATION LAW

In 1996, Turkey entered the European Union customs union and began preparing for full membership in the future. Within the broader context of lowering economic and social disparities, in 1997, the government launched the Rapid Coverage of Compulsory Education Program that increased years of compulsory schooling from five to eight. To meet the expected increase in enrollment, during 1996–2003, the government built 80,000 new classrooms, a 41 percent increase over the 1996 base, and hired 103,000 additional primary school teachers, which was a 36 percent increase over the 1996 base (Dülger 2004; State Institute of Statistics 1999; Turkish Statistical Institute 2006; also see figures 6.1a and 6.1b). Further, investment in new teachers and infrastructure varied across regions with the aim of devoting more resources to regions with low enrollment among primary school age students.

Primary school enrollment (grades 1–8) rose rapidly in the first four years of the reform: from 9.1 million in 1997 to 10.5 million in 2000 (Turkish Statistical Institute, 2006). Figure 6.2 presents the trend in gross enrollment in grades 6–8 during 1989–2004, covering eight years prior to the implementation of the Compulsory Education Law and eight years of the post-implementation period. There is a modest upward trend in enrollment in grades 6–8 during 1989–1993, followed by a leveling off during 1993–1997. Enrollment begins to rise steadily after 1997, with the implementation of the Compulsory Education Law, as cohorts mandated to remain in school reach grade 6 or progress from grades 6 to 8, reaching a plateau about four years after the policy change. Overall, during 1996–2000

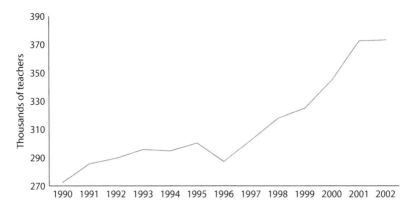

Figure 6.1a Number of primary school (grade 1–8) teachers

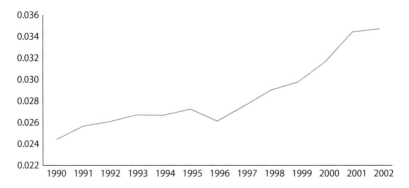

Figure 6.1b Primary school teachers per child (number of grade 1–8 teachers divided by number of children aged 6–13)

enrollment in grades 6–8 increased 1.1 million or 42 percent; and gross enrollment rate increased from 66 percent to 93 percent. Further, the gap in enrollment across the more developed western regions (e.g., Istanbul, West Marmara, and East Marmara) and less-developed eastern regions (e.g., Northeast Anatolia, Central East Anatolia, and Southeast Anatolia) declined during this period.

4. DATA

The primary data used in this study come from the Turkey Demographic and Health Surveys (TDHS) of 2003 and 2008. The TDHS collect data on demographic characteristics of each household member, including their age, sex, region and province of birth, birth place type (rural/urban), completed years of

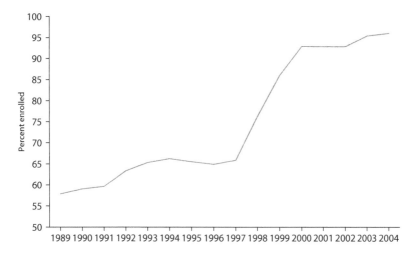

Figure 6.2 Gross enrollment rate in grades 6–8 (number of students enrolled in grades 6–8 divided by population of children aged 11–13)

schooling, and current region and province of residence. For a nationally representative sample of ever-married women aged fifteen to forty-nine, the TDHS collect data on respondent's parents' education, mother tongue,[11] and region[12] and province of residence in childhood.[13] Our analysis is based on the ever-married sample and we focus on women aged eighteen to twenty-nine at the time of the survey.[14] The variables on region of residence in childhood and cohort of childhood (when turned eleven) are used to match TDHS individual level data with the administrative data on primary school teachers (teachers for grades 1–8) per child (aged six to thirteen) by region and year, henceforth referred to as teacher-child ratio, for convenience. Data on province of residence in childhood are used to construct twenty subregions of childhood.[15] Further, the variable on subregion of residence in childhood and cohort of childhood (when turned eleven) are used to match TDHS individual level data with the administrative data on teacher-child ratio by subregion and year. The source of administrative data on primary school teachers, by subregion (and by region) and year, is Ministry of National Education's National Education Statistics. Estimates of number of children aged six to thirteen by subregion (and region) and year, come from Census 1985, 1990, and 2000; for intercensus years, these data are interpolated assuming a linear trend.[16]

The ever-married sample provides retrospective data on birth and fertility histories, including number of pregnancies, number of children born, first birth interval (age at first birth minus age at first marriage, measured in months), number of children who died before age one, number of children who died before age five, ever had a stillbirth, ever had a miscarriage, ever had induced abortion, antenatal visits, and whether the respondent uses a modern family planning method. We use data on marriage and fertility histories to construct outcome variables on age at first marriage and age at first birth and we use data on birth and fertility histories to create the outcome variables relating to child mortality and mother's fertility outcomes. Specifically, we study the following measures of child mortality: number of children deceased before the first month after birth, number of children deceased during one to twelve months after birth, number of children deceased before age one, and number of children deceased before age five; and the following measures of women's fertility: number of total births, number of pregnancies, use of contraceptives, whether the woman has knowledge of her ovulation cycle, and whether she paid an antenatal visit to a health facility during the first trimester of pregnancy.[17]

We use responses to the following questions in the ever-married sample to study the effect of education on attitudes toward women's empowerment and gender equality: Does the respondent agree/disagree that men are wiser? Does the respondent agree/disagree that a boy's education is preferable to a girl's education? Does the respondent agree/disagree if all family decisions should be made by men?[18] And finally, we study responses to a set of questions on whether wife beating is justified if she (i) wastes money, (ii) neglects children, (iii) argues with husband, and (iv) refuses sex. Appendix A provides means of these variables for ever-married women aged eighteen to twenty-two and twenty-three to twenty-nine in 2003 and 2008.

5. RESEARCH DESIGN

5.1. Effect of Compulsory Education on Schooling

Our objective is to study the effect of mother's schooling on a range of outcomes measuring fertility, child mortality, and women's empowerment. Education is endogenous to these outcomes and we use an instrumental variables methodology to address this issue. Equation (1) describes the baseline first-stage regression model to be estimated on a sample of ever-married women aged eighteen to twenty-nine using the 2008 TDHS data:

$$Edu_i = \eta_c + \eta_j + \lambda_T \ Teacher_{j\tau} * Young + \lambda \ Teacher_{j\tau}$$
$$+ \Delta X + \rho^* P_{j1996} * Cohort + e_{ijt} \tag{1}$$

Edu_i denotes the education of woman i. We use two separate measures of education: a continuous variable indicating the respondent's years of schooling and a dichotomous variable indicating whether she has eight or more years of schooling. Edu_i is modeled as a function of the respondent's cohort of childhood (η_c—a dummy variable for the year respondent turned eleven), region of childhood (η_j region where the respondent lived at age eleven), and family endowments (X) namely parental education,[19] mother-tongue (dummy variables indicating whether the mother-tongue is Turkish, Kurdish, Arabic, and other), and whether she lived in a rural area in childhood (at age eleven). The argument for including parents' schooling is that they may affect own schooling and be correlated with program intensity. The argument for excluding parents' schooling is that they may be correlated with the same unobservable factor that is correlated with own schooling. In the empirical analysis, we run models with and without these controls. Estimates were similar from the two sets of models, and for brevity, we have opted to present findings with the controls.[20]

The variable *Young* is equal to one if the respondent was born during 1986–1990, and therefore was bound by the Compulsory Education Law to complete eight years of mandatory schooling, otherwise zero. Women born during 1979–1985 are the category of comparison.[21] $Teacher_{j\tau}$ denotes the number of primary school teachers as a proportion to primary school age children (aged six to thirteen) in the region of childhood j in year τ (τ = year of birth + 11), and is a measure of the intensity of education reform by region and year.

The cohort-of-childhood dummy variables control for the national trends in schooling not related to the 1997 education reform and the region-of-childhood dummy variables control for cohort in variant region-specific unmeasured factors affecting the schooling outcome (e.g., differences across regions due to social and economic development). Parameter λ estimates the association between $Teacher_{j\tau}$ and schooling for the comparison group and $\lambda + \lambda_T$ measures the same for the treatment group (*Young*). The comparison group was not subject to the Compulsory Education Law, therefore, λ measures the effect on education of other time-varying factors correlated with the reform intensity variable $-Teacher_{j\tau}$. Assuming that these other time-varying factors correlated with the reform intensity variable had the same effect on the treatment and comparison groups, $\lambda_T (= \lambda + \lambda_T - \lambda)$ would estimate the effect of the Compulsory Education Law on the schooling outcome of the treatment group (*Young*).

Equation (1) also includes a full set of interactions of the cohort of birth dummy variables with the gross enrollment rate in grades 6–8 (P_{j1996}) in 1996, a year prior to the implementation of the Education Reform Law. The intensity of reform was likely to be greater in regions that were lagging in education in the pre-reform period (e.g., Northeast Anatolia, Central East Anatolia, and Southeast Anatolia). Inclusion of the interaction term allows us to explicitly control for variation in reform intensity associated with enrollment in the pre-reform period.

The outcome variables in equation (1) are measured as of 2008. Thus, one source of difference between the outcomes for the treatment and the comparison groups could be the difference in their ages. The identifying assumption for equation (1) is that in the absence of education reform, time-varying factors correlated with the variable $Teacher_{j\tau}$ would have the same effect on the treatment and comparison groups. Because the outcome variables are sensitive to age, this is a limiting assumption and the resulting estimates are likely to be biased. We adopt a difference-in-difference methodology to address this issue. To implement this strategy, the first-stage regression is estimated on a combined sample of ever-married women aged eighteen to twenty-nine in the TDHS 2003 and 2008 data using the following model:

$$
\begin{aligned}
Edu_{ijt} = {}& \tilde{\eta}_a + \tilde{\eta}_c + \tilde{\eta}_j + \tilde{\lambda}_T \ Teacher_{j\tau} * Young * Yr2008 \\
& + \tilde{\lambda}_y \ Teacher_{j\tau} * Young + \tilde{\lambda} \ Teacher_{j\tau} + \tilde{\rho} * P_{j1996} \\
& * Cohort + \tilde{\Delta}X + \tilde{e}_{ijt}
\end{aligned}
\tag{2}
$$

In equation (2), the symbol ~ is used to distinguish the parameters from equation (1). Equation (2) differs from equation (1) in two respects. First, equation (2) controls for a full set of age effects, denoted by $\tilde{\eta}_a$, a dummy variable for each year of age. It also includes cohort fixed effects. Thus, age-fixed effects control for nationwide trends in schooling and cohort effects control for nationwide changes specific to cohorts (e.g., the 2002 change in civil code that raised minimum marriage age for women and affected all cohorts born after 1985). Note that the 1981–1985 cohorts-of-birth appear both in the 2003 and 2008 data. These women were not covered by education reform and thus provide the counter-factual: changes in educational attainment (in the absence of education reform) during the study period.[22]

Second, equation (2) includes a three-way interaction term between $Teacher_{j\tau}$, $Young$, and a dummy variable for TDHS 2008. Thus, inclusion of the 2003 data allows estimating the effect of education reforms after controlling for age-specific (young versus older women) time-varying factors that may be correlated with the reform intensity variable. In equation (2), $\tilde{\lambda}$ captures the effect of time-varying factors correlated with the intensity of the reform on schooling and $\tilde{\lambda}_y$ allows these effects to be different for the younger and older cohorts.[23] The parameter of interest is $\tilde{\lambda}_T$ that estimates the effect of an exogenous increase in investment in primary school teachers resulting from the Compulsory Education Law on the schooling variables of Young ever-married women.

We estimate equation (2) with two alternative definitions of the geographical unit. The first is the region of childhood as specified above and the second is the subregion of childhood. In the latter case $Teacher_{j\tau}$ is measured at the subregion of childhool residence, $P_j 1996$, is gross enrollment rate in grades 6–8 at the subregional level in 1996,[24] and the analysis includes a full set of dummy variables for the twenty subregions. The advantage of the regional specification is that estimates are based on a fairly large number of women in each region. The disadvantage is that there are only twelve regions. Our design requires standard errors of regression coefficients to be obtained by clustering on the geographical unit of residence (Huber 1967). Standard errors tend to be understated if the number of clusters on which they are based is as small as twelve (Angrist and Pischke 2009).

The advantage of the subregional specification is that the number of clusters increases from twelve to twenty. Bertrand, Duflo, and Mullainathan (2004) and Angrist and Pischke (2009) argue that between forty-two and fifty clusters are required to obtain consistent estimates of standard errors that account for clustering. But Bertrand and her colleagues and Cameron, Gelbach, and Miller (2008) actually show that the rate of rejecting the null hypothesis when it is true is smaller when there are twenty clusters than when there are fifty. That suggests that twenty clusters, rather than forty-two or fifty, are sufficient. In our case, the disadvantage of the subregional model is that the estimates are based on smaller sample sizes in the geographical units than in the regional model.

5.2. Mother's Education and Child Mortality

To study the effect of mother's schooling on child mortality, we adopt an equation similar to equation (2), with two modifications: one, now the dependent variable is a measure of child mortality,[25] and two, predicted value of schooling from equation (2) replaces the three-way interaction term $Teacher_{j\tau}$ * *Young* * *Yr2008*. The second-stage regression has all the other controls of the first stage and thus the identification of the coefficient for predicted schooling depends entirely on the exclusion of the interaction term from the second-stage regression. As long as primary school teacher-child ratio ($Teacher_{j\tau}$) does not affect child health except through its effect on schooling, the IV estimate will provide the causal effect of schooling on child mortality. We estimate the structural form equations using ordinary least squares and two-stage least squares models. Throughout, standard errors are obtained by clustering on region (subregion) of residence in the region level (subregion level) analysis (Huber 1967).

Note that most of the outcomes that we study here (child mortality and other outcomes discussed below) are likely to be different for the Young and Older group of women. The difference in child mortality (and other outcomes) between these two groups of women in 2008 could be a result of higher education (resulting from the Compulsory Education Law) or due to other differences between the two cohorts (e.g., age difference). We use difference in child mortality of the two groups in the 2003 sample as the counter-factual for the difference in child mortality in the absence of any reform. In the reduced form estimates, the coefficient on the three-way interaction ($Teacher_{j\tau}$ * $Young$ * $Yr2008$) thus estimates the change in child mortality caused by an exogenous increase in investment in primary school teachers (resulting from the Compulsory Education Law) on child mortality experienced by $Young$ ever-married women.

5.3. Education, Age at Marriage and First Birth, Fertility Behaviors, Use of Health Care, and Gender Equality

Our second objective is to study the effect of women's education on their age at marriage, fertility, use of health care, and attitudes toward gender equality. A methodology similar to that discussed for child mortality outcomes is applied here. We study the following outcomes: (i) age at first marriage and age at first birth, (ii) fertility behavior such as number of pregnancies, number of children born, knowledge and utilization of family planning methods, antenatal visit during the first trimester of pregnancy, and (iii) attitudes toward gender equality. Our research methodology does not allow us to test if education affected child mortality through any of these channels e.g., via its impact on age at first marriage, age at childbirth, antenatal visits, knowledge, and use of family planning methods or attitudes toward gender equality. However, we can, and do, test if education influenced any of the aforementioned outcomes and draw inferences about the possible existence of these channels. For instance, if mother's education did not alter attitudes toward gender equality that would be evidence that changes in child outcomes that we find could not be due to changes in attitudes toward gender equality. Or if we did not find that education affected use of contraceptives, it would be unlikely that education affected the health outcomes of children, in our data, via improvement in use of contraceptives.

6. RESULTS

6.1. Effect of Compulsory Education Reform on Schooling

We begin the analysis by examining the descriptive data on the educational outcomes of the younger (aged eighteen to twenty-two) and older (aged twenty-three to twenty-nine) cohorts of the ever-married sample of women in 2003 and 2008. Figures 6.3a and 6.3b present the kernel density of years of schooling in 2003 and 2008 of the younger and older cohorts, respectively, and show that the younger cohort is far more likely to have completed at least eight years schooling in 2008 than in 2003; the corresponding difference in the proportion with eight years of schooling is modest for the older cohort. Statistics in table 6.1 show that in 2008, 34 percent of the older cohort (aged twenty-three to twenty-nine) had at least eight years of schooling. The members of the older cohort were born in 1985 or earlier and therefore they did not have to comply with the law on mandatory eight years of schooling. Among the younger cohort (aged eighteen to twenty-two), who had to comply with mandatory increase in schooling, 53 percent had eight years of schooling in 2008.

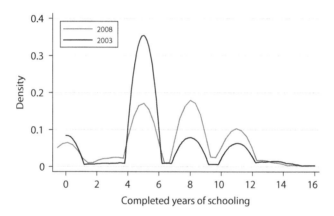

Figure 6.3a Completed years of schooling for younger cohorts (aged 18–22)

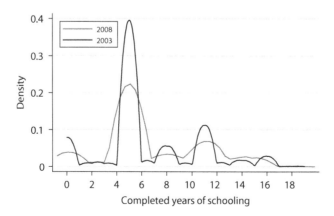

Figure 6.3b Completed years of schooling of older cohorts (aged 23–29)

The 19 percentage-points difference in the schooling variable for the two cohorts could be due to the Compulsory Schooling Law or due to other factors that caused the educational attainment of the younger and older cohorts to be different.

For a rough and crude estimate of the effect of these other factors, we compare the educational attainment of similar cohorts in the pre-policy period: in 2003, 27 percent of the younger cohort and 32 percent of the older cohort had eight years of schooling.[26] Assuming that in the absence of the compulsory schooling law, the gap in the education outcome of the younger and older cohorts in 2008 would have been the same as in 2003, we subtract the difference in the schooling outcome between the younger and older cohorts in 2003 from the difference for the two groups in 2008 to arrive at a crude difference-in-difference estimate of the effect of the Compulsory Education Law on the education outcome of the younger cohort. Our crude difference-in-difference estimate is a 24 percentage-point increase in the proportion of ever-married mothers with eight years of schooling. Table 6.1 also computes the difference-in-difference estimate of years of schooling, which is 0.83 years or a 15 percent increase over the mean for the younger group in 2003, the pre-policy period.

These crude difference-in-difference estimates assume that any increase in years of schooling of the younger cohort over-and-above the difference between the younger and older cohorts in 2003 is on account of the Compulsory Education Law. This may not be true. Indeed, there were social and economic trends correlated with the reform that may have caused increased schooling of the younger cohort. In the regression analysis that follows we control for these factors by estimating the effect of the intensity of the education reform, which

Table 6.1 Difference-in-Differences Estimates of the Association between Compulsory Education Law and Schooling of Ever-Married Women

	2008			2003			Difference-in-Difference
	Young	Older	Difference 1	Young	Older	Difference 2	
At least 8 years of schooling	0.53 (0.02)	0.34 (0.01)	0.19*** (0.02)	0.27 (0.02)	0.32 (0.01)	−0.05** (0.02)	0.24*** (0.03)
Years of schooling	6.70 (0.16)	6.68 (0.09)	0.02 (0.18)	5.65 (0.13)	6.46 (0.08)	−0.81*** (0.16)	0.83*** (0.24)
N	611	1794	2405	795	2033	2828	5233

Notes: The sample of analysis is ever-married women aged eighteen to twenty-nine in the 2003 and 2008 Turkey Demographic and Health Surveys. Women aged eighteen to twenty-two are defined as Young and women aged twenty-three to twenty-nine are defined as Older.

**$0.01 < p \leq 0.05$.

***$p \leq 0.01$.

differed across regions (and subregions) and years as specified in equation (2) and include a complete set of cohort-of-childhood dummy variables and age effects. These estimates are presented in table 6.2.

Panel 1 presents the analysis at the regional level and panel 2 at the subregional level. The intensity of the policy is measured by the number of teachers as a proportion to the number of children aged six to thirteen (or teacher-child ratio) by region in panel 1 and by subregion in panel 2. All models, in panel 1, control for respondent's age (a dummy variable for each year of age), region of residence in childhood, and cohort of childhood effects, cohort of childhood interacted with the gross enrollment rate in grades 6–8 in the region of residence in childhood in 1996, year of observation, teacher-child ratio at age eleven, the interaction of the *Young* dummy variable with teacher-child ratio at eleven, and the triple interaction term between the *Young* dummy variable, teacher-child ratio and the dummy variable for year 2008. Further controls are added sequentially in Models 2–4: Model 2 includes additional controls for the education of respondents' parents, Model 3 adds respondent's mother tongue, and Model 4 adds mother tongue and a variable for whether the respondent lived in a rural area during childhood, in addition to the controls in Model 2. Panel 2 has all the controls of panel 1, but the geographic variables and controls are at the subregional level. Standard errors in parenthesis adjust for clustering by region where the respondent lived in childhood in panel 1 and by the subregion of residence in childhood in the panel 2.

Estimates in table 6.2, model 1 suggest that a 1 percentage-point increase in teacher-child ratio, which corresponds to a 40 percent change in the mean value of teacher-child ratio, resulted in a 16 percentage-point increase in the proportion of younger ever-married women with eight or more years of schooling. Additional controls in Models 2–4 yield similar results: a 1 percentage-point increase in teacher-child ratio raised the proportion with at least eight years of schooling by 17 percentage points (Model 4, panel 1). In the first five years after the policy reform, the period relevant for this study, nationally the average teacher-child ratio increased by 0.8 percentage points. Thus, on average, the Compulsory Schooling Law raised the proportion of ever-married women with at least eight years of schooling by 14 (=17 multiplied with 0.8) percentage points. This is a 51 percent increase over the mean for the younger cohort in 2003, before the Compulsory Education law was passed. The partial F-stat for the three-way interaction term (instrumental variable) is 14 for Model 4 (panel 1). Estimates in the bottom panel are similar. Here the F-stat for the three-way interaction term is 13 (Model 4, panel 2). Estimates in panel 2 (model 4) indicate that the Compulsory Schooling law raised the proportion of ever-married

Table 6.2 Estimates of the Effect of Compulsory Years of Schooling on Ever-Married Women's Education

	Schooling = 8 Years or More				Years of Schooling			
	Model 1	Model 2	Model 3	Model 4	Model 1	Model 2	Model 3	Model 4
Panel 1: Analysis at the level of 12 regions								
Young * Teacher-child ratio (at age 11) * Year 2008	16.33**	16.68***	17.62***	17.19***	62.88	70.47*	85.52**	82.36**
	(5.96)	(4.80)	(4.80)	(4.65)	(41.42)	(33.86)	(31.74)	(31.08)
F-ratio	7.51	12.08	13.48	13.67	2.30	4.33	7.26	7.02
Panel 2: Analysis at the level of 20 subregions								
Young * Teacher-child ratio (at age 11) * Year 2008	16.76***	15.19***	16.17***	15.75***	76.18**	63.03**	78.58***	75.57**
	(4.46)	(4.32)	(4.36)	(4.30)	(34.70)	(30.31)	(29.90)	(29.61)
F-ratio	14.12	12.36	13.75	13.42	4.82	4.32	6.91	6.51
Mean of the dependent variable	0.34	0.34	0.34	0.34	6.44	6.44	6.44	6.44
Mean of teacher-child ratio (at age 11)	0.026	0.026	0.026	0.026	0.026	0.026	0.026	0.026
Model controls for:								
Mother's and father's education	No	Yes	Yes	Yes	No	Yes	Yes	Yes
Mother tongue	No	No	Yes	Yes	No	No	Yes	Yes
Childhood place of residence (rural/urban)	No	No	No	Yes	No	No	No	Yes
N	5,161	5,149	5,149	5,147	5,161	5,149	5,149	5,147

Notes: Each cell in panels 1 and 2 is based on a separate regression with respondent's schooling outcome listed in the column heading as the dependent variable. The sample of analysis is ever-married women aged eighteen to twenty-nine in the 2003 and 2008 TDHS. Women aged eighteen to twenty-two are defined as Young. Standard errors clustered on the region of childhood residence are in parentheses in panel 1 and on the subregion of childhood residence in parentheses in panel 2. F-ratios are F-statistics of the test of significance of the excluded instrument (the three-way interaction terms listed in table). In addition to the controls listed in the table, each regression controls for respondent's age (a dummy variable for each year of age), respondent's year of birth, teacher-child ratio at age eleven, region of residence at age eleven, year of childhood (age eleven) interacted with 6–8 grade gross enrollment rate in 1996 in the region of childhood, and an interaction of the Young dummy variable with teacher-child ratio in region of residence at age eleven. Regressions in panel 2 are the same as in panel 1 with one difference: all geographic variables (and controls) are measured at the subregional level. Teacher-child ratio is measured by region of childhood in panel 1 and by subregion of childhood in panel 2. Means of the teacher-child ratio at regional and subregional levels are the same at 3 decimal digits.

*0.05 < p ≤ 0.1,

**0.01 < p ≤ 0.05,

***p ≤ 0.01.

women with at least eight years of schooling by 13 percentage points (=15.8 multiplied by 0.8).

Table 6.2 also presents the first-stage estimates with years of schooling as the dependent variable. Estimated effects are positive and mostly statistically significant. These estimates suggest that a 1 percentage-point increase in the teacher-child ratio resulted in an increase in schooling by approximately 0.7 to 0.8 years. The partial F-stat for the instrumental variable for Model 4 is 7. A comparison of the results from tables 6.1 and 6.2 reveals that the simple difference-in-difference estimate that does not control for national trends in schooling over-estimates the effect of the Compulsory Schooling Law on both the schooling outcomes. Further, it appears from the F-stat estimates that we have a much better chance of detecting the effect of the dichotomous variable on eight years of schooling than the effect of the continuous variable on years of schooling on the second-stage outcomes. Therefore, henceforth the analysis is restricted to estimating the effect of schooling measured as a dichotomous variable.

Next, we estimate equation (2) with one modification: the three-way interaction term between *Young*, teacher-child ratio, and year 2008 is replaced by twelve different interactions replacing *Young* with a dummy variable indicating the age of the respondent for the twelve age categories. In figures 6.4a and 6.4b, we plot the estimated coefficients from the twelve three-way interactions. The point estimates are close to zero for women ages twenty-three to twenty-nine and turn positive and statistically significant for women ages eighteen to twenty-two. These results provide empirical justification for our construction of the treatment (*Young*) and comparison (*Older*) groups.

To test the validity of the instrument, following Duflo (2001) and Chou et al. (2010), we run regressions using equation (2) on a set of dichotomous dependent variables defined as equal to 1 if the respondent has at least "m" years of schooling, otherwise 0. In all, we run Model 4 in table 6.2 for sixteen different outcomes allowing "m" to vary from 1 to 16. The sample of analysis is ever-married women aged eighteen to twenty-nine, the same as in tables 6.1 and 6.2. Figure 6.5a presents the point estimates with regional level analysis and figure 6.5b presents point estimates with analysis at the subregional level.

The point estimates and the 95th confidence intervals of the three-way interaction term, displayed in figures 6.5a and 6.5b, show a sharp increase in the proportion of ever-married women with six, seven, and eight years of schooling. As expected, the Compulsory Schooling Law has no effect on the proportion of women with five or fewer years of schooling; estimated coefficients for dependent variables with nine or more years of schooling to sixteen

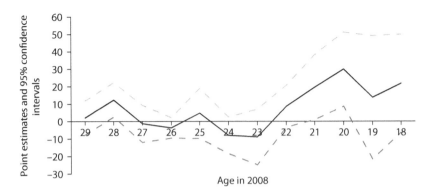

Figure 6.4a Coefficients of the interactions between age, program intensity in the region of childhood at age 11, and DHS 2008 (analysis based on twelve regions of residence in childhood)

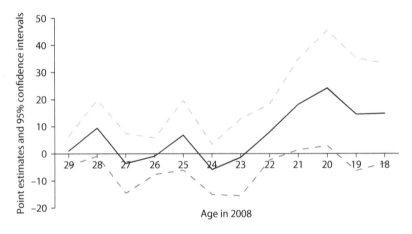

Figure 6.4b Coefficients of the interactions between age, program intensity in the region of childhood at age 11, and DHS 2008 (analysis based on twenty subregions of residence in childhood)

or more years of schooling are also modest and statistically insignificant. This is evidence that our instrumental variable, teacher-child ratio, is not capturing the effect of factors that raised education at all levels. If that were the case, the estimated coefficients for middle to secondary education or one to five years of schooling would have been positive and statistically significant. That the estimated effects on higher and lower levels of education are modest and statistically insignificant provides some evidence that our instrumental variable is valid.

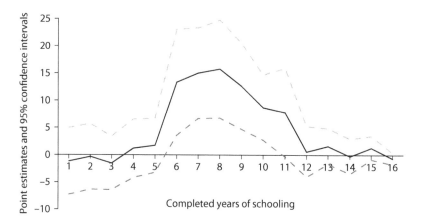

Figure 6.5a Association between the probability of completing at least "m" years of schooling and Turkey's 1997 Compulsory Education Law (analysis based on twelve regions of residence in childhood)

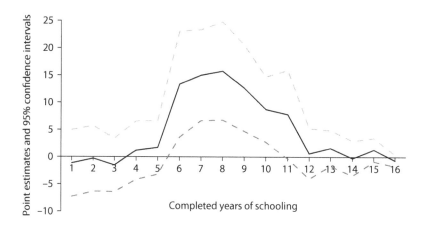

Figure 6.5b Association between the probability of completing at least "m" years of schooling and Turkey's 1997 Compulsory Education Law (analysis based on twenty subregions of residence in childhood)

6.2. Effect of Compulsory Education Reform on Fertility and Child Mortality

Table 6.3 presents the ordinary least squares (OLS) and the two-stage least squares (IV) estimates of the effect of mother's education on fertility and child mortality and the reduced form estimates of the effect of the teacher-child ratio on these outcomes. Estimates in panel 1 are based on region level analysis and estimates in

Table 6.3 Estimates of the Effect of Women's Education on Fertility and Child Mortality

	Number of Pregnancies	Number of Children Born	Number of Children Deceased before Age 1	Number of Children Deceased before Age 5	Number of Children Deceased in 1st Month after Birth	Number of Children Deceased in 1–12 Months after Birth
Panel 1: Analysis at the level of 12 regions						
OLS estimates						
Schooling = 8 years or more	−0.52***	−0.43***	−0.03**	−0.03**	−0.01	−0.01***
	(0.05)	(0.03)	(0.01)	(0.01)	(0.01)	(0.00)
Reduced form estimates						
Young * Teacher child ratio (at age 11) * Year 2008	−23.25***	−27.13***	−2.02	−3.16**	−2.24**	0.67
	(5.46)	(6.35)	(1.15)	(1.35)	(0.83)	(0.90)
IV estimates						
Schooling = 8 years or more	−1.35***	−1.58***	−0.11	−0.17*	−0.12*	0.04
	(0.46)	(0.50)	(0.07)	(0.10)	(0.07)	(0.06)
Wooldridge test statistic	5.92**	9.84***	1.25	2.82	3.81*	1.14
Panel 2: Analysis at the level of 20 subregions						
OLS estimates						
Schooling = 8 years or more	−0.51***	−0.43***	−0.03*	−0.03*	−0.01	−0.01***
	(0.04)	(0.04)	(0.01)	(0.02)	(0.01)	(0.00)

Reduced form estimates

Young * Teacher child ratio (at age 11) *	-20.17**	-19.98*	-1.69	-2.57	-1.83*	0.68
Year 2008	(5.39)	(5.83)	(1.62)	(1.88)	(0.83)	(1.24)
IV estimates						
Schooling = 8 years or more	-1.28**	-1.27***	-0.10	-0.14	-0.10*	0.04
	(0.53)	(0.48)	(0.09)	(0.11)	(0.06)	(0.07)
Wooldridge test statistic	3.52*	4.61**	0.50	1.11	3.14*	0.58
Mean of the dependent variable	1.81	1.52	0.06	0.07	0.03	0.02
N	5,147	5,147	4,228	4,228	4,228	4,228

Notes: Figures in each cell of panels 1 and 2 are based on separate regressions with column heading as the dependent variable. Standard errors clustered on the region of childhood residence are in parentheses in panel 1 and on the subregion of childhood residence are in parentheses in panel 2. The sample of analysis is ever-married women aged eighteen to twenty-nine in the 2003 and 2008 TDHS. Women aged eighteen to twenty-two are defined as Young. All regressions in panel 1 control for respondent's age (a dummy variable for each year of age), respondent's year of birth, region of residence at age eleven, parents' education, respondent's mother tongue and place of residence (urban/rural) at age eleven, year of childhood interacted with 6–8 grade gross enrollment in the region of residence in childhood in 1996, teacher-child ratio, and an interaction of the Young dummy variable with teacher-child ratio. The instrumental variable in the IV estimates is the three-way interaction between Young * Teacher-child ratio (at age eleven) * Year 2008. Regressions in panel 2 are the same as in panel 1 with one difference: all geographic variables (and controls) are measured at the subregional level.

*0.05 < *p* ≤ 0.1.

**0.01 < *p* ≤ 0.05.

***p ≤ 0.01.

panel 2 are from subregional analysis. The OLS estimates show that ever-married women aged eighteen to twenty-two with at least eight years of schooling had 0.5 fewer pregnancies, 0.4 fewer children, and 0.03 fewer deceased children (under age five) than women with less than eight years of schooling. Further, eight years of schooling is also associated with a reduced risk of child mortality.

The IV estimates are larger (in absolute levels) than the OLS estimates and suggest that a 10 percentage-point increase in proportion with eight years of schooling lowers the number of pregnancies per ever-married woman by approximately 0.13 and number of children by between 0.13 and 0.16. Further, it lowers number of deceased children before age five by 0.02 (24 percent decline over the mean of 0.07) and most of the decline is in the first month after childbirth. However, the estimate for the number of deceased children before age five is statistically insignificant in the subregional analysis. Thus, it is likely that our analyses with fewer clusters (twelve clusters in the regional analysis) underestimate the standard errors and our subregional analysis (with twenty clusters) is more reliable (Angrist and Pischke 2009; Cameron et al. 2008). Reduced form estimates also lead to the same conclusion that increased schooling resulting from the Compulsory Education Law caused a decline in fertility and lowered child mortality. The Wooldridge test statistic is often statistically significant suggesting that the OLS estimator of the same equation would yield inconsistent estimates and that the instrumental variables technique is required (Wooldridge 1995).

The combined evidence from the regional and subregional level analyses thus suggests that a 10 percentage-points increase in the proportion of ever-married women with eight years of schooling lowered the number of pregnancies per ever-married woman by approximately 0.13 and number of children per ever-married woman by between 0.13 to 0.16,[27] and there is some weak evidence that mother's education lowered child mortality.

6.3. Effect of Compulsory Education Reform on Age at First Marriage, Age at First Birth, Health-Care Use, and Fertility Behaviors

Next, we investigate the effect of women's schooling on age at first marriage and age at first birth. Models similar to those in table 6.3 are applied and the results are presented in table 6.4. The OLS estimates show that a 10 percentage points increase in the proportion of women with eight years of schooling raised age at first marriage and age at first birth by about two months (0.15 * 12). The IV estimates are similar sized and statistically significant in panel 1 but statistically insignificant in panel 2.

Table 6.4 Estimates of the Effect of Women's Education on Age at First Marriage, Age at First Birth, Health-Care Use, and Knowledge/Use of Family Planning Methods

	Age at First Marriage	Age at First Birth	Antenatal Visit During the First Trimester	Use of Modern Family Planning Methods	Knowledge of the Ovulation Cycle
Panel 1: Analysis at the level of 12 regions					
OLS estimates					
Schooling = 8 years or more	1.49***	1.40***	0.14***	0.05**	0.16***
	(0.11)	(0.11)	(0.03)	(0.02)	(0.02)
Reduced form estimates					
Young * Teacher-child ratio	26.90	29.35**	16.33**	13.92*	8.39**
(at age 11) * Year 2008	(17.41)	(12.72)	(7.33)	(7.45)	(2.97)
IV estimates					
Schooling = 8 years or more	1.56**	1.61***	0.58*	0.81**	0.48**
	(0.75)	(0.59)	(0.31)	(0.36)	(0.20)
Wooldridge test statistic	0.01	0.13	3.11	3.19	3.22
Panel 2: Analysis at the level of 20 subregions					
OLS estimates					
Schooling = 8 years or more	1.49***	1.40***	0.14***	0.05***	0.16***
	(0.10)	(0.09)	(0.03)	(0.02)	(0.02)
Reduced form estimates					
Young * Teacher-child ratio	26.91	19.67	15.40**	14.11*	8.97***
(at age 11) * Year 2008	(17.89)	(18.43)	(5.90)	(7.49)	(2.81)
IV estimates					
Schooling = 8 years or more	1.71	1.11	0.57**	0.90**	0.56**
	(1.07)	(0.92)	(0.29)	(0.45)	(0.22)
Wooldridge test statistic	0.04	0.09	3.90**	3.24*	4.61**
Mean of the dependent variable	19.59	20.64	0.67	0.39	0.25
N	5,147	4,228	1,588	5,147	5,142

Notes: Figures in each cell of panels 1 and 2 are based on separate regressions with column heading as the dependent variable. Standard errors clustered on the region of childhood residence are in parentheses in panel 1 and on the subregion of childhood residence are in parentheses in panel 2. The sample of analysis is ever-married women aged eighteen to twenty-nine in the 2003 and 2008 TDHS. Women aged eighteen to twenty-two are defined as Young. All regressions in panel 1 control for respondent's age (a dummy variable for each year of age), respondent's year of birth, region of residence at age eleven, parents' education, respondent's mother tongue and place of residence (urban/rural) at age eleven, year of childhood interacted with 6–8 grade gross enrollment in the region of residence in childhood in 1996, teacher-child ratio, and an interaction of the Young dummy variable with teacher-child ratio. The instrumental variable in the IV estimates is the three-way interaction between Young * Teacher-child ratio (at age eleven) * Year 2008. Regressions in panel 2 are the same as in panel 1 with one difference: all geographic variables (and controls) are measured at the subregional level. In regressions with whether the respondent paid an antenatal visit during the first trimester as dependent variable the sample is restricted to first births.

*0.05 < p ≤ 0.1.

**0.01 < p ≤ 0.05.

***p ≤ 0.01.

The last three columns of table 6.4 show the effect of a woman's education on her use of family planning methods, knowledge of the ovulation cycle, and whether she paid an antenatal visit during the first trimester of pregnancy. Antenatal visits are the first of many investments that women make in their children's health, cognitive development, and other aspects of life and we hypothesize that education increases these investments. In 2003, only 46 percent of young ever-married women aged eighteen to twenty-two paid at least one antenatal visit during the first trimester, 27 percent used modern family planning methods, and an even smaller proportion, 18 percent, had knowledge of their ovulation cycle. Thus, one potential channel through which education could affect fertility and child mortality is via educating women about family planning and benefits of antenatal consultations. Following previous research, we restrict the sample for the analysis on antenatal visits to first born children (Currie and Moretti 2003).[28]

The OLS estimates show that a 10 percent increase in the proportion of women with eight years of schooling increased the proportion that paid an antenatal visit in the first trimester by 1.4 percentage points, increased the proportion that used modern family planning methods by 0.5 percentage points, and the proportion with knowledge of their ovulation cycle by 1.6 percentage points. The IV estimates are much larger and suggest that a 10 percent increase in the proportion with eight years of schooling raised the proportion that paid at least one antenatal visit to a health facility during the first trimester of pregnancy by 6 percentage points, used modern family planning methods by 8–9 percentage points and those with the knowledge of their ovulation cycle by 5 percentage points. Reduced form estimates are also large and statistically significant. The Wooldridge test statistic is also statistically significant suggesting the OLS estimate is inconsistent for these outcomes and the IV technique is required.

6.4. Effect of Compulsory Education Reform on Women's Attitudes Toward Gender Equality

Our final objective is to study if increase in education resulting from the Compulsory Education Law changed women's attitudes toward gender equality. Models similar to those in tables 6.3 and 6.4 are applied and results are presented in table 6.5. The OLS estimates show that more educated women are more likely to believe in women's equality on all measures. However, the IV estimates are mostly statistically insignificant. The Wooldridge test statistic is also statistically insignificant for all of the outcomes indicating the OLS estimate is consistent for most outcomes.

Table 6.5 Estimates of the Effect of Women's Education on Her Attitudes toward Gender Equality

	Disagrees: Men Are Wiser Than Women	Disagrees: Boys' Education Is More Important Than Girls'	Disagrees: Men Should Make Decisions	Disagrees: Wife Beating Is Justified If She Wastes Money	Disagrees: Wife Beating Is Justified If She Neglects Children	Disagrees: Wife Beating Is Justified If She Argues with Husband	Disagrees: Wife Beating Is Justified If She Refuses Sex
Panel 1: Analysis at the level of 12 regions							
OLS estimates							
Schooling = 8 years or more	0.15***	0.10***	0.16***	0.12***	0.10***	0.11***	0.06***
	(0.01)	(0.02)	(0.01)	(0.01)	(0.01)	(0.01)	(0.01)
Reduced form estimates							
Young * Teacher child ratio (at age 11) * Year 2008	1.82	4.65	5.33	0.86	5.28	4.34	–4.76
	(5.77)	(5.42)	(5.82)	(3.58)	(4.42)	(2.78)	(2.88)
IV estimates							
Schooling = 8 years or more	0.11	0.27	0.31	0.05	0.31	0.25	–0.28
	(0.31)	(0.26)	(0.31)	(0.19)	(0.23)	(0.16)	(0.22)
Wooldridge test statistic	0.01	0.33	0.20	0.13	0.74	0.75	4.53*
Panel 2: Analysis at the level of 20 subregions							
OLS estimates							
At least 8 years of schooling	0.15***	0.10***	0.16***	0.11***	0.09***	0.11***	0.06***
	(0.02)	(0.02)	(0.01)	(0.01)	(0.01)	(0.01)	(0.01)
Reduced form estimates							
Young * Teacher-child ratio (at age 11) * Year 2008	4.27	5.41	6.82	–2.10	1.14	4.01	–2.61
	(5.22)	(4.36)	(4.71)	(5.34)	(3.51)	(2.44)	(2.29)

(*continued*)

Table 6.5 (*Continued*)

	Disagrees: Men Are Wiser Than Women	Disagrees: Boys' Education Is More Important Than Girls'	Disagrees: Men Should Make Decisions	Disagrees: Wife Beating Is Justified If She Wastes Money	Disagrees: Wife Beating Is Justified If She Neglects Children	Disagrees: Wife Beating Is Justified If She Argues with Husband	Disagrees: Wife Beating Is Justified If She Refuses Sex
IV estimates							
Schooling = 8 years or more	0.27	0.34	0.43	−0.13	0.07	0.26*	−0.17
	(0.30)	(0.23)	(0.31)	(0.34)	(0.21)	(0.15)	(0.17)
Wooldridge test statistic	0.15	0.87	0.84	0.57	0.01	0.89	2.69
Mean of the dependent variable	0.81	0.86	0.76	0.79	0.81	0.78	0.90
N	5,139	5,141	5,142	5,142	5,142	5,140	5,140

Notes: Figures in each cell of panels 1 and 2 are based on separate regressions with column heading as the dependent variable. Standard errors clustered on the region of childhood residence are in parentheses in panel 1 and on the subregion of childhood residence are in parentheses in panel 2. The sample of analysis is ever-married women aged eighteen to twenty-nine in the 2003 and 2008 TDHS. Women aged eighteen to twenty-two are defined as Young. All regressions in panel 1 control for respondent's age (a dummy variable for each year of age), respondent's year of birth, region of residence at age eleven, parents' education, respondent's mother tongue and place of residence (urban/rural) at age eleven, year of childhood interacted with 6–8 grade gross enrollment in the region of residence in childhood in 1996, teacher-child ratio, and an interaction of the Young dummy variable with teacher-child ratio. The instrumental variable in the IV estimates is the three-way interaction between Young * Teacher-child ratio (at age eleven) * Year 2008. Regressions in panel 2 are the same as in panel 1 with one difference: all geographic variables (and controls) are measured at the subregional level.

*0.05 < p ≤ 0.1.

***p ≤ 0.01.

The reduced form estimates are also modest and statistically insignificant. This calls into question the comparison between the OLS and IV estimates because the latter should be obtained only when the instrument has significant impacts on the outcomes of interest. Thus, we conclude that increases in schooling did not change women's attitudes toward gender equality in any substantial manner during our study period. From this we infer that the decline in fertility and child mortality observed in table 6.3 could not be on account of a change in women's attitudes toward gender inequality. On the other hand, estimates in table 6.4 suggest an increase in women's education caused an increase in age at marriage and age at first birth. We also find that increased schooling increased antenatal visits during the first trimester, improved women's use of modern contraceptive methods as well as knowledge of their ovulation cycle. Thus, it is more likely that the decline in fertility and child mortality that we observe are on account of these factors along with increase in age at first marriage and age at first childbirth.

7. CONCLUSION

In this chapter, we have used a natural experiment in Turkey to study the effect of education on women's fertility, empowerment, and their children's health. In 1997, Turkey passed the Compulsory Education Law that increased compulsory formal schooling from five to eight years. Individuals born after 1985 (who were eleven or less in 1997) were the target of the law. To accommodate the expected increase in enrollment, the government devoted additional resources on school infrastructure and to hiring new teachers and these investments varied across the subregions (and regions) of Turkey. We use the number of primary school teachers per child (aged six to thirteen) in the subregion (or region) of childhood at age eleven as an instrumental variable to predict the educational attainment of young women. The predicted education variable is then used to estimate the causal effect of education on a range of outcomes relating to child mortality, women's reproductive health, and measures of empowerment, including age at first marriage, age at first childbirth, use of contraceptives, antenatal visits, fertility outcomes, and attitudes toward gender equality.

First-stage regressions, from the subregional analysis, show that the Compulsory Schooling Law raised the proportion of ever-married women with at least eight years of schooling by 13 percentage points, which is a 48 percent increase over the mean in the pre-education reform period.

Estimates from the instrumental variables analysis suggest that a 10 percentage-point increase in proportion of ever-married women with eight years of schooling lowered the number of pregnancies and the number of children per ever-married woman by approximately 0.13. There is also some evidence of a decline in child mortality, caused by mother's education, but most of the estimated effects turn statistically insignificant in our preferred models (subregional analysis). Further, our analysis shows that a 10 percentage-points increase in the proportion with eight years of schooling raised the proportion of women making antenatal visits during the first trimester by 6 percentage points, using modern family planning methods by 8 to 9 percent and having knowledge of their ovulation cycle by 5–6 percentage points. However, we find little evidence that schooling changed women's attitudes toward gender equality.

From this we infer that the decline in fertility and child mortality (in some models) that we observe could not be on account of changes in women's attitudes toward gender inequality resulting from increased education. It is more likely that the decline in fertility and child mortality that we observe are on account of increases in age at first marriage, age at first childbirth, antenatal visits, use of contraceptive methods, and improvements in women's understanding of their ovulation cycle. It might be that attitudes are slow to change and that the content of education in classrooms is an important factor when it comes to changing attitudes.

Appendix A

DESCRIPTIVE STATISTICS

	TDHS 2003				TDHS 2008			
	Older Cohort		Younger Cohort		Older Cohort		Younger Cohort	
	Age = 23–29		Age = 18–22		Age = 23–29		Age = 18–22	
	N	Mean	N	Mean	N	Mean	N	Mean
Age at first marriage	2,033	19.81	795	18.19	1,794	20.40	611	18.21
Age at first birth	1,805	20.97	540	18.96	1,550	21.25	402	18.98
Number of pregnancies	2,033	2.17	795	1.17	1,794	1.97	611	0.98
Number of children born	2,033	1.81	795	0.99	1,794	1.64	611	0.84
Number of children deceased before age 1	1,805	0.07	540	0.06	1,550	0.05	402	0.01
Number of children deceased before age 5	1,805	0.08	540	0.07	1,550	0.06	402	0.01
Number of children deceased in first month after birth	1,805	0.04	540	0.03	1,550	0.03	402	0.01
Number of children deceased in 1–12 months after birth	1,805	0.03	540	0.03	1,550	0.02	402	0.00
Use of modern family planning methods	2,033	0.43	795	0.27	1,794	0.44	611	0.30
Knowledge of the ovulation cycle	2,032	0.29	795	0.18	1,791	0.27	609	0.18
Antenatal visit during the first trimester	507	0.71	338	0.46	494	0.75	275	0.68
Disagrees: men are wiser than women	2,030	0.78	795	0.74	1,790	0.86	610	0.85
Disagrees: boys' education is more important than girls'	2,030	0.85	795	0.80	1,792	0.91	610	0.87
Disagrees: men should make decisions	2,030	0.72	795	0.60	1,793	0.85	610	0.81
Disagrees: wife beating is justi-fied if she wastes money	2,030	0.76	795	0.67	1,793	0.88	610	0.83
Disagrees: wife beating is justi-fied if she neglects children	2,030	0.78	795	0.70	1,793	0.87	610	0.86
Disagrees: wife beating is justi-fied if she argues with husband	2,029	0.73	795	0.60	1,793	0.89	609	0.86
Disagrees: wife beating is justi-fied if she refuses sex	2,030	0.86	795	0.82	1,791	0.95	610	0.95

NOTES

Originally published as Mehmet Alper Dinçer, Neeraj Kaushal, and Michael Grossman, "Women's Education: Harbinger of Another Spring? Evidence from a Natural Experiment in Turkey," *World Development* 64 (December 2014): 243–258. We thank the Hacettepe University, Institute of Population Studies for providing us with the data used in this study, under permission for data use no. 2010/23. The views, analyses, and conclusions in this chapter are solely the responsibility of the authors.

1. See literature reviewed in Black and Devereux (2011), Card (1999), Grossman (2000, 2006), and Kaushal (2014).

2. Data on fertility and child mortality have been retrieved from http://databank .worldbank.org/.

3. See literature reviewed in Grossman (2006).

4. Similarly, researchers have applied different models to reach different conclusions. Kan and Lee (2012) apply a regression discontinuity model and find that while the change in compulsory education law in Taiwan increased women's education, it had no effect on their fertility and child mortality. However, they do not use the extensive school intensity data employed by Chou and colleagues (2010). Further, Kan and Lee's treatment groups omit a substantial number of women who were affected by the law and include some women who were not affected by it.

5. Authors' computations based on the 2008 Turkey Demographic and Health Survey.

6. In some industrialized societies, where fertility has been declining and secondary education is almost universal among women, researchers have been asking a somewhat different question: Is education or higher education an obstacle to women's fertility (Cohen, Kravdal, and Keilman 2011).

7. Cesur and Mocan (2013) investigate the impact of Compulsory Education Law on voting behavior, and Mocan (2013) studies reform's impact on wages.

8. Women's employment declined from 34 percent in 1988 to 22 percent in 2008 (World Bank 2009).

9. The Bylaw of Primary Education Institutions published in Official Gazette number 21308 on August 7, 1992, regulates school starting age in Article 14 as follows: "A child who completed 72 months at the end of the calendar year should enroll in primary school" (Authors' translation).

10. To investigate how strictly schools adhere to the provisions of the Bylaw, we used the 1999 Trends in International Mathematics and Science Study (TIMSS) for Turkey on eighth graders in school year 1998–1999 and found that 22 percent were born in 1984 and 65 percent in 1985. Further, we find that the number of eighth graders born in January 1985 is three times the number born in December 1984, whereas the number of eighth graders born in September 1985 is somewhat less than those born in August 1985. Thus, even in practice age at entry is counted as of the start of the calendar year (January 1) and not the start of the school year (September 1). Note that these students were in grade four in 1994–1995.

11. The responses to the question are as follows: Turkish, Kurdish, Arabic, and other.

12. There are twelve regions in Turkey: Istanbul, West Marmara, Aegean, East Marmara, West Anatolia, Mediterranean, Central Anatolia, West Black Sea, East Black Sea, North-eastern Anatolia, Central-eastern Anatolia, and South-eastern Anatolia.

13. The respondents are asked the region where they spent most of the time until they were twelve.

14. Restricting the sample to ever married women is likely to bias the results if education caused a reduction in marriage and reduced childbearing. Kırdar et al. (2011) investigated the impact of Compulsory Education Law (CEL) on timing of early marriage and fertility using Turkey's Demographic and Health Survey, 2008. Their results show that while CEL is associated with a delay in first marriage among girls aged seventeen or less, it does not affect the timing of first marriage for girls aged eighteen or older (Kırdar et al. 2011, 37, Table 5). This makes sense because CEL effectively increased compulsory school exit age from eleven to fourteen. It is, however, possible that CEL affected high-school (eleven years of schooling) completion rates. Because the modal age for high-school completion in Turkey is seventeen, this would affect age at first marriage for older girls. We used TDHS data to estimate the effect of CEL on high-school completion and find that CEL increased high-school completion by 3 percentage points (versus. 24 percentage points increase in completing eight years of schooling [table 6.1]). These findings suggest that the potential bias on account of restricting the sample to ever-married women is likely to be modest.

15. TURKSTAT divides the country in twenty-six subregions. We merge six small subregions with other geographically contiguous subregions within the same region to ensure that all subregions have at least one hundred observations. The twenty subregions we use are Istanbul, West Marmara, İzmir & Aydın, Manisa, Bursa, Kocaeli, West Anatolia, Antalya, Adana, Hatay, Central Anatolia, Zonguldak & Kastamonu, Samsun, Trabzon, North-eastern Anatolia, Malatya, Van, Gaziantep, Şanlıurfa, and Mardin.

16. Note that the primary source of variation in the teacher-child ratio is the increase in newly hired teachers. Thus, we do not expect the imputation to influence the findings of our analysis in any meaningful way. We, however, acknowledge that due to imputation the teacher-child ratio for intercensus years is likely to be less precise.

17. We examine number of children deceased in the first month after birth (neonatal mortality) and number of children deceased during one to twelvemonths after birth (postneonatal mortality) separately because their causes may be different. Congenital anomalies, prematurity, and complications of delivery are the causes of most neonatal deaths, whereas most postneonatal deaths are caused by infectious diseases and accidents (Chou et al. 2010).

18. There is a difference in the language used for this question in the 2003 and 2008 surveys. The question in the 2003 TDHS is: "Important family decisions should be made by men" and in 2008: "All important family decisions should be made only by men."

19. Seven dummy variables, for each parent, indicating the following categories: no education, primary drop out, primary (five years of schooling), middle school (eight years of schooling), upper secondary (eleven years), greater than eleven years of schooling, and unknown schooling.

20. Estimates without controls for parents' schooling are available upon request.

21. Our selection of the sample was partially determined by the availability of administrative data on teacher-per-child, which we had collected for 1985 and 2011. This allowed us to study seven year-of-birth cohorts of older women. For the younger cohort, we have restricted the sample to eighteen- to twenty-two-year-old women because the outcomes we study are less relevant for women less than eighteen. Thus, in each cross-section, for the younger group of women we have five year-of-birth cohorts. We also repeated the analysis with five younger and five older cohorts (young cohort: eighteen to twenty-two and older cohort: twenty-three to twenty-seven). The results remained very similar qualitatively and quantitatively.

22. Note that these controls are critical for the second-stage outcomes discussed in the next section.

23. Grade retention may cause some women in the older cohort to be subject to treatment, which will cause our estimated results of the effect of education to be downward biased. However, according to National Education Statistics grade retention for fourth graders was only 4.5 percent 1996–1997. Thus, bias on this account is likely to be small.

24. Gross enrollment rate in grades 6–8 is defined as number of students enrolled in grades 6–8 in 1996 in the region (or subregion) of childhood divided by the total population of children aged 11–13 in the region (subregion). In additional work (not presented, but available upon request), we also did the analysis with $P_{j\,1996}$ defined as primary school (1–8 grades) enrollment rate and the estimates were similar to those reported.

25. We have used the term child mortality for convenience. The actual measures are number of deceased children per ever married women with at least one childbirth.

26. In the 2003 sample, ever-married women aged eighteen to twenty-two have a lower level of education (compared to ever married women aged twenty-three to twenty-nine) because the former married earlier and stopped schooling.

27. Note that our findings do not allow for any inference regarding life-time completed fertility.

28. We do not impose the same restriction for outcomes relating to child mortality because the number of deaths in our sample is small and restricting the sample to first born will reduce our ability to detect any effects.

REFERENCES

Adler, N. E., and K. Newman. 2002. "Socioeconomic Disparities in Health: Pathways and Policies." *Health Affairs* 21(2): 60–76.

Altınay, A. G., and Y. Arat. 2007. *Violence Against Women in Turkey: A Nationwide Survey.* Punto.

Andalon, M., M. Grossman, and J. Williams. 2013. *The Effect of Schooling on Contraceptive Knowledge and Use in Mexico.* Retrieved from https://crawford.anu.edu.au /acde/events/adew-2013/papers/And-alon,M_D1.pdf.

Angrist, J. D., and W. N. Evans. 1998. "Children and Their Parents' Labor Supply: Evidence from Exogenous Variation in Family Size." *American Economic Review* 88(3): 450–477.

Angrist, J. D., and J. S. Pischke. 2009. *Mostly Harmless Econometrics: An Empiricist's Companion.* Princeton, NJ: Princeton University Press.

Atun, R., S. Aydın, S. Chakraborty, S. Sümer, M. Aran, I. Gürol, et al. 2013. "Universal Health Coverage in Turkey: Enhancement of Equity." *The Lancet* 382(9886): 65–99.

Becker, G. S., and H. G. Lewis. 1973. "On the Interaction Between the Quantity and Quality of Children." *Journal of Political Economy* 81(2): S279–S288.

Behrman, J. R., and M. R. Rosenzweig. 2002. "Does Increasing Women's Schooling Raise the Schooling of the Next Generation?" *American Economic Review* 92(1): 323–334.

Bertrand, M., E. Duflo, and S. Mullainathan. 2004. "How Much Should We Trust Differences-in-Differences Estimates?" *The Quarterly Journal of Economics* 119(1): 249–275.

Black, S. E., and P. J. Devereux. 2011. "Recent Developments in Intergenerational Mobility." In *Handbook of Labor Economics*, Volume 4, Part B, ed. D. Card and O. Ashenfelter. North Holland: 1487–1541.

Breierova, L., and E. Duflo. 2004. *The Impact of Education on Fertility and Child Mortality: Do Fathers Really Matter Less Than Mothers?* National Bureau of Economic Research working paper series No. 10513.

Cameron, A. C., J. B. Gelbach, and D. L. Miller. 2008. "Bootstrap-based Improvements for Inference with Clustered Errors." *The Review of Economics and Statistics* 90(3): 414–427.

Card, D. 1999. "The Causal Effect of Education on Earnings." In *Handbook of Labor Economics*, Volume 3, ed. D. Card and O. Ashenfelter. North Holland: 1801–1863.

Celik, Y. 2000. "The Socio-Economic Determinants of Alternative Sources of Antenatal Care in Turkey." *The International Journal of Health Planning and Management* 15(3): 221–235.

Celik, Y., and D. R. Hotchkiss.2000. "The Socio-Economic Determinants of Maternal Health Care Utilization in Turkey." *Social Science and Medicine,* 50(12): 1797–1806.

Cesur, R., and N. H. Mocan. 2013. *Does Secular Education Impact Religiosity, Electoral Participation and the Propensity to Vote for Islamic Parties? Evidence from an Education Reform in a Muslim Country.* National Bureau of Economic Research working paper series No. 19769.

Chou, S.-Y., J.-T. Liu, M. Grossman, and T. Joyce. 2010. "Parental Education and Child Health: Evidence from a Natural Experiment in Taiwan." *American Economic Journal: Applied Economics* 2(1): 33–61.

Cohen, J. E., Ø. Kravdal, and N. Keilman. 2011. "Childbearing Impeded Education More Than Education Impeded Childbearing among Norwegian Women." Paper presented at the *Proceedings of the National Academy of Sciences.*

Currie, J., and E. Moretti. 2003. "Mother's Education and the Intergenerational Transmission of Human Capital: Evidence from College Openings." *The Quarterly Journal of Economics* 118(4)" 1495–1532.

Duflo, E. 2001. "Schooling and Labor Market Consequences of School Construction in Indonesia: Evidence from an Unusual Policy Experiment." *The American Economic Review* 4(91): 795–813.

Dülger, İ. 2004. "Case Study on Turkey Rapid Coverage for Compulsory Education Pro-gram." In paper presented at the *Scaling up poverty reduction: A global learning process and conference*, Shanghai.

Fuchs, V. R. 1982. "Time Preference and Health: An Exploratory Study." In *Economic Aspects of Health*, ed. V. R. Fuchs. Chicago: University of Chicago Press: 93–120.

Görmez, Y., and S. Yiğit. 2010. "Monetary Policy under Stress: Lessons from Turkey." In paper presented at the *Monetary policy during economic crises: A comparative and historical perspective.*

Grossman, M. 2000. "The Human Capital Model." In *Handbook of Health Economics*, Volume 1A, ed. A. J. Culyer and J. P. Newhouse. North Holland: 347–408.

——. 2006. "Education and Nonmarket Outcomes." In *Handbook of the Economics of Education*, Volume 1, ed. E. A. Hanushek and F. Welch. North Holland: 577–633.

Gulesci, S., and E. Meyersson. 2014. *For the Love of the Republic: Education, Secularism, and Empowerment.* Retrieved from http://erikmeyersson.files.wordpress.com/2014/02/gulesci_meyersson_loverepub-lic.pdf.

Güneş, P. M. 2013a. *The Impact of Female Education on Fertility: Evidence from Turkey.* GCC working paper series, GCC 13–01.

——. 2013b. *The Role of Maternal Education in Child Health: Evidence from a Compulsory Schooling Law.* GCC working paper series, GCC 13–07.

Hausmann, R., L. D. Tyson, and S. Zahidi. 2012. *The Global Gender Report 2012.* World Economic Forum.

Huber, P. J. 1967. "The Behavior of Maximum Likelihood Estimates under Nonstandard Conditions." In *Proceedings of the Fifth Berkeley Symposium on Mathematical Statistics and Probability*, Volume 1, ed. L. M. LeCann and J. Neyman. Berkeley: University of California Press: 221–233).

Kaushal, N. 2014. "Intergenerational Payoffs of Education." *Future of Children* 24(1), 61–78.

Kan, K., and M. Lee. 2012. *The Effects of Education on Fertility and Child Health.* Retrieved from http://econ.ccu.edu.tw/manage/ 1369723123_a.pdf.

Kırdar, M. G., M. Dayıoğlu, and İ. Koç. 2009. *The Impact of Schooling on the Timing of Marriage and Fertility: Evidence from a Change in Compulsory Schooling Law.* Germany: University Library of Munich.

——. 2011. *The Effect of Compulsory Schooling Laws on Teenage Marriage and Births in Turkey.* Germany: University Library of Munich.

Koç, I. 2000. "Determinants of Contraceptive Use and Method Choice in Turkey. *Journal of Biosocial Science* 32(3): 329–342.

Koç, İ., M. A. Eryurt,, T. Adalı, and P. Seçkiner. 2010. Türkiye'nindemografikdönüşümü Doğurganlık, AilePlanlaması, Anne-ÇocukSağlığıveBeşYaşAltıÖlümlerdekiDeğişimler: 1968–2008 HacettepeÜniversitesiNüfusEtütleriEnstitüsü. Ankara.

Lindeboom, M., A. Llena-Nozal, and B. van Der Klaauw. 2009. "Parental Education and Child Health: Evidence from a Schooling Reform." *Journal of Health Economics* 28(1): 109–131.

McCrary, J., and H. Royer. 2011. "The Effect of Female Education on Fertility and Infant Health: Evidence from School Entry Policies Using Exact Date of Birth." *The American Economic Review* 101(1): 158–195.

Mocan, L. 2013. *The Impact of Education on Wages: Analysis of an Education Reform in Turkey.* Retrieved from http://www.aefpweb.org/sites/default/files/webform/LMocan _AEFPPaper.pdf.

Mocan, N. H., and C. Cannonier. 2012. *Empowering Women Through Education: Evidence from Sierra Leone.* National Bureau of Economic Research working paper series No. 18016.

Osili, U. O., and B. T. Long. 2008. "Does Female Schooling Reduce Fertility? Evidence from Nigeria." *Journal of Development Economics* 87(1): 57–75.

Rosenzweig, M. R., and T. P. Schultz. 1989. "Schooling, Information and Nonmarket Productivity: Contraceptive Use and Its Effectiveness." *International Economic Review* 30(2): 457–477.

State Institute of Statistics. 1999. *National Education Statistics Formal Education, 1996–1997.* Ankara: Prime Ministry, Republic of Turkey.

Turkish Statistical Institute. 2006. *National Education Statistics Formal Education 2003–04.* Ankara: Prime Ministry, Republic of Turkey.

UNDP (United Nations Development Programme). 2005. *Arab Human Development Report 2004. Towards Freedom in the Arab World.*

——. 2011. *Human Development Report 2011. Sustainability and Equity: A Better Future for All.*

Wooldridge, J. M. 1995. "Score Diagnostics for Linear Models Estimated by Two Stage Least Squares." In *Advances in Econometrics and Quantitative Economics: Essays in Honor of Professor C. R. Rao*, ed. G. S. Maddala, P. C. B. Phillips, and T. N. Srinivasan. Oxford: Blackwell: 66–87.

World Bank. 2009. *Female Labor Force Participation in Turkey: Trends, Determinants and Policy Framework.* Human Development Sector Unit Europe and Central Asia Region Report No. 48508-TR, Trans.

WHO (World Health Organization). 1995. *World Health Report 1995: Bridging the Gaps.* World Health Organization.

Zhang, S. 2012. *Mother's Education and Infant Health: Evidence from Closure of High Schools in China.* Retrieved from http://www.econ.yale.edu/conference/neudc11/papers /paper_176.pdf.

Afterword to Part 2

My four papers in this part of the book support the notion that more school-ing causes better health. To what extent does the large recent literature to which I refer in the introduction also support that hypothesis? I will answer that question with a few examples from studies that employ one of the three econometric procedures mentioned in the introduction: direct inclusion of third variables, twin differences, and instrumental variables.[1]

Before undertaking this task, I want to point out that many of the studies employ a simple conceptual and econometric framework. Contributions by Nobel Laureate James J. Heckman and his colleagues (for example, Conti and Heckman 2010; Conti, Heckman, and Urzua 2010; Savelyev 2014) are of a very different nature. They employ the framework developed by Heckman and colleagues (for example, Cuhna, Heckman, and Schennach 2010) that conceptualizes the technol-ogy of cognitive and noncognitive skill formation in childhood and adolescence as key determinants of completed schooling and health as an adult. In their frame-work, self-productivity (skills produced early in life increase skills at later stages) and dynamic complementarity (early investments raise the marginal product of later investments) interact to generate multiplier effects. Hence, investments in adolescence have much larger payoffs when earlier investments are made.

The emphasis on the key role of very early investments draws from and greatly expands on seeds in the first two papers in this section. In the first of these, I show that health status in high school is an important determinant of health status in adulthood (Grossman 1976). In the second, Shakotko, Edwards, and I (1981) report positive effects of health and cognitive development in childhood on these measures in adolescence.

In addition to providing a much more fully developed conceptual framework than the one in the two studies just mentioned, Heckman and colleagues stress the importance of a third variable that my colleagues and I did not consider: noncognitive skills. They include in these skills the "big five personality traits": conscientiousness, openness, extraversion, agreeableness, and neuroticism. Their econometric framework is much more complicated than that in the other studies I discuss or in the ones that my colleagues and I employed. It incorporates latent cognitive and personality skills, measured and unmeasured components of those skills, factor analysis to control for measured and unmeasured cognitive development, and the simultaneous estimation of outcome and measurement equations.

The studies that include hard-to-measure third variables all find positive and significant effects of completed schooling on at least some key measures of adult health and beneficial health behaviors. For example, Marjon Van Der Pol (2011) controls for time preference in the Dutch DNB Household Survey. In that survey, respondents were asked how much they would be willing to give up today to get a certain amount of money next year. Outcomes include self-rated health, cigarette smoking, body mass index (BMI), and obesity.

To cite another example, Gabriella Conti and James J. Heckman (2010) control for cognitive and noncognitive ability at age ten and health at that age in an examination of outcomes at age thirty in the 1970 British Cohort Study. These outcomes include self-rated health, daily smoking, and obesity. Conti and Heckman report positive effects of education on self-rated health and the negative effects of this variable on smoking and obesity. The education effects are more important for those with higher levels of cognitive ability, but less important for those with higher levels of noncognitive ability.

To cite a final example, Peter A. Savelyev (2014) focuses on life expectancy in the Terman Life Cycle Study of Children with High Ability. Members of this sample have IQs greater than 140, which correspond to the 99.6th percentile of the IQ distribution. They were eleven years old in 1921, were followed through 1991, and all were high school graduates. For men, graduation from college increases life expectancy at age thirty by approximately nine years compared to nongraduates. This result holds the big five personality traits (conscientiousness, openness, extraversion, agreeableness, and neuroticism) and health status (all measured at age twelve) constant. No effects are observed for women. The findings for men indicate that the favorable effects of education on health persist among those with extremely high levels of cognitive ability and are not limited to completion of primary or secondary school.

How much do the significant schooling effects fall once third variables are held constant? Given differences in outcomes, third variables, and samples in the three studies just reviewed and in others, there is no straightforward answer to this question. Van der Pol (2011) reports that the effects of schooling on self-rated health falls between 7 and 14 percent in alternative specifications once time preference is held constant. The inclusion of the latter variable has, however, no impact on the effects of schooling on smoking, BMI, and obesity. Conti and Heckman (2010), who find that the education effect is largest in the case of daily smoking, indicate a reduction of approximately 25 percent in this effect when cognitive and noncognitive skills and health at age ten are employed as regressors. Savelyev (2014) does not consider this issue. He does indicate, however, that the nine-year increase in life expectancy for college graduates compared to high school graduates mentioned above exceeds the six-year differential in that outcome between the highest and the lowest deciles of his key third variable: conscientiousness. The important message in the studies that employ direct measures of third variables is that there are few instances in which large schooling effects are reduced by a significant percentage by the these variables or in which the net effects of these variables exceed the net effects of schooling.

Results from studies that focus on twin differences have the flavor of a "point-counterpoint." Jere R. Behrman, Hans-Peter Koher, Vibeke Myrup Jensen, Dorthe Pedersen, Inge Petersen, Paul Bingley, and Kaare Christensen (2011) find no effects of differences in education on differences in adult mortality or hospitalizations in a Danish twin registry that consists of 2,500 identical (monozygotic, MZ) twin pairs. Vikesh Amin, Jere R. Behrman, and Tim D. Spector (2013) report no effects of education on obesity, smoking, and physical health in a sample of 741 female MZ twin pairs in the United Kingdom. Mia Madsen, Anne Marie Nybo Andersen, Kaare Christensen, Per Kragh Andersen, and Merete Olser (2010) indicate no overall effects in the same sample employed by Behrman et al. (2011) but negative effects in the outcomes considered by Behrman and colleagues for males born before 1935 and negative effects for cases in which there are large schooling differences within twin pairs.

The last two findings are counterpoints to the absence of schooling effects in the first two studies. Dinand Webbink, Nicholas G. Martin, and Peter M. Visscher (2010) provide another counterpoint. They report a negative impact of schooling on male obesity in 350 Australian MZ twin pairs. They do not, however, find an effect in the 350 MZ female pairs.

In three studies, Petter Lundborg and colleagues provide somewhat stronger counterpoints to the conclusion that more schooling does not cause better health in twin data (Lundborg 2013; Lundborg, Lyttkens, and Nystedt 2012; Lundborg, Nordin, and Rooth 2012). Lundborg (2013) reports effects in the expected direction of high school completion on self-rated health, chronic conditions, and exercise behavior among 347 MZ pairs in the Midlife in the United States survey. There are, however, no effects on smoking and BMI.

Lundborg, Lyttkens, and Nystedt (2012) find negative effects of schooling on mortality in a Swedish twin registry consisting of 9,000 MZ pairs. Individuals with at least thirteen years of schooling can expect to live an additional twenty-four years at age sixty compared to twenty-one years for those with less than ten years of schooling. Moreover, 84 percent of low-educated individuals lived to age seventy, compared to 90 percent of high-educated individuals. These results control for twin differences in birth weight and height.

Lundborg, Nordin, and Rooth (2012) report a negative effect of MZ twin mother's schooling on her son's health in the Swedish twin registry employed in the previous study. The finding pertains to sons who have enlisted in the military, with health measured by physical examination administered to 300 twin pairs on enlistment. There is no effect of MZ twin father's schooling on the health outcome.

Like the twin studies, the instrumental variables studies contain mixed results. Almost all of them use compulsory school reform or school entry cutoff dates as the instruments for schooling, sometimes combined with new school openings at a differential rate among areas. These studies account for a large percentage of the recent research, and I group my discussion of them by the outcomes they consider. First, I consider those in which adult mortality is the outcome. Second, I review those in which the outcome is adult health or health behaviors. Finally, I comment on those that focus on the impacts of parents' schooling on infant and adolescent health. Like the twin differences studies, the instrumental variables studies have the flavor of a point-counterpoint.

Damon Clark and Heather Royer (2013) report no effect of schooling on adult mortality in Britain. They conclude (p. 2089): "Our results . . . suggest that economic models that assume a strong causal effect of education on health ought to be carefully reconsidered." Dan Black, Yu-Chieh Hsu, and Lowell J. Taylor (2015) present a similar lack of evidence of a schooling effect in Sweden. Hans van Kippersluis, Owen O'Donnell, and Eddy van Doorslaer (2011) indicate a very different finding for men but not for women in the Netherlands. For men surviving to age eighty-one, a one-year increase in the number of years of formal schooling obtained due to compulsory school reform lowers the probability of dying before age eighty-nine by 3 percentage points relative to a baseline percentage of those who will die in that period of 50 percent. Kasey Buckles, Andreas Hagemann, Ofer Malamud, Melinda S. Morrill, and

Abigail K. Wozniak (2013, 2016) report a complementary finding for men in the United States. In their study, college completion reduces cumulative mortality by almost 30 percent relative to the mean for men ages thirty-eight to forty-nine in 1980.[2] Given the evidence in the latter two studies, the conclusion by Clark and Royer (2013) seems somewhat premature.

When adult health and health behaviors are outcomes, the evidence also is mixed. Nils Braakmann (2011) finds no effects on variety of self-rated health measures, smoking, heavy drinking, and diet in Britain. Similar findings are reported by Clark and Royer (2013). Nattavudh Powdthavee (2011) indicates a negative effect on hypertension based on physical exam in Britain. Fabrice Etilé and Andrew W. Jones (2011) indicate a negative effect on the probability of smoking and a positive effect on the probability of quitting smoking in France. Buckles et al. (2013) find negative effects on smoking, heavy drinking, and obesity; and a positive effect on exercise in the United States. Vincenzo Atella and Joanna Kopinska (2014) report negative effects on BMI and caloric intake and a positive effect on calorie expenditure in Italy.

Justin McCrary and Heather Royer (2011) fail to uncover effects of mother's schooling on low birth weight, infant mortality, maternal smoking and alcohol use during pregnancy, and prenatal care use for pregnant women in California and Texas. Petter Lundborg, Anton Nilsson, and Dan-Olof Rooth (2014) show that an increase in mothers' schooling has positive effects on their sons' physical health and height in Swedish military enlistment register data. Karen A. Grépin and Prashant Bharadwaj (2015) uncover a negative effect of mother's schooling on child mortality in Zimbabwe. A one-year increase in schooling caused by expanded access to secondary schools reduced the child mortality rate by almost 22 percent in that country.

There is enough conflicting evidence in the studies I have reviewed to warrant more research on the question of whether more schooling does in fact cause better health outcomes. Future research in this area will be especially helpful if it confronts and tries to address the following issues:

- School entry ages used by McCrary and Royer (2011) and others as instruments may not be exogenous because parents can hold their children back or petition to have them start early. Hitoshi Shigeoka (2015) finds almost 2,000 births per year shifted from a week before to a week after the school entry cutoff date in Japan.
- Why do the results of instrumental variables studies vary so much? Is it because the instruments used in different studies may affect different groups, so that local average treatment effects, rather than average treatment effects, are being obtained?

- Twin studies typically have small sample sizes. Differences in schooling between identical twins may be small. Why do identical twins obtain different amounts of schooling?
- Some instrumental variables studies find that ordinary least squares estimates are consistent. Some do not test this. Schooling is endogenous, but is it possible that a recursive model with uncorrelated errors is correct? That is, to what extent do third variables influence schooling but have no impact on health with schooling held constant?
- Studies I discussed focus on years of schooling completed; what about the quality of schooling? There is some work in this area (for example, Frisvold and Golberstein 2011), but much more could be done.
- What are the mechanisms via which schooling influences health and health behaviors? Does it provide specific health information or general knowledge that leads to better health behaviors and improved health outcomes? Alternatively, is more schooling a vehicle in the construction of a future orientation, one that is required to make decisions today that will have favorable consequences for many years to come?
- As readers may recall from the afterword to part 1, Titus Galama and Hans van Kippersluis accepted my challenge to construct a comprehensive theoretical model in which the stocks of health and knowledge are determined simultaneously. They produced an extremely rich product (Galama and van Kippersluis 2016). I have another challenge for them: specify and estimate the model in your paper. That will not be easy. It contains endogenous relationships involving schooling, health, status, and longevity; unobserved variables; and highly nonlinear relationships. Yet, as was the case in the first challenge I posed, I think the potential payoffs to this undertaking will be substantial.

NOTES

1. For a more detailed treatment of this issue, see Grossman (2015).
2. Buckles et al. (2013, 2016) do not use compulsory school reform or school entry age laws as their instrument for schooling. Instead, they employ the risk of induction into the armed services during the Vietnam War era in that capacity.

REFERENCES

Amin, Vikesh, Jere R. Behrman, and Tim D. Spector. 2013. "Does More Schooling Improve Health Outcomes and Health Related Behaviors? Evidence from U.K. Twins." *Economics of Education Review* 35(August): 134–148.

Atella, Vincenzo, and Joanna Kopinska. 2014. "Body Weight, Eating Patterns, and Physical Activity: The Role of Education." *Demography* 51(4): 1225–1249.

Behrman, Jere R., Hans-Peter Koher, Vibeke Myrup Jensen, Dorthe Pedersen, Inge Petersen, Paul Bingley, and Kaare Christensen. 2011. "Does More Schooling Reduce Hospitalization and Delay Mortality? New Evidence Based on Danish Twins." *Demography* 48(4): 1347–1375.

Black, Dan A., Yu-Chieh Hsu, and Lowell J. Taylor. 2015. "The Effect of Early-Life Education on Later-Life Mortality." *Journal of Health Economics* 44(December): 1–9.

Braakmann, Nils. 2011. "The Causal Relationship Between Education, Health and Health-Related Behaviour: Evidence from a Natural Experiment in England." *Journal of Health Economics* 30(4): 753–763.

Buckles, Kasey, Andreas Hagemann, Ofer Malamud, Melinda S. Morrill, and Abigail K. Wozniak. 2013. "The Effect of College Education on Health." Cambridge, MA: National Bureau of Economic Research Working Paper 19222.

Buckles, Kasey, Andreas Hagemann, Ofer Malamud, Melinda S. Morrill, and Abigail K. Wozniak. 2016. "The Effect of College Education on Mortality." *Journal of Health Economics* 50(December): 99-114.

Clark, Damon, and Heather Royer. 2013. "The Effect of Education on Adult Mortality: Evidence from Britain." *American Economic Review* 106(6): 2087–2120.

Conti, Gabriella, and James J. Heckman. 2010. "Understanding the Early Origins of the Education-Health Gradient: A Framework That Can Also Be Applied to Analyze Gene-Environment Interactions." *Perspectives on Psychological Science* 5(5): 585–605.

Conti, Gabriella, James J. Heckman, and Sergio Urzua. 2010. "The Education-Health Gradient." *American Economic Review* 100(2): 234–238.

Cunha, Flavio, James J. Heckman, and Susanne M. Schennach. 2010. "Estimating the Technology of Cognitive and Noncognitive Skill Formation." *Econometrica* 78(3): 883–931.

Etilé, Fabrice, and Andrew M. Jones. 2011. "Schooling and Smoking Among the Baby Boomers—An Evaluation of Education Expansion in France." *Journal of Health Economics* 30(4): 811–831.

Frisvold, David, and Ezra Golberstein. 2011. "School Quality and the Education-Health Relationship: Evidence from Blacks in Segregated Schools." *Journal of Health Economics* 30(6): 1232–1245.

Galama, Titus, and Hans van Kippersluis. 2016. "A Theory of Education, Health and Longevity." Presented at the "Human Capital and Health Behavior" conference. Gothenburg University, Sweden, May 19–20.

Grépin, Karen A., and Prashant Bharadwaj. 2015. "Maternal Education and Child Mortality in Zimbabwe." *Journal of Health Economics* 44(December): 97–117.

Grossman, Michael. 1976. "The Correlation between Health and Schooling." In *Household Production and Consumption*, ed. Nestor E. Terleckyj. Studies in Income and Wealth, Volume 40, by the Conference on Research in Income and Wealth. New York: Columbia University Press for the National Bureau of Economic Research, 147–211.

——.2015. "The Relationship Between Health and Schooling: What's New?" *Nordic Journal of Health Economics* 3(1): 7–17.

Lundborg, Petter. 2013. "The Health Returns to Schooling—What Can We Learn from Twins?" *Journal of Population Economics* 26(2): 673–701.

Lundborg, Petter, Carl Hampus Lyttkens, and Paul Nystedt. 2012. "Human Capital and Longevity: Evidence from 50,000 Twins." Working Paper 12/19, Health Econometrics and Data Group, The University of York, Great Britain.

Lundborg, Petter, Anton Nilsson, Dan-Olof Rooth. 2014. "Parental Education and Offspring Outcomes: Evidence from the Swedish Compulsory School Reform." *American Economic Journal: Applied Economics* 6(1): 253–278.

Lundborg, Petter, Martin Nordin, and Dan-Olof Rooth. 2012. "The Intergenerational Transmission of Human Capital: The Role of Skills and Health." Working Paper 2012:22, Department of Economics, School of Economics and Management, Lund University, Sweden.

Madsen, Mia, Anne Marie Nybo Andersen, Kaare Christensen, Per Kragh Andersen, and Merete Osler. 2010. "Does Educational Status Impact Adult Mortality in Denmark? A Twin Approach." *American Journal of Epidemiology* 172(2): 225–234.

McCrary, Justin, and Heather Royer. 2011. "The Effect of Female Education on Fertility and Infant Health: Evidence from School Entry Policies Using Exact Date of Birth." *American Economic Review* 101(1): 158–195.

Powdthavee, Nattavudh. 2010. "Does Education Reduce the Risk of Hypertension? Estimating the Biomarker Effect of Compulsory Schooling in England." *Journal of Human Capital* 4(2): 173–202.

Savelyev, Peter. A. 2014. "Psychological Skills, Education, and Longevity of High-Ability Individuals." Working Paper, Department of Economics. Nashville, TN: Vanderbilt University.

Shakotko, Robert A., Linda N. Edwards, and Michael Grossman. 1981. "An Exploration of the Dynamic Relationship Between Health and Cognitive Development in Adolescence." In *Contributions to Economic Analysis: Health, Economics, and Health Economics*, ed. Jacques van der Gaag and Mark Perlman. Amsterdam: North-Holland Publishing, 305–328.

Shigeoka, Hitoshi. 2015. "School Entry Cutoff Date and the Timing of Births." Cambridge, MA: National Bureau of Economic Research Working Paper 21402.

Van der Pol, Marjon. 2011. "Health, Education and Time Preference." *Health Economics* 20(8): 917–929.

van Kippersluis, Hans, Owen O'Donnell, and Eddy van Doorslaer. 2011. "Long Run Returns to Education: Does Schooling Lead to an Extended Old Age?" *Journal of Human Resources* 46(4): 695–721.

Webbink, Dinand, Nicholas G. Martin, and Peter M. Visscher. 2010. Does Education Reduce the Probability of Being Overweight? *Journal of Health Economics* 29(1): 29–38.

Determinants of Infant Health with Special Emphasis on Public Policies and Programs

PART 3

Introduction to Part 3

After I completed my 1976 paper dealing with the correlation between schooling and adult health, I turned to the determinants of infant and child health. The last three papers in the previous section are examples of my work in that area. Those three papers, however, focus on the effects of parents' schooling. The five papers in the current section are much broader. Although they all deal with infant health, they employ a rich analytical framework in which my demand for health model is combined with economic models of the family developed most notably by Gary S. Becker and H. Gregg Lewis (1973), Robert J. Willis (1973), and Becker (1981). In these models, parents maximize a utility function that depends on their own consumption, the number of children, and the quality of each child. It is natural to associate infants' health with their quality and thus to "marry" an economic approach to the family with an economic approach to the demand for health.

Why did I decide to conduct a series of studies of the determinants of infant mortality after I completed my last paper that employed measures of child health beyond the first year of life in 1981 (Shakotko, Edwards and Grossman—the second paper in the previous section)? One reason is that in the United States and the rest of the developed world, the infant mortality rate is much higher than child and teenage mortality rates—thirteen times greater than the largest of these rates in the United States in 2013. Moreover, adult age-specific death rates do not exceed the infant mortality rate until the rate at ages fifty-five to fifty-nine (Xu, Murphy, Kochanek, and Bastian 2016). In addition, relatively high infant mortality rates in areas within a given country signal poor health in all segments of the population (Fuchs 1983).

A second set of factors revolves around trends in the U.S. infant mortality rate between the mid-1950s and the early 1980s and the relative impacts of public policies, programs, and advances in medical technology in explaining these trends. During the period at issue, the infant mortality rate was characterized by a decade of relative stability followed by almost two decades of rapid decline. The rate fell by only 0.6 percent per year compounded annually between 1955 and 1964. By contrast, infant mortality dropped by 4.5 percent per year (compounded annually) between 1964 and 1982.

The period beginning in 1964 witnessed the legalization and diffusion of abortion, the widespread adoption of oral and intrauterine contraceptive techniques, and dramatic advances in neonatal science. It also witnessed the introduction and rapid growth of programs associated with President Lyndon B. Johnson's War on Poverty: Medicaid, federally subsidized maternal and infant care projects and community health centers (hereafter community health projects), federally subsidized family planning services for low-income women, and the Special Supplemental Food Program for Women, Infants, and Children (WIC program).[1] Although other researchers had pointed to these developments in explanations of the acceleration in the downward trend in infant mortality, the question had not been studied in a multivariate context prior to my work.

The infant mortality rate is defined as deaths of infants within the first year of life per thousand live births and has two components. Neonatal deaths pertain to deaths within the first twenty-seven days of life, and postneonatal deaths occur from the twenty-eighth through the 364th day of life. Low birth weight (weight less than 2,500 grams or less than 5.5 pounds) and prematurity (gestational age of less than thirty-seven weeks) are the two most important proximate causes of infant and especially of neonatal mortality. These outcomes, particularly neonatal mortality and low birth weight, are featured in this section.

The first two papers in this section are motivated by the importance of infant mortality as a key health indicator, by its trends between the mid-1950s and the early 1980s, and by the role of the developments just mentioned in those trends. My colleagues and I capitalize on variations in key determinants of neonatal mortality at a moment in time (1971 in the first paper and 1977 in the second) among counties of the United States to estimate the relative effects of each one and their contributions to the decline in that rate (Grossman and Jacobowitz 1981; Corman and Grossman 1985; Corman, Joyce, and Grossman 1987). We focus on neonatal mortality because the neonatal mortality rate was twice as large as the postneonatal mortality rate in 1982, and the former rate fell much faster than the latter rate beginning in 1964. Hence, the decline in neonatal mortality rate accounted for almost 80 percent of the decline in the infant mortality rate. Both papers apply estimated coefficients to trends in abortion availability or use, public program availability or use, and neonatal intensive care availability, to explain the downward trend in neonatal mortality from 1964 through the late 1970s or early 1980s.

Results in the two papers point to the growth in legal abortions as the single most important factor in reductions in white and black neonatal mortality rates. Increases in hospitals with neonatal intensive care units also have sizable effects for infants of both races. The extrapolations also point to the relevance of Medicaid, organized family planning clinics, the WIC program, and community health projects in accounting for reductions in the black rate. With the exception of community health projects, all these factors also are relevant for whites.

I continued to work on infant health outcomes because of the availability of data to estimate both health production functions and health demand functions. Thus I had the opportunity to make important methodological contributions to the literature on the determinants of health outcomes as well as to make important empirical contributions. In my economic formulation of the determinants of health in my 1972 *Journal of Political Economy* (Grossman 1972a) paper and in my 1972 National Bureau of Economic Research monograph (Grossman 1972b), I drew a distinction between these two outcome equations. The health production function relates health to a set of endogenous inputs or choice variables including medical care services, diet, and exercise, as well as exogenous determinants of the efficiency of the production process such as age and formal schooling completed. The health demand function relates health to income, wage rates, input prices, and efficiency variables. It is obtained by replacing the endogenous variables by their exogenous determinants and for that reason is a reduced form equation.[2] On the other hand, the production function is a structural equation because endogenous variables appear on its right-hand side.

In my NBER monograph and my 1976 paper on the correlation between health and schooling (Grossman 1976—the first paper in part 2), I focused on the estimation of health demand functions as opposed to health production functions. I did so because unobserved biological factors, such as an individual's exogenous health endowment and endowed rate of depreciation, and hard-to-measure inputs, such as the avoidance of stress, can play major roles in the determination of health outcomes. If an individual's behavior is shaped in part by knowledge of his or her endowments or if the unmeasured endogenous inputs are correlated with the included inputs, then estimation of the health technology will be biased and inconsistent.

In the specific case of infant health outcomes, women who anticipate a problematic birth outcome based on conditions unknown to the researcher may seek out more remedial medical care, whereas women with positive expectations seek out less. This adverse selection in input use is emphasized by Mark Rosenzweig and T. Paul Shultz (1983). It will understate the effect of, for example, the receipt of prenatal medical care early in the pregnancy on birth weight or survival. Rosenzweig and Schultz use adverse selection to justify the estimation of birth weight production functions by two-stage least squares. In their specification, delay in the receipt of prenatal care, maternal smoking during pregnancy, previous number of live births, and mother's age at birth are treated as endogenous inputs in a micro level dataset. Hope Corman, Theodore J. Joyce, and I use the same argument to fit neonatal mortality rate production functions in the third paper in this section (Corman, Joyce, and Grossman 1987). These functions differ from the neonatal mortality rate reduced form or demand function estimates in Corman and Grossman (1985). The primary distinction is that county-specific input availability measures in the 1985 paper are used as instruments for input use measures in the 1987 paper. Results in our 1987 paper and related results by Joyce (1987) and by Rosenzweig and Schultz (1983) point to larger input use effects when the endogeneity of use is taken into account by estimating production functions by two-stage least squares.

Adverse selection in input use, is not, however, the only source of bias due to selection. The efficacy of prenatal care, for example, may be seriously overstated if early care is but one form of healthy behavior. Pregnant women who initiate care promptly may eat more nutritiously, engage in the appropriate exercise, and use fewer drugs and other potentially harmful substances than women who begin care later. The omission of these hard-to-measure inputs tends to overestimate the impact of early prenatal care on infant health—an example of favorable selection.

Moreover, the resolution of pregnancy itself may be characterized by self-selection. With regard to this outcome, selection is favorable if women whose fetuses have poor health endowments are more likely to obtain an abortion or if women who desire to make large investments in their infants are more likely to give birth. On the other hand, selection is adverse if women who make relatively small investments are more likely to give birth.

The use of an instrumental variable approach to correct for self-selection in input use presupposes that this decision is characterized by adverse selection and ignores the problem of self-selection in the resolution of pregnancies. In the fourth paper in this section, Joyce and I (Grossman and Joyce 1990) approach the problem differently and somewhat more generally. Following James J. Heckman (1979), we treat the estimation of infant health production functions and prenatal medical care demand functions as a general problem in self-selection. Specifically, we test whether women who give birth represent a random draw from the population of women who become pregnant. The widespread use of induced abortion since its legalization by the Supreme Court in 1973 has permitted much greater choice in the number and timing of births. Thus the extent to which a failure to incorporate the choice-based nature of micro vital records into estimates of infant health production functions may bias the parameters of this function is potentially large. Joyce and I hypothesize that the unobserved factors that impact on the decision to give birth not only affect pregnancy outcomes but also condition the behavior of women who choose to give birth during pregnancy as well.

Our study is based on a cohort of pregnant women in New York City in 1984. In that year, 45 percent of all pregnancies to New York City residents ended in induced abortions. We estimate a three-equation model. The first equation is the probability of giving birth, given that a woman is pregnant. With this as our criterion equation, we test for self-selection in the infant health (measured by birth weight) production function and in the prenatal medical care demand function. Empirically, our estimates differ from those obtained by Rosenzweig and Schultz (1983) because they use micro vital records on live births alone. Not only does our methodology obviate the need to assert a priori whether adverse or favorable selection is dominant, but the sign pattern of the residual covariances indicates which type of selection characterizes both the decision to give birth and the decision to initiate prenatal care promptly.

Because our framework includes an implicit equation for the probability of becoming pregnant, we incorporate induced abortion as an alternative to traditional methods of contraception into economic models of fertility control (for example, Michael and Willis 1976; Hotz and Miller 1988). These models emphasize the use of contraception to reduce the uncertainty associated with the number and timing of births.

Induced abortion eliminates much of this uncertainty at a positive price. By assuming that the prices of contraception and abortion have unmeasured components that vary among women, we enrich the theoretical literature on the optimal number and quality of children (for example, Becker and Lewis; 1973; Willis 1973) and gain a better understanding of the earliest indicator of child quality—infant health—and the resources allocated to its production. In particular, we show that the prices of contraception and abortion, as well as the health endowment of the fetus, simultaneously influence decisions with regard to pregnancy resolutions and input selection.

Joyce and I find strong evidence of selectivity bias in the birth weight production function and prenatal demand equation among blacks but no evidence of such bias among whites. For the former group, the results suggest that the unobserved factors that raise the probability of giving birth are positively correlated with the unobserved factors that decrease delay in the initiation of prenatal care and increase birth weight. The sign patterns among the residual covariances are consistent with a model that emphasizes the cost of contraceptives. In particular, black women for whom the shadow price of contraception is relatively high are more likely to abort a pregnancy than their counterparts who face a lower shadow price and whose pregnancies were more likely to have been planned. The latter group should consume more prenatal care (delay less) and invest in other healthy behaviors that improve birth weight.

One explanation for the racial differences with respect to selectivity bias is that the shadow price of contraception is greater for blacks than it is for whites. Further, the shadow price is apt to vary more among blacks than it does among whites. Racial differences in contraceptive use and abortion in the 1980s and in more recent years are consistent with this interpretation (Guttmacher Institute 2015, 2016).

The results for blacks indicate that women who aborted would have given birth to lighter infants if they had selected the birth option and if they had had the same mean values of the observed variables in the birth weight equation as women who actually gave birth. One way to gauge the magnitude of the effect is to compare it to that of an observed risk factor for birth outcomes. Among blacks, complications due to maternal cigarette smoking reduce birth weight by 187 grams or by 5.8 percent relative to a mean of 3,184 for pregnancies not complicated by smoking. On the other hand, potential mean birth weight in the abortion sample falls short of birth weight in the birth sample by 116 grams due to unobserved inputs alone. This amounts to a differential of 3.7 percent relative to the observed mean of 3,173 for all black women in the birth sample. Thus the impact of unobserved healthy behaviors is almost two-thirds as large in absolute value as the effect of smoking. Finally, if we allow for differences in both observed and unobserved characteristics, the potential mean birth weight of women who aborted would have 140 grams less than the observed mean birth weight. This makes the impacts of unobserved healthy behaviors almost three-fourths as large as that of smoking.

As I pointed out in the introduction to this book, Joseph P. Newhouse has characterized the literature in health economics as consisting of two largely nonoverlapping streams: one dealing with the determinants of the health of the population and the other dealing with markets for health insurance and medical services. By focusing on the impact of the introduction of National Health Insurance (NHI) in Taiwan in 1995 on birth outcomes, Shin-Yi Chou,

Jin-Tan Liu, and I contribute to both streams in the last paper in this section (Chou, Grossman, and Liu 2014). There is enormous interest in the impacts of NHI on health outcomes, but the very nature of this intervention, whereby entire nations are covered universally, makes it difficult to estimate the health impacts of the change. The experience of Taiwan, however, provides a potential laboratory for overcoming these limitations. Prior to NHI, government workers possessed health insurance policies that covered prenatal medical care, newborn deliveries, neonatal care, and medical care services received by their children beyond the first month of life. Private sector industrial workers and farmers lacked this coverage. All households received coverage for the services just mentioned as of March 1995. Therefore, the introduction of NHI constitutes a natural experiment with treatment and control groups that form the basis of our empirical design. The former group consists of nongovernment-employed households, and the latter group consists of government-employed households. We expect that increases in infant health after the introduction of NHI in the treatment group will exceed corresponding increases in the control group.

Unlike in the United States, the postneonatal mortality rate in Taiwan is higher than the neonatal mortality rate. Moreover, stringent requirements for reporting births introduced in 1994 produced artificial upward trends in early infant deaths. For those reasons, we limit our analysis to postneonatal mortality.

The introduction of NHI led to reductions in this rate for infants born in farm households but not for infants born in private sector households. For the former group, the rate fell by between 0.3 and 0.6 deaths per thousand survivors or by between 8 and 16 percent. A large decline of between 3.4 and 6.8 deaths occurred for preterm infants—a drop of between 20 and 41 percent. In the pre-NHI period, the postneonatal mortality rate of farm infants was approximately 23 percent higher than the corresponding rate of private sector infants. Hence, our findings are consistent with the notion that the provision of health insurance to previously uninsured infants has larger effects on those born in poor health than on others. Our result that the effects of NHI rise in absolute value as the availability of medical care resources in the infant's county of residence rises is evidence that increases in medical care services received by infants made eligible for insurance coverage by NHI may account for at least part of the improvements in health outcomes that we observe. Farm families have lower levels of health, education, and income than private sector families and premature and low-weight infants are in worse health than other infants. Thus, taken as a set, our findings suggest that health insurance improves infant health outcomes of population subgroups characterized by low levels of education, income, and health.

NOTES

1. Federally subsidized maternal and infant care projects were authorized by the Social Security Act of 1935 but were greatly expanded by the War on Poverty. Community health centers, originally termed neighborhood health centers, were started by the Office of Economic Opportunity as part of the War on Poverty.
2. Of course, the papers in part 2 and the references in that part question the endogeneity of schooling.

REFERENCES

Becker, Gary S. 1981. *A Treatise on the Family*. Cambridge, MA: Harvard University Press.

Becker, Gary S., and H. Gregg Lewis. 1973. "On the Interaction Between the Quantity and Quality of Children." *Journal of Political Economy* 81(2, pt. 2): S279–S288.

Chou, Shin-Yi, Michael Grossman, and Jin-Tan Liu. 2014. "The Impact of National Health Insurance on Birth Outcomes: A Natural Experiment in Taiwan." *Journal of Development Economics* 111(November): 75–91.

Corman, Hope, and Michael Grossman. 1985. "Determinants of Neonatal Mortality Rates in the U.S.: A Reduced Form Model." *Journal of Health Economics* 4(3): 213–236.

Corman, Hope, Theodore J. Joyce, and Michael Grossman. 1987. "Birth Outcome Production Functions in the U.S." *Journal of Human Resources* 22(3): 339–360.

Fuchs, Victor R. 1983. *How We Live: An Economic Perspective on Americans from Birth to Death*. Cambridge, MA: Harvard University Press.

Grossman, Michael. 1972a. "On the Concept of Health Capital and the Demand for Health." *Journal of Political Economy* 80(2): 223–255.

——. 1972b. *The Demand for Health: A Theoretical and Empirical Investigation*. New York: Columbia University Press for the National Bureau of Economic Research.

——. 1976. "The Correlation Between Health and Schooling." In *Household Production and Consumption*, ed. Nestor E. Terleckyj. Studies in Income and Wealth, Volume 40, by the Conference on Research in Income and Wealth. New York: Columbia University Press for the National Bureau of Economic Research, 147–211.

Grossman, Michael, and Steven Jacobowitz. 1981. "Variations in Infant Mortality Rates among Counties of the United States: The Roles of Public Policies and Programs." *Demography* 18(4): 695–713.

Grossman, Michael, and Theodore J. Joyce. 1990. "Unobservables, Pregnancy Resolutions, and Birth Weight Production Functions in New York City." *Journal of Political Economy* 98 (5, pt. 1): 983–1007.

Guttmacher Institute. 2015. *Contraceptive Use in the United States http://www.guttmacher.org/pubs/fb_contr_use.pdf*.

Guttmacher Institute. 2016. *Facts on Induced Abortion in the United States. http://www.guttmacher.org/pubs/fb_induced_abortion.html.*Heckman, James J. 1979. "Sample Selection Bias as a Specification Error." *Econometrica* 47(1): 153–161.

Hotz, V. Joseph, and Robert A. Miller. 1988. "An Empirical Analysis of Life Cycle Fertility and Female Labor Supply." *Econometrica* 56(1): 91–118.

Joyce, Theodore J. 1987. "The Impact of Induced Abortion on Black and White Birth Outcomes." *Demography* 24(2): 229–244.

Michael, Robert T., and Robert J. Willis. 1976. "Contraception and Fertility: Household Production Under Uncertainty." In *Household Production and Consumption*, ed. Nestor E. Terleckyj. Studies in Income and Wealth, Volume 40, by the Conference on Research in Income and Wealth. New York: Columbia University Press for the National Bureau of Economic Research, 27–93.

Rosenzweig, Mark, and T. Paul Shultz. 1983. "Estimating a Household Production Function: Heterogeneity, the Demand for Health Inputs, and Their Effects on Birth Weight." *Journal of Political Economy* 91(5): 723–746.

Shakotko, Robert A., Linda N. Edwards, and Michael Grossman. 1981. "An Exploration of the Dynamic Relationship Between Health and Cognitive Development in Adolescence." In *Contributions to Economic Analysis: Health, Economics, and Health Economics*, ed. Jacques van der Gaag and Mark Perlman. Amsterdam: North-Holland Publishing, 305–328.

Willis, Robert J. 1973. "A New Approach to the Economics of Fertility Behavior." *Journal of Political Economy* 81(2, pt. 2): S14–S64.

Xu, Jiaquan, Sherry L. Murphy, Kenneth D. Kochanek, and Brigham A. Bastian. 2016. "Deaths: Final Data for 2013." *National Vital Statistics Report* 64(2). Hyattsville, MD: National Center for Health Statistics.

SEVEN

Variations in Infant Mortality Rates among Counties of the United States

The Roles of Public Policies and Programs

Michael Grossman and Steven Jacobowitz

ABSTRACT

The purpose of this paper is to shed light on the causes of the rapid decline in the infant mortality rate in the United States in the period after 1963. The roles of four public policies are considered: Medicaid, subsidized family planning services for low-income women, maternal and infant care projects, and the legalization of abortion. The most striking finding is that the increase in the legal abortion rate is the single most important factor in reductions in both white and nonwhite neonatal mortality rates. Not only does the growth in abortion dominate the other public policies, but it also dominates schooling and poverty.

From 1964 to 1977, the infant mortality rate in the United States declined at an annually compounded rate of 4.4 percent per year. This was an extremely rapid rate of decline compared to the figure of 0.6 percent per year from 1955 to 1964. The reduction in mortality proceeded at an even faster pace in the 1970s than in the late 1960s (5.2 percent per year from 1971 to 1977 versus 3.8 percent per year from 1964 to 1971).[1]

The period from 1964 to 1977 witnessed the introduction of Medicaid, maternal and infant care projects, federally subsidized family planning services for low-income women, the legalization of abortion, and the widespread adoption of oral and intrauterine contraceptive techniques. These developments have been pointed to in discussions of the cause of the acceleration in the downward trend in infant mortality (for example, Eisner et al. 1978; Lee et al. 1980), but the question has not been studied in a multivariate context. Moreover, the relative contribution of each factor has not been quantified. The purpose of this paper is to estimate the impacts of public policies and programs on infant mortality.

1. ANALYTICAL FRAMEWORK

Economic models of the family and household production developed by Becker and Lewis (1973) and Willis (1973) provide a fruitful theoretical framework to generate multivariate health outcome functions and to assess the roles of social programs and policies in these functions. Ben-Porath (1973), Ben-Porath and Welch (1976), Williams (1976), and Lewit (1977) have utilized the economic model of the family to study theoretically and empirically the determinants of birth outcomes. Following these authors, we assume that the parents' utility function depends on their own consumption, the number of births, and the survival probability. Both the number of births and the survival probability are endogenous variables. In particular, the survival probability production function depends upon endogenous inputs of medical care, nutrition, and the own time of the mother. In addition, the production function is affected by the reproductive efficiency of the mother and by other aspects of her efficiency in household production. Given the considerable body of evidence that education raises market and nonmarket productivity, one would expect more educated mothers to be more efficient producers of surviving infants.

The above model calls attention to the important determinants of the survival probability and its complement, the infant mortality rate. In general, this set of determinants is similar to that used in multivariate studies of infant mortality with different and fewer theoretical points of departure (for example, Fuchs 1974; Williams 1974; Brooks 1978; Gortmaker 1979). Moreover, the model provides a ready structure within which to interpret the effects of public programs and policies on infant mortality.[2] Thus, Medicaid and maternal and infant care projects lower the direct and indirect costs[3] of obtaining prenatal and obstetrical care, which should increase the likelihood of a favorable birth outcome and lower infant mortality. Federal subsidization of family planning services, abortion reform, and the diffusion of oral and intrauterine contraceptive techniques (the pill and the IUD) reduce the costs of birth control and increase its availability. Within the context of an economic model of the family, these developments raise the "optimal" survival probability and lower the "optimal" number of births. In addition, they will lower the observed infant mortality rate if less healthy fetuses are less likely to be conceived or more likely to be aborted.[4]

To measure the relative importance of the above factors in the recent U.S. infant mortality experience, a cross-sectional regression analysis of variations in infant mortality rates is performed among counties of the United States in 1971. This procedure capitalizes on variations in the programs at issue among counties at a moment in time. Thus, it provides a set of impact coefficients to identify the contribution of each program net of basic determinants of infant mortality such as poverty, schooling levels, and the availability of physicians. After estimating the regression, its coefficients are applied to national trends in the exogenous variables between 1964 and 1977 to "explain" the trend in infant mortality.

This methodology has a number of desirable properties. It mitigates the multicollinearity problems that almost certainly would arise in a time-series regression analysis for the United States as a whole. Moreover, the state-of-the-art in neonatology, which has changed over time and is difficult to quantify, is constant in the cross section. Finally, with the exception of abortion reform, the programs that we study are aimed at poor persons. Therefore, the appropriate way to measure their impacts is to interact the policy variables with the fraction of births to poor women. This insight is incorporated into the basic regression specification.

The last point is worth spelling out in more detail. Let d_{pj} be the infant mortality rate of babies born to poor mothers (infant deaths divided by live births) in the jth county, and let d_{nj} be the infant mortality rate of babies born to nonpoor mothers. As an identity,

$$d_j = k_j d_{pj} + (1 - k_j)d_{nj}, \tag{1}$$

where d_j is the observed infant mortality rate and k_j is the fraction of births to poor mothers. Specify behavioral equations for d_{pj} and d_{nj} as follows:

$$d_{pj} = \alpha_0 + \alpha_1 x_{pj} + \alpha_2 y_{pj} + \alpha_3 w_{pj} + \alpha_4 z_j \tag{2}$$

$$d_{nj} = \beta_0 + \beta_2 y_{nj} + \beta_3 w_{nj} + \beta_4 z_j. \tag{3}$$

In these equations, x_{pj} is a vector of policy variables that affects the mortality rate of poor babies alone such as Medicaid; $w_{ij}(i = p, n)$ is a vector of policy variables that affects both groups such as the group-specific abortion rate (legal abortions per thousand live births); y_{ij} refers to a group-specific vector of basic determinants of infant mortality such as mother's schooling; and z_j is a vector of variables that has the same value for each group such as physicians per capita. Since there are no data on income-specific mortality rates at the county level, substitute equations (2) and (3) into equation (1) to obtain

$$dj = \beta_0 + (\alpha_0 - \beta_0)k_j + \alpha_1 k_j x_{pj} + \alpha_2 k_j y_{pj} + \beta_2(1 - k_j)y_{nj}$$
$$+ \alpha_3 k_j w_{pj} + \beta_3(1 - k_j)w_{nj} + \alpha_4 k_j z_j + \beta_4(1 - k_j)z_j. \tag{4}$$

Equation (4) gives a multiple regression of d_j on eight variables (vectors): k_j, $k_j x_{pj}$, $k_j y_{pj}$, $(1 - k_j)y_{nj}$, $k_j w_{pj}$, $(1 - k_j)w_{nj}$, $k_j z_j$, and $(1 - k_j)z_j$. Attempts to estimate this equation would be plagued by severe problems of multicollinearity and by the absence of income-specific measures of certain variables such as the legal abortion rate. Therefore, we assume that the income-specific abortion rate (w_{ij}) is proportional to its weighted average ($w_{ij} = r_i w_j$). In addition, we assume that schooling of poor mothers in a given county is proportional to schooling of nonpoor mothers ($y_{pj} = sy_{nj}$). The actual equation that we fit is

$$d_j = \beta_0 + (\alpha_0 - \beta_0)k_j + \alpha_1 k_j x_{pj} + \delta_2 y_{nj} + \delta_3 w_j + \delta_4 z_j, \tag{5}$$

where δ_2 estimates $\alpha_2 k_j s + \beta_2(1 - k_j)$, δ_3 estimates $\alpha_3 k_j r_p + \beta_3(1 - k_j)r_n$, and δ_4 estimates $\alpha_4 k_j + \beta_4(1 - k_j)$. The important point to note is that we employ kj and the product of k_j and x_{pj} as independent variables in the regression. Thus, we employ a specification that explicitly recognizes that the impact on the observed infant mortality rate of policies aimed at the poor is larger the larger is the fraction of births to poor mothers ($\partial d_j / \partial x_{pj} = k_j \alpha_1$). Moreover, our specification yields a direct estimate of the impact parameter (α_1).

A more general formulation of the above model can be developed by decomposing the observed infant mortality rate in the jth county into rates associated with a variety of birth characteristics such as mother's age, mother's income, parity, birth weight, and legitimacy status of the birth:

$$d_j = \sum_{i=1}^{m} k_{ij} d_{ij}. \tag{6}$$

In this equation k_{ij} is the fraction of births in the ith category and d_{ij} is the infant mortality rate associated with that category. An example of one such category is an illegitimate, low-birth weight birth to a low-income, teenage mother with no previous live births. The policies studied here might lower the observed infant mortality rate by lowering the fraction of births in high-risk categories

(categories where d_{ij} is higher than on average) and by lowering the mortality rate in a given risk category (d_{ij}). These regression estimates incorporate both effects because there is no control here for characteristics such as the percentage of births to teenage mothers, the percentage of illegitimate births, the percentage of fourth and higher-order births, and the percentage of low-birth weight births. The percentage of births to low-income mothers is included, but as indicated below a measure is employed that varies among counties only because the percentage of the population in poverty varies among counties.

Note that some discussions of the probable impacts of abortion reform on infant mortality assume that this public policy operates solely by reducing the percentage of high-risk births, especially the percentage of low-birth weight births (for example, Lee et al. 1980). Yet abortion reform also might lower infant mortality by lowering risk-specific death rates. In particular, more prenatal and perinatal care may be allocated to pregnancies that are not aborted. Indeed, in the context of the economic model of the family outlined above (Becker and Lewis 1973; Willis 1973), it is likely that a reduction in the cost of birth control will have a larger impact on the amount of medical care demanded and therefore on the survival probability than a reduction in the price of care. The reason is that a reduction in the cost of fertility control raises the cost (price) of a birth, while a reduction in the price of medical care lowers the cost of a birth. Although both developments almost certainly will raise the optimal survival probability, a reduction in the cost of fertility control will lower the optimal birth rate, while a reduction in the price of care may increase it. This point should be kept in mind when the effects of abortion reform on infant mortality are compared to the effects of Medicaid coverage of prenatal and perinatal care services.[5]

2. EMPIRICAL SPECIFICATION

2.1. Data and Measurement of Infant Mortality

The basic data set used here is the Urban Institute's expanded version of the Area Resource File (ARF). The ARF is a county-based data service, prepared by Applied Management Sciences, Inc., for the Bureau of Health Professions, Health Resources Administration, U.S. Department of Health and Human Services. It incorporates information from a variety of sources for 3,078 counties in the United States. These counties can also be aggregated into larger geographic areas such as county groups, Standard Metropolitan Statistical Areas, and states. Demographic and socioeconomic characteristics are taken from the 1970 Census of Population. Socioeconomic characteristics of women ages fifteen to forty-nine come from the 1970 Census of Population, Women of Childbearing Age Tape. Deaths by age, race, and sex for the years 1969 through 1976 are obtained from the National Center for Health Statistics (NCHS) Mortality Tape. Births by race for those years are obtained from the NCHS Natality Tape. Health manpower and facilities come from the American Medical Association, the American Hospital Association, and other sources. We have added measures pertaining to the policies and programs discussed previously to the ARF from sources indicated in the next section.

There are two components of infant mortality: neonatal mortality and postneonatal mortality. Neonatal mortality refers to deaths of infants within the first twenty-seven days of life. Postneonatal mortality refers to deaths of infants between the ages of 28 and 364 days. Neonatal deaths are usually caused by congenital abnormalities, prematurity, and complications of delivery; while postneonatal deaths are usually caused by infectious diseases and accidents.

This empirical analysis is limited to the neonatal mortality rate, defined as neonatal deaths per thousand live births. Since the causes of the two types of infant deaths are dissimilar, socioeconomic variables and public programs are likely to have different effects on each. Specifically, these policy variables are more relevant to neonatal mortality than to postneonatal mortality. For instance, the former is considerably more sensitive to appropriate prenatal and obstetrical care than the latter (Lewit 1977). Another reason for this focus is that the neonatal mortality rate is much larger than postneonatal mortality rate; it was three times as large in 1971. Consequently, trends in the infant mortality rate are dominated by trends in the neonatal mortality rate. Obviously, one cannot hope to explain trends in the infant mortality rate without being able to explain trends in the neonatal mortality rate.

Separate regressions are fitted for white neonatal mortality and for black neonatal mortality. Black neonatal mortality rates are much higher than white rates. In a non-race-specific regression, one would enter the percentage of black births to control for race differences. But this variable would be highly correlated with the percentage of births to low-income women, schooling, and other independent variables. By fitting race-specific regressions, multicollinearity is reduced and the coefficients of the independent variables are allowed to vary between races. Linear regressions are estimated because a linear specification facilitates the aggregation of the two income-specific mortality rate functions given in the first section of this chapter into a single equation for the entire population.

Counties are used rather than states or Standard Metropolitan Statistical Areas (SMSAs) as the units of observation. SMSAs and states are very large and sometimes heterogenous. Income, schooling levels, medical resources and other variables may vary greatly within an SMSA or a state. Since counties are much more homogeneous, these problems are reduced in our research. A weakness with the use of counties is that the small size of some of these areas may mean that people may receive medical care outside the county. Moreover, the small number of births in certain counties may increase the importance of random movements or "noise" in the determination of regression coefficients.

These problems with county data are reduced by including in the regressions only counties with a population of at least 50,000 persons in 1970. A county must also have at least 5,000 blacks for inclusion in the black regressions. There are 679 counties in the white regressions and 359 counties in the black regressions. In addition to selecting large counties, we attenuate random elements by employing a three-year average of the race-specific neonatal mortality rate for the period 1970–1972 as the dependent variable and by estimating weighted regressions, where the set of weights is the square root of the race-specific number of births in 1971.

Neonatal mortality for the period 1970–1972 is studied because measures of all independent variables are available for a year in that period or for 1969. In addition, it provides an ideal time frame to estimate the impact of abortion reform because of substantial cross-sectional variations in the legal abortion rate in that period. Abortion reform proceeded at a rapid pace between 1967 and the middle of 1970. Prior to 1967 all states of the United States had laws which permitted abortion only when it was necessary to preserve a pregnant woman's life. Beginning in 1967 some states started to reform these laws to increase the number of circumstances under which abortions could be performed. The reformed statutes legalized abortions if there was a substantial risk that continuance of the pregnancy would seriously impair the physical or mental health of the woman, or that the child resulting from the pregnancy would be born with a serious physical or mental defect, or in cases of pregnancy resulting from rape or incest. By 1970, twelve states had enacted such statutes. Moreover, in 1970 four additional states enacted extremely liberal abortion laws which placed no legal restriction on the reasons for which an abortion may be obtained prior to the viability of the fetus (Centers for Disease Control 1971). After the middle of 1970, there was no significant changes in abortion law until 1973 when the Supreme Court ruled most restrictive state abortion laws unconstitutional. Concurrent with these reforms, the U.S. ratio of legal abortions per thousand live births rose from 4 in 1969 to 180 in 1972 and to 361 in 1977 (Centers for Disease Control 1971, 1972, 1974; U.S. Bureau of the Census 1980).

3. MEASUREMENT OF INDEPENDENT VARIABLES

Wherever possible, race-specific variables are employed in the regressions. Such variables are denoted with an asterisk. Except for the Medicaid and abortion measures, all variables are county-specific. Table 7.1 contains definitions, means, and standard deviations of the dependent and independent variables in the regressions.

The number of active nonfederal physicians per thousand population serves as a general proxy for the price and availability of medical care.[6] The roles of the percentage of births to poverty mothers and the percentage of women of childbearing ages who had at least a high school education were discussed above.

Note that there are no direct measures of births to poor women, either at the county or at the national level. Therefore, the estimate of the race-specific percentage of births to such women assumes that the race-specific birth rate of poor women does not vary among counties and that the race-specific birth rate of nonpoor women does not vary among counties. Under these conditions, one can compute race-specific birth rates of poor and nonpoor women by regressing the race-specific birth rate (b_j^*, the ratio of births to women ages fifteen to forty-four) on the race-specific fraction of women in poverty (π_j^*):

$$b_j^* = \gamma_0^* + \gamma_1^* \pi_j^*. \tag{7}$$

The regression intercept (γ_0^*) gives the birth rate of nonpoor women, and the sum of γ_0^* and γ_1^* gives the birth rate of poor women.[7]

After fitting the regressions for whites and blacks, the race-specific percentage of births to women in poverty is estimated as

$$PB^* - 100[(\gamma_0^* + \gamma_1^*)\pi_j^*/(\gamma_0^* | \gamma_1^* \pi_j^*)]. \tag{8}$$

It is clear that PB^* is a monotonically increasing, although nonlinear, function of the fraction of the population in poverty. Therefore, the regression coefficient of PB^* summarizes the impact of poverty on infant mortality. Since poverty and family income are highly correlated, the latter is omitted from the regression.[8]

One may question the assumption that the birth rate of poor women is the same in every county, especially since subsidized family planning services and abortion reform are likely to have substantial impacts on birth rates of poor women. The aim of this chapter, however, is to estimate reduced form, as opposed to structural, effects of public policies on infant mortality (see note 5). That is, these policies can lower the observed infant mortality rate by lowering the fraction of births in high-risk categories and by lowering the mortality rate associated with a given risk category. Since the aim is to measure both

Table 7.1 Definitions, Means, and Standard Deviations of Variables

Variable Name	Definition
Neonatal mortality 1970–1972[*]	Three-year average neonatal mortality rate for the period 1970–1972, deaths of infants less than twenty-eight days old per 1,000 live births ($\mu_w = 12.729$; $\sigma_w = 2.076$; $\mu_b = 21.477$; $\sigma_b = 3.988$)
PB[*]	Estimated percentage of births to mothers with family incomes less than the poverty level for the period 1969–1971 ($\mu_w = 21.324$; $\sigma_w = 8.388$; $\mu_b = 35.188$; $\sigma_b = 11.235$)
% ≥ HS[*a]	Percentage of women aged fifteen to forty-nine who had at least a high school education in 1970 ($\mu_w = 62.927$; $\sigma_w = 7.238$; $\mu_b = 44.096$; $\sigma_b = 8.527$)
Physicians	Active nonfederal physicians per 1,000 population in 1971 ($\mu_w = 1.505$; $\sigma_w = 0.987$; $\mu_b = 1.954$; $\sigma_b = 1.220$)
MAXPB[*]	Dichotomous variable that equals one if county is in a state that covers all first-time pregnancies to financially eligible women under Medicaid (MA) multiplied by PB[*] ($\mu_w = 7.892$; $\sigma_w = 10.850$; $\mu_b = 7.104$; $\sigma_b = 12.657$)
MUXPB[*]	Dichotomous variable that equals one if county is in a state that covers first-time pregnancies under Medicaid only if no husband present or if husband present but unemployed and not receiving unemployment compensation (MU) multiplied by PB[*] ($\mu_w = 2.810$; $\sigma_w = 7.521$; $\mu_b = 3.857$; $\sigma_b = 10.219$)
MNXPB[*]	Dichotomous variable that equals one if county is in a state that covers first-time pregnancies under Medicaid only if no husband present (MN) multiplied by PB[*] ($\mu_w = 2.284$; $\sigma_w = 7.851$; $\mu_b = 7.536$; $\sigma_b = 18.185$)
MIXPB[*]	Dichotomous variable that equals one if the county had an M and I[b] project in 1971 (MI) multiplied by PB[*] ($\mu_w = 5.339$; $\sigma_w = 9.390$; $\mu_b = 16.152$; $\sigma_b = 16.577$)
PMIBXPB[*]	Births in M and I[b] projects in 1971 as a percentage of births to women with low income (PMIB) multiplied by PB[*] ($\mu_w = 2.174$; $\sigma_w = 5.086$; $\mu_b = 8.470$; $\sigma_b = 12.670$)
UPXPB[*]	Percentage of women aged fifteen to forty-four with family income equal to or less than 150 percent of the poverty level who were served by organized family planning clinics in fiscal 1971 (UP) multiplied by PB[*] ($\mu_w = 639.506$; $\sigma_w = 521.843$; $\mu_b = 1,435.559$; $\sigma_b = 741.955$)
Abor. rate	Three-year average abortion rate for the period 1970–1972 of state in which county is located; legal abortions performed on state residents per 1,000 live births to state residents ($\mu_w = 96.607$; $\sigma_w = 80.497$; $\mu_b = 87.156$; $\sigma_b = 77.518$)
Abor. reform	Dichotomous variable that equals one if county is in a state that reformed its abortion law by 1970 ($\mu_w = 0.369$; $\sigma_w = 0.483$; $\mu_b = 0.358$; $\sigma_b = 0.480$)
IMR 66–68	Three-year average infant mortality rate for the period 1966–1968, not race or age specific ($\mu_w = 21.517$; $\sigma_w = 3.553$; $\mu_b = 24.380$; $\sigma_b = 3.867$)

Notes: Variable names ending in an asterisk (*) indicate variables that are race specific. The symbols μ_w, σ_w, μ_b, and σ_b denote the white mean, the white standard deviation, the black mean, and the black standard deviation, respectively. The white data pertain to 679 counties, while the black data pertain to 359 counties. Means and standard deviations are weighted by the race-specific number of births in 1971.

[a] Variable is available only for whites and nonwhites as opposed to whites and blacks.

[b] "M and I" refers to maternal and infant care.

mechanisms, the estimated percentage of births to low-income women, which varies among counties only because the percentage of the population in poverty varies among counties, is a superior variable to the actual percentage of such births, even if the latter were available.[9]

The policy and program measures contain variables pertaining to Medicaid coverage of prenatal and perinatal care services, maternal and infant care projects, the use of organized family planning clinics by low-income women in childbearing ages, and abortion reform. In the case of prenatal and obstetrical care services, variations among states in the treatment of first-time pregnancies under Medicaid contribute to substantial variations in the percentage of pregnant low-income women whose medical care is financed by Medicaid. In particular, nineteen states cover *no* first-time pregnancies because their aid to families with dependent children (AFDC) programs do not cover "unborn children."[10] The treatment of first-time pregnancies of low-income women under Medicaid by the state in which the county is located is described by three dichotomous variables (MN, MU, MA). MN equals one for counties in states that cover first-time pregnancies only if no husband is present. MU equals one for counties in states that provide coverage if no husband is present or if the husband is present but unemployed and not receiving unemployment insurance. MA equals one for counties in states that provide coverage to all financially eligible women, regardless of the presence or employment status of the husband. The omitted category pertains to counties in states that cover *no* first-time pregnancies because their AFDC programs do not cover unborn children.[11]

The measurement of Medicaid is imperfect because its impact on neonatal mortality depends on the percentage of second- and higher-order births covered and on the quantity and quality of services provided per birth. There are no data on these variables. In preliminary regressions, the average Medicaid payment per adult recipient in AFDC families in the state in which the county is located was included as a proxy for the quantity and quality of services. This variable had a positive and statistically insignificant effect on neonatal mortality. Its inclusion had only minor impacts on the coefficients of the other variables.

The presence of a maternal and infant care project in a county in 1971 is denoted by the dichotomous variable MI. A second measure of the impact of these projects is given by the number of births in a maternal and infant care project in 1971 as a percentage of the estimated births to low-income women in 1971 (PMIB). Both variables are employed because this program is relatively small; there were only 53 projects in 1971. The presence of a project and the number of births in it were taken from Bureau of Community Health Services (n.d.).

The impact of variations in federal, state, and local subsidization of family planning services is given by the percentage of women ages fifteen to forty-four with family incomes equal to or less than 150 percent of the poverty level who were served by organized family planning clinics in fiscal 1971 (UP). These clinics are organized by hospitals, state and local health departments, Planned Parenthood, and other agencies such as neighborhood health centers. This variable was taken from a survey conducted by the National Center for Health Statistics and by the technical assistance division of Planned Parenthood, then known as the Center for Family Planning Program Development and now known as the Alan Guttmacher Institute (Center for Family Planning Program Development 1974). It excludes family planning services delivered to low-income women by private physicians.

Dryfoos (1976) reports that almost all clients of family planning clinics use the pill or the IUD. Therefore, the percentage of low-income women who are served by these clinics is positively related to the percentage of low-income women who select the pill or the IUD as contraceptive techniques. There is no information on the use of these techniques by other women at the county or state level, but it is known that women with at least a high school education are more likely to use them. Therefore, part of the observed effect of schooling in the regressions reflects the impact of the diffusion of the pill and the IUD on neonatal mortality.

The Medicaid, maternal and infant care projects, and family planning variables are interacted with the race-specific percentage of births to women in poverty. Since PB^* is a percentage rather than a fraction, the regression coefficients must be multiplied by 100 to obtain the vector of impact parameters (α_1) associated with policies aimed at low-income women [see equations (2), (4), or (5)].

The role of abortion reform is measured by a three-year average of the legal abortion rate for the period 1970–1972 in the state in which the county is located. The measure is an average of legal abortions performed on state residents per 1,000 live births to state residents and is derived from information reported by the Centers for Disease Control (1971, 1972, 1974). It is assumed that abortions performed in the first half of a given year affect the neonatal mortality rate in the second half of that year. The computation also takes account of the extremely low legal abortion rates before the second half of 1970 in states that reformed their abortion laws in 1970. The assumptions required to estimate the abortion rate are somewhat arbitrary.[12] Therefore, in some regressions the rate is replaced by a dichotomous variable that identifies counties in states that reformed their abortion laws by the middle of 1970.

The final variable in the regressions is a three-year average of the infant mortality rate for the years 1966–1968 (IMR66-68). Theoretically, this is an important variable to include in the analysis because programs such as maternal and infant care projects and subsidized family planning clinics for low-income women were designed to service target populations with poor health indicators. Consequently, estimates of their impacts are biased toward zero if the initial level of the mortality rate is omitted from the regression. In the case of abortion reform and liberal treatment of first-time pregnancies under Medicaid, the exclusion of the lagged mortality rate might overstate their contributions to reductions in neonatal mortality. This is because most of the states that reformed their abortion laws by 1970 and enacted generous Medicaid programs were liberal states with relatively large welfare programs and probably lower than average infant mortality rates. In general, the use of the lagged rate as an independent variable controls for unmeasured determinants of infant mortality that are correlated with the included variables.

Given lags between the enactment of the programs at issue and their implementation and given lags between implementation and impacts on neonatal mortality, IMR66-68 provides an ideal control for the initial level of the mortality rate. Note also that IMR66-68 is superior to the corresponding race-specific neonatal mortality rate because the overall infant mortality rate was used to identify target populations and identifies the size of welfare programs at least as well as a race- and age-specific rate.[13] Note finally, that, to the extent that the programs at issue had an impact on mortality between 1966 and 1968, their effects are understated. Preliminary regressions (not shown) suggest that this bias is minor. When the lagged mortality rate is excluded from the regressions, the impacts of abortion reform and liberal Medicaid coverage rise in absolute value, while the impacts of family planning and the maternal and infant care program decline in absolute value. This is precisely what one would expect if the regressions with IMR66-68 provide an adequate control for the mortality rate in the period prior to the initial impact date of the programs.

4. EMPIRICAL RESULTS

Ordinary least squares regressions of white neonatal mortality rates are contained in panel A of table 7.2, and ordinary least squares regressions of black neonatal mortality rate are contained in panel B of table 7.2. For whites, the percentage of births to poor mothers has a positive and statistically significant effect on neonatal mortality, while mother's schooling has an insignificant negative effect. For blacks, the negative schooling effect is significant, but somewhat surprisingly, there is an *inverse* relationship between the percentage of births to poor black mothers and the neonatal mortality rate. For both races, the coefficient of physicians per capita is positive and not significant. Moreover, the infant mortality rate for the period 1966 to 1968 performs well as a control for the neonatal mortality rate prior to the initiation of the programs at issue and for unmeasured determinants of mortality (see regressions A1, A3, B1, and B3).

Because the poverty variable has the "wrong" sign for blacks, it is excluded in regressions A2, A4, B2, and B4. The main impact of this alternative speci-fication is to increase the absolute value of the schooling effect for whites and to reduce it for blacks. Since the coefficients of the policy variables do not change much when PB^* is omitted and since the estimation of separate poverty and schooling effects "taxes" the black data, we stress the results contained in regressions B2 and B4 in the rest of this chapter. For whites, both estimates with and without PB^* are used. In part, more specifications are used for whites because trends in white neonatal mortality dominate trends in total neonatal mortality. In particular, white births account for approximately 80 percent of all births at the national level.[14]

Table 7.2 sheds considerable light on the roles of the policy variables in neo-natal mortality outcomes. Nineteen of the twenty-eight policy coefficients have the anticipated negative signs in the four white regressions. All fourteen coeffi-cients have the anticipated negative signs in the two relevant black regressions (B2 and B4). The exceptions in the white regressions pertain to the coefficients of the variables that identify liberal coverage of first-time pregnancies under Medicaid ($MAXPB^*$, $MUXPB^*$, $MNXPB^*$). Given the high degree of intercor-relation among the variables in the regression and the imprecise measures used, the preponderance of negative effects is an important and impressive finding.

In terms of statistical significance, the hypothesis that no member of the set of policy variables has a non-zero effect on neonatal mortality always is rejected at the 1 percent level. With respect to the four specific policies, in gen-eral abortion and the use of subsidized family planning services by low-income women have significant impacts, while Medicaid and maternal and infant care projects do not.[15]

Specifically, for whites the abortion rate achieves significance at all conven-tional levels in regressions A1 and A2. A similar comment applies to the dichoto-mous variable that denotes abortion reform by the middle of 1970 in regressions A3 and A4. For blacks, abortion reform is significant at all levels in regression B4, while the abortion rate is significant at the 6 percent level, but not at the 5 percent level, in regression B2. For whites, the interaction between the per-centage of low-income women who use organized family planning clinics and the percentage of births to low-income women ($UPXPB^*$) is significant at the 5 percent level in the first three regressions and at the 6 percent level in the fourth. For blacks, $UPXPB^*$ is significant at the 5 percent level in both regressions.

Table 7.2 Ordinary Least Square Regressions of Neonatal Mortality Rates

Independent Variable	Panel A: White Regressions				Panel B: Black Regressions			
	(A1)	(A2)	(A3)	(A4)	(B1)	(B2)	(B3)	(B4)
PB*	.037 (3.00)		.042 (3.45)		-.147 (-4.14)		-.133 (-3.83)	
Physicians	.144 (1.60)	.122 (1.35)	.124 (1.37)	.097 (1.07)	.227 (1.03)	.450 (2.05)	.172 (0.79)	.393 (1.84)
% ≥ HS*	-.015 (-1.14)	-.036 (-3.13)	-.013 (-0.96)	-.037 (3.22)	-.124 (-2.93)	-.017 (-0.49)	-.137 (-3.31)	-.035 (-1.08)
MAXPB*	.004 (0.39)	.016 (1.83)	-.003 (-0.39)	.008 (1.00)	.0004 (0.00)	-.014 (-0.53)	-.007 (-0.31)	-.010 (-0.46)
MUXPB*	.003 (0.29)	.010 (1.03)	.004 (0.44)	.012 (1.24)	-.038 (-1.78)	-.033 (-1.51)	-.041 (-1.97)	-.034 (-1.61)
MNXPB*	-.006 (-0.67)	.001 (0.13)	-.002 (-0.21)	.007 (0.77)	-.010 (-0.75)	-.032 (-2.47)	-.010 (-0.73)	-.030 (-2.32)
MIXPB*	-.005 (-0.36)	-.011 (-0.87)	-.008 (-0.67)	-.017 (-1.37)	-.007 (-0.30)	-.003 (-0.15)	-.007 (-0.34)	-.005 (-0.20)
PMIBXPB*	-.022 (-1.06)	-.020 (-0.98)	-.015 (-0.76)	-.011 (-0.56)	-.033 (-1.19)	-.032 (-1.13)	-.037 (-1.35)	-.036 (-1.31)
UPXPB*	-.001 (-2.99)	-.0003 (-1.94)	-.001 (-2.80)	-.0003 (-1.58)	-.0003 (-0.86)	-.001 (-2.37)	-.0001 (-0.34)	-.001 (-1.76)
Abortion rate	-.004 (-3.25)	-.005 (-3.91)			-.009 (-2.25)	-.007 (-1.58)		
Abortion reform			-.549 (-3.43)	-.592 (-3.69)			-1.751 (-3.89)	-1.773 (-3.86)
IMR 66–68	.274 (12.34)	.280 (12.53)	.281 (12.73)	.288 (13.04)	.260 (3.98)	.240 (3.61)	.235 (3.65)	.217 (3.31)
CONSTANT	7.554	9.400	7.045	9.094	27.184	17.998	27.618	19.238
$\bar{R}^2$	.315	.307	.317	.305	.125	.084	.149	.116
F	29.38	31.05	29.54	30.80	5.64	4.30	6.70	5.68

Notes: The t-ratios are in parentheses. The critical t-ratio at the 5 percent level of significance is 1.64 for a one-tailed test. The eight F-ratios are significant at the 1 percent level.

The significance of the abortion rate is notable because this variable is neither race- or county-specific and must be computed subject to a number of somewhat arbitrary assumptions (see note 12). Therefore, it is probably subject to considerable measurement error, which biases its coefficient toward zero. The sizable and significant impacts of the dichotomous abortion reform variable strengthens confidence in the estimated coefficients of the abortion rate and confirm that the effect for blacks is larger in absolute value than that for whites.

To examine the relative contributions of schooling, poverty, and the public programs to the recent U.S. neonatal mortality experience, we apply the coefficients of regressions Al, A2, and B2 to trends in the exogenous variables between 1964 and 1977. The results of estimating the implied changes in neonatal mortality rates due to selected factors for the period 1964–1977 and for the sub-periods 1964–1971 and 1971–1977 and given in table 7.3.[16] Results for whites and nonwhites are shown because separate time series for blacks are not available.

Since there is little trend in the percentage of families in poverty after 1971 and since the definition of poverty was altered beginning in 1975, the estimates in table 7.3 assume no change in poverty or in PB^* between 1971 and 1977. In these computations, the national levels of the two maternal and infant care project measures are zero in 1964 and do not change from 1971 to 1977. The three Medicaid measures are treated in the same manner. This treatment is justified because there were few of these projects in operation prior to 1967 and almost no trend in the number of projects or the total number of births in projects after 1971 (Bureau of Community Health Services n.d.). The Medicaid program was not enacted until July 1965, and the rules governing coverage of first-time pregnancies under Medicaid did not vary between 1971 and 1977.

Our treatment of Medicaid is somewhat controversial because the percentage of Medicaid-financed births to poor women and the real quantity of medical services per birth may have risen between 1971 and 1977. Although definitive evidence on these matters is lacking, a number of observations can be made. Much of the observed decline over time in the relationship between income and physician visits, which Davis and Reynolds (1976) show was caused by Medicaid, occurred by 1971. The percentage of the poverty population that received Medicaid benefits rose by only 6 percentage points between 1970 and 1974 (Davis and Reynolds 1976; Davis and Schoen 1978). Real Medicaid benefits per recipient show no trend between 1971 and 1977 (Davis and Schoen 1978). The percentage of black mothers who started their prenatal care in the first trimester of pregnancy rose between 1969 and 1975 (Taffel 1978). Except for the last observation, this evidence justified our treatment of Medicaid. We do, however, examine the sensitivity of the results to an alternative assumption described below.

Table 7.3 Contribution of Selected Factors to Reductions in Neonatal Mortality Rates, 1964–1977

	Panel A: Whites						Panel B: Nonwhites		
	1964–1977		1964–1971		1971–1977		1964–1977	1964–1971	1971–1977
	Reg.A1	Reg.A2	Reg.A1	Reg.A2	Reg.A1	Reg.A2	Reg.B2	Reg.B2	Reg.B2
Observed reduction in neonatal mortality rate (deaths per thousand live births)	7.5		3.2		4.3		11.8	6.9	4.9
Annually compounded percentage rate of decline in neonatal mortality rate	4.9		3.2		6.9		4.6	4.4	4.9
Contribution of selected factors to observed reduction in neonatal mortality rate									
Physicians	a	a	a	a	a	a	−0.2	−0.1	−0.1
Est, poverty births (PB*)	0.4	b	0.4	b	a	c	b	b	b
% ≥ High School	0.2	0.6	0.1	0.3	0.1	0.3	0.3	0.1	0.2
Abortion rate	1.5	1.7	0.4	0.4	1.1	1.3	2.5	0.6	1.9
UPXPB*	0.6	0.2	0.3	0.1	0.3	0.1	1.4	0.8	0.6
M and I projects[d]	0.1	0.1	0.1	0.1	a	c	0.3	0.3	c
Medicaid[e]	a	−0.2	a	−0.2	a	c	0.5	0.5	c
Total explained reduction	2.8	2.4	1.3	0.7	1.5	1.7	4.8	2.2	2.6
Percentage explained	37.3	32.0	40.6	24.7	34.9	39.5	40.7	31.9	53.1

[a] Less than .1 in absolute value.
[b] Variable omitted from regression.
[c] No change in variable.
[d] Combined contribution of MIXPB* and PMIBXEB*.
[e] Combined contribution of MAXPB*, MUXPB*, and MNXPB*.

As shown in table 7.3, the actual decline in the white neonatal mortality rate between 1964 and 1977 was 7.5 deaths per thousand live births. Regression A1, which incorporates separate poverty and schooling effects, "explains" 2.8 of these deaths or 37 percent of the total reduction. Regression A2, which treats the schooling effects as the joint impact of schooling and poverty, accounts for 2.4 deaths or 32 percent of the total reduction. For nonwhites, the neonatal mortality rate fell by 11.8 deaths per thousand live births between 1964 and 1977. Regression B2 predicts a decline of 4.8 deaths or 41 percent of the observed reduction.

A striking message in table 7.3 is that the increase in the legal abortion rate is the single most important factor in reductions in both white and nonwhite neonatal mortality rates. Not only does the growth in abortion dominate the other policies, but it also dominates schooling and poverty.[17] For the entire period, the reduction in the white neonatal mortality rate due to abortion ranges from 1.5 to 1.7 deaths per thousand births. The comparable figure for nonwhites is a whopping 2.5 deaths per thousand births. When the two subperiods are examined separately, abortion makes the largest contribution except for nonwhites in the 1964–1971 period. Here it ranks second to the impact of the rise in the use of organized family planning services by low-income women. The extremely large expansion in the abortion rate in the latter period (1971–1977) provides a cogent explanation of the acceleration in the percentage rates of decline in both race-specific mortality rates and the acceleration in the absolute rate of change for whites.

The increase in the use of organized family planning services by low-income women is the second-most important factor in reductions in nonwhite neonatal mortality for the entire period (1.4 deaths per thousand live births) and the most important factor in 1964–1971 (0.8 deaths per thousand live births). For whites, the estimate of the contribution of family planning is sensitive to the inclusion in or exclusion from the regression of the percentage of births to poor women. When PB* is included, it dominates all the other factors except for abortion in the entire period and in the two subperiods. Its effect is weaker when PB* is omitted and is no larger than the impact of maternal and infant care projects in the earlier subperiod.

There is reason to believe that we understate the impact of the use of all family planning services as opposed to organized services by low-income women. This is because our measure excludes services delivered by private physicians. National trends in the percentage of low-income women serviced by private physicians contained in Family Planning Program Development (1974), Dryfoos (1976), and Cutright and Jaffe (1977) suggest that the estimates in table 7.3 should be multiplied by a factor of 1.6. This adjustment makes family planning a more important contributor to neonatal death rate reductions than maternal and infant care projects in the computations based on regression A2.

It suggests that the predicted reductions of 1.5 nonwhites deaths per thousand births and between 0.2 and 0.6 white deaths per thousand births due to family planning are conservative lower-bound estimates of the true impact.

Maternal and infant care projects have small impacts on white neonatal mortality regardless of the regression specification employed. For nonwhites the effect is somewhat more substantial; it amounts to a decline of 0.3 deaths per thousand births for the years during which the projects were expanding. Of course, the impact of these projects over the entire period is dominated by the impacts of abortion reform and family planning in part because there was no change in the size of these projects between 1971 and 1977. But suppose that the absolute increase in the size of these projects had been the same in the second subperiod as it was in the first. Then their predicted impact on the nonwhite neonatal death rate would amount to 0.6 deaths per thousand births, which still is substantially smaller than the abortion and family planning effects.

Medicaid can be dismissed as a cause of the decline in white neonatal mortality; it predicts either no change or an increase in the white death rate. In the case of nonwhites, Medicaid accounts for a reduction of 0.5 deaths per thousand live births. If the somewhat controversial assumption of no change in the program between 1971 and 1977 is relaxed in the same manner as for maternal and infant care projects, we obtain a reduction of 1.0 deaths per thousand births. This is greater than the reduction associated with maternal and infant care projects but smaller than the reductions associated with abortion reform and family planning.

To summarize, these results, when combined with information on the use of the pill and the IUD by women of all income classes, provide a coherent explanation of the U.S. neonatal experience from 1964 to 1977. After a period of relative stability, the neonatal mortality rate began to decline following 1964 as a lagged response to the extremely rapid increase in the percentage of women who used the pill and the IUD between 1961 and 1964.[18] The decline was further fueled by the increase in the percentage of low-income women who used subsidized family planning services between 1965 and 1971 and by the dramatic rise in the legal abortion rate between 1969 and 1971. The acceleration in the rate of decline in the mortality rate between 1971 and 1977 was due primarily to the literal explosion of the abortion rate in that period. These conclusions are subject to the qualification that we have no estimates of the impact of the pill and the IUD other than those inferred through the use of family planning services by low-income women. They also are subject to the qualification that we cannot estimate the contribution of advances in neonatology.

The above findings do not necessarily imply that increases in the quantity of medical care played an unimportant role in the downward trend in neonatal mortality. To be sure, the impacts of Medicaid and maternal and infant care projects are smaller than the impacts of abortion reform and family planning. But as indicated previously, this simply may mean that the quantity of medical care per birth is more responsive to a reduction in the cost of fertility control than to a reduction in the price of care.

These results with respect to the importance of the legalization of abortion in trends in infant mortality differ from those of Bauman and Anderson (1980). Using states of the United States as the units of observation, they find no relationship between changes in the legal abortion rate and changes in the fetal or infant mortality rate. Bauman and Anderson's findings differ from ours for a number of reasons. First, they do not control for other determinants of infant mortality. Second, they do not use race-specific mortality data. Third, they do not examine the impacts of abortion reform on neonatal mortality.

These results are relevant to current U.S. policy debates with respect to the financing of abortions under Medicaid and with respect to attempts by the Right to Life movement to enact a constitutional amendment that would outlaw abortion except when it is necessary to preserve a pregnant women's life. Under the Hyde Amendment, which was in effect from June 1977 until February 1980, federal funding of abortions under Medicaid was banned except in cases where the woman's life was in danger. During that period, twenty-eight states refused to pay for "medically necessary" abortions. The other twenty-two states continued to finance most abortions for Medicaid-eligible women by paying the federal share as well as the state share. As a result, the number of federally financed abortions declined from approximately 250,000 per year before 1976 to less than 3,000 in 1978 (Trussell et al. 1980). Federal funding of abortions resumed temporarily in February 1980, pending a review by the U.S. Supreme Court of a ruling by Federal District Judge John F. Dooling Jr. that declared the Hyde Amendment unconstitutional. In June 1980, the Supreme Court reversed Judge Dooling's decision and upheld the constitutionality of the Hyde Amendment.

In spite of the Hyde Amendment, the abortion rate continued to rise between 1977 and 1978. In part, this trend reflects the continued diffusion of a relatively new method of birth control. In part, it reflects a substitution of private for federal funds by roughly 80 percent of women who would have been eligible for federal financing in the absence of the amendment (Trussell et al. 1980). One can speculate, however, that the abortion rate would have risen at a more rapid rate between 1977 and 1978 in the absence of the Hyde Amendment. Given the recent Supreme Court ruling, the abortion rate for poor women probably will grow slower than otherwise and might even fall. According to these findings, this will retard the rate of decline in the neonatal mortality rate of the poor.

Taken at face value, the most striking implication of this study pertains to a constitutional ban on abortions. The current U.S. abortion rate is 400 abortions per thousand live births, while the rate in 1969 was 4 abortions per thousand live births. If a ban reduced the rate to its 1969 level, these regressions predict that the nonwhite neonatal mortality rate would rise by approximately 2.8 deaths per thousand live births or by 19 percent above its 1977 level. The white neonatal mortality rate would rise by approximately 1.8 deaths per thousand live births or by 21 percent above its 1977 level. Yet these estimates must be regarded with caution because they assume that all other factors would remain the same if a ban were enacted. In particular, to the extent that abortion is a substitute for more conventional methods of birth control, the use of these methods would not remain the same.

5. ACKNOWLEDGMENTS

Research for this chapter was supported by a grant from the Robert Wood Johnson Foundation to the National Bureau of Economic Research. We are indebted to Gary Becker, Willard Cates, Ann Colle, Joy Dryfoos, Linda Edwards, Victor Fuchs, Louis Garrison, Eugene Lewit, Robert Michael, Charlotte Muller, Cathy Schoen, and two anonymous referees for their comments on an earlier draft. In addition, we would like to thank Joy Dryfoos, Edward Duffy, Jack Hadley, and Letty Wunglueck for providing us with the data to conduct our research. This is a revision of a paper presented at the World Congress on Health Economics, Leiden University, the Netherlands, September 8–11, 1980. A preliminary version of the paper also was presented at a session sponsored by the American Economic Association and the Health Economics Research Organization at the annual meeting of the Allied Social Science Associations, Atlanta, Georgia, December 28–30, 1979. An expanded version of the paper is available on request. This version contains sources for the extrapolations in table 7.3 and a detailed description of the assumptions that underlie these extrapolations.

NOTES

Originally published as Michael Grossman and Steven Jacobowitz, "Variations in Infant Mortality Rates among Counties of the United States: The Roles of Public Policies and Programs," *Demography* 18, no. 4 (1981): 695–713. Reprinted by permission in *Economics of Health Care*, ed. Jacques van der Gaag, William B. Neenan, and Theodore Tsukahara Jr. New York: Praeger, 1982, 272–301.

1. The computations are based on data contained in U.S. Bureau of the Census (1980).

2. Descriptive and historical information concerning the programs at issue is available in the expanded version of this paper (available on request), and details on abortion reform are provided below. Briefly, Medicaid, enacted in 1965 as Title XIX of the Social Security Act of 1935, is the joint federal-state program to finance the medical care services of low-income families who are covered by the aid to families with dependent children (AFDC) program. Maternal and infant care projects originated in the 1963 amendment to Title V of the Social Security Act. The amendment provides special grants for projects designed to provide adequate prenatal and obstetrical care to reduce the incidence of mental retardation and other conditions caused by childbearing complications as well as to lower infant and maternal mortality. Federal subsidization of family planning services for low-income women originated in the 1967 amendments to the Social Security Act. Federal efforts in this area were expanded by the Family Planning Services and Population Research Act of 1970 and by the 1972 amendments to the Social Security Act. These subsidies go to family planning clinics organized by hospitals, state and local health departments, Planned Parenthood, and other agencies such as maternal and infant care projects and neighborhood health centers. The diffusion of the pill and the IUD did not result from actions by the federal government or by states. This development is important for this research, however, because it meant that an extremely effective method of birth control could be offered to low-income women by federally subsidized family planning clinics.

3. The indirect costs of obtaining a good are generated by the time spent traveling, waiting, and obtaining information about the good. The terms indirect costs and availability are used here as synonyms.

4. Eugene Lewit has emphasized to us that theoretically the direction of the effects of abortion on fertility and infant mortality may be indeterminant. For instance, abortion may substitute for other methods of birth control. Moreover, abortion reform may cause the birth rate to rise by increasing the level of sexual activity in general. In spite of these factors, we feel that the hypothesis that abortion reform lowers the infant mortality rates is very plausible. In part this is because we control for the use of family planning services in the regression analysis.

5. If abortion reform lowers infant mortality solely by reducing the fraction of high-risk births, a measure of reform such as the legal abortion rate should have no impact on infant mortality in a multiple regression that controls for the percentage of low-birth weight births. This is not the case if the medical care mechanism outlined above also is relevant. Since there is more than one mechanism via which abortion reform and the other policies can affect infant mortality and since the aim of this paper is to estimate reduced form, as opposed to structural, effects, we omit regressors such as the percentage of low-birth weight births. Another reason for adopting this strategy is that some policy variables may have differential and possibly larger impacts on death rates in high-risk categories. Therefore, a study of the mechanisms via which government policies affect infant mortality should pay careful attention to complicated interactions between the policies and the fraction of high-risk births. Such a study is important, but it is beyond the scope of this paper.

6. In preliminary regressions, the coefficient of the number of hospital beds per capita was insignificant, and its inclusion had only minor impacts on the coefficients of the other independent variables.

7. The regression equation for whites is

$$b_j^* = .064 + .169\pi_j^*, \ \bar{R}^2 = .269, \ n = 679.$$
$$(t = 15.90)$$

The regression equation for blacks is

$$b_j^* = .095 + .059\pi_j^*, \ \bar{R}^2 = .118, \ n = 359.$$
$$(t = 6.98)$$

In each regression, the dependent variable is a three-year average of the birth rate for the period 1969–1971. The regressions are weighted by the square root of the race-specific number of women ages fifteen to forty-four in 1970. The poverty variable pertains to the fraction of families below the poverty level, rather than to the fraction of women ages fifteen to forty-four. The latter variable is not available on a race-specific basis. Another reason for the use of the fraction of families in poverty is that it facilitates the trend analysis in the third section of this paper. The ratios of births per thousand women ages fifteen to forty-four implied by the regressions are 233 for poor whites, 64 for nonpoor whites, 154 for poor blacks, and 95 for nonpoor blacks.

8. In regressions not shown in the third section, median family income was included as an independent variable. Its coefficient was not significant.

9. From equation (5), the reduced form effect of x_{pj} on d_j is

$$\frac{\partial d_j}{\partial x_{pj}} = (\alpha_0 - \beta_0) \frac{\partial k_j}{\partial x_{pj}} + \alpha_1 k_j + \alpha_1 x_{pj} \frac{\partial k_j}{\partial x_{pj}}.$$

Note that

$$k_{jp}^* = \pi_j^* b_{jp}^* / b_j^*,$$

where b_{jp}^* is the race-specific birth rate of poor women in the jth county. Clearly, this variable is not held constant in our regressions. Note that reduced form effects also could be estimated by expressing k_j as a function of a set of variables, including the policy measures, in equation (5). This results in an extremely complicated functional form. Specifically, it includes the level of each policy measure, the square of that measure, and its product with each of the other measures. Such an equation is not tractable from the standpoint of estimation.

10. This list of states includes Arizona which has no Medicaid program.

11. Our information on the treatment of first-time pregnancies under Medicaid by specific state was obtained from Letty Wunglueck of the Health Care Financing Administration. Note that first-time pregnancies of young mothers who are themselves dependents in AFDC families would be covered under Medicaid in spite of the above provisions. States in one of our three categories, however, cover a larger percentage of first-time pregnancies than other states.

12. Suppose that the neonatal mortality rate (nm_{jt}) and the legal abortion rate (a_{jt}) are measured in half-year intervals. Let the relationship between the two be

$$nm_{jt} = \beta + \delta a_{jt-1}.$$

Aggregate and average this equation over three years (six half years) to obtain

$$\overline{nm}_j = \beta + \delta \overline{a}_j,$$

where

$$\overline{a}_j = \left(\sum_{t=0}^{5} a_{jt-1} \right) / 6.$$

The neonatal mortality rates pertain to the period from the first half of 1970 (70-1) to the last half of 1972 (72-2). Therefore, ignore the county subscript, and write $\overline{a}$ as

$$\overline{a} = (a69\text{-}2 + a70\text{-}1 + a70\text{-}2 + a71\text{-}1 + a71\text{-}2 + a72\text{-}1)/6.$$

We have data for $a70\text{-}2$, $a71$ (the abortion rate during the entire year of 1971), and $a72$. For states that reformed their abortion laws before 1970, we assume that $a69\text{-}2 + a70\text{-}1 = a70\text{-}2$ due to the rapid upward trend in the abortion rate during this period. We also assume that the birth rate in the first half of 1971 equaled the birth rate in the second half of 1971, so that $a71\text{-}1 + a71\text{-}2 = 2a71$. Finally, we assume $a72\text{-}1 = a72$. Hence for these states

$$\overline{a} = (1/3)(a70\text{-}2) + (1/3)(a71) + (1/6)(a72).$$

For states that reformed their laws in the middle of 1970, we assume $a69\text{-}2 = a70\text{-}1 = 0$. Hence, given the other two conditions used above,

$$\overline{a} = (1/6)\ (a70\text{-}2) + (1/3)\ (a71) + (1/6)\ (a72).$$

Since the law for New York State had no residency requirements, states near New York are treated in the same manner as New York in the computation of $\overline{a}$.

13. Age- and race-specific infant mortality rates for years prior to 1969 are not available on the Area Resource File.

14. Space limitations prevent the discussion of the effects of poverty, schooling, and physicians in detail and the presentation of additional specifications of the basic regressions. Note the following:

   (a) The variables PB* and HSP* are highly correlated for whites $(r = -.6)$ and for blacks $(r = -.8)$. The insignificant regression coefficients of HSP* in regressions A1 and A3 are due in part to multicollinearity. This phenomenon may also contribute to the black results, although the explanation is somewhat more complicated because the simple correlation between the death rate and PB* is negative.

   (b) There are few studies of the race-specific impact of poverty on infant mortality. Using a special sample of births and subsequent infant deaths taken by the National Center for Health Statistics, Gortmaker (1979) reports results similar to ours. White babies are more likely to die in poverty families than in nonpoverty families, but this relationship does not hold for black babies.

(c) The unimportance of physicians per capita in our regressions mirrors findings reported by Brooks (1978) in a study of variations in infant mortality rates among SMSAs. The coefficients of other variables are not sensitive to the exclusion of MD. The MD variable is retained because there is almost no trend in it between 1964 and 1977. Hence its retention does not cloud the forecasts and backcasts that follow.

15. For Medicaid, we always accept the hypothesis that no member of the set given by $MAXPB^*$, $MUXPB^*$, and $MNXPB^*$ has a non-zero coefficient at the 5 percent level. For maternal and infant care projects, we accept the hypothesis that no member of the set given by $MIXPB^*$ and $PMIBXPB^*$ has a non-zero coefficient in five of six cases. The exception pertains to regression A4.

16. Note that changes in the lagged mortality rate are not relevant in the forecasts and backcasts in table 7.3 because the underlying model is not a dynamic one. Rather, the lagged rate serves as a proxy for the initial level, which does not change by definition. In econometric terminology the model is one with "fixed effects" rather than one with "state dependence."

17. One might argue that we understate the impacts of schooling and poverty by holding constant an average infant mortality rate centered on the year 1967. Although it is reasonable to suppose that changes in the public policies had no impacts until after 1967, this assumption may not be reasonable in the cases of schooling and poverty. This is because the trends in these variables were continuous from 1960 to 1970. To examine the robustness of our conclusion that abortion dominates schooling and poverty, we reestimated the contributions of these variables from regressions that exclude the lagged mortality rate. Although the contribution of schooling rises relative to the contribution in table 7.3, it is still smaller than that of abortion. Note that if county-level fixed effects that lower mortality are positively correlated with schooling, we overstate the schooling coefficient by excluding the lagged mortality rate.

18. Ryder (1972) reports that in 1961 the percentage of married women under age thirty-five who used the pill stood at approximately 3 percent. By 1964, it had increased to approximately 16 percent.

REFERENCES

Bauman, K. E., and A. E. Anderson. 1980. "Legal Abortions and Trends in Fetal and Infant Mortality Rates in the United States." *American Journal of Obstetrics and Gynecology* 136: 194–202.

Becker, G. S., and H. G. Lewis. 1973. "On the Interaction between the Quantity and Quality of Children." *Journal of Political Economy* 81: S279–S288.

Ben-Porath, Yoram. 1973. "On Child Traits and the Choice of Family Size." The Maurice Falk Institute for Economic Research in Israel, Discussion Paper 731.

Ben-Porath, Y., and F. Welch. 1976. "Do Sex Preferences Really Matter?" *The Quarterly Journal of Economics* 90: 284–307.

Brooks, C. H. 1978. "Infant Mortality in SMSAs Before Medicaid: Test of a Causal Model." *Health Services Research* 13: 3–15.

Bureau of Community Health Services. n.d. "Maternity and Infant Care Projects—Statistical Summary—Fiscal Years 1969–1976." U.S. Department of Health, Education and Welfare, Public Health Service.

Centers for Disease Control. 1971, 1972, 1974. "Family Planning Evaluation: Abortion Surveillance Report, 1970–1972." U.S. Department of Health, Education and Welfare, Public Health Service.

Center for Family Planning Program Development. 1974. "Need for Subsidized Family Planning Services: United States, Each State and County, 1971." New York: Planned Parenthood—World Population.

Cutright, Phillips, and Frederick S. Jaffe. 1977. *Impact of Family Planning Programs on Fertility: The U.S. Experience.* New York: Praeger.

Davis, Karen, and Roger Reynolds. 1976. "The Impact of Medicare and Medicaid on Access to Medical Care." In *The Role of Health Insurance in the Health Services Sector*, ed. R. Rosett. New York: Neale Watson Academic Publications.

Davis, Karen, and Cathy Schoen. 1978. *Health and the War on Poverty.* Washington, D.C.: The Brookings Institution.

Dryfoos, J. G. 1976. "The United States National Family Planning Program, 1968–74". *Studies in Family Planning* 7: 80–92.

Eisner, V., M. W. Pratt, A. Hexter, M. J. Chabot, and S. Naresh. 1978. "Improvement in Infant and Perinatal Mortality in the United States, 1965–1973." *American Journal of Public Health* 68: 359–364.

Fuchs, Victor R. 1974. "Some Economic Aspects of Mortality in Developed Countries." In *The Economics of Health and Medical Care*, ed. M. Perlman. London: MacMillan.

Gortmaker, S. L. 1979. "Poverty and Infant Mortality in the United States." *American Sociological Review* 44: 280–297.

Lee, K., N. Paneth, L. M. Gartner, M. Pearlman, and L. Gruss. 1980. "Neonatal Mortality: An Analysis of the Recent Improvement in the United States". *American Journal of Public Health* 70: 15–21.

Lewit, Eugene M. 1977. "Experience with Pregnancy, the Demand for Prenatal Care, and the Production of Surviving Infants." PhD Dissertation. New York: City University of New York Graduate School.

Ryder, N. B. 1972. "Time Series of Pill and IUD Use: United States, 1961–1970." *Studies in Family Planning* 3: 233–240.

Taffel, Selma. 1978. "Prenatal Care in the United States, 1969–1975." U.S. Department of Health, Education, and Welfare, Public Health Service, National Center for Health Statistics, Vital and Health Statistics, Series 21, No. 33.

Trussell, J., J. Menken, B. L. Lindheim, and B. Vaughan. 1980. "The Impact of Restricting Medicaid Financing for Abortion." *Family Planning Perspectives* 12: "120–130.

U.S. Bureau of the Census. 1980. *Statistical Abstract of the United States, 1979.* Washington, D.C.: U.S. Government Printing Office.

Williams, Anne D. 1976. "Fertility and Reproductive Loss." PhD Dissertation. Chicago: University of Chicago.

Williams, Ronald L. 1974. "Outcome-Based Measurements of Medical Care Output: The Case of Maternal and Infant Health." PhD Dissertation. Santa Barbara: University of California at Santa Barbara.

Willis, R. 1973. "A New Approach to the Economic Theory of Fertility Behavior." *Journal of Political Economy* 81: S14–S64.

EIGHT

Determinants of Neonatal Mortality Rates in the United States

A Reduced Form Model

Hope Corman and Michael Grossman

ABSTRACT

The aim of this chapter is to contribute to an understanding of the determinants of differences in race-specific neonatal mortality rates among large counties of the United States in 1977. After estimating cross-sectional regressions, we apply their coefficients to national trends in the exogenous variables to "explain" the rapid decline in neonatal mortality since 1964. The regressions and the extrapolations point to the importance of abortion availability, neonatal intensive care availability, females' schooling levels, Medicaid, and to a lesser extent Bureau of Community Health Services projects, poverty, maternal nutrition programs and organized family planning in trends in black neonatal mortality between 1964 and 1977. They also underscore the importance of schooling, neonatal intensive care, poverty, Medicaid, maternal nutrition programs, abortion, and organized family planning clinics in trends in white neonatal mortality in those years.

1. INTRODUCTION

During the period from 1955 through 1982, the behavior of the U.S. infant mortality rate has been characterized by a decade of relative stability followed by almost two decades of rapid decline. The rate declined by only 0.6 percent per year compounded annually between 1955 and 1964. By contrast, infant mortality declined 4.5 percent per year (compounded annually) between 1964 and 1982.[1]

The trend in the infant mortality rate since 1964 has been dominated by the trend in the neonatal mortality rate (deaths of infants within the first twenty-seven days of life) for two reasons. First, the neonatal mortality rate, 8.9 deaths per thousand live births in 1979, is twice as large as the postneonatal mortality rate (deaths of infants between the ages of 28 and 364 days per thousand live births), which equaled to 4.2 in 1979. Second, the neonatal mortality rate has fallen at a faster pace than the postneonatal mortality rate since 1964 (4.6 percent per year versus 3.9 percent per year). The result of these two factors is that the decline in the neonatal mortality rate accounted for 77 percent of the reduction in the infant mortality rate during the past two decades. It follows that any attempt to explain the recent behavior of infant mortality must focus on neonatal mortality.

The period beginning in 1964 witnessed the introduction of Medicaid, maternal and infant care (M and I) projects, community health centers (CHCs, formerly called neighborhood health centers), federally subsidized family planning services for low-income women, the Special Supplemental Food Program for Women, Infants, and Children (WIC program), the legalization of abortion, the widespread adoption of oral and intrauterine contraceptive techniques, and dramatic advances in perinatal[2] and neonatal science. Although other researchers have related these developments to accelerations in the downward trends in infant and especially neonatal mortality rates (for example, Eisner et al. 1978; Kleinman et al. 1978; Lee et al. 1980; David and Siegal 1983), there have been few attempts to study this issue in a multivariate context. Moreover, there has been only one previous effort to quantify the relative contributions of at least some of these factors (Grossman and Jacobowitz 1981). Therefore, the aim of this chapter is to contribute to an understanding of the determinants of neonatal mortality rates in the United States with an emphasis on the factors just mentioned. Estimates of their effects control for such basic correlates of neonatal mortality as poverty, schooling levels, and the availability of obstetricians/gynecologists.

The aim is implemented by conducting cross-sectional regression analyses of differences in race-specific neonatal mortality rates among counties of the United States in 1977. This procedure capitalizes on variations in the public program at issue and in units that deliver sophisticated perinatal and neonatal care services among counties at a moment in time. After estimating the regressions, we apply their coefficients to national trends in the exogenous variables to 'explain' the downward trend in neonatal mortality.

2. ANALYTICAL FRAMEWORK

Economic models of the family developed by Becker and Lewis (1973) and Willis (1973) provide a fruitful theoretical framework to generate multivariate health outcome functions and to assess the roles of a variety of factors in these functions. Ben-Porath and Welch (1976), Williams (1976), Grossman and Jacobowitz (1981), Rosenzweig and Schultz (1982, 1983a, b), and Lewit (1983) have utilized the economic model of the family to study theoretically and empirically the determinants of birth outcomes. Following these authors, we assume that the parents' utility function depends on their own consumption, the number of births, and the survival probability. Both the number of births and the survival probability are endogenous variables. In particular, the survival probability production function depends upon such endogenous inputs as the quantity and quality of medical care, nutrition, and the own time of the mother. In addition, the production function is affected by the mother's efficiency in producing healthy offspring and by other aspects of her efficiency in household production. Given the considerable body of evidence that education raises market and nonmarket productivity, one would expect more educated mothers to be more efficient producers of surviving infants.

Maximization of the parents' utility function subject to production and resource constraints generates a demand function for survival in which the survival probability is related to input prices, efficiency, income, tastes, and the fixed costs of a birth. Fixed costs are costs that are independent of the survival probability. For example, Willis (1973) shows that birth control costs are negatively correlated with the fixed costs of a birth. A reduction in the cost of fertility control raises the fixed cost of a birth, reduces the optimal number of births, and raises the optimal survival probability. The interaction between the survival demand and production functions determines demand functions for medical care and other endogenous inputs. These derived demand functions depend on the same set of variables as the demand function for the probability of survival.

The above model calls attention to the important determinants of the survival probability and its complement, the neonatal mortality rate. In general, this set of determinants is similar to that used in multivariate studies of neonatal mortality with different points of departure (for example, Fuchs 1974; Williams

1974; Brooks 1978; Gortmaker 1979; Hadley 1982; Harris 1982). Moreover, the model provides a ready structure within which to interpret the impacts of the factors at issue in our research.[3] Thus, for example, Medicaid, M and I projects, and community health centers lower the direct and indirect costs[4] of obtaining medical care, which should increase the likelihood of a favorable birth outcome and lower neonatal mortality. Similar comments apply to the impacts of increases in the availability of physicians who deliver prenatal and perinatal care services and to the number of hospitals with perinatal and neonatal intensive care units, which provide constant and continuous care to critically ill newborn infants. An expansion in the percentage of eligible pregnant women served by the WIC program raises the availability of appropriate nutrition, an important nonmedical input in the production of healthy infants. Subsidization of family planning services and the diffusion and availability of abortion services reduce the cost of fertility control. Within the context of an economic model of the family, these developments raise the optimal survival probability and lower the optimal number of births. In addition, they will lower the observed infant mortality rate if less healthy fetuses are less likely to be conceived or more likely to be aborted.

The preceding ideas are formalized in the following six equation model:

$$1 - d = f_1(n, b), \quad b = f_2(m, a, c, z), \qquad (1), (2)$$

$$n = f_3(p, z, y), \quad m = f_4(p, z, y), \qquad (3), (4)$$

$$a = f_5(p, z, y), \quad c = f_6(p, z, y). \qquad (5), (6)$$

Equations (1) and (2) are production functions, while equations (3)–(6) are input demand functions. In equation (1), the probability that an infant survives the first month of life $(1 - d$, where d is the probability of death) is shown as a function of a vector of perinatal and neonatal care inputs (n) and birth weight (b).[5] Note that there is an overwhelming amount of evidence that low birth weight (less than or equal to 2,500 grams or 5.5 pounds) is the most important and most proximate endogenous risk factor in neonatal health outcomes (for example, Harris 1982; Lewit 1983). In equation (2) birth weight is a function of a vector of prenatal medical and non-medical inputs (m),[6] the use of abortion services (a), the use of contraceptive services (c), and exogenous risk and productive efficiency factors such as mother's education (z). In equations (3)–(6), the inputs are related to a vector of price and availability measures (p), socioeconomic characteristics which reflect command over resources and tastes (y), and productive efficiency and risk factors (z).

The two production functions are structural equations because they show relationships among endogenous variables. Substitution of the input demand functions into the production functions yields

$$1-d = f_7(p,\ z,y), \tag{7}$$

$$b = f_8(p, z,\ y). \tag{8}$$

These are reduced form equations because only exogenous variables appear on their right-hand sides. They may be termed demand functions for survival and birth weight. Together with the input demand functions, they constitute the reduced form of the model.[7] Although equations (1)–(8) have meaningful interpretations at the family level, our empirical analysis focuses on county-level data for the year 1977. Therefore, from now on we interpret d as the observed neonatal mortality rate and b as the percentage of low-birth-weight births.

We focus on the estimation of the reduced form neonatal mortality rate equation (7) because its coefficients are well suited for understanding the impacts of changes in policy variables and for extrapolating cross-sectional regression results to national trends in exogenous variables to 'explain' the decline in neonatal mortality. Since the reduced form mortality function contains only exogenous variables, it can be fitted by ordinary least squares.[8]

Our model calls attention to the difference between the availability and the use of services such as family planning, abortion, prenatal care, perinatal care, and neonatal care, all of which determine birth outcomes. An increase in the availability of an input lowers its price and causes the quantity demanded of that input to rise but has an ambiguous effect on the demand for some other input. For example, an increase in the availability of abortion services may reduce the use of family planning services if these methods of fertility control are substitutes. Thus, an increase in the availability of one service can affect neonatal mortality both directly and indirectly, through its effect on the use of other services. By focusing on availability rather than use, we can capture both direct and indirect effects of changes in the availability of medical services on neonatal mortality.

3. EMPIRICAL SPECIFICATION

3.1. Data and Measurement of Neonatal Mortality

The basic data set used here is the Area Resource File (ARF), a county-based data service, prepared by Applied Management Sciences, Inc., for the Bureau of Health Professions, U.S. Department of Health and Human Services. It incorporates information from different sources for the 3,077 counties of the United States. Neonatal deaths (by county of residence) by race for the years 1969 through 1978 are obtained from the National Center for Health Statistics (NCHS) Mortality Tape. Births (by county of residence) by race for those years are obtained from the NCHS Natality Tape. Health manpower data come from the American Medical Association. Data on socio-economic characteristics are taken from the "Census of Population." We have added measures pertaining to the policies and programs discussed previously from sources indicated in the appendix to this chapter (available upon request).

For reasons mentioned in the introductory section, the empirical analysis focuses on the neonatal mortality rate as opposed to the postneonatal mortality rate or the total infant death rate. Also, this strategy is adopted because most neonatal deaths are caused by congenital anomalies, prematurity, and complications of delivery. These conditions are more sensitive to improved prenatal, perinatal and neonatal care than are the infectious diseases and accidents that contribute to postneonatal mortality. Neonatal mortality may be particularly sensitive to abortion and organized family planning access for several reasons. First, women who are known to be at risk for conditions related to neonatal deaths will find it easier to prevent pregnancy. Second, for the women at risk who unexpectedly become pregnant, access to abortion services will be easier. Finally, when risks are discovered during a pregnancy, some women may choose abortion if services are accessible.

Separate regressions are fitted for white neonatal mortality and for black neonatal mortality. Black neonatal mortality rates are much higher than white rates. For example, in 1977 the black rate was almost twice as large as the white rate. In a non-race-specific regression, one would enter the percentage of black births to control for race differences. But this variable would be highly correlated with the percentage of low-income women, schooling, and other independent variables. By fitting race-specific regressions, multicollinearity is reduced and the coefficients of the independent variables are allowed to vary between races. In preliminary regressions, we tested and rejected the hypothesis that slope coefficients but not intercepts are the same for whites and blacks. Linear regressions are estimated for reasons indicated in section 3.2.

Counties are our unit of observation since they are the smallest geographic units for which aggregate national data are available. We exclude small counties from the analysis, however, for several reasons. First, some counties are so small that people may receive medical care outside the county. Second, some very small counties experience few to no neonatal deaths simply because the number of births is so small. Since our statistical techniques require mortality rates to be greater than zero and less than one, exclusion of some counties is required. Also, smaller counties have missing or unreliable data for some of the independent variables. For these reasons, we include only counties with a population of at least 50,000 in 1970. A county also has at least 5,000 blacks for inclusion in the black regressions. There are 677 counties in the white regressions and 357 counties in the black regressions.[9] The counties used in the white regressions accounted for approximately 80 percent of the white population of the United States in 1970, and the counties used in the black regressions accounted for a similar percentage of the black population of the United States in that year. In addition to selecting large counties, we attenuate random elements by employing a three-year average of the race-specific neonatal mortality rate for the period 1976–1978 as the dependent variable and by estimating weighted regressions, where the set of weights is the square root of the race-specific total number of births in the period 1976–1978.

Neonatal mortality for a three-year period centered on 1977 is studied to address the question: Do the effects that Grossman and Jacobowitz (1981) observed in 1971, particularly the large negative abortion effect, differ when data for 1977 are examined? Our approach also differs from theirs because we focus on a reduced form neonatal mortality rate equation, and we include many more determinants of neonatal mortality. For example, we are now able to measure the contribution of the rapid advances in perinatal and neonatal science since 1965.[10] These developments were accompanied by an approximately four-teen-fold increase in the number of hospitals with neonatal (defined to include perinatal) intensive care units between 1964 and 1977 (Sheridan 1983). Note that although the state-of-the-art in neonatology is fixed in the cross section, the availability of these state-of-the-art services varies considerably from one geo-graphic area to another due to regional differences in hospital construction sub-sidies (by states and the federal government), Medicaid reimbursement, federal funding of neonatal intensive care centers (under Title V of the Social Security Act), state certificate-of-need laws, and regionalization of neonatal intensive care programs.

3.2. Measurement of Independent Variables

Wherever possible, race-specific variables are employed in the regressions. Such variables are denoted with 'a'. Except for the Medicaid, WIC, and neona-tal intensive care measures, all variables are county-specific. Table 8.1 contains definitions of the dependent and independent variables in the regressions, and table 8.2 contains their means and standard deviations. Most of the independent

Table 8.1 Definitions of Variables

Variable Name	Definition
Neonatal death rate (1977)[a]	Three-year average neonatal mortality rate centered on 1977; deaths of infants fewer than 28 days old per 1,000 live births
Percent poor[a,b]	Percentage of women aged 15–44 with family income less than 200 percent of the poverty level in 1980
Percent high school educated[a,c]	Percentage of women aged 15–49 who had at least a high school education in 1970
Medicaid eligibility-1[d]	Dichotomous variable that equals one if county is in state that covered all first-time pregnancies under Medicaid to financially eligible women in the period 1976–1978
Medicaid eligibility-2[d]	Dichotomous variable that equals one if county is in state that covered first-time pregnancies under Medicaid only if no husband was present or if the husband was present but unemployed and not receiving unemployment compensation in the period 1976–1978
Medicaid eligibility-3[d]	Dichotomous variable that equals one if county is in state that covered first-time pregnancies under Medicaid only if no husband was present in the period 1976–1978
Medicaid payment for newborn	Dichotomous variable that equals one if county is in state in which Medicaid paid for newborn care under the mother's Medicaid number or did not pay for care under the mother's number but allowed pregnant women to register their 'unborn children' with Medicaid in 1981
Per capita Medicaid payment	State-specific average annual Medicaid payment per adult recipient in AFDC families in fiscal 1976
Family planning[e] clinics/1000	Number of organized family planning clinics in 1975 per 1,000 women aged 15–44 with family income less than 200 percent of the poverty level in 1975
Community health projects[e]/1000 (BCHS projects)	Sum of maternal and infant care (M and I) projects and community health centers (CHCs) in 1976 per 1,000 women aged 15–44 with family income less than 200 percent of the poverty level in 1975; numerator termed Bureau of Community Health Services (BCHS) projects
Maternal nutrition program (WIC)	State-specific percentage of eligible pregnant women served by the Special Supplemental Food Program for Women, Infants, and Children (WIC program) in 1980
Abortion providers/1000	Three-year average number of abortion providers (public hospitals, private hospitals, nonhospital clinics and office based physicians) centered on 1976 per 1,000 women aged 15–44 in 1975
Newborn intensive care hospitals/1000	Sum of state-specific number of hospitals with level II, or level III, or levels II and III neonatal intensive care units in 1979 per 1,000 women aged 15–44 in state in 1975
Neonatal death rate (1970)[a]	Three-year average neonatal mortality rate centered on 1970

[a] Variable is race-specific.

[b] Variable is available for nonblacks and blacks as opposed to whites and blacks.

[c] Variable is available for whites and nonwhites as opposed to whites and blacks.

[d] Medicaid eligibility variables characterize the eligibility of first-time pregnant women for prenatal care under Medicaid. The omitted category pertains to states that cover non-first-time pregnancies because their AFDC programs do not recognize 'unborn children.'

[e] Since numerator of this variable is not race-specific, denominator also is not race-specific. Denominator is obtained by applying the race-specific percentage of women aged 15–44 with family income less than 200 percent of the poverty level in 1980 to the race-specific number of all women aged 15–44 in 1975.

Table 8.2 Means and Standard Deviations of Dependent and Independent Variables

Variable	Raw Variable		Variables Interacted with Poverty[a]	
	Mean (1)	Standard Deviation (2)	Mean (3)	Standard Deviation (4)
Whites				
Neonatal death rate (1977)[b]	8.837	1.596		
Percent poor[b]	26.617	8.779		
Percent high school educated[b]	62.830	7.306		
Medicaid eligibility-1	0.388	0.488	0.109	0.147
Medicaid eligibility-2	0.137	0.344	0.034	0.090
Medicaid eligibility-3	0.087	0.282	0.024	0.080
Medicaid payments for newborn	0.927	0.260	0.248	0.110
Per capita Medicaid payment	453.266	142.016	119.831	56.550
Family planning clinics/1000	0.271	0.190	0.071	0.057
Community health projects/1000	0.018	0.035	0.005	0.011
Maternal nutrition program (WIC)	26.289	7.804	7.084	3.314
Abortion providers/1000	0.056	0.043		
Newborn intensive care hospitals/1000	0.011	0.004		
Neonatal death rate (1970)[b]	13.336	1.940		
Blacks				
Neonatal death rate (1977)[b]	16.387	3.303		
Percent poor[c]	54.896	9.371		
Percent high school educated[c]	44.120	8.968		
Medicaid eligibility-1	0.265	0.442	0.139	0.235
Medicaid eligbility-2	0.106	0.309	0.054	0.159
Medicaid eligibility-3	0.166	0.373	0.102	0.230
Medicaid payments for newborn	0.943	0.232	0.520	1.57
Per capita Medicaid payment	448.560	137.223	241.201	70.450
Family planning clinics/1000	0.271	0.209	0.149	0.128
Community health projects/1000	0.025	0.032	0.014	0.019
Maternal nutrition program (WIC)	26.793	7.419	14.782	5.133
Abortion providers/1000	0.056	0.036		
Newborn intensive care hospitals/1000	0.010	0.003		
Neonatal death rate (1970)[b]	22.496	4.018		

Notes: The white data pertain to 677 counties; the black data pertain to 357 counties. Means and standard deviations are weighted by the race-specific total number of births in the period 1976–1978.
[a] Where applicable, variables are multiplied by (percent poor)/100.
[b] Variable is race-specific.

variables pertain to one or more years in the 1975–1978 period. Several measures pertain to 1970, 1979, 1980, or 1981. In these cases, the assumption is made that the 1975–1978 measure is highly correlated with the one actually used. A detailed description of the variables and their sources appears in the appendix (available upon request), which also contains a discussion of preliminary regression results obtained with several additional independent variables that are not shown in section 4.

The percentage of women aged 15 to 44 with family income less than 200 percent of the poverty level in 1980 (percent poor) is a negative correlate of command over resources and is expected to have a positive regression co-efficient. As explained in section 2, the percentage of women aged fifteen to forty-nine who had at least a high school education in 1970 is a proxy for mother's efficiency in preventing undesired pregnancies, in producing healthy offspring and other aspects of efficiency in household production. The schooling variable also may serve as a proxy for the parents' preferences for healthy offspring. Whether schooling represents efficiency, tastes, or both, the neonatal mortality rate should be negatively related to it.[11]

The key public program measures at issue in this chapter pertain to Medicaid, organized family planning clinics, maternal and infant care projects, community health centers, maternal nutrition programs (WIC), abortion availability, and neonatal care availability. All of the measures are expected to have negative regression coefficients. The eligibility of low-income women who are pregnant for the first time for Medicaid coverage of their prenatal care services is reflected by three dichotomous variables. The likelihood that the newborn care received by the infant of a low-income woman will be financed by Medicaid is indicated by a dichotomous variable that equals one if a county is in a state in which Medicaid paid for newborn care under the mother's Medicaid number or did not pay for care under the mother's number but allowed pregnant women to register their unborn children with Medicaid in 1981.

There are no data on differences in the availability of Medicaid coverage of prenatal care for second- and higher-order births or on differences in the general availability of physicians to Medicaid-eligible women among states or counties. Therefore, the state-specific average annual Medicaid payment per adult recipient in Aid to Families with Dependent Children (AFDC) families in fiscal 1976 is included as a regressor. Although this variable partly reflects the use of care, it also reflects price and availability. This is because physicians in states with relatively low reimbursement schedules under Medicaid are less likely to treat Medicaid patients (Sloan, Mitchell, and Cromwell 1978).

Organized family planning's availability is given by the number of organized family planning clinics in 1975 per thousand women aged fifteen to forty-four with family income less than 200 percent of the poverty level in 1975. The denominator pertains to poor women because the clinics primarily service poor women and because the relevant public program is aimed at the poor.

Dryfoos (1976) reports that almost all clients of family planning clinics use oral or intrauterine contraceptive techniques (the pill or the IUD). Consequently, the family planning variable indicates the price and availability of these techniques to low-income women. There are no direct measures of the availability of family planning services delivered by private physicians to poor or non-poor women. Also, there is no information concerning differences in contraceptive knowledge among counties. It is likely, however, that more educated women will have better birth control information. Thus, the schooling variable may partly reflect this factor.

The extent of the maternal and infant care program and the community health center program is given by the sum of the number of Bureau of Community Health Center (BCHS) projects in the county in 1976 per thousand women aged fifteen to forty-four with family income less than 200 percent of the poverty level in 1975. The number of poor women serves as the denominator of this variable for the same reason that it serves as the denominator of the family planning measure. The two project types are aggregated in the numerator because both provide prenatal care services to low-income women.[12] The BCHS (renamed the Bureau of Health Care Delivery and Assistance in 1982), is the agency within the U.S. Department of Health and Human Services that has overall administrative responsibility for both maternal and infant care projects and community health centers.

The count of CHCs is limited to centers that were delivering services as of 1976 because the number of CHCs expanded rapidly between 1976 and 1978. Given Goldman and Grossman's (1982) evidence the CHCs affect infant mortality with a lag, the potential impacts of the new centers are not likely to be observed in our data. Note that the number of maternal and infant care projects was very stable between 1971 and 1978 (Grossman and Jacobowitz 1981).

The availability of nutritional supplements to low-income women under WIC is given by the state-specific percentage of eligible pregnant women served by WIC in 1980. Abortion availability is lagged because (Grossman and Jacobowitz's 1981) estimates suggest that abortions performed in the first half of a given year affect the neonatality mortality rate during the second half of the year.

For part of our sample period (August 1977 through December 1978), federal funding of abortions under Medicaid was banned by the Hyde Amendment except in cases where the woman's life was in danger. During that period, twenty-eight states refused to pay for medically necessary abortions. The other twenty-two states continued to finance most abortions for Medicaid-eligible women. We do not take account of this curtailment in the availability of abortion to low-income women in our regression analysis because it could have affected the neonatal mortality rate in 1978 alone. More importantly, (Cates 1981) reports that an estimated 94 percent of pregnant low-income women at risk obtained a legal abortion between August 1977 and February 1980, 65 percent with state funds and 29 percent with other sources of funding.[13] This suggests that abortion use by low-income women is very unresponsive to the money price of an abortion. It does *not* imply that abortion use is insensitive to such indirect costs as the time and money spent traveling to an abortion facility, the time spent waiting at the facility, and the time spent in obtaining information about alternative facilities. These indirect costs are likely to be very sensitive to the abortion availability measure used in the regression.

Neonatal intensive care availability is measured by the sum of the state-specific number of hospitals with level II, level III, or levels II and III neonatal intensive care units in 1979 per thousand women aged fifteen to forty-four in the state in 1975. Hospitals that provide neonatal intensive care are generally divided into three levels based on the intensity of care each is equipped to deliver. Level I hospitals provide minimal or normal newborn care, level II hospitals provide intermediate care, and level III hospitals provide the most intensive care (Budetti et al. 1981). Specific definitions of these three levels of neonatal care are contained in the recommendations of the (Committee on Perinatal Health 1977), which were developed as guidelines for the regional development of perinatal health services.

In the estimation of the availability of neonatal intensive care, the state is used as the relevant market area rather than the county. This is because many states have developed formal or informal regional referral networks for ill neonates. Under regionalization, it is possible for a newborn to be transferred out of his county of birth, suggesting that the market area for this care is larger than the county. This is in contrast to organized family planning, BCHS project, and abortion availability where regional networks do not exist. Moreover, the decision to obtain neonatal intensive care is made jointly by the physician and the mother, whereas the mother or the potential mother plays a much more important role in the decision to obtain the other services at issue. To the extent that the appropriate market area is larger than the county but smaller than the state, and to the degree mothers cross state boundaries, the neonatal intensive care variable contains measurement error. If the error is not correlated with the true value of the variable, the estimate of the availability effect is biased toward zero.

Level I hospitals are excluded from the count of neonatal intensive care hospitals since they do not provide the specialized state-of-the-art services in neonatology, referred to earlier. The count does not distinguish between level II and level III hospitals because of definitional problems in the available data.

The final variable in the regressions is a three-year average of race-specific neonatal mortality rate centered on 1970. This variable is included to control for potential reverse causality relationships that may bias the coefficients of the program measures. The reverse causality exists because some of the public programs were specifically targeted at regions with poor health indicators. For example, sites for community health centers, maternal and infant care projects, and family planning centers were selected on the basis of medical need as perceived by health planners.[14] For these programs, the availability of the program is positively related to the pre-program neonatal mortality rate. If the current and lagged mortality rates are positively related, then estimates of the impacts of these programs will be biased toward zero unless the initial level of mortality is included in the regression (assuming there is an effect). For other public programs, availability is negatively related to the pre-program neonatal mortality rate, causing the program coefficient to be overstated unless the lagged rate is included. For example, states that reformed their abortion laws by 1970 and enacted generous Medicaid programs tended to be liberal states with relatively large welfare programs and probably lower than average infant mortality rates. Thus, the dependence of program levels on the lagged mortality rate will cause a downward bias in the absolute value of a given program coefficient when the sign of the reverse causality relationship is positive and an upward bias in the absolute value of the coefficient when the sign of the reverse causality relationship is negative.

Including the lagged mortality rate may cause different biases in the coefficients. This is because of potential correlation between the lagged mortality rate and the error term. One possible source of this correlation would be a county-specific health endowment not fully measured by our independent variables. In the equation predicting the 1977 mortality rate, the unobserved health endowment would be included in the error term. Since some endowment affects the 1970 mortality rate the undesired correlation would result. We call this the serial correlation bias. Ideally, an instrumental variable procedure could eliminate the source of bias. This would require a dataset containing relevant instruments for the county mortality rates in 1970. Unfortunately, such a dataset is not available. Instead, we include the lagged mortality rate and predict the direction of the biases.

The direction of the biases depends on relationships between key variables.[15] First, because of the positive covariance between the lagged mortality rate and the error term, we expect the coefficient on the lagged mortality rate to be overstated. The direction of the biases on the coefficients on the other variables depends on the partial correlation between that variable and the lagged mortality rate. For variables where the partial correlation is negative, program effects are biased toward zero and where the partial correlation is positive, program effects are overestimated due to serial correlation bias. Most of the programs were found to have a negative partial correlation with the lagged mortality rate,[16] implying a downward bias due to serial correlation. In fact, the only program with a positive partial correlation with the lagged mortality rate for blacks and whites (and therefore expected overestimation due to serial correlation) is abortion services. In this case, the relevant partial correlation coefficients are extremely small (0.01 for whites and 0.04 for blacks), suggesting that the bias is minimal. Due to the existence of both reverse causality bias and serial correlation bias, regressions are presented with and without the lagged mortality rate in section 4.[17]

A number of programs that we study are aimed at the poor. It follows that the impacts on neonatal mortality of such programs are larger the larger is the fraction of poor women. To be specific, let d_{pj} be the neonatal mortality rate of babies born to poor mothers in the jth county, and let d_{nj} be the neonatal mortality rate of babies born to non-poor mothers. As an identity,

$$d_j = k_j d_{pj} + (1 - k_j) d_{nj}, \tag{9}$$

where d_j is the observed neonatal mortality rate and k_j is the fraction of births to poor mothers. Specify behavior equations for d_{pj}, d_{nj}, and k_j as follows:

$$d_{pj} = \alpha_0 + \alpha_1 x_{pj}, \tag{10}$$

$$d_{nj} = \beta_0, \tag{11}$$

$$k_j = \gamma_0 + \gamma_1 y_j + \gamma_2 x_{pj}. \tag{12}$$

In these equations x_{pj} is a public program availability measure that affects the mortality rate of poor babies alone, and y_j is the fraction of poor women in childbearing ages. Equation (11) contains the assumption that the mortality rate of non-poor babies does not vary among counties, but this can be modified with little loss in generality. In equation (12), a program measure such as family planning availability is allowed to affect the function of births to poor women. Presumably, α_1 and γ_2 are negative,[18] γ_1 is positive, and α_0 exceeds β_0. Substitute equations (10), (11), and (12) into equation (9) to obtain

$$d_j = \beta_0 + (\alpha_0 - \beta_0)\gamma_0 + (\alpha_0 - \beta_0)\gamma_1 y_j + [(\alpha_0 - \beta_0)\gamma_2 + \alpha_1\gamma_0]x_{pj}$$
$$+ \alpha_1\gamma_1 x_{pj} y_j + \alpha\gamma_2 x_{pj}^2. \tag{13}$$

From equation (13) the effect of x_{pj} on d_j is

$$(\partial d_j/\partial x_{pj}) = (\alpha_0 - \beta_0)\gamma_2 + \alpha_1\gamma_0 + \alpha_1\gamma_1 y_j + 2a_1\gamma_2 x_{pj}, \tag{14}$$

and this effect rises in absolute value as y_j rises,

$$(\partial^2 d_j/\partial x_{pj}\,\partial y_j) = \alpha_1 y_1. \tag{15}$$

Equation (13) gives a multiple regression of d_j on y_j, x_{pj}, $x_{pj}\,y_j$, and x^2_{pj}. With more than one public program measure, the regression has an extremely complicated functional form. Specifically, it includes the fraction of poor women, the level of each program measure, the square of that measure, its product with each of the other measures, and its product with the fraction of poor women. Such an equation is not tractable from the standpoint of estimation due to the large set of regressors and severe problems of multicollinearity. Therefore, a truncated version of equation (13) is fitted in section 4. The specification includes y_j and x_{pj} y_j.[19] In the estimation of model 2, the Medicaid, family planning, BCHS project, and WIC variables are interacted with the race-specific fraction of women aged fifteen to forty-four with family income less than 200 percent of the poverty level in 1980. The other variables are not interacted with the fraction of poor women because they reflect determinants of neonatal mortality that are relevant to the non-poor as well as the poor. The means and standard deviations of the eight interaction variables are included in columns (3) and (4) of table 8.2.

Linear regressions are estimated because a linear specification facilitates the aggregation of the two income specific mortality functions [equations (11) and (12)] into a single equation for the entire population. We choose a linear rather than a logistic functional form because the ordinary least squares (OLS) coefficients are more easily interpreted. Maddala (1983, 30) argues, in the case of large samples and probabilities not equal to zero or one, that the linear probability function, " . . . is no different in spirit from the log-linear model or the logit model. . . ." Thus, we do not sacrifice statistical appropriateness by our choice of functional form.

4. EMPIRICAL RESULTS

Ordinary least squares regressions of white neonatal mortality rates are contained in columns (1) and (2) of table 8.3, and ordinary least squares regressions of black neonatal mortality rates are contained in columns (3) and (4) of table 8.3. The regressions in columns (1) and (3) exclude the lagged neonatal mortality rate, while the regressions in columns (2) and (4) include it.

Table 8.3 Regression Results

Variable	White Neonatal Rates		Black Neonatal Rates	
	(1)	(2)	(3)	(4)
Neonatal death rate (1970)[a]		0.295 (9.61)		0.279 (6.48)
Percent high school educated[a]	−0.037 (−3.64)	−0.017 (−1.76)	−0.056 (−1.66)	−0.013 (−0.41)
Percent poor[a]	0.06 (3.58)	0.033 (2.08)	0.036 (0.99)	0.001 (0.02)
Newborn intensive care hospitals/1000	−44.196 (−2.61)	−41.033 (−2.59)	−86.196 (−1.56)	−53.875 (−1.02)
Abortion providers/1000	−3.198 (−1.99)	−3.307 (−2.20)	−16.838 (−2.94)	−18.297 (−3.38)
Family planning clinics[b]/1000	−3.605 (−3.07)	−2.745 (−2.49)	−1.910 (−1.29)	−0.532 (−0.38)
Community health centers[b]/1000	11.726 (2.04)	8.612 (1.60)	−20.515 (−2.13)	−14.220 (−1.55)
Maternal nutrition program[b]	−0.076 (−2.51)	−0.41 (−1.44)	−0.043 (−0.92)	0.020 (0.45)
Medicaid eligibility-1[b]	−1.115 (−2.10)	−0.485 (−0.97)	−0.188 (−0.20)	−0.266 (−0.31)
Medicaid eligibility-2[b]	0.562 (0.77)	0.799 (1.16)	0.627 (0.55)	1.041 (0.97)
Medicaid eligibility-3[b]	1.101 (1.35)	0.762 (0.99)	−0.355 (−0.38)	0.213 (0.24)
Medicaid payments for newborn[b]	−0.987 (−1.05)	−0.614 (−0.70)	−2.972 (−2.04)	−1.505 (−1.08)
Per capita Medicaid payment[b]	−0.01 (−0.91)	−0.01 (−0.42)	0.002 (0.94)	0.002 (0.86)
Constant	11.432 (15.30)	6.392 (7.30)	20.892 (7.67)	12.477 (4.33)
R^2	0.120	0.228	0.120	0.216
F	7.53	15.02	3.92	7.28
N	677	677	357	357

Notes: *t*-ratios are in parentheses. The critical *t*-ratios at the 5 percent level are 1.64 for a one-tailed test and 1.96 for a two-tailed test. The *F*-ratio associated each regression is significant at the 1 percent level.

[a] Variable is race-specific.

[b] These variables are interacted with the race-specific percent poor.

The basic determinants of neonatal mortality in the regressions are female schooling and female poverty levels. For whites, the schooling and poverty regression coefficients have the correct signs and are statistically significant. For blacks, these coefficients also have the correct signs although schooling is insignificant in both specifications.[20]

The six factors or public programs that have been stressed as potential contributors to the acceleration in the downward trend in neonatal mortality since 1964 are neonatal intensive care availability, abortion availability, organized family planning availability, BHCS project availability, WIC availability, and Medicaid. The regressions contain one variable pertaining to each of the five availability programs and five variables pertaining to the Medicaid financing program. Fourteen of the twenty program coefficients have the anticipated negative signs in the white regressions, including eight of the ten availability coefficients and six of the ten Medicaid coefficients. For blacks, nine of the ten availability coefficients and five of the ten Medicaid coefficients have the anticipated negative signs. BCHS project availability has the wrong sign in the two white regressions, and WIC availability has the wrong sign in the black regression that controls for the lagged neonatal mortality rate. Two of the three variables pertaining to Medicaid financing of first-time pregnancies have positive coefficients for whites and for blacks when the lagged rate is held constant. Moreover, Medicaid payments per adult recipient in AFDC families are positively related to neonatal mortality rates in the two black equations. Given the high degree of intercorrelation among the variables in the regression and the imprecise measures used, the preponderance of negative effects is an important and impressive finding.

In terms of statistical significance, the hypothesis that no member of the set of program measures has a non-zero effect on neonatal mortality always is rejected in both specifications at the 1 percent level. With respect to the five specific availability variables, for whites' neonatal intensive care, abortion and family planning are significant at the 5 percent level in both specifications. WIC is significant at the 5 percent level in the specification that omits the lagged mortality rate and at the 10 percent level in the specification that includes the lagged mortality rate.[21] In the black regressions, abortion is highly significant, and BCHS projects are significant at the 10 percent level in both specifications. Neonatal intensive care units are significant at the 6 percent level only in the specification which excludes the lagged mortality rate.

Many fewer of the five Medicaid financing variables are significant than the five availability variables. In particular, for both races there are no significant Medicaid effects either taken together or taken separately at conventional levels when the lagged neonatal mortality rate is a regressor. When the lagged rate is omitted from the white regressions, the set of Medicaid variables is significant at the 5 percent level for whites but not for blacks. These results do not necessarily imply that Medicaid is less important determinant of birth outcomes than the other programs. Rather, the results simply may reflect the imprecise Medicaid indexes.

It is notable that the black abortion and neonatal intensive care effects are two to four times larger than the corresponding white effects depending on specification. These results are important because abortion reform and advances in neonatology—unlike WIC, Medicaid, BHCS projects, and organized family planning clinics—clearly were not targeted at the poor. Yet the former two developments appear to have had their largest impact on blacks, the group in the population with the lowest income and the largest neonatal mortality rate.

To examine the relative contributions of schooling, poverty, and the program measures to the recent U.S. neonatal mortality experience, we apply the coefficients of regressions in columns (1)–(4) to trends in the exogenous variables between 1964 and 1977.[22] The extrapolations start in 1964 because that year marked the beginning of the acceleration in the downward trend in neonatal mortality. Extrapolations end in 1977 because the regressions pertain to that year. The results of estimating the implied changes in white and black neonatal mortality rates due to selected factors are shown in table 8.4.

In the period at issue the white neonatal mortality rate declined by 7.5 deaths per thousand live births, from 16.2 to 8.7. The black neonatal mortality rate declined by 11.5 deaths per thousand live births, from 27.6 to 16.1. The statistical analysis explains approximately 28 percent of the white decline on average, with a range between 23 percent and 32 percent. The statistical analysis explains 33 percent of the black decline on average, with a range between 17 percent and 48 percent.

For blacks, on average, the increase in abortion availability appears to be the single most important factor in the reduction of the neonatal mortality rate. We add a mild caveat to this result because, as discussed in section 3.2, the coefficients on abortion availability may be biased upward by a small magnitude. Even so, the growth in abortion availability appears to dominate not only the other program measures, but also trends in schooling and poverty. The estimated reduction due to abortion amounts to about one death per thousand live births or about 9 percent of the observed decline.

Schooling, Medicaid, and neonatal intensive care availability all have similar effects on the decline in black neonatal mortality—between 0.6 and 0.7 deaths per 1,000 live births. It should be noted, however, that neonatal intensive care availability is much less sensitive to the model's specification. Poverty and BCHS projects contributed between 0.20 and 0.25 fewer deaths per 1,000 live

Table 8.4 Contribution of Selected Factors to Reduction in Neonatal Mortality Rates, 1964–1977

Factor	Whites			Blacks		
	(1)	(2)	Mean Effect	(3)	(4)	Mean Effect
Schooling	0.618	0.284	0.451	1.170	0.272	0.721
Poverty	0.432	0.238	0.335	0.445	0.012	0.229
Neonatal intensive care	0.442	0.410	0.426	0.776	0.485	0.631
Abortion providers	0.178	0.185	0.182	0.943	1.025	0.984
Family planning	0.177	0.135	0.156	0.197	0.055	0.126
Community health centers	−0.059	−0.043	−0.051	0.287	0.199	0.243
Maternal nutrition program	0.538	0.290	0.414	0.636	−0.296	0.170
Medicaid[a]	0.437	0.280	0.359	1.044	0.220	0.632
Total explained reduction	2.763	1.779	2.272	5.498	1.972	3.735
Percent explained	36.8	23.7	30.3	47.8	17.1	32.5

Notes: Deaths per 1,000 live births.
[a]Combined contribution of all Medicaid variables.

births. Again, the program is less sensitive to the model's specification. Finally, family planning and the WIC program account for the smallest, but not insignificant, decline in neonatal deaths.

The results of the white extrapolations are less dramatic than those of the blacks and less clearcut. The increase in white female schooling makes the largest contribution to the decline in white neonatal mortality (about 0.5 deaths per thousand live births). The schooling factor is followed in importance by neonatal intensive care availability, poverty, and Medicaid (between 0.3 and 0.45 deaths per thousand live births each). The rise in the WIC program and abortion availability ranks as the fifth- and sixth-leading contributors (0.2 deaths per thousand live births), and the expansion in organized family planning availability ranks seventh (0.16 deaths per thousand live births). Note that the range of black effects is much larger than the range of white effects both in absolute and in relative terms. For blacks, the ratio of the largest effect to the smallest positive effect is almost 7, while for whites it equals 3. Note also that the correlation between the rankings of black and white contributions is positive but not statistically significant. The Spearman rank correlation coefficient is only 0.36. Note finally that the abortion and neonatal intensive care contributions may loom larger in white birth outcomes than the rankings suggest. This is because the estimated effects of these two factors are stable across the alternative specifications. Also note, finally, that these results focus on the differential impacts of the variables and cannot be interpreted as time series results since our analysis doesn't account for the changes in medical technology and tastes between 1964 and 1980. These changes were numerous and significant and certainly have contributed to the decline in neonatal mortality. In fact, it is not surprising that by ignoring the technological changes over time, we significantly underestimate the reduction in neonatal mortality for both whites and blacks. A time series approach could provide important additional evidence. Unfortunately, data on program measures by year were not available.

To summarize, the extrapolations point to the importance of abortion availability, female schooling, Medicaid, and neonatal intensive care availability, and to a lesser extent BCHS projects, poverty, the WIC program, and family planning in trends in black neonatal mortality between 1964 and 1977. They also underscore the importance of schooling, neonatal intensive care, poverty, Medicaid, and to a lesser extent abortion services, the WIC program, and organized family planning clinics in trends in white neonatal mortality for those years.

To the extent that very ill neonates die in the postneonatal period, one can argue that the above findings overstate the importance of neonatal intensive care availability in race-specific birth outcomes. Yet the postneonatal mortality rate has fallen every year since 1964 for both races, suggesting that this argument is not relevant. At the same time, the results do not imply that the construction and subsidization of additional neonatal intensive care units has a more favorable benefit-cost ratio than an expansion in BCHS projects for blacks if, for example, these were competing programs. Although the neonatal intensive care effect exceeds the BCHS project effect by about 0.4 deaths per thousand live births, the costs of these projects probably are smaller than the costs of constructing and maintaining sophisticated neonatal intensive care units. A similar comment applies to the 0.2 deaths per thousand live births differential between the white neonatal intensive care and organized family planning effects. Indeed, the cost of providing appropriate birth control information to poor women undoubtedly is less than the cost of providing them with prenatal and neonatal care services.

Our results can be compared to those contained in the study by Grossman and Jacobowitz (1981). Our estimates confirm Grossman and Jacobowitz's conclusion with respect to the key role of abortion in black birth outcomes. Our schooling effects are somewhat larger than theirs, which implies that this variable may operate by influencing the mix of inputs selected by families to produce healthy infants. Finally, we provide evidence of the roles of neonatal intensive care units, WIC, and BCHS projects in birth outcomes, which is not contained in their study.

Our results are relevant to the actual and potential impacts on neonatal mortality of a number of dramatic policy reversals by the Reagan Administration since the beginning of 1981. We refer to budget cutbacks which curtailed the rates of growth in such programs as WIC, Medicaid, BCHC projects, and subsidized family planning services. When inflation is taken into account, the absolute size of some of these programs declined in real terms. In spite of these cutbacks, the infant mortality rate declined from 12.6 deaths per thousand live births in 1980 to 11.2 deaths per thousand live births in 1982, and the neonatal mortality rate fell from 8.5 deaths per thousand live births in 1980 to 7.6 deaths per thousand live births in 1982.[23]

Why did the infant mortality rate continue to fall after 1980? Our results suggest that the detrimental effects of reduced spending levels for social programs may have been more than offset by the continued growth in abortion availability,[24] neonatal intensive care availability, and female schooling levels. Of course, the cutbacks may have lagged impacts on neonatal mortality. In any event our findings imply that the program reductions may have retarded the rate of decline in the neonatal mortality rate of the poor since 1980.

Our results also are relevant to the current U.S. policy debate with respect to attempts by the Right to Life movement and its supporters in Congress to outlaw abortion except when it is necessary to preserve a pregnant woman's life. During the past few years, the anti-abortion movement has tried to achieve this goal either by means of a constitutional amendment or an act of Congress. Our estimates indicate that, if these efforts are successful, neonatal mortality, especially among blacks, may fall slower than otherwise and may even rise.

NOTES

Originally published as Hope Corman and Michael Grossman, "Determinants of Neonatal Mortality Rates in the U.S.: A Reduced Form Model," *Journal of Health Economics* 4, no. 3 (1985): 213–236. Research for this paper except for Hope Corman's time was supported by Grant no. 5 R01 HD16316 from the National Institute of Child Health and Human Development to the National Bureau of Economic Research. Hope Corman's time was supported directly by the National Bureau of Economic Research. We are indebted to the following people for providing us with data: Kathleen Bajo of Ross Laboratories; Richard Bohrer, Edward Duffy, Joann Gephart and Robert Nelson of the Bureau of Health Care Delivery and Assistance, DHHS; Stephen M. Davidson of the Northwestern University Program in Hospital and Health Services Administration; Garry Davis of the American Hospital Association; Jacqueline D. Forrest and Stanley K. Henshaw of the

Alan Guttmacher Institute; and Letty Wunglueck of the Health Care Financing Administration. We are also indebted to Peter Budetti of the University of California at San Francisco Health Policy Program and to Jacqueline D. Forrest and Stanley K. Henshaw and to Joseph Newhouse and two anonymous referees for helpful comments and suggestions. Finally, we wish to thank Emil Berendt and Theodore J. Joyce for research assistance. This paper has not undergone the review accorded official NBER publications; in particular, it has not been submitted for approval by the Board of Directors.

1. The computations are based on data contained in National Center for Health Statistics (1983).

2. The perinatal period is the period around the time of birth, generally defined as from twenty weeks of gestation up to seven days of life.

3. Brief descriptive and historical information concerning these factors is as follows. Medicaid, enacted in 1965 as Title XIX of the Social Security Act of 1935, is the joint federal-state program to finance the medical care services of low-income families who are covered by the aid to families with dependent children (AFDC) program. Maternal and infant care projects originated in the 1963 amendment to Title V of the Social Security Act. The amendment provides special federal grants for projects designed to provide adequate prenatal and obstetrical care to reduce the incidence of mental retardation and other conditions caused by childbearing complications as well as to lower infant and maternal mortality. The program to create and fund community health centers was started by the Office of Economic Opportunity as part of the War on Poverty in 1965. By 1973, overall control of the centers had been shifted to the Bureau of Health Care Delivery and Assistance (formerly called the Bureau of Community Health Services), DHHS. CHCs deliver comprehensive ambulatory care, both primary and preventive, to poverty populations in medically underserved areas. The Special Supplemental Food Program for Women, Infants, and Children (WIC program) was authorized by a 1972 amendment to the Child Nutrition Act of 1966. Under the program the federal government gives cash grants to state health departments and local health clinics to provide special nutritious food supplements to low-income pregnant and lactating women, infants, and children up to four years of age who are nutritional risks. Federal subsidization of family planning services for low-income women originated in the 1967 amendments to the Social Security Act. Federal efforts in this area were expanded by the Family Planning Services and Population Research Act of 1970 and by the 1972 amendments to the Social Security Act. These subsidies go to family planning clinics organized by hospitals, state and local health departments, Planned Parenthood, and other agencies. Prior to 1967, all states of the United States had laws which permitted abortion only when it was necessary to preserve a pregnant woman's life. By the middle of 1970, sixteen states had reformed their laws to increase the number of circumstance under which abortions could be performed. In 1973 the Supreme Court ruled most restrictive state laws unconstitutional. Information on neonatal intensive care units is provided below.

4. The indirect costs of obtaining a good are generated by the time spent traveling, waiting, and obtaining information about the good. We use the terms cost and availability as synonyms. In particular, with other factors held constant, an increase in availability is associated with reductions in direct and indirect costs.

5. The variable b can be interpreted as the probability of a low-birth-weight birth.

6. Some of the nonmedical inputs, such as maternal cigarette smoking and alcohol use, have negative marginal products in the birth weight production function.

7. The input demand functions are reduced form equations because they are obtained by maximizing a utility function subject to production and resource constraints. Note that the above specification contains the restriction that prenatal care and the exogenous risk factors affect survival only through their impacts on birth weight, but this restriction does not affect the nature of the reduced form. Note also that such endogenous risk factors as mother's age at birth, parity, gestational age, and legitimacy status of the birth can be incorporated into the birth-weight production function. This would add equations for each of these factors to the reduced form but would not alter the reduced form survival equation (7). As explained below, we focus on the estimation of equation (7) in this paper.

8. Potential endogeneity problems are explored in more detail in section 3.

9. One county with a population of at least 50,000 persons in 1970 was eliminated from the sample because it was the only such county characterized as an isolated rural county with no incorporated place with a population of at least 2,500 persons in 1970. In addition, Washington, DC, was excluded because of difficulty in defining its relevant market area for neonatal intensive care (NICU) availability. For all other counties, we defined the state as the relevant NICU area. Since this was impossible for DC, we eliminated the observation. Note that although 84 percent of all births in Washington, DC, were black, DC black births accounted for less than 2 percent of all black births in the sample of 358 black counties.

10. These advances are described by the American Academy of Pediatrics (1977), the Committee on Perinatal Health (1977), and Budetti et al. (1981).

11. In the context of the household production function model of consumer behavior, the sign of the efficiency effect in a particular output demand function is ambiguous if, for example, an increase in the mother's schooling raises her productivity in the production of healthy infants by a smaller percentage than her productivity in other household activities (Grossman 1972; Michael 1972). Nevertheless, we think that it is reasonable to expect a negative schooling coefficient in the neonatal mortality rate regression.

12. A more detailed justification for the aggregation of maternal and infant care projects and community health centers is contained in the appendix, which is available on request.

13. Federal funding of abortions resumed temporarily in February 1980, pending a review by the U.S. Supreme Court of a ruling by Federal District Judge John F. Dooling, Jr., that declared the Hyde Amendment unconstitutional. In June 1980, the Supreme Court reversed Judge Dooling's decision and upheld the constitutionality of the Hyde Amendment.

14. See note 3 for detailed information.

15. The direction of the bias on the lagged mortality rate coefficient depends on the sign of the correlation between this variable and the error term. We define our regression as

$$Y = a + bX + cZ + u,$$

where Y is the 1977 neonatal mortality rate, b is a vector of coefficients on all independent variables except the lagged mortality rate, X is a vector of all independent variables except the lagged mortality rate, Z is the lagged mortality rate, c is the coefficient on Z, and u is an error term. Assuming that none of the X variables is correlated with u, the expected value of c is

$$E(c) = c + (\sigma_c^2/\sigma_u^2)E[\mathrm{cov}(Zu)].$$

Since σ_c^2 and σ_u^2 are positive, the direction of the bias depends on the sign of $E[\mathrm{cov}(Zu)]$. If this is positive, the estimated c will be biased upward and conversely. For the coefficients on the X variables,

$$E(b) = b - (\sigma_b\sigma_c/\sigma_u^2)r_{xz}E[\mathrm{cov}(Zu)],$$

where r_{xz} is the partial correlation between the X variables and Z. Since σ_b, σ_c, σ_u^2, and, in our case, $E[\mathrm{cov}(Zu)]$ are all positive, the direction of the bias depends on the sign of r_{xz}. If r_{xz} is positive, the coefficient will be biased downward (more negative) and conversely. [See Grossman (1972, 98–101) and Haitovsky (1968) for derivations of the above formulae.]

16. The majority of independent variables have negative partial correlations with the lagged mortality rate. Exceptions are poverty and abortion availability for both samples, BHCS programs for whites, Medicaid eligibility-2 for whites, and Medicaid eligibility-1 and per capita Medicaid payments for blacks. The negative partial correlations imply reduced coefficients (in absolute value) when the lagged mortality rate is included.

17. Since the partial correlations between the X variables and the lagged mortality rates are usually negative, then for most variables, the serial correlation bias causes a downward estimate (in absolute value) of the coefficient. Therefore, when the sign of the reverse causality bias is negative, inclusion of the lagged mortality rate will cause lower bound estimates of program effects and exclusion will cause upper bound estimates.

18. As indicated in section 2, the coefficient on x_{pj} in eq. (12) could be positive if the program at issue lowers the price of medical care paid by the poor and therefore lowers the cost of a birth.

19. The above approach differs from that of Grossman and Jacobowitz (1981). They estimate the fraction of births to low-income women and then fit an equation of the form $d_j = \beta_0 + (\alpha_0 - \beta_0)k_j + \alpha_1 k_j x_{pj}$. We do not adopt this procedure because we focus on the reduced form, and k_j is an endogenous variable.

20. The numerically small and statistically insignificant black schooling effect in column (4) may well reflect the serial correlation bias discussed in section 3, since there is a significant negative partial correlation between schooling and the lagged mortality rate.

21. A one-tailed test is employed because the alternative hypothesis is that each coefficient is negative.

22. The sources for the values of the independent variables in the extrapolations, and the assumptions that underlie these values, are available in the appendix to this paper, which is available on request.

23. Race-specific data are not yet available for years after 1980.

24. Recall that Cates (1981) reports that the ban on federal funding of abortions under Medicaid has had little impact on the number of abortions obtained by low-income pregnant women.

REFERENCES

American Academy of Pediatrics, Committee on Fetus and Newborn. 1977. *Standards and Recommendations for Hospital Care of New Born Infants, 1974–1977*, 6th ed. Evanston, IL: American Academy of Pediatrics.

Becker, Gary S., and H. Gregg Lewis. 1973. "On the Interaction Between the Quantity and Quality of Children." In "New Economic Approaches to Fertility, Ed. T. W. Schultz. Proceedings of a conference sponsored by the National Bureau of Economic Research and the Population Council. *Journal of Political Economy* 81, no. 2, Part II.

Ben-Porath, Yoram, and Finis Welch. 1976. "Do Sex Preferences Really Matter?" *The Quarterly Journal of Economics* 90, no. 2.

Brooks, Charles H. 1978. "Infant Mortality in SMSAs before Medicaid: Test of a Causal Model." *Health Service Research* 13, no. 1.

Budetti, Peter, et al. 1981 "Costs and Effectiveness of Neonatal Intensive Care." In *The Implications of Cost-Effectiveness Analysis of Medical Technology*. Washington, DC: U.S. Government Printing Office.

Cates, Willard, Jr. 1981 "The Hyde Amendment in Action: How Did the Restriction of Federal Funds for Abortion Affect Low-Income Women." *Journal of the American Medical Association* 246, no. 1.

Committee on Perinatal Health. 1977. "Toward Improving the Outcome of Pregnancy: Recommendations for the Regional Development of Maternal and Perinatal Health Services. White Plains, NY: National Foundation of the March of Dimes.

Corman, Hope, Theodore J. Joyce, and Michael Grossman. 1987. "Birth Outcome Production Functions in the U.S." *Journal of Human Resources* 22, no. 3.

David, Richard J., and Earl Siegel. 1983. "Decline in Neonatal Mortality, 1968 to 1977: Better Babies or Better Care." *Pediatrics* 71, no. 4.

Dryfoos, Joy G. 1976. "The United States National Family Planning Program, 1968–74." *Studies in Family Planning* 7, no. 3.

Eisner, Victor et al. 1978 "Improvement in Infant and Perinatal Mortality in the United States, 1965–1973." *American Journal of Public Health* 68, no. 4.

Fuchs, Victor R. 1974 "Some Economic Aspects of Mortality in Developed Countries." In *The Economics of Health and Medical Care*, ed. Mark Perlman. London: MacMillan.

Goldman, Fred, and Michael Grossman. 1982. "The Impact of Public Health Policy: The Case of Community Health Centers." New York: National Bureau of Economic Research Working Paper 1020.

Gortmaker, Steven L. 1979 "Poverty and Infant Mortality in the United States." *American Sociological Review* 44, no. 2.

Grossman, Michael. 1972. *The Demand for Health: A Theoretical and Empirical Investigation*. New York: Columbia University Press for the National Bureau of Economic Research.

Grossman, Michael, and Steven Jacobowitz. 1981. "Variations in Infant Mortality Rates among Counties of the United States: The Role of Public Policies and Programs." *Demography* 18, no. 4.

Hadley, Jack. 1982. *More Medical Care, Better Health?* Washington, DC: The Urban Institute.

Haitovsky, Yoel. 1968. *Simplified Formulae for Covariance B, Mimeo.* New York: NBER.

Harris, Jeffrey E. 1982. "Prenatal Medical Care and Infant Mortality." In *Economic Aspects of Health*, ed. Victor R. Fuchs. Chicago: University of Chicago Press for the National Bureau of Economic Research.

Kleinman, Joel C., et al. 1978 "A Comparison of 1960 and 1973–1974 Early Neonatal Mortality in Selected States." *American Journal of Epidemiology* 108.

Lee, Kwang-Sun, et al. 1980. "Neonatal Mortality: An Analysis of the Recent Improvement in the United States." *American Journal of Public Health* 70, no. 1.

Lewit, Eugene M. 1983. "The Demand for Prenatal Care and the Production of Healthy Infants." In *Human Capital and Development*, ed. Ismail Sirageldin, David Salkever, and Alan Sorkin. Greenwich, CT: JAI Press.

Maddala, G.S. 1983. *Limited Dependent and Qualitative Variables in Econometrics.* Cambridge: Cambridge University Press.

Michael, Robert T. 1972. *The Effects of Education on Efficiency in Consumption.* New York: Columbia University Press for the National Bureau of Economic Research.

National Center for Health Statistics. 1983. *Health.* United States, 1983, DHHS publication no. (PHS) 84–1232. Washington, DC: U.S. Government Printing Office.

Rosenzweig, Mark R., and T. Paul Schultz. 1982. "The Behavior of Mothers as Inputs to Child Health: The Determinants of Birth Weight, Gestation, and Rate of Fetal Growth." In *Economic Aspects of Health*, ed. Victor R. Fuchs. Chicago: University of Chicago Press for the National Bureau of Economic Research.

——.1983a. "Consumer Demand and Household Production: The Relationship Between Fertility and Child Mortality." *American Economic Review* 73, no. 2.

——. 1983b "Estimating a Household Production Function: Heterogeneity, the Demand for Health Inputs, and Their Effects on Birth Weight." *Journal of Political Economy* 91, no. 5.

Sheridan, John F. 1983. "The Typical Perinatal Center" *Clinics in Perinatology* 10, no. 1.

Sloan, Frank, Janet Mitchell, and Jerry Cromwell. 1978. "Physician Participation in State Medicaid Programs." *Journal of Human Resources* 13, suppl.

Williams, Anne D. 1976. "Fertility and Reproductive Loss." PhD Dissertation. Chicago, IL: University of Chicago.

Williams, Ronald L. 1974. "Outcome-based Measurements of Medical Output: The Case of Maternal and Infant Health." PhD Dissertation. Santa Barbara, CA: University of California.

Willis, Robert. 1973. "A New Approach to the Economic Theory of Fertility Behavior." In « New Economic Approaches to Fertility." Proceedings of a conference sponsored by the National Bureau of Economic Research and the Population Council. *Journal of Political Economy* 81, no. 2, Part II.

NINE

Birth Outcome Production Functions
in the United States

Hope Corman, Theodore J. Joyce,
and Michael Grossman

ABSTRACT

This chapter contains the first infant health production functions that simultaneously consider the effects of a variety of inputs on race-specific neonatal mortality rates. These inputs include the use of prenatal care, neonatal intensive care, abortion, federally subsidized organized family planning clinics, maternal and infant care projects, community health centers, and the WIC program. We place major emphasis on two-stage least squares estimation. Our results underscore the qualitative and quantitative importance of abortion, prenatal care, neonatal intensive care, and the WIC program in black and white birth outcomes.

1. INTRODUCTION

Neonatal mortality rates declined sharply in the United States. between 1964 and 1982—from 17.9 deaths of infants less than one month old per thousand live births to 7.7 deaths per thousand live births (National Center for Health Statistics 1985). For whites, the mortality rate fell by 4.9 percent per year (annually compounded), and for blacks, the rate of decline was 4.2 percent per year. During this period, there were significant changes in a number of the important health inputs related to neonatal mortality. Federally subsidized programs such as family planning clinics, community health centers (CHCs), maternal and infant care (M and I) projects, the Special Supplemental Food Program for Women, Infants and Children (WIC), and Medicaid were either expanded or implemented for the first time. In addition, the use of prenatal care grew, and there were numerous medical advances resulting in high technology neonatal intensive care units. Finally, during this period, abortion was legalized.

Since the beginning of 1981, however, budget cutbacks by the Reagan Administration have curtailed the rates of growth of such poverty-related programs as WIC, M and I projects, community health centers, subsidized family planning clinics, and Medicaid. When inflation is taken into account, the absolute sizes of some of these programs declined in real terms. The cutbacks coincide with a slowing in the decline of mortality rates, especially for blacks. For instance, from 1981 to 1982, the black neonatal mortality rate fell by 2.2 percent, and the white rate fell by 4.2 percent. These developments have caused some persons to attribute the deceleration in the rate of decline in neonatal mortality to the Reagan Administration's policies (for example, Miller 1985).

The purpose of this study is to examine the relationship between the utilization of the health inputs mentioned above and race-specific neonatal mortality in a production function context. Although a number of studies have treated subsets of these inputs,[1] none have entered them together in a multivariate birth outcome equation estimated with data covering a large percentage of all births in the United States. We use the estimates to gain insights into the causes of the rapid reduction in neonatal mortality since 1964 and the deceleration in the rate of decline in the early 1980s. Our empirical analysis is based on a cross-section of U.S. counties in 1977, with the neonatal mortality rate (deaths of infants within the first twenty-seven days of life per thousand live births) as the principal birth outcome, and with the incidence of low birth weight (2,500 grams or less) as an intermediate outcome. This allows us to examine the extent to which prenatal inputs operate directly on mortality and also allows us to examine their indirect effects on mortality rates through low birth weight.

In models developed by Harris (1982) and Rosenzweig and Schultz (1982, 1983a, 1983b), mothers with poor endowed birth outcomes will attempt to offset these unfavorable prospects by utilizing more health inputs. Thus, the decision to use the health inputs may not only affect the outcome, but the potential outcome may also affect utilization. We adopt two strategies to account for this potential reverse causality. First, major emphasis is placed on two-stage least squares estimates of the production function with prenatal care, abortion, and neonatal intensive care as endogenous (choice) variables. Second, we control for the health endowment directly, using the incidence of low birth weight as a proxy for the endowment. If birth weight is, in fact, an appropriate endowment measure, the production functions can be estimated using ordinary least squares (OLS). We then test for the appropriateness of this proxy variable approach.

2. ANALYTICAL FRAMEWORK

Following Corman and Grossman (1985) and the theoretical literature that they cite, we assume that the parents' utility function depends on their consumption, the number of births, and the survival probability of each birth (which does not vary among births in a given family). Both the number of births and the survival probability are endogenous variables. In particular, the survival probability production function depends upon such endogenous inputs as the quantity and quality of medical care, nutrition, and the own time of the mother. In addition, the production function is affected by the reproductive efficiency of the mother, including the unobserved biologically endowed probability that her infant will survive the first month of life, and other aspects of her efficiency in household production.

The preceding ideas are formalized in a structural equations model that incorporates the relationship between neonatal mortality and its most proximate determinant—low birth weight. In particular, there is an overwhelming amount of evidence that low birth weight (less than or equal to 2,500 grams or 5.5 pounds) is the most important endogenous risk factor in neonatal survival outcomes. The system of equations, which is described in detail in Corman, Joyce, and Grossman (1985), is designed to obtain estimates of the direct and indirect (through low birth weight) effects of five basic health inputs. These inputs are prenatal medical care, perinatal and neonatal care, the use of abortion services, the use of contraceptive services, and maternal cigarette smoking. The equations in the model have meaningful interpretations both at the family level and at the county level. The latter is the unit to which the empirical analysis in this chapter pertains.

The structural neonatal mortality production function in the model is

$$\pi = f_1 (n, m, a, c, b, e). \tag{1}$$

In this equation, the probability that an infant dies within the first month of life or the neonatal mortality rate at the county level (π) is shown as a vector of perinatal and neonatal care inputs (n), a vector of prenatal medical inputs (m), the use of abortion services (a), the use of contraceptive services (c), the probability that the infant is born light (b), and the infant's biological endowment (e, which rises as the endowment rises). The full model also contains structural production functions for the probability of a light (2,500 grams or less) birth or the fraction of light births in a county and for the probability of a premature birth. Substitution of these equations into equation (1) yields a quasi-structural neonatal mortality production function:

$$\pi = f_2 (n, m, a, c, s, x, e).$$

(2)

Here s is maternal cigarette smoking and x is an exogenous risk variable in birth outcomes which is measured at the county level by the number of women who are either teens or in their forties as a fraction of all women of childbearing age. By estimating both equations (1) and (2), we are able to calculate the direct and indirect (through low birth weight) effects of the basic health inputs.

In addition to the production functions, the model generates demand functions for birth weight and the five health inputs. In each of these six equations, the dependent variable is related to a vector of price and availability measures, socioeconomic characteristics that reflect command over resources and tastes, the exogenous risk measure, and the biological endowment. They are reduced form equations because only exogenous variables appear on their right-hand sides.

If the infant's biological endowment (e) were an observed variable, unbiased estimates of the production function could be obtained by ordinary least squares. Since this is not the case, the endowment must be treated as one component of the disturbance term in each equation. Hence, our model generates a recursive system of equations whose disturbance terms may be correlated. In particular, although the researcher has no information about the endowment, the mother and her physician have at least some information about it. This information is likely to lead mothers with poor endowed birth outcomes and their physicians to try to offset these unfavorable prospects by choosing a different mix of inputs than other mothers (Rosenzweig and Schultz 1981, 1982, 1983a, 1983b; Harris 1982). Under these circumstances, ordinary least squares estimates of the parameters of the production function are biased and inconsistent because the inputs are correlated with the disturbance term, which reflects in part the endowment. In particular, the effects of the inputs on favorable infant health outcomes are understated. To circumvent this problem, production functions are estimated by two-stage least squares (TSLS).

It should be noted that the biases that arise when equation (2) is estimated by ordinary least squares are likely to be more severe than the biases that arise when equation (1) is estimated in a similar manner. This is because equation (1) includes birth weight, which may be a very useful proxy for the infant's endowed probability of survival. Put differently, it is possible that the endowment has no effect on neonatal mortality with low birth weight held constant. A test of this proposition is discussed in the next section.

The model underscores the need to treat the abortion rate as an endogenous variable. This is both because abortion availability and the underlying frequency distribution of health endowments (the distribution that would be observed in the absence of abortion) vary among counties. Suppose that availability varies but the underlying frequency distribution does not. Since less healthy fetuses are more likely to be aborted, the actual health endowment of infants born in counties with high abortion rates will exceed the health endowment of infants born in counties with low abortion rates. Consequently, an expansion in the abortion rate will lower the fraction of light births. If the underlying frequency distribution of endowments varies among counties, abortion rates will be higher in counties with low underlying endowments, all other things the same, and the correlation between the abortion rate and the actual endowment is reduced and may even be negative.

Based on evidence to date, it is anticipated that abortion, contraceptive services, and prenatal care services will have their primary effect on neonatal mortality through low birth weight (for example, Institute of Medicine 1985). These inputs, however, may have sizable direct effects on newborn survival if other relevant inputs are lacking. For instance, we have no measures of the quality of prenatal and perinatal care. If these variables are positively correlated with abortion, contraception, and prenatal care, the latter inputs can have negative impacts on birth weight-specific neonatal mortality. This should be kept in mind when interpreting the results.[2]

3. EMPIRICAL IMPLEMENTATION

3.1. Data and Measurement of Variables

We have constructed the database from a variety of sources which are described in detail in Corman and Grossman (1985) and Corman, Joyce, and Grossman (1985). Counties are the units of observation because they are the smallest units for which aggregate data are available. Some counties are so small, however, that people may receive medical care outside the county. Also, small counties experience large fluctuations in birth rates simply due to random movements. These problems are reduced by including only large counties. Our sample includes counties with at least 50,000 persons in 1970, and for black regressions, at least 5,000 blacks. The 677 counties in the white regressions and 357 counties in the black regressions account for about 80 percent of the white and black populations in the United States in 1970.[3] In addition to selecting large counties, we attenuate random elements by employing three-year averages of the race-specific neonatal mortality rate and the percentage of low-birth—weight births, weighting regressions by the square root of the race-specific total number of births.

Separate regressions are fitted for white and black birth outcomes, rather than a non-race-specific equation which enters the percentage of black births. By fitting race-specific equations, we circumvent a possible source of multicollinearity, if race and input usage are correlated. Moreover, in preliminary regressions we tested and rejected the hypothesis that slope coefficients but not intercepts are the same for whites and blacks.

Table 9.1 contains definitions, means, and standard deviations of the variables used in this study. The key inputs at issue in this chapter are prenatal care, abortion, organized family planning clinic services, maternal and infant care (M and I) projects, community health centers (CHCs), WIC, and neonatal intensive care. All of these measures are expected to have negative regression coefficients in the neonatal mortality rate production function. Additional risk factors such as smoking and women in high-risk age groups are expected to have positive coefficients. Note that the use of M and I projects and CHCs is combined in one measure—Bureau of Community Health Services (BCHS) project use—because the BCHS (renamed the Bureau of Health Care Delivery and Assistance in 1982) is the agency within the U.S. Department of Health and Human Services that has overall administrative responsibility for both M and I projects and CHCs.

3.2. Estimation

Neonatal intensive care units are aimed at low-birth-weight births, and community health centers, organized family planning clinics, and the WIC program are aimed at the poor. It follows that the impact of the use of neonatal intensive care on neonatal mortality is larger, the larger the fraction of low-birth-weight births. Also, the impact of the use of inputs provided by public programs is larger the larger the fraction of poor women.[4] To account for these effects, we interact the neonatal intensive care measure with the race-specific fraction of low-birth-weight births. Under the assumption of equal use rates by white and black light neonates, the resulting variable can be interpreted as the race-specific number of inpatient days in neonatal intensive care units per birth. Similarly, the WIC

Table 9.1 Definitions of Variables

Variable Name	Definition
Neonatal mortality*	Three-year average neonatal mortality rate centered on 1977; deaths of infants fewer than 28 days old per 1,000 live births ($\mu_w = 8.837$, $\sigma_w = 1.595$, $\mu_b = 16.387$, $\sigma_b = 3.299$)
Low birth weight*	Three-year average percentage of low-birth weight (2,500 grams or less) live births centered on 1977 ($\mu_w = 5.992$, $\sigma_w = .741$, $\mu_b = 13.016$, $\sigma_b = 1.228$)
Prenatal care*[d]	Three-year average percentage of live births for which prenatal care began in the first trimester (first three months) of pregnancy centered on 1977 ($\mu_w = 78.111$, $\sigma_w = 8.290$, $\mu_b = 59.359$, $\sigma_b = 10.236$)
Abortion	Three-year average state-specific resident abortion rate centered on 1976; abortions performed on state residents per 1,000 women aged 15–44 in the state ($\mu_w = 24.969$, $\sigma_w = 8.716$, $\mu_b = 24.754$, $\sigma_b = 8.603$)
Teen family planning*[a]	Percentage of women aged 15–19 with family income less than 200 percent of the poverty level in 1975 who use organized family planning services in 1975 ($\mu_w = 35.747$, $\sigma_w = 25.265$, $\mu_b = 44.613$, $\sigma_b = 17.966$)
BCHS Projects[b]	Sum of maternity patients in maternal and infant care (M and I) projects and female users aged 15–44 of community health centers (CHCs) in 1976 per 1,000 women aged 15–44 with family income less than 200 percent of the poverty level in 1975; numerator termed Bureau of Community Health Services (BCHS) female project users ($\mu_w = 37.808$, $\sigma_w = 153.103$, $\mu_b = 54.929$, $\sigma_b = 141.517$)
WIC (maternal nutrition program)	State-specific number of eligible pregnant women served by the Special Supplemental Food Program for Women, Infants, and Children (WIC program) per 1,000 state-specific eligible women in 1980 ($\mu_w = 262.894$, $\sigma_w = 77.983$, $\mu_b = 267.931$, $\sigma_b = 74.089$)
Neonatal intensive care[b]	Sum of state-specific hospital inpatient days in Level II, or Level III, or Levels II and III neonatal intensive care units in 1979 per state-specific three-year average number of low-birth-weight births centered on 1977 ($\mu_w = 10.709$, $\sigma_w = 5.817$, $\mu_b = 11.538$, $\sigma_b = 7.395$)
Smoking	State-specific daily number of cigarettes smoked per adult 18 years and older in 1976 ($\mu_w = 7.416$, $\sigma_w = .511$, $\mu_b = 7.486$, $\sigma_b = .351$)
High-risk women*[a]	Number of women 15–19 and 40–44 as a fraction of women 15–44 in 1975 ($\mu_w = .335$, $\sigma_w = .022$, $\mu_b = .350$, $\sigma_b = .026$)
Poverty*[c]	Fraction of women aged 15–44 with family income less than 200 percent of the poverty level in 1980 $\mu_w = .266$. $\sigma_w = .877$, $\mu_b = .549$, $\sigma_b = .936$)

Notes: An asterisk (*) next to a variable means that it is race-specific. All variables are county-specific unless otherwise indicated. The symbols μ_w, σ_w, μ_b, and σ_b denote the white mean, the white standard deviation, the black mean, and the black standard deviation, respectively. Means and standard deviations are weighted by the race-specific total number of births in the period 1976–78.

[a] Variable is available for whites and nonwhites as opposed to whites and blacks.

[b] Since numerator of this variable is not race-specific, denominator also is not race-specific.

[c] Variable is available for nonblacks and blacks as opposed to whites and blacks.

[d] In counties where prenatal care was unknown for more than 50 percent of births, we consider the value as missing. Prenatal care data were missing for 83 counties in the white sample and 45 counties in the black sample. For counties with known values, prenatal care was estimated on the basis of the percentage of women employed, the percentage of women with at least a high school education, and the percentage of poor women. The coefficients were then used to generate values for the unknown counties. Note that the coefficients of production functions estimated by a two-step procedure, one that did not repredict prenatal care for the unknown counties, were almost identical to the coefficients presented in section 4.

and BCHS program measures are interacted with the race-specific fraction of women aged fifteen to forty-four with family income less than 200 percent of the poverty level, and the teenage family planning measure is interacted with the race-specific fraction of women fifteen to nineteen with family income less than 200 percent of the poverty level. The interacted teenage family planning measure gives the race-specific number of teenage users as a percentage of all race-specific teenagers. Under the assumption of equal use rates by poor white and black women, the other interacted poverty variables can be interpreted as the race-specific number of users of a given program per thousand race-specific women aged fifteen to forty-four.

The neonatal mortality equations (1) and (2) are fitted using a two-stage least squares procedure for the reasons discussed in section 2. We test for the significance of the correlation between the production function residuals and the health inputs, using Wu's T_2 statistic (Wu 1973).[5] If the null hypothesis of zero correlation between the error term and the regressors is not rejected, then OLS is an appropriate technique. For this reason, we perform OLS as well as the two-stage least squares techniques, on equations (1) and (2). A comparison of Wu statistics for equations (1) and (2) allows us to examine whether birth weight is a reasonable proxy for the health endowment. It should be noted that in both OLS and TSLS estimates of the production functions, we use a linear function form[6] and use weights appropriate for aggregate data.

In the first stage of our two-stage estimation procedure, birth weight, prenatal care, abortion, and neonatal intensive care use are predicted on the basis of variables that are used in Corman and Grossman's (1985) reduced form neonatal mortality estimates. Predicted values of these four endogenous variables are then entered into the neonatal mortality rate equations. The reduced form regressors are as follows: the race-specific fraction of high-risk women; the race-specific fraction of women aged fifteen through forty-four with family income less than 200 percent of the poverty level; the race-specific fraction of women fifteen through forty-ninewith at least a high school education; the number of hospitals with Level II or Level III neonatal intensive care units per thousand women aged fifteen through forty-four (neonatal intensive care availability); the number of abortion providers (public hospitals, private hospitals, nonhospital clinics, and office based physicians) per thousand women aged fifteen through forty-four (abortion availability); the number of organized family planning clinics per thousand women aged fifteen through forty-four with family income less than 200 percent of the poverty level (family planning availability); the number of BCHS projects per thousand women aged fifteen through forty-four with family income less than 200 percent of the poverty level (BCHS project availability); a dichotomous variable that equals one if a county is in a state that covers prenatal care for all first-time pregnancies under Medicaid to financially eligible women; a dichotomous variable that equals one if a county is in a state that covers prenatal care for first-time pregnancies under Medicaid only if no husband is present or if the husband is present but unemployed and not receiving unemployment compensation; a dichotomous variable that equals one if a county is in a state that covers prenatal care for first-time pregnancies under Medicaid only if no husband is present;[7] the likelihood that the newborn care received by the infant of a low-income woman will be financed by Medicaid measured by a dichotomous variable that equals one if a county is in a state in which Medicaid pays for newborn care under the mother's Medicaid number or does not pay for care under the mother's number but allows pregnant women to register their unborn children with Medicaid; and the average annual Medicaid payment per adult recipient in AFDC families. All of these variables are county-specific except for the neonatal intensive care and Medicaid measures which are state-specific.[8]

Ideally, in our two-stage procedure, we would treat all right-hand variables in equation (1) and all variables except the fraction of high-risk women in equation (2) as endogenous. Doing so, however, would create severe problems of multicollinearity and would tax the data to an inordinate degree. The public program input measures are all treated as exogenous in the estimation procedure. This procedure can be justified because these programs are used by poor women as opposed to all women, and the programs are relatively new. Joyce's (1985) empirical estimates of input demand functions suggest that differences in their use among counties are governed to a large extent by differences in their availability. Technically, our procedure is analogous to viewing the capital input in a firm's production function as fixed in the short run by varying among firms for historical reasons.[9] We do not estimate values for the smoking variable in a first stage because the smoking variable was already estimated on the basis of income, price, education, age, sex, and race, as described in Corman, Joyce, and Grossman (1985). Our procedure is based on the reasonable assumption that prenatal and neonatal input availability measures have zero coefficients in the cigarette demand function.[10]

Rosenzweig and Wolpin (1986) point out that it may be inappropriate to treat the availability of government funded programs such as BCHS projects and organized family planning as exogenous. They show that the government may allocate program resources systematically across areas on the basis of health endowments, thus making availability measures of such inputs endogenous. They present empirical evidence in favor of this proposition using data on the distribution of family planning and health facilities among villages in one province in the Philippines, although they do not estimate health production functions. In a separate paper, Rosenzweig and Wolpin (1984) also present evidence that women with low health endowments migrate to areas where program availability is high based on the use of a maternal and child health program in a small village in Colombia.

To examine the sensitivity of our estimated production functions to the potential endogeneity of BCHS and family planning availability, we deleted these two variables from the set of reduced form regressors. The resulting production functions were very similar to those presented in section 4. This suggests that the endogeneity of input availability may not be a problem in our data, particularly because BCHS projects and organized family planning clinics are funded in part by state and local governments. It may be more difficult to allocate resources across areas based on health endowments if more than one level of government is involved in the decision-making process. Note that the rules governing the eligibility of low-income women for Medicaid financing of prenatal care and newborn care were made solely by the states in 1977. This reduces the possibility of significant correlations between the Medicaid variables and the health endowment. Moreover, Rosenzweig and Wolpin's results pertain to less developed countries. Whether they generalize to a developed country such as the United States and to subpopulations such as teenagers is unknown.

4. RESULTS

OLS and TSLS estimates of the black and white neonatal mortality production functions are presented in table 9.2. The first set of regressions for each race (A1, A2, B1, and B2) excludes the endogenous risk factor of low birth weight. As discussed in section 1, the substitution of low birth weight by its structural determinants yields what we have termed the quasi-structural production function. The remaining regressions show the direct effect of an input on neonatal mortality by holding constant the percentage of low-birth-weight births.

The TSLS regression coefficients of prenatal care, abortion, and neonatal intensive care are substantially larger in absolute value than their corresponding OLS coefficients in the quasi-structural regressions (A1, A2, B1, and B2). The fact that this difference is greater for blacks is a noteworthy result for as Rosenzweig and Schultz (1983a) have noted, OLS and other direct correlational estimates of prenatal care's effect on early infant deaths may be seriously underestimating its true impact on infant health. For instance, the prenatal care coefficients estimated by OLS in regressions (A1) and (B1) suggest that prompt initiation of prenatal care is more effective in lowering neonatal mortality among whites than it is for blacks. The TSLS estimates reveal just the opposite [regressions (A2) and (B2)].

Table 9.2 Regression Results

	Whites				Blacks			
	A1	A2	A3	A4	B1	B2	B3	B4
	OLS	TSLS	OLS	TSLS	OLS	TSLS	OLS	TSLS
Constant	7.478 (4.98)	9.831 (5.60)	7.223 (7.24)	5.512 (1.78)	17.913 (2.97)	24.929 (3.60)	4.647 (1.87)	8.600 (1.04)
Teen family planning*	−.021 (−2.01)	−.011 (−1.03)	−.025 (−2.64)	−.014 (−1.32)	−.024 (−1.26)	−.025 (−1.27)	−.029 (−1.66)	−.024 (−1.37)
Maternal nutrition program (WIC)*	−.002 (−.78)	−.006 (−2.34)	−.002 (−1.12)	−.004 (−1.46)	−.004 (−.99)	−.009 (−2.19)	−.001 (−.44)	−.008 (−2.06)
Neonatal intensive care*[a]	−.096 (−.63)	−.467 (−.93)	−.219 (−1.48)	−1.176 (−2.26)	−.306 (−1.73)	−.475 (−.89)	−.356 (−2.22)	−.772 (−1.60)
Abortion[a]	−.029 (−4.19)	−.033 (−3.57)	−.025 (−3.72)	−.021 (−2.13)	−.044 (−1.53)	−.085 (−2.01)	−.030 (−1.51)	−.044 (−1.58)
Prenatal care*[a]	−.045 (−5.40)	−.076 (−5.14)	−.024 (−2.99)	−.016 (−.79)	−.030 (−1.69)	−.117 (−2.81)	−.008 (−.49)	−.026 (−.56)
BCHS projects*	.0003 (.23)	−.0002 (−.13)	−.002 (−1.96)	−.001 (−.82)	−.002 (−.77)	−.001 (−.42)	−.006 (−2.37)	−.002 (−.96)
Smoking[a]	.535 (4.65)	.555 (4.76)			.600 (1.06)	1.045 (1.86)		
High-risk women*	5.843 (2.05)	7.366 (2.50)			−4.263 (−.52)	−13.138 (−1.33)		
Low birth weight*[a]			.781 (9.50)	1.046 (3.78)			1.121 (8.39)	1.026 (2.18)
R^2	.108		.184		.036		.195	
F	10.16[b]	9.78[b]	21.51[b]	9.35[d]	1.64[d]	2.66[d]	12.05[b]	3.55[b]
WU test F	2.61[c]		1.57[d]		3.86[b]		.19[d]	

Notes: Asymptotic t-ratios in parentheses. The critical t-ratios at the 5 percent level are 1.64 for a one-tailed test and 1.96 for a two-tailed test. An asterisk next to a variable means it is race-specific.

[a] Endogenous in TSLS equations.
[b] Significant at the 1 percent level.
[c] Significant at the 5 percent level.
[d] Not significant at the 5 percent level.

This implies that remedial behavior among black pregnant women may be an important response to information regarding the health of the fetus.

Based on the Wu test, the null hypothesis of zero correlation between the health inputs and the disturbance term can only be accepted when the percentage of low-birth-weight births is held constant [regressions (A3), (A4), (B3), and (B4)]. This suggests that the unobserved health endowment is effectively controlled for by this endogenous risk factor. Consequently, the TSLS coefficients should be used to measure the total effect of an input on neonatal mortality, whereas the OLS estimates are appropriate when gauging an input's direct effect. Hence, further discussion of the results will focus on regressions (A2), (B2), (A3), and (B3).

All four of the aforementioned equations are significant at the 1 percent level, as indicated by F-values. For whites, in the TSLS estimate of the quasi-structural model (A2), all coefficients have their predicted signs, and five of the eight are highly significant. For the comparable black estimates (B2), seven of the eight coefficients have predicted signs, although not as many of the variables have strong significance levels. In the white OLS equation holding birth weight constant (A3), all coefficients have correct signs and have t-values greater than one in absolute value. In the comparable black equation (B3), all coefficients have correct signs, although fewer are significant as compared to the white equation. Altogether, the model works well in predicting variations in neonatal mortality rates based on medical program usage.

The effects of WIC, abortion, and prenatal care on race-specific neonatal mortality fall in absolute value when birth weight is held constant [see regressions (A2), (A3), (B2), and (B3)]. For blacks, the abortion coefficient falls 65 percent. Nevertheless, its risk-specific effect is still greater than the corresponding white one, although its significance level is only 10 percent.[11] WIC and prenatal care reduce neonatal mortality solely by reducing the percentage of low-birth-weight births. Put differently, the estimated effects are zero once the risk factors are held constant. For whites, the WIC coefficient falls by 67 percent, the abortion coefficient falls by 24 percent, and the prenatal care coefficient falls by 70 percent when the risk factor is included in the set of regressions. In spite of these reductions, the prenatal care and abortion coefficients retain their significance at the 1 percent level.

The above results imply that expansions in prenatal care use lower risk-specific death rates for whites but not for blacks. These findings suggest that the quality of prenatal care is positively related to the quality and quantity of perinatal and newborn care received by white mothers. The absence of this relationship for black women is plausible since the early initiation of prenatal care by these women is a recent phenomenon. For instance, in 1969, 72 percent of white women and 43 percent of black women started their prenatal care in the first trimester of pregnancy (Taffel 1978). The corresponding figures in 1977 were 77 percent of white women and 59 percent of black women (see table 9.1).

In the case of abortion, the above results suggest that the process of fetal selection encouraged by abortion may be improving the survivability of risk-specific births as well as reducing the incidence of low birth weight. The former effect may be the result of births being better planned or "more wanted." That is, births that are not averted may receive more of the unmeasurable inputs such as better nutrition and higher quality care that enhance the health and survivability of newborns of a given birth weight.

The sizable risk-specific BCHS project use and family planning use coefficients reflect positive relationships between these inputs and the percentage of low-birth-weight births. The BCHS result suggests that poor women who obtain prenatal care from M and I projects or community health centers probably do not start to receive care until fairly late in their pregnancies. Moreover, these women may have poorly endowed birth outcomes. Consequently, the receipt of care from BCHS projects does not lower the incidence of low birth weight, but it appears to raise the quantity and quality of perinatal and newborn care.

The same argument may apply for organized teenage family planning use. Chamie et al. (1982) report that counties that serve a high proportion of women at risk of pregnancy are more likely to provide gynecological and prenatal care than counties that serve a smaller proportion of such women. Jones, Namerow, and Philliber (1982) find that more than half of the first-time clients of a large metropolitan family planning clinic previously had been pregnant. In short, a rise in the proportion of low-income women who use organized family planning services may be indicative of a population that has been integrated into a network of prenatal and perinatal care. The births to these women may still be problematic (that is, premature or light), but with better support and care their infants are more likely to survive.

One way to gauge the magnitudes of the estimated relationships between infant health inputs and outcomes is to apply the relevant coefficients to national trends in the inputs between 1964 and 1977. This exercise allows us to shed light on the sources of the rapid decline in the U.S. neonatal mortality rate starting in 1964 by computing the contribution of each input to the downward trend in neonatal mortality. The extrapolations end in 1977 because the regressions pertain to that year. In the period at issue the white neonatal mortality rate declined by 7.5 deaths per thousand live births, from 16.2 to 8.7, or by 46 percent. The black neonatal mortality rate declined by 11.5 deaths per thousand live births, from 27.6 to 16.1, or by 42 percent.

The results of estimating the implied changes in white and black neonatal mortality rates due to trends in the inputs are shown in panels A and B

Table 9.3 Contribution of Selected Factors to Reductions in Neonatal Mortality Rates, 1964–1977

Factor	Panel A: Whites[a]			Panel B: Blacks[b]		
	Direct	Indirect	Total	Direct	Indirect	Total
Organized family planning	.191	−.107	.084	.610	−.084	.526
WIC	.143	.282	.425	.148	1.182	1.330
BCHS project use	.022	−.020	.002	.182	−.152	.030
Neonatal intensive care	.140	—	.140	.534	—	.534
Abortion	.624	.200	.824	.743	1.366	2.109
Prenatal care	.137	.297	.434	.133	1.816	1.949
Total explained reduction[c]			1.9			6.5
Percentage explained			25.3			56.5

Notes: Reduction in deaths per 1,000 live births. Negative sign denotes a predicted increase.
[a] Direct effect from regression (A3). Total effect from regression (A2). Subtraction of the former from the latter gives the indirect effect.
[b] Direct effect from regression (B3). Total effect from regression (B2). Subtraction of the former from the latter gives the indirect effect.
[c] Rounded to one decimal.

of table 9.3, respectively. The direct effect is obtained from the OLS neonatal mortality rate production function that includes birth weight as a regressor. The total effect is obtained from the TSLS estimate of the quasi-structural production function. Subtraction of the former from the latter yields the indirect effect. Thus, the indirect effect shows the reduction in the neonatal mortality rate due to an increase in one of the health inputs between 1964 and 1977 that operates via a reduction in the percentage of low-birth-weight births.[12]

For whites, the statistical analysis "explains" 25 percent of the decline in neonatal mortality. The increase in abortion makes the largest contribution to the decline (0.8 births per thousand live births) followed by prenatal care and WIC (0.4 deaths per thousand live births each) and neonatal intensive care (0.1 deaths per thousand live births). Prenatal care and WIC each have a substantial indirect effect which accounts for approximately two-thirds of the total effect of the input in question.

For blacks, the statistical analysis explains 56 percent of the decline in neonatal mortality. As in the case of whites, abortion makes the largest contribution (2.1 deaths per thousand live births) followed by prenatal care (1.9 deaths per thousand live births), WIC (1.3 deaths per thousand live births), and neonatal intensive care and organized family planning (0.5 deaths per thousand live births each). Prenatal care, WIC, and abortion have sizable indirect effects, and in each case the indirect effect is larger than the direct one.

Some caution should be exercised in interpreting the results in table 9.3 because an increase in abortion use, for example, due to an increase in abortion availability is likely to cause organized family planning use to fall. Put differently, these computations do not provide the reduced form effects that are required to evaluate fully the contributions to reductions in neonatal mortality between 1964 and 1977 of the increased availability of the inputs considered here. Nevertheless, they do provide insight with regard to the role of the expansion in the use of one input with all other inputs held constant. Caution also should be exercised because the results pertain to the actual benefits in terms of neonatal mortality of increases in the inputs in the period considered rather than to the potential benefits of future expansions. Note, however, that a ranking of the magnitude of the effect of each input based on a 10 percent increase in its 1977 value is very similar to the ranking presented in table 9.3.

A final caveat is that, although our production functions include a measure of the quantity of neonatal intensive care, they exclude a measure of its quality. Even if the state-of-the-art in neonatology is fixed in the cross-section, clearly it is not fixed over time. In light of the rapid advances in perinatal and neonatal science since 1964, we undoubtedly understate the growth in a comprehensive measure of the neonatal intensive care input.[13]

It is notable that practically all the black regression coefficients in table 9.2 and all the estimated black effects in table 9.3 exceed the corresponding white coefficients or white effects. This is a key finding because it suggests that the inputs at issue have the potential to reduce the excess mortality rate of black babies, an important goal of public health policy in the United States for a number of years. It also is notable that the combined contribution of abortion, prenatal care, and neonatal intensive care to the reduction in black neonatal mortality (4.5 deaths per thousand live births) exceeds the combined contribution of WIC, BCHS project use, and organized family planning use (1.8 deaths per thousand live births). This is an important result because the first three inputs are used by all segments of the population, while the last three are used by the poor. It implies that blacks may benefit more from developments that affect neonatal mortality rates in all segments of the population than from programs that are targeted at the poor.

5. DISCUSSION

Our results underscore the qualitative and quantitative importance of abortion and prenatal care services in black and white birth outcomes. We find that black neonatal mortality rates are more sensitive to the use of these basic health inputs than are white neonatal mortality rates. We also present evidence with respect to the potential importance of neonatal intensive care in the determination of neonatal mortality rates, particularly for blacks. Neonatal intensive care ranks fourth in importance behind prenatal care, abortion, and WIC in explaining declines in both white and black neonatal mortality between 1964 and 1977. Given the absence of cross-sectional or time-series indexes of the quality of care, the impact of neonatal intensive care undoubtedly is understated. Clearly the development of more comprehensive measures of this input deserves high priority on an agenda for future research.

These results provide suggestive, although far from definitive, explanations of the slowdown in the downward trend in neonatal mortality in the early 1980s. The abortion rate of white women reached a peak in 1980 and was stable between 1980 and 1981. The abortion rate of black and other nonwhite women peaked in 1977 and declined every year since then with the exception of 1980 (Bureau of the Census 1984). The percentage of white women who began prenatal care in their first trimester of pregnancy fell between 1980 and 1981, and the percentage of black women who began prenatal care in their first trimester fell between 1981 and 1982 (Ingram, Makuc, and Kleinman 1986). The introduction and diffusion of new techniques in neonatology slowed appreciably in the late 1970s and early 1980s (McCormick 1985).

The role of public policy in the above developments is not clear-cut. In part the recent trend in abortion may reflect the end of the diffusion of a relatively new contraceptive technique. In part, it also may reflect the Hyde Amendment which has banned federal funding of abortions under Medicaid, except in cases when the woman's life was in danger, since September 1977 (except for the months of February through August 1980). Medicaid cutbacks may have made it more difficult for pregnant low-income women to initiate prenatal care in the first trimester, although the recession of 1981–1982 also may have played a role. Our results identify the use of the WIC program as a much more important determinant of black neonatal mortality than the use of CHCs, M and I projects, or organized family planning services. Declines or modest increases in the percentage of poor black pregnant women serviced by WIC may have retarded the rate of decline in black neonatal mortality, but definitive recent trends in this statistic are not available. In summary, more research is required to provide a fuller explanation of the behavior of the U.S. neonatal mortality rate since 1980. Our study represents a useful first step in this process.

NOTES

Originally published as Hope Corman, Theodore J. Joyce, and Michael Grossman, "Birth Outcome Productions Function in the U.S." *Journal of Human Resources* 22, no. 3 (1987):

339–360. Research for this paper was supported by Grant Number 5 RO1 HD16316 from the National Institute of Child Health and Human Development to the NBER. The authors thank the following for providing data: Kathleen Bajo of Ross Laboratories; Richard Bohrer, Edward Duffy, Joann Gephart, and Robert Nelson of the Bureau of Health Care Delivery and Assistance, DHHS; Stephen M. Davidson of the Northwestern University Program in Hospital and Health Services Administration; Gary Davis of the American Hospital Association; Jacqueline D. Forrest and Stanley K. Henshaw of the Alan Guttmacher Institute; and Letty Wunglueck of the Health Care Financing Administration. They also thank Peter Budetti, Karen Davis, Jacqueline D. Forrest, Stanley K. Henshaw, Salih Neftci, Chris Robinson, David Salkever, T. Paul Schultz, John Strauss, and an anonymous referee for helpful comments and suggestions and Emil Berendt for research assistance. A longer version of this paper with more detailed descriptions of the data and the analytical model is available from the authors. This paper has not undergone the review accorded official NBER publications; in particular, it has not been submitted for approval by the Board of Directors. Any opinions expressed are those of the authors and not those of NICHD or NBER.

1. For example, see Williams 1974, 1979; Grossman and Jacobowitz 1981; Goldman and Grossman 1982; Hadley 1982; Harris 1982; Paneth et al. 1982; Rosenzweig and Schultz 1981, 1982, 1983a, 1983b; Lewit 1983; Kotelchuck et al. 1984. No study entered all variables together in a multivariate birth outcome equation estimated with data covering a large percentage of all births in the United States.

2. We use a two-stage least squares procedure to purge the observed health inputs of their correlation with the endowments. This is based on the assumption that the reduced form determinants of input utilization are not correlated with the endowment. If the reduced form regressors are correlated with the unmeasured inputs, the use of two-stage least squares does not eliminate relationships between measured and unmeasured inputs.

3. One county with a population of at least 50,000 persons in 1970 was eliminated from the sample because it was the only such county characterized as an isolated rural county, with no incorporated place, with a population of at least 2,500 persons in 1970. In addition, Washington, DC, was excluded because of difficulty of defining its relevant market area for neonatal intensive care. For all other counties, we defined the state as the relevant neonatal intensive care area. Since this was impossible for DC, we eliminated the observation. A second reason for excluding it is that Stanley K. Henshaw, who estimates resident abortion rates by states for the Alan Guttmacher Institute, informed us that figures for the states are very reliable but those for DC are very unreliable. Note that we use state-specific resident abortion rates in our analysis because county-specific resident abortion rates are not available. Note also that, although 84 percent of all births in Washington, DC, were black, DC black births accounted for less than 2 percent of all black births in the sample of 358 black counties.

4. For a more detailed explanation of this proposition see Corman, Joyce, and Grossman (1985).

5. Wu's T_2 statistic can be used to test whether a set of right-hand-side regressors is correlated with the residuals. The following description is based on the discussion by Nakamura and Nakamura (1981). Assume the following model:

$$D = HB + X_1C + u \text{ (structural equation)} \tag{F-1}$$

$$H = X_1P_1 + X_2P_2 + V = XP + V \text{ (reduced form equation)}, \tag{F-2}$$

where D is an $N \times 1$ vector of observations on the neonatal mortality rate; H is an $N \times G$ matrix of stochastic health inputs, which may also include birth weight; X_1 is an $N \times K_1$ matrix of exogenous health determinants; X_2 is an $N \times K_2$ matrix of demand determinants; u and V are $N \times 1$ and $N \times G$ matrices of disturbances; and B, C, P_1, and P_2 are $G \times 1$, $K_1 \times 1$, $K_1 \times G$, and $K_2 \times G$ matrices of unknown constants. The test of whether $E(Hu) = 0$, where E is the expected value operator, can be expressed as a test of whether u and V are correlated $[E(Vu) = 0]$. Following Hausman's (1978) derivation, equation (F-1) is rewritten as:

$$D = HB + X_1C + V\alpha + u \tag{F-3}$$

Wu's T_2 test can be expressed as a test of whether $\alpha = 0$. This is a straightforward F-test on a set of linear restrictions. Acceptance of the null hypothesis that $E(Vu) = 0$ is equivalent to the restriction that $\alpha = 0$.

6. We choose a linear rather than a logistic functional form because linear coefficients are more easily interpreted. Maddala (1983, 30) argues that a linear form is appropriate for large, aggregate probability samples such as ours. Preliminary results obtained with logistic and log-linear specifications did not differ in a qualitative sense from those presented in section 3. The linear specification rules out an investigation of the optimal input mix (the combination of inputs that minimizes the cost of producing a given level of infant health), but this is not the focus of our empirical research.

7. The omitted category for the three variables that characterize the eligibility of first-time pregnant women for prenatal care under Medicaid pertains to states that cover no first-time pregnancies because their AFDC programs do not recognize "unborn children."

8. Note that in the case of abortion and neonatal intensive care, both availability and use measures are present. In each case, own availability is a powerful prediction of own use. It has the largest t-ratio in the input demand function and therefore the highest partial correlation coefficient with the dependent variable. These results strengthen our confidence in the abortion and neonatal intensive care availability measures.

9. We do not employ public program use measures to predict prenatal care, abortion, neonatal intensive care, and birth weight in the first stage. Instead, public program availability measures are employed, except in the case of WIC where there is no availability measure. Production functions obtained with public program use measures as first stage predictors were similar to those presented in section 4.

10. Although cigarette consumption is labeled as an endogenous variable in section 4, it should be noted that the same variable is used in OLS and two-stage estimation procedures.

11. Statements concerning statistical significance in the text are based on one-tailed tests except when the estimated effect has the "wrong sign." In this case, two-tailed tests are used.

12. Consider the following model:

$$d = \alpha_0 + \alpha_1 x + \alpha_2 k$$
$$k = \beta_0 + \beta_1 x,$$

where k is the percentage of low-birth-weight births and x is any input. If Δx is the change in x between 1964 and 1977, then the direct effect is $\alpha_1 \Delta x$, the indirect effect is $\beta_1 \alpha_2 \Delta x$, and the total effect is $(\alpha_1 + \beta_1 \alpha_2)\Delta x$. Note that the indirect effect of neonatal intensive care is restricted to be zero because conceptually it is not a cause of low birth weight.

13. In addition to the caveats mentioned in the text, it should be noted that the contribution of abortion may be overstated because all states had laws that outlawed abortion except when it was necessary to preserve a pregnant woman's life in 1964. Many illegal abortions were performed in that period. If illegal abortions affected neonatal mortality, we overstate the abortion effect in table 9.3.

REFERENCES

Bureau of the Census, U.S. Department of Commerce. 1984. *Statistical Abstract of the United States.* Washington, D.C.: GPO.

Chamie, Mary, et al. 1982. "Factors Affecting Adolescents' Use of Family Planning Clinics." *Family Planning Perspectives* 14(3):126–39.

Corman, Hope, and Michael Grossman. 1985. "Determinants of Neonatal Mortality Rates in the U.S.: A Reduced Form Model." *Journal of Health Economics* 4(3): 213–36.

Corman, Hope, Theodore J. Joyce, and Michael Grossman. 1985. "Birth Outcome Production Functions in the U.S." National Bureau of Economic Research Working Paper No. 1729. Cambridge: NBER.

Goldman, Fred, and Michael Grossman. 1982. "The Impact of Public Health Policy: The Case of Community Health Centers." National Bureau of Economic Research Working Paper No. 1020. Cambridge: NBER.

Grossman, Michael, and Steven Jacobowitz. 1981. "Variations in Infant Mortality Rates Among Counties of the United States: The Roles of Public Policies and Programs." *Demography* 18(4): 695–713.

Hadley, Jack. 1982. *More Medical Care, Better Health?* Washington, D.C.: Urban Institute.

Harris, Jeffrey E. 1982. "Prenatal Medical Care and Infant Mortality." In *Economic Aspects of Health*, ed. Victor R. Fuchs. Chicago: University of Chicago Press for the National Bureau of Economic Research.

Hausman, J. 1978. "Specification Tests in Econometrics." *Econometrica* 46(6):1251–71.

Ingram, Deborah D., Diane Makuc, and Joel C. Kleinman. 1986. "National and State Trends in Use of Prenatal Care, 1970–83." *American Journal of Public Health* 76(4): 415–23.

Institute of Medicine. 1985. *Preventing Low Birth Weight.* Washington, D.C.: National Academy Press.

Jones, Judith B., Pearila B. Namerow, and Susan Philliber. 1982. "Adolescents' Use of a Hospital-Based Contraceptive Program." *Family Planning Perspectives* 14(4): 224–31.

Joyce, Theodore J. 1985. "A Structural Model of Birth Outcomes in the U.S." PhD Dissertation, City University of New York Graduate School.

Kotelchuck, Milton, et al. 1984. "WIC Participation and Pregnancy Outcomes: Massachusetts Statewide Evaluation Project." *American Journal of Public Health* 74(10):1086–92.

Lewit, Eugene M. 1983. "The Demand for Prenatal Care and the Production of Healthy Infants." In *Annual Series of Research in Human Capital and Development*, Vol. III, Ismail Sirageldin, David Salkever, and Alan Sorkin. Greenwich, Conn.: JAI Press, Inc.

Maddala, G. S. 1983. *Limited-Dependent and Qualitative Variables in Econometrics.* Cambridge: Cambridge University Press.

McCormick, Marie C. 1985. "The Contribution of Low Birth Weight to Infant Mortality and Childhood Morbidity." *The New England Journal of Medicine* 312(2): 82–90.

Miller, C. Arden. 1985. "Infant Mortality in the U.S." *Scientific American* 235(1): 31–37.

Nakamura, A., and M. Nakamura. 1981. "On the Relationship Among Several Specification Error Tests Presented by Durbin, Wu and Hausman." *Econometrica* 49(6):1583–88.

National Center for Health Statistics, U.S. Department of Health and Human Services. 1985. *Health United States* 1985. DHHS Publication No. (PHS)86-1232. Washington, D.C.: GPO.

Paneth, Nigel, et al. 1982. "Newborn Intensive Care and Neonatal Mortality in Low-Birth Weight Infants." *New England Journal of Medicine* 307(3): 149–55.

Rosenzweig, Mark R., and T. Paul Schultz. 1981. "Education and Household Production of Child Health." *Proceedings of the American Statistical Association, Social Statistics Section.* Washington, D.C.: American Statistical Association.

——. 1982. "The Behavior of Mothers as Inputs to Child Health: The Determinants of Birth Weight, Gestation, and Rate of Fetal Growth." In *Economic Aspects of Health*, ed. Victor R. Fuchs. Chicago: University of Chicago Press for the National Bureau of Economic Research.

——. 1983a. "Consumer Demand and Household Production: The Relationship Between Fertility and Child Mortality." *American Economic Review* 73(2): 38–42.

——. 1983b. "Estimating a Household Production Function: Heterogeneity, the Demand for Health Inputs, and their Effects on Birth Weight." *Journal of Political Economy* 91(5): 723–46.

Rosenzweig, Mark R, and Kenneth I, Wolpin. 1984. "Migration Selectivity and the Effects of Public Programs." Yale University Economic Growth Center Discussion Paper No. 464.

——. 1986. "Evaluating the Effects of Optimally Distributed Public Programs: Child Health and Family Planning Interventions." *American Economic Review* 76(3): 470–82.

Taffel, Selma. 1978. *Prenatal Care in the United States*, 1969–1975. U.S. Department of Health, Education, and Welfare, Public Health Service, National Center for Health Statistics, Vital and Health Statistics, Series 21, No. 33.

Williams, Ronald L. 1974. "Outcome-Based Measurements of Medical Care Output: The Case of Maternal and Infant Health." PhD Dissertation, University of California at Santa Barbara.

——. 1979. "Measuring the Effectiveness of Perinatal Medical Care." *Medical Care* 17(2): 95–110.

Wu, D. 1973. "Alternative Tests of Independence Between Stochastic Regressors and Disturbances." *Econometrica* 41(4): 733–50.

TEN

Unobservables, Pregnancy Resolutions, and Birth Weight Production Functions in New York City

Michael Grossman and Theodore J. Joyce

ABSTRACT

This chapter makes contributions to the estimation of health production functions and the economics of fertility control. We present the first infant health production functions that simultaneously control for self-selection in the resolution of pregnancies as live births or induced abortions and in the use of prenatal medical care services. We also incorporate the decision of a pregnant woman to give birth or to obtain an abortion into economic models of fertility control and use information conveyed by this decision to refine estimates of infant health production functions and demand functions for prenatal medical care.

This chapter makes contributions to two areas of investigation within the context of the household production function approach to consumer behavior (Becker 1965; Michael and Becker 1973): the estimation of health production functions and the economics of fertility control. In the former area we present the first infant health production functions that simultaneously control for self-selection (correlations between unobserved variables and observed outcomes) in the resolution of pregnancies as live births or induced abortions and in the use of prenatal medical care services. In the latter area we incorporate the decision of a pregnant woman to give birth or to obtain an abortion into economic models of fertility control and use information conveyed by this decision to refine estimates of infant health production functions and demand functions for prenatal medical care.

The concept of a health production function, originally developed by Grossman (1972), has been widely accepted and fruitfully applied. Yet, until recently, researchers have tended to emphasize reduced-form as opposed to structural estimates. The reasoning was clear. Unobserved biological factors such as an individual's exogenous health endowment and hard-to-measure endogenous inputs such as nutrition, exercise, and the avoidance of stress can play major roles in the determination of health outcomes. If an individual's behavior is shaped in part by knowledge of his or her endowment or if the unmeasured endogenous inputs are correlated with the included inputs, then estimates of the health technology will be biased.

Recent work on the economic analysis of infant health (measured by birth weight or survival) by Rosenzweig and Schultz (1982, 1983, 1988); Corman, Joyce, and Grossman (1987); and Joyce (1987) has emphasized structural estimates of the health technology. In these studies, two-stage least squares has been applied to control for the adverse selection of health inputs. In particular, Rosenzweig and Schultz have argued that women who anticipate a problematic birth based on conditions unknown to the researcher seek out more remedial care while women with positive expectations seek out less. Consequently, the association between such variables as early prenatal medical care and birth weight is understated when measured by direct correlation measures.

Adverse selection in input use is, however, only one source of bias. In the epidemiological literature, researchers have argued that favorable selection may be a more serious source of confounding (Gortmaker 1979; Institute of Medicine 1985). The efficacy of prenatal care, for example, may be seriously overstated if early care is but one form of healthy behavior. Pregnant women who initiate care promptly may eat more nutritiously, suffer less stress, engage in the appropriate exercise, and use fewer drugs and other potentially harmful substances than women who begin care late. The omission of these hard-to-measure inputs tends to overestimate the impact of early prenatal care on birth weight.

Moreover, the resolution of a pregnancy itself may be characterized by self-selection. With regard to this outcome, selection is favorable if women whose fetuses have poor health endowments are more likely to obtain an abortion or if women who desire to make relatively large investments in their infants are more likely to give birth. On the other hand, selection is adverse if women who make relatively small investments are more likely to give birth.

The use of an instrumental variable approach to correct for self-selection in input use presupposes that this decision is characterized by adverse selection and ignores the problem of self-selection in the resolution of pregnancies. In this chapter, we approach the problem differently and somewhat more generally. Following Heckman (1979), we treat the estimation of infant health production functions and prenatal medical care demand functions as a general problem in self-selection. Specifically, we test whether women who give birth represent a random draw from the population of women who become pregnant. The widespread use of induced abortion since its legalization by the Supreme Court in 1973 has permitted much greater choice in the number and timing of births. In the United States in 1983, 30 percent of all pregnancies (live births plus induced abortions) were terminated by induced abortions (Bureau of the Census 1986). Thus, potentially large biases may result from a failure to incorporate the choice-based nature of micro vital records into estimates of infant health production functions. It is our specific hypothesis that the unobserved factors that affect the decision to give birth not only affect pregnancy outcomes but also condition the behavior of women who choose to give birth during pregnancy as well.

Our study is based on a cohort of pregnant women in New York City in 1984. In that year, 45 percent of all pregnancies to New York City residents ended in induced abortions. We estimate a three-equation model. The first equation is the probability of giving birth, given that a woman is pregnant. With this as our criterion equation, we test for self-selection in the infant health (measured by birth weight) production function and in the prenatal medical care demand function. Empirically, our estimates differ from those obtained by Rosenzweig and Schultz (1982, 1983, 1988) because they use micro vital records on live births alone. Not only does our methodology obviate the need to assert a priori whether adverse or favorable selection is dominant, but the sign pattern of the residual covariances indicates which type of selection characterizes both the decision to give birth and the decision to initiate prenatal care promptly.

Since our framework includes an implicit equation for the probability of becoming pregnant, we incorporate induced abortion as an alternative to traditional methods of contraception into economic models of fertility control (e.g., Michael and Willis 1976; Hotz and Miller 1988). These models emphasize the use of contraception to reduce the uncertainty associated with the number and timing of births. Induced abortion eliminates much of this uncertainty at a positive price. By assuming that the prices of contraception and abortion have unmeasured components that vary among women, we enrich the theoretical literature on the optimal number and quality of children (e.g., Becker and Lewis 1973; Willis 1973) and gain a better understanding of the earliest indicator of child quality—infant health—and the resources allocated to its production. In particular, we show that the prices of contraception and abortion, as well as the health endowment of the fetus, simultaneously influence decisions with regard to pregnancy resolutions and input selection.

1. ANALYTICAL FRAMEWORK

Rosenzweig and Schultz (1982, 1983, 1988), Corman et al. (1987), and Joyce (1987) have generated and estimated birth outcome production functions and input and output demand functions for infant health in the context of a static economic model of the family and household production. To introduce the decision of a pregnant woman to give birth or to obtain an abortion into this model, note that a dynamic version of it implies an optimal number of children for the ith woman in year t (C_{it}^*). If C_{it} is the actual number of children that a pregnant woman will have in year t in the absence of an abortion (parity plus one), then she will give birth provided $\pi_{it} = C_{it}^* - C_{it} \geq 0$ and will abort provided $\pi_{it} < 0$.

Equations for the probability of a birth (π_i), the production function of birth weight (b_i), and the demand for prenatal medical care (m_i) are specified by equations (1)–(3). For convenience, the time subscripts and the intercepts are suppressed. The birth probability function is assumed to be linear, although later a probit specification will be used. The three equations are

$$\pi_i = \alpha_1 z_i + u_{1i}, \quad u_{1i} = \alpha_2 c_i + \alpha_3 a_i + \alpha_4 e_i, \tag{1}$$

$$b_i = \beta_1 x_i + \beta_2 m_i + u_{2i}, \, u_{2i} = \beta_3 q_i + \beta_4 e_i, \tag{2}$$

$$m_i = \gamma_1 y_i + u_{3i}, \, u_{3i} = \gamma_2 c_i + \gamma_3 a_i + \gamma_4 e_i. \tag{3}$$

In this system of equations, z_i, x_i, y_i, c_i, a_i, and e_i denote exogenous variables or vectors of variables. For instance, in the birth probability equation (1), z_i stands for such determinants of the optimal number of children and the spacing of births as family income, mother's education, and marital status. In the same equation, c_i is the cost of contraception, which is directly related to money price and indirectly related to availability and to contraceptive efficiency or knowledge. This cost also has a psychic component due to joint production (Pollak and Wachter 1975): an increase in contraceptive use lowers the probability of becoming pregnant but may also reduce the gratification yielded by sexual intercourse. The variable a_i gives the direct, indirect, and psychic costs of obtaining an abortion. The variable e_i measures the health endowment of the fetus.

Examples of members of the $\mathbf{x}_i$ vector in the birth weight production function (2) are the sex of the infant and the mother's prior fetal loss (the number of previous spontaneous abortions—including fetal deaths—that occurred after the nineteenth week of gestation). Examples of members of the $\mathbf{y}_i$ vector in the prenatal care demand function (3) are such correlates of the price of prenatal care as the presence of health insurance that finances this service and the number of prenatal care providers in the mother's area of residence. The roles of the u_{ji} ($j = 1, 2, 3$), which are linear functions of c_i, a_i, and e_i, are discussed below. In addition to prenatal care, the birth weight production function contains another endogenous input (q_i), which reflects such healthy behaviors as proper diet, appropriate exercise, and the avoidance of stress. The model includes an unspecified demand function for healthy behaviors that has the same arguments as the demand function for prenatal medical care. Finally, each of the three equations contains an unspecified random disturbance term.

A reduction in the price of contraception is expected to raise the probability of giving birth ($\alpha_2 < 0$), while an increase in the price of abortion is expected to raise this probability ($\alpha_3 > 0$). The basic force that generates these predictions is an implicit equation for the probability of becoming pregnant. Under the plausible assumption that contraception and abortion are alternative methods of birth control, a rise in the price of contraception or a decline in the price of abortion raises this probability. As these propositions imply, pregnancies to women with low costs of averting them (low contraceptive costs) may be termed "wanted" pregnancies. It also follows that a fall in the cost of contraception or abortion raises the quantity of prenatal care ($\gamma_2 < 0$, $\gamma_3 < 0$) and raises the level of the healthy behavior input. The force at work here is that a reduction in the cost of averting a pregnancy or a birth lowers the optimal number of children and raises the optimal amount of resources allocated to each birth (Becker and Lewis 1973; Willis 1973). This is another sense in which a reduction in the price of averting a birth raises the level of "wantedness."

It is very likely that women whose potential or actual fetuses have favorable health endowments demand a larger optimal number of children and are more likely to choose to give birth than women with unfavorable endowments ($\alpha_4 > 0$). Moreover, the coefficients of the endowment in the demand functions for prenatal care (γ_4) and the healthy behavior are negative because of a reallocation of resources away from infant health induced by a better endowment.[1]

Given measures of the price of contraception, the price of abortion, the health endowment of the fetus, and the healthy behavior input, one could quantify precisely the effects described above and also obtain an estimate of the coefficient of prenatal care in the birth weight production function (β_2) that controls for the endowment and healthy behaviors. Since these variables are not observed or measured imperfectly, this is not possible. Nevertheless, it still is possible to shed considerable light on their roles in reproductive outcomes. The basic idea is to include their levels and effects in the disturbance term in each equation (u_{ji}) and then to obtain estimates of the covariances between disturbance terms across equations.[2]

To be specific, assume that u_{ji} ($j = 1, 2, 3$) has a zero mean, and denote the three pairwise covariances between disturbance terms as σ_{12}, σ_{13}, and σ_{23}. Then

$$\sigma_{12} = \alpha_4 \beta_4 \sigma_e^2 + \alpha_2 \beta_3 \sigma_{qc} + \alpha_3 \beta_3 \sigma_{qa}, \tag{4}$$

$$\sigma_{13} = \alpha_4 \gamma_4 \sigma_e^2 + \alpha_2 \gamma_2 \sigma_c^2 + \alpha_3 \gamma_3 \sigma_a^2, \tag{5}$$

$$\sigma_{23} = \beta_4 \gamma_4 \sigma_e^2 + \beta_3 \gamma_2 \sigma_{qc} + \beta_3 \gamma_3 \sigma_{qa}, \tag{6}$$

where σ_j^2, ($j = e, c, a$) is the variance of variable j and σ_{qj} ($j = c, a$) is the covariance between q and j. It is assumed that e, c, and a are mutually uncorrelated and that q does not depend on e. (The conclusions reached are not sensitive to the lack of these relationships.) Recall that α_3 and α_4 are positive, while γ_2, γ_3, γ_4, σ_{qc}, and σ_{qa} are negative. Moreover, β_3 and β_4 are positive since an increase in the healthy behavior input or an increase in the health endowment of the fetus raises birth weight.

The sign patterns of the covariances identify whether the health endowment of the fetus, the cost of contraception, or the cost of abortion is the dominant unmeasured determinant of reproductive outcomes. For instance, suppose that the prices of abortion and contraception do not vary ($\sigma_c^2 = \sigma_a^2 = \sigma_{qc} = \sigma_{qa} = 0$). Then σ_{12} is positive, while σ_{13} and σ_{23} are negative. That is, an increase in the health endowment raises the probability of giving birth and birth weight (u_{1i} and u_{2i} increase), while it lowers the quantity of prenatal care demanded (u_{3i} declines). Now suppose that there is no variation in the price of abortion or in the health endowment. Then each covariance is positive. A reduction in the cost of contraception makes a birth more likely (u_{1i} rises), causes the healthy behavior input and therefore birth weight to expand (u_{2i} rises), and causes the quantity of prenatal care to grow (u_{3i} rises). Finally, if the price of abortion alone varies, σ_{12} and σ_{13} are negative, while σ_{23} is positive.[3]

The health endowment model (no variation in c or a) is the one emphasized by Rosenzweig and Schultz (1982, 1983, 1988) and by us in our previous research (Corman, Joyce, and Grossman 1987; Joyce 1987). It may be termed a model with adverse selection in input use because women who demand relatively large amounts of prenatal care have poor endowments. It also is a model with favorable selection in pregnancy resolution because women with relatively good endowments are more likely to give birth. The cost of contraception model (no variation in a or e) and the cost of abortion model (no variation in c or e) reflect favorable selection in input use because prenatal care and healthy behaviors are positively related. The cost of contraception model is characterized by favorable selection in pregnancy resolution because women with larger optimal values of m and q are more likely to give birth. The reverse holds in the cost of abortion model.[4] A unique sign pattern emerges in each model, which permits one to identify the relevant one. Moreover, identification is based solely on the signs of σ_{12} and σ_{13}, which is important because the procedure described below yields direct estimates of these two parameters.

When all three determinants vary, the sign of a given covariance is ambiguous. But their sign patterns still identify the dominant factor.[5] To summarize, the estimation of the model specified here and the pairwise covariances between its disturbance terms shed light on the qualitative and quantitative importance of hard-to-measure determinants of birth outcomes.

To estimate the three-equation model of birth outcomes, we employ procedures developed by Heckman (1979). The estimation method not only yields the covariances (σ_{12} and σ_{13}) but also recognizes that the coefficients of the birth weight production function are biased if the censored nature of the birth sample is ignored. Thus, it provides an estimate of the prenatal care coefficient (β_2) that potentially controls both for adverse selection and for favorable selection in input use. This coefficient is biased downward by adverse selection and biased upward by favorable selection in computations that ignore these factors.

Equations (1), (2), and (3) pertain to all pregnant woman, but the last two are observed only for women who give birth. These are women for whom $\pi_i \geq 0$ or $u_{1i} \geq -\alpha_1 z_i$. In such a sample, the expected value of birth weight or prenatal care is

$$E(b_i \mid \mathbf{x}_i, m_i, \pi_i \geq 0) = \beta_1 \mathbf{x}_i + \beta_2 m_i + E(u_{2i} \mid u_{1i} \geq -\alpha_1 z_i), \tag{7}$$

$$E(m_i \mid \mathbf{y}_i, \pi_i \geq 0) = \gamma_1 \mathbf{y}_i + E(u_{3i} \mid u_{1i} \geq -\alpha_1 z_i). \tag{8}$$

As emphasized by Heckman, if u_{1i} and u_{2i} are correlated, the conditional mean of u_{2i} in equation (7) is not zero, and the regressors in the equation are correlated with the disturbance term. Hence, ordinary least squares (OLS) estimates of its coefficients are biased. Exactly the same comments apply to equation (8). As we have already seen, there are good reasons to expect σ_{12} and σ_{13} to be nonzero.

Heckman has shown that unbiased estimates of equations (7) and (8) can be obtained under the assumption that the joint distributions of u_{1i}, u_{2i} and u_{1i}, u_{3i} are bivariate normal densities. His procedure is to fit the birth probability equation (1) as a probit function and to compute the inverse of the Mills ratio (λ_i) for each woman who gives birth:

$$\lambda_t = \frac{f(Q_i)}{F(Q_i)}. \tag{9}$$

Here $Q_i = \alpha_1 z_i/\sigma_1$, and f and F are, respectively, the density and distribution functions for a standard normal variable. The inverse of the Mills ratio is then inserted as a regressor in equations (7) and (8), which, after disturbance terms with zero means (υ_{2i} and υ_{3i}) are added, become

$$b_i = \beta_1 x_i + \beta_2 m_i + \left(\frac{\sigma_{12}}{\sigma_1}\right)\lambda_i + \upsilon_{2i}, \tag{10}$$

$$m_t = \gamma_1 y_i + \left(\frac{\sigma_{13}}{\sigma_1}\right)\lambda_i + \upsilon_{3i}. \tag{11}$$

Note that the coefficients of λ_i in (10) and (11) estimate σ_{12} and σ_{13}, respectively, up to a positive scale factor ($1/\sigma_1$).[6]

One conceptual issue that arises in the context of the estimation of the model pertains to the potential endogeneity of prenatal care in the birth weight production function. It is clear that m_i and the disturbance term (u_{2i}) in the birth weight production function (2) are correlated if u_{2i} is correlated with the disturbance term (u_{3i}) in the demand function for prenatal care (3). From equation (6), σ_{23} is nonzero unless $-\beta_4 \gamma_4 \sigma_e^2 = \beta_3 \gamma_2 \sigma_{qc} + \beta_3 \gamma_3 \sigma_{qa}$. Although the disturbance terms in equations (2) and (3) undoubtedly are correlated, the disturbance terms in equations (10) and (11) are less likely to be correlated because both equations include the inverse of the Mills ratio (λ_i) as a regressor. Differences in λ_i among women who give birth reflect differences in the health endowment of the fetus and the costs of contraception and abortion. Since these factors generate the correlation between disturbance terms, the biases that they introduce are reduced when λ_i is employed in the equation.

More formally, weighted (to correct for heteroskedasticity) OLS estimation of the birth weight production function is appropriate when a single factor generates the three covariances among the disturbance terms. For example, suppose that only the health endowment varies. Then each of the three pairwise correlation coefficients (ρ_{ij}) equals one in absolute value, and the coefficient of λ_i in the estimated birth weight equation ($\beta_4 \sigma_e$) differs from the coefficient of the health endowment (e) in the structural birth weight equation (β_4) only by a positive scale factor (σ_e). Now suppose that the cost of contraception model fully described the data. Then $\rho_{12} = \rho_{23} = \sigma_{qc}/\sigma_c$ and $\rho_{13} = 1$. Once again, the coefficient of λ_i in the birth weight production function $(-\beta_3\sigma_{qc}/\sigma_c)$ differs from the coefficient of the healthy behavior input (q) in the structural equation (β_3) only by a positive scale factor $(-\sigma_{qc}/\sigma_c)$. When more than one factor varies, two-stage least squares (TSLS) estimation of the production function with prenatal care treated as an endogenous variable may be appropriate. We examine this proposition by using the TSLS probit method for simultaneous equations models with selectivity developed by Lee, Maddala, and Trost (1980) and the Wu-Hausman endogeneity test (Wu 1973; Hausman 1978).

2. DATA AND ESTIMATION

Data on births and abortions are taken from New York City vital statistics in 1984. In that year there were approximately 105,000 singleton live births and 89,000 induced abortions to New York City residents. Our analysis is based on randomly chosen subsamples of the combined population of births and induced abortions. We examined 11,591 pregnancies to white, non-Hispanic women twenty years and older and 11,016 pregnancies to black, non-Hispanic women of the same age.[7] We excluded adolescents in order to minimize problems of endogeneity. This issue is discussed in greater detail below.

Data from the abortion and birth certificates were augmented with 1980 census data that had been aggregated from the census tract to the health area level. Thus, we were able to measure the race-specific percentage of persons below the poverty level by health area. New York City is divided into 352 health areas; the average health area contains between 15,000 and 25,000 residents. Other health area measures included the number of family planning clinics, abortion providers, and prenatal care clinics per 10,000 women aged fifteen to forty-four as well as a dichotomous indicator of whether the woman lived in an area served by the Supplemental Food Program for Women, Infants, and Children (WIC). A description of the variables is provided in table 10.1.

Prenatal medical care is measured by the number of months a woman delays before seeking medical care for her pregnancy. Women who received no care are assumed to have delayed ten months. This prenatal care variable is a *negative* correlate of the quantity and quality of care, while the theory developed in section 1 pertains to a *positive* correlate of care. Thus, the empirical measure of prenatal care should have a *negative* regression coefficient in the birth weight production function (equation [10]). For the same reason, the coefficient of the inverse of the Mills ratio in the prenatal care demand function (equation [11]) is *negative* in the cost of contraception model, while it is *positive* in the health endowment and cost of abortion models.

Table 10.1 Description of Variables

Birth weight	Weight of an infant in grams
Prenatal care delay	Number of months from when a woman conceived until she made her first prenatal care visit
Induced abortions	Number of previous induced abortions
Spontaneous abortions	Number of previous spontaneous abortions (including fetal deaths)
Late spontaneous abortions	Number of previous spontaneous abortions that occurred after the nineteenth week of gestation
Parity	Number of previous live births
Age 35–39	Dichotomous variable that equals one if the woman is 35–39 years of age
Age 40 and over	Dichotomous variable that equals one if the woman is 40 years or older
Education <9	Dichotomous variable that equals one if the woman completed fewer than 9 years of schooling
Education = 12	Dichotomous variable that equals one if the woman completed 12 years of schooling
Education >12	Dichotomous variable that equals one if the woman completed more than 12 years of schooling
Illegitimacy	Dichotomous variable that equals one if the woman is not married
Medicaid	Dichotomous variable that equals one if the abortion or birth was financed by Medicaid
Self-financed	Dichotomous variable that equals one if the abortion or birth was self-financed
Male	Dichotomous variable that equals one if the infant is male
Private service	Dichotomous variable that equals one if the woman's private physician delivered the birth
Narcotics	Dichotomous variable that equals one if the pregnancy was complicated by narcotics
Tobacco	Dichotomous variable that equals one if the pregnancy was complicated by smoking
Alcohol	Dichotomous variable that equals one if the pregnancy was complicated by alcohol
Family planning clinics	Number of family planning clinics per 10,000 women aged 15–44 in a health area*
Abortion providers	Number of abortion providers per 10,000 women aged 15–44 in a health area
Prenatal care clinics	Number of prenatal care clinics per 10,000 women aged 15–44 in a health area

Table 10.1 (*Continued*)

WIC center	Dichotomous variable that equals one if the woman resided in a health area district that contained an office for the Supplemental Nutrition Program for Women, Infants, and Children**
Poverty	Race-specific percentage of people below the poverty level in 1980 in a health area
λ	Inverse of the Mills ratio, which is a monotonically decreasing function of the probability of giving birth given that a woman is pregnant

* The health area is the smallest geographical area identified on the birth and abortion certificates. Data on the number of family planning clinics, abortion providers, prenatal care clinics, and WIC centers come from the Alan Guttmacher Institute and the New York City Department of Health.

** There are thirty health districts in New York City. Each contains approximately ten health areas. WIC had thirteen locations in New York City in 1983 at which women could enroll and receive food coupons. Nine of these centers also housed maternal and infant care projects. They provide prenatal and obstetrical care to poor women under the 1963 amendment to Title V of the Social Security Act.

The specification of the birth weight production function is based on the structural relationship between medical and biological inputs and the birth outcome. We treat the prenatal care demand equation and birth probability equation as reduced forms. As discussed in section 1, we apply Heckman's two-step procedure to correct for biases due to self-selection. Following Lee, Maddala, and Trost (1980), we also estimate a model in which prenatal care is treated as an endogenous input in the birth weight equation. Both models require that we impose restrictions in order to achieve identification. The birth weight equation excludes measures of income and availability. At the same time it includes the sex of the child and whether the birth was complicated by alcohol, narcotics, or tobacco, and whether the birth was delivered by a private physician. Thus, the birth weight equation easily meets the rank and order conditions for identification.

Identification of the prenatal care demand function is more problematic. Identification can be achieved via the nonlinear relationship between the inverse of the Mills ratio (λ) and the regressors in the birth probability equation. In other words, even if the vector z_i in equation (1) and the vector y_i in equation (3) contain the same set of variables, the equations are still identified. Nevertheless, the model is on firmer grounds if there are unique determinants of each equation.

We assume that the availability of family planning clinics, the availability of abortion providers, and the number of previous induced abortions have no impact on the demand for prenatal care. This is most defensible in a model in which variations in the health endowment are small, so that differences in the monetary and psychic costs of contraception and abortion are fully captured by variations in λ. Moreover, contrary to spontaneous abortions, there is little evidence that links induced abortions to subsequent reproductive difficulties (Hogue, Cates, and Tietze 1982). We include parity in the prenatal care demand equation but exclude it from the birth probability equation because the left-hand side of the latter equation is mechanically related to parity.[8] We include parity in the prenatal care demand function because it proxies experience with pregnancy and birth. In addition, parity and the number of late spontaneous abortions may control, in part, for a woman's health endowment. Finally, the availability of prenatal care clinics and WIC centers is an obvious determinant of the receipt of early prenatal care but is much less closely related to optimal family size and the decision to give birth.

Although the birth probability function is termed a reduced-form equation, certain regressors in it are potentially endogenous. Among teenagers, for instance, education may determine the probability of aborting, but years of schooling completed is clearly related to the time spent pregnant (Hofferth 1987). A similar issue occurs between Medicaid status and pregnancy resolution. Among unmarried, nulliparous adolescents, giving birth is a precondition for receiving continued support from Medicaid and additional support from welfare. Marital status is a third example. Between 1980 and 1981, 28 percent of all white first births and 8 percent of all black first births to adolescents were conceived premaritally but born inside of marriage (Hofferth and Hayes 1987, vol. 1). In short, the decision to give birth, especially among adolescents, may be determined simultaneously with the decision to complete school, apply for Medicaid, or get married (Leibowitz, Eisen, and Chow 1986). Therefore, to minimize these problems we estimate the model for women twenty years of age or more since the endogeneity of marital status, Medicaid, and education should be less relevant for these women.[9]

We treat prenatal medical care as the only endogenous variable in the birth weight production function, yet other variables in this equation could be viewed in a similar manner. These include mother's age, parity, and cigarette smoking, all of which are treated as endogenous by Rosenzweig and Schultz (1982, 1983, 1988) in the estimation of birth weight production functions in the 1967–1969 and 1980 U.S. National Natality Followback Surveys. We examine the endogeneity of prenatal care alone in the production function because we have a well-specified equation for the demand for this input. Moreover, both the birth weight production function and the prenatal care demand function must be estimated to ascertain whether the cost of contraception, the cost of abortion, or the health endowment of the fetus is the dominant unmeasured determinant of reproductive outcomes. The estimation of other equations is not essential in accomplishing this goal. Since prenatal care is the dependent variable in the demand function, it is logical to consider its endogeneity in the production function.

3. RESULTS

Empirical estimates of the birth probability equation and prenatal care demand equations are presented in table 10.2. The birth probability equation is estimated by maximum likelihood probit. Two estimates of the prenatal care demand equation are shown. The first is estimated by OLS without correcting for selection. The second employs the inverse of the Mills ratio as a regressor and adjusts the standard errors as suggested by Heckman (1979). Table 10.3 presents three estimates of the birth weight production function. The first equation is obtained by OLS with no attempt to correct for selection or endogeneity. The second specification corrects for selection but treats prenatal care as exogenous. The third uses the TSLS procedure outlined by Lee et al. (1980) to correct for the endogeneity of prenatal care as well as for selectivity.

In discussing the results, we focus on the role of sample selection bias and on the effect of prenatal care on birth weight. There is strong evidence of selectivity bias in the birth weight production function and prenatal demand equation among blacks. There is no evidence of such bias among whites. For blacks, the results suggest that the unobserved factors that raise the probability of giving birth are positively correlated with the unobserved factors that decrease delay in the initiation of prenatal care and increase birth weight.

For black women, the sign patterns among the residual covariances are consistent with a model that emphasizes the cost of contraception. In particular, black women for whom the shadow price of contraception is relatively high are more likely to abort a pregnancy than their counterparts who face a lower shadow price and whose pregnancies were more likely to have been planned. The latter group should consume more prenatal care (delay less) and invest in other healthy behaviors that improve birth weight.

One explanation for the racial differences with respect to selectivity bias is that the shadow price of contraception is greater for blacks than it is for whites. Further, the shadow price is apt to vary more among blacks than it does among whites. Racial differences in contraceptive use and abortion are consistent with this interpretation (Pratt et al. 1984; Henshaw et al. 1985; Stephen, Rindfuss, and Bean 1988).

Failure to correct for self-selection can yield biased estimates of the health technology. For example, the effect of illegitimacy rises by 50 percent in absolute value when the inverse of the Mills ratio is included in the birth weight equation for blacks. Since unmarried women are more likely to abort, those who do not abort may have lower contraceptive costs. As a result, the coefficient on illegitimacy is understated if sample selection is ignored. It should also be noted that the impact of postsecondary education falls and the incremental benefit of

Table 10.2 Birth Probability and Prenatal Care (Months of Delay) Demand for White and Black Women 20 Years and Older

	Whites				Blacks	
	Probit (1)	Prenatal Care (2)	Prenatal Care* (3)	Probit (4)	Prenatal Care (5)	Prenatal Care* (6)
Intercept	1.524 (21.73)	3.311 (33.34)	3.304 (32.93)	.836 (15.79)	4.093 (28.06)	4.197 (27.18)
Abortion providers	-.026 (-2.21)			.026 (2.06)		
Family planning clinics	-.006 (-.59)			.005 (.71)		
Prenatal care clinics		-.013 (-.87)	-.014 (-.90)	...	-.031 (-1.41)	-.034 (-1.55)
WIC center		.006 (-.14)	-.006 (-.14)	...	-.354 (-4.95)	-.355 (-4.97)
Poverty	-.204 (-2.35)	.014 (5.53)	.014 (5.49)	.0004 (.34)	.019 (5.99)	.019 (6.02)
Medicaid	.351 (6.84)	1.238 (14.44)	1.244 (14.34)	.163 (5.60)	.909 (10.38)	.882 (9.98)
Self-financed		.477 (7.24)	.476 (7.24)	...	1.169 (9.48)	1.160 (9.42)
Spontaneous abortions	.091 (2.95)			.132 (5.51)		
Induced abortions	-.560 (-31.43)			-.447 (-33.94)		
Education <9	-.548 (-4.77)	.340 (2.01)	.330 (1.94)	.461 (4.92)	-.140 (-.72)	-.193 (-.98)

	(1)	(2)	(3)	(4)	(5)	(6)
Education = 12	-.262	-.490	-.494	-.420	-.264	-.192
	(-3.97)	(-5.10)	(-5.13)	(-11.35)	(-2.69)	(-1.85)
Education >12	-.174	-.594	-.598	-.225	-.580	-.533
	(-2.60)	(-6.06)	(-6.09)	(-5.45)	(-5.25)	(-4.74)
Age 35–39	-.049	-.083	-.085	-.090	-.301	-.297
	(-1.05)	(-1.33)	(-1.36)	(-1.87)	(-2.25)	(-2.22)
Age 40 and over	-.596	-.234	-.247	-.404	-.272	-.225
	(-6.74)	(-1.57)	(-1.63)	(-4.32)	(-.98)	(-.81)
Late spontaneous abortions		-.057	-.057		-.060	-.074
		(-.25)	(-.25)		(-.30)	(-.37)
Illegitimacy	-1.915	.913	.854	-.654	.098	.214
	(-57.27)	(11.53)	(5.80)	(-22.55)	(1.23)	(2.18)
Parity		.096	.096		.174	.181
		(5.69)	(5.67)		(6.51)	(6.71)
λ			.050			-.278
			(.47)			(-2.03)
F-statistic	6,130	85.04	78.98		38.50	36.07
χ^2 statistic				2,238		
R^2	.131	.131	.131		.092	.093
Observations	11,589	7,361	7,361	11,016	4,924	4,924

Note: Asymptotic t-ratios are in parentheses.
* Corrected for selection.

Table 10.3 Birth Weight Production Functions for White and Black Women 20 Years and Older

	Whites (N = 7,361)			Blacks (N = 4,924)		
	OLS	OLS*	TSLS**	OLS	OLS*	TSLS**
Intercept	3,236.840 (86.05)	3,231.580 (85.38)	3,304.470 (42.42)	3,154.790 (93.39)	3,126.60 (188.39)	3,253.200 (31.58)
Education <9	142.706 (2.73)	135.660 (2.63)	142.112 (2.73)	51.477 (1.10)	67.109 (1.42)	61.977 (1.27)
Education = 12	47.513 (1.64)	43.615 (1.50)	31.072 (.99)	60.697 (2.60)	37.820 (1.52)	28.640 (1.09)
Education >12	71.021 (2.41)	67.472 (2.28)	50.819 (1.54)	84.098 (3.16)	68.990 (2.54)	45.821 (1.48)
Age 35–39	-32.386 (-1.72)	-33.760 (-1.79)	-36.478 (-1.92)	21.205 (.66)	19.271 (.61)	8.312 (.25)
Age 40 and over	14.816 (.33)	5.282 (.12)	-.346 (-.01)	-61.360 (-.93)	-76.584 (-1.15)	-85.518 (-1.25)
Late spontaneous abortions	-94.597 (-1.39)	-94.864 (-1.40)	-96.308 (-1.42)	-58.265 (-1.22)	-53.575 (-1.12)	-55.618 (-1.13)
Illegitimacy	-98.187 (-4.04)	-139.368 (-3.22)	-111.093 (-2.232)	-66.120 (-3.64)	-99.938 (-4.50)	-82.897 (-3.34)
Parity	25.261 (5.11)	25.215 (5.09)	28.069 (4.95)	8.324 (1.30)	6.531 (1.01)	12.306 (1.61)
Private service	34.094 (1.70)	34.204 (1.71)	32.825 (1.66)	24.975 (1.22)	20.520 (1.00)	22.615 (1.02)

Male	120.366 (10.10)	120.226 (10.09)	119.652 (10.02)	114.054 (6.79)	114.995 (6.86)	114.79 (6.64)
Tobacco	−44.615 (−.90)	−44.341 (−.89)	−42.416 (−.85)	−188.901 (−5.14)	−186.753 (−5.09)	−187.156 (−4.95)
Alcohol	248.803 (3.91)	249.147 (3.94)	253.288 (3.98)	47.816 (.48)	49.387 (.50)	55.985 (.55)
Narcotics	−356.786 (−3.86)	−361.728 (−3.91)	−362.335 (−3.91)	−325.128 (−4.52)	−334.900 (−4.66)	−352.625 (−4.79)
Prenatal care delay	−4.472 (−1.22)	−4.384 (−1.20)	−23.145 (−1.35)	−12.616 (−3.60)	−12.380 (−3.54)	−37.428 (−1.97)
λ		36.149 (1.15)	33.192 (1.05)		85.606 (2.64)	74.022 (2.16)
F-statistic	16.29	15.27		14.38	13.90	
Wu-test F***		1.49			1.18	
R^2	.030	.030		.039	.041	

Note: Asymptotic t-ratios are in parentheses.

* Corrected for selection.

** Prenatal care delay is endogenous.

*** The critical $F_{(1,\infty)}$ at the 5 percent level is 3.84.

a high school diploma becomes statistically insignificant when selectivity bias is corrected.

Our results for blacks indicate that women who aborted would have given birth to lighter infants if they had selected the birth option and if they had had the same mean values of the observed variables in the birth weight equation as women who actually gave birth. One way to gauge the magnitude of the effect is to compare it to that of an observed risk factor for birth outcomes. Among blacks, complications due to smoking reduce birth weight by 187 grams or by 5.8 percent relative to a mean of 3,184 for pregnancies not complicated by smoking. On the other hand, potential mean birth weight in the abortion sample falls short of birth weight in the birth sample by 118 grams because of unobserved inputs alone.[10] This amounts to a differential of 3.7 percent relative to the observed mean of 3,173 for all black women in the birth sample. Thus, the impact of unobserved healthy behaviors is almost two-thirds as large in absolute value as the effect of smoking. Finally, if we allow for differences in both observed and unobserved characteristics, the potential mean birth weight of women who aborted would be 140 grams less than the observed mean birth weight.

As expected, the OLS coefficients of prenatal care delay are negative. That is, the longer a woman delays between conception and her first prenatal care visit, the lighter the infant at birth. In the case of whites, each month of delay reduces birth weight by 4.4 grams, but the coefficient is not significant at the 5 percent level on a one-tailed test. The figure for blacks is 12.4, which is significant at the 5 percent level. The results for whites are almost identical to the OLS estimates obtained by Rosenzweig and Schultz (1988) with data on births to women of all races from the 1980 U.S. National Natality Followback Survey. However, Rosenzweig and Schultz emphasize the TSLS estimates, which reveal that a month's delay in the initiation of prenatal care decreases birth weight by 91 grams, a twenty-fold increase over the estimates they obtain by OLS.

When we treat prenatal care as an endogenous input, the TSLS estimate for blacks is three times greater than the coefficient obtained by OLS. The former estimate remains statistically significant at the 5 percent level. For whites the coefficient of prenatal care increases sixfold when estimated by TSLS, but the null hypothesis of no effect cannot be rejected. Although the direction of the change between the OLS and TSLS estimates is similar to that obtained by Rosenzweig and Schultz, the magnitude of the change is substantially less. Moreover, we find no empirical evidence that prenatal care should be treated as endogenous. Following Heckman (1980) and later Nakamura and Nakamura (1981), we applied a Wu test in which the residuals from the equation predicting prenatal care corrected for selection were entered as a right-hand-side regressor in the birth weight equation. We could not reject the null hypothesis of no correlation in either the white or black specifications at the 5 percent level. The relevant F statistics are presented in table 10.3.[11]

In section 2, we called attention to the potential endogeneity of Medicaid status and legitimacy status in the birth probability equation. Although data suggest that this is most relevant for white teenagers, we decided to examine the stability of our results by omitting these two variables from the birth probability equation. Their endogeneity is particularly relevant in this equation because Medicaid status and marital status can change between conception and birth. Empirically, we are forced to measure marital status, for example, of women who abort at a time shortly after conception, while we measure marital status of women who give birth at birth. These timing considerations are not relevant in the birth weight production function and in the prenatal care demand function. Therefore, legitimacy status was retained as a regressor in both equations, and Medicaid status was retained as a regressor in the demand function.

The conclusions reached in this section are not sensitive to the changes in specification discussed above. In particular, the coefficients of the inverse of the Mills ratio (not shown) remain insignificant for whites but significant for blacks in both the OLS and TSLS models. For blacks, the sign pattern of residual covariances (a positive covariance between the disturbance terms in the birth probability and birth weight equations and a negative covariance between the disturbance terms in the birth probability and prenatal care equations) remains consistent with the cost of contraception model. With regard to the magnitude of the black selection effect, the coefficient of the inverse of the Mills ratio falls by 22 percent in the OLS birth weight equation and by 14 percent in the TSLS birth weight equation. The corresponding coefficient falls by 1 percent in absolute value in the prenatal care demand function. The stability of the signs and statistical significance of the sample selection effects and the supplementary evidence that changes in marital status and Medicaid status between conception and birth are most relevant for white teenagers strengthen our confidence in the results.

In summary, recent attempts to obtain structural estimates of the infant health technology have used TSLS to control for adverse selection in input use. In this chapter, we have presented a model in which the decision to give birth among pregnant women allows for a more general form of self-selection. Because of the widespread availability and use of abortion in New York City, women who choose to give birth bring to their pregnancies a set of unobserved factors or behaviors that are associated with the increased consumption of prenatal care and increased birth weight.

We found selection to be race-specific. Only among black women is the decision to give birth correlated with healthy behavior and improved birth outcomes. This result is consistent with the interpretation that the mean shadow price of contraception and the variance in this price are greater for blacks than for whites. This suggests that in areas in which abortion availability is limited, with the price of contraception held constant, the selection process encouraged by abortion will be muted. Evidence for the latter has been reported by Corman, Joyce, and Grossman (1987) and Joyce (1987) with county-level data.

NOTES

Originally published as Michael Grossman and Theodore J. Joyce, "Unobservables, Pregnancy Resolutions, and Birth Weight Production Functions in New York City," *Journal of Political Economy* 98, no. 5, pt. 1 (1990): 983–1007. This is a condensed version of Grossman and Joyce (1988). The longer version, which contains a more detailed discussion of the empirical specification and results, is available on request. Research for this chapter was supported by grant 1 R01 HD24154 from the National Institute of Child Health and Human Development to the National Bureau of Economic Research and by grant 86–3848 from the Henry J. Kaiser Family Foundation to the NBER. We are indebted to the following people for supplying us with data without which this research could not have been undertaken: Jean Lee, Alberto Valentin, and Louise Berenson of the Division of Biostatistics, New York City Department of Health; Stanley Henshaw of the Alan Guttmacher Institute; and Marc Jacobs and Jonah Otelsberg of the City University of New York Data Service. We are also indebted to Victor Fuchs, Paul Gertler, John Mullahy, Cordelia Reimers, Sherwin Rosen, T. Paul Schultz, and an anonymous referee for helpful comments and suggestions. Finally, we wish to thank Frank Chaloupka, Pamela Mobilia, and Naci Mocan for research assistance. This chapter has not undergone the review accorded official NBER publications; in particular, it has not been submitted for approval by the Board of Directors. Any opinions expressed in the chapter are those of the authors and not those of the NBER, the NICHD, or the Kaiser Foundation.

1. An increase in the endowment is equivalent to an increase in real income. Provided that all commodities in the utility function are superior, their optimal values rise. We use the term "very likely" in the text because we do not fully take account of induced substitution between the optimal number of children and their quality (health) that occurs in the model developed by Becker and Lewis (1973).

2. To the extent that there are measured components of the price of contraception, such as mother's education or the availability of family planning clinics, these components are now included in the x_i vector. Similar comments apply to the other variables.

3. It is possible to develop a model in which variations in the price of abortion generate a positive covariance between the disturbance terms in the birth probability and prenatal care equations. Suppose that the health endowments of fetuses conceived by the same woman vary among conceptions. Each woman desires to have one child, and there are no costs of conventional fertility control methods. Abortions occur in this model to raise the health endowment of the single child in the family. An increase in the price of abortion raises the probability of giving birth and causes a substitution toward prenatal care and

away from the health endowment in the production of birth weight. Since women with lower health endowments are more likely to give birth, the disturbance terms in the birth weight and birth probability equations are negatively related even if the unmeasured input (q) rises as the price of abortion rises. The reason is that the optimal level of birth weight falls because an increase in the price of abortion raises the relative price of infant health and lowers real income. Consequently, this model can be distinguished from the cost of contraception model, even though both models produce a positive value of σ_{13}.

4. Note that adverse or favorable selection in pregnancy resolution is determined by the sign of correlation between the disturbance term in the birth probability equation and the disturbance term in the birth weight equation. Adverse or favorable selection in input use is determined by the sign of the correlation between the disturbance term in the birth weight equation and the disturbance term in the prenatal care equation. Although the procedure described below does not yield an estimate of σ_{23}, its sign can be inferred from the signs of σ_{12} and σ_{13} in a single-factor model. With more than one factor, the sign of σ_{23} can be inferred by placing reasonable restrictions on the magnitudes of certain parameters. For example, suppose that e and a vary while c does not. In addition, suppose that σ_{12} is positive. The necessary condition for σ_{23} to be negative (which is plausible since σ_{13} must be negative) is $\beta_4\gamma_4\sigma_e^2 < -\beta_3\gamma_3\sigma_{qa}$. When $\beta_4 = \beta_3$ and $\gamma_4 = \gamma_3$, this is satisfied provided $\sigma_e^2 > -\sigma_{qa}$.

5. The statement is subject to two modifications. First, the case in which the effects of the determinants exactly offset each other ($\sigma_{12} = \sigma_{13} = \sigma_{23} = 0$) cannot be distinguished from one in which each effect taken alone is zero. Second, the dominant factor is not necessarily the one with the largest variance. For example, suppose that there is no variation in the cost of abortion so that women with higher than expected probabilities of giving birth have heavier than expected babies ($\sigma_{12} > 0$). These women have larger than expected values of prenatal care ($\sigma_{13} > 0$, as predicted by the cost of contraception model) if $\alpha_2\gamma_2\sigma_c^2 > -\alpha_4\gamma_4\sigma_e^2$. The last inequality can be satisfied even if the variance in the cost of contraception is smaller than the variance in the health endowment. Moreover, the inequality may not hold even if $\sigma_c^2 > \sigma_e^2$.

6. The two-step procedure just described yields consistent, although inefficient, estimates. Efficient estimates can be obtained by maximum likelihood procedures in which the three equations are estimated simultaneously, and the residual covariances (σ_{12} and σ_{13}) are obtained directly. The maximum likelihood estimates are not presented in section 3 because they were almost identical to the two-step estimates with an exogenous prenatal care measure. When prenatal care is treated as endogenous (see below), the likelihood function is too complicated to pursue estimation methods other than the two-stage least-squares (TSLS) probit method for simultaneous equations models with selectivity developed by Lee, Maddala, and Trost (1980). For the same reason, we avoid a bivariate probit model with sample selection in which continuous birth weight is replaced by a dichotomous indicator of low birth weight (less than 2,500 grams). In particular, estimation of this model is not feasible when prenatal care is endogenous.

7. There were several reasons for choosing New York City. First, only twelve states in the United States maintain detailed information on induced abortions as part of their vital registration system (Powell-Griner 1986). Second, the large number of minorities in New York City permitted a race-specific analysis. Third, New York City birth

and induced termination certificates contain items that are not recorded in other states: specifically, how the birth and abortion were financed, whether the procedure was performed by the patient's private physician, and whether the pregnancy was complicated by alcohol, drugs, and tobacco. We do not include women whose pregnancies were terminated by spontaneous abortion. Early spontaneous abortions are poorly reported. In 1984 the reported ratio of spontaneous abortions to live births was approximately .04 in New York City. Yet data from the National Survey of Family Growth indicate that this ratio is approximately .20 (Pratt et al. 1984). Our analysis is race-specific because there are substantial differences in birth outcomes, prenatal behavior, and abortion rates between whites and blacks (Henshaw et al. 1985; Corman, Joyce, and Grossman 1987). We exclude Hispanics in order to focus on white and black differences and to make our results more comparable with those of previously published work. Moreover, it has been argued recently that Hispanics should not be lumped together because there are nontrivial differences in medical care utilization, birth outcomes, and abortions among, e.g., Puerto Ricans, Mexicans, and Cubans (Schur, Berstein, and Berk 1987).

8. That is, a woman gives birth if her optimal number of children is greater than or equal to parity plus one. Both the optimal number of children and parity (which for a given family size measures the timing and spacing of births) are governed by command over resources, prices, efficiency, tastes, marital status, and mother's age.

9. The procedure described above addresses the endogeneity of timing decisions with regard to marital status, Medicaid status, and education, but it does not address other aspects of their endogeneity in a complete life cycle model. The procedure also deals with a measurement problem in the birth probability equation that arises because Medicaid status and marital status of women who abort are measured at a time shortly after conception, while Medicaid status and marital status of women who give birth are measured at birth. In section 3, we report that our basic results are not affected by the exclusion of these two variables from the birth probability equation. We do not perform Wu-Hausman tests of their endogeneity in the other two equations or in all three equations because we lack instruments to identify equations for the probability of marriage or the receipt of Medicaid.

10. On the basis of equations (10) and (11), mean birth weight in the birth sample (b_b), potential mean birth weight for women who abort (b_a), and the mean values of prenatal care in each sample (m_b and m_a, respectively) can be written as

$$b_b = \beta_1 \mathbf{x}_b + \beta_2 m_b + \left(\frac{\sigma_{12}}{\sigma_1}\right) \lambda_b,$$

$$b_a = \beta_1 \mathbf{x}_a + \beta_2 m_a + \left(\frac{\sigma_{12}}{\sigma_1}\right) \lambda_a,$$

$$m_b = \gamma_1 \mathbf{y}_b + \left(\frac{\sigma_{13}}{\sigma_1}\right) \lambda_b,$$

$$m_a = \gamma_1 \mathbf{y}_a + \left(\frac{\sigma_{13}}{\sigma_1}\right) \lambda_a.$$

Here $\mathbf{x}_b$, y_b, $\mathbf{x}_a$, and y_a are the means of the determinants of birth weight and prenatal care in each sample; λ_b is the mean of the inverse of the Mills ratio in the birth sample; and λ_a is the mean of the inverse of the Mills ratio, defined as $-f(Q_i)/[1 - F(Q_i)]$, in the abortion sample. Thus the mean birth weight difference between those who gave birth and those who aborted had they instead given birth is

$$b_b - b_a = \beta_1(\mathbf{x}_b - \mathbf{x}_a) + \beta_2(m_b - m_a) + \left(\frac{\sigma_{12}}{\sigma_1}\right)(\lambda_b - \lambda_a).$$

The last term in this equation is positive given $\sigma_{12} > 0$. It also represents the difference in birth weight due to unobserved factors. The first two terms to the right of the equal sign capture the differences due to observed characteristics. It should be noted that some of the variables in the $\mathbf{x}_b$ vector were not observed for women who aborted. Thus to calculate the mean potential birth weight of women who aborted, we assumed that the proportion of women who used tobacco, drugs, and alcohol as well as the proportion of male infants and the proportion of women served by private physicians were the same between the two samples. To test the sensitivity of our results to this assumption, we reestimated the model excluding these five variables from the birth weight equation. The difference between the observed mean and the potential mean birth weight was not altered appreciably.

11. A comparison of our results with those of Rosenzweig and Schultz is limited for several reasons. First, our data are restricted to New York City, whereas the National Natality Survey samples women from across the country. Furthermore, we were able to estimate a race-specific model, which proved to be important. Third, the national survey excludes out-of-wedlock births. Over 57 percent of all births to black women in the United States and over 70 percent in New York occur out of wedlock (Bureau of the Census 1986). Fourth, given our focus on self-selection, we treat only prenatal care as an endogenous input, whereas Rosenzweig and Schultz treat age, parity, and smoking as additional endogenous inputs. Fifth, our specification of the birth weight production function includes mother's education, while their specification omits education. In spite of these differences, we decided to examine the extent to which a correction for sample selection attenuates the need for TSLS estimation of the black birth weight equation. We did this by excluding the correction factor (λ) from the OLS and TSLS production functions. A Wu test of the hypothesis that prenatal care is exogenous in this specification still led us to accept the null hypothesis ($F = 2.89$). To make our model more comparable with Rosenzweig and Schultz's, we also excluded education from the production function. In this specification, prenatal care is endogenous when we do not correct for sample selection ($F = 7.46$) but exogenous when we do correct for sample selection ($F = 3.49$). At the 5 percent level, the critical F ratio in each of these three tests is 3.84. When education and the correction factor are omitted from the production function, the OLS and TSLS coefficients and t-ratios of prenatal care rise in absolute value. The exclusion of education from a specification that corrects for sample selection causes the coefficients of the correction factor to rise in magnitude and statistical significance. We conclude that prenatal care can be treated as exogenous in our sample if either education or the correction factor is included in the birth weight production function. Given the

widespread availability of abortion services and the high abortion rates in New York City relative to the United States as a whole, this result may not generalize to other areas.

REFERENCES

Becker, Gary S. 1965. "A Theory of the Allocation of Time." *Econ. J.* 75: 493–517.

Becker, Gary S., and H. Gregg Lewis. 1973. "On the Interaction between the Quantity and Quality of Children." *J.P.E.* 81, no. 2, pt. 2: S279–S288.

Bureau of the Census. 1986. *Statistical Abstract of the United States.* Washington: Government Printing Office.

Corman, Hope, Theodore J. Joyce, and Michael Grossman. 1987. "Birth Outcome Production Functions in the United States." *J. Human Resources* 22: 339–60.

Gortmaker, Steven L. 1979. "Poverty and Infant Mortality in the United States." *American Sociological Rev.* 44: 280–97.

Grossman, Michael. 1972. "On the Concept of Health Capital and the Demand for Health." *J.P.E.* 80: 223–55.

Grossman, Michael, and Theodore J. Joyce. 1988. "Unobservables, Pregnancy Resolutions, and Birth Weight Production Functions in New York City." Working Paper no. 2746. Cambridge, Mass.: NBER.

Hausman, Jerry A. 1978. "Specification Tests in Econometrics." *Econometrica* 461251–71.

Heckman, James J. 1979. "Sample Selection Bias as a Specification Error." *Econometrica* 47: 153–61.

——. 1980. "Sample Selection Bias as a Specification Error with an Application to the Estimation of Labor Supply Functions." In *Female Labor Supply: Theory and Estimation*, ed. by James P. Smith. Princeton, N.J.: Princeton Univ. Press (for Rand Corp.).

Henshaw, Stanley K., Nancy J. Binkin, Ellen Blaine, and Jack C. Smith. 1985. "A Portrait of American Women Who Obtain Abortions." *Family Planning Perspectives* 17: 90–96.

Hofferth, Sandra I. 1987. "Teenage Pregnancy and Its Resolution." In *Risking the Future: Adolescent Sexuality, Pregnancy, and Childbearing*, vol. 2, ed. Sandra L. Hofferth and Cheryl D. Hayes. Washington: Nat. Acad. Press.

Hofferth, Sandra L., and Cheryl D. Hayes eds. 1987. *Risking the Future: Adolescent Sexuality, Pregnancy, and Childbearing.* 2 vols. Washington: Nat. Acad. Press.

Hogue, Carol J. R., Willard Cates, Jr., and Christopher Tietze. 1982. "The Effects of Induced Abortion on Subsequent Reproduction." *Epidemiologic Revs.* 4: 66–94.

Hotz, V. Joseph, and Robert A. Miller. 1988. "An Empirical Analysis of Life Cycle Fertility and Female Labor Supply." *Econometrica* 56: 91–118.

Institute of Medicine. 1985. *Preventing Low Birthweight.* Washington: Nat. Acad. Press.

Joyce, Theodore J. 1987. "The Impact of Induced Abortion on Black and White Birth Outcomes in the United States." *Demography* 24: 229–44.

Lee, Lung-Fei, G. S. Maddala, and Robert P. Trost. 1980. "Asymptotic Covariance Matrices of Two-Stage Probit and Two-Stage Tobit Methods for Simultaneous Equations Models with Selectivity." *Econometrica* 48: 491–503.

Leibowitz, Arleen, Marvin Eisen, and Winston K. Chow. 1986. "An Economic Model of Teenage Pregnancy Decision-Making." *Demography* 23: 67–77.

Michael, Robert T., and Gary S. Becker. 1973. "On the New Theory of Consumer Behavior." *Swedish J. Econ.* 75: 378–96.

Michael, Robert T., and Robert J. Willis. 1976. "Contraception and Fertility: Household Production under Uncertainty." In *Household Production and Consumption*, ed. Nestor E. Terleckyj. New York: Columbia Univ. Press (for NBER).

Nakamura, Alice, and Masao Nakamura. 1981. "On the Relationships among Several Specification Error Tests Presented by Durbin, Wu, and Hausman." *Econometrica* 49: 1583–88.

Pollak, Robert A., and Michael L. Wachter. 1975. "The Relevance of the Household Production Function and Its Implications for the Allocation of Time." *J.P.E.* 83: 255–77.

Powell-Griner, Eve. 1986. *Induced Terminations of Pregnancy: Reporting States, 1982 and 1983.* Monthly Vital Statistics Report, vol. 35, no. 3 (suppl.). Hyattsville, Md.: Public Health Service.

Pratt, William F.;, William D. Mosher, Christine A. Bachrach, and Marjorie C. Horn. 1984. "Understanding U.S. Fertility: Findings from the National Survey of Family Growth, Cycle III." *Population Bull.* 39.

Rosenzweig, Mark R., and T. Paul Schultz. 1982. "The Behavior of Mothers as Inputs to Child Health: The Determinants of Birth Weight, Gestation, and Rate of Fetal Growth." In *Economic Aspects of Health*, ed. Victor R. Fuchs. Chicago: Univ. Chicago Press (for NBER).

——. 1983. "Estimating a Household Production Function: Heterogeneity, the Demand for Health Inputs, and Their Effects on Birth Weight." *J.P.E.* 91: 723–46.

——. 1988. "The Stability of Household Production Technology: A Replication." *J. Human Resources* 23: 535–49.

Schur, Claudia L., Amy B. Berstein, and Marc L. Berk. 1987. "The Importance of Distinguishing Hispanic Subpopulations in the Use of Medical Care." *Medical Care* 25: 627–41.

Stephen, Elizabeth Hervey, Ronald R. Rindfuss, and Frank D. Bean. 1988. "Racial Differences in Contraceptive Choice: Complexity and Implications." *Demography* 25: 53–70.

Willis, Robert J. 1973. "A New Approach to the Economic Theory of Fertility Behavior." *J.P.E.* 81, no. 2, pt. 2: S14–S64.

Wu, De-Min. "Alternative Tests of Independence between Stochastic Regressors and Disturbances." *Econometrica* 41 (July 1973): 733–50.

ELEVEN

The Impact of National Health Insurance on Birth Outcomes

A Natural Experiment in Taiwan

Shin-Yi Chou, Michael Grossman
and Jin-Tan Liu

ABSTRACT

We estimate the impacts of the introduction of National Health Insurance (NHI) in Taiwan in March 1995 on infant survival. Prior to NHI, government workers (the control group) possessed health insurance policies with comprehensive coverage for births and infant medical care services. Private sector industrial workers and farmers (the treatment groups) lacked this coverage. All households received coverage in 1995. Since stringent requirements for reporting births introduced in 1994 produced artificial upward trends in early infant deaths, we focus on postneonatal mortality. The introduction of NHI led to reductions in this rate for infants born in farm households but not for infants born in private sector households. For the former group, the rate fell by between 0.3 and 0.6 deaths per thousand survivors or by between 8 and 16 percent. A large decline of between 3.4 and 6.8 deaths occurred for pre-term infants— a drop of between 20 and 41 percent.

1. INTRODUCTION

Improvements in infant and child health are widely accepted public health and public policy goals in most developing and developed countries. One obvious way to accomplish these goals is to provide health insurance to pregnant women, infants, and children. From the point of view of mothers and families, this policy lowers the prices of medical care services such as prenatal care, delivery, neonatal care, vaccinations, immunizations, and well-baby and child care. These price reductions should increase the quantities of services demanded. From the point of view of providers, health insurance guarantees the receipt of payment for services rendered, so that increases in supply should accompany the increased demand.

While appealing in theory, government financed or subsidized health insurance competes with a variety of other mechanisms to improve health including direct cash subsidies to families or providers, publicly supplied care, and health education campaigns to discourage such behaviors as cigarette smoking and inappropriate alcohol use. Hence, estimates of the impacts of the effects of insurance on infant and child health are key ingredients in the policy debate concerning the most efficient ways to improve health.

The extensive literature dealing with the effects of health insurance on infant and child health has reached few definitive conclusions. Given the serious challenges involved in this undertaking, these mixed results are not surprising. As emphasized by Brown, Bindman, and Lurie (1998), Kaestner (1999), and Levy and Meltzer (2008), observational or cross-sectional correlation studies throw little light on causality. On the one hand, women who anticipate a poor birth outcome or who have sick infants or children may be more likely to obtain health insurance. On the other hand, women with a propensity to avoid risk or to engage in a variety of healthy behaviors may be more likely to obtain insurance. In the first case the effect of insurance on health is understated, and in the second case it is overstated.

Studies employing experimental or quasi-experimental data have the potential to reach more definitive conclusions. Examples are the RAND Health Insurance Experiment (HIE), the introduction of NHI in Canada and Medicaid in the United States, and the Medicaid income eligibility expansions in the late 1980s and early 1990s. Even here there are problems. Subjects recruited for the HIE might already have benefited from the medical care covered by their existing policies. The widespread adoption of oral and intrauterine contraceptive devices and the reform of restrictive abortion laws coincided with the introduction of Medicaid and NHI, making it difficult to sort out the impacts of each development. Many women made eligible for Medicaid by the expansions chose not to enroll in the program (Gruber 1997), and some women switched from private insurance to Medicaid (Cutler and Gruber 1996). These factors and year-to-year changes in income in the years just before and just after the expansions make it difficult to create the appropriate treatment and control groups required to evaluate their effects.[1]

The objective of this chapter is to estimate the impacts of the introduction of NHI in Taiwan in March 1995 on the health of infants. There is enormous interest in the impacts of NHI on health outcomes, but the very nature of this intervention, whereby entire nations are covered universally, makes it difficult to estimate the health impacts of the change. The experience of Taiwan, however, provides a potential laboratory for overcoming these limitations. Prior to NHI, government workers possessed health insurance policies that covered pre-natal medical care, newborn deliveries, neonatal care, and medical care services received by their children beyond the first month of life. Private sector industrial workers and farmers lacked this coverage. All households received coverage for the services just mentioned as of March 1995. Therefore, the introduction of NHI constitutes a natural experiment with treatment and control groups that form the basis of our empirical design. The former group consists of non-government-employed households, while the latter group consists of government-employed households. We expect that increases in infant health after the introduction of NHI in the treatment group will exceed corresponding increases in the control group.

To sort out the effects of NHI from unobserved trends, we employ a difference-in-differences estimation methodology. This compares the experiences of the treatment and control groups before and after the implementation of NHI under the assumption that other temporally coincident changes are the same for the two groups. We also employ a regression framework that allows for interactions between medical resource availability and NHI.

The importance of our undertaking is highlighted by the interest in East Asia and in many other parts of the world in the promotion and expansion of universal government subsidized health insurance. There have been only two evaluations of the enactment of this type of legislation on infant health outcomes in East Asian countries to date. Gruber, Hendren, and Townsend (2014) examine the 30 Baht program implemented in Thailand in 2001. The main feature of that program was that it increased reimbursement to hospitals for treating low income patients. They find that the program led to a reduction in infant mortality among the poor of approximately 6.5 deaths per thousand live births. This finding is based on infant mortality rates by year and province that are not income-specific.

Chen and Jin (2012) examine the effects of the introduction of the National Cooperative Medical System in rural China in 2003 on mortality of children between the ages of less than one and five years old. They find no impact on this outcome. Unlike the mandatory nature of NHI in Taiwan, the program in China was implemented on a county-by-county basis. That gave local governments the option to decide when to implement it and the nature of the premium-benefit package.

By employing the Taiwan NHI experiment to evaluate the impacts of health insurance on infants, we circumvent some of the problems encountered in prior research.[2] The treatment and control groups are sharply defined by employment in the private or agricultural sector on the one hand and by employment in the government sector on the other hand. As discussed in section 6, it is difficult to switch sectors. The introduction of NHI was not accompanied by changes in birth control techniques—changes that did occur when Canada adopted NHI and when the United States introduced Medicaid. Abortion has been legal in Taiwan since 1984. Households simply had to register with the Bureau of National Health Insurance to obtain coverage, and take-up rates were nearly 100 percent. The program was mandatory, and we have mortality data for each of the three groups. One problem that we face is that the treatment and control groups have very different characteristics. We outline approaches to deal with this issue in section 6.

2. TAIWAN EXPERIENCE

Legislation authorizing National Health Insurance in Taiwan was enacted on July 19, 1994, and NHI went into effect on March 1, 1995. By the end of 1995, the percentage of the population with health insurance rose from approximately 54 percent in the month prior to implementation to approximately 92 percent (Executive Yuan, Research, Development, and Evaluation Committee 1993; Peabody et al. 1995; Bureau of National Health Insurance 1997; Chiang 1997; Chou and Staiger 2001; Chou, Liu, and Hammitt 2003; personal communication with Jack Ho of the Taiwan Council of Labor Affairs. Unless otherwise noted, the material in this section is drawn from these seven sources). Prior to NHI, dependent spouses and children and persons over the age of sixty accounted for almost all of the uninsured population, with dependent spouses and children amounting to almost 55 percent of the uninsured.

The large number of uninsured women and children prior to 1995 can be traced to the nature of the health insurance system before that year. Insurance was obtained through one of four government-sponsored health plans, three of which were tied to a person's place of employment in the government sector, the private industrial sector, or the agricultural sector. With the exception of supplementary coverage for a few selected conditions such as cancer and accidents, no private health insurance was available. The employment-based plans were Labor Insurance (LI), which covered 38 percent of the population in 1992; Government Employee Insurance (GI), which covered 8 percent of the population; and Farmers' Insurance (FI), which also covered 8 percent of the population. The fourth plan, Low-Income Households' Health Insurance (LII), was provided directly by the government and covered only 0.5 percent of the population.

LI covered individuals who were employed in the private industrial sector (hereafter termed the private sector). GI covered households in which at least one member was employed in the government sector. FI covered households in which at least one member was a farmer and a member of a local farmer's union. Coverage was mandatory for eligible persons in the three employment-based plans. Premium costs were shared by the employer, the employee, and the government in the case of LI, by the employee and the government in the case of GI, and by the farmer and the government in the case of FI. In all three sectors, the insured person's premium was a positive function of his or her income. Since farmers had the lowest income of the three groups, their premiums were very low and heavily subsidized by the government. Self-employed private sector workers could obtain LI only if they were members of an occupational union. LI, the largest of these plans, did not provide coverage for non-working spouses (almost entirely wives) and children. FI did not provide coverage for children under the age of fifteen. GI provided coverage for spouses. Effective July 1, 1992, it also provided coverage for dependent children.

In addition to these differences in coverage, GI provided much more generous benefits in the case of medical care services received by pregnant women and their very young infants. Under each of the three plans, a pregnant woman received a cash benefit for childbirth equal to two months of salary if either she or her husband was covered.[3] Typically this benefit covered the cost of delivery. A woman who underwent a difficult delivery (for example, a cesarean section) could file a claim for its costs if she was willing to forego the cash benefit under LI or FI. Women covered under GI did not have to forego this benefit. More importantly, LI and FI did not cover prenatal care services, and they also did not cover extended hospital stays of low-weight infants during the neonatal period (the first twenty-seven days of life), including the cost of neonatal intensive care. Finally, medical care services delivered to infants of LI and FI women during the postneonatal period (the period between the 28th and 364th days of life) were not covered. On the other hand, GI provided coverage, subject to a coinsurance rate of between 10 and 15 percent, for ten prenatal care visits: a first visit with a detailed physical examination and nine subsequent visits for routine checkups, an ultrasound exam around the twentieth week of pregnancy, and screening tests for hepatitis B, rubella, and syphilis around the thirty-second week of pregnancy. Moreover, neonatal care and postneonatal care received by the infant were covered regardless of where they were received.

After the introduction of NHI, nongovernment-employed households enjoyed benefits similar to those received by government-employed households prior to March 1995, with the exception that the cash benefit for childbirth received by private sector households was reduced to one month of salary. Premium costs continue to be shared in the manner described above by employers, employees, farmers, and the government, with the government continuing to pay the entire premium for low-income families and to heavily subsidize the premium for farmers.[4] Thus, the introduction of NHI constitutes a "natural experiment" in which a large number of previously uninsured pregnant women, infants, and children in a country with a population of over 21 million persons received coverage for prenatal care, delivery, neonatal care, vaccinations, immunizations, and well-baby and child care for the first time. The behavior of the two "treatment groups" (those covered by LI or FI prior to 1995) in the pre- and post-NHI periods can be compared to the behavior of the "control group" of government employed households whose health insurance coverage did not change. Table 11.1 summarizes the aspects of health insurance benefits received by pregnant women and their young infants in each of the three groups before and after the introduction of NHI.

3. CONCEPTUAL FRAMEWORK

The infant health outcome of a birth depends on a set of medical and nonmedical inputs and other determinants, all of which are endogenous. These include the quantity and quality of prenatal and neonatal care; maternal cigarette smoking, alcohol use, diet, exercise, and labor force participation during pregnancy; maternal age; the number of previous births; and decisions concerning terminations of problematic births (those with potentially poor health outcomes). The introduction of NHI may affect all of these factors. It may be tempting to argue that the policy reduces the price of medical care services delivered to pregnant women, newborns, and older infants who had no or less generous benefits prior to its enactment. If the quantity of these services demanded is inversely related to price, the quantity of services demanded by these groups should rise. If more medical care leads to better health, the groups affected should exhibit improved child health outcomes.

That argument, however, ignores effects on the other endogenous determinants of infant health just mentioned. For instance ex ante moral hazard associated with the receipt of health insurance may induce beneficiaries to reduce

Table 11.1 Insurance Benefits by Group

	Before NHI			After NHI		
Group	Government Employees	Farmers	Private Employees	Government Employees	Farmers	Private Employees
Source of health insurance[a]	GEI	FI	LI	NHI	NHI	NHI
Coverage for dependents						
Spouse	Effective in 1982	Yes if farms	No	Yes	Yes	Yes
Children	Effective in 1992	No	No	Yes	Yes	Yes
Maternity benefits						
Coverage for . . .						
Prenatal visits	Yes[b]	No	No	Yes	Yes	Yes
Cost of delivery	Yes[b]	No[c]	No[c]	Yes	Yes	Yes
Neonatal & postneonatal care	Yes[b]	No	No	Yes	Yes	Yes
Cash benefits for childbirth (months of salary)	2	2[c]	2[c]	2	2	1

[a] GEI: Government Employee Insurance; FI: Farmers' Insurance; LI: Labor Insurance; NHI: National Health Insurance.

[b] Coverage is the same for female insured or spouse

[c] A woman who underwent a difficult delivery could file a claim for its costs if she was willing to forego the cash benefit under LI or FI.

preventive nonmedical behaviors, suggesting that these behaviors and medical care are substitutes (Dave and Kaestner 2009; Kelly and Markowitz 2009/2010). In our case, pregnant women in the treatment groups may continue to smoke or to gain an excessive amount of weight. The opposite effect also is possible if new and more frequent contact with physicians promotes more healthy behaviors, a result consistent with complementarity between medical care and these behaviors.

Predictions about the impacts of the introduction of NHI also must take account of potential effects on fertility. The receipt of health insurance that covers medical care services associated with births reduces the price of a birth. Given interactions between the quantity and quality (measured by health) of children emphasized by Becker and Lewis (1973), one possible outcome is that the optimal number of children rises while the optimal health of each child falls. A related factor is that problematic births (those with potentially poor health outcomes) that previously were aborted now may be carried to term. Again, the effect could go in the opposite direction if NHI reduces fertility because it lowers the probability of an infant death and creates incentives on the part of parents to make larger investments in a smaller number of children.

We want to emphasize that our aim is to estimate the net or reduced form effect of NHI—that is, the effect that does not hold endogenous inputs constant. If the receipt of health insurance causes pregnant women to, for example, withdraw from the labor force, change smoking behavior, alcohol consumption, exercise routines, or diet patterns, decide to have more or fewer children, or give birth rather than abort a problematic birth, those effects should not be held constant in estimating the full effect of the introduction of NHI. A study that contains both the effect of NHI on infant health and its effects on medical care and the behaviors just mentioned would be of considerable importance and value, but it is beyond the scope of our chapter given that almost all of the relevant inputs are not available on Taiwanese birth certificates.[5] Because the introduction of NHI can affect many endogenous determinants of infant health in addition to medical care, its ultimate impact on this outcome is an empirical issue. That is, its effect is ambiguous on a priori grounds.[6]

4. DATA AND SAMPLE

Our two major data sources are annual birth and infant death certificates for the years 1990 through 2001. There were more than 300,000 births a year in Taiwan during this period. We link birth and death certificates through national identification numbers received by each person in Taiwan. In addition to birthweight and gestational age, birth certificates contain the following information: place of birth (hospital, clinic, other); gender; parity; mother's town of residence; mother's marital status; mother's age; mother's schooling; father's age; and father's schooling. Mother's and father's occupation and industry are also reported, but there are many missing values.[7] Instead, we create treatment and control groups by matching birth and infant death certificates to annual files that we have obtained from the Central Trust of China and from the Bureau of Labor Insurance for the years 1990–2001. Prior to the March 1995 date on which NHI became effective, the Central Trust of China administered health insurance under the GI, and the Bureau of Labor Insurance administered health insurance under LI and FI. These two organizations maintained the files containing the national identification numbers of all persons with coverage. They continued to maintain these files after March 1995 because they still are responsible for other types of insurance (for example, disability insurance, unemployment insurance, and old-age insurance).[8]

As explained in section 2, infants of parents who did not work in the government sector had much more limited health insurance than those of parents who worked in that sector in the period prior to NHI. Hence, our control group consists of births to households in which at least one parent is employed in the government sector. Treatment group I consists of birth to households in which the father works in the private sector and the mother also works in that sector or does not work. Treatment group II consists of birth to households in which the father is a farmer and the mother also is a farmer or does not work. We construct two treatment groups because farmers have lower levels of education and income than private sector workers. These factors may result in different responses to the introduction of NHI by the two groups.

There are 3,548,321 births without missing values on parental education, ages of mothers and fathers, birth date of child, and parity from 1990 to 2001. We restrict our analysis file to births of infants whose mothers were between the ages of fifteen and forty-five and fathers were between the ages of fifteen and sixty-five, which results in 3,543,389 births. After deleting births that could not be matched to any insurance administrative files, we are left with 3,471,044 observations. Finally, we delete multiple births and births to unmarried women.[9] These restrictions result in a sample of 3,340,695 from 1990 to 2001 or 94.15 percent of all births in that period. Of this sample, 384,622 births (11.51 percent) were in government-employed households; 2,665,442 (79.79 percent) were in private sector households; and 290,631 (8.70 percent) were in farm households.

The health outcome that we consider is the probability of a postneonatal death. These deaths occur between the ages of 28 and 364 days of life. We do not consider neonatal deaths, which occur within the first 27 days of life, because of a development in addition to the introduction of NHI that occurred during our sample period. Effective October 1994, child delivery institutions were mandated to report births directly to household registration offices (the source of our birth and death certificates) and to health authorities. Throughout our sample period, parents required a birth certificate completed by a physician or another hospital official to obtain national identification numbers for their infants. But prior to October 1994, some parents did not bother to report births to household registration offices if their infants died within the first twenty-seven days of life. Clearly, low-weight births resulting in neonatal deaths were most likely to go unreported. As of October 1994, delivery institutions were required to send birth certificates to household registration offices and to health authorities. Hence, the percentage of low-weight births and the neonatal mortality rate all rose after 1993 (Department of Health 1996 and personal communication with Pau-Chung Chen, M.D., of the National Taiwan University Medical College). As we discuss in detail in Chou, Grossman, and Liu (2011), the 1994 mandate makes it infeasible to treat neonatal mortality as an outcome.

Figure 11.1 shows trends in the postneonatal mortality rate from 1990 to 2001 by treatment status. That rate is defined as postneonatal deaths per thousand survivors of the neonatal period. Before the introduction of NHI, the control group had the lowest postneonatal mortality rate, followed by private sector households and then by farm households. After NHI, all groups experienced a downward trend in postneonatal morality. In interpreting trends in the figure, one should keep in mind that there are many more births in private sector households than in government sector and farm households. Hence, year-to-year changes in mortality rates in the latter two groups are subject to a considerable amount of noise.

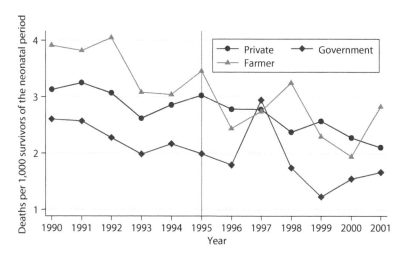

Figure 11.1 Postneonatal mortality, 1990–2001

In our primary empirical analyses in sections 6 and 7, we exclude births in 1994 and 1995 to minimize any impacts of the 1994 development on our estimates. This exclusion also is desirable because NHI was introduced on March 1, 1995, making 1996 the first full year after its introduction. Thus, our before-NHI period is 1990–1993 and after-NHI period is 1996–2001. We do, however, explore the sensitivity of our estimates to this exclusion in section 7. The restriction just mentioned results in a sample of 2,753,860 births of infants who survived the first twenty-seven days of life. Of these 313,606 (11.39 percent) were in government households; 2,201,663 (79.95 percent) were in private sector households; and 238,591 (8.66 percent) were in farm households.

5. DIFFERENCE-IN-DIFFERENCES APPROACH

5.1. Model and Implementation

To estimate the effects of NHI on infant health outcomes, we capitalize on its differential impact on the coverage and benefits of government workers and their dependents compared to other workers and their dependents. As explained in section 2, the former group had the same coverage and benefits before and after the adoption of NHI, while the latter group did not. With modifications discussed below, families with a government worker serve as the control group, and families with no government employees serve as the treatment group in a difference-in-differences (DD) estimation strategy. Health outcomes in the control group should not be affected by the introduction of NHI, while health outcomes in the treatment group should be affected. Unobserved trends may, however, impact outcomes in both groups. Examples of unmeasured time effects include advances in neonatology, diffusion of these advances, and changes in the level of air pollution. The DD methodology assumes that unobserved effects are the same for the two groups.

Our variables of interest differ at the group-year level. We have two treatment groups (private sector workers and farmers), one control group (government sector workers), and ten years of data. Four of these years (1990–1993) predate the introduction of NHI, and six (1996–2001) postdate it. Therefore, we aggregate our data into thirty group-year cells and estimate a regression of the form

$$P_{gt} = \alpha_0 + \alpha_{11}PRI_{gt} + \alpha_{12}FRM_{gt} + \alpha_{21}NHI_t * PRI_{gt} + \alpha_{22}NHI_t$$
$$* FRM_{gt} + f_t + \varepsilon_{gt}. \tag{1}$$

Here P_{gt} is the postneonatal mortality rate (deaths per thousand survivors of the neonatal period) of group g ($g = 1, 2, 3$) in year t, PRI_{gt} is an indicator variable for private sector household cell in year t, FRM_{gt} is an indicator variable for the farm sector household cell in year t, NHI_t is an indicator for the period after the implementation of NHI, f_t is a set of year fixed effects, and ε_{gt} is the disturbance term.[10] The coefficient α_{2g} on the interaction between $NHIt$ and the treatment group dummy measures the difference-in-differences for treatment group g ($g = 1, 2$).

We note a number of aspects of the estimation. First, we obtain weighted coefficients, where the set of weights is the square root of the number of neonatal survivors in each cell. Second, by aggregating to the group-year level, we correct for clustering of disturbance terms by group and year at the individual level. Third, for reasons discussed below, we omit household characteristics. Fourth, tests of significance are based on sixteen degrees of freedom. Thus, we recognize that there are a small number of degrees of freedom. Finally, to correct for serial correlation, we obtain Newey and West (1987) standard errors with an assumed lag length of 2.[11] Standard errors based on a longer lag were very similar to those presented.

The research design that we have outlined may be compromised by potential changes in the composition of the control and treatment groups in response to the introduction of NHI. It also may be compromised by interactions between baseline characteristics that vary among the three groups and trends over time. With regard to the first issue, parents who anticipate a poor birth outcome or who have sick infants or children or parents with a propensity to avoid risk or engage in a variety of healthy behaviors are more likely to obtain health insurance. Prior to the enactment of NHI, that was possible only if they were in the government sector.[12] After the enactment of NHI, the motive to enter the government sector for this reason no longer exists. To cite another example, women who married men employed in the government sector to obtain health insurance before NHI might choose to marry men employed in the industry sector after its introduction. To cite a final example, government sector wives with industry sector husbands might quit their jobs after NHI became effective. These factors suggest that there may be a time-varying unobservable that partially determines both the health outcome and membership in the treatment group.

While the incentives just mentioned do exist, a variety of factors suggest that they will have small impacts on the composition of the treatment and control groups, especially the latter, in our sample period. It is difficult to transfer from the industry or agricultural sectors to the government sector because government workers who are civil servants, must pass very demanding examinations. Government workers are better paid and enjoy more fringe benefits than industry workers and have little incentive to leave that sector.

Chou and Staiger (2001) report that turnover (both entry and exit) was very low in the government sector from 1980 to 1997 and changed little during that period. In the more recent period of 1992 through 2000, the entry rate ranged between 2.2 and 3.8 percent, while the exit rate ranged between 1.2 and 2.2 percent (Central Trust of China, 2002). Entry and exit rates were almost equal in the period before NHI, while the latter exceeded the former in the period after NHI. Note that women who were eligible for GI prior to NHI because they worked in the public sector remain in the administrative records of the Central Trust of China even if they quit their jobs after the enactment of NHI. This is because they are still eligible for old-age insurance through their previous employment. Births to these women in the post-NHI period are included in the control group.

It is possible that some women married government employees prior to 1995 to get health insurance. Given, however, that these employees account for only about 10 percent of all paid employees, the likelihood of finding a mate was small. In addition, Taiwan is characterized by a high degree of selective mating—the tendency of individuals with similar characteristics to marry. In particular in Taiwan as in most developed and developing countries, husband's and wife's years of formal schooling completed are highly correlated in a positive fashion (simple correlation coefficient = 0.50 based on birth certificates). Given that and the small size of the government sector, the odds that a woman selected at random could find a husband in the government sector to marry in order to obtain health insurance were very small.

With regard to changes in the nongovernment sectors, Chou and Staiger (2001) find that women married to nongovernment employees were less likely to work in the post-NHI period, but this does not affect the composition of the treatment group. Moreover, as pointed out in section 3, that is an endogenous response to the severance of ties between work and health insurance coverage that should not be held constant in estimating its effects on postneonatal mortality.

While turnover in the government sector was stable in the period covered by our study (1990–2001), private sector employment as a percentage of all employment rose over time and farm sector employment fell. These were not new phenomena. They have been taking place since at least 1980, while NHI became effective in 1995 (Executive Yuan, 2001). They do suggest, however, changes in unmeasured characteristics of the treatment groups over time. For example, given the growth of industries requiring computer-intensive skills (high tech industries), skill levels in the private sector may have risen over time in ways that are not fully captured by years of formal schooling completed (an observed variable in our analysis). This unmeasured variable may be correlated with propensities to avoid risk or engage in healthy behaviors, or with unobserved health endowments of infants or children.

We address this issue in a variety of ways outlined in section 5.2 with an emphasis on interactions between differences in baseline characteristics of the three groups and trends over time. Here we note that the post-NHI period covers the East Asian Financial Crisis of 1997 and 1998. Manning (2000) and Smith et al. (2002) report that some private sector workers in Indonesia coped with layoffs by moving back to family farms. Further, some young adults who otherwise would have tried to enter the private sector chose not to do so. Taiwan was not as affected by the recession as Indonesia, but a similar response could have occurred in Taiwan. If the individuals who returned to the agricultural sector or chose not to leave differed from those in farm households in the pre-NHI period, then our estimates could be biased. For example, those who returned or chose not to leave may have had higher levels of ability and higher propensities to engage in a variety of healthy behaviors.[13]

Statistics from the Executive Yuan (2013) show that the issue just outlined does not affect our empirical strategy. There was a continuous decline in employment in the agricultural sector of the Taiwanese economy from 12.85 percent in 1990 to 7.54 percent in 2001. There was no deviation from this downward trend in 1997 and 1998. Employment fell from 10.12 percent of the total in 1996 to 9.57 percent in 1997, and to 8.85 percent in 1998. At the same time, employment in the private sector rose from 56.03 percent of the total employment in 1990 to 61.45 percent in 2001. The percentage stood at 58.00 percent in 1996, 58.85 percent in 1997, and 60.07 percent in 1998.

5.2. Results

Table 11.2 contains characteristics of the control group (government sector households) and the two treatment groups (private sector households and farm households) for the entire period and for the periods before and after the introduction of NHI. Included are the percentage of births to mothers with less than ten years of schooling, the percentage of births to mothers who are less than twenty years of age, the percentage of fourth and higher-order births, and the percentage of births to mothers who reside in counties in which county-specific average household income is less than the median value of that variable in a given year. Note that family income is not available on birth and infant death certificates. Note also that we use the term births to refer to infants who survive the neonatal period since we exclude births to infants who die in the neonatal period for reasons indicated in section 4.

In terms of differences at a moment in time and trends over time, the data in table 11.2 single out mother's schooling as the most important characteristic on which to focus. For the period as a whole, 54.03 percent of births in farm households and 42.22 percent of births in private-sector households were to mothers with less than ten years of schooling. That compared to 14.37 percent in government sector households. There was no trend in this variable in the period before the enactment of NHI compared to the period after in government households. On the other hand, it fell from 50.57 percent to 36.01 percent in private sector households and from 62.62 percent to 47.02 percent in farm households. These percentage point differences swamp those in births to young mothers and higher-order births. In addition, the number of births with these characteristics is much smaller at a moment in time than the number of births to low-educated mothers in each of the three groups. Births to mothers in low-income counties are much more prevalent in farm households than in the other two types of households. There was a modest increase of approximately 6 percentage points in this variable in farm households in the post-NHI period, while it shows no trend in the private and government sectors.

The small declines in the percentage of births to mother's below the age of twenty and in the percentage of fourth- and higher-order births in farm and private sector households relative to government sector households in the post-NHI period provide some evidence that the hypothetical decline in fertility due to the introduction of NHI discussed in section 3 actually took place. Additional evidence is that the reductions in the number of children in farm and private sector families in the post-NHI period relative to the pre-NHI period were larger than in government sector families. This result is based on our analysis of the annual Survey of Income and Family Expenditure (SIFE) in Taiwan for the years 1990 through 2000. It differs somewhat from birth rates estimated from birth certificates. These rates fell more rapidly in the private sector but not in the farm sector after the introduction of NHI. Both results should be interpreted with caution because of the small number of farm and government sector families in the SIFE and because the denominators of birth rates are estimated from the latter survey.[14]

The data in table 11.2 underscore the potential benefit of running separate regressions by mother's education levels so that the treatment and control groups will be more comparable. Not only does this strategy control for mother's education, but it also allows that characteristic to interact with trends in postneonatal mortality reflected by year effects. To be complete, however, we run separate regressions by each of the three other characteristics in table 11.2.[15] The regressions by parity and mother's age incorporate at least to some extent effects due to completed family size.

Table 11.2 Baseline Characteristics by Group

	Whole Sample	Control Government Employees	Treatment I Private Employees	Treatment II Farmers
	Mean (S.D.)	Mean (S.D.)	Mean (S.D.)	Mean (S.D.)
Whole period				
Mother with <10 years of schooling	40.07% (49.00%)	14.37% (35.08%)	42.22% (49.39%)	54.03% (49.84%)
Maternal age <20	3.04% (17.17%)	0.33% (5.70%)	3.32% (17.93%)	4.00% (19.59%)
Parity >3	3.60% (18.62%)	1.50% (12.17%)	3.59% (18.61%)	6.39% (24.46%)
County family income < median	47.42% (49.93%)	34.30% (47.47%)	33.37% (47.15%)	68.94% (46.28%)
Sample size	2,753,860	313,606	2,201,663	238,591
Before NHI				
Mother with <10 years of schooling	47.54% (49.94%)	14.23% (34.93%)	50.57% (50.00%)	62.62% (48.38%)
Maternal age <20	3.26% (17.76%)	0.56% (7.46%)	3.51% (18.41%)	4.42% (20.56%)
Parity >3	4.32% (20.33%)	1.57% (12.44%)	4.37% (20.45%)	7.27% (25.96%)
County household income < median	35.62% (47.89%)	32.80% (46.95%)	32.58% (46.87%)	65.71% (47.47%)
Sample size	1,179,842	133,930	938,659	107,253
After NHI				
Mother with <10 years of schooling	34.47% (47.53%)	14.47% (35.18%)	36.01% (48.00%)	47.02% (49.91%)
Maternal age <20	2.88% (16.72%)	0.15% (3.89%)	3.18% (17.56%)	3.65% (18.75%)
Parity >3	3.06% (17.22%)	1.45% (11.97%)	3.01% (17.09%)	5.68% (23.14%)
County household income < median	37.27% (48.35%)	35.43% (47.83%)	33.97% (47.36%)	71.57% (45.11%)
Sample size	1,574,018	179,676	1,263,004	131,338

Table 11.3 contains postneonatal mortality rates (deaths per thousand survivors of the neonatal period) before and after the introduction of NHI for the treatment and control groups. Government employees, the control group, had the lowest postneonatal mortality followed by private employees and then by farmers. This ranking persisted after the introduction of NHI, although rates for all three groups fell.

For reasons just indicated, we conduct separate analyses for infants born to mothers with less than ten years of formal schooling and for infants born to mothers with ten or more years of formal schooling. Moreover, it is plausible that the impacts of increases in medical care on infant survival are larger for infants who are in poor health at birth than for other infants. Therefore, we also examine mortality outcomes for preterm infants (gestational age of less than thirty-seven weeks), full-term infants (gestational age of thirty-seven weeks or more), low-weight infants (birthweight less than 2500 g), and normal-weight infants (birthweight of 2500 g or more).

Table 11.3 contains data for each of these six groups as well as for the whole sample. The well-known differentials in infant mortality by mother's education, gestation, and birthweight emerge from these data. In general, within each category, the rankings of survival prospects were the same as in the full sample, before the introduction of NHI, and after its introduction. There are two exceptions. After the introduction of NHI, infants born to mothers with at least ten years of schooling were slightly more likely to survive in farm households than in private sector households. The same holds for premature infants and low-weight infants in farm households compared to private sector households in the post-NHI period. There are large reductions in the death rates of premature infants and low-weight infants in farm households in the post-NHI period. The former rate fell from 16.71 deaths per thousand survivors to 10.14, while the latter rate fell from 19.56 to 13.88.

Table 11.4, which is based on the data in table 11.3, shows that trends in low birthweight and prematurity—the two key indicators of initial health—were almost identical in each of the three groups when the period after the introduction of NHI is compared to the period before its introduction. Both percentages were slightly higher in each group in the period after the introduction of NHI than in the period before. These results may have been due to advances in neonatal technology that improved the survival prospects of light and premature infants. But the increase in each one was practically the same in each group. To be specific, the percentage of low-weight births rose by 0.52 percentage points in government sector households, by 0.59 percentage points in farm households, and by 0.73 percentage points in private sector

Table 11.3 Mean of Postneonatal Rate by Group and Time Period

	Whole Sample	Government Employees	Private Employees	Farmers
Whole sample				
Before NHI (1990–1993)	3.006 (1,179,842)	2.359 (133,930)	3.017 (938,659)	3.720 (107,253)
After NHI (1996–2001)	2.429 (1,574,018)	1.859 (179,676)	2.495 (1,263,004)	2.574 (131,338)
Mother's years of schooling <10				
Before NHI (1990–1993)	3.512 (560,904)	2.309 (19,055)	3.455 (474,683)	4.258 (67,166)
After NHI (1996–2001)	2.984 (542,581)	1.731 (26,003)	3.043 (454,829)	3.077 (61,749)
Mother's years of schooling ≥10				
Before NHI (1990–1993)	2.548 (618,938)	2.368 (114,875)	2.569 (463,976)	2.819 (40,087)
After NHI (1996–2001)	2.137 (1,031,437)	1.881 (153,673)	2.186 (808,175)	2.127 (69,589)
Pre-term				
Before NHI (1990–1993)	11.528 (45,283)	8.000 (5250)	11.448 (35,903)	16.707 (4,130)
After NHI (1996–2001)	10.198 (89,917)	8.258 (9,445)	10.457 (72,682)	10.141 (7,790)
Full-term				
Before NHI (1990–1993)	2.658 (1,128,469)	2.132 (128,048)	2.677 (898,071)	3.156 (102,350)
After NHI (1996–2001)	1.953 (1,479,099)	1.503 (169,683)	2.004 (1,186,449)	2.082 (122,967)
Normal birth weight				
Before NHI (1990–1993)	2.502 (1,127,300)	1.969 (128,983)	2.527 (896,326)	2.951 (101,991)
After NHI (1996–2001)	1.845 (1,496,820)	1.432 (172,511)	1.890 (1,199,774)	1.983 (124,535)
Low birth weight				
Before NHI (1990–1993)	14.745 (47,473)	13.892 (4,391)	14.260 (38,429)	19.557 (4,653)
After NHI (1996–2001)	14.093 (74,434)	12.558 (6,848)	14.288 (61,100)	13.876 (6,486)

Note: Total sample size is 2,753,860. Deaths from the 28th through the 364th day of life per thousand survivors of the first 27 days of life.

Table 11.4 Percentage of Low-Weight Births and Percentage of Premature Births by Group and Time Period

Group	Percentage of Low-Weight Births		Percentage of Premature Births	
	Before NHI	After NHI	Before NHI	After NHI
Government	3.29	3.81	3.93	5.27
Farm	4.36	4.95	3.88	5.96
Private	4.11	4.84	3.84	5.77

households. The corresponding increases in the percentage of premature births were 1.34 percentage points for government sector households, 2.08 percentage points for farm households, and 1.93 percentage points for private sector households. The slightly larger increases in farm and private households relative to government households may have been associated with incentives to give birth rather than abort a problematic birth following the introduction of NHI. In any case, none of the differences in the outcomes just noted between each of the two treatment groups and the control group is statistically significant at the 5 percent level.

Table 11.5 contains DD regression estimates of equation (1). Thirteen DDs are presented for each of the two treatment groups: one for the whole sample and one for each of twelve groups defined by mother's education (less than ten years of formal schooling versus ten or more years); pre-term infants (gestational age less than thirty-seven weeks); full-term infants (gestational age thirty-seven weeks or more); low-weight infants (birthweight less than 2500 g); normal weight infants (birthweight of 2500 g or more); mother's age at birth (less than twenty versus twenty and older); parity (first, second, or third births versus higher-order births); and residence in a county classified by county-specific average household income (less than the median of that variable for all counties in a given year versus equal to or greater than the median). None of the thirteen DDs is statistically significant for private households, and four of the coefficients are positive. The point estimate in the case of prematurity—a reduction of 1.08 deaths per thousand survivors or 9.43 percent relative to the pre-NHI mean of 11.45 deaths per thousand survivors—is substantial. But the death rate of light infants actually rose. Given that, given the large standard error associated with the reduction in the death rate of premature infants, and given the other coefficients for private sector households, there is no evidence that the introduction of NHI benefited infants born in these households.

Table 11.5 Difference-in-Differences Estimation

	Whole Sample	Years of Schooling <10	Years of Schooling ≥10	Pre-Term	Full-Term	Low Birth Weight	Normal Birth Weight
NHI * Private	0.002	0.178	0.143	−1.080	−0.024	1.485	−0.081
	(0.163)	(0.213)	(0.213)	(1.246)	(0.155)	(2.260)	(0.109)
NHI * Farmer	−0.635***	−0.589*	−0.183	−6.779**	−0.436**	−4.353	−0.422**
	(0.212)	(0.307)	(0.285)	(2.553)	(0.191)	(3.412)	(0.166)
Sample size	30	30	30	30	30	30	30

	Mothers Age <20	Mothers Age ≥20	Income < Median	Income ≥ Median	Parity >3	Parity ≤3
NHI * Private	−2.320	−0.001	−0.080	0.047	−0.335	0.030
	(3.410)	(0.157)	(0.143)	(0.209)	(0.722)	(0.168)
NHI * Farmer	−5.986	−0.514**	−0.719***	−0.709*	0.567	−0.728***
	(3.653)	(0.209)	(0.191)	(0.386)	(1.116)	(0.217)
Sample size	30	30	30	30	30	30

Note: All regressions contain 30 observations (cells), are weighted by the square root of the number of neonatal survivors in each cell, and include group and year fixed effects. The Newey-West standard errors with two lags of autocorrelation are reported in parentheses.

*** Significant at the 1 percent level (two-tailed test).
** Significant at the 5 percent level (two-tailed test).
* Significant at the 10 percent level (two-tailed test).

The story is quite different for the postneonatal mortality rate of infants born in farm families. Here twelve of the thirteen DDs are negative, three are significant at the 1 percent level, an additional four are significant at the 5 percent level, and two more are significant at the 10 percent level. Some of the negative coefficients are substantial, both in absolute and percentage terms. For the sample as a whole, the introduction of NHI lowered the postneonatal mortality rate of infants born to the wives of farmers by 0.64 deaths per thousand survivors. This is a reduction of 17.20 percent relative to the mean in the pre-NHI period of 3.72 deaths per thousand survivors. A larger absolute reduction is observed for infants born to mothers with less than ten years of education relative to those born to mothers with ten or more years of education. For the former group, the decline of 0.59 deaths per thousand survivors (a reduction of 13.85 percent relative to the pre-NHI mean of 4.26 deaths per thousand survivors) is more than three times larger than the decline of 0.18 deaths per thousand survivors for the latter group. Especially large effects are observed for pre-term and low-weight infants. In the case of prematurity, the reduction amounts to 6.78 deaths per thousand survivors or to 40.57 percent relative to the pre-NHI mean of 16.71 deaths per thousand survivors. For low-weight infants, the reduction is 4.35 deaths per thousand survivors, but it is estimated imprecisely.

We want to emphasize that each of the group-specific regressions in the table not only allows the NHI effect to interact with the characteristic at issue but also allows that characteristic to interact with the nine year effects that are obtained in each regression. We do not pursue interactions between the NHI farm coefficient and mother's age, parity, or residence in a low-income county in the remainder of the chapter. There is no evidence in table 11.5 that the coefficient for residents of low-income counties differs from the corresponding coefficient for residents of other counties. There is evidence of a larger effect for mothers below the age of twenty relative to older mothers and for first, second, or third births compared to higher-order births but births to young mothers and higher-order births account for a small percentage of all births as shown in table 11.2. Moreover, the coefficient for young mothers, while large, is not statistically significant. There is some evidence in that table of modest declines in the percentages of these births in the two treatment groups in the post-NHI period but these may be due to endogenous reductions caused by the introduction of NHI. In general, mothers with low education are more likely to give birth at young ages, more likely to have higher-order births, and more likely to have low household income. Hence, interactions between this variable and the introduction of NHI provide a convenient summary of a number of potential interactions.[16]

6. NHI AND MEDICAL TECHNOLOGY

6.1. Model and Implementation

To explore a plausible mechanism via which the legislation may have affected infant survival, we modify the model to take account of the positive effects of NHI on the adoption and use of state-of-the-art medical technology reported by Chou, Liu, and Mahhitt (2004). Our specific hypothesis, which is similar to the one proposed and explored by Currie and Gruber (1997), is that NHI will have a larger impact on the survival prospects of treatment infants if their mothers live near a hospital with more advanced technology and that this effect is larger in the period after NHI became effective for the treatment group. Put differently, both financial considerations and distance rationed intensive care services received by infants in the treatment group prior to NHI, but only distance rationed services in the period after NHI. We broaden this hypothesis to include the possibility that NHI effects are larger in areas with more medical care services in general.

Taiwan is divided into twenty-four counties, and data on medical care resources by year and county are available. Therefore, we attach these measures to the individual merged birth and infant death certificates based on the county and year in which the birth took place. Then we aggregate into 720 county-group-year cells (24 counties * 3 groups * 10 years) and estimate the following weighted regression, where the set of weights is the square root of the number of neonatal survivors in each cell:

$$P_{gjt} = \beta_0 + \beta_1 Treat_{gjt} + \beta_2 NHI_t * Treat_{gjt} + \beta_3 Q_{jt} + \beta_4 NHI_t * Q_{jt}$$
$$+ \beta_5 Treat_{gjt} * Q_{jt} + \beta_6 NHI_t * Treat_{gjt} * Q_{jt} + f_j + f_t + \varepsilon_{gjt}. \qquad (2)$$

Here j indexes counties, f_j is a set of county fixed effects, one treatment group, denoted by $Treat_{gjt}$, is assumed to simplify the exposition, and Q_{jt} is a measure of medical care availability or technology in the jth county in year t.[17] Note that the model specified by equation (2) in which a measure of the availability of intensive care in the mother's area of residence interacts with the introduction of NHI incorporates an important correlate of the introduction and diffusion of new technology. Hence, not all of the impacts of technology are assumed to be captured by time effects.

The equation contains a natural measure of the impact of NHI:

$$\beta_2 + \beta_3[(Q_{ka} - Q_{kb}) - (Q_{ca} - Q_{cb})] + \beta_4(Q_{ka} - Q_{ca}) + \beta_5(Q_{ka} - Q_{kb}) + \beta_6 Q_{ka}, \quad (3)$$

where Q_{kb} and Q_{ka} are the mean values of Q for the treatment group (denoted by the subscript k) in the period before and after NHI, respectively, and Q_{cb} and Q_{ca} are the mean values of Q for the control group (denoted by the subscript c) in the period before and after NHI, respectively. It may seem puzzling that the mean values of Q for the treatment and control groups in a given period can differ because in a given year and county, Q must have the same value for each group but the relevant national means in each year or period must be weighted by the group-specific fraction of neonatal survivors in each county. If, for example, the difference between the fraction of all treatment group survivors who were born in the jth county in year t and the corresponding fraction of all control group survivors who were born in the jth county is negatively correlated with Q_{jt}, then Q_{kt} will be smaller than Q_{ct}.[18]

Some persons may object to the comprehensive nature of the effect of NHI given by equation (3) and may prefer the more narrowly defined one given by $\beta_2 + \beta_6 Q_{ka}$. The latter estimate, however, assumes that trends in Q and its differential impacts on the treatment and control groups are unrelated to the introduction of NHI. Moreover, suppose that β_4, β_5, β_6, and $[(Q_{ka} - Q_{kb}) - (Q_{ca} - Q_{cb})]$ are zero. Does that rule out the adoption and use of state-of-the-art medical technology as a mechanism via which the introduction of NHI affected infant health? The answer is no because in the absence of this development, Q might have changed at a slower rate for the treatment group than for the control group. Indeed, there might have been no growth for the former group. Given these considerations and the high degree of collinearity among the last four variables in equation (2), we use the broad estimator of the impact of NHI given by equation (3).

We employ three alternative measures of Q at the county level divided by the county population: the number of hospitals with a pediatric department, the number of hospitals with an obstetrical department, and the total number of infant hospital beds. We aggregated individual hospital data to the county level from Hospital Registry Files and Hospital Service Files collected and maintained by the Department of Health. While none of these is a direct measure of neonatal intensive care availability or the adoption of state-of-the-art medical technology used to treat infants, each of the variables just defined is likely to be positively correlated with that measure. Moreover, they are likely to be highly correlated in a positive manner with the number of physicians who provide medical care services to infants during their first year of life.

6.2. Results

Panels A, B, and C of table 11.6 contain alternative estimates of equation(2) in which Q is given by the per capita number of hospitals with an obstetrical department, the per capita number of hospitals with a pediatric department, and the per capita number of infant hospital beds, respectively. Since these inputs are measured at the county level and interact with the NHI indicator, we adjust standard errors for clustering by county and before or after the introduction of NHI. This results in forty-eight clusters. In performing tests of the significance of regression coefficients, the cluster procedure in Stata assumes that the number of degrees of freedom equals the number of clusters minus 1. We are more conservative and set the number of degrees of freedom equal to the number of clusters minus the number of estimated parameters excluding the county fixed effects. Hence significance tests are based on 28 degrees of freedom. We also present the Newey-West standard errors for panel data with a lag length of 2 in the table. These are the ones that we employed in table 11.5. They are very similar to the clustered standard errors.[19]

As in table 11.5, we fit the weighted regressions for the whole sample and for each of the six subgroups. The set of weights is the square root of the number of neonatal survivors in each cell. In addition to reporting the coefficients of key variables, we also report the impact of NHI on farm households that emerge from equation (3) because previous results and those in table 11.6 suggest that NHI had no significant impact on private households.

Regardless of the measure of medical technology or resources employed, the estimates of equation (3) follow the same pattern as the estimates of the NHI effects in table 11.5. For farm households, all seven estimates are negative in each of the three panels in table 11.6. In each panel, the estimate for the full sample and the estimate for premature infants are significant at the 5 percent level. Note that, in assessing statistical significance, one should keep in mind that they are obtained from coefficients of highly correlated variables.

The magnitudes of the NHI effects in table 11.6 are very similar to those in table 11.5. For the sample as a whole, the reduction of 0.64 deaths per thousand in each panel is exactly the same as the reduction in table 11.5. As is the case in table 11.5, compared to the sample as a whole and to the corresponding subgroups, the effects are bigger for infants of less educated mothers, for preterm infants, and for low-weight infants. The largest effects occur for pre-term infants. They range from a reduction of 6.84 deaths per thousand survivors in panels B and C to 6.88 deaths per thousand in panel A. They all translate into the same approximate 40 percent decline relative to the pre-NHI mean of 16.71 deaths per thousand survivors that emerges in table 11.5.

For the three measures of medical inputs, only two of the twenty-one coefficients of the triple interaction (NHI * Farmer * Q) are not negative. Hence, the negative impact of NHI on the postneonatal mortality rate of infants in farm families rises in absolute value as medical inputs in the infant's county rise.

In table 11.6, all but one of the twenty-one coefficients of the interaction between the indicator for farm households and the indicator for the period after NHI are insignificant. This suggests that the impact of NHI on postneonatal mortality reflects an interaction between insurance and medical care resources that

Table 11.6 NHI and Medical Technology

	Whole Sample	Years of Schooling <10	Years of Schooling ≥10	Pre-Term	Full-Term	Low Birth Weight	Normal Birth Weight
Panel A							
Q = number of hospitals with an obstetrical department per 10,000 population							
NHI * Private * Q	-2.603	-4.376	-3.463	-30.139	-1.469	-43.998	-0.951
	(3.386)	(7.962)	(3.836)	(34.147)	(3.343)	(47.192)	(3.458)
	(3.375)	(8.423)	(3.578)	(32.996)	(3.166)	(51.108)	(3.012)
NHI * Farmer * Q	-6.124	-7.785	-9.247	-24.660	-4.900	-69.083	-3.404
	(4.748)	(7.369)	(5.352)*	(51.625)	(4.619)	(77.293)	(4.379)
	(5.434)	(10.894)	(6.159)	(50.779)	(5.138)	(76.803)	(4.724)
Private * Q	-0.065	1.149	0.095	14.158	-0.530	6.026	-0.492
	(2.945)	(6.854)	(3.086)	(17.577)	(2.866)	(28.454)	(3.098)
	(2.544)	(6.404)	(2.647)	(22.650)	(2.486)	(32.791)	(2.451)
Farmer * Q	-1.811	-4.879	4.195	-26.715	-0.595	12.717	-1.993
	(3.831)	(4.604)	(4.357)	(46.291)	(3.448)	(65.780)	(3.381)
	(4.175)	(8.008)	(4.276)	(41.514)	(3.885)	(57.884)	(3.655)
NHI * Q	1.928	4.866	1.334	31.339	0.523	51.853	0.133
	(2.696)	(7.313)	(3.076)	(25.525)	(2.897)	(41.745)	(2.988)
	(3.095)	(8.149)	(3.245)	(29.994)	(2.951)	(48.944)	(2.816)
NHI * PRI	0.381	0.826	0.637	3.405	0.183	7.898	0.050
	(0.563)	(1.362)	(0.596)	(5.065)	(0.547)	(7.079)	(0.583)
	(0.537)	(1.364)	(0.565)	(5.081)	(0.494)	(7.896)	(0.488)
NHI * Farmer	0.203	0.547	1.042	-3.258	0.227	4.998	0.038
	(0.720)	(1.052)	(0.791)	(6.928)	(0.721)	(10.488)	(0.717)
	(0.829)	(1.711)	(0.906)	(7.263)	(0.770)	(10.880)	(0.740)

Q	1.469	1.946	0.183	12.830	0.821	9.806	1.315
	(2.614)	(6.722)	(2.572)	(16.483)	(2.620)	(29.076)	(2.824)
	(2.618)	(6.593)	(2.687)	(21.265)	(2.596)	(32.800)	(2.515)

Effects of NHI on farm households

$\beta_2 + \beta_3[(Q_{ka} - Q_{kb}) - (Q_{ca} - Q_{cb})] +$
$\beta_4(Q_{ka} - Q_{ca}) + \beta_5(Q_{ka} - Q_{kb}) + \beta_6 Q_{ka}$

	−0.637	−0.590	−0.182	−6.888	−0.434	−4.488	−0.421
	(0.293)**	(0.513)	(0.382)	(2.792)**	(0.287)	(3.623)	(0.288)
	(0.289)**	(0.580)	(0.381)	(2.622)**	(0.270)	(3.584)	(0.259)

Panel B

Q = number of hospitals with a pediatric department per 10,000 population

NHI * Private * Q	0.182	−7.209	−0.263	−11.934	0.492	−43.646	1.871
	(3.532)	(7.702)	(4.107)	(31.688)	(3.647)	(41.583)	(3.833)
	(3.401)	(8.006)	(3.644)	(33.665)	(3.257)	(49.462)	(3.189)
NHI * Farmer * Q	−1.096	−8.613	−1.525	47.698	−3.935	−7.229	−0.978
	(5.786)	(6.780)	(7.033)	(42.655)	(5.388)	(64.521)	(5.246)
	(6.000)	(10.766)	(7.037)	(51.373)	(5.735)	(73.304)	(5.420)
Private * Q	−1.298	4.692	−1.250	−2.570	−1.253	12.448	−2.124
	(2.803)	(6.223)	(3.068)	(16.705)	(2.978)	(28.553)	(3.169)
	(2.511)	(5.908)	(2.657)	(23.288)	(2.518)	(34.394)	(2.492)
Farmer * Q	−3.095	2.120	−2.748	−62.238	−0.083	−12.397	−2.717
	(4.666)	(4.942)	(6.504)	(38.177)	(4.597)	(53.875)	(4.153)
	(4.591)	(7.813)	(5.954)	(39.199)	(4.548)	(54.176)	(4.238)
NHI * Q	−0.664	7.809	−1.843	17.452	−1.368	35.261	−1.959
	(2.964)	(7.055)	(3.375)	(25.608)	(3.133)	(38.336)	(3.367)
	(3.214)	(7.822)	(3.345)	(30.697)	(3.073)	(46.833)	(3.041)

(continued)

Table 11.6 *(Continued)*

	Whole Sample	Years of Schooling <10	Years of Schooling ≥10	Pre-Term	Full-Term	Low Birth Weight	Normal Birth Weight
NHI * PRI	-0.017	0.977	0.158	0.274	-0.082	6.283	-0.289
	(0.424)	(1.057)	(0.484)	(3.778)	(0.438)	(5.015)	(0.478)
	(0.402)	(1.009)	(0.430)	(4.049)	(0.380)	(6.038)	(0.387)
NHI * Farmer	-0.512	0.388	-0.041	-10.907	-0.065	-3.253	-0.326
	(0.625)	(0.921)	(0.705)	(5.130)**	(0.589)	(7.644)	(0.610)
	(0.677)	(1.315)	(0.765)	(5.705)*	(0.633)	(8.219)	(0.622)
Q	1.613	-4.270	2.028	18.114	0.905	4.279	1.590
	(2.526)	(5.922)	(2.390)	(16.624)	(2.745)	(31.655)	(2.854)
	(2.582)	(6.093)	(2.642)	(22.424)	(2.533)	(34.794)	(2.497)

Effects of NHI on farm households

$$\beta_2 + \beta_3 1[(Q_{ka} - Q_{kb}) - (Q_{ca} - Q_{cb})] + \beta_4(Q_{ka} - Q_{ca}) + \beta_5(Q_{ka} - Q_{kb}) + \beta_6 Q_{ka}$$

	Whole Sample	Years of Schooling <10	Years of Schooling ≥10	Pre-Term	Full-Term	Low Birth Weight	Normal Birth Weight
	-0.638	-0.589	-0.184	-6.835	-0.435	-4.446	-0.422
	(0.288)**	(0.505)	(0.365)	(2.807)**	(0.281)	(3.540)	(0.279)
	(0.287)**	(0.575)	(0.377)	(2.607)**	(0.268)	(3.651)	(0.256)

Panel C

Q = number of infant hospital beds per 1,000 population

	Whole Sample	Years of Schooling <10	Years of Schooling ≥10	Pre-Term	Full-Term	Low Birth Weight	Normal Birth Weight
NHI * Private * Q	0.203	0.440	-0.305	-9.635	0.795	-14.559	0.734
	(1.338)	(3.136)	(1.395)	(8.849)	(1.303)	(12.796)	(1.327)
	(1.352)	(3.382)	(1.526)	(9.451)	(1.289)	(13.996)	(1.219)
NHI * Farmer * Q	-0.217	1.289	-2.380	-2.475	-0.049	-7.540	-0.142
	(2.135)	(3.274)	(2.385)	(19.197)	(2.010)	(28.449)	(1.829)
	(2.415)	(4.748)	(2.546)	(20.964)	(2.333)	(29.229)	(2.210)

Private * Q	-1.681	-0.081	-1.043	-3.815	-1.600	2.531	-1.627
	(0.929)*	(2.984)	(0.925)	(7.591)	(0.939)*	(10.811)	(1.019)
	(0.971)*	(3.155)	(1.087)	(7.953)	(0.939)*	(10.709)	(0.953)*
Farmer * Q	-3.289*	-3.645	-0.482	-10.695	-2.962*	-3.125	-2.754*
	(1.825)*	(2.365)	(2.011)	(17.264)	(1.662)	(26.202)	(1.551)
	(1.964)*	(4.033)	(2.065)	(18.752)	(1.968)	(25.627)	(1.889)
NHI * Q	-0.201	-0.995	0.298	10.464	-0.649	19.591	-0.848
	(1.326)	(2.951)	(1.459)	(7.369)	(1.228)	(12.030)	(1.230)
	(1.278)	(3.338)	(1.427)	(8.196)	(1.211)	(13.224)	(1.153)
NHI * PRI	0.065	0.049	0.318	2.497	-0.164	6.257	-0.203
	(0.417)	(1.041)	(0.448)	(3.221)	(0.420)	(4.668)	(0.437)
	(0.406)	(1.025)	(0.442)	(3.248)	(0.382)	(5.155)	(0.371)
NHI * Farmer	-0.349	-0.698	0.489	-4.591	-0.247	-0.715	-0.243
	(0.552)	(0.947)	(0.604)	(4.760)	(0.542)	(7.699)	(0.531)
	(0.651)	(1.337)	(0.663)	(5.171)	(0.607)	(7.550)	(0.590)
Q	0.999	1.408	-0.839	8.321	0.562	-13.500	1.413
	(1.158)	(2.924)	(1.347)	(9.400)	(1.002)	(11.411)	(1.092)
	(1.156)	(3.294)	(1.336)	(10.175)	(1.091)	(13.172)	(1.070)
Effects of NHI on farm households							
$\beta_2 + \beta_3[(Q_{ka} - Q_{kb}) - (Q_{ca} - Q_{cb})] +$ $\beta_4(Q_{ka} - Q_{ca}) + \beta_5(Q_{ka} - Q_{kb}) + \beta_6 Q_{ka}$	-0.638	-0.595	-0.188	-6.844	-0.436	-4.453	-0.421
	(0.263)**	(0.512)	(0.375)	(2.701)**	(0.266)	(3.560)	(0.269)
	(0.276)**	(0.577)	(0.379)	(2.785)**	(0.261)	(3.568)	(0.250)
Sample size	719	718	719	705	719	699	719

Notes: There are 720 potential observations (cells) in each regression, but some are empty. All regressions are weighted by the square root of the number of survivors in each cell and include group, year, and county fixed effects. Standard errors, reported in the first parentheses, are adjusted for clustering by county and NHI. Standard errors, reported in the second parentheses, are the Newey-West standard errors with two lags of autocorrelation.

** Significant at the 5 percent level (two-tailed test).

* Significant at the 10 percent level (two-tailed test).

may operate to a large extent through these resources. Therefore in table 11.7, we exclude the variables NHI * Farmer and NHI * Private from equation (2) to reduce collinearity problems. We term this the "full interaction model." All twenty-one coefficients of the triple interaction (NHI * Farmer * Q) are negative in table 11.7. More importantly, eight of these coefficients are significant in table 11.7, compared to only one in table 11.6. The coefficients are largest in absolute value for pre-term and low-weight infants. The estimated effects of NHI given by equation (3) in table 11.7 are somewhat smaller and more variable than those in table 11.6. They range from 0.54 to 0.66 deaths per thousand survivors for the full sample and from 4.63 to 6.52 deaths per thousand premature survivors. But these differences are relatively small.

One might argue that the results in tables 11.6 and 11.7 reflect in part supply responses to increases in demand in the post-NHI period. For that reason, they cannot be solely attributed to the introduction of NHI. A plausible counter-argument is that in the absence of supply responses or redistribution of a fixed supply away from the control group and towards the treatment groups, the mere introduction of NHI could not impact health outcomes among the previously uninsured. Hence, the argument that the effects in tables 11.6 and 11.7 are biased would have the most degree of validity if the trends in supply in the post-NHI period were due to factors other than its introduction.

One way to evaluate the importance of the issue just raised is to examine trends in the three medical resource inputs at the national level in the pre- and post-NHI periods. The per capita number of hospitals with an obstetrical department shows no trend prior to 1995 and a slight reduction thereafter. The per capita number of hospitals with a pediatric department is essentially flat throughout the entire period. The per capita number of infant hospital beds increased by approximately 14 percent in the pre-period and by approximately 22 percent in the first few years of the post-period. But the series was flat after 1997. One point to bear in mind in evaluating the trends in the three series is that our estimates are very stable across the three of them. Another point is that the denominator of each county resource measure is the population of that county. A more appropriate denominator is the county-specific number of women between the ages of fifteen and forty-four, but that series is not available by year and county.

To address this issue in somewhat more detail, we have estimated regressions in which each medical resource measure is lagged one year. To some extent, these regressions address a concern with supply responses to the introduction of NHI or to other phenomena. The NHI estimates of equation (3) are contained in panels A and B of table 11.8. The first panel pertains to the specifications in table 11.6 (NHI * Farmer and NHI * Private included), and the second panel pertains to the specifications in table 11.7 (NHI * Farmer and NHI * Private excluded).

Table 11.7 NHI and Medical Technology, Full Interaction Model

	Whole Sample	Years of Schooling <10	Years of Schooling ≥10	Pre-Term	Full-Term	Low Birth Weight	Normal Birth Weight
Panel A							
Q = number of hospitals with an obstetrical department per 10,000 population							
NHI * Private * Q	-0.292	0.618	0.382	-9.453	-0.362	4.118	-0.647
	(1.292)	(2.772)	(1.387)	(11.433)	(1.300)	(14.991)	(1.346)
	(1.213)	(2.932)	(1.353)	(10.541)	(1.196)	(14.920)	(1.131)
NHI * Farmer * Q	-4.998	-4.654	-2.632	-48.639	-3.493	-40.262	-3.180
	(1.922)**	(3.624)	(2.714)	(21.270)**	(1.831)*	(27.747)	(1.819)*
	(1.885)**	(3.715)	(2.636)	(18.904)**	(1.772)*	(25.942)	(1.644)*
Private * Q	-1.055	-0.965	-1.580	3.471	-1.002	-16.866	-0.622
	(2.080)	(4.443)	(2.410)	(17.897)	(1.932)	(22.610)	(1.989)
	(1.827)	(4.432)	(1.955)	(17.199)	(1.731)	(25.436)	(1.635)
Farmer * Q	-2.375	-6.438	1.406	-17.482	-1.160	-2.429	-2.093
	(3.083)	(4.234)	(3.490)	(32.571)	(2.787)	(47.348)	(2.683)
	(3.108)	(5.866)	(3.523)	(30.288)	(2.898)	(44.443)	(2.662)
NHI * Q	0.015	0.310	-1.962	17.144	-0.467	10.258	-0.125
	(1.500)	(2.610)	(1.645)	(16.136)	(1.516)	(18.411)	(1.486)
	(1.667)	(3.385)	(1.909)	(16.281)	(1.596)	(20.106)	(1.499)
Q	2.295	3.893	1.658	20.010	1.252	29.682	1.427
	(1.962)	(4.653)	(2.091)	(15.259)	(1.995)	(20.433)	(1.967)
	(2.118)	(4.801)	(2.371)	(18.549)	(2.079)	(27.320)	(1.910)
Effect of NHI on farm households							
$\beta_3[(Q_{ka} - Q_{kb}) - (Q_{ca} - Q_{cb})] +$	-0.659	-0.653	-0.293	-6.518	-0.458	-4.991	-0.425
$\beta_4(Q_{ka} - Q_{ca}) + \beta_5(Q_{ka} - Q_{kb}) + \beta_6 Q_{ka}$	(0.266)**	(0.504)	(0.355)	(2.751)**	(0.259)*	(3.568)	(0.256)
	(0.261)**	(0.527)	(0.353)	(2.489)**	(0.248)*	(3.434)	(0.231)*

(continued)

Table 11.7 (*Continued*)

Panel B

Q = Number of hospitals with a pediatric department per 10,000 population

	Whole Sample	Years of Schooling <10	Years of Schooling ≥10	Pre-Term	Full-Term	Low Birth Weight	Normal Birth Weight
NHI * Private * Q	0.085	-0.168	0.909	-9.463	-0.107	3.195	-0.248
	(1.728)	(3.245)	(1.829)	(13.879)	(1.713)	(17.641)	(1.739)
	(1.596)	(3.669)	(1.782)	(13.391)	(1.566)	(18.756)	(1.461)
NHI * Farmer * Q	-5.429	-6.493	-2.059	-44.800	-4.402	-41.122	-3.441
	(2.630)**	(4.052)	(3.845)	(25.397)*	(2.587)*	(31.574)	(2.502)
	(2.472)**	(4.629)	(3.504)	(24.440)*	(2.369)*	(32.828)	(2.170)
Private * Q	-1.246	1.258	-1.818	-4.039	-0.970	-12.331	-1.118
	(1.967)	(4.204)	(2.302)	(14.952)	(1.988)	(19.071)	(2.028)
	(1.790)	(4.250)	(1.955)	(17.516)	(1.744)	(25.345)	(1.660)
Farmer * Q	-0.908	0.927	-2.374	-5.607	0.139	7.263	-1.520
	(3.588)	(4.313)	(4.543)	(27.277)	(3.505)	(35.538)	(3.327)
	(3.311)	(5.798)	(4.161)	(30.367)	(3.239)	(40.942)	(2.990)
NHI * Q	-0.218	1.643	-2.687	23.633	-0.855	0.176	-0.073
	(1.744)	(3.066)	(1.856)	(17.638)	(1.783)	(21.524)	(1.739)
	(1.885)	(3.895)	(2.126)	(16.909)	(1.812)	(21.461)	(1.682)
Q	1.408	-1.182	2.436	14.778	0.661	23.174	0.690
	(1.861)	(4.113)	(1.866)	(14.563)	(1.952)	(21.357)	(1.912)
	(2.060)	(4.631)	(2.266)	(19.341)	(1.971)	(27.711)	(1.882)
Effect of NHI on farm households							
$\beta_3[(Q_{ka} - Q_{kb}) - (Q_{ca}-Q_{cb})] +$	-0.537	-0.678	-0.174	-4.633	-0.423	-3.681	-0.360
$\beta_4(Q_{ka} - Q_{ca}) + \beta_5(Q_{ka} - Q_{kb}) + \beta_6 Q_{ka}$	(0.260)**	(0.410)	(0.345)	(2.430)*	(0.249)*	(3.094)	(0.242)
	(0.251)**	(0.488)	(0.332)	(2.397)*	(0.237)*	(3.263)	(0.219)

Panel C

Q = Number of infant hospital beds per 1000 population

NHI * Private * Q	0.392	0.596	0.576	-2.428	0.337	3.219	0.167
	(0.497)	(1.237)	(0.596)	(4.567)	(0.500)	(6.159)	(0.515)
	(0.550)	(1.509)	(0.694)	(4.732)	(0.541)	(6.518)	(0.508)
NHI * Farmer * Q	-1.583	-1.369	-0.806	-22.355	-0.836	-16.253	-0.878
	(1.020)	(1.950)	(1.609)	(12.136)*	(0.996)	(13.828)	(0.970)
	(0.984)	(2.009)	(1.555)	(11.420)*	(0.961)	(14.884)	(0.910)
Private * Q	-1.798	-0.158	-1.595	-8.807	-1.318	-9.160	-1.278
	(0.648)***	(1.671)	(0.783)**	(5.545)	(0.601)**	(7.741)	(0.611)**
	(0.700)**	(1.960)	(0.862)*	(6.131)	(0.645)**	(8.947)	(0.614)**
Farmer * Q	-2.537*	-2.343	-1.464	1.928	-2.501*	1.027	-2.313*
	(1.397)	(2.321)	(1.661)	(12.882)	(1.287)*	(16.404)	(1.230)
	(1.392)	(2.804)	(1.710)	(14.148)	(1.367)*	(18.992)	(1.314)
NHI * Q	-0.268	-0.903	-0.459	5.864	-0.227	5.330	-0.341
	(0.689)	(1.188)	(0.884)	(5.387)	(0.661)	(7.145)	(0.631)
	(0.652)	(1.590)	(0.845)	(5.450)	(0.649)	(7.302)	(0.590)
Q	1.021	1.314	-0.365	11.223	0.298	-4.334	1.099
	(0.852)	(1.836)	(1.155)	(8.398)	(0.727)	(9.295)	(0.757)
	(1.002)	(2.244)	(1.281)	(10.021)	(0.930)	(12.956)	(0.862)
Effect of NHI on farm households							
$\beta_3[(Q_{ka} - Q_{kb}) - (Q_{ca} - Q_{cb})] +$	-0.574	-0.468	-0.288	-6.012	-0.387	-4.459	-0.372
$\beta_4(Q_{ka} - Q_{ca}) + \beta_5(Q_{ka} - Q_{kb}) + \beta_6 Q_{ka}$	(0.227)**	(0.422)	(0.355)	(2.472)**	(0.225)*	(2.922)	(0.213)*
	(0.238)**	(0.458)	(0.346)	(2.281)**	(0.227)*	(3.076)	(0.210)*
Sample size	719	718	719	705	719	699	719

Notes: There are 720 potential observations (cells) in each regression, but some are empty. All regressions are weighted by the square root of the number of survivors in each cell and include group, year, and county fixed effects. Standard errors, reported in the first parentheses, are adjusted for clustering by county and NHI. Standard errors, reported in the second parentheses, are the Newey-West standard errors with two lags of autocorrelation.

*** Significant at the 1 percent level (two-tailed test).

** Significant at the 5 percent level (two-tailed test).

* Significant at the 10 percent level (two-tailed test).

The estimates in table 11.8 are very similar to the corresponding estimates in tables 11.6 and 11.7. For example, panel A suggests a reduction of 0.65 deaths per thousand survivors compared to 0.64 in table 11.6. The reduction in the case of premature births of 7.50 deaths per thousand survivors is somewhat larger than the reduction of between 6.84 and 6.89 deaths in table 11.6. Panel B of table 11.8 shows a decrease of between 0.53 and 0.68 deaths per thousand survivors compared to a decline of between 0.54 and 0.66 in table 11.7. For premature infants, the effect is again bigger when the medical resources are lagged: between 6.34 and 7.62 deaths per thousand survivors in panel B versus between 4.63 and 6.52 in table 11.7. Taken as a set, the models with lagged inputs suggest that the results in those with contemporaneous inputs are con-servative lower-bound estimates.

In summary, the estimates in tables 11.6 to 11.8 imply that the NHI effect is larger in areas in which there are more medical care inputs. Given the large number of regressors in the specifications in table 11.6 and the large degree of multicollinearity among them, we cannot conclude that the impact of NHI on postneonatal mortality reflects an interaction between insurance and med-ical care resources that operates entirely through these resources. Our results are suggestive, but definitive conclusions must await the availability of data on changes in the use of prenatal and neonatal care services and on changes in healthy and unhealthy behaviors associated with the introduction of NHI.

The estimates also imply that biases due to the endogenous choice of a household's location are not at work. To be specific, private sector families with greater concern for their infant's health could have located in areas where there were better health-care facilities. But it is extremely difficult for farm sector families to change their location. If this factor were relevant at the empirical level, it would bias the analysis for private sector families towards finding a pos-itive effect on infant survival. Yet we find no effect for private sector households and a positive effect for farm households.

7. SENSITIVITY ANALYSIS

In this section, we subject the robustness of our findings to the inclusion of data for the years 1994 and 1995, for the allowance of pre-existing trends and post-trends in postneonatal mortality for the treatment groups, and for differences in the composition of farm households compared to government households. With regard to the first two issues, we focus on alternative specifications of the regression for the whole sample in table 11.5, but the results are similar for the other regressions in that table and for those in tables 11.6 and 11.7. Recall that

Table 11.8 NHI and Medical Technology, Using Lagged Values

	Whole Sample	Years of Schooling <10	Years of Schooling ≥10	Pre-Term	Full-Term	Low Birth Weight	Normal Birth Weight
Panel A: Specification as in Table 11.6							
Q = Number of hospitals with an obstetrical department per 10,000 population							
Effect of NHI on farm households	−0.654	−0.621	−0.231	−7.510	−0.411	−5.284	−0.409
$\beta_2 + \beta_3[(Q_{ka} - Q_{kb}) - (Q_{ca} - Q_{cb})] + \beta_4(Q_{ka} - Q_{ca}) + \beta_5(Q_{ka} - Q_{kb}) + \beta_6 Q_{ka}$	(0.316)**	(0.566)	(0.497)	(2.893)**	(0.309)	(3.596)	(0.314)
	(0.332)**	(0.655)	(0.471)	(2.794)***	(0.306)	(3.636)	(0.299)
Q = Number of hospitals with a pediatric department per 10,000 population							
Effect of NHI on farm households	−0.655	−0.621	−0.233	−7.492	−0.414	−5.262	−0.410
$\beta_2 + \beta_3[(Q_{ka} - Q_{kb}) - (Q_{ca} - Q_{cb})] + \beta_4(Q_{ka} - Q_{ca}) + \beta_5(Q_{ka} - Q_{kb}) + \beta_6 Q_{ka}$	(0.308)**	(0.555)	(0.476)	(2.901)**	(0.301)	(3.700)	(0.303)
	(0.329)**	(0.652)	(0.455)	(2.790)***	(0.304)	(3.653)	(0.295)
Q = number of infant hospital beds per 1000 population							
Effect of NHI on farm households	−0.655	−0.623	−0.242	−7.490	−0.413	−5.255	−0.409
$\beta_2 + \beta_3[(Q_{ka} - Q_{kb}) - (Q_{ca} - Q_{cb})] + \beta_4(Q_{ka} - Q_{ca}) + \beta_5(Q_{ka} - Q_{kb}) + \beta_6 Q_{ka}$	(0.290)**	(0.557)	(0.493)	(2.854)**	(0.295)	(3.751)	(0.296)
	(0.321)**	(0.649)	(0.471)	(2.764)***	(0.300)	(3.661)	(0.292)
Panel B: Specification as in Table 11.7							
Q = Number of hospitals with an obstetrical department per 10,000 population							
Effect of NHI on farm households	−0.675	−0.738	−0.266	−7.616	−0.416	−6.306	−0.400
$\beta_3[(Q_{ka} - Q_{kb}) - (Q_{ca} - Q_{cb})] + \beta_4(Q_{ka} - Q_{ca}) + \beta_5(Q_{ka} - Q_{kb}) + \beta_6 Q_{ka}$	(0.274)**	(0.530)	(0.439)	(2.948)**	(0.270)	(3.692)*	(0.264)
	(0.282)**	(0.561)	(0.418)	(2.746)***	(0.264)	(3.621)*	(0.246)

(continued)

Table 11.8 *(Continued)*

	Whole Sample	Years of Schooling <10	Years of Schooling ≥10	Pre-Term	Full-Term	Low Birth Weight	Normal Birth Weight
Q = Number of hospitals with a pediatric department per 10,000 population							
Effect of NHI on farm households	−0.544	−0.765	−0.126	−6.388	−0.346	−5.604	−0.299
$\beta_3[(Q_{ka} - Q_{kb}) - (Q_{ca} - Q_{cb})] + \beta_4(Q_{ka} - Q_{ca^-} +$	(0.266)**	(0.429)*	(0.393)	(2.632)**	(0.267)	(3.247)*	(0.249)
$\beta_5(Q_{ka} - Q_{kb}) + \beta_6 Q_{ka}$	(0.264)**	(0.506)	(0.366)	(2.590)**	(0.254)	(3.353)*	(0.233)
Q = Number of infant hospital beds per 1000 population							
Effect of NHI on farm households	−0.527	−0.362	−0.270	−6.337	−0.315	−5.460	−0.287
$\beta_3[(Q_{ka} - Q_{kb}) - (Q_{ca} - Q_{cb})] + \beta_4(Q_{ka} - Q_{ca}) +$	(0.245)**	(0.460)	(0.452)	(2.487)**	(0.249)	(2.957)*	(0.237)
$\beta_5(Q_{ka} - Q_{kb}) + \beta_6 Q_{ka}$	(0.260)**	(0.501)	(0.424)	(2.380)***	(0.247)	(3.094)*	(0.232)

Notes: All regressions are weighted by the square root of the number of survivors in each cell and include group, year, and county fixed effects. Standard errors, reported in the first parentheses, are adjusted for clustering by county and NHI. Standard errors, reported in the second parentheses, are the Newey-West standard errors with two lags of autocorrelation.

*** Significant at the 1 percent level (two-tailed test).
** Significant at the 5 percent level (two-tailed test).
* Significant at the 10 percent level (two-tailed test).

we excluded the years 1994 and 1995 because of the more stringent requirements for reporting births enacted in October 1994 and because 1996 was the first full year following the introduction of NHI. The first regression in table 11.9 includes the postneonatal mortality rate in each of those two years for each of the three groups. As is the case with the other robustness checks, this has no impact on the conclusion that the introduction of NHI had no effect for private sector households. For farm households, the estimated reduction in postneonatal mortality falls from 0.64 deaths per thousand survivors to 0.49 deaths per thousand survivors.

The seven additional regressions in the table explore alternative ways of specifying pre-existing trends and in some cases post-trends on the estimated effect of NHI on the postneonatal mortality rate of infants born in farm households, including estimates that net out the trend. The regression in column 2 employs linear trends for farm and private sector households in the period before the introduction of NHI. The former coefficient is negative, while the latter coefficient is positive. Neither one is significant at conventional levels, nor the two are insignificant as a set at the 1 percent level, although they are significant at the 5 percent level (F-ratio = 3.59). Moreover, not only are the pre-existing trend coefficients insignificant, but the magnitudes of these coefficients are quite small relative to the main effect. This is important to note because it provides confidence that there is no potentially important effect introducing bias that is not picked up as a result of low power due to the small number of years in the pre-period.[20]

The net NHI effect is computed as $\alpha_{22} - 4r = -0.695 + 4 * 0.069$, where α_{22} is the coefficient of the interaction between the indicator for the years 1995 through 2001 and the indicator for infants born in farm families and r is the coefficient of the interaction between a linear trend that equals 1 in 1990 and 5 in 1994 and the indicator for farm households. This assumes that α_{22} compares the mortality rate in 1998 (the midyear of the post-NHI period) to 1990 (the first-year of the pre-NHI period). The reduction in this effect from -0.695 to -0.421 occurs because the mortality rate would have fallen by approximately 0.27 deaths per thousand survivors between 1990 and 1994 for factors that are specific to farmers.

The adjustment just mentioned assumes that the linear trend would have ended after 1994. An alternative procedure is to assume that α_{22} compares the mortality rate in 1992 (the midyear of the pre-NHI period) to the rate in 1998 and that the trend would have persisted through 1998. In that case the NHI effect becomes $-0.695 + 6 * 0.069$, which reduces the effect to 0.28 deaths per thousand survivors, with a standard error of 0.24. In our view the latter reduction is too large because it is based on an insignificant trend effect.

The regression in column 3 repeats the specification in column 2 after the years 1994 and 1995 are deleted. Each pre-trend coefficient remains insignificant at conventional levels. In addition, they are insignificant as a set at those

Table 11.9 Robustness Checks: Aggregate Data

	(1)	(2)	(3)	(4)	(5)	(6)	(7)	(8)
NHI * Private	0.080 (0.156)	0.133 (0.174)	0.113 (0.202)	0.239 (0.323)	0.022 (0.413)	0.132 (0.159)	0.066 (0.171)	-0.008 (0.184)
NHI * Farmer	-0.487** (0.200)	-0.695*** (0.230)	-0.670** (0.268)	-0.738* (0.379)	-1.062* (0.524)	-0.477** (0.192)	-0.641*** (0.208)	-0.724*** (0.237)
LinearPretrend * Private[a]		0.017 (0.029)	0.044 (0.046)	0.017 (0.031)	0.044 (0.050)			
LinearPretrend * Farmer[a]		-0.069 (0.044)	-0.014 (0.071)	-0.069 (0.046)	-0.014 (0.077)			
LinearPosttrend * Private[a]				-0.037 (0.077)	0.028 (0.100)			
LinearPosttrend * Farmer[a]				0.014 (0.100)	0.118 (0.132)			
Year92–94 * Private[b]						0.086 (0.060)		
Year92–94 * Farmer[b]						0.014 (0.178)		
Year93–94 * Private[c]							-0.031 (0.075)	
Year93–94 * Farmer[c]							-0.369*** (0.106)	
Year93 * Private[d]								-0.038 (0.076)

	(1)	(2)	(3)	(4)	(5)	(6)	(7)
Year93 * Farmer[d]	−0.487**						−0.353***
	(0.200)						(0.108)
Including data in 1994 & 1995	Yes	No	Yes	No	Yes	Yes	No
Observations	36	30	36	30	36	36	30
F-statistics on joint significance of trend variables	3.593	1.033	2.026	0.712	1.088	10.130	8.464
Reject null at 5%	Yes	No	No	No	No	Yes	Yes
Effects of NHI on farm households[e]	−0.421*	−0.635***	−0.487**	−0.635***	−0.487**	−0.273	−0.371*
	(0.206)	(0.212)	(0.200)	(0.212)	(0.200)	(0.179)	(0.210)

Note: All regressions contain 36 observations (cells), are weighted by the square root of the number of neonatal survivors in each cell, and include group and year fixed effects. The Newey-West standard errors with two lags of autocorrelation are reported in parentheses.

[a] The variable LinearPretrend is a linear trend for the years 1990 through 1994. The variable LinearPosttrend is a linear trend for the years 1995 through 2001.

[b] The variable Year92–94 is a dichotomous indicator for the years 1992, 1993, and 1994.

[c] The variable Year93–94 is a dichotomous indicator for the years 1993 and 1994.

[d] The variable Year93 is a dichotomous indicator for year 1993.

[e] See text for more details.

*** Significant at the 1 percent level (two-tailed test).

** Significant at the 5 percent level (two-tailed test).

* Significant at the 10 percent level (two-tailed test).

levels. That given, the estimated NHI effect is the one in table 11.5–0.64 deaths per thousand survivors.

The regressions in columns 4 and 5 add a linear post-trend interacted with the indicators for farm and private sector households. None of the four trend coefficients (two pre and two post for each group) is significant, and all four are insignificant as a set. Since these are "irrelevant variables," the best estimate of the NHI effect for farm households is a reduction of 0.49 deaths per thousand survivors for the whole period and 0.64 deaths per thousand survivors for the period that excludes 1994 and 1995.

The regressions in columns 6, 7, and 8 replace a linear pre-trend for each treatment group with treatment group indicators multiplied by a dichotomous indicator for the years 1992 through 1994 (column 6), a dichotomous indicator for the years 1993 and 1994 (column 7), or a dichotomous indicator for the year 1993 (column 8). The regressions in columns 6 and 7 are fit to data for the entire period, while the one in column 8 excludes 1994 and 1995. The two pre-trend coefficients are insignificant either separately or as a set in column 6. The NHI effect remains at 0.49 deaths per thousand survivors from column 1.

The picture is somewhat different in columns 7 and 8. The pre-existing effect is negative and significant for farm households, and the two pre-existing trend terms are significant as a set at the 1 percent level. As is the case in the previous estimates in table 11.9, in those in columns 7 and 8, the effect for farm households in the period before the introduction of NHI is smaller in absolute value than the corresponding coefficient in the period after its introduction. The net NHI effect falls to 0.27 deaths per thousand survivors and is estimated somewhat imprecisely in column 7.[21] The net effect is 0.37 deaths per thousand survivors in column 8 and is significant. Hence, only one of the eight estimates of the impact of the introduction of NHI on the postneonatal mortality rate of farm households is not statistically significant.

Since there are only five years of data prior to the introduction of NHI, attempts to estimate pre-existing trends, are plagued by issues related to multi-collinearity in a short time series. This compounds the problems related to the 1994 reporting requirement and the very real possibility that many births in 1995 were not affected by NHI. These factors suggest that a conservative conclusion with regard to the impact of NHI on farm households is that it reduced the post-neonatal mortality rate of infants born in these households by between 0.3 and 0.6 deaths per thousand survivors of the neonatal period or by between 8 and 16 percent relative to the pre-NHI mean of 3.7 deaths per thousand survivors. This range can be applied to the estimates for pre-term infants, low-weight infants, and infants born to mothers with less than ten years of schooling presented in previous sections of the chapter. The largest and most significant effects in tables 11.5, 11.6, and 11.7 pertain to the postneonatal mortality rate of premature infants. Based on tables 11.5 and 11.7, the reductions range from 3.4 deaths per thousand survivors to 6.8 deaths per thousand survivors or from 20 percent to 41 percent relative to the pre-NHI mean of 16.7 deaths per thousand survivors.[22]

As a final robustness check, we employ individual-level data to address concerns raised by differences between the characteristics of the treatment and control groups and changes in these characteristics over time. Our approach is to use these data to fit regressions weighted by the propensity score (Imbens 2004). The estimated probability (propensity score) of belonging to farm households compared to government households is estimated as a logistic function of continuous measures of mother's and father's years of schooling and ages. We assign individual weights equal to the probability of belonging to the opposite status group (as in McWilliams et al. 2003). For all observed characteristics, these propensity weights appear to balance the control and treatment groups extremely well. Using these weights, we fit regressions of the probability of a postneonatal death that include five mother's age dummies, six father's age dummies, five mother's education dummies, five father's education dummies, three parity dummies, year fixed effects, and county fixed effects. We limit the regressions to infants born in farm households and in government households because the estimated effects for private sector households were never significant. That is the same result that emerged in the aggregate analysis.

The results are contained in panels B and C of table 11.10. For comparative purposes, panel A of the table contains the corresponding estimates with the aggregate data and a much smaller set of covariates from table 11.5. Also for comparative purposes, all coefficients in panels B and C have been multiplied by 1,000. We limit the regressions in panels B and C to those for the full sample and for groups defined by gestation and birthweight. We do not show regressions for the two groups defined by mother's education because that variable is a key determinant of the propensity score. The weighted regression results for those two groups mirror the results for the entire sample. We do not estimate regressions for groups defined by mother's age, parity, or residence in a low-income county for reasons indicated in our discussion of the estimates in table 11.5. The regressions in panel C include interactions between year indicators and county of residence indicators. These interactions employed to capture shifts in the demand for labor from the farm sector to the private sector that may have affected the composition of the former group and may have taken place at differential rates among areas.

According to panel B, the introduction of NHI reduced the postneonatal mortality rate of infants born in farm households by 0.56 deaths per thousand survivors of the neonatal period. The corresponding estimate in panel C is larger: 0.66 deaths per thousand survivors. Both are significant at the 1 percent level.

Table 11.10 Robustness Checks: Propensity Score Weighted Regressions

	Whole Sample	Pre-Term	Full-Term	Low Birth Weight	Normal Birth Weight
Panel A. Replicate from Table 11.5					
NHI * Farmer	−0.635***	−6.779**	−0.436**	−4.353	−0.422**
	(0.212)	(2.553)	(0.191)	(3.412)	(0.166)
Sample size	30	30	30	30	30
Panel B. Propensity score weighted regressions[a,b]					
County-year interactions excluded					
NHI * Farmer	−0.561***	−8.928***	−0.312**	−4.988*	−0.370**
	(0.158)	(2.630)	(0.128)	(2.709)	(0.137)
Sample size	552,197	26,615	523,048	22,378	528,020
Panel C. Propensity score weighted regressions[a,b]					
County-year interactions included					
NHI * Farmer	−0.664***	−8.049**	−0.463***	−3.865	−0.500***
	(0.179)	(2.947)	(0.149)	(3.544)	(0.142)
Sample size	552,197	26,615	523,048	22,378	528,020

[a] All regressions include 5 mother's age dummies, 6 father's age dummies, 5 mother's education dummies, 5 father's education dummies, 3 parity dummies, year fixed effects, and county fixed effects. Standard errors, reported in parentheses, are adjusted for clustering by group and year.

[b] The propensity scores of belonging to farmers' households are estimated. Variables used to predict the propensity scores include mother's and father's years of schooling and ages.

*** Significant at the 1 percent level (two-tailed te-t).

** Significant at the 5 percent level (two-tailed test).

* Significant at the 10 percent level (two-tailed test).

The reduction in the regression with the aggregate data and with a much smaller set of covariates in panel A of 0.64 deaths per thousand survivors falls between the two declines just cited. But clearly the three estimates are very similar. The NHI effect for premature infants becomes larger in the propensity score weighted regressions: 8.93 deaths per thousand survivors in panel B and 8.05 in panel C versus 6.78 in panel A. The reductions for low-weight infants of 4.99 in panel B and 3.86 in panel C bound the reduction of 4.35 in panel A. These results buttress the conclusions that we have reached with the aggregate data. If anything, the estimates with the saturated set of covariates in panel C imply that in most cases the coefficients in panel A are conservative lower-bound estimates.[23]

8. DISCUSSION

Our results suggest that the introduction of National Health Insurance in Taiwan in 1995 led to reductions in the postneonatal mortality rate of infants born in farm households but not to infants born in private sector households. In the pre-NHI period, the postneonatal mortality rate of farm infants was approximately 23 percent higher than the corresponding rate of private sector infants. Hence, our findings are consistent with the notion that the provision of health insurance to previously uninsured infants has larger effects on those born in poor health than on others. For farm infants, we also observe bigger effects when mothers have less than ten years of education and when infants are premature or low-weight at birth. Our result that the effects of NHI rise in absolute value as the availability of medical care resources in the infant's county of residence rises is evidence that increases in medical care services received by infants made eligible for insurance coverage by NHI may account for at least part of the improvements in health outcomes that we observe. Farm families have lower levels of health, education, and income than private sector families and premature and low-weight infants are in worse health than other infants. Thus, taken as a set, our findings suggest that health insurance improves infant health outcomes of population subgroups characterized by low levels of education, income, and health.

An alternative explanation of our findings, especially the lack of an effect for infants born in private sector households, is that ex ante moral hazard associated with the receipt of health insurance may have induced women in those households to reduce preventive nonmedical behaviors or to continue to engage in these behaviors. Since these women had higher household income than those in farm households prior to the introduction of NHI, the former group probably had more contact with physicians in that period. Hence, the increase in their contact with physicians and the increase in the advice they received from physicians in the post-NHI period may have been smaller. Absent data on maternal smoking, alcohol consumption, weight gain, exercise, and prenatal care use, we cannot distinguish among the explanations just outlined.

From a policy perspective, it is important to estimate not only the size of the effect of NHI on infant health but also the mechanisms through which it operates. For example, suppose that the improvement in survival prospects experienced by infants born in farm families was due to reductions in maternal smoking in these families and that in turn was due to more frequent contact with physicians. At the same time, suppose the lack of an effect in private sector families was due to an increase in smoking by pregnant women in those families or to little or no reduction in that behavior. That would imply that physicians should be urged to counsel women in the latter households who are pregnant about the harm that they do to their fetuses by smoking. We do want to stress, however, the value of our undertaking and results. We have identified groups of infants who were affected by NHI and groups who were not. This calls attention to the need for future research that explores the mechanisms that can explain our results. It also calls attention to the characteristics of population subgroups that are most likely to benefit from large changes in health insurance coverage in developing countries.

Our results are subject to some limitations. One is that births in farm families constitute a small percentage of all births, making it somewhat difficult to evaluate the statistical significance of our findings. This factor also does not allow us to examine postneonatal mortality by cause of death or by the month in which death occurred. A second limitation is that the cash benefit received by private sector households for childbirth was reduced from two months of salary to one month. That reduction may have accounted for part of the lack of an NHI effect for that group. A final limitation is that we are not able to ascertain the impact of NHI on the neonatal mortality rate due to more stringent requirements for reporting births introduced in 1994.

We have emphasized the practical significance of the results by considering the magnitudes of the effects and their pattern in different groups in the population. For all farm households, the reduction in the postneonatal mortality rate due to the introduction of National Health Insurance of between 8 and 16 percent is a "meaningful effect." It is neither extremely large nor extremely small and pertains to the group with the highest death rate and the lowest income in the pre-NHI period. Within farm households, the larger effects for infants of mothers with low levels of education and for premature infants also underscore the plausibility of our estimates. The evidence of a positive interaction between the acquisition of health insurance and the more extensive availability of medical care inputs accomplishes the same goal.

Our results can serve as a guide to the potential impacts of large changes in health insurance coverage on infant health outcomes in developing countries. Taiwan's experience may not be directly and immediately applicable to the United States population and generalizable to that population yet it is valuable to build a body of empirical regularities about a question. When enough studies have been conducted in different settings, we can better understand how to extrapolate our knowledge to future settings.

9. ACKNOWLEDGMENTS

Research for the paper was supported by Award Number 0422665 from the National Science Foundation to the National Bureau of Economic Research. The funding source had no involvement in the study design; in the collection, analysis, and interpretation of data; in the writing of the paper; and in the decision to submit the paper for publication. The paper has had a long gestation period due to problems encountered in using Taiwanese birth and infant death certificates and to revisions in earlier files containing these certificates during the course of the research. Very preliminary versions of the paper with results that turned out to be incorrect after inconsistencies in the data were uncovered and resolved were presented at the Fifth World Congress of the International Health Economics Association and at seminars at McGill University and National Taiwan University. More recent versions of the paper with correct empirical results were presented at the Seventh World Congress of the International Health Economics Association, at the ifo/CESifo and the University of Munich Conference entitled "Empirical Health Economics" in Munich, Germany, at the 2011 annual meeting of the Allied Social Sciences Association, and at seminars at the University of Melbourne, Monash University, the University of Queensland, Emory University, the University of Chicago, the University of Maryland at Baltimore County, the University of Oregon, Oregon State University, Tokyo University, and Osaka University. We wish to thank two anonymous reviewers for their extremely helpful comments and suggestions on a previous draft of this paper. We owe a similar debt to the participants in the forums just mentioned. We also wish to thank Jason Hockenberry for research assistance.

Appendix A

Supplementary data to this article can be found online at http://dx.doi.org /10.1016/j.jdeveco.2014.08.004.

NOTES

Originally published as Shin-Yi Chou, Michael Grossman, and Jin-Tan Liu, "The Impact of National Health Insurance on Birth Outcomes: A Natural Experiment in Taiwan," *Journal of Development Economics* 111 (November 2014): 75–91.

1. The recent Oregon Health Insurance Experiment does not share the problems mentioned above, but the results to date pertain only to adults (Finkelstein et al. 2012).

2. For a detailed discussion of this research, especially studies for the United States and Canada, see Chou, Grossman, and Liu (2011).

3. Prior to NHI, women in the low-income plan received a cash benefit, but it obviously was very modest. The government did provide maternal and child care for poor women at public hospitals and clinics, but less than 1 percent of households were classified as poor.

4. After NHI became effective, the administration of medical care benefits was transferred to the Bureau of National Health Insurance. The LI, FI, and GI plans continue to administer other types of insurance such as disability, unemployment, and old-age insurance. This makes it extremely difficult to make precise comparisons of differences in health premiums before and after the introduction of NHI. That is because in the pre-period the premium covered the three other types of insurance just mentioned as well as health insurance. It is the case that the premiums paid directly by individuals for health insurance remained a positive function of income in the post-period. Hence, they were largest in the case of government workers and smallest in the case of farmers.

5. Unlike U.S. birth certificates, Taiwanese certificates do not contain such prenatal health inputs and behaviors as the month in which prenatal care began, the number of prenatal visits, and maternal cigarette smoking and alcohol use during pregnancy.

6. We are grateful to an anonymous referee for a comment that caused us to stress the ambiguous nature of the NHI effect and to emphasize its effects on endogenous determinants of infant health in addition to medical care.

7. The Taiwanese Department of Health officials have informed us that this is because very detailed information is requested

8. In the cases where no matches are made with the administrative files, we assume that the household would have been eligible for LII or would have been eligible for government-provided maternal and child health care at public clinics. Only 0.5 percent of all persons had LII in 1992, and only 0.9 percent of the population were members of low-income households in 2000 (Chou, Liu, and Hammit 2003). The type of care delivered to low income-infants may differ in important respects from that received by other children in either the treatment or control groups. Moreover, some infants and children may be incorrectly classified as members of low-income families because self-employed workers could only obtain labor insurance if they were members of an occupational union.

9. Births to unmarried women are very rare in Taiwan.

10. Since we include nine year indicators, we do not obtain a main effect for the period after the introduction of NHI.

11. We obtain standard errors using the Stata module Newey2 for panel data written by David Roodman.

12. Note that the effect should be distinguished from a change in healthy behaviors caused by NHI among women in the treatment group both before and after its enactment. We discussed the latter effect in section 3 and indicated that it should not be held constant in evaluating the net or reduced form effect of NHI.

13. We are grateful to an anonymous referee for pointing this out to us and for urging us to investigate the issue.

14. In addition, births in the private and farm sectors in years prior to 1994 are underestimated due to the reporting issues discussed in section 4.

15. The percentage of births in which father's education was less than ten years is highly correlated with the percentage of births to mothers with that level of education. For that reason, we omit it as a characteristic in table 11.2. Regressions estimated by father's education yield results that are very similar to those run by mother's education.

16. As part of the sensitivity analysis in section 7, we employ individual-level data to estimate propensity score weighted regressions with an extensive set of covariates to further address the issue of differences in the characteristics of the treatment and control groups. These regression results imply that the coefficients in table 11.5 are conservative lower-bound estimates.

17. With two treatment groups, equation (2) includes indicators for each group, interactions between each indicator and the NHI indicator, interactions between each indicator and Q_{jt}, and interactions between the NHI indicator, Q_{jt}, and each of the two treatment group indicators.

18. Let S_{kjt} be the number of neonatal survivors in the treatment group in the jth county in year t, let S_{kt} be the total number of survivors in the treatment group in all counties in that year $\left(S_{kt} = \sum_{j=1}^{24} S_{kjt} \right)$, let S_{cjt} be the number of neonatal survivors in the control group in the jth county in year t, and let S_{ct} be the total number of survivors in the control group in all counties in that year. Let w_{kjt} be the ratio of S_{kjt} to S_{kt} and let w_{cjt} be the ratio of S_{cjt} to S_{ct}. Then

$$Q_{kt} = \sum_{j=1}^{24} w_{kjt} Q_{jt}, Q_{ct} = \sum_{j=1}^{24} w_{cjt} Q_{jt}.$$

$$Q_{kt} - Q_{ct} = \sum_{j=1}^{24} (w_{kjt} - w_{cjt}) Q_{jt}.$$

19. Standard errors that are adjusted for clustering by county are very similar to those that cluster by county and before and after the introduction of NHI.

20. We are grateful to a referee for pointing this out to us.

21. With 18 degrees of freedom, it is not significant at 10 percent but is significant at 14 percent.

22. The regressions in table 11.9 for the whole sample suggest that a lower-bound estimate of the NHI effect for all farm households is one-half of the reduction contained in table 11.4. In regressions not shown, we reach a similar conclusion for the postneonatal mortality rate of premature infants in farm households.

23. The exception is the reduction in deaths per thousand low-weight survivors, which is estimated imprecisely in both panels.

REFERENCES

Becker, G. S., and H. G. Lewis. 1973. "On the Interaction Between the Quantity and Quality of Children. *J. Polit. Econ.* 81: S279–S288.

Brown, M., A. Bindman, and N. Lurie. 1998. "Monitoring the Consequences of Uninsurance: A Review of Methodologies." *Med. Care Res. Rev.* 55: 177–210.

Bureau of National Health Insurance. 1977. National Health Insurance Profile. Bureau of National Health Insurance, Taipei, Taiwan.

Central Trust of China. 2002. Statistical Data for Government Employees Insurance. Central Trust of China, Taipei, Taiwan. Available at www.exam.gov.tw/stats /stats.asp.

Chen, Y., and G. Z. Jin. 2012. "Does Health Insurance Coverage Lead to Better Health and Educational Outcomes? Evidence from Rural China." *J. Health Econ.* 31: 1–14.

Chiang, T.-L. 1997. "Taiwan's 1995 Health Care Reform." *Health Policy* 39: 225–239.

Chou, Y.-J., and D. Staiger. 2001. "Health Insurance and Female Labor Supply in Taiwan." *J. Health Econ.* 20: 187–211.

Chou, S.-Y., J.-T. Liu, and J. K. Hammitt. 2003. "National Health Insurance and Precautionary Saving: Evidence from Taiwan." *J. Public Econ.* 87: 1873–1894.

———. 2004. "National Health Insurance and Technology Adoption: Evidence from Taiwan." *Contemp. Econ. Policy* 22: 26–38.

Chou, S.-Y., M. Grossman, and J.-T. Liu. 2011. "The Impact of National Health Insurance on Birth Outcomes: A Natural Experiment in Taiwan." National Bureau of Economic Research Working Paper 16811.

Currie, J., and J. Gruber. 1997. "The Technology of Birth: Health Insurance, Medical Interventions, and Infant Health." National Bureau of Economic Research Working Paper 5985.

Cutler, D. M., and J. Gruber. 1996. "Does Public Insurance Crowd Out Private Insurance?" *Q. J. Econ.* 111: 391–430.

Dave, D. M., and R. Kaestner. 2009. "Health Insurance and Ex Ante Moral Hazard: Evidence from Medicare." *Int. J. Health Care Finance Econ.* 9: 367–390.

Department of Health, Taiwan. 1996. World Health Statistics Annual, 1996. Taiwan for the World Health Organization.

Executive Yuan. 1993. Research, Development, and Evaluation Committee Analysis and Integration Issues of Social Insurance in Taiwan. Executive Yuan, Taipei, Taiwan (in Chinese).

——. 2001. Directorate-General of Budget, Accounting and Statistics. "Man-power Survey Statistics." Executive Yuan, Taipei, Taiwan.

——. 2013. Directorate-General of Budget, Accounting and Statistics, Republic of China. http://stat.gov.tw (last accessed December 28).

Finkelstein, A., et al. 2012. "The Oregon Health Insurance Experiment: Evidence from the First Year." *Q. J. Econ.* 127: 1057–1106.

Gruber, J. 1997. "Health Insurance for Poor Women and Children in the U.S.: Lessons from the Past Decade." In *Tax Policy and the Economy*, vol. 11, ed. J. M. Poterba. Cambridge, Massachusetts: MIT Press: 169–211.

Gruber, J., N. Hendren, and R. N. Townsend. 2014. "The Great Equalizer: Health Care Access and Infant Mortality in Thailand." *Am. Econ. J.* 6: 91–107.

Imbens, G. 2004. "Nonparametric Estimation of Average Treatment Effects under Exogeneity: A Review." *Rev. Econ. Stat.* 86: 4–29.

Kaestner, R. 1999. "Health Insurance, the Quantity and Quality of Prenatal Care, and Infant Health." *Inquiry* 36: 162–175.

Kelly, I. R., and S. Markowitz. 2009/2010. "Incentives in Obesity and Health Insurance." *Inquiry* 46: 418–432.Levy, H., and D. Meltzer. 2008. "The Impact of Health Insurance on Health." *Annu. Rev. Public Health* 29: 399–409.

Manning, C. 2000. "Labour Market Adjustment to Indonesia's Economic Crisis: Context, Trends and Implications." *Bull. Indones. Econ. Stud.* 36: 105–136.

McWilliams, J. M., et al. 2003. "Impact of Medicare Coverage on Basic Clinical Services for Previously Uninsured Adults." *J. Am. Med. Assoc.* 290: 757–764.

Newey, W. K., and K. D. West. 1987. "A Simple Positive-Definite Heteroscedasticity and Autocorrelation Consistent Covariance Matrix." *Econometrica* 55: 703–708.

Peabody, J. W., et al. 1995. "Health System Reform in the Republic of China." *J. Am. Med. Assoc.* 273: 777–781.

Smith, J. P., et al. 2002. "Wages, Employment and Economic Shocks: Evidence from Indonesia." *J. Popul. Econ.* 15: 161–193.

Afterword to Part 3

My research has been guided by a philosophy in which "it is better to be the first or one of the first even if you are wrong, especially if you pick interesting topics on which to work." The large body of work that followed my research on the effects of abortion reform, WIC, Medicaid, family planning clinics, and community health projects highlights the relevance of that philosophy, even the part about being wrong.

My attribution of a number of these factors as key explanations of the decline in neonatal mortality has been questioned because almost all of the decline in that outcome has been due to improvements in birth weight–specific survival (for example, Cutler and Meara 2000). The first-order effects of most of the factors on which I focused should be on low birth weight, yet that outcome has shown little trend. Moreover, the general consensus in the clinical literature is that relatively little is known about the causes of preterm delivery, a major proximate determinant of low birth weight (see, for example, Hack and Merkatz 1995) and that most interventions designed to prevent these deliveries are not successful (see, for example, Goldenberg and Rouse 1998). This calls into question the ultimate effects of better prenatal care due to Medicaid and better nutrition due to WIC on birth weight. In addition, Alice Chen, Emily Oster, and Heidi Williams (2016) show that much of the high ranking of the U.S. infant mortality rate compared to that of other developed countries is due to the relatively high postneonatal mortality rate in the United States. But for reasons indicated in the discussion that follows, I am excited about studies that have appeared since 1990 and the areas for new investigation that they have opened. And I do have a few counterpoints to offer in my defense.

A good deal of the research to which I will refer to in this section is characterized by the use of more sophisticated econometric procedures than those employed in the first three papers in this section. These include the use of fixed-effects models in repeat cross sections, difference-in-differences procedures sometimes in the context of quasi-natural experiments, and regression discontinuity designs. Much of this body of work has focused on outcomes other than infant mortality and birth weight, although sometimes the benefits of these programs later in life are attributed to their effects at early stages in the life cycle. Unlike the attempts to deal with multiple policy determinants in the first three papers, usually the focus has been on one but with attempts to control for unmeasured factors.

Since the publication of the first paper in this section in 1981, a "cottage industry" on abortion reform and regulation has developed—one that made Steven D. Levitt rich (see below). The most proximate effects of reform and regulation are on the numbers of abortions and births. Reform in the United States led to dramatic increases in the abortion rate (abortions per thousand women ages fifteen to forty-four) and the abortion ratio (abortions per thousand pregnancies or per thousand births) followed by reductions in birthrates. From an economic perspective, the birth effects are key. As indicated in the first four papers in this section, in the economic model of the family developed by Gary S. Becker and H. Gregg Lewis (1973) and by Robert J. Willis (1973), abortion reform and subsequent increases in availability lower the costs of fertility control and raise the price of number of children. Hence, the "optimal" number of children demanded by the decision maker or makers falls and the "optimal" quality per child—measured by health, completed schooling, and lifetime earnings—rises. The latter occurs because more resources are allocated to a smaller number of children. This is the sense in which births to women with low costs of averting (low abortion or contraceptive costs) may be termed "wanted" births.[1]

To return to some empirics, there is disagreement about how much of the fertility decline that followed abortion reform was due to the 1973 Supreme Court decision in *Roe v. Wade* that ruled restrictive state laws to be unconstitutional and how much was due to early legalization of abortion by five states in 1970. For example, Jonathan Gruber, Phillip B. Levine, and Douglas Staiger (1999) estimate that birthrates in the states that legalized in 1970 fell by approximately 6 percent compared to the other states in the period from 1971 through 1973. This was followed by an additional 6 percent reduction in the other states following the *Roe* decision. Ted (Theodore J. in his earlier publications) Joyce,

Ruoding Tan, and Yuxiu Zhang (2013) revisit this issue with detailed data on abortions performed on out-of-state residents in the early legalizing states. They find a larger decline due to early legalization, especially because they show that women were willing to travel hundreds of miles to obtain a legal abortion in the period prior to the *Roe* decision. Conversely, their estimated effect of the *Roe* decision on the birthrate was smaller than that of Gruber and colleagues (1999).[2]

A related issue pertains to the relative contributions of abortion reform and the diffusion of the contraceptive pill (the Pill) to the reduction in fertility. Martha J. Bailey, Melanie Gulden, and Brad J. Hershbein (2013) summarize work by themselves and others that attributes larger effects to the diffusion of the Pill following its introduction in 1960 and the 1965 Supreme Court decision in *Griswald v. Connecticut* that declared states' regulation of such private matters as contraception unconstitutional. Some of this work uses variations in the age of majority and the expanded rights of minors across states and cohorts to identify the effects of access to the Pill on fertility among young unmarried women. Ted Joyce (2013) points out that the variable just described is likely to have a considerable amount of measurement error and may be subject to policy endogeneity. He also calls attention to the varying and unstable estimates of their effects on pill use by minors who were not subject to parental consent. Finally, his 2013 study with Tan and Zhang found that any fertility effects of the Pill were dominated by those due to abortion.

Joyce does not address Bailey's (2012) paper dealing with the effects of the introduction and diffusion of federally funded family planning clinics as part of the War on Poverty on fertility. She capitalizes on the differential rollout of these programs among counties in the late 1960s and early 1970s to show that fifteen years after a county received its first federal grant its fertility rate remained lower than in the year in which it first received that grant, net of declines in fertility in other counties in the same state. Of course, Bailey does not incorporate Joyce's insights and measures of abortion reform contained in his 2013 study with Tan and Zhang. Hence, I conclude this is a promising area for more research, especially because I could not find new estimates of the effects of family planning clinics on infant health outcomes in the literature.[3]

As opposed to the extreme liberalization of U.S. abortion policy in the late 1960s and the 1970s, the period since has been characterized by restrictions on the availability of this procedure. The most notable are state laws that require parental consent for an abortion to be obtained by a minor. The number of states with these laws increased from twelve in 1989 to thirty-eight as of 2016 (Guttmacher Institute 2016a). In addition, the Hyde Amendment has prohibited the use of federal funds for abortions under Medicaid except in cases of rape, incest, or in which the pregnant woman's life is in danger. Seventeen states use their own

Medicaid funds to pay for abortions obtained by recipients for other reasons, but the others do not do so (Guttmacher Institute 2016b). Most recently, some states have enacted laws that require doctors who perform abortions to have admitting privileges at nearby hospitals or that require stand-alone clinics, even those that perform only first-term abortions, to meet the same standards as ambulatory surgical centers. Currently, the constitutionality of these laws is under review.

Most of the research on these restrictions has focused on parental consent laws because there is a considerable amount of within-state variation in these laws over time. Joyce and colleagues (Joyce, Kaestner, and Colman 2006; Colman, Joyce, and Kaestner 2008; Colman and Joyce 2009) point out that most previous research has found that minors' abortion rates fall following the enactment of a notification law, and birthrates do not rise—a "win-win" situation. Joyce and colleagues argue that this research has serious methodological limitations. It is not able to measure cross-state travel, and it misclassifies exposure. With regard to the latter issue, three-quarters of minors who conceive at age seventeen give birth at age eighteen. This creates a bias toward finding no impact on births. In addition, minors can delay an abortion until they reach age eighteen.

Joyce and colleagues remedy these deficiencies by using data for Texas with exact dates (month, day, and year) of conception, abortion, and birth before and after the enactment of a parental notification law on January 1, 2000. They find that the abortion rate of seventeen-year-olds at conception fell by 16 percent relative to those of eighteen-year-olds due to the law. In addition, the birth rate of seventeen-year-olds at conception rose by 4 percent. Finally, abortions rose by approximately 30 percent among teens who did not reach the age of eighteen until after the first trimester of pregnancy. These second-trimester abortions involve greater health risks than first-trimester abortions. The importance of this line of research is underscored by the controversy surrounding abortion and the need of voters and policy makers to accurately assess the likely impact of parental involvement laws. I am looking forward to the results of research in progress by Kaestner and Joyce that examines the impact on teen fertility of parental involvement laws for all states, as opposed to specific states, in the period from 1989 through 2009, with confidential data on a teen's exact age in days at time of conception.

So far I have focused on the effects of abortion reform and regulation on fertility, but the very real possibility discussed previously that unwanted pregnancies and births may be affected has led to research on effects of a variety of correlates of child quality. Some of this research has followed up my investigations of the impacts of abortion on infant health outcomes. Richard G. Frank, Donna M. Strobino, Catherine A. Jackson, and David A. Salkever (1992) find no effect of the abortion rate on the fraction of low-birth-weight births in a time series of counties for the period 1975–1984. They control for the early initiation of prenatal care, which rules out a potential channel through which abortion may operate. Moreover, they treat care as endogenous, yet their first-stage model for predicting it is weak. This suggests that their estimates may be biased.

Janet Currie, Lucia Nixon, and Nancy Cole (1996) find no effects of restrictions of Medicaid funding of abortions and abortion providers in the county of residence on birth weight and the probability of low birth weight in the 1979 cohort of women in the National Longitudinal Survey of Youth for the period 1980–1989. They rely on self-reports of birth weight, which may be subject to considerable measurement error. Gruber, Levine, and Staiger (1999) report reductions in low birth weight and infant mortality in the early legalizing abortion states. David E. Kalist and Noelle A. Molinari (2006) uncover a negative effect of the abortion ratio on infant homicides in a time series of states for the period 1970–1998. Their argument in support of this result is that the abortion ratio is a negative correlate of unwanted births and that infants born unwanted are likely to live in circumstances with a higher risk of murder.

I am somewhat disappointed that no one has followed up on the sample selection model that Joyce and I estimated in our 1990 *Journal of Political Economy* paper. I was hoping that it would be possible to pool birth and abortion certificates for a number of states and for a number of different years and that this would enrich the estimates. I do think that the ability of our framework to identify and distinguish among alternative models of selection is a real plus because it is a feature that usually does not characterize these models. I take it that confidentiality issues associated with most state abortion certificates have ruled out the research I am proposing. Information on abortions as well as on births is available in the data employed by Currie, Nixon, and Cole (1996), but sample sizes are small and underreporting of abortions is extremely likely.

Studies by Joyce (1994) and by Karen Smith Conway and Partha Deb (2005) come closest to the emphasis on the role of unobservables in birth outcomes in my *Journal of Political Economy* paper with Joyce, although those two papers do not employ information conveyed by the decision to terminate a pregnancy. Joyce (1994) estimates birth weight production functions in the context of a sample selection model with endogenous switching. His prenatal care variable, based on the Kessner index, reflects three levels of care: adequate, intermediate, and inadequate. The index combines the trimester in which care began with the number of visits adjusted for gestation. He fits an ordered probit model for the level of care, which yields a correction factor to include in separate estimates of production functions for the birth weight of infants whose mothers obtain each level of care. He finds evidence of adverse selection in the sense that women who are more likely to obtain higher levels of care due to unobserved factors also are more likely to give birth to lower weight infants. He also finds diminishing returns to care: a movement from inadequate care to intermediate care has a bigger effect than a corresponding movement from intermediate care to adequate care.

Conway and Deb (2005) estimate a finite mixture model with two types of unobserved pregnancies: normal and complicated. Early prenatal care has a positive effect on birth weight for normal pregnancies but not for complicated ones. They argue that complicated births may be most likely to be premature, which is consistent with studies in the medical literature (Hack and Merkatz 1995; Goldenberg and Rouse 1998) that find early care may have little effect on this outcome.

Cristian Pop-Eleches (2006) provides dramatic evidence of the impacts of extreme restrictions on abortions on socioeconomic conditions of children born subsequently. In 1966, dictator Nicolae Ceaușescu declared abortion and family planning illegal in Romania. Birthrates doubled in 1967 because abortion had been the main method of birth control. Children born after the ban had worse education and labor market outcomes as adults. Gruber, Levine, and Staiger (1999) and Elizabeth Oltmans Anant, Gruber, Levine, and Staiger (2009) report similar outcomes for cohorts of children born in the early legalizing states in the United States. These children were less likely to live in single adult families, to live in poverty, and to receive welfare. As adults, they were more likely to graduate from college, and less likely to be on welfare and to be a single parent.

John J. Donohue III and Steven D. Levitt (2001) purport to uncover perhaps the most striking benefit of abortion legalization. If fewer unwanted children were born when abortion rates increased, they hypothesize that crime may have decreased when these children would have reached adulthood. They conclude that increased abortion access in the 1970s may explain as much as half of the decline in crime observed in the 1990s. In part, this paper led Levitt to write the hugely popular best seller titled *Freakonomics: A Rogue Economist Explores the Hidden Side of Everything* with Stephen J. Dubner in 2005.

Donohue and Levitt's results have been assessed and criticized by many economists. Joyce (2010) provides a comprehensive evaluation of the evidence and concludes that it does not support the findings. I leave the reader to consult this large and controversial literature and reach his or her own conclusions. I do, however, want to call attention to an aspect of the research by Gruber and his colleagues that has always puzzled me. First, let me identify myself as one of the "infamous" referees of the "justly famous" 1999 *Quarterly Journal of Economics* by Gruber, Levine, and Staiger. I term their paper justly famous because it anticipates and complements the even more famous 2001 *Quarterly Journal of Economics* by Donohue and Levitt. Moreover, it is the first paper in my view to provide convincing evidence that abortion reform in early legalizing states led to reductions in low birth weight and infant mortality in a design that capitalizes on within-state changes over time. So I learned a good deal from the paper and like certain aspects of it very much.

The authors present two types of estimates of the effects of abortion reform on various measures of child quality: reduced-form and structural. The former use interactions between year indicators and indicators for the early and late abortion repeal states as regressors. The latter use the variables just mentioned as instruments for the birthrate in a two-stage least squares estimation procedure. The identification restriction is that abortion reform has no impact on child quality with the birthrate held constant. The authors appeal to the Becker-Lewis quantity-quality interaction model in specifying the structural equation, but that model does not support their identification restriction. Hence, I have no problem with their reduced-form estimates, but I do have a problem with their structural estimates.

To spell out my problem in more detail, suppose that the decision maker (parent or parents) maximizes a utility function given by

$$u = u(n, q, c),$$

where n is the number of children, q is the quality of each child, and c is the decision maker's consumption. The income constraint is

$$I = \pi n q + c + F,$$

where I is income, π is the price of one unit of q, the price of c is equal to \$1, and F is the cost of fertility control. Assume that F is given by

$$F = f(n^* - n),$$

where n^* is the maximum number of children that a woman would bear in the absence of birth control, $b = n^* - n$ is the number of births averted, and f is the constant cost of averting a birth.

If a subscript denotes a first-order partial derivative and λ is the marginal utility of income, first-order conditions for n, q, and c are

$$u_n = \lambda(\pi q - f) \tag{1}$$

$$u_q = \lambda \pi n \tag{2}$$

$$u_c = \lambda. \tag{3}$$

The first two equations contain definitions of the shadow prices of n (p_n) and q (p_q): $p_n \equiv \pi q - f$ and $p_q \equiv \pi n$. Write the compensated (utility-constant) demand function for q in dln form ($Eq \equiv dln\ q$) as

$$Eq = k_q \sigma_{qq} Ep_q + k_n \sigma_{qn} Ep_n. \tag{4}$$

Here $\sigma_{qq} < 0$ is the Allen own partial elasticity of substitution in consumption of q, σ_{qn} is the Allen cross partial elasticity of substitution in consumption between

q and n, $k_q = qp_q/(qp_q + np_n + c)$ is the share of q in income evaluated at shadow prices, and k_n is the share of n in income evaluated at shadow prices. Using the definitions of p_q and p_n, one can rewrite the demand function as

$$Deq = k_q\sigma_{qq}En + (k_q\sigma_{qq} + sk_n\sigma_{qn})E\pi + (1-s)k_n\sigma_{qn}Ef. \tag{5}$$

In the last equation, $D = (1 - sk_n\sigma_{nq}) > 0$ by second-order conditions for utility maximization, and $s = \pi q/p_n > 1$, $1 - s = -f/p_n < 0$.

Equation (5) is analogous to the equation estimated by Gruber and colleagues in assessing the impact of changes in the birthrate due to abortion reform on child quality. They do this by regressing alternative measures of child quality (q) on the birthrate (which is analogous to n in my formulation). The birthrate is treated as endogenous and predicted by abortion reform, which lowers the fixed cost of averting a birth (f). But f belongs in the equation unless the elasticity of substitution in consumption between n and q (σ_{nq}) is zero.

Note that there is a similar structural equation for n as a function of q, π, and f. These two equations can be solved simultaneously to get a reduced form in which n and q depend on f and π. Hence, reduced-form regressions of n and q on these variables certainly are appropriate. The key point is that the structural equations are not identified unless rather arbitrary restrictions are imposed.

It may seem counterintuitive that an increase in f (a reduction in p_n) lowers q if $\sigma_{qn} > 0$ and raises q if $\sigma_{qn} < 0$ when n is held constant in Equation (5). While I do not have a very good intuitive explanation, I know that the algebra is correct. Ultimately, the result can be traced to substitution and/or complementarity between q, n, and the third good c. To be more specific, note

$$-k_c\sigma_{qc} = k_q\sigma_{qq} + sk_n\sigma_{qn} + (1-s)k_n\sigma_{qn}.$$

With no fixed cost ($s = 1$), the coefficient of $E\pi$ in the demand function is $-k_c\sigma_{qc}$. With a fixed cost, the coefficients of $E\pi$ and Ef can be written as $-wk_{qc}\sigma_{qc}$ and $-(1-w)k_{qc}\sigma_{qc}$, where

$$w = (k_q\sigma_{qq} + sk_n\sigma_{qn})/[k_q\sigma_{qq} + sk_n\sigma_{qn} + (1-s)k_n\sigma_{qn}].$$

I lost a lot of sleep over this issue. When I submitted my referee report in which I recommended publication after revision to Lawrence F. Katz, the journal editor in charge of the submission, I asked for his opinion on the issue I just raised. He promised to provide one but never did. I even went so far as to discuss it with Gary Becker by phone after I sent much of the above material to him. He did not have a good answer, although I had the impression that he did not have time to focus on what I did not and still do not understand. Thirteen years after the paper was published, I sent an email message to the authors in which I asked them an unrelated question about the paper and revealed myself as a referee of it. In an email message to me of March 9, 2012, Douglas Staiger replied: "I'm glad Larry [Katz] didn't push us too hard on the quantity-quality issue that you raised in your report! I vaguely recall that we responded by saying that we couldn't see any clear evidence that this [potential effects of some of the instruments in the structural equation] was going on in the data (e.g. pointing to the low-powered over-id test), but that was a bit of cop-out." Perhaps a reader of this book will be able to help me.

I would be remiss if I did not add that nothing about this review process upset me even though I was not given the opportunity to comment on a revised submission prior to its publication. I learned a lot from reviewing this and countless other papers during my professional career as an economist. One can never expect to have all of his or her questions answered. To quote Charlie Brown, "In the book of life, the answers aren't in the back."[4]

WIC and Medicaid are the two largest and most important public programs that directly aim to improve birth outcomes of infants born to poor women. These programs encourage women to obtain more prenatal medical care and to eat a more nutritious diet by reducing the price of each input. Moreover, WIC provides counseling as well as nutrition supplements, suggesting that it may encourage women to begin prenatal care earlier in their pregnancies and to stop smoking. The reverse also may hold: women who begin care early and have nutritional deficiencies may be encouraged to enroll in WIC. Finally, the subsidies and counseling services may increase financial security and reduce stress. All of these factors suggest that increases in birth weight and especially reductions in low birth weight should be the first-order effects of these programs.

In a proximate sense, birth weight and low birth weight are caused by prematurity and slow growth in utero. Premature births have gestational ages (the difference between the date of birth and the date of the mother's last menstrual cycle) of less than thirty-seven weeks. At several points, I have referred to findings in the clinical literature that relatively little is known about the causes of preterm delivery. On the other hand, fetal growth offers more scope for intervention because it is known to be linked to maternal smoking and maternal weight gain (see Joyce 1999 for a review of this evidence). Birth weight percentiles for gestational age allow one to identify infants whose fetal growth has been retarded. One convenient indicator identifies term low-weight births (weight less than 2,500 grams and gestation at least equal to thirty-seven weeks). Another reason to employ this outcome in WIC research is to avoid gestational age bias (Joyce, Racine, and Yunzal-Butler 2008). This arises because women who do not give birth prematurely have a longer period while they are pregnant to enroll in WIC. It creates a mechanical negative relationship between an indicator for participation in WIC and an indicator for a low-weight birth.

Hilary W. Hoynes and Diane Whitmore Schanzenbach (2016) review very recent studies dealing with WIC and low birth weight that use well-defined treatment and control group or differences in the adoption of the program within counties over time. I leave the reader to consult this paper and the studies they review, mainly because none of my papers in this section focuses on WIC. I do want to indicate that, in my view, the General Accounting Office reached its conclusion that "WIC works" in a 1992 report somewhat prematurely. This still remains an open issue and a fruitful area for new research.

I conclude this section with some comments on research dealing with Medicaid. Measures pertaining to this program are in the background of the first four papers in this section. Although the fifth paper deals with the effects of the introduction of National Health Insurance in Taiwan, it is very relevant for research on public financing of births, especially since low-income women constituted the group who benefited from the introduction of NHI in Taiwan.

I begin with some preliminary observations. One is a counterpoint to the argument that interventions to prevent prematurity have been unsuccessful. In a more recent review of the evidence than the one conducted by Goldenberg and Rouse (1998), Jens Ludwig and Matthew Miller (2005) are less pessimistic. They write: "Although the existing clinical evidence of a beneficial effect of isolated prenatal interventions on preterm births isn't very good, weak evidence about the efficacy of prenatal care is fundamentally different from good evidence that prenatal care is ineffective" (p. 691). Second, even if the receipt of early and appropriate care has little or no effect on the probability of a low-birth-weight birth, it may ensure that women with problematic birth outcomes deliver in hospitals that are equipped with state-of-the art neonatal intensive care facilities that can deal with the issues they confront. That is why I have argued that abortion reform and availability can affect infant mortality, with birth weight held constant. Third, the very modest declines in the percentage of low-weight births in the face of significant expansions in Medicaid coverage since the mid-1980s is not necessarily evidence that prenatal care has no impact on this outcome. After all, the percentage of births to unmarried women rose from 18 percent in 1980 to 40 percent in 2014 (Hamilton, Martin, Osterman, Curtin, and Mathews 2015). These pregnancies and births may receive significantly fewer resources than those available to married women.

In the last paper in this section, my colleagues and I point out other reasons why the reduction in the price of medical care that accompanies the provision of health insurance to previously uninsured pregnant women may not result in improvements in birth weight. For instance, ex ante moral hazard associated with the receipt of health insurance may induce beneficiaries to reduce such preventive nonmedical behaviors as attempts to quit smoking and not to gain too little or an excessive amount of weight, suggesting that these behaviors and medical care are substitutes. The opposite effect also is possible if new and more frequent contact with physicians promotes more healthy behaviors, a result consistent with complementarity between medical care and these behaviors. Moreover, the receipt of health insurance that covers medical care services associated with births reduces the price of a birth. Given interactions between the quantity and quality (measured by health) of children emphasized by Becker and Lewis (1973), one possible outcome is that the optimal number of children rises while the optimal health of each child falls. A related factor is that problematic births (those with potentially poor health outcomes) that previously were aborted now may be carried to term. Again, the effect could go in the opposite direction if the receipt of insurance reduces fertility because it lowers the probability of an infant death and creates incentives on the part of parents to make larger investments in a smaller number of children.

With these factors in mind, I highlight the effects of government financing of medical care to pregnant women in several classic studies and in several very recent ones.[5] Maria Hanratty (1996) capitalizes on the staggered adoption of NHI by the ten provinces of Canada in the period from 1962 to 1971 to assess its impacts on infant mortality and low birth weight using data for the years 1960–1975. She finds negative effects of NHI on each outcome, with a larger effect for mortality.

Janet Currie and Jonathan Gruber (1996b) capitalize on the impacts of Medicaid reforms that took place between 1984 and 1990. These reforms extended coverage to poor and near-poor pregnant women and children at varying rates among states over time and among cohorts. They find that increased eligibility has negative effects on low birth weight and infant mortality. Like Hanratty, they report larger reductions for the latter outcome than for the former.

Currie and Gruber (1996a) indicate that the expansions lowered the mortality rates of children between the ages of one and fourteen from internal and external causes considered separately. Currie and Gruber (1997, and summarized in Currie and Gruber 2001) also indicate that teenage mothers or mothers who dropped out of high school and who live near a hospital with a neonatal intensive care unit experience significant reductions in neonatal mortality relative to older or more educated mothers due to the expansions. These findings provide some evidence in support of the important role of expansions in neonatal intensive care availability and use in declines in neonatal mortality in the second and third papers in this section. The latter finding provides tentative support of my hypothesis that health insurance and prenatal care may influence infant health outcomes by making it more likely that problematic births receive the appropriate treatment at and after delivery. It also supports the result in the last paper in this section that the effects of the introduction of NHI in Taiwan rise in absolute value as the availability of medical care resources in the infant's county of residence rises.

Dhaval M. Dave, Sandra Decker, Robert Kaestner, and Kosali I. Simon (2008) and Andrew Goodman-Bacon (2015, forthcoming) criticize Currie and Gruber's estimates because they are unreasonably large in light of the small take-up rates associated with the Medicaid eligibility expansions. In addition, Dave and colleagues argue that the Currie-Gruber results are biased by omitted variables. After including state-specific time trends to control for these variables, they find that the eligibility expansions reduced the proportion of pregnant women who were uninsured by approximately 10 percent, although this decrease in uninsured was accompanied by a substantial reduction in private insurance coverage. Changes in Medicaid eligibility were associated with very small and statistically insignificant changes in prenatal care use, birth weight, and the incidence of low birth weight. In related work, Dave, Kaestner, and George L. Wehby (2015) show that increases in Medicaid eligibility were associated with increases in maternal smoking during pregnancy and reductions in weight gain during this period.

Goodman-Bacon (2015, forthcoming) takes a very different approach to estimating the effects of Medicaid than the one just described. Instead of examining the results of the expansions, he estimates the effects of the introduction of Medicaid itself during the years from 1966 through 1970 on infant mortality and child mortality (age-adjusted mortality of children ages zero through fourteen) in a time series of states for the period from 1950 to 1979. His identification strategy rests on the statutory link between the receipt of benefits under the Aid to Families with Dependent Children (AFDC) program and eligibility for Medicaid. This generated a considerable amount of variation in Medicaid eligibility across states. Moreover, nonwhite children were six times as likely to be eligible for Medicaid as white children. Hence, Bacon-Goodman compares infant and child mortality rates before and after Medicaid implementation between higher- and lower-eligibility states.

The results are striking. To quote Goodman-Bacon (2015, pp. 2–3): "After Medicaid's introduction, higher-eligibility states experienced dramatic decreases in infant and child mortality rates relative to lower-eligibility states. The effects persist for nine years and are strongest and most precise for nonwhite children who qualified for and used Medicaid. Infant mortality reductions come from improved acute care *at birth* (italics in original): they are concentrated in the first few hours of life, there are no improvements in … birth weight. Child mortality reductions come largely from improved care for infectious disease: they are largest for youngest, most susceptible children, and for causes with effective treatments in the 1960s and 1970s. Newly-entered data on public health insurance programs from 1963 to 1976 verify that welfare-based Medicaid eligibility led to meaningful increases in children's public health insurance use, the primary mechanism for the mortality effects. The estimates imply that Medicaid reduces the mortality of children who use it by 20 to 30 percent."

Goodman-Bacon's focus on effects that are more long term than birth weight and infant mortality characterize much of the newest research on the effects of policies and programs that begin in pregnancy. I have given examples of this emphasis in the context of abortion reform and organized family planning services. Hoynes and Schanzenbach (2016) summarize similar studies in the case of WIC and other programs that subsidize food purchases of low-income families. For Medicaid, Sarah R. Cohodes, Daniel S. Grossman, Samuel A. Kleiner, and Michael F. Lovenheim (2016) show that the Medicaid expansions in the 1980s and 1990s increased high school and college completion rates of affected children. David W. Brown, Amanda E. Kowalski, and Ithai Z. Lurie (2015) find that increases in cumulative Medicaid eligibility from birth to age eighteen due to the expansions led to increases in cumulative taxes paid by age twenty-eight, higher cumulative probabilities of ever attending college by that age, lower cumulative male adult mortality between the ages of eighteen and twenty-eight, and higher wages for women at that age. In a follow-up study, Goodman-Bacon (2016) finds that for whites Medicaid eligibility before age ten reduces mortality and disability and increases labor supply up to fifty years later. He attributes the lack of similar results for nonwhites to the larger increases in the use of medical care by eligible white children. Laura R. Wherry, Sarah Miller, Robert Kaestner, and Bruce D. Meyer (2015) show that more years of Medicaid eligibility in childhood due to the expansions is associated with fewer hospitalizations and emergency department visits in adulthood for blacks. They attribute the lack of an effect for whites to the smaller number of white children made eligible for Medicaid by the specific expansion that they consider.

I am excited, encouraged, and stimulated by this fascinating new research. I am stimulated because it is the "flip side" of work on the causal effect of schooling on health. It underscores that the determinants of health at very early stages in the life cycle can have long-term impacts on many outcomes at much later stages in the life cycle. Hence, it provides additional empirical support for the emphasis that James J. Heckman and colleagues place on the key role of very early childhood investments (see, for example, Cuhna, Heckman, and Schennach 2010). It also bears on David J. P. Barker's (1995) fetal origins hypothesis, which argues that events in utero and more generally at very young ages can influence health in late adulthood.

I am excited because I have not seen studies that try to incorporate more than one determinant in the same long-run outcome analysis. For instance, would it be possible to include measures pertaining to WIC, other subsidized food programs, and federally subsidized family planning programs in some of the studies just described? Most of them use their findings to obtain a cost-benefit ratio for Medicaid. It would be of great interest to know how this ratio compares to that of other programs.

Finally, I am encouraged because some of the findings that emerge support a subset of my own results. Goodman-Bacon's finding that the introduction of Medicaid had important effects on postneonatal mortality echoes a similar result in the Chou-Grossman-Liu study dealing with the introduction of NHI in Taiwan. This effect dovetails with the recommendation in the paper by Chen, Oster, and Williams (2016) that policy makers need to focus on postneonatal mortality to lower the U.S. infant mortality rate.

NOTES

1. Among pregnant women, a reduction in the price of contraception is expected to raise the probability of giving birth, whereas an increase in the price of abortion is expected to raise this probability. These predictions are derived from the determinants of the probability of becoming pregnant. Under the plausible assumption that contraception and abortion are alternative methods of birth control, a rise in the price of contraception or a decline in the price of abortion raises this probability. As these propositions imply, pregnancies to women with low costs of averting them (low contraceptive costs) may be termed "wanted" pregnancies. Note that under plausible assumptions the number of times a person has sex will rise as the cost of contraception or abortion falls in a model in which that activity enters his or her utility function and is a substitute for the number of children. If abortion is the only method of birth control or a substitute method for contraception, pregnancies rise, but abortions rise by a greater amount. More complicated models contain predictions in which pregnancies rise by more than abortions, which result in an increase in births (Akerlof, Yellen, and Katz 1996; Kane and Staiger 1996). That can happen in the simple and perhaps more fundamental model that I just specified if sex and the number of children are strong complements. Like much of my unpublished work, I developed that model while reviewing a paper for a journal. In this case, I do not recall the author or the outcome of the paper.
2. These are only two of many studies in a fairly large literature. For a summary, see Joyce et al. (2013). Research by Ted Joyce—my former student, colleague, and very good friend—plays a prominent role in this afterword. He constantly encourages me (some would say demands me) to rethink conclusions I have drawn from my past studies.
3. Martha Bailey (2013) reports that these programs led to improvements in such long-run outcomes of the children whose parents benefited from them as college completion, labor force participation, and wages.
4. The quote is from the cartoon strip *Peanuts*, by Charles M. Schulz.
5. See Thomas Buchmueller, John C. Ham, and Lara D. Shore-Sheppard (2016) for a comprehensive review of this literature as it relates to Medicaid.

REFERENCES

Akerlof, George A., Janet L. Yellen, and Michael Katz. 1996. "An Analysis of Out-of-Wedlock Childbearing in the United States." *Quarterly Journal of Economics* 111(2): 277–317.

Anant, Elizabeth Oltmans, Jonathan Gruber, Phillip B. Levine, and Douglas Staiger. 2009. "Abortion and Selection." *Review of Economics and Statistics* 91(1): 124–136.

Bailey, Martha J. 2012. "Reevaluating the Impact of U.S. Family Planning Programs on Fertility: Evidence from the War on Poverty and the Early Years of Title X." *American Economic Journal: Applied Economics* 4(1): 62–97.

Bailey, Martha J. 2013. "Fifty Years of U.S. Family Planning: New Evidence of the Long-Run Effects of Increasing Access to Contraception." *Brookings Papers on Economic Activity* Spring: 341–395.

Bailey, Martha J., Melanie Gulden, and Brad J. Hershbein. 2013. "Recent Evidence of the Broad Benefits of Reproductive Health Policy." *Journal of Policy Analysis and Management* 32(3): 888–896.

Barker, David J. P. 1995. "Fetal Origins of Coronary Heart Disease." *British Medical Journal,* 311(6998): 171–174.

Becker, Gary S., and H. Gregg Lewis. 1973. "On the Interaction Between the Quantity and Quality of Children." *Journal of Political Economy* 81(2, pt. 2): S279–S288.

Brown, David W., Amanda E. Kowalski, and Ithai Z. Lurie. 2015. "Medicaid as an Investment in Children: What Is the Long-Term Impact on Tax Receipts?" Cambridge, MA: National Bureau of Economic Research Working Paper 20835.

Buchmueller, Thomas, John C. Ham, and Laura D. Shore-Sheppard. 2016. "The Medicaid Program." In *Economics of Means-Tested Transfer Programs in the United States*, Volume 1, ed. Robert A. Moffitt. Chicago: University of Chicago Press, 21-136.

Chen, Alice, Emily Oster, and Heidi Williams. 2016. "Why Is Infant Mortality Higher in the US Than in Europe?" *American Economic Journal: Economic Policy* 8(2): 89–124.

Cohodes, Sarah R., Daniel S. Grossman, Samuel A. Kleiner, and Michael F. Lovenheim. 2016. "The Effect of Child Health Insurance on Schooling: Evidence from Public Insurance Expansions." *Journal of Human Resources* 51(3): 727-759.

Colman, Silvie, and Ted Joyce. 2009. "Behavioral Responses to Parental Involvement Laws: The Case of Delay in the Timing of Abortion Until Age 18." *Perspectives on Sex and Reproductive Health* 41(2): 119–126.

Colman, Silvie, Theodore J. Joyce, and Robert Kaestner. 2008. "Misclassification Bias in the Evaluation of Parental Involvement Laws: A Minor Oversight with a Major Impact." *American Journal of Public Health* 98(10): 1881–1885.

Conway, Karen Smith, and Partha Deb. 2005. "Is Prenatal Care Really Ineffective? Or Is the 'Devil' in the Distribution." *Journal of Health Economics* 24(3): 489–513.

Cunha, Flavio, James J. Heckman, and Susanne M. Schennach. 2010. "Estimating the Technology of Cognitive and Noncognitive Skill Formation." *Econometrica* 78(3): 883–931.

Currie, Janet, and Jonathan Gruber. 1996a. "Health Insurance Eligibility, Utilization of Medical Care, and Child Health." *Quarterly Journal of Economics* 111(2): 431–466.

Currie, Janet, and Jonathan Gruber. 1996b. "Saving Babies: The Efficacy and Cost of Recent Changes in the Medicaid Eligibility of Pregnant Women." *Journal of Political Economy* 104(6): 1263–1296.

Currie, Janet, and Jonathan Gruber. 1997. "The Technology of Birth: Health Insurance, Medical Interventions, and Infant Health." Cambridge, MA: National Bureau of Economic Research Working Paper 5985.

Currie, Janet, and Jonathan Gruber. 2001. "Public Health Insurance and Medical Treatment: The Equalizing Impact of the Medicaid Expansions." *Journal of Public Economics* 82(1): 63–89.

Currie, Janet, Lucia Nixon, and Nancy Cole. 1996. "Restrictions on Medicaid Funding of Abortions." *Journal of Human Resources* 31(1): 159–188.

Cutler, David, and Ellen Meara. 2000. "The Technology of Birth: Is It Worth It?" In *Frontiers in Health Policy Research*, Volume 3, ed. Alan M. Garber. Cambridge, MA: MIT Press, 33–68.

Dave, Dhaval M., Sandra Decker, Robert Kaestner, and Kosali I. Simon. 2008. "Re-examining the Effects of Medicaid Expansions for Pregnant Women." Cambridge, MA: National Bureau of Economic Research Working Paper 14591.

Dave, Dhaval M., Robert Kaestner, and George L. Wehby. 2015. "Does Medicaid Coverage for Pregnant Women Affect Prenatal Health Behaviors?" Cambridge, MA: National Bureau of Economic Research Working Paper 21049.

Donohue III, John J., and Steven D. Levitt. 2001. "The Impact of Legalized Abortion on Crime." *Quarterly Journal of Economics* 116(2): 379–420.

Frank, Richard G., Donna M. Strobino, Catherine A. Jackson, and David A. Salkever. 1992. "Updated Estimates of the Impact of Prenatal Care on Birthweight Outcomes by Race." *Journal of Human Resources* 24(4): 629–642.

General Accounting Office. 1992. *Early Interventions: Federal Investments like WIC Can Produce Savings*. GAO/HRD-92–18. Washington, DC: Author.

Goldenberg, Robert L., and Dwight J. Rouse. 1998. "Prevention of Premature Birth." *New England Journal of Medicine* 339(5): 313–320.

Goodman-Bacon, Andrew. 2015. "Public Insurance and Mortality: Evidence from Medicaid Implementation." Nashville, TN: Working Paper, Department of Economics, Vanderbilt University.

Goodman-Bacon, Andrew. 2016. "The Long-Run Effects of Childhood Insurance Coverage: Medicaid Implementation, Adult Health and Labor Market Outcomes." Cambridge, MA: National Bureau of Economic Research Working Paper 22899.

Goodman-Bacon, Andrew. Forthcoming. "Public Insurance and Mortality: Evidence from Medicaid Implementation." *Journal of Political Economy*.

Gruber, Jonathan, Phillip B. Levine, and Douglas Staiger. 1999. "Legalized Abortion and Child Living Circumstances: Who Is the Marginal Child." *Quarterly Journal of Economics* 114(1): 263–291.

Guttmacher Institute. 2016a. *State Policies in Brief: Parental Involvement Laws. http://www.guttmacher.org/statecenter/spibs/spib_PIMA.pdf*.

Guttmacher Institute. 2016b. *State Policies in Brief: State Funding of Abortions Under Medicaid. http://www.guttmacher.org/statecenter/spibs/spib_SFAM.pdf*.

Hack, Maureen, and Irwin R. Merkatz. 1995. "Preterm Delivery and Low Birth Weight—A Dire Legacy." *New England Journal of Medicine* 333(26): 1772–1774.

Hamilton, Brady E., Joyce A. Martin, Michelle J. K. Osterman, Sally C. Curtin, and T. J. Mathews. 2015. "Births: Final Data for 2014." *National Vital Statistics Report* 64(12). Hyattsville, MD: National Center for Health Statistics.

Hanratty, Maria J. 1996. "Canadian National Health Insurance and Infant Health." *American Economic Review* 86(1): 276–284.

Hoynes, Hilary W., and Diane Whitmore Schanzenbach. 2016. "U.S. Food and Nutrition Programs." In *Economics of Means-Tested Transfer Programs in the United States*, Volume 1, ed. Robert A. Moffitt. Chicago: University of Chicago Press, 219-301.

Joyce, Theodore. 1994. "Self-Selection, Prenatal Care, and Birthweight Among Blacks, Whites, and Hispanics in New York City." *Journal of Human Resources* 29(3): 762–794.

Joyce, Theodore. 1999. "The Impact of Augmented Prenatal Care on Birth Outcomes of Medicaid Recipients in New York City." *Journal of Health Economics* 18(1): 31–67.

Joyce, Ted. 2010. "Abortion and Crime: A Review." In *Handbook of the Economics of Crime*, ed. Bruce Benson and Paul Zimmerman. New York: Edward Elgar, 452–487.

Joyce, Ted. 2013. "How Important Was the Pill to Women's Economic Well-Being? If Roe v. Wade Were Overturned, How Might Society Change? *Journal of Policy Analysis and Management* 32(3): 879–887.

Joyce, Theodore, Robert Kaestner, and Silvie Colman. 2006. "Changes in Abortions and Births and the Texas Parental Notification Law." *New England Journal of Medicine* 354(10): 1031–1038.

Joyce, Ted, Andrew Racine, and Cristina Yunzal-Butler. 2008. "Reassessing the WIC Effect: Evidence from the Pregnancy Nutrition Surveillance System." *Journal of Policy Analysis and Management* 27(2): 277–303.

Joyce, Ted, Ruoding Tan, and Yuxiu Zhang. 2013. "Abortion Before and After *Roe*." *Journal of Health Economics* 32(3): 804–815.

Kalist, David E., and Noelle A. Molinari. 2006. "Is the Marginal Child More Likely to Be Murdered?" *Journal of Human Resources* 41(3): 611–630.

Kane, Thomas J., and Douglas Staiger. 1996. "Teen Motherhood and Abortion Access." *Quarterly Journal of Economics* 114(2): 467–506.

Levitt, Steven D., and Stephen J. Dubner. 2005. *Freakonomics: A Rogue Economist Explores the Hidden Side of Everything*. New York: HarperCollins.

Ludwig, Jens, and Matthew Miller. 2005. "Interpreting the WIC Debate." *Journal of Policy Analysis and Management* 24(4): 691–701.

Pop-Eleches, Cristian. 2006. "The Impact of an Abortion Ban on Socio-Economic Outcomes of Children: Evidence from Romania." *Journal of Political Economy* 114(4): 744–773.

Wherry, Laura R., Sarah Miller, Robert Kaestner, and Bruce D. Meyer. 2015. "Childhood Medicaid Coverage and Later Life Health Care Utilization." Cambridge, MA: National Bureau of Economic Research Working Paper 20929.

Willis, Robert J. 1973. "A New Approach to the Economics of Fertility Behavior." *Journal of Political Economy* 81(2, pt. 2): S14–S64.

The Economics of
Unhealthy Behaviors

PART 4

Introduction to Part 4

As implied by its name, the economics of unhealthy behaviors deals with the consumption of goods and associated behaviors that are harmful to health. Examples include cigarette smoking; overeating, reflected by the body mass index and by obesity; excessive alcohol consumption; and the consumption of illegal drugs.[1] These behaviors rank first, second, third, and tenth, respectively, as the leading causes of premature mortality in the United States (National Research Council 2015). Not only do consumers who engage in these behaviors harm themselves, but they also harm others. For instance, pregnant women who smoke or use cocaine may injure their fetuses, and drunk drivers may injure or kill other people. The existence of ignored internal costs (harm to self) and external costs (harm to others) explains why the governments of almost every developed country and many developing ones have chosen to intervene in the markets for these goods. Moreover, control of their consumption is a justified goal of public policy because much of the excess medical care costs associated with their consumption is borne by the state (Medicare and Medicaid) in the United States, by private health insurance, and ultimately by people who do not consume them or, in the cases of alcohol and food that is rich in calories and carbohydrates, do so in moderation.

From a positive standpoint, those who focus on economic approaches to the determinants of health outcomes need to understand the behavioral underpinnings of consumer choices pertaining to the consumption of unhealthy goods. Do decisions to consume goods with negative marginal products in the health production function conform to or violate basic propositions in economics? In particular, do they violate the "first" law in economics (or, as I once heard Gary S. Becker say, "the only law in economics"): the law of the downward sloping demand function? And how should one take account of the addictive properties of many of them: the positive relationship between past consumption and current consumption?

I made an initial attempt to deal with the demand for unhealthy goods in the last chapter of my NBER monograph in the context of a model of joint production in the household (Grossman 1972). I argued that a good such as cigarettes was demanded by at least some consumers because its positive effect on a commodity that I termed "smoking pleasure" outweighed its negative effect on health. I used the model to explain why health might have a negative income elasticity. Employing states of the United States in 1960 as the units of observation, I went so far as to run multiple regressions of the mortality rate on the price of cigarettes, which varied among states due to differences in state excise tax rates on cigarettes, and other variables. I expected a negative cigarette price effect because an increase in price would lead to less smoking and lower mortality. In some of my specifications, the price coefficient was negative, but it was not significant. Given the limited number of observations and the failure to take account of lags between reductions in smoking and improvements in health, that result was not surprising.

I did not return to this area until 1978, when I noticed a request for applications (RFA) dealing with teenage smoking from the National Institute of Child Health and Human Development. My then colleagues at the NBER and former students, Eugene M. Lewit and Douglas Coate, also saw the RFA, and we discussed applying for funding. At the time, the U.S. antismoking campaign, which began in 1964 with the issuance of the first Surgeon General's Report on Smoking and Health, was fourteen years old. The campaign had consisted primarily of policies to increase public knowledge of the harmful effects of smoking by issuing a report similar to the 1964 document on an annual basis and policies to restrict advertising by cigarette companies. The latter steps included the Fairness Doctrine of the Federal Communications Commission, which resulted in the airing of antismoking messages on radio and television from July 1, 1967, to January 1, 1971, and the Public Health Cigarette Smoking Act of 1970, which banned pro–smoking cigarettes advertising on radio and television after January 1, 1971.[2]

Despite the active antismoking campaign, the real price of a pack of cigarettes (the nominal price divided by the Consumer Price Index) declined by approximately 20 percent between 1964 and the late 1970s. The main reason was that the federal excise tax rate on cigarettes had been fixed in nominal terms at 8 cents a pack since 1951. Moreover, state excise tax rates, which like the federal tax took the form of specific excise taxes (fixed amount per pack), also had been very stable. Lewit, Coate, and I were struck by the inconsistency between the policy goal of reducing smoking and the reduction in the real price of cigarettes. It seemed to us that the relevant decision makers were ignoring the law of the downward sloping demand function. We thought it was particularly relevant to focus on the demand for cigarettes by teenagers and their responsiveness to price because the behavior at issue is one that begins early in life. Hence, policies in the form of tax hikes to raise prices and reduce smoking participation rates among youths might be the most effective way ultimately to curtail that behavior in all segments of the population.

By chance, I had been working with an individual-level dataset on teenagers that contained smoking measures and state of residence. That made it easy to append cigarette prices to it and to estimate cigarette demand functions. So, Lewit, Coate, and I felt that we had all the ingredients for a successful grant application. Indeed, we thought we were even more fortunate than I have indicated so far because the RFA to which we planned to respond also could include a component on youth alcohol consumption and excessive consumption. Not only was there an antismoking campaign under way in the United States at the time, but there was also an even newer antidrinking campaign under way.

The latter campaign was in part a reaction to an unintended consequence of the enactment of the Twenty-Sixth Amendment to the U.S. Constitution in 1971. That amendment gave eighteen-year-olds the right to vote. Shortly thereafter, the argument began to be made that if an eighteen-year-old was old enough to vote and old enough to die for his country (this was the Vietnam War era), he or she was old enough to drink alcohol. As a result, twenty-nine states lowered their legal drinking age for the purchase and consumption of alcohol from twenty-one to twenty, nineteen, or eighteen in the period from 1971 through 1975. One consequence was an increase in the motor vehicle accident mortality rate—the leading cause of death for people between the ages of one and thirty-five. This trend called attention to the involvement of alcohol in approximately one-half of all fatal crashes and stimulated an active policy to curtail alcohol abuse. Minnesota raised its legal drinking age from eighteen to nineteen in 1976, and an additional twenty-seven states had increased legal drinking ages by the time Congress passed the Federal Uniform Drinking Age Act of July 1984.[3]

As in the case of the antismoking campaign, federal and state excise tax hikes on alcoholic beverages had been ignored in the antidrinking campaign. That resulted in sharp reductions in the real prices of beer, wine, and distilled spirits. By chance, Coate had been working with a dataset that contained alcohol consumption measures for teenagers and young adults as well as state of residence. So we would be able to append alcoholic beverage prices and legal drinking ages to it, estimate demand functions for alcohol, and compare the effectiveness of a policy to raise the drinking age to twenty-one in all states to ones that raised excise tax rates by specified amounts. Moreover, we could study the impacts of these policies on motor vehicle accident mortality rates of older teenagers and young adults in a time series of state cross sections.

The outcome of our proposal, which included the components on cigarette smoking and excessive alcohol use, is depicted in the cartoon.[4] As one can see, it was not funded. That outcome was due in part to the view even among economists that the behaviors at issue were addictive and therefore highly unlikely to be sensitive to price. Despite the negative outcome, we decided to convert the proposal into one dealing with teenage smoking and the other dealing with alcohol use and motor vehicle accident mortality among older teenagers and young adults. Over the next several years, the former proposal was funded by the National Science Foundation and the latter was funded by the National Institute on Alcohol Abuse and Alcoholism, one of the National Institutes of Health. As a result of that success and the somewhat surprising results that emerged from this research that price matters in these outcomes, I have been working on the economics of unhealthy behaviors on a continuous basis ever since. I have published more papers on this topic than on the first three topics in this book,

WE HAVE READ YOUR PROPOSAL
AND ARE GIVING IT SERIOUS CONSIDERATION.

including many publications in each of the last four decades: the 1980s, 1990s, 2000s, and 2010s. That explains why the ten papers in this part of the book fall one short of the total number of eleven papers in the previous three parts.

The first paper in this part by Eugene M. Lewit, Douglas Coate, and Michael Grossman (1981) deals with teenage smoking and resulted from the National Science Foundation grant. We find that the law of the downward sloping demand function certainly holds for this behavior. Moreover, the magnitude of the response is substantial. A 10 percent increase in the price of a pack of cigarettes causes the number of teenagers who smoke to fall by 12 percent and reduces the quantity smoked by those who participate in this behavior to decline by 2 percent. These estimates imply an overall price elasticity of teenage smoking of −1.40, a much higher price elasticity than existing estimates for adults or for all segments of the population at the time.

How did we rationalize this finding? One factor is that the share of a youth's disposable income allocated to cigarettes is likely to exceed the corresponding share of an adult's income. It is well known that uncompensated (money-income constant) price elasticities rise in absolute value as this share rises. A second factor is that bandwagon or peer effects are more important in the case of youth smoking than in the case of adult smoking. That is, youths are more likely to smoke if their parents, older siblings, and peers also smoke. Hence, a price hike has both a direct effect (a youth's smoking falls, with peer smoking held constant) and an indirect effect (peer smoking falls, which also reduces a youth's smoking). The indirect effect makes the demand function more elastic. Finally, we argued that given the habitual nature of smoking, adult users, who almost always will have been users for longer periods of time than youths, might be less sensitive to price than youths. As shown below, that argument has some flaws. In any case, our results suggested that excise tax hikes, which result in price increases, might be a potent policy tool in the antismoking campaign.

The "full" price of smoking depends on the monetary value of the negative health effects of this behavior as well as on the money price of a pack of cigarettes. We are able to investigate how teenagers respond to both components because one-third of our sample was interviewed before the period in which the Fairness Doctrine was in effect (March 1, 1966, to June 30, 1967), and two-thirds were interviewed during the period of the doctrine (July 1, 1967, to March 31, 1970). As pointed out previously, the doctrine required that antismoking messages be given equal time on television and on the radio as pro-smoking messages. Stations that broadcasted the latter had to donate equal time for broadcasts of the former. Hence, the doctrine increased information about the harmful effects of smoking. We found that teenagers were approximately 3 percentage points less likely to smoke during the period in which the Fairness Doctrine was in effect than in the sixteen-month period prior to its introduction. By combining information on the number of pro- and antismoking messages aired in each year of our sample period with the amount of time each youth spent watching television, we show that the reduction could be attributed to the doctrine.

The next two papers in this part treat excessive alcohol consumption by older teenagers and young adults (Coate and Grossman 1988) and motor vehicle accident mortality in this age group (Saffer and Grossman 1987) as outcomes. Both resulted from the grant from the National Institute on Alcohol Abuse and Alcoholism. Both focus on the effects of changes in the price of beer (the drink of choice in this age group) or the state excise tax on this beverage, on one hand, and changes in the legal drinking age for the purchase and consumption of alcohol, on the other hand.

Each study finds that the outcome at issue falls as the legal drinking age or the money cost of beer rises. To gauge the magnitudes of these effects, the results are used to predict the potential effects of two policy initiatives. One is a uniform minimum legal drinking age of twenty-one in all states. That policy was being actively pursued as part of the antidrinking campaign during the sample of each study (1976–1980 in the case of Coate-Grossman and 1975–1983 in the case of Saffer-Grossman). The second policy is an increase in the federal excise tax on beer. That policy had been ignored in the campaign. The tax had been fixed in nominal terms at $0.16 on a six-pack since 1951 and would not increase until 1991. Moreover, although beer is the drink of choice among youths, the alcohol in distilled spirits was taxed three times as heavily as the alcohol in beer. The specific tax policy considered is one in which the real excise tax is indexed to the rate of inflation since 1951 and in which the rates at which the alcohol in beer and in distilled spirits are equalized.

Coate and I treat the frequency of beer consumption in a typical week in the past three months by sixteen through twenty-one-year-olds as an outcome, with an emphasis on the most frequent category of four to seven times a week. The drinking age policy would have reduced the number of youths in this category from 11 percent to 8 percent. The tax policy would have reduced this number to roughly the same percent. Saffer and I find that the drinking age policy would have reduced the motor vehicle accident mortality rate of eighteen through twenty-year-olds from 52 per 100,000 population to 48 per 100,000. The tax policy has a much larger effect, resulting in a new mortality rate of 24 deaths per 100,000. In evaluating the plausibility of these results, one should keep in mind that Coate and I did not have a measure of heavy alcohol consumption, reflected by the number of drinks consumed on a typical drinking day. One should also keep in mind that the tax policy amounted to a very large increase in the federal tax on beer. That tax would have risen by eightfold in 1978, which would have raised the nominal price of beer by almost 60 percent in that year.

Moreover, many states had legal drinking ages of twenty-one in one or more years of the sample periods. Nevertheless, the results underscore the sensitivity of potentially excessive and inappropriate (in the form of driving after drinking) alcohol consumption by youths and young adults to the money price of the beverage and to the legal drinking age. The latter is an important component of the full price because a minimum purchase age restriction makes it more difficult, although certainly not impossible, for underage drinkers to obtain alcohol. For example, they can search for sellers who are willing to violate the law, acquire fake identification cards, or obtain alcohol from older siblings or friends.

The three papers I have just summarized rebut the views of my three cartoon friends and many other individuals who refused to at least consider that potentially addictive substances might be sensitive to price. While I was verifying that demand functions for cigarettes and alcohol by youths and young adults conform to the law of their downward slope, Gary S. Becker and Kevin M. Murphy were developing a theoretical model in which addiction is a perfectly rational behavior and in which consumers who purchase goods that are addictive and that have negative health consequences take account of the future consequences of their current actions. I urge the reader not to react to this theory and to the 1988 seminal paper in the *Journal of Political Economy* that resulted from it (Becker and Murphy 1988) in the manner in which the individuals in the figure probably reacted to it. Although Becker might be termed "Mr. Rational Behavior," he published a paper in the 1962 volume of the *JPE* in which he showed that the law of the downward sloping demand function holds even in a model in which consumers are irrational in the sense that their behavior is not governed by utility maximization and in which they select goods to purchase in a random manner (Becker 1962). If the first law of economics emerges from that model, one should at least consider that testable empirical implications might emerge from a model that assumes addiction is a rational behavior and that consumers who purchase addictive goods are forward-looking.

By 1986 or 1987, Becker and Murphy had made substantial progress on their paper and were anxious to test its implications. Given the work that I had been doing on the demand for cigarettes and alcohol and my knowledge of potential data, they invited me to join them in that effort. That invitation resulted in the next four papers in this part of the book, the first two of which are coauthored with Becker and Murphy. The first, third, and fourth papers test the theory of rational addiction in the cases of cigarettes, alcohol, and cocaine, respectively. The second contains some implications of the theory that are not emphasized by Becker and Murphy in their 1988 paper.

Empirical testing of the Becker-Murphy model strips the model to its barest essentials. The two really important ingredients are the definition of an addictive good and the assumption that consumers take account of the future consequences of their current actions. A good is addictive if an increase in past consumption of that good raises current consumption because it raises the marginal utility or marginal benefit of current consumption. This is the reinforcement property of an addictive good stressed by psychologists. A harmful addiction, the focus of the ones considered in this part of the book, is one in which past consumption has detrimental effects on current utility, such as reductions in health and therefore in utility caused by cigarette smoking, excessive alcohol use, and the use of cocaine. Harmful addictions exhibit the physiological property of tolerance in the sense that the utility from a given amount of current consumption is lower when past consumption is higher. Consumers behave in a rational or farsighted manner because they take account of the effects of current consumption on future utility when they determine the optimal or utility-maximizing quantity of an addictive good in the present period.

These assumptions generate the key prediction in the model: that of intertemporal complementarity. Economists define a set of goods to be complements if a reduction in the price of one good causes consumption of all of them to rise. In the Becker-Murphy model of rational addiction, the quantities of an addictive good consumed in different periods are complements. Current and past consumption are complements because an increase in past consumption due to a reduction in past price causes the marginal benefit of current consumption and hence current consumption to rise. The current period utility function has the same form in every period, so current consumption in period t is past consumption in period $t + 1$, and an increase in current consumption raises the marginal utility of future consumption. Therefore, by symmetry, if an increase in current consumption raises the marginal utility of future consumption, an increase in future consumption must raise the marginal utility of current consumption. Hence, an increase in future consumption due to a reduction in future price causes current consumption to rise.

Becker, Grossman, and Murphy (1994) show that the Becker-Murphy model generates a demand function for consumption of an addictive good in period $t(C_t)$ of the form

$$C_t = \alpha C_{t-1} + \beta \alpha C_{t+1} + \theta P_t. \tag{1}$$

Here, (P_t) is the price of C_t. Other determinants of current period consumption are suppressed. Because α and β are positive and θ is negative, current consumption is positively related to past and future consumption (C_{t-1} and C_{t+1}, respectively) and negatively related to current price. In particular, α measures the effect of an increase in past consumption on the marginal benefit of current consumption. This parameter also measures the effect of an increase in future consumption on the marginal benefit of current consumption. The larger the value of α the greater is the degree of reinforcement or addiction. Equation (1) highlights the source of intertemporal complementarity in the rational addiction model. It arises because increases in past or future consumption (caused by reductions in past or future prices) cause current consumption to rise.

Equation (1) also implies that the short-run price elasticity, which holds past consumption constant, must be smaller than the long-run price elasticity, which allows past consumption to vary. This property does not hold in general for a non-addictive good. Hence, comparisons between the price elasticities of the two types of goods may be misleading if they are not based on long-run price elasticities. Put differently, past consumption reinforces current consumption so the price response grows over time in the case of an addictive good. For example, a price increase in 2016 would reduce consumption in 2016, which in turn would cause consumption in 2017 and in all future years to fall ceteris paribus. Indeed, the long-run price response is greater the higher the degree of addiction or reinforcement.

The parameter β in Equation (1) is the time discount factor and is equal to $1/(1 + r)$, where r is the rate of time preference for the present. Typically, economists and psychologists assume that this discount factor is smaller than one because people are impatient. They prefer to consume 100 units of a good today instead of consuming 100 units of the same good tomorrow. The smaller the time discount factor (the greater the rate of time preference for the present) the smaller is the effect of future consumption or future price on current consumption. In the case of perfectly myopic behavior in which consumers pay no attention to the future consequences of their current actions, β equals zero (r equals infinity), and future variables have no impact on current decisions. This is the sense in which a myopic model of addiction is nested within a rational model of this behavior.

Becker, Murphy, and I successfully apply the rational addiction model to the demand for cigarettes by people of all ages in the fifth paper in this section (Becker, Grossman, and Murphy 1994). Frank J. Chaloupka, Ismail Sirtalan, and I enjoy similar success in applying the model to the demand for alcohol by young adults in the sixth paper in this section (Grossman, Chaloupka, and Sirtalan 1998), as do Chaloupka and I in applying the model to the demand for cocaine by young adults in the seventh paper (Grossman and Chaloupka 1998). These three studies report negative and significant price effects, positive and significant past and future consumption effects, and larger long-run than short-run price elasticities. Short-run and long-run price elasticities of demand in these studies are −0.40 and −0.75 for cigarettes; −0.41 and −0.65 for alcohol; and −0.96 and −1.35 for cocaine.

In the fourth paper in this section, Becker, Murphy, and I show that extensions of the framework in the Becker-Murphy 1988 paper imply differential price responses by age, income, and education in the case of addictive goods (Becker, Grossman, and Murphy 1991). The total cost of addictive goods to consumers equals the sum of the good's price and the money value of the future adverse effects, such as the negative effects on earnings and health from smoking, heavy drinking, or heavy dependence on cocaine. Future costs tend to be less important for poorer, less educated, and younger consumers because they generally place a smaller monetary value on health and other harmful future effects than richer, more educated, and older consumers who have higher wage rates. Moreover, the poor, youths, and the less educated are likely to have lower time discount factors (higher rates of time preference for the present) than the rich, adults, and the more educated. It follows that the poor, youths, and the less educated are more sensitive to changes in money prices of addictive goods, whereas the middle- or upper-income classes, adults, and the more educated respond more to changes in the perceived or actual harmful consequences that take place in the future. Becker, Murphy, and I summarize existing empirical evidence as of 1991 in support of these propositions.

In the last three papers in this section, I turn my attention to the unhealthy behavior of overeating, reflected by a high body mass index and obesity. Obesity rates in the United States and the rest of the developed world remained steady from approximately 1960 until about 1980. Since then, they have increased dramatically. For example, in the United States the percentage of obese adults grew from 15 percent to 31 percent, and the percentage of obese children ages six through nineteen rose from approximately 6 percent to 16 percent between 1980 and 2000. Hence, the number of obese adults doubled, and the number of obese children almost tripled in a period of two decades. The most recent data suggest a leveling of these trends for most age groups at unacceptably high values from a public health perspective. Currently, about one out of six children and one out of three adults are obese in the United States.[5]

Obesity is a complex public health problem that is related both to individual characteristics that are genetic or acquired and to the individual's economic environment. Medical research has identified a number of potential determinants of obesity, including genetic disposition. However, the stability of obesity until about 1980 and the continuous and dramatic increase since that year suggest that genetics may not play a very prominent role in the upswing, as genetic change typically does not take place quickly.

The last three papers in this section highlight the contributions that economists can make to an understanding of the causes of obesity and to suggestions of policies to combat it. Shin-Yi Chou, Henry Saffer, and I (Chou, Grossman, and Saffer 2004) focus on the following potential determinants of this outcome: the per capita number of fast-food and full-service restaurants, the price of a meal in each type of restaurant, the price of food consumed at home, the price of cigarettes (smokers tend to gain weight when they quit), and the price of alcohol (a potential determinant given its high caloric content). We show that these variables have the expected effects on obesity and explain a considerable amount of its trend.

Chou, Inas Rashad, and I (Chou, Rashad, and Grossman 2008) estimate the effects of exposure to television fast-food restaurant advertising on children and adolescents with respect to being obese. A ban on these advertisements would reduce the number of obese children ages three to eleven in a fixed population by 18 percent and would reduce the number of obese adolescents ages twelve to eighteen by 14 percent. The elimination of the tax deductibility of this type of advertising would produce smaller declines of between 5 and 7 percent in these outcomes but would impose lower costs on children and adults who consume fast food in moderation because positive information about restaurants that supply this type of food would not be completely banned from television.

Erdal Tekin, Roy Wada, and I (Grossman, Tekin, and Wada 2014) conduct a comprehensive analysis of the effects of food prices on the body mass index (BMI) and the percentage body fat (PBF) among youths ages twelve through eighteen. Both are derived from clinical examinations. The latter is a more reliable indicator of an adverse body composition than the former because BMI has limited ability to distinguish body fat from fat-free mass. Our findings suggest that increases in the real price of one calorie in food for home consumption and the real price of fast-food restaurant food result in significant reductions in the PBF among youths. We also find that an increase in the real price of fruits and vegetables has negative consequences for these outcomes. Some of our results point to higher rates of time preference and lower expected future wage rates among nonwhite parents and youths as explanations of why minorities are more sensitive to fast food prices and less sensitive to fruits and vegetables prices than whites. These factors make individuals less sensitive to the future harmful health costs of fast food and to the future health benefits of fruits and vegetables.

My coauthors and I address extremely relevant public policy and public health issues in the papers in this part of the book. We focus on determinants of unhealthy behaviors that have been and can be manipulated at all levels of government. In many cases, we quantify the potential impacts of alternative policies to alter these behaviors. At the same time, we are careful to avoid making policy recommendations and to point out unintended consequences. For example, a cigarette excise tax hike is a tool to reduce smoking but can lead to an increase in obesity. In addition, the policy, which often has been used to raise tax revenue, actually can result in a loss of revenue if the tax is set too high. In addition, given the addictive nature of smoking, the long-run increase in revenue is likely to be considerably smaller than the short-run increase.

To cite another example, alcohol excise tax increases impose welfare costs on all segments of the population, whereas a drinking age policy is targeted at a group in the population that accounts for a disproportionate share of motor vehicle accidents and deaths. On the other hand, the enforcement and administrative costs associated with a uniform minimum legal drinking age of twenty-one may exceed those associated with the tax policy. In addition, drunk driving can be deterred by a system of severe and fairly certain punishments.

To cite a final example, a tax levied as a fixed amount per calorie in each gram of food type might be an effective tool in what is becoming a war on obesity. Such a tax would have the desirable effect of raising the relative prices of foods that are cheap sources of calories. But it might be difficult to impose and administer. An alternative policy would be to tax unhealthy foods (for example, food purchased in fast-food restaurants) and to subsidize the consumption of such healthy foods as fruits and vegetables. In light of the current debate concerning whether a diet high in fat is more or less healthy than one high in carbohydrates, attempts to distinguish between healthy and unhealthy foods may not be straightforward (Bazzano, Hu, Reynolds, Yao, Bunol, Liu, Chen, Klag, Whelton, and He 2014). As in the case of taxes on alcohol, one needs to keep in mind that taxes are blunt instruments that impose welfare costs on individuals who consume food in moderation.

In the case of adolescents, an additional issue is that parents may more easily and immediately affect the choices made by their children than the government. Indeed, some of our results point to higher rates of time preference and lower expected future wage rates among nonwhite parents and youths as explanations of why minorities are more sensitive to fast-food prices and less sensitive to fruits and vegetables prices than whites. These interpretations add to the wide range of benefits to early childhood intervention programs emphasized by James J. Heckman and colleagues (for example, Conti and Heckman 2014). These programs aim to improve the cognitive and noncognitive skills of minorities and perhaps to give them more of a future orientation as well.

NOTES

1. The body mass index (BMI) is defined as weight in kilograms divided by height in meters squared. An individual over the age of eighteen with a BMI of 25 or greater is classified as overweight, and an individual with a BMI of 30 or greater is classified as obese. A person eighteen years or younger is overweight if his or her BMI is at or above the 85th percentile based on age and gender-specific growth charts and obese if it is at or above the 95th percentile. Recently, the U.S. Centers for Disease Control has replaced the term

overweight by "risk of being overweight" and the term *obese* with "overweight" for children and youths.

2. For a discussion of other elements of the antismoking campaign as of the late 1970s, see Eugene M. Lewit, Douglas Coate, and Michael Grossman (1981). Grossman (2005) updates that discussion.

3. That legislation allowed the federal government, through its control of federal highway funds, to intercede in a legislative area traditionally reserved for states. Five percent of a state's federal highway construction fund allocation for fiscal year 1987 was withheld if that state's minimum legal drinking age was below twenty-one as of October 1, 1986, and 10 percent was withheld from each future fiscal year allocation if that state's legal drinking age remained below twenty-one. For a discussion of other elements of the antidrinking campaign as of the late 1970s, see Douglas Coate and Michael Grossman (1988). Grossman (2005) updates that discussion.

4. The cartoon appeared on page 281of a book by Alan Dundes and Carl R. Pagter titled *Never Try to Teach a Pig to Sing: Still More Urban Folklore from a Paperwork Empire.* The book was published in 1991, and the cartoon is reprinted with the permission of the publisher: Wayne State University Press, Detroit.

5. See Michael Grossman and Naci H. Mocan (2011a, 2011b) for detailed discussions of these trends.

REFERENCES

Bazzano, Lydia A., Tian Hu, Kristi Reynolds, Lu Yao, Calynn Bunol, Yanxi Liu, Chung-Shiuan Chen, Michael J. Klag, Paul K. Whelton, and Jiang He. 2014. "Effects of Low-Carbohydrate and Low-Fat Diets: A Randomized Trial." *Annals of Internal Medicine* 16(5): 309–318.

Becker, Gary S. 1962. "Irrational Behavior and Economic Theory." *Journal of Political Economy* 70(1): 1–13.

Becker, Gary S., Michael Grossman, and Kevin M. Murphy. 1991. "Rational Addiction and the Effect of Price on Consumption." *American Economic Review* 81(2): 237–241.

Becker, Gary S., Michael Grossman, and Kevin M. Murphy. 1994. "An Empirical Analysis of Cigarette Addiction." *American Economic Review* 84(3) 396–418.

Becker, Gary S., and Kevin M. Murphy. 1988. "A Theory of Rational Addiction." *Journal of Political Economy* 96(4): 675–700.

Chou, Shin-Yi, Michael Grossman, and Henry Saffer. 2004. "An Economic Analysis of Adult Obesity: Results from the Behavioral Risk Factor Surveillance System." *Journal of Health Economics* 23(3): 565–587.

Chou, Shin-Yi, Inas Rashad, and Michael Grossman. 2008. "Fast-Food Restaurant Advertising on Television and Its Influence on Childhood Obesity." *Journal of Law and Economics* 51(4): 599–618.

Coate, Douglas, and Michael Grossman. 1988. "Effects of Alcoholic Beverage Prices and Legal Drinking Ages on Youth Alcohol Use." *Journal of Law and Economics* 31(1): 145–171.

Conti, Gabriella, and James J. Heckman. 2014. "The Economics of Child Well-Being." In *Handbook of Child Well-Being*, ed. Asher Ben-Arieh, Ferran Casas, Ivar Frønes, and Jill E. Korbin. London: Springer, 363–401.

Grossman, Michael. 1972. *The Demand for Health: A Theoretical and Empirical Investigation*. New York: Columbia University Press for the National Bureau of Economic Research.

Grossman, Michael. 2005. "Individual Behaviors and Substance Use: The Role of Price." In *Substance Use: Individual Behavior, Social Interaction, Markets and Politics,* ed. Björn Lindgren and Michael Grossman. Volume 16 of *Advances in Health Economics and Health Services Research.* Amsterdam: JAI, an imprint of Elsevier Ltd., 15–39.

Grossman, Michael, and Frank J. Chaloupka. 1998. "The Demand for Cocaine by Young Adults: A Rational Addiction Approach." *Journal of Health Economics* 17(4): 427–474.

Grossman, Michael, Frank J. Chaloupka, and Ismail Sirtalan. 1998. "An Empirical Analysis of Alcohol Addiction: Results from the Monitoring the Future Panels." *Economic Inquiry* 36(1): 39–48.

Grossman, Michael, and Naci H. Mocan. 2011a. "Introduction." In *Economic Aspects of Obesity,* ed. Michael Grossman and Naci H. Mocan. Chicago: University of Chicago Press, 1–16.

Grossman, Michael, and Naci Mocan. 2011b. "The Obesity Epidemic: Causes and Current Policy Perspectives." *Baker Institute Policy Report 46.* Houston, TX: James A. Baker III Institute for Public Policy of Rice University.

Grossman, Michael, Erdal Tekin, and Roy Wada. 2014. "Food Prices and Body Fatness Among Youths." *Economics and Human Biology* 12(1): 4–19.

Lewit, Eugene M., Douglas Coate, and Michael Grossman. 1981. "The Effects of Government Regulation on Teenage Smoking." *Journal of Law and Economics* 24(3): 545–569.

National Research Council, Institute of Medicine. 2015. *Measuring the Risks and Causes of Premature Death*. Washington, DC: National Academies Press.

Saffer, Henry, and Michael Grossman. 1987. "Beer Taxes, the Legal Drinking Age, and Youth Motor Vehicle Fatalities." *Journal of Legal Studies* 16(2): 351–374.

TWELVE

The Effects of Government Regulation on Teenage Smoking

Eugene M. Lewit, Douglas Coate, and
Michael Grossman

Since the issuance of the first Surgeon General's Report on Smoking and Health in 1964,[1] the federal government has been involved in a sporadic campaign to discourage cigarette smoking. This campaign has consisted primarily of policies designed to increase public knowledge of the harmful effects of cigarette smoking and to restrict advertising by cigarette manufacturers. The major elements of this campaign have been the Fairness Doctrine of the Federal Communications Commission, which resulted in the airing of antismoking messages on radio and television from July 1, 1967, to January 1, 1971, and the Public Health Cigarette Smoking Act of 1970, which banned prosmoking cigarette advertising on radio and television after January 1, 1971.[2]

In 1968, the first full calendar year of antismoking messages, 1,300 antismoking messages were aired by the three major networks. In 1970, 1,560 messages were aired with a market value of $75 million, about one-third of the value of the prosmoking commercials.[3] The ban on broadcast cigarette advertising in 1971, however, greatly reduced the airing of antismoking messages, relegating them to the same status as other public service advertising. This has caused a number of observers to question the substitution of the broadcast advertising ban for the active antismoking campaign mounted under the Fairness Doctrine.[4]

In this chapter we present the first set of estimates of the impact of the Fairness Doctrine and advertising ban policies on the demand for cigarettes by teenagers in the United States. In addition, we examine the extent to which an increase in the federal excise tax on cigarettes would reduce teenage smoking.[5] Excise tax changes are reflected in cigarette prices and comprise an additional public policy that influences cigarette demand.[6]

Previous evaluations of the effects of government policies to discourage smoking have examined the impact of these policies on per capita cigarette consumption.[7] Fluctuations in per capita cigarette consumption reflect primarily changes in adult smoking participation rates and in the average amount of cigarettes consumed by each adult smoker. Accordingly, these studies shed little light on the impact of these policies on teenage smoking. Yet, cigarette smoking is, in part, a habitual behavior that begins early in life. Therefore, changes in teenage smoking behavior in response to government regulatory actions can have a substantial and sustained impact on aggregate smoking in the long run.[8] Moreover, age at onset of smoking is negatively correlated with the amount smoked and the incidence of negative health effects.[9]

Recent trends in smoking participation rates of teenagers are presented in table 12.1. Comparable trends for the adult cohorts that comprise the parents of these teenagers are presented in table 12.2. Note that the percentage of teenagers who smoke increased between 1968 and 1970, and the percentage of girls who smoke rose between 1970 and 1974. On the other hand, the percentage of adults who smoke declined between 1966 and 1970 and between 1970 and 1975.[10] These trends underscore another reason for studying teenagers in the context of the antismoking campaign. Supporters of the advertising ban have pointed to the increase in teenage smoking rates between 1968 and 1970 as

Table 12.1 Percentage of Youths Ages Twelve to Eighteen Who Are Current Regular Smokers, 1968–1979

Year	Both Sexes	Boys	Girls
1968	11.5	14.7	8.4
1970	15.2	18.5	11.9
1972	14.4	15.7	13.3
1974	15.6	15.8	15.3
1979	11.7	10.7	12.7

Source: Data are from the National Clearinghouse for Smoking and Health and National Institute of Education, as reported in Dorothy E. Green, "Teenage Smoking: Immediate and Long-Term Patterns" (1979).

Table 12.2 Percentage of Adults Who Are Current Regular Smokers by Age and Sex, 1966–1975

Year	Males			Females		
	25–34	35–44	45–54	25–34	35–44	45–54
1966	59.9	59.0	53.8	45.1	40.6	42.0
1970	46.7	48.6	43.1	40.3	38.8	36.1
1975	43.9	47.1	41.1	35.4	36.4	32.8

Source: Data are from the National Clearinghouse for Smoking and Health, as reported in Jeffrey E. Harris, "Cigarette Smoking in the United States, 1950–1978," in *Smoking and Health: Report of the Advisory Committee to the Surgeon General of the Public Health Service* (1979).

evidence that, whatever the impact of the Fairness Doctrine on aggregate cigarette consumption, the doctrine was not effective in the case of teenagers.[11] Ignored in this argument is the important point that the Fairness Doctrine went into effect on July 1, 1967. Therefore, smoking rates in 1968 pertain to rates in the second half of the first year and first half of the second year of the doctrine. Thus, the data in table 12.1 do not allow one to compare teenage smoking in the period *before* the Fairness Doctrine to smoking *during* the doctrine.

Our empirical research in this chapter is based on Cycle III of the U.S. Health Examination Survey (HES III). This is a national sample of 6,768 noninstitutionalized youths aged twelve to seventeen conducted in the period 1966–1970.[12] Since one-third of the sample was interviewed before the period of the Fairness Doctrine (March 1, 1966–June 30, 1967), while two-thirds of the sample were interviewed during the period of the doctrine (July 1, 1967–March 31, 1970),[13] we are able to present the first multivariate evaluation of the Fairness Doctrine on teenage smoking. In addition, since some of our estimated equations include the number of pro- and antismoking messages seen by each youth, we are able to make predictions about the potential impacts of the advertising ban.

Previous studies have examined the effects of the Fairness Doctrine and the advertising ban on per capita cigarette consumption in the context of time-series cigarette demand functions.[14] Hamilton, Warner, and Doran conclude that the Fairness Doctrine had a significant negative effect on per capita consumption. Hamilton and Doran also find that the advertising ban may actually have encouraged consumption because the airing of antismoking messages fell dramatically after 1970. On the other hand, Ippolito, Murphy, and Sant conclude that the effects reported in the other studies can be attributed solely to a lagged response to the surgeon general's report of 1964.[15]

Not only do these four time-series studies present conflicting conclusions regarding the effects of the Fairness Doctrine and the advertising ban, but their conclusions are somewhat suspect because in all the studies the Fairness Doctrine is modeled as a dichotomous variable. In addition, Warner and Ippolito, Murphy, and Sant exclude procigarette advertising in their empirical work. In this chapter, we develop and include in our estimated demand functions a time series on the number of antismoking messages aired on television between the last half of 1967 and first quarter of 1970.[16] We also incorporate measures of procigarette advertising in our pooled time-series cross-section demand functions. Moreover, we focus on a group, teenagers, who might be most susceptible to both types of mass persuasion.

We also present the first estimates of the responsiveness of smoking by teenagers to variations in the price of cigarettes. This is possible because of cross-sectional differences in the price of cigarettes, primarily due to differences in state excise tax rates. Interstate variations in cigarette prices are substantial— retail cigarette prices are approximately 50 percent higher in the high-tax states than in the low-tax states (Tobacco Tax Council, various years).

As summarized by Lewit and Coate, estimates of the price elasticity of demand for cigarettes by adults range from −.1 to −1.5, with the best estimate being approximately −.4.[17] We investigate the price elasticity of demand for cigarettes by teenagers, in part, because these previous estimates primarily reflect adult smoking behavior. Given the habitual nature of smoking, adult users, who almost always will have been users for longer periods of time than youths, might be much less sensitive to price than youths. In addition, bandwagon or peer effects (discussed in more detail below) are believed to be much more important in the case of youth smoking than in the case of adult smoking. As shown by Leibenstein, the presence of these effects increases the price elasticity of demand in absolute value.[18]

1. METHODOLOGY

To examine the effects of the price of cigarettes and the Fairness Doctrine on teenage smoking, we use Cycle III of the HES III to estimate demand functions for cigarette smoking by teenagers. The HES III is a random sample of 6,768 youths between the ages of twelve and seventeen that was conducted between March 1966 and March 1970 by the National Center for Health Statistics. It contains complete medical and health behavior histories of the youths provided by the youths and their parents, information on family socioeconomic characteristics, birth certificate information, a school report with data on school performance and classroom behavior provided by teachers and other school officials, scores on psychological (including IQ and achievement) tests, and objective measures of health from physical examinations. The physical examinations and the psychological tests were administered by the Public Health Service. Information on cigarette smoking was obtained directly from the youths as part of the health behavior questionnaire. Parents were not present during the interviews with the youths and were not informed about the smoking responses of their children.

Information on the date of the examination enables us to divide the sample into youths interviewed before the Fairness Doctrine and youths interviewed during the Fairness Doctrine. Information on the city and state of residence of each youth and on the date of the examination enables us to add a measure of the price of cigarettes to the data set. The resulting series incorporates variations in price due to variations in state and municipal excise and retail sales tax rates. It also incorporates variations in price due to trends over time between 1966 and 1970.

Within the context of the HES sample, the most general way to specify a demand function for smoking by teenagers is

$$y_{ijt} = a_0 + a_1 p_{jt} + a_2 d_{jt} + a_3 x_{ijt} + a_4 s_{ijt}$$
$$+ a_5 \bar{y}_{jt} + a_6 f_t + a_7 t + \varepsilon_{ijt}. \tag{1}$$

The dependent variable in equation (1) can be either the amount smoked by the ith youth in the jth locality in period t or the probability that the youth smokes. The independent variables include two measures of the price of cigarettes: the actual retail price of cigarettes (p_{jt}) and the difference between the "own price" of cigarettes and the "low price" (d_{jt}), which is described below. Additional independent variables are a vector of family and youth characteristics (x_{ijt}) such as family income, family size, mother's labor force status, absence of father from the household, parents' schooling, age of youth, sex of youth, and race of youth; parents' smoking (s_{ijt}); the mean smoking participation rate or the mean quantity smoked by all youths in the jth locality ($\bar{y}_{jt}$); a vector of variables pertaining to the Fairness Doctrine (f_t); time (t); and a random disturbance term ε_{ijt}).

The definition and measurement of the variables in equation (1) are discussed in the next section. Here we make a few general comments on the roles of certain variables. Lewit and Coate have pointed out that difficulties arise in defining the relevant measure of the price of cigarettes in a cross section because smokers in a high-price area might purchase cigarettes in border areas with lower prices.[19] This phenomenon arises because cross-sectional variations in cigarette prices reflect primarily variations in state and municipal excise and sales taxes. To deal with this problem, we have added two price series to the HES: own price (price in city and state of residence) and low price.[20] If a youth lives within twenty miles of a lower-price area, low price equals the price in that area. If a youth does not reside within twenty miles of such a border area, low price is set equal to own price.

The incentive to travel to lower-price border areas to buy cigarettes is greater the greater is the difference between own price and low price. Therefore, the most flexible method to control for the border phenomenon (out-of-area purchases) is to enter own price and the difference between own and low price as separate independent variables in the demand functions. With the own-area price held constant, an increase in the price differential reflects a reduction in the border-area price and should cause cigarette smoking to increase. Note that the twenty-mile distance is selected to compute the low price of cigarettes because the purchase of cigarettes within twenty miles of residence is likely to be incidental to the purpose of travel. Although the incentive to make purchases or to have friends or fellow employees make purchases is positively related to the difference between own price and low price, the lack of direct data on travel costs presents no problem if purchases of cigarettes are incidental to the main purpose of the trip.

Although Lewit and Coate find that the border phenomenon is an important consideration in estimating the price elasticity of demand for adult smokers,[21] there is less reason to believe that it presents a problem in the case of teenagers. This is because the quantity of cigarettes smoked by teenagers generally is very small, so that the incentive to search for low-priced cigarettes is reduced. Moreover, the amount of incidental travel by teenagers in the HES sample is likely to be small because most of them are below minimum legal driving ages. In our estimated equations, however, we enter both own price and the difference between own and low price to minimize measurement error problems and determine empirically the importance of border crossing by teenagers.

Both time (t) and specific variables pertaining to the Fairness Doctrine, such as the number of antismoking messages aired on television in a given year (f_t), enter the demand function. This is because there may be underlying trends in teenage smoking that are unrelated to the Fairness Doctrine. In practice, since the HES spans a short period of time, these underlying trends cannot be estimated and t must be omitted from the equation. This means that the impact of the Fairness Doctrine variables may reflect in part developments not related to the doctrine. Given the plausible assumption of an underlying upward trend, the omission of time biases the coefficients of the Fairness Doctrine variables toward zero.[22]

The main empirical regularity in youth smoking research by sociologists and psychologists is that youths are more likely to smoke if their parents, siblings, and peers also smoke.[23] Hence, the demand curve for youth smoking is subject to "bandwagon effects," to use the term coined by Leibenstein.[24] An alternative explanation of these effects is that youths obtain cigarettes "free of charge" or at reduced rates from their parents, older siblings, and peers.

In the demand function specified by equation (1), the mean smoking rate in the locality ($\bar{y}_{jt}$) is a proxy for sibling and peer smoking. We refer to it as the "smoking environment" of a particular youth and treat its impact in the context of a well-known model of externalities in consumption.[25] To be specific, aggregation of equation (1) over the n_j youths in the jth locality yields

$$
\bar{y}_{jt} = \left(\frac{a_0}{1-a_5}\right) + \left(\frac{a_1}{1-a_5}\right)p_{jt} + \left(\frac{a_2}{1-a_5}\right)d_{jt}
$$

$$
+ \left(\frac{a_3}{1-a_5}\right)\bar{x}_{jt} + \left(\frac{a_4}{1-a_5}\right)\bar{s}_{jt} + \left(\frac{a_6}{1-a_5}\right)f_t
$$

$$
+ \left(\frac{a_7}{1-a_5}\right)t + \left(\frac{1}{1-a_5}\right)\bar{\varepsilon}_{jt}, \tag{2}
$$

where bars over variables denote means.

Equation (1) is a structural demand function, while equation (2) is a reduced form. Since a_5 is assumed to be positive and smaller than one, the absolute value of a given reduced-form coefficient exceeds the absolute value of the corresponding structural coefficient.[26] Clearly, the reduced-form coefficients are more relevant than the structural coefficients in assessing the impact on youth smoking of price and the Fairness Doctrine. Since we have no independent measure of $\bar{y}_{jt}$, we estimate equation (1) with this variable omitted. We interpret the resulting coefficients as reduced-form effects.[27]

In addition to omitting $\bar{y}_{jt}$ from equation (1), we omit parents' smoking because there is no information on this variable in the data. If parents' smoking has no trend, its exclusion presents no problems. As in the case of peer smoking, the coefficients of the price and Fairness Doctrine variables in the teenage demand function can be interpreted as reduced-form effects. Put differently, a policy to curb youth smoking by raising the federal excise tax rate on cigarettes would raise the price of cigarettes paid by youths and their parents, which would discourage smoking by both groups. Therefore, in evaluating the impact of such a policy, parents' smoking should not be held constant (included in the regression).

The situation is somewhat different if there is a trend in parents' smoking. To see this, write the parents' demand function as

$$
s_{ijt} = b_0 + b_1 p_{jt} + b_2 d_{jt} + b_3 z_{ijt} + b_4 f_t + b_5 t, \tag{3}
$$

where z_{ijt} is a vector of parents' characteristics and the disturbance term is suppressed. Substitute equation (3) into equation (1) and ignore variables other than p_{jt}, f_t, and t:

$$y_{ijt} = a_0 + (a_1 + b_1 a_4) p_{jt} + (a_6 + b_4 a_4) f_t + (a_7 + b_5 a_4) t. \qquad (4)$$

If equation (4) is fitted with t omitted, the parameter estimate of f_t is biased. But the direction of the bias is indeterminant if a_7 is positive while b_5 is negative. Given these signs, estimation problems may not be serious because biases due to the omission of time are mitigated by biases due to the omission of parents' smoking.

2. EMPIRICAL IMPLEMENTATION

Equation (1) with s_{ijt}, t, and $\bar{y}_{jt}$ omitted is estimated using Cycle III data for white or black youths who live with either both of their parents or with their mothers only. Youths of other races and from other kinds of families are eliminated in order to produce a more homogeneous sample. The omitted observations account for a small percentage of the total sample. Observations are also deleted if there are missing data. The final sample size is 5,308. Table 12.3 contains means of the dependent and selected independent variables for the whole sample, for the sample interviewed before the Fairness Doctrine went into effect, and for the sample interviewed during the period of the Fairness Doctrine.

Two measures of smoking behavior are examined: whether or not the youth is a current smoker (SMOKEP) and the number of packs of cigarettes smoked per day (QSMOKE). Of these two measures, we believe that smoking participation is the more important. As indicated previously, most youthful smokers will remain smokers as adults, and age at onset of smoking is negatively correlated with the amount smoked in adulthood and the incidence of negative health effects. Smoking participation is a dichotomous variable that assumes the value of one for current smokers. The number of packs of cigarettes smoked per day assumes one of five possible values: 0, .25, .75, 1.50, or 2.50. In spite of this, the method of estimation is ordinary least squares. Previous research with the HES sample by Grossman revealed almost no differences between ordinary least-squares estimates and logit estimates obtained by the method of maximum likelihood.

Our smoking variables are obtained directly from youths. Because youths may underreport their cigarette use,[28] our smoking measures may be inaccurate. If any such response error is uncorrelated with the independent variables in the demand function for cigarettes, coefficients will be unbiased, although their standard errors will be inflated. If all youths underreport smoking by a constant factor of proportionality, slope coefficients and their standard errors are biased downward by this factor, leaving statistical tests of significance and elasticities unaffected.

Table 12.3 Sample Means of Selected Variables

Variable	Total Sample (N = 5,308)	Before Fairness Doctrine (N = 1,814)	During Fairness Doctrine (N = 3,494)
SMOKEP	.131	.146	.124
QSMOKE	.068	.070	.067
PRICE	31.298	29.817	32.067
PDIF	.816	.809	.820
FAIR	.658	...	...
T1	.243	...	.369
T2	.252	...	.383
T3	.163	...	.248
TV	2.860	2.685	2.951
TV × FAIR	1.942	...	2.951
TV × Tl	.698	...	1.061
TV × T2	.760	...	1.553
TV × T3	.484	...	.735
PROTV	212,889.514	200,605.088	219,267.290
ANTITV	2,127.631	...	3,309.724
ANTITVS	12,354,502.896	...	18,768,658.000
PRTVFAIR	144,333.065	...	219,267.290

In the two models outlined above, the existence of response error essentially presents no problems for the statistical analysis. Response error only becomes a problem if it is systematic or correlated with some or all of the independent variables in the demand function. To be specific, Warner argues that underreporting has increased over time "due to increases in the perceived personal threat or social stigma associated with smoking."[29] Given this argument, one would expect reported teenage smoking rates to have fallen continuously during the period of the Fairness Doctrine. In fact, the trends in table 12.1 and our own empirical results presented in section 3 indicate that this was not the case.

The Tax Burden on Tobacco, published by the Tobacco Tax Council, is the source for annual state-specific price series on cigarettes. Price is measured in cents per pack adjusted for municipal excise and retail sales taxes. The own price of cigarettes is deflated by a state- and time-specific cost-of-living index to obtain the own relative price of cigarettes (PRICE). Similarly, the difference between the own price and the low price is divided by the cost-of-living index to obtain the relative price difference (PDIF). The interstate price index was developed for the year 1967 by Fuchs, Michael, and Scott.[30] Cross-sectional price indexes for years covered by the HES other than 1967 are developed by assuming that year-to-year percentage changes for each state equal the year-to-year percentage change in the Bureau of Labor Statistics' Consumer Price Index for the United States as a whole.[31]

Family background characteristics included in the demand functions are real family income (money family income divided by the cost-of-living index), the number of persons in the household twenty years of age or less (a proxy for the number of children in the family), mother's schooling, father's schooling, absence of father from the household,[32] whether or not the mother works full time, and whether or not the mother works part time. Youth characteristics included in the demand functions are age, race, sex, student status, whether the youth works for pay during the school year, the number of hours worked per week during the school year, whether or not the youth works part time during school vacations, whether or not the youth works full time during school vacations, whether or not the youth receives an allowance, region of residence, and size of place of residence.

Some of the above variables indicate the youth's command over real resources, others are determinants of parents' smoking, and others have been shown to be important determinants of youth smoking in studies by psychologists and sociologists.[33] It is important to control for region and size of place of residence because the HES is a nationally representative sample for the period 1966–1970 but not for each year of this period. In addition, the inclusion of size of place of residence controls for cross-sectional differences in the cost of living that are not reflected in the state price index. We do not present or discuss the effects of parental and youth characteristics on youth smoking in section 3. But it should be realized that all estimated price and Fairness Doctrine effects control for (hold constant) the effects of these variables.[34]

A number of alternative specifications and variables are used to estimate the impacts of the Fairness Doctrine. The simplest specification is one with a dichotomous variable that identifies youths who were interviewed during the period of the doctrine (FAIR). A second specification distinguishes among four groups of youths: those interviewed during the first year of the Fairness Doctrine (T1 = 1), those interviewed during the second year of the doctrine (T2 = 1), those interviewed during the third year of the doctrine (T3 = 1), and those interviewed before the doctrine went into effect (the omitted category).[35]

Our other specifications capitalize in various ways on information on the number of hours per day that the youth reports he spends watching television (TV). Advertising on television was the main source of exposure of youths to cigarette advertising prior to the banning of such advertisements on January 1,

1971. Most other cigarette advertising occurs in the adult print media and via sample cigarettes. Youths have only limited exposure to these sources.

Based on time-series analysis, Hamilton, Schmalensee, and Doran have shown procigarette advertising to have at best a weak positive impact on per capita consumption of cigarettes in the aggregate.[36] These findings do not conflict with the contention of the cigarette industry that most advertising is directed toward interbrand competition and little at stimulating total consumption per se. It is reasonable to suppose, however, that procigarette advertising may have a different and perhaps larger effect on a youth who does not currently smoke or who has been experimenting with this behavior than it does on an adult. In particular, even if advertisements are directed toward interbrand competition, they may give youths the impression that smoking is an "attractive adult behavior." Presumably, the antismoking messages aired on television during the Fairness Doctrine, which stressed the health hazards posed by smoking, should work against the impact of procigarette advertising on teenage smoking.

To test the above notions, we estimate a multiple regression in which two of the independent variables are the amount of time spent watching television per day (TV) and the product of this variable and the Fairness Doctrine dummy (TV × FAIR). According to our hypotheses, the coefficient of TV should be positive, and the coefficient of TV × FAIR should be negative.[37] In a modification of this specification, TV × FAIR is replaced by interactions between TV and each of the three years of the Fairness Doctrine (TV × T1, TV × T2, TV × T3).

Our final specifications of the Fairness Doctrine combine the individual data on TV watching reported by each youth with aggregate time series on the number of prosmoking and antismoking messages aired on television for the years 1965–1970. To be specific, let PRO be the number of prosmoking messages aired on television in the twelve months preceding the data on which a given youth was interviewed. Similarly, let ANTI be the number of antismoking messages aired on television in the same twelve-month period.[38] Then we compute the product of PRO and TV (PROTV) and the product of ANTI and TV (ANTITV). These variables are proxies for the number of pro- or antismoking messages that a youth saw as opposed to the number aired. The rationale is that the ratio of messages seen to messages aired is positively related to the amount of time spent watching television. We estimate cigarette demand functions with PROTV and ANTITV as two of the independent variables. Nonlinear specifications are explored in which the square of ANTITV (ANTITVS) and the product of PROTV and the Fairness Doctrine dummy (PRTVFAIR) are included. These are discussed in more detail when the results are presented.

The time series on antismoking messages is taken from Rimer.[39] These are based on reports made by the three networks (NBC, ABC, and CBS) to the producers of the antismoking messages: the American Heart Association, the American Cancer Society, the American Lung Association, and the U.S. Public Health Service. Undeflated outlays on TV advertising by cigarette companies are taken from Doran.[40] This series is deflated by the median price (cost) of a twenty-second spot announcement on network owned and operated TV stations, which was obtained from Standard Rate and Data, Incorporated.

3. RESULTS

Estimated effects of the responsiveness of teenage smoking to the price of cigarettes and to the Fairness Doctrine are discussed in this section. Before presenting the full set of estimates, we explore the appropriateness of our specification of the border phenomenon (the purchase of cigarettes at a price lower than the own locality price), which relies on the use of the difference between the own price and the low price (if it is positive) as an independent variable. Three alternative price effects from smoking participation regressions are presented in panel A of table 12.4. The corresponding price effects from quantity-smoked regressions are presented in panel B. Each regression includes all family and youth characteristics mentioned in section 2 but excludes variables related to the Fairness Doctrine. Regression (1) includes the price difference (PDIF), while regression (2) omits it. Regression (3) is estimated using a subsample of youths in which the price difference is zero (the border price is either equal to or larger than the own price).

In all three specifications price elasticities at the mean are substantial; in most cases they exceed one in absolute value. Moreover, the elasticities in the table are the appropriate ones to use in evaluating the impacts of an increase in the federal excise tax on cigarettes or an increase in price due to an increase in input prices. In these situations the own price and the low price rise by the same amount, and the difference between them remains the same.[41]

One explanation of the large price elasticities in table 12.4 is that they may incorporate income effects as well as substitution effects. We do hold constant real family income and proxies for the amount of discretionary income that a youth can spend on his own consumption, such as whether or not he works for pay. But in the absence of a perfect measure of a youth's real income, the estimated price effect is something other than a pure (utility-constant) price effect.

It should be noted that the price elasticity of the number of cigarettes smoked by youths who smoke is relatively small. Let Q be the quantity smoked

Table 12.4 Regression Coefficients of the Price of Cigarettes and the Price Difference, Alternative Specifications and Samples

Variable	Total Sample (N = 5,308)		Sample in Which PDIF = 0 (N = 2,974)
	Regression 1	Regression 2	Regression 3
Panel A. Smoking-participation regressions:			
PRICE	−.006	−.005	−.004
	(−4.60)	(−4.48)	(−2.87)
Elasticity at mean	−1.43	−1.19	−.97
PDIF	.004	...	...
	(1.14)	...	...
Adjusted R^2	.10357	.10352	.10639
Panel B. Quantity-smoked regressions:			
PRICE	−.003	−.003	−.003
	(−3.74)	(−3.86)	(−2.83)
Elasticity at mean	−1.44	−1.44	−1.42
PDIF	.001	...	...
	(.28)	...	...
Adjusted R^2	.10623	.10639	.10187

Note: *t*-ratios in parentheses. The critical *t*-ratios at the 5 percent level are 1.64 for a one-tailed test and 1.96 for a two-tailed test. The *F*-ratio associated with each regression (not shown) is statistically significant at the 1 percent level of significance.

by youths who smoke, and interpret smoking participation as the probability that a given youth smokes. Hence

$$\text{QSMOKE} = (\text{SMOKEP})\,(Q), \tag{5}$$

and

$$\frac{\partial \ln Q}{\partial \ln \text{PRICE}} = \frac{\partial \ln \text{QSMOKE}}{\partial \ln \text{PRICE}} - \frac{\partial \ln \text{SMOKEP}}{\partial \ln \text{PRICE}}. \tag{6}$$

The estimates of the elasticity on the left-hand side of the last equation are −.01 in regression (1), −.25 in regression (2), and −.45 in regression (3).

In all regressions the own relative price of cigarettes (PRICE) has a negative and statistically significant regression coefficient. The regression coefficient of the price difference has the anticipated positive sign, but it is not significant. The own price effects are stable across alternative specifications. They are identical in panel B and range from −.004 to −.006 in panel A. A principal message of table 12.4 is clear: The border phenomenon is not an important issue in the estimation of youth cigarette demand functions. This finding is consistent with the notions that youths are less mobile than adults and have less incentive to search for lower-priced cigarettes because youths typically smoke much less than adults.

Seven alternative regressions for assessing the impacts of the Fairness Doctrine on smoking participation are shown in table 12.5. The corresponding regressions for assessing the impacts of the doctrine on the quantity smoked are shown in table 12.6. The regression coefficients associated with the price of cigarettes and the price difference also are given. As in table 12.4, the regressions in tables 12.5 and 12.6 include all family and youth characteristics. An inspection of the price effects in the two new tables reveals that the conclusions reached with respect to these effects are not altered when the Fairness Doctrine variables are added to the regressions. In particular, the own price coefficients are negative and significant, while the price-difference coefficients are positive and not significant. In addition, elasticities at the mean always exceed one. The smoking participation elasticity of approximately −1.20 is nearly five times larger than the implied elasticity of quantity smoked by those who smoke of −.25.

An overview of the impacts of the Fairness Doctrine in the seven alternative specifications indicates that, whatever the impacts of the doctrine on smoking participation, it has little or no impact on the quantity smoked. For this reason and because of the importance of smoking participation as a behavioral variable, we focus on the results of table 12.5 in the remainder of this section.

In regression (1), the coefficient of the dichotomous variable that identifies youths who were interviewed during the period of the Fairness Doctrine (FAIR) is negative and significant. It indicates that during the period of the doctrine the teenage smoking rate was 3.0 percentage points smaller than in the sixteen-month period prior to the doctrine (March 1966–June 1967). Time trends in smoking participation during the Fairness Doctrine period itself are explored in regression (2). As shown by the coefficient of T1, the smoking rate fell by 5.2 percentage points during the first year of the doctrine. The rate rose by 3.1 percentage points in the second year (given by the difference between the coefficient of T2 and that of T1) and declined by .5 percentage points in the third year relative to the second (the coefficient of T3 minus that of T2).

Clearly, the above findings suggest that the Fairness Doctrine had its largest impact in the first year of its existence. Put differently, the introduction of the doctrine represented a "shock" to the underlying upward trend in teenage smoking in the mid-1960s and early 1970s. But by the second year of the doctrine, the trend factor began to dominate the shock. This scenario mirrors the shocks to aggregate time trends in smoking due to antismoking developments

Table 12.5 Selected Coefficients, Smoking-Participation Regressions, Total Sample

Panel A. Regressions 1–4

Variable	Regression Number			
	1	2	3	4
PRICE	−.005	−.005	−.005	−.005
	(−3.83)	(−3.86)	(−4.03)	(−3.92)
Elasticity at mean	−1.19	−1.19	−1.19	−1.19
PDIF	.002	.004	.003	.004
	(.72)	(1.12)	(.94)	(1.10)
FAIR	−.030	…	…	…
	(−2.76)			
T1	…	−.052	…	…
		(−3.59)		
T2	…	−.021	…	…
		(−1.52)		
T3	…	−.026	…	…
		(−1.61)		
TV	…	…	.011	.011
			(2.83)	(2.83)
TV × FAIR	…	…	−.008	…
			(−2.55)	
TV × T1	…	…	….	−.012
				(−2.75)
TV × T2	…	…	…	−.009
				(−2.17)
TV × T3	…	…	…	−.005
				(−1.01)
Adjusted R^2	.10470	.10525	10479	.10487

Panel B. Regressions 5–7

Variable	Regression Number		
	5	6	7
PRICE	−.006	−.005	−.005
	(−4.55)	(−4.30)	(−3.96)
Elasticity at mean	−1.43	−1.19	−1.19
PDIF	.004	.003	.004
	(1.07)	(.88)	(1.06)
PROTV	.678D-07	.581D-07	.131D-06
	(1.56)	(1.32)	(2.48)

Table 12.5 (*Continued*)

	Panel B. Regressions 5–7		
	Regression Number		
Variable	5	6	7
ANTITV	−.801D-06	−.816D-05	−.116D-06
	(−.45)	(−1.70)	(−.00)
ANTITVS	...	.931D-09	.411D-09
		(1.66)	(.69)
PRTVFAIR	...	...	−.153D-06
			(−2.48)
Adjusted R^2	.10364	.10394	.10481

Note: *t*-ratios in parentheses. The critical *t*-ratios at the 5 percent level are 1.64 for a one-tailed test and 1.96 for a two-tailed test. The *F*-ratio associated with each regression (not shown) is statistically significant at the 1 percent level of significance.

Table 12.6 Selected Coefficients, Quantity-Smoked Regressions, Total Sample

	Panel A. Regressions 1–4			
	Regression Number			
Variable	1	2	3	4
PRICE	−.003	−.003	−.003	−.003
	(−3.51)	(−3.63)	(−3.59)	(−3.60)
Elasticity at mean	−1.44	−1.44	−1.44	−1.44
PDIF	.005D-01	.002	.006D-01	.001
	(.19)	(.80)	(.24)	(.58)
FAIR	−.004	...	...	...
	(−.54)			
T1	...	−.026	...	...
		(−2.59)		
T2	...	.007	...	...
		(.74)		
T3	...	−.001	...	...
		(−.10)		
TV	...	...	.005D-01	.006D-01
			(.18)	(.22)
TV × FAIR	...	...	−.008D-01	...
			(−.34)	
TV × T1	...	...	...	−.005
				(−1.72)

(*continued*)

Table 12.6 (*Continued*)

	Panel A. Regressions 1–4			
	Regression Number			
Variable	1	2	3	4
TV × T2	...	...	...	007D-01 (.08)
TV × T3	...	...	...	.001 (.39)
Adjusted R^2	.10611	.10771	.10591	.10651

	Panel B. Regressions 5–7		
	Regression Number		
Variable	5	6	7
PRICE	−.003 (−3.87)	−.003 (−3.82)	−.003 (−3.59)
Elasticity at mean	−1.44	−1.44	−1.44
PDIF	.001 (.51)	.001 (.49)	.002 (.61)
PROTV	−.002D-05 (−.72)	−.002D-05 (−.74)	.001D-05 (.30)
ANTITV	.002D-03 (1.34)	.001D-03 (.36)	.005D-03 (1.21)
ANTITVS	...	.006D-08 (.16)	−.002D-07 (−.42)
PRTVFAIR	...	...	−.007D-05 (−1.63)
Adjusted R^2	.10621	.10604	.10632

Note: t-ratios in parentheses. The critical t-ratios at the 5 percent level are 1.64 for a one-tailed test and 1.96 for a two-tailed test. The F-ratio associated with each regression (not shown) is statistically significant at the 1 percent level of significance.

that are modeled and estimated by Ippolito, Murphy, and Sant[42] and by Lewit, Coate, and Grossman (in progress). The decline in smoking participation in the first year of the Fairness Doctrine is dramatic evidence that smoking behavior can change drastically when the rate of change in antismoking information is extremely large. The coefficients of T2 and T3 indicate that the impact of anti-smoking messages is subject to diminishing returns. For teenagers, the effects of the doctrine in its second and third years are dominated by the trend.[43]

Our findings also are consistent with trends in teenage smoking in the surveys conducted by the National Clearinghouse for Smoking and Health (NCSH) that are shown in table 12.1. According to the NCSH surveys, the teenage smoking rate rose by 3.7 percentage points between 1968 and 1970. According to regression (2), the teenage smoking rate rose by 2.6 percentage points between the first and third years of the Fairness Doctrine (the coefficient of T3 minus that of T1). The two estimates differ because the NCSH survey includes eighteen-year-olds, because our estimate controls for variables that may have changed between 1968 and 1970, and because the two time periods (1968 and 1970 versus the first and third years of the Fairness Doctrine) are not exactly the same. It is important to note that the increase in teenage smoking between 1968 and 1970 or between the first and third years of the Fairness Doctrine does not indicate that the antismoking messages failed to discourage smoking by teenagers, as claimed by the proponents of the advertising ban.[44] Based on our first regression, teenage smoking was 3.0 percentage points smaller during the Fairness Doctrine than it was in the sixteen months prior to the doctrine. Based on the second regression, the doctrine was associated with a 3.4 percentage point reduction in smoking.[45]

The five additional regressions in table 12.5 try to identify mechanisms via which the Fairness Doctrine reduced teenage smoking. In regression (3) the number of hours per week spent watching television (TV) has a positive and significant impact on the probability of smoking. On the other hand, the interaction between TV watching and the Fairness Doctrine dummy variable has a negative and significant impact on this probability. Although TV watching has a positive impact on the probability of smoking during the Fairness Doctrine period (given by the sum of the coefficients of TV and TV × FAIR), the effect is much weaker than in the predoctrine period. To be specific, a one hour per week increase in TV watching raises the smoking probability by 1.1 percentage points in the predoctrine period. The comparable increase in the during period is .3 percentage points. The weaker effect in the latter period reflects the presence of antismoking messages on TV. The effect is positive rather than negative, in part, because the number of prosmoking messages exceeded the number of antismoking messages throughout the period of the Fairness Doctrine.

In regression (4), we model the initial shock and diminishing effect process by interacting TV with each of the three years of the Fairness Doctrine (TV × T1, TV × T2, TV × T3). The coefficients of all these interactions are negative and, for the first two periods, significant. Moreover, an increase in TV watching has a slight negative effect on the probability of smoking in the first year of the Fairness Doctrine.

In regressions (5), (6), and (7), the proxies for the number of pro- and antismoking messages seen are entered (PROTV and ANTITV).[46] In regression (5) the coefficient of PROTV has the anticipated positive sign, and the coefficient of ANTITV has the anticipated negative sign. Neither coefficient, however, is statistically significant. In the sixth regression we include the square of ANTITV (ANTITVS) as an additional independent variable. This is an attempt to capture elements of a model with an initial shock followed by a diminishing effect. It is particularly important to allow the number of antismoking messages aired to have a nonlinear effect because both TV watching and the number of messages aired rose throughout the period of the Fairness Doctrine. The finding that the coefficient of ANTITV is negative and significant, while the coefficient of ANTITVS is positive and significant, is consistent with the hypothesized diminishing effect of antismoking messages. The model is refined further in regression (7) by allowing procigarette advertising to have a different effect in the Fairness Doctrine period than in the predoctrine period.[47] Consistent with a priori notions, the coefficient of PROTV is positive and significant, while that of the interaction between PROTV and the Fairness Doctrine dummy (PRTV-FAIR) is negative and significant. The coefficients of ANTITV and ANTITVS have the appropriate signs but are not significant.

Clearly, the four measures of pro- and antismoking messages seen in regression (7) are highly correlated. One cannot expect all four variables to achieve statistical significance. The finding that all three have the appropriate signs in regression (6) and all four have the appropriate signs in regression (7) is consistent with our expectations.

Panel A of table 12.7 summarizes the implied impacts of the Fairness Doctrine on teenage smoking participation rates from each of the seven regressions in table 12.5. The procedure simply is to predict smoking participation in the periods before and during the doctrine based on the regression coefficients and on the mean values in each period of the Fairness Doctrine variables.[48] The computations reveal that we have specified a plausible mechanism by which the Fairness Doctrine reduced teenage smoking. In particular, regressions (3), (4), and (7) account for between 2.1 percentage points and 2.7 percentage points of

Table 12.7 Percentage Point Impacts of the Fairness Doctrine and the Advertising Ban on Teenage Smoking Participation Rates

			Regression Number			
1	2	3	4	5	6	7
A. Fairness Doctrine impacts:						
−3.0	−3.4	−2.1	−2.7	−.1	−.8	−2.4
B. Advertising ban impacts:						
...	...	−.9	−.2	−1.2	−.4	−.3
				(−2.0)	(−.6)	(.0)

the 3.0–3.4-percentage-point reduction predicted by the simple trend equations [regressions (1) and (2)]. Note that equation (4) does a better job of explaining the trend than those that enter the proxy for antismoking messages seen and allow it to have a diminishing effect. We believe that this is because even the nonlinear specification does not fully capture the initial shock caused by the messages.

Panel B of table 12.7 contains the predicted impact of the advertising ban on further changes in teenage smoking from regressions (3)–(7). In the first two predictions, it is assumed that the effects of TV watching disappear after the end of the Fairness Doctrine. In the last three predictions, it is assumed that the number of antismoking messages aired falls to zero after the end of the doctrine. Although the antismoking messages did not disappear entirely after 1970, the number aired declined by almost 80 percent relative to the number aired in 1969. Moreover, in the postdoctrine period many of the messages were aired at times when youths are extremely unlikely to be viewing television.[49] The figures in parentheses show how the last three estimates are altered when the number of anti-smoking messages aired during the ban equals 20 percent of the 1969 value.[50] The predicted declines in teenage smoking after the end of the Fairness Doctrine are modest. They suggest that the ban was not a particularly effective policy instrument to curtail teenage smoking in a post-Fairness Doctrine environment. Of course, since small declines in smoking rather than increases are shown in panel B, one can argue that the advertising ban was no worse a policy than the Fairness Doctrine. In particular, our extrapolations suggest that the ban should have discouraged teenage smoking. This is in contrast to the findings by Hamilton and Doran that the ban should have increased per capita cigarette consumption in the aggregate.[51] Our results differ from those of Hamilton and Doran in part because we include an explicit measure of exposure to antismoking messages in our regressions. Moreover, we focus on teenagers, whose responses to pro- and antismoking messages are likely to differ from adults' responses.

A full cost-benefit analysis of the Fairness Doctrine, the advertising ban, or an increase in the federal excise tax on cigarettes vis-à-vis teenage smoking is beyond the scope of this chapter. Similarly, we cannot provide a definitive statement with regard to the relative merits of an active antismoking policy versus a policy of laissez-faire. But based on our results, we can highlight a number of policy-relevant facts and insights:

1. Teenage price elasticities of demand for cigarettes are large. The smoking participation elasticity equals −1.2, and the quantity smoked elasticity equals −1.4. This result is consistent with Lewit and Coate's finding that smoking by young adults ages twenty through twenty-four is much more responsive to price than smoking by older adults.[52] It follows that, if future reductions in youth smoking

are desired, an increase in the federal excise tax is a potent policy to accomplish this goal. Such a policy may also be an effective way to curb the detrimental health effects of smoking in the long run without substantially harming the cigarette industry in the short run. Since youth and young adult price elasticities are much larger than adult price elasticities, while adult smokers account for the bulk of cigarette sales, a substantial excise tax increase would substantially reduce smoking participation by young new smokers but leave industry sales largely unchanged. Given the evidence that individuals are considerably less likely to initiate smoking after age twenty-five, it is quite possible that the cohort of young smokers who never began to smoke as a result of the tax increase would never become regular smokers. As a consequence, over a period of several decades, aggregate smoking and its associated detrimental health effects would decline substantially.

2. The contention of the proponents of the advertising ban that the Fairness Doctrine failed in the case of teenagers is incorrect. According to our results, the doctrine had a substantial negative impact on teenage smoking participation rates. We also have evidence that the mechanism at work was the responsiveness of teenagers to antismoking messages that stress the health hazards posed by smoking. This calls into question Evans's argument that teenagers are not sensitive to such messages.[53]

3. Between 1970 and 1974, smoking participation by teenagers rose by 0.4 percentage points (see table 12.1). Based on the computations in panel B of table 12.7 we predict a reduction of approximately 0.6 percentage points over this period due to the advertising ban.[54] Why did the percentage of teenagers who smoke rise rather than fall? The obvious answer is that our forecast assumes no changes in the determinants of teenage smoking except for variables related to the Fairness Doctrine. Smoking rates may have risen because an underlying upward trend in this behavior dominated developments related to the advertising ban. But there is a more obvious explanation. Between 1970 and 1974, the relative price of cigarettes declined by roughly 6 percent due to a rapid increase in the Consumer Price Index accompanied by no change in the federal excise tax rate. Our regression results suggest that this should have caused the smoking rate to rise by 1.0 percentage point. The net extrapolation, based on these two competing factors, is an increase of .4 percentage points, which coincides with the observed increase.[55]

4. As shown in table 12.1, the teenage smoking rate peaked in 1974; it declined from 15.6 percent in that year to 11.7 percent in 1979. It is still too early to explain the apparent reversal in trend or the differential trends for boys and girls.[56] It is plausible to hypothesize, however, that the trend reversal represents in part a lagged response to the downward trend in adult smoking participation rates reported in table 12.2.

NOTES

Originally published as Eugene M. Lewit, Douglas Coate, and Michael Grossman, "The Effects of Government Regulation on Teenage Smoking," *Journal of Law and Economics* 24, no. 3 (1981): 545–569. This is a revised version of a paper presented at a conference on Consumer Protection Regulation sponsored by the Center for the Study of the Economy and the State of the University of Chicago, December 5–6, 1980. Research for the paper was supported by grant no. DAR-80 14959 from the National Science Foundation to the National Bureau of Economic Research and by grant no. HS 03738 from the National Center for Health Services Research to the College of Medicine and Dentistry of New Jersey, New Jersey Medical School. We are indebted to Lee Benham and Rodney Smith for helpful comments on an earlier draft. This paper has not undergone the review accorded official NBER publications; in particular, it has not been submitted for approval by the board of directors.

1. The 1964 surgeon general's report officially was titled "Smoking and Health: Report of the Advisory Committee to the Surgeon General of the Public Health Service."

2. Other federal government policies designed to discourage smoking included the requirement, beginning in July 1966, of a health warning in all cigarette advertising and on every package and the strengthening of this warning at the time of the imposition of the advertising ban in 1971. In addition, the Federal Trade Commission began monitoring the tar and nicotine content of various brands of cigarettes in 1967. Subsequently, the cigarette industry voluntarily agreed to include the FTC measurements in all advertising. Finally, federal agencies have required the separation of smokers and nonsmokers in vehicles in interstate passenger transportation, and many state and local governments have required the provision of no smoking areas in public places.

3. Irving Rimer, "The Impact of Broadcasting," in *Second World Conference on Smoking and Health* (R. G. Richardson ed. 1972); Gideon Doran, *The Smoking Paradox* (1979).

4. For example, James L. Hamilton, "The Demand for Cigarettes: Advertising, the Health Scare, and the Cigarette Advertising Ban," 54 *Rev. Econ. and Stat.* 401 (1972); Doran, *supra* note 3; Kenneth E. Warner, "The Effects of the Anti-Smoking Campaign on Cigarette Consumption," 67 *Am. J. Pub. Health* 645 (1977).

5. Arguments for government intervention in the cigarette market are derived from the assumptions of externalities in consumption (the health of some persons enters the utility function of others); externalities in production (smoking by some may harm the health of others); lack of complete information about the health effects of smoking, particularly among youth; and moral hazard in the markets for life and health insurance (premiums paid by smokers do not fully reflect their higher probabilities of illness and death). In this paper we do not evaluate these assumptions.

6. Although the federal excise tax on cigarettes has remained at eight cents per pack for the last twenty-five years, there have been several attempts to increase it in recent years because of the concern over the health effects of cigarette smoking. Moreover, there is evidence that some states increased their cigarette taxes as a result of the antismoking publicity that followed the issuance of the surgeon general's report in 1964. In 1965 there were twenty-three state and local cigarette tax increases compared with no more than a dozen

in any of the preceding fourteen years. I. L. Kellner, "The American Cigarette Industry: A Reexamination" (1973) (unpublished PhD dissertation, New School for Social Research).

7. Hamilton, *supra* note 4; Warner, *supra* note 4; Doran, *supra* note 3; Richard A. Ippolito, R. Dennis Murphy, and Donald Sant, "Consumer Responses to Cigarette Health Information" (FTC, Bureau Econ. Staff Report 1979).

8. Among adults who smoke, 95 percent began to smoke between the ages of twelve and twenty-one (Centers for Disease Control and National Cancer Institute, Adult Use of Tobacco—1975 [1976]).

9. For example, see E. Cuyler Hammond, "Smoking in Relation to the Death Rates of 7 Million Men and Women" (Nat'l Cancer Inst. Monograph No. 19, 1966); and Ippolito, Murphy, and Sant, *supra* note 7.

10. The 1979 figures in table 12.1 reveal dramatic reductions in teenage smoking between 1974 and 1979. When the data are examined by age and sex, smoking participation rates for boys declined by almost 25 percent for twelve- to sixteen-year-olds and by 38 percent for seventeen- to eighteen-year-olds. For girls, participation rates between 1974 and 1979 increased slightly for those seventeen to eighteen years old and declined slightly for those twelve to fourteen years old. Smoking by girls ages fifteen to sixteen fell, however, by almost 42 percent after rising by almost 110 percent between 1968 and 1974. The extent to which these dramatic trend reversals and inconsistencies are due to sampling variability, an increase in underreporting over time, or other factors is not known. Teenage smoking rates from the U.S. National Surveys on Drug Abuse conducted by the National Institute on Drug Abuse (NIDA) in 1974, 1976, and 1977 suggest that smoking rates have not fallen as rapidly as the figures in table 12.1 suggest. The NIDA surveys also show that the rates tend to fluctuate somewhat from year to year. See Herbert I. Abelson, Patricia M. Fishburne, and Ira Cisin, "The National Survey on Drug Abuse: 1977," Volume I, Main Findings (Nat'l Inst. on Drug Abuse, HEW Pub. No. [ADM] 78–618, 1977); Ira Cisin, Judith Miller, and Adele Harrell, "Highlights from the National Survey on Drug Abuse: 1977" (HEW Pub. No. [ADM] 78–620, 1978).

11. For example, Richard I. Evans, "Smoking in Children; Developing a Social Psychological Strategy of Deterrence," 5 *Preventive Medicine* 122 (1976); Ellen R. Gritz, "Smoking: The Prevention of Onset," in *Research on Smoking Behavior* (Murray E. Jarvik et al. eds.) (Nat'l Inst. on Drug Abuse Research Monograph 17, 1977).

12. A full description of the sample, the sampling technique, and the data collection is presented in "Plan and Operation of a Health Examination Survey of U.S. Youths 12–17 Years of Age" (National Center for Health Statistics, 1974).

13. HES III ended after the first quarter of 1970. Hence it has no data on teenage smoking in the last three quarters of the last year of the Fairness Doctrine.

14. Hamilton, *supra* note 4; Warner, *supra* note 4; Doran, *supra* note 3; and Ippolito, Murphy, and Sant, *supra* note 7.

15. Warner does not consider explicitly the effect of the advertising ban.

16. In research in progress, we are estimating time-series cigarette demand functions that include the number of antismoking messages aired on television between the last half of 1967 and 1979.

17. Eugene M. Lewit and Douglas Coate, "The Potential for Using Excise Taxes to Reduce Smoking" (Sept. 1980) (paper presented at annual meeting of Allied Social Science Ass'ns, Denver, Colo.).

18. For a discussion of bandwagon effects, see Harvey Liebenstein, Bandwagon, Snob, and Veblen, "Effects in the Theory of Consumer Demand," 64 *Q. J. Econ.* 183 (1950). In addition, note that price effects are not unrelated to the antismoking campaign because price may be interpreted broadly to incorporate both the nominal price of cigarettes and the indirect cost of consuming them. The latter pertains to the perceived cost of the health hazards associated with smoking. Developments such as the antismoking campaign presumably raise the perceived cost. The interaction between the money price of a package of cigarettes (p) and the perceived cost of the health risks of smoking (z) in the demand function for cigarettes is highlighted by specifying the quantity smoked (y) as a function of the "full" price of cigarettes ($\pi = p + z$): $y = g(\pi) = g(p + z)$. Note that an increase in the perceived cost of smoking alters the elasticity of smoking with respect to money price, although the direction of the effect is ambiguous. For example, suppose that the elasticity of smoking with respect to full price is constant. Then $\ln y = \alpha - \eta \ln \pi, - (\partial \ln y / \partial \ln p) \equiv e = p (p + z)^{-1}$ η; and $(\partial e / \partial z) = -p (p + z)^{-1}\eta$; and $(\partial e / \partial z) = -p (p + z)^{-2}\eta < 0$. On the other hand, if the demand function has a constant slope, rather than a constant elasticity, e rises in absolute value as z rises: $y = \beta - \beta_1 \pi = \beta - \beta_1 p - \beta_1 z$, $e = \beta_1 p y^{-1}$, $(\partial e / \partial z) = -\beta_1 p y^{-2}$ $(\partial y / \partial z) = \beta_1^2 p y^{-2} > 0$. If neither the slope nor the elasticity is constant, the impact of an increase in z on the money price elasticity is indeterminant.

19. Lewit and Coate, *supra* note 17.

20. The low-price border area may lie within the state of residence because cigarettes are subject to municipal excise taxes and municipal retail sales taxes at different rates (some zero) within the same state. All of these are included in the own- and low-price variables.

21. Lewit and Coate, *supra* note 17. For a similar finding in the context of alcohol consumption, see Rodney T. Smith, "The Legal and Illegal Markets for Taxed Goods: Pure Theory and an Application to State Government Taxation of Distilled Spirits," 19 *J. Law and Econ.* 393 (1976).

22. Smoking participation by adult males increased dramatically during World War II. The diffusion of the smoking habit among females has lagged behind that of males. Between 1955 and 1966, smoking rates of males who were eligible for military service in World War II declined. On the other hand, smoking rates by females in the same age cohorts as these males increased. Jeffrey E. Harris, "Cigarette Smoking in the United States, 1950–1978," in *Smoking and Health: Report of the Advisory Committee to the Surgeon General of the Public Health Service* (1979).

23. See, for example, Joseph D. Matarazzo and Ruth G. Matarazzo, "Smoking," in *Int'l Encyclopedia of Soc. Sci.* 335 (1968); Richard R. Lanese, Franklin R. Banks, and Martin D. Keller, "Smoking Behavior in a Teenage Population: A Multivariate Conceptual Approach," 62 *Am. J. Pub. Health* 807 (1972); Dorothy E. Green, "Teenage Smoking: Immediate and Long-Term Patterns" (1979) (prepared for Nat'l Inst. of Education).

24. Leibenstein, *supra* note 18.

25. *Id.;* and Gary S. Becker, *Economic Theory* (1971).

26. If a_5 exceeds one, cigarette smoking is a bandwagon good with an upward-sloping market demand curve. This is inconsistent with a stable equilibrium because the supply function is assumed to be infinitely elastic in the estimation procedure.

27. Empirically, $\bar{y}_{jt}$ could be obtained by computing means for each sampling site in the HES. This procedure was not adopted because the means would be based on a small number of observations in a significant percentage of the sites. Essentially, with $\bar{y}_{jt}$ omitted, the coefficients of (1) can differ from those of (2) only in the sense that the solved and estimated-reduced form differ due to sampling variability.

28. See, for example, Richard I. Evans, William B. Hansen, and Maurice B. Mittlemark, "Increasing the Validity of Self-Reports of Smoking Behavior in Children," 62 *J. Applied Psychology* 521 (1977).

29. Kenneth E. Warner, "Possible Increases in the Underreporting of Cigarette Consumption," 73 *J. Am. Stat. Ass'n* 314 (1978).

30. Victor R. Fuchs, Robert T. Michael, and Sharon R. Scott, "A State Price Index" (Nat'l Bureau Econ. Research Working Paper No. 320, Feb. 1979).

31. Demand functions estimated with a cost-of-living index that varies over time but not among states (not shown) do not differ significantly from those presented in section 3.

32. For youths who are not currently living with their fathers, the father's schooling is coded at the race-specific mean of the sample for which the father's schooling is reported. Alternative coding schemes would alter the regression coefficient of absence of father but not alter the coefficients of the other independent variables.

33. See, for example, Matarazzo and Matarazzo, *supra* note 23; Lanese, Banks, and Keller, *supra* note 23; and Green, *supra* note 23.

34. In general, our findings with respect to the impacts of family and youth characteristics are consistent with those of other studies. In particular, smoking is negatively related to mother's and father's schooling and positively related to the number of persons in the family twenty years of age or less. Moreover, a youth is more likely to smoke and to smoke larger amounts if he is not a student, if he works during the school year, if he works during school vacations, if his mother works full time, and if his father is absent from the household. Boys smoke more than girls, whites smoke more than blacks, and older youths smoke more than younger youths. These results strengthen our confidence in the validity and reliability of the HES smoking measures.

35. The first year of the Fairness Doctrine is July 1, 1967–June 30, 1968. The second year is July 1, 1968–June 30, 1969. The third year is July 1, 1969–March 31, 1970. Since the HES ended in March 1970, we have no data for the last quarter of the third year.

36. Hamilton, *supra* note 4; Richard Schmalensee, *The Economics of Advertising* (1972); and Doran, *supra* note 3.

37. It should be noted that the relationship between TV watching and smoking may reflect causality in both directions. In part, it also may reflect the role of omitted "third variables."

38. Time series for PRO and ANTI are available on an annual rather than on a monthly basis. Therefore, if a youth was interviewed, for example, on April 1, 1966, PRO for that youth equals three-fourths of its 1965 value plus one-fourth of its 1966 value. A similar

weighting scheme is used to compute ANTI. Clearly, ANTI equals zero for all youths who were interviewed before the Fairness Doctrine went into effect.

39. Rimer, *supra* note 3.

40. Doran, *supra* note 3, gives total outlays on TV and radio advertising by cigarette companies. We multiplied his series by the ratio of TV expenditures by all advertisers to the sum of TV and radio expenditures (Bureau of Census 1980). As indicated by the data, the same ratio for each year between 1965 and 1970 is appropriate.

41. These are not the appropriate elasticities to use in evaluating the effect on teenage smoking of an increase in state or local excise taxes. In these cases, even a small increase in the local tax rate can result in a substantial increase in the price difference if border-area taxes are not also increased. As a result, some of the deterrent effects of a state or local tax increase may be mitigated. Of course, to predict the percentage reduction in cigarette consumption caused by a 1 percent increase in any excise tax, one has to know the share of the tax in total price as well as the price elasticity of demand.

42. Ippolito, Murphy, and Sant, *supra* note 7.

43. The findings are inconsistent with the hypothesis of a continuous downward trend in teenage smoking during the Fairness Doctrine period due to an upward trend in underreporting.

44. Evans, *supra* note 11; and Gritz, *supra* note 11.

45. This is a weighted average of the coefficients of T1, T2, and T3. The weights are the number of youths interviewed in each year of the Fairness Doctrine relative to all youths interviewed during the period of the doctrine.

46. Regressions (5), (6), and (7) do not allow for cumulative or lagged antismoking effects, except to the extent that current TV watching probably is positively related to prior TV watching. We do not try to "tease out" lagged effects, in part because we have a very short time series and because we do not believe them to be important in the case of teenage smokers.

47. In regressions not shown, we allowed for a diminishing proadvertising effect by including the square of PROTV as an independent variable. There was no evidence of a nonlinear effect.

48. Consider regression (3): $\text{SMOKEP} = a_0 + a_1\text{TV} + a_2(\text{TV} \times \text{FAIR})$. Then $\text{SMOKEP}_D - \text{SMOKEP}_B = (a_1 + a_2)\overline{\text{TV}}_D - a_1\overline{\text{TV}}_B$, where the subscripts D and B denote the periods during and before the doctrine and bars over variables denote means.

49. For reasons of confidentiality, we do not reveal the source of this information.

50. These figures also incorporate an upward trend in TV watching due to an increase in the percentage of families with television sets.

51. Hamilton, *supra* note 4; Doran, *supra* note 3.

52. Lewit and Coate, *supra* note 17.

53. Evans, *supra* note 11.

54. This figure is an average of six of the eight estimates in panel B of table 12.7. The smallest and largest figures are omitted from the average.

55. Smoking rates also may have risen because of changes in family-background characteristics. For instance, the percentage of mothers who work full time and the percentage

of youths who live with their mothers only rose. Rough computations suggest, however, that, given the sizes of the observed changes, their impacts on smoking were minimal. Moreover, there are factors that go in the other direction: family size fell and parents' schooling rose. Note also that the reduction in teenage smoking from 1970 to 1972 (see table 12.1) occurred in a period in which the relative price of cigarettes rose.

56. In preliminary research, we find that the Fairness Doctrine variables have larger effects on smoking participation rates of boys than on smoking participation rates of girls.

Beer Taxes, the Legal Drinking Age,
and Youth Motor Vehicle Fatalities

THIRTEEN

Henry Saffer and Michael Grossman

1. INTRODUCTION AND BACKGROUND

Since the mid-1970s, the federal government of the United States and various state and local governments have been involved in a campaign to reduce deaths from motor vehicle accidents by discouraging alcohol abuse. One major element of this campaign has been the upward trend in state minimum legal ages for the purchase and consumption of alcoholic beverages. This trend began with the increase in the legal drinking age in Minnesota from eighteen to nineteen years of age in 1976, and an additional twenty-seven states had increased legal drinking ages by the time Congress passed the Federal Uniform Drinking Age Act of July 1984.[1] This legislation allows the federal government, through its control of federal highway funds, to intercede in a legislative area traditionally reserved for states. Five percent of a state's federal highway construction fund allocation for the fiscal year 1987 was withheld if the minimum legal drinking age was below twenty-one years on October 1, 1986, and 10 percent will be withheld from each future fiscal year allocation in which its drinking age is below twenty-one. To date, nineteen states have passed laws complying with the act, and a total of forty-two states now have a minimum drinking age of twenty-one. A second major effect of the antidrinking campaign is evidenced by more severe penalties for conviction of drunken driving, by the allocation of additional resources for apprehension of drunk drivers, and by the easing of standards required for conviction.

One policy that has been virtually ignored by federal and state governments in the antidrinking campaign is increased taxation of alcoholic beverages. By raising prices, this policy could, in effect, lower alcoholic beverage consumption and motor vehicle mortality. Instead, the federal excise tax rates on liquor (distilled spirits), beer, and wine remained constant in nominal terms between November 1, 1951, and the end of fiscal 1985. During this period the federal government taxed liquor at the rate of $10.50 per proof gallon (one gallon of 100 proof liquor, which is the equivalent of 50 percent alcohol by volume), beer at the rate of $0.29 per gallon (approximately 4.5 percent alcohol by volume), and wine at the rate of $0.17 per gallon (11.6–21 percent alcohol by volume).[2]

Partly as a result of the stability of the federal excise taxes and the modest increases in state and local excise taxes, the real price of alcoholic beverages (the nominal price divided by the consumer price index [CPI]) has declined substantially over time. Between 1960 and 1980, the real price of liquor fell by 48 percent; the real price of beer fell by 27 percent; and the real price of wine fell by 20 percent. While twenty-nine states raised the legal drinking age during 1976–1984, real alcoholic beverage prices continued to fall: 27 percent for liquor, 12 percent for beer, and 19 percent for wine.[3] Thus, if alcohol abuse is sensitive to price, a government policy of declining real excise tax levels actually may be exacerbating this problem.[4]

A primary purpose of this chapter is to investigate the responsiveness of motor vehicle death rates of youths aged fifteen through twenty-four to variations in the cost of beer as reflected by differences in state excise tax rates on beer. We provide evidence for this important age group on the extent to which declining real beer excise taxes have contributed to increases in fatal motor vehicle crashes and on the extent to which increases in real beer taxes can serve as a potent instrument in the antidrinking campaign. We also examine the effect of an increase in the legal drinking age on youth motor vehicle deaths. Our empirical research is based on a time series analysis of state cross sections for the period 1975–1981. Logit motor vehicle death rate regressions are obtained for three age groups: youths aged fifteen through seventeen, youths aged eighteen through twenty, and youths aged twenty-one through twenty-four. During the period at issue, fifteen states raised their legal drinking age, and twenty-one states raised their nominal excise tax rate on beer. Moreover, there were substantial differences in both variables at each moment in time among states.

We focus on teenagers and young adults in the context of the antidrinking campaign because motor vehicle accident mortality is the leading cause of death of persons under the age of thirty-five, and alcohol is involved in over half of these fatal accidents. In 1979, persons under the age of twenty-five accounted for 22 percent of all licensed drivers but 38 percent of all drivers involved in fatal accidents.[5] These figures are even more dramatic than they appear because members of the young driver group do not drive nearly as much as older drivers.[6] In 1980, the motor vehicle accident mortality rate of persons between the ages of fifteen and twenty-four was forty-five deaths per 100,000 population.[7] This figure was approximately twice as large as either the crude motor vehicle death rate or any other age-specific motor vehicle death rate.

Research on the responsiveness of youth motor vehicle deaths to the cost of beer is particularly timely in the light of proposals to correct the erosion in the real value of the federal excise tax rates on all forms of alcoholic beverages since 1951 and to prevent future erosion by indexing tax rates to the rate of inflation or by converting to an ad valorem alcoholic beverage excise tax system.[8] Moreover, although beer is the drink of choice among youths who drink alcoholic beverages,[9] the alcohol in liquor is taxed three times as heavily as the alcohol in beer. This has led to suggestions to equalize the tax rates on the alcohol in all forms of alcoholic beverages by raising the tax on beer.[10] Research on the sensitivity of youth alcohol use to legal drinking ages is also valuable given the adverse reaction to federal uniform drinking legislation.[11] This study will help explain the significance of the volatility of state minimum drinking age laws in the 1970s and 1980s and the effectiveness of these laws in reducing death rates in the affected populations.

One of the basic aims of our research is to compare the effect of a uniform minimum age of twenty-one for the purchase of beer in all states on the motor vehicle accident mortality rate of eighteen- through twenty-year-olds with that of one or more of the policies to raise the federal excise tax on beer described above. Before turning to a technical discussion of how these relations should be measured, we note that an effectively enforced prohibition of beer consumption in this age group clearly should have a larger influence on their motor vehicle accident mortality than an increase in the excise tax on beer. This issue is not clear-cut at the empirical level only because of the problem of evasion. Underage youths can obtain beer from their older siblings or friends. In addition, they can purchase fake identification cards or buy beer in stores that do not bother to demand proof of age. This type of evasion simply is not possible with an excise tax hike, so that the responsiveness of youths to the price of beer determines the change in its consumption and therefore the motor vehicle death rate. Given Coate and Grossman's evidence that youthful beer drinkers are very sensitive to price, the excise tax policy could well dominate the drinking age policy.[12]

There have been no previous studies of the effects of beer taxes on youth motor vehicle fatalities. Cook, however, finds that states that raised their excise tax rates on liquor between 1960 and 1974 experienced below-average increases or above-average reductions in motor vehicle deaths of persons of all ages, relative to states that did not increase their tax rates.[13] Statistically significant short-run increases in youth motor vehicle deaths have been reported in selected states that lowered their legal drinking age in the early 1970s, and significant short-run reductions in fatalities have been reported in selected states that raised their legal drinking age in the late 1970s or early 1980s.[14] While this research is valuable, it is state specific and thus cannot be generalized to the population of all youths in the United States. More definitive estimates are contained in studies by McCornac and by Cook and Tauchen, both of which employ time-series analyses of state cross sections for the forty-eight contiguous states of the United States.[15] Cook and Tauchen use data for the period 1970–1977, while McCornac uses data for the period 1970–1975. Both studies conclude that a uniform minimum drinking age of twenty-one in the mid-1970s would have saved a substantial number of lives.

The research reported here differs from that by Cook and Tauchen and by McCornac in two important respects. First, McCornac and Cook and Tauchen deal with a period during which there was a downward trend in the legal drinking age. In particular, between 1970 and 1975, twenty-nine states lowered their drinking age to conform with a federal shift in the voting age from twenty-one to eighteen in 1970. On the other hand, as noted previously, our study deals with a period in which fifteen states raised their drinking age. Second, we consider the effects of beer taxes on youth motor vehicle fatalities.

Our attempt to compare the excise tax and legal drinking age policies is particularly valuable because Males argues that an increase in the drinking age may simply redistribute fatal motor vehicle crashes from younger to older youths.[16] His hypothesis is that twenty-one-year-olds in a state with a legal drinking age of eighteen, for example, may have more knowledge of the amount of alcohol they can safely consume shortly before driving than similar youths in a state with a legal drinking age of twenty-one (the "experience" effect). He presents evidence in support of this hypothesis based on univariate comparisons of states that did and did not raise their legal drinking age in the 1975–1983 period. Since all youths must pay the higher alcoholic beverage prices associated with excise tax hikes, this factor is not relevant in evaluating the tax policy.

2. ANALYTICAL FRAMEWORK

The model employed in this chapter consists of two equations. One is a technical relationship or a production function in which the probability that a youth will experience a fatal motor vehicle accident (π) is positively related to his consumption of alcohol (y) and which also depends on a vector of additional variables (z):

$$\pi = \pi(y, z). \tag{1}$$

Examples of members of the z vector include highway density in the state in which the youth resides and the general quality and state of repair of the motor vehicle that he drives. The second equation is a behavioral relationship or a demand function for alcohol:

$$y = y(p, x). \tag{2}$$

In this equation, p is the price of alcohol, and x is a vector whose members include the youth's command of real resources, the prices of substitute goods, and tastes or preferences.

Substitution of equation (2) into equation (1) yields a reduced-form probability of death equation:

$$\pi = \pi(p, x, z). \tag{3}$$

Equation (3) is termed a reduced-form equation because alcohol consumption, an endogenous right-hand-side variable in equation (1), has been replaced by its exogenous determinants. Of course, the demand function for alcohol also is a reduced-form equation.

Our empirical aim in this chapter is to estimate equation (3) using data for states of the United States. This aim is facilitated by aggregating the equation over the n_j youths in the jth state and by interpreting the resulting probability of death as the observed motor vehicle mortality rate. The principal hypothesis tested is that youth alcohol consumption is negatively related to its price, and therefore the youth motor vehicle accident mortality rate is negatively related to the price of alcohol. In testing this hypothesis, we define price broadly as the sum of the direct cost of alcohol and the indirect cost that must be incurred to obtain it. In particular, the indirect cost of obtaining alcohol for a person under the age of twenty-one should be lower in states where the legal drinking age is eighteen as opposed to twenty-one. Thus, subject to certain modifications in section 3, the money price of alcohol and the legal drinking age play symmetrical roles in the reduced-form motor vehicle mortality equation.

3. EMPIRICAL IMPLEMENTATION

The dataset employed here is a time-series study of state cross sections and consists of the forty-eight contiguous states of the United States for the years 1975–1981. Hence there are 336 observations in each regression estimated in section 4. Alaska and Hawaii were omitted from the dataset because several important variables were missing for these two states. The District of Columbia was omitted because it is a much smaller physical area than any of the forty-eight states, and it is likely that many of its motor vehicle accidents involve nonresidents. Table 13.1 contains definitions, means, and standard deviations of the variables in the dataset. A detailed description of the variables and their sources appears in an appendix to this chapter (available on request). The appendix also includes a discussion of the theoretical roles of variables other than the real beer tax, the beer legal drinking age, and the "drinking sentiment" measures in the estimated mortality equations. In addition, it includes comments on preliminary results obtained with several variables that are not listed in table 13.1.

Separate motor vehicle accident mortality regressions are obtained for three age groups: youths aged fifteen through seventeen, youths aged eighteen through twenty, and youths aged twenty-one through twenty-four.[17] This is because the legal drinking age ranges from eighteen through twenty-one. Consequently, fifteen-, sixteen-, and seventeen-year-olds are illegal drinkers in all states, while twenty-one-, twenty-two-, twenty-three-, and twenty-four-year-olds are legal drinkers in all states. It follows that youths between the ages of eighteen and twenty should be most affected by differences in the drinking age. Formally, we rejected the hypothesis that slope coefficients are the same for the three age groups. Since the death rate differs among the three groups, this hypothesis was tested under the assumption that the intercepts are not the same.

Youths between the ages of fifteen and seventeen and between the ages of twenty-one and twenty-four are not excluded entirely from the analysis because they have higher motor death rates than any other age group except for eighteen- to twenty-year-olds. Thus, it is of interest to assess the effects on these death rates of differences in the cost of alcohol. A second consideration is that persons aged twenty-one through twenty-four or aged fifteen through seventeen may be passengers in cars driven by youths aged eighteen through twenty and may die in crashes caused by these drivers.

A third reason for not limiting the analysis to youths aged eighteen through twenty is that differences in the legal drinking age can affect motor vehicle fatalities of young teenagers and older youths. Since peers are a common source of alcohol,[18] the indirect cost of obtaining alcohol for persons younger than eighteen is lower in states where the legal drinking age is eighteen as opposed

Table 13.1 Definitions, Means, and Standard Deviations of Variables

Variable	Definition, Mean, Standard Deviation
Motor vehicle death rate	Deaths due to motor vehicle accidents per 100,000 population: ages fifteen to seventeen, mean = 31.581, SD = 8.794; ages eighteen to twenty, mean = 51.468, SD = 12.934; ages twenty-one to twenty-four, mean = 41.921, SD = 11.401.
Real beer tax	Sum of federal and state excise taxes on a case of twenty-four twelve-ounce cans of beer divided by CPI (1967 = 1), mean = .518, SD = .240.
Beer legal drinking age	Minimum legal age in years for the purchase and consumption of beer, alcoholic content more than 3.2 percent, mean = 19.404, SD = 1.391.
Border age	Sums of differences between own-state legal drinking age and bordering states' legal drinking ages (if positive) multiplied by fractions of population living in border counties, mean = .208, SD = .389.
Real income	Money per capita personal income divided by CPI (1967 = 1), expressed in thousands of dollars, mean = 3.830, SD = .447.
Vehicle miles traveled	Vehicle miles traveled in millions of miles per licensed driver, mean = .011, SD = .001.
Young drivers	Number of licensed drivers aged twenty-four or younger as a fraction of the population aged fifteen to twenty-four, mean = .726, SD = .090.
Inspection of motor vehicles	Dichotomous variable that equals one if inspection of motor vehicles is required every year, mean = .548, SD = .498.
Mormon	Fraction of population who are Mormons, mean = .012, SD = .059.
Southern Baptist	Fraction of population who are Southern Baptists, mean = .074, SD = .098.
Catholic	Fraction of population who are Catholics, mean = .210, SD = .127.
Protestant	Fraction of population who are Protestants (excludes Southern Baptists and Mormons), mean = .199, SD = .080.
Residents of "wet" counties	Fraction of the population who reside in fully or partially "wet" counties (counties that permit the sale of alcoholic beverages), mean = .967, SD = .084.

Note: Data pertain to the forty-eight contiguous states of the United States for the years 1975–1981. Means and standard deviations of the death rates are weighted by the age-specific number of persons in the category at issue by state and year. Means and standard deviations of all other variables are weighted by the number of persons aged fifteen through twenty-four by state and year.

to nineteen, twenty, or twenty-one. To the extent that age at onset of alcohol consumption and current alcohol use are negatively related,[19] an increase in the legal drinking age can lower the motor vehicle death rate of twenty-one- to twenty-four-year-olds (the "consumption" effect). A factor that goes in the opposite direction is the "experience" effect discussed in section 1.

Studies of the effect of changes in legal drinking ages in individual states or in a small number of states by Williams et al., by Douglass, and by Wagenaar employ one or more of the following outcome measures: (1) nighttime fatal accidents involving youthful drivers; (2) nighttime single-vehicle fatal accidents involving youthful drivers; and (3) nighttime single-vehicle fatal accidents involving youthful male drivers.[20] On the other hand, our outcome measure, like the one used by Cook and Tauchen, is more comprehensive. We adopt it for reasons given by Cook and Tauchen. They point out: "In evaluating alternative minimum drinking age legislation, it is desirable to have as comprehensive a measure of the associated social costs as possible. For example, from the evaluation viewpoint, it is more useful to know the effect of MLDA [minimum legal drinking age] change on total fatalities than nighttime fatal crashes.... The Douglass-Wagenaar 'three factor surrogate'—nighttime single vehicle crashes involving male drivers—is only remotely related to any natural indicator of social costs."[21] Thus we have chosen not to employ single-vehicle nighttime fatal accidents as an outcome measure because the policy variables at issue may affect single-vehicle daytime fatal crashes and multivehicle fatal crashes at all times of the day or night.

Our outcome measure, like Cook and Tauchen's, is incomplete in that it omits auto fatalities of persons under age fifteen or greater than age twenty-four caused by youthful drivers. Cook and Tauchen summarize data that indicate, however, that most of the victims of fatal crashes involving youthful drivers are the drivers themselves or youthful passengers in their vehicles. Motor vehicle deaths by age were provided to us by the National Highway Traffic Safety Administration (NHTSA) and come from unpublished data in NHTSA's Fatal Accident Reporting System. Deaths pertain to state of occurrence rather than to state of residence.

The key independent variables in the model are the legal drinking age and the price of alcohol. Both pertain to beer because of its popularity among youths. Moreover, Coate and Grossman report that the consumption of beer by youths is inversely related to the price of beer and to the minimum legal age for its purchase and consumption.[22] They also report that the magnitudes of these effects are substantial. On the other hand, the consumption of liquor or wine by youths is much less sensitive to the relevant beverage-specific price or legal drinking age, and Coate and Grossman find that youths substitute nonalcoholic beverages or other items such as leisure, rather than liquor or wine, for beer when the price of beer rises.

Youths who reside in a state with a high legal drinking age may be able to purchase and consume alcohol in a border state with a lower legal drinking age. In turn they may be killed in motor vehicle accidents that occur when they are returning from the border state. To deal with the border phenomenon (out-of-state purchases), we note that the more youthful residents of the jth state are affected by it, the greater the difference between the legal drinking age in that state (a_j) and the legal drinking age in the border state (a_k, $k \neq j$), provided this difference is positive. In addition, the border effect is larger, as the fraction of the population of state j that live in counties that border on state $k(f_j)$ increases. Hence we define the border age variable (b_j) as

$$b_j = f_j(a_j - a_k), \quad \text{if } a_j > a_k;$$
$$b_j = 0, \quad \text{if } a_j < a_k, \tag{4}$$

and include it as a regressor. With the resident-state legal drinking age held constant, an increase in the border variable reflects a reduction in a_k or an increase in f_j, both of which should cause the motor vehicle fatality rate to rise.[23]

If motor vehicle deaths pertain to the state of residence, the measure of b_j given above captures all elements of the border phenomenon. In our data, however, deaths are tabulated by state of occurrence. Nevertheless, b_j still is a perfect indicator of the border phenomenon provided youths who travel from state j to state k to drink are killed in accidents that occur within the boundary of state j. To the extent that some residents of state j die in state k, certain modifications of the border variable may be desirable. We do not pursue such modifications in this chapter, but we indicate in section 4 how the results are affected when the border variable is omitted from the regressions.[24]

The cost of beer is given by the sum of the federal and state excise tax rates on a case of twenty-four twelve-ounce cans of beer divided by the annual CPI (1967 = 1) for the United States as a whole. Deflation by the CPI is required to take account of trends in the prices of other goods between 1975 and 1981. All regressions include dichotomous variables for each year except 1981. Therefore, the measure of the real or relative price of beer just defined is an accurate indicator of the true relative price, provided the relative price of beer exclusive of tax does not vary from state to state. This last condition is satisfied because the time variables account for any trend in the real price of beer exclusive of tax.

It should be stressed that the state excise tax is a preferable regressor to the price of beer if the price exclusive of tax varies among states because the supply curve of beer slopes upward. The reason is that an outward shift in the demand function for beer simultaneously raises the price of beer, the quantity of beer consumed, and the motor vehicle mortality rate. Consequently, the coefficient of the price of beer in the mortality equation is understated in absolute value if the equation is estimated by ordinary least squares because price is positively correlated with the disturbance term. In our context, the tax also is superior to the price because the policy simulations performed in section 4 require reduced form as opposed to structural parameter estimates.[25]

To take account of the potential role of "drinking sentiment" in the endogenous determination of beer excise tax rates, legal drinking ages, and alcohol consumption, the fractions of the population who are Mormons, Southern Baptists, Catholics, and Protestants (excluding Southern Baptists and Mormons) and the fraction of the population who reside in "wet" counties (counties that permit the sale of alcoholic beverages) are included in one specification of the motor fatality equations. Drinking sentiment refers to cultural and taste variables that may either encourage or discourage alcohol consumption. For example, antidrinking sentiment should be relatively widespread in states in which those religious groups that oppose the use of alcohol, such as Mormons and Southern Baptists, are prevalent. Antidrinking sentiment should also be an important force in states in which a higher-than-average fraction of the population reside in "dry" counties (counties that prohibit the sale of alcoholic beverages). These states may enact high alcoholic beverage excise tax rates as part of the political process. In this situation, the tax coefficients that emerge from regressions that omit drinking sentiment overstate in absolute value the true parameters. On the other hand, states in which prodrinking sentiment is prevalent (antidrinking sentiment is weak) and alcohol consumption is large may enact high excise tax rates because the taxation of alcoholic beverages is an attractive source of revenue. In this case, the tax effects are understated if drinking sentiment is excluded from the regressions. Similar comments can be made with respect to drinking age effects that do not control for drinking sentiment.[26]

The role of drinking sentiment is considered in detail by Coate and Grossman in the context of a formal econometric model.[27] They emphasize the point made above, namely, tax and legal drinking age effects are not necessarily overstated in absolute value when drinking sentiment is omitted from the regression model. This is particularly true if omitted proxies for drinking sentiment are correlated with those included. Our strategy here is to fit a set of regressions that excludes the religion variables and the fraction of the population who reside in wet counties and then to construct a second set of regressions that includes these variables.[28]

An alternative estimation strategy to control for hard-to-measure variables, such as drinking sentiment, is to employ dichotomous variables for forty-seven of the forty-eight states. Each dichotomous variable identifies a specific state. This is the strategy adopted by Cook and Tauchen in their study of youth motor vehicle fatalities described in section 1. In fact, the only other independent variables in their model are the legal drinking age and dichotomous variables for seven of the eight years of their time series. Our approach, on the other hand, is to work with a more fully specified model of the determinants of youth motor vehicle accident mortality rates. This is because a model with state dummies has the potential of creating severe problems of multicollinearity. Nevertheless, we view a model with state dummy variables as a reasonable alternative to the one that we stress, and we present one regression for each of the three age groups that includes dichotomous variables for forty-seven of the forty-eight states. Since this specification is viewed as an alternative way to control for drinking sentiment, the religion variables and the fraction of the population residing in wet counties are omitted from it.

The actual motor vehicle mortality rate (π_{ijt})—defined as deaths per person rather than per 100,000 persons in the ith age group in the jth state in year t—ranges between zero and one. Therefore, a logistic functional form for the death rate is selected because it imposes this constraint. The equation is specified as

$$\pi_{ijt} = \left\{ 1 + \exp\left[-\alpha_i + \sum_{k=1}^{m} (-\beta_{ik})(x_{jtk}) - u_{ijt} \right] \right\}^{-1}, \tag{5}$$

where x_{jtk} is the value of the kth independent variable in the jth state in year t and u_{ijt} is the disturbance term. By solving for the logarithm of the odds of death from a motor vehicle accident relative to survival or death from other causes ($\pi_{ijt}/[1 - \pi_{ijt}]$), one transforms the logistic function into a linear equation:

$$\ln[\pi_{ijt}/(1 - \pi_{ijt})] = \alpha_i + \sum_{k=1}^{m} \beta_{ik} x_{jtk} + u_{ijt}, \tag{6}$$

which is called the logit function. The logit coefficient β_{ik} is the percentage change in the odds of motor vehicle mortality for a one-unit change in x_{jtk}.

Maddala shows that a regression estimate of equation (6) should employ weighted least squares.[29] The weights are given by $[n_{ijt}\pi_{ijt}(1 - \pi_{ijt})]^{1/2}$, where n_{ijt} is the number of youths in the ith age group in the jth state in year t. This weighted least-squares regression method is employed in section 4.

4. RESULTS

Weighted least-squares regression estimates of logit motor vehicle mortality equations for youths aged fifteen through seventeen, eighteen through twenty, and twenty-one through twenty-four are contained in panels A, B, and C, respectively, of table 13.2. Three regressions are shown in each panel.

Table 13.2 Weighted Least Squares Estimates of Logit Motor Vehicle Accident Mortality Equations

Independent Variable	Panel A: Ages 15–17 (Regression Number)			Panel B: Ages 18–20 (Regression Number)			Panel C: Ages 21–24 (Regression Number)		
	(2-A1)	(2-A2)	(2-A3)	(2-B1)	(2-B2)	(2-B3)	(2-C1)	(2-C2)	(2-C3)
Real beer tax	−.144	−.177	−.261	−.296	−.327	−.319	−.246	−.326	−.470
	(−3.05)	(−3.49)	(−1.54)	(−5.94)	(−6.16)	(−2.09)	(−4.41)	(−5.89)	(−3.07)
Beer legal drinking age	.009	.003	−.046	−.037	−.045	−.069	−.001	−.016	−.064
	(1.13)	(.33)	(−2.39)	(−4.56)	(−5.12)	(−3.96)	(−.09)	(−1.82)	(−3.72)
Border age	−.015	.019	.016	.025	.069	.118	.033	.120	.142
	(−.55)	(.65)	(.25)	(.88)	(2.22)	(2.08)	(1.06)	(3.87)	(2.51)
Real income	−.198	−.268	.081	−.121	−.204	.372	−.135	−.264	.232
	(−7.43)	(−7.82)	(.67)	(−4.47)	(−5.95)	(3.56)	(−4.52)	(−7.47)	(2.20)
Vehicle miles traveled	84.807	91.234	47.613	82.159	89.988	34.196	83.522	89.745	54.497
	(12.52)	(11.54)	(2.78)	(12.04)	(11.26)	(2.26)	(10.95)	(10.78)	(3.64)
Young drivers	1.436	1.302	.542	1.330	1.226	.683	1.418	1.317	.775
	(14.01)	(11.65)	(1.72)	(12.75)	(10.83)	(2.43)	(12.19)	(11.22)	(2.71)
Inspection of motor vehicles	−.022	−.050	.079	−.034	−.066	.036	−.032	−.085	.072
	(−1.09)	(−2.32)	(1.18)	(−1.65)	(−3.00)	(.58)	(−1.37)	(−3.78)	(1.16)
Mormon	…	−.377	…	…	−.444	…	…	−.767	…
		(−2.19)			(−2.48)			(−4.26)	…

Southern Baptist	...	...	−.068 (−.33)	...	...	−.120 (−.57)	...	...	−.050 (−.23)
Protestant	...	...	−.300 (−2.28)	...	...	−.449 (−3.37)	...	...	−.951 (−6.87)
Catholic	...	...	−.226 (−1.84)	...	...	−.224 (−1.80)	...	...	−.431 (−3.36)
Residents of wet counties	...	...	.572 (4.14)	...	...	.577 (3.91)	...	...	.901 (5.86)
R^2	.690	.711	.838	.605	.634	.845	.584	.665	.865
F	55.21	43.38	23.68	37.93	30.54	24.93	34.78	34.93	29.49

Note: Logit coefficients and *t*-ratios are shown in parentheses. The critical *t*-ratios at the 5 percent level are 1.64 for a one-tailed test and 1.96 for a two-tailed test. The *F*-ratio associated with each equation is significant at the 1 percent level. Each equation includes intercept and dichotomous variables for the years 1975–1980. Regressions 2-A3, 2-B3, and 2-C3 include dichotomous variables for forty-seven of the forty-eight states.

The first omits the religion variables and the fraction of the population who reside in wet counties, while the second includes these measures of drinking sentiment. The third regression excludes the five drinking sentiment variables but includes dichotomous variables for forty-seven of the forty-eight states. The logit coefficients of the state variables are not presented. Each of the three regressions contains an intercept and dichotomous variables for the years 1975–1980. The intercepts and the coefficients of the time variables are omitted from the tables.

Focusing on the first two regressions in each panel, one sees that all logit coefficients of the real beer tax are negative and statistically significant at the 5 percent level of significance or better.[30] At the point of means, the elasticity of the death rate with respect to the real beer tax is –.09 for the youngest age group and –.17 for the other two age groups.[31] Data contained in Coate and Grossman indicate that the sum of the federal and state excise tax on a case of beer accounted for 13 percent of the retail price of beer inclusive of tax on average in the period 1975–1981.[32] Suppose that the beer industry is competitive and has an infinitely elastic supply curve, so that a tax increase is fully passed on to consumers. Then the elasticity of the motor vehicle death rate with respect to the real price of beer would equal –0.7 for fifteen- through seventeen-year-olds and –1.3 for eighteen- through twenty-year-olds and twenty-one- through twenty-four-year-olds.

How reasonable are elasticities that range from –0.7 to –1.3? Cook estimates an elasticity of the motor vehicle death rate of persons of all ages with respect to the price of liquor of –0.7.[33] Thus our elasticities appear to be quite reasonable. This is particularly true because Coate and Grossman present arguments that suggest that youth price elasticities of demand for alcoholic beverages may be larger in absolute value than the corresponding adult price elasticities.[34]

Based on the first two regressions in panels A–C, the only negative and statistically significant legal drinking age coefficients pertain to youths aged eighteen through twenty. These are extremely plausible results because eighteen- through twenty-year-olds should be most affected by differences in the drinking age, which ranges from eighteen to twenty-one. The border age coefficients have the appropriate positive signs for the middle age group in regressions 2-B1 and 2-B2. In the latter model the coefficient is significant.

The above conclusions are not altered when the border age is omitted from the regressions. As shown by the first two regression specifications in table 13.3, the legal drinking age coefficients remain significant for youths aged eighteen through twenty. But the coefficients are not significant for the two other groups.[35] The drinking age coefficient in regression 3–2 is almost 30 percent smaller in absolute value than the corresponding coefficient in regression 2-B2,

Table 13.3 Logit Coefficients of Beer Legal Drinking Age, Border Age Omitted

	Regression Number		
	(3–1)	(3–2)	(3–3)
Ages fifteen through seventeen	.007	.006	−.044
	(.99)	(.92)	(−2.49)
Ages eighteen through twenty	−.033	−.033	−.055
	(−4.91)	(−4.75)	(−3.41)
Ages twenty-one through twenty-four	.004	.005	−.048
	(.57)	(.62)	(−2.95)

Notes: *t*-ratios in parentheses. First equation excludes religion and residents of wet counties. Second equation includes these variables. Third equation omits religion and residents of wet counties but includes dichotomous variables for forty-seven of the forty-eight states.

indicating that the magnitude of the estimated effect is somewhat sensitive to the inclusion or exclusion of the border age. The parameter estimates of the other regressors (not shown in table 13.3) are very similar to the corresponding estimates in panels A–C of table 13.2.

The income and highway variables prove to be important determinants of youth motor vehicle death rates. The income effect is negative, suggesting that higher-income persons or their offspring are safer drivers and operate motor vehicles that are in better physical condition than lower-income persons. These factors dominate the presumed positive relation between income and the demand for alcohol. Based on the second regression in each panel, the income elasticities are similar in magnitude to the price elasticities: −1.0 for the youngest age group, −0.8 for the middle age group, and −1.0 for the oldest age group.

An increase in the number of vehicle miles traveled per licensed driver or in the fraction of youths aged fifteen through twenty-four who are licensed drivers raises each of the three age-specific death rates. The elasticity of the death rate with respect to the number of vehicle miles traveled per licensed driver is unity for each age group. A similar comment applies to the magnitude of the elasticity of the death rate with respect to the fraction of youths aged fifteen through twenty-four who are licensed drivers. These results underscore the plausibility of our empirical specification because they imply that deaths per miles traveled by licensed drivers do not depend on miles traveled per licensed driver or on the fraction of licensed drivers.[36] States that require compulsory inspection of motor vehicles every year have lower death rates than other states. Except for the middle age group, this effect is significant only when the drinking sentiment measures are held constant.

Comparing the first and second regressions in each panel of table 13.2, one sees that the signs, significance levels, and magnitudes of the tax and legal drinking age effects are not in general affected by the inclusion of the drinking sentiment proxies. If anything, the significant coefficients become larger in absolute value when the religion variables and the fraction of the population residing in wet counties are added to the set of regressors. This is an important finding because it means that increases in the beer tax and the legal drinking age play the dominant role in reducing consumption of beer and, through it, road deaths. The cultural factors are therefore less important than the financial and legal variables. The estimated income and highway coefficients also are not sensitive to the inclusion of the sentiment variables, with the exception of the inspection coefficient noted above.

With regard to the drinking sentiment measures themselves, the coefficient of the fraction of persons who reside in wet counties always is positive and significant. The results for the religion variables are less clear-cut. Death rates are lower in states where Mormons and Southern Baptists are prevalent, although the effect with Southern Baptists never is significant. But death rates also fall as the fraction of the population who are Protestants or Catholics rises. This result is puzzling because Coate and Grossman find that the frequency of beer consumption by youths is positively related to the prevalence of Protestants and Catholics in their area of residence.[37] We offer no explanation of the finding. We note, however, that our conclusions with respect to the tax and legal drinking age effects are not altered when the religion variables or the fraction of the population who reside in wet counties are omitted from the drinking sentiment vector.

The third regression in panels A–C of table 13.2 includes dichotomous variables for forty-seven of the forty-eight states. The tax effects rise in absolute value when the state dummies are held constant, except for the middle age group where the coefficient is virtually unchanged. Thus, the negative tax effects that we report are quite robust. In particular, they cannot be attributed to unmeasured state-specific variables, indicating that the state excise tax rate on beer has an independent effect on the motor vehicle accident mortality rate of youths.

The specification with the state dummies exhibits a number of peculiarities. All three income effects become positive, and two of the positive coefficients are significant. The coefficients pertaining to vehicle miles traveled per driver and to the fraction of youths who have drivers' licenses are greatly reduced. The sign of the inspection coefficient switches from negative to positive. The drinking age effect for eighteen-through twenty-year-olds, which was negative and significant in the second regression model, rises by slightly more than 50 percent in absolute value. The drinking age coefficient for fifteen- through seventeen-year-olds switches signs from positive to negative and becomes significant. For the oldest age group, the negative drinking age coefficient rises by a factor of four and becomes significant. These results suggest that a model with state dummies is overdetermined and plagued by multicollinearity. The implausible nature of the estimates that emerge from this specification provides a justification for not emphasizing it.

To evaluate the potential effects of the federal excise tax and legal drinking age policy initiatives discussed in section 1, we simulate their effects on youth motor vehicle accident mortality rates. Specifically, first we compute the "actual" mortality rate for a given age group by predicting the mortality probability for the jth state in year $t(\hat{\pi}_{ijt})$ based on the logit coefficients and the actual values of the independent variables (x_{Jtk}) for that observation (see equation [5]). Then we obtain the actual death rate as a weighted average of the 336 computed probabilities (forty-eight states times seven years) multiplied by 100,000. The weight is the fraction of the total population of all youths in the ith age group in the period 1975–1981 who reside in the jth state in year t.[38] Next we vary one or more of the independent variables by a certain amount, recompute each $\hat{\pi}_{ijt}$, and average to obtain to the "new" mortality rate. The simulations are restricted to eighteen- through twenty-year-olds because public policy with respect to the legal drinking age focuses on this age group. Simulations based on the second regression model in table 13.2 are emphasized, but simulations based on the third regression model are also presented for comparative purposes.

The legal drinking age policy pertains to a uniform minimum age of twenty-one for the purchase of beer in all states. This policy is simulated by setting the legal drinking age equal to twenty-one for each of the 336 observations in the regression and by setting the border age variable equal to zero. The resulting mortality rate is the one that would have been observed if the legal drinking age had been twenty-one in all states throughout the period 1975–1981.

Three federal excise tax policies are considered. The first indexes the federal excise tax rate on a case of beer, which has been fixed at $0.64 in nominal terms since 1951, to the rate of inflation since 1951. It is termed the inflation tax policy. Under it, the real beer tax in the jth state in year $t(q_{jt})$ becomes

$$q_{jt} = [r_{jt} + (\$0.64)(c_{t,51})] / (c_{t,67}), \tag{7}$$

where r_{jt} is the state excise tax rate in nominal terms, $c_{t,51}$ is the CPI in year t relative to 1951, and $c_{t,67}$ is the CPI in year t relative to 1967. The second tax policy raises the excise tax on a case of beer from $0.64 to $2.09 to equalize the rates at which the alcohol in beer and liquor are taxed (see note 4). It is termed the alcohol tax equalization policy. In this simulation the real beer tax is given by

$$q^*_{jt} = (r_{jt} + \$2.09) / (c_{t,67}).\tag{8}$$

The third tax policy combines the first two and is termed the combined tax policy. The real beer tax becomes

$$q'_{jt} = [r_{jt} + (\$2.09)(c_{t,51})] / (c_{t,67}).\tag{9}$$

The resulting simulation shows the mortality rate that would have prevailed if the excise tax rate on beer had been fixed in real as opposed to nominal terms during the 1975–1981 period and if the alcohol in beer had been taxed as heavily as the alcohol in liquor.

Note that substantial tax hikes are involved in the last three simulations. Indexation of the nominal federal excise tax on beer to the rate of inflation produces a tax on a case of beer in 1978 (the midyear of the sample period) that is 2.5 times larger than the actual tax. Equalization of the tax on the alcohol in beer with that on the alcohol in liquor produces a beer tax that is 3.3 times as large as the actual tax. Both policies combined amount to an approximately eightfold increase in the federal beer tax in 1978, which would have raised the nominal price of beer by roughly 60 percent in that year.[39]

Table 13.4 contains the results of the simulations. The figures in panel A are obtained from the regression model with the religion variables and the residents of wet counties. Those in panel B are obtained from the regression model with the state dummy variables.

Based on panel A, a uniform legal drinking age of twenty-one throughout the period would have reduced the death rate of youths ages eighteen through twenty (fifty-two deaths per 100,000 population based on the actual values of all independent variables) by four deaths per 100,000 population. This represents an 8 percent decline in the number of youths who would have died in motor vehicle crashes. The corresponding reduction in panel B is 12 percent.

More dramatic declines are produced by the excise tax policies. Since these results are not sensitive to the regression model used, we focus on the results in panel A. The number of deaths falls by 9 per 100,000 population if the federal excise tax rises at the rate of inflation, which represents a 15 percent decline in the number of lives lost in fatal crashes. The policy that taxes the alcohol in beer and liquor at the same rates has a slightly bigger effect. It saves eleven lives per 100,000 population, which represents a 21 percent reduction in the number of lives lost. The combination of both tax policies causes the mortality rate to fall by twenty-eight deaths per 100,000 population, which represents a whopping 54 percent reduction.

It is notable that a 12 percent increase in the price of beer that accompanies the inflation tax policy appears to have a larger effect than a uniform drinking age of twenty-one, even when the 12 percent drinking age effect from panel B is used

Table 13.4 Predicted Effects of Imposition of Uniform Legal Drinking Age of Twenty-One or Increase in Federal Excise Tax on Beer on Motor Vehicle Accident Mortality Rate of Eighteen- to Twenty-Year-Olds

	Actual	Drinking Age Policy	Inflation Tax Policy	Alcohol Tax Equaliza-tion Policy	Combined Tax Policy
Panel A: Model with religion variables and residents of wet counties (regression 2-B2):					
Death rate	52.04	47.76	44.16	41.16	24.06
Absolute change	...	4.28	7.88	10.88	27.98
Percentage change	...	8.22	15.14	20.91	53.77
Panel B: Model with state dummies (regression 2-B3):					
Death rate	51.72	45.32	44.06	41.12	24.34
Absolute change	...	6.40	7.66	10.60	27.38
Percentage change	...	12.37	14.81	20.49	52.94

Note: Death rate and absolute change are expressed in terms of deaths per 100,000 population. Absolute change equals the actual death rate minus the death rate predicted by one of the four policies at issue. Percentage change equals the absolute change divided by the actual death rate and multiplied by 100.

in the comparison. In part, this conclusion is reached because many states had legal drinking ages of twenty-one in one or more years of the period. Therefore, we have simulated the death rates of eighteen- through twenty-year-olds under the assumption of a uniform drinking age of eighteen. Based on the regression model with the antidrinking sentiment measures, the mortality rate in the latter simulation exceeds the one in the simulation with a drinking age of twenty-one by seven deaths per 100,000 population. The corresponding differential in the regression with the state dummies is ten deaths per 100,000 population. The former differential but not the latter is smaller than the eight-deaths-per-100,000-population reduction produced by the policy to adjust the beer tax for inflation.

Our preferred regression model indicates that 8 percent fewer youths would have died in motor vehicle crashes if the drinking age had been twenty-one in all states during the period 1975–1981. On the other hand, Cook and Tauchen's results suggest that the drinking age policy would have lowered the death rate by approximately 4 percent during the period 1970–1977.[40] In part our estimate is larger than their estimate because they do not control for the border age. Indeed, we predict a reduction of 5 percent when the border age is omitted from the regression. Our figure also may exceed Cook and Tauchen's because the mean drinking age may have been higher in their sample period than in ours.

To summarize the qualitative results of the logit equations, negative and statistically significant real beer tax effects are obtained for youths aged fifteen through seventeen, eighteen through twenty, and twenty-one through twenty-four. Negative and statistically significant legal drinking age effects are obtained for youths aged eighteen through twenty. These results cannot be attributed to the omission of drinking sentiment from the estimating equation because we control for this phenomenon by including as regressors religion measures and the fraction of the population who reside in counties that permit the sale of alcohol.

Quantitatively, the enactment of a uniform drinking age of twenty-one in all states would have reduced the number of eighteen- through twenty-year-olds killed in motor vehicle crashes by 8 percent in the period 1975–1981. A policy that fixed the federal beer tax in real terms since 1951 would have reduced the number of lives lost in fatal crashes by 15 percent, while a policy that taxed the alcohol in beer at the same rate as the alcohol in liquor would have lowered the number of lives lost by 21 percent. A combination of the two tax policies would have caused a 54 percent decline in the number of youths killed.

The preceding figures suggest that, if reductions in youth motor vehicle accident deaths are desired, both a uniform drinking age of twenty-one and an increase in the federal excise tax rate on beer are effective policies to accomplish this goal. They also suggest that the tax policy may be more potent than the drinking age policy. Indeed, according to our computations, the lives of 1,022 youths aged eighteen through twenty would have been saved by the inflation excise tax policy in a typical year during the period 1975–1981, while the lives of 555 youths would have been saved by the drinking age policy.

It does not follow that we have provided enough evidence to justify the approximately eightfold (thirteen fold based on the 1984 CPI) increase in the federal excise tax on beer that is implicit in the most comprehensive tax policy. Excise tax hikes impose welfare costs on all segments of the population, while a drinking age policy is targeted at the group in the population that accounts for a disproportionate share of motor vehicle accidents and deaths. On the other hand, the enforcement and administrative costs associated with a uniform minimum drinking age of twenty-one may exceed those associated with the tax policy. Moreover, our results indicate that an excise tax increase lowers death rates of youths between the ages of fifteen and seventeen and between the ages of twenty-one and twenty-four. These benefits do not accompany a rise in the drinking age. In addition, the tax policy may reduce fatal crashes involving adults. Of course, a substantial tax hike may greatly stimulate the demand for illegally produced beer suggesting that we have overestimated the impact of an eightfold increase in the federal excise tax on beer.

Finally, Becker has shown that the optimal way for a society to deter offenses is via a system of severe and fairly certain punishments.[41] In the case of drunk driving, these might take the form of loss of driving privileges for long periods of time, mandatory community service, enrollment in alcohol rehabilitation programs, and prison sentences for repeat offenders. Of course, youthful drunk drivers may respond to an increase in the penalty for this offense only if the probabilities of apprehension and conviction are nontrivial. If substantial resources must be allocated to raising these probabilities, the excise tax policy may be preferable to or complementary with a system of severe penalties. In conclusion, more research is required to formulate the best mix of policies to deal with youth motor vehicle accident mortality. Our study represents a useful step in this process.

NOTES

Originally published as Henry Saffer and Michael Grossman, "Beer Taxes, the Legal Drinking Age, and Youth Motor Vehicle Fatalities." *Journal of Legal Studies* 16, no. 2 (1987): 351–374. Research for this paper was supported by grant 5 R01 AA05849 from the National Institute on Alcohol Abuse and Alcoholism to the National Bureau of Economic Research. We are indebted to the National Highway Traffic Safety Administration for providing us with motor vehicle deaths by age, sex, year, and state. We wish to thank Dennis McCornac for designing the database used in this project and for supervising its construction. We also wish to thank Gary Becker, Philip Cook, Gilbert Ghez, and an anonymous referee for helpful comments and Frank Chaloupka, Emil Berendt, and Theodore Joyce for research assistance. This paper has not undergone the review accorded official NBER publications; in particular, it has not been submitted for approval by the Board of Directors.

1. Public Law 98–363.
2. The federal excise tax rate on distilled spirits was raised from $10.50 per proof gallon to $12.50, effective October 1, 1985, as part of the Deficit Reduction Act of 1984.
3. U.S. Dep't Labor, Bur. Labor Statistics, Monthly Labor Review (various issues).
4. Philip J. Cook and George Tauchen, "The Effect of Liquor Taxes on Heavy Drinking," 13 *Bell J. Econ.* 379 (1982).
5. The above figures were taken from U.S. Dep't Transportation, Nat'l Highway Traffic Safety Administration, Fatal Accident Reporting System, 1981 (1983).
6. Robert B. Voas and John Moulden, "Historical Trends in Alcohol Use and Driving by Young Americans, in Minimum-Drinking-Age Laws: An Evaluation" 59 (Henry Wechsler ed.1980).
7. U.S. Dep't Health and Human Services, Public Health Service, Nat'l Center for Health Statistics, Mortality, pt. A, vol. 2 in Vital Statistics of the United States, 1980 (1984).
8. For example, Allan Luks, *Will America Sober Up?* (1983); Philip J. Cook, "Increasing the Federal Alcohol Excise Tax," in *Toward the Prevention of Alcohol Problems: Government,*

Business, and Community Action 24 (Dean R. Gerstein ed. 1984); Gary S. Becker, "Don't Raise the Drinking Age, Raise Taxes," *Business Week*, November 25, 1985, at 21; and Michael Jacobson and Mark Albion, "Raising Alcohol Taxes Is the Way to Cut Drinking and the Debt," *Wash. Post*, August 11, 1985, at L2. Under an ad valorem alcoholic beverage excise tax system, the tax rate would be set at a fixed proportion of wholesale price.

9. Douglas Coate and Michael Grossman, "Effects of Alcoholic Beverage Prices and Legal Drinking Ages on Youth Alcohol Use," 31 *J. Law Econ.* 145 (1988).

10. For example, Jeffrey E. Harris, "More Data on Tax Policy," in Gerstein ed., *supra* note 8, at 33; and Jacobson and Albion, *supra* note 8. Under the federal excise tax on liquor of $10.50 per gallon of liquor (50 percent alcohol by volume) in effect prior to October 1, 1985, one gallon of alcohol in liquor was taxed at a rate of $21. Since the federal excise tax on beer is $0.29 per gallon and since one gallon of beer contains 4.5 percent alcohol by volume, the tax rate on one gallon of alcohol in beer is $6.44. The alcohol in liquor is taxed fifteen times as heavily as the alcohol in wine, and the proposals mentioned here also contain provisions to correct this distortion.

11. Originally, the penalties imposed on states with a drinking age below twenty-one by the Federal Uniform Drinking Age Act of 1984 were scheduled to expire at the end of fiscal year 1988. In response to this provision, Texas and Nebraska adopted laws that called for a revocation of the twenty-one drinking age as soon as the legislation expired. See Insurance Institute for Highway Safety, 20 Highway Loss Status Rep. 1 (1985). To counteract these laws, the federal legislation was made permanent in 1986.

12. Coate and Grossman, *supra* note 9. They also present theoretical reasons why youthful drinkers are likely to be more sensitive to price than adults.

13. Philip J. Cook, "The Effect of Liquor Taxes on Drinking, Cirrhosis, and Auto Accidents," in *Alcohol and Public Policy: Beyond the Shadow of Prohibition* 255 (Mark H. Moore and Daniel R. Gerstein eds. 1981).

14. For example, Allan F. Williams et al., "The Legal Minimum Drinking Age and Fatal Motor Vehicle Crashes," 4 *J. Legal Stud.* 219 (1975); Allan F. Williams et al., "The Effect of Raising the Legal Minimum Drinking Age on Involvement in Fatal Crashes," 12 *J. Legal Stud.* 169 (1983); and Alexander C. Wagenaar, *Alcohol, Young Drivers, and Traffic Accidents* (1983).

15. Dennis C. McCornac, "The Effects of Government Regulation on Teenage Motor Vehicle Mortality" (Working Paper No. 1030, Nat'l Bur. Economic Research, 1982); and Philip J. Cook and George Tauchen, "The Effect of Minimum Drinking Age Legislation on Youthful Auto Fatalities," 1970–1977, 13 *J. Legal Stud.* 169 (1984).

16. Mike A. Males, "The Minimum Purchase Age for Alcohol and Young-Driver Fatal Crashes: A Long-Term View," 15 *J. Legal Stud.* 181 (1986).

17. The male death rate is approximately three times as large as the female death rate for the cohort of persons aged fifteen through twenty-four. Sex-specific regressions are not presented because we tested and accepted the hypothesis that slope coefficients but not intercepts are the same for males and females. Since there is almost no variation in the fraction of fifteen- through twenty-four-year-olds who are females across states, this variable is not included as a regressor.

18. Howard T. Blane and Linda E. Hewitt, "Alcohol and Youth: An Analysis of the Literature" (report prepared for the Nat'l Institute on Alcohol Abuse and Alcoholism 1977).

19. J. Valley Rachai et al., "The Extent and Nature of Adolescent Alcohol Use: The 1974 and 1978 National Sample Survey" (National Technical Information Service 1980).

20. Williams et al., *supra* note 14 (both studies); Richard L. Douglass, "The Legal Drinking Age and Traffic Casualties: A Special Case of Changing Alcohol Availability in a Public Health Context," in Wechsler ed., *supra* note 6, at 93; and Wagenaar, *supra* note 14.

21. Cook and Tauchen, *supra* note 15, at 174–175.

22. Coate and Grossman, *supra* note 9.

23. Suppose that there are m border states, each of which has a lower drinking age than state j. Then b_j becomes

$$b_j = \sum_{k=1}^{m} f_{jk}(a_j - a_k).$$

24. If residents of state j who drink in state k are as likely to die in that state as in state j, b_k could be set equal to b_j rather than to zero. Given more than one border state and little information about the precise location of accidents involving youths who leave their state of residence to drink, the construction of an appropriate border variable becomes somewhat arbitrary.

25. Cook and Tauchen, *supra* note 4, present a similar argument in the context of the estimation of demand functions for liquor. The transactions price of a single leading brand of medium-priced, nationally sold beer is available for two unidentified major markets in each state for the years 1976, 1977, and 1978. See Stanley I. Ornstein and Dominique M. Hanssens, "Alcohol Control Laws and the Consumption of Distilled Spirits and Beer," 12 *J. Consumer Research* 200 (1985); and Coate and Grossman, *supra* note 9. In addition to the reasons given above, this price is not used here because it would have to be predicted for the years 1975, 1979, 1980, and 1981 from a regression that includes dichotomous variables for forty-seven of the forty-eight contiguous states. This would create severe problems of multicollinearity in the motor vehicle mortality regression model specified below that includes dichotomous variables for the states. Note that state excise tax rates on wine and liquor are poor proxies for the prices of wine and liquor in control (monopoly) states because such states derive most of their revenue from the sale of wine and liquor from the price markups rather than from the excise taxes. This comment does not apply to state excise tax rates on beer because beer is sold privately in monopoly states.

26. Although it might appear as if the drinking age effect is overstated, this need not be the case. For example, adult voters in a state with a vocal minority that opposes alcohol consumption may enact a high legal drinking age to prevent the minority from campaigning to raise alcohol excise tax rates. To cite another illustration, the high mortality rate in a state where prodrinking sentiment is widespread may result in the enactment of a high legal drinking age.

27. Coate and Grossman, *supra* note 9.

28. An alternative approach to the problem discussed above is to estimate a simultaneous-equations model of the joint determination of the legal drinking age, the beer tax, and the motor vehicle accident mortality rate. This approach is pursued by Henry Saffer and Michael Grossman, "Drinking Age Laws and Highway Mortality Rates: Cause and Effect," 25 *Economic Inquiry* 403 (1987). Although our results are quite sensitive to alternative specifications, they suggest that the tax and legal drinking age effects presented here are conservative lower-bound estimates. Moreover, the relative ranking of the two estimates is not affected by biases associated with endogeneity.

29. G. S. Maddala, *Limited-Dependent and Qualitative Variables in Econometrics* (1983).

30. Statements concerning statistical significance in the text are based on one-tailed tests except when the direction of the effect is unclear on a priori grounds or when the estimated effect has the "wrong sign." In the latter cases, two-tailed tests are used. When no significance level is indicated, it is assumed to be 5 percent.

31. These elasticities are based on the second regression in each panel. The formula for the elasticity (ε_i) is

$$\varepsilon_i = \beta_{ik}(1 - \pi_{ijt})x_{jtk},$$

where x_{jtk} is the real beer tax and β_{ik} is its logit coefficient. We evaluate ε_i at the weighted sample means of π_{itk}, and x_{jtk} (see table 13.1). Note that the mean death rates in table 13.1 must be divided by 100,000 before the elasticities are computed.

32. Coate and Grossman, *supra* note 9.

33. Cook, *supra* note 13.

34. Coate and Grossman, *supra* note 9.

35. The negative legal drinking age coefficient for the twenty-one- through twenty-four-year-olds in regression 2-C2 is not significant at the 5 percent level for a two-tailed test. This is the appropriate test because the experience factor suggests a positive effect, while the consumption factor suggests a negative effect (see section 3). Since the age coefficient is negative, our results, like those of Cook and Tauchen, *supra* note 15, do not support the experience hypothesis proposed by Males, *supra* note 16.

36. Strictly speaking, the above proposition holds for the following logarithmic regression model:

$$\ln(d_{ij}/m_{ij}) = \alpha_i + \beta_i x_j.$$

Here d_{ij} is the number of deaths in the ith age group in the jth state, m_{ij} is the number of miles traveled by licensed drivers in this age group, x_j is the vector of exogenous variables, and time subscripts are suppressed. As an identity,

$$m_{ij} \equiv n_{ij} w_{ij} \bar{m}_{ij},$$

where n_{ij} is the number of persons in the ith age group, w_{ij} is the fraction who are licensed drivers, and $\bar{m}_{ij}$ is the number of miles driven per licensed driver. Therefore,

$$\ln \pi_{ij} \equiv \ln(d_{ij}/n_{ij}) = \alpha_i + \beta_i x_j + \ln w_{ij} + \ln \bar{m}_{ij}.$$

The last steps in the derivation are to assume that

$$\bar{m}_{ij} = s_i \bar{m}_j,$$

$$w_{ij} = v_i w_{1524j},$$

where $\bar{m}_j$ denotes the number of miles driven by licensed drivers of all ages divided by the number of licensed drivers of all ages in the jth state, w_{1524j} is the fraction of licensed drivers ages fifteen through twenty-four, and the factors of proportionality (s_i and v_i) do not vary among states.

37. Coate and Grossman, *supra* note 9.

38. That is, the actual death rate $(\tilde{\pi}_i)$ is given by

$$\bar{\pi}_i = 100,000 \sum_{t=1}^{7} \sum_{j=1}^{48} f_{ijt} \hat{\pi}_{ijt},$$

where

$$f_{ijt} = n_{ijt} \bigg/ \left(\sum_{t=1}^{7} \sum_{j=1}^{48} n_{ijt} \right).$$

As shown by table 13.4, $\bar{\pi}_i$ differs from the corresponding mean in table 13.1. This is because the logit regression does not necessarily pass through the point of weighted arithmetic means. But the difference is very small; in a given regression model it is always less than one death per 100,000 population.

39. Since the excise tax and legal drinking age increases are nonmarginal and the logit functions are nonlinear, the simulations are employed to evaluate their effects. This is preferable to computing marginal price or legal drinking age effects at the point of means or for each observation and then multiplying by the change in the policy variable at issue.

40. We computed the 4 percent figure based on Cook and Tauchen, *supra* note 15, table 5, at 186.

41. Gary G. Becker, "Crime and Punishment: An Economic Approach," 76 *J. Pol. Econ.* 169 (1968). In Becker's model, a system of monetary fines is optimal in most situations. Since teenagers involved in serious automobile accidents presumably would not have enough resources to pay an adequate fine, other punishments for drunk driving are required.

FOURTEEN

Effects of Alcoholic Beverage Prices and Legal Drinking Ages on Youth Alcohol Use

Douglas Coate and Michael Grossman

1. INTRODUCTION AND BACKGROUND

Since the mid-1970s, the federal government of the United States and various state and local governments have been involved in a campaign to reduce deaths from motor vehicle accidents by discouraging alcohol abuse. One major effect of this campaign has been the upward trend in state minimum legal ages for the purchase and consumption of alcoholic beverages. This trend began with the increase in the legal drinking age in Minnesota from eighteen to nineteen years of age in 1976. An additional twenty-seven states had increased legal drinking ages by the time Congress passed the Federal Uniform Drinking Age Act of July 1984.[1] This legislation allows the federal government, through its control of federal highway funds, to intercede in a legislative area traditionally reserved for states. Five percent of a state's federal highway construction fund allocation for the fiscal year 1987 has been withheld if that state's minimum legal drinking age was below twenty-one on October 1, 1986, and 10 percent will be withheld from each future fiscal year allocation if that state's drinking age remains below twenty-one. To date, twenty-seven states have passed laws complying with the act, and only Wyoming has failed to raise its minimum drinking age to twenty-one.[2] A second major element of the antidrinking campaign is reflected by more severe penalties for conviction of drunk driving, the allocation of additional resources to apprehend drunk drivers, and the easing in the standards required for conviction.

One policy that has been virtually ignored by the federal and state governments in the antidrinking campaign is increased taxation of alcoholic beverages which, by raising prices, would lower alcoholic beverage consumption and motor vehicle mortality. Instead, the federal excise tax rates on liquor (distilled spirits), beer, and wine remained constant in nominal terms between November 1, 1951, and the end of fiscal 1985. During this period, the federal government taxed liquor at the rate of $10.50 per proof gallon (one gallon of 100-proof liquor, which is the equivalent of 50 percent alcohol by volume), beer at the rate of $.29 per gallon (approximately 4.5 percent alcohol by volume), and wine at the rate of $.17 per gallon (between 11.6 percent and 21 percent alcohol by volume).[3]

Partly as a result of the stability of the federal excise taxes and the modest increases in state and local excise taxes, the real price of alcoholic beverages (the nominal price divided by the Consumer Price Index) has declined substantially over time. Between 1960 and 1980, the real price of liquor fell by 48 percent, the real price of beer fell by 27 percent, and the real price of wine fell by 20 percent. While twenty-nine states raised the legal drinking age from 1976 through 1984, real alcoholic beverage prices continued to fall: 27 percent for liquor, 12 percent for beer, and 19 percent for wine.[4] Thus, if alcohol abuse is sensitive to price, a government policy of declining real excise tax levels actually may be exacerbating this problem.[5]

A primary purpose of this article is to investigate the sensitivity of alcoholic beverage consumption, particularly excessive consumption, to price among sixteen- through twenty-one-year-olds in the United States. We provide evidence for this important age group on the extent to which declining real alcoholic beverage excise taxes have contributed to increases in youth drinking and on the extent to which increases in real alcoholic beverage excise taxes can serve as a potent instrument in the antidrinking campaign. We also examine the effect of an increase in the legal drinking age on youth alcohol use. Our empirical research is based on the second National Health and Nutrition Examination Survey (NHANES II), which was conducted by the National Center for Health Statistics (NCHS) between February 1976 and February 1980. It capitalizes on substantial differences in legal drinking ages among states in the period of NHANES II and on substantial differences in the prices of alcoholic beverages among states that were due primarily to differences in state excise tax rates on these beverages.

We focus on teenagers and young adults in the context of the antidrinking campaign because motor vehicle accidents are the leading cause of death of persons under the age of thirty-five, and alcohol is involved in over half of these fatal accidents. In 1984, persons under the age of twenty-five accounted for 20 percent of all licensed drivers but constituted 35 percent of all drivers involved in fatal accidents.[6] These figures are even more dramatic than they appear because members of the young driver group do not drive nearly as much as older drivers.[7] We also focus on youths because alcohol abuse in adolescence appears to be associated with alcohol abuse in adult life.[8] Thus, policies to prevent the onset of this behavior in adolescents might be the most effective means to reduce it in all segments of the population.

Research on the responsiveness of youth alcohol use to alcoholic beverage prices is particularly timely in light of proposals to correct the erosion since 1951 in the real value of the federal excise rates on all forms of alcoholic beverages and in light of proposals to prevent future erosion by indexing tax rates to the rate of inflation or by converting to an ad valorem alcoholic beverage excise tax system.[9] Moreover, although beer is the drink of choice among youths who drink alcoholic beverages (see section 2), the alcohol in liquor is taxed three times as heavily as the alcohol in beer. This has led to suggestions to equalize the tax rates on the alcohol in all forms of alcoholic beverages by raising the tax on beer.[10] In addition, this study complements the one by Saffer and Grossman,[11] which reports dramatic reductions in youth motor vehicle accident mortality rates in response to increases in real state excise tax rates on beer. Research on the sensitivity of youth alcohol use to legal drinking ages is also valuable given the adverse reaction to federal uniform drinking legislation[12] and the volatility of state minimum drinking ages in the 1970s and 1980s.

One of the basic aims of our research is to compare the effect of a uniform minimum age of twenty-one for the purchase of alcohol in all states on youth alcohol use with that of one or more of the policies to raise the federal excise tax rates on alcohol beverages described above. Before turning to a technical discussion of how these relations should be measured, we note that an effectively enforced prohibition of alcohol consumption in this age group clearly should have a larger effect on their consumption than an increase in excise tax rates. This issue is not clear-cut at the empirical level only because of the problem of evasion. Underage youths can obtain alcohol from their older siblings or friends. In addition, they can purchase fake identification cards or buy alcohol in stores that do not bother to demand proof of age. This type of evasion simply is not possible with an excise tax hike, so that the responsiveness of youths to the price of alcohol determines the change in its consumption.

Aside from our study with Arluck[13] described below, there has been no research on the price sensitivity of youth alcohol use and no investigation of the long-run effects of differences in legal drinking ages in recent nationally representative samples. Statistically significant short-run increases in alcohol consumption by youths have been reported in selected states or provinces of Canada that lowered their legal drinking age in the early 1970s, and significant short-run reductions in consumption have been reported in selected states that raised their legal drinking age in the late 1970s or early 1980s.[14] Grossman, Coate, and Arluck[15] found that the incidence of heavy drinking and frequent drinking by youths falls as alcoholic beverage prices or legal drinking ages rise. These results are based on the first National Health and Nutrition Examination Survey (NHANES I), conducted by NCHS between May 1971 and June 1974, and pertain to youths of ages sixteen through twenty-one who reside in large metropolitan areas.

Studies that use time series or state cross sections to estimate price elasticities of alcoholic beverages[16] employ per-capita consumption by all age groups as the dependent variable. Therefore, the estimated price elasticities primarily reflect adult drinking behavior and cannot be used to predict how youths would respond to excise tax and price changes. As pointed out above, however, it is especially important to focus on youths in the context of the antidrinking campaign.

It should be noted that, even if adult price elasticities are relatively small (inelastic) in absolute value, this need not be the case for youth price elasticities. Given the habitual nature of alcohol abuse, adult users, who almost always will have been users for longer periods of time than youths, may be much less sensitive to price than youths. In addition, the fraction of disposable income that a youthful drinker spends on alcohol probably exceeds the corresponding fraction of an adult drinker. It is well known that the uncompensated (income-constant) price elasticity of a good rises as the fraction of income spent on that good rises. Finally, bandwagon or peer effects are much more important in the case of youth drinking than in the case of adult drinking. That is, youths are more likely to drink if their peers also drink.[17] As shown by Leibenstein and by Lewit, Coate, and Grossman,[18] the presence of bandwagon or peer effects increases the price elasticity of demand.[19]

2. METHODOLOGY

2.1. Data and Subsample Selection

To examine the effects of alcohol prices and legal drinking ages on youth alcohol use, we have used NHANES II to estimate demand functions for alcohol consumption by youths. The NHANES II is a national probability sample of the civilian, noninstitutionalized population of the United States with some oversampling of low-income persons, preschool children, and the elderly. The survey was conducted by NCHS between February 1976 and February 1980 and contains approximately 21,000 persons between the ages of six months and seventy-four years. These persons were selected from sixty-four primary sampling units, which consist of one or more counties. Each person in the survey was given a detailed physical examination. A variety of information on medical and health histories, family socioeconomic characteristics, and diet patterns also was obtained. Data on alcohol use for the past three months were collected for persons from ages twelve through seventy-four. These data were acquired on the date on which the physical examination was given as one component of a food frequency interview.[20]

We have limited our demand function estimates to sixteen- through twenty-one-year-olds because of our interest in the sensitivity of alcohol consumption of older youths to price and to legal drinking age. Youths below the age of sixteen are excluded from the demand functions because they cannot legally drive in most states. Youths aged sixteen and seventeen are illegal drinkers in all states, but they are included in the demand functions because it is likely to be easier (less costly) for them to obtain alcoholic beverages in a state with a legal drinking age of eighteen than in one with a higher legal drinking age.[21] Twenty-one-year-olds are legal drinkers in all states, but they are not excluded from the demand functions because twenty-one-year-olds in states with a legal drinking age of eighteen will have been legal drinkers for a longer period of time than youths in states with a legal drinking age of nineteen, twenty, or twenty-one. This may have an effect on their consumption of alcoholic beverages. Although the sixteen through twenty-one age range is somewhat arbitrary, demand functions estimated with youths of slightly different ages (fifteen through twenty or sixteen through twenty) yield results that are very similar to those presented in section 3.

Alcoholic beverage prices and legal drinking ages have been added to the NHANES II survey based on a given youth's place of residence (primary sampling unit) from sources indicated in section 2.3. Since beer prices for the state of Hawaii were not available and since beer is the drink of choice among youths who consume alcoholic beverages (see section 2.2), youths residing in Honolulu, Hawaii, were excluded. After deleting observations with missing data, we obtained a final sample of 1,761 youths aged sixteen through twenty-one living in sixty-three of the sixty-four NHANES II primary sampling units.[22]

2.2. Measurement of Alcohol Use

The NHANES II alcohol use measures for the final sample of 1,761 youths are summarized by the percentage distributions of beverage-specific drinking frequencies in the past three months in panel A of table 14.1. These measures pertain to the number of drinking occasions per week in the past three months. Information about the number of drinks consumed in total or on a typical drinking occasion was not obtained. The figures in table 14.1 highlight the popularity of beer among teenagers and young adults. Approximately 57 percent of all youths drank beer in the past three months, while only 39 percent drank liquor and only 32 percent drank wine. Moreover, 11 percent of youths drank beer four to seven times a week, while fewer than 1 percent drank liquor or wine that often.

The beverage-specific number of drinking occasions in the past three months is a categorical variable in NHANES II, and the four categories shown in table 14.1 (four to seven times a week, one to three times a week, less than once a week, and never) are employed as outcome measures in demand functions estimated by multivariate techniques described in section 2.4.[23] Here it is important to note that the use of a categorical variable allows us to examine the determinants of beverage-specific drinking participation and infrequent, fairly frequent, and frequent participation simultaneously. It also permits the effect of prices and legal drinking ages on these outcomes to differ. In addition, if more alcohol is consumed per drinking occasion as the number of occasions rises, true consumption would not be linearly related to a continuous drinking-frequency measure. To take account of this nonlinearity, a categorical variable would be preferable to a continuous one even if the latter were available.

The number of drinking occasions per week is closely related to, and in a majority of cases probably coincides with, the number of drinking days per week. Under this interpretation, the most frequent drinking category identifies youths who consumed alcohol at least every other day in the past three months. Given the age cohort studied here, this is a very reasonable indicator of frequent consumption.

Information on alcohol consumption was obtained directly from youths in NHANES II. Parents were not present during the interviews with the youths and were not informed about the alcohol responses of their children. Nevertheless, there is a possibility that youths may report their alcohol use with error.[24] If any such response error is uncorrelated with the independent variables in the demand function for alcohol, coefficients will be unbiased, although their standard errors will be inflated. In this case, the existence of response error essentially presents no problem for the statistical analysis. Response error becomes a problem only if it is systematic or correlated with some or all of the variables in the demand functions.

The validity of the NHANES II alcohol measures is underscored by referring to the related problem of the measurement of cigarette smoking by adolescents. Williams and Gillies have reviewed the literature on self-reported smoking behavior of adolescents and have concluded "that teenagers probably do report 'truthfully' about their smoking behavior when anonymous questionnaires are used."[25] An additional consideration is that the drinking questions

Table 14.1 Variables Employed in Empirical Analysis

Panel A. Percentage distributions of beverage-specific drinking frequencies in past three months[a]

	Outcome Category			
Beverage	4–7 Times a Week	1–3 Times a Week	Less than Once a Week	Never
Beer	11.07	27.43	18.57	42.93
Liquor	.85	13.57	24.48	61.10
Wine	.85	9.20	22.37	67.58

Panel B. Definitions, means, and standard deviations of independent variables[b]

Variable Name	Definition
Real price of beer (1967 dollars)	Price of a package of six 12-ounce cans of a leading brand of beer divided by CPI, 1967 = 1 (mean = 1.027, SD = .116)
Real price of liquor (1967 dollars)	Price of Seagram's 7-Crown, 80 proof (40% alcohol), fifth-size bottle (four-fifths of a quart), divided by CPI, 1967 = 1 (mean = 2.941, SD = .309)
Beer legal drinking age (months)	Minimum legal age for purchase and consumption of beer, alcoholic content 3.2% or less (mean = 228.572, SD = 16.092)
Liquor legal drinking age (months)	Minimum legal age for purchase and consumption of liquor (mean = 234.835, SD = 17.651)
Border age	Dichotomous variable that equals 1 if youth lives within 20 miles of a state with a lower legal drinking age than his state of residence, computed separately for beer and liquor but assumed the same value for each beverage (mean = .197, SD = .398)
Mormon	Percentage of population who are Mormons in youth's primary sampling unit (mean = 1.585, SD = 8.323)
Southern Baptist	Percentage of population who are Southern Baptists in youth's primary sampling unit (mean = 7.955, SD = 13.179)
Catholic	Percentage of population who are Catholics in youth's primary sampling unit (mean = 19.161, SD = 15.708)
Protestant	Percentage of population who are Protestants in youth's primary sampling unit, excludes Southern Baptists and Mormons (mean = 20.465, SD = 8.389)

[a]Sample size is 1,761. For each beverage, the four cell entries give the percentage of all youths in each outcome category.

[b]SD denotes standard deviation.

were included as a small part of a much larger survey that was focused on very different issues. Gordon and Kannel argue that this improves the quality of reports of alcohol consumption.[26]

To be sure, it is possible that heavy consumers of alcoholic beverages are more likely to underreport their consumption than are other persons.[27] If heavy users are more likely to be found in areas with low prices or low legal drinking ages, estimates of the demand parameters of these variables are biased toward zero. This is another reason for the use of a categorical rather than a continuous drinking measure. In particular, the former does not assume a linear relation between true and reported consumption. Moreover, youths are unlikely to be found in one of the four outcome categories used here rather than in another as a result of reporting error.

2.3. Measurement of Independent Variables

Panel B of table 14.1 contains definitions, means, and standard deviations of the key independent variables in the demand functions. In addition to the variables listed in panel B, all demand functions include as regressors the youth's age in months on the date of his or her NHANES II examination, a dichotomous variable that identifies blacks, a dichotomous variable that identifies females, and real family income (family monetary income divided by the Consumer Price Index). We do not present or discuss the effects of these variables on alcohol use in section 3. But it should be realized that all estimated price and legal drinking age effects control for (hold constant) the effects of these variables.[28] We have used a relatively sparse set of independent variables because Arluck found that the coefficients of interest in NHANES I demand functions are not sensitive to the inclusion of additional family background and youth characteristics. They also do not change much when state-specific measures of the availability and regulation of alcohol are added to the set of independent variables.[29]

The minimum legal ages in months for the purchase of beer (alcoholic content 3.2 percent or less by weight) and liquor were taken from Wagenaar's (1981/1982) extremely painstaking and definitive compilation for every state for the years 1970 through 1981.[30] Each NHANES II youth was assigned beverage-specific legal drinking ages in his state of residence as of the midmonth of the three-month period culminating on the date of his examination. In principle, this algorithm takes account of the upward trend in state legal drinking ages during the period of the NHANES II examinations. In fact, only two NHANES II primary sampling units—Dakota, Minnesota, and Hennepin, Minnesota— are in a state that raised its legal drinking age during a three-month period culminating on the date of the examination or before that period. All other states that raised their legal drinking age did so after the NHANES II examinations in those states were completed.[31]

Youths who reside in a state with a high legal drinking age may be able to purchase alcohol in a border state with a lower legal drinking age. To deal with this phenomenon, we created a dichotomous variable that equals one for youths who live within twenty miles of a state with a lower legal drinking age than the one in their state of residence. With the own-state legal drinking age held constant, the coefficient of the border age variable in the demand functions should be positive.

An alternative model of drinking age effects results when the two variables just defined are replaced by dichotomous variables that identify youths who are illegal drinkers in their own state but legal drinkers in the border state. This model is less flexible than the one that we used because it does not recognize that evasion of drinking age laws by an illegal drinker is easier (less costly) the closer the person is to the legal drinking age in his state of residence or in the border state. Consider two eighteen-year-olds who are identical in all respects except that one resides in a state with a legal drinking age of nineteen, while the other resides in a state with a drinking age of twenty-one. Since peers are a common source of alcohol,[32] the indirect cost of obtaining alcohol is likely to be lower for the first youth than for the second. Moreover, it should be easier for an eighteen-year-old to pass for nineteen than for twenty-one.

Our specification also is preferable to the alternative model because it allows for the negative relation that frequently has been reported between age at onset of alcohol consumption and current use.[33] Put differently, current use is expected to be positively related to the number of years that a youth has been a legal drinker. Thus, a twenty-year-old in a state with a legal drinking age of eighteen should not be constrained by the specification to consume the same quantity of alcohol as an otherwise identical youth in a state with a drinking age of twenty.

Since the youth's age is included as an independent variable, the specification employed here is equivalent to one in which alcohol use (y) depends on the youth's age (a), the difference between the legal drinking age and age ($x_1 = d - a$), and a vector of additional variables (x_2):

$$y = \alpha_0 + \alpha_1 a + \alpha_2 x_1 + \alpha_3 x_2. \tag{1}$$

Substitute the definition of x_1 into this equation to obtain

$$y = \alpha_0 + (\alpha_1 - \alpha_2)a + \alpha_2 d + \alpha_3 x_2. \tag{2}$$

The coefficient of x_1 in the first equation is identical to the coefficient of d in the second equation. A dichotomous variable identifying illegal drinkers cannot be added to equation (2) because of multicollinearity. Consequently, for the reasons given above, our specification has more desirable properties than the one in which the drinking age is replaced by the illegal drinker identifier.

The beer price variable pertains to the transactions price of a single leading brand of medium-priced, nationally sold beer. The specific brand is confidential. Prices are reported in two unidentified major markets in each state (one in the cases of Rhode Island and the District of Columbia) in January and July of 1976, 1977, and 1978 and in January of 1979. The data were obtained by Stanley Ornstein[34] and kindly made available to us.

Monthly prices for each state from January 1976 through January 1979 were obtained by linear interpolation of state-specific price series, computed by averaging the two prices for each state at a moment in time. Monthly prices for the period February 1979 through January 1980 were predicted from a regression of the state price on the state excise tax rate, time (a continuous variable), and dichotomous variables for all contiguous states except one.[35] The beer price of the midmonth in the three month period for which alcoholic beverage consumption was reported was then assigned to each subject.[36] To take account of trends in the prices of other goods during the four-year period of NHANES II, the monthly beer price is divided by the annual Consumer Price Index (CPI, 1967 = 1) to obtain the real or relative price of beer.[37]

The real price of liquor is given by the price of Seagram's 7-Crown (a blended whiskey) divided by the CPI. This price is selected because Seagram's 7-Crown was the leading brand of liquor in the United States during the period of NHANES II, and its price commonly is used as a standard in the liquor industry. It was obtained from the annual survey of the retail prices of eight leading brands of distilled spirits in each state conducted by the Distilled Spirits Council of the United States and kindly made available to us by Gary Marshall.[38]

There were no data available on wine prices by state for the period of NHANES II. As a result, wine demand functions are not presented in the following section.

To take account of the potential role of "drinking sentiment" in the endogenous determination of alcoholic beverage prices, legal drinking ages, and alcohol consumption, the percentages of the population in a youth's primary sampling unit who are Mormons, Southern Baptists, Catholics, and Protestants (excluding Southern Baptists and Mormons) are included in some specifications of the demand functions. Drinking sentiment refers to cultural and taste variables that may either encourage or discourage alcohol consumption. For example, antidrinking sentiment should be relatively widespread in states where religious groups that oppose the use of alcohol, such as Mormons and Southern Baptists, are prevalent. These states may enact high alcoholic beverage excise tax rates as part of the political process. In this situation, the price coefficients that emerge from demand functions that omit drinking sentiment overstate in absolute value the true parameters. On the other hand, states in which prodrinking sentiment is prevalent (antidrinking sentiment is weak) and alcohol consumption is high may enact high excise tax rates because the taxation of alcoholic beverages is an attractive source of revenue. In this case, the price effects are understated if drinking sentiment is excluded from the demand functions.[39]

The preceding issue is illuminated with reference to an econometric model of the determinants of beer consumption, both at the aggregate (state or county) level and at the individual level (available on request). The price of beer, the legal drinking age, drinking sentiment, and beer consumption are treated as endogenous. The model is recursive rather than simultaneous, but the disturbance terms in the price and demand equations, for example, are correlated. This is because drinking sentiment is not observed. Instead, it must be replaced by a vector of observable variables whose elements in the state model include the state-specific equivalents of the religion measures in table 14.2 and a disturbance term.

Biases arise if the demand function is estimated by ordinary least squares because the disturbance terms in that equation and the price equation share a common element: the unobserved component of drinking sentiment. It is shown, however, that the importance of omitted variables bias is greatly reduced when individual demand functions are estimated with drinking sentiment omitted. This is because an individual consumer's beer consumption depends on his drinking sentiment, while the tax on beer or its price depends on the average value of drinking sentiment in the relevant market area. Therefore, the correlation between price (a state or county variable) and drinking sentiment is much weaker in micro data than in aggregate data.

The above conclusion is important because no measures of an individual's religious preference are available in NHANES II, and two-stage least squares estimation of demand functions with price treated as endogenous is not feasible. Some demand functions are obtained with the four primary sample-specific religion variables listed in table 14.2. These results should, however, be interpreted with caution because the price of beer or liquor is specific to the state rather than to the primary sampling unit. Given errors of measurement in price and correlations between true price and the religion variables, price coefficients are biased toward zero and religion coefficients are biased away from zero. Therefore, we wish to reemphasize that price effects are not necessarily overstated in absolute value when drinking sentiment is excluded from the demand functions. We also wish to reemphasize that the most relevant religion measure is the youth's own religious preference. In theory, this variable is more closely related

Table 14.2 Maximum Likelihood Estimates of Multinomial Logit Beer Frequency Equations[a]

	Outcome Category		
Independent Variable	4–7 Times a Week	1–3 Times a Week	Less Than Once a Week
Panel A. Religion variables excluded:			
Real price of beer	−1.790	−1.209	−.587
	(−2.12)	(−2.19)	(−1.01)
Beer legal drinking age	−.024	−.015	−.008
	(−3.69)	(−3.24)	(−1.62)
Border age	.196	.366	.279
	(.74)	(2.01)	(1.43)
x^2	383.77		
Panel B. Religion variables included:			
Real price of beer	−1.028	−.987	−.714
	(−1.12)	(−1.57)	(−1.07)
Beer legal drinking age	−.019	−.008	−.001
	(−2.63)	(−1.68)	(−.28)
Border age	−.079	.994	.008
	(−.27)	(.51)	(.04)
Mormon	−.026	−.010	−.019
	(−1.38)	(−1.16)	(−1.58)
Southern Baptist	−.031	−.021	−.014
	(−3.09)	(−3.23)	(−1.98)
Catholic	.013	.015	.012
	(1.48)	(2.47)	(1.79)
Protestant	.028	.035	.039
	(1.91)	(3.44)	(3.62)
x^2	464.18		

[a]Logit coefficients and asymptotic *t*-ratios in parentheses are shown. The critical asymptotic *t*-ratios at the 5 percent level are 1.64 for a one-tailed test and 1.96 for a two-tailed test. The x^2 associated with each equation is significant at the 1 percent level. Each equation includes three intercepts and the following additional independent variables: age of youth in months, race of youth, sex of youth, and real family income.

to the youth's consumption of alcohol but less closely related to price than the community religion variables that are actually employed as regressors.

The religion variables pertain to 1980, and were taken from a survey conducted by the National Council of Churches of Christ and the Glenmary Research Center.[40] Jews are included with nonchurch members in the omitted category because the size of the Jewish population was significantly underestimated in the survey. The religion measures pertain to the youth's primary sampling unit of residence rather than to his state of residence because the former are better predictors of the youth's actual religion.

An alternate specification of drinking sentiment results when the religion measures are replaced by average alcohol use by persons over the age of twenty-one in the youth's primary sampling unit of residence. Adult drinking practices should be influenced by the same underlying sentiments that influence youthful drinking practices, all other things being equal. This is an indirect effect that is associated with the ecology of the social drinking environment.

We have rejected the above specification of drinking sentiment on theoretical, econometric, and empirical grounds. Theoretically, an increase in price will reduce adult consumption. Thus, a rise in price will curtail youth consumption directly and indirectly via its effect on adult consumption. We are concerned with the total price effect, whereas the youth price coefficient from a model that includes adult drinking gives the difference between the youth and adult price effects.[41] To be sure, we could obtain one set of results with adult consumption as a regressor and a second set that excludes that control. The first set of results could be used to isolate the other effect of interest in our research, the legal drinking age. The econometric problem here, however, is that the disturbance term in the youth demand function is correlated with adult alcohol use (see note 41). Empirically, NHANES II is representative of the population of the United States, but it is not representative of the population of each primary sampling unit. Thus, it is inappropriate to estimate mean alcohol consumption by adults in a given community from the sample.

Although youths are more likely to drink if their peers also drink, it is inappropriate to include peers' consumption of alcohol in the demand functions. This is because peer behavior is an endogenous rather than an exogenous variable in a more broadly defined model of drinking. That is, peer behavior is determined by such a model rather than by factors not specified by the model. For instance, suppose that one is evaluating a policy to curtail youth drinking by raising the federal excise tax rate on beer. An increase in the tax would raise the price of beer paid by youths and their peers, which would discourage consumption by both groups. Therefore, in evaluating the effect of such a policy, peers' beer consumption should not be held constant (included in the demand equation).

2.4. Estimation Techniques

The beverage-specific frequency of drinking in the past three months consists of four outcome categories (see table 14.1). Therefore, multinomial logit equations are fitted by the method of maximum likelihood. In the case of beer, let π_{i1}, π_{i2},

$\pi_i 3$, and π_{i4} be the probabilities that the ith youth consumes beer four to seven times a week, one to three times a week, less than once a week, and never, respectively. The probability of the kth outcome (π_{ik}, $k = 1, 2, 3$) is

$$\pi_{ik} = \pi_{i4} \exp\left(\alpha_k + \sum_{t=1}^{n} \beta_{kt} x_{it}\right), \tag{3}$$

where x_{it} is the value of the tth independent variable for the ith youth. The logarithm of the odds of category k relative to category 4 is

$$\ln(\pi_{ik} / \pi_{i4}) = \alpha_k + \sum_{t} \beta_{kt} x_{it}. \tag{4}$$

The logit coefficient β_{kt} shows the percentage change in the odds of category i relative to no beer participation for a one unit change in x_{it}. The marginal effect of x_{it} on π_{ik} is

$$(\partial \pi_{ik} / \partial x_{kt}) = \pi_{ik} \beta_{kt} - \pi_{ik} \sum_{k=1}^{3} \pi_{ik} \beta_{kt}. \tag{5}$$

Multinomial logit estimation methods are discussed in detail by Maddala.[42] Here it is important to emphasize several features of our estimates. The measures of drinking frequency are ordered categorical variables, but we do not use the ordered logit model. This is because that model does not allow for nonlinear and possibly nonmonotonic effects of the independent variables on the outcomes at issue.

Since the beer frequency equation, for example, contains non-beer drinkers (the omitted category), it gives an estimate of the effect of each independent variable on the probability of no beer participation.[43] We do not model beer consumption as a two-stage process in which youths first determine whether they will drink beer and then determine the frequency of beer consumption, given participation. In the two-stage model, nonbeer participants would be excluded from the equation for frequency. We do not use this model because it is appropriate only when the determinants of participation differ from those of frequency. This condition is not satisfied in our research.[44]

3. RESULTS

Table 14.2 contains maximum likelihood estimates of multinomial logit beer frequency equations. Logit coefficients and their asymptotic t-ratios are shown.[45] An equation that excludes the four religion measures is presented in panel A of the table, while an equation that includes them is presented in panel B. In the discussion of these results, youths who drink beer four to seven times a week are termed frequent drinkers; those who drink one to three times a week are termed fairly frequent drinkers; and those who drink less than once a week are termed infrequent drinkers.

In the beer frequency equation in panel A, the logit coefficients of the real price of beer and the legal drinking age all are negative and are statistically significant at the 5 percent level of significance or better, except in the infrequent drinking category.[46] The border legal age coefficients have the appropriate positive signs, but only the coefficient pertaining to fairly frequent drinking is significant.

There is a perfect rank correlation between the absolute values of the price and legal drinking age coefficients and the number of drinking occasions represented by each outcome category. That is, the logit coefficient of price in the frequent drinking category exceeds the corresponding coefficient in the fairly frequent category. In turn, the latter exceeds the logit coefficient of price in the infrequent category. In general, this guarantees that an increase in price lowers the probabilities of frequent and fairly frequent drinking. Indeed, the price elasticities of the probabilities of frequent and fairly frequent beer consumption are substantial: −1.18 and −0.59, respectively. The price elasticity of the probability of infrequent drinking is positive and very small (0.05), which indicates that the probability of infrequent drinking rises (but by a smaller percentage than that of nonparticipation) as the real price of beer rises. The positive price elasticity of the probability of nonparticipation of 0.65 is relatively large.[47]

The price and legal drinking age effects retain their negative signs and relative rankings when the religion variables are included as regressors (see panel B, table 14.2), but the significant coefficients in the equation in panel A are reduced in absolute value. In percentage terms these reductions range from 47 percent for the legal drinking age coefficient associated with the fairly frequent outcome category to 18 percent for the price coefficient in the same category. The two significant legal drinking age coefficients in panel A retain their significance in panel B. The price coefficients, however, lose their significance at the 5 percent level, although the t-ratio associated with each coefficient exceeds one in absolute value. The price elasticities are still relatively large: −0.53 for the probability of frequent drinking, −0.48 for the probability of fairly frequent drinking, −0.20 for the probability of infrequent drinking, and 0.53 for the probability of no drinking. For all practical purposes, there are no border age effects when the religion variables are held constant. The frequency of beer consumption is negatively related to the percentage of Mormons or Southern Baptists in the primary sampling unit, while it is positively related to the percentage of Catholics or Protestants.

Recall from section 3.3 that the price and legal drinking age coefficients are likely to be conservative lower-bound estimates of the true parameters with the religion variables included in the demand equations. Also, the corresponding coefficients obtained without controlling for religion are not necessarily upper-bound estimates of the true parameters. In light of these considerations, the findings that the real beer price coefficients retain their signs and relative rankings, and that the beer legal drinking age coefficients retain their signs, rankings, and statistical significance, are impressive and important.

Fewer negative and significant price and legal drinking age effects emerge from the demand functions for liquor (not shown) than from the demand functions for beer. Moreover, the negative liquor price elasticities are smaller in absolute value than the corresponding beer price elasticities. For these reasons, and because beer is the most popular alcoholic beverage among youths, we focus on the frequency of beer consumption in the remainder of this article.

In logit equations not shown, the real price of liquor was included in the demand functions for beer. No evidence of substitution between beer and liquor was revealed by these equations. In most cases, the cross price effect was negative (suggesting complementarity) but not significant. This finding is probably not an artifact of multicollinearity; the simple correlation coefficient between the price of beer and liquor is positive but not substantial ($r = .19$).

To evaluate the potential effect of the federal excise tax and legal drinking age policy initiatives discussed in section 1, we simulate their effects on the frequency of beer consumption by youths. Specifically, we first compute the "actual" percentage distribution of the frequency of beer consumption (four to seven times a week, one to three times a week, less than once a week, and never) by predicting the four outcome probabilities (π_{ik}) for each youth based on the logit coefficients and the actual value of each independent variable (x_{it}) for that youth (see equation [3] and the second equation in note 43 *supra*). Next, we average each of the four outcome probabilities over all youths. Then we vary one or more of the independent variables by a certain amount, recompute each π_{ik} and average a given probability over all youths. This gives a "new" percentage distribution.

The legal drinking age policy pertains to a uniform minimum age of twenty-one for the purchase of beer in all states. This policy is simulated by setting the beer legal drinking age equal to twenty-one for each youth in our NHANES II sample and by setting the border age variable equal to zero. The resulting distribution shows the percentage distribution of the frequency of beer consumption that would have been observed if the legal drinking age had been twenty-one throughout the period of the NHANES II survey (February 1976–February 1980).

Three federal excise tax policies are considered. The first indexes the federal excise tax on a six-pack of beer, which has been fixed at $.16 in nominal terms since 1951, to the rate of inflation since 1951. It is termed the inflation tax policy. Under it, the real price of beer in 1967 dollars faced by an NHANES II youth examined in year t becomes

$$p_t^* = [p_t - \$.16 + (\$.16)(c_{t,51})] / (c_{t,67}),$$
(6)

where p_t is the actual money price faced by the youth, $c_{t,51}$ is the CPI in year t relative to 1951, and $c_{t,67}$ is the CPI in year t relative to 1967. The second tax policy raises the excise tax on a six-pack of beer from $.16 to $.52 to equalize the rates at which the alcohol in beer and liquor are taxed (see note 10 *supra*). It is termed the alcohol tax equalization policy. In this simulation the real beer price is given by

$$p_t' = (p_t - \$.16 + \$.52) / (c_{t,67}).$$
(7)

The third tax policy combines the first two and is termed the combined tax policy. The real beer price is given by

$$\hat{p}_t = [p_t - \$.16 + (\$.52)(c_{t,51})] / (c_{t,67}).$$
(8)

The resulting simulation contains the percentage distribution of beer consumption that would have prevailed if the excise tax had been indexed to the rate of inflation since 1951 during the period of NHANES II and if the alcohol in beer had been taxed as heavily as the alcohol in liquor.

Each tax policy simulation assumes that a tax increase is fully passed on to consumers or that the beer industry is competitive and has an infinitely elastic supply curve. The inflation excise tax policy causes the price of beer to rise by approximately 12 percent in the sample period. The alcohol tax equalization policy involves an 18 percent increase in price. Both policies combined amount to a substantial rise of 57 percent in the price of beer.[48] Although the price of beer rises relative to the price of liquor, our demand function estimates suggest that youths would not substitute liquor for beer. Thus, cross price effects are assumed to be zero in the simulations.

Table 14.3 contains the results of the simulations. Two simulations of each policy are presented. The first is based on the beer demand function that excludes the religion variables, while the second is based on the beer demand function that includes the religion variables.

According to panels A and B of table 14.3, the number of youths who drink beer frequently (11 percent of all youths on the basis of actual values of all

Table 14.3 Predicted Effects of Imposition of a Uniform Legal Drinking Age of Twenty-One or Increase in Federal Excise Tax on Beer on Frequency of Beer Consumption

Outcome Category	Actual Percentage Distribution	New Percentage Distribution	Percentage Change in Number of Youths in Each Category[a]
	Panel A. Uniform legal drinking age of 21, religion variables excluded		
4–7 times a week	10.99	7.84	−28.66
1–3 times a week	27.74	23.48	−15.36
Less than once a week	18.78	18.21	−3.04
Never	42.49	50.47	+ 18.78
	Panel B. Uniform legal drinking age of 21, religion variables included		
4–7 times a week	11.43	8.40	−26.51
1–3 times a week	27.27	25.24	−7.44
Less than once a week	18.51	19.96	+ 7.83
Never	42.78	46.40	+ 8.46
	Panel C. Inflation tax policy, religion variables excluded		
4–7 times a week	10.99	9.83	−10.56
1–3 times a week	27.74	26.15	−5.73
Less than once a week	18.78	18.81	+ .16
Never	42.49	45.21	+ 6.40
	Panel D. Inflation tax policy, religion variables included		
4–7 times a week	11.43	10.97	−4.02
1–3 times a week	27.27	26.00	−4.66
Less than once a week	18.51	18.06	−2.43
Never	42.78	44.97	+ 5.12
	Panel E. Alcohol tax equalization policy, religion variables excluded		
4–7 times a week	10.99	9.21	−16.20
1–3 times a week	27.74	25.27	−8.90
Less than once a week	18.78	18.80	+ .11
Never	42.49	46.72	+ 9.96
	Panel F. Alcohol tax equalization policy, religion variables included		
4–7 times a week	11.43	10.70	−6.39
1–3 times a week	27.27	25.29	−7.26
Less than once a week	18.51	17.80	−3.84
Never	42.78	46.21	+ 8.02

(*continued*)

Table 14.3 (*Continued*)

Outcome Category	Actual Percentage Distribution	New Percentage Distribution	Percentage Change in Number of Youths in Each Category[a]
	Panel G. Combined tax policy, religion variables excluded		
4–7 times a week	10.99	6.15	−44.04
1–3 times a week	27.74	20.13	−27.43
Less than once a week	18.78	18.29	−2.61
Never	42.49	55.43	+ 30.45
	Panel H. Combined tax policy, religion variables included		
4–7 times a week	11.43	9.19	−19.60
1–3 times a week	27.27	21.25	−22.08
Less than once a week	18.51	16.11	.−12.97
Never	42.78	53.45	+ 24.94

[a]Column 2 minus column 1 divided by column 1 and multiplied by 100.

independent variables) or fairly frequently (28 percent of all youths, which is an average of the actual percentages in panels A and B) falls substantially in response to the enactment of a uniform legal drinking age of twenty-one in all states. To be precise, the number of frequent beer drinkers falls by 29 percent in panel A and by 27 percent in panel B. At the same time, the number of fairly frequent beer drinkers falls by 15 percent in the former panel and by 7 percent in the latter panel. These declines imply increases in the number of youths who do not drink beer (43 percent of all youths) that range from 8 percent to 19 percent. If averages of the figures in the last columns of panels A and B are taken as "best estimates," then the drinking-age policy causes the number of youths who drink beer four to seven times a week to fall by 28 percent and the number who drink beer one to three times a week to fall by 11 percent. Simultaneously, the number of infrequent beer drinkers rises by 2 percent and the number of nonparticipants rises by 14 percent.

Either of the two excise tax policies taken alone produces smaller declines in the number of frequent or fairly frequent beer drinkers than the drinking age policy. On the basis of the best estimates (averages of the figures in the last columns of panels C and D), the inflation tax policy causes the number of youths in the former category to decline by 8 percent and the number of youths in the latter category to fall by 6 percent. The corresponding reductions under the alcohol tax equalization policy are 11 percent and 8 percent (see panels E and F).

Under the combined tax policy, the incidence of excessive drinking falls dramatically (see panels G and H). To be specific, the numbers of youths who drink beer four to seven times a week, one to three times a week, and less than once a week fall by 32 percent, 24 percent, and 8 percent, respectively.[49] Simultaneously, the number of youths who do not drink beer rises by 28 percent.

Although the combined tax policy has somewhat larger effects on the rates of frequent and fairly frequent beer consumption than the drinking age policy, it probably is more notable that both policies have sizable negative effects on these measures of beer consumption. Put differently, the negative responses are not limited to the probability of infrequent drinking. Indeed, that probability rises under the drinking age policy. It falls under the tax policy but by a smaller percentage amount than the other two probabilities. Even the absolute reduction in the infrequent drinking rate (1 percentage point on average) is smaller than the absolute reductions in the fairly frequent and frequent rates (seven percentage points and four percentage points, respectively).

4. SUMMARY

To summarize, our results suggest that the frequency of the consumption of beer, the most popular alcoholic beverage among youths, is inversely related to the real price of beer and to the minimum legal age for its purchase and consumption. The negative price and legal drinking age effects are by no means limited to reductions in the fraction of youths who consume beer infrequently (less than once a week). Instead, the fractions of youths who consume beer fairly frequently (one to three times a week) and frequently (four to seven times a week) fall more in absolute or percentage terms than the fraction of infrequent drinkers when price or the drinking age rises. These are striking findings because frequent and fairly frequent drinkers are likely to be responsible for a large percentage of youth motor vehicle accidents and deaths.

With regard to the magnitude of the effects at issue, a federal policy that simultaneously taxes the alcohol in beer and liquor at the same rates and offsets the erosion in the real beer tax since 1951 would have reduced the number of youths who drink beer frequently (approximately 11 percent of all youths) by 32 percent during the period of NHANES II and would have reduced the number of fairly frequent beer drinkers (approximately 28 percent of all youths) by 24 percent. The enactment of a minimum uniform drinking age of twenty-one in all states would have reduced the number of frequent drinkers by 28 percent and the number of fairly frequent drinkers by 11 percent. These figures suggest that, if reductions in youth alcohol use and abuse are desired, both a uniform drinking age of twenty-one and an increase in the federal excise tax rate on beer are effective policies to accomplish this goal.[50]

They also suggest that the tax policy may be more potent than the drinking age policy.

It does not follow that we have provided enough evidence to justify the approximately eightfold (thirteenfold on the basis of the 1984 CPI) increase in the federal excise tax on beer that serves as the basis of the above computations. Excise tax hikes impose welfare costs on all segments of the population, while a drinking age policy is targeted at the group in the population that accounts for a disproportionate share of motor vehicle accidents and deaths. On the other hand, the enforcement and administrative costs associated with a uniform minimum drinking age of twenty-one may exceed those associated with the tax policy. Moreover, an excise tax increase may reduce excessive alcohol consumption by adults as well as by youths. Of course, a substantial tax hike may stimulate the demand for illegally produced beer, suggesting that we have overestimated the effect of an eightfold increase in the federal excise tax on beer unless the legal and illegal prices are the same.

Finally, Becker has shown that the optimal way for a society to deter offenses is via a system of severe and fairly certain punishments.[51] In the case of drunk driving, these might take the form of loss of driving privileges for long periods of time, mandatory community service, enrollment in alcohol rehabilitation programs, and prison sentences for repeat offenders. Of course, youthful drunk drivers may respond to an increase in the penalty of this offense only if the probabilities of apprehension and conviction are nontrivial. If substantial resources must be allocated to raising these probabilities, the excise tax policy may be preferable to or complementary with a system of severe penalties. Moreover, severe and certain punishments for drunk driving do not address the problems caused by the link between youth alcohol abuse and adult alcohol abuse. In conclusion, more research is required to formulate the best mix of policies to deal with youth alcohol abuse. Our study represents a useful first step in this process.

NOTES

Originally published as Douglas Coate and Michael Grossman, "Effects of Alcoholic Beverage Prices and Legal Drinking Ages on Youth Alcohol Use," *Journal of Law and Economics* 31, no. 1 (1988): 145–171. Research for this article was supported by grant 5 R01 AA05849 from the National Institute on Alcohol Abuse and Alcoholism to the National Bureau of Economic Research. We are indebted to Gary Marshall for providing us with data on the price of Seagram's 7-Crown and to Stanley I. Ornstein for providing us with data on the price of a leading brand of beer. We wish to thank Gary S. Becker, Philip J. Cook, Michael Jacobson, Patrick King, Kevin M. Murphy, Stanley I. Ornstein, and an anonymous referee for helpful comments. We also wish to thank Frank

Chaloupka and Emil Berendt for research assistance. This article has not undergone the review accorded official NBER publications; in particular, it has not been submitted for approval by the Board of Directors.

1. Federal Uniform Drinking Age Act Pub. L. No. 98–363 (1984).

2. The increases in the legal drinking age documented above represent a dramatic reversal of the downward trend between 1970 and 1975. In that period, twenty-nine states lowered their drinking age to conform with a federal shift in the voting age from twenty-one to eighteen in 1970.

3. The federal excise tax rate on distilled spirits was raised from $10.50 per proof gallon to $12.50, effective October 1, 1985, as part of the Deficit Reduction Act of 1984.

4. U.S. Dep't of Labor, Bureau of Labor Statistics, Monthly Labor Review (various issues).

5. Philip J. Cook and George Tauchen, "The Effect of Liquor Taxes on Heavy Drinking," 13 *Bell J. Econ.* 379 (1982).

6. The above figures were taken from U.S. Dep't of Transportation, Nat'l Highway Traffic Safety Administration, Fatal Accident Reporting System, 1984 (1986).

7. Robert B. Voas and John Moulden, "Historical Trends in Alcohol Use and Driving by Young Americans, in Minimum-Drinking Age Laws: An Evaluation" 59 (Henry Wechsler ed. 1980).

8. Howard T. Blane and Linda E. Hewitt, "Alcohol and Youth: An Analysis of the Literature" (report prepared for the Nat'l Inst. on Alcohol Abuse and Alcoholism, 1977); J. Valley Rachal et al., "The Extent and Nature of Adolescent Alcohol Use: The 1974 and 1978 National Sample Survey," Nat'l Technical Information Service (1980).

9. For example, Allan Luks, *Will America Sober Up?* (1983); Philip J. Cook, "Increasing the Federal Excise Tax," in *Toward the Prevention of Alcohol Problems: Government, Business, and Community Action* 24 (Dean R. Gerstein ed. 1984); Gary S. Becker, "Don't Raise the Drinking Age, Raise Taxes," *Bus. Week*, November 25, 1985, at 21; Michael Jacobson and Mark Albion, "Raising Alcohol Taxes Is the Way to Cut Drinking and the Debt," *Wash. Post*, August 11, 1985, at L2. Under an ad valorem alcoholic beverage excise tax system, the tax rate would be set at a fixed proportion of wholesale price.

10. For example, Jeffrey E. Harris, "More Data on Tax Policy," in Gerstein, *supra* note 9, at 33; Jacobson and Albion, *supra* note 9. Under the federal excise tax on liquor of $10.50 per gallon of liquor (50 percent alcohol by volume) in effect prior to October 1, 1985, one gallon of alcohol in liquor was taxed at a rate of $21.00. Since the federal excise tax on beer is $.29 per gallon, and since one gallon of beer contains 4.5 percent alcohol by volume, the tax rate on one gallon of alcohol in beer is $6.44. The alcohol in liquor is taxed fifteen times as heavily as the alcohol in wine, and the proposals mentioned here also contain provisions to correct this distortion.

11. Henry Saffer and Michael Grossman, "Beer Taxes, the Legal Drinking Age, and Youth Motor Vehicle Fatalities," *16 J. Legal Stud.* 351 (1987).

12. Originally, the penalties imposed on states with a drinking age below twenty-one by the Federal Uniform Drinking Age Act of 1984 were scheduled to expire at the end of fiscal 1988. In response to this provision, Texas and Nebraska adopted laws that called for a revocation of the twenty-one drinking age as soon as the legislation expired. See Insurance

Inst. for Highway Safety, 20 The Highway Loss Status Report 1 (1985). To counteract these laws, the federal legislation was made permanent in 1986. South Dakota challenged the constitutionality of the 1984 Federal Uniform Drinking Age Act in a suit before the Supreme Court, South Dakota v. Dole, No. 86–260 (December 1986), which was supported by eight additional states. In June 1987, the Court ruled against South Dakota.

13. Michael Grossman, Douglas Coate, and Gregory M. Arluck, "Price Sensitivity of Alcoholic Beverages in the United States," in Control Issues in Alcohol Abuse Prevention: Strategies for Communities 169 (Harold D. Holder ed. 1987).

14. For example, Reginald G. Smart and Michael S. Goodstadt, "Effects of Reducing the Legal Alcohol-Purchasing Age on Drinking and Drinking Problems," 38 *J. Stud. Alcohol* 1313 (1977); Alexander C. Wagenaar, *Alcohol, Young Drivers, and Traffic Accidents* (1983). Stephen A. Maistro and J. Valley Rachai, "Indications of the Relationship among Adolescent Drinking Practices, Related Behaviors, and Drinking-Age Laws," in Wechsler, *supra* note 7, at 155, have studied the effects of differences in legal drinking ages among states on teenage alcohol use in a 1978 national drinking survey. Their research is limited to youths who are almost all below the lowest legal drinking age of eighteen and is conducted in a univariate context.

15. Grossman, Coate, and Arluck, *supra* note 13.

16. For example, Stanley I. Ornstein, "Control of Alcohol Consumption through Price Increases," 41 *J. Stud. Alcohol* 807 (1980); Stanley I. Ornstein and Dominique M. Hanssens, "Alcohol Control Laws and the Consumption of Distilled Spirits and Beer," 12 *J. Consumer Res.* 200 (1985).

17. For example, Blane and Hewitt, *supra* note 8 and Rachai et al., *supra* note 8.

18. Harvey Liebenstein, "Bandwagon, Snob, and Veblen Effects in the Theory of Consumer Behavior," 64 *Q. J. Econ.* 183 (1950); Eugene M. Lewit, Douglas Coate, and Michael Grossman, "The Effects of Government Regulation on Teenage Smoking," 24 *J. Law and Econ.* 545 (1981).

19. In a penetrating economic analysis of rational addiction over the life cycle, Gary S. Becker and Kevin M. Murphy, "A Theory of Rational Addiction," 96 *J. Political Econ.* 675 (1986), show that the effect of habit formation or peer pressure on price responsiveness depends on whether the price variation is permanent or temporary, whether the magnitude of the effect is measured by the slope or the elasticity, and whether the outcome pertains to the probability of consuming the addictive good or to consumption given participation. In certain cases, adults can be more responsive to price than youths in their model, while in other cases the reverse holds.

20. The NHANES II is described in detail in U.S. Dep't of Health and Human Services, Nat'l Center for Health Statistics, Plan and Operation of the Second Health and Nutrition Examination Survey, 1976–80 (1981).

21. Philip J. Cook and George Tauchen, "The Effects of Minimum Drinking Age Legislation on Youthful Auto Fatalities, 1970–77," 13 *J. Legal Stud.* 169 (1984).

22. Of the variables employed in the demand functions, the only ones with missing values are alcohol use and family income. In each case the number of observations with missing values is very small.

23. The actual beverage-specific frequency measure in NHANES II has more categories than those given in table 14.1. The complete set of outcomes is never, less than once a week, 1–6 times a week (each of the 6 outcomes can be reported), and 1–24 times a day (each of the 24 outcomes can be reported). We collapse these 32 outcomes into 4 because, as indicated in the text, the number of drinks consumed per drinking occasion is likely to rise as the number of occasions rises and because very frequent consumers are likely to underreport. In addition, it is possible that respondents in the 1–24 times a day categories drink every day and are indicating the number of drinks consumed per day or on a typical drinking day. For these reasons, we do not form a separate category of 7 or more times a week. We have experimented with several alternative categorical variables and have found that the demand function estimates are similar to those presented in section 3.

24. Past surveys of alcohol use by all segments of the population have been criticized because of apparent under-reporting. If national alcoholic beverage sales data are compared to national consumption estimates that are based on survey data, underreporting by survey respondents appears to range between 20 percent and 50 percent. For discussions of under reporting, see Lorraine Midanik, "The Validity of Self-reported Alcohol Consumption and Alcohol Problems: A Literature Review," 77 *Brit. J. Addiction* 357 (1982); and J. Michael Polich, "The Validity of Self-Reports in Alcoholism Research," 7 *Addictive Behaviors* 123 (1982). For reasons indicated, underreporting is not likely to be a problem in our research.

25. Ruth Williams and Pam Gillies, "Do We Need Objective Measures to Validate Self-Reported Smoking?" 98 *Pub. Health London* 297 (1984).

26. Tavia Gordon and William B. Kannel, "Drinking and Its Relation to Smoking, BP, Blood Lipids and Uric Acid," 143 *Archives Internal Medicine* 1366 (1983).

27. Midanik, *supra* note 24; Polich, *supra* note 24.

28. Briefly, the results indicate that the frequency of alcohol use rises sharply with age. Males drink more frequently than females, and whites drink more frequently than blacks. Real family income is not a significant determinant of youth alcohol use.

29. Gregory M. Arluck, "Economic and Other Factors in Youth Alcohol Use" (unpublished PhD dissertation, City Univ. New York Graduate School 1987). The availability and regulatory measures considered by Arluck include the per capita number of establishments that are licensed to sell alcoholic beverages, a dichotomous variable that indicates whether off-premise alcoholic beverage stores are state owned and operated, a dichotomous variable that indicates whether drug and grocery stores can sell alcoholic beverages, and a dichotomous variable that indicates whether billboard advertising of alcoholic beverages is allowed. All of them pertain to the state in which a given youth resides. Arluck's results are based on ordinary least squares regressions. It is beneficial for us to limit the set of independent variables because the estimation techniques that we employ (see section 3.4) are computer intensive.

30. Alexander C. Wagenaar, "Legal Minimum Drinking Age Changes in the United States: 1970–1981," 6 *Alcohol Health and Res. World* 21 (1981/82). In the case of beer, a few states have two legal drinking ages. One age is for beer that contains 3.2 percent or less alcohol by weight, and the second and higher age is for beer that contains more than 3.2

percent alcohol by weight. We use the former variable, but it is very highly correlated with the latter. The beer and liquor legal drinking ages also are highly correlated (the latter is always greater than or equal to the former) and cannot be included in the same demand equation. If beer and liquor were substitutes, an increase in the liquor legal drinking age should increase the demand for beer. Studies summarized by Ornstein, *supra* note 16, however, find almost no substitution among alcoholic beverages. Additional evidence on this lack of substitution is reported in section 3.

31. This statement also pertains to the border legal drinking age variable described below. Minnesota raised its legal drinking age from eighteen to nineteen effective September 1, 1976. The legislation contained a grandfather clause that exempted youths who were eighteen years of age as of August 31, 1976, from the new act. This clause is taken into account in our legal drinking age variables for Minnesota youths.

32. Blane and Hewitt, *supra* note 8.

33. For example, Rachai et al., *supra* note 8.

34. See Ornstein and Hanssens, *supra* note 16.

35. Specifically, let t be a time counter that starts at zero in January 1979 and ends at twelve in January 1980, and let p_{jt} be the price of beer in the jth state in month t. Then $p_{jt} = p_{j0} + bt$, where b is the monthly time trend from the regression. The regression employs annual price data, with the price in 1976, for example, defined as an average of the prices in January 1976, July 1976, and January 1977. Annual data are used because state excise tax rates on beer are very stable over time. Moreover, when a state raises its tax rate, beer prices may rise gradually rather than instantaneously. Indeed, the increase may begin before the actual date on which the tax rate is scheduled to rise. The regression is estimated for a cross section of the contiguous states of the United States for the years 1976, 1977, and 1978. Each observation is weighted by the square root of the population of the state in a given year. The annual trend obtained from the regression is converted to a monthly trend by dividing it by 12.

36. The earliest NHANES II examination was conducted on February 20, 1976, and the latest was conducted on February 27, 1980. Therefore, the midmonth dates are January 1976 through January 1980.

37. Although we have specified real income-real price demand functions, we interpret the estimated price effects as uncompensated (money income-constant) rather than compensated (utility-constant) substitution effects. One consideration is that family income may be a very imperfect measure of a youth's command of real resources. A second consideration is that the CPI measures the cost of living of a four-person family. Expenditure patterns and thus the cost-of-living index of that unit are likely to be very different from those of a youth between the ages of sixteen and twenty-one. For the same reason, seasonal patterns in a youth's cost-of-living index may be very different from seasonal patterns in the CPI. Consequently, we do not deflate the monthly beer price by the monthly CPI. In preliminary research we estimated demand functions with money family income, the money price of beer, and a monthly time trend (a proxy for the youth's CPI) as regressors. The price effects in this specification were very similar to those reported in section 3.

38. Distilled Spirits Council of the United States, Price per Fifth for Selected Types and Brands of Liquor in Control and License States (various years). The seven additional

brands are Old Crow (bourbon), Old Grand-Dad (bonded whiskey), Dewar's (scotch), Smirnoff (vodka), Bacardi (rum), Canadian Club (whiskey), and Beefeater (gin). The prices of the eight brands all are highly correlated in a positive direction. In a time series of state cross sections for the period of NHANES II, the lowest pairwise correlation coefficient is .73. The correlation coefficient between the price of Seagram's 7-Crown and an unweighted average of the prices of the eight brands is .94. Recently, sales of Bacardi and Smirnoff have overtaken sales of Seagram's 7-Crown. In this context, note that the correlation coefficients between the price of Seagram's 7-Crown and the prices of Bacardi and Smirnoff are .92 and .93, respectively.

39. Similar comments can be made with respect to drinking age effects that do not control for drinking sentiment. Although it might appear as if the drinking age effect is overstated, this need not be the case. For example, the high youth motor vehicle accident mortality rate in a state where prodrinking sentiment is widespread may result in the enactment of a high legal drinking age.

40. Bernard Quinn et al., *Churches and Church Membership in the United States, 1980* (1982).

41. Suppose that the youth and adult demand functions are, respectively,

$$y = \alpha_0 + \alpha_1 p + \alpha_2 s + u,$$
$$z = \beta_0 + \beta_1 p + \beta_2 s + w.$$

Here, p is price, s is drinking sentiment, and u and w are disturbance terms that are not correlated with p and s. Note that adult drinking (z) may have a direct effect on youth drinking (y), with drinking sentiment held constant, for the same reason that youth consumption responds to the behavior of peers (see, for example, Blane and Hewitt, *supra* note 8, and Rachai et al., *supra* note 8). In that case, the first equation should be interpreted as a reduced form. Solve the second equation for s, substitute the result into the first equation, and assume that α_2 equals β_2 to obtain

$$y = \alpha_0 - \alpha_0 + (\alpha_1 - \beta_1)p + z + u - w.$$

If e denotes the composite disturbance term in the last equation ($e = u - w$) and σ_w^2 denotes the variance of w, the covariance between e and z is

$$\text{cov}(e, z) = -\sigma_w^2.$$

More generally, if $\alpha_2 \neq \beta_2$, $e = u - (\beta_2/\alpha_2)w$, and

$$\text{cov}(e, z) = -(\beta_2 / \alpha_2)\sigma_w^2.$$

42. G. S. Maddala, *Limited-Dependent and Qualitative Variables in Econometrics* (1983).

43. Since

$$\sum_{k=1}^{4} \pi_{ik} = 1,$$

$$\pi_{i4} = \left[1 + \sum_{k=1}^{3} \exp\left(\alpha_k + \sum_{t=1}^{n} \beta_{kt} x_{it}\right)\right]^{-1},$$

and

$$\left(\partial \pi_{i4} / \partial x_{it}\right) = -\sum_{k=1}^{3}\left(\partial \pi_{ik} / \partial x_{it}\right).$$

44. For a discussion of the two-stage model, see Daniel McFadden, "Conditional Logit Analysis of Qualitative Choice Behavior," in *Frontiers of Econometrics* 105 (Paul Zarembka ed. 1973). An estimation issue in addition to those discussed above arises because NHANES II is a stratified cluster sample rather than a simple random sample. Consider an ordinary least squares regression in this context. If the regression is fit under the assumption of simple random sampling, regression coefficients are unbiased, but their *t*-ratios are overstated. A computer program called SURREG estimates unbiased *t*-ratios for ordinary least squares regressions—*t*-ratios that account for sample design effects. See Michael M. Holt, *SURREG: Standard Errors of Regression Coefficients from Sample Survey Data, Research Triangle Inst.* (1977). There is, however, no SURREG equivalent of a logit model. This suggests that the asymptotic *t*-ratios (the ratios of logit coefficients to their standard errors) shown in section 3 may be biased upward. There is, however, a factor that goes in the opposite direction. We employ a relatively sparse set of regressors; standard errors would fall if this set were expanded. Recall that Arluck, *supra* note 29, finds that the coefficients of interest in the demand functions are not sensitive to the inclusion of additional independent variables.

45. The ratios of logit coefficients to their standard errors do not have student's *t*-distribution. These ratios do, however, have an asymptotic normal distribution. Therefore, the *t*-test is an asymptotic one.

46. Statements concerning statistical significance in the text are based on one-tailed tests except when the direction of the effect is unclear on a priori grounds or when the estimated effect has the "wrong sign." In the latter cases, two-tailed tests are used. In particular, the own price and legal drinking effects are expected to be negative, and the border legal age effects are expected to be positive. When no significance level is indicated, it is assumed to be 5 percent for a one-tailed test.

47. On the basis of equation (5), the elasticity of π_{ik} with respect to x_{it} is

$$\varepsilon_{ikt} = \left(\beta_{kt} - \sum_{k=1}^{3}\pi_{ik}\,\beta_{kt}\right)x_{it}.$$

This elasticity is computed for each youth in the sample by first predicting π_{ik} from equation (3) and the second equation in note 43. The resulting figures are averaged over all youths to obtain the elasticity reported in the text. Note that, since each of the three logit coefficients of price is negative, the marginal price effect (see equation [5]) and the elasticity will be negative if

$$\left|\beta_{kt}\right| > \left|\sum_{k=1}^{3}\pi_{ik}\,\beta_{kt}\right|.$$

Clearly, the above inequality must hold with respect to the largest β_{kt}. Given the range of the estimated π_{ik} and the values of β_{kt} in our sample, the inequality also is satisfied with respect to the second-largest logit coefficient of price in a majority of cases.

48. The percentage increases in price pertain to the actual mean price of beer in the NHANES II sample ($1.03 per six-pack in 1967 dollars) compared to the new mean price under each of the three tax policies. Since the excise tax and legal drinking age increases are nonmarginal and the logit functions are nonlinear, the simulations are employed to evaluate their effects. This is preferable to computing marginal price or legal drinking age effects at the point of means or for each individual and then multiplying by the change in the policy variable at issue. Note that the actual percentage distribution of the frequency beer consumption in table 14.3 differs from the corresponding "observed" distribution in table 14.1. The latter contains, for example, the mean of a dichotomous variable that equals one if a youth is a frequent beer drinker. These differences emerge because a multinomial logit equation, unlike a multiple regression, does not necessarily pass through the point of means of the sample. But they are very small. In particular, the difference between an outcome probability in table 14.1 and the corresponding probability in table 14.3 is always less than 1 percentage point in absolute value.

49. Although the elasticity of the probability of infrequent beer consumption with respect to the real price of beer is positive, the probability of infrequent beer drinking falls as the excise tax rises. This is because the probability of infrequent drinking is not a monotonically increasing function of price (see equation [5]).

50. Some caution should be exercised in applying the results of the drinking age simulation to the Federal Uniform Drinking Age Act because the mean legal drinking age was closer to twenty in July 1984 than to the NHANES II mean of nineteen. On the other hand, as pointed out in section 1, a long-term prohibition of purchases of alcoholic beverages by persons below the age of twenty-one is not a fait accompli given the adverse reaction to the Federal Uniform Drinking Age Act. Therefore, the figures given above probably are reasonable to use in a long-term evaluation of the drinking age policy.

51. Gary S. Becker, "Crime and Punishment: An Economic Approach," 76 *J. Pol. Econ.* 169 (1968). In Becker's model, a system of monetary fines is optimal in most situations. Since teenagers involved in serious automobile accidents presumably would not have enough resources to pay an adequate fine, other punishments for drunk driving are required.

Rational Addiction and the Effect of Price on Consumption

FIFTEEN

Gary S. Becker, Michael Grossman, and Kevin M. Murphy

L egalization of such substances as marijuana, heroin, and cocaine surely will reduce the prices of these harmful addictive drugs. By the law of the downward-sloping demand function, their consumption will rise. But by how much? According to conventional wisdom, the consumption of these illegal addictive substances is not responsive to price.

However, conventional wisdom is contradicted by Becker and Murphy's (1988) theoretical model of rational addiction. The Becker-Murphy (B-M) analysis implies that addictive substances are likely to be quite responsive to price. In this chapter, we summarize B-M's model of rational addiction and the empirical evidence in support of it. We use the theory and evidence to draw highly tentative inferences concerning the effects of legalization of currently banned substances on consumption in the aggregate and for selected groups in the population.

Addictive behavior is usually assumed to involve both "reinforcement" and "tolerance." Reinforcement means that greater past consumption of addictive goods, such as drugs or cigarettes, increases the desire for present consumption. But tolerance cautions that the utility from a given amount of consumption is lower when past consumption is greater.

These aspects of addictive behavior imply several restrictions on the instantaneous utility function

$$U(t) = u[c(t), S(t), y(t)], \qquad (1)$$

where $U(t)$ is utility at t, $c(t)$ is consumption of the addictive good, $y(t)$ is a nonaddictive good, and $S(t)$ is the stock of "addictive capital" that depends on past consumption of c and on life-cycle events. Tolerance is defined by $\partial u/\partial S = u_s < 0$, which means that addictions are harmful in the sense that greater past consumption of addictive goods lowers current utility. Stated differently, higher $c(t)$ lowers future utility by raising future values of S.

Reinforcement ($dc / dS > 0$) requires that an increase in past use raises the marginal utility of current consumption: ($\partial^2 u / \partial c \partial S = u_{cs} > 0$). This is a sufficient condition for myopic utility maximizers who do not consider the future consequences of their current behavior. But rational utility maximizers also consider the future harmful consequences of their current behavior. Reinforcement for them requires that the positive effect of an increase in $S(t)$ on the marginal utility of $c(t)$ exceeds the negative effect of higher $S(t)$ on the future harm from greater $c(t)$.

Becker-Murphy (p. 680) show that a necessary and sufficient condition for reinforcement near a steady state (where $c = \delta S$) is

$$(\sigma + 2\delta)u_{cs} > -u_{ss}, \qquad (2)$$

where u_{cs} and u_{ss} are local approximations near the steady state, σ is the rate of time preference, and δ is the rate of depreciation on addictive capital. Reinforcement is stronger, the bigger the left-hand side is relative to the right-hand side. Clearly, $u_{cs} > 0$ is necessary if u is concave in $S(u_{ss} < 0)$; that is, if tolerance increases as S increases.

It is not surprising that addiction is more likely for people who discount the future heavily (a higher σ) since they pay less attention to the adverse consequences. Addiction to a good is also stronger when the effects of past consumption depreciate more rapidly (δ is larger), for then current consumption has smaller negative effects on future utility. The harmful effects of smoking, drinking, and much drug use do generally disappear within a few years after a person stops the addiction unless vital organs, such as the liver, get irreversibly damaged.

Reinforcement as summarized in equation (2) has the important implication that the consumption of an addictive good at different times are complements. Therefore, an increase in either past or expected future prices decreases current

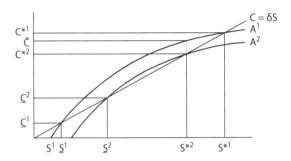

Figure 15.1

consumption. The relation between these effects of past and future prices depends on both time preference and the depreciation rate.

Figure 15.1 illustrates several implications of our approach to addiction, where $S(t)$ is measured along the horizontal axis and $c(t)$ along the vertical one. The line $c = \delta S$ gives all possible steady states where c and S are constant over time. The positively sloped curves A^1 give the relation between c and S for an addicted consumer who has a particular utility function, faces given prices of c and y, and has a given wealth. The initial stock (S^0) depends on past consumption and past life-cycle experience. Both c and S grow over time when S^0 is in the interval where A^1 is above the steady-state line, and both fall over time when S^0 is in the intervals where A^1 is below the steady-state line.

Figure 15.1 shows clearly why the degree of addiction is very sensitive to the initial level of addictive capital. If S^0 is below $\underline{S}^1$ in the figure, a rational consumer eventually lays off the addictive good. But if S^0 is above $\underline{S}^1$, even a rational consumer becomes addicted, and ends up consuming large quantities of the addictive good.

The curve A^1 intersects the steady-state line at two points: $\underline{c}^1 = \delta\underline{S}^1$, and $c^{*1} = \delta S^{*1}$. Other relevant points are where $c = 0$ and $S \le S^1$. The second point and third set of points are locally stable. If initially $c = 0$, $S \le S^1$, and a divorce or other events raise the stock of addictive capital to a level below $\underline{S}^1$, c may become positive, but eventually the consumer again refrains from consuming c. Similarly, if initially $c = c^{*1} = \delta S^{*1}$, c falls at first if say finding a good job lowers S from S^{*1} to a level $> \underline{S}^1$. But c then begins to rise over time and returns toward c^{*1}. The other steady state, $\underline{c}^1 = \delta\underline{S}^1$, is locally and globally unstable: even small changes in S cause cumulative movements toward $c = 0$ or $c = c^{*1}$.

Unstable steady states are an important part of the analysis of rational addictions, for they explain why the same person is sometimes heavily addicted to cigarettes, drugs, or other goods, and yet at other times lays off completely.

Suppose the consumer starts out at $c*^1 = \delta S*^1$, and experiences favorable events that lower his stock of addictive capital below $\underline{S}^1$, the unstable steady state with A^1. The consumer goes from being strongly addicted to eventually giving up c entirely. If A^1 is very steep when S is below the unstable steady state (if reinforcement is powerful in this interval), consumers would quit their addiction "cold turkey" (see the more extended analysis in B-M).

To analyze rational addicts' responses to changes in the cost of addictive goods, suppose they are at $c*^2 = \delta S*^2$ along A^2, and that a fall in the price of c raises the demand curve for c from A^2 to A^1. Consumption increases at first from $c*^2$ to $\hat{c}$, and then c grows further over time since $\hat{c}$ is above the steady-state line. Consumption grows toward the new stable steady state at $c*^1 = \delta S*^1$. This shows that long-run responses to price changes exceed short-run responses because initial increases in consumption of addictive goods cause a subsequent growth in the stocks of addictive capital, which then stimulates further growth in consumption.

Since the degree of addiction is stronger when A is steeper, and since long-run responses to price changes are also greater when A is steeper, strong addictions do not imply weak price elasticities. Indeed, if anything, rational addicts respond more to price changes in the long run than do nonaddicts.[1] The short-run change is smaller than the long-run change because the stock of addictive capital is fixed. Even in the short run, however, rational addicts respond to the anticipated growth in future consumption since future and current consumption of addictive goods are complements for them. But the *ratio* of short- to long-run responses does decline as the degree of addiction increases.[2]

The presence of unstable steady states for highly addictive goods means that the full effect of a price change on consumption could be much greater for these goods than the change between stable steady states given in note 1. Households with initial consumption capital between $\underline{S}^2$ and $\underline{S}^1$ in figure 15.1 would be to the left of the unstable steady state at $\underline{S}^2$ when price equals p^2, but they would be to the right of the unstable steady state at $\underline{S}^1$ when price equals p^1. A reduction in price from p^2 to p^1 greatly raises the long-run demand by these households because they move from low initial consumption to a stable steady state with a high level of consumption.

The total cost of addictive goods to consumers equals the sum of the good's price and the money value of any future adverse effects, such as the negative effects on earnings and health of smoking, heavy drinking, or dependence on crack. Either a higher price of the good (due perhaps to a larger tax) or a higher future cost (due perhaps to greater information about health hazards) reduces consumption in both the short and long run.

It is intuitively plausible that as price becomes a bigger share of total cost, long-run changes in demand induced by a given percentage change in the money price get larger *relative* to the long-run changes induced by an equal percentage change in future costs (see our 1991 paper, fn. 3). Money price tends to be relatively more important to poorer and younger consumers, partly because they generally place a smaller monetary value on health and other harmful future effects.

Poorer and younger persons also appear to discount the future more heavily (this is suggested by the theoretical analysis in Becker 1990). It can be shown that addicts with higher discount rates respond more to changes in money prices of addictive goods, whereas addicts with lower rates of discount respond more to changes in the harmful future consequences.[3]

These implications of rational addiction can be tested with evidence on the demand for cigarettes, heavy consumption of alcohol, and gambling. In Becker, Grossman and Murphy (1994), we fit models of rational addiction to cigarettes to a time-series of state cross sections for the period 1955–1985. We find a sizable long-run price elasticity of demand ranging between −.7 and −.8, while the elasticity of consumption with respect to price in the first year after a permanent price change (the short-run price elasticity) is about −.4. Smoking in different years appear to be complements: Cigarette consumption in any year is lower when both future prices and past prices are higher.

Frank Chaloupka (1991) analyzes cigarette smoking over time by a panel of individuals. He finds similar short- and long-run price elasticities to those we estimate, and that future as well as past increases in cigarette prices reduce current smoking. He also finds that smoking by the less educated responds much more to changes in cigarette prices than does smoking by the more educated; a similar result has been obtained by Joy Townsend (1987) with British data. Eugene Lewit et al. (1981) and Lewit and Douglas Coate (1982) report that youths respond more than adults to changes in cigarette prices. By contrast, the information that began to emerge in the early 1960s about the harmful long-run effects of smoking has had a much greater effect on smoking by the rich and more educated than by the poor and less educated (see Farrell and Fuchs 1982, for the United States; Townsend 1987 for Britain).

Philip Cook and George Tauchen (1982) examine variations in death rates from cirrhosis of the liver (a standard measure of heavy alcohol use), as well as variations in per capita consumption of distilled spirits in a time-series of state cross sections for 1962–1977. They find that state excise taxes on distilled spirits have a negative and statistically significant effect on the cirrhosis death rate. Moreover, a small increase in prices in a state's excise tax lowers death rates by a larger percentage than it lowers per capita consumption.

Pamela Mobilia (1990) applies the rational addiction framework to the demand for gambling at horse racing tracks. Her data consist of a U.S. time-series of racing track cross sections for the period 1950–1986 (tracks over time are the units of observation). She measures consumption by the real amount bet per person attending (handle per attendant), and price by the takeout rate (the fraction of the total amount bet that is retained by the track). Her findings are similar to those in the rational addictive studies of cigarettes. The long-run price elasticity of demand for gambling equals −.7 and is more than twice as large as the short-run elasticity of −.3. Moreover, an increase in the current takeout rate lowers handle per attendant in both past and future years.

The evidence from smoking, heavy drinking, and gambling rather strongly supports our model of rational addiction. In particular, long-run price elasticities are sizable and much bigger than short-run elasticities, higher future as well as past prices reduce current consumption, lower-income persons respond more to changes in prices of addictive goods than do higher-income persons, whereas the latter respond more to changes in future harmful effects, and younger persons respond more to price changes than older persons. It seems reasonable to us that what holds for smoking, heavy drinking, and gambling tends to hold also for drug use, although direct evidence is not yet available, and many experts on drugs would be skeptical. Lacking the evidence, we simply indicate what to expect from various kinds of price changes if responses of drug addicts are similar to those of persons addicted to other goods.

To fix ideas, consider a large permanent reduction in the price of drugs (perhaps due to partial or complete legalization) combined with much greater efforts to educate the population about the harm from drug use. Our analysis predicts that much lower prices could significantly expand use even in the short run, and it would surely stimulate much greater addiction in the long run. Note, however, that the elasticity of response to large price changes would be less than that to modest changes if the elasticity is smaller at lower prices.

The effects of a fall in drug prices on demand would be countered by the education program. But since drug use by the poor would be more sensitive to the price fall than to greater information about harmful longer-run effects, drug addiction among the poor is likely to become more important relative to addiction among the middle classes and rich. For similar reasons, addiction among the young may rise more than that among other segments of the population.

A misleading impression about the reaction to permanent price changes may have been created by the effects of temporary police crackdowns on drugs, or temporary federal "wars" on drugs. Since temporary policies raise current but not future prices (they would even lower future prices if drug inventories are built up during a crackdown period), there is no complementary fall in current use from a fall in future use. Consequently, even if drug addicts are rational, a temporary war that greatly raised street prices of drugs may well have only a small effect on drug use, whereas a permanent war could have much bigger effects, even in the short run.

Clearly, we have not provided enough evidence to evaluate whether or not the use of heroin, cocaine, and other drugs should be legalized. A cost-benefit analysis of many effects is needed to decide between a regime in which drugs are legal and one in which they are not. What this chapter shows is that the permanent reduction in price caused by legalization is likely to have a substantial positive effect on use, particularly among the poor and young.

NOTES

Our research has been supported by the Lynde and Harry Bradley Foundation through the Center for the Study of the Economy and the State, University of Chicago, and by the Hoover Institution.

1. Becker-Murphy show (equation [18], p. 685) that the long-run response between stable steady states to a permanent change in p_c is $dc*/dp_c = \mu/\alpha_{cc}B'$, where μ is the marginal utility of wealth. The term B' measures the degree of addiction, where B' ranges between 1 (no addiction) and 0 for an addictive good that has a stable steady state.

2. One can show that a rational addict's short-run response to a permanent change in p_c equals $dc_s/dp_c = -(\lambda/\delta)(dc*/dp_c)$, where $-\delta \leq \lambda \leq 0$, and λ is larger when the degree of addiction is stronger (see B-M, 679–80). Therefore, the ratio of the short- to long-term response gets smaller as the degree of addiction (measured by λ) is larger. But one can also show that dc_s/dp_c itself gets larger as the degree of addiction increases.

3. If u is concave, $-\delta^2 u_{cc} - u_{ss} > 2\delta u_{cs}$. This implies that either or both of the following inequalities hold: $-u_{ss}/\delta^2 > u_{cs}/\delta$, and $-u_{cc} > u_{cs}/\delta$. We assume both hold. The second inequality states that an increase in c between steady states reduces the marginal utility of c by more than the increase in S raises it. The first inequality assumes that the increase in S has a larger effect on its marginal utility than does the increase in c.

   The absolute value of the long-run change in c induced by a change in p_c is raised by an increase in σ if $-u_{ss} > \delta u_{cs}$. Similarly, the absolute value of the long-run change in c with respect a change in future costs is reduced by an increase in σ if $-u_{cc}\delta > u_{cs}$. (For more details, see our 1991 paper, fn. 4).

REFERENCES

Becker, Gary S. 1990. "Optimal Discounting of the Future," Department of Economics, University of Chicago.

Becker, Gary S., Michael Grossman, and Kevin M. Murphy. 1994. "An Empirical Analysis of Cigarette Addiction." *American Economic Review* 84: 396–418.

——. 1991. "Rational Addiction and the Effect of Price on Consumption." Working Paper, Center for the Study of the Economy and the State, University of Chicago.

Becker, Gary S., and Kevin M. Murphy. 1988. "A Theory of Rational Addiction." *Journal of Political Economy* 96: 675–700.

Chaloupka, Frank J. 1991. "Rational Addictive Behavior and Cigarette Smoking." *Journal of Political Economy* 99: 722–742.

Cook, Philip J., and George Tauchen. 1982. "The Effect of Liquor Taxes on Heavy Drinking." *Bell Journal of Economics* 13: 379–390.

Farrell, Phillip, and Victor R. Fuchs. 1982. "Schooling and Health: The Cigarette Connection." *Journal of Health Economics* 1: 217–230.

Lewit, Eugene M., and Douglas Coate. 1982. "The Potential for Using Excise Taxes to Reduce Smoking." *Journal of Health Economics* 1: 121–145.

Lewit, Eugene M., Douglas Coate, and Michael Grossman. 1981. "The Effects of Government Regulation on Teenage Smoking" *Journal of Law and Economics* 24: 545–569.

Mobilia, Pamela. 1990. "An Economic Analysis of Addictive Behavior: The Case of Gambling." Unpublished doctoral dissertation, City University of New York.

Townsend, Joy L. 1987. "Cigarette Tax, Economic Welfare and Social Class Patterns of Smoking." *Applied Economics* 19: 355–365.

An Empirical Analysis
of Cigarette Addiction

SIXTEEN

Gary S. Becker, Michael Grossman, and
Kevin M. Murphy

ABSTRACT

To test a model of rational addiction, we examine whether lower past and future prices for cigarettes raise current cigarette consumption. The empirical results tend to support the implication of addictive behavior that cross price effects are negative and that long-run responses exceed short-run responses. Since the long-run price elasticity of demand is almost twice as large as the short-run price elasticity, the long-run increase in tax revenue from an increase in the federal excise tax on cigarettes is considerably smaller than the short-run increase.

In Becker and Murphy (1988), a theoretical model was developed in which utility-maximizing consumers may become "addicted" to the consumption of a product, and the key empirical predictions were outlined. In the Becker-Murphy framework consumers are rational or farsighted in the sense that they anticipate the expected future consequences of their current actions. This chapter uses that framework to analyze empirically the demand for cigarettes. The data consist of per capita cigarette sales (in packs) annually by state for the period 1955–1985. The empirical results indicate that smoking is addictive.

The Becker-Murphy model follows Harl E. Ryder, Jr., and Geoffrey M. Heal (1973), George J. Stigler and Becker (1977), Marcel Boyer (1978, 1983), Frans Spinnewyn (1981), and Lawrence R. Iannaccone (1986) by considering the interaction of past and current consumption in a model with utility-maximizing consumers. The main feature of these models is that past consumption of some goods influences their current consumption by affecting the marginal utility of current and future consumption. Greater past consumption of harmfully addictive goods such as cigarettes stimulates current consumption by increasing the marginal utility of current consumption more than the present value of the marginal harm from future consumption. Therefore, past consumption is reinforcing for addictive goods.

This chapter tests the model of rational addiction by considering the response of cigarette consumption to a change in cigarette prices. We examine whether lower past and future prices for cigarettes raise current cigarette consumption. The empirical results tend to support the implication of addictive behavior that cross price effects are negative and that long-run responses exceed short-run responses.

We find that a 10-percent permanent increase in the price of cigarettes reduces current consumption by 4 percent in the short run and by 7.5 percent in the long run. In contrast, a 10-percent increase in price for only one period decreases consumption by only 3 percent. In addition, a one-period price increase of 10 percent decreases consumption in the previous period by approximately 0.6 percent and decreases consumption in the subsequent period by 1.5 percent. These estimates illustrate the importance of the intertemporal linkages in cigarette demand implied by addictive behavior. We are not able to test other implications of the Becker-Murphy model such as abrupt quitting behavior by cold turkey.

In myopic models of addictive behavior, past consumption stimulates current consumption, but individuals ignore the future when making consumption decisions. We show that these models imply that past prices have negative effects on current consumption, but that they imply that there is no effect of anticipated future prices on current consumption. Since rational models always exhibit the symmetry of (compensated) cross price effects implied by optimizing behavior, testing for the effects of future prices on current consumption distinguishes rational models of addiction from myopic models. The results strongly reject myopic behavior, while they tend to support the model of rational addiction. However, some results cannot readily be explained by rational addiction.

The cigarette industry raised the price of cigarettes in 1982 as well as in 1983 when the federal excise tax on cigarettes increased. The industry also raised cigarette prices throughout the 1980's presumably in anticipation of a continuing fall in smoking. Such pricing is inconsistent with perfect competition, but it is consistent with monopoly power in the cigarette industry if cigarette smoking is addictive. Since other evidence also suggests that the industry has monopoly power, this pricing policy is further testimony to the effect of addictive behavior on aggregate cigarette consumption, because a monopolist will take account of the effect of current price on the demand for future consumption.

Our results are relevant to government regulation of the cigarette industry. Since the first Surgeon General's Report on Smoking and Health in 1964, the federal government and state governments have carried out policies to increase public knowledge about the harmful effects of smoking, to restrict advertising by cigarette manufacturers, and to create no-smoking areas in public places and in the workplace. These policies will induce monopolistic producers to raise current prices because the decline in future demand that they cause reduces the gains from maintaining a lower price to stimulate future consumption. This indirect effect of the antismoking campaign in the form of higher prices has not been taken into account in evaluations of the campaign (e.g., Kenneth E. Warner 1986).

Our results also are relevant in estimating the potential revenue yield of an increase in the federal excise tax rate on cigarettes to help finance national health-care reform or to reduce the federal deficit. Given the addictive nature of smoking, consumption of cigarettes is positively related to past consumption. For example, a price hike in 1993 due to an increase in the federal excise tax rate would reduce consumption in 1993, which would cause consumption in 1994 and in all future years to fall. Since we find that the long-run price elasticity is almost twice as large as the short-run price elasticity, the long-run increase in tax revenue would be considerably smaller than the short-run increase.

1. THE BASIC MODEL

Most empirical analyses of consumption deal with single-period models or assume time-separable utility. By definition, single-period models cannot deal with the dynamics of consumption behavior, and the usual two-stage budgeting property of time-separable models precludes any dynamics other than those arising from dynamic wealth changes and aggregate consumption effects. Since addictions imply linkages in consumption of the same good over time, it is essential to relax the additive-separability assumption in order to model consumption of addictive goods.

The simplest way to relax the separability assumption is to allow utility in each period to depend on consumption in that period and consumption in the previous period. In particular, following Boyer (1978, 1983), we consider a model with two goods and current-period utility in period t given by a concave utility function

$$U(Y_t, C_t, C_{t-1}, e_t). \qquad (1)$$

Here C_t is the quantity of cigarettes consumed in period t, C_{t-1} is the quantity of cigarettes consumed in period $t - 1$, Y_t is the consumption of a composite commodity in period t, and e_t reflects the impact of unmeasured life-cycle variables on utility. Individuals are assumed to be infinite-lived and to maximize the sum of lifetime utility discounted at the rate r.

If the composite commodity, Y, is taken as numeraire, if the rate of interest is equal to the rate of time preference, and if the price of cigarettes in period t is denoted by P_t, then the consumer's problem is

$$\max \sum_{t=1}^{\infty} \beta^{t-1} U(C_t, C_{t-1}, Y_t, e_t) \qquad (2)$$

such that $C_0 = C^0$ and

$$\sum_{t=1}^{\infty} \beta^{t-1}(Y_t + P_t C_t) = A^0$$

where $\beta = 1/(1 + r)$. We ignore any effect of C on earnings, and hence on the present value of wealth (A^0), and we also ignore any effect of C on the length of life and all other types of uncertainty. The initial condition for the consumer in period 1, C^0, measures the level of cigarette consumption in the period prior to that under consideration.

The associated first-order conditions are

$$U_y(C_t, C_{t-1}, Y_t, e_t) = \lambda \qquad (3a)$$

$$U_1(C_t, C_{t-1}, Y_t, e_t) + \beta U_2(C_{t+1}, C_t, Y_{t+1}, e_{t+1}) = \lambda P_t. \qquad (3b)$$

Equation (3a) is the usual condition that the marginal utility of other consumption in each period, U_y, equals the marginal utility of wealth, λ. Equation (3b) implies that the marginal utility of current cigarette consumption, U_1, plus the discounted marginal effect on next period's utility of today's consumption, U_2, equals the current price multiplied by the marginal utility of wealth. In the case of a harmfully addictive good such as cigarettes, U_2 is negative, although the model that we develop simply assumes that this term is not zero. That is, the predictions contained in this section also are valid in the case of beneficial addiction ($U_2 > 0$).

Since with perfect certainty the marginal utility of wealth, λ, is constant over time, variations in the price of cigarettes over time trace out marginal utility of wealth-constant demand curves for Y and C. In the time-separable case, these demand curves depend only on the current price (P_t) and the marginal utility of wealth, but with nonseparable utility, they depend on prices in all periods through the effects of past and future prices on past and future consumption.

To illustrate, consider a utility function that is quadratic in Y_t, C_t, and e_t. By solving the first-order condition for Y_t and substituting the result into the first-order condition for C_t, we get a linear difference equation that determines current cigarette consumption as a function of past and future cigarette consumption, the current price of cigarettes, P_t, and the shift variables e_t and e_{t+1}:

$$C_t = \theta C_{t-1} + \beta \theta C_{t+1} + \theta_1 P_t + \theta_2 e_t + \theta_3 e_{t+1} \tag{4}$$

where

$$\theta_1 = \frac{u_{yy}\lambda}{(u_{11}u_{yy} - u_{1y}^2) + \beta(u_{22}u_{yy} - u_{2y}^2)} < 0$$

$$\theta_2 = \frac{-(u_{yy}u_{1e} - u_{1y}u_{ey})}{(u_{11}u_{yy} - u_{1y}^2) + \beta(u_{22}u_{yy} - u_{2y}^2)}$$

$$\theta_3 = \frac{-\beta(u_{yy}u_{2e} - u_{2y}u_{2e})}{(u_{11}u_{yy} - u_{1y}^2) + \beta(u_{22}u_{yy} - u_{2y}^2)}$$

where lowercase letters denote the coefficients of the quadratic utility function, and the intercept is suppressed

Since θ_1 is negative by concavity of U, equation (4) implies that increases in the current price decrease current consumption, C_t, when the marginal utility of wealth, past consumption, and future consumption are fixed.[1] The effects of changes in future or past consumption on current consumption depend only on the sign of the term θ. When θ is positive, forces that increase past or future consumption, such as lower past or future cigarette prices, also increase current consumption. In contrast, when θ is negative, greater past or future consumption decreases current consumption. Hence current and past consumption are complements if and only if

$$\theta = \frac{-(u_{12}u_{yy} - u_{1y}u_{2y})}{(u_{11}u_{yy} - u_{1y}^2) + \beta(u_{22}u_{yy} - u_{2y}^2)} > 0. \tag{5}$$

Since past consumption reinforces current consumption when behavior is addictive, we say that a good is addictive if and only if an increase in past consumption leads to an increase in current consumption holding current prices, e_t, e_{t+1}, and the marginal utility of wealth fixed. A good is more addictive when the reinforcement from past consumption is greater. This definition means that a good is addictive if $\theta > 0$, and the degree of addiction is greater when θ is larger.

Equation (4) is the basis of the empirical analysis in this chapter. Cigarette consumption in period t is a function of cigarette consumption in periods $t - 1$ and $t + 1$, the current price of cigarettes (P_t), and the unobservables e_t and e_{t+1}. Ordinary-least-squares estimation of equation (4) would lead to inconsistent estimates of the parameters of interest. The unobserved errors, e_t, that affect utility in each period are likely to be serially correlated; even if these variables are uncorrelated, the same error e_t directly affects consumption at all dates through the optimizing behavior implied by equation (4). Positive serial correlation in the unobserved effects incorrectly implies that past and future consumption positively affect current consumption, even when the true value of θ is zero.

Fortunately, the specification in equation (4) suggests a way to solve this endogeneity problem, since it implies that current consumption is independent of past and future prices when C_{t-1} and C_{t+1} are held fixed. That is, any effect of past or future prices must come through their effects on C_{t-1} or C_{t+1}. Provided that the unobservables are uncorrelated with prices in these periods, past and future prices are logical instruments for C_{t-1} and C_{t+1}, since past prices directly affect past consumption, and future prices directly affect future consumption. Therefore, our empirical strategy is to estimate θ and θ_1, the main parameters of equation (4), by using past and future price variables as instruments for past and future consumption.

These estimates can be used to derive short- and long-run demand elasticities for cigarettes and to derive cross price elasticities between cigarette consumption levels at different points in time that test how important addiction is to aggregate cigarette consumption. It is intuitively clear from equation (4) that a fall in the current price of cigarettes, P_t, increases current consumption, C_t, which will increase cigarette consumption at time $t + 1$ when θ is positive. Similarly, if this fall in P_t is anticipated in period $t - 1$, the rise in C_t also stimulates a rise in consumption at time $t - 1$. In addition, a permanent fall in price has a larger effect on current consumption than does a temporary fall in price, since a permanent fall in price combines a fall in the current price with a fall in all future prices.

These and other results can be seen more formally by solving the second-order difference equation in (4). The solution and the various price effects in the model are contained in Appendix A. The solution results in an equation in which consumption in period t depends on prices in all periods. This equation determines the sign of the effects of changes in the price of cigarettes in period τ on cigarette consumption in period t. These effects are temporary in nature since prices in other periods are held constant. The temporary own or current price effect must be negative. The sign of the cross price effect depends entirely on the sign of the coefficient of past consumption (θ) in equation (4). The goods in any two consecutive periods are complements (i.e., negative cross price effects) if and only if θ is positive.

Since an increase in past consumption increases current consumption if a good is addictive, fully anticipated price effects must exceed completely unanticipated price effects in absolute value. The latter describes a price change in period t that is not anticipated until that period, so that past consumption is not affected. The former describes a price change in period t that is anticipated as of the planning date, so that past consumption is affected.

In addition to the own price effects, cross price effects, and the difference between anticipated and unanticipated price effects, there are important differences between long- and short-run responses to permanent price changes in the context of addiction. The short-run price effect describes the response to a change in price in period t and all future periods that is not anticipated until period t. The long-run price effect pertains to a price change in *all* periods. Since C_{t-1} remains the same if a price change is not anticipated until period t, the long-run price effect must exceed the short-run price effect. In addition, the long-run price effect must exceed the fully anticipated temporary own price effect.

The differences between long-run and short-run, temporary and permanent, and anticipated and unanticipated price changes are greater when there is a greater degree of addiction or complementarity (i.e., when θ is larger). The cross price effects, and hence the differences between these various elasticities, are small when θ is close to zero. The simplicity of a time-separable model then would make it superior to the addiction model. However, if θ is quite different from zero, a time-separable model is likely to give highly misleading predictions about both the short-run and long-run response of consumption to changes in prices.

2. A MYOPIC MODEL OF ADDICTION

While the model presented in Becker and Murphy (1988) shows that addictive behavior can be successfully modeled in a rational-choice framework, many previous researchers have considered nonrational or myopic models of addiction and habit formation (see e.g., Robert A. Pollak 1970, 1976; Menahem E. Yaari 1977). We cannot hope to develop an empirical framework that encompasses the structures used in all nonrational models, but this section presents a myopic model related to those suggested in the literature. Even this sample model highlights an important empirical distinction between myopic and nonmyopic models.

To maintain as much similarity to the previous model as possible, we use the same utility function and the same assumptions about the goods Y and C. The key distinction is that myopic individuals fail to consider the impact of current consumption on future utility and future consumption. Analytically, this corresponds to individuals using a first-order condition that does not contain the future effect βU_2.

Differences between myopic and rational behavior are highlighted by solving the myopic first-order condition for C_t to get the myopic equivalent of equation (4). The major difference between equation (4) and the myopic equation is that the latter is entirely backward-looking. Current consumption depends only on current price, lagged consumption, the marginal utility of wealth, and current events. Current consumption is independent of both future consumption, C_{t+1}, and future events, e_{t+1}. Because of these distinctions, myopic models and rational models have different implications about responses to future changes. In particular, rational addicts increase their current consumption when future prices are expected to fall, but myopic addicts do not.

Empirically, the difference between the two equations provides a clear test between rational and myopic addiction. Myopic behavior implies that the coefficient on instrumented future consumption should be zero, while the rational model implies that it should have the same sign as the coefficient on lagged consumption (the sizes differ only by the discount factor). Future price (and consumption) changes have no impact on the current consumption of a myopic addict, but they have significant effects on the current consumption of a rational addict.

3. DATA AND EMPIRICAL IMPLEMENTATION

The data consist of a time series of state cross sections covering the period from 1955 through 1985. We assume that per capita cigarette consumption in these data reflects the behavior of a representative consumer. To be sure, we cannot study the decision to start or quit smoking, given the aggregate nature of the data. But Becker and Murphy's (1988) treatment of unstable steady states indicates that the same forces that govern consumption of an addictive good, given participation, also govern these decisions. For example, the quit probability in period t is positively related to current price and negatively related to

Table 16.1 Definitions, Means, and Standard Deviations (SD) of Variables

Variable	Definition (Mean, SD)
C_t	Per capita cigarette consumption in packs in fiscal year t, as derived from state tax-paid sales (mean = 126.171, SD = 31.794)
P_t	Average retail cigarette price per pack in January of fiscal year t in 1967 cents (mean = 29.812, SD = 3.184)
income	Per capita income on a fiscal-year basis, in hundreds of 1967 dollars (mean = 31.439, SD = 8.092)
ℓdtax	Index, which measures the incentives to smuggle cigarettes long distance from Kentucky, Virginia, or North Carolina. The index is positively related to the difference between the state's excise tax and the excise taxes of the exporting states (mean = 0.160, SD= 15.572)
sdtexp	Index, which measures short-distance (export) smuggling incentives. The index is a weighted average of differences between the exporting state's excise tax and excise taxes of neighboring states, with weights based on border populations (mean = −0.828, SD = 1.847)
sdtimp	Index, which measures short-distance (import) smuggling incentives in a state. Similar to sdtexp (mean = 0.494, SD = 0.792)
tax	Sum of state and local excise taxes on cigarettes in 1967 cents per pack (mean = 6.582, SD = 2.651)

consumption in periods $t - 1$ and $t + 1$. However, it depends on where a person starts from and the magnitude of these changes in price and consumption.

Table 16.1 contains definitions, means, and standard deviations of the primary variables in the dataset (see Appendix B for a detailed discussion of the data). All prices, taxes, and income measures were deflated to 1967 dollars with the consumer price index for all goods. State- and year-specific cigarette prices were obtained from the Tobacco Tax Council (1986). The consumption data were taken from the same source and pertain to per capita tax-paid cigarette sales (in packs). A number of studies have used these data to estimate cigarette demand functions. The most recent one, which contains a review of past research, is by Badi H. Baltagi and Dan Levin (1986). None of them contains the refined measures of incentives for short- and long-distance smuggling of cigarettes across state lines that we employ (see below) or considers how addiction affects the estimates.

Cigarette sales are reported on the basis of a fiscal year running from July 1 through June 30. Therefore, real per capita income also is on a fiscal-year basis, and the retail price of a pack of cigarettes pertains to January of the year at issue. The price is given as a weighted-average price per pack, using national weights for type of cigarette (regular, king, 100-mm) and type of transaction (carton, single pack, machine). It is inclusive of federal, state, and municipal excise taxes and state sales taxes imposed on cigarettes.

There are 1,581 potential observations in the dataset (fifty states and the District of Columbia times thirty-one years). Missing sales and price data in nine states in certain years reduce the actual number of observations to 1,517. There are no gaps in the state-specific price and sales series. That is, if one of these variables is reported in year t, it is reported in all future years. Note that states are deleted *only* in years for which data are missing.

The existence of state excise taxes on cigarettes provides much of the empirical leverage required to estimate the parameters of cigarette demand. Cigarette tax rates vary greatly across states at a point in time and within a given state over time. For example, for the period of our sample, the average tax level (in 1967 dollars) is 6.4 cents per pack, or about 21 percent of the average retail price of 30 cents. The range of tax rates also is substantial. A rate one standard deviation above the mean is 6 cents higher than a rate one standard deviation below the mean. This difference is 20 percent of the average retail price. The variation in retail prices due to differences in taxes across states and over time within a state helps identify the impact of price changes on consumption.

The state and time-series data have several pitfalls. In particular, the diffusion of new information about the health hazards of smoking may have greatly affected smoking over the period of our sample. To incorporate such effects, we use time-specific dummy variables. Unfortunately, the coefficients of these time variables also contain the responses in aggregate consumption to national changes in the price of cigarettes.

In addition, states differ in demographic composition, income, and other variables that are correlated with smoking. Our estimates of price effects would be biased if these differences are also correlated with tax or price differentials across states. To mitigate this bias, we estimate all specifications with real per capita income and fixed state effects (dichotomous variables for each state except one).

The measure of cigarette smoking refers to per capita sales within states, which can differ from per capita consumption within states. When adjacent states have significantly different tax policies, there is an obvious incentive to smuggle cigarettes across states. We constructed three measures that attempt to correct for both short-distance and long-distance smuggling. The short-distance smuggling variables use tax differentials between surrounding states together with information on the proportion of individuals living within 20 miles of neighboring states that have lower cigarette tax rates (for imports) or higher tax rates (for exports). The long-distance smuggling measure uses the difference between a state's tax and the tax in each of the states of Kentucky,

North Carolina, and Virginia. These three states account for almost all of the cigarettes produced in the United States, based on value added and had the three lowest excise tax rates in the country starting in fiscal 1967.

The demand function developed in section 1 of this chapter is one that holds the marginal utility of wealth constant. In a model with perfect foresight, the marginal utility of wealth is fixed over time but varies among individuals and therefore among states. Thus, the state dummies capture this variation. The coefficients of the time dummies reflect in part the effects of unanticipated growth in wealth, which cause the marginal utility of wealth to change over time. We assume that deviations in real per capita income around state- and time-specific means follow a random walk, or more generally a first-order autoregressive process. In these cases unanticipated state-specific changes in real wealth over time, or deviations in real wealth from state- and time-specific means, are determined fully by deviations in real per capita income from state- and time-specific means. Put differently, with the state and time dummies held constant, the coefficient of real per capita income reflects forces associated with state-specific changes in the marginal utility of wealth over time.[2]

4. EMPIRICAL RESULTS

Our estimation strategy is to begin with the myopic model. We then test the myopic model by testing whether future prices are significant predictors of current consumption as they would be in the rational-addiction model, but not under the myopic framework. Since consumers base their current consumption decisions on expected future price under the rational-addiction framework, the actual future price suffers from the classical errors-in-variable problem in which the measurement error is uncorrelated with expected future price and all other variables in the equation. Under the null hypothesis of the myopic framework, our coefficient estimate is still unbiased and represents a valid test of the myopic model.

The first three columns of table 16.2 contain two-stage least-squares (TSLS) estimates of myopic models of addiction, while the last column contains an ordinary least-squares (OLS) estimate. Past consumption is treated as an endogenous variable in the first three columns because of the high likelihood that the unobserved variables that affect current utility (e_t) are serially correlated.[3] The instruments used in column (i) consist of past price (P_{t-1}) plus the other explanatory variables in the model. Column (ii) adds the current and one-period lag values of the state cigarette tax to the instruments, and column (iii) further adds two additional lags of the price and tax variables. State excise taxes are used as instruments in some of the models for reasons indicated below.[4] The table also contains F ratios resulting from De-Min Wu's (1973) test of the hypothesis that OLS estimates are consistent. Since this hypothesis always is rejected, we stress the TSLS results.

According to the parameter estimates of the myopic model presented in table 16.2, cigarette smoking is inversely related to current price and positively related to income.[5] The highly significant effects of the smuggling variables (ℓdtax, sdimp, and sdexp) indicate the importance of interstate smuggling of cigarettes. The positive and significant past-consumption coefficient is consistent with the hypothesis that cigarette smoking is an addictive behavior. The parameter estimates in the table are quite stable across the three alternative sets of instruments for past consumption.

When the one-period lead of price is added to the TSLS models in table 16.2, its coefficient is negative and significant at all conventional levels. The absolute t-ratio associated with the coefficient of this variable is 5.06 in model (i), 5.54

Table 16.2 Estimates of Myopic Models of Addiction, Dependent Variable $= C_t$ (Asymptotic t Statistics in Parentheses)

Independent Variable	2SLS			OLS
	(i)	(ii)	(iii)	(iv)
C_{t-1}	0.478	0.502	0.602	0.755
	(12.07)	(14.68)	(21.43)	(64.84)
P_t	−1.603	−1.538	−1.269	−0.860
	(10.12)	(10.48)	(9.74)	(8.33)
Y_t	0.942	0.903	0.741	0.493
	(7.61)	(7.71)	(6.96)	(5.44)
ℓdtax	−0.240	−0.233	0.212	−0.160
	(7.33)	(7.40)	(7.22)	(6.17)
sdtimp	−1.541	−1.514	−1.372	−1.228
	(5.04)	(5.09)	(4.97)	(4.84)
sdtexp	−3.659	−3.544	−3.059	−2.328
	(13.24)	(13.88)	(13.71)	(13.15)
R^2	0.969	0.970	41.61	0.979
Wu F ratio	84.76	94.42	0.976	—
N	1,415	1,415	1,371	1,415

Notes: Intercepts are not shown. Regressors include state and year dummy variables. Columns (i)–(iii) give two-stage least squares (2SLS) estimates with C_{t-1} treated as endogenous. Column (iv) gives an ordinary least-squares (OLS) estimate. The instruments in column (i) consist of the one-period lag of price plus the other explanatory variables in the model. Column (ii) adds the current and one-period lag values of the state cigarette tax to the instruments, and column (iii) further adds two additional lags of the price and tax variables. The Wu F ratios pertain to tests of the hypothesis that the OLS models corresponding to the first three columns are consistent. They all are significant at the 1-percent level.

in model (ii), and 6.45 in model (iii). These results suggest that decisions about current consumption depend on future price. They are inconsistent with a myopic model of addiction, but consistent with a rational model of this behavior in which a reduction in expected future price raises expected future consumption, which in turn raises current consumption. While these tests soundly reject the myopic model, they do not provide definitive evidence in support of the rational-addiction model outlined above because they do not impose the constraint that the future-price effect works solely through future consumption. Nevertheless, they suggest that consumers do consider future prices in their current consumption decisions and hence that it is worth trying to obtain structural estimates of rational-addiction demand functions.

Two strategies can be pursued in fitting the rational-addiction model. One is to use the actual future price as an instrument for future consumption. The problem with this strategy is that the forecast error in future price creates a downward bias in the coefficient of future consumption. The second strategy is to restrict the set of instruments to lagged values of prices and taxes. This is a common general strategy in estimating the effects of expected future variables.

There are two problems with the second strategy. First, consumers have a good deal of information concerning the state-specific future price of cigarettes, because this price depends to a large extent on the future state excise tax rate on cigarettes. Excise tax hikes are announced in advance and receive a good deal of publicity as a result of delays in the legislative process. Moreover, most states raise their excise tax rates in response to revenue shortfalls (see e.g., Eugene E. Lewit 1982). Hence, it is plausible that tax hikes are anticipated even before the corresponding bills are introduced in state legislatures. Phrased differently, if consumers have information concerning future prices and taxes, then one is losing valuable information by discarding these variables as instruments.

Second, past prices and taxes simply are not good predictors of the future price. Consider a regression of the future price on all the exogenous variables in the demand function, the one-period lag of the price, the one-period lag of the tax, and the current tax. At the 1-percent level, the last three variables are not significant as a set in the regression ($F = 3.0$, compared to a critical F ratio of 3.8). Addition of a second lag of the price and the tax does not improve matters because the F statistic falls to 2.0, compared to a critical F of 3.0. Even these computed F ratios are, however, biased upward because the real issue is whether past prices and taxes are significant predictors of future price net of their contribution to the prediction of past consumption. When predicted past consumption is added to the regressions just described, the F statistics fall to 0.1 and 1.5, respectively.

Charles R. Nelson and Richard Startz (1990) have shown that the use of a poor instrument (an instrument that explains little of the variation in an endogenous right-hand-side variable) can produce a large bias in the estimated coefficient of the endogenous variable relative to its standard error. They state (p. S139), "In the context of estimating stochastic Euler equations, we would particularly caution against the use of lagged changes in consumption or lagged stock returns as instruments for current values...." In our case, this implies even more caution against the use of past prices as instruments for future consumption. Therefore, our preferred estimation strategy uses future price directly as a predictor of future consumption; but we present results both for this strategy and for the one that restricts the instruments to past prices and taxes.

Table 16.3 tests the rational-addiction model directly by estimating equation (4) with past and future consumption treated as endogenous variables and with future prices included in the set of instruments. The instruments used in column (i) consist of past and future prices (P_{t-1} and P_{t+1}, respectively) plus the other explanatory variables in the model. Column (ii) adds the current and one-period lag values of the state cigarette tax to the instruments, column (iii) further adds the one-period lead value of the tax, and column (iv) further adds two additional lags of the price and tax variables. As indicated above, state excise taxes are used as instruments in some of the models because consumers may have more knowledge about taxes, especially future taxes, than about future prices.[6] Column (v) presents an OLS estimate of the rational-addiction model. As in table 16.2, the Wu test rejects the hypothesis that OLS coefficients are consistent.

The estimated effects of past and future consumption on current consumption are significantly positive in the four TSLS models in table 16.3, and the estimated price effects are significantly negative in all cases.

The positive and significant past consumption coefficient is consistent with the hypothesis that cigarette smoking is an addictive behavior. The positive and significant future consumption coefficient (though downward-biased) is consistent with the hypothesis of rational addiction and inconsistent with the hypothesis of myopic addiction.

Table 16.4 uses the TSLS estimates from table 16.3 to compute the elasticity of cigarette consumption with respect to various price changes defined in section 1 and Appendix A at the sample means of price and consumption. Estimates of the long-run response to a permanent change in price in the first row range from −0.73 to −0.79 (average equals −0.75) and are at the high end of those in the literature that omit past and future consumption from the demand function. More important are the significant cross price effects. A 10-percent unanticipated reduction in current price leads to an increase of between 1.4 percent and

Table 16.3 Estimates of Rational Models of Addiction, Dependent Variable = C_t
(Asymptotic t Statistics in Parentheses)

Independent Variable	2SLS				OLS
	(i)	(ii)	(iii)	(iv)	(v)
C_{t-1}	0.418	0.373	0.443	0.481	0.485
	(8.88)	(9.18)	(11.72)	(14.58)	(36.92)
C_{t+1}	0.135	0.236	0.169	0.228	0.423
	(2.45)	(5.04)	(3.79)	(5.87)	(28.61)
P_t	−1.388	−1.230	−1.227	−0.971	−0.412
	(8.94)	(9.11)	(9.11)	(8.36)	(4.98)
Y_t	0.837	0.761	0.746	0.608	0.302
	(7.34)	(7.44)	(7.31)	(6.72)	(4.21)
ℓdtax	−0.188	−0.150	−0.164	−0.127	−0.022
	(5.42)	(4.82)	(5.30)	(4.50)	(1.05)
sdtimp	−1.358	−1.222	−1.266	−1.090	−0.748
	(4.82)	(4.70)	(4.88)	(4.63)	(3.73)
sdtexp	−3.218	−2.892	−2.914	−2.401	−1.347
	(11.37)	(11.84)	(11.96)	(11.58)	(9.39)
R^2	0.975	0.978	0.978	0.983	0.987
Wu F ratio	87.15	85.13	82.63	46.62	—
N	1,415	1,415	1,415	1,371	1,415

Notes: Intercepts are not shown. Regressors include state and year dummy variables. Columns (i)–(iv) give two-stage least-squares (2SLS) estimates with C_{t-1} and C_{t+1} treated as endogenous. Column (v) gives an ordinary least-squares (OLS) estimate. The instruments in column (i) consist of the one-period lag and lead of price plus the other explanatory variables in the model. Column (ii) adds the current and one-period lag values of the state cigarette tax to the instruments; column (iii) further adds the one-period lead of the tax; and column (iv) further adds two additional lags of the price and tax variables. The Wu F ratios pertain to tests of the hypothesis that the OLS models corresponding to the first four columns are consistent. They all are significant at the 1-percent level.

1.6 percent in next period's consumption (see row 5, which assumes that the price change is not anticipated until the current period) and to a 0.5–0.8-percent increase in the previous period's consumption (see row 4, which assumes that the price change is not anticipated until the previous period).

These estimates imply that a 10-percent decline in cigarette prices causes a short-run increase in cigarette consumption of 4 percent (see row 6), which is only about 50 percent of the estimated long-run response of 7.5 percent. Finally, a 10-percent temporary increase in the current price of cigarettes would decrease current consumption by 3.5 percent if it is anticipated (see row 2) and by 3 percent if it is unanticipated (see row 3). Each of these responses is less than half of the long-run response of approximately 7.5 percent.

Table 16.4 Price Elasticities for Two-Stage Least-Squares Models (Approximate t Statistics in Parentheses)

Elasticity	(i)	(ii)	(iii)	(iv)
Long-run	−0.734	−0.743	−0.747	−0.788
	(13.06)	(12.43)	(12.43)	(10.67)
Own price:				
Anticipated	−0.373	−0.361	−0.346	−0.306
	(10.73)	(11.13)	(10.86)	(9.87)
Unanticipated	−0.349	−0.322	−0.316	−0.262
	(9.97)	(10.09)	(10.10)	(9.20)
Future price, unanticipated	−0.050	−0.084	−0.058	−0.068
	(2.37)	(4.90)	(3.70)	(5.14)
Past price, unanticipated	−0.155	−0.133	−0.152	−0.144
	(8.99)	(8.01)	(9.80)	(9.43)
Short-run	−0.407	−0.436	−0.387	−0.355
	(9.34)	(9.51)	(9.69)	(8.80)

Clearly, the estimates indicate that cigarettes are addictive, that past and future changes significantly impact current consumption. This evidence is inconsistent with the hypothesis that cigarette consumers are myopic. Still, the estimates are not fully consistent with rational addiction, because the point estimates of the discount factor (β) are implausibly low: the ratio of the estimated coefficient of future consumption to the estimated coefficient of past consumption in the TSLS models in table 16.3 ranges from 0.31 to 0.64. These discount factors correspond to interest rates ranging from 56.3 percent to 222.6 percent. However, as we already indicated, uncertainty about future prices could account for the implausibly high interest rates implied by our estimates.

Although the OLS coefficients in column (v) of table 16.3 are not consistent, they provide further support for the hypotheses that smoking is addictive (the coefficient of past consumption is positive and significant) and that consumers are rational (the coefficient of future consumption is positive, significant, and smaller than the coefficient of past consumption). The long-run price elasticity in the OLS model is −1.06, and the short-run elasticity is −0.34. The implied discount factor of 0.87 (interest rate of 14.9 percent) is quite reasonable. We return to the issue of inferring the discount factor from the estimates at the end of this section.

Table 16.5 contains estimates of rational-addiction demand functions that exclude the one-period lead value of price and the one-period lead value of the excise tax from the set of instruments. Model (i) in table 16.5 employs the

Table 16.5 Two-Stage Least-Squares Estimates of Rational-Addiction Models, Future Price and Tax Excluded from Set of Instruments, Dependent Variable = C_t (Asymptotic t Statistics in Parentheses)

Independent Variable	Model		
	(i)	(ii)	(iv)
C_{t-1}	−0.235	0.139	0.109
	(1.03)	(2.25)	(1.69)
C_{t+1}	1.601	0.737	0.887
	(3.75)	(6.62)	(8.55)
P_t	0.865	−0.472	−0.164
	(1.39)	(2.33)	(0.89)
Y_t	−0.217	0.397	0.258
	(−0.67)	(3.19)	(2.14)
ℓdtax	0.393	0.038	0.115
	(2.30)	(0.77)	(2.39)
sdtimp	0.630	−0.559	−0.297
	(0.86)	(1.94)	(0.98)
sdtexp	1.571	1.325	−0.631
	(1.20)	(3.33)	(1.75)
R^2	0.926	0.979	0.976
Wu F ratio	39.35	51.85	42.36
N	1,371	1,415	1,371

Notes: Intercepts are not shown. Regressors include state and year dummy variables. C_{t-1} and C_{t+1} are treated as endogenous. The instruments in model (i) consist of the first and second lag of price plus the other explanatory variables in the model. Model (ii) adds the current and one-period lag values of the state cigarette tax to the instruments and deletes the second lag of price, and model (iv) further adds two additional lags of the price and tax variables. The Wu F ratios pertain to tests of the hypothesis that the OLS estimates corresponding to the first three columns are consistent. They all are significant at the 1-percent level.

exogenous variables in the demand function and the first and second lag of price as instruments. Like the first model in table 16.3, it is exactly identified. The last two models in table 16.5 correspond to models (ii) and (iv) in table 16.3 after future variables are deleted from the instruments. The last model in table 16.5 is labeled model (iv) because it corresponds to model (iv) in table 16.3.[7] As in table 16.3, the Wu test rejects the hypothesis that OLS yields consistent estimates.[8]

The coefficients in table 16.5 are very different from those in table 16.3. The current-price and lagged-consumption coefficients fall dramatically, and the future-consumption coefficients rise dramatically (as Nelson and Startz [1990] would predict) when future variables are not used as instruments.

The estimates in table 16.5 still offer some support for the rational-addiction model, because the coefficient of future consumption is positive and significant. But the point estimates of the discount factor now are too high rather than too low: 5.30 in model (ii) and 8.14 in model (iv).[9] These discount factors correspond to negative interest rates of −81 percent and −88 percent, respectively.

The results in table 16.5 are less supportive of the rational and myopic addiction models than are the results in table 16.3. First, the implied discount factors in table 16.5 are less plausible than those in table 16.3. Second, the price coefficient in the first model in table 16.5 is positive, and the corresponding coefficient in the third model, while negative, is not significant. Third, the estimate of the degree of addiction (θ), which is given by the coefficient of past consumption, in the second model in table 16.5, is approximately one-third as large as the estimates of this parameter in table 16.3. As a result, the short-run price elasticity of −0.76 in the second model in table 16.5 is only 15-percent smaller than the long-run price elasticity of −0.90, while the short-run price elasticity is 50-percent smaller than the long-run price elasticity in all the models in table 16.3. Finally, the estimates in table 16.3 are much more stable across alternative sets of instruments than those in table 16.5.

One way to choose between the estimates in tables 16.3 and 16.5 is to perform Hausman tests (Jerry A. Hausman 1978) of the hypothesis that future prices and taxes are legitimate estimates. Under the null hypothesis of perfect foresight (no measurement error in future prices), the estimates in both tables are consistent, but those in table 16.3 are more efficient. Under the alternative hypothesis of measurement error in future prices, only the estimates in table 16.5 are consistent. Therefore, Hausman's procedure amounts to a Wald test of the hypothesis that the coefficients in the second model in table 16.5 are the same as the coefficients in the second or third model in table 16.3, and that the coefficients in the third model in table 16.3 are the same as those in the corresponding model in table 16.3.

The computed χ^2 statistics associated with these three tests are 24.4, 48.9, and 56.2, respectively. The first test has one degree of freedom since one instrument is excluded when future price is deleted. The second and third tests have two degrees of freedom since two instruments are excluded when the future price and the future tax are deleted. At the 1-percent level, the critical value of χ^2 is 6.6 in the first test and 9.2 in the second and third tests. Since the computed χ^2 always greatly exceeds the critical value, the hypothesis that future values are legitimate instruments is rejected by this test given the maintained hypothesis that the past variables themselves are excluded from the demand equation.

However, before too much weight is placed on this rejection, one should recall the problems associated with the estimates in table 16.5 that are not taken into account by the Hausman test. In particular, by limiting the set of instruments to poor predictors of future price and, therefore, to poor predictors of future consumption, it becomes difficult to sort out the past and future consumption effects. This is reflected in part by the dramatic increase in the standard errors of the past- and future-consumption coefficients, suggesting that the degree of multicollinearity rises when the future price and tax are not employed as instruments.

Therefore, it is useful to look at other ways to choose between the estimates in tables 16.3 and 16.5. One way is to examine what happens if the true structural demand function was slightly different. Suppose that the second lag of consumption belongs in the true model with a coefficient of 0.1 or 0.2. When the first model in table 16.3 is reestimated with either of these constraints imposed, the coefficient of future consumption remains unchanged at 0.14.[10] When the first model in table 16.5 is reestimated with a constraint of 0.1 on the second lag of consumption, the coefficient of future consumption falls from 1.60 to 1.26. This coefficient drops even further to 0.88 when a constraint of 0.2 is used.

Similar results emerge with model (iv) in tables 16.3 and 16.5. Since these models are overidentified, they can be estimated by including the second lag of consumption as an endogenous right-hand-side variable with no constraint imposed on its coefficient. When model (iv) in table 16.3 is fit in this fashion, the coefficient of future consumption falls slightly from 0.23 to 0.20. With an imposed constraint of 0.1, this coefficient equals 0.22, and with a constraint of 0.2, it equals 0.21. The same exercises applied to model (iv) in table 16.5 result in future consumption coefficients of 0.72, 0.80, and 0.72, respectively. These values should be compared to the coefficient of 0.89 in the table.

Although we have only considered the effect on the future-consumption coefficient, the results are similar when variations in the current-price coefficient are examined. In each case, models that use future prices and future taxes as instruments are much less sensitive to changes in the specification of the structural demand function than those that exclude these instruments. This is not surprising since the future-price variable provides variation that is correlated with future consumption and not highly correlated with potentially omitted past price and consumption variables.

A final way to choose between the estimates in tables 16.3 and 16.5 is to simulate the impact of overstating the covariance between expected future price and expected future consumption. Consider the exactly identified model estimated in the first column in table 16.3. Let c be current consumption, f be expected future consumption, ℓ be the first lag of consumption, p be expected future price, z be past price, and σ_{ij} be the covariance between any two of these variables net of all other variables in the demand function (current price, income, the three smuggling measures, and the state and time dummies).[11] If f and p were observed, the two-stage least-squares coefficients of future consumption (θ_f) and past consumption (θ_ℓ) would be

$$\theta_f = (\sigma_{cp}\sigma_{\ell z} - \sigma_{\ell p}\sigma_{cz}) / (\sigma_{fp}\sigma_{\ell z} - \sigma_{\ell p}\sigma_{fz}) \tag{6}$$

$$\theta_\ell = (\sigma_{cz}\sigma_{fp} - \sigma_{fz}\sigma_{cp}) / (\sigma_{fp}\sigma_{\ell z} - \sigma_{\ell p}\sigma_{fz}). \tag{7}$$

Let π be actual future price and let a be actual future consumption. Note that $\pi = p + u$ and $a = f + \varepsilon$, where the forecast error in future consumption (ε) is negatively related to the forecast error in future price (u). Since u is uncorrelated with current or past variables, the only covariance that is affected when π replaces p and a replaces f is that between π and a. In particular,

$$\sigma_{fp} = k\sigma_{a\pi} \qquad k = [1 - (\sigma_{\varepsilon u} / \sigma_{a\pi})]. \tag{8}$$

Presumably, k is less than 1. Therefore, if $\sigma_{a\pi}$ rather than σ_{fp} is used in equations (10) and (11), the coefficient of future consumption and the ratio of the coefficient of future consumption to the coefficient of past consumption are understated.

Table 16.6 presents estimates of θ_f, θ_ℓ, and the ratio of the long-run price elasticity to the short-run price elasticity for alternative assumed values of k. As long as k is at least as large as 0.75 (the forecast error covariance is no larger than 25 percent of the total covariance), the true estimates are similar to those in the first column of table 16.3. These latter estimates assume that $k = 1$, or that the forecast error covariance is zero. Not surprisingly, if one attempts to reconcile the large divergence between the estimates in tables 16.3 and 16.5 and 5 based only on imperfect information concerning future prices, it is necessary to assume that the forecast error covariance is extremely (and in our view unreasonably) large. We have already pointed out a better way to reconcile these estimates. This is to use the empirical fact that past prices and taxes are poor predictors of future prices and relatively good predictors of potentially omitted past effects. This makes these variables poor predictors of future consumption.

The conclusions to be drawn from these tests of the estimates in tables 16.3 and 16.5 depend on one's priors. If one believes that the structural demand function is correctly specified, and that the errors in forecasting future cigarette prices are enormous, then the estimates in table 16.5 are preferable. However, if one believes that the structural demand function is misspecified—if only slightly—and that consumers do have relevant information to forecast future cigarette prices, then the estimates in table 16.3 are clearly preferable. For the

Table 16.6 Future Consumption Coefficient (θ_f), Past Consumption Coefficient (θ_ℓ), and Ratio of Long-Run to Short-Run Price Elasticity, Corrected for Forecast Error

k	θ_f	θ_ℓ	Ratio of Long-Run to Short-Run Price Elasticity
1.000	0.135	0.418	1.803
0.750	0.179	0.399	1.762
0.500	0.268	0.360	1.676
0.400	0.336	0.330	1.608
0.333	0.407	0.299	1.535

Notes: In the first column, k is the ratio of the partial covariance between expected future consumption and expected future price to the partial covariance between actual future consumption and actual future price, with current price, income, the three smuggling measures, and the state and time dummies held constant.

reasons already given, we prefer the second interpretation, which is supportive of the rational-addiction model. It should be noted that none of the models in either table supports the myopic-addiction model. In fact, the results in table 16.5 reject the rational model because they imply that consumers put *too much* weight on future consumption.

Even if the rational-addiction model is accepted, it is not possible to infer the discount rate reliably from these cigarette data. One approach is simply to impose the discount factor a priori. We do this in table 16.7, by imposing six alternative discount factors ranging from 0.70 to 0.95 (interest rates ranging from 5.3 percent to 42.9 percent) in estimating models (ii) and (iv). That is, we constrain the coefficient of future consumption to equal β multiplied by the estimated coefficient of past consumption. We impose this constraint both in the specifications that include the future price and the future tax as instruments, and in the specifications that exclude these variables as instruments.

The table presents price coefficients, past-consumption coefficients, long-run price elasticities, and short-run price elasticities that emerge from the restricted estimates. The marginal significance level of the restriction, based on a Lagrange multiplier (LM) test, also is indicated. Regardless of the discount factor imposed, the long-run price elasticities are very similar to each other and to those in table 16.4. The same comment applies to the short-run price elasticities. Moreover, the specifications that employ the future price and the future tax as instruments yield elasticities that are almost identical to those that exclude these two instruments.[12]

Discount factors of 0.85 and 0.90 are very similar to the discount factor of 0.87 implied by the OLS regression in table 16.5. Yet the application of the Wu test to the constrained estimates in table 16.7 that impose these discount factors rejects the hypothesis that OLS is consistent. When the imposed discount factor

Table 16.7 Current Price Coefficients, Lagged Consumption Coefficients, Long-Run Price Elasticities, and Short-Run Price Elasticities in Restricted Models

β	Model	Panel A: Future Price or Future Price and Future Tax Included as Instruments					Panel B: No Future Variables Included as Instruments				
		Marginal Significance Level of Restriction	P_t	C_{t-1}	Long-Run Price Elasticity	Short-Run Price Elasticity	Marginal Significance level of Restriction	P_t	C_{t-1}	Long-Run Price Elasticity	Short-Run Price Elasticity
0.70	(ii)	0.727	−1.220	0.360	−0.742	−0.445	0.000	−1.105	0.385	−0.755	−0.426
	(iv)	0.054	−0.925	0.426	−0.792	−0.395	0.000	−0.822	0.449	−0.820	−0.376
0.75	(ii)	0.548	−1.214	0.351	−0.743	−0.452	0.000	−1.084	0.378	−0.756	−0.430
	(iv)	0.021	−0.919	0.415	−0.792	−0.404	0.000	−0.803	0.440	−0.824	−0.384
0.80	(ii)	0.400	−1.208	0.342	−0.742	−0.458	0.000	−1.063	0.372	−0.759	−0.436
	(iv)	0.008	−0.913	0.404	−0.790	−0.413	0.000	−0.781	0.432	−0.829	−0.391
0.85	(ii)	0.285	−1.203	0.334	−0.743	−0.465	0.000	−1.044	0.366	−0.763	−0.442
	(iv)	0.003	−0.908	0.394	−0.791	−0.421	0.000	−0.761	0.424	−0.833	−0.398
0.90	(ii)	0.199	−1.199	0.326	−0.743	−0.472	0.000	−1.025	0.359	−0.761	−0.446
	(iv)	0.001	−0.904	0.385	−0.795	−0.431	0.000	−0.743	0.416	−0.837	−0.405
0.95	(ii)	0.136	−1.196	0.318	−0.743	−0.478	0.000	−1.007	0.353	−0.763	−0.451
	(iv)	0.000	−0.901	0.375	−0.791	−0.439	0.000	−0.725	0.409	−0.845	−0.414

Notes: All price and lagged consumption coefficients and all elasticities are statistically significant at all conventional levels of confidence. For panel A, the instruments in model (ii) are the one-period lag of price, the one-period lead of price, the current state excise tax, the one-period lag of the tax, and the exogenous variables in the demand function. Model (iv) adds the one-period lead of the tax and the two-period lags of the tax and price to the set of instruments. For panel B, the instruments in model (ii) are the one-period lag of price, the current tax, the one-period lag of the tax, and the exogenous variables in the demand function. Model (iv) adds the two-period lags of the tax and price to the set of instruments. The marginal significance levels of the restrictions are based on a Lagrange multiplier (LM) test.

is 0.85, the F ratios in panel A are 167.5 in model (ii) and 77.8 in model (iv). The corresponding F ratios in panel B are 72.3 and 27.7. When the imposed discount factor is 0.90, the F ratios in panel A are 167.5 in model (ii) and 78.0 in model (iv). The corresponding F ratios in panel B are 68.0 and 25.2. All are significant at the 1-percent level. The eight models in table 16.7 with discount factors of 0.85 and 0.90 imply an average long-run price elasticity of −0.78 and an average short-run price elasticity of −0.44. We are more confident in these estimates than in the long-run elasticity of −1.06 and the short-run elasticity of −0.34 associated with the OLS regression in table 16.3.

The results in tables 16.3, 16.5, and 16.7 suggest that the data are not rich enough to pin down the discount factor with precision. This is not surprising. Estimates of consumer discount factors from studies of aggregate consumption, the consumption of specific goods, or the consumption of leisure over time vary considerably. Some of these estimates imply extremely high interest rates, while others imply very low and even negative interest rates (e.g., Hansen and Singleton 1983; Mankiw et al. 1985; Hotz et al. 1988; Bover 1991; Epstein and Zin 1991). Nevertheless, it is reassuring that our estimates of the basic parameters of the model are not sensitive to the choice of alternative discount factors. Moreover, in the specifications with the future price and tax as instruments, we cannot reject the hypothesis (at the 1-percent level) that the discount factor is as high as 0.90 or 0.95 in two of four cases. Finally, when we compensate for the narrow set of instruments that results from the deletion of future variables by imposing a discount factor, the estimates of short-run and long-run price elasticities are not sensitive to the instruments used to obtain them.

Frank Chaloupka (1991) provides further evidence in support of a model of cigarette addiction in a micro dataset: the second National Health and Nutrition Examination Survey. Using measures of cigarette consumption in three adjacent periods, he fits demand functions similar to those in table 16.3. He finds a short-run price elasticity (−0.20) that is less than half of the long-run price elasticity of −0.45. His significant future-consumption coefficient is further evidence against myopic addiction.

5. MONOPOLY AND ADDICTION

The organization of the cigarette industry has been studied frequently and shown to be highly concentrated (Bain 1968; Sumner 1981; Appelbaum 1982; Geroski 1983; Porter 1986). Two companies (R. J. Reynolds and Philip Morris) account for about 70 percent of U.S. output, and the studies just cited conclude in general that cigarette companies have significant monopoly power. Discussions of pricing by cigarette companies have not paid attention to the habitual aspects of cigarette smoking, even though that greatly affects optimal monopoly pricing and other company policies.

To illustrate the relation between pricing and addiction, elsewhere we develop a simple monopoly pricing model (see Becker et al. 1990; also see the extensions of our analyses by Gary Fethke and Raj Jagannathan [1991] and by Mark H. Showalter [1991]). The main implications are quite intuitive. In each period a monopolist sets a price where marginal revenue is below marginal cost, as long as consumption is addictive and future prices tend to exceed future marginal costs due to the monopoly power. The reason is that future profits are higher when current consumption is larger and current price is lower, because greater current consumption raises future consumption. As it were, a monopolist may lower price to get more consumers "hooked" on the addictive good. The optimal marginal revenue is lower relative to marginal cost when the good is more addictive, future demand is stronger, and future price minus cost is bigger. With a sufficiently large positive effect on future demand of a lower current price, a monopolist might choose a current price that is below current cost, or a price in the inelastic region of demand.

This analysis, which incorporates addiction into pricing policy, may be helpful in understanding the rise in cigarette prices in recent years. Much of the drop in demand for cigarettes since 1981 documented by Jeffrey E. Harris (1987) and others is due to greater information about health hazards, restrictions imposed on smoking in public places, and the banning of cigarette advertising on radio and television. Several studies have commented about the apparent paradox that cigarette companies have been posting big profits while smoking is declining and have documented the faster rise in cigarette prices than in apparent costs (see Harris 1987; Dunkin et al. 1988). Indeed, according to Stephen J. Adler and Alix M. Freedman (1990, 1), "One of the great magic tricks of market economics ... [is] how to force prices up and increase profits in an industry in which demand falls by tens of billions of cigarettes each year."

Incorporation of the addictive aspects of smoking into the analysis resolves this paradox if cigarette companies have some monopoly power. An increase in current prices would raise cigarette companies' profits in the short run if they were pricing below the current profit-maximizing point (in order to raise future demand through the addictive effect of greater current smoking). Addictive behavior can also explain why current prices rise: the decline in future demand for smoking reduces the gains from maintaining a lower price to stimulate future consumption.

Incorporation of the addictive aspects of smoking also leads to a test of whether the cigarette industry is oligopolistic or competitive. If smokers are addicted and if the industry is oligopolistic, an expected rise in future taxes and hence in future prices induces a rise in current prices even though current demand falls when future prices are expected to increase. This cannot happen in simple models of competitive behavior.

A higher federal excise tax on cigarettes was widely expected to go into effect at the beginning of 1983—an example of an instance where consumers had prior information about future tax increases. Cigarette prices increased sharply not only in 1983, but also prior to the tax increase during 1982. The price increase in 1982 has been taken as evidence that "the tax increase served as a focal point [or coordinating device] for an oligopolistic price increase" (Harris 1987, 101). That is possible, but a price increase in 1982 may have occurred even if oligopolistic cigarette producers had no such coordinating problems, because the higher future cigarette tax reduced future demand and, hence, the gain from lowering current price.

Appendix A

SOLUTION OF DIFFERENCE EQUATION AND PRICE EFFECTS

The solution of the difference equation (4) is

$$
\begin{aligned}
C_t = & \frac{1}{\theta \phi_1 [\phi_2 - \phi_1]} \sum_{s=1}^{\infty} \phi_1^s h(t + s) \\
& + \frac{1}{\theta \phi_2 [\phi_2 - \phi_1]} \sum_{s=0}^{\infty} \phi_2^{-s} h(t - s) \\
& + \frac{1}{\phi_2^i} \left(C^0 - \frac{1}{\theta \phi_1 [\phi_2 - \phi_1]} \sum_{s=1}^{\infty} \phi_1^s h(s) \right)
\end{aligned}
\tag{A1}
$$

where

$$
h(t) = \theta_0 + \theta_1 P_{t-1} + \theta_2 e_{t-1} + \theta_3 e_t
$$

$$
\phi_1 = \frac{1 - (1 - 4\theta^2 \beta)^{1/2}}{2\theta}
$$

$$
\phi_2 = \frac{1 + (1 - 4\theta^2 \beta)^{1/2}}{2\theta}
$$

with $4\theta^2 \beta < 1$ for stability.

Equation (Al) determines the sign of the effects of changes in the price of cigarettes in period τ on cigarette consumption in period t. These effects, which are temporary in nature since prices in other periods are held constant, are

$$\frac{dC_t}{dP_\tau}\bigg|_{\tau>t} = \frac{\theta_1\phi_1^{\tau-t}}{\theta[\phi_2-\phi_1]}\left[1-\left(\frac{\phi_1}{\phi_2}\right)^t\right] \lessgtr 0 \qquad \text{(A2a)}$$

$$\text{as } \theta \gtrless 0$$

$$\frac{dC_t}{dP_\tau}\bigg|_{\tau<t} = \frac{\theta_1\phi_2^{\tau-t}}{\theta[\phi_2-\phi_1]}\left[1-\left(\frac{\phi_1}{\phi_2}\right)^\tau\right] \lessgtr 0 \qquad \text{(A2b)}$$

$$\text{as } \theta \gtrless 0$$

$$\frac{dC_t}{dP_t} = \frac{\theta_1}{\theta[\phi_2-\phi_1]}\left[1-\left(\frac{\phi_1}{\phi_2}\right)^t\right] < 0. \qquad \text{(A2c)}$$

To obtain the completely unanticipated price effect, set t or τ on the right-hand side of equation (A2) equal to 1. To obtain the fully anticipated price effect, let t or τ approach infinity.

The effect on consumption in period t of a permanent reduction in price beginning in period t, which we denote as dC_t/dP_t*, is given by

$$\frac{dC_t}{dP_t^*} = \frac{\theta_1[1-(\phi_1/\phi_2)^t]}{\theta(1-\phi_1)(\phi_2-\phi_1)}. \qquad \text{(A3)}$$

With t equal to 1, the equation gives the effect on current consumption of a completely unanticipated permanent reduction in price. This effect is

$$\frac{dC_t}{dP_t^*} = \frac{\theta_1}{\theta(1-\phi_1)\phi_2}. \qquad \text{(A4)}$$

Equation (A4) shows the short-run price effect, defined as the impact on consumption of a reduction in current price and all future prices, with past consumption held constant.

Finally, the effect of a permanent reduction in price in *all* periods on consumption in period t is

$$\frac{dC_t}{dP} = \frac{\theta_1\phi_2^{-t}}{\theta(\phi_2-\phi_1)}\times\left[\frac{\phi_2^t}{\phi_2-1}-\frac{1-\phi_1^t}{1-\phi_1}\right]+\frac{\theta_1[1-(\phi_1/\phi_2)^t]}{\theta(1-\phi_1)(\phi_2-\phi_1)}. \qquad \text{(A5)}$$

The limit of equation (A5) as t goes to infinity equals the long-run effect of a permanent reduction in price:

$$\frac{dC_\infty}{dP} = \frac{\theta_1}{\theta(1-\phi_1)(\phi_2-1)}. \qquad \text{(A6)}$$

Appendix B

DATA

Cigarette sales were missing for nine states in the years specified below:

Alaska, 1955–1959
Hawaii, 1955–1960
California, 1955–1959
Colorado, 1955–1964
Maryland, 1955–1958
Missouri, 1955
North Carolina, 1955–1969
Oregon, 1955–1966
Virginia, 1955–1960.

The price of cigarettes was missing for Alaska and Hawaii in each year in which sales were missing. In addition, price was not reported for the former state in 1960 and for the latter state in 1961.

The state excise tax on a pack of cigarettes is a weighted average of the tax rates in effect during the fiscal year, where the weights are the fraction of the year each rate was in effect. The Tobacco Tax Council gives the price of cigarettes as of November. The price used in our regressions in fiscal year t equals five-sixths of the price in November of year $t - 1$ plus one-sixth of the price in November of year t, adjusted for changes in the state excise tax rate during the fiscal year. In particular, the state excise tax as of the date of the price was subtracted from the price, the average price exclusive of tax was computed from the preceding formula; and the average excise tax was added back to the price. The algorithm was modified in certain years in which price was reported in October. The price variable published by the Tobacco Tax Council (1986) excludes municipal excise taxes imposed on cigarettes by one or more municipalities in certain states. We created a state-specific average municipal excise tax rate (the sum of revenues from municipal cigarette excise taxes for the state as reported by the Tobacco Tax Council [various years] divided by state cigarette sales in packs) and added this variable to the price. Note that the state excise tax rate defined in table 16.1 and used as an instrumental variable for past and future consumption in tables 16.2, 16.3, 16.5, and 16.7 is inclusive of the average municipal excise tax rate.

In every state except Hawaii and New Hampshire, the excise tax on cigarettes was a specific tax (fixed amount per pack) during our sample period. In Hawaii the tax was 40 percent of the wholesale price throughout the period. In New

Hampshire the tax was 42 percent of retail price until fiscal 1976. Equivalent taxes per pack in these two states were computed by the Tobacco Tax Council.

Short-distance smuggling or casual bootlegging refers to out-of-state purchases by residents of a neighboring state with a higher excise tax. The short-distance importing and exporting incentive measures are used as separate regressors because consumption in an importing state (defined as sales plus imports) depends on the difference between the own state and the out-of-state price or tax. Consumption in an exporting state does not depend on this difference. Of course, both imports and exports respond to the tax difference. Long-distance smuggling or organized bootlegging refers to systematic attempts to ship cigarettes from North Carolina, Virginia, or Kentucky to other states. These cigarettes are sold at the retail prices prevailing in the relevant states without paying the excise tax, which is imposed at the wholesale level. Consumption in the importing state does not depend on the difference between that state's tax and the tax in North Carolina, Virginia, or Kentucky. Hence, long-distance importing and exporting incentives can be summarized by a single variable since imports summed over all states in a given year must equal exports summed over all states in that year. Given the definitions of the three smuggling variables in table 16.1, their regression coefficients all should be negative.

The effects of short-distance casual smuggling are measured by two variables: one for imports and one for exports. The importing variable is

$$\text{sdtimp}_i = \sum_j k_{ij}(T_i - T_j)$$

where k_{ij} is the fraction of the population of state i (the higher-tax state) living within 20 miles of state i (the lower-tax state), and T_i and T_j are the cigarette excise tax rates in each state. The weights are computed from the 1970 Census of Population (Bureau of the Census 1973), and the summation is taken over neighboring states with lower tax rates. This is equivalent to setting the tax differential equal to zero if $T_i \leq T_j$. The exporting variable is given by

$$\text{sdtexp}_i = \sum_j k_{ji}(T_i - T_j)(\text{POP}_j / \text{POP}_i)$$

where k_{ji} is the fraction of the higher-taxed state's population living within 20 miles of the exporting state (state i) and POP_j denotes the population of state j. Here the summation is taken over neighboring states with higher tax rates. This is equivalent to setting the tax differential equal to zero if $T_i \geq T_j$. The reason that the population ratio is used in the export variable is that *total* exports from state i to state j should depend on the part of the population of state j living near state i or POP_j multiplied by k_{ji}. Since the dependent variable in the regression model is state-specific per capita sales, the population of state i enters the denominator.

The tax differentials in the preceding formulas include or exclude municipal excise taxes depending on the border area at issue. The population figures are year-specific. They were taken from the 1960, 1970, and 1980 Censuses of Population for census years and from the Bureau of the Census (1985) for other years (see the reference just cited for the complete list of sources). For noncensus years, the population was given as of July 1, and for census years, it was given as of April 1. The latter was interpolated to July 1 using state-specific exponential-growth trends between, for example, April 1, 1980, and July 1, 1981. Then population in fiscal year t was defined as a simple average of population as of July 1 in years $t - 1$ and t.

The construction of the long-distance smuggling variable is based on several assumptions. It is assumed that Virginia and North Carolina share the long-distance exporting to all states in the Northeast and Southeast as well as any state within 500 miles of either. All Western states within 1,000 miles of Kentucky are assumed to import from Kentucky. States more than 1,000 miles from Kentucky, Virginia, or North Carolina are assumed to do no long-distance smuggling. The long-distance smuggling variable based on these assumptions is given by

$$\ell\mathrm{dtax}_i = (T_i - T_{KY}) \qquad \text{if importing from Kentucky}$$

$$= z_{NC}(T_i - T_{NC}) + z_{VA}(T_i - T_{VA})$$

if importing from North Carolina and Virginia

$$= \sum_j (T_{KY} - T_j)(POP_j / POP_{KY}) \quad \text{for Kentucky}$$

$$= z_i \left[\sum_j (T_i - T_j)(POP_j / POP_i) \right]$$

for $i = $ NC, VA.

The weights used for states that import from North Carolina and Virginia are the shares of value added accounted for by each in the production of cigarettes in these two states combined. That is,

$$z_{NC} = \frac{(\text{value added in NC})}{(\text{value added in NC} + \text{value added in VA})}.$$

Note that total imports from Kentucky, North Carolina, or Virginia to state i depend on the population of i, which cancels when imports are expressed on a per capita basis. If state i's excise tax was lower than the exporting state's excise tax, which occurred in a few states prior to fiscal 1967, the tax difference was set equal to zero.

State-specific money-per-capita income in fiscal year t is a simple average of money-per-capita income in calendar years $t - 1$ and t. The consumer price index in fiscal year t, which is not state-specific, is defined in a similar manner. Per capita income by state was taken from the Bureau of Economic Analysis (various years).

NOTES

Originally published as Gary S. Becker, Michael Grossman, and Kevin M. Murphy, "Rational Addiction and the Effect of Price on Consumption," *American Economic Review* 81, no. 2 (1991): 237–241. Also published in *Searching for Alternatives: Drug Control Policy in the United States*, ed. Melvyn B. Krauss and Edward P. Lazear. Stanford, CA: Hoover Institution Press, 1991, 77–86. Funding for this research was supported by a grant from the Bradley Foundation to the Center for the Study of the Economy and the State of the University of Chicago. We are indebted to Eugene M. Lewit, David Merriman, three anonymous referees, and the participants in seminars at the University of Chicago, Columbia University, Harvard University, the University of Kentucky, the Federal Trade Commission, the City University of New York Graduate School, Colgate University, Pennsylvania State University, and the State University of New York at Albany for helpful comments and suggestions. We thank Frank Chaloupka, Brooks Pierce, Robert Tamura, Ahmet E. Kocagil, Geoffrey F. Joyce, Patricia De Vries, and Ismail Sirtalan for research assistance. This paper has not undergone the review accorded official NBER publications; in particular, it has not been submitted for approval by the Board of Directors.

1. Price effects that do not hold past and future consumption constant are considered later in the paper.

2. The coefficient of current price (θ_1) in equation (4) depends on the parameters of the utility function, the discount factor, and the marginal utility of wealth. Strictly speaking, price should be interacted with any variable that determines the marginal utility of wealth. Such an equation is not tractable from the standpoint of estimation due to its large set of regressors and potential for creating severe problems of multi-collinearity. Our procedure, which captures variations in the marginal utility of wealth but not interactions between the determinants of this variable and price, may be viewed as a linear approximation to the true model. Essentially, we estimate the price coefficient associated with the marginal utility of wealth evaluated at its mean value. Technically, if the marginal utility of C_t does not depend on Y_t, the only coefficient in equation (4) that depends on the

marginal utility of wealth is the coefficient of current price. That coefficient equals $\lambda\alpha$, where α equals $1/(u_{11} + \beta u_{22})$. Suppressing subscripts and variables other than current price and the constant, this equation can be written as

$$C = \theta_0 + \alpha\lambda P.$$

As an identity,

$$\lambda P = \bar{\lambda}\bar{P} + v\bar{\lambda} + w\bar{P} + vw$$

where a bar over a variable denotes a mean, v equals the deviation of P from its mean, and w equals the deviation of λ from its mean. If vw approaches zero,

$$C = \theta_0 + \alpha\bar{\lambda}\bar{P} + \alpha\bar{\lambda}P + \alpha\bar{P}\lambda.$$

3. In the rational-addiction model, C_{t-1} depends on e_t through the optimizing behavior implied by the first-order conditions. Therefore, past consumption must be treated as an endogenous variable in estimating this model even if e_t is not serially correlated.

4. Since the regressions in table 16.2 are reestimated after adding future price, models (i) and (ii) contain 1,415 (1,517–102) observations. Fewer than fifty-one observations are lost when the second lag of price is introduced, due to the pattern of missing price data. In particular, seven states have missing cigarette sales but known prices in certain years.

5. The residuals from several of the models in table 16.2 were examined for autocorrelation. The algorithm assumed a common time-series error structure among states, and no autocorrelations for lag lengths greater than ten. The first ten autocorrelation coefficients were obtained and were used to compute a variance-covariance matrix of regression coefficients (var) of the form

$$\text{var} = (\hat{Z}'\hat{Z})^{-1}\hat{Z}'V\hat{Z}(\hat{Z}'\hat{Z})^{-1}$$

where V is the variance-covariance matrix of the disturbance term and

$$\hat{Z} - [\hat{Y}X_1].$$

The last equation specifies a matrix of the predicted values of the endogenous variables ($\hat{Y}$) and exogenous variables (X_1) in the structural demand function for current consumption. Standard errors of regression coefficients based on this algorithm (available from the authors upon request) were very similar to those that did not correct for autocorrelation. In most cases the corrected standard error was *smaller* than the corresponding uncorrected standard error. The same comment applies to the estimates in tables 16.3 and 16.5. The regression residuals also were examined for cross-sectional heteroscedasticity due to averaging over an unequal number of people in each state. This analysis suggested that there were no efficiency gains to weighting by the square root of the state population.

6. Inclusion of the future price as well as the future tax allows for the possibility that consumers have additional information about the price exclusive of tax or about the relationship between the price inclusive of tax and the tax.

7. Models (ii) and (iii) in table 16.3 are the same when future variables are deleted from the instruments.

8. An OLS demand function is not presented in table 16.5 because it is identical to the one in table 16.3.

9. We do not compute the discount factor in model (i) because the coefficient of past consumption has the wrong sign.

10. The coefficient in table 16.3 is 0.135. The same coefficient is 0.139 in a model that omits the second lag of consumption but is estimated on the reduced sample that results when the constraint is imposed.

11. That is, c, f, ℓ, p, and z are residuals from, for example, a regression of actual current consumption on the exogenous variables in the demand function.

12. When future variables are used as instruments, the restriction is not significant (the imposed discount factor is valid) at the 1-percent level in eight out of twelve cases, and it is not significant at the 5-percent level in seven out of twelve cases. On the other hand, when future variables are not used as instruments, the restriction is significant in every case at any conventional level of confidence. These results are to be expected since the estimates in table 16.5 imply discount factors that exceed 1.

REFERENCES

Adler, Stephen J., and Alix M. Freedman. 1990. "Tobacco Suit Exposes Ways Cigarette Firms Keep the Profits Fat." *Wall Street Journal* 5: 1.

Appelbaum, Elie. 1982. "The Estimation of the Degree of Oligopoly Power." *Journal of Econometrics* 19(2/3): 287–299.

Bain, Joe S. 1968. *Industrial organization,* 2nd Ed. New York: Wiley.

Baltagi, Badi H., and Dan Levin. 1986. "Estimating Dynamic Demand for Cigarettes Using Panel Data: The Effects of Bootlegging, Taxation and Advertising Reconsidered." *Review of Economics and Statistics* 68(1): 148–155.

Becker, Gary S., Michael Grossman, and Kevin M. Murphy. 1990. "An Empirical Analysis of Cigarette Addiction." National Bureau of Economic Research (Cambridge, MA) Working Paper No. 3322.

Becker, Gary S., and Kevin M. Murphy. 1988. "A Theory of Rational Addiction." *Journal of Political Economy* 96(4): 675–700.

Bover, Olympia. 1991. "Relaxing Intertemporal Separability: A Rational Habits Model of Labor Supply Estimated from Panel Data." *Journal of Labor Economics* 9(1): 85–100.

Boyer, Marcel. 1978. "A Habit Forming Optimal Growth Model." *International Economic Review* 19(3): 585–609.

——. 1983. "Rational Demand and Expenditures Patterns under Habit Formation." *Journal of Economic Theory* 31(1): 27–53.

Bureau of the Census, U.S. Department of Commerce. 1973. *1970 Census of population. Volume I: Characteristics of the population,* Part 1: "United States Summary," Section 1,

Washington, DC: U.S. Government Printing Office. (Comparable sources used for data from the 1960 and 1980 *Censuses of population.*)

——. 1985. *Current population reports: Population estimates and projections,* Series P–25, No. 970. Washington, DC: U.S. Government Printing Office. (Also No. 957, 1984; No. 460, 1971; No. 304, 1965.)

Bureau of Economic Analysis, U.S. Department of Commerce. Various years. *Survey of current business,* Washington, DC: U.S. Government Printing Office.

Chaloupka, Frank. 1991. "Rational Addictive Behavior and Cigarette Smoking." *Journal of Political Economy* 99(4): 722–742.

Dunkin, Amy, Michael Oneal, and Kevin Kelly. 1988. "Beyond Marlboro Country." *Business Week*: 54–58.

Epstein, Larry G., and Stanley E. Zin. 1991. "Substitution, Risk Aversion, and the Temporal Behavior of Consumption and Asset Returns: An Empirical Analysis." *Journal of Political Economy* 99(2): 263–86.

Fethke, Gary, and Raj Jagannathan. 1991. "Monopoly Pricing with Habit Formation." Working paper, Department of Economics, University of Iowa.

Geroski, Paul A. 1983. "Some Reflections on the Theory and Application of Concentration Indices." *International Journal of Industrial Organization* 1(1): 79–94.

Hansen, Lars Peter, and Kenneth J. Singleton. 1983. "Stochastic Consumption, Risk Aversion, and the Temporal Behavior of Asset Returns." *Journal of Political Economy* 91(2): 249–265.

Harris, Jeffrey E. 1987. "The 1983 Increase in the Federal Cigarette Excise Tax." In Lawrence H. Summers, ed., *Tax Policy and the Economy,* Vol. 1. Cambridge, MA: MIT Press: 87–111.

Hausman, Jerry A. 1978. "Specification Tests in Econometrics." *Econometrica* 46(6): 1251–1271.

Hotz, V. Joseph, Finn E. Kytdland, and Guilherme L. Sedlacek. 1988. "Intertemporal Preferences and Labor Supply." *Econometrica* 56(2): 335–360.

Iannaccone, Lawrence R. 1986. "Addiction and Satiation." *Economics Letters* 21(1): 95–99.

Lewit, Eugene M. 1982. "The Interstate Market for Smuggled Cigarettes." Unpublished manuscript presented at the annual meetings of the American Economic Association, New York.

Mankiw, N. Gregory, Julio J. Rotemberg, and Lawrence H. Summers. 1985. "Intertemporal Substitution in Macroeconomics." *Quarterly Journal of Economics* 100(1):2 225–51.

Nelson, Charles R., and Richard Startz. 1990. "The Distribution of the Instrumental Variables Estimator and Its *t*-Ratio When the Instrument Is a Poor One." *Journal of Business* 63(1), Part 2: S125–S140.

Pollak, Robert A. 1970. "Habit Formation and Dynamic Demand Functions." *Journal of Political Economy* 78(4), Part I: 745–763.

——. 1976. "Habit Formation and Long-Run Utility Functions." *Journal of Economic Theory* 13(2): 272–297.

Porter, Robert H. 1986. "The Impact of Government Policy on the U.S. Cigarette Industry." In Pauline M. Ippolito and David T. Scheffman, eds., *Empirical Approaches to Consumer Protection Economics.* Washington, DC: Federal Trade Commission:4 447–81.

Ryder, Harl E., Jr., and Geoffrey M. Heal. 1973. "Optimum Growth with Intertemporally Dependent Preferences." *Review of Economic Studies* 40(1): 1–33.

Showalter, Mark H. 1991. "Monopoly Behavior with Intertemporal Demands." PhD Dissertation, Massachusetts Institute of Technology.

Spinnewyn, Frans. 1981. "Rational Habit Formation." *European Economic Review* 15(1): 91–109.

Stigler, George J., and Gary S. Becker. 1977. "De Gustibus Non Est Disputandum." *American Economic Review* 67(1): 76–90.

Sumner, Daniel A. 1981. "Measurement of Monopoly Behavior: An Application to the Cigarette Industry." *Journal of Political Economy* 89(5): 1010–1019.

Tobacco Tax Council. 1986. *The Tax Burden on Tobacco: Historical Compilation,* Vol. 20. Richmond, VA: Tobacco Tax Council.

——. Various years. *Municipal Tax Surveys.* Richmond, Virginia: Tobacco Tax Council.

Warner, Kenneth E. 1986. *Selling Smoke: Cigarette Advertising and Public Health.* Washington, DC: American Public Health Association.

Wu, De-Min. 1973. "Alternative Tests of Independence between Stochastic Regressors and Disturbances." *Econometrica* 41(4) 733–750.

Yaari, Menahem E. 1977. "Consistent Utilization of an Exhaustible Resource, or How To Eat an Appetite-Arousing Cake." Working paper, Center for Research on Mathematical Economics and Game Theory, Hebrew University.

SEVENTEEN

An Empirical Analysis
of Alcohol Addiction

Results from the Monitoring
the Future Panels

Michael Grossman, Frank J. Chaloupka,
and Ismail Sirtalan

ABSTRACT

In a panel of young adults, we find that alcohol consumption is addictive in the sense that increases in past or future consumption cause current consumption to rise. The positive and significant future consumption effect is consistent with the hypothesis of rational addiction. The long-run price elasticity is approximately 60 percent larger than the short-run price elasticity and twice as large as the elasticity that ignores addiction. Thus, a tax hike policy to curtail consumption or abuse may not have a favorable cost-benefit ratio unless it is based on the long-run price elasticity.

1. INTRODUCTION

This chapter aims to refine and enrich the empirical literature dealing with the price sensitivity of alcohol consumption by incorporating insights provided by Becker and Murphy's (1988) theoretical model of rational addictive behavior. Their model emphasizes the interdependency of past, current, and future consumption of an addictive good. In addition, we reexamine the relative potency of excise tax and drinking age hikes as policy instruments to curtail alcohol abuse by young adults. Our study is unique in that it addresses these issues in a panel of individuals. The panel is formed from the nationally representative cross-sectional surveys of high school seniors conducted each year since 1975 by the Institute for Social Research of the University of Michigan. The members of the panel range in age from seventeen through twenty-nine. Since Grant et al. (1991) report that the prevalence of alcohol dependence and abuse is highest in this age range, addictive models of alcohol consumption may be more relevant to this sample than to a representative sample of the population of all ages. By testing for rational addiction, we address the issue of whether teenagers and young adults ignore the internal costs of alcohol use and abuse and whether these costs should be considered in formulating public policy.

Rachal et al. (1980) demonstrate a positive relationship between alcohol abuse at early and later stages of the life cycle, indicating that excessive consumption is an example of an addictive behavior. Yet the substantial empirical literature on the demand for alcohol does not incorporate insights from the Becker-Murphy theoretical model of this behavior.[1] The main element of this and other models of addiction is that an increase in past consumption of an addictive good raises the marginal utility of current consumption and therefore raises current consumption. A key feature of the Becker-Murphy model which distinguishes it from other models of addictive behavior is that addicts are rational or far-sighted in the sense that they anticipate the expected future consequences of their current actions. This is in sharp contrast to myopic models of addiction in which consumers ignore the effects of current consumption on future utility when they determine the optimal or utility-maximizing quantity of an addictive good in the present period.

The Becker-Murphy model predicts intertemporal complementarity of consumption or negative cross price effects and a long-run own price elasticity of demand which exceeds the short-run elasticity (the former allows past consumption to vary while the latter does not). This model has been successfully applied to the addictive behavior of cigarette smoking in published research by Chaloupka (1991); Keeler, Hu, Barnett, and Manning (1993); and Becker, Grossman, and Murphy (1994). These three studies report negative and significant price effects, positive and significant past and future consumption effects, and long-run elasticities which are larger than short-run price elasticities.

We find that alcohol consumption by young adults is addictive in the sense that increases in past or future consumption cause current consumption to rise. The positive and significant future consumption effect is consistent with the hypothesis of rational addiction and inconsistent with the hypothesis of myopic addiction. The long-run elasticity of consumption with respect to the price of beer (the alcoholic beverage of choice by young adults) is approximately 60 percent larger than the short-run price elasticity and twice as large as the elasticity that ignores addiction.

2. ANALYTICAL FRAMEWORK

Following Becker, Grossman, and Murphy (1994), we assume that consumers maximize a lifetime utility function given by

$$V = \sum_{t=1}^{\infty} \beta^{t-1} U(Y_t, C_t, C_{t-1}, e_t). \tag{1}$$

Here Y_t is consumption of a nonaddictive good at time or age t, C_t is consumption of an addictive good (alcohol in our case) at age t, C_{t-1} is alcohol consumption at age $t-1$, e_t reflects the effects of unmeasured life cycle variables on utility, and β is the time discount factor [$\beta = 1/(1+r)$, where r is the rate of time preference for the present]. An increase in lagged alcohol consumption (C_{t-1}) lowers utility if the addiction is harmful ($\partial U/\partial C_{t-1} < 0$), while an increase in the lagged consumption raises utility if the addiction is beneficial ($\partial U/\partial C_{t-1} > 0$). Presumably, the partial derivative just defined is negative, although the model simply assumes that this term is nonzero. Regardless of the nature of the addiction, an increase in past consumption must raise the marginal utility of C_t in order for an increase in past consumption of C to increase current consumption.

When the utility function is quadratic and the rate of time preference for the present is equal to the market rate of interest, equation (1) generates a structural demand function for consumption of C of the form

$$C_t = \theta C_{t-1} + \beta\theta C_{t+1} + \theta_1 P_t + \theta_2 e_t. \tag{2}$$

Here P_t is the price of C_t, and the intercept is suppressed. Since θ is positive and θ_1 is negative, current consumption is positively related to past and future consumption (C_{t-1} and C_{t+1}, respectively) and negatively related to current price. In particular, θ measures the effect of an increase in past consumption on the marginal utility of current consumption. By symmetry, it also measures the effect of an increase in future consumption on the marginal impact of current consumption on next period's utility. The larger the value of θ the greater is the degree of reinforcement or addiction.

Equation (2) is the basis of the empirical analysis in this chapter. Note that ordinary least squares estimation of the equation might lead to biased estimates of the parameters of interest. The unobserved variables that affect utility in each period are likely to be serially correlated. Even if these variables are uncorrelated, C_{t-1} and C_{t+1} depend on e_t through the optimizing behavior. These relationships imply that an ordinary least squares estimation of the equation might incorrectly imply that past and future consumption affect current consumption, even when the true value of θ is zero. Fortunately, the specification in equation (2) suggests a way to solve the endogeneity problem. The equation implies that current consumption is independent of past and future prices when past and future consumption are held constant; any effect of past or future prices on current consumption must come through their effects on past or future consumption. Provided that the unobservables are uncorrelated with prices in these periods, past and future prices are logical instruments for past and future consumption, since past prices directly affect past consumption, and future prices directly affect future consumption. Therefore, the empirical strategy amounts to estimating equation (2) by two-stage least squares, with past and future prices serving as instrumental variables for past and future consumption. This strategy can be modified when measures of some of the life cycle events that affect utility and therefore partially determine e_t, such as marital status and unemployment, are available. Then current marital status, for example, is a relevant regressor in the structural demand function given by equation (2), and past and future marital status are instruments for past and future consumption.

The statistical significance of the coefficient of future consumption provides a direct test of a rational model of addiction against an alternative model in which consumers are myopic. In the latter model they fail to consider the impact of current consumption on future utility and future consumption. That is, the myopic version of equation (2) is entirely backward looking. In this version, current consumption depends only on current price, lagged consumption, the marginal utility of wealth (which is one of the determinants of the current price coefficient), and current events. Because of these distinctions, myopic models and rational models have different implications about responses to future changes. In particular, rational addicts increase their current consumption when future prices are expected to fall, but myopic addicts do not.

Equation (2) implies that there are important differences between long- and short-run responses to permanent price changes (price changes in more than one period) in the case of addiction. The short-run price effect describes the response to a change in price in period t and all future periods that is not anticipated until period t. The long-run price effect pertains to a price change in *all* periods. Since C_{t-1} remains the same if a price change is not anticipated until period t, the long-run price effect must exceed the short-run price effect.[2]

3. DATA AND EMPIRICAL IMPLEMENTATION

Every spring since 1975, the University of Michigan's Institute for Social Research has conducted a nationally representative random sample of between 15,000 and 19,000 high school seniors as part of the Monitoring the Future research program. These surveys, which are described in detail by Johnston, O'Malley, and Bachman (1993), focus on the use of illegal drugs, alcohol, and cigarettes. Starting with the class of 1976, a sample of approximately 2,400 individuals in each senior class has been chosen for follow-up. Individuals reporting the use of marijuana on twenty or more occasions in the past thirty days or the use of any other illegal drug at least once in the past thirty days in their senior year are selected with a higher probability (by a factor of three). The 2,400 selected respondents are divided into two groups of 1,200 each; one group is surveyed on even-numbered calendar years, while the other group is surveyed on odd-numbered calendar years. As a result of this design, one group is resurveyed for the first time one year after baseline (the senior year in high school), while the other group is resurveyed for the first time two years after baseline. Subsequent follow-ups are conducted at two-year intervals for both groups.

We estimate alcohol demand functions using ten of the twenty panels formed from the high school senior surveys conducted from 1976 through 1985. We limit the panels to those in which the first follow-up occurred two years after baseline, so that each follow-up was conducted at two-year intervals. The last follow-up in our dataset, which contains approximately 12,000 persons, took place in 1989. We have between one and five observations on each person since we require information on current, past, and future consumption of alcohol. Since an annual measure of consumption is used in the regressions, past consumption coincides with the second annual lag and future consumption coincides with the second annual lead.

Information on county identifiers at base line and at each follow-up allowed us to augment the dataset with alcoholic beverage prices from the *Inter-City Cost of Living Index*, published quarterly by the American Chamber of Commerce Researchers Association (ACCRA) (various years) for between 250 and 300 cities since the first quarter of 1968. ACCRA collects information on the prices of a number of consumer goods including beer, wine, and distilled spirits. In addition to prices, the ACCRA constructs a city-specific cost of living index for each of the cities with an average for all cities in a given quarter and year equal to one.

The baseline survey is conducted between March 15 and April 30 and takes place in the youth's high school. The follow-up surveys are mailed to the home addresses of respondents during the weeks of April 1–15. Respondents are requested to return the surveys promptly but do not always do so. Consequently, we assume that the annual alcohol consumption measure described below, which pertains to consumption during the last year, reflects consumption in the first two quarters of the year in which the survey was conducted (year t) and the last two quarters of the previous year (year $t - 1$). Thus, the current annual price of alcohol described below is computed as a simple average of the prices over these four quarters. The second annual lead and lag, which are employed extensively in the regressions in section 4, are given as a simple average of the price in the first two quarters of year $t + 2$ and the last two quarters of year $t + 1$ (second annual lead) and as a simple average of the price in the first two quarters of year $t - 2$ and the last two quarters of year $t - 3$ (second annual lag). The current, past, and future prices are annual averages of quarterly prices rather than prices as of a certain month within the year. Thus, they account fully for state excise tax changes that take place during the twelve-month period for which consumption is measured.

The price assigned to each person comes from the ACCRA survey city nearest the person's county of residence. Similar comments apply to the computation of lags and leads of the price. For persons with different county residence codes in survey years t and $t + 2$, prices from the third quarter of year t through the fourth quarter of year $t + 1$ are computed as simple averages of the prices in each county. Since much of the cross-sectional variation in alcoholic beverage prices is due to variations in state excise tax rates on these beverages, persons are never matched to ACCRA cities outside their state of residence. This results in the deletion of some observations because not all states are represented in a given ACCRA survey.

Data on the consumption of specific alcoholic beverages (beer, wine, and distilled spirits) are not collected for four-fifths of the Monitoring the Future respondents. Therefore, the price of beer is used as the measure of the price of alcohol. This price is selected because beer is the most heavily consumed alcoholic beverage and because beer is the beverage of choice among teenagers and young adults. The specific price used is the price of a six-pack (six 12-ounce cans) of Budweiser or Schlitz. All quarterly nominal beer prices are averaged over the four relevant quarters to obtain the current annual nominal price of beer and the second annual lead and lag of the price. These prices are converted to real prices by dividing them by a year- and city-specific cost of living index. This index is the ACCRA city-specific cost of living index multiplied by the quarterly CPI for the United States as a whole (1982–1984 = 1) and then averaged over the four relevant quarters.

A sample of 21,420 person-years or person follow-ups is employed in the empirical analysis. It is obtained by deleting persons who failed to respond to at least three consecutive questionnaires (including baseline) and by deleting observations for which the number of drinks of alcohol in the past year, the current real price of beer, or current real annual earnings are missing. Given three observations per person on average, there are approximately 7,140 respondents in the final sample.

The number of drinks of alcohol consumed in the past year is the dependent variable in all regressions in section 4. This variable is given by the product of the number of drinking occasions during the last twelve months and the number of drinks consumed on a typical drinking occasion. The number of drinking occasions is an ordered categorical variable with seven outcomes: 0 occasions, 1–2 occasions, 3–5 occasions, 6–9 occasions, 10–19 occasions, 20–39 occasions, and 40 or more occasions. It is converted into a continuous variable by assigning midpoints to the closed intervals and a value of 50 to the open-ended interval.

The number of drinks on a typical drinking occasion is inferred from the response to the question: "On the occasions that you drink alcoholic beverages, how often do you drink enough to feel pretty high?" The response categories are none of the occasions, few of the occasions, half of the occasions, most of the occasions, and nearly all of the occasions. We assume that the second response category corresponds to 25 percent of all occasions, that the fourth corresponds to 75 percent of all occasions, and that the fifth corresponds to 100 percent of all occasions. We also assume that four drinks must be consumed to feel pretty high. Persons in the first response category are assumed to consume 1.5 drinks on a typical drinking occasion. Persons in the second category are assumed to consume $.75 \times 1.5 + .25 \times 4 = 2.125$ drinks on a typical occasion. Persons in third category are assigned a value of $.5 \times 1.5 + .5 \times 4 = 2.75$. Persons in the fourth category are assigned a value of $.25 \times 1.5 + .75 \times 4 = 3.375$, and persons in the fifth category are given a value of four drinks on a typical occasion.

The minimum legal drinking age for the purchase and consumption of low alcohol beer is a partial determinant of the full price of alcohol, especially for underage youths. Since no state has ever had a legal drinking age greater than twenty-one, the drinking age is multiplied by a dichotomous variable that equals one for persons twenty-one years of age or younger. In addition to the own-state minimum legal drinking age, a dichotomous indicator equal to one if a respondent resides in a county within 25 miles of any state with a lower legal drinking age is employed as a regressor. It is interacted with the dichotomous indicator for persons whose age is less than or equal to twenty-one for the same reason that the drinking age is interacted with this indicator. The border age variable is included in the model to capture potential border crossings by youths from states with high drinking ages to nearby lower age states to obtain alcohol. With the own-state legal drinking age held constant, the coefficient of the border age variable in the demand function should be positive.

A variety of independent variables were constructed from the demographic and socio-economic information collected in the surveys. These include sex;

race (black or other); age (dichotomous indicators for ages 19, 21, 23, and 25); real annual earnings; years of formal schooling completed; college student status (full-time, half-time, or less than half-time); work status (full-time, part-time, or unemployed); religious participation (infrequent or frequent); marital status (married, engaged, or separated or divorced); and the respondent's number of children. Finally, all models include dichotomous variables for nine of the ten cohorts (the high school senior classes of 1976 through 1984). The time-varying variables serve as proxies for life-cycle variables that affect the marginal utility of current consumption.

Given the nature of the panel, we estimate equation (2) with the second lag of the annual number of drinks of alcohol as the measure of past consumption and the second lead of the annual number of drinks of alcohol as the measure of future consumption. Since past consumption and future consumption are endogenous, the equation is fitted by two-stage least squares (TSLS). The instruments consist of the exogenous variables in the model, the second lag of the annual real beer price, the second lead of the annual real beer price, the second annual lags of the two measures pertaining to the legal drinking age (legal drinking age × age ≤21 and lower border drinking age indicator × age ≤21), and the second leads and the second lags of all time-varying socioeconomic variables. These include real annual earnings, years of formal schooling completed, college student status, work status, religious participation, marital status, and number of children. The second leads of the two measures pertaining to the legal drinking age are not used as instruments because the values of these two variables are zero except at the first follow-up.

A problem with the use of leads and lags of the socioeconomic variables as instruments is that these variables may not be exogenous. While plausible arguments can be made for the endogeneity of all of them, the real issue is which ones are most likely to be caused by alcohol consumption or correlated with the disturbance term in the structural alcohol demand function given by equation (2). In our view, religious participation, marital status, and number of children are more likely to fall into the latter category. Therefore, demand functions are obtained with and without these variables.

4. EMPIRICAL RESULTS

Panel A of table 17.1 contains price, legal drinking age, and border age coefficients from standard alcohol demand functions that ignore addictive behavior. In particular, past and future consumption are excluded from these estimates. The regression in column 1 omits religious participation, marital status, and number of children, while the regression in column 2 includes these variables.

The most important findings in these regressions are the negative and significant price and legal drinking age effects and the positive and significant border age effect. The magnitude, but not the significance, of the price coefficient is sensitive to the inclusion of religious participation, marital status, and number of children. In particular, the price coefficient is cut in half when these variables are added to the set of regressors. At the weighted (to correct for oversampling of illegal drug users at baseline) sample means of consumption (60.630 drinks in the past year) and price ($2.789 in 1982–1984 dollars for a six-pack of Budweiser or Schlitz), the price elasticity of demand equals –0.38 in the first regression and –0.20 in the second regression. The first estimate may be influenced by omitted variables bias, while the second may be influenced by simultaneous equations bias. Therefore, we regard these two figures as bracketing the true estimate. We consider their average of –0.29 as the benchmark price elasticity that emerges from a demand function for the number of drinks of alcohol in the past year that ignores addictive behavior, but we realize that the reader may want to use the range in comparing the nonaddictive and addictive estimates.

Panel B of table 17.1 tests the rational addiction model directly by estimating the structural demand function given by equation (2). The first two columns contain TSLS regression coefficients of past consumption, future consumption, price, and the two drinking age variables from models in which past consumption (the second annual lag of consumption) and future consumption (the second annual lead of consumption) are endogenous. Religious participation, marital status, and number of children are excluded from the first regression and included in the second. The last two columns contain the corresponding ordinary least squares (OLS) coefficients. Panel B also contains F-ratios resulting from Wu's (1973) test of the hypothesis that the regressors are exogenous and thus that the OLS estimates are consistent.

In the model with religious participation, marital status, and number of children, the ex-ogeneity of the regressors is rejected. In the model without these variables, the Wu test is inconclusive. The F-ratio of 3.18 is significant at the 5 percent level but not at the 1 percent level. Given these results and the potential endogeneity of religious participation, marital status, and number of children, it is useful to consider the OLS regressions as well as the TSLS regressions in evaluating the findings.

The estimated effects of past and future consumption on current consumption are significantly positive in the four regressions in panel B, and the estimated price and legal drinking age effects are significantly negative in all cases. The positive and significant past consumption coefficient is consistent with the

Table 17.1 Selected Coefficients from Demand Functions for Annual Number of Drinks of Alcohol

Panel A: Non-Addictive Demand Functions		
(n = 21,420)	(1)[a]	(2)[b]
Price	−8.158	−4.303
	(−6.48)	(−3.55)
Legal drinking age × age ≤21	−1.106	−1.217
	(−2.55)	(−2.92)
Lower border drinking age indicator × age ≤21	7.789	7.323
	(5.73)	(5.61)
R^2	0.104	0.176
Price elasticity	−0.375	−0.198

	Panel B: Structural Demand Functions			
	Two–Stage Least Squares		Ordinary Least Squares	
(n = 18,473)	(1)[a]	(2)[b]	(3)[a]	(4)[b]
Past consumption	0.254	0.274	0.346	0.339
	(4.37)	(8.18)	(60.07)	(58.69)
Future consumption	0.656	0.345	0.474	0.454
	(9.12)	(11.14)	(76.30)	(72.60)
Price	−2.470	−2.155	−2.663	−1.744
	(2.40)	(2.24)	(−2.84)	(−1.87)
Legal drinking age × age ≤21	−1.038	−1.131	−1.015	−1.059
	(3.12)	(3.44)	(−3.14)	(−3.30)
Lower border drinking age indicator × age ≤21	1.597	3.379	2.139	2.203
	(1.42)	(3.24)	(2.12)	(2.21)
R^2	0.191	0.292	0.568	0.576
Wu *F*-ratio	3.417	16.945	—	—
Long-run price elasticity	−1.265	−0.260	−0.681	−0.386
Short-run price elasticity	−0.857	−0.181	−0.384	−0.225

Notes: Asymptotic *t*-statistics in parentheses. All regressions include gender, race, age, real annual earnings, years of formal schooling completed, work status, college student status, and cohort indicators. Price elasticities computed at weighted sample means of price and consumption.
[a] Religious participation, marital status, and number of children excluded.
[b] Religious participation, marital status, and number of children included.

hypothesis that alcohol consumption is an addictive behavior. The positive and significant future consumption coefficient is consistent with the hypothesis of rational addiction and inconsistent with the hypothesis of myopic addiction.

Clearly, the estimates indicate that alcohol consumption is addictive in the sense that past and future changes significantly impact current consumption. This evidence is inconsistent with the hypothesis that alcohol consumers are myopic. Still, the estimates are not fully consistent with rational addiction because the estimates of the discount factor (β)—given by the ratio of the coefficient of future consumption to the coefficient of past consumption—are implausibly high. The implied discount factor is 2.58 in the first regression, 1.26 in the second regression, 1.37 in the third regression, and 1.34 in the fourth regression. These discount factors correspond to negative interest rates of −61 percent, −20 percent, −27 percent, and −26 percent, respectively.

We imposed a discount factor of 0.95 (interest rate of 5 percent) a priori and reestimated the four regressions in panel B of table 17.1. The price and legal drinking age coefficients in these models are extremely close to their unconstrained counterparts. These results, combined with the detailed analysis in Becker, Grossman, and Murphy (1994), suggest that data on alcohol consumption or cigarette smoking are not rich enough to pin down the discount factor with precision even if the rational addiction model is accepted.

At the weighted sample means of consumption and price, the long-run price elasticity of demand ranges from −0.26 to −1.26 (average equals −0.65) in panel B. The short-run elasticity ranges from −0.18 to −0.86 (average equals −0.41). The ratio of the long-run elasticity to the corresponding short-run elasticity is more stable. It varies from 1.44 to 1.77 (average equals 1.60). This ratio should be compared to a ratio of approximately 1.91 in the case of rational addiction demand functions for cigarettes reported by Chaloupka (1991) and by Becker, Grossman, and Murphy (1994). Becker, Grossman, and Murphy (1991) show that the ratio of the long-run price elasticity to the short-run price elasticity rises as the degree of addiction, measured by the coefficient of past consumption, rises. Thus, our results suggest that alcohol consumption is somewhat less addictive than cigarette smoking.

Nevertheless, the long-run elasticity of demand for the number of drinks of alcohol in the past year is substantially larger than the short-run elasticity. The average long-run price elasticity of −0.65 also is more than twice as large as the benchmark price elasticity of −0.29 that emerges from the demand functions in panel A that ignore addiction. Indeed, the average short-run elasticity is almost 40 percent larger than the benchmark elasticity.

Our results bear on efforts to reduce youth alcohol abuse by raising the legal drinking age or by raising the federal excise tax rate on beer. The former policy was actively pursued by the federal government and state governments in the late 1970s and the 1980s. It resulted in a uniform minimum drinking age of twenty-one in all states as of July 1988. Increased taxation of beer—the alcoholic beverage of choice among youth and young adults—has been virtually ignored in the antidrinking campaign. Between November 1951 and January 1991, the federal excise tax rate on beer was fixed in nominal terms at 16 cents per six-pack. Moreover, despite the popularity of beer, the alcohol in distilled spirits currently is taxed twice as heavily as the alcohol in beer, and the alcohol in spirits was taxed three times as heavily as the alcohol in beer prior to October 1985.[3] Due in part to the stability of the federal beer tax and the modest increases in state beer taxes, the real price of beer declined by 20 percent between 1975 and 1990.

We use the four regression models in panel B of table 17.1 to simulate the effects of drinking age changes and federal beer tax excise tax hikes on the annual number of drinks of alcohol consumed by nineteen year olds in the mid years of our sample—1982 and 1983. This age group consumed sixty-two drinks per year in the period at issue (this is the weighted mean). The average legal drinking age was 19.6, and 19 percent of the sample lived within 25 miles of a state with a lower drinking age.

If the drinking age had been twenty-one in all states in 1982 and 1983 (which means that the border age indicator would have been zero for all youth), nineteen year olds would have consumed approximately 11 fewer drinks of alcohol in the long run. This is an average of the four long-run declines predicted by the regression models in panel B and amounts to an 18 percent reduction relative to the mean of 62. If the federal beer tax had been indexed to the rate of inflation in the Consumer Price Index since 1951, consumption would have declined by six drinks or by 10 percent. If the beer tax were raised to equalize the rates at which the alcohol in beer and liquor are taxed and if beer and liquor taxes both were indexed to the inflation rate, consumption would have fallen by 26 drinks per year or by more than 40 percent.

The impact of the combined tax policy is more than twice as large as the impact of the drinking age policy. In part, this is because a number of states had raised the drinking age to twenty-one by 1982 or 1983. Therefore, to put these two policies in perspective, suppose that the drinking age had been eighteen (the historical minimum in any state) in all states in the years at issue. Then consumption would have risen by eight drinks per year. Put differently, the effect of going from a minimum legal drinking age of eighteen to one of twenty-one amounts to a reduction of nineteen drinks per year or slightly more than 30 percent relative to the mean of 62. Thus, the reduction in consumption associated with the combined tax policy exceeds that associated with the maximum increase in the drinking age by approximately 37 percent. These computations agree with conclusions reached by Grossman, Coate, and Arluck (1987); Coate and Grossman (1988); Kenkel (1993); and Grossman, Chaloupka, Saffer, and Laixuthai (1994) with regard to the effectiveness of beer tax hikes. The absolute magnitudes of the effects in these studies differ from those in our study because the outcomes differ and because our estimates are obtained in the context of a model of rational addiction.

Our evaluations of policies that would increase the federal excise tax on beer in order to curtail teenage and young adult alcohol abuse extend previous evaluations in two important ways. First, we find that the long-run price elasticity of consumption with respect to the price of beer is approximately 60 percent larger than the short-run elasticity and twice as large as the elasticity that ignores addiction. Thus, forecasts of reductions in consumption in this age group would be considerably understated if they were not based on the long-run elasticity. Put differently, a tax hike to curtail abuse may have an unfavorable cost-benefit ratio based on the short-run price elasticity or the price elasticity that ignores addiction, while the same policy may have a very favorable cost-benefit ratio based on the long-run price elasticity.

Second, we find evidence that alcohol consumption decisions made by teenagers and young adults exhibit rational or farsighted behavior in the sense that current consumption is positively related to future consumption. This suggests that at least some of the internal effects or costs of alcohol abuse are not ignored costs that can be used to justify government intervention. If consumers take into account the future costs that they impose upon themselves by abusing alcohol, then the case for higher taxes or other policies to curtail abuse must be based solely on the harm that abusers do to third parties. This conclusion is tentative because we have focused on a measure of alcohol use rather than on a measure of abuse and because certain aspects of moderate current alcohol consumption may raise future utility by lowering the risk of heart disease or by improving social interactions at bars, clubs, and parties. Future research could clarify these issues by directly considering measures of abuse in the context of rational addiction.

NOTES

Originally published as Michael Grossman, Frank J. Chaloupka, and Ismail Sirtalan, "An Empirical Analysis of Alcohol Addiction: Results from the Monitoring the Future Panels," *Economic Inquiry* 36, no. 1 (1998): 39–48. This is a condensed version of Grossman, Chaloupka, and Sirtalan (1996). The longer version contains a detailed discussion of the model, data, and empirical results. It also considers a number of estimation issues and performs a variety of sensitivity analyses. In particular, we show that the choice between weighted regressions (to correct for oversampling of illegal drug users at baseline) and unweighted regressions is moot because the two sets of estimates are very similar. We also present results with alternative values for the open-ended alcohol drinking frequency category of 40 or more occasions in the past year of 45, 55, 60, 65, 70, 80, 90, 100, 200, and 300 (a value of 50 is used in the paper). The slope coefficient of the price of beer rises in absolute value as the value assigned to the open-ended category rises, but tests of significance and long- and short-run price elasticities are not affected. In addition, results with alternative assumptions about the number of drinks of alcohol that it takes to get pretty high are shown to be very similar to those in the paper. Finally, estimates obtained from a two-stage least squares fixed-effects model in which all time-varying variables are transformed into deviations from person-specific means and time-invariant variables are deleted confirm the estimates presented in the paper.

Research for this paper was supported by grant 5 R01 AA08359 from the National Institute on Alcohol Abuse and Alcoholism to the National Bureau of Economic Research. We are extremely grateful to Patrick M. O'Malley, Senior Research Scientist at the University of Michigan's Institute for Social Research, for providing us with the Monitoring the Future panels and for agreeing to attach county identifiers to our tapes. We also are extremely grateful to Jerome J. Hiniker, Senior Research Associate at ISR, for creating the computer programs that produced these tapes. Part of the paper was written while Grossman was a visiting scholar at the Catholic University of Louvain in Belgium, and he wishes to acknowledge the financial support provided by that institution. We are indebted to Gary S. Becker, Randall K, Filer, Robert J. Kaestner, Theodore E. Keeler, Donald S. Kenkel, Lee A. Lillard, John Mullahy, Kevin M. Murphy, William S. Neilson, Jon P. Nelson, Thomas R. Saving, Frank C. Wykoff, Gary A. Zarkin, and two anonymous referees for helpful comments and suggestions. Preliminary versions of the paper were presented at the 1995 meeting of the American Economic Association and the 1994 meeting of the Western Economic Association and at seminars at Brigham Young University, the Catholic University of Louvain, Charles University in Prague, the University of Chicago, Erasmus University in Rotterdam, the Rand Corporation, the Stockholm School of Economics, and the United States Military Academy at West Point. We are indebted to the participants in those meetings and seminars for comments and suggestions. Finally, we wish to thank Patricia Kocagil, Hadassah Luwish, Geoffrey Joyce, Sandy Grossman, Esel Yazici, and Sara Markowitz for research assistance. This paper has not undergone the review accorded official NBER publications; in particular, it has not been submitted for approval by the Board of Directors.

1. For a review of this literature, see Leung and Phelps (1993). For recent contributions, see Baltagi and Griffin (1995) and Manning, Blumberg, and Moulton (1995).
2. These results can be seen more formally by solving the second-order difference equation in equation (2). The solution, which is contained in Becker, Grossman, and Murphy (1994), results in an equation in which consumption in period t depends on prices and

life-cycle variables in all periods. Formulas for the long-run and short-run price effects also are contained in the paper just cited.

3. Prior to October 1, 1985, the federal excise tax on distilled spirits amounted to $10.50 per gallon of spirits (50 percent alcohol by volume) or $21.00 per gallon of alcohol in spirits. The beer tax of 16 cents per six-pack is equivalent to a tax of $.29 per gallon. Since one gallon of beer contains 4.5 percent alcohol by volume, this amounts to a tax of $6.44 on one gallon of alcohol in beer. Between October 1, 1985, and January 1, 1991, the federal tax rate on spirits was $12.50 per gallon or $25.00 per gallon of alcohol in spirits. On January 1, 1991, the federal beer tax rate doubled to $.58 per gallon, and the spirits tax rose by 8 percent to $13.50 per gallon.

REFERENCES

American Chamber of Commerce Researchers Association. Various years. *Inter-City Cost of Living Index.* Louisville, Kentucky.

Baltagi, Badi H., and James M. Griffin. 1995. "A Dynamic Model for Liquor: The Case for Pooling." *Review of Economics and Statistics*: 545–554.

Becker, Gary S., Michael Grossman, and Kevin M. Murphy. 1991. "Rational Addiction and the Effect of Price on Consumption." *American Economic Review*: 237–241.

——. 1994. "An Empirical Analysis of Cigarette Addiction." *American Economic Review*: 396–418.

Becker, Gary S., and Kevin M. Murphy. 1988. "A Theory of Rational Addiction." *Journal of Political Economy*: 675–700.

Chaloupka, Frank J. 1991. "Rational Addictive Behavior and Cigarette Smoking." *Journal of Political Economy*: 722–742.

Coate, Douglas, and Michael Grossman. 1988. "Effects of Alcoholic Beverage Prices and Legal Drinking Ages on Youth Alcohol Use." *Journal of Law and Economics*: 145–171.

Grant, Bridget F., Thomas C. Hartford, Patricia Chou, Roger Pickering, Deborah A. Dawson, Frederick S. Stinson, and John Noble. 1991. "Prevalence of DSM-III-R Alcohol Abuse and Dependence." *Alcohol Health & Research World* 15(1): 91–96.

Grossman, Michael, Frank J. Chaloupka, Henry Saffer, and Adit Laixuthai. 1994. "Alcohol Price Policy and Youths: A Summary of Economic Research." *Journal of Research on Adolescence* 4(2): 347–64.

Grossman, Michael, Frank J. Chaloupka, and Ismail Sirtalan. 1996 "An Empirical Analysis of Alcohol Addiction: Results from the Monitoring the Future Panels." National Bureau of Economic Research Working Paper No. 5200.

Grossman, Michael, Douglas Coate, and Gregory M. Arluck. 1987. "Price Sensitivity of Alcoholic Beverages in the United States." In *Control Issues in Alcohol Abuse Prevention: Strategies for States and Communities*, ed. Harold D. Holder. Greenwich, Conn.: JAI Press, Inc.: 169–198.

Johnston, Lloyd D., Patrick M. O'Malley, and Jerald G. Bachman. 1993. *National Survey Results from the Monitoring the Future Study,* 1975–1992. NIH Publication No. 93-3597/98. Washington, D.C.: U.S. Government Printing Office.

Keeler, Theodore E., Teh-wei Hu, Paul G. Barnett, and Willard G. Manning. 1993. "Taxation, Regulation, and Addiction: A Demand Function for Cigarettes Based on Time-Series Evidence." *Journal of Health Economics*: 1–18.

Kenkel, Donald S. 1993. "Drinking, Driving, and Deterrence: The Social Costs of Alternative Policies." *Journal of Law and Economics*: 877–913.

Leung, Siu Fai, and Charles E. Phelps. 1993. "'My Kingdom for a Drink ....?' A Review of the Price Sensitivity of Demand for Alcoholic Beverages." In *Economic and Socioeconomic Issues in the Prevention of Alcohol-Related Problems*, ed. Gregory Bloss and Michael Hilton. National Institute on Alcohol Abuse and Alcoholism Research Monograph 25. NIH Publication No. 93–3513. Washington, D.C.: U.S. Government Printing Office: 1–32.

Manning, Willard G., Linda Blumberg, and Lawrence H. Moulton. 1995. "The Demand for Alcohol: The Differential Response to Price." *Journal of Health Economics*: 123–148.

Rachal, J. Valley, L. Lynn Guess, Robert L. Hubbard, Stephen A. Maisto, Elizabeth R. Cavanaugh, Richard Waddell, and Charles H. Benrud. 1980. "The Extent and Nature of Adolescent Alcohol Abuse: The 1974 and 1978 National Sample Surveys." Prepared for the National Institute on Alcohol Abuse and Alcoholism. Springfield, Virginia: U.S. National Technical Information Service.

Wu, De-Min. 1973. "Alternative Tests of Independence between Stochastic Regressors and Disturbances." *Econometrica*: 733–750.

The Demand for Cocaine
by Young Adults

A Rational Addiction Approach

Michael Grossman and Frank J. Chaloupka

EIGHTEEN

ABSTRACT

This chapter applies the rational addiction model to the demand for cocaine by young adults in the Monitoring the Future panel. The price of cocaine is added to this survey from the Drug Enforcement Administration's System to Retrieve Information from Drug Evidence. Results suggest that annual participation and frequency of use given participation are negatively related to the price of cocaine. In addition, current participation (frequency) is positively related to past and future participation (frequency). The long-run price elasticity of total consumption (participation multiplied by frequency given participation) of −1.35 is substantial.

1. INTRODUCTION

The period from the late 1980s to the present has witnessed a lively debate concerning the costs and benefits of legalization of such substances as cocaine, marijuana, and heroin. Legalization of these harmfully addictive goods surely will reduce their prices. By the law of the downward-sloping demand function, their consumption will rise. Prices will also fall and consumption will rise if these substances remain illegal, but resources allocated to enforcement activities are permanently lowered. But by how much will consumption rise? According to conventional wisdom, which is adopted by some proponents of legalization, the consumption of these illegal addictive substances is not very responsive to price. Opponents of legalization argue that consumption may be quite responsive to price based in part on research on the demand for two widely used legal addictive substances—alcohol and cigarettes—particularly by teenagers and young adults (for example, Grossman 1993).

The theoretical model of addictive behavior of Becker and Murphy (1988), which assumes that addicts behave rationally, allows for the possibility that addictive goods may be responsive to price in the long run. Their model emphasizes the interdependency of past, current, and future consumption of an addictive good. The main element of this and other models of addictive behavior is that an increase in past consumption of an addictive good raises the marginal utility of current consumption and therefore raises current consumption. A key feature of the Becker-Murphy model that distinguishes it from other models of addictive behavior is that addicts are rational or farsighted in the sense that they anticipate the expected future consequences of their current actions. This is in contrast to myopic models of addiction in which consumers ignore the effects of current consumption on future utility when they determine the optimal or utility-maximizing quantity of an addictive good in the present period. The Becker-Murphy model predicts intertemporal complementarity of consumption or negative cross price effects. This model and myopic addiction models predict that the long-run own price elasticity of demand should exceed the short-run elasticity (the former allows past consumption to vary while the latter does not). Hence, the conventional wisdom may be correct for short-run price changes but not for long-run price changes.

The purpose of this chapter is to inform the debate on legalization by providing estimates of the price elasticity of demand for cocaine consumption in the context of the rational addiction model. These estimates also are useful in evaluating policies such as crop reduction and criminal justice that raise price. There are few previous empirical studies in this area, and no previous attempts to study the demand for illegal drugs with a panel of individuals in the context of rational addiction because data on prices and quantities consumed of illegal drugs have been difficult to acquire. The data employed in this study consist of the panel formed from the nationally representative cross-sectional surveys of high school seniors conducted each year since 1975 by the Institute for Social Research of the University of Michigan as part of the Monitoring the Future research program. The members of the panel range in age from seventeen through twenty-nine. Since the prevalence of cocaine consumption is highest in this age range, and few people initiate use after age twenty-nine (National Institute on Drug Abuse 1991), information on the responsiveness to price in this segment of the population is crucial in evaluating the impacts of alternative price policies in all segments of the population.

We find that cocaine consumption by young adults is addictive in the sense that increases in past or future consumption cause current consumption to rise. The positive and significant future consumption effect is consistent with the hypothesis of rational addiction and inconsistent with the hypothesis of myopic addiction. The long-run price elasticity of −1.35 is substantial and approximately 40 percent larger than the short-run price elasticity.

2. PRIOR STUDIES

There are few published studies on the effects of price on the use of cocaine, marijuana, heroin, or other illegal drugs; and no published studies that investigate price effects in nationally representative micro panel data. Nisbet and Vakil (1972) report a price elasticity of demand for marijuana ranging from −0.36 to −1.51 in an anonymous mail survey of students at the University of California at Los Angeles. Silverman and Spruill (1977) estimate the price elasticity of demand for heroin in an indirect manner from the relationship between crime and the price of heroin in a monthly time series of forty-one neighborhoods in Detroit and obtain an elasticity of −0.27. DiNardo (1993) finds that cocaine participation in the past month by high school seniors does not respond to the price of cocaine price in a time series of state cross sections for the years 1977–1987. Van Ours (1995) examines the demand for opium in Indonesia from 1923 through 1938. By allowing present consumption to depend on past consumption, his study is the only one to explicitly allow for addiction. van Ours obtains a substantial long-run elasticity of −1.00, which is approximately 40 percent larger than the short-run price elasticity.

The Becker and Murphy (1988) rational addiction model has been applied successfully to the demand for cigarettes by Chaloupka (1991), Keeler et al. (1993), and Becker et al. (1994). It also has been applied successfully to the demand for alcohol by Grossman et al. (1998). All these studies report negative and significant price effects, positive and significant past and future consumption effects, and larger long-run than short-run price elasticities.

3. ANALYTICAL FRAMEWORK

Following Becker et al. (1994), we assume that consumers maximize a lifetime utility function given by:

$$V = \sum_{t=1}^{\infty} \beta^{t-1} U(Y_t, C_t, C_{t-1}, e_t) \tag{1}$$

Here Y_t is consumption of a nonaddictive good at time or age t, C_t is consumption of an addictive good (cocaine in our case) at age t, C_{t-1} is cocaine consumption at age $t-1$, e_t reflects the effects of measured and unmeasured life cycle variables on utility, and β is the time discount factor [$\beta = 1/(1+r)$, where r is the rate of time preference for the present]. An increase in lagged cocaine consumption (C_{t-1}) lowers utility if the addiction is harmful ($\partial U/\partial C_{t-1} < 0$), while an increase in lagged consumption raises utility if the addiction is beneficial ($\partial U/\partial C_{t-1} > 0$).[1] In this chapter, presumably, the partial derivative just defined is negative, although the model simply assumes that this term is nonzero. Regardless of the nature of the addiction, an increase in past consumption must raise the marginal utility of C_t in order for an increase in past consumption of C to increase current consumption.

When the utility function is quadratic and the rate of time preference for the present is equal to the market rate of interest, equation (1) generates an equation of motion for current consumption, which we term a structural demand function, of the form:[2]

$$C_t = \theta \, C_{t-1} + \beta \theta \, C_{t+1} + \theta_1 P_t + \theta_2 e_t \tag{2}$$

Here P_t is the price of C_t, and the intercept is suppressed. Since θ is positive and θ_1 is negative, current consumption is positively related to past and future consumption (C_{t-1} and C_{t+1}, respectively) and negatively related to current price. In particular, θ measures the effect of an increase in past consumption on the marginal utility of current consumption. By symmetry, it also measures the effect of an increase in future consumption on the marginal impact of current consumption on next period's utility. The larger the value of θ, the greater is the degree of reinforcement or addiction.

Equation (2) is the basis of the empirical analysis in this chapter. Note that ordinary least squares (OLS) estimation of the equation might lead to biased estimates of the parameters of interest. The unobserved variables that affect utility in each period are likely to be serially correlated. Even if these variables are uncorrelated, C_{t-1} and C_{t+1} depend on e_t through the optimizing behavior.

These relationships imply that an OLS estimation of the equation might incorrectly imply that past and future consumption affect current consumption, even when the true value of θ is zero.

Fortunately, the specification in equation (2) suggests a way to solve the endogeneity problem. The equation implies that current consumption is independent of past and future prices when past and future consumption are held constant; any effect of past or future prices on current consumption must come through their effects on past or future consumption. Provided that the unobservables are uncorrelated with prices in these periods, past and future prices are logical instruments for past and future consumption, since past prices directly affect past consumption, and future prices directly affect future consumption. Therefore, the empirical strategy amounts to estimating equation (2) by two-stage least squares (TSLS), with past and future prices serving as instrumental variables for past and future consumption. This strategy can be modified when measures of some of the life cycle events that affect utility and therefore partially determine e_t, such as marital status and unemployment, are available. Then current marital status, for example, is a relevant regressor in the structural demand function given by equation (2), and past and future marital status are instruments for past and future consumption.

The statistical significance of the coefficient of future consumption provides a direct test of a rational model of addiction against an alternative model in which consumers are myopic. The latter model fails to consider the impact of current consumption on future utility and future consumption. That is, the myopic version of equation (2) is entirely backward looking. Because of this distinction, myopic models and rational models have different implications about responses to future changes. In particular, rational addicts increase their current consumption when future prices are expected to fall, but myopic addicts do not.

Equation (2) implies intertemporal complementarity or negative cross price elasticities between cocaine consumption at various points in time. These effects pertain to changes in the price of cocaine in period τ on consumption in period t. They are temporary in nature since prices in other periods are held constant. For example, a reduction in price in period $t + 1$ (P_{t+1}) with prices in all other periods held constant will increase consumption in that period. In turn, C_t will rise since $\beta\theta$ is positive.

Equation (2) also implies that there are important differences between long- and short-run responses to permanent price changes (price changes in more than one period) in the case of addiction. The short-run price effect describes the response to a change in price in period t and all future periods that is not anticipated until period t. The long-run price effect pertains to a price change in all periods. Since C_{t-1} remains the same if a price change is not anticipated until period t, the long-run price effect must exceed the short-run price effect. In addition, the short-run price effect must exceed the temporary current price effect since the latter holds future prices constant.[3]

4. DATA AND EMPIRICAL IMPLEMENTATION

4.1. Sample

Each year since 1975, the University of Michigan's Institute for Social Research has conducted a nationally representative random sample of between 15,000 and 19,000 high school seniors during the months of March and April as part of the Monitoring the Future research program. These surveys, which are described in detail by Johnston et al. (1995), focus on the use of illegal drugs, alcohol, and cigarettes. Starting with the class of 1976, a sample of approximately 2400 individuals in each senior class has been chosen for follow-up at two-year intervals. Individuals reporting the use of marijuana on twenty or more occasions in the past thirty days or the use of any other illegal drugs in the past thirty days in their senior year are selected with a higher probability (by a factor of 3).

We estimate cocaine demand functions using the panels formed from the high school senior surveys conducted from 1976 through 1985. The last follow-up in our dataset, which contains approximately 22,800 persons, took place in 1989. We have between one and five observations on each person since we require information on current, past, and future consumption of cocaine. Since an annual measure of consumption is used in the regressions, past consumption coincides with the second annual lag and future consumption coincides with the second annual lead.

Although Monitoring the Future obtains information on the use of a variety of illegal drugs, we limit the empirical analysis to cocaine for several reasons. Cocaine prices (described in more detail in section 4.2) are available for many more areas and are based on much larger samples than the prices of other illegal drugs. Moreover, cocaine was the second most widely used illegal substance next to marijuana during the sample period.

One problem with the Monitoring the Future panels is that persons who dropped out of high school prior to March of their senior year are excluded. Dropouts may have different cocaine consumption patterns than persons who remain in school. Nevertheless, the Monitoring the Future sample is the longest nationally representative panel with information on cocaine consumption in the age group that has the highest rate of cocaine use. Panel retention rates have been very high.

In the first follow-up after high school, approximately 82 percent of the persons selected for follow-up have returned questionnaires. The 1988 panel retention from the class of 1976 was between 71 and 74 percent (Johnston et al. 1989).

4.2. Cocaine Prices

Information on county identifiers at baseline and at each follow-up allowed us to augment the dataset with cocaine prices from the System to Retrieve Information from Drug Evidence (STRIDE) maintained by the Drug Enforcement Administration (DEA) of the U.S. Department of Justice. DEA and FBI agents and state and local police narcotics officers purchase illicit drugs on a regular basis in order to apprehend dealers. Taubman (1991) argues that DEA agents must make transactions at close to the street price of cocaine in order to make an arrest because an atypical price can cause suspicion on the part of dealers.

Information on the date and city of the purchase, its total cost, total weight in grams, and purity (as a percentage) is recorded in STRIDE. There are 139 cities in STRIDE with usable data for the period from 1977 through 1991. Following DiNardo (1993) and Caulkins (1994), we obtained the price of 1 g of pure cocaine by year and city from a regression of the natural logarithm of the total purchase cost on the natural logarithm of weight, the natural logarithm of purity, dichotomous variables for each city and year except one, and interactions between the year variables and dichotomous variables for eight of the nine Census of Population divisions. The regression is based on over 25,000 purchases.

The cost of a purchase is more likely to be governed by the user's perception of purity than by its actual value (Caulkins 1994). Since purchasers are likely to have imperfect information about purity, the coefficient of the logarithm of actual purity is biased downward given that the difference between the logarithms of perceived and actual purity is not correlated with the logarithm of perceived purity. Thus, we use the other regressors in the total cost equation as instruments for purity. To identify the model, the coefficient of the natural logarithm of predicted purity is constrained to equal the coefficient of the natural logarithm of weight.[4] The price of 1 g of pure cocaine is then given as the antilogarithm of the sum of the intercept, the relevant city coefficient, and the relevant time-division coefficient. The money price is converted to a real price by dividing it by the annual Consumer Price Index for the U.S. as a whole (1982–1984 = 1).

Several things should be noted about the methodology just described. First, it eliminates variations in the price or unit cost of cocaine due to variations in weight and purity. Second, the resulting year- and city-specific price is akin to a geometric mean. Hence, the influence of outliers is mitigated. Finally, we experimented with alternative specifications of the total cost regression. In one specification, interactions between time and Census division were eliminated. In a second, purity was treated as exogenous with an unconstrained coefficient. In a third, purity was deleted as a regressor, but its predicted value was included as an independent variable in the cocaine demand function. The estimates presented in section 5 are not sensitive to these alternative specifications of the total cost regression.

To match DEA cities to Monitoring the Future counties, we assigned each to its Metropolitan Statistical Area, Central Metropolitan Statistical Area, or Primary Metropolitan Statistical Area (whichever was smaller). For any county where a match could not be made, price was defined as a population-weighted average of price in all DEA cities in that county's state. The second annual lag and the second annual lead of the real price of cocaine, which are employed as instruments in TSLS regression models, were added to the panels in the same manner. Changes of residence to a different county by panel members during the sample period were taken into account when the prices were added.

Although our sample period includes the widespread introduction of crack cocaine in late 1985 or early 1986, we do not distinguish between the price of crack and the price of powder cocaine. Crack's reputation for being less expensive than powder is due primarily to the smaller quantity at which it is retailed (Caulkins 1995). Caulkins (1997) finds that the price per pure gram of crack is the same as the price per pure gram of powder cocaine. Crack cocaine gives a more intense but shorter high than powder cocaine. If quantity is defined as the product of intensity and duration, it is not clear which type of cocaine is more or less expensive.

The full price of consuming cocaine consists of three components: (1) the money price; (2) the monetary value of the travel and waiting time required to obtain cocaine; and (3) the monetary value of the expected penalties for possession or use (the probability of apprehension and conviction multiplied by the fine or the monetary value of the prison sentence). We assume that variations in cocaine prices among cities can be used to trace out a demand function because they reflect differences in the three components of the full price among cities. Put differently, larger transportation costs, stiffer fines and prison terms imposed on dealers, and higher probabilities of apprehension and conviction cause the supply function of cocaine, which we assume to be infinitely elastic, to shift upward and raise the money price of cocaine. To the extent that the number of dealers in the market falls, travel and waiting costs also rise. The full price will also increase if the expected penalty for possession and use is positively related to the expected penalty for selling cocaine. Since the direct and indirect price of obtaining cocaine are likely to be positively correlated, consumers may respond to changes in money prices even if they have imperfect knowledge about these prices.[5]

4.3. Measurement of Variables

Table 18.1 contains definitions, means, and standard deviations of variables that are employed in the regression analyses in section 5. They are based on the sample of 38,885 person–years or person–follow-ups that result by deleting persons who failed to respond to at least three consecutive questionnaires (including baseline) and by deleting observations for which the use of cocaine in the past year, the real price of cocaine, and real annual earnings are missing. Given three observations per person on average, there are approximately 12,962 respondents in the final sample.

There are no missing values for age, male, black, and other race/ethnicity. Missing values for the other variables listed in the table are replaced by panel- and strata-specific means. Recall that there are two strata for each panel. One consists of persons who used marijuana twenty or more times in the past thirty days or used another illegal drug in the past thirty days at baseline, and the other consists of persons who did not exhibit these illegal drug use patterns at baseline. The means and standard deviations in the table were weighted to correct for oversampling—by a factor of three—of persons in the illegal drug stratum.

Panel members report the number of occasions in the past year on which they used cocaine. This is an ordered categorical variable with seven outcomes: 0 occasions, 1–2 occasions, 3–5 occasions, 6–9 occasions, 10–19 occasions, 20–39 occasions, and 40 or more occasions. Since many persons did not use cocaine in the past year, two dependent variables are considered. One is a dichotomous variable that identifies users (termed cocaine participation), and the second gives frequency of use (number of occasions) conditional on positive participation. Cocaine participation has a weighted mean of 15.9 percent. Since the unweighted mean is 23.0 percent, the sample of positive users contains 8926 observations (person–years). Cocaine frequency is converted into a continuous variable by assigning midpoints to the closed intervals and a value of 50 to the open-ended interval.[6]

Monitoring the Future did not distinguish between the use of crack cocaine and the use of other forms of cocaine until the 1986 baseline survey (not included in our sample) and the 1987 follow-up survey. In that follow-up and in the 1988 and 1989 follow-ups, two-fifths of the respondents were asked separate questions on crack and powder cocaine. These answers have been aggregated to form indicators of the use of any form of cocaine

Table 18.1 Definitions, Means, and Standard Deviations of Variables

Cocaine participation (0.159, 0.320)
: Dichotomous variable that equals 1 if respondent used cocaine at least once in the past year

Cocaine frequency given positive participation (9.195, 8.963)
: Number of occasions in past year on which respondent used cocaine

Price (286.557, 117.204)
: Price of one pure gram of cocaine in 1982–1984 dollars[a]

Legal drinking age * age ≤21 (12.093, 8.409)
: Minimum legal age in years for purchase and consumption of beer, alcoholic content 3.2% or less (legal drinking age); multiplied by a dichotomous variable that equals 1 if respondent is 21 years of age or younger (age ≤21)[a]

Lower border drinking age indicator * age ≤21 (0.099, 0.261)
: Dichotomous variable that equals 1 if respondent resides in a county within 25 miles of a state with a lower legal drinking age (lower border age indicator); multiplied by a dichotomous variable that equals 1 if respondent is 21 years of age or younger

Marijuana decriminalization indicator (0.330, 0.411)
: Dichotomous variable that equals 1 if respondent resides in a state in which incarceration and heavy fines are not penalties for most marijuana possession offenses

Male (0.438, 0.434)
: Dichotomous indicator

Black (0.091, 0.252), Other race/ethnicity (0.068, 0.221)
: Dichotomous variables that identify African Americans or blacks (Black) and American Indians, Puerto Ricans or other Latin Americans, Mexican Americans or Chicanos, or Orientals or Asian Americans (Other race/ethnicity); omitted category pertains to whites

Real earnings (7447.845, 5880.433)
: Real earnings in the past calendar year in 1982–1984 dollars; money earnings divided by a year- and city-specific cost of living index

Years of completed schooling (13.357, 1.355)
: Years of formal schooling completed

Full-time college student (0.334, 0.410)
: Dichotomous indicators; omitted category pertains to persons not attending school in March of the survey year

(continued)

Table 18.1 (*Continued*)

Half-time college student (0.037, 0.164)	—
Less than half-time college student (0.054, 0.196)	—
Working full-time (0.530, 0.428)	Dichotomous indicators that pertain to first full week of March of the survey year; omitted category identifies respondents not in the labor force
Working part-time (0.215, 0.352)	—
Unemployed (0.031, 0.149)	—
Infrequent religious participation (0.410, 0.428)	Dichotomous variables that identify respondents who rarely attend religious services (infrequent religious participation) and who attend services at least once or twice a month (frequent religious participation), respective omitted category pertains to respondents who never attend religious services
Frequent religious participation (0.487, 0.435)	—
Married (0.255, 0.381)	Dichotomous indications; omitted category pertains to single respondent
Engaged (0.084, 0.242)	—
Separated or divorced (0.024, 0.134)	—
Number of children (0.229, 0.499)	Respondent's number of children

Note: Means and standard deviations in parentheses. First figure is mean, second figure is standard deviation. Means and standard deviations are weighted by the inverse of the probability of selection; equivalent to multiplying values of a given variable from the illegal drug stratum by one-third. Basic set of independent variables also includes dichotomous variables for ages 18 through 26 and for years 1978 through 1986. Sample size is 38,885 except for cocaine frequency given positive participation where the sample size is 8926.

[a] See text for more details.

and the frequency of use by means of an algorithm developed by the Institute for Social Research.

To account for the possibility that cocaine and alcohol or cocaine and marijuana are substitutes or complements, we include the minimum legal drinking age for the purchase and consumption of low-alcohol beer (described in detail in Chaloupka et al. 1993) and a dichotomous variable that identifies respondents of states that have decriminalized the possession of marijuana. Since no state has ever had a legal drinking age greater than twenty-one, the drinking age is multiplied by a dichotomous variable that equals one for persons twenty-one years of age or younger.

In addition to the own-state minimum legal drinking age, a dichotomous indicator equal to one if a respondent resides in a county within 25 miles of a state with a lower legal drinking age is employed as a regressor. This variable is interacted with the dichotomous indicator for persons whose age is less than or equal to twenty-one for the same reason that the drinking age is interacted with this indicator. The border age variable is included in the model to capture potential border crossings by youths from states with high drinking ages to nearby lower age states to obtain alcohol. With the own-state legal drinking age held constant, the coefficient of the border age variable in the demand function should be negative if alcohol and cocaine are substitutes (the own-legal drinking age coefficient is positive in this case) and positive if they are complements (the own-legal drinking age coefficient is negative in this case).

A variety of independent variables were constructed from the demographic and socioeconomic information collected in the surveys. These include nine dichotomous age indicators (ages eighteen through twenty-six); sex; race (black or other); real annual earnings; years of formal schooling completed; college student status (full-time, half-time, or less than half-time); work status (full-time, part-time, or unemployed); religious participation (infrequent or frequent); marital status (married, engaged, or separated or divorced); and the respondent's number of children. Finally, all models include dichotomous variables for nine of the ten years covered by current consumption (1978 through 1986). The time-varying variables serve as proxies for life-cycle variables that affect the marginal utility of current consumption.

4.4. Estimation Issues

We estimate separate equations for participation and for frequency given positive participation. This is an application of Cragg's (Cragg 1971) two-part model for an outcome (cocaine consumption) with many nonparticipants or zero values.

We prefer it to Heckman's (Heckman 1979) sample selection procedure or to the adjusted tobit version of Heckman's procedure (van de Ven and van Praag 1981) because the two-part model is more robust to violations of the normality assumption and because the sample selection model is not well-behaved if the regressors in the selection and primary equations are identical (Manning et al. 1987; Leung and Yu 1996). Linear probability models for participation and linear models for frequency given participation are obtained. The TSLS participation equations correspond to the simultaneous equations linear probability model of Heckman and MaCurdy (1985).

Given the nature of the panels, we estimate the participation version of equation (2) with the second lag of participation as the measure of past consumption and the second lead of participation as the measure of future consumption. Similarly, we estimate the equation for frequency conditional on positive use with the second lag of frequency as the measure of past consumption and the second lead of frequency as the measure of future consumption.[7] The instruments for past and future consumption in TSLS estimation consist of the exogenous variables in the structural demand function for current consumption, the second lag of the annual real cocaine price, the second lead of the annual real cocaine price, the second annual lag and lead of the marijuana decriminalization indicator, the second annual lags of the two measures pertaining to the legal drinking age (legal drinking age * age ≤21 and lower border drinking age indicator * age ≤21), and the second leads and the second lags of all time-varying socioeconomic variables. These include real annual earnings, years of formal schooling completed, college student status, work status, religious participation, marital status, and number of children. The second leads of the two measures pertaining to the legal drinking age are not used as instruments because the values of these two variables are zero except at the first follow-up.

The simple version of the rational addiction model outlined in section 3 implies that the parameters of the participation and frequency given participation equations are the same. That is, it implies that the tobit model (Tobin 1958) is appropriate. We do not use the tobit model because so little is known about the demand for cocaine. Therefore, we do not want to constrain the parameters of price and other variables to be the same for the two outcomes. Moreover, underreporting of cocaine frequency is likely to be more of a problem than underreporting of cocaine participation (see below for more details). Since the rational addiction demand function given by equation (2) pertains to a continuous outcome, the parameter estimates of the participation equation should be viewed as first-order approximations.

Reported cocaine use in the Monitoring the Future cohort of young adults between the ages of eighteen and twenty-seven may underestimate actual use by all persons in this cohort in the U.S. as a whole for two reasons. First, use may be underreported. Second, persons who dropped out of high school prior to March of their senior year are excluded. These persons are more likely to end up in groups with higher than average cocaine use such as criminals and the homeless than persons who graduated from high school.[8]

No definitive conclusions can be reached with regard to whether price effects or elasticities are biased by the above two factors. A number of studies have shown that reported cigarette or alcohol consumption in survey data is smaller than actual consumption measured by national sales (for example, Coate and Grossman 1988; Wasserman et al. 1991). Wasserman et al. (1991) indicate that researchers usually assume that smoking participation is measured accurately, while the number of cigarettes smoked is underreported. Although there is no direct evidence to support this assumption, Marquis et al. (1981) find that self-reports of alcohol abstention are highly valid. Thus, it is likely that cocaine participation is more accurately reported than frequency given positive participation. This justifies considering them as separate outcomes.

There are no studies concerning whether response error in self reports of alcohol or cigarette consumption is systematic or correlated with variables that enter the demand functions for these substances. The same is true for cocaine. If linear demand functions are employed and the response error is random, coefficients are unbiased, although their standard errors are inflated. Elasticities evaluated at sample means are overstated because reported mean consumption is too small. An offsetting factor is that Midanik (1982) and Polich (1982) find that heavier consumers of alcoholic beverages are more likely to underreport their consumption than other persons. If the same pattern holds for cocaine and if heavy users are more likely to be found in areas with low prices, the estimated price parameter in the demand function is biased downward.

In the specific case of Monitoring the Future, Johnston and O'Malley (1985) argue that underreporting is reduced because the baseline survey is conducted in a high school setting. Clearly, parents are not present and are not informed of the responses. Followup questionnaires are mailed directly to the respondents. They also argue that self-reported illegal drug use has a high degree of construct validity in their data because it is correlated with a host of other variables in predictable ways. Finally, they point out that missing data rates on the illegal drug use questions are only slightly above average, even though respondents are instructed to skip these items if they cannot answer them honestly.

With regard to the absence of high school dropouts, Johnston and O'Malley (1985) summarize studies by themselves and others showing that dropouts have higher rates of illegal drug use and younger ages of initiation than in-school students. They also show that adjustment of baseline prevalence rates (illegal drug use participation rates at age seventeen) for the higher participation rates of dropouts has a minor effect on overall rates since only 15 percent of the relevant cohort are dropouts. Of course, the difference in the use of illegal drugs between dropouts and high school graduates may increase beyond age seventeen. If price and consumption slope coefficients in the demand function for dropouts are the same as for high school graduates, parameter estimates of these slopes are not biased by omitting dropouts. The price elasticity of demand of graduates is larger than that of dropouts since the former group consumes less.

If slope coefficients differ between dropouts and graduates, no conclusions can be reached with regard to the nature of the biases. Thus, the most cautious approach to our empirical analysis and results is to limit conclusions to persons who were in high school in March of their senior year. Note that persons from the illegal drug stratum are not more likely to drop out as the panel ages. Thus, our estimates are not biased because heavy users of illegal drugs who did not drop out of high school are more likely to leave the panel as it ages.

The real price of cocaine contains measurement error for several reasons. First, the price data pertain to the DEA survey city nearest to the respondents county of residence rather than to the city or town in which the respondent actually resides. Second, the respondent may have imperfect information concerning the market price and the quality (purity) of the purchase, which creates a difference between this price and the perceived price that governs his or her consumption. Third, the future price employed assumes that respondents who moved fully anticipated the move. Random measurement error in an independent variable biases its coefficient and t-ratio toward zero. Thus, the price coefficients and the t-ratios of the price coefficients in section 5 are conservative lower-bound estimates, although the coefficients and associated t-ratios of other variables may be overstated.

We estimate a rational addiction model of cocaine consumption by assuming perfect foresight and using the actual future price and the actual future values of the socioeconomic variables as instruments for future consumption. Becker et al. (1994) adopt this same strategy. They point out that individuals' forecast errors in future price and other future variables create a downward bias in the coefficient of future consumption because these factors introduce random measurement error into the predicted value of future consumption.

An additional problem with the use of leads of socioeconomic variables as instruments is that these variables may not be exogenous. For example, assume that the unmeasured life cycle variable (e_t) in the demand function given by equation (2) causes current cocaine consumption to rise. This shock to current consumption also may lower future earnings and reduce the probability of marriage in the future. With a single socioeconomic variable, the predicted value of future consumption and e_t will be correlated. But with more than one socioeconomic variable, there may be offsetting forces that attenuate or eliminate the correlation between predicted future consumption and e_t. To anticipate the results in section 5, earnings have a positive effect on consumption, while married persons consume less than other persons. The first factor creates a negative correlation between predicted consumption and e_t, while the second factor creates a positive correlation.

We acknowledge that the assumption of perfect foresight in the rational addiction model and the use of future socioeconomic variables as instruments are controversial and may create biases. We deal with these issues in two ways. First, we estimate a myopic as well as a rational model of cocaine addiction. In the former model, future consumption is deleted from the demand function and future variables are deleted as instruments. Second, we examine the sensitivity of the results to the exclusion of current values of the socioeconomic variables from the demand functions and past and future values of these variables from the set of instruments.

Given the panel nature of the sample, the disturbance terms of a given person are likely to be correlated over time. Disturbance terms of different people within the same county also may be correlated. Grossman et al. (1998) find that Huber (1967) standard errors, which take account of these correlations, are no larger than uncorrected standard errors in their study of rational addiction demand functions for alcohol in the Monitoring the Future panels. We observed a similar phenomenon in preliminary estimates of demand functions for cocaine. Thus, the standard errors in section 5 are not corrected for intra-person or intra-cluster (county) correlations. We also found that the choice between weighted regressions (to correct for oversampling of illegal drug users at baseline) and unweighted regressions is moot because the two sets of estimates are very similar. The same finding is reported by Grossman et al. (1998).

5. EMPIRICAL RESULTS

5.1. Basic Estimates

Tables 18.2 and 18.3 test the rational addiction model of cocaine consumption by estimating structural demand functions given by equation (2) for cocaine participation (table 18.2) and for frequency of cocaine use given positive participation (table 18.3). The first and third columns of each table contain TSLS regressions in which past and future participation or past and future frequency

Table 18.2 Structural Demand Functions, Dependent Variable = Participation[a], Rational Addiction Model

	Two-Stage Least Squares	Ordinary Least Squares	Two-Stage Least Squares	Ordinary Least Squares
Price	−0.000132 (−4.63)	−0.000151 (−5.86)	−0.000151 (−2.51)	−0.000174 (−6.72)
Past participation	0.381 (10.09)	0.377 (85.93)	0.206 (1.19)	0.389 (89.01)
Future participation	0.449 (14.16)	0.408 (95.38)	0.662 (5.36)	0.423 (99.69)
Marijuana decriminalization	0.008 (2.13)	0.008 (2.29)	0.014 (2.53)	0.013 (3.74)
Legal drinking age * age ≤21	0.004 (2.36)	0.004 (2.55)	0.005 (2.36)	0.005 (2.94)
Lower border drinking age indicator * age ≤21	0.008 (1.48)	0.010 (1.89)	0.006 (0.92)	0.011 (1.89) (2.01)
Real earnings	4.47E-07 (1.47)	4.91E-07 (1.63)		
Years of completed schooling	−0.0001 (−0.11)	−0.001 (−0.43)		
Full-time college student	−0.007 (−1.46)	−0.008 (−1.57)		
Half-time college student	0.002 (0.20)	0.002 (0.27)		
Less than half-time college student	−0.004 (−0.51)	−0.003 (−0.46)		
Working full-time	−0.002 (−0.37)	−0.002 (−0.48)		
Working part-time	−0.001 (−0.25)	−0.001 (−0.30)		
Unemployed	0.013 (1.35)	0.013 (1.41)		
Infrequent religious participation	−0.012 (−2.38)	−0.014 (−2.66)		
Frequent religious participation	−0.052 (−7.24)	−0.061 (−11.63)		
Married	−0.050 (−9.18)	−0.056 (−12.17)		
Engaged	−0.011 (−1.84)	−0.013 (−2.36)		
Separated or divorced	−0.002 (−0.18)	−0.002 (−0.23)		
Number of children	−0.008 (−2.23)	−0.008 (−2.37)		

Elasticities				
Long-run	-1.400	-1.264	-2.057	-1.667
Short-run	-0.716	-0.675	-1.551	-0.847
Temporary current	-0.304	-0.336	-0.325	-0.395
R^2	0.181	0.486	0.059	0.480
Hausman χ^2	3.815		4.853	
Basmann F-ratio	2.637		1.808	
F-ratio, instruments for past participation	24.880		11.977	
F-ratio, instruments for future participation	33.823		22.142	
N	38,885	38,885	38,885	38,885

[a] Asymptotic t-statistics in parentheses, and intercepts not shown. All regressions include dichotomous variables for male, black, other race/ethnicity, ages 18 through 26, and years 1978 through 1986. For Hausman test, critical values of χ^2 (2) are 5.99 at 5 percent and 9.21 at 1 percent. For Basmann test, critical values of $F(32, \infty)$ are 1.45 at 5 percent and 1.67 at 1 percent for models including socioeconomic variables, and critical values of $F(4, \infty)$ are 2.37 at 5 percent and 3.32 at 1 percent for models excluding socioeconomic variables. For test of instruments, critical values of $F(34, \infty)$ are 1.43 at 5 percent and 1.65 at 1 percent for models including socioeconomic variables, and critical values of $F(6, \infty)$ are 2.09 at 5 percent and 2.80 at 1 percent for models excluding socioeconomic variables.

Table 18.3 Structural Demand Functions, Dependent Variable = Frequency[a], Rational Addiction Model

	Two-Stage Least Squares	Ordinary Least Squares	Two-Stage Least Squares	Ordinary Least Squares
Price	-0.008076 (-3.13)	-0.005469 (-2.51)	-0.008388 (-1.84)	-0.005098 (-2.34)
Past frequency	0.218 (2.51)	0.313 (29.56)	-0.160 (-0.53)	0.316 (29.79)
Future frequency	0.225 (3.95)	0.302 (31.94)	0.560 (2.28)	0.311 (33.01)
Marijuana decriminalization	0.250 (0.89)	0.203 (0.75)	0.636 (1.53)	0.190 (0.70)
Legal drinking age * age ≤21	0.149 (1.03)	0.144 (1.00)	0.235 (1.38)	0.151 (1.05)
Lower border drinking age indicator * age ≤21	0.455 (1.03)	0.283 (0.66)	0.274 (0.51)	0.206 (0.48)
Real earnings	8.69E-05 (3.59)	7.91E-05 (3.35)		
Years of completed schooling	-0.366 (-3.13)	-0.257 (-2.51)		
Full-time college student	-1.324 (-3.34)	-1.199 (-3.10)		
Half-time college student	-1.132 (-1.76)	-1.191 (-1.88)		
Less than half-time college student	-1.037 (-1.92)	-1.075 (-2.05)		
Working full-time	-0.532 (-1.25)	-0.362 (-0.88)		
Working part-time	-0.212 (-0.52)	-0.164 (-0.41)		
Unemployed	0.020 (0.03)	0.084 (0.12)		
Infrequent religious participation	0.013 (0.04)	0.045 (0.14)		
Frequent religious participation	-1.007 (-2.34)	-0.711 (-1.81)		
Married	-2.658 (-6.05)	-2.414 (-5.85)		
Engaged	-1.588 (-3.39)	-1.474 (-3.25)		
Separated or divorced	-0.383 (-0.51)	-0.266 (-0.36)		
Number of children	-0.147 (-0.44)	-0.094 (-0.29)		

Elasticities				
Long-run	−0.452	−0.443	−0.435	−0.427
Short-run	−0.348	−0.288	−0.500	−0.275
Temporary current	−0.265	−0.191	−0.241	−0.179
R^2	0.045	0.240	0.015	0.232
Hausman χ^2	4.077		2.495	
Basmann F-ratio	1.191		0.261	
F-ratio, instruments for past frequency	4.074		3.299	
F-ratio, instruments for future frequency	7.665		3.954	
N	8,926	8,926	8,926	8,926

[a]Asymptotic t-statistics in parentheses, and intercepts not shown. All regressions include dichotomous variables for male, black, other race/ethnicity, ages 18 through 26, and years 1978 through 1986. For Hausman test, critical values of χ^2 (2) are 5.99 at 5 percent and 9.21 at 1 percent. For Basmann test, critical values of $F_{(32, \infty)}$ are 1.45 at 5 percent and 1.67 at 1 percent for models including socioeconomic variables, and critical values of $F_{(4, \infty)}$ are 2.37 at 5 percent and 3.32 at 1 percent for models excluding socioeconomic variables. For test of instruments, critical values of $F_{(34, \infty)}$ are 1.43 at 5 percent and 1.65 at 1 percent for models including socioeconomic variables, and critical values of $F_{(6, \infty)}$ are 2.09 at 5 percent and 2.80 at 1 percent for models excluding socioeconomic variables.

are treated as endogenous. The model in the first column includes current values of the socioeconomic variables in the structural demand function and past and future values of these variables as instruments in the first stage. The model in the third column deletes past and future values of the socioeconomic variables as instruments in the first stage and omits current values of these measures as exogenous variables in the structural equation and in the first stage. Thus, in column 3, the only instruments for past and future consumption are the past and future price, the past and future marijuana decriminalization indicator, the past legal drinking age, and the past lower border drinking age indicator. The second and fourth columns contain the OLS regressions corresponding to the TSLS regressions in the first and third columns, respectively.

The tables also contain χ^2 statistics resulting from the test of the hypothesis of Hausman (1978) that OLS estimates are consistent, F-ratios resulting from the test of Basmann (1960) that the overidentification restrictions are valid, and F-ratios pertaining to the tests that the instruments for past and future consumption are significant as a set in the first stage. Thus, the F-ratio of 24.88 (with degrees of freedom 32, infinity) for the instruments for past participation in the first column of table 18.2 is obtained by testing the hypothesis that the coefficients of the following measures are significant as a set in the reduced form regression for past participation: past price, future price, past marijuana decriminalization, future marijuana decriminalization, past drinking age, past border drinking age, past socioeconomic variables, and future socioeconomic variables.

The first stage regressions for past and future participation are shown in table A1 in the Appendix, and the first stage regressions for past and future frequency are shown in table A2 in the Appendix. The explanatory power of these first stage regressions is modest. When the socioeconomic variables are included as instruments, the R^2 values are 0.11 for past participation, 0.12 for future participation, 0.08 for past frequency, and 0.06 for future frequency. When the socioeconomic variables are excluded as instruments, the R^2 values are 0.04 for past and future participation, 0.06 for past frequency, and 0.02 for future frequency. Despite these low values, the F-ratios associated with the instruments are all significant at 1 percent. Moreover, the large magnitudes of these ratios indicate that the TSLS estimates are not biased because the instruments are weakly correlated with the endogenous explanatory variables (Bound et al. 1995; Staiger and Stock 1997). The pairwise simple correlation coefficients between past, current, and future price are positive and extremely large. They range between 0.91 and 0.93. Despite these large correlations, the past, future, and current price coefficients are negative in the reduced form, as predicted by the rational addiction model, except that the current price coefficient is positive when future frequency is the outcome and the socioeconomic variables are excluded. In addition, when past participation or past frequency is the dependent variable, the past price coefficient is significant at the 1 percent level. When future participation or future frequency is the dependent variable, the future price coefficient is significant at the 1 percent level.

According to the Hausman test, the consistency of the OLS estimates is accepted, primarily because the low explanatory power of the first stage regressions results in large TSLS standard errors of the coefficients of past and future consumption relative to the OLS standard errors of these coefficients. Nevertheless, it is useful to consider all the estimates in the two tables because they are fairly similar and because the consistency of OLS is rejected in some of the alternative specifications discussed later. According to the Basmann test, the overidentification restrictions are valid except in the participation demand function that includes the socioeconomic variables (column 1 of table 18.2).

The estimated effects of past and future participation on current participation are positive in the four regressions in table 18.2 and are significant, except for the past participation coefficient in the TSLS model that omits the socioeconomic variables. The estimated cocaine price effects are significantly negative in the participation demand functions. The same comments apply to the past frequency, future frequency, and cocaine price coefficients in the four regressions in table 18.3, except that the past frequency coefficient in the TSLS model that omits the socioeconomic variables is negative and not significant.

The ratio of the coefficient of future consumption to the coefficient of past consumption provides an estimate of the discount factor (β). Since the rational addiction demand function given by equation (2) pertains to a continuous outcome, the implied discount factors in table 18.3 are on somewhat firmer grounds than those in table 18.2. The discount factor is 1.03 in the first frequency regression in table 18.3, 0.96 in the second regression, and 0.98 in the fourth. A meaningful estimate cannot be obtained from the third regression because the coefficient of past frequency is negative. These discount factors correspond to interest rates of −3 percent, 4 percent, and 2 percent, respectively.[9]

All but two of the regressions in tables 18.2 and 18.3 imply unreasonable discount factors because the coefficient of future consumption typically is larger than the coefficient of past consumption. But the coefficient of future consumption is significantly greater than the coefficient of past consumption in only two of eight cases, the two OLS participation equations. We imposed a discount factor of 0.95 (interest rate of 5 percent) a priori and re-estimated the eight regressions in tables 18.2 and 18.3. The price coefficients and price elasticities (discussed in more detail below) in these models are extremely close to their unconstrained counterparts. These results, combined with the detailed analysis in Becker et al.

(1994) and in Grossman et al. (1998) suggest that data on cocaine, cigarette, or alcohol consumption may not be rich enough to pin down the discount factor with precision even if the rational addiction model is accepted.

Are these results consistent with addiction and rational addiction? If one focuses on the signs and significance of the coefficients and is willing to accept the consistency of OLS, the answer is yes. In these models, the positive effect of past consumption is consistent with the hypothesis that cocaine consumption is an addictive good. The positive effect of future consumption is consistent with the hypothesis of rational addiction and not consistent with the hypothesis of myopic addiction. If one uses the same criteria but prefers to use the TSLS estimates, the answer is yes in the models that employ past and future socioeconomic variables as instruments. If one wants to exclude these variables because they are potentially endogenous, the past consumption effects are not significant and the past frequency effect is negative. These results conflict with the notion of addiction. On the other hand, the future consumption effects are positive and significant, which support rational addiction.

One problem with the TSLS models that exclude the socioeconomic variables is that the degree of precision falls when the set of instruments is restricted because exogenous variation falls. This is reflected by the increase in the standard errors of the TSLS coefficients of past and future consumption. This makes it difficult to sort out past and future consumption effects. To highlight this point, we estimate myopic models of cocaine addiction in table 18.4 for participation and in table 18.5 for frequency. This exercise also allows the reader to compare price elasticities of demand that emerge from the two models. In the myopic model, future participation or future frequency is excluded from the structural demand function, and all future variables are excluded as instruments. The models in columns 1–4 in tables 18.4 and 18.5 correspond to the models in columns 1–4 in tables 18.2 and 18.3. The only difference is that in tables 18.4 and 18.5, all future variables are omitted both as regressors and instruments. The first stage regressions for past participation and past frequency are shown in table A3 in the Appendix.

The coefficients of past consumption in tables 18.4 and 18.5 are much larger than the corresponding coefficients in tables 18.2 and 18.3. These results indicate that cocaine is an addictive behavior. They also support the proposition that imprecise nature of the TSLS past and future consumption coefficients makes it somewhat difficult to sort out the separate effects of these variables, particularly when the set of instruments is curtailed. The significance of the eight future consumption coefficients in tables 18.2 and 18.3 suggests that additional insights into the demand for cocaine can be gained by allowing consumption to depend on future variables.

Table 18.4 Structural Demand Functions, Dependent Variable = Participation[a], Myopic Model

	Two-Stage Least Squares	Ordinary Least Squares	Two-Stage Least Squares	Ordinary Least Squares
Price	−0.000233 (−7.20)	−0.000235 (−8.23)	−0.00023 (−3.16)	−0.00028 (−9.68)
Past participation	0.565 (16.72)	0.560 (127.42)	0.685 (5.59)	0.592 (136.40)
Marijuana decriminalization	0.007 (1.69)	0.007 (1.76)	0.012 (2.02)	0.015 (3.97)
Legal drinking age * age ≤21	0.005 (2.51)	0.005 (2.57)	0.005 (2.04)	0.006 (3.16)
Lower border drinking age indicator * age ≤21	0.022 (3.55)	0.023 (3.67)	0.021 (2.55)	0.025 (3.94)
Real earnings	6.67E-07 (1.98)	6.73E-07 (2.01)		
Years of completed schooling	−0.004 (−2.47)	−0.004 (−2.50)		
Full-time college student	−0.007 (−1.23)	−0.007 (−1.26)		
Half-time college student	0.007 (0.77)	0.007 (0.77)		
Less than half-time college student	−0.003 (−0.35)	−0.003 (−0.34)		
Working full-time	−0.008 (−1.49)	−0.008 (−1.49)		
Working part-time	−0.003 (−0.58)	−0.003 (−0.58)		
Unemployed	0.009 (0.81)	0.009 (0.83)		
Infrequent religious participation	−0.015 (−2.63)	−0.015 (−2.74)		
Frequent religious participation	−0.102 (−12.09)	−0.103 (−17.79)		
Married	−0.092 (−15.76)	−0.093 (−18.30)		
Engaged	−0.037 (−5.83)	−0.037 (−5.84)		
Separated or divorced	−0.005 (−0.44)	−0.005 (−0.44)		
Number of children	−0.005 (−1.29)	−0.005 (−1.36)		

(continued)

Table 18.4 (*Continued*)

	Two-Stage Least Squares	Ordinary Least Squares	Two-Stage Least Squares	Ordinary Least Squares
Elasticities				
Long-run	−0.965	−0.961	−1.315	−1.237
Short-run	−0.420	−0.424	−0.415	−0.505
R^2	0.143	0.366	0.050	0.347
Hausman χ^2	0.0261		0.572	
Basmann F-ratio	3.559		1.602	
F-ratio, instruments for past participation	37.044		12.378	
N	38,885	38,885	38,885	38,885

[a] Asymptotic t-statistics in parentheses, and intercepts not shown. All regressions include dichotomous variables for male, black, other race/ethnicity, ages 18 through 26, and years 1978 through 1986. For Hausman test, critical values of χ^2 (1) are 3.84 at 5 percent and 6.64 at 1 percent. For Basmann test, critical values of $F(17, \infty)$ are 1.62 at 5 percent and 1.97 at 1 percent for models including socioeconomic variables, and critical values of $F(3, \infty)$ are 2.60 at 5 percent and 3.78 at 1 percent for models excluding socioeconomic variables. For test of instruments, critical values of $F(18, \infty)$ are 1.61 at 5 percent and 1.94 at 1 percent for models including socioeconomic variables, and critical values of $F(4, \infty)$ are 2.37 at 5 percent and 3.32 at 1 percent for models excluding socioeconomic variables.

Table 18.5 Structural Demand Functions, Dependent Variable = Frequency[a], Myopic Model

	Two-Stage Least Squares	Ordinary Least Squares	Two-Stage Least Squares	Ordinary Least Squares
Price	−0.010272 (−3.83)	−0.009197 (−4.00)	−0.010353 (−2.27)	−0.008749 (−3.79)
Past frequency	0.311 (3.27)	0.385 (35.16)	0.285 (1.08)	0.392 (35.73)
Marijuana decriminalization	0.122 (0.41)	0.068 (0.24)	0.130 (0.37)	0.045 (0.16)
Legal drinking age * age ≤21	0.123 (0.81)	0.115 (0.76)	0.140 (0.89)	0.124 (0.81)
Lower border drinking age indicator * age ≤21	0.658 (1.43)	0.599 (1.32)	0.582 (1.17)	0.503 (1.10)
Real earnings	9.40E-05 (3.71)	9.09E-05 (3.64)		
Years of completed schooling	−0.517 (−4.44)	−0.483 (−4.48)		
Full-time college student	−1.542 (−3.75)	−1.513 (−3.71)		
Half-time college student	−1.113 (−1.65)	−1.144 (−1.71)		
Less than half-time college student	−1.282 (−2.28)	−1.353 (−2.45)		
Working full-time	−0.630 (−1.42)	−0.551 (−1.28)		
Working part-time	−0.193 (−0.45)	−0.161 (−0.38)		
Unemployed	−0.164 (−0.22)	−0.163 (−0.22)		
Infrequent religious participation	0.158 (0.45)	0.206 (0.59)		
Frequent religious participation	−1.155 (−2.54)	−1.012 (−2.44)		
Married	−3.188 (−7.27)	−3.151 (−7.25)		
Engaged	−1.962 (−4.08)	−1.971 (−4.11)		
Separated or divorced	−0.298 (−0.38)	−0.213 (−0.28)		
Number of children	−0.010 (−0.03)	0.048 (0.14)		

(continued)

Table 18.5 (*Continued*)

	Two-Stage Least Squares	Ordinary Least Squares	Two-Stage Least Squares	Ordinary Least Squares
Elasticities				
Long-run	−0.464	−0.466	−0.448	−0.449
Short-run	−0.320	−0.287	−0.268	−0.273
R^2	0.040	0.152	0.019	0.138
Hausman χ^2	0.613		0.167	
Basmann F-ratio	1.941		0.075	
F-ratio, instruments for past frequency	6.655		3.929	
N	8,926	8,926	8,926	8,926

[a]Asymptotic t-statistics in parentheses, and intercepts not shown. All regressions include dichotomous variables for male, black, other race/ethnicity, ages 18 through 26, and years 1978 through 1986. For Hausman test, critical values of χ^2 (1) are 3.84 at 5 percent and 6.64 at 1 percent. For Basmann test, critical values of $F_{(17, \infty)}$ are 1.62 at 5 percent and 1.97 at 1 percent for models including socioeconomic variables, and critical values of $F_{(3, \infty)}$ are 2.60 at 5 percent and 3.78 at 1 percent for models excluding socioeconomic variables. For test of instruments, critical values of $F_{(18, \infty)}$ are 1.61 at 5 percent and 1.94 at 1 percent for models including socioeconomic variables, and critical values of $F_{(4, \infty)}$ are 2.37 at 5 percent and 3.32 at 1 percent for models excluding socioeconomic variables.

The long-run, short-run, and temporary current price elasticities of participation or frequency given positive participation are shown at the bottom of tables 18.2 and 18.3. They are computed at the weighted sample means of price, participation, and frequency using equations contained in Becker et al. (1994). The long-run participation price elasticity is substantial. It ranges from −1.26 to −2.01 with a mean of −1.60. The short-run participation price elasticity ranges from −0.68 to −1.55 (average equals −0.95). Thus, the average long-run participation elasticity is approximately 60 percent larger than the average short-run elasticity.

Frequency conditional on positive use is not as sensitive to price as participation. The long-run elasticity is −0.44, and the short-run elasticity is −0.35.[10] The unconditional price elasticities, defined as the sum of the relevant participation and frequency elasticities, are quite large: −2.04 in the long-run and −1.30 in the short-run. The unconditional temporary current price elasticity is −0.56. It is smaller than the short-run price elasticity because future prices are held constant.

In the myopic model, the unconditional long-run and short-run elasticities also are substantial. The former equals −1.58, and the latter equals −0.73. These elasticities are smaller than those that emerge from the rational model, although the differences are not statistically significant.

There is some evidence in tables 18.2 through 18.5 that cocaine and marijuana are complements in consumption, while cocaine and alcohol are substitutes. Both cocaine participation and frequency are higher in states that decriminalized marijuana than in other states, although the frequency coefficients are not statistically significant. Another interpretation of this finding is that the expected penalty for cocaine use is smaller in states that decriminalized marijuana. An increase in the legal drinking age raises cocaine participation and use, although again, the frequency effects are not significant. While the coefficient of the lower border age drinking indicator has the wrong sign (it should be negative since the own drinking age effect is positive), the sign and significance of the drinking age coefficient itself are not altered when the border age measure is deleted. But the conclusion that cocaine and alcohol are substitutes must be tempered because states with higher drinking ages may allocate more resources to enforcement of drinking age laws and less resources to apprehending and convicting cocaine users and dealers.

By estimating rational and myopic cocaine demand functions by OLS and TSLS with and without socioeconomic variables, we have presented results for eight different specifications in this subsection. Supportive evidence of rational addiction is presented because the coefficient of future consumption always is positive and significant. Regardless of the specification employed, the long-run price elasticity of consumption (participation multiplied by frequency given participation) is substantial. This elasticity is larger in absolute value in the rational specification than in the myopic specification (−2.04 vs. −1.58). Although this difference is not statistically significant, the test is complicated by the imprecision with which either elasticity is estimated since the rational addiction elasticity is a nonlinear function of three coefficients and the myopic elasticity is a nonlinear function of two coefficients.

The choice between the specification that includes the socioeconomic variables and the one that omits them depends on a trade-off between an increase in omitted variables bias (omitting potential determinants of current consumption) and a reduction in simultaneous equations bias (omitting potentially endogenous variables). This trade-off arises because current values of the time-varying socioeconomic variables are excluded from the structural demand function for current consumption when past and future values of these variables are excluded from the set of instruments. Omitted variables bias is present in the regressions in tables 18.4 and 18.5 if current socioeconomic variables have causal effects on current consumption and are correlated with past consumption, future consumption, and the current price. Simultaneous equations bias is present in the regressions in tables 18.2 and 18.3 if current consumption of cocaine has causal effects on the current socioeconomic variables or if a shock to current consumption has impacts on future values of the socioeconomic variables.[11] On balance, we prefer the estimates with the socioeconomic variables because they minimize omitted variables bias and yield a long-run price elasticity of demand that can be viewed as a lower bound. There is no evidence that the relatively large elasticity in this specification is due to the choice of instruments and the inclusion of potentially endogenous variables in the structural demand function since the price elasticity becomes larger in absolute value when the socioeconomic variables are deleted. We realize, however, that the reader may have different views on these issues, and we have given equal weight to both sets of estimates in discussing the results.

5.2. Sensitivity Analysis

In table 18.6, we examine the robustness of the price and consumption effects in the rational addiction model by estimating TSLS fixed-effects models. Using this technique, we transform all time-varying variables into deviations from person-specific means and delete time-invariant variables and cases where there is only one observation for a given person from the regression. This approach is equivalent to including a dummy variable for each person in an untransformed specification and controls for unobserved heterogeneity. Since the Hausman

Table 18.6 Price and Consumption Coefficients, Two-Stage Least Squares Fixed-Effects Structural Demand Functions[a], Rational Addiction Models

	Socioeconomic Variables Included	Socioeconomic Variables Excluded
Panel A: Participation		
Price	−0.000151 (−2.85)	−0.000165 (−2.84)
Past participation	0.210 (3.68)	−0.038 (−0.09)
Future participation	0.283 (4.05)	0.245 (1.14)
R^2	0.023	0.013
Hausman χ^2	94.542	9.258
Basmann F-ratio	2.520	5.196
F-ratio, instruments for past participation	15.753	2.996
F-ratio, instruments for future participation	11.528	12.900
N	35,494	35,494
Elasticities		
Long-run	−0.536	−0.375
Short-run	−0.416	−0.389
Temporary current	−0.290	−0.295

(*continued*)

Table 18.6 (*Continued*)

	Socioeconomic Variables Included	Socioeconomic Variables Excluded
Panel B: Frequency given positive participation		
Price	−0.004207 (−0.76)	−0.005842 (−1.06)
Past frequency	0.250 (2.07)	−0.401 (−1.33)
Future frequency	0.256 (2.64)	0.293 (0.79)
R^2	0.029	0.017
Hausman χ^2	49.547	2.710
Basmann F-ratio	3.040	2.981
F-ratio, instruments for past frequency	4.404	3.765
F-ratio, instruments for future frequency	5.932	2.312
N	7,763	7,763
Elasticities		
Long-run	−0.265	−0.164
Short-run	−0.194	−0.224
Temporary current	−0.141	−0.165

[a]Asymptotic t-statistics in parentheses, and intercepts not shown. For Hausman test, critical values of χ^2 (2) are 5.99 at 5 percent and 9.21 at 1 percent. For Basmann test, critical values of $F(32, \infty)$ are 1.45 at 5 percent and 1.67 at 1 percent for models including socioeconomic variables, and critical values of $F(4, \infty)$ are 2.37 at 5 percent and 3.32 at 1 percent for models excluding socioeconomic variables. For test of instruments, critical values of $F(3, \infty)$ at 5 percent and 1.65 at 1 percent for models including socioeconomic variables and critical values of $F(6, \infty)$ are 2.09 at 5 percent and 2.80 at 1 percent for models excluding socioeconomic variables.

tests strongly reject the consistency of OLS, only the TSLS coefficients are presented in the table.

The results in the specification that includes the socioeconomic variables (column 1 of table 18.6) confirm those in tables 18.2 and 18.3. The past and future consumption coefficients are positive and significant. The current price coefficients are negative, although the frequency effects are not significant. The specification that excludes the socioeconomic variables is less supportive because the future consumption effects are not significant and the past consumption effects are negative. The unconditional price elasticities are smaller than those in tables 18.2 and 18.3: −0.67 in the long-run, −0.61 in the short-run, and −0.44 in the case of a temporary current price change.

Which of the two sets of estimates is preferable? As pointed out in section 4.4, the real price of cocaine contains random measurement error for a variety of reasons. The downward biases in the price coefficient and its t-ratio due to this factor are exacerbated in the fixed-effects model in table 18.6 (Griliches 1979; Griliches and Hausman 1986). Thus, the estimates in Table 8.6 are not necessarily superior to those in tables 18.2 and 18.3. Despite our misgivings about the fixed-effects model, we summarize the magnitudes of the price elasticities by averaging over the two models. This gives a long-run unconditional price elasticity of −1.35, a short-run price elasticity of −0.96, and a temporary current price elasticity of −0.50. We view these figures as conservative lower-bound estimates.

6. DISCUSSION

We find that cocaine consumption is quite sensitive to its price. A permanent 10 percent reduction in price would cause the number of cocaine users to grow by approximately 10 percent in the long-run and would increase the frequency of use among users by a little more than 3 percent. Total or unconditional frequency would rise by almost 14 percent in a fixed population in the long-run and by slightly less than 10 percent in the short-run. Surely, both proponents and opponents of drug legalization should take account of this increase in consumption in debating their respective positions.

A good deal of caution, however, must be exercised in extrapolating our findings to a regime in which cocaine consumption is legal. One consideration is that the response to the large price cut caused by legalization would be smaller than the one suggested by our estimates if the price elasticity of demand is smaller at lower prices because the demand function is linear or because the linear form that we have employed is an approximation to a concave demand function. A second consideration is that government tax policies could counteract part of the price cut, and government education policies could be used to increase knowledge about the harmful effects of cocaine consumption. A third factor is that forbidden fruit is attractive, particularly to the young (Friedman 1989). A factor that goes in the opposite direction is that legalization may stimulate consumption by removing the stigma associated with cocaine consumption.

A misleading impression about the reaction to permanent price changes may have been created by the effects of temporary police crackdowns on drugs or temporary federal wars on drugs. Since temporary policies raise current but not future prices (they would even lower future prices if drug inventories are built up during the crackdown period), there is no complementary fall in current use from a fall in future use. Consequently, even if drug addicts are rational, a temporary war that greatly raised the street price of cocaine may well only have a small effect on drug use, whereas a permanent war could have much bigger effects. For example, according to our estimates, a 10 percent price hike for one year would reduce total cocaine consumption by approximately 5 percent, whereas a permanent 10 percent price hike would lower consumption by 14 percent.

Clearly, we have not provided enough evidence to evaluate whether or not the use of cocaine should be legalized. A cost-benefit analysis of many effects is needed to decide between a regime in which cocaine is legal and a regime in which it is not. What we have shown is that the permanent reduction in price caused by legalization is likely to have a substantial positive effect on use, particularly among young adults.

ACKNOWLEDGEMENTS

This is a condensed version of Grossman and Chaloupka (1997). The longer version, which is available on request, contains a discussion of trends in the price of cocaine and in cocaine consumption over time and an analysis of variations in the price of cocaine among cities for the year 1991. Research for this chapter was supported by grant 5 R01 DA07533 from the National Institute on Drug Abuse to the National Bureau of Economic Research. We are extremely grateful to Patrick J. O'Malley, Senior Research Scientist at the University of Michigan's Institute for Social Research, for providing us with selected data from the Monitoring the Future panels and for variance-covariance matrixes containing illegal drug use and illegal drug prices. We also are extremely grateful to Jerome J. Hiniker, Senior Research Associate at ISR, for creating the computer programs that produced these tapes. We wish to thank Charles C. Brown, Professor of Economics at the University of Michigan and Senior Research Scientist at ISR, for supervising preliminary research with our database and for penetrating comments on earlier drafts of this chapter. We owe a special debt to Carolyn G. Hoffman, Chief of the Statistical Analysis Unit of the U.S. Department of Justice Drug Enforcement Administration, for providing us with illegal drug prices from STRIDE. Part of the research for this chapter was completed while Grossman was a visiting scholar at the Institute for Research on Economics and Society (IRES) at the Catholic University of Louvain in Belgium, and he wishes to acknowledge the financial support provided by that institution. We are indebted to Gary S. Becker, Warren J. Bickel, Jonathan P. Caulkins, Richard Clayton, David M. Cutler, Jack E. Henningfield, Theodore J. Joyce, Robert Kaestner, Matthew E. Kahn, Mark A.R. Kleiman, John R. Lott, Jr., Willard G. Manning, Jacob Mincer, John Mullahy, Kevin M. Murphy, Derek Neal, Joseph P. Newhouse, Robert Ohsfeldt, Solomon W. Polachek, William Rhodes, Sherwin Rosen, Henry Saffer, Robert H. Topel, Joseph Tracey, and three anonymous referees for helpful comments and suggestions. Preliminary versions of this chapter were presented at the 1997 meeting of the American Economic Association, the 1996 Western Economic Association International Conference, the 1996 International Health Economics Association Conference, the 1996 Pacific Rim Allied Economic Organization Conference and at seminars at the University of Chicago, the City University of New York Graduate School, the University of Colorado at Denver, Columbia University, Johns Hopkins University, the Rand Corporation, Rutgers University at Newark, and the State University of New York at Binghamton. We are indebted to the participants in those conferences and seminars for comments and suggestions. Finally, we wish to thank Sara Markowitz, Ismail Sirtalan, Timothy Perry, Patricia Kocagil, and Abeni Crooms for research assistance. This chapter has not undergone the review accorded official NBER publications; in particular it has not been submitted for approval by the Board of Directors.

Appendix Table A1 Rational Addiction Model First Stage Regressions, Participation

	Dependent Variables = Past Participation	Dependent Variables = Future Participation	Dependent Variables = Past Participation	Dependent Variables = Future Participation
Price	-0.000206 (-3.55)	-0.0000034 (-0.06)	-0.00025 (-4.22)	-0.000045 (-0.73)
Past price	-0.000117 (-2.80)	-0.000048 (-1.12)	-0.00014 (-3.15)	-0.000065 (-1.45)
Future price	-0.000205 (-2.93)	-0.000599 (-8.36)	-0.00029 (-4.01)	-0.000723 (-9.68)
Marijuana decriminalization	0.004 (0.31)	0.005 (0.37)	0.010 (0.68)	0.012 (0.82)
Legal drinking age * age ≤21	-0.004 (-1.05)	0.0004 (0.11)	-0.0005 (-0.13)	0.004 (0.96)
Lower border drinking age indicator * age ≤21	0.024 (2.44)	0.023 (2.32)	0.026 (2.56)	0.028 (2.67)
Past marijuana decriminalization	0.001 (0.05)	-0.011 (-0.97)	0.007 (0.61)	-0.005 (-0.44)
Past legal drinking age * age ≤21	0.012 (4.24)	0.004 (1.35)	0.012 (4.26)	0.004 (1.35)
Past lower border drinking age indicator * age ≤21	0.020 (2.35)	0.026 (2.95)	0.022 (2.47)	0.030 (3.24)
Future marijuana decriminalization	0.016 (1.48)	0.007 (0.65)	0.022 (1.94)	0.015 (1.29)
Real earnings	-4.330E-07 (-0.93)	2.770E-07 (0.58)		
Years of completed schooling	-0.0005 (-0.13)	-0.003 (-0.68)		
Full-time college student	-0.007 (-0.96)	-0.006 (-0.79)		
Half-time college student	0.005 (0.41)	0.007 (0.66)		
Less than half-time college student	0.014 (1.52)	0.003 (0.35)		
Working full-time	-0.001 (-0.14)	-0.016 (-2.31)		
Working part-time	-0.005 (-0.83)	-0.009 (-1.35)		

Unemployed	0.029 (2.42)	−0.004 (−0.34)
Married	−0.038 (−4.44)	−0.039 (−4.41)
Engaged	0.001 (0.16)	−0.007 (−0.90)
Separated or divorced	0.011 (0.73)	0.002 (0.10)
Number of children	0.002 (0.33)	0.009 (1.26)
Infrequent religious participation	−0.004 (−0.54)	−0.001 (−0.14)
Frequent religious participation	−0.064 (−6.91)	−0.071 (−7.46)
Past real earnings	3.553E-06 (6.66)	1.849E-06 (3.39)
Past years of completed schooling	0.005 (1.33)	−0.003 (−0.81)
Past full-time college student	0.004 (0.49)	0.001 (0.07)
Past half-time college student	0.018 (1.38)	0.002 (0.14)
Past less than half-time college student	−0.005 (−0.43)	0.023 (1.97)
Past working full-time	0.010 (1.51)	0.012 (1.90)
Past working part-time	0.003 (0.47)	0.007 (1.27)
Past unemployed	0.029 (2.13)	0.036 (2.58)
Past married	−0.099 (−11.53)	−0.025 (−2.80)
Past engaged	−0.004 (−0.48)	0.012 (1.51)
Past separated or divorced	0.007 (0.40)	0.004 (0.21)
Past number of children	−0.029 (−4.06)	0.015 (2.01)
Past infrequent religious participation	−0.031 (−3.95)	0.008 (0.95)
Past frequent religious participation	−0.107 (−12.23)	−0.027 (−3.00)

(continued)

Appendix Table A1 (*Continued*)

	Dependent Variables = Past Participation	Dependent Variables = Future Participation	Dependent Variables = Past Participation	Dependent Variables = Future Participation
Future real earnings	2.240E-07 (0.57)	4.640E-07 (1.16)		
Future years of completed schooling	-0.007 (-2.20)	-0.003 (-0.87)		
Future full-time college student	-0.004 (-0.48)	-.019 (-2.49)		
Future half-time college student	0.010 (0.91)	-0.001 (-0.10)		
Future less than half-time college student	0.013 (1.50)	0.003 (0.31)		
Future working full-time	-0.001 (-0.18)	-0.009 (-1.23)		
Future working part-time	-0.008 (-1.18)	-0.006 (-0.84)		
Future unemployed	0.019 (1.42)	0.012 (0.87)		
Future married	-0.029 (-4.24)	-0.111 (-16.05)		
Future engaged	-0.008 (-1.00)	-0.050 (-6.48)		
Future separated or divorced	0.017 (1.40)	0.008 (0.63)		
Future number of children	0.010 (2.11)	-0.016 (-3.30)		
Future infrequent religious participation	-0.0004 (-0.05)	-0.009 (-1.23)		
Future frequent religious participation	-0.056 (-6.53)	-0.119 (-13.53)		
R^2	0.092	0.119	0.032	0.039
F-ratio	53.547	72.078	40.860	50.825
N	38,885	38,885	38,885	38,885

Note: Other regressors include dichotomous indicators of age, year, race, and sex.

Appendix Table A2 Rational Addiction Model First Stage Regressions, Frequency

	Dependent Variables = Past Frequency	Dependent Variables = Future Frequency	Dependent Variables = Past Frequency	Dependent Variables = Future Frequency
Price	−0.005261 (−1.27)	−0.0011940 (−0.26)	−0.00589 (−1.42)	0.000297 (0.06)
Past price	−0.007337 (−2.56)	−0.002973 (−0.93)	−0.00744 (−2.58)	−0.003184 (−0.98)
Future price	−0.00324 (−0.69)	−0.020239 (−3.90)	−0.00272 (−0.58)	−0.021315 (−4.04)
Marijuana decriminalization	−0.386 (−0.47)	0.053 (0.06)	−0.278 (−0.34)	0.038 (0.04)
Legal drinking age * age ≤21	−0.324 (−1.49)	−0.178 (−0.74)	−0.320 (−1.46)	−0.275 (−1.12)
Lower border drinking age indicator * age ≤21	0.493 (0.83)	0.225 (0.34)	0.510 (0.85)	0.393 (0.58)
Past marijuana decriminalization	0.047 (0.07)	−0.275 (−0.36)	−0.047 (−0.07)	−0.226 (−0.29)
Past legal drinking age * age ≤21	0.390 (2.24)	0.083 (0.43)	0.445 (2.54)	0.176 (0.90)
Past lower border drinking age indicator * age ≤21	0.591 (1.14)	0.960 (1.67)	0.413 (0.80)	0.876 (1.50)
Future marijuana decriminalization	1.204 (1.85)	−0.200 (−0.28)	1.187 (1.81)	−0.198 (−0.27)
Real earnings	−3.353E−05 (−1.16)	2.500E−05 (0.78)		
Years of completed schooling	−0.3555 (−1.56)	−0.469 (−1.85)		
Full-time college student	−0.465 (−1.01)	−1.135 (−2.22)		
Half-time college student	0.371 (0.56)	0.097 (0.13)		
Less than half-time college student	0.975 (1.79)	−0.651 (−1.07)		
Working full-time	−1.062 (−2.44)	−0.944 (−1.95)		
Working part-time	−0.459 (−1.09)	−0.262 (−0.56)		
Unemployed	−0.003 (−0.00)	−1.097 (−1.35)		

(continued)

Appendix Table A2 (*Continued*)

	Dependent Variables = Past Frequency	Dependent Variables = Future Frequency	Dependent Variables = Past Frequency	Dependent Variables = Future Frequency
Married	0.260 (0.45)	0.651 (1.02)		
Engaged	−0.011 (−0.02)	0.314 (0.56)		
Separated or divorced	−0.316 (−0.34)	0.897 (0.86)		
Number of children	0.559 (1.19)	1.391 (2.66)		
Infrequent religious participation	−0.482 (−1.17)	−0.036 (−0.08)		
Frequent religious participation	−0.901 (−1.65)	−0.657 (−1.08)		
Past real earnings	1.640E-04 (5.01)	5.659E-05 (1.55)		
Past years of completed schooling	0.103 (0.45)	−0.518 (−2.05)		
Past full-time college student	−0.939 (−1.93)	−1.748 (−3.23)		
Past half-time college student	−0.139 (−0.18)	−0.075 (−0.08)		
Past less than half-time college student	−0.744 (−1.12)	0.072 (0.10)		
Past working full-time	0.414 (1.01)	−0.501 (−1.09)		
Past working part-time	−0.275 (−0.72)	0.372 (0.88)		
Past unemployed	0.609 (0.73)	0.598 (0.64)		
Past married	−2.713 (−4.31)	−0.747 (−1.07)		
Past engaged	−0.285 (−0.53)	1.058 (1.76)		
Past separated or divorced	−0.380 (−0.34)	0.297 (0.24)		
Past number of children	−0.980 (−1.97)	0.355 (0.64)		
Past infrequent religious participation	−0.826 (−1.98)	0.810 (1.75)		

Variable	(1)	(2)	(3)
Past frequent religious participation	−2.514 (−4.98)	1.123 (2.00)	
Future real earnings	2.123E-05 (0.88)	3.976E-05 (1.47)	
Future years of completed schooling	0.169 (0.91)	0.157 (0.76)	
Future full-time college student	−0.295 (−0.62)	−1.759 (−3.33)	
Future half-time college student	0.016 (0.02)	−1.261 (−1.68)	
Future less than half-time college student	−0.421 (−0.83)	−1.441 (−2.57)	
Future working full-time	−0.545 (−1.21)	−0.170 (−0.34)	
Future working part-time	−0.496 (−1.02)	−0.282 (−0.52)	
Future unemployed	−0.339 (−0.42)	0.962 (1.08)	
Future married	−0.017 (−0.04)	−4.199 (−8.81)	
Future engaged	−0.436 (−0.93)	−2.296 (−4.42)	
Future separated or divorced	0.796 (1.09)	−0.880 (−1.09)	
Future number of children	−0.464 (−1.42)	−1.432 (−3.94)	
Future infrequent religious participation	1.000 (2.59)	0.359 (0.84)	
Future frequent religious participation	1.076 (2.13)	−2.411 (−4.29)	
R^2	0.054	0.061	0.056
F-ratio	6.942	7.878	17.088
N	8,926	8,926	8,926
R^2			0.020
F-ratio			5.794
N			8,926

Note: Other regressors include dichotomous indicators of age, year, race, and sex.

Appendix Table A3 Myopic Model First Stage Regressions

	Dependent Variables = Past Participation	Dependent Variables = Past Participation	Dependent Variables = Past Frequency	Dependent Variables = Past Frequency
Price	−0.00029 (−5.79)	−0.00038 (−7.23)	−0.00701 (−2.02)	−0.00731 (−2.09)
Past price	−0.000156 (−3.88)	−0.00019 (−4.43)	−0.007545 (−2.69)	−0.00777 (−2.75)
Marijuana decriminalization	0.019 (1.73)	0.027 (2.43)	0.510 (0.76)	0.606 (0.90)
Legal drinking age * age ≤21	−0.004 (−1.21)	−0.001 (−0.33)	−0.323 (−1.48)	−0.323 (−1.48)
Lower border drinking age indicator * age ≤21	0.026 (2.69)	0.027 (2.65)	0.561 (0.94)	0.543 (0.91)
Past marijuana decriminalization	0.002 (0.20)	0.010 (0.92)	0.263 (0.39)	0.173 (0.26)
Past legal drinking age * age ≤21	0.013 (4.43)	0.013 (4.43)	0.379 (2.18)	0.446 (2.56)
Past lower border drinking age indicator * age ≤21	0.020 (2.30)	0.022 (2.47)	0.575 (1.12)	0.384 (0.74)
Real earnings	−4.160E-07 (−0.96)		−2.520E-05 (−0.94)	
Years of completed schooling	−0.005 (−1.72)		−0.234 (−1.23)	
Full-time college student	−0.017 (−2.69)		−0.341 (−0.83)	
Half-time college student	0.003 (0.32)		0.428 (0.66)	
Less than half-time college student	0.014 (1.53)		0.969 (1.80)	
Working full-time	0.001 (0.10)		−1.109 (−2.62)	
Working part-time	−0.005 (−0.86)		−0.490 (−1.18)	
Unemployed	0.033 (2.78)		−0.113 (−0.16)	
Married	−0.054 (−7.62)		0.220 (0.45)	
Engaged	−0.010 (−1.41)		−0.033 (−0.07)	

	(1)	(2)	(3)	(4)
Separated or divorced	0.020 (1.42)			0.056 (0.07)
Number of children	0.010 (1.84)			0.236 (0.58)
Infrequent religious participation	−0.007 (−1.00)			−0.103 (−0.27)
Frequent religious participation	−0.096 (−11.41)			−0.428 (−0.86)
Past real earnings	3.557E-06 (6.71)			1.660E-04 (5.10)
Past years of completed schooling	0.003 (0.83)			0.161 (0.73)
Past full-time college student	0.003 (0.37)			−0.898 (−1.87)
Past half-time college student	0.016 (1.25)			−0.147 (−0.19)
Past less than half-time college student	−0.005 (−0.48)			−0.760 (−1.14)
Past working full-time	0.009 (1.47)			0.395 (0.96)
Past working part-time	0.002 (0.43)			−0.270 (−0.71)
Past unemployed	0.031 (2.22)			0.570 (0.68)
Past married	−0.101 (−11.74)			−2.723 (−4.33)
Past engaged	−0.005 (−0.63)			−0.322 (−0.60)
Past separated or divorced	0.011 (0.58)			−0.359 (−0.32)
Past number of children	−0.028 (−3.97)			−1.031 (−2.09)
Past infrequent religious participation	−0.033 (−4.29)			−0.566 (−1.40)
Past frequent religious participation	−0.122 (−14.35)			−2.199 (−4.48)
R^2	0.088	0.031	0.053	0.056
F-ratio	65.831	42.885	8.625	18.122
N	38,885	38,885	8,926	8,926

Note: Other regressors include dichotomous indicators of age, year, race, and sex.

NOTES

Originally published as Michael Grossman and Frank J. Chaloupka, "The Demand for Cocaine by Young Adults: A Rational Addiction Approach," *Journal of Health Economics* 17, no. 4 (1998): 427–474.

1. These are particular definitions of harmful and beneficial addiction in the sense that they pertain to the effects of past consumption on current utility. Past consumption also might affect such variables as the current wage rate and current hours of work. We rule out these effects in outlining the theory but consider them when we discuss the roles of time-varying socioeconomic variables as determinants and consequences of consumption in sections 4 and 5.

2. For a derivation of equation (2), including formulas that relate the parameters in the demand function to those in the underlying utility function, see Becker et al. (1994). Equation (2) assumes no interaction between C_t and e_{t+1} in the current period utility function at time $t + 1$. That is, it assumes that $\partial^2 U/\partial e_{t+1}\partial C_t = 0$. This does not mean that changes in future life cycle variables (e_{t+1}) have no effects on current consumption. Instead, it means that these effects operate through future consumption. It is analogous to the assumption that a change in future price affects current consumption through its impact on future consumption.

3. These results can be seen more formally by solving the second-order difference in equation (2). The solution, which is contained in Becker et al. (1994), results in an equation in which consumption in period t depends on prices and life-cycle variables in all periods. Formulas for the long-run, short-run, and temporary current price effects also are contained in the paper just cited.

4. In this regression, the coefficient of the logarithm of weight times predicted purity equals 0.724, with a standard error of 0.002. Hence, the coefficient is significantly less than 1, indicating that the cost of a pure gram falls as the number of pure grams rises. This means that price cannot be obtained by simply dividing total cost by the product of weight and purity.

5. Even if the supply function of cocaine is not infinitely elastic, young adults can be viewed as price takers if they represent a small fraction of all illegal drug users. If this is not the case and the supply function slopes upward, we understate the price coefficient or elasticity in the demand function in absolute value. If the supply function slopes downward due to externalities (the greater is market consumption, the smaller is the probability of catching a given dealer), the price coefficient or elasticity in the demand function is overstated. Suppose that the demand function is linear in full price ($\pi = p + f$, where f is the expected penalty imposed on users), and suppose that $f = \alpha + kp$, $k > 0$, $\alpha \geq 0$. If f is omitted from the demand function, the elasticity of consumption with respect to p is less than or equal to the elasticity of consumption with respect to π as α is greater than or equal to zero.

6. To examine the sensitivity of the results to the value assigned to the open-ended interval, we assigned alternative values of 45, 55, 60, 65, 70, 80, 90, 100, 200, and 300 to this category. The absolute value of the slope coefficient of price rises as the value assigned to the open-ended category rises, but elasticities and tests of significance are not affected.

7. The sample of positive current users includes persons whose past or future values of use can be zero. In fact, the weighted means of past and future participation are 64 percent and 69 percent, respectively.

8. In a personal communication, Patrick M. O'Malley informed us that Monitoring the Future does attempt to survey panel members who are imprisoned. These attempts are not very successful, and the reliability of data obtained from prison inmates is very questionable since their correspondence can be read by prison officials.

9. The same computations applied to the participation equations yield discount factors ranging from 3.21 to 1.08 and negative interest rates ranging from −68 percent to −7 percent.

10. In the remainder of this section, all elasticities mentioned in the text are averages of those that emerge from the four alternative specifications of a given non-addictive, rational, or myopic model.

11. In the former case, the disturbance term in the structural demand function is correlated with the current socioeconomic variables. In the latter case, this disturbance term is correlated with the predicted value of future consumption.

REFERENCES

Basmann, R. L. 1960. "On Finite Sample Distributions of Generalized Classical Linear Identifiability Test Statistics." *J. Am. Stat. Assoc.* 55: 650–659.

Becker, G. S., and K. M. Murphy. 1988. "A Theory of Rational Addiction." *J. Political Econ.* 96: 675–700.

Becker, G. S., M. Grossman, and K. M. Murphy. 1994. "An Empirical Analysis of Cigarette Addiction." *Am. Econ. Rev.* 84: 396–418.

Bound, J., D. A. Jaeger, and R. M. Baker. 1995. "Problems with Instrumental Variables Estimation When the Correlation Between the Instruments and the Endogenous Explanatory Variable Is Weak." *J. Am. Stat. Assoc.* 90: 443–450.

Caulkins, J. P. 1994. *Developing Price Series for Cocaine*. Santa Monica, CA: RAND.

——. 1995. "Domestic Geographic Variation in Illicit Drug Prices." *J. Urban Econ.* 37: 38–56.

——. 1997. "Is Crack Cheaper Than (Powder) Cocaine?" *Addiction* 92: 1437–1443.

Chaloupka, F. J. 1991. "Rational Addictive Behavior and Cigarette Smoking." *J. Political Econ.* 99: 722–742.

Chaloupka, F. J., H. Saffer, and M. Grossman. 1993." Alcohol-Control Policies and Motor-Vehicle Fatalities." *J. Legal Studies*: 161–186.

Coate, D., and M. Grossman. 1988. "Effects of Alcoholic Beverage Prices and Legal Drinking Ages on Youth Alcohol Use." *J. Law Econ.* 31: 145–171.

Cragg, J. G. 1971. "Some Statistical Models for Limited Dependent Variables with Application to the Demand for Durable Goods." *Econometrica* 39: 829–844.

DiNardo, J. 1993. "Law Enforcement, the Price of Cocaine, and Cocaine Use". *Math. Comput. Modeling* 17: 53–64.

Friedman, M. 1989. An open letter to Bill Bennett. *Wall Street Journal*: A16.

Griliches, Z. 1979. "Sibling Models and Data in Economics: Beginnings of a Survey." *J. Political Econ.* 87: S37–S64.

Griliches, Z., and J. A. Hausman. 1986. "Errors in Variables in Panel Data". *J. Econ.* 31: 93–118.

Grossman, M. 1993. "The Economic Analysis of Addictive Behavior." In *Economic and Socioeconomic Issues in the Prevention of Alcohol-related Problems*, ed. G. Bloss and M. Hilton , U.S. Government Printing Office, Washington, DC: 91–124.

Grossman, M., and F. J. Chaloupka. 1997. "The Demand for Cocaine by Young Adults: A Rational Addiction Approach." National Bureau of Economic Research Working Paper No. 5713, revised.

Grossman, M., F. J. Chaloupka, and I. Sirtalan. 1998. "An Empirical Analysis of Alcohol Addiction: Results from the Monitoring the Future Panels." *Econ. Inquiry* 36: 39–48.

Hausman, J. A. 1978. "Specification Tests in Econometrics." *Econometrica* 46: 1251–1271.

Heckman, J. J. 1979. "Sample Selection Bias as a Specification Error." *Econometrica* 47: 153–161.

Heckman, J. J., and T. E. MaCurdy. 1985. "A Simultaneous Equations Linear Probability Model." *Can. J. Econ.* 18: 28–37.

Huber, P. J. 1967. "The Behavior of Maximum Likelihood Estimates under Nonstandard Conditions." Fifth Berkeley Symposium on Mathematical Statistics and Probability. Berkeley, CA: University of California Press: 221–233.

Johnston, L. D., and P. M. O'Malley. 1985. "Issues of Validity and Population Coverage in Student Surveys of Drug Abuse." In *Self-report Methods of Estimating Drug Use: Meeting Current Challenges to Validity*, ed. B. A. Rouse, N. J. Kozel, and L. G. Richards. Rockville, MD: National Institute on Drug Abuse: 31–54.

Johnston, L. D., P. M. O'Malley, and J. G. Bachman. 1989. "Drug Use, Drinking, and Smoking: National Survey Results from High School, College, and Young Adult Populations, 1975–1988." Washington, DC: U.S. Government Printing Office.

———. 1995. "National Survey Results on Drug Use from the Monitoring the Future Study, 1975–1994." Washington, DC: U.S. Government Printing Office.

Keeler, T. E., T. Hu, P. G. Barnett, and W. G. Manning. 1993. "Taxation, Regulation, and Addiction: A Demand Function for Cigarettes Based on Time-Series Evidence." *J. Health Econ.* 12: 1–18.

Leung, S. F., and S. Yu. 1996. "On the Choice Between Sample Selection and Two-Part Models." *J. Econ.* 71: 197–229.

Manning, W. G., Duan, N., Rogers, W. H., 1987. Monte Carlo evidence on the choice between sample selection and two-part models. *J. Econ.* 35: 59–82.

Marquis, K. H., N. Duan, M. S. Marquis, and J. M. Polich. 1981. *Response Errors in Sensitive Survey Topics: Estimates, Effects, and Correction Options, R-2710/2-HHS*. Santa Monica, CA: The RAND, Santa Monica, CA.

Midanik, L. 1982. "The Validity of Self-Reported Alcohol Consumption and Alcohol Problems." *Br. J. Addiction* 77: 357–368.

National Institute on Drug Abuse, U.S. Department of Health and Human Services. 1991. "National Household Survey on Drug Abuse: Main Findings 1990." Rockville, MD: U.S. Department of Health and Human Services.

Nisbet, C. T., and F. Vakil. 1972. "Some Estimates of Price and Expenditure Elasticities of Demand for Marijuana Among U.C.L.A. Students." *Rev. Econ. Stat.* 54: 473–475.

Polich, J. M. 1982. "The Validity of Self-Reports in Alcoholism research." *Addictive Behav.* 7: 123–132.

Silverman, L. P., and N. L. Spruill. 1977. "Urban Crime and the Price of Heroin." *J. Urban Econ.* 4: 80–103.

Staiger, D., and J. A. Stock. 1997. "Instrumental Variables Regression with Weak Instruments." *Econometrica* 65: 557–586.

Taubman, P. 1991. "Externalities and Decriminalization of Drugs." In *Drug Policy in the United States*, ed. M. B. Krauss and E. P. Lazear. Stanford, CA: Hoover Institution Press: 90–111.

Tobin, J. 1958. "Estimation of relationships for Limited Dependent variables." *Econometrica* 26: 24–36.

van de Ven, W. P., and B. M. van Praag. 1981. "Risk Aversion and Deductibles in Private Health Insurance: Application of an Adjusted Tobit Model to Family Health Care Expenditures." In *Health, Economics, and Health Economics*, ed. J. van der Gaag and M. Perlman. North-Holland, Amsterdam: 125–148.

van Ours, J. C. 1995. "The Price Elasticity of Hard Drugs: The Case of Opium in the Dutch East Indies, 1923–1938." *J. Political Econ.* 103: 261–279.

Wasserman, J., W. G. Manning, J. P. Newhouse, and J. P. Winkler. 1991. "The Effects of Excise Taxes and Regulations on Cigarette Smoking." *J. Health Econ.* 10: 43–64.

An Economic Analysis of
Adult Obesity

*Results from the Behavioral Risk
Factor Surveillance System*

Shin-Yi Chou, Michael Grossman,
and Henry Saffer

NINETEEN

ABSTRACT

This chapter examines the factors that may be responsible for the 50 percent increase in the number of obese adults in the United States since the late 1970s. We employ the 1984–1999 Behavioral Risk Factor Surveillance System, augmented with state level measures pertaining to the per capita number of fast-food and full service restaurants, the prices of a meal in each type of restaurant, food consumed at home, cigarettes, alcohol, and clean indoor air laws. Our main results are that these variables have the expected effects on obesity and explain a substantial amount of its trend.

1. INTRODUCTION

Since the late 1970s, the number of obese adults in the United States has grown by over 50 percent. This chapter examines the factors that may be responsible for this rapidly increasing prevalence rate. We focus on societal forces which may alter the cost of nutritional and leisure time choices made by individuals and specifically consider the effect of changes in relative prices, which are beyond the individual's control, on these choices. The principal hypothesis to be tested is that an increase in the prevalence of obesity is the result of several economic changes that have altered the lifestyle choices of Americans. One important economic change is the increase in the value of time, particularly of women, which is reflected by the growth in their labor force participation rates and in their hours of work. The reduction in home time has been associated with an increase in the demand for convenience food (food requiring minimal preparation time) and consumption in fast-food restaurants. Home time also has fallen and the consumption of the two types of food just mentioned has risen because the slow growth in income among certain groups has increased their labor market time.

Another important change is the rise in the real cost of cigarette smoking due to increases in the money price of cigarettes, the diffusion of information concerning the harmful effects of smoking, and the enactment of state statutes that restrict smoking in public places and in the workplace. This relative price change may have reduced smoking, which tends to increase weight. A final set of relative price changes revolves around the increasing availability of fast-food, which reduces search and travel time and changes in the relative costs of meals consumed in fast-food restaurants, full-service restaurants, and meals prepared at home. Some of the changes just mentioned, especially the growth in the availability of fast-food restaurants, may have been stimulated by increases in the value of female time.

To study the determinants of adult obesity and related outcomes, we employ micro-level data from the 1984–1999 Behavioral Risk Factor Surveillance System (BRFSS). These repeated cross sections are augmented with state level measures pertaining to the per capita number of restaurants, the prices of a meal in fast-food and full-service restaurants, the price of food consumed at home, the price of cigarettes, clean indoor air laws, and the price of alcohol (a potential determinant of weight outcomes given the high caloric content of beer, wine, and distilled spirits). Our main results are that these variables have the expected effects on obesity and explain a substantial amount of its trend. These findings control for individual-level measures of age, race, household income, years of formal schooling completed, and marital status.

2. BACKGROUND

The significance of research on obesity and sedentary lifestyle is highlighted by the adverse health outcomes and costs associated with these behaviors and by the level and growth of obesity rates. According to McGinnis and Foege (1993) and Allison et al. (1999), obesity and sedentary lifestyles result in over 300,000 premature deaths per year in the United States. By comparison, the mortality associated with tobacco, alcohol and illicit drugs is about 400,000, 100,000, and 20,000 deaths per year, respectively. Wolf and Colditz (1998) estimate that in 1995 the costs of obesity were US$ 99.2 billion, which was 5.7 percent of the total costs of illness. Public financing of these costs is considerable since approximately half of all health care is paid by the federal government and state and local governments.

Until recently, obesity in the United States was a fairly rare occurrence. Obesity is measured by the body mass index (BMI), also termed Quetelet's index, and defined as weight in kilograms divided by height in meters squared (kg/m^2). According to the World Health Organization (1997) and National Heart, Lung, and Blood Institute, National Institutes of Health (1998), a BMI value of between 20 and 22 kg/m^2 is "ideal" for adults regardless of gender in the sense that mortality and morbidity risks are minimized in this range. Persons with BMI ≥ 30 kg/m^2 are classified as obese.

Trends in the mean body mass index of adults ages eighteen years of age and older and the percentage who are obese between 1959 and 2000 are presented in table 19.1. These data come from heights and weights obtained from physical examinations conducted in the First National Health Examination Survey (NHES I) between 1959 and 1962, the First National Health and Nutrition Examination Survey (NHANES I) between 1971 and 1975, the Second National Health and Nutrition Examination Survey (NHANES II) between 1976 and 1980,

Table 19.1 Trends in Body Mass Index and the Percentage Obese, Persons 18 Years of Age and Older

Survey	Period	Body Mass Index[a]	Percentage Obese[b]
NHES I[c]	1959–1962	24.91	12.73
NHANES I	1971–1975	25.14	13.85
NHANES II	1976–1980	25.16	13.95
NHANES III	1988–1994	26.40	21.62
NHANES 99	1999–2000	27.85	29.57

Note: The surveys are as follows: First National Health Examination Survey (NHES I), First National Health and Nutrition Examination Survey (NHANES I), Second National Health and Nutrition Examination Survey (NHANES II), Third National Health and Nutrition Examination Survey (NHANES III), and National Health and Nutrition Examination Survey 1999–2000 (NHANES 99). Survey weights are employed in all computations.

[a] Weight in kilograms divided by height in meters squared. Actual weights and heights are used in calculation.

[b] Percentage with body mass index ≥ 30 kg/m^2.

[c] In computations with NHES, 2 lbs. are subtracted from actual weight since examined persons were weighed with clothing.

the Third National Health and Nutrition Examination Survey (NHANES III) between 1988 and 1994, and the National Health and Nutrition Examination Survey 1999–2000 (NHANES 99).[1] Note the extremely modest upward trends in the two outcomes in table 19.1 until the period between 1978 (the midyear of NHANES II) and 1991 (the midyear of NHANES III). In that thirteen-year period, the percentage obese rose from approximately 14 to 22 percent. Absent any increase in population, this implies that the number of obese Americans grew by roughly 55 percent. At the same time, BMI rose by 1.24 kg/m^2 or by 5 percent, which represents a six pound weight gain for a woman or man of average height. The corresponding figures between 1960–1961 (the midyear of NHES I) and 1978 were a 10 percent increase in the number of obese persons, and a 1 percent increase in BMI. Data from the most recent NHANES survey suggest that the sharp upward trend in obesity between NHANES II and III continued through the year 2000.

The trends in table 19.1 are important because the stability of BMI in the two decades between NHES I and NHANES II is masked in longer-term trends in this variable between 1864 and 1991 presented by Costa and Steckel (1997).[2] They include NHES I and NHANES III in their time series but do not include NHANES I and NHANES II. Philipson and Posner (1999), Philipson (2001), and Lakdawalla and Philipson (2002) use Costa and Steckel's time series as the point of departure of a penetrating analysis in which increases in BMI over time are caused by reductions in the strenuousness of work. Lakdawalla and Philipson (2002) show that BMI is negatively related to an index of job strenuousness in repeated cross sections from the National Health Interview Survey for the period 1976–1994 and in the National Longitudinal Survey of Youth (NLSY) for the period from 1982 to 1998. This important finding confirms their explanation of the long-term trend in BMI. Yet it sheds little light on the trend between NHANES II and NHANES III because the job strenuousness measure was very stable in the periods that they consider.

Trends in aggregate time series data and four studies by economists (Cawley 1999; Ruhm 2000; Lakdawalla and Philipson 2002; Cutler et al. 2003) provide some insights concerning the causes of the upward trend in obesity. The shift from an agricultural or industrial society to a post-industrial society emphasized by Philipson (2001) in his economic analysis of obesity has been accompanied by innovations that economize on time previously allocated to the nonmarket or household sector. One such innovation has economized on time spent in food preparation at home and is reflected by the introduction of convenience food for consumption at home and by the growth of fast-food and full-service restaurants. The growth in restaurants, particularly fast-food restaurants, has been dramatic. According to the *Census of Retail Trade*, the per capita number of fast-food restaurants doubled between 1972 and 1997, while the per capita number of full-service restaurants rose by 35 percent (Bureau of the Census 1976, 2000). Fast-food and convenience food are inexpensive and have a high caloric density (defined as calories per pound) to make them palatable (Schlosser 2001). Total calories consumed rises with caloric density if the reduction in the total amount of food consumed does not fully offset the increase in density. Mela and Rogers (1998) report that this occurs in many cases.

The increasing prevalence of convenience food and fast-food is part of the long-term trend away from the labor-intensive preparation of food at home prior to consumption. But it also can be attributed in part to labor market developments since 1970 that have witnessed declines or slow growth in real income of certain groups and increases in hours of work and labor force participation rates by most groups, especially women (see Chou et al. 2002 for a detailed discussion of these trends). The data show that more household time is going to market work. There is correspondingly less time and energy available for home and leisure activities such as food preparation and active leisure. The increases in hours worked and labor force participation rates, and declines or modest increases in real income experienced by certain groups appear to have stimulated the demand for inexpensive convenience and fast-food, which has increased caloric intakes. At the same time, the reduction in the time available for active leisure has reduced calories expended.

The final trend that we wish to call attention to is the anti-smoking campaign, which began to accelerate in the early 1970s. Individuals who quit smoking typically gain weight (Pinkowish 1999). The real price of cigarettes rose by 164 percent between 1980 and 2001 (Orzechowski and Walker 2002). This large increase resulted in part from four federal excise tax hikes, a number of state tax hikes and the settlement of the state lawsuits filed against cigarette makers to recover Medicaid funds spent treating diseases related to smoking. The period since the late 1970s also has been characterized by a dramatic increase in the percentage of the population residing in states that have enacted clean indoor air laws that restrict smoking in public places and in the workplace. For example, in 1980, 6 percent of the population resided in states that restrict smoking in the workplace. By 1999, this figure stood at 42 percent (Centers for Disease Control and Prevention [CDC] website http://www2.cdc.gov/nccdph/osh/state).

Very recent contributions to the determinants of obesity by economists have focused on the roles of unemployment, job strenuousness, and prices of food prepared at home. Ruhm (2000) finds that body mass index and obesity are inversely related to state unemployment rates in repeated cross sections from the Behavioral Risk Factor Surveillance System for the years 1987–1995. His interpretation of these results is that the value of time is negatively related to the unemployment rate. Cawley (1999) reports that BMI is negatively related to the real price of groceries in the National Longitudinal Survey of Youth for the period from 1981 to 1996. His price variable incorporates variations over time and among the four major geographic regions of the United States. Cawley is careful to note that more expensive food does not always contain more calories than cheaper food and that consumers can substitute towards inexpensive, caloric food when this overall price index rises.

Using the same NLSY panel employed by Cawley, Lakdawalla, and Philipson (2002) also find a negative effect of a price of food at home measure that varies by city and year on BMI. They control for unmeasured time effects but do not control for unmeasured area effects. Moreover, their methodology assumes that each individual faces an upward sloping average or marginal cost function of food. This differs from the standard assumption that consumers are price takers. Cutler et al. (2003) present evidence that reductions in the time costs of preparing meals at home for certain groups in the population contribute to an increase in BMI for those groups. They attribute the reduction in the daily time allocated to meal preparation (their measure of the time cost) to technological advances. Their results are based on very aggregate data and do not directly take account of the growth in fast-food and full-service restaurants.

We extend the research just summarized by considering many more potential determinants of BMI and obesity, especially those with significant trends. This is important in attempting to explain the growth in obesity since the late 1970s. Although job strenuousness, unemployment, grocery prices, and the time required to prepare a meal at home are important determinants of BMI and obesity, trends in the first two variables cannot account for the increase in obesity. Moreover, a focus on the role of food at home prices including time costs ignores the dramatic shift away from the consumption of meals at home during the past 30 years.

3. ANALYTICAL FRAMEWORK

In Chou et al. (2002), we develop a simple behavioral model of the determinants of obesity using standard economic tools. Obesity is a function of an individual's energy balance over a number of time periods or ages. The energy balance in a given period is the difference between calories consumed and expended in that period. In addition to this cumulative energy balance, age, gender, race, ethnicity, and genetic factors unique to an individual help determine weight outcomes by influencing the process by which energy balances are translated into changes in body mass. A behavioral model of obesity must explain the determinants of calories consumed and calories expended.

Since no one desires to be obese, it is useful to consider obesity as the byproduct of other goals in the context of Becker's (1965) household production function model of consumer behavior. This model provides a framework for studying the demand for caloric intakes and expenditures because it recognizes that consumers use goods and services purchased in the market together with their own time to produce more fundamental commodities that enter their utility functions. Three such commodities are health, which depends in part by consuming the appropriate diet and engaging in physical exercise, the enjoyment of eating palatable food, and the entertainment provided by dining with family and friends in restaurants or at home.

Households consume the ingredients in food via meals, and meals are produced with inputs of food and time. Time enters the production of meals in a variety of ways. Obviously, it is required to consume the food, but it also is required to obtain and prepare it. The production of meals at home is the most intensive in the household's own time, while the production of meals in restaurants is the least intensive in that time. For a given quality, food consumed in restaurants is more expensive than prepared food consumed at home, which in turn is more expensive than food prepared and consumed at home.

The other variable in the energy balance equation is caloric expenditure. Calories are expended at work, doing home chores, and at active leisure. Calories expended at work depend on the nature of the occupation as emphasized by Lakdawalla and Philipson (2002). Individuals who work more hours in the market will substitute market goods for their own time in other activities. An increase in hours of work raises the price of active leisure and generates a substitution effect that causes the number of hours spent in this activity to fall. An increase in hours of work also lowers the time allocated to household chores.

These considerations suggest reduced form equations or demand functions for calories consumed and expended and for cigarette smoking. The last variable is included because smokers have higher metabolic rates than nonsmokers. They also consume fewer calories than nonsmokers, so that cigarette consumption is a partial indicator of caloric intakes in previous periods, which we do not explicitly model. The demand functions depend on a set of variables specified below and consisting mainly of prices and income. Substitution of these equations into the structural equation for BMI or for the probability of being obese yields a reduced form equation for the outcome at issue.

Reduced form determinants include hours of work or the hourly wage rate; family income; a vector of money prices including the prices of convenience foods, the prices of meals consumed at fast-food and at full-service restaurants, the prices of food requiring significant preparation time, the price of cigarettes, and the price of alcohol; years of formal schooling completed; and marital status. With regard to the roles of variables not discussed so far, with hours of work held constant, an increase in income expands real resources. If health is a superior commodity (a commodity whose optimal value rises as income rises with prices held constant) and if an individual weighs less than his or her recommended weight, the demand for calories grows. Even for consumers at or above recommended weight, calorie consumption increases if palatable food and food consumed at "upscale" full-service restaurants are rich in calories.

Reductions in convenience food prices, fast-food restaurant prices, and certain full-service restaurant prices, or increases in the prices of foods requiring significant preparation time raise calorie consumption by inducing a substitution towards higher caloric intakes. It is conceivable that the demand for active leisure may rise, although we consider this offset to the potential increase in obesity to be unlikely. The price vector is not limited to food prices because cigarette smoking is associated with lower weight levels, as previously noted. Restrictions on smoking in public places and in the workplace raise the "full price" of smoking by increasing the inconvenience costs associated with this behavior. Trends in the enactment of clean indoor air laws also may reflect increased information about the harmful effects of smoking. The price of alcohol also is included because alcohol has a high caloric content. The empirical evidence that increased alcohol consumption contributes to weight gain is, however, mixed (for example, Prentice 1995; Kahn et al.,1997). Years of formal schooling completed may increase efficiency in the production of a variety of household commodities, expand knowledge concerning what constitutes a healthy diet, and make the consumer more future oriented. Marital status may affect the time available for household chores and active leisure in a variety of ways.

Consumption of meals in restaurants requires travel and in some cases waiting time. Hence, the full price of a meal in a restaurant should reflect this component as well as the money price. Travel and waiting time should fall as the per capita number of restaurants in the consumer's area of residence rises. Therefore, we include the per capita numbers of fast-food and full-service restaurants in our empirical analysis. This is particularly important because we do not have direct measures of wage rates or hours of work. Restaurants, particularly fast-food restaurants, should locate in areas in which consumers have relatively high time values.

Consequently, the availability of these restaurants in a particular area is a negative correlate of travel and waiting time and a positive correlate of the value that consumer's place on their time.

4. EMPIRICAL IMPLEMENTATION

To investigate the determinants of body mass index and obesity, we employ repeated cross sections from the Behavioral Risk Factor Surveillance System for the years 1984–1999. The BRFSS consists of annual telephone surveys of persons of age eighteen years and older conducted by state health departments in collaboration with the CDC. Fifteen states participated in the first survey in 1984. The number of participating states grew to thirty-three in 1987, to forty-five in 1990, and to all fifty-one states (including the District of Columbia) in 1996.[3] The average number of interviews per state ranged from approximately 800 in 1984 to 1,800 in 1990, and to 3,000 in 1999. These state stratified cluster samples are used by CDC to make national and state-specific estimates of the prevalence of lifestyle indicators and behavioral factors that contribute to positive or negative health outcomes.

Definitions, means, and standard deviations of all variables employed in the regressions in section 5 are contained in table 19.2. Except where noted, they are based on the sample of 1,111,074 that emerges when observations with missing values are deleted. The means and standard deviations in the table and those cited in the text are computed based on BRFSS sampling weights and are representative of the population at large. CDC makes national estimates from the BRFSS beginning in 1990 when forty-five states participated in the survey. To maximize variation in the state-specific regressors, we include data for all years in the regressions. Preliminary results obtained when the sample was restricted to the years 1987–1999 were fairly similar to those obtained for the entire period. The weights are not employed in the regression estimates since DuMouchel and Duncan (1983) and Maddala (1983, 171–173) have shown that this is not required in the case of exogenous stratification.[4]

Self-reported data on height and weight allow us to construct the body mass index of each respondent and indicators of whether he or she is obese. It is well known that self-reported anthropometric variables contain measurement error with heavier persons more likely to underreport their weight. Therefore, we employ procedures developed by Cawley (1999) to correct for these errors. The Third National Health and Nutrition Examination Survey contains both actual weight and height from physical examinations and self-reported weight and height. For persons eighteen years of age and older in NHANES III, we regress actual weight on reported weight and the square of reported weight. We also regress actual height on reported height and the square of reported height. These regressions are estimated separately for eight groups: white male non-Hispanics, white female non-Hispanics, black male non-Hispanics, black female non-Hispanics, Hispanic males, Hispanic females, other males, and other females.[5]

Table 19.2 Definitions, Means, and Standard Deviations of Variables

Variable	Definition	Mean and Standard Deviation
Body mass index	Weight in kilograms divided by height in meters squared	26.015 (4.959)
Obese	Dichotomous variable that equals 1 if body mass index ≥ 30 kg/m^2	0.175 (0.380)
Black non-Hispanic	Dichotomous variable that equals 1 if respondent is black but not Hispanic	0.092 (0.288)
Hispanic	Dichotomous variable that equals 1 if respondent is Hispanic	0.085 (0.279)
Other race	Dichotomous variable if respondent's race is other than white or black	0.033 (0.179)
Male	Dichotomous variable that equals 1 if respondent is male	0.499 (0.500)
Some high school	Dichotomous variable that equals 1 if respondent completed at least 9 years but less than 12 years of formal schooling	0.092 (0.289)
High school graduate	Dichotomous variable that equals 1 if respondent completed exactly 12 years of formal schooling	0.330 (0.470)
Some college	Dichotomous variable that equals 1 if respondent completed at least 13 years but less than 16 years of formal schooling	0.262 (0.440)
College graduate	Dichotomous variable that equals 1 if respondent graduated from college	0.263 (0.440)
Married	Dichotomous variable that equals 1 if respondent is married	0.613 (0.487)
Divorced	Dichotomous variable that equals 1 if respondent is divorced or separated	0.089 (0.284)
Widowed	Dichotomous variable that equals 1 if respondent is widowed	0.066 (0.249)
Household income	Real household income in thousands of 1982–1984 dollars	29.460 (24.627)
Age	Age of respondent	43.381 (17.119)
Restaurants	Number of fast-food restaurants and full-service restaurants per 10,000 persons in respondent's state of residence[a]	13.252 (1.529)
Fast-food price	Real fast-food meal price in respondent's state of residence in 1982–1984 dollars[a]	2.903 (0.220)
Full-service restaurant price	Real full-service restaurant meal price in respondent's state of residence in 1982–1984 dollars[a]	5.971 (1.172)

(*continued*)

Table 19.2 *(Continued)*

Variable	Definition	Mean and Standard Deviation
Food at home price	Real food at home price in respondent's state of residence in 1982–1984 dollars: weighted average of prices of 13 food items, weights are shares of each item in total food expenditures based on expenditure patterns of mid-management (middle-income) households[a]	1.258 (0.121)
Cigarette price	Real cigarette price in respondent's state of residence in 1982–1984 dollars[a]	1.287 (0.257)
Alcohol price	Real alcohol price in respondent's state of residence in 1982–1984 dollars: weighted average of prices of pure ounce of ethanol in beer, wine, and spirits; weights are shares of each item in total alcohol consumption[a]	1.065 (0.170)
Private	Dichotomous variable that equals 1 if smoking is prohibited in private workplaces in respondent's state of residence	0.343 (0.475)
Government	Dichotomous variable that equals 1 if smoking is prohibited in state and local government workplaces in respondent's state of residence	0.564 (0.496)
Restaurant	Dichotomous variable that equals 1 if smoking is prohibited in restaurants in respondent's state of residence	0.546 (0.498)
Other	Dichotomous variable that equals 1 if smoking is prohibited in other public places such as elevators, public transportation, and theaters in respondent's state of residence	0.688 (0.463)

Note: Standard deviations are in parentheses. Sample size is 1,111,074. BRFSS sample weights are used in calculating the mean and standard deviation.
[a]See text for more details.

The coefficients from these regressions are combined with the self-reported BRFSS data to adjust height and weight and to compute BMI and the obesity indicator.[6] These two measures are employed as alternative dependent variables. Given the large sample size, we fit linear probability models rather than logit or probit models when obese is the outcome.

The corrected mean values of BMI and obese in the BRFSS all exceed values computed from reported weight and height. For BMI, the corrected figure is 26.01 kg/m^2, and the uncorrected figure is 25.40 kg/m^2. According to the corrected data, 17.54 percent of the population is obese, compared to an uncorrected figure of 13.75 percent. The simple correlation coefficient between corrected and uncorrected BMI exceeds 0.99. The simple correlation coefficients between the corrected and uncorrected obesity indicator is smaller (0.86) but still very substantial.

The trends in corrected BMI and the corrected percentages of the population obese in the BRFSS are plotted in figure 19.1. The values of BMI and obese are computed based on BRFSS sampling weights which produce nationally representative figures as of 1990. Between 1984 and 1999, BMI increased by 2.13 kg/m^2 or by 9 percent, and the number of obese adults more than doubled. While the algorithm for adjusting self-reported weight and height does raise BMI and obesity, the adjusted levels are still lower than those obtained from actual heights and weights in NHANES. For example, 24.00 percent of the population was obese in 1999 based on the BRFSS compared to 29.57 percent based on NHANES 99.[7] Nevertheless, annual rates of change in the BRFSS appear to be comparable to those in NHANES. This holds even though the BRFSS data prior to 1990 may not be nationally representative. For example, in the thirteen-year period spanned by the mid-years of NHANES II and NHANES III, BMI grew at an annually compounded rate of 0.4 percent per year, and the percentage obese grew at an annually compounded rate of 3.4 percent per year. The corresponding increases in the fifteen-year period spanned by the BRFSS were 0.5 percent per year for BMI and 5.3 percent per year for obesity.[8]

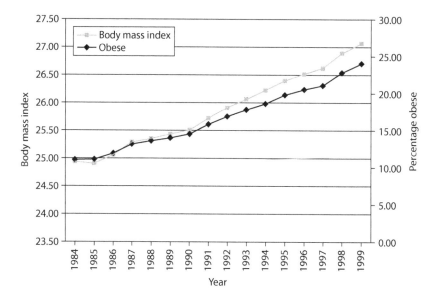

Figure 19.1 Trends in body mass index and percentage obese, persons 18 years of age and older, "Behavioral Risk Factor Surveillance System, 1984–1999"

The roles of all the independent variables in table 19.2 in body mass and obesity outcomes were discussed in section 3. Therefore, in the remainder of this section, we discuss the definitions and sources of the variables that are appended to the BRFSS based on state of residence and survey year.[9]

The number of fast-food restaurants and the number of full-service restaurants are taken from the 1982, 1987, 1992, and 1997 *Census of Retail Trade* (Bureau of the Census 1986, 1989, 1994, 2000). For other years, these variables are obtained from interpolations and extrapolations of state-specific logarithmic time trends. Except for 1999, the Bureau of the Census classifies establishments based on the Standard Industrial Classification (SIC) system.[10] Fast-food restaurants correspond to refreshment places (SIC category 5812/40). These are establishments primarily selling limited lines of refreshments and prepared food items. Included are establishments which prepare pizza, barbecued chicken, and hamburgers for consumption either on or near the premises or for "take-home" consumption. Full-service restaurants are restaurants and lunchrooms (SIC category 5812/10). They are establishments engaged in serving prepared food selected by the patron from a full menu. Waiter or waitress service is provided, and the establishment has seating facilities for at least fifteen patrons. The distinction between fast-food and full-service restaurants made by the Bureau of the Census is not clear-cut. In particular, many full-service restaurants serve the type of high-caloric and inexpensive food that is offered by fast-food restaurants. In preliminary regressions, the coefficients of the two types of restaurants were very similar. Therefore, we summed the fast-food and full-service restaurants and employ the per capita number in the regressions in section 5.

The full-service restaurant price pertains to the average cost of a meal in this type of restaurant and was taken from the same source as the number of full-service restaurants. The *Census of Retail Trade* contains data on the number of restaurants whose average cost of a meal falls in specific categories by state. The categories are less than US$ 2.00, 2.00–4.99, 5.00–6.99, 7.00–9.99, 10.00–14.99, 15.00–19.99, 20.00–29.99, and 30.00 and over. We assigned midpoints to the closed end categories, an average cost of US$ 1.50 to the smallest category, and an average cost of US$ 45.00 to the highest category. We then computed price as a weighted average of the average cost in each category, where the weights are the number of restaurants in each category in the state. The use of midpoints and the failure to adjust for quality imply that the restaurant price variable suffers from measurement error. In addition, the price in 1982, which is required to obtain estimates for 1984, 1985, and 1986, is based on much broader average cost categories than those in 1987.[11]

The fast-food price and the food at home price come from prices in the *ACCRA Cost of Living Index*, published quarterly by the American Chamber of

Commerce Researchers Association (ACCRA various years), for between 250 and 300 cities. Three fast-food prices are reported by this source: a McDonald's Quarter-Pounder with cheese, a thin crusted cheese pizza at Pizza Hut or Pizza Inn, and fried chicken at Kentucky Fried Chicken or Church's. We obtained quarterly state-specific prices as population-weighted averages of the city prices and then averaged over the four quarters in a given year to get annual prices.

The ACCRA collects prices of fifty-nine different items and also reports the weight of each item in the typical budget of a household whose head holds a mid-management position. The budget shares of each of the three fast-food items were equal to each other in the period from 1984 to 1999. Therefore, the fast-food price employed in the regressions is a simple average of the three ACCRA fast-food prices divided by the annual Bureau of Labor Statistics Consumer Price Index (CPI) for the United States as a whole (1982–1984 = 1). All other money prices and money income in the regressions are deflated by the CPI.[12]

The food at home price is constructed from thirteen food prices obtained by ACCRA. As in the case of fast-food prices, we obtained quarterly state-specific prices as population-weighted averages of the city prices and then averaged over the four quarters in a given year to get annual prices. The final food at home price is a weighted average of these thirteen prices, where the weights are the average expenditure shares of these items as reported by the ACCRA during the years from 1984 to 1999. Since the weights are fixed over time, the resulting price is a Laspeyres food at home price level.[13]

The price of alcohol also is taken from the ACCRA survey. It is given as a weighted average of the prices of beer, wine, and distilled spirits. This price is constructed by converting beer, wine, and distilled spirits prices into the price per ounce of pure ethanol in each beverage. These three prices were then averaged using the national fractions of total ethanol consumption accounted for by each beverage in 1990 as weights.

The price of cigarettes is taken from the *Tax Burden on Tobacco* (Orzechowski and Walker 2002; formerly published by the Tobacco Institute). The price in this source is given as a weighted average price per pack, using national weights for each type of cigarette (regular, king, 100 mm) and type of transaction (carton, single pack, machine). It is inclusive of federal and state excise taxes.[14] The clean indoor air regulations (private, government, restaurant, and other) are taken from the Centers for Disease Control and Prevention website http://www2.cdc.gov/nccdph/osh/state.

The main aim of the empirical analysis in the next section is to see how much of the trend in the prevalence of the percentage of the population that is obese and in body mass index can be accounted for by the state-specific variables just defined. We accomplish this aim by multiplying the coefficients of all regressors by national trends in these variables between 1984 and 1999 and between 1960–1961 (the midyear of NHES I) and 1978 (the midyear of NHANES II). We go part of the way towards a full fixed-effects specification by including a set of dichotomous variables for each state except one in all regressions. Hence we control for unmeasured determinants of obesity that vary among states but do not vary over time. These unmeasured determinants may be correlated with the state-specific variables.

We allow the coefficients of the state-specific variables to be determined by within-state variation over time and by national variation over time. That is, we do include trend terms in the regressions. In preliminary research we found that the multicollinearity between trend measures and the state-specific variables made it very difficult to disentangle their separate effects. Moreover, the effects of adding states to the BRFSS over time confound the interpretation of trend terms. We realize that the omission of trend measures is controversial and limits our ability to interpret estimated relationships as being causal. We do think that it is illuminating to investigate what proportion of the recent dramatic increase in obesity can be explained by changes in our variables without a trend. We also think it is illuminating to see how well we can backcast weight outcomes between 1960–1961 and 1978.[15] A conservative interpretation of our goal is that we seek to explain trends in an accounting, rather than in a causal, sense.

5. RESULTS

Table 19.3 contains ordinary least squares regressions of body mass index and the probability of being obese, for persons eighteen years of age and older. Robust or Huber (1967) standard errors, which allow for state/year clustering, are obtained.[16] In preliminary regressions we found evidence that most of the continuous variables had nonlinear effects. Therefore, we employ a quadratic specification for each of these variables. Recent research by economists dealing with obesity estimates separate models by gender, race, and in some cases ethnicity (for example, Averett and Korenman 1996; Lakdawalla and Philipson 2002; Cawley 2004). We do not pursue this approach because the studies at issue focus on the relationship between obesity and labor market outcomes specific to an individual. We do not directly consider this relationship. Moreover, our aim is to provide an explanation of general trends in obesity rather than in trends for specific groups in the population.

The two regressions in the table have low explanatory power, with R^2 ranging from 4 to 8 percent. The main reason for this result is that body mass index and obesity have large genetic components. In this context it should be

Table 19.3 Body Mass Index and Obese Regressions, Persons 18 Years of Age and Older

Independent Variable	Dependent Variable: BMI	Dependent Variable: Obese
Black	1.638 (57.58)	0.089 (43.67)
Hispanic	0.737 (26.09)	0.027 (14.01)
Other race	−0.406 (−7.14)	−0.017 (−4.98)
Male	0.890 (54.41)	−0.003 (−2.53)
Some high school	−0.110 (−3.50)	−0.011 (−4.46)
High school graduate	−0.503 (−17.21)	−0.043 (−19.42)
Some college	−0.572 (−19.17)	−0.049 (−21.23)
College graduate	−1.150 (−35.68)	−0.084 (−34.29)
Married	0.187 (11.99)	0.004 (3.33)
Divorced	−0.411 (−19.86)	−0.029 (−20.27)
Widowed	0.262 (10.00)	0.010 (5.26)
Household income	−0.035 (−32.95)	−0.003 (−35.65)
Household income squared	0.0002 (23.18)	0.0000 (26.39)
Age	0.346 (165.73)	0.018 (114.52)
Age squared	−0.003 (−153.92)	−0.0002 (−110.67)
Restaurants (full-service + fast-food)	0.631 (9.41)	0.037 (8.02)
Restaurants squared	−0.011 (−5.17)	−0.001 (−4.23)
Fast-food restaurant price	−1.216 (−1.67)	−0.034 (−0.58)
Fast-food restaurant price squared	0.135 (1.13)	0.002 (0.20)
Full-service restaurant price	−0.687 (−4.28)	−0.047 (−3.83)
Full-service restaurant price squared	0.050 (3.97)	0.003 (3.57)
Food at home price	−6.462 (−3.37)	−0.530 (−4.28)
Food at home price squared	2.244 (3.12)	0.191 (4.12)
Cigarette price	0.486 (1.37)	0.032 (1.32)
Cigarette price squared	0.009 (0.08)	0.001 (0.11)
Alcohol price	1.140 (1.29)	0.145 (2.35)
Alcohol price squared	−0.734 (−1.93)	−0.080 (−2.98)
Private	0.015 (0.38)	0.0004 (0.13)
Government	0.115 (1.63)	−0.0000 (0.00)
Restaurant	−0.020 (−0.36)	0.001 (0.21)
Other	0.054 (0.97)	0.008 (1.96)
R^2	0.081	0.041
F-statistic	1212.21	593.94
Sample size	1,111,074	1,111,074

Note: All regressions include state dummies. The t-ratios are in parentheses. Huber (1967) or robust standard errors on which they are based allow for state/year clustering. Intercepts are not shown.

emphasized that our aim is to explain the increasing prevalence of obesity rather than to explain why a given individual is obese. This perspective is important because genetic characteristics of the population change slowly, while the incidence of obesity has increased rapidly. To be sure, some individual characteristics, such as years of formal schooling completed, may be correlated with genetic determinants of weight outcomes.[17] But there is little reason to believe that the state-specific variables that we consider are correlated with heredity. Of course, the regression disturbance term also may reflect tastes for different types of food. Our working hypothesis is that the mix of food consumption changes over time due to changes in prices and related determinants rather than to changes in tastes.

Focusing on the effects of the individual characteristics, one sees that age has an inverted U-shaped effect. BMI peaks at an age of approximately fifty-seven, while the probability of being obese peaks at an age of forty-five years.[18] Black non-Hispanics and Hispanics have higher values of both outcomes than whites, while persons of other races have lower values. Males have higher BMI levels than females, but females are more likely to be obese. Married and widowed persons have higher levels of BMI than single (never married) and divorced individuals. These relations carry over to the prevalence of obesity.

Years of formal schooling completed and real household income have negative effects on BMI and the probability of being obese. There is little evidence that the schooling effect falls as the amount of schooling rises. Differentials between college graduates and those who attended college but did not graduate are almost as large as differentials between the latter group and persons who did not attend high school. Graduation from college appears to maximize the probability that BMI is in the range that minimizes mortality and morbidity risks since the differentials between those with some college and those who are high school graduates are small

Although the negative effect of household income on BMI or obesity falls as income rises, the effect remains negative throughout almost all the observed income range. At weighted sample means, the income elasticity of body mass index is modest (−0.03). The impact of income on the probability of being obese is more substantial. Evaluated at sample means, a 10 percent increase in income is associated with a 0.5 percentage point decline in the percentage obese from 17.5 to 17.0 percent. In a fixed population, the number of obese people falls by 2 percent. It should be noted that the magnitude of the income effect may be overestimated due to the reverse causality from obesity to income (Averett and Korenman 1996; Cawley 2004).

Despite the relatively large number of state-specific variables in the set and the considerable amount of intercorrelations among them, most of their coefficients have the expected signs and are statistically significant. Regardless of the outcome considered, the per capita number of restaurants and the real price of cigarettes have positive and significant effects at weighted sample means. Along the same lines, the real fast-food restaurant price, the real food at home price and the real full-service restaurant price have negative and significant effects at weighted sample means.

The effects of the clean indoor air laws do not show a consistent pattern. Restrictions on cigarette smoking in restaurants have no role in weight outcomes. This is surprising because these restrictions are most likely to encourage a substitution of food for cigarettes. One possible explanation is that smokers substitute consumption of food at home for consumption in restaurants in states that restrict smoking at the latter site. Restrictions in state and local government workplaces are associated with higher levels of BMI and higher prevalence rates of obesity, but the coefficients are not significant. Private workplace restrictions never are significant and are associated with higher levels of BMI and obesity. Restrictions in elevators, public transportation, and theaters (reflected by the dichotomous indicator other) raise both weight outcomes, with the obesity effect achieving significance.

The absence of a clear pattern in the effects of clean indoor air laws may reflect in part their endogeneity. Evans et al. (1999) find that workplace smoking bans have very large negative effects on smoking participation. Moore (2001) reports this relationship reflects the underlying preferences of workers and employers rather than a direct causal process. In our context, state fixed effects may control for unobserved forces that influence smoking, obesity, and the enactment of clean indoor air laws.

Table 19.4 contains elasticities of BMI with respect to the continuous state-specific variables at the points of weighted sample means. It also contains percentage point changes in the probability of being obese associated with 10 percent changes in the state-specific variables.[19] As in the case of income, the elasticity of body mass index with respect to any of these variables is modest. The largest elasticity of 0.17 pertains to the per capita number of restaurants. This elasticity is six times larger than the absolute value of the income elasticity. When the probability of being obese is the outcome, the effects in table 19.4 are much more substantial. For example, a 10 percent increase in the number of restaurants increases the probability of being obese by 1.4 percentage points. Put differently, evaluated at sample means, a 10 percent increase in the per capita number of restaurants is associated with a growth in the percentage obese from 17.5 to 18.9 percent. In a fixed population, the number of obese people rises by 8 percent. Note, however, that national or state-specific time varying unobservable changes in the demand for caloric intakes might be correlated with changes in obesity and the number of restaurants. In that case, the impact of the fast-food restaurants may be overestimated.

Table 19.4 Elasticities of Body Mass Index and Percentage Point Change in the Probability of Being Obese with Respect to Selected Variables

Independent Variable	Body Mass Index	Obesity Probability[a]
Restaurants	0.173	1.390
Fast-food restaurant price	−0.048	−0.650
Full-service restaurant price	−0.021	−0.667
Food at home price	−0.039	−0.622
Cigarette price	0.025	0.445
Alcohol price	−0.017	−0.271

Note: Computed at weighted sample means.
[a] Figures in the second column show 100 times the change in the probability of being obese associated with a 10 percent change in a given independent variable. See note 18 for more details.

With regard to the three direct food price variables, the greatest response to BMI occurs when the real fast-food restaurant price varies. The elasticity of BMI with respect to this price is −0.05. When obesity is the outcome, the fast-food and full-service restaurant price effects are about the same. A 10 percent increase in each price is associated with a 0.7 percentage point decrease in the percentage obese. Like Cawley (1999) and Lakdawalla and Philipson (2002), we find that weight outcomes rise when food at home prices decline. The elasticity of BMI with respect to this price is larger in absolute value than the full-service restaurant price elasticity but smaller than the fast-food price elasticity. When obesity is the outcome, the magnitude of the food at home price effect is slightly smaller than those of the other two food prices.

The positive cigarette price effects in table 19.4 indicate substitution between calories and nicotine. The magnitude of the cigarette price effect in the obesity equation is approximately two-thirds as large as any of the three food price effects in that equation. The elasticity of BMI with respect to the cigarette price is larger than full-service restaurant price elasticity. These results point to an unintended consequence of the antismoking campaign. In particular, state and federal excise tax hikes and the settlement of state Medicaid lawsuits have caused the real price of cigarettes to rise substantially. Our findings suggest that this development contributed to the upward trend in obesity. Finally, the negative alcohol price effects in table 19.4 imply that calories and alcohol are complements. The magnitudes of these effects, however, are the smallest among the variables that we consider.

The large elasticities with regard to the per capita number of restaurants emerge from models that hold the real fast-food restaurant price and the real full-service restaurant price constant. A simple supply and demand model predicts that these two variables should be negatively correlated if the demand function for restaurants is more stable than the supply function and positively correlated if the supply function is more stable. Only a minor change in the restaurant elasticity occurs when the price variables are deleted, implying that the supply function is very elastic. The reader should keep in mind that the per capita number of restaurants is employed as a proxy for the travel time and waiting time costs involved in obtaining meals at these eating places.

The main purpose of this chapter is to gain an understanding of the factors associated with the stability in obesity between the early 1960s and the late 1970s and the rapid increase since that time. Table 19.5 addresses the latter issue by examining how well selected models predict the increases in obesity and related outcomes between 1984 and 1999. The estimates in table 19.5 are based on regression models in table 19.3. The procedure simply is to multiply the change in a given variable between the initial and terminal year by the coefficient of that variable. In the cases of race/ethnicity, schooling, marital status, the clean indoor air laws, and variables in quadratic form, predicted changes associated with related variables (married, divorced, and widowed in the case of marital status) are summed to form a single factor. Note that national values of state-specific variables in 1984 are population-weighted averages of values

Table 19.5 Impacts of Selected Factors on Body Mass Index and Percentage Obese, Persons 18 Years of Age and Older, 1984–1999

Factor	Body Mass Index Observed Change = 2.13	Obese Observed Change[a] = 12.99
Race/ethnicity	0.08	0.36
Schooling	−0.06	−0.42
Marital status	−0.03	−0.13
Age	0.23	1.14
Household income	−0.08	−0.49
Restaurants	1.40	8.37
Fast-food restaurant price	0.09	0.47
Full-service restaurant price	0.05	0.33
Food at home price	0.14	0.95
Cigarette price	0.48	3.24
Alcohol price	0.01	0.09
Clean indoor air laws	0.09	0.54
Total predicted change	2.38	14.25

[a] In percentage points.

for all states rather than for states in the BRFSS in that year. Note also that our conclusions are not altered when 1987 or 1990 is taken as the initial year.

During the period at issue BMI rose from 24.94 to 27.07 kg/m^2, and the percentage of the population obese rose from 11.05 to 24.04 percent. Our regression models slightly overpredict both outcomes. Race/ethnicity, schooling, marital status, and household income contribute little to an understanding in the behavior of obesity over time. Indeed, the last three variables predict reductions in obesity. This is because schooling, real household income, and the fraction of the population divorced grew in the period at issue, while the fraction of the population married declined.

The increase in the per capita number of restaurants makes the largest contribution to trends in weight outcomes, accounting for 61 percent of the actual growth in BMI and 65 percent of the rise in the percentage obese. The real price of cigarettes ranks second, with a contribution roughly one-third as large as that due to restaurants. The three real food prices considered fell during the period at issue, causing the weight outcomes to rise. Taken alone, the decline in each price was modest and explains little of the trend. The largest contribution is made by the food at home price and contributes 7 percent to the trends in BMI and obesity. A somewhat different picture emerges if the three food price effects are aggregated into a single component. The contribution of this component is between one-half and three-fifths as large as that of the cigarette price and accounts for approximately 12 percent of the trend in weight outcomes. The rising prevalence of clean indoor air laws has about the same impact as the reduction in the fast-food restaurant price. The slight reduction in the price of alcohol has the smallest impact on the growth in BMI and the rise in the percentage obese.

As shown in table 19.1, BMI and the percentage obese were very stable between 1960 1961 (the midyear of NHES I) and 1978 (the midyear of NHANES II). We conclude by applying our estimated regression coefficients to trends in exogenous variables between those two years in an attempt to explain why weight outcomes did not rise in that eighteen-year period. The results of this exercise are contained in table 19.6. Since a consistent series on household income is not available over this period, median family income is used in its place. This variable as well as marital status and schooling are taken from the Bureau of the Census (various years). The initial year values of the number of fast-food and full-service restaurants are averages of the figures reported in the 1958 and 1963 Census of Business (Bureau of the Census 1961, 1966). Effects due to fast-food and full-service restaurant prices are omitted because there are no measures of these prices in 1960. Trends in the food at home and alcohol prices are based on the series in the Consumer Price Index (Bureau of the Census various years).

Table 19.6 Impacts of Selected Factors on Body Mass Index and Percentage Obese, Persons 18 Years of Age and Older (NHES I and NHANES II)

Factor	Body Mass Index Observed Change = 0.25	Obese Observed Change[a] = 1.22
Schooling	−0.18	−1.39
Marital status	−0.02	−0.10
Age	−0.07	−0.33
Family income	−0.20	−1.54
Restaurants	0.22	1.29
Food at home price	−0.02	−0.03
Cigarette price	0.00	−0.02
Alcohol price	0.04	1.17
Clean indoor air laws	0.01	0.22
Total predicted change	−0.22	−0.74

[a]In percentage points.

Our model predicts very small reductions in the outcomes compared to the very small increases that actually took place. On the other hand, Chou et al. (2002) show that backcasts with a model that replaces the state-specific variables with trend terms fails to explain the stability of weight outcomes between 1960 and 1978. That specification predicts much larger increases in these outcomes than the very modest ones that actually occurred. The main reason for the success of the model with state-specific variables is that the per capita number of full-service restaurants fell between 1960 and 1978. While more credence might be given to this result if the per capita number of fast-food restaurants declined, the distinction between these two types of restaurants is not "hard and fast." Some full-service restaurants serve the high caloric food offered by fast-food restaurants. Hence the growth of both types of restaurants after 1978 but the growth in only one type before that year is the explanation that we offer for the stability in obesity between 1960 and 1978 and its expansion after 1978.

Our explanation is subject to several caveats. Trends in cigarette prices account for little of the trend in obesity because the real cigarette price in 1960 was almost the same as the real price in 1978. If, however, a year in the mid-1960s had been selected as the initial year, the real price of cigarettes would have fallen, and the predicted negative cigarette price component would have been larger in absolute value. More importantly, adult smoking participation rates fell between 1960 and 1978 as well as after that year. Absolute declines in the two periods were very similar (Public Health Service 1996). Obesity should have increased in both periods due to this factor alone. Our model appears to be missing a variable that can account for the reduction in smoking in the earlier period since the increasing prevalence of clean indoor air laws has small effects. This suggests that it also is missing a variable that can offset the positive impact of declines in smoking on obesity.

6. SUMMARY

In this chapter, we have examined the extent to which relative price variations determine variations in body mass index and obesity among adults and the extent to which changes in relative prices over time contribute to an understanding of trends in weight outcomes. The set of relative prices includes state level measures pertaining to the per capita number of restaurants, the price of a meal in fast-food and full-service restaurants, the price of food consumed at home, the price of cigarettes, the price of alcohol, and clean indoor air laws. Our main results are that these variables have the expected effects on obesity and explain a substantial amount of its trend. These findings control for individual-level measures of household income, years of formal schooling completed, and marital status.

Three results stand out. The first is the large positive effects associated with the per capita number of restaurants and the importance of trends in this variable in explaining the stability of obesity between 1960 and 1978 and the increase since 1978. A literal interpretation of this result implicates fast-food and full-service restaurants as culprits in undesirable weight outcomes. But a very different interpretation emerges if one recognizes that the growth in these restaurants, and especially fast-food restaurants, is to a large extent a response to the increasing scarcity and increasing value of household or nonmarket time. In a fuller model that perhaps treated restaurant availability as endogenous, labor market attachment would have indirect effects that operate through restaurant availability.

The second and related result is that downward trends in food prices account for part of the upward trend in weight outcomes. In one sense this simply verifies the law of the downward sloping demand function. But there are more subtle aspects of this finding since the location in which food is consumed appears to matter. In particular, technological innovations and the realization of economies of scale that led to reductions in the real fast-food restaurant price may have been stimulated in part by efforts to accommodate the increased demand for consumption of food away from home.

The third result that stands out is the positive cigarette price effect. This result points to an unintended consequence of the anti-smoking campaign. In particular, state and federal excise tax hikes and the settlement of state Medicaid lawsuits have caused the real price of cigarettes to rise substantially. Our findings suggest that this development contributed to the upward trend in obesity.

In a sense, all three findings underscore the price that must be paid to achieve goals that in general are favored by society. Expanded labor market opportunities for women have resulted in significant increases in families' command of real resources and higher living standards. Cigarette smoking is the largest cause of premature death, and declines in this behavior have obvious health benefits. Our results suggest that these two factors contribute to the rising prevalence of obesity. Whether public policies should be pursued that offset this ignored consequence of previous actions to discourage smoking and increase market opportunities depends on the costs and benefits of these policies.

The reduced form approach to the determinants of obesity in this chapter would be complemented and enriched by a structural approach in which caloric intake, energy expenditure, and cigarette smoking are treated as endogenous determinants of weight. A study that takes this approach deserves high priority on an agenda for future research.

ACKNOWLEDGEMENTS

Research for this chapter was supported by grant number 5R01 DK54826 from the National Institute of Diabetes and Digestive and Kidney Diseases to the National Bureau of Economic Research. We are indebted to Inas Rashad and Neeraj Kaushal for research assistance. We also are indebted to Anna M. Jacobson for advice with regard to data on fast-food and full-service restaurants in the Census of Retail Trade. We wish to thank David B. Allison, Joseph P. Newhouse, and two anonymous referees for helpful comments and suggestions. Preliminary versions of this chapter were presented at the Third Annual International Health Economics Association Conference, the 23rd Annual Association for Public Policy Analysis & Management Research Conference, the RAND Corporation, the Leonard Davis Institute at the University of Pennsylvania, the Johns Hopkins University School of Hygiene and Public Health, the Centers for Disease Control and Prevention, the National Task Force on the Prevention and Treatment of Obesity, and the United States Department of Agriculture Economics of Obesity Workshop. We are grateful to the participants in those conferences, seminars, and workshops for comments and suggestions. This chapter has not undergone the review accorded official NBER publications; in particular, it has not been submitted for approval by the Board of the Directors. Any opinions expressed are those of the authors and not those of NIDDKD or NBER.

NOTES

Originally published as Shin-Yi Chou, Michael Grossman, and Henry Saffer, "An Economic Analysis of Adult Obesity: Results from the Behavioral Risk Factor Surveillance System," *Journal of Health Economics* 23, no. 3 (2004): 565–587.

1. The figures in table 19.1 are based on our computations with these surveys. They differ slightly from published estimates because we consider a somewhat broader age range and because we include pregnant women. The exclusion of pregnant women and persons below the age of twenty years has almost no impact on levels or trends.

2. Costa and Steckel (1997) and Fogel and Costa (1997) show that the long-term increase in BMI is the major "proximate cause" of the long-term reduction in mortality and morbidity in the United States and other countries. This finding is analogous to the key role played by birthweight in infant survival outcomes. Of course, the studies just cited recognize that BMI is endogenous.

3. The states in the BRFSS in 1984 were Arizona, California, Idaho, Illinois, Indiana, Minnesota, Montana, North Carolina, Ohio, Rhode Island, South Carolina, Tennessee, Utah, West Virginia, and Wisconsin. In 1985, Connecticut, the District of Columbia, Florida, Georgia, Kentucky, Missouri, New York, and North Dakota entered the survey. Alabama, Hawaii, Massachusetts, and New Mexico joined in 1986. Maine, Maryland, Nebraska, New Hampshire, South Dakota, Texas, and Washington joined in 1987. Iowa, Michigan, and Oklahoma joined in 1988. Oregon, Pennsylvania, and Vermont joined in 1989. Colorado, Delaware, Louisiana, Mississippi, and Virginia joined in 1990. Alaska, Arkansas, and New Jersey joined in 1991. Kansas and Nevada joined in 1992. Wyoming joined in 1994. The first year in which all fifty states and the District of Columbia were in the BRFSS was 1996 because Rhode Island, which joined the survey in 1984, was not in it in 1994 and because the District of Columbia, which joined in 1985, was absent in 1995.

4. Nevertheless, we also estimated weighted regressions in preliminary analysis and obtained results similar to those in the unweighted regressions.

5. The other category consists of persons who are not white, black, or Hispanic and primarily includes Asians, Pacific Islanders, Native Americans, and Eskimos. The number of people in this category is very small.

6. We eliminated the extremely small number of BRFSS respondents with an uncorrected BMI of <11 or >140 kg/m^2.

7. The latter figure is taken from table 19.1. That figure and all other data in table 19.1 are based on actual heights and weights in NHANES.

8. The more rapid growth rate in obesity in the BRFSS is not a function of the small number of states in that survey in 1984. Between 1991 and 1999, obesity grew at an annually compounded rate of 5.4 percent per year in the BRFSS. The corresponding growth rate in NHANES between NHANES III and NHANES 99 was 3.6 percent per year.

9. Starting in 1989, county of residence codes are contained in the BRFSS. These codes, however, are missing for many respondents.

10. In 1997, the Bureau of the Census replaced the SIC system with the North American Classification System (NAICS). A discussion of the algorithm employed to estimate fast-food and full-service restaurants in that year is available on request.

11. In that year, the categories are less than US$ 2.00, 2.00–4.99, 5.00–9.99, and 10.00 and over.

12. The ACCRA reports a cost of living index for each city, which can be employed to compute a state-specific cost of living index. We chose not to do this because the index reflects cost differentials among areas for households whose heads hold mid-management positions. Clearly, these households have higher incomes than those headed by clerical workers or by average urban consumers. In particular, homeownership costs are more heavily weighted than they would be if the index reflected clerical workers' or average urban consumers' standards of living.

13. A detailed description of the food at home price is available on request. The same comment applies to the alcohol price defined further.

14. Starting in 1990, the source contains two price series: one that includes generic brands and one that excludes these brands. For purposes of comparability, the series that excludes generic brands is employed. The two price series are extremely highly correlated.

15. Regressions with linear and quadratic trend terms are presented and discussed in Chou et al. (2002).

16. Standard errors of state-specific variables computed by clustering by state do not differ dramatically from those computed by clustering by state/year and do not lead to different results with regard to statistical significance. We emphasize results with state/year clustering because state clustering distorts the standard errors of the state dummies. The number of restaurants and the full-service restaurant price in some years are obtained from interpolations and extrapolations. Empirically, the standard deviation of a given variable in a year in which it is predicted is very similar to its standard deviation in a surrounding year in which it is available. This obviates the need to adjust standard errors for the presence of predicted values in some years.

17. Suppose that u is an unobserved determinant of schooling and g an unobserved determinant of obesity. An increase in u, which might represent mental ability, raises schooling; while an increase in g, which might represent the genetic propensity towards obesity, raises this outcome and BMI. If g and u are negatively correlated, the schooling coefficient in an obesity or BMI regression is biased away from zero in a negative direction. The reverse holds if u and g are positively correlated. Trends in schooling over periods as short as three or four decades are unlikely to be explained by trends in u. But some caution should be exercised when cross-sectional regression coefficients are applied to these trends. For a detailed analysis of the roles of heredity and the environment in schooling, body mass, and wage outcomes in the US based on data in the Minnesota Twin Registry, see Behrman and Rosenzweig (2001).

18. According to Stevens et al. (1987) the relative mortality associated with greater BMI declines with age. Therefore, an adjustment for this factor would produce a peak in BMI at an earlier age.

19. Let π be the probability of being obese and let x be a continuous regressor. We fit an equation of the form $\pi = \alpha x + \beta x^2$, where the intercept and other independent variables are suppressed. Hence, $(\partial \pi / \partial (\ln x)) = (\alpha + 2\beta x)x$, and $100\partial \pi = 100(\alpha + 2\beta x)x \, \partial(\ln x)$. Column 2 of table 19.2 contains estimates of $100\partial \pi$ evaluated at the mean of x and a value of $\partial(\ln x)$ equal to 0.10.

REFERENCES

Allison, D. B., K. R. Fontaine, J. E. Manson, J. Stevens, and T. B. VanItallie. 1999. "Annual deaths Attributable to Obesity in the United States." *Journal of the American Medical Association* 282: 1530–1538.

American Chamber of Commerce Researchers Association (ACCRA). Various years. ACCRA Cost of Living Index. Arlington, VA: ACCRA.

Averett, S., and S. Korenman. 1996. "The Economic Reality of the Beauty Myth." *Journal of Human Resources* 31: 304–330.

Becker, G. S. 1965. "A theory of the Allocation of Time." *Economic Journal* 75 493–517.

Behrman, J. R., and M. R. Rosenzweig. 2001. "The Returns to Increasing Body Weight." Philadelphia, PA: Department of Economics, University of Pennsylvania Working Paper.

Bureau of the Census, U.S. Department of Commerce. 1961, 1966, 1958, and 1963. Census of Business. Washington, DC: U.S. Government Printing Office.

Bureau of the Census, U.S. Department of Commerce. 1976, 1986, 1989, 1994, and 2000. 1972, 1982, 1987, 1992, and 1997 Census of Retail Trade. Washington, DC: U.S. Government Printing Office.

Bureau of the Census, U.S. Department of Commerce. Various years. Statistical Abstract of the United States. Washington, DC: U.S. Government Printing Office.

Cawley, J. 1999. "Rational Addiction, the Consumption of Calories, and Body Weight." Ph Dissertation. Chicago, IL: University of Chicago.

——. 2004. "The Impact of Obesity on Wages." *Journal of Human Resources* 39: 452–474.

Chou, S.-Y., M. Grossman, and H. Saffer. 2002. "An Economic Analysis of Adult Obesity: Results from the Behavioral Risk Factor Surveillance System." Cambridge, MA: National Bureau of Economic Research Working Paper 9247.

Costa, D. L., and R. H. Steckel. 1997. "Long-Term Trends in Health, Welfare, and Economic Growth in the United States." In *Health and Welfare During Industrialization*, ed. R. H. Steckel and R. Floud. Chicago: University of Chicago Press: 47–89.

Cutler, D. M., E. L. Glaeser, and J. M. Shapiro. 2003. "Why Have Americans Become More Obese?" *Journal of Economic Perspectives* 17: 93–118.

DuMouchel, W., and G. J. Duncan. 1983. "Using Sample Survey Weights in Multiple Regression Analysis of Stratified Samples." *Journal of the American Statistical Association* 78: 535–543.

Evans, W., M. C. Farrelly, and E. Montgomery. 1999. "Do Workplace Smoking Bans Reduce Smoking?" *American Economic Review* 89: 728–747.

Fogel, R. W., and D. L. Costa. 1997. "A Theory of Technophysic Evolution, with Some Implications for Forecasting Population, Health Care, and Pension Costs." *Demography* 34: 49–66.

Huber, P. J. 1967. "The Behavior of Maximum Likelihood Estimates Under Nonstandard Conditions." In *Proceedings of the Fifth Berkeley Symposium on Mathematical Statistics and Probability*. Berkeley, CA: University of California Press: 221–233.

Kahn, H. S., L. M. Tatham, C. Rodriguez, E. E. Calle, M. JU. Thun, and C. W. Heath Jr. 1997. "Stable Behaviors Associated with Adults' 10-Year Change in Body Mass Index and Likelihood of Gain at the Waist." *American Journal of Public Health* 87: 747–754.

Lakdawalla, D., and T. Philipson. 2002. "The Growth of Obesity and Technological Change: A Theoretical and Empirical Investigation." Cambridge, MA: National Bureau of Economic Research Working Paper 8965.

Maddala, G. S. 1983. *Limited-Dependent and Qualitative Variables in Econometrics*. Cambridge, UK: Cambridge University Press.

McGinnis, J. M., and W. H. Foege. 1993. "Actual Causes of Death in the United States." *Journal of the American Medical Association* 270: 2207–2212.

Mela, D. J., and P. J. Rogers. 1998. *Food, Eating and Obesity: The Psychobiological Basis of Appetite and Weight Control*. London: Chapman & Hall.

Moore, M. J. 2001. "The Political Economy of Workplace Smoking." Charlottesville, VA: Darden Graduate School of Business Administration, University of Virginia Working Paper.

National Heart, Lung, and Blood Institute, National Institutes of Health. 1998. "Clinical Guidelines on the Identification, Evaluation, and Treatment of Overweight and Obesity in Adults—The Evidence Report." *Obesity Research* 6 (Suppl. 2): 51S-215S.

National Institute of Diabetes and Digestive and Kidney Diseases (NIDDKD). 1996. *Statistics Related to Overweight and Obesity*. NIH Publication no. 96–4158. Washington, DC: U.S. Government Printing Office.

Orzechowski, W., and R. Walker. 2002. *The Tax Burden on Tobacco*, vol. 36. Arlington, VA: Orzechowski and Walker.

Philipson, T. 2001. "The World-Wide Growth in Obesity: An Economic Research Agenda." *Health Economics* 10: 1–7.

Philipson, T., and R. A. Posner. 1999. "The Long-Run Growth in Obesity as a Function of Technological Change." Cambridge, MA: National Bureau of Economic Research Working Paper 7423.

Pinkowish, M. D. 1999. "Hand in Glove: Smoking Cessation and Weight Gain." *Patient Care* 33: 134.

Prentice, A. M. 1995. "Alcohol and Obesity." *International Journal of Obesity* 19 (Suppl. 5): 44–50.

Public Health Service, U.S. Department of Health and Human Services. 1996. Health United States 1995. Washington, DC: U.S. Government Printing Office.

Ruhm, C. J. 2000. "Are Recessions Good for Your Health?" *Quarterly Journal of Economics* 115: 616–650.

Schlosser, E. 2001. *Fast Food Nation: The Dark Side of the All-American Meal*. Boston: Houghton Mifflin.

Stevens, J., J. Cai, E. R. Pamuk, D. F. Williamson, M. J. Thun, and J. L. Wood. 1987. "The Effects of Age on the Association Between Body-Mass Index and Mortality." *New England Journal of Medicine* 338: 1–7.

Wolf, A., and G. Colditz. 1998. "Current Estimates of the Economic Cost of Obesity in the United States." *Obesity Research* 6: 97–106.

World Health Organization. 1997. *Obesity: Preventing and Managing the Global Epidemic*. Geneva: World Health Organization.

Fast-Food Restaurant Advertising on Television and Its Influence on Childhood Obesity

Shin-Yi Chou, Inas Rashad,
and Michael Grossman

ABSTRACT

Childhood obesity is an escalating problem around the world that is especially detrimental as its effects carry on into adulthood. In this chapter we employ the 1979 Child–Young Adult National Longitudinal Survey of Youth and the 1997 National Longitudinal Survey of Youth to estimate the effects of television fast-food restaurant advertising on children and adolescents with respect to being overweight. A ban on these advertisements would reduce the number of overweight children ages three to eleven in a fixed population by 18 percent and would reduce the number of overweight adolescents ages twelve to eighteen by 14 percent. The elimination of the tax deductibility of this type of advertising would produce smaller declines of between 5 and 7 percent in these outcomes but would impose lower costs on children and adults who consume fast food in moderation because positive information about restaurants that supply this type of food would not be completely banned from television.

1. INTRODUCTION

Childhood obesity around the world, and particularly in the United States, is an escalating problem that has received much attention of late. In less than thirty years, the prevalence of overweight children and adolescents in the United States has more than doubled. In the 1963–1970 period, 4 percent of children ages six to eleven years and 5 percent of adolescents age twelve to nineteen were defined as being overweight. The percentage of children who are overweight more than tripled by 1999, reaching 13 percent. For adolescents, the incidence of overweight has nearly tripled in the same period, reaching 14 percent (U.S. Department of Health and Human Services 2001).

Each author is affiliated with the National Bureau of Economic Research. Research for this chapter was supported by grant 1R01 DK54826 from the National Institute of Diabetes and Digestive and Kidney Diseases (NIDDKD) to the National Bureau of Economic Research (NBER). We are indebted to Sam Peltzman and a referee for very helpful comments on a previous draft. Preliminary versions of the chapter were presented at the Fifth World Congress of the International Health Economics Association, the 2006 Public Policies and Child-Well Being conference sponsored by the Andrew Young School of Policy Studies at Georgia State University, the 2007 Allied Social Sciences Association conference, and seminars at a number of universities and at the Centers for Disease Control and Prevention. We wish to thank the participants in those conferences and seminars for helpful comments and suggestions. We also wish to thank Silvie Colman and Ryan Conrad for research assistance. The views expressed herein are those of the authors and do not necessarily reflect the views of NBER or NIDDKD.

An investigation of the nongenetic determinants of obesity among children and adolescents is an important input in designing prevention policies. On the simplest level, weight gain is caused by more energy intake than energy expenditure over a long period of time. The problem of energy imbalance is not purely due to genetics since our genes have not changed substantially during the past two decades. Researchers have tended to focus on environmental factors such as the availability of highly palatable and calorie-dense fast food to promote high energy intake as well as the appeal of television, video games, and computers to discourage energy expenditure. Potentially, television viewing has two effects: reductions in physical activity and increases in fast-food consumption associated with exposure to advertisements of this product.

How the commercial advertising of foods contributes to the prevalence of obesity among children and adolescents is still an ongoing debate. Despite the lack of evidence showing a direct linkage between television food advertising and childhood obesity, several industrialized countries such as Sweden, Norway, and Finland have banned commercial sponsorship of children's programs. Sweden also does not permit any television advertising targeting children under the age of 12 (Kaiser Family Foundation 2004).

In the United States, most recently, companies such as Kraft Foods have decided to curb advertising aimed at children in an effort to encourage better eating habits (Mayer 2005). The Institute of Medicine 2006 report entitled *Food Marketing to Children and Youth: Threat or Opportunity* indicated that there is compelling evidence linking food advertising on television and increases in childhood obesity. Some members of the committee that wrote the report recommended congressional regulation of television food advertisements aimed at children, but the report also said that the final link that would definitively prove that children had become fatter by watching food commercials aimed at them cannot be made.

The purpose of this chapter is to explore the causal relationship between exposure to fast-food restaurant advertising on television and childhood obesity. We employ two individual-level datasets: the National Longitudinal Survey of Youth 1997 for adolescents ages twelve to eighteen and the Child–Young Adult National Longitudinal Survey of Youth 1979 for children ages 3–11. The data for fast-food restaurant advertising on television are appended to the individual-level data by metropolitan area and year. We employ several different specifications, and most results show a positive and statistically significant impact of fast-food restaurant advertising on television on body mass index and on the probability of being overweight for children and adolescents.

2. BACKGROUND

Obesity is measured by the body mass index (BMI), also termed Quetelet's index, and is defined as weight in kilograms divided by height in meters squared. Persons eighteen years of age and older with a BMI greater than or equal to 30 kg/m^2 are classified as obese. An overweight child or adolescent (the term obese is reserved for adults) is defined as one having a BMI at or above the 95th percentile based on age- and gender-specific growth charts for children and adolescents in the second and third National Health Examination Surveys (NHES II and NHES III), which were conducted between 1963 and 1965 and between 1966 and 1970, respectively, and from the first, second, and third National Health and Nutrition Examination Surveys (NHANES I, NHANES II, and NHANES III), which were conducted between 1971 and 1974, 1976 and 1980, and 1988 and 1994, respectively.

Trends in the mean BMI of persons ages three to eleven (hereafter termed children) and the percentage overweight between 1963 and 2000 are presented in table 20.1. Similar data for persons ages twelve to eighteen

Table 20.1 Trends in Body Mass Index and the Percentage of Overweight Persons 3–11 Years of Age

				Males Only		Females Only	
Survey	Period	BMI	Overweight[a]	BMI	Overweight[a]	BMI	Overweight[a]
NHES II	1963–65	16.63	4.24	16.57	4.00	16.68	4.50
NHANES I	1971–74	16.44	5.33	16.46	5.74	16.42	4.92
NHANES II	1976–80	16.64	7.33	16.64	7.22	16.64	7.44
NHANES III	1988–94	17.15	10.59	17.09	10.25	17.22	10.95
NHANES 99	1999–2000	17.37	14.26	17.38	14.74	17.36	13.76

Note: The surveys are as follows: National Health Examination Survey II (NHES II), National Health and Nutrition Examination Survey I (NHANES I), National Health and Nutrition Examination Survey II (NHANES II), National Health and Nutrition Examination Survey III (NHANES III), and National Health and Nutrition Examination Survey 1999–2000 (NHANES 99). NHES II pertains to children 6–11 years of age. Survey weights are employed in all computations. Body mass index (BMI) is weight in kilograms divided by height in meters squared. Actual weights and heights are used in calculations.
[a] Percentage with BMI equal to or greater than the 95th percentile based on Centers for Disease Control and Prevention (2007) growth charts.

(hereafter termed adolescents or teenagers) are presented in table 20.2. These data come from heights and weights obtained from physical examinations conducted in NHES II and III, in NHANES I, II, and III, and in 1999–2000 NHANES (NHANES 99). Both tables show dramatic increases in the percentage of overweight children and teenagers between 1978 (the midyear of NHANES II) and 2000. This percentage doubled for children and almost tripled for teenagers.

In the period during which childhood obesity increased so drastically, trends in the amount of time spent watching television and exposure to food advertising by children and adolescents were not clear-cut. Around 1950, only 2 percent of households in the United States had television sets; by the early 1990s, 98 percent of households owned at least one, and over 60 percent had cable television (Huston et al. 1992). Yet the average amount of time children spent watching television fell from about 4 hours a day in the late 1970s to 2 hours and 45 minutes a day in 1999 before rising to 3 hours and 20 minutes a day in 2005 (Zywicki, Holt, and Ohlaysen 2004; Powell, Szczypka, and Chaloupka 2007).

According to estimates made by Kunkel (2001), in the late 1970s, children viewed an average of about 20,000 commercials aired on television per year. The number increased to 30,000 per year in the late 1980s and to more than 40,000 per year in the late 1990s, possibly because programs or commercials became shorter over time. Holt et al. (2007), on the other hand, estimate that

Table 20.2 Trends in Body Mass Index and the Percentage of Overweight Persons 12–18 Years of Age

Survey	Period	BMI	Overweight[a]	Males Only BMI	Males Only Overweight[a]	Females Only BMI	Females Only Overweight[a]
NHES I, III	1959–62, 1966–70	20.61	4.45	20.47	4.50	20.76	4.40
NHANES I	1971–74	20.97	6.82	20.81	6.83	21.13	6.82
NHANES II	1976–80	21.03	5.63	20.92	5.39	21.16	5.89
NHANES III	1988–94	22.11	10.62	21.95	11.48	22.28	9.72
NHANES 99	1999–2000	22.82	14.75	22.52	15.03	23.13	14.45

Note: The surveys are as follows: National Health Examination Survey I and III (NHES I, III), National Health and Nutrition Examination Survey I (NHANES I), National Health and Nutrition Examination Survey II (NHANES II), National Health and Nutrition Examination Survey III (NHANES III), and National Health and Nutrition Examination Survey 1999–2000 (NHANES 99). NHES I was used for adolescents of age 18, while NHES III was used for those between the ages of 12 and 17. Survey weights are employed in all computations. Body mass index (BMI) is weight in kilograms divided by height in meters squared. Actual weights and heights are used in calculations.

[a] Percentage with BMI equal to or greater than the 95th percentile based on Centers for Disease Control and Prevention (2007) growth charts.

the number of television advertisements viewed by children actually declined between 1977 and 2004. They also report that, while the number of television food advertisements viewed by children decreased between those two years, the number of restaurant and fast-food advertisements viewed increased. The last trend is consistent with the increase in the share of fast-food restaurant advertising in total food product advertising from 5 percent in 1980 to 28 percent in 1997 (Gallo 1999).

While most prior studies have confirmed correlations between television watching and obesity in children, few studies have looked at the effect that fast-food restaurant advertising on television per se might have on childhood obesity (see Chou, Rashad, and Grossman [2007] for a review of both types of studies). Consumer behavior in response to advertising could be explained using Becker and Murphy (1993), which presents a model in which a brand's advertising level interacts with consumption in the consumer's utility function. In this model, by treating advertising as a complementary good, consumers may simply derive more utility from consuming a more advertised good.

More generally, fast-food restaurants would not choose to advertise if advertising did not increase the demand for their products. Unless fast-food demand perfectly crowds out demand for other foods that are equal in calories, body weight will increase since consumers will never choose to perfectly offset the increased food demand with more exercise. Of course, it may be the case that most advertising is directed toward competition among restaurants and little at stimulating consumption per se (see, for example, Schmalensee 1972). In summary, the effect of television advertising on childhood obesity is complex, dealing with the interplay among the characteristics of the children, the attitudes of their parents, and environmental settings. Our empirical study attempts to isolate the effect of fast-food restaurant advertising on television on obesity in children and adolescents.

3. DATA

The microlevel dataset that we use for adolescents ages twelve to eighteen is the National Longitudinal Survey of Youth 1997 (hereafter NLSY97). This is a nationally representative sample of the U.S. population ages twelve to sixteen as of December 31, 1996. The initial sample in 1997 consists of 8,984 respondents who originated from 6,819 unique households. Two subsamples make up the NLSY97 cohort. The first is a nationally representative sample of 6,748 respondents born between 1980 and 1984. The second consists of 2,236 over-sampled black and Hispanic respondents for that age group. The survey has collected extensive information about youth labor market behavior and educational experiences over time. Round 1 of the NLSY97, which took place in 1997, contains a parent questionnaire that generates information about the youth's family background and history. Only 7,942 youth respondents (out of 8,984) have information available from a parent interview. The NLSY97 also contains information on time use including the amount of time spent in the prior week watching television from youth ages twelve to fourteen in round 1.[1]

We pool three rounds of NLSY97 for the analysis: 1997 ($N = 8,984$), 1998 ($N = 8,386$), and 1999 ($N = 8,209$).[2] Before any state-level or advertising data are appended to the NLSY97, the pooled sample size is 14,852 when observations with missing values are deleted. Note that a large percentage of observations are dropped because of the missing values for television-watching time. This question is not asked of youth over the age of fourteen in 1997 (round 1), and it is not asked after that year. Therefore, we assume that the 1997 values also apply to 1998 and 1999.

We also use the matched mother-child data from the National Longitudinal Survey of Youth 1979 (hereafter NLSY79) for children ages three to eleven. The NLSY79 is a nationally representative sample of 12,686 individuals, of whom 6,283 are women who were fourteen to twenty-two years old when they were first surveyed in 1979. In 1986, biennial interviews of all children born to female respondents began, making up the Child and Young Adult File. We use three survey years of data, 1996, 1998, and 2000. The television-watching variable is available in each of these years.

We obtained fast-food restaurant television advertising data from special tabulations performed for us by Competitive Media Reporting (CMR), the largest provider of advertising tracking services in the United States. CMR was formed in 1992 by combining several advertising tracking and broadcast proof-of-performance companies. The tabulations that CMR supplied to us have exposure information and dollar expenditures for a wide array of fast-food restaurant chains in the United States from 1996 to 1999.[3] The exposure variable equals the annual number of seconds of fast-food restaurant messages aired on television. This variable is then divided by a factor of $(60 \times 60 \times 52)$, or 187,200, to convert it into the weekly number of hours of fast-food restaurant advertising messages aired.

The unit of observation for the variable just described is the designated market area (DMA), which is similar to a metropolitan statistical area (MSA). The DMA is a region composed of counties (and occasionally split counties) that defines a television market. Thus, the advertising data were appended to our individual records by DMA and year.[4] Out of about 210 DMAs, the top 75 (in terms of television households) are contained in the CMR database and used in our study. As a consequence, our final sample sizes, when the advertising data are appended, are 6,034 person-years for respondents ages three to eleven (NLSY79) and 7,069 person-years for respondents ages twelve to eighteen (NLSY97).[5]

Note that network television, syndicated television, and cable network television advertising are not included in our data because they have no local variation. National advertising effects cannot be obtained in the specifications that we employ since they contain dichotomous year indicators. Spot television advertising has local variation and is reported by year and by market area by CMR. That is the type of advertising that we consider.

An important conceptual issue that arises in measuring the impact of exposure to advertising on consumer behavior is whether the effect on any one consumer depends on the total number of hours of advertising aired on television in the consumer's DMA or on the per capita number of hours aired. This depends on whether advertising is treated as a public good. Public goods are nonexcludable and nonrejectable. If street signs are public goods, then a billboard showing an ad, for example, can be viewed as a public good (or a public "bad" if over-provided). This is not as straightforward with advertisements on television, which could be excludable (unless everyone owns a television set) or rejectable (as one can turn the channel if one chooses to do so).

The advertising literature seems to be mixed with regard to using total exposure or this variable per capita.[6] The most compelling justification for total exposure is that two consumers cannot eat the same apple, but two consumers can watch the same advertisement. The most compelling justification for the per capita specification is that there are more television stations in larger market areas. This lowers the probability that two consumers will see the same advertisement in a larger market even if they spend the same amount of time watching television. Because the first factor seems to us to be more important than the second (two consumers in the same market area certainly can view the same advertisement no matter how large the area), we emphasize results with total exposure. In preliminary research, we found that results for per capita exposure were similar to those with total exposure.

To control for other factors that might affect caloric intake and caloric expenditure, we also include state-level variables that are appended to the individual data by state and year. These variables are the number of fast-food restaurants, the number of full-service restaurants, the price of a meal in each type of restaurant, an index of food-at-home prices, the price of cigarettes, and clean-indoor-air laws. Detailed descriptions of their sources, definitions, and roles in equations for weight outcomes can be found in Chou, Grossman, and Saffer (2004). Discussions of their estimated effects in the regressions are contained in Chou, Rashad, and Grossman (2007).

4. EMPIRICAL IMPLEMENTATION

We employ height and weight measures in NLSY79 and in NLSY97 to construct two dependent variables: BMI and an indicator that equals one if the child or adolescent is overweight. Given the large sample size, we fit linear probability models rather than logit or probit models when the overweight indicator is the outcome. Our most inclusive regression model is

$$Y_{ijt} = \gamma_0 + \gamma_1 \ln S_{ijt} + \gamma_2 \ln T_{ijt} + \beta_1 X_{ijt} + \beta_2 M_{ijt} + \beta_3 Z_{ijt} + \mu_j + v_t + \varepsilon_{ijt}. \quad (1)$$

In this equation, the dependent variable (Y_{ijt}) is the weight outcome (BMI or overweight) for person i in DMA j surveyed in year t. The regressors are the natural logarithm of the number of hours of spot television fast-food restaurant advertising messages seen per week ($\ln S_{ijt}$); the natural logarithm of the number of hours per week spent watching television ($\ln T_{ijt}$); a vector of demographic variables for children or adolescents, including age, race, and gender (X_{ijt}); a vector of variables containing mother's employment status, household income, a dummy for missing income, and dummy variables indicating whether the mother is overweight (BMI of 25 kg/m² or greater) or obese (M_{ijt}); a vector of state-specific variables including the per capita number of fast-food restaurants, the per capita number of full-service restaurants, the real cigarette price, dichotomous indicators for clean-indoor-air laws, the real full-service restaurant price, the real food-at-home price, and the real fast-food restaurant price (Z_{ijt}); and vectors indicating DMA (μ_j) and year (υ_t). The disturbance term is ε_{ijt}.

Whether the mother is overweight or obese helps to partially capture the genetic component that determines a child's BMI. The effect of food advertising on children and adolescents also depends on the resources allocated by parents for food consumption by the family, parental response to their children's food purchase requests, and parental control of their food consumption. We include family income and mother's employment status to control for parental influence on children's and adolescents' food consumption.

Our main variable of interest is the number of hours of spot television fast-food restaurant advertising messages seen per week (S_{ijt}). We compute this as

$$S_{ijt} = p_{ijt} A_{jt}, \tag{2}$$

where A_{jt} is the number of hours of messages aired per week and p_{ijt} is the probability that a given child or adolescent saw one hour of advertising. In turn, this probability is estimated as

$$p_{ijt} = KT_{ijt}/168, \tag{3}$$

where T_{ijt} is the number of hours per week that the child or adolescent watches television, 168 equals the total number of hours in a week, and K is a positive constant that presumably is smaller than one. This assumes that the ratio of hours of advertising seen to hours of advertising aired is proportional to the ratio of hours of television seen to hours available for all activities including sleep.

The assumption that K is smaller than one is reasonable since messages are aired on more than one television channel, and an individual can watch only one channel at a time. Given that assumption, p_{ijt} is less than one even in the unlikely event that the individual spends all of his or her time watching television. From now on, we ignore K and set p_{ijt} equal to $T_{ijt}/168$. Since we employ the natural logarithm of S_{ijt} as a regressor (see below for a justification), only the regression intercept is affected by this treatment.

An advantage of the specification given by equation (1) is that it allows the amount of time spent watching television to have an effect on weight outcomes that is independent of the number of hours of fast-food restaurant advertising messages seen.

Both S_{ijt} and T_{ijt} are entered in natural logarithms for several reasons. First, both variables are positively skewed. By employing natural logarithms, we mitigate the influence of outliers in determining regression coefficients. In addition, we allow the marginal effect of each variable on BMI or obesity to be nonlinear and to diminish as the variable increases. Preliminary analyses revealed evidence in support of this type of nonlinearity.

Finally, given the definition of S_{ijt} in equations (2) and (3), equation (1) can be rewritten as

$$Y_{ijt} = \gamma_0 - \gamma_1 \ln 168 + \gamma_1 \ln A_{jt} + (\gamma_1 + \gamma_2) \ln T_{ijt}$$
$$+ \beta_1 X_{ijt} + \beta_2 M_{ijt} + \beta_3 Z_{ijt} + \mu_j + \nu_t + \varepsilon_{ijt}. \tag{4}$$

At first glance, $\alpha \equiv \gamma_1 + \gamma_2$ should exceed γ_1 since that coefficient and γ_2 are positive. Both S_{ijt} and T_{ijt} are, however, measured with error in the equations that generate equation (4). The amount of time that children spend watching television is based on estimates reported by their mothers in NLSY79, except that this information is obtained directly from ten- and eleven-year-olds. In NLSY97, the information is reported by adolescents and is available only in the first year of the panel. Clearly, our estimate of the probability that a given child saw a certain message is subject to error.

Given the issues just raised, we begin by estimating equation (4) and testing the hypothesis that α equals γ_1. This is useful because it may be unrealistic to try to obtain separate estimates of γ_1 and γ_2. Moreover, both television-viewing time and advertising may be endogenous. More overweight children may be more sedentary and thus watch more television, and advertising may be determined simultaneously with consumption in fast-food restaurants. We lack instruments to treat both variables as endogenous but can explore one in which $\ln T_{ijt}$ is omitted from equation (1). That is equivalent to constraining the coefficient of $\ln A_{jt}$ to equal the coefficient of $\ln T_{ijt}$.

By including DMA or area effects, we control for time-invariant unmeasured factors that are correlated with television advertising and weight outcomes. For example, fast-food restaurants may choose to place more advertisements in areas in which residents have a higher than average taste for high-calorie foods, and hence a larger percentage of the population is overweight. Since the children of overweight parents are more likely to be overweight than the children of normal-weight parents, advertising effects are biased if area effects are omitted.

Although an individual fixed-effects model controls for DMA fixed effects if individuals do not move, we estimate a DMA fixed-effects model for several reasons. First, as explained above, the amount of time spent watching television in the NLSY97 is available only in the first year of the panel and cannot be used as a regressor with individual fixed effects. Second, the key unobservables governing area-level advertising decisions are characteristics pertaining to the population of the area. Since an individual picked at random in an area with a strong taste for dining in fast-food restaurants is likely to share the tastes of the area, the area indicator reflects that factor.

The last factor is important because the area fixed effects model is more efficient than the individual fixed effects model. This is true because the former model involves the estimation of far fewer parameters. Indeed, preliminary results revealed similar point estimates of advertising coefficients but larger standard errors in individual fixed effects models compared with area fixed effects models.[7] We do account for the panel nature of the data and for the measurement of at least one component of the advertising variable at the area level by clustering by DMAs in obtaining standard errors of regression coefficients. This allows the disturbance term (ε_{ijt}) to be correlated for the same person over time and to be correlated among different persons in the same DMA both at a moment in time and over time.

Means and standard deviations for the NLSY79 and NLSY97 datasets are reported in tables 20.3 and 20.4. These means and the regressions in the next section employ the NLSY sampling weights. In NLSY79, heights and weights are obtained from measurements taken by interviewers for approximately 75 percent of the sample. The remainder of the height and weight data are reported by mothers. All of our regression models for this sample include a dichotomous indicator that equals one if BMI and overweight are based on mothers' reports since they are more likely to result in errors in BMI and the classification of overweight status. In NLSY97, heights and weights are reported by adolescents.

The average BMIs are 17.62 and 22.10 kg/m^2 for children ages three to eleven and adolescents ages twelve to eighteen, respectively. Moreover, 15.8 percent of the children (NLSY79) and 10.3 percent of the adolescents (NLSY97) are overweight. All of these figures except for the last one are comparable to those from NHANES 99 in tables 20.1 and 20.2. To be specific, adolescents are 40 percent more likely to be overweight in NHANES 99 than in NLSY97. Almost all of this difference results because adolescent girls are twice as likely to be overweight in NHANES 99 than in NLSY97. Undoubtedly, this reflects a reluctance by adolescent girls to report their true weight.

Inclusion of a gender indicator in NLSY97 regressions controls for the source of response error just described. Of course, one cannot decompose the gross difference in overweight status between adolescent males and females or the difference net of other regressors into a component due to response error and

Table 20.3 Definitions, Means, and Standard Deviations of Dependent Variables

| Variable | Definition | Ages 3–11 | | | Ages 12–18 | | |
		Whole	Male	Female	Whole	Male	Female
Body mass index	Weight (kg) divided by height (m²)	17.62 (4.67)	17.70 (4.51)	17.53 (4.84)	22.10 (4.44)	22.54 (4.58)	21.65 (4.24)
Overweight	Equals 1 if BMI is ≥ the 95th percentile	.158 (.365)	.176 (.381)	.140 (.347)	.103 (.304)	.135 (.342)	.070 (.255)
Sample size	Person-year	6,034	3,087	2,947	7,069	3,665	3,404

Note: Data for ages 3–11 are from the National Longitudinal Survey of Youth 1979. Data for ages 12–18 are from the National Longitudinal Survey of Youth 1997. Standard deviations are in parentheses. BMI = body mass index.

Table 20.4 Definitions, Means, and Standard Deviations of Explanatory Variables

Variable	Definition	Ages 3–11		Ages 12–18	
ln(TV Time)	Time spent by child watching television (hours/week; in logs)	2.966	(.788)	2.650	(.805)
ln(Messages aired)	Hours of fast-food restaurant advertising messages aired per week in respondent's DMA (in logs)	1.194	(.361)	1.269	(.383)
ln(Messages seen)	Hours of fast-food restaurant advertising messages seen per week in respondent's DMA (in logs)	−.964	(.861)	−1.205	(.911)
Age	Respondent's age (in years)	7.259	(2.532)	14.769	(1.400)
Hispanic	Equals one if respondent is Hispanic	.060	(.237)	.111	(.315)
Black non-Hispanic	Equals one if respondent is black but not Hispanic	.123	(.329)	.155	(.362)
Other race	Indicates if respondent's race is other than white, black, or Hispanic	…		.012	(.111)
Male	Equals one if respondent is male	.513	(.500)	.511	(.500)
Family income	Real household income (1982–1984 $10,000s)	7.062	(10.180)	5.474	(4.193)
Income missing	Equals one if family income is missing	.034	(.180)	.132	(.339)
Weight reported by mother	Equals one if weight is reported by mother	.282	(.450)	…	
Height reported by mother	Equals one if height is reported by mother	.232	(.422)	…	
Mother overweight	Equals one if mother's BMI ≥25 kg/m^2	.482	(.500)	.493	(.500)
Mother obese	Equals one if mother's BMI ≥30 kg/m^2	.218	(.413)	.209	(.407)
Mother employed	Equals one if mother is employed	.693	(.461)	.708	(.455)
Yr98	Equals one if year = 1998	.341	(.474)	.333	(.471)
Yr99	Equals one if year = 1999	…		.343	(.475)
Yr00	Equals one if year = 2000	.293	(.455)	…	
Fast-food restaurants	Fast-food restaurants per 10,000 persons in respondent's state of residence	7.116	(.564)	7.226	(.491)
Full-service restaurants	Full-service restaurants per 10,000 persons in respondent's state of residence	7.144	(.925)	7.232	(1.000)
Cigarette price	Real cigarette price in respondent's state of residence (1982–1984 dollars)	2.486	(.532)	2.523	(.495)
Government	Equals one if smoking is prohibited in government workplaces in respondent's state of residence	.882	(.323)	.863	(.344)
Private	Equals one if smoking is prohibited in private workplaces in respondent's state of residence	.550	(.498)	.452	(.498)
Restaurant	Equals one if smoking is prohibited in restaurants in respondent's state of residence	.680	(.466)	.654	(.476)
Other	Equals one if smoking is prohibited in other public places in respondent's state of residence	.923	(.266)	.923	(.267)
Full-service restaurant price	Real full-service restaurant meal price in respondent's state of residence (1982–1984 dollars)	8.991	(1.867)	9.258	(1.975)
Fast-food restaurant price	Real fast-food restaurant meal price in respondent's state of residence (1982–1984 dollars)	4.529	(.266)	4.558	(.250)
Food-at-home price	Real food-at-home price in respondent's state of residence (1982–1984 dollars)	2.011	(.230)	2.025	(.266)
N, person-year		6,034		7,069	

Note: Data for ages 3–11 are from the National Longitudinal Survey of Youth 1979. Data for ages 12–18 are from the National Longitudinal Survey of Youth 1997. Standard deviations are in parentheses. DMA = designated market area; BMI = body mass index.

a component due to other factors. But as long as response error is uncorrelated with variables other than gender and as long as gender is not correlated with these variables, regression coefficients of these variables are unbiased, although their standard errors are inflated. Hence, the t-ratios on which tests of significance are based are conservative lower-bound estimates.

If reporting errors result in a constant percentage reduction in BMI, all slope coefficients involving this outcome, including those associated with fast-food advertising, are understated. When the probability of being overweight is the outcome, the bias is less obvious even if, as we hypothesize, overweight girls are more likely to be found in areas with relatively large amounts of fast-food advertising on television. That depends on the distribution of girls around the overweight cutoff among areas and the degree to which response error in percentage terms is correlated with true weight. If too few girls are classified as overweight in areas with relatively large amounts of advertising, the associated coefficients are conservative lower-bound estimates. Note that all percentage changes in BMI and in the number of overweight children and adolescents computed from regression results in sections 5 and 6 employ NHANES 99 means. If slope coefficients are unbiased, this corrects for the upward bias in the absolute value of the impact of a change in advertising on the percentage change in the number of overweight adolescents that would result if NLSY97 means were employed in the computations.

5. RESULTS

Table 20.5 presents results in which BMI is the dependent variable for children ages three to eleven and for adolescents age twelve to eighteen. Table 20.6 contains similar results in which the probability of being overweight is the dependent variable. Regressions are also run separately by gender because the results of Chow tests (not shown) indicate significant differences between male and female slope coefficients in most specifications.[8] Pooled regressions are presented for completeness, for the interest of the reader, because they are based on more observations than the gender-specific regressions and because of the response errors associated with weight outcomes of adolescent girls discussed in the previous section. Moreover, the policy initiatives that we consider in the next section are not gender specific. In almost all cases, the advertising coefficient in a given regression is a simple average of the corresponding gender-specific coefficients. Hence, the pooled coefficient can be used to evaluate the impact of the policy at issue.

In all specifications, individual characteristics and DMA and year fixed effects, are included. In specification (1) in each table, we include both the

Table 20.5 Regression Results: Dependent Variable Is Body Mass Index

	Specification (1)			Specification (2)		
	Whole	Male	Female	Whole	Male	Female
Ages 3–11:						
ln(Messages aired)	.232 (.763)	.066 (.155)	.544 (1.175)	...	...	...
ln(TV time)	.278** (3.118)	.283* (2.211)	.285** (2.386)	...	...	...
ln(Messages seen)	...	...	...	.276** (3.211)	.272* (2.169)	.297** (2.493)
T-test on equality of coefficient[a]	.885	.617	.576			
R^2	.146	.174	.156	.146	.174	.156
N	6,034	3,087	2,947	6,034	3,087	2,947
Ages 12–18:						
ln(Messages aired)	.266+ (1.630)	.381+ (1.365)	.117 (.557)	...	...	...
ln(TV time)	.474** (4.479)	.556** (4.049)	.380** (3.274)	...	...	...
ln(Messages seen)	...	...	...	.463** (4.721)	.547** (4.280)	.367** (3.367)
T-test on equality of coefficient[a]	.346	.606	.298			
R^2	.193	.191	.236	.193	.191	.236
N	7,069	3,665	3,404	7,069	3,665	3,404

Note: Data for ages 3–11 are from the National Longitudinal Survey of Youth (NLSY) 1979. Data for ages 12–18 are from the National Longitudinal Survey of Youth 1997. All regressions are weighted by NLSY sampling weights. *T*-ratios are reported in parentheses. Regressions are clustered by designated market area (DMA). All coefficients are adjusted for individual characteristics, state variables, DMA fixed effects, and year fixed effects. Individual variables include age, black non-Hispanic, Hispanic, other race (NLSY97 only), male, family income, missing income dummy, mother employed, mother obese, mother overweight, mother reported for weight and height reported by mothers (as opposed to actual measurements; NLSY79 only). State variables include the per capita number of fast-food restaurants, per capita number of full-service restaurants, real cigarette price, dummies for clean-indoor-air laws, real full-service restaurant price, real food-at-home price, and real fast-food restaurant price.

[a] The null hypothesis is that the coefficient of log(messages aired) is equal to the coefficient of log(TV time).

+ Significant at the 10 percent level (one-tailed test).

* Significant at the 5 percent level (one-tailed test).

** Significant at the 1 percent level (one-tailed test).

natural logarithm of television-watching time (ln T) and the natural logarithm of fast-food restaurant advertising messages aired on television (ln A) as explanatory variables. We find a positive and significant relationship between television-viewing time and BMI or the probability of being overweight, except when the probability that adolescent females are overweight is the outcome.[9] All twelve coefficients of advertising messages aired are positive, but only two of the six coefficients are significant when BMI is the outcome. Five of the six coefficients are, however, significant when overweight is the outcome. As is the case for television-viewing time, the exception pertains to adolescent girls.

In each of the twelve specification (1) regressions in tables 20.5 and 20.6, we test the hypothesis that the coefficient of the log of television time is equal to the coefficient of the log of messages aired. In each case, we accept the hypothesis that the two coefficients are the same. Therefore, we estimate a second model (specification [2] in each table) in which the log of messages aired and the log of television time are omitted but the log of messages seen is included. As pointed out in section 3, this is equivalent to constraining the coefficient of the log of television time to equal the coefficient of the log of messages aired. In this specification, all twelve coefficients are positive and significant.

To gauge the magnitudes of the effects at issue, we focus on the regressions in table 20.6 in which the probability of being overweight is the dependent variable. This outcome is a negative correlate of health, while BMI is a positive correlate for children and adolescents who are below their ideal weight. Moreover, the coefficients of the log of messages seen are smaller than the coefficients of the log of messages aired in table 20.6, while the reverse holds in table 20.5. Hence, the coefficients in specification (2) of table 20.6 may be viewed as conservative lower-bound estimates.

We employ an increase in the number of messages seen equal to its coefficient of variation in the actual variable rather than in its natural logarithm. On average, children and youths view approximately half an hour per week of fast-food advertising messages. Since the coefficient of variation of this variable is approximately equal to one in each regression, our computations reveal the impacts of an increase in exposure to this type of advertising of half an hour per week.[10] Note that this increase can occur if a given child is exposed to an additional half an hour of advertising, if more children are exposed to the same amount of advertising, or by a combination of these two changes.

For boys ages three to eleven, increasing exposure to fast-food advertising by half an hour per week will increase the probability of being overweight by 2.2 percentage points. This translates to a 15 percent increase in the number of

Table 20.6 Regression Results: Dependent Variable Is Overweight

	Specification (1)			Specification (2)		
	Whole	Male	Female	Whole	Male	Female
Ages 3–11:						
ln(Messages aired)	.052* (2.302)	.058+ (1.565)	.049+ (1.545)	...	...	...
ln(TV time)	.025** (3.319)	.030** (2.560)	.021* (2.111)	...	...	...
ln(Messages seen)	...	...	...	.026** (3.670)	.032** (2.729)	.023* (2.314)
T-test on equality of coefficient[a]	.260	.464	.412	...	...	...
R^2	.088	.102	.102	.088	.102	.102
N	6,034	3,087	2,947	6,034	3,087	2,947
Ages 12–18:						
ln(Messages aired)	.021* (1.967)	.028* (1.846)	.014 (.822)	...	...	...
ln(TV time)	.021** (3.071)	.036** (3.414)	.009 (1.224)	...	...	...
ln(Messages seen)	...	...	...	.021** (3.316)	.036** (3.555)	.009+ (1.383)
T-test on equality of coefficient[a]	.961	.650	.805	...	...	...
R^2	.100	.108	.127	.100	.108	.127
N	7,069	3,665	3,404	7,069	3,665	3,404

Note: Data for ages 3–11 are from the National Longitudinal Survey of Youth (NLSY) 1979. Data for ages 12–18 are from the National Longitudinal Survey of Youth 1997. All regressions are weighted by NLSY sampling weights. *T*-ratios are reported in parentheses. Regressions are clustered by designated market area (DMA). All coefficients are adjusted for individual characteristics, state variables, DMA fixed effects, and year fixed effects. Individual variables include age, black non-Hispanic, Hispanic, other race (NLSY97 only), male, family income, missing income dummy, mother overweight, mother obese, mother employed, and dummies for weight and height reported by mothers (as opposed to actual measurements; NLSY79 only). State variables include the per capita number of fast-food restaurants, per capita number of full-service restaurants, real cigarette price, dummies for clean-indoor-air laws, real full-service restaurant price, real food-at-home price, and real fast-food restaurant price.

[a] The null hypothesis is that the coefficient of log(messages aired) is equal to the coefficient of log(TV time).

+ Significant at the 10 percent level (one-tailed test).

* Significant at the 5 percent level (one-tailed test).

** Significant at the 1 percent level (one-tailed test).

overweight boys in a fixed population.[11] The corresponding figures for girls ages three to eleven are a 1.6 percentage point, or 12 percent, increase in the number of overweight girls in a fixed population. For adolescent boys and girls ages twelve to eighteen, we obtain an increase of 2.5 percentage points (17 percent) for boys and an increase of .6 percentage points (4 percent) for girls.

We have subjected the sensitivity of our results to alternative specifications and to estimation by two-stage least squares methodology. These analyses pertain to the second model in tables 20.5 and 20.6. We summarize them here and present and discuss them in detail in Chou, Rashad, and Grossman (2007). The first alternative specification omits DMA fixed effects and state variables. The second specification adds DMA fixed effects, while the third adds state variables and linear DMA-specific trends. In general, the coefficients of the log of messages seen are very stable across these alternative specifications. One might be concerned if the effects became smaller as more location-specific variables were included because that might be evidence of omitted-variables bias. In fact, that is not the case. Hence, these estimates strengthen our confidence in those emphasized in tables 20.5 and 20.6.

In the two-stage least squares models, the price of advertising (measured in dollars per seconds of messages aired) and the number of households with a television in the DMA serve as instruments.[12] They have the expected signs in the first stage and pass overidentification tests. Moreover, the F-statistics resulting from the test of the significance of the two instruments as a set range from 15 to 76, which suggests that the instrumental variables estimates are not biased because the instruments are highly correlated with the endogenous explanatory variable. Most important, the results suggest that the variable for messages seen is not endogenous. All the Durbin-Wu-Hausman tests of the consistency of ordinary least squares are accepted, regardless of the sample.

6. DISCUSSION

The investigation of the causal relationship between fast-food restaurant advertising and body weight among children and adolescents is important when forming policies to cope with the rapid increase in obesity rates. Overall, our results show a strong positive effect of exposure to fast-food restaurant advertising on the probability that children and adolescents are overweight. As indicated in section 1, there is conflicting evidence on trends in television and commercial viewing by children and youths since 1980. Hence, it would be premature to point to our findings as a partial explanation of the upward trend in obesity. Our results can, however, be used to estimate the impact of a fast-food restaurant advertising ban on television on childhood obesity. A complete advertising ban on television would reduce the number of overweight children ages three to eleven in a fixed population by 18 percent.[13] The impact of this policy for adolescents ages twelve to eighteen amounts to a smaller decline of 14 percent. These computations underestimate the impact of a complete advertising ban on television because they are based on local or spot television advertising and ignore advertising associated with network, syndicated, and cable television because they have no local variation. On the other hand, the computations could overestimate the impact of an advertising ban because we ignore advertising in other media (that is, radio, magazines, outdoor, newspaper).

Another policy option is to eliminate food advertising as ordinary business expenses that reduce taxable corporate income. Since the corporate income tax rate is 35 percent, elimination of the tax deductibility of food advertising costs is equivalent to increasing the price of advertising by about 54 percent. On the basis of our results, this elimination of tax deductibility would reduce fast-food restaurant messages seen on television by 40 and 33 percent for children and adolescents, respectively, and would reduce the number of overweight children and adolescents by 7 and 5 percent, respectively.[14] These declines are smaller than would be the case with an advertising ban, but the tax policy would impose lower welfare costs on children and adults who consume fast food in moderation because positive information about restaurants that supply this type of food would not be banned completely from television.

Clearly, we have not provided enough information to fully evaluate the two policies just discussed. Indeed, we have not addressed the larger issue of whether the government should intervene in the food purchase decisions of its citizens. In the case of children, one justification for government intervention is that society as a whole may reap substantial current and future production and consumption benefits from improvements in children's health. The case is strengthened because overweight children are extremely likely to become obese adults and because children are less likely to have information about the consequences of their actions or to heavily discount these consequences. The case is weakened because parents may more easily and immediately affect the choices made by their children than can the government.

In addition, one would need to consider the degree of government involvement that is merited and the costs of alternative policies if some intervention appears to be worthwhile. Hence, more research is required to evaluate the effectiveness of these policies and others. Our study should be viewed as one of many inputs in this process.

NOTES

Originally published as Shin-Yi Chou, Inas Rashad, and Michael Grossman, "Fast-Food Restaurant Advertising on Television and Its Influence on Childhood Obesity," *Journal of Law and Economics* 51, no. 4 (2008): 599–618.

1. Out of 8,984, only 5,419 youth respondents were between the ages of 12 and 14 in round 1. Thus, 40 percent of our sample was dropped because of the missing values for television-watching time.

2. We do not use the year 2000 for National Longitudinal Survey of Youth 1997 (NLSY97) because our advertising data are from 1996–1999.

3. The corporations we chose for this analysis that we believed best reflected the fast-food industry were A&W Restaurants Inc., AFC Enterprises, Allied Domecq Plc., Arthur Treachers Inc., Carrols Corp, Chester Fried Chicken Restaurants, Chick-Fil-A Inc., Cici Enterprises Inc., Cke Restaurants Inc., Culver Franchising System Inc., Diageo Plc., Dominos Pizza Inc., Fatboys Franchise Systems Inc., Foodmaker Inc., Galardi Group, Hungry Howies Pizza & Subs Inc., Ich Corp, In-N-Out Burgers Inc., Inno-Pacific Holdings Inc., Krispy Kreme Doughnut Corp, Krystal Co, Leeann Chin, Little Caesars Enterprises Inc., Long John Silvers Inc., McDonalds Corp, Panda Express, Papa Ginos Inc., Papa Johns Intl Inc., Quality Dining Inc., Ranch 1, Rax Restaurants Inc., Showbiz Pizza Time Inc., Sizzler Intl Inc., Sonic Corp, Speedy Burgers Inc., TCBY Enterprises Inc., Triarc Cos Inc., Tricon Global Restaurants Inc. (now Yum! Brands and responsible for KFC, Pizza Hut, Taco Bell, and Long John Silver's), Wendy's Intl Inc., Whataburger Inc., and White Castle System Inc.

4. We append 1999 advertising data to 2000 NLSY79 data by designated market area (DMA).

5. A DMA is always larger than the corresponding metropolitan statistical area (MSA) because the market reached by a television station exceeds the MSA in which it is located. Our matching algorithm employs information on the specific counties that are included in each DMA.

6. For example, Saffer (1997), Tellis and Weiss (1995), and Tellis, Chandy, and Thaivanich (2000) use advertising only, while Saffer and Dave (2006) use exposure per capita.

7. This comparison could only be done for NLSY79 because we could not estimate individual fixed effects models for NLSY97.

8. These tests allow the intercept to vary by gender.

9. We evaluate the significance of advertising and television coefficients with one-tailed tests since the alternative hypothesis is that these coefficients are positive.

10. To be specific, we compute the percentage-point increase in the percentage of children or adolescents who are overweight as $100\gamma_1 \ln(1 + \Delta S/\overline{S})$, where γ_1 is the regression the coefficient of $\ln S$, $\overline{S}$ is the mean of S, and $\Delta S/\overline{S}$ is set equal to the coefficient of variation. Note that the antinatural logarithm of the mean of the log of S is the geometric mean and is measured in the same units as S—namely, hours per week. But the antilog of the standard deviation of $\ln S$ is not measured in hours per week. Bland and Altman (1996) indicate that calculation of the standard deviation of a variable after it has been transformed to natural

logarithms requires taking the difference between each log observation and the log of the geometric mean. Since the difference between the log of two numbers is the log of their ratio, it is a dimensionless pure number. For that reason and because an increase in messages seen of half an hour per week is a meaningful magnitude to consider, we base our computations on arithmetic means and the corresponding standard deviations. Note that if messages seen incorporates the constant ($K < 1$) in equation (3), then $S^* = KS$. Clearly, the coefficient of variation of S^* equals the coefficient of variation of S.

11. We use the means from the National Health and Nutrition Examination Survey 1999 (NHANES 99) dataset to compute the percentage change.

12. According to *Advertising Age* (Endicott 2005 S19), spending on television advertising by restaurants accounted for 6 percent of all television-advertising spending in 2004. Of course, advertising spending by fast-food restaurants in that medium was even less. This justifies our a priori assumption that the price of a fast-food restaurant advertisement is exogenous.

13. Calculations use specification (2) in table 20.6 and means for the percentage of overweight persons from NHANES 99. The number of advertising messages seen is assumed to decline from its age- and gender-specific mean to zero. Since we employ the log of messages seen in the regressions, we compute the marginal effect of S at the mean ($\gamma_1/\overline{S}$) and then multiply this effect by $\overline{S}$. Of course, that is equivalent to computing the effect of a ban as γ_1. This is an underestimate since the effect of S on the probability of being overweight rises as S declines. In our view, this source of bias is less relevant than those discussed in the text. Since both the mean and the standard deviation of S are approximately equal to half an hour per week, the reduction in S associated with the ban is roughly equal to the increase employed in the computations in section 5.

14. These computations employ specification (2) in table 20.6 and the reduced-form advertising price coefficients for each age group from the first stage of our instrumental variables models. To be specific, let γ_1 be the coefficient of the log of messages seen in the regression for percentage of overweight persons, let β be the coefficient of price in the regression for the log of messages seen, let p be the mean price of a message seen, and let t be the corporate tax rate. Then the reduction in the percentage of overweight persons due to the elimination of the tax deductibility of advertising is $100\gamma_1\beta pt/(1 - t)$.

REFERENCES

Becker, Gary S., and Kevin M. Murphy. 1993. "A Simple Theory of Advertising as a Good or Bad." *Quarterly Journal of Economics* 108: 941–964.

Bland, J. Martin, and Douglas G. Altman. 1996. "Transformations, Means, and Confidence Intervals." *British Medical Journal* 312: 1079.

Centers for Disease Control and Prevention. 2007. *2000 CDC Growth Charts: United States.* http://www.cdc.gov/growthcharts.

Chou, Shin-Yi, Michael Grossman, and Henry Saffer. 2004. "An Economic Analysis of Adult Obesity: Results from the Behavioral Risk Factor Surveillance System." *Journal of Health Economics* 23: 565–587.

Chou, Shin-Yi, Inas Rashad, and Michael Grossman. 2007. "Fast-Food Restaurant Advertising on Television and Its Influence on Childhood Obesity." Cambridge, Mass: National Bureau of Economic Research Working Paper No. 11879. Revised.

Endicott, R. Craig. 2005. "Fiftieth Annual 100 Leading National Advertisers." *Advertising Age.* June 27: S1, S19.

Gallo, Anthony E. 1999. "Food Advertising in the United States." In *America's Eating Habits: Changes and Consequences*, ed. Elizabeth Frazao. Washington, D.C.: U.S. Department of Agriculture.

Holt, Debra J., Pauline M. Ippolito, Debra M. Desrochers, and Christopher R. Kelley. 2007. *Children's Exposure to TV Advertising in 1977 and 2004: Information for the Obesity Debate.* Bureau of Economics Staff Report. Washington, D.C.: Federal Trade Commission.

Huston, Aletha C., Edward Donnerstein, Halford Fairchild, Norma D. Feshbach, Phyllis A. Katz, John P. Murray, Eli A. Rubinstein, Brian L. Wilcox, and Diana M. Zuckerman. 1992. *Big World, Small Screen: The Role of Television in American Society.* Lincoln: University of Nebraska Press.

Institute of Medicine. 2006. *Food Marketing to Children and Youth: Threat or Opportunity?* Washington, D.C.: National Academies Press.

Kaiser Family Foundation. 2004. *The Role of Media in Childhood Obesity.* Menlo Park, Calif.: Kaiser Family Foundation.

Kunkel, Dale. 2001. "Children and Television Advertising." In *Handbook of Children and the Media*, ed. Jerome L. Singer. Thousand Oaks, Calif.: Sage Publications.

Mayer, Caroline. 2005. "Kraft to Curb Snack Food Advertising." *Washington Post*, January 12: E1.

Powell, Lisa M., Glen Szczypka, and Frank J. Chaloupka. 2007. "Exposure to Food Advertising on TV among Children." *Archives of Pediatrics and Adolescent Medicine* 161: 553–560.

Saffer, Henry. 1997. "Alcohol Advertising and Motor Vehicle Fatalities." *Review of Economics and Statistics* 79: 431–442.

Saffer, Henry, and Dhaval Dave. 2006. "Alcohol Advertising and Alcohol Consumption by Adolescents." *Health Economics* 15: 617–637.

Schmalensee, Richard. 1972. *The Economics of Advertising.* Amsterdam: North-Holland.

Tellis, Gerald J., Rajesh K. Chandy, and Patana Thaivanich. 2000. "Which Ad Works, When, Where, and How Often? Modeling the Effects of Direct Television Advertising." *Journal of Marketing Research* 37: 32–46.

Tellis, Gerald J., and Doyle L. Weiss. 1995. "Does TV Advertising Really Affect Sales? The Role of Measures, Models, and Data Aggregation." *Journal of Advertising* 24: 1–12.

U.S. Department of Health and Human Services. 2001. National Center for Health Statistics. *Overweight among U.S. Children and Adolescents.* Washington, D.C.: Government Printing Office.

Zywicki, Todd J., Deborah Holt, and Maureen K. Ohlaysen. 2004. "Obesity and Advertising Policy." *George Mason Law Review* 12: 979–1011.

Food Prices and Body Fatness among Youths

Michael Grossman, Erdal Tekin, and Roy Wada

ABSTRACT

We examine the effect of food prices on clinical measures of obesity, including body mass index (BMI) and percentage body fat (PBF) measures derived from bioelectrical impedance analysis (BIA) and dual energy X-ray absorptiometry (DXA), among youths ages twelve through eighteen in the National Health and Nutrition Examination Survey. This is the first study to consider clinically measured levels of body composition rather than BMI to investigate the effects of food prices on obesity outcomes among youths classified by gender and race/ethnicity. Our findings suggest that increases in the real price per calorie of food for home consumption and the real price of fast-food restaurant food lead to improvements in obesity outcomes among youths. We also find that a rise in the real price of fruits and vegetables leads to increased obesity. Finally, our results indicate that measures of PBF derived from BIA and DXA are no less sensitive and in some cases more sensitive to the prices just mentioned than BMI, and serve an important role in demonstrating that rising food prices (except fruit and vegetable prices) are indeed associated with reductions in obesity rather than with reductions in body size proportions alone.

1. INTRODUCTION

The prevalence of childhood obesity has increased at an alarming rate in the United States over the last three decades. Since the mid-1970s, the proportion of children aged twelve to nineteen who are obese has grown from 5.0 to 18.1 percent and has grown more rapidly among non-Hispanic black adolescents than among Hispanic or non-Hispanic white adolescents (Ogden et al. 2010a,b). The growing prevalence and the racial/ethnic disparities in childhood obesity are of major concern to public health, given that obese children are more likely to develop health problems, such as high blood pressure, hypertension, gallbladder disease, and Type 2 diabetes as early as adolescence (Serdula et al. 1993; Freedman et al. 1999, 2007; Hill et al. 2006). Furthermore, obese children are more likely to experience negative long-term psychological and labor market outcomes ranging from poor self-esteem and depression to discrimination and lower wages (Daniels 2006; Mocan and Tekin 2011; Dietz 1998; Strauss 2000). Wang and Dietz (2002) estimate that hospital expenditures related to childhood obesity rose from $35 million in the late-1980s to $127 million (in 2001 constant dollars) in the late-1990s. Both the Institute of Medicine (2004) and *Healthy People 2020* (U.S. Department of Health and Human Services 2010) identify the prevention of childhood obesity, particularly among disadvantaged groups, as a top public health priority.

Public interventions for improving child and adolescent health typically take the form of policies that limit access and provide price incentives and disincentives (Grossman 2005). Raising price through taxation has been shown to be highly effective at reducing substance use among adolescents (e.g., Grossman 2005; Brownell and Frieden 2009; Engelhard et al. 2009). Likewise, selective applications of taxation and subsidies may shift food consumption away from unhealthy food and toward healthier alternatives (Cawley 2010; Powell and Chaloupka 2009). The falling real cost of food has been suspected of being a contributing factor in the recent epidemic of obesity (e.g., Lakdawalla and Philipson 2002; Chou et al. 2004, 2008). In general, empirical studies that recently examined the effects of prices on obesity (e.g., Chou et al. 2004, 2008; Rashad et al. 2006; Powell and Yanjun 2007; Powell 2009; Powell et al. 2007; Auld and Powell 2009; Sturm and Datar 2005) found larger and more significant effects than studies that examined the effects of food taxes (Powell et al. 2009; Fletcher et al. 2010).

These studies typically attach location and year-specific prices or taxes to a variety of micro datasets and further include location and year fixed effects in regression analyses. The geographic unit of analysis is mostly states, but several studies focus on counties, cities, or even zip codes. These price variables usually include price indices of meals in fast-food and full-service restaurants, and an index of the price of food prepared at home. Prices of foods for consumption at home are decomposed into prices of foods with low energy densities, defined as low calories per pound of consumption (for example, fruits and vegetables) and those with high energy densities (for example, fast food). There is reasonably consistent evidence that fruit and vegetable prices, particularly non-starch variety, are associated with lower weight outcomes while fast-food prices are associated with higher weight outcomes for the adolescent population (Powell et al. 2013). These effects tend to be larger for minorities, children in lower-income families, and children whose mothers have less than a high school education. Some, but not all, of these results are based on BMI-measures of obesity calculated from self- or parental-reports of height and weight. A child or youth is classified as obese if his or her BMI is at or above the 95th percentile based on age- and gender-specific growth charts.

However, none of the results just mentioned are based on clinically measured levels of body fatness. The standard measure used in these studies is based on BMI, which is defined as weight in kilograms divided by height in meters squared. The advantage of BMI is that it is easy to calculate and readily available from many social science datasets but its reliability for use in epidemiological studies has come into question recently. Some of the weak or mixed results found by studies using BMI may be due to its limited ability to correctly distinguish body fat from lean body mass (e.g., Yusuf et al. 2004, 2005; Romero-Corral et al. 2006, 2007). Since it is body fat (and not fat-free mass) that is responsible for the detrimental health effects of obesity, several studies caution against a sole reliance on BMI and point to a need for using direct measures of body composition in obesity studies (e.g., Smalley et al. 1990, Romero-Corral et al. 2006).

Furthermore, the inability of BMI to correctly distinguish body fat from lean body mass could result in cases of false positives (Wada 2007). That is, the previously documented relationship between BMI and food prices may be due in part to the relationship between these prices and lean body mass or external body size proportions rather than body fatness per se. Thus, it is not enough to document that rising food prices lead to smaller body size without investigating whether they lead to lower body fatness. The possibility of false positives through reductions in lean body mass is an important consideration for public health and nutrition policy given that proposed food taxes may possibly increase childhood hunger and malnutrition instead of reducing childhood obesity (Zhang et al. 2013).

These concerns of reliability and false positives are particularly relevant for children and adolescents due to the gender differences in physical growth as well as the gender and racial differences in the association of BMI with a child's body fatness (e.g., Daniels et al. 1997). Consequently, several studies tested whether measures other than BMI can be used as valid measures for the detection of the degree of obesity in obese children and adolescents. Widhalm et al. (2001) used regression methods to assess the relationship between the percentage body fat and BMI along with several demographic characteristics from a sample of 105 obese boys and 99 obese girls. The authors concluded that BMI provides only limited insight to the degree of obesity for children ages ten and over. Skybo and Ryan-Wenger (2003) recommend the use of body fat percentage for identification of overweight status in school-age children.

Another related limitation of the previous studies is using BMI calculated from self-reported values of height and weight may induce its own bias. Previous studies show considerable evidence of misreporting in weight and height (Rowland 1989; Gorber et al. 2007). In an effort to determine the degree of agreement between self-reported and measured values of height and weight, Gorber et al. (2007) reviewed sixty-four studies and concluded that there was evidence for under-reporting for weight and BMI and over-reporting for height that varies between men and women.

In this paper, we use clinically obtained body composition measures to conduct a comprehensive analysis of the effects of various food prices on body fatness among youths ages twelve through eighteen and compare the sensitivity of our findings against results using BMI. This is the first study to consider clinically measured levels of body composition to investigate the effects of food prices on body fatness among youths. The body composition measure that we employ is the percentage body fat (PBF).[1] The PBF measure is derived from three separate sources, two of which rely upon BIA and one of which relies upon DXA. We also employ clinically measured height and weight to estimate the effects of prices on BMI. We employ data from the restricted-use versions of NHANES to merge various county-level time-varying price variables.

Our findings have implications for the optimal targeting of public policies designed to prevent or reduce childhood obesity, including the extent to which changes in farm, tax, and subsidy policies might affect consumption patterns. Furthermore, the precision of alternative body fat measurements for the quantification of body fat and the correct identification of the degree of obesity in youths are important for the assessment of risk factors associated with obesity and its detection among youths. The rest of the paper is laid out as follows. We discuss our data and the way body fat measures are constructed in section 2. We describe the empirical methodology in section 3 and summarize our results in section 4. We provide a brief conclusion in section 5.

2. DATA

The data for the empirical analyses are drawn from several waves of the National Health and Nutrition Examination Survey (NHANES), a program of the National Center for Health Statistics (NCHS).[2] The NHANES is a series of cross-sectional nationally representative surveys designed to assess the health and nutritional status of adults and children in the United States. The surveys are unique in that they combine interviews and physical examinations administered by trained nurses and technicians. The NHANES is ideal for the purposes of our chapter because it is the only set of nationally representative health surveys that contains measures of body composition (body fat and fat-free mass) or information necessary for calculating these measures. In the NHANES surveys, these measures were obtained by using readings from BIA and DXA. In this chapter, we use data from NHANES 1999–2000, NHANES 2001–2002, and NHANES 2003–2004 since all three measures of obesity outcomes we use are available only in these rounds.

2.1. Construction of Measures of Percentage Body Fat and Obesity

Body composition has long been used by nutritionists and physiologists for the purpose of studying nutrition, physical growth, and physical performance (Forbes 1999). However, recent improvements in clinical measurements and the rising tide of obesity have led to a renewed interest in body composition. In multivariate analyses, body composition has been shown to perform significantly better in explaining individual variations in strength, health, and physical performance than body size (Björntorp 2001; Institute of Medicine 2004). Furthermore, it has been demonstrated that fat-free mass (FFM) has a positive effect on health and physical performance, while body fat (BF) has a negative effect (e.g., Heitmann et al. 2000; Allison et al. 2002). One potential obstacle to widespread adoption of body composition in studying obesity is that it is considerably more difficult and costly to obtain than BMI. However, advancements in various measurement technologies have reduced the cost of obtaining measures of body composition considerably, which has led to their incorporation in the NHANES.

Increasingly available alternative methods of measuring obesity and physical fitness include body composition derived from BIA and DXA.[3] Although clinical researchers have been using these alternative measures for some time, social scientists have only recently begun to take advantage of them in studying obesity, primarily due to the lack of clinical data in large-scale social science datasets. Exceptions include Burkhauser and Cawley (2008), Johansson et al. (2009), and Wada and Tekin (2010), who studied labor market outcomes by using direct measurements or developing a method for imputing body composition in social science datasets. In a recent paper, Grossman et al. (2012) examine the effects of fast-food restaurant advertising on television on the body composition of adolescents as measured by percentage body fat and assess the sensitivity of these effects compared to using conventional measures of obesity based on BMI.

One particular methodology developed by clinical investigators to measure body composition is based on BIA (Kushner et al. 1990; Roubenoff et al. 1995; Sun et al. 2005; Chumlea et al. 2002). In BIA, body composition is estimated by measuring the electrical resistance of a body to a weak electrical current (National Institutes of Health 1994). FFM registers a lower electrical resistance due to its high water content, but in contrast, BF does not conduct electricity well (Chumlea et al. 2002; Sun et al. 2005). The observed electrical resistance is then converted into FFM by entering it into a predetermined equation obtained from a multiple regression analysis along with a set of easily acquired characteristics of individuals such as weight, height, age, and gender. Once FFM is predicted, BF is computed from the following identity:

$$BF \equiv W - FFM. \tag{1}$$

One advantage of BIA-based measures over DXA is the availability of population-specific prediction equations for the former that address population differences in body density and body fat distribution patterns. We make use of two specific prediction equations for FFM with resistance values found in the NHANES 1999–2000, NHANES 2001–2002, and NHANES 2003–2004. One of the prediction equations was developed by Chumlea et al. (2002) for particular use with the NHANES III, while the other was developed by Boileau (1996) for use with youths. For males, Chumlea's prediction equation is

$$FFM = -10.678 + 0.262 \text{ weight} + \frac{0.652 \text{ height}^2}{\text{resistance}} + 0.015 \text{ resistance}, \tag{2}$$

where resistance is obtained from BIA. The corresponding equation for females is

$$FFM = -9.529 + 0.168 \text{ weight} + \frac{0.696 \text{ height}^2}{\text{resistance}} + 0.016 \text{ resistance}. \tag{3}$$

Boileau's equation, which he developed specifically to measure FFM in children ages eight through sixteen, is

$$\text{FFM} = 4.138 + \frac{0.657 \text{ height}^2}{\text{resistance}} + 0.16 \text{ weight} - 1.31 \text{ male}, \tag{4}$$

where male is a binary indicator that takes on the value of 1 if the individual is a male, and 0 otherwise.

Finally, we constructed PBF measures of obesity from DXA as an alternative to the two BIA-based measures of PBF described above. As opposed to BIA, DXA does not rely on a specific prediction equation and yields direct measures of body fat and fat-free mass. However, the DXA instrument used in the NHANES survey relies on the algorithms based on adult proportions of body composition that may limit their accuracy in children and adolescents (Wong et al. 2002), which is another reason for using both the BIA and DXA measures in this study. Despite this limitation, DXA is one of the most widely adopted methods of measuring body composition (Centers for Disease Control 2008). DXA has long been used as a method to measure bone mineral content and bone mineral density and considered to be a highly reliable method because of its precision, accuracy, and low radiation exposure (Njeh et al. 1999; Wahner and Fogelman 1994; World Health Organization 1994; Genant et al. 1996).[4] It is also increasingly being used as a criterion method for body composition assessment for children (Cameron et al. 2004; Eisenmann et al. 2004; Elberg et al. 2004; Frisard et al. 2005; Okasora et al. 1999; Lazzer et al. 2008; Eisenkölbl et al. 2001). Recent scientific developments in the DXA hardware along with fan-beam technology have led to new software development for a body composition assessment, which has allowed its incorporation into large surveys (Tylavsky et al. 2003).

In DXA, a complete body scan is administered with two low dose X-rays absorbed at different rates of energies by bone and soft tissue mass. The participants are positioned supine on the tabletop with their feet in neutral position and hands flat by their side. Each administered scan of the NHANES subjects was analyzed by the Radiology Department at the University of California, San Francisco using special software, standard radiologic techniques, and specific protocols developed for the NHANES to produce assessments of various body components, such as bone mineral content and density, fat mass, lean mass with and without bone mineral content, and percentage body fat.[5] Because DXA was collected multiple times per person, all estimations associated with DXA were carried out using a multiple-imputation methodology as recommended by the NHANES technical documentation (NCHS 2008).

In addition to these three PBF measures developed by body composition analyses based on BIA and DXA, we also estimate all of our models using clinically measured BMI. Typically, an indicator of obesity is employed as an additional outcome. The indicator is equal to one if a youth's BMI is at or above the 95th percentile based on age- and gender-specific CDC growth charts. We do not employ that indicator because PBF is a continuous measure and because obesity cutoffs based on PBF are not well developed.[6]

2.2. Food Prices

We make use of three separate measures of county- and year-specific food prices in our analysis. These are the real price per calorie of food consumed at home, the real price of fast food consumed in restaurants, and the real price of fruits and vegetables consumed at home. These prices are obtained from the Council of Community and Economic Research (C2ER) Cost of Living Index, which has been published quarterly since 1968 for between 250 and 300 cities.[7] Researchers have made extensive use of the C2ER prices in studying obesity (Chou et al. 2004, 2008; Powell 2009).

The C2ER collected prices of forty-four different items during the period spanned by our NHANES data (1999–2004) and also reported the weight of each item in the typical budget of a household whose head holds a mid-management position. Included were the prices of twenty-one foods for consumption at home and three food items sold by fast-food restaurants for consumption on or off the premise.[8] We computed annual averages of each price and developed an algorithm to assign a relevant set of prices to each of the 3,114 counties in the United States. In a number of cases, counties were assigned prices based on the prices of the geographically nearest within-state county for which price data were available. The measurement was based on the distance from the geographic center point of one county to another.

The twenty-one foods for consumption at home were used to construct a Laspeyres index of the price per calorie of food for home consumption. The index is given by

$$L_{ijt} = \frac{\sum_{i=1}^{21} \pi_{ijt} C_{ib}}{\sum_{i=1}^{21} \pi_{ib} C_{ib}}. \tag{5}$$

In this equation π_{ijt} is the price per calorie of food type i in county j in year t, C_{ib} is total calories consumed from food type i in the base year (b) in the United States as a whole, and π_{ib} is the price per calorie of food type i in the base year in the United States as a whole. The index can be rewritten as

$$L_{ijt} = \frac{\sum_{i=1}^{21} (\pi_{ijt}/\pi_{ib})\pi_{ib}C_{ib}}{\sum_{i=1}^{21} \pi_{ib}C_{ib}}. \tag{6}$$

Let p_{ib} be the price per gram of food type i in the base year in the United States as a whole, let q_{ib} be the number of calories in one gram of that food type, and let X_{ib} be the number of grams consumed. Then

$$\pi_{ib} = \left(\frac{p_{ib}}{q_{ib}}\right) \tag{7}$$

$$C_{ib} = q_{ib}X_{ib} \tag{8}$$

$$\pi_{ib}C_{ib} = P_{ib}X_{ib} \tag{9}$$

$$\frac{\pi_{ib}C_{ib}}{\sum_{i=1}^{21} \pi_{ib}C_{ib}} = \frac{P_{ib}X_{ib}}{\sum_{i=1}^{21} P_{ib}X_{ib}} = k_{ib}. \tag{10}$$

Note that k_{ib} in the last equation is the fraction of total food outlays spent on food item i in the base year in the United States as a whole.

Given equation (10), equation (6) can be rewritten as

$$L_{ijt} = \sum_{i=1}^{21} k_{ib}\left(\frac{\pi_{ijt}}{\pi_{ib}}\right) = \sum_{i=1}^{21} k_{ib}\left(\frac{p_{ijt}}{p_{ib}}\right)\left(\frac{C_{ib}}{C_{it}}\right). \tag{11}$$

Equation (11) contains the reasonable assumption that the number of calories in one gram of each food item does not vary among counties in a given year. The U.S. Department of Agriculture National Nutrient Database reports the number of calories in one gram of each food item at a moment in time for the United States as a whole. There are, however, no data on variations in C_i over time. Therefore, we make a second reasonable assumption that C_i is the same in each year. This yields the final formula for L_{ijt}:

$$L_{ijt} = \sum_{i=1}^{21} k_{ib}\left(\frac{p_{ijt}}{p_{ib}}\right) = \sum_{i=1}^{21} k_{ib}r_{ijt}. \tag{12}$$

In equation (12), $r_{ijt} = p_{ijt}/p_{ib}$ is a simple price relative: the price of item i in county j in year t relative to the price of that item in the base period in the United States as a whole.

Equation (12) indicates that a Laspeyres index of the price per calorie of food for home consumption coincides with a Laspeyres index of the price of food for home consumption. We compute it by first expressing each of the twenty-one food items as a simple price relative in which the denominator is the average nationwide nominal price of that item in 2000.[9] We take the fractions of food outlays spent on each food item (k_{ib}) for the same year. We then deflate by the annual Bureau of Labor Statistics Consumer Price Index (CPI, 2000 = 1) for all goods and services for the United States as a whole to convert the price per calorie into real terms.

In addition to the price just described, we include a fast-food restaurant price in all of our models. That price is computed from the prices of a McDonald's Quarter-Pounder with cheese, a thin-crusted cheese pizza at Pizza Hut or Pizza Inn, and fried chicken at Kentucky Fried Chicken or Church's. In each case, the price is expressed as a simple relative as in equation (12). Then a weighted average of these simple price relatives is computed, where the weights are the shares of outlays on each item in total outlays on the three combined in 2000. The resulting price is deflated by the CPI. Finally, we compute a fruit and vegetable price from a subset of the prices of six items purchased for consumption at home: potatoes, bananas, lettuce, peas, peaches, and corn. The methodology is the same as that employed for the fast-food price. Simple price relatives are obtained and then averaged using as weights the shares of each item in total expenditures on fruits and vegetables in 2000. Finally the resulting price is deflated by the CPI.

3. EMPIRICAL IMPLEMENTATION

Our goal is to estimate the effects of various types of food prices on obesity outcomes of youths. To accomplish this goal, we specify a two-way fixed effects OLS regression equation in the following form:

$$Y_{ijt} = \alpha_0 + \alpha_1 \text{Realcala}_{ijt} + \alpha_2 \text{Realfast}_{ijt} + \alpha_3 Z_{ijt} + \mu_t + v_j + \varepsilon_{ijt}. \quad (13)$$

In equation (13), Y_{ijt} is one of the obesity outcomes for youth i in county j surveyed in year t. The key regressors are the price per calorie of food for home consumption (Realcala_{ijt}) and the real price of food sold by fast-food restaurants (Realfast_{ijt}). The vector Z_{ijt} consists of youth and household specific characteristics. These include indicators for race and ethnicity, age in months, indicators for the ratio of income to the family's appropriate poverty threshold (less than 1.35, between 1.35 and 3, and between 3 and 5, and income missing) indicators for the living situation of the youth (in a married household, in a household headed with a female, in a household headed by a male, and living situation missing), household size, indicators for the education of the household head (less than eighth grade, ninth through eleventh grade, high school or GED, some college, college or higher).

The equation also includes two-way fixed effects consisting of year fixed effects, μ_t, that account for unmeasured variables that vary over time at the national level and that are correlated with obesity outcomes and their determinants and county fixed effects, v_j, to account for time-invariant, area-specific unmeasured factors that are correlated with the prices and weight. For example, locations with a high proportion of minority and low-income populations may have a higher concentration of fast-food restaurants, which may push the price of food in these restaurants down. These areas may also have a higher concentration of obese individuals if low socio-economic status and poverty are positively associated with obesity. Then a failure to control for county fixed effects may result in a biased estimate of the effect of food prices on youth obesity. Finally, the variable ε_{ijt} is an idiosyncratic error term.

We predict that α_1 and α_2 should be negative. We realize, however, that the effects of increases in the two food prices are not unambiguous. For example, an increase in the price per calorie of food consumed at home can lead to an increase in food consumed at fast-food restaurants. To cite another example, dense convenience food prepared and consumed at home could rise in response to an increase in the price of fast food obtained in restaurants. Since we employ body composition rather than the consumption of certain foods as outcomes, our estimates will reflect these types of substitutions. In that sense, they are more informative than a regression in which the only outcome is fast-food restaurant consumption or consumption of convenience food. Note that the identification of the two price coefficients in the regression comes from within county changes in prices over time.

Obviously not all foods are unhealthy in the sense that increases in their consumption lead to weight gains. Therefore, we also estimate a version of equation (13), in which the calorie price is replaced by the fruits and vegetables price. We continue to include the fast-food restaurant price in that specification. Here our prediction is that the coefficient of the fruits and vegetables price should be positive. This reflects a substitution away from "healthy" foods and toward "unhealthy" foods in response to an increase in the price of the former. The specification takes into account an important point made by Auld and Powell (2009). They show that an increase in the price of foods with high energy densities (for example, food consumed at fast-food restaurants), with the price of foods with low energy densities (for example, fruits and vegetables) held constant, will result in a reduction in total calories consumed if the price of dense food is cheaper per calorie consumed than the price of non-dense food also per calorie consumed.

The Auld–Powell model highlights another reason why the signs of the price coefficients in equation (13) are ambiguous. In that equation, the price per calorie of food for home consumption is held constant when the price of food consumed in fast-food restaurants varies. But that does not guarantee that the prices of dense and non-dense food consumed at home are fixed. Moreover, when the price of per calorie of food consumed at home varies, with the price of fast-food restaurant food held constant, prices of dense and non-dense food may be changing. In theory, one would want to include the calorie prices of many different types of food in the regression. Multicollinearity among these prices makes that approach infeasible, however. Inter-correlations among the three prices that we do use are fairly high. That is another reason for the two alternative specifications, and also is a reason for interpreting the results with caution.

We estimate all of our models separately for males and females because Chumlea's measure is based on formulae developed separately for each gender. Furthermore, body structures may exhibit major differences in size, shape, composition, and function during puberty. For example, most girls begin puberty between the ages of nine and thirteen, while most boys experience puberty later between the ages of ten and sixteen. This suggests that a pooled specification may not fully account for gender-specific differences in body growth. Finally, in light of the well-known health disparities between whites and minorities, we also present estimates from regressions that are estimated separately for each gender and race/ethnicity combination. While Chumlea et al. (2002) did not find significant differences by race/ethnicity in their sample, they cautioned that such differences are often found by other studies. Doing so will allow us to assess the extent to which the food price-body composition relationship differs by race/ethnicity, as well as to account for potential PBF measurement errors associated with race/ethnicity.

It is also important to note that, just as with any dependent variable, our three measures of PBF contain measurement errors. They are of special concern because PBF pertains to *interior* measurement of the human body that, despite significant improvements in instrumentation, is constructed with the help of predictive equations or algorithms with underlying assumptions. However, random measurement error in the dependent variable inflates standard errors but does not bias the estimated coefficients, and the measurement errors associated with PBF are unlikely to be correlated with food prices except possibly through correlations with third unobserved factors, which are addressed in this chapter through the use of two-way fixed effects in our estimation.

4. RESULTS

Definitions, means and standard deviations of all variables used in the empirical analysis are reported in table 21.1. Means and standard deviations are weighted using the medical examination sampling weights provided in the NHANES. Note that nonwhites are oversampled, which is why there are more observations for nonwhites in the columns that contain data by gender and race/ethnicity.

All three measures of PBF indicate that females possess a higher percentage of their total weight as body fat than males. Furthermore, the means for PBF from the measures developed from the prediction equations of Boileau and Chumlea are very close to each other. Those generated by DXA are somewhat larger, but not far from the other two measures of PBF. Note that both Boileau and Chumlea are based on BIA, while DXA is based on X-ray imaging. While the PBF figures are indicative of a higher percentage body fat among females than males, this pattern does not hold if we focus on BMI. Nonwhites have higher values of PBF than whites for both males and females. One exception to this pattern is DXA measured for males, where the difference is quite small. While the differences are perhaps not as striking as one might expect, nonwhite adolescents and especially adults exhibit higher rates of obesity than whites (Flegal et al. 2012; Ogden et al. 2012). Since obese youths are likely to become obese adults, this motivates, in part, the gender and race/ethnicity-specific regression analysis later in this section.

Additionally, the means for control variables follow patterns that are usually consistent with one's expectations. For example, heads in households where minority children live are more likely to have lower education, more likely to be in poverty, less likely to be married, and more likely to be female.

Table 21.2 presents pairwise correlations among our outcome measures. Consistent with the means presented in table 21.1, there is a high degree of correlation among our three body composition measures. For example, the four gender and race/ethnicity-specific correlation coefficients between PBF from Boileau and Chumlea are at least as large as 0.98. The eight pairwise correlations between the PBF measure from DXA and the PBF measures from Boileau and Chumlea are somewhat lower, ranging from 0.83 to 0.92. The twelve pairwise correlation coefficients between BMI and each measure of PBF are smaller, falling into an interval from 0.67 through 0.88. Similar conclusions hold within each of the four gender-majority/minority-specific groups.

We present our regression results in tables 21.3 through 21.5. In table 21.3, columns 1 and 2 show the results for all males and columns 3 and 4 show them for all females. Columns 1 and 3 present estimates from the model specifications that include the real price per calorie of food for home consumption and

Table 21.1 Descriptive Statistics

	All Races		Whites		Nonwhites	
Variable	Males	Females	Males	Females	Males	Females
PBF-Boileau[b]	19.847	29.401	19.306	28.371	20.916	31.355
	(9.359)	(8.575)	(9.262)	(8.574)	(9.467)	(8.238)
PBF-Chumlea[b]	20.322	31.024	19.815	30.055	21.329	32.862
	(7.777)	(8.410)	(7.686)	(8.385)	(7.865)	(8.154)
PBF-DXA[b]	24.158	33.742	24.344	33.522	23.793	34.188
	(7.872)	(7.082)	(7.642)	(6.976)	(8.298)	(7.279)
BMI	23.171	23.465	23.021	22.935	23.457	24.465
	(5.474)	(5.692)	(5.259)	(5.260)	(5.866)	(6.307)
Price per calorie of food for home consumption	1.056	1.057	1.041	1.044	1.085	1.082
	(0.136)	(0.139)	(0.135)	(0.142)	(0.134)	(0.129)
Price of fast food	1.010	1.013	1.008	1.011	1.015	1.017
	(0.074)	(0.074)	(0.0717)	(0.0723)	(0.0779)	(0.0775)
Price of fruits and vegetables	1.029	1.033	1.013	1.017	1.061	1.062
	(0.153)	(0.158)	(0.156)	(0.164)	(0.143)	(0.142)
White	0.663	0.652	—	—	—	—
	(0.473)	(0.477)				
Black	0.153	0.158	—	—	0.454	0.454
	(0.360)	(0.365)			(0.498)	(0.498)
Hispanic	0.184	0.190	—	—	0.546	0.546
	(0.388)	(0.393)			(0.498)	(0.498)
Age	15.836	15.829	15.87	15.86	15.77	15.76
	(2.302)	(2.268)	(2.309)	(2.256)	(2.287)	(2.293)
$0.00 \leq PIR^{a} < 1.85$	0.433	0.450	0.333	0.356	0.630	0.627
	(0.480)	(0.480)	(0.460)	(0.462)	(0.459)	(0.463)
$1.85 \leq PIR \leq 3.00$	0.180	0.184	0.180	0.192	0.179	0.170
	(0.371)	(0.374)	(0.375)	(0.381)	(0.365)	(0.359)
$3.00 < PIR \leq 5.00$	0.387	0.365	0.487	0.452	0.191	0.203
	(0.476)	(0.469)	(0.492)	(0.486)	(0.372)	(0.384)
PIR is missing	0.062	0.070	0.0463	0.0647	0.0927	0.0797
	(0.241)	(0.255)	(0.210)	(0.246)	(0.290)	(0.271)
Household size	4.328	4.306	4.167	4.165	4.646	4.570
	(1.387)	(1.354)	(1.295)	(1.264)	(1.503)	(1.472)
Household head married	0.636	0.609	0.695	0.663	0.520	0.507
	(0.456)	(0.461)	(0.436)	(0.445)	(0.471)	(0.473)

(*continued*)

Table 21.1 (*Continued*)

Variable	All Males	All Females	Whites Males	Whites Females	Nonwhites Males	Nonwhites Females
Household head female	0.418	0.491	0.368	0.452	0.516	0.564
	(0.493)	(0.500)	(0.482)	(0.498)	(0.500)	(0.496)
Household head male	0.582	0.509	0.632	0.548	0.484	0.436
	(0.493)	(0.500)	(0.482)	(0.498)	(0.500)	(0.496)
Household head living situation missing	0.099	0.107	0.0916	0.106	0.115	0.109
	(0.299)	(0.309)	(0.289)	(0.308)	(0.319)	(0.312)
HH education < 8th grade	0.083	0.086	0.0394	0.0405	0.170	0.171
	(0.267)	(0.272)	(0.184)	(0.185)	(0.365)	(0.369)
HH education: 9–11 grade	0.150	0.151	0.0966	0.101	0.253	0.246
	(0.348)	(0.351)	(0.288)	(0.293)	(0.424)	(0.424)
HH education: high school/GED	0.270	0.280	0.276	0.295	0.257	0.251
	(0.435)	(0.442)	(0.441)	(0.449)	(0.424)	(0.425)
HH education: some college	0.300	0.301	0.333	0.325	0.234	0.255
	(0.451)	(0.452)	(0.467)	(0.463)	(0.411)	(0.429)
HH education: college or higher	0.198	0.182	0.255	0.239	0.0857	0.0769
	(0.393)	(0.381)	(0.433)	(0.422)	(0.268)	(0.259)
Year: 1999	0.111	0.110	0.0974	0.0986	0.138	0.130
	(0.314)	(0.312)	(0.297)	(0.298)	(0.345)	(0.337)
Year: 2000	0.185	0.182	0.184	0.166	0.187	0.213
	(0.388)	(0.386)	(0.388)	(0.372)	(0.390)	(0.410)
Year: 2001	0.193	0.194	0.208	0.212	0.165	0.160
	(0.395)	(0.395)	(0.406)	(0.409)	(0.371)	(0.366)
Year: 2002	0.163	0.169	0.157	0.164	0.173	0.177
	(0.369)	(0.371)	(0.364)	(0.371)	(0.378)	(0.381)
Year: 2003	0.168	0.173	0.158	0.167	0.189	0.184
	(0.374)	(0.378)	(0.365)	(0.373)	(0.391)	(0.387)
Year: 2004	0.180	0.173	0.196	0.192	0.148	0.136
	(0.384)	(0.378)	(0.397)	(0.394)	(0.355)	(0.343)
Observations[b]	3,348	3,084	898	827	2,450	2,257

Notes: Standard deviations are in parentheses. Means and standard deviations are weighted using the NHANES sampling weights. All the prices are in real terms. Household head is abbreviated HH.

[a]PIR stands for poverty-income ratios.

[b]Because observation sizes differ slightly by the outcome, the mean and the observations sizes are reported for BMI, which had the maximum observation size. Observations sizes for PBF-Boileau, PBF-Chumlea, PBF-DXA are slightly less. They are available from authors upon request.

Table 21.2 Pairwise Correlations among Body Fat and BMI Measures

	PBF-Boileau	PBF-Chumlea	BMI	PBF-DXA
All males				
PBF-Boileau	1.000			
PBF-Chumlea	0.987	1.000		
BMI	0.797	0.787	1.000	
PBF-DXA	0.827	0.857	0.681	1.000
All females				
PBF-Boileau	1.000			
PBF-Chumlea	0.983	1.000		
BMI	0.826	0.890	1.000	
PBF-DXA	0.887	0.910	0.847	1.000
White males				
PBF-Boileau	1.000			
PBF-Chumlea	0.986	1.000		
BMI	0.802	0.786	1.000	
PBF-DXA	0.829	0.863	0.671	1.000
White females				
PBF-Boileau	1.000			
PBF-Chumlea	0.984	1.000		
BMI	0.835	0.897	1.000	
PBF-DXA	0.898	0.921	0.861	1.000
Nonwhite males				
PBF-Boileau	1.000			
PBF-Chumlea	0.988	1.000		
BMI	0.790	0.792	1.000	
PBF-DXA	0.841	0.867	0.702	1.000
Nonwhite females				
PBF-Boileau	1.000			
PBF-Chumlea	0.981	1.000		
BMI	0.811	0.882	1.000	
PBF-DXA	0.881	0.902	0.828	1.000

Notes: Sample sizes for pairwise correlations range between 2,865 and 3,023 for males, 1,949 and 2,759 for females, 772 and 898 for white males, 577 and 827 for white females, 2,098 and 2,453 for nonwhite males, and 1,372 and 2,258 for nonwhite females. Correlations are weighted using the NHANES sampling weights.

the real price of food sold by fast-food restaurants. Columns 2 and 4 show estimates from the model specifications that replace the real price of per calorie of food for home consumption with the real price of fruits and vegetables. Finally, table 21.3 contains four panels, each presenting the price estimates for one of the outcomes: PBF based on Boileau, PBF based on Chumlea, PBF based on DXA, and BMI.[10] Note that all the regressions are weighted using the appropriate sampling weights and the standard errors are clustered by county.[11] This allows the error term to be correlated among different youths in the same county both at a moment in time and over time.

Focusing on the first panel (PBF-Boileau), we find that the price per calorie of food consumed at home is associated with a decrease in PBF for both genders, but the male estimate is smaller in magnitude than the female estimate and is not statistically significant. Evaluated at sample means, the male elasticity of −0.87 is slightly larger in absolute value than the female elasticity of −0.76. That is a 10 percent increase in the price per calorie of food for home consumption lowers PBF for males by approximately 9 percent and lowers PBF for females by approximately 8 percent.

The fast-food restaurant price coefficient in the first panel is sensitive to the specific model that is being estimated. When the price per calorie of food consumed at home is held constant, the coefficient is negative and significant for both genders (see columns 1 and 3). On the other hand, the coefficient is smaller and not significant but still negative when the price of fruits and vegetables is held constant (see columns two and four). These results are due in part to multicollinearity, and we interpret them with caution. Here and in the remainder of the chapter, we summarize the magnitude of the fast-food price effect based on an average elasticity implied by the two specifications.[12] For males the figure is −1.73 and for females, it is −0.76. When PBF is measured by the Boileau formula, the coefficient on the price of fruits and vegetables is positive for both genders (see columns 2 and 4 of panel 1) but significant only for females. The female elasticity of 0.88 is larger than the male elasticity of 0.72.

Taken as a whole, the results in the first panel of table 21.3 suggest that the price of healthy food, measured by the price of fruits and vegetables, is a more important determinant of female PBF than of male PBF. When this price rises by 10 percent, PBF rises by 9 percent for females but by 7 percent for males, and the estimate is significant only for females. On the other hand, the price per calorie of food consumed at home or in fast-food restaurants plays a more important role, as reflected by elasticities, in male than in female body fatness. For example, a 10 percent reduction in the price of fast-food restaurant food is associated with a 17 percent increase in PBF for males, which is much larger than the 8 percent reduction for females. This result and the corresponding

Table 21.3 Estimates of the Effect of Food Prices on Body Composition by Gender

	All Males		All Females	
PBF-Boileau				
Price per calorie	−16.436 (11.765)		−21.063* (11.900)	
Elasticity	[−0.874]		[−0.755]	
Price of fast food	−38.742** (14.924)	−29.383 (18.205)	−29.441* (16.141)	−14.818 (15.044)
Elasticity	[−1.970]	[−1.490]	[−1.010]	[−0.509]
Price of fruits and vegetables		13.839 (15.673)		25.079* (12.795)
Elasticity		[0.717]		[0.878]
R^2	0.114	0.113	0.213	0.213
Observations	2,993	2,993	2,759	2,759
PBF-Chumlea				
Price per calorie	−16.515 (10.040)		−24.636* (12.634)	
Elasticity	[−0.857]		[−0.837]	
Price of fast food	−28.825*** (10.609)	−20.886 (13.329)	−23.396 (16.868)	−7.575 (15.459)
Elasticity	[−1.430]	[−1.030]	[−0.762]	[−0.246]
Price of fruits and vegetables		9.687 (12.847)		25.720* (13.217)
Elasticity		[0.490]		[0.854]
R^2	0.110	0.110	0.1989	0.198
Observations	3,002	3,002	2,759	2,759
PBF-DXA				
Price per calorie	−15.650* (8.198)		−22.520** (11.088)	
Elasticity	[−0.684]		[−0.707]	
Price of fast food	−21.770** (9.029)	−14.600 (11.196)	16.182 (17.627)	34.553* (18.340)
Elasticity	[−0.910]	[−0.610]	[0.484]	[1.032]
Price of fruits and vegetables		7.403 (8.952)		26.623** (11.811)
Elasticity		[0.315]		[0.819]
R^2	0.125	0.125	0.150	0.160
Observations	3,368	3,368	2,257	2,257

(*continued*)

Table 21.3 (Continued)

	All Males		All Females	
BMI				
Price per calorie	−22.020*** (4.547)		−11.618 (8.364)	
Elasticity	[−1.000]		[−0.523]	
Price of fast food	−22.109*** (4.446)	−17.378** (7.462)	−4.744 (8.579)	4.585 (6.803)
Elasticity	[−0.963]	[−0.757]	[−0.204]	[0.198]
Price of fruits and vegetables		−4.978 (6.277)		17.862** (6.846)
Elasticity		[−0.221]		[0.786]
R^2	0.138	0.137	0.152	0.153
Observations	3,351	3,351	3,085	3,085

Notes: All regressions are weighted using the NHANES sampling weights. Standard errors in parentheses are clustered at the county level. All the prices are in real terms. Elasticities reported in brackets are computed at sample means.

* Statistical significance at the 10 percent level.
** Statistical significance at the 5 percent level.
*** Statistical significance at the 1 percent level.

result for the food at home price may reflect a greater willingness of girls to substitute toward healthy food when the price of unhealthy food rises.

In general, the results for the other three outcomes (PBF-Chumlea, PBF-DXA, and BMI) tell a similar story. Male calorie price elasticities range from −0.68 in the case of PBF-DXA to −1.00 in the case of BMI. The corresponding range for female elasticities is −0.52 for BMI to 0.84 for PBF-Chumlea. Male fast-food price elasticities range from −0.76 (PBF DXA) to −1.49 (PBF-Boileau). Female fast-food price elasticities are all negative only for the Boileau-PBF and Chumlea-PBF (−0.76 for the former and −0.50 for the latter). The only negative and significant effect of this variable for females is obtained in the model that includes the price per calorie in food consumed at home. The price of fruits and vegetables never has a significant effect on male PBF. For females, the effect always is positive and significant, and the elasticities lie in a fairly tight range from 0.79 for BMI to 0.88 for PBF-Boileau.

In tables 21.4 and 21.5, we investigate whether the effects of food prices on PBF differ between adolescents from different racial and ethnic backgrounds. To do this, we estimate our gender-specific models for whites in the former table and for nonwhites (blacks and Hispanics) in the latter table. Before these results are discussed, it is useful to point to some factors that might generate differences.

Table 21.4 Estimates of the Effect of Food Prices on Body Composition, Whites, by Gender

	White Males		White Females	
PBF-Boileau				
Price per calorie	−58.178** (25.055)		−21.036 (56.854)	
Elasticity	[−3.130]		[−0.771]	
Price of fast food	−77.68** (19.681)	−6.773 (34.035)	−53.001** (24.538)	−5.299 (37.582)
Elasticity	[−4.050]	[−0.353]	[−1.880]	[−0.188]
Price of fruits and vegetables		68.24** (26.236)		58.551* (34.790)
Elasticity		[3.576]		[2.090]
R^2	0.171	0.173	0.261	0.263
Observations	807	807	754	754
PBF-Chumlea				
Price per calorie	−58.494*** (16.321)		−35.780 (56.704)	
Elasticity	[−3.070]		[−1.230]	
Price of fast food	−64.407*** (16.634)	−3.167 (26.613)	−50.057* (25.448)	6.183 (36.804)
Elasticity	[−3.270]	[−0.160]	[−1.670]	[0.207]
Price of fruits and vegetables		49.720** (22.276)		59.697* (33.670)
Elasticity		[2.537]		[2.012]
R^2	0.162	0.163	0.246	0.247
Observations	811	811	754	754
PBF-DXA				
Price per calorie	−37.198 (22.933)		−41.502 (61.212)	
Elasticity	[−1.590]		[−1.290]	
Price of fast food	−31.046* (17.540)	17.33 (18.675)	−81.770** (31.294)	−41.472 (73.402)
Elasticity	[−1.280]	[0.717]	[−2.450]	[−1.240]
Price of fruits and vegetables		48.29** (19.401)		13.896 (37.155)
Elasticity		[2.001]		[0.422]
R^2	0.168	0.170	0.221	0.221
Observations	902	902	652	652

(*continued*)

Table 21.4 (*Continued*)

	White Males		White Females	
BMI				
Price per calorie	−31.888*** (8.988)		−31.492 (35.265)	
Elasticity	[−1.440]		[−1.430]	
Price of fast food	−21.792** (9.664)	6.224 (12.300)	−18.869 (16.953)	27.027 (17.215)
Elasticity	[−0.953]	[0.272]	[−0.831]	[1.190]
Price of fruits and vegetables		16.892 (12.223)		45.164** (13.914)
Elasticity		[0.744]		[2.002]
R^2	0.221	0.221	0.206	0.209
Observations	898	898	827	827

Notes: All regressions are weighted using the NHANES sampling weights. Standard errors in parentheses are clustered at the county level. All the prices are in real terms. Elasticities reported in brackets are computed at sample means.

* Statistical significance at the 10 percent level.
** Statistical significance at the 5 percent level.
*** Statistical significance at the 1 percent level.

An overarching consideration is that nonwhite youths come from families with lower incomes than white youths. To be sure, such proxies for family income, the education of the head of the household, and indicators for income to poverty ratios are included as regressors. But these variables are held constant at lower levels for nonwhites than for whites in the estimation of food price effects. Hence, in a fundamental sense, differences in price effects can be traced to interactions between family income and price.[13]

Components that contribute to the "full" price of consuming food in addition to the money price may also contribute to differences in observed money price elasticities between youths from low-income families and other youths. One of these components is the time price. Shopping time (the sum of the time spent traveling to and from a food outlet and waiting in line to pay for the purchase) is required to obtain food for consumption at home. Travel and waiting time also are required to consume food at restaurants. The time price of food consumption, defined as time required to purchase and consume it multiplied by the value of time, is negatively related to the per capita availability of food outlets. A one percent change in the money price of food amounts to a smaller percentage change in the full price and hence to a smaller percentage change in consumption the larger the time price component.

Table 21.5 Estimates of the Effect of Food Prices on Body Composition, Nonwhites, by Gender

	Nonwhite Males		Nonwhite Females	
PBF-Boileau				
Price per calorie	−21.106***		−33.477***	
	(5.753)		(8.191)	
Elasticity	[−1.090]		[−1.154]	
Price of fast food	−35.546***	−36.131***	0.981	9.622
	(7.488)	(10.515)	(11.148)	(10.872)
Elasticity	[−1.720]	[−1.750]	[0.032]	[0.312]
Price of fruits and vegetables		−15.579*		12.151
		(8.144)		(8.761)
Elasticity		[−0.790]		[0.412]
R^2	0.114	0.114	0.154	0.151
Observations	2,186	2,186	2,005	2,005
PBF-Chumlea				
Price per calorie	−17.675**		−37.907***	
	(5.961)		(7.766)	
Elasticity	[−0.899]		[−1.240]	
Price of fast food	−27.530***	−27.668***	3.193	12.306
	(5.302)	(8.017)	(12.281)	(11.363)
Elasticity	[−1.310]	[−1.310]	[0.099]	[0.380]
Price of fruits and vegetables		−11.761*		11.297
		(6.448)		(9.697)
Elasticity		[−0.585]		[0.365]
R^2	0.113	0.112	0.145	0.141
Observations	2,191	2,191	2,005	2,005
PBF-DXA				
Price per calorie	−17.82***		−11.04	
	(4.521)		(8.741)	
Elasticity	[−0.812]		[−0.351]	
Price of fast food	−30.14***	−29.81***	29.21*	39.36***
	(5.659)	(7.566)	(16.255)	(13.743)
Elasticity	[−1.280]	[−1.270]	[0.866]	[1.166]
Price of fruits and vegetables		−11.29		27.79***
		(7.219)		(9.034)
Elasticity		[−0.503]		[0.875]
R^2	0.153	0.152	0.166	0.167
Observations	2,466	2,466	1,605	1,605

(*continued*)

Table 21.5 (*Continued*)

	Nonwhite Males		Nonwhite Females	
BMI				
Price per calorie	-22.381***		-14.206**	
	(4.085)		(5.964)	
Elasticity	[-1.030]		[-0.628]	
Price of fast food	-26.633***	-25.542***	-0.626	3.997
	(4.209)	(7.830)	(7.339)	(5.686)
Elasticity	[-1.150]	[-1.100]	[-0.026]	[0.166]
Price of fruits and vegetables		-11.754*		9.968
		(6.566)		(6.681)
Elasticity		[-0.531]		[-0.433]
R^2	0.109	0.107	0.122	0.122
Observations	2,453	2,453	2,258	2,258

Notes: All regressions are weighted using the NHANES sampling weights. Standard errors in parentheses are clustered at the county level. All the prices are in real terms. Elasticities reported in brackets are computed at sample means.

* Statistical significance at the 10 percent level.

** Statistical significance at the 5 percent level.

*** Statistical significance at the 1 percent level.

Another component of the full price of food consumption is the monetary value of the future health consequences of that consumption. This component is positive in the case of food served in fast-food restaurants and acts as a tax on its consumption. On the other hand, the component is negative in the case of fruits and vegetables and acts as a subsidy to its consumption. A one percent change in money price results in a larger percentage in full price the smaller are the future health costs or the larger are the future health benefits.

The time price of consuming food is likely to be smaller for low-income families who have lower wage rates and hence a lower value of time. This effect is reinforced if fast-food restaurants are more likely to locate in poor areas, but weakened if supermarkets and grocery stores are less likely to locate in these areas. While previous research has documented these locational patterns, Lee (2012) finds that both fast-food restaurants and large-scale grocery stores are more prevalent in poor neighborhoods.[14] These considerations suggest that minorities may be more sensitive to fast-food restaurant prices while leaving differences in the sensitivity of responses to fruit and vegetable prices an open issue.

Future costs should be less important to parents and youths in poorer, less educated families, and future benefits should be more important to parents and youths in richer, more-educated families. Future costs and benefits are smaller for poor parents who have low wage rates and plausibly expect their children to have low wage rates as adults. Another factor is that the poor and the less educated are likely to have lower time discount factors (higher rates of time preference for the present) than the rich and more educated (Becker and Mulligan 1997). Variations in the evaluation of future costs and benefits imply larger fast-food price elasticities for the poor but smaller fruit and vegetable price elasticities.

Turning to the results in tables 21.4 and 21.5, one sees that that the eight fruit and vegetable price coefficients are positive for whites and six of the eight coefficients are significant. In table 21.4, for white females, the elasticity is approximately 2 for BMI, and PBF-Boileau and PBF-Chumlea, while it is lower at 0.42 for PBF-DXA. The range for white males is from 0.74 for BMI to 3.58 for PBF-Boileau. The pattern is very different for nonwhites in table 21.5. Only one coefficient is positive and significant (female PBF-DXA), and all four male coefficients are negative. These results are consistent with an explanation that stresses higher rates of time preference for the present and lower expected future wage rates among nonwhite youths and their parents than among white youths.

The fast-food price results tell a somewhat similar story, although here the evidence is less conclusive. Focusing on a comparison of white and nonwhite males, one sees that the eight fast-food restaurant coefficients are negative and significant for the latter group, while only four of the eight coefficients are negative and significant for the former group. Moreover, two of the coefficients are positive (for BMI and PBF-DXA) for white males. As previously indicated, we summarize the magnitude of the fast-food price effect based on an average elasticity implied by the two specifications that we estimate because the elasticity is overstated in the first specification and understated in the second (see note 12). The average elasticity range for nonwhites (between −1.12 for BMI and −1.74 for PBF-Boileau) is much tighter than for whites (between −0.28 in the case of PBF-DXA and −2.20 in the case of PBF-Boileau). These findings are consistent with the lower future costs and benefits hypothesis, but they also are consistent with an explanation that stresses lower time costs for nonwhite youths or their parents.

For both white and nonwhite females, the price of fast food plays a much less important role in body composition outcomes than for white and nonwhite males. Only one of the nonwhite female coefficients is negative. Two of the eight coefficients are positive for white females, and only three of the six negative coefficients are significant. These results mirror the gender difference in the fast-food restaurant price obtained from non-race specific regressions. It is puzzling, however, that the price elasticity for nonwhite females is never negative.

Finally, male body composition outcomes continue to be more responsive to changes in the price per calorie of food consumed at home than female outcomes when separate estimates are obtained for whites and nonwhites. While the elasticities are bigger for white males than for nonwhite males, the coefficients on which they are based are estimated more precisely for the latter group. For example, the PBF-DXA coefficient is not significant for white males. A similar conclusion emerges when the estimates for white and nonwhite females are compared. Except in the case of PBF-Boileau, the white female elasticity is bigger than the nonwhite female elasticity. But the calorie price coefficient is never significant for the former group, while three of the four coefficients are significant for the latter group.

A possible explanation for gender differences in price responsiveness and estimation precision may lie in adolescent food purchasing patterns. One recent study showed that, after controlling for socioeconomic factors, caloric intake from fast-food restaurants is significantly higher among males than females for adolescents (about 320 kcal larger) but not for children (Appendix D, Powell et al. 2012). This is a considerably large difference given that an average female adolescent might consume 2,050 kcal to an average adolescent male consuming 2,250 kcal per day. The lack of similar gap for children suggests an important role of food purchases made by adolescents away from home.

Very limited information is available on adolescent spending patterns on food items but one study of young adolescents in the United States found that food items account for 27 percent of their weekly outlays, with males spending an additional 5 percent compared to females (Alhabeeb 1996). Therefore, adolescent males with higher expenditure and caloric intake from fast-food items may be more responsive to the fast-food price than adolescent females. A corollary suggests that adolescent females may be more responsive to the price per calorie of food for home consumption than to the price of fast food when compared to males. We find such patterns in table 21.3 for PBF measures where males are more sensitive to the price of fast food while females are more sensitive to the price per calorie of food for home consumption. The patterns are mixed among white females in table 21.4 but hold for nonwhite females in table 21.5.

5. CONCLUSIONS

The proportion of children who are obese has reached epidemic levels in the last three decades. The rising prevalence of childhood obesity is a source of major concern among public health officials because of the well-documented health problems tied to obesity for both children and adults. There are a large number of policy efforts under way to stop or reverse this trend. For example, the Child Nutrition and Women Infants and Children (WIC) Reauthorization Act of 2004 required that all local education agencies participating in the National School Lunch Program create local wellness policies no later than July 2006. The Kids Walk-to-School Program developed by the Centers for Disease Control and Prevention (CDC) aims to increase opportunities for daily physical activity by encouraging children to walk to and from school in groups accompanied by adults. An increasing number of schools are limiting access to foods high in fats and sugars by banning soda machines and snack bars in cafeterias and school stores. The School Breakfast and the National School Lunch programs are two federal entitlement programs that provide nutritionally balanced, low-cost or free breakfasts and lunches to millions of children each school day.

Regulating the prices of healthy and unhealthy foods is a promising option for influencing obesity outcomes among youths. Previous studies of the analysis of the effect of prices on obesity outcomes of youths have exclusively used BMI or BMI-based indicators of obesity. However, obesity is defined as excess of body fat, and it is body fat (and not fat-free mass) that is responsible for the detrimental health effects of obesity. Therefore, an increasing number of studies point to the limitation of BMI in distinguishing fat from fat-free mass. They caution against a sole reliance on BMI and point to a need for developing alternative measures of obesity.

In this study, we consider alternative measures of obesity based on body composition rather than a BMI-based measure to investigate the effects of food prices on obesity among children and to assess their performance relative to BMI. In particular, we estimate the effects of the prices of various types of food on percentage body fat outcomes derived from BIA and DXA using data from various waves of NHANES. We also examine whether the effects of food prices on these outcomes differ between nonwhite and white adolescents and motivate this analysis by the lower socioeconomic background that characterizes nonwhites.

Our findings suggest that increases in the real price per calorie of food for home consumption and the real price of fast-food restaurant food lead to improvements in body composition outcomes among youths. We also find that a rise in the price of fruits and vegetables leads to increased obesity. The former effects are more important for males compared to females, for nonwhite males compared to white males and in the case of the calorie price for nonwhite females compared to white females. The "healthy food" price effect, reflected by the price of fruits and vegetables, is more important for whites compared to nonwhites.

There are two important implications of our study. One pertains to future research with such measures of body composition as the PBF and the other pertains to public policy. With regard to the first issue, many of our estimates suggest that the PBF is at least as sensitive to prices as BMI and in some instances more sensitive to prices than BMI, especially for adolescent females in our sample. Had we solely relied on BMI, we would have mistakenly concluded that increased fast-food prices have no impact on adolescent female obesity. There is also the issue of false positives. By using measures of PBF as outcomes, we exclude the possibility that the previously documented negative effects of increased food prices on obesity could have been driven by reductions in FFM or the muscularity component of BMI. This is an important finding for public health and nutrition policy because it demonstrates that increases in food prices (except fruit and vegetable prices) are indeed associated with reductions in body fat composition rather than with reductions in body size proportions alone.

Given that, it would be useful to employ an obesity indicator defined by PBF as an additional outcome. We have placed this issue on an agenda for future research because obesity cutoffs based on PBF result in an implausibly large percentage of youths being classified as obese. For example, Boreham et al. (1997) classify adolescent boys with PBF greater than 20 percent as obese and adolescent girls with PBF greater than 24 percent as obese. Grossman et al. (2012) show that if these cutoffs are applied to their NLSY97 data, approximately 50 percent of males and 90 percent of females are classified as obese. Even if the cutoffs for adults recommended by the National Institute of Diabetes and Digestive and Kidney Diseases (2006) for adults of greater than 25 percent for males and greater than 30 percent for females are used, approximately 22 percent of males and 60 percent of females are identified as obese. The development of more reasonable cutoffs deserves high priority on an agenda for future research. Part of that undertaking should involve an examination of the characteristics of individuals classified as obese by one measure but not the other and vice versa. It would be valuable to compare various cutoff points, including ones that result in the same percentage of obese youths as BMI cutoffs, to examine their effects on estimation outcomes.

With regard to the policy implications of our research, "fat taxes" or taxes on foods with high caloric content have received a considerable amount of recent attention in the so-called "war on obesity." One specific version is a tax on sugar-sweetened beverages (soda). Research summarized by Grossman and Mocan (2011) finds that soda taxes have very modest effects on calories consumed from soda on BMI. Indeed, Fletcher et al. (2010) find the modest decline in soda-based calories is completely offset by increases in the consumption of other high-calorie drinks such as juice and milk. Our results do not directly speak to the potential impacts of a soda tax, but they do suggest that a tax on meals purchased in fast-food restaurants or a subsidy to the consumption of fruits and vegetables would lead to better obesity outcomes among adolescents.

These findings take account of any adverse effects due to substitution toward or away from other food items in response to taxes and subsidies.

Of course, we also find that an increase in the price per calorie of food regardless of its source would improve obesity outcomes. Clearly, a food tax could be imposed to increase the price per calorie. If it took the form of a specific excise tax (fixed amount per calorie in a gram of each food type), it would have the desirable effect of raising the relative prices of foods that are cheap sources of calories. An ad valorem tax (fixed percentage of price) would not have that effect because it would not alter the relative price of dense food. But the latter tax would be much easier to impose and administer. Taken at face value, our results suggest that such a tax might be an effective tool in the war on obesity.

A good deal of caution is required here. Taxes are blunt instruments that impose significant welfare costs on individuals who consume food in moderation. Moreover, in the case of adolescents, an additional issue is that parents may more easily and immediately affect the choices made by their children than the government. Indeed, some of our results point to higher rates of time preference and lower expected future wage rates among nonwhite parents and youths as explanations of why minorities are more sensitive to fast-food prices and less sensitive to fruits and vegetables prices than whites. These interpretations add to the wide range of benefits to early childhood intervention programs emphasized by Heckman and colleagues (for example, Conti and Heckman 2012). These programs aim to improve the cognitive and non-cognitive skills of minorities and perhaps to give them more of a future orientation as well. Hence, we view our contribution as an input into the policy debate concerning the most effective ways to reverse the upward trend in obesity. We have shown that selective taxes or subsidies may be able to accomplish part of this goal. We also have shown that uniform increases or decreases in the price of food do have the expected impacts on body weight. An integrated approach to nutrition could be more focused and effective than the current approach used by the federal and states governments in taxing and subsidizing nutritional goods and allocating food stamps, which currently involves little or no consideration of the impact of these decisions on youth obesity. We leave it to others to evaluate the external costs and benefits of policies to combat obesity.

ACKNOWLEDGMENTS

Research for this chapter was supported by grant #65068 from the Robert Wood Johnson Foundation to the National Bureau of Economic Research. This chapter was presented at the Eighth World Congress of the International

Health Economics Association and at the Sixth Annual Meeting of the Robert Wood Johnson Foundation Healthy Eating Research Program. We are grateful to John Cawley who discussed our chapter at the first forum just mentioned, to the other participants in both forums, and to Jesse Margolis and three anonymous referees for helpful comments and suggestions. We also wish to thank Jesse, Ryan Conrad, and Ben Padd for research assistance. We are indebted to Karen Davis, formerly a health scientist at the National Center for Health Statistics Research Data Center (RDC); Stephanie Robinson, a health scientist at the NCHS RDC; Frances McCarty, a senior service fellow at the NCHS RDC; and Frank Limehouse, RDC Administrator at the Chicago Bureau of the Census RDC, for their assistance in helping us to gain access to and work with restricted files from the National Health and Nutrition Examination Survey at the Chicago RDC. The findings and conclusions in this chapter are those of the author(s) and do not necessarily represent the views of the Research Data Center, the National Center for Health Statistics, or the Centers for Disease Control and Prevention.

NOTES

Originally published as Michael Grossman, Erdal Tekin, and Roy Wada, "Food Prices and Body Fatness among Youths," *Economics and Human Biology* 12, no. 1 (2014): 4–19.

1. Note that $PBF \equiv 100 \times \frac{BF}{W} \equiv 100 \times \frac{W - FFM}{W}$, where W is weight, BF is body fat, and FFM is fat-free mass.

2. See http://www.cdc.gov/nchs/nhanes.htm for more information.

3. See http://www.cdc.gov/nchs/data/nhanes/bc.pdf for more information.

4. See http://www.cdc.gov/nchs/data/nhanes/dxa/dxa_techdoc.pdf for more information on DXA.

5. Hologic software version 8:26:a3 is used to administer the scans (Centers for Disease Control and Prevention 2008). More detail on the NHANES DXA examination and protocol features can be found at http://www.cdc.gov/nchs/data/nhanes/dxa/dxx_c.pdf.

6. See section 5 for more details.

7. C2ER was formerly referred to as ACCRA and before that as the American Chamber of Commerce Researchers Association.

8. The twenty-one prices of foods for consumption at home pertain to the following items: a pound of t-bone steak, a pound of ground beef, a pound of Jimmy Dean or similar sausage, a pound of whole chicken, a 6-ounce can of tuna, a half gallon of milk, a dozen large eggs, a 1-pound tub of butter, 8 ounces of Kraft parmesan, a 10-pound sack of potatoes, a pound of bananas, a head of iceberg lettuce, a 24-ounce loaf of white bread, a 12-ounce can of coffee, a 4-pound bag of sugar, an 18-ounce box of Kellogg's corn flakes, a 16-ounce can of peas, a 30-ounce can of peaches, a 3-pound can of Crisco

shortening, a 16-ounce can of corn, and a 2-liter bottle of Coke. The fast-food restaurant prices are specified in the text.

9. Each simple price relative is adjusted so that the trend in it between 1988 and 2006 is the same as the trend in the comparable item in the Bureau of Labor Statistics Consumer Price Index.

10. In the interest of space, we only provide a discussion of the price coefficients in the paper. However, the estimates on other covariates are usually consistent with those documented in the relevant literature. The full results for the models with each of the outcomes are available from the authors upon request.

11. Note that the sample sizes in the four panels of table 21.3 vary with the outcome variables, depending on the availability of these outcome measures in various NHANES rounds. In order to assess whether the differences in the price effects in the table are due to the differences in the sample sizes, we investigated the results for all these models limiting the analyses to the same sample size. These results are very similar to those presented here and are available from the authors upon request.

12. We average the two elasticities because the pattern of partial correlations among the prices suggest that the fast-food price coefficient is overstated in absolute value in the first model and understated in the second model. To be specific, let P_1 be the price per calorie of food consumed at home (excluding fruits and vegetables), let P_2 be the price of fast food, let P_3 be the price of fruits and vegetables, and let Y be PBF or BMI. Suppose that the correct specification is $Y = \alpha_1 P_1 + \alpha_2 P_2 + \alpha_3 P_3$, $\alpha_1 < 0, \alpha_2 < 0, \alpha_3 > 0$. Note that a vector of other right-hand side variables, x, is suppressed. Our two empirical specifications are $Y = a_1 P_1 + a_2 P_2$ and $Y = b_2 P_2 + b_3 P_3$. Let E denote the expected value operator. Then $Ea_2 = \alpha_2 + \alpha_3 c_{32.1x}$ and $Eb_2 = \alpha_2 + \alpha_1 d_{12.3x}$, where $c_{32.1x}$ is the coefficient of P_2 in a regression of P_3 on P_1, P_2, and x; and $d_{12.3x}$ is the coefficient of P_2 in a regression of P_1 on P_2, P_3, and x. Our empirical results indicate that the coefficients from the price regressions, $c_{32.1x}$ and $d_{12.3x}$, are negative. A priori one might expect them to be positive if food prices move in the same direction. But it should be kept in mind that $c_{32.1x}$ and $d_{12.3x}$ are partial regression coefficients that hold a number of other variables constant including P_1 or P_3 and county and year dichotomous indicators.

13. We do not estimate separate regressions by gender, race, and income because the resulting estimates would be based on a small number of observations in each group.

14. Lee's data are at the census-track level, but it is not clear how many tracts are represented.

REFERENCES

Alhabeeb, M. J. 1996. "Teenagers' Money, Discretionary Spending and Saving." *Financial Counseling and Planning* 7: 123–132.

Allison, D. B., S. K. Zhu, M. Plankey, M. S. Faith, and M. Heo. 2002. "Differential associations of Body Mass Index and Adiposity with All-Cause Mortality Among Men in the

First and Second National Health and Nutrition Examination Surveys (NHANES I and NHANES II) Follow-Up Studies." *International Journal of Obesity* 26(3): 410–416.

Auld, M. C., and L. M. Powell. 2009. "Economics of Food Energy Density and Adolescent Body Weight." *Economica* 76(304): 719–740.

Becker, G. S., and C. B. Mulligan. 1997. "The Endogenous Determination of Time Preference." *Quarterly Journal of Economics* 112(3): 729–758.

Björntorp, P. 2001. "Do Stress Reactions Cause Abdominal Obesity and Comorbidities?" *Obesity Reviews* 2(2): 73–86.

Boileau, R. A. 1996. "Body Composition Assessment in Children and Youths." *Encyclopedia of Sports Medicine*. The Child and Adolescent Athlete, International Olympic Committee, vol. VI. Blackwell Science, Cambridge, MA: 523–537.

Boreham, C. A., J. Twisk, and J. Savage. 1997. "Physical Activity, Sports Participation, and Risk Factors in Adolescents." *Medicine and Science in Sports and Exercise* 29(6): 788–793.

Brownell, K., and T. R. Frieden. 2009. "Ounces of Prevention—The Public Policy Case for Taxes on Sugared Beverages." *New England Journal of Medicine* 360(18): 1805–1808.

Burkhauser, R. V., and J. Cawley. 2008. "Beyond BMI: The Value of More Accurate Measures of Fatness and Obesity in Social Science Research." *Journal of Health Economics* 27(2): 519–529.

Cameron, N., P. L. Griffiths, M. M. Wright, C. Blencowe, N. C. Davis, J. M. Pettifor, and S. N. Norris. 2004. "Regression Equations to Estimate Percentage Body Fat in African Prepubertal Children Aged 9 Y." *American Journal of Clinical Nutrition* 80(1): 70–75.

Cawley, J. 2010. "The Economics of Childhood Obesity." *Health Affairs* 29(3): 364–371.

Centers for Disease Control and Prevention. 2008. National Health and Nutrition Examination Survey 2003–2004. Documentation, Code-book, and Frequencies: Dual-Energy X-ray Absorptiometry. January. Available at: http://www.cdc.gov/nchs/data/nhanes/dxa/dxx_c.pdf.

Chou, S. Y., M. Grossman, and H. Saffer. 2004. "An Economic Analysis of Adult Obesity: Results from the Behavioral Risk Factor Surveillance System." *Journal of Health Economics* 23(3): 565–587.

Chou, S. Y., I. Rashad, and M. Grossman. 2008. "Fast-Food Restaurant Advertising on Television and Its Influence on Childhood Obesity." *Journal of Law & Economics* 51(4): 599–618.

Chumlea, W. C., S. S. Guo, R. J. Kuczmarski, K. M. Flegal, C. L. Johnson, S. B. Heymsfield, H. C. Lukaski, K. Friedl, and V. S. Hubbard. 2002. "Body Composition Estimates from NHANES III Bioelectrical Impedance Data." *International Journal of Obesity* 26(12): 1596–1609.

Conti, G., and J. J. Heckman. 2012. "The Economics of Child Well-Being." In: National Bureau of Economic Research Working Paper No. 18466.

Daniels, S. R. 2006. "The Consequences of Childhood Overweight and Obesity." *The Future of Children* 16(1): 47–67.

Daniels, S. R., P. R. Khoury, and J. A. Morrison. 1997. "The Utility of Body Mass Index as a Measure of Body Fatness in Children and Adolescents: Differences by Race and Gender." *Pediatrics* 99(6): 804–807.

Dietz, W. H. 1998. "Health Consequences of Obesity in Youth: Childhood Predictors of Adult Disease." *Pediatrics* 101(3 Pt 2): 518–525.

Eisenkölbl, J., M. Kartasurya, and K. Widhalm. 2001. "Underestimation of Percentage Fat Mass Measured by Bioelectrical Impedance Analysis Compared to Dual Energy X-Ray Absorptiometry Method in Obese Children." *European Journal of Clinical Nutrition* 55(6): 423–429.

Eisenmann, J. C., K. A. Heelan, and G. J. Welk. 2004. "Assessing Body Composition Among 3- to 8-Year-Old Children: Anthropometry, BIA, and DXA." *Obesity Research* 12(10): 1633–1640.

Elberg, J., J. R. McDuffie, N. G. Sebring, et al. 2004. "Comparison of Methods to Assess Change in Children's Body Composition." *The American Journal of Clinical Nutrition* 80(1): 64–69.

Engelhard, C., A. Garson, and S. Dorn. 2009. *Reducing Obesity: Policy Strategies from the Tobacco Wars.* Washington, DC: The Urban Institute.

Flegal, K. M., M. D. Carroll, B. K. Kitt, and C. L. Ogden. 2012. "Prevalence of Obesity and Trends in the Distribution of Body Mass Index Among US Adults." *Journal of the American Medical Association* 307(5): 491–497.

Fletcher, J. M., D. E. Frisvold, and N. Tefft. 2010. "The Effects of Soft Drink Taxes on Child and Adolescent Consumption and Weight Outcomes." *Journal of Public Economics* 94(11–12): 967–974.

Forbes, A. 1999. "Body Composition: Influence of Nutrition, Physical Activity, Growth and Aging." In *Modern Nutrition in Health and Disease*, 9th ed. Baltimore: Williams and Wilkins: 789–809.

Freedman, D. S., W. H. Dietz, S. R. Srinivasan, and G. S. Berenson. 1999. "The Relation of Overweight to Cardiovascular Risk Factors Among Children and Adolescents: The Bogalusa Heart Study." *Pediatrics* 103(6 Pt 1): 1175–1182.

Freedman, D., Z. Mei, S. Srinivasan, G. Berenson, and W. Dietz. 2007. "Cardiovascular Risk Factors and Excess Adiposity Among Overweight Children and Adolescents: The Bogalusa Heart Study." *Journal of Pediatrics* 150(1): 12–17.e2.

Frisard, M. I., F. L. Greenway, and J. P. Delany. 2005. "Comparison of Methods to Assess Body Composition Changes During a Period of Weight Loss." *Obesity Research* 13(5): 845–854.

Genant, H. K., K. Engelke, T. Fuerst, C-C. Güer, S. Grampp, S. T. Harris, M. Jergan, T. Lang, Y. Lu, S. Majumdar, A. Mathur, and M. Takada. 1996. "Noninvasive Assessment of Bone Mineral and Structure: State of The Art." *Journal of Bone and Mineral Research* 11(6): 707–730.

Gorber, S., M. Connor Tremblay, D. Moher, and B. Gorber. 2007. "A Comparison of Direct Vs. Self-Report Measures for Assessing Height, Weight, and Body Mass Index: A Systematic Review." *Obesity Reviews* 8(4): 307–326.

Grossman, M. 2005. "Individual Behaviors and Substance Use: The Role of Price." In *Substance Use: Individual Behaviors, Social Interactions, Markets and Politics*, Volume 16, of Advances in Health Economics and Health Services Research, ed. B. Lindgren and M. Grossman. Elsevier, Amsterdam: 15–39.

Grossman, M., and N. Mocan. 2011. "The Obesity Epidemic: Causes and Current Policy Perspectives." Baker Institute Policy Report, vol. 46. Rice University: James A. Baker III Institute for Public Policy: 1–11.

Grossman, M., E. Tekin, and R. Wadea. 2012. "Fast-Food Restaurant Advertising on Television and Its Influence on Youth Body Composition." In National Bureau of Economic Research Working Paper No. 18640, December.

Heitmann, B. L., H. Erikson, B. M. Ellsinger, K. L. Mikkelsen, and B. Larsson. 2000. "Mortality Associated with Body Fat, Fat-Free Mass and Body Mass Index Among 60-Year-Old Swedish Men–A 22-Year Follow-Up: The Study of Men Born in 1913." *International Journal of Obesity* 24(1): 33–37.

Hill, J. O., V. A. Catenacci, and H. R. Wyatt. 2006. "Obesity: Etiology." In *Modern Nutrition in Health and Disease*, 9th ed., ed. M. Shils et al. Baltimore: Williams and Wilkins: 1013–1028.

Institute of Medicine, 2004. *Preventing Childhood Obesity: Health in the Balance.* Washington, DC: National Academies Press.

Johansson, E., P. Böckerman, U. Kiiskinen, M. Heliövaara. 2009. "Obesity and Labour Market Success in Finland: The Difference Between Having a High BMI and Being Fat." *Economics and Human Biology* 7(1): 36–45.

Kushner, R. F., A. Kunigk, M. Alspaugh, P. T. Andronia, C. A. Leitch, and D. A. Schoeller. 1990. "Validation of Bioelectrical-Impedance Analysis as a Measurement of Change in Body Composition in Obesity." *American Journal of Clinical Nutrition* 52(2): 219–223.

Lakdawalla, D., and T. Philipson. 2002. "The Growth of Obesity and Technological Change: A Theoretical and Empirical Examination." In National Bureau of Economic Research Working Paper No. 8946.

Lazzer, S., G. Bedogni, F. Agosti, A. De Col, D. Mornati, and A. Sartorio. 2008. "Comparison of Dual Energy X-Ray Absorptiometry, Air Displacement Plethysmography and Bioelectrical Impedance Analysis for the Assessment of Body Composition in Severely Obese Caucasian Children and Adolescents." *British Journal of Nutrition* 100(4): 918–924.

Lee, H. 2012. "The Role of Local Food Availability in Explaining Obesity Risk Among Young School-Aged Children." *Social Science & Medicine* 74(8): 1193–1203.

Mocan, N. H., and E. Tekin. 2011. "Obesity, Self-Esteem and Wages." In *Economic Aspects of Obesity*, ed. M. Grossman and N. Mocan. University of Chicago Press: 349–380.

National Center for Health Statistics. 2008. Technical Documentation for the 1999–2004 Dual Energy X-Ray Absorptiometry (DXA) Multiple Imputation Data File. http://www.cdc.gov/nchs/data/nhanes/dxa/ dxa_techdoc.pdf.

National Institute of Diabetes and Digestive and Kidney Diseases. 2006. Weight Control Information Network. http://win.niddk.nih.gov/publications/understanding.htm#distribution.

National Institutes of Health. 1994. "Bioelectrical Impedance Analysis in Body Composition Measurement." In National Institutes of Health Technology Assessment Conference Statement, December 12–14. http://consensus.nih.gov/1994/1994Bioelectic ImpedanceBody-ta015PDF.pdf.

Njeh, C. F., T. Fuerst, D. Hans, G. M. Blake, and H. K. Genant. 1999. "Radiation Exposure in Bone Mineral Density Assessment." *Applied Radiation and Isotopes* 50(1): 215–236.

Ogden, C. L., and M. Carroll. 2010a. "Prevalence of Obesity Among Children and Adolescents: United States, Trends 1963–1965 Through 2007–2008." National Center for Health Statistics, Centers for Disease Control and Prevention.

Ogden, C. L., M. D. Carroll, L. R. Curtin, M. M. Lamb, and K. M. Flegal. 2010b. "Prevalence of High Body Mass Index in US Children and Adolescents, 2007–2008." *JAMA: The Journal of the American Medical Association* 303(3): 242–249.

Ogden, C. L., M. D. Carroll, B. K. Kit, and K. M. Flegal. 2012. "Prevalence of Obesity and Trends in Body Mass Index Among US Children and Adolescents, 1999–2010." *Journal of the American Medical Association* 307(5): 483–490.

Okasora, K., R. Takaya, M. Tokuda, Y. Fukunaga, T. Oguni, H. Tanaka, K. Konishi, and H. Tamai. 1999. "Comparison of Bioelectrical Impedance Analysis and Dual Energy X-Ray Absorptiometry for Assessment of Body Composition in Children." *Pediatrics International* 41(2): 121–125.

Powell, L. M. 2009. "Fast Food Costs and Adolescent Body Mass Index: Evidence from Panel Data." *Journal of Health Economics* 28(5): 963–970.

Powell, L. M., and F. J. Chaloupka. 2009. "Food Prices and Obesity: Evidence and Policy Implications for Taxes and Subsidies." *Milbank Quarterly* 87(1): 229–257.

Powell, L. M., F. J. Chaloupka, and Y. Bao. 2007. "The Availability of Fast-Food and Full-Service Restaurants in the United States: Associations with Neighborhood Characteristics." *American Journal of Preventative Medicine* 33(4 Suppl.): S240-S245.

Powell, L. M., J. Chriqui, and F. J. Chaloupka. 2009. "Associations Between State-Level Soda Taxes and Adolescent Body Mass Index." *Journal of Adolescent Health* 45(3): S57-S63.

Powell, L. M., J. Chriqui, T. Khan, R. Wada, and F. Chaloupka. 2013. "Assessing the Potential Effectiveness of Food and Beverage Taxes and Subsidies for Improving Public Health: A Systematic Review of Prices, Demand and Weight Outcomes." *Obesity Reviews* 14(2): 110–128.

Powell, L. M., B. T. Nguyen, and E. Han. 2012. "Energy Intake from Restaurants: Demographics and Socioeconomics, 2003–2008." *American Journal of Preventive Medicine* 43(5): 498–504.

Powell, L. M., and B. Yanjun. 2007. "Food Prices, Access to Food Outlets and Child Weight Outcomes." Presented at the Seventh World Congress of the International Health Economics Association, Copenhagen, Denmark.

Rashad, I., S.-Y. Chou, and M. Grossman. 2006. "The Super Size of America: An Economic Estimation of Body Mass Index and Obesity in Adults." Eastern Economic Journal 32(1, Winter): 133–148.

Romero-Corral, A., V. M. Montori, V. K. Somers, J. Korinek, R. J. Thomas, T. G. Allison, F. Mookadam, and F. Lopez-Jimenez. 2006. "Association of Bodyweight with Total Mortality and with Cardiovascular Events in Coronary Artery Disease: A Systematic Review of Cohort Studies." *The Lancet* 368(9536): 666–678.

Romero-Corral, A., V. K. Somers, J. Sierra-Johnson, M. D. Jensen, R. J. Thomas, R. W. Squires, T. J. Allison, J. Korinek, and F. Lopez-Jimenez. 2007. "Diagnostic Performance of Body Mass Index to Detect Obesity with Coronary Artery Disease." *European Heart Journal* 28(17): 2087–2093.

Roubenoff, R., G. E. Dalla, and P. W. Wilson. 1995. "Predicting Body Fatness: The Body Mass Index vs. Estimation by Bioelectrical Impedance." *American Journal of Public Health* 85(8 Pt): 1063.

Rowland, M. L. 1989. "Reporting Bias in Height and Weight Data." *Statistical Bulletin* 70(2): 2–11.

Serdula, M. K., D. Ivery, R. Coates, D. S. Freedman, D. F. Williamson, and T. Byers. 1993. "Do Obese Children Become Obese Adults? A Review of the Literature." *Preventive Medicine* 22(2): 167–177.

Skybo, T., and N. Ryan-Wenger. 2003. "Measures of Overweight Status in School-Age Children." *The Journal of School Nursing* 19(3): 172–180.

Smalley, K. J., A. N. Knerr, Z. V. Kendrick, J. A. Colliver, and O. E. Owen. 1990. "Reassessment of Body Mass Indices." *American Journal of Clinical Nutrition* 52(3): 405–408.

Strauss, R. S. 2000. "Childhood Obesity and Self-Esteem." *Pediatrics* 105(1): e15.

Sturm, R., and A. Datar. 2005. "Body Mass Index in Elementary School Children, Metropolitan Area Food Prices and Food Outlet Density." *Public Health* 119(12): 1059–1068.

Sun, G., C. R. French, G. R. Martin, B. Younghusband, R. C. Green, Y. G. Xie, M. Mathews, J. R. Barron, D. G. Fitzpatrick, W. Gulliver, and H. Zhang. 2005. "Comparison of Multifrequency Bioelectrical Impedance Analysis with Dual-Energy X-Ray Absorptiometry for Assessment of Percentage Body Fat in a Large, Healthy Population." *American Journal of Clinical Nutrition* 81(1): 74–78.

Tylavsky, F., T. Lohman, B. A. Blunt, D. A. Schoeller, T. Fuerst, J. A. Cauley, M. C. Nevitt, M. Visser, and T. B. Harris. 2003. "QDR 4500A DXA Overestimates Fat-Free Mass Compared with Criterion Methods." *Journal of Applied Physiology* 94(3): 959–965.

U.S. Department of Health and Human Services. 2010. *Healthy People 2020.* HHS announces the nation's new health promotion and disease prevention agenda. Press release: http://www.healthypeople.gov/2020/about/DefaultPressRelease.pdf.

Wada, R. 2007. "Obesity and Physical Fitness in the Labor Market." PhD Dissertation. Andrew Young School of Policy Studies, Georgia State University

Wada, R., and E. Tekin. 2010. "Body Composition and Wages," *Economics and Human Biology* 8(2): 242–254.

Wahner, H. W., and I.Fogelman. 1994. *The Evaluation of Osteoporosis: Dual Energy X-ray Absorptiometry in Clinical Practice.* London: Martin Dunitz Ltd.

Wang, G., and W. H. Dietz. 2002. "Economic Burden of Obesity in Youths Aged 6 to 17 Years: 1979–1999." *Pediatrics* 109(5): e81-e86.

Widhalm, K., K. Schönegger, C. Huemer and A. Auterith. 2001. "Does the BMI Reflect Body Fat in Obese Children and Adolescents? A Study Using the TOBEC Method." *International Journal of Obesity* 25(2): 279–285.

World Health Organization. 1994. *Assessment of fracture risk and its application to screening for post menopausal osteoporosis.* Report of a WHO study group. World Health Organ Technical Report Series 843: 1–129.

Wong, W. W., A. C. Hergenroeder, J. E. Stuff, N. F. Butte, E. O. Smith, and K. JU. Ellis. 2002. "Evaluating Body Fat in Girls and Female Adolescents: Advantages and Disadvantages of Dual-Energy X-Ray Absorptiometry." *American Journal of Clinical Nutrition* 76(2): 384–389.

Yusuf, S., S. Hawken, S. Ounpuu, L. Bautista, M-G. Franzosi, P. Commerford, C. C. Lang, Z. Rumboldt, C. L. Onen, L. Lisheng, S. Tanomsup, P. Wangai Jr., F. Razak, A. M. Sharma, and S. S. Anand. 2004. "Effect of Potentially Modifiable Risk Factors Associated with Myocardial Infarction in 52 Countries (The INTERHEART Study): A Case-Control Study." *The Lancet* 364(9438): 937–952.

Yusuf, S., S. Hawken, S. Ounpuu, L. Bautista, M-G. Franzosi, P. Commerford, C. C. Lang, Z. Rumboldt, C. L. Onen, L. Lisheng, S. Tanomsup, P. Wangai Jr., F. Razak, A. M. Sharma, S. S. Anand, and INTERHEART Study Investigators. 2005. "Obesity and the Risk of Myocardial Infarction in 27,000 Participants from 52 Countries: A Case-Control Study." *The Lancet* 366(9497): 1640–1649.

Zhang, Q., S. Jones, C. J. Ruhm, and M. Andrews. 2013. "Higher Food Prices May Threaten Food Security Status Among American Low–Income Households with Children." *Journal of Nutrition* 143: 1659–1665.

Afterword to Part 4

$\mathbf{M}$y three cartoon friends and I suspect many other people, including a number of economists, have been greatly surprised by the emergence of the economics of unhealthy behaviors as a major subfield of health economics during the past four decades. Not only have health economists applied their tools to the determinants of these behaviors, but they also have studied their consequences on such labor market outcomes as completed schooling, hours worked, wage rates, and earnings. The very significant interest in this area is reflected in part by two very recent, comprehensive, and detailed survey papers (Cawley and Ruhm 2012; Cawley 2015). Given these two papers and my focus on determinants, I emphasize key contributions in areas that are most closely related to the ten papers included in this part of the book. I also emphasize new and promising research issues in these areas that excite me.

I coauthored two studies that found very large price elasticities of demand for cigarettes: −1.40 for teenagers and −0.75 for people of all ages (mainly adults). Have these estimates stood the test of time? Not surprisingly, the answer is no. Most studies that followed my two reported smaller elasticities. John Cawley and Christopher J. Ruhm (2012) report an average price elasticity of −1.09 for teenagers and young adults based on thirty studies and an average price elasticity of −0.40 for people of all ages (mainly adults) based on 155 studies.[1] Despite these differences, almost all of the studies that followed mine support the important conclusions that the demand function for cigarettes slopes downward and that teenagers are more sensitive to price than adults.

Because most individuals who smoke consume a large number of ciga-rettes, the decision to participate in this behavior is a key outcome on which to focus. At young ages, participation mainly reflects the decision to start smoking. Jonathan Gruber and Jonathan Zinman (2001) report a smoking participation price elasticity of −0.67 for high school seniors. Donna B. Gilleskie and Kole-man S. Strumpf (2005) and Christopher Carpenter and Philip J. Cook (2008) estimate this price elasticity as −0.41 and −0.56, respectively, for teenagers. These estimates are smaller than my figure of −1.20 but are still substantial.

Few adults decide to begin to smoke, so the decision to quit smoking is a key outcome at older ages. Stratford Douglas (1998) finds that quit decisions by adult smokers are positively related to the price of cigarettes. I did not consider this outcome in the two cigarette smoking papers in this section, but I did treat the decision to quit smoking by pregnant women in a paper with Greg Colman and Ted Joyce (Colman, Grossman, and Joyce 2003). This is a particularly important decision because smoking by these women accounts for one in five low-weight babies and is the most important modifiable risk factor for poor pregnancy out-comes. Based on smoking status three months prior to conception and three months prior to delivery, we find that a 10 percent increase in price increases the probability that a pregnant woman quits smoking by 10 percent. We estimate that a 30-cent increase in the tax on a package of cigarettes would have the same effect on quit rates as enrolling women in prenatal smoking cessation programs.

Michael J. Moore (1996) and Sara Markowitz (2014) provide even more dramatic evidence of the responsiveness of some of the most serious conse-quences of smoking to taxes. Moore (1996) finds that state cigarette excise tax increases lead to decreases in mortality due to heart disease, cancer, and asthma. Markowitz (2014) reports that increases in state excise tax rates on cigarettes are associated with fewer fires caused by smoking and injuries and deaths resulting from cigarette fires.

Perhaps it is inevitable that some very recent research has questioned what has become the conventional wisdom concerning the downward slope of the cigarette demand function. Kevin Callison and Robert Kaestner (2014) find that for adults the association between state tax hikes and either smoking partici-pation or smoking intensity is negative, small, or not statistically significant. Benjamin Hansen, Joseph J. Sabia, and Daniel I. Rees (2017) report similar results for teenagers. This evidence is contradicted in research for adults by Chad Cotti, Erik Nesson, and Nathan Tefft (2016) and by Johanna Catherine Maclean, Asia Sikora Kessler, and Donald S. Kenkel (2016). A similar con-tradiction in research for teenagers is reported by Jidong Huang and Frank J.

Chaloupka IV (2012). Clearly, a reconciliation of these results should be placed on an agenda for future research.

Studies that focus on Electronic Nicotine Delivery Systems (ENDS), of which e-cigarettes constitute the most common subproduct, deserve an even more prominent position on an agenda for future research. ENDS are a non-combustible alternative to smoking. As opposed to smoking cigarettes, the use of ENDS, termed vaping, delivers nicotine to the user without exposing that person to tar—the substance in cigarettes responsible for most of its harm. Only recently introduced into the U.S. market, ENDS have been aggressively pro-moted, and use is increasing rapidly among both adults and youths. This has generated an extremely contentious policy debate concerning the regulation of ENDS. At the heart of this regulatory debate are fundamental questions regard-ing whether ENDS will draw cigarette smokers away from a dangerous habit or lure new initiates into tobacco use and lead to a new generation of nicotine addicts. Although ENDS are not a completely safe alternative to cigarettes, in April 2016 the Royal College of Physicians (2016) in Great Britain issued a report urging smokers to switch to ENDS. A few weeks later, the European Court of Justice, Europe's highest court, found that the European Union had the right to regulate ENDS including banning advertising (Jolly 2016). At approx-imately the same time, the U.S. Food and Drug Administration (2016), which was given the authority to regulate ENDS by the 2009 Family Protection and Tobacco Control Act, announced regulations that would ban the sale of ENDS products to minors at the national level and would require all ENDS products that were not commercially marketed prior to February 15, 2007, to gain FDA approval. ENDS advertisements were not banned on television, but the approval process can be quite lengthy. Thus it has the potential to eliminate many current producers and result in significant price increases.

From an economics research perspective, the key issue is whether ENDS and cigarettes are substitutes or complements. They are substitutes if an increase in the price of ENDS, or the enactment of a regulation that makes it more dif-ficult to acquire the product (for example, a minimum purchase age law), or that bans its advertising, increases the demand for cigarettes. The two goods are complements if the reverse holds. Proponents of the policies being pursued by the FDA and by the European Union assume that ENDS and cigarettes are complements, whereas proponents of the recommendations made by the Royal College of Surgeons assume they are substitutes. Yet almost nothing is known about this issue. Abigail S. Friedman (2015) and Michael F. Pesko, Jenna M. Hughes, and Fatima S. Faisal (2016) find that state bans on ENDS sales to minors raise smoking rates among youths ages twelve to seventeen in two dif-ferent datasets. These studies do not use recent data, do not examine the effects of advertising, and do not verify that the use of ENDS was affected in states with higher minimum purchase age laws. In addition, they obviously do not deal with the behavior of adult smokers.

Given the gaps in this literature, Dhaval Dave, Henry Saffer, Donald S. Kenkel, Gregory Colman, Michael Pesko, and I have begun the first comprehensive analyses of the extent to which advertising of ENDS in magazines and on TV (constituting almost 90 percent of media ad spending), and ads in social media affects patterns of ENDS use among both adults and youths, as well as transitions between ENDS use and smoking behaviors, including initiation, cessation, and relapse among former smokers. In addition, we will examine the effects of ENDS prices, cigarette taxes, and other regulatory variables on the demand for ENDS and on transitions to and from other nicotine products. Our research, which is funded by a grant from the National Institute on Drug Abuse to the National Bureau of Economic Research and which began in March 2016, employs six large-scale national datasets.

Alcohol and cigarettes are not linked to adverse health outcomes in the same way. There is overwhelming evidence that smoking has detrimental health effects. One can usually focus on whether and how much an individual smokes because these measures are highly correlated with the smoking-related costs of interest. With alcohol, the situation is more complex. Unlike cigarettes, many people regularly consume small quantities of alcohol. Most individuals who consume alcohol do not harm themselves or others; indeed, moderate alcohol consumption has been shown to lower the risk of coronary heart disease in men. Instead, the adverse effects of alcohol spring from the overuse or misuse of this substance. Examples include cirrhosis of the liver, drunk driving crashes, workplace accidents, various forms of violent behavior, risky sexual behavior, and failure to complete college.

Given these complexities, it is notable that studies conducted in the 1990s and early 2000s find that the overuse of alcohol and its negative consequences fall as the cost of alcohol rises.[2] These include consumption of five or more drinks in a row on a single occasion (termed binge drinking) or the number of days in a specified period in which an individual engaged in that behavior (Kenkel 1993;Cook and Moore 2001); cirrhosis mortality (Saffer 1991); workplace accidents (Ohsfeldt and Morrissey 1997); violent crime (Cook and Moore 1993b); spouse abuse (Markowitz 2000); failure to complete college (Cook and Moore 1993a); and sexually transmitted diseases (Chesson, Harrison, and Kassler 2000).

Not all of the evidence is supportive. For example, Thomas S. Dee (1999) and Dee and William N. Evans (2001) report that the negative effects of the state excise tax on beer on youth drinking and motor vehicle accident mortality disappear or become implausibly large once state fixed effects and state-specific time trends are included as regressors. Their findings can be attributed to the relative stability of the beer tax within states over time. Therefore, it is difficult to distinguish the effects of the beer tax from that of unobserved state effects, some of which may vary over time (for example, overall drinking sentiment).

Sara Markowitz, Erik Nesson, Eileen Poe-Yamagata, Curtis Florence, Partha Deb, Tracy Andrews, and Sarah Beth L. Barnett (2014) confront this problem in their recent study of the effects of the cost of alcohol in criminal victimization. They employ data in a time period in which state taxes on all three types of alcoholic beverages were very stable. This rules out the inclusion of state fixed effects as regressors. Their solution is to employ the price of beer contained in data collected by the Council for Community and Economic Research (C2ER and formerly known as the American Chamber of Commerce Research Association, https://www.c2er.org/). That source also contains wine prices and before 2005 distilled spirits prices. It has been criticized, however, for relying on a single beer, wine, or distilled spirits product with only a few observations per city (Ruhm, Jones, McGeary, Kerr, Terza, Greenfield, and Pandian 2012; Markowitz and colleagues 2014). Given these issues, Markowitz and colleagues interpret their results with caution. They do find negative effects of the beer price on alcohol or drug-related assault victimizations. In most cases, however, the effects are only statistically significant at the 10 percent level.

Given the issues just discussed, I am very excited by two recent developments that will facilitate new research on the effects of the cost of alcohol on a variety of outcomes. One is the occurrence of two extremely large increases in state alcohol excise tax rates: one in Illinois in 2009 and the other in Washington /state in 2012. The second is the emergence of the Nielsen Retail Scanner Data as an alternative source of alcohol beverage prices (https://research.chicagobooth. edu/nielsen/datasets/scanner-data.aspx). This source covers more than 35,000 retail outlets in fifty-two U.S. markets in forty-two states from 2006 to the present. It includes the product purchased, the quantity purchased, and the value of the transaction. This allows for construction of precise information on units sold and prices. I give examples of the type of research that can be undertaken as part of my discussion of new research on obesity and rational addiction below.

In the area of the determinants of the consumption of unhealthy food and obesity, I refer the reader to the detailed surveys of this literature by Cawley and Ruhm (2012) and by Cawley (2015). Instead, I want to call your attention to two brand new papers that have greatly stimulated me and to a very promising area for new research. The papers are by Charles J. Courtemanche, Joshua C. Pinkston, Christopher J. Ruhm and George Wehby (2016) and by Charles J. Courtemanche, Rusty Tchernis, and Benjamin Ukert (2016). Both confirm results in my study of the factors accounting for the rapid increase in BMI and obesity in the United States since 1980 with Shin-Yi Chou and Henry Saffer (Chou, Grossman, and Saffer 2004, the eighth paper in this section). My colleagues and I explored this issue in the Behavioral Risk Factor Surveillance System (BRFSS). We augmented these individual-level surveys with state-specific variables for the period from 1984 through 1999. Courtemanche, Pinkston, Ruhm, and Wehby (2016) studied the same issue in the BRFSS for the period from 1990 through 2010 and with a more detailed approach to account for the effects of unmeasured variables. They also extend our analysis by considering class II/III obesity (BMI ≥35, also known as severe obesity) as an outcome and by estimating effects at various quantiles of the BMI distribution. After controlling for demographic characteristics and state and year fixed effects, they find that changes in state-level economic variables account for approximately 40 percent of the rise in BMI and obesity, 60 percent of the increase in severe obesity, and half of the rise in the 90th percentile of BMI. Within this set, Courtemanche and colleagues report that variables related to caloric intake, especially restaurant and very large discount grocery store densities, are the main sources of the rapid rise in obesity in the United States since 1990.

The set of variables that Courtemanche and colleagues find to be important in explaining trends in obesity is similar to the set that my colleagues and I found to be important. Moreover, although we did not consider discount grocery store density, we found that restaurant density was the key driver in explaining trends in our sample period. In turn, the growth in restaurants and large supermarkets can be traced to attempts to economize on what may be termed the ultimate scarce resource—the own time of the consumer. The findings by Courtemanche and colleagues of large effects among the heaviest individuals are especially powerful because they highlight the key relevance of economics in an area that in the past was reserved for other disciplines.

In our 2004 study, Chou, Saffer, and I found that an increase in the price of cigarettes was associated with an increase in obesity. We explained that finding because smokers tend to gain weight when they reduce the number of cigarettes smoked or quit this behavior altogether. Jonathan Gruber and Michael Frakes (2006) and Charles Courtemanche (2009) show, however, that this finding is sensitive to alternative specifications. In a fascinating new study, Courtemanche, Tchernis, and Ukert (2016) use randomized treatment assignment as an instrument for smoking and estimate that quitting this behavior leads to a long-run average weight gain of 1.5–1.7 BMI units or 11–12 pounds at the average height. These magnitudes are significantly larger than those in studies that do not account for the endogeneity of smoking. Their results imply that the reduction in smoking accounts for 14 percent of the increase in obesity in recent decades.

The findings by Courtemanche and colleagues in the two studies just discussed as well as those in the study by Saffer, Chou, and me underscore the idea that public policy can have unintended consequences. Oftentimes, there is a trade-off involving goals that society favors such as more workforce participation by women and fewer smokers. Expanded workforce participation by women has increased families' command over real resources and increased equality of opportunity. At the same time, the value of time has risen, which has promoted the growth of restaurants and large discount grocery stores. Cigarette smoking is still the largest cause of premature death, and excise tax hikes and other policies to reduce this behavior have obvious health benefits. But these policies also may lead to an increase in obesity.

The imposition of higher and in some cases new taxes on soda is receiving a considerable amount of attention as a method to reduce obesity. For example, in June 2016, Philadelphia imposed a tax of 1.5 cents for every ounce of sugary drink sold by distributors. It amounts to a tax of approximately 30 cents for a 20-ounce drink or $2.16 for a twelve-pack, which typically sells for between $3 and $6 at the retail level. If the tax is fully passed on to consumers, the price hike will be enormous. Although the impacts on consumption potentially are quite large, Philadelphia residents can travel to nearby parts of the state or to New Jersey or Delaware to purchase soda. Along the same lines, a tax enacted by one state should have smaller effects on consumption than a tax enacted by the United States as a whole because residents of the state that enacted the tax who live near border states can travel to those states to purchase soda.

Previous research on the effects of taxes on soft drinks in the United States provides little guidance for predicting the effects of the imposition of such a large tax (see, for example, Fletcher, Frisvold, and Tefft 2010a, 2010b). This research, which typically finds no impacts of taxes on consumption or weight outcomes, relies primarily on whether or not purchases of soda are subject to or exempt from retail sales taxes. Some states of exempt purchases of food from such a tax, and others include it. Of those states that exempt food, some states require that soda be taxed. In a model with state and time fixed effects, soda tax effects are estimated from small within-state changes in retail taxes over time, combined with differences in the way in which soda is treated in the food exemption. Hence, variations in the tax are small, resulting in little power to detect effects.

The situation would be very different if a state imposed a tax as large as the one being considered by Philadelphia. The experience in Mexico is an example. In January 2014, Mexico imposed a 1 peso per liter sales tax on sugar-sweetened beverages. If fully shifted to consumers, the tax would amount to a roughly 10 percent price increase on soft drinks. M. Arantxa Colchero, Juan Carlos Salgado, Mishel Unar-Munguía, Mariana Molina, Shuwen Ng, and Juan Angel

Rivera-Dommarco (2015) find that full-shifting actually did occur. Colchero, Barry M. Popkin, Juan A. Rivera, and Shu Weng Ng (2016) report that the imposition of the tax lowered purchases of taxed beverages by an average of 6 percent in the twelve months following its enactment, implying a short-run price elasticity of −0.60. The rate of decrease relative to pretax trends reached 12 percent in December of 2014, suggesting that the long-run impact of the tax may exceed 6 percent. Given the proclivity of U.S. states to enact tax policy in a nonuniform fashion, the Nielsen Retail Scanner Data could be used to evaluate the imposition of soda taxes by a subset of states, using difference-in-differences and synthetic control methodologies.[3]

The only paper in this section that deals with the demand for illegal drugs is the one by Frank J. Chaloupka and me on cocaine (Grossman and Chaloupka 1998, the seventh paper in this section.) I do not, however, want to give the reader the mistaken impression that the demand for illegal drugs is an unimportant issue in the economics of unhealthy behaviors. Indeed, it certainly is not the case that public policy has eradicated the use of cocaine, heroin, marijuana, and opium by making their consumption illegal, just as it has not eradicated underage drinking by making it illegal.

In addition to Chaloupka and me, a number of other investigators have verified that the law of the downward sloping demand function holds for illegal drugs. The U.S. investigators on whose research I focus compute prices based on purchases of cocaine, heroin, and marijuana made by drug enforcement agents to apprehend drug dealers as recorded in the System to Retrieve Information from Drug Evidence (STRIDE) maintained by the Drug Enforcement Administration (DEA) of the U.S. Department of Justice (*http://www.dea.gov/resource-center/stride-data.shtml*). Information on the date and city of purchase, its total cost, weight in grams, and purity as a fraction is recorded. For each purchase, the price of one pure gram of the substance in question is computed as total cost divided by the product of weight and purity. A year- and city-specific average of these prices has then been added to a number of datasets that contain measures of participation in the consumption of illegal drugs and in some cases the frequency of use.[4] Ilyana Kuziemko and Steven D. Levitt (2004) have found that increases in the prices within areas over time are positively related to the certainty of punishment, as measured by per capita drug offense arrests, and the severity of punishment, as measured by the fraction of drug arrests that result in the criminal's being sentenced to prison.

Studies published from 1999 through 2006 report cocaine participation price elasticities that range from −0.30 to −0.59 (Saffer and Chaloupka 1999; Dave 2006, 2008). The corresponding range for heroin participation price elasticities in these three studies is from −0.20 to −0.89. For marijuana, the price elasticities fall between −0.20 and −0.46 (Pacula, Grossman, Chaloupka, O'Malley, Johnston, and Farrelly 2001; Williams, Pacula, Chaloupka, and Wechsler 2004; Grossman 2005).

Most surveys of illegal drug use are deficient because the measures are self-reported and because certain groups of heavy users such as the homeless and criminals are excluded. Therefore, I want to call attention to Dave's 2006 and 2008 studies. In the first, he employs the rates of cocaine- and heroin-related hospital emergency department visits per capita as outcomes. In the second, he uses the percentage of arrestees testing positive for these substances based on urine analyses as outcomes. Clearly, these measures suffer from none of the deficiencies of those in household surveys. His estimated cocaine participation elasticities are −0.44 in the first study and −0.30 in the second. The corresponding heroin price elasticities are −0.31 and −0.20, respectively. Although these estimates are smaller than those reported by Saffer and Chaloupka, they certainly are not zero.

Todd Olmstead, Sheila M. Alessi, Brendan Kline, Rosalie Liccardo Pacula, and Nancy M. Petry (2015) present even more dramatic evidence of potentially large price elasticities for illegal drugs. They employ a highly novel and imaginative research design to estimate the price elasticity of demand for heroin in a sample of regular users. Their design has two components. In the first, longitudinal information about real-world heroin demand (actual price and actual quantity consumed at daily intervals for each user) is collected. Demand functions estimated with this component capitalize on random variation in the price over time that occurs in markets for illegal drugs. The second component employs experimentally induced variations in price and the resulting quantities that users indicate that they would consume. Quite remarkably, demand functions estimated in both components reveal that the conditional price elasticity of demand for heroin (the elasticity of consumption give participation) is approximately −0.80.

As a result of the 2012, 2014, and 2016 elections, eight U.S. states—Alaska, Oregon, Colorado, Washington, California, Massachusetts, Maine, and Nevada—legalized the use of marijuana for recreational purposes. Moreover, laws enacted by an additional twenty-four states since 1996 have legalized marijuana use for medical purposes. These developments have encouraged investigations of the impacts of these laws on marijuana use, alcohol use, and motor vehicle accident mortality. The laws reduce the price of marijuana, including the component that reflects fines and other penalties, and should lead to an increase in its use. They may reduce the use of alcohol if that substance and marijuana are substitutes, and they may increase the use of alcohol if the two substances are complements. If alcohol and marijuana are substitutes, they also have the potential to reduce motor vehicle accident mortality, because simulator and driver-course studies show that impairments due to alcohol increase the risk of a collision, whereas impairments due to the use of marijuana do not. Drivers under the influence of marijuana reduce their speed, avoid risky maneuvers, and increase "following distances." Drivers under the influence of alcohol behave in the opposite manner (Kelly, Darke, and Ross 2004; Sewell, Poling, and Sofuoglu 2009).

Using data from the period from 1990 through 2010, D. Mark Anderson, Benjamin Hansen, and Daniel I. Rees (2013) find that use of marijuana rose and alcohol-related traffic fatalities fell by 13 percent in the thirteen states that enacted medical marijuana laws during the sample period. At the same time, consumption of alcohol, including binge drinking, fell. These findings, which pertain to adults, are consistent with the notion that alcohol and marijuana are substitutes; reductions in the price of marijuana lead to increases in its use and reductions in the use of alcohol. The authors found no evidence that marijuana use by youths increased. In a subsequent paper using a larger dataset, the same authors again find no effect on use by teenagers (Anderson, Hansen, and Rees 2015).

Rosalie Liccardo Pacula, David Powell, Paul Heaton, and Eric Sevigny (2015) focus on policy differences among states that have adopted medical marijuana laws and analyze the effects of these laws on all outcomes considered in the studies just discussed. These dimensions include whether states require patient registry systems, whether states permit home cultivation, whether states legally allow dispensaries, and whether states make allowance for "pain" rather than only for specific medical conditions. They show that inclusion of these dimensions clouds the sharp results in the studies by Anderson, Hansen, and Rees. Pacula and her colleagues are unable to draw firm conclusions with regard to the effects of the laws on marijuana use, alcohol use, and alcohol-involved fatal crashes.

To complicate the picture even further, Heifei Wen, Jason M. Hockenberry, and Janet R. Cummings (2015) employ a dataset not used in previous studies and find that the enactment of medical marijuana laws is associated with an increase in the probability of use by youths and adults. Frequency of use and binge drinking increased among adults but not youths. I hope these disparate findings will be better understood as data for longer periods of time become available, which suggests that this is a very fruitful area for new research.

In addition to creating new research opportunities, I am optimistic that developments in the marijuana market will lead to renewed interest in evaluations of a regime in which the production and consumption of a number of currently banned substances are fully legal but their use is discouraged by taxation. Monetary taxes have been considered a poor substitute for a drug war because excise taxes have been assumed to be unable to reduce drug use by as much as a war on drugs. The argument is that producers could always choose to go "underground" and sell illegally if a monetary tax made legal prices higher than underground prices.

Gary S. Becker, Kevin M. Murphy, and I show, however, that the market price of cocaine with a monetary excise tax could be greater than the price induced by a war on drugs, even when producers could ignore the monetary tax and produce illegally underground (Becker, Murphy, and Grossman 2006). The reason is that the government could allocate resources to preventing production in the illegal market. In effect, it imposes a nonmonetary tax in this market whose expected value exceeds the tax in the legal market. In certain circumstances, we conclude that the threat of imposing a cost on illegal producers that is above the excise tax if they produce legally is sufficient to discourage illegal production. Hence, the threat does not have to be carried out on a large scale and is much less costly to implement than a war on drugs in a regime in which drugs are illegal.

Excise taxes imposed on producers or consumers of drugs play the same role in a regime in which drugs are legal as expected penalties imposed on producers and consumers when drugs are illegal. Both raise the full price of consumption and reduce the quantity demanded. But excise taxes are simply transfers, whereas penalties and efforts to enforce and evade them use real resources. Hence, social welfare potentially is greater in a regime in which drugs are legal and taxed. Tax revenue could be redistributed to the population in a lump sum fashion or used to fund drug treatment and prevention programs. In the long run, legalization might lead to a lower level of consumption than the present situation.

To address the problem of consumption by youths, legalization and taxation could be combined with minimum purchase age laws already in place for alcohol and cigarettes. Even if these laws are partially evaded, the higher money price of cocaine that might characterize the legalization regime might be a very powerful deterrent to youth consumption. Legalization eliminates the current expected penalty costs imposed on users. The latter costs are much higher for adults than youths because adults place a higher value on their time than youths and because youths are much more likely to heavily discount the future effects of their current decisions.

Hence, an increase in money price accompanied by the elimination of prison terms, community service, and the acquisition of a police record for possession would raise the full or effective price of drugs faced by youths even if this price falls for adults.

I conclude this afterword with some comments about rational addiction. I am sure that my three cartoon friends would have predicted that a topic with such an oxymoronic name would have withered and died by this time. That, however, has not happened, possibly because Gary S. Becker and Kevin M. Murphy are the best and second best economists, respectively, who I have had the privilege to know. In studies appearing after the three rational addiction papers in this section, José M, Labeaga (1999); Badi H. Baltagi and James M. Griffin (2001); José Julián Escario and Jose Alberto Molina (2001); and Aju J. Fenn, Frances Antonovitz, and John R. Schroeter (2001); and Lien Nguyen, Gunnar Rosenqvist, and Markku Pekurinen (2012) confirm the key predictions of the rational addiction model in the case of cigarettes. Baltagi and Griffin (2002) do the same in the case of alcohol. All five studies report negative current price effects, positive past and future consumption effects, and larger long-run than short-run price elasticities of demand.

More indirect evidence in support of rational addiction is available as well. Audrey Laporte, Alfia Karimova, and Brian Ferguson (2010) show that current consumption of cigarettes is more responsive to future consumption at lower quantiles of the current consumption distribution than at higher quantiles. On the other hand, current consumption is more responsive to past consumption at higher quantiles than at lower quantiles. These results are to be expected because heavier smokers are more addicted to this behavior and are likely to discount the future more heavily (to have higher rates of time preference for the present). Vinish Shrestha (2015) reports that the price elasticity of demand for alcohol is largest at the 90th quantile of the current consumption distribution. This supports two predictions of the rational addiction model. An increase in the degree of addiction should increase the price elasticity of demand, and the higher discount rates that characterize addictive consumers should make them more price sensitive. Charles J. Courtemanche, Garth Heutel, and Patrick McAlvanah (2015) present direct evidence of interactions between impatience (high discount factors) and incentives (price changes) in weight outcomes. They find that the body mass index of people around the age of forty-five who discount the future heavily based on survey responses is more sensitive to the price of food than the body mass index of other consumers.

Not everything has been "smooth sailing" for proponents of the rational addiction model. I myself have been involved in one study that does not support Shrestha's result of a larger price elasticity for heavier consumers of alcohol (Saffer, Dave, and Grossman 2016). Both studies employ data prior to the large alcohol excise tax hikes that occurred after 2008 and that were mentioned previously. Information for more recent years could be combined with the Nielsen Retail Scanner Data to resolve these conflicting findings.

The rapidly growing field of behavioral economics poses the most serious challenge to the rational addiction model. That is not surprising because economists in that field question many of the foundations that underlie rational decision making by utility maximizing consumers and profit maximizing firms (for example, Camerer, Lowenstein, and Rabin 2011). One of the first assumptions to be challenged is that of exponential discounting. That assumption, which plays an important role in rational addiction models, implies that individuals apply the same discount factor to consumption one period hence relative to today as they do to consumption two periods hence relative to one period hence. Behavioral economists argue that it is more reasonable to assume that individuals apply a smaller discount rate (a larger rate of time preference for the present) to consumption one period hence relative to today. Jonathan Gruber and Botond Köszegi (2001) show that a model with this aspect cannot be distinguished from a rational addiction model, although future price effects become smaller and the scope for government intervention becomes larger.

In contrast to the single agent decision-making process employed in rational economic models and some behavioral economic models with hyperbolic discounting, a more common model in behavioral economics contains a process characterized by more than one decision-making process. Most often, the latter model uses the analytically convenient fiction of two distinct neurological systems that act simultaneously to produce a single decision (for example, Kahneman and Frederick 2002; O'Donoghue and Rabin 1999, 2001; Bernheim and Rangel 2004). It emanates from neuroeconomics, a subfield of behavioral economics. These neurological systems have been given different labels such as system 1 and system 2 (Kahneman and Frederick 2002), but I will adopt terminology developed by Henry Saffer (see Saffer, Dave, and Grossman 2016) and refer to them as the heuristic system and the rational system. Prices are very relevant to the rational system but not to the heuristic system, which pays much more attention to external cues such as those provided by advertising. When consumption choices involving goods that are potentially harmful and addictive are made, the hedonic system is assumed to dominate the rational system for some individuals.

Until four or five years ago, I did not pay attention to the challenges to rational addiction posed by the neuroeconomics approach. This was mainly because empirical evidence in support of it typically takes the form of laboratory experiments with a small number of people that does not generalize to the population at large and introspection. But Henry Saffer—my former student, colleague, and very good friend—has been persistent in encouraging me (some might say demanding me) to rethink my position and to engage in research with him that would evaluate the empirical relevance of the two competing models. Our study of the demand for alcohol with Dave referred to above (Saffer, Dave, and Grossman 2016) is an example of that line of research. We do not confirm a prediction of the rational addiction model that heavier consumers of alcohol have a larger price elasticity of demand than lighter consumers, although problems with the price data previously discussed may be responsible for this finding. We do find that heavier drinkers are more responsive to advertising than lighter drinkers, which is in line with decisions made by the heuristic system. That result is, however, also consistent with a larger demand for the informational content of advertising by individuals who consume large quantities of the good in question.

Recently, Robert Kaestner—my former student, colleague, and very good friend—pointed out to me that when mistakes made by heuristic decision making become large, profit-making firms will see opportunities to offer solutions and share the benefits with consumers. This suggests that challenges posed to standard microeconomic frameworks posed by neuroeconomics may not be as serious as one may think. Bob always has very good insights and to some extent I agree with him. But I also agree with Henry that it is important to devise empirical tests that can distinguish between the two frameworks.

Here is one suggestion, which comes from the newly emerging field of genoeconomics (for example, Benjamin, Chabris, Glaeser, Gudnason, Harris, Laibson, Launer, and Purcell 2008). That field emphasizes interactions between genes and the environment in the determination of outcomes of interest to economists. Given evidence that future-oriented behavior is determined at least to some extent by genetic factors and that these factors are connected to addiction in other ways (for example, Benjamin et al. 2008; National Academy of Sciences 2010; Mitchell 2011; Saffer 2014), studies that pursue interactions between genes and prices in demand functions for addictive substances have, in my view, great promise.

To my knowledge, only two studies have addressed gene-price interactions. Both deal with cigarettes and present conflicting evidence. Jason D. Boardman (2009) shows that genetic influences on cigarette smoking by adolescents are weaker in states with higher cigarette excise tax rates. That is, the positive effect of genetic variants on smoking is weakened by higher taxes. This supports the rational model. On the other hand, Jason M. Fletcher (2012) finds that the negative effect of price on smoking is weaker in adults with a genetic predisposition toward this behavior. Boardman's study is based on one cross-sectional dataset, and Fletcher's is based on a short repeat cross section. Neither study controls for individual-specific fixed effects that may be correlated with taxes and smoking. Clearly, this is a fruitful area for new research, especially because a number of datasets, including the Health and Retirement Study conducted by the National Institute on Aging and the University of Michigan (*http://hrsonline.isr.umich.edu*), contain detailed genome-wide association measures.

NOTES

1. I average the elasticities that Cawley and Ruhm report separately for teenagers and young adults because each one, and especially the former, is based on a small number of studies.
2. See Cawley and Ruhm (2012) for a survey of estimates of the price elasticity of demand for alcohol.
3. See Joshua D. Angrist and Jörn-Steffen Pischke (2009) for the former methodology, and Alberto Abadie, Alexis Diamond, and Jens Hainmueller (2010) for the latter.
4. The computation of prices by city and year is more complicated than the procedure described in the text, and a different source is employed in two of the first two marijuana studies discussed below. See Grossman and Chaloupka (1998) and the marijuana studies for details.

REFERENCES

Abadie, Alberto, Alexis Diamond, and Jens Hainmueller. 2010. "Synthetic Control Methods for Comparative Case Studies: Estimating the Effect of California's Tobacco Control Program." *Journal of the American Statistical Association* 105(490): 493–505.

Anderson, D. Mark, Benjamin Hansen, and Daniel I. Rees. 2013. "Medical Marijuana Laws, Traffic Fatalities, and Alcohol Consumption." *Journal of Law and Economics* 56(2): 333–369.

Anderson, D. Mark, Benjamin Hansen, and Daniel I. Rees. 2015. "Medical Marijuana Laws and Teen Marijuana Use." *American Law and Economics Review* 17(2): 495–528.

Angrist, Joshua D., and Jörn-Steffen Pischke. 2009. *Mostly Harmless Econometrics*. Princeton, NJ: Princeton University Press.

Baltagi, Badi H., and James M. Griffin. 2001. "The Econometrics of Rational Addiction: The Case of Cigarettes." *Journal of Business and Economic Statistics* 19(4): 449–454.

Baltagi, Badi H., and James M. Griffin. 2002. "Rational Addiction to Alcohol: Panel Data Analysis of Liquor Consumption." *Health Economics* 11(6): 485–491.

Becker, Gary S., Kevin M. Murphy, and Michael Grossman. 2006. "The Market for Illegal Goods: The Case of Drugs." *Journal of Political Economy* 114(1): 38–60.

Benjamin, Daniel J., Christopher F. Chabris, Edward L. Glaeser, Vilmundur Gudnason, Tamura B. Harris, David I. Laibson, Lenore Launer, and Shaun Purcell. 2008. "Genoeconomics." In *Biosocial Surveys*, ed. Maxine Weinstein, James W. Vaupel, and Kenneth W. Wachter. Washington, DC: National Academies Press, 304–335.

Bernheim, Douglas, and Antonio Rangel. 2004. "Addiction and Cue-Triggered Decision Processes." *American Economic Review* 94(5): 1558–1590.

Boardman, Jason D. 2009. "State-Level Moderation of Genetic Tendencies to Smoke." *American Journal of Public Health* 99(3): 480–486.

Callison, Kevin, and Robert Kaestner. 2014. "Do Higher Tobacco Taxes Reduce Adult Smoking? New Evidence of the Effect of Recent Cigarette Tax Increases on Adult Smoking." *Economic Inquiry* 52(1): 155–172.

Camerer, Colin F., George Lowenstein, and Matthew Rabin. (Editors). 2011. *Advances in Behavioral Economics*. Princeton, NJ: Princeton University Press.

Carpenter, Christopher, and Philip J. Cook. 2008. "Cigarette Taxes and Youth Smoking: New Evidence from National, State, and Local Youth Risk Behavior Surveys." *Journal of Health Economics* 27(2): 287–299.

Cawley, John. 2015. "An Economy of Scales: A Selective Review of Obesity's Economic Causes, Consequences, and Solutions." *Journal of Health Economics* 43(September): 244–268.

Cawley, John, and Christopher J. Ruhm. 2012. "The Economics of Risky Behaviors." In *Handbook of Health Economics*, Volume 2, ed. Mark V. Pauly, Thomas G. McGuire, and Pedro Pita Barros. Amsterdam: Elsevier Science B.V., North-Holland Publishing, 95–199.

Chesson, Harrell, Paul Harrison, and William J. Kassler. 2000. "Sex Under the Influence: The Effect of Alcohol Policy on Sexually Transmitted Disease Rates in the United States." *Journal of Law and Economics* 43(1): 215–238.

Chou, Shin-Yi, Michael Grossman, and Henry Saffer. 2004. "An Economic Analysis of Adult Obesity: Results from the Behavioral Risk Factor Surveillance System." *Journal of Health Economics* 23(3): 565–587.

Colchero, M. Arantxa, Barry M. Popkin, Juan A. Rivera, and Shu Weng Ng. 2016. "Beverage Purchases from Stores in Mexico Under the Excise Tax on Sugar Sweetened Beverages: Observational Study." *British Medical Journal* 352(h6704): 1–10.

Colchero, M. Arantxa, Juan Carlos Salgado, Mishel Unar-Munguía, Mariana Molina, Shuwen Ng, and Juan Angel Rivera-Dommarco. 2015. "Changes in Prices After an Excise Tax to Sweetened Sugar Beverages Was Implemented in Mexico: Evidence from Urban Areas." *PLOS ONE* 10(12): e0144408, 1–11.

Colman, Greg, Michael Grossman, and Ted Joyce. 2003. "The Effect of Cigarette Excise Taxes on Smoking Before, During and After Pregnancy." *Journal of Health Economics* 22(6): 1053–1072.

Cook, Philip J., and Michael J. Moore. 1993a. "Drinking and Schooling." *Journal of Health Economics* 12(4): 411–430.

Cook, Philip J., and Michael J. Moore. 1993b. "Economic Perspectives on Reducing Alcohol-Related Violence." In *Alcohol and Interpersonal Violence: Fostering Multidisciplinary Perspectives*, ed. Susan E. Martin. National Institute on Alcohol Abuse and Alcoholism Research Monograph No. 24. Washington, DC: US Government Printing Office, 193–211.

Cook, Philip J., and Michael J. Moore. 2001. "Environment and Persistence in Youthful Drinking Patterns." In *Risky Behavior Among Youth: An Economic Analysis,* ed. Jonathan Gruber. Chicago: University of Chicago Press, 375–437.

Cotti, Chad, Erik Nesson, and Nathan Tefft. 2016. "The Effects of Tobacco Control Policies on Tobacco Products, Tar, and Nicotine Purchases: Evidence from Household Panel Data." *American Economic Journal: Economic Policy* 8(4): 103–123.

Courtemanche, Charles J. 2009. "Rising Cigarette Prices and Rising Obesity: Coincidence or Unintended Consequence?" *Journal of Health Economics* 28(4): 781–98.

Courtemanche, Charles, Garth Heutel, and Patrick McAlvanah. 2015. "Impatience, Incentives, and Obesity." *The Economic Journal* 125(582): 1–31.

Courtemanche, Charles J., Joshua C. Pinkston, Christopher J. Ruhm, and George Wehby. 2016. "Can Changing Economic Factors Explain the Rise in Obesity?" *Southern Economic Journal* 82(4): 1266–1310.

Courtemanche, Charles, Rusty Tchernis, and Benjamin Ukert. 2016. "The Effect of Smoking on Obesity: Evidence from a Randomized Trial." Cambridge, MA: National Bureau of Economic Research Working Paper 21937.

Dave, Dhaval. 2006. "The Effects of Cocaine and Heroin Price on Drug-Related Emergency Department Visits." *Journal of Health Economics* 25(2): 311–333.

Dave, Dhaval. 2008. "Illicit Drug Use Among Arrestees, Prices and Policy. *Journal of Urban Economics* 63(2): 694–714.

Dee, Thomas S. 1999. "State Alcohol Policies, Teen Drinking, and Traffic Fatalities." *Journal of Public Economics* 72(2): 289–315.

Dee, Thomas S., and William N. Evans. 2001. "Teens and Traffic Safety." In *Risky Behavior Among Youth: An Economic Analysis,* ed. Jonathan Gruber. Chicago: University of Chicago Press, 121–166.

Douglas, Stratford. 1998. "The Duration of the Smoking Habit." *Economic Inquiry* 36(1): 49–64.

Escario, José Julián, and Jose Alberto Molina. 2001. "Testing for the Rational Addiction Hypothesis in Spanish Tobacco Consumption." *Applied Economics Letters* 8(4): 211–15.

Fenn, Aju J., Frances Antonovitz, and John R. Schroeter. 2001. "Cigarettes and Addiction Information: New Evidence in Support of the Rational Addiction Model." *Economics Letters* 72(1): 39–45.

Fletcher, Jason M. 2012. "Why Have Tobacco Control Policies Stalled? Using Genetic Moderation to Examine Policy Impacts." *PLOS ONE* 7(12): e50576, 1–6.

Fletcher, Jason M., David E. Frisvold, and Nathan Tefft. 2010a. "Can Soft Drink Taxes Reduce Population Weight?" *Contemporary Economic Policy* 28(1): 23–35.

Fletcher, Jason M., David E. Frisvold, and Nathan Tefft. 2010b, "The Effects of Soft Drink Taxes on Child and Adolescent Consumption and Weight Outcomes." *Journal of Public Economics* 94(11–12): 967–974.

Friedman, Abigail S. 2015. "How Does Electronic Cigarette Access Affect Adolescent Smoking?" *Journal of Health Economics* 44(December): 300–308.

Gilleskie, Donna B., and Koleman S. Strumpf. 2005. "The Behavioral Dynamics of Youth Smoking." *Journal of Human Resources* 40(4): 822–866.

Grossman, Michael. 2005. "Individual Behaviors and Substance Use: The Role of Price." In *Substance Use: Individual Behavior, Social Interaction, Markets and Politics,* ed. Björn Lindgren and Michael Grossman. Volume 16 of *Advances in Health Economics and Health Services Research.* Amsterdam: JAI, an imprint of Elsevier Ltd., 15–39.

Grossman, Michael, and Frank J. Chaloupka. 1998. "The Demand for Cocaine by Young Adults: A Rational Addiction Approach." *Journal of Health Economics* 17(4): 427–474.

Gruber, Jonathan, and Michael Frakes. 2006. "Does Falling Smoking Lead to Rising Obesity?" *Journal of Health Economics* 25(2): 183–197.

Gruber, Jonathan, and Botond Köszegi. 2001. "Is Addiction 'Rational'? Theory and Evidence." *Quarterly Journal of Economics* 116(4): 1261–1303.

Gruber, Jonathan, and Jonathan Zinman. 2001. "Youth Smoking in the United States: Evidence and Implications." In *Risky Behavior Among Youths: An Economic Analysis*, ed. Jonathan Gruber. Chicago: University of Chicago Press, 69–120.

Hansen, Benjamin, Joseph J. Sabia, and Daniel I. Rees. 2017. "Have Cigarette Taxes Lost Their Bite: New Estimates of the Relationship Between Cigarette Taxes and Youth Smoking." *American Journal of Health Economics* 3(1): 60–75.

Huang, Jidong, and Frank J. Chaloupka IV. 2012. "The Impact of the 2009 Tobacco Excise Tax Increase on Youth Tobacco Use." Cambridge, MA: National Bureau of Economic Research Working Paper 18026.

Jolly, David. 2016. "European Court of Justice Upholds Strict Rules on Tobacco." *New York Times*, May 4:B1.

Kahneman, Daniel, and Shane Frederick. 2002. "Representativeness Revisited: Attribute Substitution Intuitive Judgment." In *Heuristics and Biases: The Psychology of Intuitive Judgment*, ed. Thomas Gilovich, Dale Griffin, and Daniel Kahneman. New York: Cambridge University Press, 49–81.

Kelly, Erin, Shane Darke, and Joanne Ross. 2004. "A Review of Drug Use and Driving: Epidemiology, Impairment, Risk Factors, and Risk Perceptions." *Drug and Alcohol Review* 23(3): 319–344.

Kenkel, Donald S. 1993. "Drinking, Driving, and Deterrence: The Effectiveness and Social Costs of Alternative Policies." *Journal of Law and Economics* 36(2): 877–913.

Kuziemko, Ilyana, and Steven D. Levitt. 2004. "An Empirical Analysis of Imprisoning Drug Offenders." *Journal of Public Economics* 88(9–10): 2043–2066.

Labeaga, José M. 1999. "A Double-Hurdle Rational Addiction Model with Heterogeneity: Estimating the Demand for Tobacco." *Journal of Econometrics* 93(1), 49–72.

Laporte, Audrey, Alfia Karimova, and Brian Ferguson. 2010. "Quantile Regression Analysis of the Rational Addiction Model: Investigating Heterogeneity in Forward-Looking Behavior." *Health Economics* 19(9): 1063–1074.

Maclean, Johanna Catherine, Asia Sikora Kessler, and Donald S. Kenkel. 2016. "Cigarette Taxes and Older Adults: Results from the Health and Retirement Study." *Health Economics* 25(4): 424–438.

Markowitz, Sara. 2000. "The Price of Alcohol, Wife Abuse, and Husband Abuse." *Southern Economic Journal* 67(2): 279–303.

Markowitz, Sara. 2014. "Where There's Smoke There's Fire: The Effects of Smoking Policies on the Incidence of Fires in the USA." *Health Economics* 23(11): 1353–1373.

Markowitz, Sara, Erik Nesson, Eileen Poe-Yamagata, Curtis Florence, Partha Deb, Tracy Andrews, and Sarah Beth L. Barnett. 2014. "Estimating the Relationship Between Alcohol Policies and Criminal Violence and Victimization." *German Economic Review* 13(4): 416–435.

Mitchell, Suzanne H. 2011. "The Genetic Basis of Delay Discounting and Its Genetic Relationship to Alcohol Dependence." *Behavioural Processes* 87(1): 10–17.

Moore, Michael J. 1996. "Death and Tobacco Taxes." *RAND Journal of Economics* 27(2): 415–428.

National Academy of Sciences, Committee on Population. 2010. "Using Genome-Wide Association Studies (GWAS) to Explore Fundamental Questions About Aging in the Health and Retirement Study (HRS) Sample: Summary of an Expert Meeting." *http://www.nia.nih.gov /ResearchInformation/ExtramuralPrograms/BehavioralandSocial Research/Genetics.htm.*

Nguyen, Lien, Gunnar Rosenqvist, and Markku Pekurinen. 2012. *Demand for Tobacco in Europe: An Econometric Analysis of 11 Countries for the PPACTE Project*, Report 6. Helsinki, FI: National Institute for Health and Welfare.

O'Donoghue, Ted, and Matthew Rabin. 1999. "Doing It Now or Later." *American Economic Review* 89(1): 103–124.

O'Donoghue, Ted, and Matthew Rabin. 2001. "Choice and Procrastination." *Quarterly Journal of Economics* 116(1): 121–160.

Ohsfeldt, Robert L., and Michael A. Morrissey. 1997. "Beer Taxes, Workers' Compensation and Industrial Injury." *Review of Economics and Statistics* 79(1): 155–160.

Olmstead, Todd A., Sheila M. Alessi, Brendan Kline, Rosalie Liccardo Pacula, and Nancy M. Petry. 2015. "The Price Elasticity of Demand for Heroin: Matched Longitudinal and Experimental Evidence." *Journal of Health Economics* 41(May): 59–71.

Pacula, Rosalie Liccardo, Michael Grossman, Frank J. Chaloupka, Patrick M. O'Malley, Lloyd D. Johnston, and Matthew C. Farrelly. 2001. "Marijuana and Youth." In *Risky Behavior Among Youth: An Economic Analysis,* ed. Jonathan Gruber. Chicago: University of Chicago Press, 271–326.

Pacula, Rosalie Liccardo, David Powell, Paul Heaton, and Eric L. Sevigny. 2015. "Assessing the Effects of Medical Marijuana Laws on Marijuana Use: The Devil is in the Details." *Journal of Policy Analysis and Management* 34(1): 7–31.

Pesko, Michael F., Jenna M. Hughes, and Fatima S. Faisal. 2016. "The Influence of Electronic Cigarette Age Purchasing Restrictions on Adolescent Tobacco and Marijuana Use." *Preventive Medicine* 87(June): 207–212.

Royal College of Physicians. 2016. *Nicotine without Smoke: Tobacco Harm Reduction*. London: Royal College of Physicians.

Ruhm, Christopher J., Alison Snow Jones, Kerry Anne McGeary, William C. Kerr, Joseph V. Terza, Thomas K. Greenfield, and Ravi S. Pandian. 2012. "What U.S. Data Should Be Used to Measure the Price Elasticity of Demand for Alcohol?" *Journal of Health Economics* 31(6): 851–862.

Saffer, Henry. 1991. "Alcohol Advertising Bans and Alcohol Abuse: An International Perspective." *Journal of Health Economics* 10(1): 65–80.

Saffer, Henry. 2014. "Self-Regulation and Health." Cambridge, MA: National Bureau of Economic Research Working Paper 20483.

Saffer, Henry, and Frank J. Chaloupka. 1999. "Demographic Differentials in the Demand for Alcohol and Illegal Drugs." In *The Economic Analysis of Substance Use and Abuse: An Integration of Econometric and Behavioral Economic Research,* ed. Frank J. Chaloupka, Michael Grossman, Warren K. Bickel, and Henry Saffer. Chicago: University of Chicago Press, 187–212.

Saffer, Henry, Dhaval Dave, and Michael Grossman. 2016. "A Behavioral Economic Model of Alcohol Advertising and Price." *Health Economics* 25(7): 816–828.

Sewell, R. Andrew, James Poling, and Mehmet Sofuoglu. 2009. "The Effect of Cannabis Compared with Alcohol on Driving." *American Journal on Addictions* 18(3): 185–193.

Shrestha, Vinish. 2015. "Estimating the Price Elasticity of Demand for Different Levels of Alcohol Consumption Among Young Adults." *American Journal of Health Economics* 1(2): 224–254.

U.S. Food and Drug Administration. 2016. "Deeming Tobacco Products to Be Subject to the Federal Food, Drug, and Cosmetic Act, as Amended by the Family Smoking Prevention and Tobacco Control Act; Restrictions on the Sale and Distribution of Tobacco Products and Required Warning Statements for Tobacco Products; Final Rule." *Federal Registrar*, May 10.

Wen, Heifei, Jason M. Hockenberry, and Janet R. Cummings. 2015. "The Effect of Medical Marijuana Laws on Adolescent and Adult Use of Alcohol, Marijuana, and Other Substances." *Journal of Health Economics* 42(July): 64–80.

Williams, Jenny, Rosalie Liccardo Pacula, Frank J. Chaloupka, and Henry Wechsler. 2004. "Alcohol and Marijuana Among College Students: Economic Complements or Substitutes?" *Health Economics* 13(9): 825–843.

Reflections

I have not completed my career in economics research, so I do not think that a concluding section of this book would be appropriate. Instead, I would like to reflect on two issues. One pertains to the current status of the field of health economics relative to its status in the mid-1960s. The second deals with implications of the papers in the book for recent trends in opioid use and mortality as well as differences in mortality among certain groups in the population.

When I began to work on my PhD dissertation in the fall of 1966, health economics was not recognized as a field by the American Economic Association. Very few universities offered courses in that subject. Columbia University certainly did not. There were no specialty journals in health economics, no associations of health economists, no conferences devoted to the field, and no advertisements in *Job Openings for Economists* (a publication of the American Economic Association) for teaching positions in health. Indeed, I am a member of the first cohort of economists to list health economics as a primary specialty. Other members of that cohort include Joseph P. Newhouse, Mark V. Pauly, David Salkever, and Frank A. Sloan.

Five decades later the situation is very different. Health economics has been recognized as a major field by the American Economic Association for some time. Virtually every major PhD program in economics offers at least one course in health, and courses in this subject are given at the undergraduate and master's level in most universities and colleges as well. As a result, *Job Openings for Economists* is filled with academic job postings that require health as a field. A number of economics field journals are devoted to health including the *Journal of Health Economics*, *Health Economics*, the *American Journal of Health Economics*, the *European Journal of Health Economics*, and the *International Journal of Health Care Finance and Economics*. A typical issue of the best general journals in economics contains one or more papers on health. There are a number of associations of health economists, the two most prominent of which are the International Association of Health Economists (iHEA) and the American Society of Health Economists (ASHEcon). Each of these associations holds a biennial conference. The most recent ones have attracted more than a thousand participants. I am delighted by the rapid growth in the field of health economics. It is compelling evidence that the theoretical, empirical, and policy issues that health economists have addressed over the past fifty years are important and that practitioners have made profound contributions to an understanding of these issues.

Very recent research on trends and differentials in mortality among certain segments of the population highlights the continued relevance of the economic perspective of determinants of the health of the population found in the papers in this book. Anne Case and Angus Deaton (2015) call attention to the startling upward trend in the all-cause mortality of middle-aged white non-Hispanic men and women in the United States between 1999 and 2013. Individuals with no more than a high school education were hit the hardest, with an increase in their mortality rate of 134 deaths per one hundred thousand population in the period at issue. Gina Kolata and Sarah Cohen (2016) report that the trend extended to young white adults ages twenty-five to thirty-four, especially for those with less than a high school education. These trends resulted in the first increase in the age-adjusted death rate in a decade between 2014 and 2015 (Ahmad 2016).

What caused this striking trend? The studies just cited and others point to expansions in deaths from external causes, mainly drug overdoses and suicides. In turn, the growth in these causes of death has been traced to the explosion in the abuse and misuse of such prescription opioids as oxycodone and hydrocodone (Manchikanti, Fellows, Ailinani, and Pampati 2010; Meldrum 2016). Marcia L. Meldrum points to evidence from selected studies in the 1980s that these pain relievers were not addictive as the reason why the total number of opioid prescriptions dispensed by U.S. retail pharmacies has grown so much since the early 1990s. Unfortunately, they are addictive, and users have increasingly turned to theft, purchases from a friend or relative, "doctor shopping" (obtaining prescriptions from multiple providers without a given provider being aware of the other prescriptions), and "pill mills" (physicians operating from pain clinics and prescribing the drugs in an inappropriate manner). Users also have turned to heroin, an illegal opioid that typically can produce the same effect as OxyContin at one-fourth the price (Meldrum 2016).

The papers in parts 2 and 4 of this book provide important insights with regard to the developments just documented. The evidence in my studies and those by others is that the demand for legal and illegal addictive substances is quite sensitive to price. Hence, it can explain why individuals addicted to "pain killers" have turned to heroin and may have increased the quantity they demand as a result of its lower price. These studies also can account for the protective effect of education, reflected by the much larger effect of the opioid epidemic on the mortality rate of the less educated. Those with more schooling are likely to have been the first to have acquired knowledge of the harmful effects of opioid abuse in part because of their future orientation.

Finally, the papers in parts 2 and 4 lay the groundwork for the brand new project by my colleagues Henry Saffer and Dhaval Dave on the effects of state laws that target prescription drug abuse. As usual, Henry is getting involved in a key issue in health economics at a very early stage. Together with Dhaval and Anca Cotet-Grecu, he plans to investigate whether these laws have the intended consequences and reduce treatment admissions, hospital emergency department visits, and deaths due to abuse of opioid prescription drugs—possibly by substantial amounts—or whether the reductions are small or nonexistent due to substitution to heroin. That would be another example of unintended consequences, one similar to the finding that policies that curtail cigarette smoking may have led to an increase in obesity. Whatever Henry and his colleagues find, I am sure they will be striking and will open up a whole new area for future research.

One fascinating study to undertake would be a comparative study of the cocaine epidemic of the 1980s and the current opioid prescription drug epidemic. From a historical perspective, the two epidemics have similar origins. As Frank J. Chaloupka, Charles C. Brown, and I describe, cocaine use was fairly widespread in the United States from the late 1880s until the early 1900s when many states enacted criminal prohibitions (Grossman, Chaloupka, and Brown 1996). This process culminated in a federal ban under the 1914 Harrison Act (Musto 1973), and the drug virtually disappeared from use until the early 1970s. Apparently, so did the knowledge about the harm that it can do. In August 1974 Dr. Peter Bourne, who later served as President Jimmy Carter's science advisor, stated: "Cocaine, once a component of many tonics and of Coca-Cola, is probably the most benign of illicit drugs currently in widespread use. The number of people seeking treatment as a result of cocaine use is for all practical purposes zero" (as quoted by Peter Kerr 1986, B6). In the 1980 edition of the *Comprehensive Textbook of Psychiatry*, the main psychiatric textbook in the United States, Dr. Lester Grinspoon and James B. Bakalar wrote: "If it is used no more than two or three times a week, cocaine creates no serious problems…. At present, chronic cocaine use does not usually appear as a medical problem" (pp. 1621–1622).

Chaloupka, Brown, and I show that the resulting rapid increase in cocaine use and its negative consequences in the 1980s and early 1990s was not reversed by the federal War on Drugs, which was begun by President Richard P. Nixon and greatly expanded by President Ronald Reagan. That was because the real price of cocaine declined dramatically from 1975 through the early 2000s (Grossman, Chaloupka, and Brown 1996; Grossman and Chaloupka 1998; Grossman 2005). Instead, the impacts of such developments as efforts by the Partnership for a Drug-Free America to publicize the harmful effects of cocaine and the dramatic drug deaths in June 1986 of the basketball star Len Bias and the football star Don Rogers appear to have had much bigger effects. I encourage studies that would provide more definitive evidence regarding factors that reversed the cocaine epidemic and that may reverse the prescription opioid drug abuse epidemic. I wonder whether such studies can answer the question of whether the United States and other developed countries are doomed to experience cycles in the use of harmfully addictive substances.

Not all the news concerning recent trends in U.S. mortality is bad. Janet Currie and Hannes Schwandt (2016) document large reductions in mortality for children and young adults below age twenty between 1990 and 2010. These reductions were largest in poorer counties. Referring to a study by Currie and Maya Rosin-Slater (2015), the authors point to the probable roles of a number of public programs discussed in part 3 of this book including Medicaid, WIC, and community health programs. Currie and Schwandt's findings highlight the high value of a new study that would estimate the effects of these programs and others on mortality in the relevant age groups with a focus on poor children and with an attempt to compute a cost-benefit ratio for each program. I proposed that type of study in the afterword to part 3.

I want to conclude by commenting on a study by Raj Chetty, Michael Stepner, Sarah Abraham, Shelby Lin, Benjamin Scuder, Nicholas Turner, Augustin Bergeron, and David Cutler (2016) that has attracted a considerable amount of attention. Using very recent U.S. data at the county level, the authors document that higher income was positively correlated with greater longevity throughout the income distribution. They also find that between 2001 and 2014 life expectancy grew by the largest amount in the top 5 percent of the income distribution, which resulted in an increase in inequality in life expectancy.

In an accompanying editorial on this paper, Nobel Laureate Angus Deaton points out that part of the relationship between income and mortality reflects causality from poor health to income, a relationship that serves as a key foundation for my human capital approach to the demand for health in part 1 of this book (Deaton 2016). Even more important, he writes: "for policy, it is important to consider the role of education or factors, such as forward-looking behavior, that are correlated with education. Indeed, it is possible that much of the correlation is attributable to a combination of (1) reverse causality from health to income throughout the life course; (2) the effects of parental incomes on child health and child education, which in turn have profound effects on those children's health and income in adulthood; and (3) the direct causal effects of education and cognitive function on health and on income, working through better behaviors, greater thought for the future, and a better ability to deal with the health care system" (p. 1705). Deaton's editorial underscores themes that run throughout part 2 and indeed throughout all parts of this book. The positive relationship between more schooling and better health is one of the most fundamental relationships in health economics. It is natural to explore complementarities between these two most important forms of human capital. Research that investigates the causal nature of the relationship and the mechanisms via which schooling influences health has played and should continue to play an extremely prominent role in the literature that explores the determinants of the health of the population from an economic perspective.

REFERENCES

Ahmad, Farida B. 2016. "Quarterly Provisional Estimates for Selected Indicators of Mortality, 2014-Quarter 2, 2016." *National Vital Statistics System, Vital Statistics Rapid Release Program*. Hyattsville, MD: National Center for Health Statistics.

Case, Anne, and Angus Deaton. 2015. "Rising Morbidity and Mortality in Midlife Among White Non-Hispanic Americans in the 21st Century." *Proceedings of the National Academy of Sciences* 112(49): 15078–15083.

Chetty, Raj, Michael Stepner, Sarah Abraham, Shelby Lin, Benjamin Scuder, Nicholas Turner, Augustin Bergeron, and David Cutler. 2016. "The Association Between Income and Life Expectancy in the United States, 2001–2014." *Journal of the American Medical Association* 315(16): 1751–1766.

Currie, Janet, and Maya Rossin-Slater. 2015. "Early-Life Origins of Lifecycle Wellbeing: Research and Policy Implications." *Journal of Policy Analysis and Management* 34(1): 208–242.

Currie, Janet, and Hannes Schwandt. 2016. "Inequality in Mortality Decreased Among the Young While Increasing for Older Adults, 1990–2010." *Science* 352(6286): 708–712.

Deaton, Angus. 2016. "Editorial: On Death and Money History, Facts, and Explanations." *Journal of the American Medical Association* 315(16): 1703–1705.

Grinspoon, Lester, and James B. Bakalar. 1980. "Drug Dependence: Nonnarcotic Agent." In *Comprehensive Textbook of Psychiatry*, Volume 2, Third Edition, ed. Harold I. Kaplan, Alfred M. Freedman, and Benjamin J. Sadock. Baltimore: Williams and Wilkins, 1614–1629.

Grossman, Michael. 2005. "Individual Behaviors and Substance Use: The Role of Price." In *Substance Use: Individual Behavior, Social Interaction, Markets and Politics,* ed. Björn Lindgren and Michael Grossman. Volume 16 of *Advances in Health Economics and Health Services Research.* Amsterdam: JAI, an imprint of Elsevier Ltd., 15–39.

Grossman, Michael, and Frank J. Chaloupka. 1998. "The Demand for Cocaine by Young Adults: A Rational Addiction Approach." *Journal of Health Economics* 17(4): 427–474.

Grossman, Michael, Frank J. Chaloupka, and Charles B. Brown. 1996. "The Demand for Cocaine by Young Adults: A Rational Addiction Approach." Cambridge, MA: National Bureau of Economic Research Working Paper 5713.

Kerr, Peter. 1986. "Anatomy of the Drug Issue: How, After Years, It Erupted." *New York Times* November 17: A1, B6.

Kolata, Gina, and Sarah Cohen. 2016. "Drug Overdoses Propel Mortality Rates of Young Whites." *New York Times* January 16: C1.

Manchikanti, Laxmaiah, Bert Fellows, Hary Ailinani, and Vidyasagar Pampati. 2010. "Therapeutic Use, Abuse, and Non-Medical Use of Opioids: A Ten-Year Prospective." *Pain Physician* 13(5): 401–435.

Meldrum, Marcia L. 2016. "Editorial: The Ongoing Opioid Prescription Epidemic: Historical Context." *American Journal of Public Health* 106(8): 1365–1366.

Musto, David F. 1973. *The American Disease: Origins of Narcotics Control.* New Haven, CT: Yale University Press.

Index

Ingram Content Group UK Ltd.
Milton Keynes UK
UKHW011018210523
422048UK00003B/48